Frommer's

D1220473

New England

12th Edition

*by Herbert Bailey Livesey, Paul Karr,
Marie Morris, Laura M. Reckford*

Here's what the critics say about Frommer's:

"Amazingly easy to use. Very portable, very complete."
—*Booklist*

"Detailed, accurate, and easy-to-read information for all price ranges."
—*Glamour Magazine*

"Hotel information is close to encyclopedic."
—*Des Moines Sunday Register*

"Frommer's Guides have a way of giving you a real feel for a place."
—*Knight Ridder Newspapers*

WILEY
Wiley Publishing, Inc.

Published by:

Wiley Publishing, Inc.

111 River St.
Hoboken, NJ 07030-5774

ISBN 0-7645-6764-0

Editor: Kathleen Warnock
Production Editor: M. Faunette Johnston
Cartographer: Roberta Stockwell
Photo Editor: Richard Fox
Production by Wiley Indianapolis Composition Services

Front cover photo: Vermont country road
Back cover photo: New Hampshire: Fisherman in canoe

For information on our other products and services or to obtain technical support, please contact our Customer Care Department within the U.S. at 800/762-2974, outside the U.S. at 317/572-3993 or fax 317/572-4002.

Wiley also publishes its books in a variety of electronic formats. Some content that appears in print may not be available in electronic formats.

Manufactured in the United States of America

5 4 3 2

Contents

4 Boston & Cambridge

78

by Marie Morris

5 Side Trips from Boston: Lexington & Concord, the North Shore & Plymouth

145

by Marie Morris

6 Cape Cod

193

by Laura M. Reckford

12 New Hampshire   531

by Paul Karr

13 Maine   579

by Paul Karr

Appendix: New England in Depth   663

by Paul Karr

Index   674

List of Maps

About the Authors

Paul Karr (chapters 2, 3, 11–13, and appendix) is also the author of *Frommer's Nova Scotia, New Brunswick & Prince Edward Island; Frommer's Portable Maine Coast; Frommer's Vermont, New Hampshire & Maine* and *Frommer's Canada.* He has edited Frommer's guides to The Bahamas, Jamaica, London, Paris, San Antonio, and San Francisco; edited and updated Irreverent Guides to Rome, Vancouver, and Seattle; and authored *Vancouver & Victoria For Dummies.*

Herbert Bailey Livesey (chapters 8–10) is a native New Yorker and a former NYU administrator. After leaving his career in higher education, he worked briefly as an artist before devoting himself to writing full time. He is the author of several travel guides, nine books on education and sociology, and a novel.

Marie Morris (chapters 4 and 5) is a native New Yorker and a graduate of Harvard, where she studied history. She has worked for the *New York Times, Boston* magazine, and the *Boston Herald,* and is also the author of *Frommer's Boston.* She lives in Boston.

Laura M. Reckford (chapters 6 and 7) is a writer and editor who lives on Cape Cod. Formerly the managing editor *of Cape Cod Life Magazine,* she has also been on the editorial staffs of *Good Housekeeping Magazine* and *Entertainment Weekly.*

An Invitation to the Reader

In researching this book, we discovered many wonderful places—hotels, restaurants, shops, and more. We're sure you'll find others. Please tell us about them, so we can share the information with your fellow travelers in upcoming editions. If you were disappointed with a recommendation, we'd love to know that, too. Please write to:

Frommer's New England, 12th Edition
Wiley Publishing, Inc. • 111 River St. • Hoboken, NJ 07030-5774

An Additional Note

Please be advised that travel information is subject to change at any time—and this is especially true of prices. We therefore suggest that you write or call ahead for confirmation when making your travel plans. The authors, editors, and publisher cannot be held responsible for the experiences of readers while traveling. Your safety is important to us, however, so we encourage you to stay alert and be aware of your surroundings. Keep a close eye on cameras, purses, and wallets, all favorite targets of thieves and pickpockets.

Other Great Guides for Your Trip:

Frommer's Vermont, New Hampshire & Maine
Frommer's New England's Best Loved Driving Tours
Frommer's Portable Maine Coast
Frommer's Wonderful Weekends from New York City
Frommer's Cape Cod, Nantucket & Martha's Vineyard
Frommer's Boston
Frommer's Irreverent Guide to Boston

Frommer's Star Ratings, Icons & Abbreviations

Every hotel, restaurant, and attraction listing in this guide has been ranked for quality, value, service, amenities, and special features using a **star-rating system.** In country, state, and regional guides, we also rate towns and regions to help you narrow down your choices and budget your time accordingly. Hotels and restaurants are rated on a scale of zero (recommended) to three stars (exceptional). Attractions, shopping, nightlife, towns, and regions are rated according to the following scale: zero stars (recommended), one star (highly recommended), two stars (very highly recommended), and three stars (must-see).

In addition to the star-rating system, we also use **seven feature icons** that point you to the great deals, in-the-know advice, and unique experiences that separate travelers from tourists. Throughout the book, look for:

Finds	Special finds—those places only insiders know about
Fun Fact	Fun facts—details that make travelers more informed and their trips more fun
Kids	Best bets for kids, and advice for the whole family
Moments	Special moments—those experiences that memories are made of
Overrated	Places or experiences not worth your time or money
Tips	Insider tips—great ways to save time and money
Value	Great values—where to get the best deals

The following **abbreviations** are used for credit cards:

AE	American Express	DISC	Discover	V	Visa
DC	Diners Club	MC	MasterCard		

Frommers.com

Now that you have the guidebook to a great trip, visit our website at **www.frommers.com** for travel information on more than 3,000 destinations. With features updated regularly, we give you instant access to the most current trip-planning information available. At Frommers.com, you'll also find the best prices on airfares, accommodations, and car rentals—and you can even book travel online through our travel booking partners. At Frommers.com, you'll also find the following:

- Online updates to our most popular guidebooks
- Vacation sweepstakes and contest giveaways
- Newsletter highlighting the hottest travel trends
- Online travel message boards with featured travel discussions

What's New in New England

BOSTON & CAMBRIDGE In 2004, the **Big Dig,** Boston's massive highway-construction job (now in its 16th year) turned for home. The $14.6 billion Central Artery/Third Harbor Tunnel project (its formal name) moved from tunnel and bridge construction to demolition of the elevated expressway. The parks, surface roads, and buildings that will replace the hideous green structure will be in the works when you visit.

Boston's MBTA (© **617/222-3200;** www.mbta.com) transit authority raised fares on all of its train, bus, and ferry lines in 2004.

Significantly, in 2004 Massachusetts enacted a **smoking ban** in all state workplaces, restaurants, bars, and nightclubs.

Changes were afoot in Boston's hotel mix, as well. The Irish brand Jurys Doyle has opened its first U.S. property outside Washington, D.C., the **Jurys Boston Hotel,** 350 Stuart St. (© **866/JD-HOTELS;** www.jurys doyle.com).

Tours of storied **Fenway Park,** 4 Yawkey Way (© **617-226-6666;** www.redsox.com), are now available year-round.

The **Boston Tea Party Ship & Museum** (© **617/338-1773;** www. bostonteapartyship.com) closed after a fire in 2001 but is set to reopen in spring or summer of 2005; if you wish to visit, call ahead to ensure it's open.

Dreams of Freedom, a museum of immigration not far from the Freedom Trail, has closed.

In 2004, James Levine replaced Seiji Ozawa as music director of the **Boston** Symphony Orchestra (© 617/266-1492 or 617/CONCERT for program information; www.bso.org).

Finally, a decrepit Theater District landmark was transformed into the **Opera House,** 539 Washington St. (© **617/880-2400**), which reopened in 2004 with a splashy production of *The Lion King.*

SIDE TRIPS FROM BOSTON Salem's **Peabody Essex Museum,** East India Square (© **800/745-4054** or 978/745-9500; www.pem.org), has attracted international attention with its new wing, which incorporates an 18th-century home imported from China and reassembled in America.

CAPE COD Major renovation work on the **Salt Pond Visitors' Center** (© **508/255-3421**) in Eastham is expected to be completed by the fall of 2004. The visitor center will be closed during the renovation, but visitors will still be able to walk the trails and obtain maps at a temporary visitor booth. If you're traveling onward to Provincetown, visit the Province Lands Visitors Center (© **508/487-1256**), with similar displays and programs.

MARTHA'S VINEYARD & NANTUCKET For those going to Martha's Vineyard, check out the new fast ferry from Rhode Island to Oak Bluffs that makes the trip in 90 minutes and avoids Cape Cod traffic jams. **Vineyard Fast Ferry Company** (© **401/295-4040;** www.vineyard fastferry.com) runs this seasonal high-speed catamaran, called *Millennium,* which leaves from Quonset Point in

North Kingston. The round-trip cost is $48 for adults and $36 for children.

Another new option for Vineyard vacationers is a high-speed ferry from **New Bedford** to the island. For schedule and fare details, contact the **Steamship Authority** (© **508/477-8600** or www.steamshipauthority.com).

The **Whaling Museum** (13 Broad St., Nantucket; © **508/228-1894**), one of the region's top attractions, is undergoing a major renovation that should be completed by fall of 2004. Some exhibits will be displayed at the Friends Meeting House, an 1838 historic property at 7 Fair St., during the renovation. For details, call © **508/228-1894.**

A new Nantucket inn, **The Veranda House** at 3 Step Lane (© **508/228-0695;** www.theverandahouse.com), is a superb renovation of a historic building. The owners have remade this 20-room inn into a stylish version of a classic guesthouse. The inn is located in a quiet neighborhood, a short walk from the center of town.

After a fire destroyed the 200-year-old Tisbury Inn in Vineyard Haven in 2001, the fate of the property was uncertain. But it reopened last year as the **Mansion House Inn** (9 Main St., Vineyard Haven; © **800/332-4112** or 508/693-2200), a luxury 32-room inn. The three-story building is once again a community hub, with a restaurant, health club, and shops. See chapter 7 for details.

CENTRAL & WESTERN MASSACHUSETTS Shakespeare & Company, 70 Kemble St. (© **413/637-1199**) has completed its move to a new complex closer to Lenox center. With two new theaters, it has expanded its season, now running from May to December.

In Northampton, the **Smith College Museum of Art,** Elm Street and Bedford Terrace (© **413/585-2760**), has completed a 3-year renovation and expansion, enhancing its reputation as one of New England's finest college museums.

A grand Art Deco cinema in Great Barrington, the **Mahaiwe,** Main Street and Taconic Avenue (© **413/644-9040**), is being transformed into a year-round performing arts center. One of its first tenants was the Berkshire Opera Company.

The largest town in the southern Berkshires, Great Barrington also continues to underscore its desirability as a dining mecca with the opening of several new restaurants, including the snappy bistro **Pearl's,** 47 Railroad St. (© **413/528-7767**), the giddily eclectic **Helsinki Tea Company,** 284 Main St. (© **413/528-3394**), and contemporary Italian **Verdura,** 44–47 Railroad St. (© **413/528-8969**).

CONNECTICUT To the surprise of many, Westport's ultra-luxurious **Inn at National Hall,** 2 Post Rd. (© **203/221-1351**), appears to be on its last legs, as evidenced by a closed dining room and reduced staff.

In April 2003, the **Aldrich Museum of Contemporary Art,** 258 Main St. (© **203/438-4519**) in Ridgefield, closed to begin massive renovation to the existing building and construction of large new galleries. Its mission has been changed from the exhibition of 20th-century painters and sculptors to the showcasing of works less than 5 years old.

After remaining shuttered for over 2 years, the **Toll Gate Hill Inn,** 571 Torrington Rd. (© **860/567-1233**) in Litchfield, has reopened. The restaurant, in the 1745 tavern, has already become a dining destination.

Kent, home to a prominent prep school of the same name, is roiled in controversy over the recent federal recognition of the local Schaghticoke tribe. While the tiny Indian nation hasn't decided what it will do with that status, many townspeople worry that a casino is in their near future.

> **Tips** **Marrying in Massachusetts**
>
> On May 17, 2004 the state of Massachusetts began issuing marriage licenses to same-sex couples, setting off a wave of gays and lesbians traveling to the Bay State to wed. For more information about obtaining a marriage license in Massachusetts, visit the state website at www.state. ma.us/sec/cis/cismrg/mrgidx.htm. For more about planning gay and lesbian weddings in Massachusetts and Vermont civil unions, see p. 40.

The **Florence Griswold Museum,** 96 Lyme St. (© **860/434-5542**) in Old Lyme, is famed as the turn-of-the-last-century residence of painters who became known as the American Impressionists. Construction of a large new gallery behind the original house has now been completed.

One of Mystic's favorite lodging places, the **Inn at Mystic,** Routes 1 and 27 (© **800/237-2415**), has completed a major overhaul of its honored restaurant, **Flood Tide.** Also in Mystic, the once-musty **Whaler's Inn,** 20 E. Main St. (© **800/243-2588**), has new owners, who have added rooms and rehabilitated old ones in the five structures that comprise the inn.

Smoking is now banned in public places throughout the state, including bars and restaurants.

RHODE ISLAND Providence's dining scene continues to bloom. New owners of **The Gatehouse,** 4 Richmond Sq. (© **401/521-9229**), having updated the menu and redecorated the entire property, opened the riotously popular **Mill's Tavern,** 101 N. Main St. (© **401/272-3331**), attracting a good-looking crowd of young and middle-age professionals. A block away is the artsy **XO Café,** 125 N. Main St. (© **401/273-9090**), where the menu urges, "Life is short, order dessert first."

A fading resort hotel at the north end of Newport's famed Cliff Walk has been infused with copious amounts of money and planning to become the deluxe **Chanler,** 117 Memorial Blvd. (© **401/847-1300**). A boutique hotel with only 20 units and every reasonable service and facility, it leaped to the front of the line of local hostelries.

Rhode Island hasn't legislated against smoking—yet—leaving the decision to restaurateurs and innkeepers. In practice, this means smokers often find themselves confined to bars and porches.

VERMONT   The **Vermont Historical Society Museum,** 109 State St. (© **802/828-2291**), near the Vermont State House in Montpelier, has reopened after extensive renovation and expansion.

The **American Museum of Fly Fishing** (© **802/362-3300**) in Manchester had closed at press time. It is scheduled to reopen at a location near the famous Orvis store (which stocks a wide variety of fishing equipment), perhaps in 2004.

Two of the Connecticut River Valley's most interesting eateries closed in 2003. The African restaurant **Karibu Tulé** in White River Junction and the French **La Poule à Dents** in Norwich each bid their fans adieu.

Middlebury's **Swift House Inn,** 25 Stewart Lane (© **802/388-9925**), has been purchased by owners who bring a new spirit to the place (as well as renovations and a reopened dining room). Expect the experience here to get better and better.

NEW HAMPSHIRE   The biggest news here was the collapse of the **Old Man of the Mountains** in Franconia

Notch during a 2003 storm. There are no plans at present to reconstruct the famous rock profile, long identified with New Hampshire.

On New Castle Island just outside Portsmouth, the resort **Wentworth by the Sea,** P.O. Box 860, Wentworth Rd. (© **866/240-6313**), has reopened after being boarded up for years, and it's now the classiest lodging on the New Hampshire coast. There are more than 160 rooms, with 17 additional luxury units to come in 2004; there's also a full-service spa, two pools, and a wonderful dining room.

In the lakes region, Meredith's sprawling, classy **Inns at Mills Falls,** 312 Daniel Webster Hwy. (© **800/622-6455**), is expanding—again. The new Church Landing facility opens in 2004 with 58 luxury rooms and suites in Adirondack style, fitted into a converted church right on the lakeshore. The facility will also incorporate a conference center and upscale health club.

Finally, the White Mountains' **Bretton Woods Resort,** Route 302, Bretton Woods (© **800/258-3320**), has added Olympic medalist Bode Miller to its ski facility's staff, tapping Miller to be director of skiing. A new section of runs at the resort known as Rosebrook features "Bode's Run," an expert trail partly designed by Miller.

MAINE On the southern coast of Maine, Peter and Kate Morency have renovated and updated the former Seascapes fine-dining restaurant in Cape Porpoise; it's now known as the **Pier 77 Restaurant,** 77 Pier Rd. (© **207/967-8500**), but still serves a Continental menu.

In 2003, Kennebunk's esteemed **White Barn Inn,** 37 Beach Ave. (© **207/967-2321**), acquired a handful

of cottages on the tidal Kennebunk River, a bit down the road from the main inn, and will shortly be developing a wharf on that site to encourage boating interests. The cottages are cozy, nicely equipped with modern kitchens and bathrooms, and will continue to see future upgrades. The inn's restaurant was recently selected as one of America's top inn restaurants by readers of *Travel + Leisure* magazine.

Two major hotels cut their ribbons in Portland's Old Port section in 2003. The luxury **Portland Harbor Hotel,** 468 Fore St. (© **888/798-9090**), based around a central garden and in the heart of the neighborhood's dining and nightlife, offers top-of-the-line accommodations and services. And the Hilton chain unveiled a new waterfront **Hilton Garden Inn,** 65 Commercial St. (© **207/780-0780**), across from the city's ferry dock.

There's hotel news in Bar Harbor, too. Converted from a family-style motel into luxury waterside accommodations, the **Harborside Hotel & Marina,** 55 West St. (© **800/328-5033**), features whale-watching, a lobster restaurant, and stunning ocean views from the dining room and many of the luxury rooms.

The popular Bar Harbor B&B **Sunset on West,** however, has been sold and is now a private residence.

Also in Bar Harbor, the **Abbe Museum**—Maine's largest Native American museum—has created a new year-round annex (© **207/288-3519**) at 26 Mt. Desert St., in the heart of downtown, greatly adding to its exhibit space and accessibility. The original museum location, inside Acadia National Park, also remains open from May to October.

The Best of New England

One of the greatest challenges of traveling in New England is choosing from an abundance of superb restaurants, accommodations, and attractions. Where to start? Here's an entirely biased list of our favorite destinations and experiences. Over years of traveling through the region, we've discovered that these are places worth more than just a quick stop—they're all worth a major detour.

1 The Best of Small-Town New England

- **Marblehead** (Mass.): The "Yachting Capital of America" has major picture-postcard potential, especially in summer, when the harbor fills with boats of all sizes. From downtown, a short distance inland, make your way toward the water down the narrow, flower-dotted streets. The first glimpse of blue sea and sky is breathtaking. See "Marblehead," in chapter 5.

- **Chatham** (Cape Cod, Mass.): Located on the "elbow" of the Cape, Chatham is proof that Main Street, U.S.A, is alive and well. Families throng here to enjoy the beach and to browse through shops brimming with upscale gifts. In summer, visitors and locals gather every Friday night for festive outdoor concerts, while the looming Chatham Lighthouse, built in 1828, keeps a close eye on the Atlantic. See "The Lower Cape," in chapter 6.

- **Edgartown** (Martha's Vineyard, Mass.): For many visitors, Edgartown *is* Martha's Vineyard, its regal captains' houses and manicured lawns a symbol of a more refined way of life. The old-fashioned Fourth of July parade harks back to small-town America, as hundreds line Main Street cheering the loudest for the floats with the most heart. See "Martha's Vineyard," in chapter 7.

- **Oak Bluffs** (Martha's Vineyard, Mass.): Stroll down Circuit Avenue in Oak Bluffs with a Mad Martha's ice-cream cone and then ride the Flying Horses Carousel. This island harbor town is full of fun for kids and parents. Don't miss the colorful "gingerbread" cottages behind Circuit Avenue. Oak Bluffs also has great beaches, bike paths, and the Vineyard's best nightlife. See "Martha's Vineyard," in chapter 7.

- **Stockbridge** (Mass.): Norman Rockwell made a famous painting of the main street of this, his adopted hometown. Facing south, it uses the southern Berkshires as backdrop for the sprawl of the Red Lion Inn and the other late-19th-century buildings that make up the commercial district. Then as now, they service a beguiling mix of unassuming saltboxes and Gilded Age mansions that have sheltered farmers, artists, and aristocrats since the days of the French and Indian Wars. See "The Berkshires," in chapter 8.

- **Washington** (Conn.): A classic, with a Congregational church facing a village green surrounded by clapboard colonial houses—all of

New England

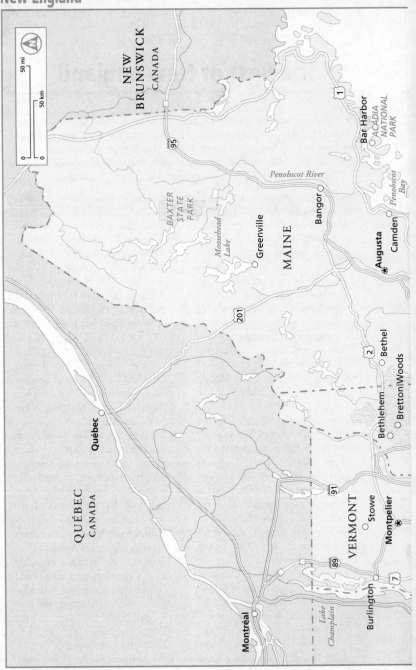

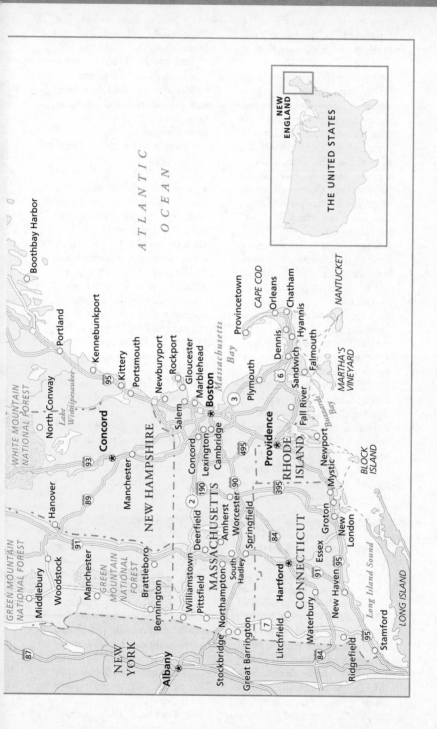

them with black shutters. See "The Litchfield Hills," in chapter 9.

- **Essex** (Conn.): A widely circulated survey voted Essex tops on its list of the 100 best towns in the United States. That judgment is largely statistical, but a walk past white-clapboard houses on this unspoiled waterfront on this active stretch of the Connecticut River rings all the bells. There is not an artificial note, a cookie-cutter franchise, nor a costumed docent to muddy its near-perfect image. See "The Connecticut River Valley," in chapter 9.

- **Grafton** (Vt.): Grafton was once a down-at-the-heels mountain town slowly being reclaimed by termites and the elements. A wealthy family took it on as a pet project, and has lovingly restored the village to its former self—even burying the electric lines to reclaim the landscape. It doesn't feel like a living-history museum; it just feels right. See "Brattleboro & the Southern Green Mountains," in chapter 11.

- **Woodstock** (Vt.): Woodstock has a stunning village green, a whole range of 19th-century homes, woodland walks leading just out of town, and a settled, old-money air. This is a good place to explore on foot or by bike, or to just sit and watch summer unfold. See "Woodstock," in chapter 11.

- **Montpelier** (Vt.): This is the way all state capitals should be: slow-paced, small enough so you can walk everywhere, and full of shops that still sell nails and strapping tape. Montpelier also shows a more sophisticated edge, with its Culinary Institute, an art house movie theater, and several fine bookshops. But at heart it's a small town, where you just might run into the governor at the corner store. See "Exploring Montpelier & Barre," in chapter 11.

- **Hanover** (N.H.): It's the perfect college town: the handsome brick buildings of Dartmouth College, a tidy green, a small but select shopping district, and a scattering of good restaurants. Come in the fall and you'll be tempted to join in the touch football game on the green. See "Hanover & Environs," in chapter 12.

- **Castine** (Maine): Soaring elm trees, a peaceful harborside setting, plenty of grand historic homes, and a few good inns make this a great spot to soak up some of Maine's coastal ambience off the beaten path. See "The Blue Hill Peninsula," in chapter 13.

2 The Best Places to See Fall Foliage

- **Walden Pond State Reservation** (Concord, Mass.): Walden Pond is hidden from the road by the woods where Henry David Thoreau built a small cabin and lived from 1845 to 1847. When the leaves are turning and the trees are reflected in the water, it's hard to imagine why he left. See p. 155.

- **Bash-Bish Falls State Park** (Mass.): Head from the comely village of South Egremont up into the forested hills of the southwest corner of Massachusetts. The roads, which change from macadam to gravel to dirt and back, wind between crimson clouds of sugar maples and white birches feather-stroked against banks of black evergreens. The payoff is a three-state view from a promontory above a 50-foot cascade notched into a bluff, with carpets of russet and gold stretching all the way to the Hudson River. See p. 327.

- **The Litchfield Hills** (Conn.): Route 7, running south to north through the rugged northwest corner of Connecticut, roughly along the course of the Housatonic River, explodes with color in the weeks before and after Columbus Day. Leaves drift down to the water and whirl down the foaming river. See "The Litchfield Hills," in chapter 9.

- **I-91** (Vt.): An interstate? Don't scoff (the traffic can be terrible on narrow state roads). If you like your foliage viewing wholesale, cruise I-91 from Brattleboro to Newport. You'll be overwhelmed with gorgeous terrain, from the gentle Connecticut River Valley to the sloping hills of the Northeast Kingdom. See chapter 11.

- **Route 100** (Vt.): Route 100 winds the length of Vermont from Readsboro to Newport. It's the major north-south route through the center of the Green Mountains, and it's surprisingly undeveloped along most of its length.

You won't have it to yourself along the southern stretches on autumn weekends, but as you head farther north, you'll leave the crowds behind. See chapter 11.

- **Crawford Notch** (N.H.): Route 302 passes through this scenic valley, where you can see the brilliant red maples and yellow birches high on the hillsides. In fall, Mount Washington, in the background, is likely to be dusted with an early snow. See "The White Mountains," in chapter 12.

- **Camden** (Maine): The dazzling fall colors that cover the rolling hills are reflected in Penobscot Bay on the east side, and in the lakes on the west. Ascend the peaks for views out to the color-splashed islands in the bay. Autumn usually comes a week or so later on the coast, so you can stretch out your viewing pleasure. See "Penobscot Bay," in chapter 13.

3 The Best Ways to View Coastal Scenery

- **Strolling Around Rockport** (Mass.): The town surrounds the small harbor and spreads out along the rugged, rocky coastline of Cape Ann. From the end of Bearskin Neck, the view is spectacular—fishing and pleasure boats in one direction, roaring surf in the other. See "Cape Ann," in chapter 5.

- **Getting Back to Nature on Plum Island** (Mass.): The Parker River National Wildlife Refuge, in Newburyport, offers two varieties of coastal scenery: picturesque salt marshes packed with birds and other animals, and gorgeous ocean beaches where the power of the Atlantic is evident. See "Newburyport, Ipswich & Plum Island," in chapter 5.

- **Biking or Driving the Outer Cape** (Mass.): From Eastham

through Wellfleet and Truro, all the way to Provincetown, Cape Cod's outermost towns offer dazzling ocean vistas and a number of exceptional bike paths, including the Province Lands, just outside Provincetown, that are bordered by spectacular swooping dunes. See "The Outer Cape," in chapter 6.

- **Heading "Up-Island" on Martha's Vineyard** (Mass.): Many visitors never venture beyond the port towns of Vineyard Haven, Oak Bluffs, and Edgartown. Though each has its charms, the scenery actually gets more spectacular "up-island," in towns like Chilmark, where you'll pass moorlike meadows and family farms surrounded by stone walls. Follow State Road and the scenic Moshup Trail to the westernmost tip of the island, where you'll experience the dazzling colored cliffs of Aquinnah and the quaint fishing port of Menemsha. See "Martha's Vineyard," in chapter 7.

- **Cruising Newport's Ocean Drive** (R.I.): After a tour of the fabulously overwrought "cottages" of the hyper-rich that are strung along Bellevue Avenue, emerging onto the shoreline road that dodges the spray of the boiling Atlantic is a cleansing reminder of the power of nature over fragile monuments to the conceits of men. To extend the experience, take a 3½-mile hike along the Cliff Walk that skirts the edge of the bluff commanded by the largest mansions. See "Newport," in chapter 10.
- **Sitting in a Rocking Chair** (Maine): The views are never better than when you're caught unawares—such as suddenly looking up from an engrossing book on the front porch of an oceanside inn. Throughout the Maine chapter, look for mention of inns right on the water, such as Black Point Inn (p. 596), Grey Havens (p. 606), Samoset Resort (p. 619),

Inn on the Harbor (p. 629), and the Claremont (p. 649).
- **Hiking Monhegan Island** (Maine): The village of Monhegan is clustered around the harbor, but the rest of this 700-acre island is all picturesque wildlands, with miles of trails crossing open meadows and winding along rocky bluffs. See "Mid–Coast Maine," in chapter 13.
- **Driving the Park Loop Road at Acadia National Park** (Maine): This is the region's premier ocean drive. You'll start high along a ridge with views of Frenchman Bay and the Porcupine Islands, then dip down along the rocky shores to watch the surf crash against the dark rocks. Plan to do this 20-mile loop at least twice to get the most out of it. See p. 634.
- **Cruising on a Windjammer** (Maine): See Maine as it was first seen for centuries—from the ocean looking inland. A handsome fleet of sailing ships departs from various harbors along the coast, particularly Rockland and Camden. Spend from a night to a week exploring the dramatic shoreline. See p. 618.

4 The Best Places to Rediscover America's Past

- **Paul Revere House** (Boston, Mass.): We often study the history of the American Revolution through stories of governments and institutions. At this little home in the North End, you'll learn about a real person. The self-guided tour is particularly thought provoking, allowing you to linger on the artifacts that hold your interest. Revere had 16 children with two wives, supported them with his thriving silversmith's trade—and put the whole operation in jeopardy with his role in the events that led to the Revolutionary War. See p. 123.
- **Old State House** (Boston, Mass.): Built in 1713, the once-towering Old State House is dwarfed by modern skyscrapers. It stands as a reminder of British rule (the exterior features a lion and a unicorn) and its overthrow—the Declaration of Independence was read from the balcony, which overlooks a traffic island where a circle of bricks represents the site of the Boston Massacre. See p. 122.
- **Faneuil Hall** (Boston, Mass.): Although Faneuil Hall is best known nowadays as a shopping destination, if you head upstairs, you'll be transported back in time.

In the second-floor auditorium, park rangers talk about the building's role in the Revolution. Tune out the sound of sneakers squeaking across the floor, and you can almost hear Samuel Adams (his statue is out front) exhorting the Sons of Liberty. See p. 123.

- **"Old Ironsides"** (Boston, Mass.): Formally named the USS *Constitution,* the frigate was launched in 1797 and made a name for itself battling Barbary pirates and seeing action in the War of 1812. Last used in battle in 1815, it was periodically threatened with destruction until a complete renovation in the late 1920s started its career as a floating monument. The staff includes sailors on active duty who wear 1812 dress uniforms. See p. 123.

- **North Bridge** (Concord, Mass.): British troops headed to Concord after putting down the uprising in Lexington, and the bridge (a replica) stands as a testament to the Minutemen who fought here. The Concord River and its peaceful green banks give no hint of the bloodshed that took place. On the path in from Monument Street, placards and audio stations provide a fascinating narrative. See "Concord," in chapter 5.

- **Plymouth Rock** (Plymouth, Mass.): Okay, it's a fraction of its original size and looks like something you might find in your garden. Nevertheless, Plymouth Rock makes a perfect starting point for exploration. Close by is the *Mayflower II,* a replica of the alarmingly small original vessel. The juxtaposition reminds you of what a dangerous undertaking the Pilgrims' voyage was. See "Plymouth," in chapter 5.

- **Sandwich** (Mass.): The oldest town on Cape Cod, Sandwich was founded in 1637. Glassmaking brought notoriety and prosperity to this picturesque town in the 19th century. Visit the Sandwich Glass Museum for the whole story, or tour one of the town's glassblowing studios. Don't leave without visiting the 76-acre Heritage Museums and Gardens, which has a working carousel, a sparkling antique-car collection, and a wonderful collection of Americana. See "The Upper Cape," in chapter 6.

- **Nantucket** (Mass): It looks like the whalers just left, leaving behind their grand houses, cobbled streets, and a gamut of enticing shops offering luxury goods from around the world. The Nantucket Historical Association owns more than a dozen properties open for tours, and the Whaling Museum is one of the most fascinating sites in the region. Tourism may be rampant, but not its tackier side effects, thanks to stringent preservation measures. See "Nantucket," in chapter 7.

- **Deerfield** (Mass.): Arguably the best-preserved colonial village in New England, Deerfield has scores of houses dating back to the 17th and 18th centuries. None of the clutter of modernity has intruded here. Fourteen houses on the main avenue can be visited through tours conducted by the organization known as Historic Deerfield. See "The Pioneer Valley," in chapter 8.

- **Newport** (R.I.): A key port of the clipper trade long before the British surrendered their colony, Newport retains abundant recollections of its maritime past. In addition to its great harbor, clogged with cigarette boats, tugs, ferries, and majestic sloops, the City by the Sea has kept three distinctive enclaves preserved: the waterside homes of colonial seamen, the hillside Federal houses of port-bound merchants, and the ostentatious mansions of America's post–Civil War industrial and financial grandees. See "Newport," in chapter 10.

- **Plymouth** (Vt.): President Calvin Coolidge was born in this high upland valley, and the state has done a superb job preserving his hometown village. You'll get a good sense of the president's roots, but also gain a greater understanding of how a New England village works. See p. 487.

- **Shelburne Museum** (Shelburne, Vt.): Think of this sprawling museum as New England's attic. Located on the shores of Lake Champlain, the Shelburne features not only the usual exhibits of quilts and early glass, but also whole buildings preserved like specimens in formaldehyde. Look for the lighthouse, the railroad station, and the stagecoach inn. This is one of northern New England's "don't miss" destinations. See p. 518.

- **Portsmouth** (N.H.): Portsmouth is a salty coastal city that just happens to boast some of the most impressive historic homes in New England. Start at Strawbery Banke, a historic compound of 42 buildings dating from 1695 to 1820. Then visit the many other grand homes in nearby neighborhoods, like the house John Paul Jones occupied while building his warship during the Revolution. See "Portsmouth & the Sea Coast," in chapter 12.

- **Victoria Mansion** (Portland, Maine): Donald Trump had nothing on the Victorians when it came to excess. You'll see Victorian decorative arts at their zenith in this Italianate mansion built during the Civil War years by a prosperous hotelier. It's open to the public for tours in summer and also puts on outstanding Christmas-season programs in December. See p. 594.

5 The Best Literary Landmarks

- **Concord** (Mass.): Concord is home to a legion of literary ghosts. The homes of Ralph Waldo Emerson, Nathaniel Hawthorne, Henry David Thoreau, and Louisa May Alcott are popular destinations, and look much as they did during the "flowering of New England" in the mid–19th century. See "Concord," in chapter 5.

- **Salem** (Mass.): Native son Nathaniel Hawthorne might still feel at home here. A hotel and a boulevard bear his name, the Custom House where he reputedly found an embroidered scarlet "A" still stands, and his birthplace is open for tours. It has been moved into the same complex as the House of the Seven Gables, a cousin's home that inspired the classic novel. See "Salem," in chapter 5.

- **The Outer Cape** (Mass.): In the late 19th and early 20th centuries, the communities at the far end of the Cape—Wellfleet, Truro, and particularly Provincetown—were a veritable headquarters of Bohemia. Henry David Thoreau walked the 28 miles from Eastham to Provincetown and wrote about it in *Cape Cod*. Distinguished literati such as Edna St. Vincent Millay, Mary McCarthy, Edmund Wilson, Tennessee Williams, Norman Mailer, and many others have also taken refuge among the dunes here. See "The Outer Cape," in chapter 6.

- **The Frost Place** (Franconia Notch, N.H.): Two of the most famous New England poems—"The Road Not Taken" and "Stopping by Woods on a Snowy Evening"—were composed by Robert Frost at this farm just outside of Franconia. Explore the woods and read the verses posted along the pathways, then tour the farmhouse where Frost lived with his family. See p. 574.

- **The Mark Twain House** (Hartford, Conn.): This house is a memorable example of the Victorian Gothic style. Sam Clemens lived in these 19 rooms from 1874 and 1891, and though he complained of persistent money problems, it contains stained glass panels by Louis Comfort Tiffany and one of the first telephones. (Twain loved gadgets, and was said to be the author of the first novel written on a typewriter.) See p. 382.

6 The Best Activities for Families

- **Exploring the Museum of Fine Arts** (Boston, Mass.): Parents hear "magnificent Egyptian collections," but kids think: "Mummies!" Even the most hyper youngster manages to take it down a notch in these quiet, refined surroundings, and the collections at the MFA simultaneously tickle visitors' brains. See p. 119.

- **Visiting the Museum of Science** (Boston, Mass.): Built around demonstrations, experiments, and interactive displays that never feel like homework, this museum is wildly popular with kids—and adults. Explore the exhibits, and then take in a show at the planetarium or the Mugar Omni Theater. Before you know it, everyone will have learned something, painlessly. See p. 120.

- **Catching a Free Friday Flick at the Hatch Shell** (Boston, Mass.): Better known for the Boston Pops's Fourth of July concert, the Esplanade is also famous for family films (like *The Wizard of Oz* or *Pocahontas*) shown on Friday nights in summer. The lawn in front of the Hatch Shell turns into a giant, carless drive-in as hundreds of people picnic and wait for dark. See p. 138.

- **Visiting the Heritage Museums and Gardens** (Cape Cod, Mass.): This site with museum buildings spread over 76 acres will delight both children and adults. Kids will especially love the gleaming antique cars, the collections of soldiers and Native American clothing, and the 1912 carousel that offers unlimited rides. Outdoor concerts free with admission take place most Sunday afternoons in season. See p. 197.

- **Whale-Watching off Provincetown** (Cape Cod, Mass.): Boats leave MacMillan Wharf for the 8-mile journey to Stellwagen Bank National Marine Sanctuary, a rich feeding ground for several types of whales. Nothing can prepare you for the thrill of spotting these magnificent creatures feeding, breaching, and even flipper slapping. The best outfit in town is the *Dolphin* Fleet (© 800/826-9300), which is affiliated with the Center for Coastal Studies. See p. 249.

- **Deep-Sea Fishing:** Charter fishing boats these days usually have high-tech fish-finding gear—imagine how your kids will react to reeling in one big bluefish after another. The top spots to mount such an expedition are Barnstable Harbor or Rock Harbor in Orleans, on Cape Cod; Point Judith, at the southern tip of Rhode Island; and the Maine coast. See chapters 6, 10, and 13, respectively.

- **Riding the Flying Horses Carousel in Oak Bluffs** (Martha's Vineyard, Mass.): Some say this is the oldest carousel in the country, but your kids might not notice the genuine horsehair, sculptural details, or glass eyes. They'll be too busy trying to grab the brass ring to win a free ride. After your ride, stroll around the town of Oak Bluffs. Children will be enchanted with the "gingerbread" houses, a carryover from the 19th-century revivalist movement. See p. 274.

- **Biking Nantucket** (Mass.): Short, flat trails crisscross the island, and every one leads to a beach. The shortest rides lead to Children's Beach, with its own playground, and Jetties Beach, with a skate park and watersports equipment for rent; older kids will be able to make the few miles to Surfside and Madaket. See "Nantucket," in chapter 7.

- **Learning to Ski at Jiminy Peak** (Mass.): More than 70% of Jiminy Peak's trails are geared toward beginners and intermediates, making it one of the premier places to learn to ski in the East. The mountain is located in the heart of the Berkshires, near Mount Greylock. See p. 346.

- **Visiting Mystic Seaport and Mystic Aquarium** (Conn.): The double-down winner in the family-fun sweepstakes has to be this combination: performing dolphins and whales, full-rigged tall ships, penguins and sharks, and river rides on a perky little 1906 motor launch. These are the kinds of G-rated attractions that have no age barriers. See p. 397.

- **Exploring the Lake Champlain Bikeway** (Burlington, Vt.): A lovely bike path follows the shores of the lake on an abandoned railbed. Efforts to link up this trail with others to the north include two new bike ferries that span rivers and causeway gaps. Lakeshore beaches and leafy parks dot the route. See p. 519.

- **Visiting the Montshire Museum of Science** (Norwich, Vt.): This handsome children's museum, in a soaring, barnlike space on the Vermont–New Hampshire border, has interactive exhibits that put the wonder back into science. Afterward, stroll the nature trails along the Connecticut River. See p. 483.

- **Riding the Mount Washington Cog Railway** (Crawford Notch, N.H.): It's fun! It's terrifying! It's a great glimpse into history. Kids love this ratchety climb to the top of New England's highest peak aboard trains that were specially designed to scale the mountain in 1869. As a technological marvel, the railroad attracted tourists by the thousands a century ago. They still come to marvel at the sheer audacity of it all. See p. 567.

- **Exploring Monhegan Island** (Maine): Kids from 8 to 12 especially enjoy overnight excursions to Monhegan Island. The mailboat from Port Clyde is rustic and intriguing, and the hotels are an adventure. Leave at least an afternoon to sit atop the high, rocky bluffs scouting the glimmering ocean for whales. See "The Mid-Coast Maine," in chapter 13.

7 The Best Country Inns

- **Hawthorne Inn** (Concord, Mass.; ⓒ **978/369-5610**): Everything here—the 1870 building, the garden setting a stone's throw from the historic attractions, the antiques, the eclectic decorations, the accommodating innkeepers—is top of the line. See p. 156.

- **Longfellow's Wayside Inn** (Sudbury, Mass.; ☎ **800/339-1776**): A gorgeous inn, an unusual setting, excellent food, the imprimatur of a distinguished New England author, nearly 300 years of history, and the schoolhouse the little lamb followed Mary to. What's not to like? See p. 157.

- **Captain's House Inn** (Chatham, Cape Cod, Mass.; ☎ **800/315-0728**): An elegant country inn dripping with good taste, this is among the best small inns in the region. Most rooms have fireplaces, elegant paneling, and antiques; they're sumptuous yet cozy. This could be the ultimate spot to enjoy Chatham's Christmas Stroll festivities. See p. 231.

- **Charlotte Inn** (Edgartown, Martha's Vineyard, Mass.; ☎ **508/627-4751**): Edgartown tends to be the most formal enclave on Martha's Vineyard, and this compound of exquisite buildings is by far the fanciest address in town. The rooms are distinctively decorated: One boasts a baby grand, another its own thematic dressing room. The conservatory restaurant, **L'étoile**, is among the finest you'll find this side of France. See p. 276.

- **Mayflower Inn** (Washington, Conn.; ☎ **860/868-9466**): Not a tough call at all for this part of the region: Immaculate in taste and execution, the Mayflower is as close to perfection as any such enterprise is likely to be (points off for whiffs of excess pretension). A genuine Joshua Reynolds hangs in the hall. See p. 367.

- **Griswold Inn** (Essex, Conn.; ☎ **860/767-1776**): "The Griz" has been accommodating sailors and travelers as long as any inn in the country, give or take a decade. In all that time, it has been a part of life and commerce in the lower Connecticut River Valley, always ready with a mug of suds, a haunch of beef, and a roaring fire. The walls are layered with nautical paintings and memorabilia, and there's music every night in the schoolhouse-turned-tavern. See p. 389.

- **The Equinox** (Manchester Village, Vt.; ☎ **800/362-4747**): This is southern Vermont's grand resort, with nearly 200 rooms in a white-clapboard compound that seems to go on forever. The rooms are pleasant enough, but the real draws are the grounds and the resort's varied activities—it's set on 2,300 acres with pools, tennis courts, an 18-hole golf course, and even its own mountainside. Tried everything on vacation? How about falconry classes or backcountry driving at the Range Rover school? See p. 467.

- **Windham Hill Inn** (West Townshend, Vt.; ☎ **800/944-4080**): Welcome amenities such as air-conditioning in the rooms and a conference room in the barn have been added, while preserving the charm of this 1823 farmstead. It's at the end of a remote dirt road in a high upland valley, and guests are welcome to explore 160 private acres on a network of walking trails. See p. 475.

- **Jackson House Inn** (Woodstock, Vt.; ☎ **800/448-1890**): Constant improvements and the meticulous attention to service have made this a longtime favorite for visitors to Woodstock. The meals are stunning, the guest rooms the very picture of antique elegance. The only downside? It fronts a sometimes noisy road. See p. 479.

- **Twin Farms** (Barnard, Vt.; ☎ **800/894-6327**): Just north of Woodstock may be the most elegant inn in New England. Its rates are a tad breathtaking, but guests are certainly pampered here. Novelist Sinclair Lewis once lived on this 300-acre farm, and today it's an aesthetic retreat that offers serenity and exceptional food. See p. 481.

- **The Pitcher Inn** (Warren, Vt.; ℂ 888/867-8424): Even though this place was built in 1997, it's possessed of the graciousness of a longtime, well-worn inn. It combines traditional New England form and scale with modern and luxe touches, plus a good dollop of whimsy. See p. 500.

- **Basin Harbor Club** (Vergennes, Vt.; ℂ 800/622-4000): Established in 1886, this lakeside resort has the sort of patina that only comes with age. It's a classic old-fashioned family resort, with golf, boating on Lake Champlain, jackets-required dining, evening lectures on the arts, and even a private airstrip. Bring books and board games, and re-learn what summer's all about. See p. 520.

- **Balsams Grand Resort Hotel** (Dixville Notch, N.H.; ℂ 800/255-0600): The designation "country inn" is only half correct.

You've got plenty of country—it's set on 15,000 acres in northern New Hampshire. But this resort is more castle than inn. The Balsams has been offering superb hospitality and gracious comfort since 1866. It has two golf courses, miles of hiking trails, and, in winter, its own downhill and cross-country ski areas. See p. 578.

- **White Barn Inn** (Kennebunkport, Maine; ℂ 207/967-2321): Many of the White Barn's staff hail from Europe, and guests are treated with a Continental graciousness that's hard to match. Rooms, suites, and cottages here are all a delight, and the meals (served in the barn) are among the best in Maine. See p. 589.

- **The Claremont** (Southwest Harbor, Maine; ℂ 800/244-5036): The 1884 Claremont is a Maine classic. This waterside lodge has everything a Victorian resort should, including sparely decorated rooms, creaky floorboards in the halls, great views of water and mountains, and a perfect croquet pitch. See p. 649.

8 The Best Moderately Priced Accommodations

- **Newbury Guest House** (Boston, Mass.; ℂ 800/437-7668) and **Harborside Inn** (Boston, Mass.; ℂ 888/723-7565): These sister properties would be good deals even if they weren't ideally located—the former in the Back Bay, the latter downtown. Rates at the Guest House even include breakfast. See p. 99 and p. 93.

- **Harvard Square Hotel** (Cambridge, Mass.; ℂ 800/458-5886): Smack in the middle of Cambridge's most popular destination, this hotel is a comfortable place to stay in a great location. See p. 104.

- **Pilgrim Sands Motel** (Plymouth, Mass.; ℂ 800/729-7263): The

ocean views and two pools (indoor and outdoor) make this a great deal, whether you're immersing yourself in Pilgrim lore or passing through on the way from Boston to Cape Cod. See p. 192.

- **Isaiah Hall B&B Inn** (Dennis, Cape Cod, Mass.; ℂ 800/736-0160): Nestled amid oak trees in Dennis, this B&B has been welcoming visitors for more than 50 years. The inn and its gregarious owner are popular with actors starring in summer stock at the nearby Cape Playhouse. Guests enjoy country-cozy rooms and a communal breakfast. See p. 220.

- **Nauset House Inn** (East Orleans, Cape Cod, Mass.; © 508/255-2195): This romantic 1810 farmhouse is like a sepia-toned vision of old Cape Cod. Recline in a wicker divan surrounded by fragrant flowers while the wind whistles outside. Better yet, stroll to Nauset Beach and take a quiet walk as the sun sets. Your genial hosts also prepare one of the finest breakfasts in town. See p. 336.
- **Hopkins Inn** (New Preston, Conn.; © 860/868-7295): This yellow farmhouse bestows the top view of Lake Waramaug, at its best on soft summer days when robust Alpine dishes can be taken out on the terrace. The somewhat spartan rooms don't tempt winding-down guests with either phones or TVs. See p. 368.
- **Bee and Thistle Inn** (Old Lyme, Conn.; © 800/622-4946): Known for decades for its cuisine, this 1756 house also has a detached cottage and 11 pretty guest rooms, two of which have fireplaces. Easily one of the area's most romantic weekend getaways, there are musicians underscoring the mood in the dining rooms on weekends. See p. 388.
- **Inn at the Mad River Barn** (Waitsfield, Vt.; © 800/631-0466): It takes a few minutes to adapt to the spartan rooms and no-frills accommodations here. But you'll soon discover that the real action takes place in the living room and dining room, where skiers relax and chat after a day on the slopes, and share heaping helpings at mealtime. See p. 499.
- **Thayers Inn** (Littleton, N.H.; © 800/634-8179): This old-fashioned downtown inn has 48 eclectic rooms and a whole lot of relaxed charm. Ulysses S. Grant and Richard Nixon slept here, among others. Rooms start at just $45 if you're willing to share a bathroom; from $65 for a private bathroom. See p. 577.
- **Philbrook Farm Inn** (Shelburne, N.H.; © 603/466-3831): Come here if you're looking for a complete getaway. The inn has been taking in travelers since the 1850s, and the owners know how to do it right. The farmhouse sits on 1,000 acres between the Mahoosuc Mountains and the Androscoggin River, and guests can hike or relax with equal aplomb. See p. 578.
- **Franciscan Guest House** (Kennebunk, Maine; © 207/967-4865): No daily maid service, cheap paneling on the walls, and industrial carpeting. What's to like? Plenty, including the location (on the lush riverside grounds of a monastery), price (doubles from $65), and a great Lithuanian-style breakfast spread in the morning. You can bike to the beach or walk to Dock Square in Kennebunkport. See p. 588.
- **Driftwood Inn & Cottages** (Bailey Island, Maine; © 207/833-5461): Where else can you find rooms at the edge of the rocky Maine coast for $80? This classic shingled compound dates from 1910 and mostly offers rooms with shared bathrooms—but it's worth that small inconvenience for the views alone. See p. 605.

9 The Best Restaurants

- **Legal Sea Foods** (Boston, Mass., and other locations; © 617/266-6800): Newcomers ask where to go for fresh seafood, then react suspiciously when I recommend a world famous restaurant instead of a local secret. No, it's no secret—but it's a wildly successful chain for a reason. See p. 112.

- **Rialto** (Cambridge, Mass.; ℰ **617/661-5050**): This is a don't-miss destination if your plans include fine dining. The contemporary setting is a great match for chef Jody Adams's inventive cuisine, and the service is efficient without being too familiar—surely a draw for the visiting celebrities who flock here. See p. 113.

- **Chester** (Provincetown, Cape Cod, Mass.; ℰ **508/487-8200**): A singular dining experience awaits beyond the colonnaded portico of this Commercial Street restaurant. Chester specializes in local seafood, meats, and vegetables prepared simply yet with a flourish, and the service is exceptional. See p. 254.

- **L'étoile** (Edgartown, Martha's Vineyard, Mass.; ℰ **508/627-5187**): The most exemplary dining experience on Martha's Vineyard can be found in this exquisite conservatory at the Charlotte Inn. The nouvelle cuisine offerings vary seasonally, but the chef consistently dazzles with a menu of delicacies flown in from everywhere. See p. 284.

- **Òran Mór** (Nantucket, Mass.; ℰ **508/228-8655**): Climb up the stairs of this historic building and prepare yourself for an extravagant dining experience. Chef/owner Peter Wallace has created an intimate setting for his creative international cuisine, served with utmost professionalism. The best sommelier on the island will assist you in choosing a wine to go with your elegant meal. See p. 302.

- **Truc Orient Express** (West Stockbridge, Mass.; ℰ **413/232-4204**): The artists who live in this funky Berkshires hamlet like to seek out something outside the prevailing red-sauce and red meat modes. They find it in this converted warehouse, with eye-opening Thai, Vietnamese, and Southeast Asian dishes that rarely emerge from kitchens this far west of Ho Chi Minh City. Tastes range from delicate to sinus-clearing. See p. 335.

- **Union League Café** (New Haven, Conn.; ℰ **203/562-4299**): This august setting of arched windows and high ceilings is more than a century old and was long the sanctuary of an exclusive club. It still looks good, but the tone has been lightened into an approximation of a Lyonnaise brasserie. The menu observes the southern French tastes for curry, olive oil, pastas, lamb, and shellfish. See p. 378.

- **Scales & Shells** (Newport, R.I.; ℰ **401/846-3474**): Ye who turn aside all ostentation, get yourselves hence. There's nary a frill nor affectation anywhere near this place, and because the wide-open kitchen is right at the entrance, there are no secrets, either. What we have here are marine critters mere hours from the depths, prepared and presented free of any but the slightest artifice. This might well be the purest seafood joint on the southern New England coast. See p. 440.

- **Chantecleer** (Manchester Center, Vt.; ℰ **802/362-1616**): Swiss chef Michel Baumann has been turning out dazzling dinners here since 1981, and the kitchen hasn't gotten stale in the least. The dining room in an old barn is magical, the staff helpful and friendly. It's a great spot for those who demand top-notch Continental fare but don't like the fuss of a fancy restaurant. See p. 469.

- **T. J. Buckley's** (Brattleboro, Vt.; ℰ **802/257-4922**): This tiny diner on a dark side street serves up outsize tastes prepared by talented chef Michael Fuller. Forget about stewed-too-long diner fare; get in your mind big tastes blossoming from the freshest of ingredients prepared just right. See p. 473.

- **Jackson House Inn** (Woodstock, Vt.; *©* **800/448-1890**): Situated in a modern addition to an upscale country inn, the Jackson House Inn serves meals that are ingeniously conceived, deftly prepared, and artfully arranged. The three-course meals cost around $55, and offer excellent value at that. See p. 479.

- **Hemingway's** (Killington, Vt.; *©* **802/422-3886**): Killington seems an unlikely place for a serious culinary adventure, yet Hemingway's will meet the loftiest expectations. The menu changes frequently to ensure only the freshest of ingredients. If it's available, be sure to order the wild mushroom and truffle soup. See p. 491.

- **White Barn Inn** (Kennebunkport, Maine; *©* **207/967-2321**): The setting, in an ancient, rustic barn, is magical. The tables are set with floor-length tablecloths, and the chairs feature imported Italian upholstery. The food? To die for. Start with lobster spring rolls, then enjoy entrees such as roasted duck with juniper sauce or Maine lobster over fettuccine with a cognac coral butter sauce. See p. 589.

- **Fore Street** (Portland, Maine; *©* **207/775-2717**): Fore Street is one of New England's most celebrated restaurants—the place was listed as one of *Gourmet* magazine's 100 best restaurants in 2001, and the chef has been getting lots of press elsewhere as well. His secret? Simplicity, and lots of it. Some of the most memorable meals are prepared over an applewood grill. See p. 598.

10 The Best Local Dining Experiences

- **Durgin-Park** (Boston, Mass.; *©* **617/227-2038**): A meal at this landmark restaurant might start with a waitress dropping a handful of cutlery in front of you and saying, "Here, give these out." The surly service usually seems to be an act, but it's so much a part of the experience that some people are disappointed when the waitresses are nice (as they often are). In any case, it's worked since 1827. See p. 110.

- **Woodman's of Essex** (Essex, Mass.; *©* **800/649-1773**): This busy North Shore institution is not for the faint of heart—or the hard of artery, unless you like eating corn and steamers while everyone around you is gobbling fried clams and onion rings. The food at this glorified clam shack is fresh and delicious, and a look at the

organized pandemonium behind the counter is worth the (reasonable) price. See p. 171.

- **The Bite** (Menemsha, Martha's Vineyard, Mass.; *©* **508/645-9239**): This is your quintessential "chowdah" and clam shack, serving up exceptional chowder, potato salad, and fried fish. Those in the know bring their picnic dinner over to nearby Menemsha Beach, where the sunsets are awesome. See p. 285.

- **Louis' Lunch—The Very First (Well, Probably) Burgers** (New Haven, Conn.; *©* **203/562-5507**): Not a lot of serious history has happened in New Haven, but boosters claim it was here that hamburgers were invented in 1900. This little luncheonette lives on, moved from its original site in order to save it. The patties are freshly ground daily, thrust into vertical grills, and served on white toast. Garnishes are tomato, onion, and cheese. No ketchup and no fries, so don't even ask. See p. 378.

- **Wooster Street Pizza** (New Haven, Conn.): New Haven's claim to America's first pizza is a whole lot shakier, but it has few equals as purveyor of the ultra-thin, charred variety of what they still call "apizza" in these parts, pronounced "ah-peetz." Old-timer **Frank Pepe's,** 157 Wooster St. (© **203/865-5762**), is usually ceded top rank among the local parlors, but it is joined by such contenders as **Sally's,** 237 Wooster St. (© **203/624-5271**) and the upstart brewpub **Brü Rm,** 254 Crown St. (© **203/495-1111**). See p. 378 and 379.

- **Abbott's Lobster in the Rough** (Noank, Conn.; © **860/536-7719**): Places like this frill-free shack abound along more northerly reaches of the New England coast, but here's a little bit o' Maine a Sunday drive from Manhattan. Shore dinners rule, so roll up sleeves, tie on napkins and feedbags, dive into bowls of chowder and platters of boiled shrimp and steamed mussels, and dunk hot lobster chunks in pots of drawn butter. See p. 400.

- **Johnnycakes and Stuffies** (R.I.): Sooner or later, most worthy regional food faves become known to the wider world (witness Buffalo wings). The Ocean State still clutches a couple of taste treats within its borders. "Johnnycakes" are flapjacks made with cornmeal, which come small and plump or wide and lacy, depending upon family tradition. "Stuffies" are the baby-fist-size quahog (*KWAH*-og or *KOE*-hog) clams barely known elsewhere in New England. The flesh is chopped up, combined

with minced bell peppers and breadcrumbs, and packed back into both halves of the shell. See chapter 10.

- **Blue Benn Diner** (Bennington, Vt.; © **802/442-5140**): This 1945 Silk City diner has a barrel ceiling, acres of stainless steel, and a vast menu. Don't overlook specials scrawled on paper and taped all over the walls. And leave room for a slice of delicious pie, such as blackberry, pumpkin, or chocolate cream. See p. 463.

- **Al's** (South Burlington, Vt.; © **802/862-9203**): This is where Ben and Jerry go to eat french fries—as does every other potato addict in the state. See p. 522.

- **Lou's** (Hanover, N.H.; © **603/643-3321**): Huge crowds flock to Lou's, just down the block from the Dartmouth campus, for breakfast on weekends. Fortunately, breakfast is served all day here, and the sandwiches on fresh-baked bread are huge and delicious. See p. 547.

- **Becky's** (Portland, Maine; © **207/773-7070**): Five different kinds of home fries on the menu? It's breakfast nirvana at this local institution on the working waterfront. It's a favored hangout of fishermen, high-school kids, businessmen, and just about everyone else. See p. 600.

- **Silly's** (Portland, Maine; © **207/772-0117**): Hectic and fun, this tiny, informal, kitschy restaurant serves up delicious finger food, like pita wraps, hamburgers, and pizza. The milkshakes alone are worth the detour. See p. 600.

- **Fisherman's Friend** (Stonington, Maine; © **207/367-2442**): This is a lively and boisterous kind of place, where you'll get your fill of both local color and what may be Maine's most succulent lobster stew. See p. 630.

11 The Best of the Performing Arts

- **Symphony Hall** (Boston, Mass.; ℭ 617/266-1492): Home to the Boston Symphony Orchestra, the Boston Pops, and other local and visiting groups and performers, this is a perfect (acoustically and otherwise) destination for classical music. See p. 138.

- **Hatch Shell** (Boston, Mass.; ℭ 617/727-5215): This amphitheater on the Charles River Esplanade plays host to free music and dance performances and films almost every night in summer. Around the Fourth of July, the Boston Pops provide the entertainment. Bring a blanket to sit on. See p. 138.

- **Boston's Theater District:** The area's performance spaces are in the midst of a nearly unprecedented boom, and this is the epicenter. Previews and touring companies of Broadway hits, local music and dance troupes, and other productions of every description make this part of town hop every night. See p. 140.

- *The Nutcracker* (Boston, Mass.; ℭ 617/695-6955 for tickets): New England's premier family-oriented holiday event is Boston Ballet's extravaganza. When the Christmas tree grows through the floor, even fidgety preadolescents forget that they think they're too cool to be here. See p. 139.

- **The Comedy Connection at Faneuil Hall** (Boston, Mass.; ℭ 888/398-5100): Even in the Athens of America, it's not all high culture. The biggest national names and the funniest local comics take the stage at this hot spot. See p. 141.

- **The Berkshire Theatre Festival** (Stockbridge, Mass.; ℭ 413/298-5576): An 1887 "casino" and converted barn mount both new and classic plays from June to late August in one of the prettiest towns in the Berkshires. Name artists on the order of Joanne Woodward and Dianne Wiest are often listed as actors and directors in the annual playbill. See p. 333.

- **The Jacob's Pillow Dance Festival** (Becket, Mass.; ℭ 413/243-0745): Celebrated dancer/choreographer Martha Graham made this her summertime performance space for decades. Guest troupes are among the world's best, often including Dance Theatre of Harlem, the Merce Cunningham Dance Company, and the Paul Taylor Company, supplemented by repertory companies working with jazz, flamenco, or world music. See p. 336.

- **Tanglewood Music Festival** (Lenox, Mass.; ℭ 617/266-1492 in Boston, 413/637-5165 in Lenox): By far the most dominating presence on New England's summer cultural front, the music festival that takes place on this magnificent Berkshires estate is itself in thrall to the Boston Symphony Orchestra (BSO). While the BSO reigns, room is made for such guest soloists as Jessye Norman and Itzhak Perlman as well as practitioners of other forms, from jazz (Dave Brubeck) to folk (James Taylor) and the Boston Pops. See p. 338.

- **The Williamstown Theatre Festival** (Williamstown, Mass.; ℭ 413/597-3400): Classic, new, and avant-garde plays are all presented during the June-through-August season at this venerable festival. There are two stages, one for works by established playwrights, the smaller second venue for less mainstream or experimental plays. There is usually a Broadway headliner on hand; Frank

Langella has been a frequent presence. See p. 350.

- **The Norfolk Chamber Music Festival** (Norfolk, Conn.; © **860/542-3000**): A century-old "Music Shed" on the Ellen Battell Stoeckel Estate in this Litchfield Hills town shelters such important chamber performance groups as the Tokyo String Quartet and the Vermeer Quartet. Young professional musicians perform morning recitals. See p. 373.

- **Summer in Newport** (R.I.): From Memorial Day to Labor Day, only a scheduling misfortune will deny visitors the experience of an outdoor musical event. In calendar order, the highlights (well short of all-inclusive) are the July Newport Music Festival, the August Ben & Jerry's Folk Festival and JVC Jazz Festival, and the Waterfront Irish Festival in September. See p. 426.

12 The Best Destinations for Antiques Hounds

- **Charles Street** (Boston, Mass.): Beacon Hill is one of the city's oldest neighborhoods, and at the foot of the hill is a thoroughfare that's equally steeped in history. Hundreds of years' worth of furniture, collectibles, and accessories jam the shops along its 5 blocks. See p. 82.

- **Main Street, Essex** (Mass.): The treasures on display in this North Shore town run the gamut, from one step above yard sales to one step below nationally televised auctions. Follow Route 133 west of Route 128 through downtown and north almost all the way to the Ipswich border. See "Cape Ann," in chapter 5.

- **Route 6A: The Old King's Highway** (Cape Cod, Mass.): Antiques buffs, as well as architecture and country-road connoisseurs, will have a field day along scenic Route 6A. Designated a Regional Historic District, this former stagecoach route winds through a half dozen charming villages and is lined with scores of antiques shops. The largest concentration is in Brewster, but you'll find good pickings all along this meandering road, from Sandwich to Orleans. See chapter 6.

- **Brimfield Antique and Collectible Shows** (Brimfield, Mass.): This otherwise undistinguished town west of Sturbridge erupts with three monster shows every summer, in mid-May, mid-July, and early September. Upward of 6,000 dealers set up tented and tabletop shops in fields around town. Call © **800/628-8379** for details, and book room reservations far in advance. See p. 310.

- **Sheffield** (Mass.): This southernmost town in the Berkshires is home to at least three dozen dealers in collectibles, Americana, military memorabilia, English furniture of the Georgian period, silverware, and weather vanes . . . even antique birdhouses. Most of them are strung along Route 7, with a worthwhile detour west along Route 23 in South Egremont. See p. 327.

- **Woodbury** (Conn.): More than 30 dealers along Main Street offer a diversity of precious treasures, near-antiques, and simply funky old stuff. American and European furniture and other pieces are most evident, but there are forays into crafts and assorted whimsies as well. Pick up the directory of the Woodbury Antiques Dealers Association, available in most shops. See p. 365.

- **Newfane and Townshend** (Vt.): A handful of delightful antiques shops are hidden in and around these picture-perfect towns. But the real draw is the Sunday flea market, held just off Route 30 north of Newfane, where you never know what might turn up. See p. 474.

- **Portsmouth** (N.H.): Picturesque downtown Portsmouth is home to a half dozen or so antiques stores and some fine used-book shops. For more meaty browsing, head about 25 miles northwest on Route 4 to Northwood, where a dozen good-size shops flank the highway. See "Portsmouth & the Seacoast," in chapter 12.

- **Route 1, Kittery to Scarborough** (Maine): Antiques scavengers delight in this 37-mile stretch of less-than-scenic Route 1. Antiques minimalls and high-class junk shops alike are scattered all along the route, though there's no central antiques zone. See "The Southern Maine Coast," in chapter 13.

2

Planning Your Trip to New England

by Paul Karr

This chapter provides most of the nuts-and-bolts information you'll need before setting off for New England. Browse through this section before you hit the road to ensure you've touched all the bases.

1 The Regions in Brief

BOSTON Oliver Wendell Holmes dubbed Boston the "Hub of the Universe," and the label stuck. Today, "The Hub" is the region's largest and most vibrant city. This alluring metropolis of historic and modern buildings, world-class museums, and top-notch restaurants is an important stop for travelers on any trip to New England.

CAPE COD & THE ISLANDS The ocean is writ large on Cape Cod, a low peninsula with miles of sandy beaches and grassy dunes that whisper in the wind. The carnival-like atmosphere of Provincetown is a draw, as are the genteel charms of Martha's Vineyard and Nantucket, two islands just offshore.

THE PIONEER VALLEY Extending through Massachusetts along the Connecticut River, the area takes its name from the early settlers who arrived here in the 17th century. Among the many picturesque towns is unspoiled Historic Deerfield.

THE BERKSHIRES Massachusetts's rolling hills at the state's western edge are home to historic old estates, graceful villages, and an abundance of festivals and cultural events, including the Tanglewood Music Festival and Jacob's Pillow Dance Festival.

THE LITCHFIELD HILLS The historic northwest corner of Connecticut has sleepy villages, hidden hiking trails, and a surfeit of New England charm—all just a couple of hours from New York City.

THE CONNECTICUT COAST The eastern coast is home to the historic towns of Mystic and New London, where you can get a glimpse of the shipbuilding trade at the Mystic Seaport museum and the Navy submarine base in nearby Groton.

NEWPORT, RHODE ISLAND AREA The lifestyles of the truly rich and famous are on parade in Newport, once home to the likes of the Astors and Vanderbilts. A tour of the oceanfront mansions never fails to astonish.

GREEN MOUNTAINS Extending the length of Vermont from Massachusetts to Canada, this mostly gentle chain of forested hills and low mountains offers great hiking, scenic backroad drives, fantastic inns, and superb bicycling.

WHITE MOUNTAINS Since the mid–19th century, New Hampshire's White Mountains have drawn travelers to its windswept peaks and forests dotted with glacial boulders and clear,

New England's Regions

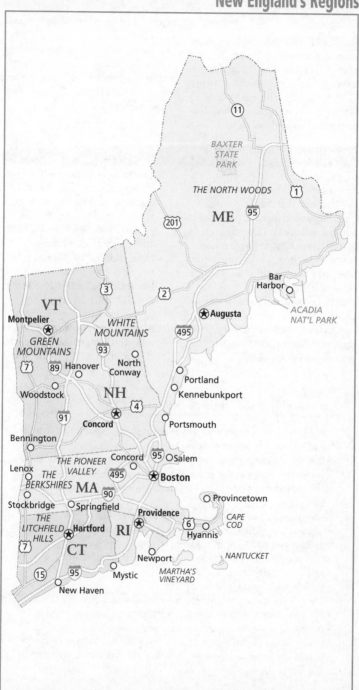

rushing streams. New England's best backcountry hiking and camping are found here.

COASTAL MAINE Maine's rocky coast is the stuff of legend, art, and poetry. The southern coast features most of the state's beaches; farther "Down East," you'll find rocky headlands and Acadia National Park, New England's only national park.

MAINE'S NORTH WOODS Consisting of millions of acres of uninhabited terrain, the North Woods is almost entirely owned by timber companies that harvest trees to feed their mills. Within this vast tree plantation are pockets of undisturbed wildlands that recall the era when Thoreau made his way north.

2 Visitor Information

Chamber addresses and phone numbers are provided for each region in the chapters that follow. If you're a highly organized traveler, you'll call in advance and ask for information to be mailed to you long before you depart. If you're like the rest of us, you'll swing by when you reach town and hope the office is still open.

All six New England states are pleased to send out general visitor information packets and maps to those who call or write ahead. Here's the contact information:

- **Connecticut Office of Tourism,** Department of Economic and Community Development, 505 Hudson St., Hartford, CT 06106 (© **800/282-6863** or 860/270-8080; www.ctbound.com).
- **Maine Office of Tourism,** P.O. #59 State House Station, Augusta, ME 04333 (© **888/624-6345** or 207/287-5711; www.visitmaine. com).
- **Massachusetts Office of Travel and Tourism,** State Transportation Building, 10 Park Plaza,

Destination: New England—Red Alert Checklist

- Did you make sure to book advance reservations for popular tours and restaurants you don't want to miss?
- Did you make sure your favorite attractions are open? Especially if you're traveling early or late in the season, you should call ahead for opening and closing hours if you have your heart set on seeing certain places.
- Do you have a safe, accessible place to store money?
- Did you bring identification that could entitle you to discounts, such as AAA and AARP cards, student IDs, and so on?
- Did you bring emergency drug prescriptions and extra glasses and/or contact lenses?
- Do you have your credit card PINs?
- If you have an E-ticket, do you have documentation?
- Did you leave a copy of your itinerary with someone at home?
- If renting a car, have you checked your insurance and credit card policies to see what's covered? You may be able to save money by declining the extra insurance (collision damage waiver) offered by the rental agency.

Suite 4510, Boston, MA 02116 (© **800/227-6277** or 617/973-8500; www.mass-vacation.com).
- **New Hampshire Division of Travel and Tourism,** 172 Pembroke Rd. (P.O. Box 1856), Concord, NH 03302 (© **800/386-4664** or 603/271-2665; www.visitnh.gov).
- **Rhode Island Department of Economic Development,** 1 West

Exchange St., Providence, RI 02903 (© **800/556-2484** or 401/277-2601; www.visitrhodeisland.com).
- **Vermont Department of Tourism,** Drawer 33, 6 Baldwin St., Montpelier, VT 05633 (© **800/837-6668** or 802/828-3237; www.travel-vermont.com).

3 Money

ATMS

ATMs (automated teller machines) are easy to find in New England's more populated areas and in regions that cater to tourists. The machines are even making their way to the smaller villages, but don't count on finding them in the more remote parts of the region. Stock up on cash when you can.

ATMs are linked to a network that most likely includes your bank at home. The **Cirrus** (© **800/424-7787;** www.mastercard.com) and **PLUS** (© **800/843-7587;** www.visa.com) networks span the globe; look at the back of your bank card to see which network you're on, then call or check online for ATM locations at your destination. Be sure you know your personal identification number (PIN) before you leave home and be sure to find out your daily withdrawal limit before you depart. Also keep in mind that many banks impose a fee every time a card is used at a different bank's ATM (rarely more than $1.50). On top of this, the bank from which you withdraw cash may charge its own fee. To compare banks' ATM fees within the U.S., use

www.bankrate.com. For international withdrawal fees, ask your bank.

TRAVELER'S CHECKS

Traveler's checks are something of an anachronism from the days before the ATM made cash accessible at any time. Traveler's checks used to be the only sound alternative to traveling with dangerously large amounts of cash. They were as reliable as currency, but, unlike cash, could be replaced if lost or stolen.

These days, traveler's checks are less necessary because most cities have 24-hour ATMs that allow you to withdraw small amounts of cash as needed. However, keep in mind that you will likely be charged an ATM withdrawal fee if the bank is not your own, so if you're withdrawing money every day, you might be better off with traveler's checks—provided that you don't mind showing identification every time you want to cash one.

You can get traveler's checks at almost any bank. **American Express** offers denominations of $20, $50, $100, $500, and (for cardholders

---

Tips **Small Change**

When you change money, ask for some small bills or loose change. Petty cash will come in handy for tipping and public transportation. Consider keeping the change separate from your larger bills, so that it's readily accessible and you'll be less of a target for theft.

Tips Saving Money on Accommodations

Budget travelers might be in for a bit of sticker shock in New England. Boston is one of the nation's more expensive cities when it comes to hotels, and in midsummer, there's simply no such thing as a cheap room in popular areas like Cape Cod, Newport, or Bar Harbor. To save money, consider these alternatives:

- **Travel in the off season.** At summer destinations, inexpensive rooms are often available in April, May, November, and early December. Granted, it's a bit bleak then, but you can find good deals if you're just looking for a quiet retreat. The best "off-season" period to my mind is September. The weather is great, and many lodgings cut prices between the summer and foliage seasons.
- **Commute from lower-priced areas.** If you're willing to drive a half hour or an hour to reach prime destinations, you can often find cheaper lodging in less glamorous settings. Chain hotels ring the Boston area, and Bangor, Maine, is within striking distance of Acadia National Park. Study a map and be creative.
- **Camp out.** You can often find camping at both public and private campgrounds near popular attractions, with prices ranging from $9 to $25 per night. That's especially true in the northern three states, where you can often find camping within a short drive of even major cities.

---

only) $1,000. You'll pay a service charge ranging from 1% to 4%. You can also get American Express traveler's checks over the phone by calling ⓒ 800/221-7282; Amex gold and platinum cardholders who use this number are exempt from the 1% fee.

Visa offers traveler's checks at Citibank locations nationwide, as well as at several other banks. The service charge ranges between 1.5% and 2%; checks come in denominations of $20, $50, $100, $500, and $1,000. Call ⓒ 800/732-1322 for information. AAA members can obtain Visa checks without a fee at most AAA offices or by calling ⓒ 866/339-3378. **MasterCard** also offers traveler's checks. Call ⓒ 800/223-9920 for a location near you.

If you choose to carry traveler's checks, be sure to keep a record of their serial numbers separate from your checks in the event that they are stolen or lost. You'll get a refund faster if you know the numbers.

CREDIT CARDS

Credit cards are a safe way to carry money, they provide a convenient record of all your expenses, and they generally offer good exchange rates. You can also withdraw cash advances from your credit cards at banks or ATMs, provided you know your PIN. If you've forgotten yours, or didn't even know you had one, call the number on the back of your credit card and ask the bank to send it to you. It usually takes 5 to 7 business days, though some banks will provide the number over the phone if you tell them your mother's maiden name or some other personal information.

For tips and telephone numbers to call if your wallet is stolen or lost, go to "Lost & Found," in the Fast Facts section of this chapter.

4 When to Go

The well-worn joke about New England's weather is that the region has just two seasons: winter and August. There's a kernel of truth to that, especially in the north, but it's mostly a canard to keep outsiders from moving here. In fact, the individual seasons are among those elements that make New England so distinctive.

SUMMER Peak summer season runs from July 4th to Labor Day, when crowds surge into New England's tourist areas in the mountains and along the coast. Summers are verdant and lush, and in the mountains, warm (rarely hot) days are the rule, followed by cool nights. Along the coast, ocean breezes keep temperatures down; Cape Cod and the Islands, for example, are generally 10 degrees cooler than the mainland in summer.

The weather typically follows the winds. Southerly breezes bring haze, heat, and humidity. Northwest winds bring cool weather and knife-sharp vistas. These systems tend to alternate, often with rain between them, and the change from hot to cool will sometimes occur in a matter of minutes. Rain is never far away—some days it's a quick afternoon thunderstorm; other times it's a steady drizzle that brings a 4-day soaking. Travelers should come prepared.

For most of the region, especially the coastal areas, midsummer is the prime season for travel. Expect to pay premium prices at hotels and restaurants except near the empty ski resorts of northern New England, where you can often find bargains. Also be aware that early summer (generally mid-May through June) brings out voracious black flies and mosquitoes, especially in the North Country. Outdoorsy types are better off waiting until July before heading into the deep woods.

AUTUMN In northern New England, don't be surprised to smell the tang of fall approaching as early as mid-August. Fall comes early, puts its feet up on the couch, and stays for a time. The foliage season begins in earnest in the northern part of the region by the third week in September; in the south, it reaches its peak by mid- to late October. The change in seasons in southern Connecticut runs 3 to 4 weeks behind northern Maine. And the higher elevations of the Green and White mountains start to feel wintry a month or so before coastal locations.

Fall in New England is one of America's great natural spectacles, with miles of rolling hills blanketed with brilliant reds and stunning oranges. Along winding country roads you'll find heaps of pumpkins for sale beneath blazing red sugar maples, and crisp apples available by the bushel.

Keep in mind that this is the most popular time of year to travel—bus tours fill the roads and hotels throughout October. Advance reservations are essential; you can also expect to pay a foliage premium of $20 or more at many inns.

WINTER New England winters are like wine—some years are good, some lousy. During a good season, plenty of light, fluffy snow covers the woods and ski slopes, and exploring the forest on snowshoes or cross-country skis is a magical experience.

During the *other* winters, the weather brings a nasty mélange of rain and sleet. It's bone-numbing cold, and bleak, bleak, bleak. Look into the eyes of the residents on the streets during this time. They are all thinking about the Caribbean.

The higher you go and the farther north you head, the better your odds of finding snow and avoiding rain. Winter coastal vacations can be spectacular (nothing beats cross-country skiing at the edge of the pounding surf), but it's a high-risk venture that could yield rain rather than snow.

Ski areas naturally are crowded during the winter months, especially so during school vacations, when most resorts tend to hike their rates.

SPRING New England is famous for its elusive spring, which some residents claim lasts only a weekend or so, typically around mid-May, but sometimes as late as June. One day the ground is muddy, the trees are barren, and gritty snow is piled in shady hollows. The next day, temperatures are in the 80s, trees are blooming, and kids are swimming in the lakes. It's a little weird, frankly. Travelers must be very alert if they want to experience spring in New England. Spring is also known as the mud season, and a time when many innkeepers and restaurateurs close up for a few weeks for either vacation or renovation.

Be aware that New England is home to hundreds of colleges, universities, and prep schools. As graduation nears (mid- to late May and early June), the region is afflicted with unusually high hotel occupancy rates in towns near schools. As always, it's best to book rooms well in advance.

Burlington, Vt.'s Average Temperatures (°F/°C)

	Jan	Feb	Mar	Apr	May	June	July	Aug	Sept	Oct	Nov	Dec
Avg. High	25/-4	27/-3	38/3	53/12	66/19	76/24	80/27	78/26	69/21	57/14	44/7	30/-1
Avg. Low	8/-13	9/-13	21/-6	33/1	44/7	54/12	59/15	57/14	49/9	39/4	30/-1	15/-9

Boston's Average Temperatures (°F/°C)

	Jan	Feb	Mar	Apr	May	June	July	Aug	Sept	Oct	Nov	Dec
Avg. High	36/2	38/3	43/6	54/12	67/19	76/24	81/27	79/26	72/22	63/17	49/9	40/4
Avg. Low	20/-7	22/-6	29/-2	38/3	49/9	58/14	63/17	63/17	56/13	47/8	36/2	25/-4

NEW ENGLAND CALENDAR OF EVENTS

January

New Year's and First Night Celebrations, regionwide. Boston, Mass.; Portland, Maine; Providence, R.I.; Hartford, Conn.; Portsmouth, N.H.; Burlington, Vt.; and many other cities and towns, including on Cape Cod and Martha's Vineyard, celebrate the coming of the New Year with an abundance of festivities. Check with local chambers of commerce for details. New Year's Eve.

February

U.S. National Toboggan Championships, Camden, Maine. This is a raucous and lively athletic event where being overweight is actually an advantage. Held at the toboggan chute of the Camden Snow Bowl. Call ℂ **207/236-3438.** Early February.

Dartmouth Winter Carnival, Hanover, N.H. Huge and elaborate ice sculptures grace the village green during this festive celebration of winter, which includes numerous sporting events and other winter-related activities. Call ℂ **603/646-1110.** Mid-February.

Stowe Derby, Stowe, Vt. The oldest downhill/cross-country ski race in the nation pits racers who scramble from the wintry summit of Mount Mansfield into the village on the Stowe Recreation path. Call ℂ **802/253-7704.** Late February.

March

New England Spring Flower Show, Dorchester, Mass. This annual harbinger of spring presented by the Massachusetts Horticultural Society (✆ **617/536-9280**) draws huge crowds starved for a glimpse of green. Second or third week in March.

St. Patrick's Day/Evacuation Day, Boston, Mass. (Parade, South Boston; celebration, Faneuil Hall Marketplace). The 5-mile parade salutes the city's Irish heritage and the day British troops left Boston in 1776. Head to Faneuil Hall Marketplace for music, dancing, food, and plenty of Irish spirit. Call ✆ **800/888-5515.** March 17.

Maine Boatbuilders Show, Portland, Maine. More than 200 exhibitors and 9,000 boat aficionados gather as winter fades to make plans for the coming summer. A great place to meet boatbuilders and get ideas for your dream craft. Call ✆ **207/774-1067.** Mid- to late March.

April

Patriot's Day, Boston area (Paul Revere House, Old North Church, Lexington Green, Concord's North Bridge), Mass. The events of April 18 and 19, 1775, which signified the start of the Revolutionary War, are commemorated and reenacted. Participants dressed as Paul Revere and William Dawes ride to Lexington and Concord to warn the Minutemen that "the regulars are out" (not that "the British are coming"— most colonists considered themselves British). Mock battles are fought at Lexington and Concord. Call the Lexington Visitor Center (✆ **781/862-1450**) or the Concord Chamber of Commerce (✆ **978/369-3120**). Third Monday in April; a state holiday in Massachusetts and Maine.

Boston Marathon, from Hopkinton to Boston, Mass. International stars and local amateurs run in the world's oldest and most famous marathon. The noon start means elite runners hit Boston around 2pm; weekend runners stagger across the Boylston Street finish line as late as 4 hours after that. Call the Boston Athletic Association (✆ **617/236-1652;** www.bostonmarathon.org). Patriot's Day, the third Monday in April.

Sugarbush Celebration, Waitsfield, Vt. Ski-related events herald the end of the season. A barbecue and après-ski party are featured. Call ✆ **800/53-SUGAR** or 802/583-6789. Mid-April.

Daffodil Festival, Nantucket, Mass. Spring's arrival is trumpeted with masses of yellow blooms adorning everything in sight, including a cavalcade of antique cars. Call ✆ **508/228-1700.** Late April.

May

Brimfield Antique and Collectible Show, Brimfield, Mass. Up to 6,000 dealers fill several fields near this central Massachusetts town, with similar fairs in July and September. Call ✆ **800/628-8379** or 508/347-2761, or go to www.brimfieldshow.com. Mid-May.

Cape Maritime Week, Cape Cod, Mass. A multitude of cultural organizations mount special events—such as lighthouse tours—highlighting the region's nautical history. Call ✆ **508/362-3828.** Mid-May.

Lilac Festival, Shelburne, Vt. See the famed lilacs (more than 400 bushes) at the renowned Shelburne Museum when they're at their most beautiful. Call ✆ **802/985-3346.** Mid-May to late May.

MooseMainea, Greenville, Maine. A variety of low-key events, from an antique-car show to a black-fly festival, are staged deep in the heart of moose territory. But the real attraction is the possibility of spotting one of the gangly beasts on a forest safari. Call © **888-876-2778** or 207/695-2702. Late May to mid-June.

Figawi Sailboat Race, Hyannis (on Cape Cod) to Nantucket, Mass. The largest and wildest sailboat race on the East Coast. Intensive partying in Hyannis and on Nantucket surrounds this popular event. Call © **508/771-3333.** Late May.

June

Old Port Festival, Portland, Maine. A block party in the heart of Portland's historic district with live music, food vendors, and activities for kids. Call © **207/772-6828.** Early June.

Yale-Harvard Regatta, on the Thames River in New London, Conn. One of the oldest collegiate rivalries in the country. Call © **617/495-4848.** Early June.

Taste of Hartford, Hartford, Conn. One of New England's largest outdoor festivals, where many area restaurants serve up their specialties. You'll also get a "taste" of local music, dance, magic, and comedy. Call © **860/728-3089.** Early June.

Market Square Weekend, Portsmouth, N.H. This lively street fair attracts 300 vendors and revelers from throughout southern New Hampshire and Maine into downtown Portsmouth to dance, listen to music, sample food, and enjoy summer's arrival. Call © **603/436-3988.** Early June.

Motorcycle Week, Loudon and Weirs Beach, N.H. Tens of thousands of bikers descend on the Lake Winnipesaukee region early each summer to compare their machines and cruise the strip at Weirs Beach. The Gunstock Hill Climb and the Loudon Classic race are the centerpieces of the week's activities. Call © **603/366-2000.** Early June.

***Boston Globe* Jazz & Blues Festival,** Boston, Mass. Big names and rising stars of the jazz world appear at lunchtime, after-work, evening, and weekend events, some of which are free. For the current schedule, call © **617/267-4301,** or go to www.boston.com/jazzfest. Third week in June.

Stowe Garden Festival, Stowe, Vt. This 3-day event celebrates the joys of making the earth bloom, with offerings as diverse as resort garden tours, brunch talks, and seminars on gardening topics by experts. Call © **800/247-8693.** Last week in June.

Whatever Family Festival, Augusta, Maine. A community celebration to mark the cleaning up of the Kennebec River, culminating in a race involving all manner of watercraft, some more seaworthy than others. Call © **207/623-4559.** Late June to early July.

Jacob's Pillow Dance Festival, Becket, Mass. The oldest dance festival in America features everything from ballet to modern dance and jazz. For a season brochure, call © **413/243-0745.** Late June through August.

Williamstown Theater Festival, Williamstown, Mass. This nationally distinguished festival presents everything from the classics to uproarious comedies and contemporary works. Scattered among the drama are readings and cabarets. Call © **413/597-3399.** Late June through August.

July

Tanglewood Music Festival, near Lenox, Mass. The Boston Symphony Orchestra makes its summer home at this fine estate, bringing symphonies, chamber groups, and soloists to the Berkshire Hills. Call the Tanglewood Concert Line at *©* **413/637-1666** (July and Aug only) or Symphony Hall at *©* **617/266-1492;** or go to www.bso.org. July through August.

Boston Harborfest, downtown Boston (along Boston Harbor and the Harbor Islands), Mass. The city puts on its Sunday best for the Fourth of July, which has become a gigantic weeklong celebration of Boston's maritime history and an excuse to get out and have fun. Events include concerts, tours, cruises, fireworks, the Boston Chowderfest, and the annual turnaround of the USS *Constitution.* Call *©* **617/227-1528.** First week in July.

Boston Pops Concert and Fireworks Display, Hatch Memorial Shell on the Esplanade, Boston, Mass. Independence Week culminates in the famous Boston Pops' Fourth of July concert. People wait from dawn 'til dark for the music to start. The program includes Tchaikovsky's *1812 Overture* with actual cannon fire that segues into the fireworks. Call *©* **617/727-5215.** July 4th.

Independence Day, regionwide. Communities throughout New England celebrate the Fourth of July with parades, cookouts, road races, and fireworks. Contact local chambers of commerce for details. July 4th.

Wickford Art Festival, Wickford, R.I. More than 200 artists gather in this quaint village for one of the East Coast's oldest art festivals. Wickford is the ancestral home of author John Updike and is said to be the setting for his book *The Witches of Eastwick.* Call *©* **401/294-6840,** or go to www.wickford art.org. Weekend after July 4th.

Newport Music Festival, Newport, R.I. Chamber-music concerts are held inside Newport's opulent mansions. Call *©* **401/846-1133.** Second and third weeks in July.

Brimfield Antique and Collectible Show, Brimfield, Mass. Up to 6,000 dealers fill several fields near this central Massachusetts town, with similar fairs in May and September. Call *©* **800/628-8379** or 508/347-2761, or go to www. brimfieldshow.com. Mid-July.

Friendship Sloop Days, Rockland, Maine. This 3-day event is a series of boat races that culminates in a parade of sloops. Call *©* **207/596-0376.** Mid-July.

Vermont Quilt Festival, Northfield, Vt. Displays are only part of the allure of New England's largest (and oldest) quilt festival. You can also attend classes and have your heirlooms appraised. See descriptions at www.vqf.org, or call *©* **802/485-7092** for more information. Mid-July.

Revolutionary War Days, Exeter, N.H. Learn all you need to know about the War of Independence during this historic community festival, which features a Revolutionary War encampment and dozens of re-enactors. Call *©* **603/772-2411.** Mid-July.

Barnstable County Fair, East Falmouth (on Cape Cod), Mass. An old-time county fair complete with rides, food, and livestock contests. Call *©* **508/563-3200.** Late July.

Marlboro Music Festival, Marlboro, Vt. This is a popular 6-week series of classical concerts featuring talented student musicians and seasoned artists performing in the peaceful hills outside of Brattleboro. Call ☎ **802/254-2394** (or ☎ 215/569-4690 in winter) for information. Weekends from July to mid-August.

Maine Lobster Festival, Rockland, Maine. Fill up on the local harvest at this event marking the importance and delectability of Maine's favorite crustacean. Enjoy a boiled lobster or two, and take in the ample entertainment during this informal waterfront gala. Call ☎ **207/596-0376.** Late July to early August.

August

Southern Vermont Art & Craft Fair, Manchester, Vt. More than 200 artisans show off their fine work at this popular festival, which also features creative food and good music. Held on the grounds of Hildene, a grand historic home. Call ☎ **802/362-2100.** Early August.

Newport Folk Festival. Newport, R.I. Thousands of music lovers congregate at Fort Adams State Park for a heavy dose of performances on an August weekend. It's one of the nation's premier festivals. Call ☎ **401/847-3700,** or go to www. newportfolk.com. Early August.

Annual Star Party, St. Johnsbury, Vt. The historic Fairbanks Museum and Planetarium hosts special events and shows, including nightviewing sessions during the Perseid Meteor Shower. Call ☎ **802/748-2372.** Mid-August.

Wild Blueberry Festival, Machias, Maine. A festival marking the harvest of the region's wild blueberries. Eat to your heart's content. Call ☎ **207/794-3543** or 207/255-6665. Mid-August.

JVC Jazz Festival. Newport, R.I. This 3-day jazz festival brings together some of the best in the music industry to play for a sizzling weekend at Fort Adams State Park. Call ☎ **401/847-3700.** Mid-August.

Martha's Vineyard Agricultural Fair, West Tisbury, Mass. An old-fashioned country fair featuring horse pulls, livestock shows, musicians, and woodsman contests, along with plenty of carnival action. Call ☎ **508/693-4343.** Third weekend in August.

Blue Hill Fair, Blue Hill, Maine. A classic country fair just outside one of Maine's most elegant villages. Call ☎ **207/374-3701.** Late August.

September

Windjammer Weekend, Camden, Maine. Come visit Maine's impressive fleet of old-time sailing ships, which host open houses throughout the weekend at this scenic harbor. Call ☎ **207/236-4404.** Labor Day weekend.

Brimfield Antique and Collectible Show, Brimfield, Mass. Up to 6,000 dealers fill several fields near this central Massachusetts town, with similar fairs in May and July. Call ☎ **800/628-8379** or 508/347-2761, or go to www.brimfield show.com. Early September.

Vermont State Fair, Rutland, Vt. All of Vermont seems to show up for this grand event, with a midway, live music, and plenty of agricultural exhibits. Call ☎ **802/775-5200.** Early September.

Providence Waterfront Festival, Providence, R.I. Musical performances are the highlight of this weekend event, especially the jazz festival on Sunday. A food court and children's tent round out the activities. Call ☎ **401/621-1992.** Weekend after Labor Day.

Norwalk Oyster Festival, Norwalk, Conn. This waterfront festival celebrates Long Island Sound's seafaring past. Highlights include oyster-shucking and slurping contests, harbor cruises, concerts, and fireworks. Call © **203/838-9444.** Weekend after Labor Day.

Convergence International Festival of the Arts, Providence, R.I. Various Providence arts organizations pull together for this week-long citywide event, which includes sculptural installations, musical performances, and other arts events. Call © **401/621-1992.** Mid-September.

Eastern States Exhibition, West Springfield, Mass. "The Big E" is New England's largest agricultural fair with a midway, games, rides, rodeo and lumberjack shows, country-music stars, and lots of eats. Call © **413/737-2443.** Mid- to late September.

Provincetown Arts Festival, Provincetown (on Cape Cod), Mass. One of the country's oldest art colonies celebrates its past and present with local artists opening their studios. It's a great opportunity for collecting 20th-century works. Call © **508/487-3424.** Late September.

Common Ground Country Fair, Unity, Maine. A sprawling, old-time state fair with a twist: The emphasis is on organic foods, recycling, and wholesome living. Call © **207/568-4142.** Late September.

October

Fall Foliage Festival, St. Johnsbury, Vermont. A cornucopia of events in Vermont's northeast corner heralds the arrival of the foliage season. Be the first to see colors at their peak. Call © **802/748-3678.** Early October.

Fryeburg Fair, Fryeburg, Maine. Cotton candy, tractor pulls, live music, and huge vegetables and barnyard animals at Maine's largest agricultural fair. There's also harness racing in the evening. Call © **207/985-3268.** One week in early October.

Mystic Chowderfest, Mystic, Conn. A festival of soup served from bubbling cauldrons set on wood fires. Call © **860/572-5315.** Mid-October.

Harvest Day, Canterbury, N.H. A celebration of the harvest season, Shaker style. Lots of autumnal exhibits and children's games. Call © **603/783-9511.** Mid-October.

Cranberry Harvest Festival, Nantucket, Mass. Tour scenic cranberry bogs and local inns just when foliage is at its burnished prime. Call © **508/228-1700.** Mid-October.

Head of the Charles Regatta, Boston and Cambridge, Mass. High school, college, and post-collegiate rowing teams and individuals—some 4,000 in all—race in front of hordes of fans along the banks of the Charles River. This event always seems to fall on the crispest, most picturesque Sunday of the season. Call the Metropolitan District Commission Harbor Master (© **617/727-0537**) for information. Late October.

November

Brookfield Holiday Craft Exhibition & Sale, Brookfield, Conn. Thousands of unique, elegant, and artful gifts are displayed in gallery settings on three floors of a restored grist mill. Call © **203/775-4526.** Mid-November through late December.

Thanksgiving Celebration, Plymouth, Mass. The holiday that put Plymouth on the map is observed with a "stroll through the ages," showcasing 17th- and 19th-century Thanksgiving preparations in historic homes. Nearby Plimoth

Plantation, where the colony's first years are re-created, wisely offers a Victorian Thanksgiving feast (reservations required). Call Plymouth Visitor Information (© 800/872-1620) or the Plimoth Plantation (© 508/746-1622). Thanksgiving Day.

Victorian Holiday, Portland, Maine. From late November until Christmas, Portland decorates its Old Port in a Victorian Christmas theme. Enjoy the window displays, take a free hayride, and listen to costumed carolers sing. Call © 207/772-6828 or 207/780-5555. Late November to Christmas.

December

Christmas Tree Lighting, Prudential Center, Boston, Mass. Carol singing precedes the lighting of a magnificent tree from Nova Scotia—an annual expression of thanks from the people of Halifax for Bostonians' help in fighting a devastating fire more than 70 years ago. Call the Greater Boston Convention & Visitors Bureau (© 888/SEE-BOSTON or 617/536-4100). Early December.

Christmas Prelude, Kennebunkport, Maine. This scenic coastal village greets Santa's arrival in a lobster boat, and marks the coming of

Christmas with street shows, pancake breakfasts, and tours of the town's splendid inns. Call © 207/967-0857. Early December.

Candlelight Stroll, Portsmouth, N.H. Historic Strawbery Banke gets in a Christmas way with old-time decorations and more than 1,000 candles lighting the 10-acre grounds. Call © 603/433-1100. First two weekends in December.

Boston Tea Party Reenactment, Congress Street Bridge, Boston, Mass. Chafing under British rule, the colonists rose up on December 16, 1773, to strike a blow where it would cause real pain—in the pocketbook. Call © 617/338-1773. Mid-December.

Woodstock Wassail Celebration, Woodstock, Vt. Enjoy classic English grog, along with parades and dances at this annual event. Call © 802/457-3555. Mid-December.

Christmas Eve and Christmas Day, festivities throughout New England. In Newport, R.I., several of the great mansions offer tours; Mystic, Conn., has a program of Christmas festivities; Nantucket, Mass., features carolers in Victorian garb, art exhibits, and tours of historic homes. December 24 and 25.

5 Travel Insurance

Check your existing insurance policies and credit card coverage before you buy travel insurance. You may already be covered for lost luggage, cancelled tickets or medical expenses. The cost of travel insurance varies widely, depending on the cost and length of your trip, your age, health, and the type of trip you're taking.

TRIP-CANCELLATION INSURANCE Trip-cancellation insurance helps you get your money back if you have to back out of a trip, if you have

to go home early, or if your travel supplier goes bankrupt. Allowed reasons for cancellation can range from sickness to natural disasters to the State Department declaring your destination unsafe for travel. (Insurers usually won't cover vague fears, though, as many travelers discovered who tried to cancel their trips in October 2001 because they were wary of flying.) In this unstable world, trip-cancellation insurance is a good buy if you're getting tickets well in advance—who knows what the state of the world, or of your airline, will be in 9 months? Insurance policy details vary, so read the fine print—and especially make sure that your airline or cruise line is on the list of carriers covered in case of bankruptcy. For information, contact one of the following insurers: **Access America** (℡ 866/807-3982; www.accessamerica.com); **Travel Guard International** (℡ 800/826-4919; www.travelguard.com); **Travel Insured International** (℡ 800/243-3174; www.travel insured.com); and **Travelex Insurance Services** (℡ 888/457-4602; www.travelex-insurance.com).

MEDICAL INSURANCE Most health insurance policies cover you if you get sick away from home—but check, particularly if you're insured by an HMO. If you require additional medical insurance, try **MEDEX International** (℡ 800/527-0218 or 410/453-6300; www.medexassist. com) or **Travel Assistance International** (℡ 800/821-2828; www. travelassistance.com; for general information on services, call the company's Worldwide Assistance Services, Inc., at ℡ 800/777-8710).

LOST-LUGGAGE INSURANCE On domestic flights, checked baggage is covered up to $2,500 per ticketed passenger. On international flights (including U.S. portions of international trips), baggage is limited to approximately $9.05 per pound, up to approximately $635 per checked bag. If you plan to check items more valuable than the standard liability, see if your valuables are covered by your homeowner's policy, get baggage insurance as part of your comprehensive travel-insurance package or buy Travel Guard's "BagTrak" product. Don't buy insurance at the airport, as it's usually overpriced. Be sure to take any valuables or irreplaceable items with you in your carry-on luggage, as many valuables (including books, money, and electronics) aren't covered by airline policies.

If your luggage is lost, immediately file a lost-luggage claim at the airport, detailing the luggage contents. For most airlines, you must report delayed, damaged, or lost baggage within 4 hours of arrival. The airlines are required to deliver luggage, once found, directly to your house or destination free of charge.

6 Health & Safety

STAYING HEALTHY

You shouldn't face any serious health risks when traveling in New England, though you may find yourself at higher risk when exploring the outdoors, particularly the backcountry. Those planning longer outdoor excursions may find a first-aid kit with basic salves and medicines handy to have along. Those traveling mostly in towns and villages should have little trouble finding a local pharmacy to stock up on common medicines (like calamine lotion or aspirin) to aid with minor ailments.

If you suffer from a chronic illness, consult your doctor before your departure. For conditions like epilepsy, diabetes, or heart problems, wear a **Medic Alert Identification Tag** (℡ 800/825-3785; www.medic alert.org), which will immediately alert doctors to your condition and give them access to your records through Medic Alert's 24-hour hotline.

Pack **prescription medications** in your carry-on luggage, and carry prescription medications in their original containers, with pharmacy labels—otherwise they won't make it through airport security. Also bring along copies of your prescriptions in case you lose your pills or run out. Don't forget an extra pair of contact lenses or prescription glasses.

A few things to watch for when venturing off the beaten track:

POISON IVY   The shiny, three-leafed plant is common throughout the region. If touched, you may develop a nasty, itchy rash. If you're unfamiliar with what poison ivy looks like, ask at a ranger station or visitor center for more information. Many have posters or books to help with identification.

GIARDIA   That crystal-clear stream coursing down a backcountry peak may seem as pure as pure gets, but consider the possibility that it may be contaminated with animal feces. Giardia cysts may be present in some streams and rivers; when ingested by humans, the cysts can result in diarrhea and weight loss. Symptoms may not surface until well after you've left the backcountry. Carry your own water for day trips, or bring a small filter (available at most sporting-goods shops) to treat backcountry water. Failing that, at least boil water or treat it with iodine before using it for cooking, drinking, or washing. If you detect symptoms, see a doctor immediately.

LYME DISEASE   Lyme disease has been a growing problem in New England since 1975, when the disease was identified in Lyme, Conn. It's transmitted by tiny deer ticks—smaller than the more common, relatively harmless wood ticks. Look for a bull's-eye shaped rash, 3 to 8 inches in diameter; it may feel warm but usually doesn't itch. Symptoms include muscle and joint pain, fever, and fatigue. If left untreated, heart damage may occur. It's more easily treated in early phases than later, so it's best to seek medical attention as soon as any symptoms are noted.

RABIES   Since 1989, rabies has been spreading northward from New Jersey through New England. The disease is spread by animal saliva and is especially prevalent in skunks, raccoons, bats, and foxes. It is fatal if left untreated in humans. Infected animals tend to display erratic and aggressive behavior. The best advice is to keep a safe distance between yourself and any wild animal you may encounter. If bitten, wash the wound as soon as you can and immediately seek medical attention. Treatment is no longer as painful as it once was, but still involves a series of shots.

7 Specialized Travel Needs

TRAVELERS WITH DISABILITIES

Prodded by the Americans with Disabilities Act, a growing number of inns and hotels are retrofitting some of their rooms for guests with special needs. Outdoor-recreation areas, especially on state and federal lands, are also providing more trails and facilities for those who've been effectively barred in the past. Accessibility is improving regionwide, but improvements are far from universal. When in doubt, call ahead to ensure that you'll be accommodated.

The U.S. National Park Service offers a **Golden Access Passport** that gives free lifetime entrance to all properties administered by the National Park Service—national parks, monuments, historic sites, recreation areas, and national wildlife refuges—for persons who are blind or permanently disabled, regardless of age. You may pick up a Golden Access Passport at any NPS entrance fee area by showing proof of medically determined disability and eligibility for receiving benefits under federal law. Besides free entry, the Golden Access Passport also offers a 50% discount on federal-use fees charged for such facilities as camping, swimming, parking, boat launching, and tours. For more information, go to www.nps.gov/fees_passes.htm or call ℂ **888/467-2757.**

Many travel agencies offer customized tours and itineraries for travelers with disabilities. **Flying Wheels Travel** (ℂ **507/451-5005;** www. flyingwheelstravel.com) offers escorted tours and cruises that emphasize sports and private tours in minivans with lifts. **Accessible Journeys** (ℂ **800/846-4537** or 610/521-0339; www.disabilitytravel.com) caters specifically to slow walkers and wheelchair travelers and their families and friends.

Organizations that offer assistance to disabled travelers include **Moss-Rehab** (www.mossresourcenet.org), which provides a library of accessible-travel resources online; the **Society for Accessible Travel and Hospitality** (ℂ **212/447-7284;** www.sath.org; annual membership fees: $45 adults, $30 seniors and students), which offers a wealth of travel resources for all types of disabilities and informed recommendations on destinations, access guides, travel agents, tour operators, vehicle rentals, and companion services; and the **American Foundation for the Blind** (ℂ **800/232-5463;** www.afb.org), which provides information on traveling with Seeing Eye dogs.

For more information specifically targeted to travelers with disabilities, the community website **iCan** (www. icanonline.net/channels/travel/index. cfm) has destination guides and several regular columns on accessible travel. Also check out the magazine *Emerging Horizons* ($15 per year, $20 outside the U.S.; www.emerging horizons.com); **Twin Peaks Press** (ℂ **360/694-2462;** http://disability bookshop.virtualave.net/blist84.htm), offering travel-related books for travelers with special needs; and *Open*

World Magazine, published by the Society for Accessible Travel and Hospitality (subscription: $18 per year, $35 outside the U.S.).

SENIOR TRAVEL

Mention the fact that you're a senior citizen when you make your travel reservations. Although all of the major U.S. airlines except America West have cancelled their senior discount and coupon book programs, many hotels still offer discounts for seniors. In most cities, people over the age of 60 qualify for reduced admission to theaters, museums, and other attractions, as well as discounted fares on public transportation.

New England offers older travelers a wide array of activities and discounts. It's wise to request a discount at hotels or motels when booking the room, not when you arrive. Members of **AARP** (formerly known as the American Association of Retired Persons), 601 E St. NW, Washington, DC 20049 (ℂ **800/424-3410** or 202/434-2277; www.aarp.org), get discounts on hotels, airfares, and car rentals. AARP offers members a wide range of benefits, including *AARP: The Magazine* and a monthly newsletter. Anyone over 50 can join.

The **U.S. National Park Service** offers a **Golden Age Passport** that gives seniors 62 years or older lifetime entrance to all properties administered by the National Park Service—national parks, monuments, historic sites, recreation areas, and national wildlife refuges—for a one-time processing fee of $10, which must be purchased in person at any NPS facility that charges an entrance fee. Besides free entry, a Golden Age Passport also offers a 50% discount on federal-use fees charged for such facilities as camping, swimming, parking, boat launching, and tours. For more information, go to www.nps.gov/fees_passes.htm or call ℂ **888/467-2757.**

Many reliable agencies and organizations target the 50-plus market. **Elderhostel** (© 877/426-8056; www.elderhostel.org) arranges study programs for those aged 55 and over (and a spouse or companion of any age) in the U.S. and in more than 80 countries around the world. Most courses last 5 to 7 days in the U.S. (2–4 weeks abroad), and many include airfare, accommodations in university dormitories or modest inns, meals, and tuition. **ElderTreks** (© 800/741-7956; www.eldertreks.com) offers small-group tours to off-the-beaten-path or adventure-travel locations, restricted to travelers 50 and older.

Recommended publications offering travel resources and discounts for seniors include: the quarterly magazine *Travel 50 & Beyond* (www.travel50andbeyond.com); *Travel Unlimited: Uncommon Adventures for the Mature Traveler* (Avalon); *101 Tips for Mature Travelers,* available from Grand Circle Travel (© 800/221-2610 or 617/350-7500; www.gct.com); *The 50+ Traveler's Guidebook* (St. Martin's Press); and *Unbelievably Good Deals and Great Adventures That You Absolutely Can't Get Unless You're Over 50* (McGraw-Hill).

GAY & LESBIAN TRAVELERS

Provincetown, on the tip of Cape Cod, is one of the first and still one of the most famous gay resort communities. Gay entrepreneurs and politicians are well represented in the town, and much of the nightlife revolves around gay culture.

Outside of Provincetown, New England isn't exactly a hotbed of gay culture, although there are noted pockets, like Ogunquit, Maine (see www.gayogunquit.com). Providence, Boston, and Burlington tend to be very welcoming to alternative lifestyles. For a small city, Portland has an active gay population and hosts a

sizable gay pride festival early each summer.

Vermont became the first state in the nation (in 2000) to permit same-sex couples to be joined in civil union—at that point, the closest thing to gay marriage available (though the state of Massachusetts has since begun to allow same-sex marriages). One needn't be a state resident to establish a civil union; many same-sex couples have traveled here, paid their $20 fee, and exchanged legally recognized vows before a judge or clergy member, even though such unions may not be recognized outside of Vermont. A good guide to the law is found at www.sec.state.vt.us/municipal/civil_mar.htm.

Vermont has a fine monthly newsletter covering gay, lesbian, and bisexual issues and happenings called *Out in the Mountain* (on the Web at www.mountainpridemedia.org). It's free at many Vermont bookstores and other shops.

For a more detailed directory of gay-oriented enterprises in New England, track down a copy of **The Pink Pages,** published by KP Media (66 Charles St., #283, Boston, MA 02114). The price is $8.95, plus $2 shipping and handling. Call © 617/423-1515 or visit the firm's website at **www.pinkweb.com**, which also contains much of the information in the published version.

More adventurous souls should consider linking up with the **Chiltern Mountain Club,** P.O. Box 407, Boston, MA 02117 (© 888/831-3100 or 617/556-7774; www.chiltern.org), an outdoor-adventure club for gays and lesbians; about two-thirds of its 1,200 members are men. The club organizes trips to northern New England throughout the year.

For more general information about gay travel, the following resources are helpful:

The **International Gay & Lesbian Travel Association (IGLTA)** (℗ **800/448-8550** or 954/776-2626; www.iglta.org) is the trade association for the gay and lesbian travel industry, and offers an online directory of gay- and lesbian-friendly travel businesses; go to their website and click on "Members."

Many agencies offer tours and travel itineraries specifically for gay and lesbian travelers. **Above and Beyond Tours** (℗ **800/397-2681;** www.abovebeyondtours.com) is the exclusive gay and lesbian tour operator for United Airlines. **Now, Voyager** (℗ **800/255-6951;** www.nowvoyager.com) is a well-known San Francisco–based gay-owned and operated travel service. The following travel guides are available at most travel bookstores and gay and lesbian bookstores: *Out and About* (℗ **800/929-2268** or 415-644-8044; www.outand\about.com), which offers guidebooks and a newsletter 10 times a year packed with solid information; *Spartacus International Gay Guide* (Bruno Gmunder Verlag) and *Odysseus: The International Gay Travel Planner* (Odysseus Enterprises Ltd.), both good, annual English-language guidebooks focused on gay men; the *Damron* guides (Damron Company), with separate, annual books for gay men and lesbians.

FAMILY TRAVEL

Be sure to ask about family discounts when visiting attractions. Many places offer a flat family rate that is cheaper than paying for each ticket individually. Some parks and beaches charge by the car rather than the head.

Be aware that a number of inns cater to couples and prefer that children be over a certain age. We note in this guide the recommended age where restrictions apply, but it's still best to ask first just to be safe.

Recommended destinations for families include Boston, with its plethora of museums; Cape Cod, with its miles of famous beaches and dunes; and Martha's Vineyard, with bike paths, beaches, and kid-scaled architecture in the cottage section of Oak Bluffs. Other destinations good for kids are Weirs Beach on New Hampshire's Lake Winnipesaukee, Hampton Beach on New Hampshire's tiny coast, and York Beach and Acadia National Park in Maine.

North Conway, N.H., also makes a good base for exploring with younger kids. The town has lots of motels with pools, and there are nearby train rides, aquaboggans, streams for splashing around, easy hikes, and the always-entertaining StoryLand. Excellent children's museums are located in Mystic, Boston, Portsmouth, Portland, and Norwich.

Several specialized guides offer more detailed information for families on the go. Try *The Unofficial Guide to New England & New York with Kids* (Wiley Publishing, Inc.), *Fun Places to Go With Children in New England* (Chronicle Books, 1998), and *Great Family Vacations Northeast* (Globe Pequot, 2001). *How to Take Great Trips with Your Kids* (The Harvard Common Press, 1995) is full of good general advice that can apply to travel anywhere.

FOR TRAVELERS WITH PETS

No surprise: Some places allow pets; some don't. We've noted hotels and inns that allow pets (it doesn't hurt to inquire, even if the pet policy isn't explicitly mentioned in these pages), but we still don't recommend showing up with a pet in tow unless you've cleared it over the phone first. Note that many establishments have only one or two rooms (often a cottage or room with exterior entrance) set aside for guests traveling with pets, and they won't be happy to meet Fido if the pet rooms are already occupied. Also expect a surcharge of $10 or $20 to pay for the extra cleaning.

An excellent resource is **www.petswelcome.com**, which dispenses medical tips, names of animal-friendly lodgings and campgrounds, and lists of kennels and veterinarians. Also check out *The Portable Petswelcome. com: The Complete Guide to Traveling with Your Pet* (Howell, 2001). Another resource is *Pets-R-Permitted Hotel, Motel & Kennel Directory: The Travel Resource for Pet Owners Who Travel* (Annenberg Communications, 1997).

Note that summer may not be the best time to fly with your pet: Many airlines will not check pets as baggage in the hotter months. The ASPCA discourages travelers from checking pets as luggage at any time, as storage conditions on planes are loosely monitored, and fatal accidents are not unprecedented. Your other option is to ship your pet with a professional carrier, which can be expensive.

Note: Dogs are prohibited on hiking trails and must be leashed at all times on federal lands administered by the National Park Service. Pets are allowed to hike off-leash in the White Mountains National Forest in New Hampshire and the Green Mountains National Forest in Vermont.

8 Planning Your Trip Online

SURFING FOR AIRFARES

The "big three" online travel agencies, **Expedia.com, Travelocity.com,** and **Orbitz.com** sell most of the air tickets bought on the Internet. (Canadian travelers should try expedia.ca and Travelocity.ca; U.K. residents can go for expedia.co.uk and opodo.co.uk.) Each has different business deals with the airlines and may offer different fares on the same flights, so it's wise to shop around. Expedia and Travelocity will also send you **e-mail notification** when a cheap fare becomes available to your favorite destination. Of the smaller travel agency websites, **Side-Step** (www.sidestep.com) has gotten the best reviews from Frommer's authors. It's a browser add-on that purports to "search 140 sites at once," but in reality only beats competitors' fares as often as other sites do.

Also remember to check **airline websites,** especially those for low-fare carriers such as Southwest, JetBlue, AirTran, WestJet, or Ryanair, whose fares are often misreported or simply missing from travel agency websites. Even with major airlines, you can often shave a few bucks from a fare by booking directly through the airline and avoiding a travel agency's transaction fee. But you'll get these discounts only by **booking online:** Most airlines now offer online-only fares that even their phone agents know nothing about. For the websites of airlines that fly to and from your destination, go to "Getting There," later in this chapter.

Great **last-minute deals** are available through free weekly e-mail services provided directly by the airlines. Most of these are announced on Tuesday or Wednesday and must be purchased online. Most are only valid for travel that weekend, but some (such as Southwest's) can be booked weeks or months in advance. Sign up for weekly e-mail alerts at airline websites or check sites that compile comprehensive lists of last-minute specials, such as **Smarter Living** (smarterliving.com). For last-minute trips, **site59.com** in the U.S. and **lastminute.com** in Europe often have better deals than the major-label sites.

If you're willing to give up some control over your flight details, use an **opaque fare service** like **Priceline** (www.priceline.com; www.priceline.co.uk for Europeans) or **Hotwire** (www.hotwire.com). Both offer rock-bottom prices in exchange for travel

Frommers.com: The Complete Travel Resource

For an excellent travel-planning resource, we highly recommend **Frommers.com** (www.frommers.com). We're a little biased, of course, but we guarantee that you'll find the travel tips, reviews, monthly vacation giveaways, and online-booking capabilities thoroughly indispensable. Among the special features are our popular **Message Boards,** where Frommer's readers post queries and share advice (sometimes even our authors show up to answer questions); **Frommers.com Newsletter,** for the latest travel bargains and insider travel secrets; and **Frommer's Destinations Section,** where you'll get expert travel tips, hotel and dining recommendations, and advice on the sights to see for more than 3,000 destinations around the globe. When your research is done, the **Online Reservations System** (www.frommers.com/book_a_trip) takes you to Frommer's preferred online partners for booking your vacation at affordable prices.

on a "mystery airline" at a mysterious time of day, often with a mysterious change of planes en route. The mystery airlines are all major, well-known carriers—and the possibility of being sent from Philadelphia to Chicago via Tampa is remote; the airlines' routing computers have gotten a lot better than they used to be. But your chances of getting a 6am or 11pm flight are pretty high. Hotwire tells you flight prices before you buy; Priceline usually has better deals than Hotwire, but you have to play their "name our price" game. If you're new at this, the helpful folks at **BiddingForTravel** (www.biddingfortravel.com) do a good job of demystifying Priceline's prices. Priceline and Hotwire are great for flights within North America and between the U.S. and Europe.

For much more about airfares and savvy air-travel tips and advice, pick up a copy of *Frommer's Fly Safe, Fly Smart* (Wiley Publishing, Inc.).

SURFING FOR HOTELS

Shopping online for hotels is easier in New England than it is in the rest of the world. Of the "big three" sites, **Expedia** may be the best choice,

thanks to its long list of specials. **Travelocity** runs a close second. Hotel specialist sites **hotels.com** and **hotel discounts.com** are also reliable. An excellent free program, **TravelAxe** (www.travelaxe.net) can help you search multiple sites at once, even ones you may never have heard of.

Priceline and Hotwire are even better for hotels than for airfares; with both, you're allowed to pick the neighborhood and quality level of your hotel before offering up your money. Priceline's hotel product even covers Europe and Asia, though it's much better at getting five-star lodging for three-star prices than at finding anything at the bottom of the scale. *Note:* Hotwire overrates its hotels by one star—what Hotwire calls a four-star is a three-star anywhere else.

Helpfully, most resorts, inns, and hotels throughout New England operate their own websites with online booking resources.

SURFING FOR RENTAL CARS

For booking cars online, the best deals are usually found at rental-car company sites, although all the major online travel agencies also offer rental-car reservations services. Price-line and Hotwire work well for rental cars, too; the only "mystery" is which major rental company you get, and for most travelers the difference between Hertz, Avis, and Budget is negligible.

9 The 21st-Century Traveler

INTERNET ACCESS AWAY FROM HOME

Travelers have any number of ways to check their e-mail and access the Internet on the road. Of course, using your own laptop—or even a PDA (personal digital assistant) or electronic organizer with a modem—gives you the most flexibility. But even if you don't have a computer, you can still access your e-mail and even your office computer from cybercafes.

WITHOUT YOUR OWN COMPUTER

It's hard nowadays to find a city that *doesn't* have a cybercafe. Although there's no definitive directory for cybercafes—these are independent businesses, after all—three places to start looking are at **www.cybercaptive. com**, **www.netcafeguide.com**, and **www.cybercafe.com**. You may have a harder time finding access in New England's small towns, though most **public libraries** in the region offer Internet access free or for a small charge; you may need to surrender your driver's license or car keys as collateral during the session. Avoid **hotel business centers,** which often charge exorbitant rates.

To retrieve your e-mail, ask your **Internet Service Provider (ISP)** if it has a Web-based interface tied to your existing e-mail account. If your ISP doesn't have such an interface, you can use the free **mail2web** service (www. mail2web.com) to view and reply to your home e-mail. For more flexibility, you may want to open a free, Web-based e-mail account with **Yahoo! Mail** (http://mail.yahoo.com). (Microsoft's Hotmail is another popular option, but Hotmail has severe spam problems.) Your home ISP may be able to forward your e-mail to the Web-based account automatically.

If you need to access files on your office computer, look into a service called **GoToMyPC** (www.gotomypc. com). The service provides a Web-based interface for you to access and manipulate a distant PC from anywhere—even a cybercafe—provided your "target" PC is on and has an always-on connection to the Internet (such as with Road Runner cable). The service offers top-quality security, but if you're worried about hackers, use your own laptop rather than a cybercafe to access the GoToMyPC system.

WITH YOUR OWN COMPUTER

Major Internet Service Providers (ISP) have **local access numbers** around the world, allowing you to go online by simply placing a local call. Check your ISP's website or call its toll-free number and ask how you can use your current account away from home, and how much it will cost.

If you're traveling outside the reach of your ISP, the **iPass** network has dial-up numbers in most of the world's countries. You'll have to sign up with an iPass provider, who will then tell you how to set up your computer for your destination(s). For a list of iPass providers, go to www.ipass. com and click on "Reseller Locator." Under "Select a Country" pick the country that you're coming from, and under "Who is this service for?" pick "Individual." One solid provider is **i2roam** (www.i2roam.com; © **866/ 811-6209** or 920/235-0475).

Wherever you go, bring a **connection kit** of the right power and phone adapters, a spare phone cord, and a spare Ethernet network cable.

Most business-class hotels throughout the world offer dataports for laptop modems, and a few thousand hotels in the U.S. and Europe now offer high-speed Internet access using an Ethernet network cable. You'll have to bring your own cables either way, so **call your hotel in advance** to find out what the options are.

Many business-class hotels in the U.S. also offer a form of computer-free Web browsing through the room TV set. We've successfully checked AOL, Yahoo! Mail, and Hotmail on these systems.

If you have an 802.11b/**Wi-fi** card for your computer, several commercial companies have made wireless service available in airports, hotel lobbies, and coffee shops, primarily in the U.S. **T-Mobile Hotspot** (www.t-mobile. com/hotspot) serves up wireless connections at more than 1,000 Starbucks coffee shops nationwide. **Boingo** (www.boingo.com) and **Wayport** (www.wayport.com) have set up networks in airports and high-class hotel lobbies. IPass providers (see above) also give you access to a few hundred wireless hotel lobby setups. Best of all, you don't need to be staying at the Four Seasons to use the hotel's

network; just set yourself up on a nice couch in the lobby. Unfortunately, the companies' pricing policies are byzantine, with a variety of monthly, per-connection, and per-minute plans.

Community-minded individuals have also set up **free wireless networks** in major cities around the world. These networks are spotty, but you get what you (don't) pay for. Each network has a home page explaining how to set up your computer for their particular system; start your explorations at www.personaltelco.net/index.cgi/ WirelessCommunities.

USING A CELLPHONE ACROSS THE U.S.

Just because your cellphone works at home doesn't mean it'll work elsewhere in the country (thanks to our nation's fragmented cellphone system). It's a good bet that your phone will work in major cities. But take a look at your wireless company's coverage map on its website before heading out— T-Mobile, Sprint, and Nextel are particularly weak in rural areas such as New England. And there's no carrier that will get a signal deep in the back-country of, for example, the Green or White Mountains. If you need to stay

Online Traveler's Toolbox

Veteran travelers usually carry some essential items to make their trips easier. Following is a selection of online tools to bookmark:

Veteran travelers usually carry some essential items to make their trips easier. Following is a selection of online tools to bookmark and use:

- **Visa ATM Locator** (www.visa.com), for locations of PLUS ATMs worldwide, or **MasterCard ATM Locator** (www.mastercard.com), for locations of Cirrus ATMs worldwide.
- **Intellicast** (www.intellicast.com) and **Weather.com** (www.weather. com). These sites provide weather forecasts for all 50 states and for cities around the world.
- **MapQuest** (www.mapquest.com) and **Yahoo! Maps** (maps.yahoo. com). These are the best of the mapping sites; in seconds, from an input address, they return a map and detailed driving directions.

in touch at a destination where you know your phone won't work, **rent** a phone that does from **InTouch USA** (© **800/872-7626;** www.intouch global.com) or from a rental car location, but beware that you'll pay $1 a minute or more for airtime.

If you're venturing deep into remote areas, you may want to consider renting a **satellite phone ("satphones"),** which are different from cellphones in that they connect to satellites rather than ground-based towers. A satphone is more costly than a cellphone but works where there's no cellular signal and no towers. Unfortunately, you'll pay at least $2 per minute to use the phone, and it only works where you can see the horizon (that is, usually not indoors). In North America, you can rent Iridium satellite phones from **RoadPost** (www.road post.com; © **888/290-1606** or 905/ 272-5665). InTouch USA (see above) offers a wider range of satphones but at higher rates. As of this writing,

satphones were amazingly expensive to buy, so don't even think about it.

If you're not from the U.S., you'll be appalled at the poor reach of our **GSM (Global System for Mobiles) wireless network,** which is used by much of the rest of the world. Your phone will probably work in most major U.S. cities; it definitely won't work in many rural areas. (To see where GSM phones work in the U.S., check out www.t-mobile.com/coverage/ national_popup.asp.) And you may or may not be able to send SMS (text messaging) home—something Americans tend not to do anyway, for various cultural and technological reasons. (International budget travelers like to send text messages home because it's much cheaper than making international calls.) Assume nothing—call your wireless provider and get the full scoop. In a worst-case scenario, you can always rent a phone; InTouch USA delivers to hotels.

10 Getting There

BY PLANE

Airlines serving New England include **American** (© 800/433-7300; www. aa.com), **Comair** (© 800/354-9822; www.comair.com), **Continental** (© 800/525-0280; www.continental. com), **Delta** (© 800/221-1212; www. delta.com), **JetBlue** (© 800/538-2583; www.jetblue.com), **Northwest** (© 800/225-2525; www.nwa.com), **Pan Am** (© 800/359-7262; www.fly panam.com), **Southwest** (© 800/ 435-9792; www.southwest.com), **United** (© 800/241-6522; www. united.com), and **US Airways** (© 800/428-4322; www.usair.com).

Carriers to Cape Cod and the Islands include several of the above, plus **Cape Air/Nantucket Air** (© 800/ 352-0714 or 508/771-6944) and **Island Airlines** (© 800/248-7779 or 508/775-6606). Charter flights

throughout the region are offered by Cape Air/Nantucket Air, as well as by **Cape Flight Limited** (© 508/775-8171) and **King Air Charters** (© 800/ 247-2427).

The traditional gateways to New England have been Boston, New York City, and Montréal. Major commercial carriers also serve Hartford, Conn. (Bradley International); Burlington, Vt.; and Bangor and Portland, Maine. Note that if you're heading to southwest Vermont or northwest Massachusetts, the closest major airport is Albany, N.Y.

In the last few years, Providence, R.I., and Manchester, N.H., have grown in prominence thanks to the arrival of **Southwest** and other airlines, which have brought competitive, low-cost airfares and improved service. Manchester in particular has

Driving Distances

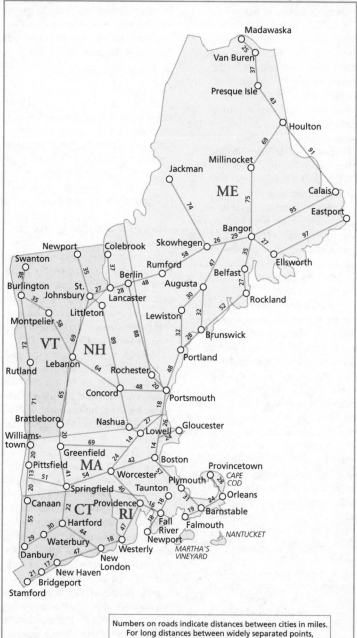

Numbers on roads indicate distances between cities in miles.
For long distances between widely separated points,
add all intervening mileages.

gone from a sleepy backwater airport to a bustling destination serving an increasing number of flights.

Pan Am, once a dominant (then bankrupt) air carrier, and now back to life (under the auspices of entrepreneurs who purchased the name) and operating out of Manchester and Portsmouth, N.H., also serving Bangor, Maine; and Worcester, Mass. Pan Am connects to a limited but growing roster of airports, including Baltimore, Maryland; Myrtle Beach, South Carolina; and Sanford, Florida. Call ✆ **800/359-7262** or book flights at **www.flypanam.com**.

Upstart discounter **JetBlue** offers direct service between Burlington, Vermont, and New York City's LaGuardia Airport, with onward connections. For more information, call ✆ **800/538-2583** or check online at **www.jetblue.com**.

Travelers should note that Boston's Logan Airport can be very congested. Following the September 11, 2001, terrorist attacks, increased security has led to periodic but massive delays during check-in and screening. With far fewer flights, the smaller airports (such as Bangor and Burlington) have not been subject to such wholesale disruptions. No matter what airport you use, remember that new security measures allow travelers in the U.S. only one carry-on bag, plus one personal bag (such as a purse or briefcase). At press time, Pan Am disallows all carry-ons except for a purse or wallet. The Transportation Security Administration (TSA) has also issued a list of newly restricted carry-on items. Knives, box cutters, corkscrews, straight razors, metal scissors, ice picks, golf clubs, baseball bats, pool cues, hockey sticks, and ski poles are not permitted as carry-on items. Permitted items include nail clippers, nail files, tweezers, eyelash curlers, safety razors (including disposable razors), syringes (with documented proof of

medical need), and walking canes and umbrellas (which must be inspected first). For more information, go to www.tsa.gov. Note that your airline may have additional restrictions; call ahead to avoid problems.

GETTING THROUGH THE AIRPORT

With the federalization of airport security, security procedures at U.S. airports are more stable and consistent than ever. Generally, you'll be fine if you arrive at the airport **1 hour** before a domestic flight; if you show up late, tell an airline employee and she'll probably whisk you to the front of the line.

Bring a **current, government-issued photo ID** such as a driver's license or passport. Keep your ID at the ready to show at check-in, the security checkpoint, and sometimes even the gate. (Children under 18 do not need photo IDs for domestic flights, but the adults checking in with them should have them.)

In 2003, the TSA phased out **gate check-in** at all U.S. airports. Passengers with e-tickets can still beat the ticket-counter lines by using **electronic kiosks** or **online check-in.** Ask your airline which alternatives are available, and if you're using a kiosk, bring the credit card you used to book the ticket or your frequent-flier card. If you're checking bags or looking to snag an exit-row seat, you will be able to do so using most airlines' kiosks; again, call your airline for up-to-date information. **Curbside check-in** is also a good way to avoid lines, although a few airlines still ban curbside check-in; call before you go.

Security checkpoint lines are getting shorter than they were during 2001 and 2002, but some doozies remain. If you have trouble standing for long periods of time, tell an airline employee; the airline will provide a wheelchair. Speed up security by **not** wearing metal objects such as big belt buckles. If you've got metallic body parts, a note from your doctor can prevent a long chat with the security screeners. Keep in mind that only **ticketed passengers** are allowed past security, except for folks escorting disabled passengers or children.

Federalization has stabilized **what you can carry on** and **what you can't.** The general rule is that sharp things are out, nail clippers are okay, and food and beverages must be passed through the X-ray machine—but that security screeners can't make you drink from your coffee cup. Bring food in your carry-on rather than checking it, as explosive-detection machines used on checked luggage have been known to mistake food (especially chocolate, for some reason) for bombs. Travelers in the U.S. are allowed one carry-on bag, plus a "personal item" such as a purse, briefcase, or laptop bag. Carry-on hoarders can stuff all sorts of things into a laptop bag; as long as it has a laptop in it, it's still considered a personal item. The Transportation Security Administration (TSA) has issued a list of restricted items; check its website (www.tsa.gov/public/index.jsp) for details.

At press time, the TSA is also recommending that you **not lock your checked luggage** so screeners can search it by hand if necessary. The agency says to use plastic "zip ties," which can be bought at hardware stores and can be easily cut off.

FLYING FOR LESS: TIPS FOR GETTING THE BEST AIRFARE

Passengers sharing the same airplane cabin rarely pay the same fare. Travelers who need to purchase tickets at the last minute, change their itinerary at a moment's notice, or fly one-way often get stuck paying the premium rate. Here are some ways to keep your airfare costs down.

- Passengers who can book their ticket **long in advance,** who can **stay over Saturday night,** or who **fly midweek** or **at less-trafficked hours** will pay a fraction of the full fare. If your schedule is flexible, say so, and ask if you can secure a cheaper fare by changing your flight plans.

- You can also save on airfares by keeping an eye out in local newspapers for **promotional specials** or **fare wars,** when airlines lower prices on their most popular routes. You rarely see fare wars offered for peak travel times, but if you can travel in the off-months, you may snag a bargain.

- Search **the Internet** for cheap fares (see "Planning Your Trip Online").

- **Consolidators,** also known as bucket shops, are great sources for international tickets, although they usually can't beat the Internet on fares within North America. Start by looking in Sunday newspaper travel sections; U.S. travelers should focus on the *New York Times, Los Angeles Times,* and *Miami Herald.* **Beware:** Bucket shop tickets are usually nonrefundable or have stiff cancellation penalties, often as high as 50% to 75% of the price, and some put you on charter airlines with questionable safety records.

Several reliable consolidators are worldwide and available on the Net. **STA Travel** is now the world's leader in student travel, thanks to their purchase of Council Travel. It also offers good fares for travelers of all ages. **ELTExpress (Flights. com) (© 800/TRAV-800;** www. eltexpress.com) started in Europe and has excellent fares worldwide, but particularly to that continent. It also has "local" websites in 12 countries. **FlyCheap (© 800/FLY-CHEAP;** www.1800flycheap.com)

Travel in the Age of Bankruptcy

At press time, two major U.S. airlines were struggling in bankruptcy court and most of the rest weren't doing very well either. To protect yourself, **buy your tickets with a credit card,** as the Fair Credit Billing Act guarantees that you can get your money back from the credit card company if a travel supplier goes under (and if you request the refund within 60 days of the bankruptcy). **Travel insurance** can also help, but make sure it covers against "carrier default" for your specific travel provider. And be aware that if a U.S. airline goes bust mid-trip, a 2001 federal law requires other carriers to take you to your destination (albeit on a space-available basis) for a fee of no more than $25, provided you rebook within 60 days of the cancellation.

is owned by package-holiday megalith MyTravel and so has especially good access to fares for sunny destinations. **Air Tickets Direct** (© 800/778-3447; www. airticketsdirect.com) is based in Montréal and leverages the currently weak Canadian dollar for low fares; it'll also book trips to places that U.S. travel agents won't touch, such as Cuba.

- Join **frequent-flier clubs.** Accrue enough miles, and you'll be rewarded with free flights and elite status. It's free, and you'll get the best choice of seats, faster response to phone inquiries, and prompter service if your luggage is stolen, your flight is canceled or delayed, or if you want to change your seat. You don't need to fly to build frequent-flier miles—**frequent-flier credit cards** can provide thousands of miles for doing your everyday shopping.
- For many more tips about air travel, including a rundown of the major frequent-flier credit cards, pick up a copy of *Frommer's Fly Safe, Fly Smart* (Wiley Publishing, Inc.).

BY CAR

From the south, **I-95** is the major interstate highway serving Connecticut, Rhode Island, Massachusetts, and Maine. The least stressful route (with fewer tractor-trailers) from New York to Boston is via Hartford, Conn., using **I-84** and the **Massachusetts Turnpike.** The easiest approach to northern New England from southern New England is along one of the three main interstate highway corridors. **I-91** heads more or less due north from Hartford along the Vermont–New Hampshire border, then angles through northern Vermont. **I-93** departs from I-95 near Boston, and then cuts through New Hampshire to connect with I-91 near St. Johnsbury, Vt. For Maine, take I-95 north; it parallels the southern Maine coast before veering inland.

If scenery is your priority, the most picturesque way to enter New England is from the west. The most scenic way to arrive in northern Vermont is to drive **I-87** to Exit 34 near Port Kent on Lake Champlain, then catch the car ferry across the lake to Burlington. For a more southern route, take one of the smaller state highways that cross from New York State into Connecticut or Massachusetts. These routes, while often slow, take you through rolling hills and farmland and are exceptionally scenic.

Be aware that the interstates out of New York and Boston can be sluggish on Friday afternoons and evenings in summer, especially along the routes leading to Cape Cod and Maine. A handful of choke points (particularly the Bourne and Sagamore bridges to Cape Cod and the Maine tollbooths on I-95) can back up for miles. North Conway, N.H., is also famed for its nightmarish weekend traffic, especially during foliage season.

BY TRAIN

Amtrak (✆ 800/872-7245; www.amtrak.com) operates Northeast Direct service from Newport News, Va., to Boston via Washington, Baltimore, Philadelphia, and New York City. North of New Haven, Conn., the line divides into two branches, both of which reunite in Boston. Stops along the Hartford branch include Springfield and Worcester; stops on the Providence, R.I., branch include New London, Mystic, and Kingston. The route through Providence is about 15 minutes faster.

Train service to northern New England is very limited. **Amtrak's Vermonter** departs Washington, D.C., with stops in Baltimore, Philadelphia, and New York before following the Connecticut River northward. Stops in Vermont include Brattleboro, Bellows Falls, Claremont (New Hampshire), White River Junction, Randolph, Montpelier, Waterbury, Burlington/Essex Junction, and St. Albans. A bus connection takes passengers on to Montreal. The **Ethan Allen Express** departs New York and travels northward up the Hudson River Valley and into the Adirondacks before veering over to Vermont and terminating at Rutland. Buses continue on to Killington and northward to Middlebury and Burlington.

After more than a decade of delays, Amtrak finally relaunched rail service to Maine in December 2001, restoring a line that had been discontinued in the 1960s. The **Down Easter** operates between North Station in Boston and Portland, with intermediate stops at Haverhill, Massachusetts; Exeter, Durham, and Dover, New Hampshire; and Wells, Saco, and Old Orchard Beach, Maine. Travel time is about 2 hours and 45 minutes between Boston and Portland, with that duration expected to decrease as track upgrades are completed. Bikes may be loaded and off-loaded at Boston, Wells, and Portland. Four trips daily are offered.

For rail service between New York and Connecticut, try the cheaper **Metro North** (✆ 800/METRO-INFO or 212/532-4900; www.mta.nyc.ny.us/mnr) service, which runs commuter trains connecting towns from New Haven to New York City.

BY BUS

Bonanza (✆ 800/556-3815 or 617/720-4110) operates largely in Connecticut. **Concord Trailways** (✆ 800/639-3317; www.concordtrailways.com) serves New Hampshire and Maine, including some smaller towns in the Lake Winnipesaukee and White Mountains areas. **Greyhound** (✆ 800/231-2222 or 617/526-1810) is nationwide, and serves many destinations in New England. **Peter Pan** (✆ 800/343-9999 or 617/426-7838) serves western Massachusetts and Connecticut. **Plymouth & Brockton** (✆ 508/746-0378) serves Massachusetts's south shore and onward to Cape Cod. And **Vermont Transit** (✆ 800/451-3292; www.vermonttransit.com) is affiliated with Greyhound and serves Vermont, New Hampshire, and Maine with frequent departures from Boston.

11 The Active Vacation Planner

Don't let New England's outsized reputation for quaint villages and pastoral landscapes obscure another fact: It's also a superb destination for outdoor adventures.

Of course, New England isn't the Rockies—you won't find endless acres of wilderness populated by grizzlies and bighorn sheep. But you may be surprised at the amount of undeveloped terrain. While the three northern states are the least densely populated and offer the best chances for slipping away from the crowds, you'll still find plenty of outdoor opportunities throughout the region.

The state and regional chapters that follow offer a number of tips on specific adventures (such as biking trips and kayaking tours). This section offers a general overview, as well as contact information for guided tours and recreation specialists.

For more detailed information on where to go and what to do in New England's backcountry, see *Frommer's Great Outdoor Guide to New England.* The **Appalachian Mountain Club** (© 617/523-0636; www.outdoors. org) publishes a number of definitive guides to hiking and boating in the region. An exhaustive collection of regional outdoor guidebooks for sale can be found at **www.mountain wanderer.com**.

OUTFITTERS & ORGANIZED TOURS Reputable resources for New England excursions include the following:

Appalachian Mountain Club (© 603/466-2727; www.outdoors. org), New England's largest outdoor club, hosts workshops and tours throughout the year, many based out of its Pinkham Notch compound in New Hampshire's White Mountains. (Other workshops are held at Mount Greylock in the Massachusetts Berkshires.) One- to 5-day classes range from introductory rock climbing to identifying wild mushrooms to tracking wild animals; tours include backcountry canoeing and hiking trips.

Away.com, one of the best managed of the outdoor-adventure websites, has extensive trip-planning information for those seeking thrills; packaged tours are also available online. Adventure specialists promptly answer any queries you might have. You can search by state and activity.

Backroads (© 800/462-2848 or 510/527-1555; www.backroads.com), the venerable Berkeley-based retailer of packaged soft-adventure trips, offers multi-sport trips to Maine (biking, walking, and sea kayaking), as well as biking and walking excursions through Vermont. This is one of the higher-end outfitters; accommodations typically consist of luxe inns.

Elderhostel (© 877/426-8056; www.elderhostel.org) has a number of excellent programs in New England (and throughout the world) for those over 55 (or traveling with someone who is); many offerings focus on learning about the outdoors through hiking, kayaking, canoeing, and more. Accommodations vary, but the price is right— averaging $500 for 6 days, including meals and instruction. Courses are so popular that catalogs are distributed via a lottery system to ensure that everyone gets an even shot at signing up for the classes most in demand.

Gorp Travel (www.gorp.com), one of the first online resources for outdoor adventure, also offers dozens of adventure packages around the globe. It's now part of the away.com network (see above); more than 100 New England trips are listed, ranging from 1-day canoe excursions in Connecticut to 6-day kayaking and hiking trips along the Maine coast. Overnights typically find travelers at upscale inns.

L.L.Bean (© 888/552-3261; www. llbean.com), the region's premier outdoor retailer, offers workshops on activities ranging from ice climbing to sporting clays. The outdoor discovery program features a 3-day fly-fishing school, 3-day canoe and kayak symposiums, and a weekend cross-country ski workshop, among many other programs.

Sierra Club (© 415/977-5500; www.sierraclub.org/chapters), the venerable environmental organization, has chapters in all six New England states. All host outings ranging from area hikes and bike rides to ice-skating parties open to nonmembers. To view a schedule of upcoming events, visit the website and follow links by state.

Zoar Outdoor (© 800/532-7483; www.zoaroutdoor.com), an all-purpose adventure center on Route 2 (the Mohawk Trail) in western Massachusetts, is a great destination for river sports, including white-water rafting and kayaking, as well as rock climbing. Ask about the family adventure packages.

ALPINE SKIING New England's most challenging alpine ski resorts are located in the three northernmost states, although western Massachusetts also offers skiing that's popular with families. All of the major ski areas offer packages (including accommodations and lift tickets); see the state or regional chapters that follow for resort contact information.

Moguls Ski and Snowboard Tours (© 800/666-4857; www.skimoguls. com) sells packaged ski vacations in Maine, New Hampshire, and Vermont.

For information on resorts and current ski conditions, contact **Ski Maine Association** (© 207/761-3774; www. skimaine.com), **Ski New Hampshire** (© 800/887-5464, or 603/745-9396 in N.H.; www.skinh.com), or **Ski Vermont** (© 802-223-2439; www.ski vermont.com).

BACKPACKING Contact the **Appalachian Mountain Club** (see above) for information on trail guidebooks and organized backpacking trips in the White Mountains and beyond. Contact information for ranger stations in the Green and White mountains national forests is in chapters 11 and 12.

Appalachian Trail Conference (© 304/535-6331; www.atconf.org) is the best single source for information on hiking New England's premier long-distance pathway, which passes through five of the region's six states. (Rhode Island is the exception.) This nonprofit organization publishes detailed trail guides for every step along the route.

Green Mountain Club, on Route 100 between Waterbury and Stowe (© 802/244-7037; www.green mountainclub.org), is the best source of information on Vermont's Long Trail, the oldest long-distance hiking trail in the nation. The club publishes the definitive *Long Trail Guide.* The information center and bookstore are open Monday through Friday, usually until about 5pm.

Baxter State Park (© 207/723-5140; www.baxterstateparkauthority. com) consists of more than 200,000 wild acres in the north-central part of Maine. The park maintains about 180 miles of backcountry hiking trails and more than 25 backcountry sites, some accessible only by canoe. Most hikers coming to the park are intent on ascending 5,267-foot Mount Katahdin, but dozens of other peaks are well worth scaling, and just traveling through the deep woods hereabouts is a sublime experience. Reservations, which can be made by mail or in person (but not by phone), are required for backcountry camping; many of the best spots fill up shortly after the first of the year.

Note: Backcountry camping is not permitted at Acadia National Park in Maine.

BIKING With its human scale and quiet back roads, New England offers great opportunities for road bikers and mountain bikers alike. Bikes are easy to rent throughout the region, and bike shops are great sources of information on the best routes. Look for tips in the regional chapters that follow.

Bike Riders (📞 800/473-7040; www.bikeriderstours.com), out of Boston, runs excellent 6-day tours of Martha's Vineyard and Nantucket, as well as other excursions around New England, Canada, and Europe.

The **Massachusetts Bicycle Coalition** (📞 617/542-2453; www.mass bike.org) strives to improve the biking experience around the state through the development of bikeways. The group's website offers information on state bikeways and numerous links to local bike groups.

Organized inn-to-inn bike tours through the rolling hills of Vermont are a great way to see the countryside by day while relaxing in luxury at night. Tours are typically self-guided, with luggage transferred for you each day by vehicle. Try **Bike Vermont** (📞 800/257-2226 or 802-457-3553; www.bikevt.com), **Country Inns Along the Trail** (📞 800/838-3301 or 802-326-2072; www.inntoinn.com), or **Vermont Bicycle Touring** (VBT; 📞 800/245-3868; www.vbt.com). VBT also offers three trips in Maine, including a 6-day Acadia trip with some overnights at the grand Claremont Hotel.

Bike the Whites (📞 877/854-6535; www.bikethewhites.com) offers self-guided biking tours between three inns in the White Mountains, with each day involving a relaxed 20 miles of biking. Luggage is shuttled from inn to inn.

BIRDING Each state has one or more birding hot lines, which offer recorded announcements of recent unusual sightings: Cape Cod (📞 508/349-9464); Western Massachusetts (📞 413/253-2218); Eastern Massachusetts (📞 781/259-8805); Connecticut (📞 203/254-3665); Rhode Island (📞 401/949-3870); Vermont (📞 802/457-2779); New Hampshire (📞 603/224-9900); and Maine (📞 207/781-2332).

Many experienced birders sign up for whale-watching trips to view pelagic birds; some birder-only trips are scheduled, usually in conjunction with a statewide birding group. For tips on upcoming offshore birding expeditions in Massachusetts, see **www.neseabirds.com**.

The **Maine Audubon Society** (📞 207/781-2330; www.maine audubon.org) offers a series of superb in-depth bird-watching workshops each summer on a beautiful 333-acre island in Mucongus Bay, just northeast of Pemaquid Point. The highlight is a boat trip to an offshore island to see nesting puffins.

CANOEING **Upper Valley Land Trust** (📞 603/643-6626; www.uvlt. org) has established a network of primitive campsites along the Connecticut River; canoeists can paddle and portage its length and camp along the riverbanks. Two of the campsites are accessible by car.

Battenkill Canoe Ltd. (📞 800/421-5268 or 802/362-2800; www. battenkill.com) runs 2- to 6-night canoeing and walking excursions in Vermont. Nights are spent at inns.

The **Allagash Wilderness Waterway**, in Maine, is considered by many to be the region's premier canoe trip. Some 80 campsites are spaced along the nearly 100-mile route, which includes a 9-mile stretch of Class I to II white water. For a map and brochure, contact the **Maine Bureau of Parks and Lands'** northern region office at 106 Hogan Road, Bangor, ME 04401 (📞 207/941-4014).

The Allagash is also served by several outfitters, including **Allagash Canoe Trips** (📞 207/237-3077; www. allagashcanoetrips.com), which leads 5- to 9-day excursions. Bring a sleeping bag; everything else is taken care of.

See also Appalachian Mountain Club and Zoar Outdoor, under "Outfitters & Organized Tours," above.

CROSS-COUNTRY SKIING

Western Massachusetts Cross Country Ski Areas Association (no phone; www.xcskimass.com) produces a website with current ski conditions, upcoming events, and information on the association's eight members.

For a free brochure listing all cross-country facilities in Vermont, contact the **Vermont Department of Travel and Tourism** (© 800/VERMONT). Or log on to www.vermontvacation. com/recreation and click on "X-C Skiing" for a full list and links.

The **Catamount Trail Association** (© 802/864-5794; www.catamount-trail.org) oversees the 200-mile Catamount Trail, which runs the length of Vermont.

Ski New Hampshire (© 800/887-5464, or 603/745-9396 in N.H.; www.skinh.com) offers current information on conditions at cross-country ski resorts, as well as assistance in finding a resort that's suited to your skills and interests.

The **Maine Nordic Ski Council** (© 800/754-9263; www.mnsc.com) prepares a recorded guide to conditions at cross-country ski areas throughout the state; it's updated Fridays in winter. Or go to the website and click on "Snow Conditions."

DEEP-SEA FISHING

Ports up and down the New England coast are home to charter fishing boats; inquire with the chamber of commerce at your destination for more information. Other resources include the following:

Cape Cod Charter Association (© 508/945-6052; www.capecod outdoors.com) books fishing trips on various charter boats sailing from the Cape and the Islands.

Rhode Island Party & Charter-boat Association (© 401/737-5812; www.rifishing.com) is a good contact for setting up trips from this state. Many of the boats sail from bustling Port Judith.

Fish-Maine.com (© 207/273-3474; www.fish-maine.com) manages a website featuring information and links to about three dozen charter boats based along the Maine coast and rivers.

FRESHWATER FISHING

Housatonic Anglers (© 860/672-4457; www.housatonicanglers.com) offers 3-day fly-fishing classes in summer and fall on the scenic Housatonic River in Connecticut. Ask also about guide services and the guest cottages located on 14 private acres along the river.

Orvis Company Store, in Manchester, Vt. (© 888/235-9763 or 802/362-3750; www.orvis.com), sells the company's well-regarded equipment and features small ponds to try out gear before you buy. Orvis also offers top-rated fly-fishing classes in Vermont and on Cape Cod, during which an expert will critique your technique and offer pointers.

Maine Professional Guides Association (© 207/751-3797; www.maineguides.com) represents dozens of registered guides, who pass stringent proficiency tests before being licensed. The website features links to numerous Maine guide services.

Maine Sporting Camps Association (no phone; www.mainesporting camps.com) represents some 50 traditional backcountry lodges scattered in the more remote sections of the state. Fishing guides are often available for hire by the day.

See also L.L.Bean, under "Outfitters and Organized Tours," above, for fly-fishing equipment and workshops.

HIKING

Hikers have dozens of specialized guidebooks to choose from, each offering detailed information on thousands of trails that wind through New England hills and mountains. Local bookstores are amply stocked with guides, which can also be ordered in advance through Amazon.com or other online booksellers. See

"Backpacking," above, for additional information on regional trails.

Country Walkers (© 800/464-9255 or 802/244-1387; www.country walkers.com) has a glorious color catalog (more like a wishbook) outlining supported walking trips around the world, among them 4- or 5-night tours in coastal Maine and north-central Vermont. Trips include all meals and lodging at appealing inns.

New England Hiking Holidays (© 800/869-0949 or 603/356-9696; www.nehikingholidays.com) offers an extensive inventory of options, including weekend trips in the White Mountains as well as more extended excursions to the Maine coast and Vermont. Trips typically involve moderate day hiking coupled with nights at comfortable lodges.

HORSEBACK RIDING Horse rentals.com (© 877/446-7730; www. horserentals.com) features a directory of stables that offer horse rentals and guided trail rides in all six New England states.

Kedron Valley Stables (© 800/225-6301 or 802/457-1480) runs 4- to 6-day trips in the Green Mountains of Vermont. You'll be guided through secluded woods and historic towns like South Woodstock, Tyson, and Window, staying at inns and eating at wonderful country restaurants.

Vermont Icelandic Horse Farm (© 802/496-7141; www.icelandic horses.com) leads 2- to 5-day trips on tiny Icelandic ponies, which move at a steady gait without much rocking—much like driving with good shocks.

SAILING JWorld Sailing School (© 800/343-2255 or 401/849-5492; www.jworldschool.com) is a performance sailing school founded in Newport, R.I., in 1981. (It also has locations in Key West, Annapolis, and San Diego.) Offerings include a 5-day learn-to-sail course; each class has just four students and includes 6-hour days on the water.

Winds of Ireland (© 800/458-9301 or 802/863-5090; www.windsof ireland.net), in South Burlington, Vt. on "New England's West Coast" (Lake Champlain, that is), charters six Hunters and a Catalina ranging from 28 to 41 feet.

Maine Windjammer Association (© 800/807-9463; www.sailmaine coast.com) is a consortium of more than a dozen handsome vintage and replica sailing ships that take passengers on crewed trips of 3 and 6 days. Most are based in the Camden and Rockland area. An array of excursions are available.

Hinckley Yacht Charters (© 800/492-7245 or 207/244-5008; www. hinckleycharters.com) is on the southwestern shores of Mount Desert Island in Maine, and features more than 20 of the internationally famous boats available for weekly rental (from $2,525) to qualified sailors. Those without experience should contact **Hinckley Crewed Charters** (© 800/504-2305 or 207/244-0122; www. hinckleyyacht.com) for information on fully outfitted charters.

SEA KAYAKING Adventure Learning (© 800/649-9728 or 978/346-9728; www.adventure-learning. com) offers 1-day sea-kayaking workshops and tours, including a whale-watching paddle that departs from Newburyport, Mass.

Collinsville Canoe & Kayak (© 860/693-6977; www.cckstore. com), in Collinsville, Conn., leads 4- to 6-hour trips around some of the appealing lakes and estuaries of coastal Connecticut. Lessons and rentals are also available.

Maine Island Trail Association (© 207/596-6456 or 207/761-8225; www.mita.org) oversees the nation's first long-distance water trail. Established in 1987, this 325-mile waterway winds along the coast from Portland to Machias, and incorporates some 70 state- and privately owned

Spas for Sybarites

New England's Puritan work ethic and its inhabitants' preference for austere forms of recreation (fly-fishing in Apr, ice-skiing in Jan) don't necessarily mean that sybarites will be left out in the cold. Spas have made some inroads in New England, and now offer guests the sort of pampering that the Pilgrims would have found altogether bewildering. Below is a sampling of some reputable spas in the region.

Canyon Ranch, 165 Kemble St., Lenox, MA 01240 (© **800/742-9000;** www.canyonranch.com), is the region's premier spa. It's in the Berkshires at the Bellefontaine mansion, an extraordinary 1897 replica of a palace at Versailles. The spa mixes athletic and outdoor endeavors with nutritional dining, and tops it all off with massages and other body work, including mud treatments, relexology, shiatsu, and herbal wraps. The rates are not for the budget-minded (a 3-night stay for two typically runs more than $2,100), but they do include treatments, gratuities, and other activities that are priced separately at many other spas.

Kripalu Center for Yoga and Health, P.O. Box 793, Lenox, MA 01240 (© **800/967-3577;** www.kripalu.org/programguide.html), is a superb destination for those who use "quest" as a verb. The emphasis is on spirit and soul, with weekend retreats offering programs such as "Raw Juice Fasting" and "The Practice of Thai Yoga Massage." It's in the Berkshires on the grounds of a former Jesuit seminary, and the accommodations range from dormitories to rather spartan private rooms. (Make your own bed.) The center publishes an extensive bulletin of classes and events; you can browse upcoming programs on the website.

Norwich Inn & Spa, 607 W. Thames St., Rte. 32, Norwich, CT 06369 (© **800/ASK-4-SPA;** www.norwichinnandspa.com), is an intimate retreat in a brick Georgian mansion on 40 acres not far from Mystic. It offers a long list of services, such as invigorating loofah scrubs, clay wraps, and thalassotherapy, a seawater-based treatment. It also has tennis courts and an 18-hole golf course next door.

Topnotch at Stowe, Mountain Road, Stowe, VT 05672 (© **800/ 451-8686** or 802-253-8585; www.topnotch-resort.com), is considered a resort spa rather than a destination spa, but it has an attractive indoor pool and fitness facility situated on 120 acres near Stowe's ski area and is near great summer hiking trails. A variety of treatments are available, and there's easy access to year-round outdoor activities, like hiking in the Green Mountains and horseback riding on superb local trails. Spa and non-spa meals are served in the elegant on-site restaurant.

islands along the route. Members of the association, a nonprofit group, help maintain and monitor the islands and in turn are granted permission to visit and camp on them provided they follow certain restrictions. Membership is $45 per year.

Maine Island Kayak Co. (© **800/ 796-2373** or 207/766-2373; www.sea-kayak.com) has a fleet of seaworthy kayaks it employs on camping trips up and down the Maine coast. The firm has a number of 2- and 3-night expeditions each summer, and the staff has plenty of experience training novices.

Maine Sport Outfitters (© 800/722-0826 or 207/236-8797; www.mainesport.com) offers rentals and guided tours from a convenient Penobscot Bay location.

See also L.L.Bean, under "Outfitters and Organized Tours," earlier in this chapter, for information on the store's kayak classes and symposia.

SNOWMOBILING VAST, the **Vermont Association of Snow Travelers** (© 802/229-0005; www.vtvast.org), produces a helpful newsletter and can help point you and your machine in the right direction. **Snowmobile Vermont** (© 860/916-0937; www.snowmobilevt.com) runs another website of links to clubs.

The **New Hampshire Snowmobile Association** (© 603/224-8906; www.nhsa.com) provides information on the nearly 6,000 miles of groomed trails that lace the state, including information on how to register your machine (mandatory) through any of the 248 off-highway recreational-vehicle agents. For current trail conditions, call © 603/743-5050 or go to the website.

The **Maine Snowmobile Association** (© 207/622-6983; www.mesnow.com) has information on more than 12,000 miles of maintained snowmobile trails. The website lists current conditions, sled-friendly accommodations, and outfitters.

WHITE-WATER RAFTING The region's big-water rivers are in northern and western Maine, but white-water rafting trips are available in Massachusetts, Vermont, and Connecticut as well.

North American Whitewater Expeditions (© 800/727-4379 or 207/663-4430; www.nawhitewater.com) runs early-spring trips on Connecticut's Housatonic River and Vermont's West River, as well as summer trips in Maine.

Raft Maine (© 800/723-8633 or 207/824-3694; www.raftmaine.com) is a trade association of white-water outfitters running descents on Maine rivers, including the Penobscot, Kennebec, and Dead. See chapter 13 for more information on the rivers.

See also Zoar Outdoor under "Outfitters and Organized Tours," earlier in this section for information on rafting rivers in western Massachusetts.

12 Getting Around New England

BY CAR New England airports all host national car rental chains. Useful phone numbers include: **Avis** (© 800/831-2847), **Budget** (© 800/527-0700), **Enterprise** (© 800/325-8007), **Hertz** (© 800/654-3131), **National** (© 800/227-7368), **Rent-A-Wreck** (© 800/535-1391), and **Thrifty** (© 800/367-2277).

Before you drive off in a rental car, be sure you're insured. The basic insurance coverage offered by most car-rental companies, known as the **Loss/Damage Waiver (LDW)** or **Collision Damage Waiver (CDW),** can cost $20 per day or more. It usually covers the full value of the vehicle with no deductible if an outside party causes

damage to the car. In all states but California, you will probably be covered in case of theft as well. Liability coverage varies according to company policy and state law, but the minimum is usually at least $15,000. If you are at fault in an accident, however, you will be covered for the full replacement value of the car but not for liability.

Most major credit cards provide some degree of coverage as well—provided they were used to pay for the rental. Terms vary widely, however, so be sure to call your credit card company directly before you rent. The credit card will cover damage or theft of a rental car for the full cost of the vehicle. If you already have insurance, your credit card will provide secondary coverage—which basically covers your deductible. Credit cards will not cover liability.

The speed limit on interstate highways in the region is generally 65 mph, although this is reduced to 55 mph near cities. State highways are a less formal network, and the speed limits vary. Watch for speed limits to drop as you approach a town; that's where the local police can lurk in search of speeders.

If you're a connoisseur of back roads and off-the-beaten-track exploring, **DeLorme Atlases** are invaluable. They offer an extraordinary level of detail, right down to logging roads and public boat launches on small ponds. DeLorme's headquarters and map store (© **888/227-1656**) is in Yarmouth, Maine, but its products are widely available at bookshops and convenience stores throughout the region.

BY BUS   See "Getting There," earlier in this chapter, for a list of bus companies serving New England. While express bus service to major cities and tourist areas is quite good, quirky schedules and routes between regional destinations may send you miles out of the way and increase trip time significantly.

13 Tips on Accommodations

What's the difference between an inn and a B&B? The difference narrows by the day. Until relatively recently, inns were always full-service affairs, whereas B&Bs consisted of private homes with an extra bedroom or two and a homeowner looking for some extra income. A few of these old-style B&Bs still exist, but they seem to be fading to the margins, in large part driven by the fact that Americans generally don't want to share bathrooms with other guests.

Today, the only difference between an inn and a B&B is that inns serve dinner (and sometimes lunch), whereas B&Bs provide breakfast only. At least that's the distinction we employ for this guide. Readers shouldn't infer that B&Bs in this guide are necessarily more informal or in any way inferior to a full-service inn. Indeed, many of the B&Bs listed have the air of gracious inns that have accidentally overlooked dinner.

B&Bs today are mostly professionally run affairs, where guests enjoy sumptuous breakfasts, attentive service, private bathrooms (we note exceptions in our reviews), and a common area that's separate from the owner's living quarters.

As innkeeping evolves into the more complex and demanding "hospitality industry," you're bound to bump up against more restrictions, rules, and regulations. It's always best to ask in advance to avoid unpleasant surprises.

A few notes on recent trends:

SMOKING   Smokers looking to light up are being edged out the door to smoke on front lawns and porches. It's no different in the region's inns and B&Bs than in other public spaces. A decade or two ago, only a handful of places prohibited smoking. Today, the great majority of inns and B&Bs have banned smoking within their buildings entirely, and some have even exiled smokers from their property—front lawn included.

Frommer's has stopped mentioning whether smoking is allowed or not in inns because it has rapidly become a non-issue—almost everyone has banned it. Assume that no smoking is allowed at any of the accommodations listed in this guide. (As in other regions, the larger, more modern hotels—say a Radisson or Holiday Inn—will have guest rooms set aside for smokers.) If being able to smoke in your room or the lobby is paramount to your vacation happiness, be sure to inquire first. Likewise, if you're a nonsmoker who finds the smell of cigarette smoke obnoxious in the extreme, it also wouldn't hurt to ask and make sure you're at a fully smoke-free establishment.

ADDITIONAL GUESTS The room rates published in this guide are for two people sharing a room. Many places charge $10 and up for each extra guest sharing the room. Don't assume that children traveling with you are free; ask first about extra charges. Also don't assume that all places are able to accommodate children or extra guests; the rooms at some inns are quite cozy and lack space for a cot. Ask first if you don't want to end up four to a bed.

MINIMUM STAY It's become increasingly common for inns to require guests to book a minimum of 2 nights or more during busy times. These times typically include weekends in summer (or in winter near ski areas), holiday periods, and the fall foliage season. These policies are mentioned in the following pages when known, but they're in constant flux, so don't be surprised if you're told you need to reserve an extra day when you make reservations.

Note that minimum-stay policies typically apply only to those making advance reservations. If you stop by an inn on a Saturday night and find a room available, innkeepers won't make you stay a second night. Also, thanks to erratic travel planning, the occasional stray night sometimes becomes available during minimum-stay periods. Don't hesitate to call and ask if a single night is available when planning your itinerary.

DEPOSITS Many establishments now require guests to provide a credit card number to hold a room. What happens if you cancel? Some places have a graduated refund—cancel a

week in advance, and you'll be charged for 1 night's stay; cancel a day in advance, and you're charged for your whole reserved stay—unless they can fill the room. Then you'll be charged for half. Other places are quite generous about refunding your deposit. It's more than a bit tedious to figure it all out, and the policies can often seem irrational.

Most hotels and inns are fair and will scrupulously spell out their cancellation policy when you make reservations, but always ask about it before you divulge your credit card number, and, if possible, ask to have it e-mailed, faxed, or sent to you before you agree to anything.

PETS Sometimes yes, sometimes no. Always ask.

SERVICE CHARGES Rather than increase room rates in the face of rising competition, many lodgings are increasingly tacking on unpublicized fees to guests' bills. Most innkeepers will tell you about these when you reserve or check in; the less scrupulous will surprise you at checkout. In our opinion, this is not a welcome trend.

The most common surcharge is an involuntary "service charge" of 10% to 15%. Coupled with state lodging taxes (even "sales-tax-free" New Hampshire has an 8% levy), that bumps the cost of a bed up by nearly 25%. (The rates listed in this guide don't include service charges or sales tax.)

Other charges might include a pet fee (as much as $10 per day extra), a foliage-season surcharge ($10 or more per room), or a "resort fee."

SAVING ON YOUR HOTEL ROOM

The **rack rate** is the maximum rate that a hotel charges for a room. Hardly anybody pays this price, however. To lower the cost of your room:

- **Ask about special rates or other discounts.** Always ask whether a room less expensive than the first one quoted is available, or whether any special rates apply to you. You may qualify for corporate, student, military, senior, or other discounts. Mention membership in AAA, AARP, frequent-flier programs, or trade unions, which may entitle you to special deals as well. Find out the hotel policy on children—do kids stay free in the room or is there a special rate?

- **Dial direct.** When booking a room in a chain hotel, you'll often get a better deal by calling the individual hotel's reservation desk than at the chain's main number.
- **Book online.** Many hotels offer Internet-only discounts, or supply rooms to Priceline, Hotwire, or Expedia at rates much lower than the ones you can get through the hotel itself.
- **Remember the law of supply and demand.** Resort hotels are most crowded and therefore most expensive on weekends, so discounts are usually available for midweek stays. Business hotels in downtown locations are busiest during the week, so you can expect big discounts over the weekend. Many hotels have high-season and low-season prices, and booking the day after "high season" ends can mean big discounts.
- **Look into group or long-stay discounts.** If you come as part of a large group, you should be able to negotiate a bargain rate, since the hotel can then guarantee occupancy in a number of rooms. Likewise, if you're planning a long stay (at least 5 days), you might qualify for a discount. As a general rule, expect 1 night free after a 7-night stay.
- **Avoid excess charges and hidden costs.** When you book a room, ask whether the hotel charges for

parking. Use your own cellphone, pay phones, or prepaid phone cards instead of dialing direct from hotel phones, which usually have exorbitant rates. And don't be tempted by the room's minibar offerings: Most hotels charge through the nose for water, soda, and snacks. Finally, ask about local taxes and service charges, which can increase the cost of a room by 15% or more. If a hotel insists upon tacking on a surprise "energy surcharge" that wasn't mentioned at check-in or a "resort fee" for amenities you didn't use, you can often make a case for getting it removed.

- Carefully consider your hotel's meal plan. If you enjoy eating out and sampling the local cuisine, it makes sense to choose a **Continental Plan (CP),** which includes breakfast only, or a **European Plan (EP),** which doesn't include any meals and allows you maximum flexibility. If you're more interested in saving money, opt for a **Modified American Plan (MAP),** which includes breakfast and one meal, or the **American Plan (AP),** which includes three meals. If you must choose a MAP, see if you can get a free lunch at your hotel if you decide to do dinner out.
- **Book an efficiency.** A room with a kitchenette allows you to cook your own meals. This is a big money saver, especially for families on long stays.

LANDING THE BEST ROOM

Somebody has to get the best room in the house. It might as well be you. You can start by joining the hotel's frequent-guest program, which may make you eligible for upgrades. A hotel-branded credit card usually gives it owner "silver" or "gold" status in frequent-guest programs for free.

Always ask about a corner room. They're often larger and quieter, with more windows and light, and they often cost the same as standard rooms. When you make your reservation, ask if the hotel is renovating; if it is, request a room away from the construction. Ask about nonsmoking rooms, rooms with views, rooms with twin, queen- or king-size beds. If you're a light sleeper, request a quiet room away from vending machines, elevators, restaurants, bars, and discos. Ask for one of the rooms that has been most recently renovated or redecorated.

If you aren't happy with your room when you arrive, say so. If another room is available, most lodgings will be willing to accommodate you.

In resort areas, particularly in warm climates, ask the following questions before you book a room:

- What's the view like? Cost-conscious travelers may be willing to pay less for a back room facing the parking lot, especially if they don't plan to spend much time in their room.
- Does the room have air-conditioning or ceiling fans? Do the windows open? If they do, and the nighttime entertainment takes place alfresco, you may want to find out when show time is over.
- What's included in the price? Your room may be moderately priced, but if you're charged for beach chairs, towels, sports equipment, and other amenities, you could end up spending more than you bargained for.
- How far is the room from the beach and other amenities? If it's far, is there transportation to and from the beach.

FAST FACTS: New England

American Express American Express offers travel services, including check cashing and trip planning, through a number of affiliated agencies in the region. Call ✆ **800/221-7282** for the nearest location.

Embassies/Consulates See chapter 3, "For International Visitors."

Emergencies In the event of an emergency, find any phone and dial ✆ **911**. You do not need a coin to make this call from a pay phone. If this fails, dial "0" (zero) and tell the operator you need to report an emergency.

Internet Access Many public libraries have free terminals with Web access, allowing travelers to check their e-mail through a Web-based e-mail service such as Yahoo! or Hotmail. Internet cafes have come and gone in the last few years; it's best to ask around locally, or check **www.netcafeguide.com** or **www.cybercafe.com**.

Liquor Laws The legal age to consume alcohol is 21. In Maine, New Hampshire, and Vermont, liquor is sold at government-operated stores only; in Connecticut, Massachusetts, and Rhode Island, liquor is sold in privately owned shops. Restaurants that don't have liquor licenses sometimes allow patrons to bring in their own. Ask first.

Lost & Found Be sure to notify all of your credit card companies the minute you discover your wallet has been lost or stolen, and file a report at the nearest police precinct. Your credit card company or insurer may require a police report number or record of the loss. Most credit card companies have an emergency toll-free number to call if your card is lost or stolen; they may be able to wire you a cash advance immediately or deliver an emergency credit card in a day or two. Visa's U.S. emergency numbers are ⓒ **800/847-2911** or 410/581-9994. American Express cardholders and traveler's check holders should call ⓒ **800/221-7282.** MasterCard holders should call ⓒ **800/307-7309** or 636/722-7111. For other credit cards, call the toll-free number directory at ⓒ **800/555-1212.**

If you need emergency cash over the weekend when all banks and American Express offices are closed, you can have money wired to you via **Western Union** (ⓒ 800/325-6000; www.westernunion.com).

Identity theft or fraud are potential complications of losing your wallet, especially if you've lost your driver's license along with your cash and credit cards. Notify the major credit-reporting bureaus immediately; placing a fraud alert on your record may protect you against liability for criminal activity. The three major U.S. credit-reporting agencies are **Equifax** (ⓒ **800/766-0008**; www.equifax.com), **Experian** (ⓒ **888/397-3742**; www.experian.com), and **TransUnion** (ⓒ **800/680-7289**; www.transunion.com). Finally, if you've lost all forms of photo ID, call your airline and explain the situation; they might allow you to board the plane if you have a copy of your passport or birth certificate and a copy of the police report you've filed.

Maps All five states offer free maps at well-stocked visitor information centers; ask at the counter if you don't see them. For incredibly detailed maps, consider purchasing one or more of the DeLorme atlases, which depict every road and stream, along with many hiking trails and access points for canoes. DeLorme's headquarters and map store (ⓒ **800/561-5105** or 800/642-0970) are in Yarmouth, Maine, but their products are available at bookstores and convenience stores throughout the region.

Newspapers/Magazines The *Boston Globe, Wall Street Journal,* and *New York Times* are distributed throughout New England, although they can sometimes be hard to find in more remote villages. Almost every small town has a daily or weekly newspaper covering local happenings. These are good sources of information for events and restaurant specials.

Taxes Current state sales taxes (as of 2004): Connecticut, 6% (12% on lodging); Maine, 5% (7% on lodging, 10% on auto rentals); Massachusetts, 5% (local sales taxes may also apply on lodging); New Hampshire, no general sales tax but 8% tax on lodging and dining; Rhode Island, 7% (plus 5% surtax on lodging); and Vermont, 6% (9% on lodging and dining, 10% on alcohol served in restaurants).

Time All of New England is in the eastern time zone, the same as New York. All states shift to daylight savings time (1 hr. ahead) on the first Sunday in April, and back to standard time on the last Sunday in October.

3

For International Visitors

by Paul Karr

Most of the general information you'll need to ensure a pleasant trip can be found in chapter 2, "Planning Your Trip to New England." Some aspects of U.S. laws, customs, and culture that might be perplexing to visitors from overseas are covered in this chapter.

1 Preparing for Your Trip

ENTRY REQUIREMENTS

Check at any U.S. embassy or consulate for current information and requirements. You can also obtain a visa application and other information online at the **U.S. State Department**'s website, at **www.travel.state.gov**.

VISAS The U.S. State Department has a **Visa Waiver Program** allowing citizens of certain countries to enter the United States without a visa for stays of up to 90 days. At press time these included Andorra, Australia, Austria, Belgium, Brunei, Denmark, Finland, France, Germany, Iceland, Ireland, Italy, Japan, Liechtenstein, Luxembourg, Monaco, the Netherlands, New Zealand, Norway, Portugal, San Marino, Singapore, Slovenia, Spain, Sweden, Switzerland, and the United Kingdom. Citizens of these countries need only a valid passport and a round-trip air or cruise ticket in their possession upon arrival. If they first enter the United States, they may also visit Mexico, Canada, Bermuda, and/or the Caribbean islands and return to the United States without a visa. Further information is available from any U.S. embassy or consulate. Canadian citizens may enter the United States without visas; they need only proof of residence.

Citizens of all other countries must have (1) a valid passport that expires at least 6 months later than the scheduled end of their visit to the United States, and (2) a tourist visa, which may be obtained without charge from any U.S. consulate.

To obtain a visa, the traveler must submit a completed application form (either in person or by mail) with a 1½-inch-square photo, and must demonstrate binding ties to a residence abroad. Usually you can obtain a visa at once or within 24 hours, but it may take longer during the summer rush from June through August. If you cannot go in person, contact the nearest U.S. embassy or consulate for directions on applying by mail. Your travel agent or airline office may also be able to provide you with visa applications and instructions. The U.S. consulate or embassy that issues your visa will determine whether you will be issued a multiple- or single-entry visa and any restrictions regarding the length of your stay.

British subjects can obtain up-to-date visa information by calling the **U.S. Embassy Visa Information Line** (© **0891/200-290**) or by visiting the "Consular Services" section of the American Embassy London's website at www.usembassy.org.uk.

Tips Prepare to Be Fingerprinted

Starting in January 2004, many international visitors traveling on visas to the United States will be photographed and fingerprinted at Customs in a new program created by the Department of Homeland Security called **US-VISIT.** Non-U.S. citizens arriving at airports and on cruise ships must undergo an instant background check as part of the government's ongoing efforts to deter terrorism by verifying the identity of incoming and outgoing visitors. Exempt from the extra scrutiny are visitors entering by land or those from 28 countries (mostly in Europe) that don't require a visa for short-term visits. For more information, go to the Homeland Security website at **www.dhs.gov/dhspublic.**

Irish citizens can obtain up-to-date visa information through the **Embassy of the USA Dublin,** 42 Elgin Rd., Dublin 4, Ireland (© **353/1-668-8777**) or by checking the "Consular Services" section of the website at www.usembassy.ie.

Australian citizens can obtain up-to-date visa information by contacting the **U.S. Embassy Canberra,** Moonah Place, Yarralumla, ACT 2600 (© **02/ 6214-5600**) or by checking the U.S. Diplomatic Mission's website at http:// usembassy-australia.state.gov/consular.

Citizens of **New Zealand** can obtain up-to-date visa information by contacting the **U.S. Embassy New Zealand,** 29 Fitzherbert Terrace, Thorndon, Wellington (© **644/472-2068**), or get the information directly from the "Services to New Zealanders" section of the website at http:// usembassy.org.nz.

MEDICAL REQUIREMENTS

Unless you're arriving from an area known to be suffering from an epidemic (particularly cholera or yellow fever), inoculations or vaccinations are not required for entry into the United States. If you have a medical condition that requires **syringe-administered medications,** carry a valid signed prescription from your physician— the Federal Aviation Administration (FAA) no longer allows airline passengers to pack syringes in their carry-on baggage without documented proof of medical need. If you have a disease that requires treatment with **narcotics,** you should also carry documented proof with you—smuggling narcotics aboard a plane is a serious offense that carries severe penalties in the U.S.

For **HIV-positive visitors,** requirements for entering the United States are somewhat vague and change frequently. According to the latest publication of *HIV and Immigrants: A Manual for AIDS Service Providers,* the Immigration and Naturalization Service (INS) doesn't require a medical exam for entry into the United States, but INS officials may stop individuals because they look sick or because they are carrying AIDS/HIV medicine.

If an HIV-positive noncitizen applies for a nonimmigrant visa, the question on the application regarding communicable diseases is tricky no matter which way it's answered. If the applicant checks "no," INS may deny the visa on the grounds that the applicant committed fraud. If the applicant checks "yes" or if INS suspects the person is HIV-positive, it will deny the visa unless the applicant asks for a special waiver for visitors. This waiver is for people visiting the United States for a short time, to attend a conference, for instance, to visit close relatives, or to receive medical treatment. It can be a confusing situation. For up-to-the-minute information, contact **AIDSinfo** (© **800/448-0440,** or

301/519-6616 outside the U.S.; www. aidsinfo.nih.gov) or the **Gay Men's Health Crisis** (© 212/367-1000; www.gmhc.org).

DRIVER'S LICENSES Foreign driver's licenses are mostly recognized in the U.S., although you may want to get an international driver's license if your home license is not written in English.

PASSPORT INFORMATION

Safeguard your passport in an inconspicuous, inaccessible place like a money belt. Make a copy of the critical pages, including the passport number, and store it in a safe place, separate from the passport itself. If you lose your passport, visit the nearest consulate of your native country as soon as possible for a replacement. Passport applications are downloadable from the websites listed below.

Note that the International Civil Aviation Organization (ICAO) has recommended a policy requiring that *every* individual who travels by air have his or her own passport. In response, many countries are now requiring that children must be issued their own passport to travel internationally, where before those under 16 or so may have been allowed to travel on a parent or guardian's passport.

FOR RESIDENTS OF CANADA

You can pick up a passport application at 1 of 28 regional passport offices or most travel agencies. Canadian children who travel must have their own passport. However, if you hold a valid Canadian passport issued before December 11, 2001, that bears the name of your child, the passport remains valid for you and your child until it expires. Passports cost C$85 for those 16 years and older (valid 5 years), C$35 children 3 to 15 (valid 5 years), and C$20, children under 3 (valid 3 years). Applications, which must be accompanied by two identical passport-sized photographs and proof of Canadian citizenship, are available at travel agencies throughout Canada or from the central **Passport Office,** Department of Foreign Affairs and International Trade, Ottawa, ON K1A 0G3 (© 800/567-6868; www. ppt.gc.ca). Processing takes 5 to 10 days if you apply in person, or about 3 weeks by mail.

FOR RESIDENTS OF THE UNITED KINGDOM

As a member of the European Union, you need only an identity card, not a passport, to travel to other EU countries. However, if you already possess a passport, it's always useful to carry it. To pick up an application for a standard 10-year passport (5-year passport for children under 16), visit the nearest Passport Office, major post office, or travel agency. You can also contact the **United Kingdom Passport Service** at © 0870/571-0410, or visit its website at www.passport.gov.uk. Passports are £33 for adults and £19 for children under 16, with an additional £30 fee if you apply in person at a Passport Office. Processing takes about 2 weeks (1 week if you apply at the Passport Office).

FOR RESIDENTS OF IRELAND

You can apply for a 10-year passport, costing €57, at the **Passport Office,** Setanta Centre, Molesworth Street, Dublin 2 (© 01/671-1633; www. irlgov.ie/iveagh). Those under age 18 and over 65 must apply for a €12 3-year passport. You can also apply at 1A South Mall, Cork (© 021/272-525) or over the counter at most main post offices.

FOR RESIDENTS OF AUSTRALIA

You can pick up an application from your local post office or any branch of Passports Australia, but you must schedule an interview to present your application materials. Call the **Australian Passport Information Service** at ℂ **131-232,** or visit the government website at www.passports.gov.au. Passports for adults are A$144 and for those under 18 are A$72.

FOR RESIDENTS OF NEW ZEALAND

You can pick up a passport application at any New Zealand Passports Office or download it from their website. Contact the **Passports Office** at ℂ **0800/225-050** in New Zealand or 04/474-8100, or log on to www.passports.govt.nz. Passports for adults are NZ$80 and for children under 16 NZ$40.

CUSTOMS
WHAT YOU CAN BRING IN

Every visitor more than 21 years of age may bring in, free of duty, the following: (1) 1 liter of wine or hard liquor; (2) 200 cigarettes, 100 cigars (but not from Cuba), or 3 pounds of smoking tobacco; and (3) $100 worth of gifts. These exemptions are offered to travelers who spend at least 72 hours in the United States and who have not claimed them within the preceding 6 months. It is altogether forbidden to bring into the country foodstuffs (particularly fruit, cooked meats, and canned goods) and plants (vegetables, seeds, tropical plants, and the like). Foreign tourists may bring in or take out up to $10,000 in U.S. or foreign currency with no formalities; larger sums must be declared to U.S. Customs on entering or leaving, which includes filing form CM 4790. For more specific information regarding U.S. Customs, contact your nearest U.S. embassy or consulate, or the **U.S. Customs** office (ℂ **202/927-1770** or www.customs.ustreas.gov).

WHAT YOU CAN TAKE HOME

U.K. citizens returning from a non-EU country have a Customs allowance of: 200 cigarettes; 50 cigars; 250g of smoking tobacco; 2 liters of still table wine; 1 liter of spirits or strong liqueurs (over 22% volume); 2 liters of fortified wine, sparkling wine or other liqueurs; 60cc (ml) perfume; 250cc (ml) of toilet water; and £145 worth of all other goods, including gifts and souvenirs. People under 17 cannot have the tobacco or alcohol allowance. For more information, contact HM Customs & Excise at ℂ **0845/010-9000** (from outside the U.K., 020/8929-0152), or consult their website at www.hmce.gov.uk.

For a clear summary of **Canadian** rules, request the booklet *I Declare,* issued by the **Canada Customs and Revenue Agency** (ℂ **800/461-9999** in Canada, or 204/983-3500; www.ccra-adrc.gc.ca). Canada allows its citizens a C$750 exemption, and you're allowed to bring back duty-free one carton of cigarettes, 1 can of tobacco, 40 imperial ounces of liquor, and 50 cigars. In addition, you're allowed to mail gifts to Canada valued at less than C$60 a day, provided they're unsolicited and don't contain alcohol or tobacco (write on the package "Unsolicited gift, under $60 value"). All valuables should be declared on the Y-38 form before departure from Canada, including serial numbers of valuables you already own, such as expensive foreign cameras. *Note:* The C$750 exemption can only be used once a year and only after an absence of 7 days.

The duty-free allowance in **Australia** is A$400 or, for those under 18, A$200. Citizens age 18 and over can bring in 250 cigarettes or 250 grams of loose tobacco, and 1,125 milliliters of alcohol. If you're returning with valuables you already own, such as foreign-made cameras, you should file form B263. A helpful brochure available from Australian consulates or Customs offices is *Know Before*

You Go. For more information, call the **Australian Customs Service** at ℭ **1300/363-263,** or log on to www.customs.gov.au.

The duty-free allowance for **New Zealand** is NZ$700. Citizens over 17 can bring in 200 cigarettes, 50 cigars, or 250 grams of tobacco (or a mixture of all three if their combined weight doesn't exceed 250g); plus 4.5 liters of wine and beer, or 1.125 liters of liquor. New Zealand currency does not carry import or export restrictions. Fill out a certificate of export, listing the valuables you are taking out of the country; that way, you can bring them back without paying duty. Most questions are answered in a free pamphlet available at New Zealand consulates and Customs offices: *New Zealand Customs Guide for Travellers, Notice no. 4.* For more information, contact **New Zealand Customs,** The Customhouse, 17–21 Whitmore St., Box 2218, Wellington (ℭ **0800/428-786** or 04/473-6099; www.customs.govt.nz).

HEALTH INSURANCE

Although it's not required of travelers, health insurance is highly recommended. Unlike many European countries, the United States does not usually offer free or low-cost medical care to its citizens or visitors. Doctors and hospitals are expensive, and in most cases will require advance payment or proof of coverage before they render their services. Policies can cover everything from the loss or theft of your baggage and trip cancellation to the guarantee of bail in case you're arrested. Good policies will also cover the costs of an accident, repatriation, or death. See "Health & Safety," in chapter 2 for more information. Packages such as **Europ Assistance's "Worldwide Healthcare Plan"** are sold by European automobile clubs and travel agencies at attractive rates. **Worldwide Assistance Services, Inc.**

(ℭ **800/821-2828;** www.worldwide assistance.com) is the agent for Europ Assistance in the United States.

Though lack of health insurance may prevent you from being admitted to a hospital in nonemergencies, don't worry about being left on a street corner to die: The American way is to fix you now and bill the living daylights out of you later.

INSURANCE FOR BRITISH TRAVELERS Most big travel agents offer their own insurance and will probably try to sell you their package when you book a holiday. Think before you sign. **Britain's Consumers' Association** recommends that you insist on seeing the policy and reading the fine print before buying travel insurance. **The Association of British Insurers** (ℭ **020/7600-3333;** www.abi.org.uk) gives advice by phone and publishes *Holiday Insurance,* a free guide to policy provisions and prices. You might also shop around for better deals: Try **Columbus Direct** (ℭ **020/7375-0011;** www.columbusdirect.net).

INSURANCE FOR CANADIAN TRAVELERS Canadians should check with their provincial health plan offices or call **Health Canada** (ℭ **613/957-2991;** www.hc-sc.gc.ca) to find out the extent of their coverage and what documentation and receipts they must take home in case they are treated in the United States.

MONEY

CURRENCY The U.S. monetary system is very simple: The most common **bills** are the $1 (colloquially, a "buck"), $5, $10, and $20 denominations. There are also $2 bills (seldom encountered), $50 bills, and $100 bills (the last two are usually not welcome as payment for small purchases). All the paper money was recently redesigned, making the famous faces adorning them disproportionately large. The old-style bills are still legal tender.

There are seven denominations of coins: 1¢ (1 cent, or a penny); 5¢ (5 cents, or a nickel); 10¢ (10 cents, or a dime); 25¢ (25 cents, or a quarter); 50¢ (50 cents, or a half dollar); the new gold-colored "Sacagawea" coin worth $1; and, prized by collectors, the rare, older silver dollar.

Note: The "foreign-exchange bureaus" so common in Europe are rare even at airports in the United States, and nonexistent outside major cities. It's best not to change foreign money (or traveler's checks denominated in a currency other than U.S. dollars) at a small-town bank, or even a branch in a big city; in fact, leave any currency other than U.S. dollars at home—it may prove a greater nuisance to you than it's worth.

Also note that Canadian dollars are often accepted in Maine, New Hampshire, and Vermont (all of which border Canada), although it's generally easier to use Canadian currency closer to the border. Most hotels and many restaurants will accept Canadian currency at a discount close to its current trading value. Increasingly common in border towns on the Canadian side are ATMs (automated teller machines) that dispense U.S. dollars from your Canadian account.

TRAVELER'S CHECKS   Though traveler's checks are widely accepted, make sure that they're denominated in U.S. dollars, as foreign-currency checks are often difficult to exchange. The three traveler's checks that are most widely recognized—and least likely to be denied—are **Visa, American Express,** and **Thomas Cook.** Be sure to record the numbers of the checks, and keep that information in a separate place in case they get lost or stolen. Most businesses are pretty good about taking traveler's checks, but you're better off cashing them in at a bank (in small amounts, of course) and paying in cash. *Remember:* You'll need identification, such as a driver's license or passport, to change a traveler's check.

CREDIT CARDS & ATMS   Credit cards are the most widely used form of payment in the United States: **Visa** (Barclaycard in Britain), **MasterCard** (Eurocard in Europe, Access in Britain, Chargex in Canada), **American Express, Diners Club, Discover,** and **Carte Blanche.** There are, however, a handful of stores and restaurants that do not take credit cards, so be sure to ask in advance. Most businesses display a sticker near their entrance to let you know which cards they accept. (*Note:* Businesses may require a minimum purchase, usually around $10, to use a credit card.)

It is strongly recommended that you bring at least one major credit card. You must have a credit or charge card to rent a car. Hotels and airlines usually require a credit card imprint as a deposit against expenses, and in an emergency a credit card can be priceless.

You'll find **automated teller machines (ATMs)** at banks and shopping areas in New England's cities and towns. Some ATMs will allow you to draw U.S. currency against your bank and credit cards. Check with your bank before leaving home, and remember that you will need your personal identification number (PIN) to

Travel Tip
Be sure to keep a copy of all your travel papers separate from your wallet or purse, and leave a copy with someone at home should you need it faxed in an emergency.

do so. Most accept Visa, MasterCard, and American Express, as well as ATM cards from other U.S. banks. Expect to be charged up to $3 per transaction, however, if you're not using your own bank's ATM.

One way around these fees is to ask for cash back at grocery stores that accept ATM cards and don't charge usage fees. Of course, you'll have to purchase something first.

ATM cards with major credit card backing, known as "debit cards," are now a commonly acceptable form of payment in most stores and restaurants. Debit cards draw money directly from your checking account. Some stores enable you to receive "cash back" on your debit card purchases as well.

SAFETY

GENERAL SUGGESTIONS Although New England is generally very safe and friendly, urban areas such as Boston tend to be less safe than those in Europe or Japan. You should always stay alert. If you're in doubt about which neighborhoods are safe, don't hesitate to make inquiries with the hotel front desk staff or the local tourist office.

Avoid deserted urban areas, especially at night, and don't go into public parks after dark unless there's a concert or similar occasion that will attract a crowd.

Avoid carrying valuables with you on the street, and keep expensive cameras or electronic equipment bagged up or covered when not in use. If you're using a map, try to consult it inconspicuously—or better yet, study it before you leave your room. Hold onto your pocketbook, and place your billfold in an inside pocket. In theaters, restaurants, and other public places, keep your possessions in sight.

Always lock your room door—don't assume that once you're inside the hotel you are automatically safe

and no longer need to be aware of your surroundings. Hotels are open to the public, and in a large hotel, security may not be able to screen everyone who enters.

DRIVING SAFETY Driving safety is important, too, and carjacking is not unprecedented. Question your rental agency about personal safety and ask for a traveler-safety brochure when you pick up your car. Obtain written directions—or a map with the route clearly marked—from the agency showing how to get to your destination. (Many agencies now offer the option of renting a cellphone for the duration of your car rental; check with the rental agent when you pick up the car. Otherwise, contact **InTouch USA** at 🕿 **800/872-7626** or www.intouch usa.com for short-term cellphone rental.) And, if possible, arrive and depart during daylight hours.

If you drive off a highway and end up in a dodgy-looking neighborhood, leave the area as quickly as possible. If you have an accident, even on the highway, stay in your car with the doors locked until you assess the situation or until the police arrive. If you're bumped from behind on the street or are involved in a minor accident with no injuries, and the situation appears to be suspicious, motion to the other driver to follow you. Never get out of your car in such situations. Go directly to the nearest police precinct, well-lit service station, or 24-hour store.

Park in well-lit and well-traveled areas whenever possible. Always keep your car doors locked, whether the vehicle is attended or unattended. Never leave any packages or valuables in sight. If someone attempts to rob you or steal your car, don't try to resist the thief/carjacker. Report the incident to the police department immediately by calling 🕿 **911.**

SIZE CONVERSION CHART

Women's Clothing

American	4	6	8	10	12	14	16
French	34	36	38	40	42	44	46
British	6	8	10	12	14	16	18

Women's Shoes

American	5	6	7	8	9	10
French	36	37	38	39	40	41
British	4	5	6	7	8	9

Men's Suits

American	34	36	38	40	42	44	46	48
French	44	46	48	50	52	54	56	58
British	34	36	38	40	42	44	46	48

Men's Shirts

American	14½	15	15 ½	16	16 ½	17	17½
French	37	38	39	41	42	43	44
British	14 ½	15	15 ½	16	16 ½	17	17½

Men's Shoes

American	7	8	9	10	11	12	13
French	39½	41	42	43	44½	46	47
British	6	7	8	9	10	11	12

2 Getting to the United States

Most international travelers come to New England from Canada, via Boston's Logan Airport, or via one of the three New York City–area airports. Dozens of airlines serve New York and Boston airports from overseas. But because New York gets far more air traffic from abroad, the fares there and back are often more competitive. Some helpful numbers (all in London) include: **Air Canada** (© 0181/759-2636), **American Airlines** (© 0181/572-5555), **British Airways** (© 0345/222-111), **Continental** (© 01293/776-464), **Delta** (© 0800/414-767), **United** (© 0845/844-4747), and **Virgin Atlantic** (© 0293/747-747).

Those coming from Latin America, Asia, Australia, or New Zealand will probably arrive in New England through gateway cities like Miami, Los Angeles, or San Francisco, clearing Customs before connecting onward. Airports with regularly scheduled flights into the region include—in addition to Boston—Hartford, Conn.; Providence, R.I.; Portland, Maine; Manchester, N.H.; and Burlington, Vt. Albany, N.Y., is another option, especially if your destination is southern Vermont. See "Getting There," in chapter 2.

Bus service is fairly extensive throughout the region, and you can connect to all major cities and many smaller ones through hubs in Boston or New York. Most buses leave Boston from **South Station,** 700 Atlantic Ave., and New York from the **Port Authority Bus Terminal,** Eighth Avenue and 42nd Street.

Travelers seeking to explore more remote regions such as the Litchfield Hills, the Berkshires, or the White Mountains are advised to rent a car. Cars may be easily rented at most airports and at many in-town locations in larger cities. See chapter 2 for a listing of phone numbers for car rental firms.

AIRLINE DISCOUNTS The smart traveler can find numerable ways to reduce the price of a plane ticket simply by taking time to shop around. For example, overseas visitors can take advantage of the APEX (Advance Purchase Excursion) reductions offered by all major U.S. and European carriers. For more money-saving airline advice, see "Getting There," in chapter 2. For the best rates, compare fares and be flexible with the dates and times of travel.

IMMIGRATION AND CUSTOMS CLEARANCE Visitors arriving by air, no matter what the port of entry, should cultivate patience and resignation before setting foot on U.S. soil. Getting through immigration control can take as long as 2 hours on some days, especially on summer weekends, so be sure to carry this guidebook or something else to read. This is especially true in the aftermath of the World Trade Center attacks, when security clearances have been considerably beefed up at U.S. airports

---

FAST FACTS: **For the International Traveler**

Automobile Organizations Auto clubs will supply maps, suggested routes, guidebooks, accident and bail-bond insurance, and emergency road service. The **American Automobile Association (AAA)** is the major auto club in the United States. If you belong to an auto club in your home country, inquire about AAA reciprocity before you leave. You may be able to join AAA even if you're not a member of a reciprocal club; to inquire, call AAA (© **800/222-4357**). AAA is actually an organization of regional auto clubs; so look under "AAA Automobile Club" in the White Pages of the telephone directory. AAA has a nationwide emergency road service telephone number (© 800/AAA-HELP).

Business Hours Offices are usually open weekdays from 9am to 5pm. Banks are open weekdays from 9am to 3pm or later and sometimes Saturday mornings. Stores typically open between 9 and 10am and close between 5 and 6pm from Monday through Saturday. Stores in shopping complexes or malls tend to stay open late: until about 9pm on weekdays and weekends, and many malls and larger department stores are open on Sundays.

Climate See "When to Go," in chapter 2.

Currency & Currency Exchange See "Entry Requirements" and "Money" under "Preparing for Your Trip," earlier.

Drinking Laws The legal age for purchase and consumption of alcoholic beverages is 21; proof of age is required and often requested at bars, nightclubs, and restaurants, so it's always a good idea to bring ID when you go out. Beer and wine often can be purchased in supermarkets, but liquor laws vary from state to state.

Do not carry open containers of alcohol in your car or any public area that isn't zoned for alcohol consumption. The police can fine you on the spot. And, no matter what your age, state laws in New England are notoriously harsh on those who drive drunk.

Driving A current overseas license is valid on U.S. roads. If your license is in a language other than English, it's recommended that you obtain an International Driver's Permit from the AAA affiliate or other automobile organization in your own country prior to departure (see "Automobile Organizations," above).

Drivers may make a right turn at a red light, provided that they first stop fully and confirm that no other driver is approaching from the left. At some intersections, signs prohibit such a turn.

Electricity Like Canada, the United States uses 110 to 120 volts AC (60 cycles), compared to 220 to 240 volts AC (50 cycles) in most of Europe, Australia, and New Zealand. If your small appliances use 220 to 240 volts, you'll need a 110-volt transformer and a plug adapter with two flat parallel pins to operate them here. Downward converters that change 220–240 volts to 110–120 volts are difficult to find in the United States, so bring one with you.

Embassies/Consulates All embassies are located in the nation's capital, Washington, D.C. Some consulates are located in major U.S. cities, and most nations have a mission to the United Nations in New York City. If your country isn't listed below, call for directory information in Washington, D.C. (© **202/555-1212**) or log on to **www.embassy.org/embassies**.

A handful of countries maintain consulates in Boston, including Canada, 3 Copley Place, Suite 400 (© 617/262-3760); Great Britain, Federal Reserve Plaza, 600 Atlantic Ave., 25th floor (© 617/248-9555); Ireland, 535 Boylston St. (© 617/267-9330); and Israel, 1020 Statler Office Building, 20 Park Plaza (© 617/535-0200). For other countries, contact directory assistance (© 617/555-1212).

Emergencies Call © **911** to report a fire, call the police, or get an ambulance anywhere in the United States. This is a toll-free call. (No coins are required at public telephones.)

If you encounter serious problems, contact the **Traveler's Aid International** (© **202/546-1127**; www.travelersaid.org) to help direct you to a local branch. This nationwide, nonprofit, social-service organization geared to helping travelers in difficult straits offers services that might include reuniting families separated while traveling, providing food and/or shelter to people stranded without cash, or even emotional counseling. If you're in trouble, seek them out.

Gasoline Petrol is known as gasoline (or simply "gas") in the United States, and petrol stations are known as both gas stations and service stations. Gasoline costs about half as much here as it does in Europe (about $2.00 per gallon at press time), and taxes are already included in the printed price. One U.S. gallon equals 3.8 liters or .85 Imperial gallons.

Gasoline is widely available throughout the region, with the exception of the North Woods region of Maine, where you can travel many miles without seeing a filling station. Gas tends to be cheaper farther to the south and in larger town and cities; you're better off filling up before setting off into remote or rural areas. (The exception is in Connecticut, where state taxes drive the price of gasoline to above the regional average.)

Many of the filling stations in New England have both "self-serve" and "full-service" pumps; look for signs as you pull up. The full-service pumps are slightly more expensive per gallon, but an attendant will pump your gas and check your oil. (You might have to ask for this.) The self-serve pumps often have simple directions posted on them. If you're at all confused, ask anyone who happens to be around for instructions.

Holidays Banks, government offices, post offices, and many stores, restaurants, and museums are closed on the following legal national holidays: January 1 (New Year's Day), the third Monday in January (Martin Luther King, Jr. Day), the third Monday in February (Presidents' Day, Washington's Birthday), the last Monday in May (Memorial Day), July 4 (Independence Day), the first Monday in September (Labor Day), the second Monday in October (Columbus Day), November 11 (Veterans' Day/Armistice Day), the fourth Thursday in November (Thanksgiving Day), and December 25 (Christmas). Also, the Tuesday following the first Monday in November is Election Day and is a federal government holiday in presidential-election years (every 4 years, next in 2004).

In Maine and Massachusetts, Patriot's Day is celebrated on the third Monday in April. Banks, government offices, and post offices are closed on these holidays. Shops are sometimes open, but assume almost all will be closed on Thanksgiving and Christmas.

Languages Some of the larger hotels may have multilingual employees, but don't count on it. Outside of the cities, English is the only language spoken. The exception is along the Canadian border and in some Maine locales (including Old Orchard Beach), where French is commonly spoken, or at least understood.

Legal Aid If you are "pulled over" for a minor infraction (such as speeding), never attempt to pay the fine directly to a police officer; this could be construed as attempted bribery, a much more serious crime. Pay fines by mail, or directly into the hands of the clerk of the court. If accused of a more serious offense, say and do nothing before consulting a lawyer. Here the burden is on the state to prove a person's guilt beyond a reasonable doubt, and everyone has the right to remain silent, whether he or she is suspected of a crime or actually arrested. Once arrested, a person can make one telephone call to a party of his or her choice. Call your embassy or consulate.

Mail If you aren't sure what your address will be in the United States, mail can be sent to you, in your name, c/o General Delivery at the main post office of the city or region where you expect to be. (Call ⓒ 800/ 275-8777 for information on the nearest post office.) The addressee must pick up mail in person and must produce proof of identity (driver's license, passport, and so on). Most post offices will hold your mail for up to one month, and are open Monday to Friday from 8am to 6pm, and Saturday from 9am to 3pm.

Virtually every small town and village has a post office. Mail may also be deposited at mailboxes, located on many streets and intersections. Mailboxes are blue with a white eagle logo and carry the inscription U.S. Mail. If your mail is addressed to a U.S. destination, don't forget to add the five-digit postal code (or zip code), after the two-letter abbreviation of the state to which the mail is addressed. This is essential to prompt delivery.

At press time, domestic postage rates were 23¢ for a postcard and 37¢ for a letter. For international mail, a first-class letter of up to one-half ounce costs 80¢ (60¢ to Canada and Mexico); a first-class postcard costs 70¢ (50¢ to Canada and Mexico); and a preprinted postal aerogramme costs 70¢.

Measurements See the chart on the inside front cover of this book for details on converting metric measurements to U.S. equivalents.

Newspapers/Magazines Overseas newspapers and magazines are commonly found in Boston and Cambridge, but are harder to track down elsewhere in New England. Your best bet is to check in the phone book for Borders or Barnes & Noble, two of the largest chain bookstores in New England.

Taxes The United States has no value-added tax (VAT) or other indirect tax at the national level. There is a sales tax (typically 5%–7%) added to the price of goods and some services in New England. New Hampshire does not have any sales tax on goods, but does levy an 8% tax on hotel rooms and restaurant meals.

Telephone, Telegraph, Telex & Fax The telephone system in the United States is run by private corporations, so rates, especially for long-distance service and operator-assisted calls, can vary widely. Generally, hotel surcharges on long-distance and local calls are astronomical, so you're usually better off using a **public pay telephone,** which you'll find clearly marked in most public buildings and private establishments as well as on the street. Convenience grocery stores and gas stations always have them. Many convenience groceries and packaging services sell **prepaid calling cards** in denominations up to $50; these can be the least expensive way to call home. Many public phones at airports now accept American Express, MasterCard, and Visa credit cards. **Local calls** made from public pay phones in most locales cost either 35¢ or 50¢. Pay phones do not accept pennies, and few will take anything larger than a quarter.

You may want to look into leasing a cellphone for the duration of your trip.

Most long-distance and international calls can be dialed directly from any phone. **For calls within the United States and to Canada,** dial 1 followed by the area code and the seven-digit number. **For other international calls,** dial 011 followed by the country code, city code, and the telephone number of the person you are calling.

Calls to area codes **800, 888, 877,** and **866** are toll-free. However, calls to numbers in area codes **700** and **900** (chat lines, bulletin boards, "dating" services, and so on) can be very expensive—usually a charge of 95¢ to $3 or more per minute, and they sometimes have minimum charges that can run as high as $15 or more.

For **reversed-charge or collect calls,** and for person-to-person calls, dial 0 (zero, not the letter O) followed by the area code and number you want; an operator will then come on the line, and you should specify that you are calling collect, or person-to-person, or both. If your operator-assisted call is international, ask for the overseas operator.

For **local directory assistance** ("information"), dial 411; for long-distance information, dial 1, then the appropriate area code and 555-1212.

Telegraph and telex services are provided primarily by Western Union. You can bring your telegram into the nearest Western Union office (there are hundreds across the country) or dictate it over the phone (✆ 800/ 325-6000). You can also telegraph money, or have it telegraphed to you, very quickly over the Western Union system, but this service can cost as much as 15% to 20% of the amount sent.

Most hotels have **fax machines** available for guest use (be sure to ask about the charge to use it). Many hotel rooms are even wired for guests' fax machines. A less expensive way to send and receive faxes may be at stores such as **The UPS Store** (formerly Mail Boxes Etc.), a national chain of retail packing service shops. (Look in the Yellow Pages directory under "Packing Services.")

There are two kinds of telephone directories in the United States. The so-called **White Pages** list private households and business subscribers in alphabetical order. The inside front cover lists emergency numbers for police, fire, ambulance, the Coast Guard, poison-control center, crime-victims hotline, and so on. The first few pages will tell you how to make long-distance and international calls, complete with country codes and area codes. Government numbers are usually printed on blue paper within the White Pages. Printed on yellow paper, the so-called **Yellow Pages** list all local services, businesses, industries, and houses of worship according to activity with an index at the front or back. (Drugstores/ pharmacies and restaurants are also listed by geographic location.) The Yellow Pages also include city plans or detailed area maps, postal zip codes, and public transportation routes.

Time All of New England is in the eastern time zone, the same as New York. All states shift to daylight savings time (1 hr. ahead) on the first Sunday in April, and back to standard time on the last Sunday in October.

Tipping Tips are a very important part of certain workers' income, and gratuities are the standard way of showing appreciation for services provided. (Tipping is certainly not compulsory if the service is poor!) In hotels, tip **bellhops** at least $1 per bag ($2–$3 if you have a lot of luggage) and tip the **chamber staff** $1 to $2 per day (more if you've left a disaster area for him or her to clean up). Tip the **doorman** or **concierge** only if he or she has provided you with some specific service (for example, calling a cab for you or obtaining difficult-to-get theater tickets). Tip the **valet-parking attendant** $1 every time you get your car.

In restaurants, bars, and nightclubs, tip **service staff** 15% to 20% of the check, tip **bartenders** 10% to 15%, tip **checkroom attendants** $1 per garment, and tip **valet-parking attendants** $1 per vehicle.

As for other service personnel, tip **cab drivers** 15% of the fare; tip **sky-caps** at airports at least $1 per bag ($2–$3 if you have a lot of luggage); and tip **hairdressers** and **barbers** 15% to 20%.

Toilets You won't find public toilets or "restrooms" on the streets in most U.S. cities, but they can be found in hotel lobbies, bars, restaurants, museums, department stores, railway and bus stations, and service stations. Large hotels and fast-food restaurants are probably the best bet for good, clean facilities. If possible, avoid the toilets at parks and beaches, which tend to be dirty; some may be unsafe. Restaurants and bars in resorts or heavily visited areas may reserve their restrooms for patrons. Some establishments display a notice indicating this. You can ignore this sign or, better yet, avoid arguments by paying for a cup of coffee or a soft drink, which will qualify you as a patron.

4

Boston & Cambridge

by Marie Morris

Boston embodies contrasts and contradictions—it's blue blood and blue collar, Yankee and Irish, home to budget-conscious graduate students and free-spending computer wizards. Rich in colonial history and 21st-century technology, it's a living landmark that's putting on a new face. The 15-year, $14.6-billion highway-construction project known as the "Big Dig" will be wrapping up when you visit. The last stages incorporate parks, open space, surface roads, and new buildings on the downtown waterfront, mending the scar left when traffic on Interstate 93 moved into a state-of-the-art tunnel and the old elevated expressway came down.

Cambridge and Boston are so close that many people believe they're the same—a notion both cities' residents and politicians are happy to dispel. Cantabrigians are often considered more liberal and better educated than Bostonians, which is another idea that's sure to get you involved in a heated discussion. Harvard dominates Cambridge's history and geography, but there's more to the city than just the university.

Take a few days (or weeks) to get to know the Boston area, or use it as a gateway to the rest of New England. Here's hoping your experience is memorable and delightful.

1 Orientation

ARRIVING

BY PLANE The major domestic carriers that serve Boston's Logan International Airport are **AirTran** (© 800/247-8726), **American** (© 800/433-7300), **America West** (© 800/235-9292), **ATA** (© 800/225-2995), **Continental** (© 800/523-3273), **Delta** (© 800/221-1212), **Frontier** (© 800/432-1359), **JetBlue** (© 800/538-2583), **Midwest** (© 800/452-2022), **Northwest** (© 800/225-2525), **United** (© 800/241-6522), and **US Airways** (© 800/428-4322). Many major international carriers also fly into Boston.

Southwest (© 800/435-9792) and several other major carriers serve **T. F. Green Airport,** in the Providence suburb of Warwick, RI (© 888/268-7222; www.pvd-ri.com), and New Hampshire's **Manchester International Airport** (© 603/624-6556; www.flymanchester.com). **Bonanza** (© 888/751-8800; www.bonanzabus.com) offers bus service from T. F. Green to Boston's South Station; the fare is $19 one-way, $34 round-trip. Allow at least 90 minutes. From Manchester, **Vermont Transit** (© 800/552-8737; www.vermonttransit.com) runs buses to South Station; some continue to Logan. The fare is $12 one-way, $23 round-trip. Allow 60 to 90 minutes.

Logan Airport is in East Boston at the end of the Sumner, Callahan, and Ted Williams tunnels, 3 miles across the harbor from downtown. Each terminal has ATMs, Internet kiosks, pay phones with dataports, fax machines, and information booths (near baggage claim). Terminals C and E have bank branches that handle currency exchange; A (which was closed for construction at press time) and C have children's play spaces.

The Massachusetts Port Authority, or **MassPort** (© **800/23-LOGAN;** www. massport.com), coordinates airport transportation. Access to the city is by subway (the "T"), cab, and boat. The **subway** is fast and cheap—10 minutes to downtown and $1.25 for a token (good for 1 ride). Free **shuttle buses** run from each terminal to the Airport station on the Blue Line of the T daily from 5:30am to 1am. The Blue Line stops at State Street and Government Center, downtown points where you can exit or transfer (free) to the other lines.

A **cab** from the airport to downtown or the Back Bay costs about $20 to $27. The ride into town takes 10 to 45 minutes, depending on traffic and the time of day. If you must travel during rush hour or on Sunday afternoon, allow extra time, or plan to take the subway or water shuttle (and pack accordingly).

The trip to the downtown waterfront (near cab stands and several hotels) in a weather-protected **boat** takes 7 minutes, dock to dock. The free no. 66 shuttle bus connects all terminals to the Logan ferry dock. At press time, the only company providing year-round service is **Harbor Express** (© **617/222-6999;** www.harborexpress.com), which runs to Long Wharf. It operates every 20 minutes Monday through Friday from 7am to 8pm (to 11pm on Fri), less frequently on weekends. Hours are shorter in the winter. The one-way fare is $10.

From April through mid-October, the **City Water Taxi** (© **617/422-0392;** www.citywatertaxi.com) connects a dozen stops on the harbor, including the airport ferry dock. The flat fare is $10. Call ahead from the dock for pickup.

Some hotels have **limousines** or **shuttle vans;** ask when you make your reservations. To arrange private service, call ahead for a reservation, especially at busy times. Your hotel can recommend a company, or try **Carey Limousine Boston** (© **800/336-4646** or 617/623-8700) or **Commonwealth Limousine Service** (© **800/558-LIMO** outside Mass., or 617/787-5575).

BY CAR   Boston is 218 miles from New York; driving time is about 4½ hours. From Washington, it takes about 8 hours to cover the 468 miles; the 992-mile drive from Chicago takes around 21 hours.

Driving to Boston is not difficult, but between the cost of parking and the hassle of traffic, the savings on airfare may not be worth the aggravation. If you're thinking of using the car to get around town, think again—you won't need one to explore Boston and Cambridge.

The major highways are **I-90,** the Massachusetts Turnpike ("Mass. Pike"), an east-west toll road that runs from Logan Airport to the New York State Thruway; **I-93/U.S. 1,** which extends north to Canada; and **I-93/Route 3,** the Southeast Expressway, which connects with the south, including Cape Cod. **I-95** (Mass. Rte. 128) is a beltway about 11 miles from downtown that connects to I-93 and to highways in Rhode Island, Connecticut, and New York to the south and New Hampshire and Maine to the north.

To reach Cambridge, take **Storrow Drive** or **Memorial Drive** (on either side of the Charles River). The Mass. Pike's Allston/Brighton exit connects with Storrow Drive. It has a Harvard Square exit; cross the Anderson Bridge to John F. Kennedy Street to reach the square. Memorial Drive intersects with Kennedy Street; turn away from the bridge to reach the square.

AAA (© **800/AAA-HELP;** www.aaa.com) provides members with maps, itineraries, and other information, and arranges free towing if you break down. The privately operated Mass. Pike arranges its own towing; if you break down, wait in your car until a patrol arrives. To reach the state police from a cellphone, call ⓒ *77.

BY TRAIN   Boston has three rail centers: **South Station,** on Atlantic Avenue; **Back Bay Station,** on Dartmouth Street across from the Copley Place mall; and **North Station,** on Causeway Street near the FleetCenter. **Amtrak** (ⓒ **800/ USA-RAIL** or 617/482-3660; www.amtrak.com) serves all three. Each train station is also a rapid-transit station. See the "Boston Transit" map on p. 85.

Amtrak serves Boston from the south and from Portland, Maine. **Acela Express** high-speed service has cut trip time from New York to just under 4 hours and from Washington to about 6 hours. Standard Northeast Corridor service takes 4 to 5 hours and 8 hours, respectively.

South Station is a stop on the Red Line, which runs to Cambridge by way of Park Street, the hub of the **subway** (ⓒ **800/392-6100** outside Mass., or 617/222-3200; www.mbta.com). At Park Street you can connect to the Green, Blue, and Orange lines. The Orange Line links Back Bay Station with Downtown Crossing (where there's a walkway to Park St. station) and other points. The **commuter rail** serves Ipswich, Rockport, and Fitchburg from North Station, and points south and west of Boston, including Plymouth, from South Station.

BY BUS   The **South Station Transportation Center,** on Atlantic Avenue next to the train station, is the city's bus-service hub. It's served by regional and national lines, including **Greyhound** (ⓒ **800/231-2222** or 617/526-1801; www.greyhound.com), **Bonanza** (ⓒ **800/556-3815** or 617/720-4110; www.bonanzabus.com), and **Peter Pan** (ⓒ **800/237-8747** or 617/426-8554; www.peterpanbus.com).

VISITOR INFORMATION

BEFORE YOU LEAVE HOME   Contact the **Greater Boston Convention & Visitors Bureau,** 2 Copley Place, Suite 105, Boston (ⓒ **888/SEE-BOSTON** or 617/536-4100; 0171/431-3434 in the U.K.; fax 617/424-7664; www.bostonusa.com). It offers a comprehensive information kit ($10) with a planner, guidebook, map, and coupons; and a *Kids Love Boston* guide ($5). Free smaller planners for specific seasons or events are often available.

The **Cambridge Office for Tourism,** 18 Brattle St., Cambridge (ⓒ **800/ 862-5678** or 617/441-2884; fax 617/441-7736; www.cambridge-usa.org), distributes information about Cambridge.

The **Massachusetts Office of Travel and Tourism,** 10 Park Plaza, Suite 4510, Boston (ⓒ **800/227-6277** or 617/973-8500; fax 617/973-8525; www.massvacation.com), distributes the *Getaway Guide,* a free magazine with information on attractions and lodgings, a map, and a seasonal calendar.

An excellent resource for travelers with disabilities is **VSA Arts Massachusetts** (ⓒ **617/350-7713;** TTY 617/350-6836; www.vsamass.org). Its comprehensive website includes general access information and specifics on more than 200 arts and entertainment facilities.

IN PERSON   The **Boston National Historic Park Visitor Center,** 15 State St. (ⓒ **617/242-5642;** www.nps.gov/bost), across the street from the Old State House and the State Street T, is a good place to start exploring. National Park Service rangers staff the center and lead free tours of the Freedom Trail. The audiovisual show provides basic information on 16 historic sites on the trail. The center is wheelchair accessible and has restrooms; it is open daily from 9am to 5pm.

The Freedom Trail begins at the **Boston Common Information Center,** 146 Tremont St., on the Common. The center is open Monday through Saturday from 8:30am to 5pm, Sunday from 9am to 5pm. The **Prudential Information Center,** on the main level of the Prudential Center, is open Monday through Friday from 8:30am to 6pm, Saturday and Sunday from 10am to 6pm. The **Greater Boston Convention & Visitors Bureau** (© **888/SEE-BOSTON** or 617/536-4100) operates both centers.

There's an outdoor information booth at **Faneuil Hall Marketplace** between Quincy Market and the South Market Building. It's staffed in the spring, summer, and fall from 10am to 6pm Monday through Saturday, noon to 6pm Sunday.

In Cambridge, there's an **information kiosk** (© **800/862-5678** or 617/497-1630) in the heart of Harvard Square, near the T entrance at the intersection of Mass. Ave., John F. Kennedy Street, and Brattle Street. It's open Monday through Saturday from 9am to 5pm, Sunday from 1 to 5pm.

CITY LAYOUT

Parts of Boston reflect the city's original layout, a seemingly haphazard plan that can disorient even longtime residents. Old Boston abounds with alleys, dead ends, one-way streets, streets that change names, and streets named after extinct geographical features. On the plus side, every "wrong" turn **downtown,** in the **North End,** or on **Beacon Hill** is a chance to see something you might otherwise have missed.

FINDING AN ADDRESS   There's no rhyme or reason to the street pattern, compass directions are virtually useless, and there aren't enough street signs. The best way to find an address is to call ahead and ask for directions, including landmarks, or leave time for wandering around. If the directions involve a T stop, be sure to ask which exit to use—most stations have more than one.

STREET MAPS   Free maps of downtown Boston and the transit system are available at visitor centers around the city. *Where* and other tourism-oriented magazines, available free at most hotels, include maps of central Boston and the T. *Streetwise Boston* ($5.95) and *Artwise Boston* ($5.95) are sturdy, laminated maps available at most bookstores.

The Big Deal About the Big Dig

In a city with glorious water views, historic architecture, and gorgeous parks, the most prominent physical feature over the past decade has been a giant highway-construction project. The $14.6-billion Central Artery/Third Harbor Tunnel Project, better known as **the Big Dig,** transformed I-93 from an elevated expressway into a tunnel—without closing the road though downtown Boston. Its hallmark is the gorgeous Leonard P. Zakim Bunker Hill Memorial Bridge over the Charles River (north of North Station).

When the last major piece, the southbound tunnel, opened in 2004, drivers all over New England cheered, and even the most pessimistic observers admitted that the new road improved traffic flow. During your visit, the Big Dig will be winding down, replacing the expressway with parks, surface roads, and new buildings. To learn more, visit www.bigdig.com, or just go for a walk downtown.

BOSTON NEIGHBORHOODS IN BRIEF

See the map on p. 90 to locate these areas. When Bostonians say **"downtown,"** they usually mean the first six neighborhoods defined here.

The Waterfront This narrow area along **Atlantic Avenue** and **Commercial Street,** once filled with wharves and warehouses, now boasts luxury condos, marinas, restaurants, offices, and hotels. Also here are the New England Aquarium and departure points for harbor cruises and whale watches.

The North End One of the city's oldest neighborhoods has been an immigrant stronghold for much of its history. It's now less than half Italian-American, but you'll still hear Italian spoken and find many Italian restaurants, *caffès,* and shops. **Hanover Street** is the main street of the North End, which lies between Faneuil Hall Marketplace and the Waterfront. Clubs and restaurants cluster on and near **Causeway Street** in the **North Station** area (between N. Washington St. and Beacon Hill), but don't wander the side streets alone late at night.

Faneuil Hall Marketplace & Haymarket Employees aside, Boston residents tend to be scarce at Faneuil Hall Marketplace (also called Quincy Market). An irresistible draw for out-of-towners and suburbanites, the cluster of restored market buildings adjacent to the North End is the city's most popular attraction. **Haymarket,** along Blackstone Street, is home to an open-air produce market on Friday and Saturday.

Government Center Here, modern design strays into the red-brick facade of traditional Boston architecture. Across **Cambridge Street** from Beacon Hill, Government Center is home to state and federal office towers, Boston City Hall, and a central T stop.

Financial District In the city's banking, insurance, and legal center, skyscrapers surround the landmark Custom House Tower. This area is frantic during the day and practically empty at night. **State Street** separates it from Faneuil Hall Marketplace.

Downtown Crossing The Freedom Trail runs through this shopping and business district east of Boston Common, which hops during the day and slows at night. The intersection that gives Downtown Crossing its name is where Winter Street becomes Summer Street at **Washington Street,** the most "main" street downtown.

Beacon Hill Narrow, tree-lined streets and architectural showpieces make up this residential area near the State House. **Charles Street** is the main drag of "the Hill." Two of the city's loveliest and most exclusive spots are here: Mount Vernon Street and Louisburg Square (pronounced "Lewis-burg," and home to John Kerry). Massachusetts General Hospital is off **Cambridge Street.** On the south side, **Beacon Street** borders Boston Common, as does **Park Street,** which is just 1 block long (but looms large in the geography of the **T**).

Charlestown One of the oldest areas of Boston is where you'll see the Bunker Hill Monument and USS *Constitution* ("Old Ironsides"). Yuppification has brought some diversity to the mostly white residential neighborhood, but pockets remain that have earned their reputation for insularity. To get here, follow **North Washington Street** from the North End.

South Boston Waterfront (Seaport District) The city's newest neighborhood has several names; these are the most popular. Across

Fort Point Channel from downtown, it's where you'll find the World Trade Center, Seaport Hotel, Fish Pier, federal courthouse, Museum Wharf, Boston Convention & Exhibition Center, and a lot of construction.

Chinatown The fourth-largest Chinese community in the country abounds with Asian restaurants, groceries, and other businesses. As the "Combat Zone," or red-light district, has nearly disappeared, Chinatown has expanded to fill the area between Downtown Crossing and the Mass. Pike extension. Its main street is **Beach Street.** Also in this neighborhood, the tiny **Theater District** extends about 1½ blocks in each direction from the intersection of Tremont and Stuart streets; be careful here at night after the crowds thin out.

South End Cross **Huntington Avenue** or Stuart Street to reach this landmark district packed with Victorian row houses and little parks. Known for its ethnic, economic, and cultural diversity, as well as its galleries and boutiques, the South End has a large gay community and some of the city's best restaurants. Main thoroughfares include **Tremont** and **Washington streets,** which originate downtown, and **Columbus Avenue.** *Note:* Don't confuse the South End with South Boston, a residential neighborhood across I-93.

Back Bay Fashionable since its creation out of landfill over a century ago, the Back Bay overflows with gorgeous architecture and chic shops. It extends from **Arlington Street,** in the plush area near the

Public Garden, to the student-dominated sections near Massachusetts Avenue, or **Mass. Ave.** Unlike downtown, it's laid out in a grid. The main streets include the prime shopping areas of **Boylston** and **Newbury streets** and largely residential Commonwealth Avenue, or **Comm. Ave.,** and **Beacon Street.** The cross streets go in alphabetical order.

Huntington Avenue Landmarks dot the "Avenue of the Arts" (or, with a Boston accent, "Otts"). Not a formal neighborhood, Huntington Avenue is where you'll find Symphony Hall (at the corner of **Mass. Ave.**), Northeastern University, and the Museum of Fine Arts. Parts of Huntington can be a little risky; if you're leaving the museum at night, grab a cab or the Green Line, and travel in a group.

Kenmore Square The landmark white-and-red Citgo sign above the intersection of **Comm. Ave., Beacon Street,** and **Brookline Avenue** tells you you're approaching Kenmore Square. Boston University students throng its shops, bars, restaurants, and clubs. The college-town atmosphere goes out the window when the Red Sox are in town and baseball fans flock to Fenway Park, 3 blocks away.

Cambridge The backbone of Boston's neighbor across the Charles River is **Mass. Ave.,** which originates in Roxbury and extends into Cambridge, Arlington, and Lexington, 9 miles away. The Red Line subway parallels Mass. Ave. in the areas you're likeliest to visit, around the following T stops: **Kendall/MIT, Central, Harvard,** and **Porter.**

2 Getting Around

It's impossible to say this often enough: When you reach your hotel, *leave your car in the garage and walk or use public transportation.* If you must drive in town, ask at the front desk for a route around or away from post–Big Dig construction.

Tips **Late-Night Transit**

The MBTA's **Night Owl** bus service operates until 2:30am on Friday and Saturday nights on popular bus routes and on supplemental routes that parallel subway lines. The fare is $1.50 in coins. For information and schedules, contact the MBTA (© **800/392-6100** outside Mass., or 617/222-3200; www.mbta.com).

BY PUBLIC TRANSPORTATION

The Massachusetts Bay Transportation Authority, or **MBTA** (© **800/392-6100** outside Mass., or 617/222-3200; www.mbta.com), is known as the "T," and its logo is the letter in a circle. It runs subways, trolleys, buses, and ferries in Boston and many suburbs, as well as the commuter rail. Its website includes maps, schedules, and other information.

Newer stations on the Red, Blue, and Orange lines are wheelchair accessible; the Green Line is being converted. All T buses have lifts or kneelers; call © **800/LIFT-BUS** for information. To learn more, call the **Office for Transportation Access** (© **617/222-5438** or TTY 617/222-5854).

The **Boston Visitor Pass** (© **877/927-7277** or 617/222-5218; www.mbta.com) includes unlimited travel on the subway and local buses (but not the Night Owl), in commuter rail zones 1A and 1B, and on two ferries. The cost is $7.50 for 1 day (so tokens are cheaper for fewer than six trips), $18 for 3 days, and $35 for 7 days. The $17 **weekly combo pass** covers subways and buses but not ferries, and is good only from Sunday through Saturday. You can buy a pass in advance by phone or online, or when you arrive at the Airport T station, South Station, Back Bay Station, or North Station. They're also for sale at the Government Center and Harvard T stations; the Boston Common, Prudential Center, and Faneuil Hall Marketplace information centers; and some hotels.

BY SUBWAY & TROLLEY   Red, Blue, and Orange line trains and Green Line trolleys make up the **subway** system, which runs partly aboveground. (The commuter rail to the suburbs is purple on system maps and is sometimes called the Purple Line; the Silver Line is a fancy name for the bus line that connects downtown with Roxbury.) The local fare is $1.25—you'll need a token—and can be as much as $3 for some surface line extensions. Transfers are free. Route and fare information and timetables are available through the website and at centrally located stations. Service begins around 5:15am and ends around 12:30am. On New Year's Eve, closing time is 2am and service is free after 8pm. A sign on the token booth in every station gives the time of the last train in either direction.

The oldest system in the country, the T dates to 1897. The Green Line is the most unpredictable—leave early if you're taking it to a vital appointment. Note that downtown stops are so close together that walking is often faster. The system is generally safe, but always watch out for pickpockets, especially during the holiday season.

BY BUS   T buses and "trackless trolleys" (buses with electric antennae) provide service around town and to and around the suburbs. The local bus fare is 90¢; express buses are $2.20 and up. Exact change is required. You can use a token, but you won't get change. Important local routes include **no. 1** (Mass. Ave. from Dudley Sq. in Roxbury through the Back Bay and Cambridge to Harvard Sq.);

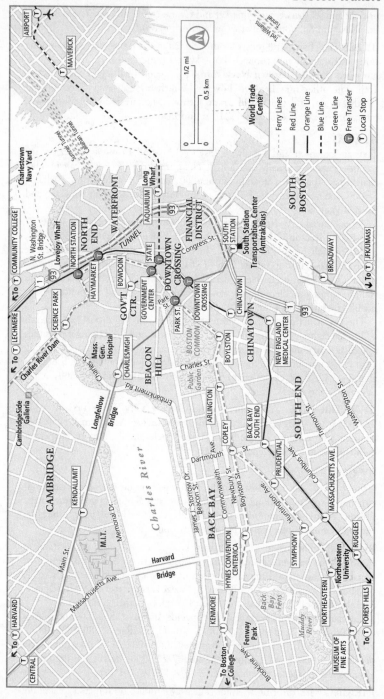

nos. 92 and **93** (between Haymarket and Charlestown); and **no. 77** (Mass. Ave. from Harvard Sq. north to Porter Sq. and Arlington).

BY FERRY   Two useful routes (both included in the T visitor pass) run on the Inner Harbor. The first connects **Long Wharf** (near the New England Aquarium) and the **Charlestown Navy Yard**—it's a good final leg of the Freedom Trail. The other runs between **Lovejoy Wharf,** off Causeway Street behind North Station, and the **World Trade Center.** The fare is $1.50. Visit www. mbta.com or call ℂ **617/227-4321** for information.

BY TAXI

Taxis are expensive and not always easy to flag—find a cabstand or call a dispatcher. Stands are usually near hotels. There are also busy ones at Faneuil Hall Marketplace (on North St. and in front of 60 State St.), South Station, Back Bay Station, and on either side of Mass. Ave. in Harvard Square, near the Coop and Au Bon Pain.

To call ahead, try the **Independent Taxi Operators Association** (ℂ 617/ 426-8700), **Boston Cab** (ℂ **617/262-2227**), **Town Taxi** (ℂ **617/536-5000**), or **Metro Cab** (ℂ **617/242-8000**). In Cambridge, call **Ambassador Brattle** (ℂ **617/492-1100**) or **Yellow Cab** (ℂ **617/547-3000**). Boston Cab can dispatch a wheelchair-accessible vehicle; advance notice is recommended. If you want to report a problem or have lost something in a cab, call the police department's **Hackney Hot Line** (ℂ **617/536-8294**).

The fare structure: the first quarter mile (when the flag drops), $1.75; each additional eighth of a mile, 30¢. Wait time is extra, and the passenger pays tolls as well as a total of $6.50 in fees on trips entering and leaving Logan. Charging a flat rate is not allowed in the city; the police department publishes a list (available at www.massport.com/logan) of distances to the suburbs that establishes the flat rate for those trips.

BY WATER TAXI   From April to mid-October, **City Water Taxi** (ℂ 617/ 422-0392; www.citywatertaxi.com) provides on-call service in small boats that connects a dozen stops on the Inner Harbor, including the airport. It operates daily from 7am to 7pm. The fare is $10.

BY CAR

If you plan to visit only Boston and Cambridge, you do not need a car. Construction, expensive parking, daredevil drivers, and confusing geography make Boston in particular a motorist's nightmare. If you arrive by car, park at the hotel and walk or use public transit. For day trips, you'll probably want a car.

RENTALS   The major car-rental firms have offices at Logan Airport and in Boston; some have other area branches. Boston levies a $10 surcharge on car rentals that goes toward the construction of a new convention center. If you're traveling at a busy time, especially during foliage season, reserve well in advance. Most agencies offer shuttle service from the airport to their offices.

Companies with offices at the airport include **Alamo** (ℂ 800/327-9633), **Avis** (ℂ 800/831-2847), **Budget** (ℂ 800/527-0700), **Dollar** (ℂ 800/800-4000), **Hertz** (ℂ 800/654-3131), and **National** (ℂ 800/227-7368). **Enterprise** (ℂ 800/325-8007) and **Thrifty** (ℂ 800/367-2277) are nearby but not on the grounds; leave time for the shuttle ride.

PARKING   It's difficult to find your way around Boston and practically impossible to park in some areas. Most spaces on the street are metered (and patrolled until 6pm on the dot Mon–Sat), have strict time limits, or both. Rates vary (usually $1 an hour downtown); bring plenty of quarters. Time limits range from 15 minutes to 2 hours. The penalty is a $40 ticket, but should you blunder into a tow-away zone, retrieving the car will take at least $100 and a lot of running around. The city tow lot is at 200 Frontage Rd., South Boston (© 617/635-3900).

It's best to leave the car in a garage or lot and walk. A full day at most lots costs no more than $25, but some downtown facilities charge as much as $35. Some restaurants offer discounts at nearby garages; ask when you make reservations.

The city-run **Boston Common Garage,** off Charles Street (© 617/954-2096), accepts vehicles under 6 feet, 3 inches tall. The **Prudential Center Garage** (© 617/267-1002) has entrances on Boylston Street, Huntington Avenue, and Exeter Street, and at the Sheraton Boston Hotel. Parking is discounted if you buy something at the Shops at Prudential Center and have your ticket validated. The **Copley Place Garage,** off Huntington Avenue (© 617/375-4488), offers a similar deal. Many businesses in Faneuil Hall Marketplace validate parking at the **75 State St. Garage** (© 617/742-7275).

Good-size garages downtown are at **Government Center,** off Congress Street (© 617/227-0385); **Sudbury Street** off Congress Street (© 617/973-6954); the **New England Aquarium** (© 617/723-1731); and **Zero Post Office Square,** in the Financial District (© 617/423-1430). In the Back Bay, there's a large garage near the Hynes Convention Center on **Dalton Street** (© 617/247-8006).

DRIVING RULES   When traffic permits, you may turn right at a red light after stopping, unless a sign says otherwise. Seat belts are mandatory for adults and children, children under 12 may not ride in the front seat, and infants and children under 5 must be in car seats. Pedestrians in the crosswalk and vehicles already in a rotary (traffic circle or roundabout) have the right of way.

FAST FACTS: Boston & Cambridge

American Express   The main local office is at 1 State St. (© 617/723-8400), opposite the Old State House. Other offices are in the Back Bay, 432 Stuart St., around the corner from Back Bay Station (© 617/236-1331), and in Cambridge, 39 John F. Kennedy St., Harvard Square (© 617/868-2600).

Area Codes   Eastern Massachusetts has eight area codes: Boston proper, **617** and **857;** immediate suburbs, **781** and **339;** northern and western suburbs, **978** and **351;** southern suburbs, **508** and **774.** *Note:* To complete a local call, you must dial all 10 digits.

Car Rentals   See "Getting Around," above.

Dentists   Ask at your hotel's front desk or try the **Massachusetts Dental Society** (© 800/342-8747 or 508/651-7511; www.massdental.org).

Doctors   Your hotel concierge should be able to help you. Hospital referral services include **Brigham and Women's** (© 800/294-9999), **Massachusetts General** (© 800/711-4MGH), and **Tufts–New England Medical Center** (© 617/636-9700). An affiliate of Mass. General, **MGH Back Bay,** 388 Comm. Ave. (© 617/267-7171), offers walk-in service and honors most insurance plans.

Drinking Laws The legal drinking age is 21. In many bars, particularly near college campuses, and at sporting events, you will probably be asked for ID. Some suburban towns, notably Rockport, are "dry."

Embassies/Consulates See "Fast Facts: For the International Traveler," in chapter 3.

Emergencies Call © **911** for fire, ambulance, or police. For the state police, call © **617/523-1212** or, from a cellphone, © ***77**.

Hospitals **Massachusetts General Hospital,** 55 Fruit St. (© **617/726-2000**), and **Tufts–New England Medical Center,** 750 Washington St. (© **617/636-5000**), are closest to downtown. In Cambridge are **Mount Auburn Hospital,** 330 Mt. Auburn St. (© **617/492-3500**), and **Cambridge Hospital,** 1493 Cambridge St. (© **617/498-1000**).

Hot Lines AIDS Hotline (© **800/590-2437** or 617/451-5155); Poison Control (© **800/682-9211**); Rape Crisis (© **617/492-7273**); and Travelers Aid Society (© **617/542-7286**).

Information See "Visitor Information," earlier in this chapter. For directory assistance, dial © **411**.

Internet Access The ubiquitous **Kinko's** charges 10¢ to 20¢ a minute. Locations include 2 Center Plaza, Government Center (© **617/973-9000**); 187 Dartmouth St., Back Bay (© **617/262-6188**); and 1 Mifflin Place, off Mount Auburn Street near Eliot Street, Harvard Square (© **617/497-0125**). **Tech Superpowers,** 252 Newbury St., third floor (© **617/267-9716**; www.newburyopen.net), offers access by the hour ($5/hour; $3 minimum) and free wireless access at many spots near its offices.

Newspapers/Magazines The daily papers are the *Boston Globe* and *Boston Herald*. The "Calendar" section of the Thursday *Globe* and the "Edge" section of the Friday *Herald* contain extensive cultural listings. The arts-oriented *Boston Phoenix*, published on Thursday, has entertainment and restaurant listings.

Where, a free monthly magazine, contains information on shopping, nightlife, attractions, museums, and galleries. Newspaper boxes around both cities dispense the free weekly *Phoenix* and *Tab*, and the biweekly *Improper Bostonian* and *Stuff@Night. Boston* magazine is a lifestyle-oriented monthly.

Pharmacies Downtown Boston has no 24-hour pharmacy. The pharmacy at the **CVS** at 155–157 Charles St. (© **617/523-1028**), next to the Charles/MGH Red Line T stop, is open until midnight. The pharmacy at the **CVS** at the Porter Square Shopping Center, off Mass. Ave. in Cambridge (© **617/876-5519**), is open 24 hours. Some emergency rooms can fill your prescription at the hospital's pharmacy.

Police Call © **911** for emergencies. For the state police, call © **617/523-1212** or, from a cellphone, © ***77**.

Restrooms The visitor center at 15 State St. has public restrooms, as do most tourist attractions, hotels, department stores, shopping centers, coffee bars, and public buildings. Free-standing, self-cleaning pay toilets (25¢) occupy eight locations downtown, including City Hall Plaza and Commercial Street at Snowhill Street, near the Freedom Trail.

Safety On the whole, Boston and Cambridge are safe cities for walking. As in any urban area, stay out of parks (including Boston Common, the Public Garden, and the Esplanade) at night unless you're in a crowd. Areas to avoid at night include Boylston Street between Tremont and Washington, and Tremont Street from Stuart to Boylston. Try not to walk alone late at night in the Theater District and around North Station. Public transportation is busy and safe, but service stops between 12:30 and 1am.

Smoking Massachusetts bans smoking in all workplaces, including clubs, bars, and restaurants. Take it outside—you'll have plenty of company.

Taxes The 5% sales tax does not apply to food, prescription drugs, newspapers, or clothing that costs less than $175; the tax on meals and takeout food is 5%. The lodging tax in Boston and Cambridge is 12.45%.

Taxis See "Getting Around," earlier in this chapter.

Transit Info Call © **617/222-3200** for the T (subways, local buses, commuter rail), and © **800/23-LOGAN** for MassPort (airport transportation).

3 Where to Stay

During the roaring 1990s, sky-high occupancy rates sparked a boom in hotel construction. Now that those establishments are open, the supply is up and demand is down, so prices have held steady or even dropped. Still, you'll need to do some planning, especially at busy times. Rates at most downtown hotels are lower on weekends than on weeknights, when business and convention travelers fill rooms; leisure hotels offer discounts during the week. If you don't mind cold and the possibility of snow, aim for January through March, when you'll find great deals, especially on weekends.

It's always a good idea to make a reservation, especially during foliage season. The area is also busy during spring and fall conventions, July and August vacations, and college graduation season (May and early June).

Before you rule out a hotel because of its location, consult a map. Especially downtown, neighborhoods are so small that the borders are somewhat arbitrary. The division to consider is **downtown** vs. **the Back Bay** vs. **Cambridge** and not, say, Downtown Crossing vs. the Financial District. For example, if your interests lie primarily in Cambridge, the Back Bay is not the most convenient place to stay. But if your companion has business downtown and you have the Newbury Street shopping bug, the Theater District may be a good compromise.

The state **hotel tax** is 5.7%. Boston and Cambridge (like Worcester and Springfield) add a 2.75% convention-center tax to the 4% city tax, bringing the total tax to 12.45%.

The Convention & Visitors Bureau **Hotel Hot Line** (© **800/777-6001**) can help make reservations even at the busiest times. It's staffed Monday through Friday until 8pm, Saturday and Sunday until 4pm. If you're driving from the west, stop at the Mass. Pike's Natick rest area and try the **reservations service** at the visitor center.

BED-AND-BREAKFASTS   Most lodgings require a minimum stay of at least 2 nights. The following organizations can help you find a B&B:

Boston Accommodations

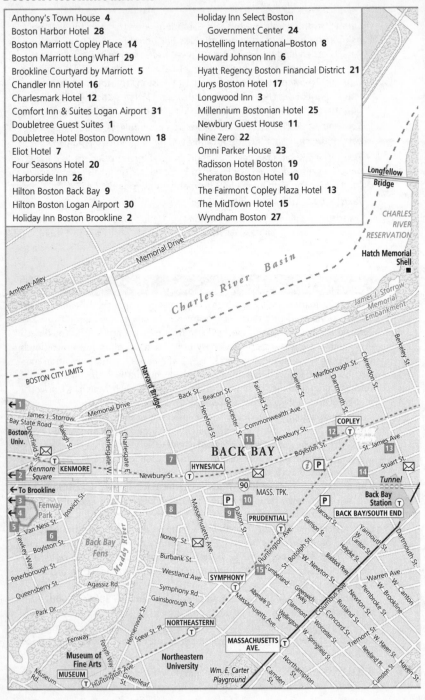

Anthony's Town House **4**
Boston Harbor Hotel **28**
Boston Marriott Copley Place **14**
Boston Marriott Long Wharf **29**
Brookline Courtyard by Marriott **5**
Chandler Inn Hotel **16**
Charlesmark Hotel **12**
Comfort Inn & Suites Logan Airport **31**
Doubletree Guest Suites **1**
Doubletree Hotel Boston Downtown **18**
Eliot Hotel **7**
Four Seasons Hotel **20**
Harborside Inn **26**
Hilton Boston Back Bay **9**
Hilton Boston Logan Airport **30**
Holiday Inn Boston Brookline **2**

Holiday Inn Select Boston
    Government Center **24**
Hostelling International–Boston **8**
Howard Johnson Inn **6**
Hyatt Regency Boston Financial District **21**
Jurys Boston Hotel **17**
Longwood Inn **3**
Millennium Bostonian Hotel **25**
Newbury Guest House **11**
Nine Zero **22**
Omni Parker House **23**
Radisson Hotel Boston **19**
Sheraton Boston Hotel **10**
The Fairmont Copley Plaza Hotel **13**
The MidTown Hotel **15**
Wyndham Boston **27**

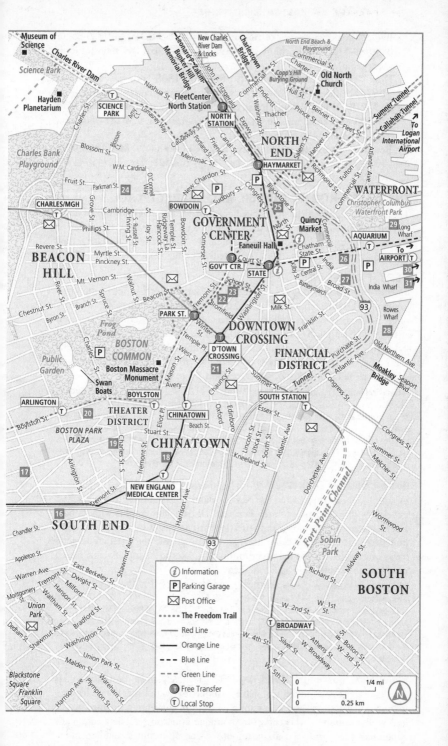

- **Bed & Breakfast Agency of Boston** (*©* **800/248-9262** or 617/720-3540, 0800/89-5128 from the U.K.; fax 617/523-5761; www.boston-bnb agency.com).
- **Host Homes of Boston** (*©* **800/600-1308** outside Mass. or 617/244-1308; fax 617/244-5156; www.hosthomesofboston.com).
- **Bed & Breakfast Reservations North Shore/Greater Boston/Cape Cod** (*©* **800/832-2632** outside Mass., 617/964-1606 or 978/281-9505; fax 978/281-9426; www.bbreserve.com).
- **Bed & Breakfast Associates Bay Colony** (*©* **888/486-6018,** 0800/731-3553 from the U.K., or 617/720-0522; fax 781/455-6745; www.bnbboston.com).

THE WATERFRONT & FANEUIL HALL MARKETPLACE

These areas are convenient to the Financial District and other downtown destinations, but not as handy if you plan to spend a lot of time in the Back Bay or Cambridge. *Tip:* Ask for a room on a high floor—you'll want to be as far as possible from the construction that has succeeded the Big Dig.

VERY EXPENSIVE

Boston Harbor Hotel ★★★   The Boston Harbor Hotel is one of the finest in town, an excellent choice for both business and leisure travelers. The 16-story brick building is within walking distance of downtown and the waterfront attractions. Each plush guest room is a luxurious combination of bedroom and living area, with mahogany furnishings and comfortable chairs. Rooms with city views are less expensive than those that face the harbor. The best units are suites with private terraces and dazzling water vistas.

Rowes Wharf (entrance on Atlantic Ave.), Boston, MA 02110. *©* 800/752-7077 or 617/439-7000. Fax 617/330-9450. www.bhh.com. 230 units. $295–$595 double; from $465 suite. Extra person $50. Children under 18 stay free in parent's room. Weekend packages available. AE, DC, DISC, MC, V. Valet parking $22–$34; self-parking $17–$30. T: Red Line to South Station or Blue Line to Aquarium. Pets accepted. **Amenities:** Restaurant (New England); cafe; bar; 60-ft. indoor lap pool; well-appointed health club and spa; concierge; courtesy car; business center; 24-hr. room service; in-room massage; babysitting; laundry service; dry cleaning; video rentals. *In room:* A/C, TV, high-speed Internet access ($10/day), minibar, hair dryer, robes.

Boston Marriott Long Wharf ★   The landmark Marriott's chief appeal is its location, a stone's throw from the New England Aquarium. It attracts business travelers with its proximity to the Financial District, and families with its pool and easy access to downtown and waterfront attractions. Rooms and bathrooms underwent extensive renovation in 2002. Rooms close to the water afford good views of the wharves and the waterfront; units closer to Atlantic Avenue have a newly peaceful post–Big Dig atmosphere.

296 State St. (at Atlantic Ave.), Boston, MA 02109. *©* 800/228-9290 or 617/227-0800. Fax 617/227-2867. www.marriottlongwharf.com. 400 units. Apr–Nov $249–$450 double; Dec–Mar $159–$279 double; $450–$490 suite year-round. Weekend packages available. AE, DC, DISC, MC, V. Parking $34. T: Blue Line to Aquarium. **Amenities:** Restaurant (seafood); cafe and lounge; bar and grill; indoor pool; exercise room; Jacuzzi; game room; concierge; tour desk; 24-hr. business center; limited room service; laundry service; same-day dry cleaning. *In room:* A/C, TV, high-speed Internet access ($10/day), coffeemaker, hair dryer, iron, safe, umbrella.

Millennium Bostonian Hotel ★★   The relatively small Bostonian offers excellent service and features that make it competitive with larger hotels. It's popular with business travelers who want a break from convention-oriented giants, and with vacationers who enjoy the boutique atmosphere. The traditionally appointed guest rooms contain top-of-the-line furnishings and amenities.

They're soundproofed, an important feature in this busy location. Half of the units have French doors that open onto small balconies; the plushest rooms are suites with working fireplaces or Jacuzzis.

At Faneuil Hall Marketplace, 26 North St., Boston, MA 02109. ✆ **800/343-0922** or 617/523-3600. Fax 617/523-2454. www.millennium-hotels.com/boston. 201 units. $245–$420 double; $265–$450 deluxe double; $500–$775 suite. Extra person $20. Children under 18 stay free in parent's room. Weekend, spa, and other packages available. AE, DC, DISC, MC, V. Valet parking $35. T: Orange Line to Haymarket, or Green or Blue Line to Government Center. **Amenities:** Restaurant (contemporary American); lounge; small fitness room; access to nearby health club ($10); in-room exercise equipment delivery on request; concierge; car-rental desk; business center; 24-hr. room service; in-room massage; babysitting; laundry service; same-day dry cleaning. *In room:* A/C, TV w/pay movies, high-speed Internet access ($10/day), minibar, hair dryer, iron, safe, umbrella, robes.

MODERATE

Harborside Inn ★★   Under the same management as the Newbury Guest House in the Back Bay, the Harborside Inn offers a similar combination of location and (for this neighborhood) value. The renovated 1858 warehouse is near Faneuil Hall Marketplace, the harbor, and the Financial District. The nicely appointed guest rooms have hardwood floors, Oriental rugs, and Victorian-style furniture. They surround a skylit atrium; city-view units are more expensive but can be noisier. Still, they're preferable to the interior rooms, whose windows open only to the atrium. Units on the top floors of the eight-story building have lower ceilings but better views.

185 State St. (between Atlantic Ave. and the Custom House Tower), Boston, MA 02109. ✆ **888/723-7565** or 617/723-7500. Fax 617/670-6015. www.harborsideinnboston.com. 54 units. $120–$210 double; $235–$310 suite. Extra person $15. Packages and long-term rates available. Rates may be higher during special events. AE, DC, DISC, MC, V. Off-site parking $20; reservation required. T: Blue Line to Aquarium or Orange Line to State. **Amenities:** Restaurant (international bistro); access to nearby health club ($15); concierge; limited room service; laundry service; dry cleaning. *In room:* A/C, TV, wireless Internet access ($10/day), hair dryer, iron.

AT THE AIRPORT
EXPENSIVE

Hilton Boston Logan Airport ★★   This hotel smack in the middle of the airport draws most of its guests from meetings, conventions, and canceled flights. Walkways lead directly to Terminals A (close, but under construction) and E (distant). The hotel is convenient for business travelers, and an excellent fallback for vacationers who don't mind a short commute to downtown. Guest rooms are tastefully furnished; the best units, on higher floors of the 10-story building, afford sensational views. Soundproofing throughout the hotel, which opened in 1999, is excellent. The closest competition, the Hyatt Harborside, is farther from the T but right at the ferry dock.

85 Terminal Rd., Logan International Airport, Boston, MA 02128. ✆ **800/HILTONS** or 617/568-6700. Fax 617/568-6800. www.hiltonbostonloganairport.com. 599 units. $149–$399 double; from $500 suite. Children under 19 stay free in parent's room. Weekend and other packages from $159 per night. AE, DC, DISC, MC, V. Valet parking $20; self-parking $18. T: Blue Line to Airport, then take shuttle bus. Pets accepted. **Amenities:** Restaurant (American); Irish pub; coffee counter; indoor lap pool; health club and spa; 24-hr. shuttle bus to airport destinations (including car-rental offices and ferry dock); business center; 24-hr. room service; laundry service; same-day dry cleaning. *In room:* A/C, TV/VCR w/pay movies, high-speed Internet access ($10/day), minibar, coffeemaker, hair dryer, iron.

MODERATE

Comfort Inn & Suites Logan Airport   Although it loses points for the misleading name—the airport is about 3½ miles south—the well-equipped Comfort Inn ranks high in other areas. The eight-story hotel, which opened in 2001, offers a good range of amenities, including free high-speed Internet access and local phone calls, continental breakfast, and an indoor pool. The somewhat inconvenient location translates to reasonable rates, and the North Shore is easily accessible if you plan to take a day trip.

85 American Legion Hwy. (Rte. 60), Revere, MA 02151. © 800/228-5150, 888/283-9300 (local toll-free), or 781/485-3600. Fax 781/485-3601. www.comfortinnboston.com. 208 units. $79–$199 double; $99–$229 suite. Rates include continental breakfast. Senior and AAA discounts available. AE, DC, DISC, MC, V. Free parking. T: Blue Line to Airport, then take shuttle bus. Small pets accepted ($10/day). **Amenities:** Restaurant (Italian/American); lounge; indoor pool; exercise room; shuttle to subway and airport; business center; limited room service; coin-op laundry; laundry service; same-day dry cleaning. *In room:* A/C, TV w/pay movies, high-speed Internet access, coffeemaker, hair dryer, iron.

FINANCIAL DISTRICT
VERY EXPENSIVE

Wyndham Boston ★★   This meticulously designed luxury hotel draws business travelers during the week and leisure travelers on weekends. The 14-story building is near Faneuil Hall Marketplace and the waterfront, but not all that close (by downtown standards) to the T. The spacious guest rooms have 9½-foot ceilings that make them feel even larger. The best units, on the upper floors, have great views of the harbor and downtown. Soundproofing throughout makes the whole building exceptionally quiet. The closest competitor, literally and figuratively, is the Langham, which is less convenient to public transit but has a pool.

89 Broad St., Boston, MA 02110. © 800/WYNDHAM or 617/556-0006. Fax 617/556-0053. www.wyndham. com. 362 units. Double $149–$399 weekdays, $129–$249 weekends; suite $224–$474 weekdays, $204–$324 weekends. Children under 13 stay free in parent's room. Weekend, family, and other packages available. AE, DC, DISC, MC, V. Valet parking $32. T: Blue or Orange Line to State, or Red Line to South Station. **Amenities:** Restaurant (California/Italian); bar; fitness center; concierge; business center; 24-hr. room service. *In room:* A/C, TV w/pay movies, high-speed Internet access ($10/day), minibar, coffeemaker, hair dryer, iron, safe, umbrella, robes.

DOWNTOWN CROSSING & BEACON HILL

The **Holiday Inn Select Boston Government Center,** 5 Blossom St., at Cambridge Street (© 800/HOLIDAY or 617/742-7630), offers all the features you'd expect of the international chain, including a heated outdoor pool.

VERY EXPENSIVE

Hyatt Regency Boston Financial District ★ *Value*   This centrally located 22-story hotel lives two lives. It's a busy convention and business destination during the week, and its excellent weekend packages make it a magnet for sightseers. Hyatt took over the former Swissôtel Boston in 2003 and plans renovations from late 2004 into 2005; be sure to request a room away from the work zone. Guest rooms are large enough to hold sitting areas, a desk, and a settee; they have king-size or European twin-size beds. Ask for a unit on a high floor; this neighborhood was ugly even before construction began all along nearby Washington Street.

1 Ave. de Lafayette (off Washington St.), Boston, MA 02111. © 800/223-1234 or 617/912-1234. Fax 617/451-0054. www.hyattregencyboston.com. 500 units. $189–$375 double; $300–$450 suite. Extra person $25. Children under 12 stay free in parent's room. AE, DC, DISC, MC, V. Valet parking $34; self-parking $26. T: Red Line to Downtown Crossing, or Green Line to Boylston. **Amenities:** Restaurant (American/Continental); bar; 52-ft. indoor pool; health club; Jacuzzi; sauna; concierge; tour desk; business center; 24-hr. room service; massage; babysitting; laundry service; same-day dry cleaning; executive-level rooms. Rooms for travelers with disabilities are available. *In room:* A/C, TV/VCR w/pay movies, dataport, coffeemaker, hair dryer, iron, robes.

Nine Zero ★   Sleek and sophisticated, Nine Zero feels almost like a transplant from New York or L.A. The decent-size guest rooms and oversize bathrooms contain opulent appointments, including luxurious linens, down comforters, cordless two-line phones, and extensive business features. The contemporary boutique atmosphere distinguishes the 19-story hotel from the more old-fashioned establishments that dominate this market. This neighborhood is convenient for both business and leisure travelers: It's within walking distance of most downtown destinations, and 2 blocks from the subway to Cambridge.

90 Tremont St. (near Bromfield St.), Boston, MA 02108. ℂ 866/NINE-ZERO or 617/772-5800. Fax 617/772-5810. www.ninezerohotel.com. 189 units. $289–$500 double; $500–$1,800 suite. Packages available. AE, DC, DISC, MC, V. Valet parking $32. T: Red or Green Line to Park St. Pets accepted. **Amenities:** Restaurant (progressive French); bar; exercise room; access to nearby health club ($10); concierge; tour desk; business center; 24-hr. room service; in-room massage; babysitting; laundry service; same-day dry cleaning. *In room:* A/C, TV w/pay movies, high-speed Internet access, minibar, coffeemaker, hair dryer, iron, safe, umbrella, robes, radio w/CD player.

EXPENSIVE

Omni Parker House ⟨★⟩   The Parker House offers a great combination of nearly 150 years of history and extensive renovations. It has been in continuous operation longer than any other hotel in America, since 1856. Since the detail-oriented Omni chain took over in the late 1990s, the hotel has been upgraded throughout. Guest rooms, a patchwork of more than 50 configurations, aren't huge, but they are thoughtfully laid out and nicely appointed. Business travelers can book a room with an expanded work area, while sightseers can economize by requesting a smaller, less expensive unit.

60 School St., Boston, MA 02108. ℂ 800/THE-OMNI or 617/227-8600. Fax 617/742-5729. www.omni hotels.com. 552 units (some w/shower only). $119–$179 double; $139–$339 deluxe double; $179–$349 executive double; $189–$389 suite. Children under 18 stay free in parent's room. Weekend packages and AARP discount available. AE, DC, DISC, MC, V. Valet parking $27; self-parking $20. T: Green or Blue Line to Government Center, or Red Line to Park St. Pets under 25 lbs. accepted ($50). **Amenities:** Restaurant (New England); 2 bars; exercise room; access to nearby health club ($20); children's programs; concierge; tour desk; business center; 24-hr. room service; babysitting; laundry service; same-day dry cleaning. *In room:* A/C, TV w/pay movies and Nintendo, high-speed Internet access, minibar, coffeemaker, hair dryer, iron, robes.

CHINATOWN/THEATER DISTRICT
EXPENSIVE

Radisson Hotel Boston ⟨★★⟩   The construction-bound neighborhood isn't the most attractive, so this hotel can be a pleasant surprise. It's convenient to both the Back Bay and downtown, and the guest rooms are among the largest in the city, each with a private balcony and sitting area. The well-maintained hotel is popular with business travelers, tour groups, and families. The best units are the executive-level rooms on the top five floors of the 24-story building.

200 Stuart St. (at Charles St. S.), Boston, MA 02116. ℂ 800/333-3333 or 617/482-1800. Fax 617/451-2750. www.radisson.com/bostonma. 356 units (some w/shower only). $159–$359 double. Extra person $20; cot $20; cribs free. Children under 18 stay free in parent's room. Weekend, theater, and other packages available. AE, DC, DISC, MC, V. Valet parking $21; self-parking $19. T: Green Line to Boylston, or Orange Line to New England Medical Center. **Amenities:** Cafe; Stuart Street Playhouse (ℂ 617/426-4499), a small professional theater; indoor pool; exercise room; concierge; business center; limited room service; in-room massage; laundry service; same-day dry cleaning. *In room:* A/C, TV w/pay movies, coffeemaker, hair dryer, iron.

MODERATE

Doubletree Hotel Boston Downtown ⟨★⟩ ⟨*Value*⟩   Within walking distance of both downtown and the Back Bay, the relatively new Doubletree (it opened in 2000) is a better deal than most competitors in either neighborhood. The six-story building is a former high school, with high ceilings and compact, well-designed rooms. Ask for a unit that faces away from busy Washington Street, and your view will be of a cityscape rather than the hospital across the street. Don't confuse this hotel with its all-suite corporate sibling in Cambridge (p. 99). This Doubletree adjoins the Wang YMCA of Chinatown, and room rates include access to its extensive facilities.

821 Washington St., Boston, MA 02111. ✆ 800/222-TREE or 617/956-7900. Fax 617/956-7901. www. downtownboston.doubletree.com. 267 units (some w/shower only). $129–$299 double; $189–$359 suite. Extra person $10. Children under 17 stay free in parent's room. Weekend and other packages, AAA, AARP, and military discounts available. AE, DC, DISC, MC, V. Valet parking $30. T: Orange Line to New England Medical Center. **Amenities:** Restaurant and lounge (American/Asian); cafe; access to adjoining YMCA with Olympic-size pool; concierge; business center; room service until 11:30pm; same-day dry cleaning; executive-level rooms. *In room:* A/C, TV w/pay movies, wireless Internet access ($10/day), minibar, coffeemaker, hair dryer, iron, safe.

BACK BAY/SOUTH END
VERY EXPENSIVE

Eliot Hotel ★★★   This exquisite hotel combines the flavor of Yankee Boston with European-style service and amenities. On tree-lined Comm. Ave., it feels more like a classy apartment building than a hotel, with a romantic atmosphere that belies the top-notch business features. Every unit is a spacious suite with antique furnishings. French doors separate the living rooms and bedrooms, and bathrooms are outfitted in Italian marble. The 1925 building is near Boston University and MIT (across the river), and the location contrasts pleasantly with the bustle of Newbury Street, a block away.

370 Comm. Ave. (at Mass. Ave.), Boston, MA 02215. ✆ 800/44-ELIOT or 617/267-1607. Fax 617/536-9114. www.eliothotel.com. 95 units. $235–$415 1-bedroom suite for 2; $450–$750 2-bedroom suite. Extra person $20. Children under 18 stay free in parent's room. AE, DC, MC, V. Valet parking $28. T: Green Line B, C, or D to Hynes/ICA. Pets accepted. **Amenities:** Restaurant (eclectic); sashimi bar; access to nearby health club; concierge; business center; 24-hr. room service; in-room massage; babysitting; laundry service; dry cleaning. *In room:* A/C, TV/DVD w/pay movies, fax/printer, high-speed Internet access ($15/day), minibar, hair dryer, iron, umbrella, robes.

The Fairmont Copley Plaza Hotel ★★   The "grande dame of Boston" is a true grand hotel. Built in 1912, the six-story Renaissance Revival building faces Copley Square. Already known for superb service, the Copley Plaza has enjoyed a renaissance of its own since becoming a Fairmont property in 1996. In 2004 it completed a $29-million renovation and redecoration of the spacious guest rooms. The traditional furnishings reflect the elegance of the opulent public spaces. Rooms that face the lovely square afford better views than those that overlook busy Dartmouth Street.

138 St. James Ave., Boston, MA 02116. ✆ 800/441-1414 or 617/267-5300. Fax 617/247-6681. www. fairmont.com/copleyplaza. 383 units. From $249 double; from $429 suite. Extra person $30. Weekend and other packages available. AE, DC, MC, V. Valet parking $32. T: Green Line to Copley, or Orange Line to Back Bay. Pets up to 20 lbs. accepted. **Amenities:** 2 restaurants (steakhouse, American); bar; lounge; exercise room; concierge; courtesy car; business center; 24-hr. room service; laundry service; same-day dry cleaning. *In room:* A/C, TV w/pay movies, high-speed Internet access ($15/day), minibar, hair dryer, iron, safe, umbrella, robes.

Four Seasons Hotel ★★★   Many hotels offer exquisite service, a beautiful location, elegant guest rooms and public areas, a terrific health club, and wonderful restaurants. But no other hotel in Boston—indeed, in New England—combines every element of a luxury hotel as seamlessly as the Four Seasons. If I were traveling with someone else's credit cards, I'd head straight here. The 16-story brick-and-glass building (the hotel occupies eight floors) blends traditional and contemporary style. The best units overlook the Public Garden; city views from the back of the hotel aren't as desirable. Children receive bedtime snacks and toys, and can ask at the concierge desk for duck food to take to the Public Garden. Small pets even enjoy a special menu and amenities.

200 Boylston St., Boston, MA 02116. © **800/332-3442** or 617/338-4400. Fax 617/423-0154. www.four seasons.com. 274 units. $425–$815 double; from $1,600 1-bedroom suite; from $2,200 2-bedroom suite. Weekend packages available. AE, DC, DISC, MC, V. Valet parking $36. T: Green Line to Arlington. Pets under 15 lb. accepted. **Amenities:** Restaurant (see review of Aujourd'hui under "Where to Dine," later in this chapter); Bristol Lounge (see "Bars & Lounges," later in this chapter); 51-ft. pool; health club and spa; concierge; tour desk; car-rental desk; limo to downtown; business center; 24-hr. room service; in-room massage; babysitting; laundry service; same-day dry cleaning. In room: A/C, TV w/pay movies, high-speed Internet access ($10/day), minibar, coffeemaker, hair dryer, iron, safe, umbrella, robes.

EXPENSIVE

The largest convention hotel in New England is the 1,147-unit **Boston Marriott Copley Place,** 110 Huntington Ave., Boston, MA 02116 (© **800/228-9290** or 617/236-5800; www.copleymarriott.com). Part of the Copley Place shopping complex, it offers complete business features and a good-size pool.

Hilton Boston Back Bay ★★   Across the street from the Prudential Center complex, the Hilton is primarily a business hotel, but families also find it convenient. Rooms in the 26-story tower are large, soundproofed, and furnished in modern style. The weekend packages, especially in winter, can be a great deal. The closest competitor is the Sheraton, across the street. It's three times the Hilton's size (which generally means less personalized service), has a better pool, and books more vacation and function business.

40 Dalton St., Boston, MA 02115. © **800/874-0663**, 800/HILTONS, or 617/236-1100. Fax 617/867-6104. www.hiltonbostonbackbay.com. 385 units (some w/shower only). $179–$295 double; from $450 suite. Extra person $20; rollaway $20. Children stay free in parent's room. Packages and AAA discount available. AE, DC, DISC, MC, V. Valet parking $26; self-parking $17. T: Green Line B, C, or D to Hynes/ICA. Pets accepted. **Amenities:** Restaurant (American/Continental); bar; indoor pool; fitness center; concierge; courtesy car; 24-hr. business center; limited room service; laundry service; same-day dry cleaning. In room: A/C, TV w/pay movies, high-speed Internet access ($10/stay), minibar, coffeemaker, hair dryer, iron.

Jurys Boston Hotel ★★   In the former Boston Police Headquarters building, the Irish chain caters to both business and leisure travelers. The 1925 limestone-and-brick structure now holds dramatic public areas and plush accommodations. The luxurious guest rooms have nice touches such as a work area with an ergonomic chair, good-size bathrooms, and windows that open but also muffle street noise. Still, light sleepers will want to face away from busy Berkeley Street. Opened in 2004, this is Jurys Doyle's first U.S. property outside Washington, D.C.; while the brand establishes itself in this market, you might be able to score a deal.

350 Stuart St. (at Berkeley St.), Boston, MA 02116. © **866/JD-HOTELS** or 617/266-7200. Fax 617/266-7203. www.jurysdoyle.com. 220 units (some w/shower only). $155–$435 double; $275–$575 1-bedroom suite; $475–$775 2-bedroom suite. Children under 16 stay free in parent's room. Extra person $20. Weekend, family, and other packages from $155 per night. AE, DC, DISC, MC, V. Valet parking $32. T: Orange Line to Back Bay or Green Line to Arlington or Copley. **Amenities:** Restaurant (American); Irish bar; coffee and wine bar; exercise room; access to nearby health club ($10); concierge; business center; 24-hr. room service; laundry service; same-say dry cleaning. In room: A/C, TV w/pay movies, wireless Internet access, fridge, hair dryer, iron, safe, umbrella, robes.

Sheraton Boston Hotel ★   Its central location, range of accommodations, convention and function facilities, direct access to the Hynes Convention Center and the Prudential Center complex, and huge pool make this 29-story hotel one of the most popular in the city. Because it's so big, it often has rooms available when smaller properties are full. If you're on a budget, though, you may be able to get a better deal elsewhere; shop around. A $110-million overhaul in

2001 upgraded the entire property. The fairly large guest rooms are decorated in sleek contemporary style and contain Starwood's signature pillow-top beds. Units on higher floors afford gorgeous views, especially to the west and north.

39 Dalton St., Boston, MA 02199. © **800/325-3535** or 617/236-2000. Fax 617/236-1702. www.sheraton. com/boston. 1,215 units. $129–$409 double; from $309 suite. Children under 17 stay free in parent's room. Weekend packages available. 25% discount for students, faculty, and retired persons with ID, depending on availability. AE, DC, DISC, MC, V. Valet parking $35; self-parking $32. T: Green Line E to Prudential, or B, C, or D to Hynes/ICA. Dogs under 40 lb. accepted with prior approval. **Amenities:** Restaurant (New England); lounge; heated indoor/outdoor pool; health club; Jacuzzi; sauna; concierge; airport shuttle; business center; limited room service; laundry service; same-day dry cleaning. *In room:* A/C, TV w/pay movies, high-speed Internet access ($10/day), coffeemaker, hair dryer, iron, robes.

MODERATE

Chandler Inn Hotel ⭐ *Value*   The comfortable, unpretentious Chandler Inn is a bargain for its location, just 2 blocks from the Back Bay. Guest rooms have individual climate control and tasteful contemporary-style furniture. Each unit holds a queen or double bed or two twin beds, without enough room to squeeze in a cot. Bathrooms are tiny, and the one elevator in the eight-story inn can be slow, but the staff is welcoming and helpful. This is a gay-friendly hotel—Fritz, the bar next to the lobby, is a neighborhood hangout—that often books up early.

26 Chandler St. (at Berkeley St.), Boston, MA 02116. © **800/842-3450** or 617/482-3450. Fax 617/542-3428. www.chandlerinn.com. 56 units. Apr–Dec $139–$169 double; Jan–Mar $129–$139 double. Children under 12 stay free in parent's room. AE, DC, DISC, MC, V. No parking. T: Orange Line to Back Bay. Pets under 25 lb. accepted with prior approval. **Amenities:** Lounge; access to nearby health club ($10). *In room:* A/C, TV, dataport, hair dryer.

Charlesmark Hotel ⭐⭐ *Value*   In an excellent location overlooking the Boston Marathon finish line, the Charlesmark has a boutique feel and great prices. It's both luxurious and—literally, not figuratively—no frills. The contemporary design evokes a yacht, using custom furnishings to pack plenty of comfort into compact spaces. Rooms have pillow-top mattresses and enough room to hold a comfortable chair. The amenities don't challenge the perks of the large hotels in this neighborhood, but they're more than sufficient for most business or leisure travelers—rates include continental breakfast, access to a computer in the lobby, and local phone calls.

655 Boylston St. (between Dartmouth and Exeter sts.), Boston, MA 02116. © **617/247-1212.** Fax 617/247-1224. www.thecharlesmark.com. 33 units (most w/shower only). $99–$249 double. Rates include continental breakfast. Children under 12 stay free in parent's room. AE, DC, DISC, MC, V. Self-parking $32 in nearby garage. T: Green Line to Copley. Pets accepted with prior approval. **Amenities:** Access to nearby health club ($10); laundry service. *In room:* A/C, TV, high-speed Internet access, mini-fridge, hair dryer.

The MidTown Hotel ⭐ *Value*   Even without free parking and an outdoor pool, this centrally located two-story hotel would be a good deal for families and budget-conscious businesspeople; it also books a lot of tour groups. It's on a busy street within walking distance of Symphony Hall and the Museum of Fine Arts. The well-maintained rooms are large, bright, and attractively outfitted, although bathrooms are on the small side. Some units have connecting doors that allow families to spread out. The best rooms are on the side of the building that faces away from Huntington Avenue.

220 Huntington Ave., Boston, MA 02115. © **800/343-1177** or 617/262-1000. Fax 617/262-8739. www. midtownhotel.com. 159 units. $89–$209 double. Extra person $15. Children under 18 stay free in parent's room. Packages and AAA, AARP, and government employee discount available, subject to availability. AE, DC DISC, MC, V. Free parking (1 car per room). T: Green Line E to Prudential, or Orange Line to Mass. Ave. **Amenities:** Restaurant (breakfast only); heated outdoor pool; access to nearby health club ($10); concierge;

tour desk; airport shuttle; salon; babysitting; laundry service; dry cleaning. *In room:* A/C, TV w/pay movies, dataport, coffeemaker, hair dryer, iron.

Newbury Guest House ★★ *Value*   After just a little shopping in the Back Bay, you'll appreciate what a find this cozy inn is: a bargain on Newbury Street. It's a pair of brick town houses built in the 1880s and combined into a refined guesthouse. It offers comfortable furnishings, a pleasant staff, nifty architectural details, and a buffet breakfast served in the dining room, which adjoins a brick patio. Rooms are modest in size but nicely appointed. Since opening in 1991, it has operated near capacity all year, drawing business travelers during the week and sightseers on weekends. At these prices in this location, there's only one caveat: Reserve early.

261 Newbury St. (between Fairfield and Gloucester sts.), Boston, MA 02116. ⓒ **800/437-7668** or 617/437-7666. Fax 617/670-6100. www.newburyguesthouse.com. 32 units (some w/shower only). $140–$195 double. Winter discounts and packages available. Rates include continental breakfast. Extra person $15. Rates may be higher during special events. Minimum 2 nights on weekends. AE, DC, DISC, MC, V. Parking $15 (reservation required). T: Green Line B, C, or D to Hynes/ICA. **Amenities:** Access to nearby health club ($15); 24-hr. room service. *In room:* A/C, TV, high-speed Internet access, hair dryer, iron.

INEXPENSIVE

Hostelling International–Boston   This hostel near the Berklee College of Music and Symphony Hall caters to students, youth groups, and other travelers in search of comfortable, no-frills lodging. Accommodations are dorm-style, with six beds per room; there are also a couple of private units. The air-conditioned hostel has two kitchens, 19 bathrooms, and a large common room. It provides linens, or you can bring your own; sleeping bags are not permitted. The enthusiastic staff organizes free and inexpensive cultural, educational, and recreational programs.

12 Hemenway St., Boston, MA 02115. ⓒ **800/909-4776** or 617/536-9455. Fax 617/424-6558. www.boston hostel.org. 205 beds. Members of Hostelling International–American Youth Hostels $32 per bed; nonmembers $35 per bed. Members $87 per private unit; nonmembers $93 per private unit. Children 3–12 half-price; children under 3 free. Rates include continental breakfast. MC, V. T: Green Line B, C, or D to Hynes/ICA. **Amenities:** Airport shuttle; coin laundry; Internet access (fee). *In room:* A/C, lockers, no phone.

OUTSKIRTS & BROOKLINE

Staying in this area means commuting to downtown Boston. Because of the unwieldy public transit connections, it's not a great choice if your destination is Cambridge.

EXPENSIVE

Doubletree Guest Suites ★★ *Value*   This hotel is one of the best deals in town—every unit is a two-room suite. Overlooking the Charles River, the hotel is near Cambridge and the riverfront bike path, but not in a real neighborhood. Van service to and from attractions and business areas in Boston and Cambridge makes the location easier to handle. The large, attractively furnished suites surround a 15-story atrium. Most bedrooms have a king-size bed and writing desk. Each living room contains a sofa bed and dining table. The Hyatt Regency Cambridge, the hotel's nearest rival, is more convenient but generally more expensive.

400 Soldiers Field Rd., Boston, MA 02134. ⓒ **800/222-TREE** or 617/783-0090. Fax 617/783-0897. www. doubletree.com. 308 units. $129–$309 double. Extra person $20. Children under 18 stay free in parent's room. Packages and AARP and AAA discounts available. AE, DC, DISC, MC, V. Parking $20. Pets accepted with prior approval; $250 deposit. **Amenities:** Restaurant (American); lounge; Scullers Jazz Club (see below); indoor pool; exercise room; free access to nearby health club; Jacuzzi; sauna; concierge; shuttle service;

24-hr. business center; limited room service; coin laundry; laundry service; same-day dry cleaning. *In room:* A/C, TV w/pay movies and Sony PlayStation, high-speed Internet access ($10/day), minibar, fridge, coffeemaker, hair dryer, iron.

MODERATE

Many options in this price range and area are chain hotels, including the **Brookline Courtyard by Marriott,** 40 Webster St., Brookline (✆ **866/296-2296,** 800/321-2211, or 617/734-1393), **Holiday Inn Boston Brookline,** 1200 Beacon St., Brookline (✆ **800/HOLIDAY** or 617/277-1200), and the **Howard Johnson Inn,** 1271 Boylston St., Boston (✆ **800/654-2000** or 617/267-8300).

INEXPENSIVE

Anthony's Town House   The Anthony family has operated this four-story brownstone guesthouse since 1944, and a stay here feels like a visit to Grandma's. Many patrons are Europeans accustomed to accommodations with shared bathrooms, but budget-minded Americans won't be disappointed. Each floor has three high-ceilinged rooms furnished in Queen Anne or Victorian style, plus a bathroom with enclosed shower. The large front rooms have bay windows. The guesthouse is 1 mile from Kenmore Square, about 15 minutes from downtown by T, and 2 blocks from a busy commercial strip.

1085 Beacon St., Brookline, MA 02446. ✆ **617/566-3972.** Fax 617/232-1085. www.anthonystownhouse. com. 12 units (none w/private bathroom). $68–$98 double. Extra person $10. Weekly rates and winter discounts available. No credit cards. Limited free parking. T: Green Line C to Hawes St. *In room:* A/C, TV, no phone.

Longwood Inn   In a residential area 3 blocks from the Boston-Brookline border, this three-story Victorian guesthouse offers comfortable accommodations at modest rates. Guests have the use of a full kitchen, dining room, and TV lounge. There's one apartment with a private bathroom, kitchen, and balcony. Tennis courts, a running track, and a playground at the school next door are open to the public. Public transportation is easily accessible, and the Longwood Medical Area and busy Coolidge Corner neighborhood are within walking distance.

123 Longwood Ave., Brookline, MA 02446. ✆ **617/566-8615.** Fax 617/738-1070. www.longwood-inn.com. 22 units, 17 w/private bathroom (some w/shower only). Apr–Nov $89–$109 double; Dec–Mar $69–$89 double. 1-bedroom apt (sleeps 4-plus) $99–$119. Weekly rates available. AE, DISC, MC, V. Free parking. T: Green Line D to Longwood, or C to Coolidge Corner. *In room:* A/C.

CAMBRIDGE
VERY EXPENSIVE

The Charles Hotel ★★★   This nine-story brick hotel a block from Harvard Square has been *the* place for business and leisure travelers in Cambridge since it opened in 1985. Much of its fame derives from its excellent restaurants, jazz bar, and day spa; the service is equally impeccable. In the posh guest rooms, the style is contemporary country, with custom adaptations of early American Shaker furniture. The austere design contrasts with the indulgent amenities, which include down quilts and Bose Wave radios; bathrooms contain telephones and TVs.

1 Bennett St., Cambridge, MA 02138. ✆ **800/882-1818** outside Mass., or 617/864-1200. Fax 617/864-5715. www.charleshotel.com. 293 units. $229–$599 double; $279–$4,000 suite. Extra person $20. Weekend packages available. AE, DC, MC, V. Valet and self-parking $28. T: Red Line to Harvard. Pets under 25 lb. accepted. **Amenities:** 2 restaurants (including Rialto, p. 113); bar; Regattabar jazz club (p. 142); access to adjacent health club with pool, Jacuzzi, and exercise room; adjacent spa and salon; concierge; car-rental desk; business center; 24-hr. room service; in-room massage; babysitting; laundry service; same-day dry cleaning. *In room:* A/C, TV/DVD, high-speed Internet access ($11/day), minibar, hair dryer, iron, safe, umbrella, robes.

Royal Sonesta Hotel ★★ *Kids*   This luxurious hotel is in a curious location—it's close to only a few things but convenient to everything. Features for both businesspeople and families, from the business center to Wi-Fi access throughout the building to the indoor/outdoor pool with retractable roof, are excellent. The CambridgeSide Galleria mall and the Museum of Science are nearby, and it's actually closer to Boston than to Harvard Square. MIT and Kendall Square are 10 minutes away on foot. Most of the spacious rooms have lovely views of the river or the city. (Higher prices are for better views.) Everything is custom designed in modern yet comfortable style. The closest competition is the Hotel Marlowe, across the street, which offers less extensive fitness options (there's no pool) and fewer river views.

5 Cambridge Pkwy., Cambridge, MA 02142. © **800/SONESTA** or 617/806-4200. Fax 617/806-4232. www. sonesta.com/boston. 400 units (some w/shower only). $239–$279 standard double; $259–$299 superior double; $279–$319 deluxe double; $339–$1,000 suite. Extra person $25. Children under 18 stay free in parent's room. Weekend, family, and other packages available. AE, DC, DISC, MC, V. Valet and self-parking $19. T: Green Line to Lechmere; 10-min. walk. Pets accepted with prior approval. **Amenities:** Restaurant (northern Italian); cafe; indoor/outdoor pool; health club and spa; bike rental (seasonal); concierge; courtesy van; business center; limited room service; massage; laundry service; dry cleaning. *In room:* A/C, TV w/pay movies and Sony PlayStation, wireless Internet access ($10/day), minibar, coffeemaker, hair dryer, iron, safe, umbrella.

EXPENSIVE

Hotel Marlowe ★★ *Kids*   Hotel Marlowe is the first Northeast property of Kimpton Boutique Hotels, best known for the beloved Hotel Monaco brand. It opened in 2003 in a new eight-story building adjacent to the CambridgeSide Galleria mall and around the corner from the Museum of Science. It's chic yet comfortable, with abundant amenities for both businesspeople and leisure travelers. The elegantly decorated guest rooms are good size, with enough room to hold a work desk and armchair. They overlook the river (across the busy boulevard), a small canal, or the landscaped courtyard/driveway that shields the lobby from the street. The Marlowe's closest competition is the Royal Sonesta Hotel, across the street, which is more expensive but has a pool and health club.

25 Edwin H. Land Blvd., Cambridge, MA 02141. © **800/825-7040**, 800/KIMPTON, or 617/868-8000. Fax 617/868-8001. www.hotelmarlowe.com. 236 units (some w/shower only). $189–$349 double; from $389 suite. Extra person $25. Rates include morning coffee and tea, evening cocktail reception, and use of bikes. Children under 18 stay free in parent's room. Weekend, family, and other packages available. AARP and AAA discounts available. AE, DC, DISC, MC, V. Valet parking $28; self-parking $20. T: Green Line to Lechmere or Red Line to Kendall. Pets accepted. **Amenities:** Restaurant (American brasserie); bar; exercise room; concierge; business center; 24-hr. room service; laundry service; same-day dry cleaning. *In room:* A/C, TV w/pay movies and Sony PlayStation, high-speed Internet access, minibar, coffeemaker, hair dryer, iron, safe, umbrella, robes.

Sheraton Commander Hotel ★   This six-story hotel in the heart of Cambridge's historic district opened in 1927, and it's exactly what you'd expect of a traditional hostelry within sight of the Harvard campus. The colonial-style decor begins in the elegant lobby and extends to the guest rooms, which are attractively furnished and well maintained. Ask the pleasant front-desk staff for a room facing Cambridge Common; even if you aren't on a (relatively) high floor, you'll have a decent view. The Sheraton Commander doesn't have the cachet and amenities of the Charles Hotel—but it doesn't have the Charles's prices, either.

16 Garden St., Cambridge, MA 02138. © **800/325-3535** or 617/547-4800. Fax 617/868-8322. www. sheratoncommander.com. 175 units. $139–$385 double; $295–$750 suite. Extra person $20. Children under 18 stay free in parent's room. Weekend packages and AAA and AARP discounts available. AE, DC, DISC, MC, V. Valet parking $18. T: Red Line to Harvard. **Amenities:** Restaurant (American); lounge; exercise room;

Cambridge Accommodations & Dining

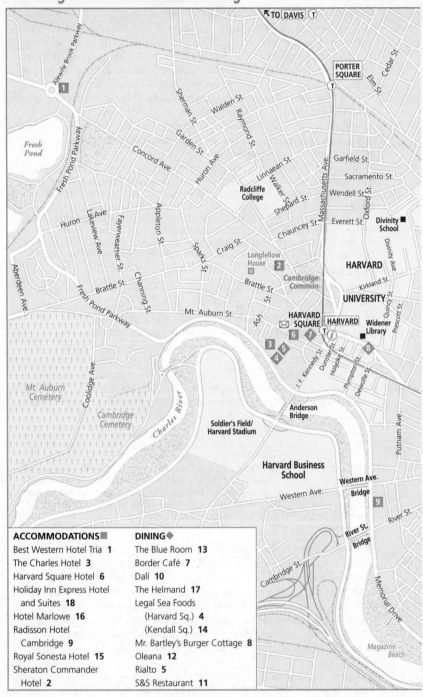

TO DAVIS ⓣ

PORTER SQUARE ⓣ

Fresh Pond

Alewife Brook Parkway

1

Fresh Pond Parkway

Sherman St.

Walden St.

Raymond St.

Garden St.

Concord Ave.

Huron Ave.

Linnaean St.

Walker St.

Shepard St.

Garfield St.

Sacramento St.

Wendell St.

Everett St.

Chauncey St.

Massachusetts Ave.

Oxford St.

Divinity School ■

Radcliffe College

Huron

Lakeview Ave.

Fayerweather St.

Appleton St.

Sparks St.

Craig St.

Longfellow House ■

2

Cambridge Common

HARVARD UNIVERSITY

Kirkland St.

Divinity Ave.

Quincy St.

Prescott St.

Aberdeen Ave.

Brattle St.

Channing St.

Fresh Pond Parkway

Mt. Auburn St.

Brattle St.

Ash St.

Ash St.

HARVARD SQUARE

✉ **6** **7**

HARVARD ⓣ

ⓘ

Widener Library ■

Coolidge Ave.

3

5

4

J. F. Kennedy St.

Dunster St.

Holyoke St.

Plympton St.

8

DeWolfe St.

Mt. Auburn Cemetery ✝

Cambridge Cemetery ✝

Charles River

Soldier's Field/ Harvard Stadium

Anderson Bridge

Putnam Ave.

Harvard Business School

Western Ave.

Western Ave. Bridge

9

River St.

River St. Bridge

Cambridge St.

Memorial Drive

Magazine Beach

ACCOMMODATIONS ■
Best Western Hotel Tria **1**
The Charles Hotel **3**
Harvard Square Hotel **6**
Holiday Inn Express Hotel
 and Suites **18**
Hotel Marlowe **16**
Radisson Hotel
 Cambridge **9**
Royal Sonesta Hotel **15**
Sheraton Commander
 Hotel **2**

DINING ◆
The Blue Room **13**
Border Café **7**
Dalí **10**
The Helmand **17**
Legal Sea Foods
 (Harvard Sq.) **4**
 (Kendall Sq.) **14**
Mr. Bartley's Burger Cottage **8**
Oleana **12**
Rialto **5**
S&S Restaurant **11**

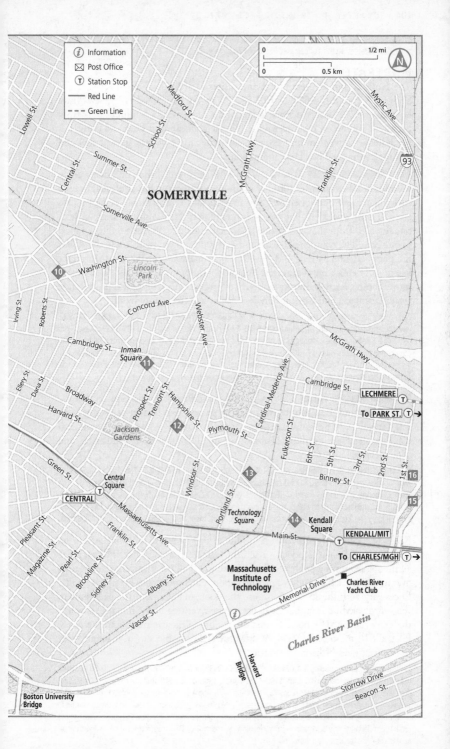

Information
Post Office
Station Stop
Red Line
Green Line

0   1/2 mi
0   0.5 km
N

Lowell St.
Medford St.
School St.
Mystic Ave.
Summer St.
Central St.
McGrath Hwy.
Franklin St.
93

SOMERVILLE

Somerville Ave.

Washington St.
Lincoln Park
10

Concord Ave.
McGrath Hwy.

Irving St.
Roberts St.
Cambridge St.
Inman Square
11
Webster Ave.
Cambridge St.
LECHMERE T

Ellery St.
Dana St.
Broadway
Prospect St.
Tremont St.
Hampshire St.
Cardinal Medeiros Ave.
Fulkerson St.
To PARK ST. T →

Harvard St.
Jackson Gardens
12
Plymouth St.
6th St.
5th St.
3rd St.
2nd St.
1st St.
16

Green St.
Windsor St.
13
Binney St.
15

CENTRAL T
Central Square
Massachusetts Ave.
Portland St.

Pleasant St.
Franklin St.
Technology Square
14
Kendall Square
KENDALL/MIT T

Magazine St.
Pearl St.
Brookline St.
Sidney St.
Albany St.
Main St.
To CHARLES/MGH T →

Vassar St.
Massachusetts Institute of Technology
Memorial Drive
Charles River Yacht Club

i

Charles River Basin

Harvard Bridge

Boston University Bridge

Storrow Drive
Beacon St.

concierge; business center; limited room service; laundry service; dry cleaning. *In room:* A/C, TV w/pay movies, high-speed Internet access, coffeemaker, hair dryer, iron, umbrella.

MODERATE

The **Holiday Inn Express Hotel and Suites,** 250 Msgr. O'Brien Hwy., Cambridge (© **888/887-7690** or 617/577-7600; fax 617/354-1313; www.bristol hotels.com), is a limited-service lodging on a busy street a 5-minute walk from Lechmere station on the Green Line. The neighborhood is busy and noisy, but the hotel is convenient and economical—rates for a double start at $99 and include continental breakfast and parking.

Best Western Hotel Tria ★ This four-story establishment underwent a $3-million renovation in 2003. It offers a sophisticated blend of chain-motel convenience and boutique-hotel features—such as a "soap menu." Guest rooms are spacious, with sleek but comfy contemporary furnishings, and are at least one floor up from the busy street. Room rates include 30 free minutes of local phone calls. The commercial neighborhood is nothing to write home about, but the pool and free parking and breakfast help make up for the less-than-scenic location. There's a restaurant next door and a shopping center with a 10-screen movie theater nearby. Boston is about a 15-minute drive or a 30-minute T ride away; Lexington and Concord are less than a half-hour away by car.

220 Alewife Brook Pkwy., Cambridge, MA 02138. © **866/333-8742** or 617/491-8000. Fax 617/491-4932. www.hoteltria.com. 69 units. Mid-Mar to Oct $129–$299 double; Nov to mid-Mar $109–$159 double. Extra person $10. Rates include continental breakfast. Rates may be higher during special events. Children under 16 stay free in parent's room. AE, DC, MC, V. Free parking. T: Red Line to Alewife, 10-min. walk. Pets accepted; reservation required; $20 fee. **Amenities:** Indoor pool; exercise room; Jacuzzi; tour desk; shuttle service; same-day dry cleaning. *In room:* A/C, TV, dataport, coffeemaker, hair dryer, iron, robes.

Harvard Square Hotel ★ Smack in the middle of Harvard Square, this six-story brick hotel is a favorite with visiting parents and budget-conscious business travelers. The unpretentious guest rooms are relatively small but comfortable; some overlook Harvard Square. The front desk handles fax and copy services.

110 Mount Auburn St., Cambridge, MA 02138. © **800/458-5886** or 617/864-5200. Fax 617/864-2409. www.doubletree.com. 73 units. $129–$209 double. Extra person $10. Children under 17 stay free in parent's room. Corporate rates and AAA and AARP discounts available. AE, DC, DISC, MC, V. Parking $25. T: Red Line to Harvard. **Amenities:** Dining privileges at the Harvard Faculty Club; free access to nearby health club; car-rental desk; laundry service; dry cleaning. *In room:* A/C, TV, dataport, fridge, coffeemaker, hair dryer, iron, umbrella.

Radisson Hotel Cambridge ★ This former Howard Johnson hotel is an attractive, modern 16-story tower across the street from the Charles River. It has an indoor swimming pool, and Radisson replaced all the furniture when it took over in 2000. Each room has a picture window, and some have private balconies. Prices vary with the size of the room, the floor, and the view; the panorama of the Boston skyline from higher floors on the river side of the building is worth the extra money. The hotel is near the major college campuses and the Mass. Pike. It's 10 minutes by car from downtown Boston but not near public transit—leave time for the hotel shuttle.

777 Memorial Dr., Cambridge, MA 02139. © **800/333-3333** or 617/492-7777. Fax 617/492-6038. www. radisson.com/cambridgema. 205 units. $109–$269 double. Extra person $10. Rollaway $20. Cribs free. Children under 18 stay free in parent's room. Packages and AARP and AAA discounts available. AE, DC, DISC, MC, V. Parking $10. **Amenities:** 2 restaurants (Japanese, Greek); indoor pool; exercise room; concierge; shuttle to Harvard, Central, and Kendall squares and Massachusetts General Hospital; business center; room service until 10pm; laundry service; same-day dry cleaning. *In room:* A/C, TV w/pay movies, high-speed Internet access, coffeemaker, hair dryer, iron.

4 Where to Dine

Travelers from around the world relish the variety of skillfully prepared seafood available in the Boston area. Lunch is an excellent, economical way to check out a fancy restaurant without breaking the bank. At restaurants that accept reservations, it's always a good idea to make them, particularly for dinner.

WATERFRONT
EXPENSIVE

A branch of **Legal Sea Foods,** at 255 State St. (✆ **617/227-3115**), sits across from the New England Aquarium. See "Back Bay," later in this section.

Sel de la Terre ✿✿ PROVENÇAL   A stone's throw from Boston Harbor, Sel de la Terre is a taste of southern France. The subtly flavorful food—scallops handled so gently that they're still sweet, juicy roasted chicken, salmon with truffled cauliflower purée—relies on fresh local ingredients. The restaurant attracts a go-go business-lunch crowd (dinner is calmer). The unusual pricing structure feels like a deal when you're tucking into a generous portion of roasted lamb, less of a bargain if you're eating pasta. Whatever you're eating, try the sublime *pommes frites.* Now that the expressway has come down, there's seasonal outdoor seating; the boulangerie at the entrance sells out-of-this-world breads.

255 State St. ✆ 617/720-1300. www.seldelaterre.com. Reservations recommended. Main courses $15 lunch, $24 dinner; sandwiches (lunch only) $8.50. Children's menu $7. AE, DC, DISC, MC, V. Mon–Fri 11:30am–2:30pm; Sat–Sun 11am–3:30pm; daily 5–10pm. Valet and validated parking available at dinner. T: Blue Line to Aquarium.

THE NORTH END

Many North End restaurants don't serve dessert, but you can satisfy your sweet tooth at a *caffè*. Favorites include **Caffè dello Sport,** 308 Hanover St. (✆ **617/ 523-5063**), and **Caffè Vittoria,** 296 Hanover St. (✆ **617/227-7606**). There's also table service at **Mike's Pastry,** 300 Hanover St. (✆ **617/742-3050**), which is better known for its bustling takeout business.

VERY EXPENSIVE

Mamma Maria ✿✿✿ NORTHERN ITALIAN   In a town house overlooking North Square and the Paul Revere House, the best restaurant in the North End offers innovative seasonal cuisine and a level of sophistication that's unusual for this casual neighborhood. The menu changes seasonally, and portions are more than generous. Fork-tender *osso buco* is almost enough for two, but you'll want it all for yourself. You can't go wrong with main-course pastas, either, and the fresh seafood specials are uniformly marvelous. The pasta, bread, and desserts are homemade, and the shadowy, whitewashed rooms make this a popular spot for getting engaged.

3 North Sq. ✆ 617/523-0077. www.mammamaria.com. Reservations recommended. Main courses $19–$35. AE, DC, DISC, MC, V. Sun–Thurs 5–9:30pm; Fri–Sat 5–10:30pm. Closed 1 week in Jan. Valet parking available. T: Green or Orange Line to Haymarket.

MODERATE

Billy Tse Restaurant CHINESE/PAN-ASIAN/SUSHI   This casual spot on the edge of the Italian North End serves excellent renditions of the usual Chinese dishes and especially good fresh seafood. The Thai- and Vietnamese-influenced selections are just as enjoyable. Main dishes range from nine kinds of fried rice to the house special noodles, topped with shrimp, calamari, and scallops in a scrumptious sauce. Be sure to ask about daily specials.

Boston Dining

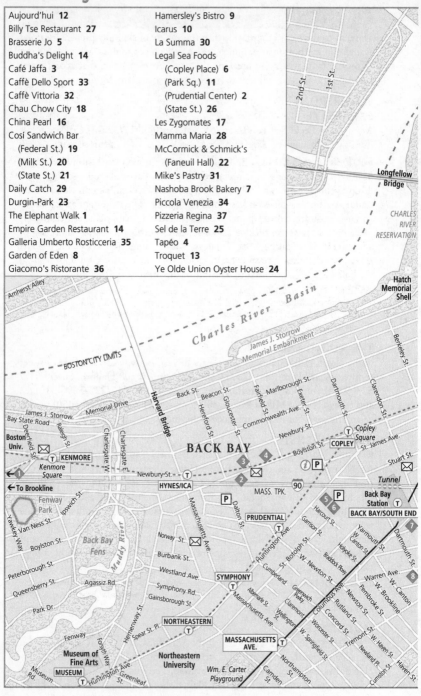

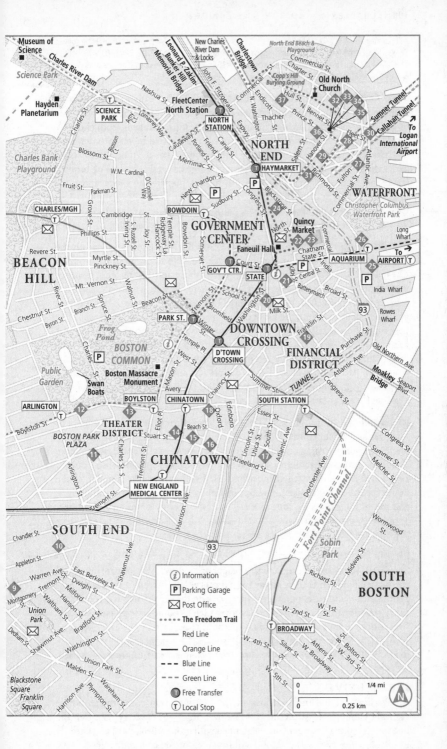

240 Commercial St. ℂ 617/227-9990. Reservations recommended for dinner on weekends. Main courses $7–$33 (most items less than $17); lunch specials $6–$8; sushi from $3.75. AE, DC, DISC, MC, V. Mon–Thurs 11:30am–11:30pm; Fri–Sat 11:30am–midnight; Sun 11:30am–11pm. T: Green or Orange Line to Haymarket, or Blue Line to Aquarium.

Daily Catch ⭐ SOUTHERN ITALIAN/SEAFOOD This storefront restaurant is about the size of a large kitchen (it seats just 20), but it packs a wallop—of garlic. A North End favorite for over 30 years, it has excellent food, chummy service, and very little elbowroom. The surprisingly varied menu includes Sicilian-style calamari (squid stuffed with bread crumbs, raisins, pine nuts, parsley, and garlic), fresh clams, squid-ink pasta puttanesca, and a variety of broiled, fried, and sautéed fish and shellfish. All food is prepared to order, and some dishes arrive still in the frying pan.

323 Hanover St. ℂ 617/523-8567. Reservations not accepted. Main courses $12–$19. No credit cards. Sun–Thurs 11:30am–10pm; Fri–Sat 11:30am–11pm. T: Green or Orange Line to Haymarket.

Giacomo's Ristorante ⭐⭐ ITALIAN/SEAFOOD The line snakes out the door and down the street, especially on weekends. No reservations, cash only, a tiny dining room with an open kitchen—what's the secret? Terrific food, plenty of it, and the "we're-all-in-this-together" atmosphere. To start, try fried calamari or mozzarella with excellent marinara sauce. Take the chef's advice or put together your own main dish from the list of daily ingredients on a board on the wall. The best suggestion is salmon and sun-dried tomatoes in tomato cream sauce over fettuccine. Non-seafood offerings such as butternut squash ravioli are equally memorable. Service is friendly but incredibly swift. (Those hungry people want your seat.) After a 40-minute dinner, dessert at a *caffè* is practically a necessity.

355 Hanover St. ℂ 617/523-9026. Reservations not accepted. Main courses $11–$18. No credit cards. Mon–Thurs 5–10pm; Fri–Sat 5–10:30pm; Sun 4–10pm. T: Green or Orange Line to Haymarket.

La Summa ⭐ SOUTHERN ITALIAN Away from the restaurant rows of Hanover and Salem streets, La Summa maintains a cozy neighborhood atmosphere. It's worth seeking out for wonderful homemade pasta and desserts; more elaborate entrees are scrumptious, too. Try any seafood special, lobster ravioli, *pappardelle e melanzane* (eggplant strips tossed with ethereal fresh pasta), or the house special—veal, chicken, sausage, shrimp, artichokes, pepperoncini, olives, and mushrooms in white-wine sauce. Desserts, especially tiramisu, are terrific.

30 Fleet St. ℂ 617/523-9503. Reservations recommended. Main courses $11–$24. AE, DC, DISC, MC, V. Mon–Sat 4:30–10:30pm; Sun 2–10:30pm. T: Green or Orange Line to Haymarket.

Piccola Venezia ITALIAN Piccola Venezia's glass front wall faces the Freedom Trail—a touristy location with a neighborhood feel. Portions are large, and the homey food tends to be heavy on red sauce. Spaghetti and meatballs, eggplant rolatini, and pasta puttanesca are always on the menu. This is a good place to try traditional Italian-American favorites such as home-style polenta, *baccala* (reconstituted salt cod), or the house specialty, tripe.

263 Hanover St. ℂ 617/523-3888. Reservations recommended for dinner. Main courses $11–$21; lunch specials $5–$10. AE, DISC, MC, V. Daily 11am–10pm (lunch Mon–Fri until 4pm). T: Green or Orange Line to Haymarket.

INEXPENSIVE

An excellent eat-and-run spot just off the Freedom Trail is the cafeteria-style **Galleria Umberto Rosticceria,** 289 Hanover St. (ℂ **617/227-5709**). Join the line for tasty pizza, *arancini* (a rice ball filled with ground beef, peas, and cheese), or calzones. Lunch is served Monday through Saturday; cash only.

> **Tips** **It's Nothing Personal**
>
> State law requires the scary disclaimer that appears on menus to alert you
> to the potential danger of eating raw or undercooked meat (such as rare
> burgers), seafood (raw oysters, for instance), poultry, or eggs.

Pizzeria Regina ★★ PIZZA Regina's looks like a movie set, but it's the real
thing. Busy waitresses weave through the boisterous dining room, delivering
peerless pizza hot from the brick oven. The list of toppings includes nouveau
ingredients such as sun-dried tomatoes, but that's not authentic. House-made
sausage, maybe some pepperoni, and a couple of beers—now, *that's* authentic.

11½ Thacher St. ✆ 617/227-0765. www.pizzeriaregina.com. Reservations not accepted. Pizza $9–$16. No
credit cards. Mon–Thurs 11am–11:30pm; Fri–Sat 11am–midnight; Sun noon–11pm. T: Green or Orange Line
to Haymarket.

FANEUIL HALL MARKETPLACE & FINANCIAL DISTRICT

The **food court** at Faneuil Hall Marketplace is a great place to pick up picnic
fare. Eat here, or cross under the Expressway and pass the Marriott to reach the
plaza at the end of Long Wharf. Or head to the left of the hotel and dine in
Christopher Columbus Waterfront Park.

EXPENSIVE

The national chain **McCormick & Schmick's Seafood Restaurant** has a
branch at Faneuil Hall Marketplace in the North Market Building (✆ 617/
720-5522).

Les Zygomates ★★ FRENCH/ECLECTIC Tucked away near South Station, this delightful bistro and wine bar is worth seeking out. It offers a great
selection of wines by the bottle, glass, and 2-ounce "taste." The efficient staff will
guide you toward a good accompaniment for chef-owner Ian Just's delicious
food. Roasted salmon is toothsome; smoked pork chop with brandy-and-*cidre*
reduction is succulent. For dessert, try not to fight over the lemon mousse.
There's live jazz (in its own dining room) nightly.

129 South St. ✆ 617/542-5108. www.winebar.com. Reservations recommended. Main courses $9–$14
lunch, $17–$26 dinner; prix fixe $15 lunch, $29 dinner. AE, DC, DISC, MC, V. Mon–Fri 11:30am–1am (lunch
until 2pm, dinner until 10:30pm); Sat 6pm–1am (dinner until 11:30pm). Valet parking available at dinner. T:
Red Line to South Station.

Ye Olde Union Oyster House ★ NEW ENGLAND/SEAFOOD America's
oldest restaurant in continuous service, the Union Oyster House opened in
1826. Its tasty New England fare is popular with tourists on the adjacent Freedom Trail as well as savvy locals. They're not here for anything fancy; the best
bets are simple, classic preparations. Try oyster stew or a cold seafood sampler of
oysters, clams, and shrimp. Follow with a broiled or grilled dish such as scrod or
salmon, or perhaps fried seafood or grilled pork loin. A "shore dinner" (chowder, steamers, lobster, corn, and dessert) is an excellent introduction to local
favorites. *Tip:* A plaque marks John F. Kennedy's favorite booth (no. 18), where
he often read the Sunday papers.

41 Union St. (between North and Hanover sts.). ✆ 617/227-2750. www.unionoysterhouse.com. Reservations recommended. Main courses $10–$21 lunch, $16–$30 dinner. Children's menu $5–$11. AE, DC, DISC,
MC, V. Sun–Thurs 11am–9:30pm (lunch until 5pm); Fri–Sat 11am–10pm (lunch until 6pm). Union Bar daily
11am–midnight (lunch until 3pm, late supper until 11pm). Validated and valet parking available. T: Green or
Orange Line to Haymarket.

MODERATE

Durgin-Park ★★ *Kids* NEW ENGLAND   For huge portions of delicious food, a rowdy atmosphere where CEOs share tables with students, and famously cranky waitresses, Bostonians have flocked to Durgin-Park since 1827. Approximately 2,000 people a day join the line that stretches down a flight of stairs to the first floor of Faneuil Hall Marketplace's North Market building, and everyone's disappointed when the waitresses are nice (as they often are). They come for prime rib the size of a hubcap, piles of fried seafood, fish dinners broiled to order, and bounteous portions of roast turkey. Steaks and chops are broiled on an open fire over wood charcoal. This is the place to try Boston baked beans. For dessert, the strawberry shortcake is justly celebrated.

340 Faneuil Hall Marketplace. ✆ 617/227-2038. www.durgin-park.com. Reservations accepted for parties of 15 or more. Main courses $7–$25; specials $19–$40. AE, DC, DISC, MC, V. Daily 11:30am–2:30pm; Mon–Sat 2:30–10pm; Sun 2:30–9pm. Validated parking available. T: Green or Blue Line to Government Center, or Orange Line to Haymarket.

INEXPENSIVE

Cosí Sandwich Bar ★ ITALIAN/ECLECTIC   Flavorful fillings on delectable bread make Cosí a downtown lunch favorite. This location, right on the Freedom Trail, makes a delicious refueling stop. Tasty Italian flatbread is filled with your choice of meat, fish, vegetables, cheese, and spreads. The more fillings you choose, the more you pay; the total can climb, so don't go wild if you're on a budget. Other branches are at 14 Milk St., near Downtown Crossing (✆ 617/426-7565), and 133 Federal St. (✆ 617/292-2674), which has patio seating.

53 State St. (at Congress St.). ✆ 617/723-4447. Sandwiches $6–$9; soups and salads $3–$7. AE, DC, MC, V. Mon–Thurs 7am–6pm; Fri 7am–5pm. T: Orange or Blue Line to State.

CHINATOWN/THEATER DISTRICT

The best way to sample Chinese food is by trying **dim sum,** the traditional midday meal featuring a variety of appetizer-style dishes. It's especially popular on weekends, when the variety of offerings is greatest. Our favorite dim sum is at **Empire Garden Restaurant,** also known as Emperor's Garden, 690–698 Washington St., 2nd floor (✆ 617/482-8898); other good destinations are **China Pearl,** 9 Tyler St., 2nd floor (✆ 617/426-4338), and **Chau Chow City,** 83 Essex St. (✆ 617/338-8158).

VERY EXPENSIVE

Troquet ★★ NEW AMERICAN/WINE BAR   The second-floor dining room at Troquet (French slang for "small wine cafe") overlooks Boston Common, and the ground floor is a lounge that serves "creative cocktails" and small plates. Troquet offers 40-plus wines by the 2- or 4-ounce glass and hundreds more by the bottle. Because the markup is lower than usual, sampling several selections is surprisingly affordable. The menu and the helpful staff can recommend pairings; you'll want just the right thing to complement the exceptional cuisine, which emphasizes seasonal ingredients and never overwhelms the wine.

140 Boylston St. ✆ 617/695-9463. Reservations recommended. Main courses $21–$36. AE, DC, DISC, MC, V. Dining room Tues–Sat 5–10:30pm; lounge daily 5pm–1am (food available until midnight). T: Green Line to Boylston.

INEXPENSIVE

Buddha's Delight ★ VEGETARIAN/VIETNAMESE   Fresh, healthful, cheap, and filling—what's not to like? Buddha's Delight serves "chicken," "pork," and even "lobster"—in quotes because the chefs substitute fried and barbecued tofu and gluten for meat, poultry, fish, or dairy (some beverages have condensed milk) to create more-than-reasonable facsimiles of traditional dishes. Between pondering how they do it and savoring the strong, clear flavors, you might not miss your usual protein. To start, try fried "pork" dumplings or a delectable salad. Move on to "shrimp" with rice noodles, any of the house specialties, or excellent chow fun.

5 Beach St. ✆ 617/451-2395. Main courses $6–$13; lunch specials $6.50. MC, V. Sun–Thurs 11am–9:30pm; Fri–Sat 11am–10:30pm. T: Orange Line to Chinatown.

SOUTH END
VERY EXPENSIVE
Hamersley's Bistro ⋆ ECLECTIC   This is the place that put the South End on Boston's culinary map, a pioneering restaurant that's both classic and contemporary. One of its many claims to fame is its status as a Julia Child favorite. The seasonal menu offers entrees noted for their emphasis on local ingredients and classic techniques. The signature roast chicken with garlic is a bit tame, but cassoulet with pork, duck confit, and garlic sausage is a gorgeously executed combination of flavors and textures. The kitchen also has a way with fish— perhaps sea scallops with spring vegetables and lemon sauce. The wine list is excellent, and there's seasonal outdoor seating.

553 Tremont St. ✆ 617/423-2700. www.hamersleysbistro.com. Reservations recommended. Main courses $24–$39; tasting menu varies. AE, DISC, MC, V. Mon–Fri 6–10pm; Sat 5:30–10pm; Sun 5:30–9:30pm. Closed 1 week in Jan. Valet parking available. T: Orange Line to Back Bay.

Icarus ⋆⋆ AMERICAN   This shamelessly romantic subterranean restaurant offers every element of a great dining experience. Chef and co-owner Christopher Douglass uses choice local ingredients to create imaginative dishes. The menu changes regularly—you might start with braised exotic mushrooms on polenta, or perhaps succulent lobster salad. Move on to pine-nut-and-lemon-crusted lamb chops served with lamb osso buco, or a scrumptious seafood special. Save room for dessert; the seasonal fruit sorbets are especially delicious.

3 Appleton St. ✆ 617/426-1790. www.icarusrestaurant.com. Reservations recommended. Main courses $24–$33. AE, DC, DISC, MC, V. Mon–Thurs 6–10pm; Fri 6–10:30pm; Sat 5:30–10:30pm; Sun 5:30–10pm. Valet parking available. T: Green Line to Arlington or Orange Line to Back Bay.

MODERATE
Garden of Eden SANDWICHES/FRENCH   Almost as well known for its people-watching as for its cuisine, Garden of Eden sits on a busy corner on the South End's main drag. It's a good place to go for neighborhood gossip as well as tasty food served at communal tables (and on the patio in good weather). You can order everything from breakfast to cappuccino with a delectable pastry to a full meal. The unusual sandwiches on fresh-baked bread are especially popular—the namesake sandwich of mesclun, red onion, blue cheese, and (of course) apples on a baguette is delicious. Dinner entrees are satisfying French country comfort food—coq au vin, yummy macaroni and cheese, chicken pot pie, and the like.

571 Tremont St. ✆ 617/247-8377. www.goeboston.com. Sandwiches and salads $5–$9.50; main courses $5.50–$15. AE, DC, DISC, MC, V. Mon–Fri 7am–11pm; Sat–Sun 7:30am–11pm. T: Orange Line to Back Bay.

INEXPENSIVE
Nashoba Brook Bakery ⋆ SANDWICHES   This little neighborhood cafe serves baked goods so scrumptious you'll wish the South End were your neighborhood. The soups, salads, breads, and pastries make a reverse commute every day from the original location in suburban Concord (p. 157). Everything is fresh

and delicious, especially the sandwiches—like ham and cheese with the tasty addition of apple slices—on incredible artisan breads.

288 Columbus Ave. © 617/236-0777. www.slowrise.com. Most items less than $6. MC, V. Mon–Fri 7am–6pm; Sat 8am–5pm; Sun 8am–4pm. T: Orange Line to Back Bay.

BACK BAY
VERY EXPENSIVE

Aujourd'hui ★★★ CONTEMPORARY AMERICAN　　On the second floor of the city's premier luxury hotel, the most beautiful restaurant in town offers incredible service and food to its special-occasion and expense-account clientele, and is coming off of a renovation that saw it reopening in June, 2004. Yes, the cost is astronomical, but how often is it true that you get what you pay for? Here, it is. The menu encompasses basic hotel dining room offerings and creations that characterize an inventive kitchen, and the wine list is excellent. Entrees might include baked halibut with tamarind-glazed beets, veal chop with polenta "fries," and (always) a lobster option. The dessert menu includes picture-perfect soufflés and homemade sorbets.

In the Four Seasons Hotel, 200 Boylston St. © 617/351-2071. Reservations recommended (required on holidays). Main courses $21–$30 lunch, $35–$45 dinner; Sun buffet brunch $58 adults, $28 children. (At press time, restaurant had not reopened after renovation. Call to confirm open hours and prices). AE, DC, DISC, MC, V. Mon–Fri 6:30–11am, Sat 7am–noon; Mon–Fri 11:30am–2pm, Sun brunch 11:30am–2pm; Mon–Sat 5:30–10pm, Sun 6–10pm. Valet parking available. T: Green Line to Arlington.

EXPENSIVE

The Spanish tapas restaurant **Dalí** (p. 114) has a Back Bay outpost called **Tapéo,** at 266 Newbury St. (© **617/267-4799**).

Legal Sea Foods ★★★ SEAFOOD　　The food at "Legal's" isn't the fanciest, cheapest, or trendiest. It's the freshest, and management's commitment to that policy has produced a thriving chain (and a private seafood-processing plant). The menu includes regular selections plus whatever looked good at the market that morning, prepared in every imaginable way. It's all splendid. The clam chowder is famous, the fish chowder lighter but equally good. There's even a terrific wine list. I suggest the Prudential Center branch because it takes reservations (at lunch only), a deviation from a long tradition.

In the Prudential Center, 800 Boylston St. © 617/266-6800. www.legalseafoods.com. Reservations recommended at lunch, not accepted at dinner. Main courses $7–$15 lunch, $14–$35 dinner; lobster priced daily. AE, DC, DISC, MC, V. Mon–Thurs 11am–10:30pm; Fri–Sat 11am–11:30pm; Sun noon–10pm. T: Green Line B, C, or D to Hynes/ICA or E to Prudential. Also at 255 State St. © 617/227-3115. T: Blue Line to Aquarium. 36 Park Sq. (between Columbus Ave. and Stuart St.). © 617/426-4444. T: Green Line to Arlington. Copley Place, 2nd level. © 617/266-7775. T: Orange Line to Back Bay or Green Line to Copley. 1 Bennett St., behind the Charles Hotel, Cambridge. © 617/491-9400. T: Red Line to Harvard. 5 Cambridge Center, Cambridge. © 617/864-3400. T: Red Line to Kendall/MIT.

MODERATE

Brasserie Jo ★ REGIONAL FRENCH　　One of the most discriminating diners we know lit up like a marquee on hearing that Boston has a branch of this Chicago favorite. The food is classic—fresh baguettes, Alsatian onion tart, *choucroute, coq au vin*—but never boring. The house beer, an Alsace-style draft, is a good accompaniment. This casual, all-day brasserie and bar is a good bet before or after the symphony or during a shopping break. The only drawback is the noise level, which is high at busy times.

In the Colonnade Hotel, 120 Huntington Ave. © 617/425-3240. www.brasseriejoboston.com. Reservations recommended for dinner. Main courses $6–$15 lunch, $15–$27 dinner; *plats du jour* $18–$32. AE, DC, DISC,

MC, V. Mon–Fri 6:30am–11pm; Sat 7am–11pm; Sun 7am–10pm; late-night menu daily until 1am. Valet and garage parking available. T: Green Line E to Prudential.

INEXPENSIVE

Café Jaffa MIDDLE EASTERN A long, narrow brick room with a glass front, Café Jaffa looks more like a snazzy pizza place than the excellent Middle Eastern restaurant it is. Reasonable prices, high quality, and large portions draw crowds for traditional dishes such as falafel, baba ghanoush, and hummus, as well as burgers and steak tips. For dessert, try the baklava if it's fresh (give it a pass if not).

48 Gloucester St. © 617/536-0230. Main courses $5–$16. AE, DC, DISC, MC, V. Mon–Thurs 11am–10:30pm; Fri–Sat 11am–11pm; Sun 1–10pm. T: Green Line B, C, or D to Hynes/ICA.

KENMORE SQUARE

MODERATE

The Elephant Walk ★★ FRENCH/CAMBODIAN France meets Cambodia on the menu at this madly popular spot 4 blocks from Kenmore Square. Many Cambodian dishes have part-French names, such as *poulet dhomrei* (chicken with Asian basil, bamboo shoots, fresh pineapple, and kaffir lemongrass) and *curry de crevettes* (shrimp curry with picture-perfect vegetables). Or try *loc lac,* fork-tender beef cubes in addictively spicy sauce. On the French side, you'll find classics like filet mignon with pommes frites. The pleasant staff will help out if you need guidance.

900 Beacon St. © 617/247-1500. www.elephantwalk.com. Reservations recommended for dinner Sun–Thurs; not accepted Fri–Sat. Main courses $7–$26 lunch, $11–$27 dinner. AE, DC, DISC, MC, V. Mon–Fri 11:30am–2:30pm; Sun–Thurs 5–10pm; Fri–Sat 5–11pm. Valet parking available at dinner. T: Green Line C to St. Mary's St.

CAMBRIDGE

The Red Line runs from downtown Boston to Harvard Square. Many of the restaurants listed here can be reached on foot from there. To go in search of inexpensive ethnic food, head for Central and Inman squares.

Note: See the "Cambridge Accommodations & Dining" map on p. 102 for the locations of the restaurants reviewed below.

VERY EXPENSIVE

Rialto ★★★ MEDITERRANEAN This is my favorite Boston-area restaurant. It attracts a chic crowd, but it's not such a scene that out-of-towners will feel left behind. The dramatic but comfortable room has floor-to-ceiling windows overlooking Harvard Square. Chef Jody Adams's menu changes regularly, and main courses are so good that you might as well close your eyes and point. Tuscan-style steak with portobello-and-arugula salad is wonderful, and any seafood is a guaranteed winner—say, seared scallops with braised leeks and wild and farmed mushrooms. For dessert, seasonal sorbets are a great choice.

In the Charles Hotel, 1 Bennett St. © 617/661-5050. www.rialto-restaurant.com. Reservations recommended. Main courses $22–$37. AE, DC, MC, V. Mon–Fri 5:30–10pm; Sat 5:30–11pm; Sun 5:30–9pm. Bar Sun–Thurs 5pm–midnight; Fri–Sat 5pm–1am. Valet and validated parking available. T: Red Line to Harvard.

EXPENSIVE

Legal Sea Foods has branches in Harvard Square and in Kendall Square; see "Back Bay," above.

The Blue Room ★★ ECLECTIC The Blue Room sits below plaza level in an office-retail complex, a slice of foodie paradise in high-tech heaven. The cuisine is a rousing combination of top-notch ingredients and aggressive flavors, the service excellent, and the crowded dining room not as noisy as it looks. Main courses tend to be roasted, grilled, or braised, with at least one well-conceived vegetarian choice. Roast chicken, served with garlic mashed potatoes, is world-class. Seafood is always a good choice, and pork "osso bucco" will make you think twice the next time you skip over pork on a menu to get to steak. In warm weather, there's patio seating.

1 Kendall Sq. ☎ 617/494-9034. www.theblueroom.net. Reservations recommended. Main courses $18–$24. AE, DC, DISC, MC, V. Sun–Thurs 5:30–10pm; Fri–Sat 5:30–11pm; Sun brunch 11am–2:30pm. Validated parking available. T: Red Line to Kendall/MIT; 10-min. walk.

Dalí ★★★ SPANISH   The bar at this festive restaurant fills with people cheerfully waiting an hour or more for a table. The payoff is authentic Spanish food, notably tapas. Entrees include excellent paella, but most people come in a group and explore the three dozen or more tapas offerings, all perfect for sharing. They include delectable garlic potatoes, salmon balls with not-too-salty caper sauce, pork tenderloin with blue goat cheese, and delicious sausages. The staff sometimes seems rushed, but never fails to supply bread for sopping up juices, and sangria for washing it all down. Finish with excellent flan, or try the rich *tarta de chocolates*.

The owners of Dalí also run **Tapéo,** 266 Newbury St. (☎ **617/267-4799**), between Fairfield and Dartmouth streets in Boston's Back Bay.

415 Washington St., Somerville. ☎ 617/661-3254. www.DaliRestaurant.com. Reservations not accepted. Tapas $3–$8.50; main courses $17–$24. AE, DC, MC, V. Daily summer 6–11pm; winter 5:30–11pm. T: Red Line to Harvard; follow Kirkland St. to intersection of Washington and Beacon sts. (20 min. walk or $5 cab ride).

Oleana ★★ MEDITERRANEAN   Both casual neighborhood eatery and culinary travelogue, Oleana occupies a welcoming space outside Inman Square. The seasonal menu might include traditional Portuguese clams *cataplana*, with sausage in an aromatic tomatoey broth; almond-fried chicken, a great contrast of crunchy crust and juicy flesh; or spicy tuna, in a perfectly matched peppery sauce that trades intense heat for intense flavor. Service is polished, portions generous, and the dessert menu heavy on house-made ice cream. In warm weather, there's seating on the lovely patio.

134 Hampshire St., Inman Sq. ☎ 617/661-0505. www.oleanarestaurant.com. Reservations recommended. Main courses $17–$24; vegetarian tasting menu $38. AE, MC, V. Sun–Thurs 5:30–10pm; Fri–Sat 5:30–11pm. Free parking. T: Red Line to Central; 10-min. walk.

MODERATE

Border Cafe TEX-MEX/CAJUN   This unbelievably crowded restaurant has been a Harvard Square favorite for nearly 20 years. Patrons loiter at the bar while waiting for a table, enhancing the festival atmosphere. Portions are generous, and the beleaguered staff keeps the chips and salsa coming. Try the excellent chorizo appetizer, seafood enchiladas, or popcorn shrimp. Fajitas for one or two, sizzling noisily, are also popular. Ask to be seated downstairs if you want to be able to hear your companions.

32 Church St. ☎ 617/864-6100. Reservations not accepted. Main courses $7–$15. AE, MC, V. Daily 11am–11pm. T: Red Line to Harvard.

The Helmand ★ AFGHAN   Never exactly a secret, the Helmand enjoyed a burst of publicity when the manager's brother took over the provisional government of Afghanistan, and it's hardly had a slow night since. Unusual cuisine, an elegant setting, and reasonable prices had already made this spacious spot near the CambridgeSide Galleria mall a local favorite. Afghan food is vegetarian friendly; many non-veggie dishes use meat as one element rather than the centerpiece. *Aushak,* pasta pockets filled with leeks or potatoes and topped with split-pea-and-carrot sauce, also comes with meat sauce. Other entrees include stews like *deygee kabob,* an excellent mélange of lamb, yellow split peas, onion, and red peppers. For dessert, don't miss the Afghan version of baklava.

143 First St. ℂ 617/492-4646. Reservations recommended. Main courses $12–$20. AE, MC, V. Sun–Thurs 5–10pm; Fri–Sat 5–11pm. T: Green Line to Lechmere.

INEXPENSIVE

Mr. Bartley's Burger Cottage ★★ AMERICAN   Great burgers and the best onion rings in the world make Bartley's a perennial favorite with a cross section of Cambridge. The 40-plus-year-old family business is a high-ceilinged, crowded room plastered with signs and posters. Anything you can think of to put on ground beef is available, from American cheese to grilled pineapple. Good dishes that don't involve meat include veggie burgers and creamy, garlicky hummus.

1246 Mass. Ave. ℂ 617/354-6559. www.mrbartleys.com. Most items under $9. No credit cards. Mon–Sat 11am–9pm. T: Red Line to Harvard.

S&S Restaurant ★★ DELI   *Es* is Yiddish for "eat," and this Cambridge classic is as straightforward as its name ("eat and eat"). Founded in 1919 by the current owners' great-grandmother, the wildly popular brunch spot draws huge crowds at busy times on weekends. It looks contemporary, but the brunch offerings are traditional: pancakes, waffles, fruit salad, fantastic omelets. You'll also find traditional deli items (corned beef, pastrami, potato pancakes, blintzes), and breakfast anytime. Arrive early for brunch, or plan to spend a good chunk of your Saturday or Sunday people-watching and getting hungry. Or dine on a weekday and soak up the neighborhood atmosphere.

1334 Cambridge St., Inman Sq. ℂ 617/354-0777. www.sandsrestaurant.com. Main courses $4–$14. AE, MC, V. Mon–Wed 7am–11pm; Thurs–Fri 7am–midnight; Sat 8am–midnight; Sun 8am–10pm (brunch Sat–Sun until 4pm). T: Red Line to Harvard, then no. 69 (Harvard–Lechmere) bus to Inman Sq. Or Red Line to Central; 10-min. walk on Prospect St.

5 Seeing the Sights in Boston

If you concentrate on the included attractions, a **CityPass** offers great savings in money and time. It's a booklet of tickets to the Harvard Museum of Natural History, Kennedy Library, Museum of Fine Arts, Museum of Science, New England Aquarium, and Prudential Center Skywalk. The price (at press time, $34 for adults, $20 for children 3–17) represents a 50% savings for adults who visit all six attractions, and having a ticket means you can go straight to the entrance without waiting in line. The passes, good for 9 days from the date of purchase, are on sale at participating attractions, at the Boston Common and Prudential Center visitor centers, through the **Greater Boston Convention & Visitors Bureau** (ℂ **800/SEE-BOSTON;** www.bostonusa.com), and through www.citypass.com.

The **Go Boston Card** (ℂ **617/848-5900;** www.gobostoncard.com) includes admission to more than 30 Boston-area museums and attractions, dining and shopping discounts, a guidebook, and a 2-day Beantown Trolley ticket. You'll want to do some careful planning before you invest in this card—it costs $39 for 1 day, $69 for 2 days, $89 for 3 days, $109 for 5 days, with discounts for children and for winter travelers—but if you strategize wisely, it's a great value. The

Boston Attractions

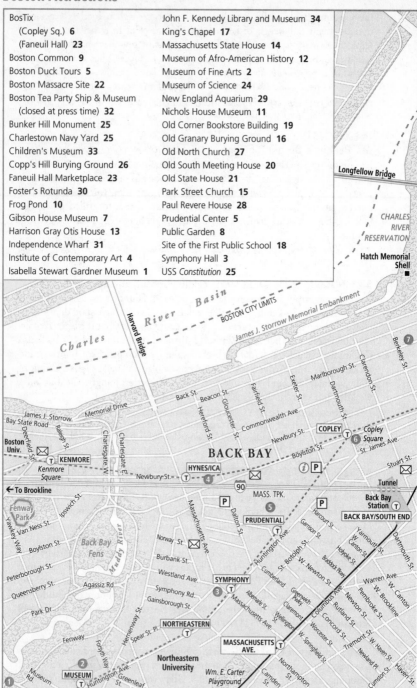

Longfellow Bridge

CHARLES RIVER RESERVATION

Hatch Memorial Shell

River Basin

BOSTON CITY LIMITS

Charles

Harvard Bridge

James J. Storrow Memorial Embankment

James J. Storrow Memorial Drive
Bay State Road

Back St.

Beacon St.

Marlborough St.

Clarendon St.

Berkeley St.

Fairfield St.

Exeter St.

Dartmouth St.

Gloucester St.

Hereford St.

Commonwealth Ave.

Newbury St.

COPLEY

Copley Square

St. James Ave.

Boston Univ.

Raleigh St.

Deerfield St.

Memorial Drive

Charlesgate W.

Charlesgate E.

KENMORE

Kenmore Square

Newbury St.

HYNES/ICA

Boylston St.

BACK BAY

Stuart St.

Tunnel

← To Brookline

90

MASS. TPK.

Back Bay Station

BACK BAY/SOUTH END

Fenway Park

Ipswich St.

Yawkey Way

Van Ness St.

Boylston St.

Peterborough St.

Queensberry St.

Park Dr.

Back Bay Fens

Muddy River

Agassiz Rd.

Massachusetts Ave.

Norway St.

Burbank St.

Westland Ave.

SYMPHONY

Symphony Rd.

Gainsborough St.

Dalton St.

PRUDENTIAL

Harcourt St.

Garrison St.

Huntington Ave.

St. Botolph St.

W. Newton St.

Cumberland St.

Greenwich St.

Claremont Pkwy.

Albemarle St.

Wellington St.

Columbus Ave.

Warren Ave.

Montgomery St.

Pembroke St.

W. Brookline

Newton St.

Rutland St.

Concord St.

Worcester St.

W. Springfield St.

Yarmouth St.

W. Canton St.

Holyoke St.

Braddock Pkwy.

Dartmouth St.

W. Canton St.

Tremont St.

W. Newton St.

W. Haven St.

Newland Pl.

Haven St.

Northampton St.

Camden St.

Cumston St.

NORTHEASTERN

MASSACHUSETTS AVE.

Fenway

Forsyth Way

Hemenway Ave.

Spear St. Pl.

Northeastern University

Wm. E. Carter Playground

Museum Rd.

MUSEUM

Huntington Ave.

Greenleaf St.

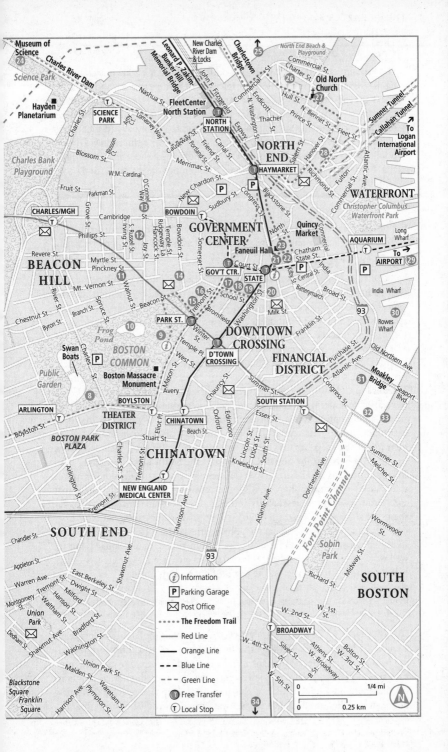

Museum of
Science
Science Park

Charles River Dam

Hayden
Planetarium

24

**Charles Bank
Playground**

New Charles
River Dam
& Locks

Charlestown
Bridge

North End Beach &
Playground

25

Commercial St.

Charter St. **26** Old North
Church **27**

Hull St. N. Bennet St. Fleet St.

Sumner Tunnel

Callahan Tunnel

To
Logan
International
Airport

SCIENCE
PARK

Nashua St.

Lomasney Way

FleetCenter
North Station

**NORTH
STATION**

Charles St.

Blossom St.

Blossom
Ct.

W.M. Cardinal

Fruit St.

Parkman St.

CHARLES/MGH

Cambridge St.

Phillips St.

Revere St.

**BEACON
HILL**

Myrtle St.

Pinckney St.

Mt. Vernon St.

Chestnut St.

Byron St.

Branch St.

Spruce St.

ARLINGTON

Boylston St.

Causeway St.

Canal St.

Portland St.

Friend St.

Merrimac St.

New Chardon St.

Sudbury St.

Congress St.

BOWDOIN

13

Bowdoin St.

Somerset St.

Temple St.

Ridgway La.

Hancock St.

Joy St.

S. Russell St.

Irving St.

12

11

Walnut St.

River St.

**GOVERNMENT
CENTER**

Faneuil Hall

GOV'T CTR.

14

Beacon St.

15

16 Tremont St.

17

18 19

School St.

Court St.

Bromfield

PARK ST.

Winter
St.

9

Temple Pl.

West St.

Mason St.

Avery

10

Frog
Pond

**BOSTON
COMMON**

Swan
Boats

Boston Massacre
Monument

Public
Garden

8

BOYLSTON

**THEATER
DISTRICT**

Stuart St.

Eliot Pl.

CHINATOWN

Beach St.

Charles St. S.

Tremont St.

Arlington St.

Tremont St.

**NEW ENGLAND
MEDICAL CENTER**

SOUTH END

Chandler St.

Appleton St.

Warren Ave.

East Berkeley St.

Dwight St.

Tremont St.

Milford

Hanson St.

Bradford St.

Union Park St.

Washington St.

Malden St.

Wareham St.

Plympton St.

Harrison Ave.

**Blackstone
Square
Franklin
Square**

Union
Park

Shawmut Ave.

Dedham St.

Montgomery
St.

Waltham St.

Waltham St.

Shawmut Ave.

John F. Fitzgerald Expwy.

Leonard P. Zakim
Bunker Hill
Memorial Bridge

New Charles
River Dam
& Locks

N. Washington St.

Endicott St.

Thacher St.

Prince St.

Salem St.

Hanover St.

**NORTH
END**

HAYMARKET

P

Blackstone St.

North St.

Richmond St.

Fulton

Commercial St.

Atlantic Ave.

Commercial St.

WATERFRONT

Christopher Columbus
Waterfront Park

28

Quincy
Market

Chatham
State St.

India St.

Clinton St.

Central St.

Broad St.

Batterymarch

Milk St.

AQUARIUM

T

Long
Wharf

**To
AIRPORT 29**

India Wharf

30

Rowes
Wharf

21 22

23

20

P

P

P

STATE

**DOWNTOWN
CROSSING**

**D'TOWN
CROSSING**

**FINANCIAL
DISTRICT**

Franklin St.

Purchase St.

Atlantic Ave.

Congress St.

Summer St.

Old Northern Ave.

31

Moakley
Bridge

Seaport
Blvd.

32

33

Summer St.

Melcher St.

Wormwood
St.

**SOUTH
BOSTON**

SOUTH STATION

T

Chauncy St.

Essex St.

Kneeland St.

Lincoln St.

Utica St.

South St.

Oxford

Edinboro

Dorchester Ave.

Atlantic Ave.

Fort Point Channel

Sobin
Park

Richard St.

W. 2nd St.

W. 1st
St.

BROADWAY

T

W. 4th St.

Silver St.

W. 3rd St.

Athens St.

W. Broadway

Bolton St.

A St.

B St.

W. 5th St.

34

CHINATOWN

T

**BOSTON PARK
PLAZA**

**BOSTON
COMMON**

93

93

Legend	
i	Information
P	Parking Garage
✉	Post Office
•••••	**The Freedom Trail**
——	Red Line
——	Orange Line
---	Blue Line
---	Green Line
T	Free Transfer
T	Local Stop

0   1/4 mi

0   0.25 km

N

Kids Up, Up & Away: A Great View

The **Prudential Center Skywalk** ★★, on the 50th floor of 800 Boylston St. (© 617/859-0648), offers a 360-degree view of Boston and beyond. When it's clear, you can see as far as the mountains of New Hampshire and the beaches of Cape Cod. Away from the windows, interactive audiovisual exhibits chronicle the city's history. Open 10am to 10pm daily (call before visiting; the space sometimes closes for private events). Admission is $7 for adults, $4 for seniors and children 4 to 10. Adults must show an ID to enter the Prudential Tower. T: Green Line E to Prudential or B, C, or D to Hynes/ICA.

Go Boston Card is available through the website; at the Transportation Building, 16 Charles St. S.; at many concierge desks; and as part of some hotel packages.

THE TOP ATTRACTIONS

Faneuil Hall Marketplace ★★ *Kids*   Since Boston's most popular attraction opened in 1976, cities all over the country have imitated the "festival market" concept. The complex of shops, food counters, restaurants, bars, and public spaces is such a magnet for tourists and suburbanites that you could be forgiven for thinking that the only Bostonians in the crowd are employees.

The five-structure complex sits on brick-and-stone plazas that teem with crowds shopping, eating, performing, watching performers, and people-watching. In warm weather, it's busy from just after dawn until well past dark. **Quincy Market** (you'll hear the whole complex called by that name) is the central Greek Revival–style building; its central corridor is an enormous food court. On either side, glass canopies cover full-service restaurants as well as pushcarts that hold everything from crafts created by New England artisans to hokey souvenirs. Here you'll also see a bar that exactly replicates the set of the TV show *Cheers.* In the plaza between the **South Canopy** and the South Market building is an **information kiosk,** and throughout the complex you'll find an enticing mix of chain stores and unique shops. On summer evenings, people fill the tables that spill outdoors from the restaurants and bars. One constant since the year after the original market opened (in 1826) is **Durgin-Park,** a traditional New England restaurant with traditionally crabby waitresses (p. 110). **Faneuil Hall** ★ itself—nicknamed the "Cradle of Liberty"—sometimes gets overlooked, but it's well worth a visit. National Park Service rangers give free 20-minute talks every half-hour from 9am to 5pm in the second-floor auditorium.

Between North, Congress, and State sts. and I-93. © 617/523-1300. www.faneuilhallmarketplace.com. Marketplace Mon–Sat 10am–9pm; Sun noon–6pm. Food court opens earlier; some restaurants close later. T: Green or Blue Line to Government Center, Orange Line to Haymarket, or Blue Line to Aquarium or State.

The Institute of Contemporary Art   Across from the Hynes Convention Center, the ICA mounts rotating exhibits of 20th- and 21st-century art, including painting, sculpture, photography, and video and performance art. The institute also offers films, lectures, music, video, poetry, and educational programs for children and adults. Check at this location for updates on the ICA's new home, at Fan Pier on the South Boston waterfront, scheduled to open in 2006.

955 Boylston St. © 617/266-5152. www.icaboston.org. Admission $7 adults, $5 seniors and students, free for children under 12; free to all Thurs 5–9pm. Tues–Wed and Fri noon–5pm; Thurs noon–9pm; Sat–Sun 11am–5pm. T: Green Line B, C, or D to Hynes/ICA.

Isabella Stewart Gardner Museum ★★ Isabella Stewart Gardner (1840–1924) was an incorrigible individualist long before such behavior was acceptable for a woman in polite Boston society, and her iconoclasm paid off for art lovers. "Mrs. Jack" designed her exquisite home in the style of a 15th-century Venetian palace and filled it with European, American, and Asian painting and sculpture. You'll see works by Titian, Botticelli, Raphael, Rembrandt, Matisse, and Mrs. Gardner's friends James McNeill Whistler and John Singer Sargent. Titian's magnificent *Europa* is one of the most important Renaissance paintings in the United States. In preparing *Frommer's Boston,* I took an unscientific poll of Boston-area travel experts, and the Gardner was the most popular museum.

The building holds a hodgepodge of furniture and architectural details imported from European churches and palaces. The pièce de résistance is the magnificent skylit courtyard, filled year-round with fresh flowers from the museum greenhouse. A special exhibition gallery features two or three changing shows a year, often by contemporary artists in residence.

280 The Fenway. ✆ **617/566-1401.** www.gardnermuseum.org. Admission $11 adults Sat–Sun, $10 adults Mon–Fri; $7 seniors; $5 college students; free for children under 18 and adults named Isabella w/ID. Tues–Sun, some Mon holidays 11am–5pm. T: Green Line E to Museum.

John F. Kennedy Library and Museum ★★ *Kids* The Kennedy era springs to life at this dramatic library, museum, and research complex overlooking Dorchester Bay. It captures the 35th president's accomplishments in sound and video recordings as well as fascinating displays of memorabilia and photos. Far from being a static experience, it changes regularly, with temporary shows and reinterpreted displays that highlight and complement the permanent exhibits. A visit begins with a 17-minute film about Kennedy's early life. The exhibits start with the 1960 campaign and end with a tribute to Kennedy's legacy. There's a film about the Cuban Missile Crisis, along with displays on Attorney General Robert F. Kennedy, the civil-rights movement, the Peace Corps, the space program, First Lady Jacqueline Bouvier Kennedy, and the Kennedy family.

Columbia Point. ✆ **877/616-4599** or 617/929-4500. www.jfklibrary.org. Admission $10 adults; $8 seniors, college students, and youths 13–17; free for children under 13. Surcharges may apply for special exhibitions. Daily 9am–5pm (last film at 3:55pm). T: Red Line to JFK/UMass, then free shuttle bus, which runs every 20 min. By car, take Southeast Expwy. (I-93/Rte. 3) south to Exit 15 (Morrissey Blvd./JFK Library), turn left onto Columbia Rd., and follow signs to free parking lot.

Museum of Afro-American History ★★ *Kids* The final stop on the **Black Heritage Trail** (p. 121) has the most comprehensive information on the history and contributions of blacks in Boston and Massachusetts. It occupies the recently restored **Abiel Smith School** (1834), the first American public grammar school for African-American children, and the 1806 **African Meeting House,** 8 Smith Court. Once known as the "Black Faneuil Hall," it offers an informative audiovisual presentation and schedules lectures, concerts, and church meetings.

46 Joy St. ✆ **617/725-0022.** www.afroammuseum.org. Free admission; donations encouraged. Memorial Day to Labor Day daily 10am–4pm; winter Mon–Sat 10am–4pm. T: Red or Green Line to Park St.

Museum of Fine Arts ★★★ *Kids* One of the world's great museums, the MFA works constantly to become even more accessible and interesting. The museum's not-so-secret weapon in its quest is a powerful one: its magnificent collections. Every installation reflects a curatorial attitude that makes even those who go in with a feeling of obligation leave with a sense of discovery and wonder.

That includes children, who can launch a scavenger hunt, admire the mummies, or participate in family-friendly programs scheduled year-round.

The MFA is especially noted for its **Impressionist paintings** ★★★ (including 43 Monets), Asian and Old Kingdom Egyptian collections, classical art, Buddhist temple, and medieval sculpture and tapestries. The American and European paintings and sculpture are a remarkable assemblage of timeless works that may seem as familiar as the face in the mirror or as unexpected as a comet. There are also magnificent holdings of prints, photography, furnishings, and decorative arts, including the finest collection of Paul Revere silver in the world. The museum has two restaurants, a cafe, and a cafeteria. Pick up a floor plan at the information desk, or take a free **guided tour** (weekdays except Mon holidays at 10:30am and 1:30pm; Wed at 6:15pm; and Sat at 10:30am and 1pm).

None of this comes cheap: The MFA's admission fees are among the highest in the country. A Boston CityPass (see the introduction to this section) is a great deal if you plan to visit enough of the other included attractions.

Tip: The Huntington Avenue entrance is usually much less busy than the West Wing lobby—though farther from the gift shop, restaurants, and garage. To use it, walk back along Huntington Avenue when you leave the T, enter from the driveway, and stop to take in the John Singer Sargent murals.

465 Huntington Ave. ✆ 617/267-9300. www.mfa.org. Admission $15 adults, $13 seniors and students when entire museum is open ($13 and $11, respectively, when only West Wing is open); $5 children under 18 on school days before 3pm, otherwise free. Admission good for 2 visits within 30 days. Voluntary contribution ($15 suggested) Wed 4–9:45pm. Surcharges may apply for special exhibitions. Free admission for museum shop, library, restaurants, and auditoriums. Entire museum Sat–Tues 10am–4:45pm; Wed 10am–9:45pm; Thurs–Fri 10am–5pm. West Wing only Thurs–Fri 5–9:45pm. T: Green Line E to Museum or Orange Line to Ruggles.

Museum of Science ★★★ *(Kids)*　For the ultimate pain-free educational experience, head to the Museum of Science. The demonstrations, experiments, and interactive displays introduce facts and concepts so effortlessly that everyone learns something. Take a couple of hours or a whole day to explore the permanent and temporary exhibits, most of them hands-on and all of them great fun. Among the hundreds of exhibits, you might find out how much you'd weigh on the moon, battle urban traffic (in a computer model), or climb into a space module. Activity centers focus on fields of interest—natural history (with live animals), computers, and the human body—as well as interdisciplinary approaches. **Investigate!** teaches visitors to think like scientists, analyzing questions through activities such as sifting through an archaeological dig. **Science in the Park** uses familiar tools such as playground equipment and skateboards to look at Newtonian physics.

The separate-admission theaters are worth planning for, even if you're skipping the exhibits. Buy all your tickets at once, not only because it's cheaper but also because shows sometimes sell out. Tickets are for sale in person and, subject to a service charge, over the phone and online (www.tickets.mos.org). The **Mugar Omni Theater** ★★★, which shows IMAX movies on a five-story screen, is an intense experience. The **Charles Hayden Planetarium** ★★ takes you into space with daily star shows as well as shows on special topics that change several times a year. On weekends, rock-music laser shows take over.

Many fascinating interactive exhibits from the defunct Computer Museum now delight patrons of the Museum of Science. The most popular is **Virtual Fish-Tank** ★★★, which uses 3D computer graphics and character-animation software to allow visitors to program their own virtual fish. You can even "build" fish at home (through www.virtualfishtank.com) and launch them at the museum.

Science Park, off O'Brien Hwy. on bridge between Boston and Cambridge. (℗ 617/723-2500. www.mos.org. Admission to exhibit halls $13 adults, $11 seniors, $10 children 3–11. Mugar Omni Theater, Hayden Planetarium, or laser shows $8.50 adults, $7.50 seniors, $6.50 children 3–11. Discounted combination tickets available. July 5–Labor Day Sat–Thurs 9am–7pm, Fri 9am–9pm; day after Labor Day to July 4 Sat–Thurs 9am–5pm, Fri 9am–9pm. T: Green Line to Science Park.

New England Aquarium ★ *Kids*   This entertaining complex is home to more than 15,000 fish and aquatic mammals. At busy times, it seems to contain at least that many people—try to make this your first stop of the day, especially on weekends. You'll want to spend at least half a day, and afternoon crowds can make getting around painfully slow. Also consider buying a Boston CityPass (p. 115); it allows you to skip the ticket line, which can be uncomfortably long. The **Simons IMAX Theatre** ★★★, which has its own hours and admission fees, is worth planning ahead for, too. It shows 3D films that concentrate on the natural world.

The focal point of the main building is the four-story, 200,000-gallon **Giant Ocean Tank.** It holds a replica of a Caribbean coral reef, a vast assortment of sea creatures, and, twice a day, scuba divers who feed the sharks. Other exhibits focus on freshwater and tropical specimens, the Aquarium Medical Center, denizens of the Amazon, a wide variety of jellyfish, and the ecology of Boston Harbor. The hands-on **Edge of the Sea** exhibit contains a tide pool with sea stars, sea urchins, and horseshoe crabs. The aquarium runs naturalist-led **harbor tours** daily in spring, summer, and fall. Discounts are available when you combine a visit to the aquarium with an IMAX film, harbor tour, or whale watch (see "Organized Tours," below).

Central Wharf. (℗ 617/973-5200. www.newenglandaquarium.org. Admission $16 adults, $14 seniors, $9 children 3–11. Harbor tours $13 adults, $10 seniors and college students, $9 children 3–18. Free admission for outdoor exhibits, cafe, and gift shop. July to Labor Day Mon–Thurs 9am–6pm, Fri–Sun and holidays 9am–7pm; day after Labor Day to June Mon–Fri 9am–5pm, Sat–Sun and holidays 9am–6pm. Simons IMAX Theatre: (℗ 866/815-4629 or 617/973-5206. Tickets $9 adults, $7 seniors and children 3–11. Daily 10am–9pm. T: Blue Line to Aquarium.

THE FREEDOM TRAIL ★★★

A line of red paint or red brick on the sidewalk, the 3-mile Freedom Trail links 16 historic sights. Markers identify the stops, and plaques point the way from one to the next. The trail begins at **Boston Common,** where the Information Center, 146 Tremont St., distributes pamphlets that describe a self-guided tour.

The Freedom Trail Foundation (℗ **617/357-8300;** www.thefreedomtrail. org) rents handheld digital audio players, for use with or without headphones, that allow visitors to take a narrated tour of the trail at their own pace. The 2-hour narrative includes interviews, sound effects, and music. Players rent for $15 each, with group rates available.; they're available at the Boston Common Visitor Center.

You can also explore the **Black Heritage Trail** ★★ from here. Stops include stations on the Underground Railroad and homes of famous citizens as well as the African Meeting House, the oldest standing black church in the country. A 2-hour guided tour starts at the visitor center at 46 Joy St. (℗ **617/742-5415;** www.nps.gov/boaf), daily in summer and by request at other times.

As you follow the Freedom Trail, you'll come to the **Boston National Historic Park Visitor Center,** 15 State St. (℗ **617/242-5642;** www.nps.gov/bost). From here, rangers lead free tours of the heart of the trail from mid-April to November, and sometimes in the winter. An audiovisual show provides basic information on the stops. The wheelchair-accessible center has restrooms and a bookstore. It's open daily from 9am to 5pm.

The hard-core history fiend who peers at every artifact and reads every plaque along the trail will wind up at Bunker Hill some 4 hours later, weary but rewarded. The family with restless children will probably appreciate the enforced efficiency of the 90-minute ranger-led tour.

Space doesn't permit detailing every stop on the trail, but here's a concise listing:

- **Boston Common.** In 1634, when their settlement was just 4 years old, the town fathers paid the Rev. William Blackstone £30 for this property. In 1640, it was set aside as common land. Be sure to stop at Beacon and Park streets, where a **memorial** ★★★ designed by Augustus Saint-Gaudens celebrates Col. Robert Gould Shaw and the Union Army's 54th Massachusetts Colored Regiment, who fought in the Civil War. You may remember the story of the first American army unit made up of free black soldiers from the movie *Glory*.

- **Massachusetts State House** (© 617/727-3676; www.mass.gov/statehouse). Charles Bulfinch designed the "new" State House, and Gov. Samuel Adams laid the cornerstone of the state capitol in 1795. Free tours (guided and self-guided) leave from the second floor Monday through Friday from 10am to 3:30pm; check ahead to see whether weekend hours have been reinstated.

- **Park Street Church,** 1 Park St. (© 617/523-3383; www.parkstreet.org). The plaque at the corner of Tremont Street describes this Congregational church's storied past. In July and August, it's open for tours Tuesday through Saturday from 9am to 3:30pm. Year-round Sunday services are at 8:30am, 11am, 4pm, and 6pm.

- **Old Granary Burying Ground.** This cemetery, established in 1660, contains the graves of Samuel Adams, Paul Revere, John Hancock, and the wife of Isaac Vergoose, believed to be the "Mother Goose" of nursery-rhyme fame. It's open daily from 9am to 5pm (until 3pm in winter).

- **King's Chapel,** 58 Tremont St. (© 617/523-1749). Completed in 1754, this church was built by erecting the granite edifice around the existing wooden chapel. The **burying ground** (1630), facing Tremont Street, is the oldest in Boston. It's open daily from 8am to 5:30pm (until 3pm in winter).

- **Site of the First Public School.** Founded in 1634, the school is commemorated with a colorful mosaic in the sidewalk on (of course) School Street. Inside the fence is the 1856 statue of **Benjamin Franklin,** the first portrait statue erected in Boston.

- **Old Corner Bookstore Building,** 3 School St. Built in 1718, it's on a plot of land that was once home to the religious reformer Anne Hutchinson.

- **Old South Meeting House,** 310 Washington St. (© 617/482-6439; www.oldsouthmeetinghouse.org). Originally built in 1670 and replaced by the current structure in 1729, it was the starting point of the Boston Tea Party. It's open daily, April to October from 9:30am to 5pm, November to March from 10am to 4pm. Admission is $5 for adults, $4 for seniors, and $1 for children 6 to 18.

- **Old State House** ★, 206 Washington St. (© 617/720-1713; www.boston history.org). Built in 1713, it served as the seat of colonial government in Massachusetts before the Revolution, and as the state capitol until 1797. It houses the Bostonian Society's fascinating **museum** of the city's history, open daily from 9am to 5pm. Admission is $5 for adults, $4 for seniors and students, and $1 for children 6 to 18.

- **Boston Massacre Site.** On a traffic island in State Street, across from the T station under the Old State House, a ring of cobblestones marks the place where the skirmish took place on March 5, 1770.
- **Faneuil Hall** ★ (℗ **617/242-5675;** www.ns.gov/bost). Built in 1742, and enlarged using a Charles Bulfinch design in 1805, it was a gift to the city from the merchant Peter Faneuil. National Park Service rangers give free 20-minute talks every half-hour from 9am to 5pm in the second-floor auditorium.
- **Paul Revere House** ★★★, 19 North Sq. (℗ **617/523-2338;** www.paulreverehouse.org). The oldest house in downtown Boston (built around 1680) presents history on a human scale. It's open April 15 through October daily from 9:30am to 5:15pm; November through April 14 from 9:30am to 4:15pm (closed Mon Jan–Mar). Admission is $3 for adults, $2.50 for seniors and students, and $1 for children 5 to 17.
- **Old North Church** ★, 193 Salem St. (℗ **617/523-6676;** www.old north.com). Paul Revere saw a signal in this church's steeple and set out on his "midnight ride." Officially named Christ Church, this is the oldest church building in Boston (1723). It's open daily from 9am to 5pm; a $3 donation is requested. Free tours of the church begin every 15 minutes. The 50-minute behind-the-scenes tour ($8 adults, $5 children under 17) includes visits to the steeple and the crypt. The quirky gift shop and museum, in a former chapel, are also open daily from 9am to 5pm. Sunday services (Episcopal) are at 9 and 11am.
- **Copp's Hill Burying Ground,** off Hull Street. The second-oldest cemetery (1659) in the city, it contains the graves of Cotton Mather and Prince Hall, who established the first black Masonic lodge. It's open daily from 9am to 5pm (until 3pm in winter).
- **USS** *Constitution* ★★, Charlestown Navy Yard (℗ **617/242-5670;** www.oldironsides.com). Active-duty sailors in 1812 dress uniforms give free tours of "Old Ironsides" daily between 10am and 3:30pm. The **USS** *Constitution* **Museum** ★ (℗ **617/426-1812;** www.ussconstitution museum.org) is open daily, May through October 15 from 9am to 6pm, October 16 through April from 10am to 5pm. Admission is free; donations are encouraged.
- **Bunker Hill Monument** (℗ **617/242-5641;** www.nps.gov/bost), Charlestown. The 221-foot granite obelisk honors the memory of the men who died in the Battle of Bunker Hill on June 17, 1775. A punishing flight of 294 stairs leads to the top. National Park Service rangers staff the monument, which is usually open daily from 9am to 4:30pm (call ahead in late 2004 and 2005 to see whether ongoing renovations have affected open hours). Admission is free.

> **Tips** **Out to Sea**
>
> A fun way to return to downtown from Charlestown is on the **ferry** that connects the Navy Yard to Long Wharf (near the Aquarium) or Lovejoy Wharf (near North Station). It costs $1.50 and is included in the MBTA Boston Visitor Pass.

HOUSE MUSEUMS

The most fascinating historic home in Boston is the **Paul Revere House** (see above). To see three other interesting residences, you must take a guided tour. Check ahead for open days and hours

Finds **Eyes in the Skies**

For a smashing view of the airport, the harbor, and the South Boston waterfront, stroll along the water or Atlantic Avenue to Northern Avenue. On either side of this intersection are buildings with free observation areas. Be ready to show an ID. The first, on the 14th floor of Independence Wharf, 470 Atlantic Ave., is open daily from 11am to 5pm. Foster's Rotunda, on the ninth floor of 30 Rowes Wharf, in the Boston Harbor Hotel complex, is open Monday to Friday from 11am to 4pm.

On Beacon Hill, you'll find two houses as notable for their architecture as for their occupants. Charles Bulfinch designed both. Tours of the 1796 **Harrison Gray Otis House** ☆☆, 141 Cambridge St. (© **617/227-3956;** www.spnea. org), discuss post-Revolutionary social, business, and family life. The 1804 **Nichols House Museum** ☆, 55 Mount Vernon St. (© **617/227-6993;** www. nicholshousemuseum.org), holds beautiful antique furnishings collected by several generations of the Nichols family. Admission is $5.

Nearby, in the Back Bay, the **Gibson House Museum,** 137 Beacon St. (© **617/267-6338;** www.thegibsonhouse.org), is a lavishly decorated 1859 brownstone that embodies the word "Victorian." Admission is $5.

PARKS & GARDENS

The best-known park in Boston is the spectacular **Public Garden** ☆☆☆, bordered by Arlington, Boylston, Charles, and Beacon streets. Something lovely is in bloom at the country's first botanical garden at least half of the year. For 5 months, the lagoon is home to the celebrated **Swan Boats** (© **617/522-1966;** www.swanboats.com). The pedal-powered vessels—the attendants pedal, not the passengers—come out of hibernation on the Saturday before Patriot's Day (the third Mon of Apr). They operate in summer daily from 10am to 5pm; in spring daily from 10am to 4pm; and from Labor Day to mid-September Monday through Friday from noon to 4pm and Saturday and Sunday from 10am to 4pm. The 15-minute ride costs $2.50 for adults, $1.50 for seniors, and $1 for children under 16.

The most spectacular garden is the **Arnold Arboretum** ☆☆, 125 Arborway, Jamaica Plain (© **617/524-1718;** www.arboretum.harvard.edu). One of the oldest parks in the United States, founded in 1872, it is open daily from sunrise to sunset. Admission is free. Its 265 acres contain more than 15,000 ornamental trees, shrubs, and vines from all over the world. Lilac Sunday, in May, is the only time picnicking is allowed. To get here, take the Orange Line to Forest Hills and follow signs to the entrance.

ORGANIZED TOURS

WALKING TOURS ☆☆   From May to October, the nonprofit **Boston by Foot** ☆☆ (© **617/367-2345,** or 617/367-3766 for recorded info; www.boston byfoot.com), conducts excellent historical and architectural tours that focus on neighborhoods or themes. The rigorously trained volunteer guides encourage questions. Buy tickets ($10 adults, $8 children 6–12) from the guide; reservations are not required. The 90-minute tours take place rain or shine.

The **Society for the Preservation of New England Antiquities** (© **617/ 227-3956;** www.spnea.org) offers a fascinating 2-hour tour that describes life in the mansions and garrets of Beacon Hill in 1800. "Magnificent and Modest"

($10) starts at the Harrison Gray Otis House, 141 Cambridge St., at 11am on Saturdays from mid-May to October. The price includes a tour of the Otis House; reservations are recommended.

The **Boston Park Rangers** (© 617/635-7383; www.ci.boston.ma.us/parks) offer free guided walking tours. The best-known focus is the **Emerald Necklace,** a loop of green spaces designed by pioneering landscape architect Frederick Law Olmsted. They include Boston Common, the Public Garden, the Commonwealth Avenue Mall, the Muddy River in the Fenway, Olmsted Park, Jamaica Pond, the Arnold Arboretum, and Franklin Park. Call for schedules.

The nonprofit **Boston History Collaborative** (© 617/350-0358; www.bostonhistorycollaborative.org) coordinates several heritage trails. Presented as guided and self-guided walking tours, longer excursions by bus and boat, and copiously documented websites, they focus on maritime history (www.bostonbysea.org), immigration (www.bostonfamilyhistory.net), literary history (www.Lit-Trail.org), and inventions (www.innovationodyssey.com).

TROLLEY TOURS   Because Boston is so pedestrian friendly, a trolley tour isn't the best choice for the able-bodied and unencumbered making a long visit. But if you're short on time, unable to walk long distances, or traveling with children, a trolley tour can be worth the money. The narrated tour can give you an overview before you focus on specific attractions, or you can use your all-day pass to hit as many places as possible in 8 hours or so.

The various companies cover the major attractions and offer informative narratives in their 90- to 120-minute tours. Most offer free reboarding if you want to visit the sites. Tickets cost $20 to $24 for adults, $12 or less for children (at press time, Old Town Trolleys was offering free admission for children under 12). Boarding spots are at hotels, historic sites, and tourist information centers. Each company paints its cars a different color. Orange-and-green **Old Town Trolleys** (© 617/269-7150; www.trolleytours.com) are the most numerous. Historic Tours of America owns Old Town as well as Minuteman Tours, which runs blue **Boston Trolley Tours** (© 617/867-5539; www.historictours.com). **Freedom Trail Trolleys** (© 800/343-1328 or 781/968-6100; www.bostontrolley.com) say "Gray Line" but are red, and **CityView Luxury Trolleys**

Kids Boston by Duck

The most unusual and enjoyable way to see Boston is with **Boston Duck Tours** ★★★ (© 800/226-7442 or 617/267-DUCK; www.bostonducktours.com). The tours, offered from April to November, are pricey but great fun. Sightseers board a "duck," a reconditioned World War II amphibious landing craft, on the Huntington Avenue side of the Prudential Center. The 80-minute narrated tour begins with a quick but comprehensive jaunt around the city. Then the duck lumbers down a ramp, splashes into the Charles River, and takes a spin around the basin. Tickets cost $24 for adults, $21 for seniors and students, $14 for children 3 to 11, and $3 for children under 3. Tours run every 30 to 60 minutes from 9am to a half-hour before sunset. You can buy tickets online or in person (at the Prudential Center, the Museum of Science, and Faneuil Hall). Try to buy same-day tickets early in the day, or ask about the limited number of tickets available 5 days in advance. Reservations are not accepted (except for groups of more than 15). No tours December through March.

(✆ 617/363-7899; www.cityviewtrolleys.com) are silver. The **Discover Boston Trolley Tours** (✆ 617/742-0767) vehicle is white, and narration is available translated into Japanese, Spanish, French, German, and Italian.

SIGHTSEEING CRUISES ★★   The season runs from April to October, with spring and fall offerings often restricted to weekends. If you're prone to seasickness, check the size of the vessel (larger equals more comfortable) before buying tickets.

Boston Harbor Cruises, 1 Long Wharf (✆ **877/733-9425** or 617/227-4321; www.bostonharborcruises.com), is the largest company. Ninety-minute historic sightseeing cruises, which tour the Inner and Outer harbors, depart daily at 11am, 1pm, 3pm, and 6 or 7pm (the sunset cruise), with extra excursions at busy times. Tickets are $18 for adults, $16 for seniors, and $13 for children under 12. The 45-minute USS *Constitution* cruise takes you around the Inner Harbor and docks at the Charlestown Navy Yard so you can visit "Old Ironsides." Tours leave Long Wharf hourly from 10:30am to 4:30pm, and on the hour from the Navy Yard from 11am to 5pm. Tickets are $12 for adults, $11 for seniors, and $9 for children. The same company offers service to Georges Island, where free water-taxi service to the rest of the Boston Harbor Islands is available (see "A Vacation in the Islands," later in this chapter).

Massachusetts Bay Lines operates the **Boston Steamship Company** (✆ **617/ 542-8000;** www.bostonsteamship.com), which offers 55-minute harbor tours. Cruises leave from Rowes Wharf on the hour from 11am to 6pm (till 5pm after Labor Day; the price is $11 for adults, $8 for children 5 to 12 and seniors. Children under 5 are free. The 90-minute sunset cruise ($17 for adults, $13 for children and seniors) leaves at 7pm (6pm after Labor Day).

The **Charles Riverboat Company** (✆ **617/621-3001;** www.charlesriverboat. com) offers 75-minute narrated cruises around the lower Charles River basin. Boats leave the CambridgeSide Galleria mall five times a day daily from June to August, and weekends in April, May, and September. Sunset cruises run daily; call for times. Tickets cost $11 for adults, $9 for seniors, and $6 for children 2 to 12.

WHALE-WATCHING ★★   For information on Cape Ann excursions, see "A Whale of an Adventure," in chapter 5.

The **New England Aquarium** (p. 121) runs whale-watching trips (✆ **617/ 973-5277**) daily from May to mid-October and on weekends in April and late October. They travel several miles out to Stellwagen Bank, the feeding ground for whales as they migrate from Newfoundland to Provincetown. Allow 3½ to 5 hours. Tickets are $29 for adults, $24 for seniors and college students, $23 for youths 12 to 18, and $18 for children 3 to 11. Children must be at least 3 years old and 30 inches tall. Reservations are strongly recommended; you can also buy tickets online.

With its on-board exhibits and vast experience, the Aquarium offers the best whale-watches in Boston. If they're booked, try **Boston Harbor Cruises** (✆ 617/227-4321; www.bostonharborcruises.com), which has a high-speed catamaran; Massachusetts Bay Lines' **Beantown Whale Watch** (✆ 617/542- 8000; www.beantownwhalewatch.com); and, on weekends only, **A. C. Cruise Line** (✆ 617/261-6633; www.accruiseline.com).

ESPECIALLY FOR KIDS

Destinations with something for every family member include **Faneuil Hall Marketplace** (✆ 617/523-1300) and the **Museum of Fine Arts** (✆ 617/267- 9300), which offers special weekend and after-school programs. Hands-on exhibits and large-format films are the headliners at the **New England Aquarium** (© 617/973-5200) and the **Museum of Science** (© 617/723-2500). A **Red Sox game** (see "Spectator Sports," later in this chapter) is another sure-fire kid pleaser.

The allure of seeing people the size of ants draws young visitors to the **Prudential Center Skywalk** (© 617/236-3318). They can see actual ants—though they might prefer dinosaurs—at the Museum of Comparative Zoology, part of the **Harvard Museum of Natural History** (© 617/495-3045; see "Exploring Cambridge," below).

Older children who have studied American history will enjoy a visit to the **John F. Kennedy Library and Museum** (© 617/929-4523). Middle-schoolers who enjoyed Esther Forbes's *Johnny Tremain* might get a kick out of the **Paul Revere House** (© 617/523-2338). Young visitors who have read Robert McCloskey's children's classic *Make Way for Ducklings* will relish a visit to the **Public Garden,** as will fans of E. B. White's *The Trumpet of the Swan,* who certainly will want to ride on the **Swan Boats.** Considerably less tame and much longer are **whale watches** (see "Organized Tours," above, and "A Whale of an Adventure," in chapter 5); **sightseeing cruises** fall somewhere in the middle.

The **Boston Tea Party Ship & Museum** (© 617/338-1773; www.boston teapartyship.com) closed after a fire in late 2001 and is currently scheduled to reopen in 2005. Call ahead to see whether the complex has reopened; it makes an entertaining stop on the way to or from the Children's Museum. The season runs from March to November.

The walking-tour company **Boston by Foot** ★★ (© 617/367-2345, or 617/367-3766 for recorded info; www.bostonbyfoot.com) has a special program, **Boston by Little Feet,** geared to children 6 to 12. The 1-hour walk gives a child's-eye view of the architecture along the Freedom Trail and of Boston's role in the American Revolution. Children must be accompanied by an adult. Tours ($8 per person) run May through October and meet at the statue of Samuel Adams on the Congress Street side of Faneuil Hall, Saturday at 10am, Sunday at 2pm, and Monday at 10am, rain or shine.

The **Historic Neighborhoods Foundation,** 99 Bedford St. (© 617/426-1885; www.historic-neighborhoods.org), offers a 90-minute "Make Way for Ducklings" tour ($8 for adults, $6 for children 12 and under). It follows the path of the Mallard family described in Robert McCloskey's famous book, and ends at the Public Garden. Reservations are required.

Children's Museum ★★ *Kids*   A delightful destination for kids under 11, the Children's Museum is great fun for adults, too. Children can stick with the family or wander on their own. The centerpiece of the renovated warehouse building is a two-story-high maze, the **New Balance Climb & Construction Zone,** which incorporates motor skills and problem-solving. The hands-on exhibits include, among many others, **Grandparents' Attic,** a souped-up version of playing dress-up at Grandma's; physical experiments (such as creating giant soap bubbles); and **Boats Afloat,** which has an 800-gallon play tank and a replica of the bridge of a working boat. A special room, **Playspace,** is packed with toys and activities for children under 4 and their caregivers. Check ahead for information on traveling exhibitions, participatory plays, and other special programs.

300 Congress St. (Museum Wharf). © 617/426-8855. www.bostonkids.org. Admission $9 adults, $7 seniors and children 2–15, $2 children age 1, free for children under 1; Fri 5–9pm $1 for all. Sat–Thurs 10am–5pm; Fri 10am–9pm. T: Red Line to South Station. Walk north on Atlantic Ave. 1 block (past Federal Reserve Bank), turn right onto Congress St., walk 2 blocks (across bridge). Call for information on discounted parking.

6 Exploring Cambridge

Harvard Square is a people-watching paradise of students, instructors, commuters, and sightseers. Restaurants and stores pack the three streets that radiate from the center of the square and the streets that intersect them. On weekend afternoons and evenings year-round, you'll hear music and see street performers. To get away from the urban bustle, stroll down to the paved paths along the Charles River.

From Boston, take the Red Line toward Alewife. In Cambridge, the subway stops at Kendall/MIT, and Central, Harvard, and Porter squares. If you're staying in or visiting the Back Bay, a longer and more colorful route is the no. 1 bus (Harvard–Dudley), which runs along Mass. Ave.

By car from Boston, follow Mass. Ave., or take Storrow Drive along the south bank of the river to the Harvard Square exit. Memorial Drive runs along the north side of the river near MIT, Central Square, and Harvard. Traffic in and around Harvard Square is almost as bad as in downtown Boston. Once you get to Cambridge, park the car and walk.

HARVARD UNIVERSITY

Harvard is the oldest college in the country, and if you suggest aloud that it's not the best, you may encounter the attitude that inspired the saying, "You can always tell a Harvard man, but you can't tell him much." The university encompasses the college and 10 graduate and professional schools in more than 400 buildings around Boston and Cambridge. Free student-led tours of the main campus leave from the **Events & Information Center,** in Holyoke Center, 1350 Mass. Ave. (© **617/495-1573**), during the school year twice a day weekdays and once on Saturday (except during vacations), and during the summer four times a day Monday through Saturday. Call for exact times; reservations aren't necessary. You're also free to wander on your own. The Events & Information Center has maps, illustrated booklets, and self-guided walking-tour directions. You might want to check out the university's website, www.harvard.edu.

The **Harvard Hot Ticket** ($10 adults, $8 seniors and students) covers admission to the art and natural history museums. It's good for 1 year and is available at the museums and at the Harvard Collections store in Holyoke Center, 1350 Mass. Ave.

Harvard Museum of Natural History and Peabody Museum of Archaeology & Ethnology *Kids* These fascinating museums house the university's collections of items and artifacts related to the natural world. The world-famous academic resource offers interdisciplinary programs and exhibitions that tie in elements of all the associated fields. On weekends, staffed "Investigation Stations" help visitors learn through hands-on activities. You'll certainly find something interesting here, be it a dinosaur skeleton, a hunk of meteorite, a Native American artifact, or the world-famous Glass Flowers.

The centerpiece of the **Botanical Museum,** the **Glass Flowers** are 3,000 models of more than 840 plant species devised between 1887 and 1936 by the German father-and-son team of Leopold and Rudolph Blaschka. You may have heard about them, and you may be skeptical, but it's true: They look real. Children love the **Museum of Comparative Zoology** , where dinosaurs share space with preserved and stuffed insects and animals that range in size from butterflies to giraffes. The **Peabody Museum** boasts the **Hall of the North American Indian,** where artifacts representing 10 cultures are on display, and is home to the only surviving artifacts positively attributed to the Lewis

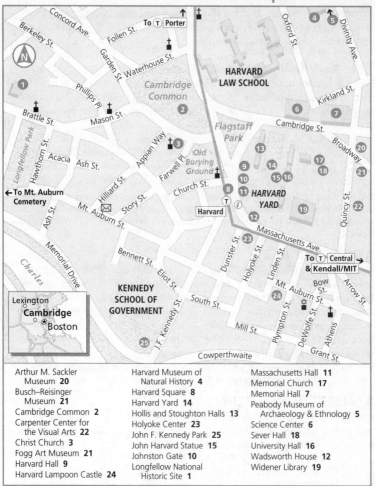

Arthur M. Sackler
  Museum **20**
Busch–Reisinger
  Museum **21**
Cambridge Common **2**
Carpenter Center for
  the Visual Arts **22**
Christ Church **3**
Fogg Art Museum **21**
Harvard Hall **9**
Harvard Lampoon Castle **24**

Harvard Museum of
  Natural History **4**
Harvard Square **8**
Harvard Yard **14**
Hollis and Stoughton Halls **13**
Holyoke Center **23**
John F. Kennedy Park **25**
John Harvard Statue **15**
Johnston Gate **10**
Longfellow National
  Historic Site **1**

Massachusetts Hall **11**
Memorial Church **17**
Memorial Hall **7**
Peabody Museum of
  Archaeology & Ethnology **5**
Science Center **6**
Sever Hall **18**
University Hall **16**
Wadsworth House **12**
Widener Library **19**

and Clark expedition. The **Mineralogical Museum** is the most specialized but can be as interesting as the others, especially if gemstones hold your interest.

Museum of Natural History: 26 Oxford St. ℰ 617/495-3045. www.hmnh.harvard.edu. Peabody Museum: 11 Divinity Ave. ℰ 617/496-1027. www.peabody.harvard.edu. Admission to both $7.50 adults, $6.50 seniors and students, $5 children 3–18; free to all Sun until noon year-round and Wed 3–5pm Sept–May. Daily 9am–5pm. T: Red Line to Harvard. Cross Harvard Yard, keeping John Harvard statue on right, and turn right at Science Center. First left is Oxford St.

Harvard University Art Museums ⚐ The Harvard art museums house some 160,000 works in three collections. The exhibit spaces also serve as teaching and research facilities. You can take a 1-hour guided tour of the Fogg weekdays at 11am, of the Busch-Reisinger weekdays at 1pm (both year-round), or of the Sackler at 2pm weekdays September through June, Wednesday only in July and August.

The **Fogg Art Museum,** 32 Quincy St., near Broadway, centers on an impressive 16th-century Italian stone courtyard. Each of the 19 galleries holds something different—17th-century Dutch and Flemish landscapes, 19th-century British and American paintings and drawings, French paintings and drawings from the 18th century through the Impressionist period, contemporary sculpture, and changing exhibits.

The **Busch-Reisinger Museum,** in Werner Otto Hall (enter through the Fogg), is the only museum in North America devoted to the art of northern and central Europe, specifically Germany. The early-20th-century collections include works by Klee, Feininger, Kandinsky, and artists and designers associated with the Bauhaus.

The **Arthur M. Sackler Museum,** 485 Broadway, at Quincy Street, houses Asian, ancient, Islamic, and Later Indian art. You'll see internationally renowned Chinese jades, superb Roman sculpture, Greek vases, Korean ceramics, Japanese woodblock prints, and Persian miniature paintings and calligraphy.

32 Quincy St. and 485 Broadway. ℂ 617/495-9400. www.artmuseums.harvard.edu. Admission to all three museums $6.50 adults, $5 seniors and students, free for children under 18; free to all until noon Sat. Mon–Sat 10am–5pm; Sun 1–5pm. T: Red Line to Harvard. Cross Harvard Yard diagonally from the T station and cross Quincy St.

A HISTORIC HOUSE

Longfellow National Historic Site ✮   The books and furniture inside the yellow mansion have remained intact since the poet Henry Wadsworth Longfellow died here in 1882. During the siege of Boston in 1775 and 1776, the house served as the headquarters of Gen. George Washington, with whom Longfellow was fascinated. On the absorbing tour—the only way to see the house—you'll learn about the history of the building and its famous occupants.

105 Brattle St. ℂ 617/876-4491. www.nps.gov/long. Guided tours $3 adults, free for children under 17. Call ahead to confirm hours and tour times. May–Oct Wed–Sun 10am–4:30pm. Tours 10:30am, 11:30am, 1, 2, 3, and 4pm. Closed Nov–Apr. T: Red Line to Harvard, then follow Brattle St. about 7 blocks; house is on the right.

A CELEBRATED CEMETERY

Dedicated in 1831, **Mount Auburn Cemetery** ✮, 580 Mt. Auburn St. (ℂ 617/547-7105), was the first of America's rural, or garden, cemeteries. Since the day it opened, Mount Auburn has been a popular place to retreat and reflect. The graves of Henry Wadsworth Longfellow, Oliver Wendell Holmes, James Russell Lowell, Winslow Homer, and many other prominent New Englanders are here. In season, you'll see gorgeous flowering trees and shrubs. The cemetery is open daily from 8am to dusk; there is no admission fee. Pets, picnicking, and jogging are not allowed. Bus routes no. 71 and 73 start at Harvard station and stop near the gates; they run frequently on weekdays, less often on weekends. From Harvard Square by car (5 min.) or on foot (30 min.), take Mount Auburn Street or Brattle Street west; just after they intersect, the gate is on the left. Stop at the office to pick up brochures and a map or to rent the 60-minute audio tour ($5; a $15 deposit is required), which you can play in your car or on a portable tape player. The **Friends of Mount Auburn Cemetery** conduct workshops and coordinates walking tours. Call the main number for topics, schedules, and fees.

A STROLL AROUND CAMBRIDGE

To explore Harvard and the surrounding area, begin your walk in **Harvard Square.** Town and gown meet at this lively intersection, where you'll get a taste of the improbable mix of people drawn to the crossroads of Cambridge.

Start at the Harvard T station, with the **Harvard Coop** at your back. Walk half a block, crossing Dunster Street. To your right is **Holyoke Center,** an administration building designed by the Spanish architect Josep Luis Sert, the dean of the university's Graduate School of Design from 1953 to 1969, and a disciple of Le Corbusier.

Across the street is **Wadsworth House,** 1341 Mass. Ave., a yellow wood structure built in 1726 as a residence for Harvard's fourth president. Its claim to fame is a classic: George Washington slept here. Turn left and follow the outside of the brick wall along Mass. Ave. to another T entrance. Pass through **Johnston Gate,** which guards the oldest part of **Harvard Yard.** "The Yard" was just a patch of grass with grazing animals when Harvard College was established in 1636 to train young men for the ministry. The Continental Army, under Washington's command, spent the winter of 1775 to 1776 here.

With Johnston Gate at your back, to your right is **Massachusetts Hall** (1720), the university's oldest surviving building. It houses the president's office and rooms for first-year students. To your left is **Harvard Hall** (1765), a classroom building. The matching side-by-side buildings behind Harvard Hall are **Hollis** and **Stoughton halls.** Hollis dates to 1763 and has been home to many students who went on to great fame, among them Ralph Waldo Emerson, Henry David Thoreau, and Charles Bulfinch.

Across the Yard is **University Hall,** the college's main administration building, designed by Bulfinch and constructed in 1812 and 1813. It's the backdrop of the **John Harvard statue** ★★, one of the most photographed objects in the Boston area. Designed by Daniel Chester French in 1884, it's known as the "Statue of Three Lies" because the inscription reads "John Harvard—Founder—1638." In fact, the college was established in 1636; Harvard (one of many people involved) wasn't the founder, but donated money and his library; and this isn't John Harvard, anyway. No portraits of him survive, so the model was, according to various accounts, either his nephew or a student. Walk over to the statue and join the throng of tourists posing for pictures with the benevolent-looking gentleman.

Walk around University Hall into the adjoining quadrangle; you're leaving the "Old Yard" for the "New Yard," where commencement and other university-wide ceremonies take place. On your right is **Widener Library,** the centerpiece of the world's largest university library system. It was built in 1913 as a memorial to Harry Elkins Widener, a 1907 Harvard graduate who died when the *Titanic* sank in 1912. Legend has it that he was unable to swim 50 yards to a lifeboat, and his mother donated $2 million for the library on the condition that every undergraduate pass a 50-yard swimming test.

Facing the library is **Memorial Church,** built in 1931 and topped with a tower and weather vane 197 feet tall. You're welcome to look around this Georgian Revival–style edifice unless services are going on. The entrance is on the left. The south wall, toward the Yard, lists the names of Harvard graduates who died in World Wars I and II, Korea, and Vietnam. One is Joseph P. Kennedy, Jr., '38, JFK's oldest brother.

Continue across the Yard onto Quincy Street. To your right is the curvilinear **Carpenter Center for the Visual Arts,** 24 Quincy St. Designed by the Swiss-French architect **Le Corbusier,** along with the team of Sert, Jackson, and Gourley, it was constructed from 1961 to 1963. It's the only Le Corbusier building in North America.

Re-enter the Yard, pass Memorial Church, and turn right. Follow the path out of the Yard to the **Science Center,** Zero Oxford St. The 10-story monolith supposedly resembles a Polaroid camera. (Edwin H. Land, founder of Cambridge-based Polaroid Corporation, was one of its main benefactors.) Sert also designed this structure, which was built from 1970 to 1972.

To your right as you face the Science Center is **Memorial Hall,** a Victorian structure built from 1870 to 1874. The hall of memorials (enter from Kirkland or Cambridge sts.) is a transept where you can read the names of the Harvard men who died fighting for the Union during the Civil War—but not those who died for the Confederacy.

With the Science Center behind you and "Mem Hall" to your left, turn right, and follow the walkway for the equivalent of a block and a half as it curves around to the right. The **Harvard Law School** campus is on your right. Carefully cross Mass. Ave. to **Cambridge Common.** Memorials and plaques dot this well-used plot of greenery and bare earth. Turn left and head back toward Harvard Square; after a block or so you'll walk near or over **horseshoes** embedded in the concrete. This is the path William Dawes, Paul Revere's fellow alarm-sounder, took from Boston to Lexington on April 18, 1775.

Turn right onto Garden Street and find **Christ Church,** Zero Garden St. The oldest church in Cambridge, it was designed by Peter Harrison of Newport, Rhode Island (also the architect of King's Chapel in Boston), and opened in 1761. Note the square wooden tower. Inside the vestibule you can still see bullet holes made by British muskets.

With the church at your back, turn right and return to Mass. Ave. Turn right again, then walk 2 blocks into the middle of the square and 1 more block on John F. Kennedy Street. Turn left onto Mount Auburn Street. Stay on the left side of the street as you cross Dunster, Holyoke, and Linden streets.

The corner of Mount Auburn and Linden streets is a good vantage point for viewing the **Harvard Lampoon Castle,** designed by Wheelwright & Haven in 1909. Listed on the National Register of Historic Places, this is the home of Harvard's undergraduate humor magazine, the *Lampoon.* The main tower looks like a face, with windows as the eyes, nose, and mouth, topped by what looks like a miner's hat.

Follow Mount Auburn Street back to John F. Kennedy Street and turn left. Cross the street at some point, and follow it toward the Charles River, almost to Memorial Drive. On your right is **John F. Kennedy Park** and the adjacent Graduate School of Government. Walk away from the street to the fountain, engraved with excerpts from the president's speeches. This is an excellent place to take a break and plan the rest of your day.

7 Spectator Sports & Getting Outside

SPECTATOR SPORTS

Boston's reputation as a great sports town derives in part from the days when at least one pro team was one of the world's best. In 2002 and 2004, the New England Patriots (who play in suburban Foxboro) continued that tradition by winning the Super Bowl. Although the other pro teams haven't enjoyed that level of success recently, passions run deep. That enthusiasm also applies to college sports, particularly hockey, in which the Division I schools are fierce rivals.

BASEBALL   No other experience in sports matches watching the **Boston Red Sox** play at **Fenway Park** ★★★, which they do from April to early October, and later if they make the playoffs. The quirkiness of the oldest park in the major leagues (1912) and the fact that (at press time) the team last won the World Series in 1918 only add to the Fenway mystique. The team changed hands in 2002, and the new owners have invested so much in the existing structure—including building seats above the legendary left-field wall—that rumors of its impending demolition have quieted down.

The Fenway Park **ticket office** (© **877/REDSOX-9**, or 617/482-4SOX for touch-tone ticketing; www.redsox.com) is at 4 Yawkey Way, off Brookline Avenue. Tickets go on sale in February; order early. Prices start at $18. Forced to choose between tickets for a low-numbered grandstand section (say, 10 or below) and less expensive bleacher seats, go for the bleachers and the better view. Throughout the season, a limited number of standing-room tickets and (if you're lucky) returned tickets go on sale the day of the game. Take the Green Line B, C, or D to Kenmore or D to Fenway.

Tours (© **617/236-6666**) are offered on the hour from 9am to 4pm (or 3 hr. before game time, whichever is earlier) daily, year-round. There are no tours on holidays or before day games. The cost is $10 for adults, $9 for seniors, and $8 for children under 15.

BASKETBALL   Sixteen NBA championship banners hang in the FleetCenter, testimony to the history of the **Boston Celtics.** Unfortunately, the most recent is from 1986. The Celtics play from early October to April or May; when a top contender is visiting, you may have trouble getting tickets. Prices are as low as $10 for some games and top out at $150. For information, call the **FleetCenter** (© **617/624-1000**; www.nba.com/celtics); for tickets, contact **Ticketmaster** (© **617/931-2000**; www.ticketmaster.com). To reach the FleetCenter, take the Green or Orange Line to North Station. *Note:* Spectators may not bring any bags, including backpacks and briefcases, into the arena.

FOOTBALL   The **New England Patriots** (© **800/543-1776**; www.patriots. com) were playing to sellout crowds even before they won the Super Bowl in 2002 and 2004. The Pats play from August to December or January at Gillette Stadium on Route 1 in Foxboro, about a 45-minute drive south of the city. Tickets sell out well in advance. Call or check the website for information on individual ticket sales and public-transit options.

HOCKEY   The **Boston Bruins** are exciting but expensive to watch. Tickets often sell out early despite being among the priciest ($19–$155) in the league. For information, call the **FleetCenter** (© **617/624-1000**; www.bostonbruins. com); for tickets, call **Ticketmaster** (© **617/931-2000**; www.ticketmaster.com). To reach the FleetCenter, take the Green or Orange Line to North Station. *Note:* Spectators may not bring any bags, including backpacks and briefcases, into the arena.

Economical fans will be pleasantly surprised by the quality of local **college hockey** *. Even for sold-out games, standing-room tickets are usually available shortly before game time. Local teams include **Boston College,** Conte Forum, Chestnut Hill (© **617/552-3000**); **Boston University,** Walter Brown Arena, 285 Babcock St., through January 2005, then Agganis Arena, 928 Commonwealth Ave. (© **617/353-3838**); **Harvard University,** Bright Hockey Center, North Harvard Street, Allston (© **617/495-2211**); and **Northeastern University,** Matthews Arena, St. Botolph Street (© **617/373-4700**).

THE MARATHON   Every year on Patriot's Day (the third Mon in Apr), the **Boston Marathon** ★★★ rules the roads from Hopkinton to Copley Square in Boston. An especially nice place to watch is tree-shaded Comm. Ave. between Kenmore Square and Mass. Ave., but you'll be in a crowd wherever you stand, particularly near the finish line in front of the Boston Public Library. For information about qualifying, contact the **Boston Athletic Association** (© **617/ 236-1652**; www.bostonmarathon.org).

Finds A Vacation in the Islands

Majestic ocean views, hiking trails, historic sights, rocky beaches, nature walks, campsites, and picnic areas abound in New England. The **Boston Harbor Islands** (✶✶ (© 617/223-8666; www.bostonislands.com) have them all. Their unspoiled beauty makes a welcome break from the urban landscape 45 minutes to the west, but they're not well known, even to many longtime Bostonians. Bring a sweater or jacket, and note that fresh water is available only on Georges Island. (Management strongly suggests that you bring your own.)

Thirty islands dot the Outer Harbor, and at least a half dozen are open to the public. Ferries run to the **Georges Island,** home of Fort Warren (1834), which held Confederate prisoners during the Civil War. You can investigate on your own or take a ranger-led tour. The island has a visitor center, refreshment area, fishing pier, picnic area, and wonderful view of Boston's skyline. Allow at least half a day, longer if you plan to take the free water taxi to **Lovell, Gallops, Peddocks, Bumpkin,** or **Grape Island,** all of which have picnic areas and campsites.

Boston Harbor Cruises (© 617/227-4321; www.bostonharborcruises. com) serves Georges Island from Long Wharf; the trip takes 45 minutes, and tickets cost $10 for adults, $9 for seniors, and $7 for children under 12. Cruises depart daily at 10am, noon, 2pm, and 4pm in spring and fall, and daily on the hour from 10am to 5pm in summer. Water taxis and admission to the islands are free.

The Boston Harbor Islands National Recreation Area (www.nps.gov/boha) is the focus of a public-private project designed to make the islands more interesting and accessible. For more information, visit the website, consult the staff at the **kiosk on Long Wharf,** or contact the **Friends of the Boston Harbor Islands** (© 617/740-4290; www.fbhi.org).

ROWING   In late October, the **Head of the Charles Regatta** ✶ (© 617/868-6200;** www.hocr.org) attracts some 4,000 oarsmen and oarswomen. The largest crew event in the country draws hundreds of thousands of spectators who socialize and occasionally even watch the action.

GETTING OUTSIDE

The **Department of Conservation & Recreation** (www.state.ma.us/dcr) oversees activities on the state's public lands. (The DCR's Division of Urban Parks & Recreation replaced the Metropolitan District Commission, a name that survives on many signs.) The incredibly helpful website describes properties and activities, and has a planning area to help you make the most of your time.

BEACHES   The beaches in Boston proper are not worth the trouble. Boston Harbor water is not only bone-chilling, but also subject to being declared unsafe for swimming. If you want to swim, book a hotel with a pool. If you want the sand-between-your-toes experience, hit the beach on the North Shore or at Walden Pond in Concord. See chapter 5 for information on suburban beaches.

BIKING   Even expert cyclists who feel comfortable with Boston's layout will be better off in Cambridge, which has bike lanes, or on the area's many bike paths. The 18-mile **Dr. Paul Dudley White Charles River Bike Path** follows the river from the Museum of Science to Watertown and back. You can enter and exit at many points along the way. Bikers share the path with lots of pedestrians, joggers, and in-line skaters. On summer Sundays from 11am to 7pm, **Memorial Drive** from Central Square to west Cambridge is closed to cars.

State law requires that children under 12 wear helmets. Bicycles are forbidden on buses and the Green Line, and on other lines during rush hours.

Most rental shops charge around $5 per hour or $25 per day. They include **Back Bay Bicycles,** 366 Comm. Ave., near Mass. Ave. (© **617/247-2336;** www.backbaybicycles.com), and **Community Bicycle Supply,** 496 Tremont St., near East Berkeley Street (© **617/542-8623;** www.communitybicycle.com). Across the river, try **Cambridge Bicycle,** 259 Mass. Ave., near MIT (© **617/ 876-6555;** www.oldroads.com/cb.html), or **Ata Cycle,** 1773 Mass. Ave., near Porter Square (© **617/354-0907;** www.atabike.com). For more information, contact **MassBike** (© **617/542-2453;** www.massbike.org).

GOLF   The **Massachusetts Golf Association** (© **781/449-3000;** www.mga links.org) represents more than 310 courses around the golf-mad state. Given a choice, play on a weekday, when you'll find lower prices and smaller crowds than on weekends.

One of the best public courses in the area, **Newton Commonwealth Golf Course,** 212 Kenrick St., Newton (© **617/630-1971;** www.sterlinggolf.com), is a challenging 18-hole Donald Ross design. It's 5,305 yards from the blue tees, par is 70, and greens fees are $28 weekdays, $35 weekends. Within the city limits is the legendary 6,009-yard **William J. Devine Golf Course,** in Franklin Park, Dorchester (© **617/265-4084;** www.sterlinggolf.com). As a Harvard student, Bobby Jones sharpened his game on the 18-hole, par-70 course. Greens fees are $26 weekdays, $34 weekends. Less challenging but with more of a neighborhood feel is 9-hole, par-35 **Fresh Pond Golf Course,** 691 Huron Ave., Cambridge (© **617/349-6282;** www.freshpondgolf.com). The 3,161-yard layout adjoins the Fresh Pond Reservoir (there's water on four holes) and charges $19, or $29 to go around twice, on weekdays; $23 and $36 on weekends.

GYMS   The concierge at your hotel can recommend a health club. Hotels with good health clubs (see "Where to Stay," earlier in this chapter) include the Boston Harbor Hotel, the Four Seasons Hotel, the Hilton Boston Logan Airport, and the Royal Sonesta Hotel. The best combination of facilities and value is at the **Wang YMCA of Chinatown,** 8 Oak St. W., off Washington Street (© **617/426-2237**), close to downtown; or the **Central Branch YMCA,** 316 Huntington Ave. (© **617/536-7800**), near Symphony Hall. A day pass costs $10.

ICE-SKATING   The rink at the Boston Common **Frog Pond** (© **617/635-2120**) is an extremely popular cold-weather destination. It's an open surface with an ice-making system and a clubhouse. Admission is $3 for adults and free for children under 14; skate rental costs $7 for adults, $5 for kids. Try to go on a weekday; huge crowds descend on weekends.

IN-LINE SKATING   Unless you're confident of your ability and your knowledge of Boston traffic, stay off the streets. A favorite car-free spot is the **Esplanade,** between the Back Bay and the Charles River. It continues onto the bike path that runs to Watertown and back, but once you leave the Esplanade, the pavement isn't totally smooth. Your best bet is to wait for a summer Sunday, when **Memorial Drive** in Cambridge closes to cars. It's a perfect surface. The **InLine Club of Boston** offers event and safety information on its website (www.sk8net.com).

Expect to pay about $15 for rentals. Try the **Beacon Hill Skate Shop,** 135 Charles St. S. (✆ **617/482-7400**), not far from the Esplanade, or **Blades Board & Skate,** 38 John F. Kennedy St., Cambridge (✆ **617/491-4244;** www.blades. com), near Memorial Drive.

JOGGING The **Dr. Paul Dudley White Charles River Bike Path** (see "Biking," above) is the area's busiest jogging trail. It's so popular because it's car-free (except at intersections), scenic, and generally safe. The bridges along the river allow for circuits of various lengths, but be careful around abutments, where you can't see far ahead. Don't jog at night, and try not to go alone. Visit the DCR website (www.state.ma.us/dcr) to view a map that gives distances. If the river's not convenient, check with the concierge or desk staff at your hotel for a map with suggested routes.

SAILING The best deal in town is **Community Boating, Inc.,** 21 David Mugar Way, on the Esplanade (✆ **617/523-1038;** www.community-boating. org). It's open April through November, and the fleet includes 13- to 23-foot sailboats as well as windsurfers and kayaks. Visitors pay $100 for 2 days of unlimited use in the Charles River basin.

TENNIS Public courts are available throughout the city at no charge. Well-maintained courts near downtown that seldom get busy until after work are along the Southwest Corridor Park in the South End (there's a nice one near **W. Newton St.**) The courts on **Boston Common** and in **Charlesbank Park,** overlooking the river next to the bridge to the Museum of Science, are more crowded during the day.

8 Shopping

Boston-area shopping represents a tempting blend of classic and contemporary. Boston and Cambridge boast tiny boutiques and sprawling malls, esoteric bookshops and national chain stores, classy galleries and snazzy secondhand-clothing outlets.

Note: Massachusetts has no sales tax on clothing priced below $175 or on food. All other items are taxed at 5% (as are restaurant meals and takeout food). The state no longer prohibits stores from opening before noon on Sunday, but many still wait until noon or don't open at all—call ahead before setting out.

BACK BAY This is New England's premier shopping district. Dozens of classy galleries, shops, and boutiques make **Newbury Street** ✦✦✦ a world-famous destination. Nearby, a weatherproof walkway across Huntington Avenue links upscale **Copley Place** (✆ **617/375-4400**) and the **Shops at Prudential Center** (✆ **800/SHOP-PRU**). This is where you'll find the tony department stores **Neiman Marcus** (✆ **617/536-3660**), **Lord & Taylor** (✆ **617/262-6000**), and **Saks Fifth Avenue** (✆ **617/262-8500**).

If you're passionate about art, set aside a couple of hours for strolling along Newbury Street. Besides being a prime location for upscale boutiques, it boasts an infinite variety of styles and media in the dozens of art galleries at street level and on the higher floors. (Remember to look up.) Most galleries are open Tuesday through Sunday from 10 or 11am to 5:30 or 6pm. For specifics, pick up a copy of the free monthly *Gallery Guide* at businesses along Newbury Street.

DOWNTOWN **Faneuil Hall Marketplace** (✆ **617/523-1300**) is the busiest attraction in Boston not only for its smorgasbord of food outlets, but also for its shops, boutiques, and pushcarts. Although it has more upscale chain outlets than only-in-Boston shops, it's a fun experience.

If the hubbub here is too much for you, stroll over to **Charles Street,** at the foot of Beacon Hill. A short but commercially dense (and picturesque) street, it's home to perhaps the best assortment of gift and antiques shops in the city. Be sure to check out the contemporary home accessories at **Koo De Kir,** 65 Chestnut St., just off Charles (© **617/723-8111;** www.koodekir.com); the well-edited selection at **Upstairs Downstairs Antiques,** 93 Charles St. (© **617/ 367-1950**), and the engagingly funky gifts at **Black Ink,** 101 Charles St. (© **617/723-3883**).

One of Boston's oldest shopping areas is **Downtown Crossing.** Now a traffic-free pedestrian mall along Washington, Winter, and Summer streets near Boston Common, it's home to two major department stores (**Filene's** and **Macy's**); tons of smaller clothing, shoe, and music stores; food and merchandise pushcarts; and outlets of two major bookstore chains, **Barnes & Noble** and **Borders. Filene's Basement** ★★★, 426 Washington St. (© **617/542-2011**), is a New England legend. The famed automatic markdown policy (25% off the already-discounted price after 2 weeks on the selling floor, up to 75% after 7 weeks) applies only here, at the flagship store. We happen to love this sort of thing, but you may find that battling the crowds isn't worth the payoff—the selling floors are pretty wild at busy times.

CAMBRIDGE   The bookstores, boutiques, and T-shirt shops of **Harvard Square** lie about 15 minutes from downtown Boston by subway. Despite the neighborhood association's efforts, chain stores have swept over the Square. You'll find a mix of national and regional outlets, and more than a few persistent independent retailers. They include the delightful children's store **Calliope,** 33 Brattle St. (© **617/876-4149**); **Colonial Drug,** 49 Brattle St. (© **617/864-2222**), which stocks hard-to-find perfume and other high-end cosmetics; and

---

Finds **By the Book**

Bookworms flock to Cambridge; Harvard Square in particular caters to general and specific audiences. Check out the basement of the **Harvard Book Store,** 1256 Mass. Ave. (© **800/542-READ** outside 617, or 617/661-1515; www.harvard.com), for great deals on remainders and used books; and **WordsWorth Books,** 30 Brattle St. (© **800/899-2202** or 617/ 354-5201; www.wordsworth.com), for a huge discounted selection. Up the street, children's books have their own store at **Curious George Goes to WordsWorth,** 1 John F. Kennedy St. (© **617/498-0062;** www. curiousg.com). Barnes & Noble runs the book operation at the **Harvard Coop,** 1400 Mass. Ave. (© **617/499-2000;** www.thecoop.com), which stocks textbooks, academic works, and a large general selection.

Two excellent Boston stores with huge selections of used merchandise are the **Avenue Victor Hugo Bookshop,** 353 Newbury St. (© **617/ 266-7746;** www.avenuevictorhugobooks.com), in the Back Bay, and the **Brattle Book Shop,** 9 West St. (© **800/447-9595** or 617/542-0210; www. brattlebookshop.com), near Downtown Crossing. Also near Downtown Crossing are **Barnes & Noble,** 395 Washington St. (© **617/426-5184;** www.barnesandnoble.com), and **Borders,** 24 School St. (© **617/557-7188;** www.borders.com). There's also a **Borders** (© **617/679-0887**) at the CambridgeSide Galleria mall.

Oona's, 1210 Mass. Ave. (© **617/491-2654**), a trove of lovely "experienced" clothing and accessories.

For a less generic experience, walk along **Mass. Ave.** in either direction to the next T stop. The stroll takes about an hour. Heading north toward Porter Square, be sure to stop at **Joie de Vivre,** 1792 Mass. Ave. (© **617/864-8188**), a top-notch gift shop, and the retro home-accessories emporium **Abodeon,** 1713 Mass. Ave. (© **617/497-0137**). Going southeast to Central, pop into **Pearl Art & Craft Supplies,** 579 Mass. Ave. (© **617/547-6600**), an excellent link in the national discount chain.

And if you just can't manage without a trip to a mall, head to East Cambridge. Take the Green Line to Lechmere, or the Red Line to Kendall/MIT and the free shuttle bus to the **CambridgeSide Galleria,** 100 CambridgeSide Place (© **617/621-8666**).

9 Boston & Cambridge After Dark

For up-to-date entertainment listings, consult the "Calendar" section of the Thursday *Boston Globe,* the "Edge" section of the Friday *Boston Herald,* or the Sunday arts sections of both papers. Three free publications, available at newspaper boxes around town, publish nightlife listings: the *Boston Phoenix,* the *Stuff@Night* (a *Phoenix* offshoot), and the *Improper Bostonian.* The *Phoenix* website (www.bostonphoenix.com) archives the paper's season preview issues; especially before a summer or fall visit, it's a worthwhile planning tool.

GETTING TICKETS   Some companies and venues sell tickets over the phone or online; many will refer you to a ticket agency. The major agencies that serve Boston, **Ticketmaster** (© **617/931-2000;** www.ticketmaster.com), **Next Ticketing** (© **617/423-NEXT;** www.nextticketing.com), and **Tele-charge** (© **800/ 447-7400** or TTY 888/889-8587; www.telecharge.com), calculate service charges per ticket, not per order. To avoid the fee—and possible losses if your plans change and you can't get your money back—visit the box office in person. If you wait until the day before or day of a performance, you'll sometimes have access to tickets that were held back and have just gone on sale.

DISCOUNT TICKETS   Visit a **BosTix** (© **617/482-2849;** www.bostix.org) booth at Faneuil Hall Marketplace (on the south side of Faneuil Hall) or in Copley Square (at the corner of Boylston and Dartmouth sts.). Same-day tickets to musical and theatrical performances are half price, subject to availability. Credit cards are not accepted, and there are no refunds or exchanges. Check the board or the website for the day's offerings. The booths, which are also Ticketmaster outlets, are open Tuesday through Saturday from 10am to 6pm (half-price tickets go on sale at 11am), Sunday from 11am to 4pm. The Copley Square location is also open Monday from 10am to 6pm.

THE PERFORMING ARTS

The city's premier classical performance venue is **Symphony Hall,** 301 Mass. Ave. (© **617/266-1492;** www.bso.org), which turned 100 in 2000. It plays host to other notable groups and artists when the Boston Symphony Orchestra and the Boston Pops are away. The **Hatch Shell** on the Esplanade (© **617/727-5215**) is an amphitheater best known as the home of the Pops' Fourth of July concerts. On summer nights, free music and dance performances and films take over the stage to the delight of crowds on the lawn.

Other venues that attract big-name visitors include the **Berklee Performance Center,** 136 Mass. Ave. (© **617/747-8890;** www.berkleebpc.com); the newly expanded **Boston Center for the Arts,** 539 Tremont St. (© **617/426-2787;** www.bcaonline.org); the **Cutler Majestic Theatre,** 219 Tremont St. (© **617/ 824-8000;** www.maj.org); **Jordan Hall,** 30 Gainsborough St. (© **617/585- 1260;** www.newenglandconservatory.edu/jordanhall); and **Sanders Theatre,** 45 Quincy St., Cambridge (© **617/496-2222;** www.fas.harvard.edu/~memhall).

THE MAJOR COMPANIES

In addition to the companies listed below, the **Boston Lyric Opera** (© **617/ 542-6772** or 617/542-4912; www.blo.org) performs classical and contemporary works. The season runs from October to May. Performances are at the **Shubert Theatre,** 265 Tremont St., and tickets cost $33 to $152.

Boston Ballet ✸✸ Boston Ballet's reputation seems to jump a notch every time someone says, "So it's not just *The Nutcracker.*" The country's fourth-largest dance company performs the holiday staple from Thanksgiving to New Year's. During the rest of the season (Oct–May), it presents an eclectic mix of classic ballets and contemporary works. Because the Wang was originally a movie theater, the pitch of the seats makes the top two balconies less than ideal for ballet— paying more for a better seat is a good investment. *Note:* Other Boston Ballet productions will stay at the Wang, but *The Nutcracker* is moving. In 2004, performances will be at the **Colonial Theatre,** 106 Boylston St. After that, the **Opera House,** 539 Washington St., will play host to the spectacular show. 19 Clarendon St. © **617/695-6955** or 800/447-7400 (Tele-charge). www.bostonballet.com. Performances at the Wang Theatre, 270 Tremont St. (box office Mon–Sat 10am–6pm). Tickets $23–$73. Student rush tickets (1 hr. before curtain) $12.50, except for The Nutcracker. T: Green Line to Boylston.

Boston Pops ✸✸ From May to July, members of the BSO lighten up. Tables and chairs replace the floor seats at Symphony Hall, and drinks and light refreshments are served. The Pops play a range of music from light classical to show tunes to popular music, often with celebrity guest stars. Performances are Tuesday through Sunday evenings. Special holiday performances in December ($20–$95) usually sell out well in advance, but it can't hurt to check. The regular season ends with a week of free outdoor concerts at the Hatch Shell on the Esplanade along the Charles River. It includes the traditional Fourth of July concert. Symphony Hall, 301 Mass. Ave. (at Huntington Ave.). © **617/266-1492** or 617/CONCERT (program information). SymphonyCharge © 888/266-1200 (outside 617) or 617/266-1200. www.bso.org. Tickets $37–$69 for tables; $16–$43 for balcony seats. T: Green Line E to Symphony, or Orange Line to Mass. Ave.

Boston Symphony Orchestra ✸✸✸ The Boston Symphony, one of the world's greatest, was founded in 1881. In 2004, James Levine replaced Seiji Ozawa as music director, one classical music superstar replacing another. You might want to schedule your trip to coincide with a particular performance, or with a visit by a celebrated guest artist or conductor. The season runs from October to April, with performances most Tuesday, Thursday, and Saturday evenings; Friday afternoons; and some Friday evenings. Explanatory talks (included in the ticket price) begin 30 minutes before the curtain. If you can't get tickets in advance, check at the box office for returns from subscribers 2 hours before showtime. A limited number of rush tickets are available on the day of the performance for Tuesday and Thursday evening and Friday afternoon programs. Some Wednesday evening and Thursday morning rehearsals are open to the public. Symphony Hall, 301 Mass. Ave. (at Huntington Ave.). © **617/266-1492** or 617/ CONCERT (program information). SymphonyCharge © 888/266-1200 (outside 617) or 617/266- 1200. www.bso.org. Tickets $26–$95. Rush tickets $8 (on sale 9am Fri, 5pm Tues and Thurs). Rehearsal tickets $16. T: Green Line E to Symphony, or Orange Line to Mass. Ave.

THEATER & PERFORMANCE ART

Boston is one of the last cities for pre-Broadway tryouts, allowing an early look at a classic (or classic flop) in the making. It's also a popular destination for touring companies of established hits. You'll find most of the shows headed to or coming from Broadway in the **Theater District,** at the **Colonial Theatre,** 106 Boylston St. (© **617/426-9366**); the **Opera House,** 539 Washington St. (© **617/880-2400**); the **Shubert Theatre,** 265 Tremont St. (© **617/482-9393**); the **Wang Theatre,** 270 Tremont St. (© **617/482-9393;** www.wangcenter.org); and the **Wilbur Theater,** 246 Tremont St. (© **617/423-4008**). The promoter often is **Broadway in Boston** (© **617/880-2400;** www.broadwayinboston.com).

The excellent local theater scene boasts the **Huntington Theatre Company,** which performs at the Boston University Theatre, 264 Huntington Ave. (© **617/266-0800;** www.huntington.org), and the **American Repertory Theatre,** which makes its home at Harvard University's Loeb Drama Center, 64 Brattle St., Cambridge (© **617/547-8300;** www.amrep.org).

The off-Broadway performance-art sensation **Blue Man Group** is a trio of cobalt-colored entertainers who use music, percussion, food, and audience participants—props include social commentary, Twinkies, marshmallows, breakfast cereal, toilet paper, and lots of blue paint. Older children and teenagers enjoy the mayhem as much as adults. Shows are at the **Charles Playhouse,** 74 Warrenton St. (© **617/426-6912;** www.blueman.com), in the Theater District. Tickets are $53 and $43 at the box office and through Ticketmaster (© **617/931-ARTS**).

THE CLUB & MUSIC SCENE

The Boston-area club scene changes constantly, and somewhere out there is a good time for everyone. Check the "Calendar" section of the Thursday *Globe,* the *Phoenix,* the "Edge" section of the Friday *Herald, Stuff@Night,* or the *Improper Bostonian* while you're planning.

Bars close at 1am, clubs at 2am. The subway shuts down between 12:30 and 1am; Night Owl bus service operates until 2:30am on Friday and Saturday (see "Late-Night Transit," on p. 84). The drinking age is 21; a valid driver's license or passport is required as proof of age. The law is strictly enforced, especially near college campuses (in other words, practically everywhere). Be prepared to show ID if you appear to be younger than 35 or so, and try to be patient while the amazed 30-year-old ahead of you fishes out a license.

Big-name rock and pop artists play the **FleetCenter,** 150 Causeway St. (© **617/624-1000;** www.fleetcenter.com), when it's not in use by the Bruins (hockey), the Celtics (basketball), the circus (in Oct), and touring ice shows. Concerts are in the round or on the arena stage.

Finds **Boston Common Culture**

An excellent summer diversion is a free, top-quality performance on historic Boston Common. Bring a picnic, spread out a blanket, and enjoy the sunset. The **Commonwealth Shakespeare Company** (© **617/532-1252**; www.commonwealthshakespeare.org) performs Tuesday through Sunday nights in July and early August. The **Boston Landmarks Orchestra** (© **617/520-2200**; www.landmarksorchestra.org) schedules classical concerts in parks around town, including the Common, on weekend afternoons and evenings in July and August.

> **Finds** **The Classiest Pickup Joint in Town**
>
> On the first Friday of each month, the **Museum of Fine Arts,** 465 Huntington Ave. (© **617/267-9300**; www.mfa.org), becomes a spirited nightlife destination. From 5:30 to 9:30pm, music, a cash bar, and a crowd of 20- and 30-somethings liven up the galleries. General admission to the museum ($13 after 5pm) includes admission to "firstfridays."

COMEDY

The Comedy Connection at Faneuil Hall ★★　The oldest original comedy club in town (established in 1978) draws top-notch talent from near and far. There's one show Sunday through Thursday, two shows Friday and Saturday. The cover seldom tops $15 during the week, but jumps for a big name appearing on a weekend. Quincy Market (2nd floor, off the rotunda). © **617/248-9700.** www.comedyconnectionboston.com. Cover $12–$40. T: Green or Blue Line to Government Center or Orange Line to Haymarket. Validated parking available.

The Comedy Studio ★★★ *Finds*　Nobody here is a sitcom star—yet. With a stellar reputation for searching out undiscovered talent, the no-frills Comedy Studio draws connoisseurs, students, and network scouts. Sketches and improv spice up the standup. Shows Tuesday through Sunday nights. At the Hong Kong restaurant, 1236 Mass. Ave., Cambridge. © **617/661-6507.** www.thecomedystudio.com. Cover $7–$10. T: Red Line to Harvard.

DANCE CLUBS

Avalon ★★★　A cavernous multilevel space with a spectacular light show, Avalon is either great fun or sensory overload. Friday is **"Avaland,"** with national and international names in the DJ booth and costumed house dancers on the floor. On Saturday (suburbanites' night out), expect more mainstream dance hits. Concerts (John Mayer and Ani DiFranco have played recently) usually start in the early evening. The dress code calls for jackets and shirts with collars, and no jeans or athletic wear. Open Thursday (international night) through Sunday (gay night) from 10pm to 2am. 15 Lansdowne St. © **617/262-2424.** www.avalonboston.com. Cover $5–$20. T: Green Line B, C, or D to Kenmore.

The Roxy ★★　This former hotel ballroom boasts excellent DJs and live music, a huge dance floor, a stage, and a balcony. Occasional concerts and boxing cards take good advantage of the sight lines. No jeans or athletic shoes. Open from 9pm to 2am Thursday through Saturday, plus some Wednesdays and Sundays. In the Tremont Boston hotel, 279 Tremont St. © **617/338-7699.** www.roxyplex.com. Cover $10–$20. T: Green Line to Boylston or Orange Line to New England Medical Center.

FOLK & ECLECTIC

Club Passim ★★　Joan Baez, Suzanne Vega, and Tom Rush all started out in this legendary basement coffeehouse. There's live music nightly, and coffee and food (but no alcohol) until 10:30pm. Open Sunday through Thursday from 11am to 11pm, Friday and Saturday until midnight. 47 Palmer St., Cambridge. © **617/492-7679.** www.clubpassim.org. Cover $5–$25; most shows $12 or less. T: Red Line to Harvard.

Johnny D's Uptown Restaurant & Music Club ★★★ *Finds*　This family-owned establishment draws a congenial post-collegiate-and-up crowd for performers on international tours as well as local acts. The music ranges from zydeco to rock, blues to ska. It's only two stops past Harvard Square on the Red Line (about a 15-min. ride at night). Open daily from 11:30am to 1am. Brunch starts at 9am on weekends; dinner runs from 4:30 to 9:30pm Tuesday through Saturday, with lighter fare until 11pm. 17 Holland St., Davis Sq., Somerville. ⦿ **617/776-2004** or 617/776-9667 (concert line). www.johnnyds.com. Cover $2–$16, usually $5–$10. T: Red Line to Davis.

JAZZ & BLUES

On summer Fridays at 7pm, the **Waterfront Jazz Series** (⦿ **617/635-3911**) brings amateurs and professionals to Christopher Columbus Park, on the waterfront, for a refreshing interlude of free music and cool breezes. On summer Thursdays at 6pm, the **Boston Harbor Hotel** (⦿ **617/439-7000**) stages performances on the "Blues Barge," which floats in the water behind the hotel. The *Boston Globe* **Jazz & Blues Festival** (⦿ **617/267-4301;** www.boston.com/jazzfest) is usually scheduled for the third week of June. Constellations of jazz and blues stars appear, often outdoors. The festival wraps up with a free Sunday program at the Hatch Shell.

Regattabar ★★★   The Regattabar's lineup of local and international artists is often considered the best in the area—a title that Scullers (see below) is happy to dispute. McCoy Tyner, Irma Thomas, and Rebecca Parris have appeared recently. The third-floor room holds about 200 and, unfortunately, can get a little noisy. Buy tickets in advance from Concertix or try your luck at the door an hour before showtime. In the Charles Hotel, 1 Bennett St., Cambridge. ⦿ **617/661-5000.** Concertix: ⦿ 617/876-7777. Tickets $12–$35. T: Red Line to Harvard.

Scullers Jazz Club ★★★   Overlooking the Charles River, Scullers is a lovely room that books top singers and instrumentalists—recent notables include Abbey Lincoln, Arturo Sandoval, and Bobby Short. Patrons tend to be more hard-core and quieter than the crowds at the Regattabar, but it really depends on who's performing. The box office is open Monday through Saturday from 11am to 6:30pm. Ask about dinner and overnight packages. In the Doubletree Guest Suites hotel, 400 Soldiers Field Rd. ⦿ **617/562-4111.** www.scullersjazz.com. Tickets $12–$50. Validated parking available.

Wally's Cafe ★   This Boston institution, near a busy corner in the South End, opened in 1947. It draws a notably diverse crowd—black, white, straight, gay, affluent, indigent—and features nightly live music by local ensembles, students and instructors from the Berklee College of Music, and (on occasion) internationally renowned musicians. 427 Mass. Ave. ⦿ **617/424-1408.** www.wallyscafe.com. 1-drink minimum. T: Orange Line to Mass. Ave.

ROCK & ALTERNATIVE

The Middle East ★★★   The best rock club in the area books an impressive variety of progressive and alternative acts in two rooms (upstairs and downstairs) every night. Showcasing top local talent as well as bands with international reputations, it's a popular hangout that gets crowded, hot, and *loud.* 472–480 Mass. Ave., Central Sq., Cambridge. ⦿ **617/864-EAST** or 617/931-2000 (Ticketmaster). www.mideastclub.com. Cover $7–$15. T: Red Line to Central.

Paradise Rock Club ★   Hard by the Boston University campus, the medium-size Paradise draws enthusiastic, student-intensive crowds for top local rock and alternative performers. You might see national names or locals who aren't ready to headline a big show. 967 Comm. Ave. ⦿ **617/562-8800,** or 617/423-NEXT for tickets. http://boston.cc.com. T: Green Line B to Pleasant St.

> **Tips Bowled Over**
>
> The hottest nightlife destination in town is, of all things, a bowling alley. **Kings,** 10 Scotia St. ((C) **617/266-2695;** www.backbaykings.com), is a 25,000-square-foot complex in a former movie theater. It has 20 bowling lanes (four of them private) and an eight-table billiards room. Open until 2am daily; patrons must be 21 after 6pm. The complex includes a branch of the Cambridge restaurant **Jasper White's Summer Shack.** Scotia Street is off Dalton Street, across from the Hynes Convention Center.

Toad (★★ (Value   Essentially a bar with a stage, this narrow space attracts a savvy three-generation clientele with big local names and no cover. Toad enjoys good acoustics but not much elbow room—a plus when restless musicians wander into the crowd. 1912 Mass. Ave., Cambridge. (C) **617/497-4950** (info line). T: Red Line to Porter.

T. T. the Bear's Place (★   This no-frills spot generally attracts a young crowd, but 30-somethings will feel comfortable, too. Bookings range from cutting-edge alternative rock to ska to up-and-coming pop acts. New bands predominate early in the week, with more established artists on weekends. Open Sunday and Monday from 7pm to midnight, Tuesday through Saturday from 6pm to 1am. 10 Brookline St., Cambridge. (C) **617/492-0082** or 617/492-BEAR (concert line). www.ttthe bears.com. Cover $3–$15, usually $10 or less. T: Red Line to Central.

BARS & LOUNGES

The Black Rose   Purists might sneer at the Black Rose's touristy location, but performers don't. Sing along with the authentic entertainment at this jam-packed pub and restaurant at the edge of Faneuil Hall Marketplace. 160 State St. (C) **617/742-2286.** www.irishconnection.com. Cover $3–$5. T: Orange or Blue Line to State.

Bristol Lounge (★★★   An elegant room with cushy seating and a fireplace, the Bristol is an oasis anytime, and features a fabulous dessert buffet on week-end nights. There's live jazz every evening, and food until 11:30pm (12:30am on Fri and Sat). In the Four Seasons Hotel, 200 Boylston St. (C) **617/351-2037.** T: Green Line to Arlington.

Casablanca (★★   Students and professors jam this legendary Harvard Square watering hole, especially on weekends. It offers an excellent jukebox, excellent food, and excellent eavesdropping. 40 Brattle St., Cambridge. (C) **617/876-0999.** T: Red Line to Harvard.

Cheers (Beacon Hill)   Try to hide your shock when you enter "the *Cheers* bar" and it looks nothing like the bar on the TV show. (A spin-off in Faneuil Hall Marketplace fills that niche—see the next listing.) This really is a neighborhood bar, but it's far better known for attracting legions of out-of-towners, who find good pub grub and plenty of souvenirs. 84 Beacon St. (C) **617/227-9605.** www.cheersboston.com. T: Green Line to Arlington.

Cheers (Faneuil Hall Marketplace)   Blatantly but good-naturedly courting fans of the sitcom, this bar centers on an area that exactly replicates the set of the TV show. Go ahead, you know you want to. Quincy Market Building, South Canopy. (C) **617/227-0150.** www.cheersboston.com. Cover $5 for live entertainment. T: Green or Blue Line to Government Center, or Orange Line to Haymarket.

DeLux Cafe *✦* Ultracool but never obnoxious about it, the DeLux is one of the classiest dives around. The funky decor, selection of microbrews, and veggie-friendly ethnic menu attract a cross-section of the South End, from off-duty chefs to yuppies. 100 Chandler St. ℂ **617/338-5258**. T: Orange Line to Back Bay.

Flat Top Johnny's *✦✦* A spacious, loud room with a bar and 12 red-topped pool tables, Flat Top Johnny's has a funky neighborhood feel despite being in a rather sterile office-retail complex. Open weekdays noon to 1am, weekends 3pm to 1am. 1 Kendall Sq., Cambridge. ℂ **617/494-9565**. www.flattopjohnnys.com. Pool $10/hr. Sun–Thurs, $12/hr. Fri–Sat. T: Red Line to Kendall/MIT.

The Fours One of Boston's best and best-known sports bars, the Fours is about one football field away from the FleetCenter. Festooned with sports memorabilia and TVs, it's a madhouse before Celtics and Bruins games—and a promising place to pick up an extra ticket. 166 Canal St. ℂ **617/720-4455**. T: Green or Orange Line to North Station.

Grendel's Den *✦* A vestige of pre-franchise Harvard Square, this cozy subterranean space is *the* place to celebrate turning 21. Recent grads and grad students dominate, but Grendel's has been so popular for so long that it also gets its share of Gen Y's parents. 89 Winthrop St., Cambridge. ℂ **617/491-1050**. www.grendelsden.com. T: Red Line to Harvard.

Hard Rock Cafe *Kids* This link in the chain is a fun one—just ask the other tourists in line with you. The bar is shaped like a guitar, and the stained-glass windows glorify rock stars. Memorabilia of Jimi Hendrix, Elvis Presley, Madonna, local favorites Aerosmith and the Cars, and others decorates the walls. 131 Clarendon St. ℂ **617/424-ROCK**. www.hardrock.com. T: Orange Line to Back Bay or Green Line to Copley.

John Harvard's Brew House *✦✦* This subterranean Harvard Square hangout pumps out terrific English-style brews in a clublike setting and prides itself on its food. 33 Dunster St., Cambridge. ℂ **617/868-3585**. www.johnharvards.com. T: Red Line to Harvard.

Mr. Dooley's Boston Tavern *✦✦* Sometimes an expertly poured Guinness is all you need. If one of the nicest bartenders in the city pours it, so much the better. This Financial District spot offers many imported beers on tap, live music, and a menu of pub favorites. 77 Broad St. ℂ **617/338-5656**. www.somers pubs.com. Cover $3–$5 Fri–Sat. T: Orange Line to State or Blue Line to Aquarium.

The Purple Shamrock This rowdy, fun place near Faneuil Hall Marketplace attracts wall-to-wall 20-somethings with DJs and cover bands. 1 Union St. ℂ **617/ 227-2060**. www.irishconnection.com. Cover $3–$6 Thurs–Sat. T: Green or Blue Line to Government Center, or Orange Line to Haymarket.

Top of the Hub *✦✦✦* The 52nd-story view of greater Boston from this appealing lounge is especially lovely at sunset. There's music and dancing nightly. Dress is casual but neat. Prudential Center, 800 Boylston St. ℂ **617/536-1775**. T: Green Line E to Prudential.

Side Trips from Boston: Lexington & Concord, the North Shore & Plymouth

by Marie Morris

Besides being, in the words of Oliver Wendell Holmes, "the hub of the solar system," Boston is the hub of a network of wonderful day trips and longer excursions. The destinations in this chapter are lively communities where you'll find sights and attractions of great beauty and historical significance. Exploring can take as little as half a day or as long as a week or more.

WEST OF BOSTON If time is short, combine a visit to Cambridge (see chapter 4) with a trip to Lexington and Concord for a hefty dose of American history. The route that Paul Revere took out of Boston on April 18, 1775, is tough to follow—he started by crossing the harbor in a rowboat, for one thing—but his fellow rider William Dawes cut through Harvard Square. Both proceeded to warn the colonists that British troops were on the march.

NORTH OF BOSTON Great prosperity came to eastern Massachusetts after the Revolution, as the new nation took advantage of the lifting of British trade barriers. Today, the spoils of the China trade adorn mansions and public edifices in seaside locales such as Marblehead, Salem, and Cape Ann. Fishing is still an important industry, but these days the area caters more to commuters and tourists than to those who make their living from the sea. A worthwhile detour from the north or west is Lowell, a once-decrepit mill town where tourism is now the largest industry.

SOUTH OF BOSTON The communities between Boston and Cape Cod are mostly commuter suburbs. The prime sightseeing destination is Plymouth, one of the oldest permanent European settlements in North America. It's a pleasant place where

---

Tips Planning Pointers

If you have a few days to explore and history is your main motivation, consider approaching the area in roughly chronological order. Start in Plymouth with the Pilgrims, and then move on to Lexington and Concord to learn about the rebellious colonists. Finally, visit the North Shore and Cape Ann, which flourished after the Revolution. If you lack the time or inclination to make your own arrangements, consider an escorted tour. One reliable company is Gray Line's **Brush Hill Tours**, 435 High St., Randolph (© **800/343-1328** or 781/986-6100; www.grayline.com).

you can walk in the footsteps of the Pilgrims—and of the countless out-of-towners who flock here in summer and at Thanksgiving. Farther south, the old whaling port of New Bedford makes an interesting detour.

1 Lexington ★

9 miles NW of downtown Boston; 6 miles NW of Cambridge; 6 miles E of Concord

A country village turned prosperous suburb, Lexington takes great pride in its history. It's a pleasant town with some engaging destinations, but it lacks the atmosphere and abundant attractions of nearby Concord. Being sure to leave time for a tour of the Buckman Tavern, you can schedule as little as a couple of hours to explore downtown Lexington, possibly en route to Concord. A visit can also fill a half or full day. The town contains part of Minute Man National Historical Park, which is definitely worth a visit.

The shooting phase of the Revolutionary War started here, with a skirmish on the town green. It began when British troops clashed with local militia members, who were known as "Minutemen" for their ability to assemble on short notice. British soldiers marched from Boston to Lexington late on April 18, 1775. Tipped off, Paul Revere and William Dawes rode ahead to sound the warning. They did their job so well that the alarm came long before the advancing forces. The Lexington Minutemen, under the command of Capt. John Parker, got the word shortly after midnight, but the redcoats were still several hours away. The colonists repaired to their homes and the Buckman Tavern. Five hours later, some 700 British troops under Major Pitcairn arrived.

A tense standoff ensued. Three times Pitcairn ordered them to disperse, but the patriots—fewer than 100, and some accounts say 77—refused. Parker called: "Stand your ground. Don't fire unless fired upon, but if they mean to have a war, let it begin here!" Finally the captain, perhaps realizing as the sky grew light how badly outnumbered his men were, gave the order to fall back.

As the Minutemen began to scatter, a shot rang out. One British company charged into the fray, and the colonists attempted to regroup as Pitcairn tried unsuccessfully to call off his troops. Nobody knows who started the shooting, but when it was over, eight militia members, including a drummer boy, lay dead, and 10 were wounded.

ESSENTIALS

GETTING THERE   From downtown Boston, take Storrow or Memorial Drive to Route 2. Follow Route 2 from Cambridge through Belmont, exit at Route 4/225, and follow signs to downtown Lexington. Or take Route 128 (I-95) to Exit 31A and follow signs. If it's not rush hour, allow about 35 minutes. **Massachusetts Avenue** (the same "Mass. Ave." you saw in Boston and Cambridge) runs through the center of town. There's metered parking on the street and in several municipal lots, and free parking at the National Heritage Museum and the National Historical Park.

Tips **Poetry in Motion**

Before you visit Lexington and Concord, you might want to read **"Paul Revere's Ride,"** Henry Wadsworth Longfellow's classic but historically questionable poem that dramatically chronicles the events of April 18 and 19, 1775.

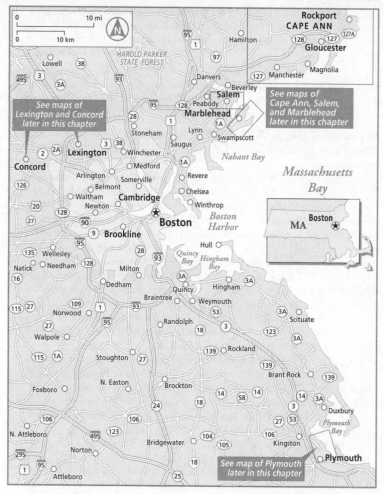

The **MBTA** (© **800/392-6100** outside Mass., or 617/222-3200; www.mbta. com) runs bus routes no. 62 (Bedford) and 76 (Hanscom) to Lexington from Alewife station, the last stop on the Red Line. The one-way fare is 90¢; the trip takes about 25 minutes. Buses operate Monday through Saturday every hour during the day and every half-hour during rush periods. There's no Sunday service. There's no public transit between Lexington and Concord.

VISITOR INFORMATION The Chamber of Commerce **visitor center,** 1875 Mass. Ave. (© **781/862-2480;** www.lexingtonchamber.org), distributes maps and information. The **Greater Merrimack Valley Convention & Visitors Bureau** (© **800/443-3332** or 978/459-6150; www.merrimackvalley.org) includes Lexington.

GETTING AROUND Downtown Lexington is easily negotiable on foot, and most of the attractions are within walking distance. If you prefer not to walk to the Munroe Tavern and the National Heritage Museum (see below), buses no. 62 and 76 pass by on Mass. Ave.

The **Liberty Ride** (✆ **781/862-0500,** ext. 702; www.libertyride.us) is a narrated tour that connects the local attractions. It operates from 10am to 5pm daily April through October; check ahead to confirm that it's running before you plan on it. The fare (good for a full day) is $10 for adults, $5 for children 5 to 17.

SPECIAL EVENTS   Patriots Day, a state holiday observed on the third Monday in April, commemorates the start of the Revolution. Celebrations include a re-enactment of the battle and other festivities.

EXPLORING THE HISTORIC SITES

Minute Man National Historical Park is in Lexington, Concord, and Lincoln (see "Concord," below).

Start your visit to Lexington at the **visitor center,** on the town common or "Battle Green." It's open daily from 9am to 5pm (10am–4pm Dec–Mar). A diorama and accompanying narrative illustrate the Battle of Lexington. The *Minuteman* **statue** (1900) on the green is of Capt. John Parker, who commanded the militia. The **Old Revolutionary Monument** (1799) marks the grave of seven of the eight colonists who died in the conflict, which the **Line of Battle Boulder** commemorates. The **Memorial to the Lexington Minutemen** bears the names of the men who fell in the battle. Across Mass. Ave., near Clarke Street, is the **Old Belfry,** a reproduction of the freestanding bell that sounded the alarm the day of the battle. **Ye Olde Burying Ground,** at the west end of the green, dates to 1690 and contains Parker's grave. A stop at the visitor center and a walk around the monuments takes about half an hour, and gives a good sense of what went on here and why the participants are still held in such high esteem.

Three important destinations in Lexington were among the country's first historic houses when their restoration began in the 1920s. The **Lexington Historical Society** (✆ **781/862-1703;** www.lexingtonhistory.org) operates all three. Currently headquartered in the Munroe Tavern, the society is in the process of restoring a building on Depot Square (downtown, off Mass. Ave. near the Battle Green) that will hold exhibits, offices, and a gift shop.

The **Buckman Tavern** *ⓡⓡ*, 1 Bedford St. (✆ **781/862-5598**), built around 1710, is the only building still on the green that was here on April 19, 1775. If time is short and you have to pick just one house to visit, this is it. The interior has been restored to approximate its appearance on the day of the battle. You'll see the original bar and front door, which has a hole in it from a British musket ball. The Minutemen gathered here to wait for word of British troop movements, and brought their wounded here after the conflict. On the excellent tour, costumed guides describe the history of the building and its inhabitants, explain the battle, and discuss colonial life.

Within walking distance is the **Hancock-Clarke House,** 36 Hancock St. (✆ **781/861-0928**). Samuel Adams and John Hancock, who had left Boston several days earlier upon learning that the British were after them, were sleeping here (or trying to) when Revere arrived. They fled to nearby Woburn. Built around 1698 by Hancock's grandfather and lavishly improved by his uncle, the house, restored and furnished in colonial style, contains the Historical Society's museum.

The British took over the **Munroe Tavern** *ⓡ*, 1332 Mass. Ave. (about 1 mile east of the green), to use as their headquarters and field hospital. The taproom ceiling still has a bullet hole made by a careless soldier. The 1690 building holds many fascinating artifacts. The furniture, carefully preserved by the Munroe

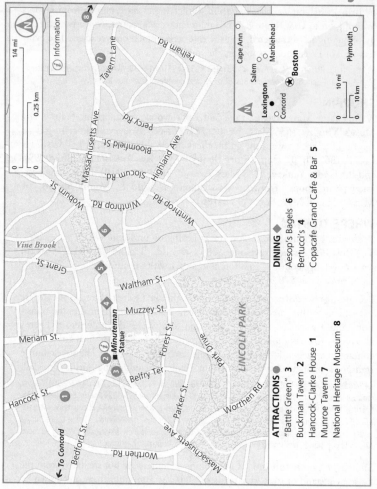

DINING ◆
Aesop's Bagels **6**
Bertucci's **4**
Copacafe Grand Cafe & Bar **5**

ATTRACTIONS ●
"Battle Green" **3**
Buckman Tavern **2**
Hancock-Clarke House **1**
Munroe Tavern **7**
National Heritage Museum **8**

family, includes the table and chair where President Washington dined in 1789. The historically accurate gardens at the rear (free admission) are beautifully planted and maintained.

All three houses are open for guided tours April through October, Monday through Saturday from 10am to 5pm and Sunday from 1 to 5pm. The Buckman Tavern is also open in late March and November. Admission for adults is $5 per house, $8 for two houses, $12 for all three; for seniors, $7 for two houses, $11 for all three; for children 6 to 16, $3 per house, $5 for two, $7 for three. The last tour starts 30 minutes before closing time; tours take 30 to 45 minutes. Call for information about group tours, which are offered by appointment.

National Heritage Museum ★★ *Kids* This fascinating museum explores history through popular culture. It makes an entertaining complement to the colonial focus of the rest of the town. The installations in the six exhibition spaces change regularly; you can start with another dose of the Revolution, the permanent exhibit *Lexington Alarm'd.* Other topics have ranged from George Washington to U.S. Route 1 to metal lunchboxes. Lectures, concerts, and family programs are also offered, and the cafe serves lunch on weekdays. The Scottish Rite of Freemasonry sponsors the museum.

33 Marrett Rd., Rte. 2A (at Mass. Ave.). (C) **781/861-6559** or 781/861-9638. www.monh.org. Free admission. Mon–Sat 10am–5pm; Sun noon–5pm. Bus: 62 or 76 from downtown Lexington to Rte. 2A.

SHOPPING

A stroll along **Mass. Ave.** near the center of town won't disappoint. Start at **The Muse's Window,** 1656 Mass. Ave. (C) **781/274-6873**), an excellent crafts gallery. As you head back toward the green, check out **Waldenbooks,** 1713 Mass. Ave. (C) **781/862-7870**); **Upper Story Books,** 1730 Mass. Ave. (C) **781/862-0999**); and the **Crafty Yankee,** 1838 Mass. Ave. (C) **781/861-1219**). One of the best-known yarn shops in eastern Massachusetts is **Wild & Woolly Studio,** 7A Meriam St., off Mass. Ave. (C) **781/861-7717**).

WHERE TO STAY

Bedford is 15 minutes from downtown Lexington on Route 4/225, across I-95. The **Boston/Bedford Travelodge,** 285 Great Rd., Bedford (C) **781/275-6120; www.travelodge.com**), is an affordable motel with an outdoor pool. A double room runs about $79 in high season.

Renaissance Bedford Hotel ⭐   The sights in Lexington and Concord are convenient to this three-story, lodge-style hotel, which neatly makes the transition from a weekday business destination to a weekend family resort. There's also plenty to do without leaving the property. The well-maintained guest rooms contain oversize work desks; larger units have king-size beds. The hotel shuttle transports guests to destinations within 5 miles, including the Burlington Mall.

44 Middlesex Tpk., Bedford, MA 01730. (C) **800/228-9290** or 781/275-5500. Fax 781/275-3042. www. renaissancehotels.com. 284 units. Sun–Thurs $159–$249 double; Fri–Sat $99–$229 double. Extra person $15. Children under 19 stay free in parent's room. Weekend packages and senior and AAA discounts available. AE, DC, DISC, MC, V. **Amenities:** Restaurant (eclectic); lounge; indoor pool; indoor/outdoor tennis courts; fitness center; Jacuzzi; sauna; shuttle; business center; 24-hr. room service; laundry service; dry cleaning. *In room:* A/C, TV w/pay movies, high-speed Internet access, minibar, coffeemaker, hair dryer, iron.

Sheraton Lexington Inn   Overlooking the interstate but sheltered from the noise by a stand of trees, this two-story hotel is 5 minutes from downtown by car. It offers the chain's usual amenities, including pillow-top beds; some units have high-speed Internet access. Rooms are large enough to hold a wing chair or couch, and some have balconies. It's a decent choice for families, and popular with travelers who have business on the Route 128 high-tech corridor.

727 Marrett Rd. (Exit 30B off I-95), Lexington, MA 02173. (C) **800/325-3535** or 781/862-8700. Fax 781/863-0404. www.sheraton.com. 119 units. $89–$219 double; $199–$369 suite. Extra person $10. AAA and AARP discounts available. AE, DC, DISC, MC, V. **Amenities:** Restaurant (American); lounge; outdoor pool; exercise room; business center; limited room service. *In room:* A/C, TV, dataport, coffeemaker, iron.

WHERE TO DINE

If you're not continuing to Concord, which has more interesting dining options, Lexington offers some pleasant choices. The fresh soups and sandwiches at the cafe at the **National Heritage Museum** (see above) make it a popular spot for lunch on weekdays. **Bertucci's,** 1777 Mass. Ave. (C) **781/860-9000**), is a branch of the family-friendly pizzeria chain. **Aesop's Bagels,** 1666 Mass. Ave. (C) **781/674-2990**), is a good place to pick up a light meal. **Copacafe Grand Cafe & Bar,** 1727 Mass. Ave. (C) **978/862-6622; www.copacafelex.com**), serves luscious pastries, and excellent coffee daily from early morning through early evening.

2 Concord

18 miles NW of Boston; 15 miles NW of Cambridge; 6 miles W of Lexington

Concord (say "conquered") revels in its legacy as a center of groundbreaking thought and its role in the country's political and intellectual history. A visit can easily fill a day; if your interests are specialized or time is short, a half-day excursion is reasonable. For an excellent overview of town history, start your visit at the **Concord Museum.**

After just a little time in this lovely town, you may find yourself adopting the local attitude toward two of its most famous residents: Ralph Waldo Emerson, who comes across as a well-respected uncle figure, and Henry David Thoreau, everyone's favorite eccentric cousin. Long before they wandered the countryside, the first official battle of the Revolutionary War took place at the North Bridge, now part of Minute Man National Historical Park. By the middle of the 19th century, Concord was the center of the Transcendentalist movement. Homes of Emerson, Thoreau, Nathaniel Hawthorne, and Louisa May Alcott are open to visitors, as is the authors' final resting place, Sleepy Hollow Cemetery.

ESSENTIALS

GETTING THERE   From Lexington (10 min. by car), take Route 2A west from Mass. Ave. (Rte. 4/225) at the National Heritage Museum; follow the BATTLE ROAD signs. From Boston and Cambridge (30–40 min.), take Route 2 into Lincoln and stay in the right lane. Where the main road makes a sharp left, go straight onto Cambridge Turnpike, and follow signs to HISTORIC CONCORD. To go directly to Walden Pond, use the left lane, take what's now Route 2/2A another mile or so, and turn left onto Route 126. There's parking throughout town and at the attractions.

The **commuter rail** (© 800/392-6100 outside Mass., or 617/222-3200; www.mbta.com) takes about 45 minutes from North Station in Boston, with a stop at Porter Square in Cambridge. The round-trip fare is $10. The station is about ¾ of a mile over flat terrain from the town center. There is no bus service from Boston to Concord, and no public transit between Concord and Lexington.

VISITOR INFORMATION   The **Chamber of Commerce,** 100 Main St., Suite 310–12 (© 978/369-3120; www.concordmachamber.org), maintains a visitor center at 58 Main St., behind Middlesex Savings Bank, 1 block south of Monument Square. It's open daily 9:30am to 4:30pm from April through October; public restrooms in the same building are open year-round. Guided walking tours are available on weekends. Weekday and group tours are available by appointment. The community (**www.concordma.com**) and town (**www.concordnet. org**) websites include visitor information. You can also contact the **Greater Merrimack Valley Convention & Visitors Bureau** (© 800/443-3332 or 978/459-6150; www.merrimackvalley.org).

GETTING AROUND   Major attractions are within walking distance of downtown. If you're trying to stop everywhere in a day or are visiting Walden Pond or Great Meadows, you'll need a car.

SEEING THE SIGHTS

LITERARY LANDMARKS & HISTORIC ATTRACTIONS

Concord Museum ★★ (Kids)   Just when you're (understandably) suspecting that everything interesting in this area started on April 18, 1775, and ended the next day, this superb museum sets you straight. It's a great place to start your visit to the town. The **History Galleries** ★★ explore the question "Why Concord?"

Artifacts, murals, films, maps, documents, and other presentations illustrate the town's role as a Native American settlement, Revolutionary War battleground, 19th-century intellectual center, and focal point of the 20th-century historic preservation movement. One of the lanterns that signaled Paul Revere from the Old North Church is on display. You'll also see the contents of Ralph Waldo Emerson's study and a large collection of Henry David Thoreau's belongings. Pick up a **family activity pack** 🛆 as you enter and use the games and reproduction artifacts (including a quill pen and powder horn) to give the kids a hands-on feel for life in the past.

Cambridge Tpk. at Lexington Rd. 🕐 **978/369-9609** (recorded info) or 978/369-9763. www.concordmuseum. org. Admission $8 adults, $7 seniors and students, $5 children under 16. June–Aug daily 9am–5pm; Apr–May and Sept–Dec Mon–Sat 9am–5pm, Sun noon–5pm; Jan–Mar Mon–Sat 11am–4pm, Sun 1–4pm. Follow Lexington Rd. out of Concord Center and bear right at museum onto Cambridge Tpk.; entrance is on left. Parking allowed on road.

The Old Manse 🛆

The engaging history of this home touches on the military and the literary, but it's mostly the story of a family. The Rev. William Emerson built the Old Manse in 1770 and watched the Battle of Concord from his yard. For almost 170 years, the house was home to his widow, her second husband, their descendants, and two famous friends. Nathaniel Hawthorne and his bride, Sophia Peabody, moved in after their marriage in 1842 and stayed for 3 years. As a wedding present, Henry David Thoreau sowed the vegetable garden for them. This is also where William's grandson Ralph Waldo Emerson wrote the essay "Nature." Today, you'll see mementos and memorabilia of the Emerson and Ripley families and of the Hawthornes, who scratched notes on two windows with Sophia's diamond ring.

269 Monument St. (at North Bridge). 🕐 **978/369-3909.** www.thetrustees.org. Guided tour $7.50 adults, $6.50 seniors and students, $5 children 6–12, $22 families. Mid-Apr to Oct Mon–Sat 10am–5pm, Sun and holidays noon–5pm (last tour at 4:30pm). Closed Nov to mid-Apr. From Concord Center, follow Monument St. to North Bridge parking lot (on right); Old Manse is on left.

Orchard House 🛆🛆🛆 *Kids*

Little Women (1868), Louisa May Alcott's best-known and most popular work, was written and set at Orchard House. Seeing the family home brings the Alcotts to life for legions of female visitors and their pleasantly surprised male companions. Fans won't want to miss the excellent tour, copiously illustrated with heirlooms. Serious buffs can check in advance for information on special events and holiday programs, some of which require reservations.

Louisa's father, the writer and educator Amos Bronson Alcott, created Orchard House by joining and restoring two homes. The family lived here from 1858 to 1877, socializing in the same circles as Emerson, Thoreau, and Hawthorne. Other relatives served as the models for the characters in *Little Women*. Anna ("Meg"), the eldest, was an amateur actress, and May ("Amy") a talented artist. Elizabeth ("Beth"), a gifted musician, died before the family moved to this house. Their mother, the social activist Abigail May Alcott, frequently assumed the role of breadwinner—Bronson, Louisa wrote in her journal, had "no gift for money making."

Note: Call before visiting; an extensive preservation project is under way and may be continuing when you're here.

399 Lexington Rd. 🕐 **978/369-4118.** www.louisamayalcott.org. Guided tour $8 adults, $7 seniors and students, $5 children 6–17, $20 families. Apr–Oct Mon–Sat 10am–4:30pm, Sun 1–4:30pm; Nov–Mar Mon–Fri 11am–3pm, Sat 10am–4:30pm, Sun 1–4:30pm. Closed Jan 1–15. Follow Lexington Rd. out of Concord Center and bear left at Concord Museum; house is on left. Overflow parking across the street.

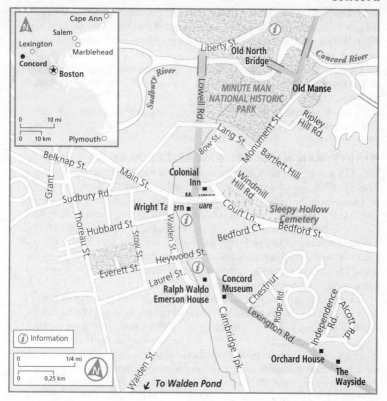

Ralph Waldo Emerson House

This house offers an instructive look at the days when a philosopher could attain the status we now associate with rock stars. Emerson, also an essayist and poet, lived here from 1835 until his death, in 1882. He moved here after marrying his second wife, Lydia Jackson, whom he called "Lydian"; she called him "Mr. Emerson," as the staff still does. The tour gives a good look at his personal side and at the fashionably ornate interior decoration of the time. You'll see original furnishings and some of Emerson's personal effects.

28 Cambridge Tpk. ℂ **978/369-2236.** Guided tours $6 adults, $4 seniors and students. Call to arrange group tours (10 people or more). Mid-Apr to Oct Thurs–Sat 10am–4:30pm, Sun 2–4:30pm. Closed Nov to mid-Apr. Follow Cambridge Tpk. out of Concord Center; just before Concord Museum, house is on right.

Sleepy Hollow Cemetery

Follow the signs for AUTHOR'S RIDGE and climb the hill to the graves of some of the town's literary lights, including the Alcotts, Emerson, Hawthorne, and Thoreau. Emerson's bears no religious symbols, just an uncarved quartz boulder. Thoreau's grave is nearby; at his funeral, in 1862, his old friend Emerson concluded his eulogy with these words: ". . . wherever there is knowledge, wherever there is virtue, wherever there is beauty, he will find a home."

Entrance on Rte. 62 W. ℂ **978/318-3233.** www.concordnet.org. Daily 7am to dusk, weather permitting. Call ahead for wheelchair access. No buses allowed.

The Wayside

The Wayside was Nathaniel Hawthorne's home from 1852 until his death, in 1864. The Alcotts also lived here (the girls called it "the yellow house"), as did Harriett Lothrop, who wrote the *Five Little Peppers* books under the pen name Margaret Sidney and owned most of the current furnishings. The Wayside is part of Minute Man National Historical Park, and the fascinating 45-minute ranger-led tour illuminates the occupants' lives and the house's crazy-quilt architecture. The exhibit in the barn (free admission) consists of audio presentations and figures of the authors. Call ahead to double-check hours, which are subject to change.

455 Lexington Rd. ℂ 978/369-6975. www.nps.gov/mima/wayside. Guided tour $4 adults, free for children under 17. May–Oct Thurs–Tues 10am–4:30pm. Closed Nov–Apr. Follow Lexington Rd. out of Concord Center past Concord Museum and Orchard House. Parking across the street.

MINUTE MAN NATIONAL HISTORICAL PARK ☆☆

This 970-acre park preserves the scene of the first Revolutionary War battle, on April 19, 1775. Encouraged by their victory at Lexington, the British continued to Concord in search of stockpiled arms (which the colonists had already moved). Warned of the advance, the Minutemen crossed the North Bridge, evading the "regulars" standing guard, and awaited reinforcements on a hilltop. The British searched nearby homes and burned any guns they found, and the colonials, seeing the smoke, mistakenly thought the soldiers were burning the town. The gunfire that ensued, the opening salvo of the Revolution, is remembered as "the shot heard round the world."

The park is open daily year-round. A visit can take as little as half an hour—for a jaunt to the North Bridge (a reproduction)—or as long as half a day (or more), if you stop at both visitor centers and perhaps participate in a ranger-led program. Travelers in 2004–2005 may not be able to cross the bridge, because it's scheduled for replacement—which should also be quite interesting. To reach the bridge from Concord Center, follow Monument Street until you see the parking lot on the right. Walk a short distance to the bridge, stopping along the unpaved path to read and hear the narratives. On one side of the bridge is a plaque commemorating the British soldiers who died in the Revolutionary War. On the other side is Daniel Chester French's *Minute Man* statue, engraved with a stanza of the poem Emerson wrote for the dedication ceremony in 1876.

You can also start at the **North Bridge Visitor Center** ☆, 174 Liberty St., off Monument Street (ℂ **978/369-6993**; www.nps.gov/mima), which overlooks the Concord River and the bridge. A diorama and video illustrate the Battle of Concord; exhibits include uniforms, weapons, and tools of colonial and British soldiers. Park rangers lead programs and answer questions. Outside, picnicking is allowed, and the scenery (especially the fall foliage) is lovely. The center is open daily from 9am to 5:30pm (until 4pm in winter).

At the Lexington end of the park, the **Minute Man Visitor Center** ☆ (ℂ **781/862-7753**; www.nps.gov/mima), off Route 2A, about ½-mile west of I-95 Exit 30B, is open daily from 9am to 5pm (until 4pm in winter). The park includes the first 4 miles of the Battle Road, the route the defeated British troops took as they left Concord. At the visitor center, you'll see a fascinating multi-media program on the Revolution, informational displays, and a 40-foot mural illustrating the battle. On summer weekends, rangers lead tours of the park—call ahead for times. The **Battle Road Trail**, a 5½-mile interpretive path, carries pedestrian, wheelchair, and bicycle traffic. Panels and granite markers display information about the area's military, social, and natural history.

Also on the park grounds, on Old Bedford Road, is the **Hartwell Tavern.** Costumed interpreters demonstrate daily life on a farm and in a tavern in colonial days. It's open from 9:30am to 5pm, daily June through August and weekends only in April, May, September, and October. Admission is free.

NEARBY SIGHTS

DeCordova Museum and Sculpture Park ⋆⋆   Indoors and out, this museum shows the work of American contemporary and modern artists, with an emphasis on living New England residents. The main building, on a leafy hilltop, overlooks a pond and the public sculpture park. The museum also has a roof garden and a sculpture terrace. Picnicking is allowed in the sculpture park; bring your lunch or buy it at the cafe (open Tues–Sun 11am–3pm). Free tours of the main galleries start at 1pm Wednesday and Sunday year-round; sculpture-park tours run May through October on Saturday and Sunday at 1pm.

51 Sandy Pond Rd., Lincoln. ⓒ 781/259-8355. www.decordova.org. Museum: $6 adults; $4 seniors, students, and children 6–12. Tues–Sun and Mon holidays 11am–5pm. Sculpture park: Free admission. Daily daylight hours. From Rte. 2 east, take Rte. 126 south to Baker Bridge Rd. (1st left after Walden Pond). When it ends, go right onto Sandy Pond Rd.; museum is on left. From I-95, take Exit 28B, follow Trapelo Rd. 2½ miles to Sandy Pond Rd., then follow signs.

Gropius House ⋆   Architect Walter Gropius (1883–1969), founder of the Bauhaus school of design, built this home for his family in 1938. Having taken a job at the Harvard Graduate School of Design, he worked with Marcel Breuer to design the hilltop house, now maintained by the Society for the Preservation of New England Antiquities. He used traditional materials such as clapboard, brick, and fieldstone, with components then seldom seen in domestic architecture, including glass blocks and welded steel. Breuer designed many of the furnishings, which were made for the family at the Bauhaus. Decorated as it was in the last decade of Gropius's life, the house affords a revealing look at his life, career, and philosophy.

68 Baker Bridge Rd., Lincoln. ⓒ 781/259-8098. www.spnea.org. Admission $10, SPNEA members and residents of Lincoln free. Tours on the hour June–Oct 15 Wed–Sun 11am–4pm; Oct 16–May Sat–Sun 11am–4pm. From Rte. 2 east, take Rte. 126 south to left on Baker Bridge Rd. (1st left after Walden Pond); house is on right. From I-95, take Exit 28B, follow Trapelo Rd. to Sandy Pond Rd., go left onto Baker Bridge Rd.; house is on left.

WILDERNESS RETREATS

The titles of Henry David Thoreau's first two published works can serve as starting points: *A Week on the Concord and Merrimack Rivers* (1849) and *Walden* (1854).

To see the area from water level, there's no need to take a week; 2 hours or so should suffice. Rent a **canoe** ⋆ at the **South Bridge Boathouse,** 496 Main St. (ⓒ **978/369-9438**), just over half a mile west of the center of town, and paddle to the North Bridge and back. Rates are about $12 per hour on weekends, less on weekdays.

At **Walden Pond State Reservation** ⋆⋆, 915 Walden St., Rte. 126 (ⓒ **978/369-3254;** www.state.ma.us/dem/parks/wldn.htm), a pile of stones marks the site of the cabin where Thoreau lived from 1845 to 1847. Today the picturesque reservation is an extremely popular destination for walking (a path circles the pond), swimming, and fishing. Although crowded, it's well preserved and insulated from development, making it less difficult than you might expect to imagine Thoreau's experience. Call for the schedule of interpretive programs. No dogs or bikes are allowed. Parking costs $5. In good weather, the lot fills early every day—call before setting out, as the rangers turn away visitors if the park has reached capacity (1,000). To get here from Concord Center, take Walden Street (Rte. 126) south, cross Route 2, and follow signs to the parking lot.

Another Thoreau haunt, an especially popular destination for birders, is **Great Meadows National Wildlife Refuge** ⊛, Weir Hill Road, Sudbury (© **978/443-4661;** http://greatmeadows.fws.gov). The Concord portion of the 3,400-acre refuge includes 2½ miles of walking trails around man-made ponds that attract abundant wildlife. More than 200 species of native and migratory birds have been recorded. The refuge is open daily from sunrise to sunset; admission is free. Follow Route 62 (Bedford St.) east out of Concord Center for 1⅓ miles, then turn left onto Monsen Road.

SHOPPING

Downtown Concord, off **Monument Square,** is a terrific shopping destination. Here you'll find the **Concord Toy Shop,** 4 Walden St. (© **978/369-2553**); the **Grasshopper Shop,** 36 Main St. (© **978/369-8295**), which carries women's clothing and accessories; jewelry and art at **Catseye,** 48 Monument Sq. (© **978/369-8377**); and the **Concord Bookshop,** 65 Main St. (© **978/371-2672**). The compact shopping district in **West Concord,** along Route 62, boasts the old-fashioned **West Concord 5 & 10,** 106 Commonwealth Ave. (© **978/369-9011**), which carries everything from light bulbs to lace.

WHERE TO STAY

The **Best Western at Historic Concord,** 740 Elm St. (© **800/528-1234,** 800/780-7234, or 978/369-6100), is just off Route 2, about 2 miles from the center of town. The motel has a fitness room and a seasonal outdoor pool. Doubles go for $119 to $149, which includes continental breakfast.

Concord's Colonial Inn ⊛   The main building of the Colonial Inn has overlooked Monument Square since 1716. Like many historic inns, it's not luxurious, but it is comfortable and centrally located. Additions since it became a hotel in 1889 have left the inn large enough to offer modern conveniences (including wireless Internet access) and small enough to feel friendly. It's popular with businesspeople as well as vacationers, especially during foliage season. The 15 original guest rooms—one of which (no. 24) supposedly is haunted—are in great demand. Reserve early if you want to stay in the main inn, which is decorated (surprise, surprise) in colonial style. Rooms in the 1970 Prescott House have country-style decor, and four freestanding buildings hold one-, two-, and three-bedroom suites suitable for long-term stays.

Two lounges serve light meals; sit on the porch and you'll have a front-row seat for the action on Monument Square. The lovely restaurant serves salads, sandwiches, and pasta at lunch, and traditional American fare at dinner. Afternoon tea is served Friday through Sunday; reservations required (© **978/369-2373**).

48 Monument Sq., Concord, MA 01742. © **800/370-9200** or 978/369-9200. Fax 978/371-1533. www.concordscolonialinn.com. 56 units (some w/shower only). Apr–Oct $195–$205 main inn, $159–$189 Prescott House; Nov–Mar $165 main inn, $145 Prescott House. AE, DC, DISC, MC, V. **Amenities:** Restaurant (American), 2 lounges, bar with live jazz and blues on weekends; access to nearby health club ($10); concierge; tour desk; business center; same-day dry cleaning. *In room:* A/C, TV/DVD, wireless Internet access, coffeemaker, hair dryer, iron.

Hawthorne Inn ⊛⊛   This is the quintessential country inn. Built around 1870, it sits on a tree-shaded property across the street from Nathaniel Hawthorne's home, the Wayside. Antiques and handmade quilts enhance the rooms, which aren't huge but are meticulously maintained and gorgeously decorated. Original art is on display throughout, and there's a small pond in the peaceful garden. Personable innkeepers Gregory Burch and Marilyn Mudry, who have been in business for more than 20 years, acquaint interested guests with the philosophical, spiritual, military, and literary aspects of Concord's history.

462 Lexington Rd., Concord, MA 01742. ℭ **978/369-5610**. Fax 978/287-4949. www.concordmass.com. 7 units (some w/shower only). $165–$315 double. Rates include continental breakfast. Extra person $20. Off-season discounts available. AE, DISC, MC, V. From Concord Center, take Lexington Rd. ¼ mile east; inn is on right. *In room:* A/C.

A HISTORIC INN NEARBY

Longfellow's Wayside Inn 🌶🌶 Worth a visit even if you're not spending the night, this delightful institution dates to 1716 and got its name when Henry Wadsworth Longfellow published *Tales of a Wayside Inn* in 1863. Part of a non-profit educational and charitable trust, it claims to be the country's oldest operating inn. All 10 guest rooms are attractively decorated and furnished with antiques, but only two (the most popular, of course) are in the original building. Reserve as early as possible.

In addition to being a popular wedding and honeymoon destination, the inn is the centerpiece of what amounts to a tiny theme park. Buildings on the 106-acre property include the Redstone School of "Mary Had a Little Lamb" fame, a wedding chapel, and a working gristmill. The mill stone grinds the wheat flour and cornmeal used in the inn's baked goods. Old grindstones dot the lawn, a pleasant spot for sunbathing.

In the rambling **dining rooms** 🌶, costumed staff members dish up generous portions of traditional New England fare, which often incorporates produce grown at the inn. The menu changes daily; favorite choices include prime rib, lobster casserole, and strawberry shortcake. You'll see lots of families—this seems to be *the* place for grandparents' birthdays. Food is served Monday through Saturday from 11:30am to 3pm and 5 to 9pm, Sunday from noon to 8pm (dinner menu only). Main courses are $9 to $15 at lunch, $18 to $30 at dinner. Reservations are recommended, especially on weekends.

Wayside Inn Rd., Sudbury, MA 01776. ℭ **800/339-1776** or 978/443-1776. Fax 978/443-8041. www.wayside. org. 10 units (some w/shower only). Summer $122–$155 double. Rates include breakfast. Extra person $15. Packages and off-season discounts available. AE, DC, DISC, MC, V. Closed July 4, Dec 25. From Main St. in Concord, follow Sudbury Rd. to Rte. 20 west; 11 miles after passing I-95, bear right onto Wayside Inn Rd.; inn is on the right. *In room:* A/C.

WHERE TO DINE

See also the **Colonial Inn** and **Longfellow's Wayside Inn,** above. For basic to lavish picnic provisions, stop in downtown Concord at the **Cheese Shop,** 25–31 Walden St. (ℭ **978/369-5778**).

Nashoba Brook Bakery & Café 🌶 AMERICAN   The enticing variety of artisan breads, baked goods, pastries, and from-scratch soups, salads, and sandwiches makes this airy cafe a popular destination throughout the day. The industrial-looking building off West Concord's main street backs up to little Nashoba Brook, which is visible through the glass back wall. Order and pick up at the counter, then grab a seat along the window or near the children's play area. Or order takeout—this is great picnic food.

152 Commonwealth Ave., West Concord. ℭ **978/318-1999**. www.slowrise.com. Sandwiches $5–$6; salads $6–$8 per pound. Mon–Sat 8am–8pm. From Concord Center, follow Main St. (Rte. 62) west, across Rte. 2; bear right at traffic light in front of train station and go 3 blocks. For overflow parking, turn right onto Commonwealth Ave. and right onto Winthrop St.

Tips **North of Boston: Road Rules**

For convenience and flexibility, drive if you can. The trip from Boston to Cape Ann on I-93 and Route 128 takes about an hour. A more leisurely excursion on Routes 1A, 129, and 114 allows you to explore Marblehead and Salem. You can also follow Route 1 to I-95 and Route 128, but don't attempt it during rush hour. To take Route 1A, leave downtown through the Callahan or Ted Williams Tunnel. If you miss the entrance and wind up on I-93, follow signs to Route 1 and pick up Route 1A in Revere. The **North of Boston Convention & Visitors Bureau** (© 800/742-5306 or 978/977-7760; www.northofboston.org) publishes a visitor guide that covers many destinations in this chapter.

---

3 Marblehead ★★★

15 miles NE of Boston; 4 miles SE of Salem

Like an attractive person with a great personality, Marblehead has it all. Scenery, history, architecture, and shopping combine to make it one of the area's most popular day trips for both locals and visitors. The narrow streets of historic "Old Town" lead down to the magnificent harbor that helps make this the self-proclaimed "Yachting Capital of America." The homes along the way have plaques bearing the dates of construction as well as the names of the builders and original occupants—a history lesson without any studying.

Many of the houses have stood since before the Revolutionary War, when Marblehead was a center of merchant shipping. Two historic homes are open for tours. Allow at least a full morning to visit Marblehead, but be flexible, because you may want to hang around.

ESSENTIALS

GETTING THERE   From Boston, take Route 1A north until you see signs in Lynn for Swampscott and Marblehead. Take Lynn Shore Drive to Route 129, and follow it into Marblehead. Or take I-93 or Route 1 to Route 128, then Route 114 through Salem into Marblehead. Except at rush hour, allow 35 to 40 minutes. Parking is tough, especially in Old Town—grab the first spot you see.

MBTA (© 800/392-6100 outside Mass., or 617/222-3200; www.mbta.com) bus no. 441/442 runs from Haymarket (Orange or Green Line) in Boston to downtown Marblehead. During weekday rush periods, bus no. 448/449 connects Marblehead to Downtown Crossing. The trip takes about an hour; the one-way fare is $3.45.

VISITOR INFORMATION   The **Marblehead Chamber of Commerce,** 62 Pleasant St. (© 781/631-2868; www.marbleheadchamber.org or www.visit marblehead.com), is open Monday through Friday from 9am to 5pm. The **information booth** (© 781/639-8469) on Pleasant Street near Spring Street is open May through October, daily from noon to 5pm.

GETTING AROUND   Wear good walking shoes—the car or bus can get you to Marblehead, but it can't negotiate many of the narrow streets of Old Town. The downtown area is fairly compact and moderately hilly.

SPECIAL EVENTS   Sailing regattas take place all summer. **Race Week,** in mid- to late July, draws competitors from across the country. During the **Christmas Walk,** on the first weekend in December, Santa Claus arrives by lobster boat.

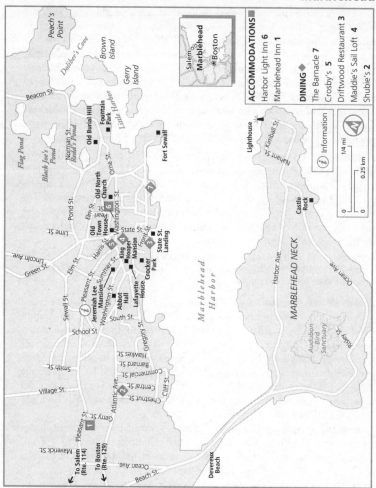

ACCOMMODATIONS ■
Harbor Light Inn **6**
Marblehead Inn **1**

DINING ◆
The Barnacle **7**
Crosby's **5**
Driftwood Restaurant **3**
Maddie's Sail Loft **4**
Shubie's **2**

EXPLORING THE TOWN

A stroll through the winding streets of **Old Town** ★★★ invariably leads to shopping, snacking, or gazing at something picturesque, be it the harbor or a beautiful home. Be sure to spend some time in **Crocker Park** ★★, on the water off Front Street. Especially in warm weather, when boats jam the harbor, the view is breathtaking. The park has benches and allows picnicking. The view from **Fort Sewall,** at the other end of Front Street, is just as mesmerizing. The ruins of the fort, built in the 17th century and rebuilt late in the 18th, are another excellent picnic spot.

Just inland, the **Lafayette House** is a private home at the corner of Hooper and Union streets. Legend has it that one corner of the first floor was chopped off in 1824 to allow Lafayette's carriage to negotiate the turn. In Market Square, on Washington Street near State Street, is the **Old Town House,** a public meeting and gathering place since 1727.

By car or bicycle, the swanky residential community of **Marblehead Neck** ✦ is worth a look. Follow Ocean Avenue across the causeway. Here you can visit the **Audubon Bird Sanctuary** (✆ **800/AUDUBON** or 781/259-9500; www.mass audubon.org); look for the tiny sign at the corner of Risley Ave. Admission is $3 for adults, $2 for seniors and children 3 to 12. Or continue to **Castle Rock** for another eyeful of scenery. At the end of "the Neck," at Harbor and Ocean avenues, is **Chandler Hovey Park,** which has a (closed) lighthouse and a panoramic view. Many inns and B&Bs provide bikes for guests' use; to rent, visit **Marblehead Cycle,** 25 Bessom St., 1 block off Pleasant Street (✆ **781/631-1570;** www. marbleheadcycle.com). Bikes go for $14 for a half day, $20 for a full day.

Abbot Hall A 5-minute stop here (look for the clock tower) is just the ticket if you want to be able to say you did some sightseeing. The town offices and Historical Commission share Abbot Hall with Archibald M. Willard's famous painting *The Spirit of '76* ✦, on display in the Selectmen's Meeting Room. The thrill of recognizing the ubiquitous drummer, drummer boy, and fife player is the main reason to stop here. Cases in the halls contain objects and artifacts from the Historical Society's collections.

Washington Sq. ✆ **781/631-0528.** Free admission. Year-round Mon–Tues and Thurs 8am–5pm, Wed 7:30am–7:30pm, Fri 8am–1pm; May–Oct also open Fri 1–5pm, Sat 9am–6pm, Sun 11am–6pm. From the historic district, follow Washington St. up the hill.

Jeremiah Lee Mansion ✦✦ The prospect of seeing original hand-painted wallpaper in an 18th-century home is reason enough to visit this house, built in 1768 for a wealthy merchant and considered an extraordinary example of pre-Revolutionary Georgian architecture. Original rococo carving and other details complement historically accurate room arrangements, and ongoing restoration and interpretation by the Marblehead Museum & Historical Society place the 18th- and 19th-century furnishings and artifacts in context. The friendly guides welcome questions and are well versed in the history of the home. The lawn and gardens are open to the public.

Across the street is a visitor center that houses two galleries; one shows changing exhibits and the other folk art by the noted primitivist painter J. O. J. Frost, a Marblehead native. The society sponsors **summer walking tours** of Marblehead. Call ahead to see if your schedules match.

✆ **781/631-1768.** Mansion: 161 Washington St. Guided tours $5 adults, $4.50 seniors and students. June to mid-Oct Mon–Sat 10am–4pm. Closed mid-Oct to May. Historical Society: 170 Washington St. Free admission. Year-round Tues–Fri 10am–4pm, June–Oct also open Sat 10am–4pm. Follow Washington St. until it curves right and heads uphill toward Abbot Hall; mansion is on right.

King Hooper Mansion Shipping tycoon Robert Hooper got his nickname because he treated his sailors so well, but it's easy to think he was called "King" because he lived like royalty. Around the corner from the home of Jeremiah Lee (whose sister was the second of Hooper's four wives), the 1728 King Hooper Mansion gained a Georgian addition in 1745. The period furnishings, although not original, give a sense of the life of an 18th-century merchant prince, from the wine cellar to the third-floor ballroom. The building houses the headquarters of the Marblehead Arts Association, which stages exhibits, schedules special events, and runs a gift shop that sells members' work. The mansion has a lovely garden; enter through the gate at the right of the house.

8 Hooper St. ✆ **781/631-2608.** www.marbleheadarts.org. Donation requested for tour. Tues–Sat 10am–4pm; Sun 1–5pm. Call ahead; no tours during private parties. Where Washington St. curves at the foot of hill near Lee Mansion, look for the colorful sign.

SHOPPING 😊😊

One of Marblehead's claims to fame is its excellent retail scene. Shops, boutiques, and galleries abound in **Old Town** and on **Atlantic Avenue** and the east end of **Pleasant Street.**

The most unusual shop in town is **Antiquewear,** 82 Front St. (✆ 781/639-0070; http://users.primushost.com/~antiquew), near the town pier. It sells 19th-century buttons ingeniously fashioned into women's and men's jewelry of all descriptions. Other good stops include **Arnould Gallery,** 111 Washington St. (✆ 781/631-6366); **Artists & Authors,** 108 Washington St. (✆ 781/639-0400; www.artists-authors.com), which carries rare books and fine art; **Cargo Unlimited,** 82 Washington St. (✆ 781/631-1112; www.cargounlimited.com), for home furnishings and accessories; **Erlich Gallery,** 96 Washington St. (✆ 781/631-1202); **Lavender Home & Table,** 7 Pleasant St. (✆ 781/639-2238), which specializes in French country wares; and the **Marblehead Toy Shop,** 44–48 Atlantic Ave. (✆ 781/631-9900).

WHERE TO STAY

The accommodations listings of the **Chamber of Commerce** (✆ 781/631-2868; www.marbleheadchamber.org) include many of the town's innumerable inns and B&Bs. Contact the chamber or consult one of the agencies listed in chapter 4 under "Accommodations."

Harbor Light Inn 😊😊   Two Federal-era mansions make up this gracious inn, a stone's throw from the Old Town House. From the wood floors to the 1729 beams (in a 3rd-floor room) to the swimming pool, it's both historic and relaxing. Rooms are comfortably furnished in period style, with some lovely antiques; most have canopy or four-poster beds. Eleven have working fireplaces, and five of those have double Jacuzzis. The best rooms, on the top floor at the back of the building (away from the street), have gorgeous harbor views. If you don't book one, you can still take in the scenery from the roof deck. Undeniably romantic, the inn also attracts business travelers during the week.

58 Washington St., Marblehead, MA 01945. ✆ 781/631-2186. Fax 781/631-2216. www.harborlightinn.com. 21 units (some w/shower only). $125–$245 double; $195–$295 suite. Rates include breakfast. Corporate rate available midweek. 2- to 3-night minimum weekends and holidays. AE, MC, V. Free parking. **Amenities:** Heated outdoor pool; access to nearby health club ($5); airport shuttle. *In room:* A/C, TV/VCR, wireless Internet access, hair dryer, iron, umbrella, robes.

Marblehead Inn 😊 *(Kids)*   This 1872 Victorian mansion just outside the historic district is an all-suite inn. It's not as convenient and romantic as the Harbor Light Inn, but offers better amenities and a more family-friendly atmosphere. Each attractive unit contains a living room, bedroom, and workstation. This is a good choice for businesspeople making an extended stay as well as families, who can make good use of the self-catering kitchenette. (Breakfast provisions are supplied.) Most suites have Jacuzzis, and some have fireplaces and small patios.

264 Pleasant St. (Rte. 114), Marblehead, MA 01945. ✆ 800/399-5843 or 781/639-9999. Fax 781/639-9996. www.marbleheadinn.com. 10 units (some w/shower only). $129–$219 double. Rates include continental breakfast. Extra person $25. Children under 10 stay free in parent's room. Winter discounts and long-term rates available. 2- to 3-night minimum weekends and holidays. AE, MC, V. Free parking. *In room:* A/C, TV, fax, dataport, kitchenette, coffeemaker, hair dryer.

A SEASIDE INN NEARBY

Diamond District Bed & Breakfast 😊😊   This comfortable Georgian-style mansion, built in 1911 as a private home, attracts both business and leisure travelers. The Atlantic is a block away; the 3-mile public beach (a good place to burn off the inn's generous breakfast) is popular for jogging, skating, and biking as well as swimming. It's visible from many of the good-size rooms, tastefully decorated with elaborate Victorian touches. The best are third-floor units with ocean views and Jacuzzis. Two rooms have cozy electric fireplaces. The large living room and porch overlook houses on Lynn Shore Drive and, just past them, the ocean. The whirlpool spa, on the back lawn, also has a water view.

The **1882 Stewart House,** across the street (away from the water), contains a common living room, a double room, two doubles that share a bathroom (a good choice for families), and a tiny single room.

142 Ocean St., Lynn, MA 01902. © 800/666-3076 or 781/599-4470. Fax 781/599-5122. www.diamond districtinn.com. 15 units, 13 with private bathroom (some w/shower only). $135–$265 double. Rates include breakfast. Extra person $20. Winter discounts available. 2-night minimum on holiday, summer, and fall weekends. AE, DC, DISC, MC, V. Take Rte. 1A north to signs for Swampscott/Marblehead; after rotary, take Lynn Shore Dr. north, past 2 lights and Christian Science Church. Turn left onto Wolcott Rd., then right onto Ocean St.; inn is on the right. **Amenities:** Outdoor whirlpool. *In room:* A/C, TV, dataport.

WHERE TO DINE

You can stock up for a picnic at a number of places in Old Town. **Crosby's,** 118 Washington St. (© **781/631-1741**), is a full-service market with a large prepared-food section. **Shubie's,** 32 Atlantic Ave. (© **781/631-0149**), carries a good selection of specialty foods.

The Barnacle SEAFOOD   This unassuming spot affords a shorebird's-eye view of the harbor from the deck, the counter, and the crowded dining room. The food is tasty and plentiful. It's not innovative, but it is fresh—the restaurant's lobster boat delivers daily—and popular with local residents, which is always a good sign. The chowder and fried seafood are terrific. This is an agreeable place to quaff a beer and watch the boats.

141 Front St. © 781/631-4236. Reservations not accepted. Main courses $5–$15 lunch, $13–$18 dinner. DISC, MC, V. Sun–Thurs 11:30am–9pm; Fri–Sat 11:30am–10pm (lunch until 4pm). Closed Tues in winter.

Driftwood Restaurant ☆ DINER/SEAFOOD   At the foot of State Street next to Clark Landing (the town pier) is an honest-to-goodness local hangout. Join the crowd at a table or the counter for generous portions of breakfast (served all day) or lunch. Try pancakes or hash, chowder or a seafood "roll" (a hotdog bun filled with, say, fried clams or lobster salad). The house specialty, served on weekends and holidays, is fried dough, which is exactly as delicious and indigestible as it sounds.

63 Front St. © 781/631-1145. Main courses $3–$10; breakfast items under $7. No credit cards. Daily 5:30am–2pm.

Maddie's Sail Loft SEAFOOD   Less than a block from the harbor, Maddie's is a friendly tavern that serves good steaks as well as excellent fresh seafood. The strong drinks are another attraction, especially during the summer boating season; this (or, alas, one of the private yacht clubs) is the place to search for that cute sailor you saw down by the water. There's live jazz on Thursday nights and a lively local scene year-round.

15 State St. © 781/631-9824. Main courses $9–$16. No credit cards. Mon–Sat 11:45am–2pm and 5–10pm; Sun 11:45am–4pm. Bar open until 11:30pm.

4 Salem ☆☆

16 miles NE of Boston; 4 miles NW of Marblehead

Settled in 1626 (4 years before Boston) and later known around the world as a center of merchant shipping, Salem is internationally famous today for a 7-month

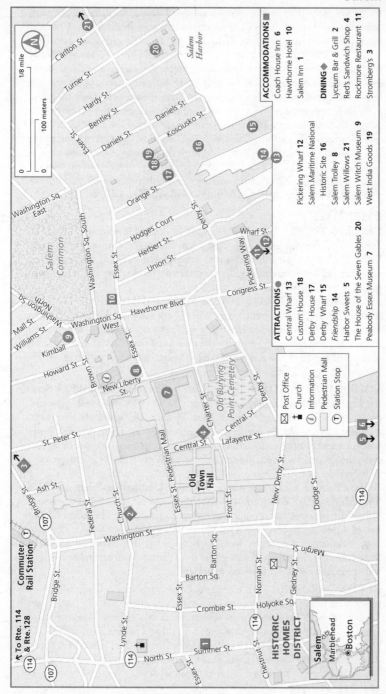

Salem

ACCOMMODATIONS ■
Coach House Inn **6**
Hawthorne Hotel **10**
Salem Inn **1**

DINING ◆
Lyceum Bar & Grill **2**
Red's Sandwich Shop **4**
Rockmore Restaurant **11**
Stromberg's **3**

ATTRACTIONS ●
Central Wharf **13**
Custom House **18**
Derby House **17**
Derby Wharf **15**
Friendship **14**
Harbor Sweets **5**
The House of the Seven Gables **20**
Peabody Essex Museum **7**
Pickering Wharf **12**
Salem Maritime National Historic Site **16**
Salem Trolley **8**
Salem Willows **21**
Salem Witch Museum **9**
West India Goods **19**

Post Office
Church
Information
Pedestrian Mall
Station Stop

Salem Harbor

Salem Common

Old Burying Point Cemetery

Old Town Hall

HISTORIC HOMES DISTRICT

Commuter Rail Station

To Rte. 114 & Rte. 128

Salem
Marblehead
●Boston

1/8 mile
100 meters

episode in 1692. The witchcraft trials led to 20 deaths, centuries of notoriety, countless lessons on the evils of prejudice, and innumerable bad puns ("Stop by for a spell" is a favorite slogan). Today, the city abounds with witch-associated attractions. Most are historically accurate, but you'll also see a fair number of goofy souvenirs and opportunistic tourist traps. An excellent antidote is the **Peabody Essex Museum.** Salem is a family-friendly destination that's worth at least a half-day visit, perhaps after a stop in Marblehead; it can easily fill a day.

Visitors concentrating on wall-to-wall witches will miss another important part of the city's history. Salem's merchant vessels circled the globe in the 17th and 18th centuries, returning laden with treasures. The city peaked between the Revolutionary War and the War of 1812, with the opening of the China trade—many overseas merchants even believed that Salem was an independent country. One reminder of that era, a replica of the 1797 East Indiaman tall ship *Friendship,* is anchored near the Salem Maritime National Historic Site.

ESSENTIALS

GETTING THERE From Marblehead, take Route 114 west into downtown Salem. From Boston, take I-93 or Route 1 to Route 128, then Route 114 east. Or take Route 1A north from Boston, being careful in Lynn, where the road turns left and immediately right. There's metered street parking and a reasonably priced garage opposite the visitor center.

From Boston, the **MBTA** (© **800/392-6100** outside Mass., or 617/222-3200; www.mbta.com) runs commuter trains from North Station and bus no. 450 from Haymarket (Orange or Green Line). The train is more comfortable but runs less frequently. It takes 30 to 35 minutes; the round-trip fare is $7.50. The station is about 5 blocks from the downtown area. The one-way fare for the 35- to 55-minute bus trip is $3.45.

VISITOR INFORMATION A good place to start is the **National Park Service Regional Visitor Center,** 2 New Liberty St. (© **978/740-1650;** www.nps.gov/sama), open daily from 9am to 5pm. Exhibits highlight early settlement, maritime history, and the leather and textiles industries. The center distributes brochures and pamphlets, including one that describes a walking tour of the historic district, and has an auditorium where a free film on Essex County provides an overview.

The Office of Tourism & Cultural Affairs, **Destination Salem** (© **877/SALEM-MA** or 978/744-3663; www.salem.org), and the Chamber of Commerce collaborate on a free visitor guide that includes a good map. The **Salem Chamber of Commerce,** 63A Wharf St. (© **978/744-0004;** www.salem-chamber.org), maintains a rack of brochures and pamphlets at its office on Pickering Wharf. It's open Monday through Friday from 9am to 5pm. Salem has an excellent community website, **www.salemweb.com**.

GETTING AROUND In the congested downtown area, walking is the way to go. If it's hot or you plan lots of sightseeing, you might prefer to ride. **Salem Trolley** (© **508/744-5469;** www.salemtrolley.com) offers a 1-hour narrated tour and unlimited reboarding at any of its 12 stops. The tour starts at the Essex Street side of the visitor center. It operates from 10am to 5pm (last tour at 4pm), daily April through October; check ahead for November hours. Tickets ($10 for adults, $9 seniors, $5 children 5–14) are good all day.

SPECIAL EVENTS The city's month-long Halloween celebration, **Haunted Happenings** 🌟🌟, includes parades, parties, tours, and a ceremony on the big day. During **Heritage Days,** a weeklong event in mid-August, the city celebrates its multicultural history with musical and theatrical performances, a parade, and fireworks.

EXPLORING SALEM

The **historic district** extends well inland from the waterfront; ask at the visitor center for the walking-tour pamphlet. Many 18th-century houses, some with original furnishings, still stand. Ship captains lived near the water at the east end of downtown, in relatively small houses crowded close together. The captains' employers, the shipping-company owners, built their homes away from the water (and the accompanying aromas). Many lived on the grand thoroughfare of **Chestnut Street** ✸✸, now a National Historic Landmark.

By car or trolley, the **Salem Willows** (© 978/745-0251) amusements are 5 minutes away; many signs point the way. The strip of rides and snack bars has a honky-tonk air, and the waterfront park is a good place to bring a picnic and wander along the shore. Admission is free; metered parking is available. To enjoy the great view without the arcades and rides, have lunch one peninsula over at **Winter Island Park.**

The House of the Seven Gables ✸ *Kids*   Nathaniel Hawthorne's cousin lived here, and stories and legends of the house and its inhabitants inspired his 1851 book. If you haven't read the eerie novel, don't let that keep you away—begin with the audiovisual program, which tells the story. The house, built by Capt. John Turner in 1668, holds six rooms of period furniture, including pieces referred to in the book, and a secret staircase. Tours include a visit to Hawthorne's birthplace and descriptions of what life was like for the house's 18th-century inhabitants. The costumed guides can get a little silly as they mug for young visitors, but they're well versed and eager to answer questions. Also on the grounds, overlooking Salem Harbor, are period gardens, the **Retire Beckett House** (1655), **the Hooper-Hathaway House** (1682), and a counting house (1830).

54 Turner St. © **978/744-0991**. www.7gables.org. Guided tour of house and grounds $11 adults, $9.90 seniors, $7.15 children 5–12, free for children under 5. Surcharges may apply for special exhibitions. Nov–June daily 10am–5pm; July–Oct daily 10am–7pm. Closed 1st 3 weeks of Jan. From downtown, follow Derby St. east 3 blocks past Derby Wharf.

Peabody Essex Museum ✸✸ *Kids*   The Peabody Essex is gaining a national reputation for its collections of art and cultural artifacts. Though sometimes overshadowed by Salem's every-witch-way reputation, the museum's encyclopedic collections offer an engaging look at nearly 4 centuries in a fascinating seaport. A huge expansion project completed in 2003 created new galleries and added an 18th-century Qing dynasty house that was shipped from China and reassembled. The new wing, designed by Moshe Safdie, allows the museum to display a significant proportion of its holdings for the first time.

The permanent collections blend "the natural and artificial curiosities" Salem's sea captains and merchants brought back from around the world with the local artifacts of the county historical society. The well-planned displays help you understand the significance of each item, and interpretive materials (including interactive and hands-on activities) get children involved. You might see objects related to the history of the port of Salem (including gorgeous furniture), the whaling trade, the witchcraft trials, and East Asian art. Portraits of area residents include Charles Osgood's omnipresent rendering of Nathaniel Hawthorne.

Trying Times: The Salem Witch Hysteria

The Salem witch trials took place in 1692, a product of Old World superstition, religious control of government, and plain old boredom.

The crisis began quietly in Salem Village (now the town of Danvers). The Rev. Samuel Parris's household included his 9-year-old daughter, Elizabeth, her cousin Abigail, and a West Indian slave named Tituba who told stories to amuse the girls during the long, harsh winter. Entertained by tales of witchcraft, sorcery, and fortune-telling, the girls and their friends began to act out the stories, claiming to be under a spell, rolling on the ground and wailing. The settlers—aware that thousands of people in Europe had been executed as witches in the previous centuries—took the behavior seriously.

At first, only Tituba and two other women were accused of casting spells. The infighting typical of the Puritan theocracy surfaced soon enough, and an accusation of witchcraft became a handy way to settle a score. Anyone "different" was a potential target, from the elderly to the deaf to the poor. A special court convened in Salem proper, and although the girls recanted, the trials began. Defendants had no counsel, and pleading not guilty or objecting to the proceedings was considered equivalent to a confession. From March 1 to September 22, of the more than 150 people who were accused, 27 were convicted.

In the end, 19 people went to the gallows, and one man who refused to plead, Giles Corey, was pressed to death by stones piled on a board on his chest. Finally, cooler heads prevailed. Leading cleric Cotton Mather and his father, Harvard president Increase Mather, led the call for tolerance. With the jails overflowing, the court called off the trials and freed the remaining prisoners, including Tituba.

The episode's lessons about open-mindedness and tolerance have echoed through the years. Salem was the backdrop for Arthur Miller's 1953 play *The Crucible*. It is both a story about the witch trials and an allegory about the McCarthy Senate hearings—another kind of witch hunt in a time when those lessons needed to be taught again.

Sign up for a fascinating tour of one of the museum's 10 historic houses. They include the 1804 **Gardner-Pingree House** ★★, a magnificent Federal mansion where a notorious murder was committed in 1830. You can also take a gallery tour or select from about a dozen pamphlets that describe self-guided tours.

East India Sq. © 800/745-4054 or 978/745-9500. www.pem.org. Admission $13 adults, $11 seniors, $9 students, free for children under 17. Surcharges may apply for special exhibitions. Fri–Wed 10am–5pm, Thurs 10am–9pm. Take Hawthorne Blvd. to Essex St., following signs for visitor center. Enter on Essex St. or New Liberty St.

Salem Maritime National Historic Site ★ *Kids*   An entertaining introduction to Salem's seagoing history, this complex includes an exciting attraction: a real live ship. The *Friendship* ★★ is a full-size replica of a 1797 East Indiaman merchant vessel, a three-masted 171-footer that disappeared during the War of 1812. The guided ranger tour includes a tour of the ship.

Central Wharf holds a warehouse (ca. 1800) that houses the orientation center. Tours, which vary seasonally, expand on Salem's maritime history. Yours might include the Derby House (1762), a wedding gift to shipping magnate Elias Hasket Derby from his father, and the Custom House (1819). Legend (myth, really) has it that this is where Nathaniel Hawthorne was working when he found an embroidered scarlet "A." If you prefer to explore on your own, you can see the free film at the orientation center and wander around Derby Wharf, the West India Goods Store, the Bonded Warehouse, the Scale House, and Central Wharf.

174 Derby St. ℭ 978/740-1660. www.nps.gov/sama. Free admission. Guided tour $5 adults, $3 seniors and children 6–15. Daily 9am–5pm. Take Derby St. east; just past Pickering Wharf, Derby Wharf is on the right.

Salem Witch Museum ★★ (Kids)   This is one of the most memorable attractions in eastern Massachusetts—it's both interesting and scary. The main draw of the museum (a former church) is a three-dimensional audiovisual presentation with life-size figures. The show takes place in a huge room lined with displays that are lighted in sequence. The 30-minute narration tells the story of the witchcraft trials and the accompanying hysteria. The well-researched presentation tells the story accurately, if somewhat overdramatically. One of the victims was crushed to death by rocks piled on a board on his chest—smaller kids may need a reminder that he's not real.

19½ Washington Sq., on Rt. 1A. ℭ 978/744-1692. www.salemwitchmuseum.com. Admission $7 adults, $6 seniors, $4.50 children 6–14. Daily July–Aug 10am–7pm; Sept–June 10am–5pm; check ahead for Oct hours. Follow Hawthorne Blvd. to the northwest corner of Salem Common.

SHOPPING

Pickering Wharf, at the corner of Derby and Congress streets (ℭ **978/740-6990;** www.pickeringwharf.com), is a waterfront complex of boutiques, restaurants, and condos. It's popular for strolling, snacking, and shopping, and the central location makes it a local landmark.

Several shops specialize in witchcraft accessories. Bear in mind that Salem is home to many practicing witches who take their beliefs very seriously. The **Broom Closet,** 3–5 Central St. (ℭ **978/741-3669**), and **Crow Haven Corner,** 125 Essex St. (ℭ **978/745-8763**), stock everything from crystals to clothing.

Shops throughout New England sell the chocolate confections of **Harbor Sweets** ★★, Palmer Cove, 85 Leavitt St., off Lafayette Street (ℭ **978/745-7648**). The retail store overlooks the floor of the factory. The deliriously good sweets are expensive, but candy bars and small assortments are available. Closed Sunday.

WHERE TO STAY

The busiest and most expensive time of year is **Halloween week;** reserve well in advance if you plan to travel anytime in October.

Most major chains are represented on or near Route 1 north of I-95, within 30 minutes of downtown Salem. The **Clipper Ship Inn,** 40 Bridge St., Rte. 1A (ℭ **978/745-8022**), is a comfortable, modern motel northeast of downtown. Doubles in high season run $120 to $160.

Coach House Inn   Built in 1879 for a ship's captain, this welcoming inn is 2 blocks from the harbor and a 20-minute walk or 5-minute drive from downtown. The three-story mansion was renovated in 2002. The good-size guest rooms are elegantly furnished in traditional style. All have high ceilings, and most have (nonworking) fireplaces. Breakfast arrives at your door in a basket.

284 Lafayette St. (Routes 1A and 114), Salem, MA 01970. 📞 **800/688-8689** or 978/744-4092. Fax 978/745-8031. www.coachhousesalem.com. 11 units, 9 with private bathroom (2 w/shower only). $80–$98 double with shared bathroom; $95–$155 double with private bathroom; $160–$198 suite. Rates include continental breakfast. 2- to 3-night minimum weekends and holidays. AE, DISC, MC, V. Free parking. *In room:* A/C, TV, coffeemaker.

Hawthorne Hotel 🎯   This historic hotel, built in 1925, is both convenient and comfortable. It attracts vacationers and business travelers, and is popular for functions. The six-story building is centrally located and well maintained, with a traditional atmosphere. The guest rooms are attractively furnished and adequate in size. The best units, on the Salem Common (north) side of the building, have better views than rooms that face the street. Ask to be as high up as possible, as the neighborhood is busy.

18 Washington Sq. W. (at Salem Common), Salem, MA 01970. 📞 **800/729-7829** or 978/744-4080. Fax 978/745-9842. www.hawthornehotel.com. 89 units (some w/shower only). $104–$204 double; $204–$309 suite. Extra person $12. Children under 16 stay free in parent's room. Off-season and senior discounts, weekend and other packages available. 2-night minimum May–Oct weekends. AE, DC, DISC, MC, V. Limited self-parking. Pets accepted ($15). **Amenities:** Restaurant (American); tavern; exercise room; access to nearby heath club ($5–$8); concierge; airport shuttle; room service until 10pm; laundry service; same-day dry cleaning. *In room:* A/C, TV, dataport, hair dryer, iron.

Salem Inn 🎯🎯   The Salem Inn, which consists of three properties, occupies the comfortable niche between too-big hotel and too-small B&B. Its clientele includes honeymooners as well as sightseers and families, and the variety of

---

Milling Around: A Trip to Lowell

A 19th-century textile center that later fell into disrepair, Lowell is a 21st-century success story. A city built around restored mills and industrial canals will never be a glamorous vacation spot, but thousands of visitors a year find Lowell a fascinating and rewarding destination. The sights concentrate on the history of the Industrial Revolution and the textile industry. They include boardinghouses where the "mill girls" lived; the workers, some as young as 10 years old, averaged 14-hour days weaving cloth on power looms.

Start at the **Lowell National Historical Park Visitor Center,** 246 Market St. (📞 **978/970-5000;** www.nps.gov/lowe), open daily from 9am to 5pm. Rangers lead free programs and tours, and canal cruises and free trolley tours operate in summer. Ask for a map of the area, and use it to find your way around downtown. Two interesting museums are within walking distance: the **American Textile History Museum,** 491 Dutton St. (📞 **978/441-0400;** www.athm.org), and the **New England Quilt Museum** 🎯, 18 Shattuck St. (📞 **978/452-4207;** www.nequilt museum.org). For more information, consult the **Greater Merrimack Valley Convention & Visitors Bureau,** 9 Central St., Suite 201, Lowell (📞 **800/443-3332** or 978/459-6150; www.merrimackvalley.org).

To drive to Lowell, take Route 3 or I-495 to the Lowell Connector and follow signs north to Exit 5B and the historic district. The **commuter rail** (📞 **800/392-6100** outside Mass., or 617/222-3200; www. mbta.com) from Boston's North Station takes about 45 minutes and costs $11 round-trip.

rooms means the innkeepers can make a good match of guest and accommodations. Rooms are large and tastefully decorated; some have fireplaces, canopy beds, and whirlpool baths. The best units are the honeymoon and family suites in the 1874 Peabody House. Guests of all three houses can relax in the peaceful rose garden at the rear of the main building.

7 Summer St. (Rte. 114), Salem, MA 01970. © **800/446-2995** or 978/741-0680. Fax 978/744-8924. www. SalemInnMA.com. 41 units (some w/shower only). Nov–Sept $119–$149 double; $169–$229 suite. Oct $180–$210 double; $220–$285 suite. Rates include continental breakfast. 2- to 3-night minimum during holidays and special events. AE, DC, DISC, MC, V. Free parking. Pets accepted by prior arrangement ($15–$25/night). *In room:* A/C, TV, coffeemaker, hair dryer, iron.

WHERE TO DINE

Pickering Wharf has a food court as well as a link in the **Victoria Station** (© **978/744-7644**) chain, with a great view of the marina from the deck.

Lyceum Bar & Grill ★★ CONTEMPORARY AMERICAN   The elegance of the Lyceum's dining rooms matches the quality of the food, which attracts local businesspeople and out-of-towners. Grilling is a favorite cooking technique—try the signature marinated grilled portobellos. They're available as an appetizer and scattered throughout the menu—say, in delectable pasta with chicken, red peppers, and Swiss chard in wine sauce, or with beef tenderloin, red pepper sauce, and garlic mashed potatoes. Spicy vegetable lasagna is also tasty. Save room for one of the traditional yet sophisticated desserts—the brownie sundae is out of this world.

43 Church St. (at Washington St.). © **978/745-7665**. www.lyceumsalem.com. Reservations recommended. Main courses $7–$12 lunch, $17–$27 dinner. AE, DISC, MC, V. Mon–Fri 11:30am–3pm; Sun brunch 11am–3pm; daily 5:30–10pm.

Red's Restaurant NEW ENGLAND   Locals and visitors feel equally comfortable at this no-frills hangout. Hunker down at the counter or a table and be ready for your waitress to call you "dear" as she brings you pancakes and eggs at breakfast, or soup (opt for chicken over chowder) and a burger at lunch or dinner.

15 Central St. © **978/745-3527**. www.redssandwichshop.com. Most items under $7. No credit cards. Mon–Sat 5am–9pm; Sun 6am–1pm.

Rockmore Restaurant ★ SEAFOOD/AMERICAN   If you're going to eat at a restaurant with a gimmick, it might as well be a good gimmick. This is: It's on a float in the middle of Salem Harbor. The Rockmore serves burgers, sandwiches, and fresh seafood in an extremely casual atmosphere, usually to local boaters. The food is fine, but nobody's here for the food. (Did we mention it's on a *float?*) If you're not traveling by boat, ferry service is available from the year-round **Rockmore Dry Dock** restaurant, 94 Wharf St., Pickering Wharf.

Salem Harbor. © **978/740-1001**. Main courses $8–$16. AE, DISC, MC, V. Memorial Day to Labor Day daily 11am–10pm, weather permitting.

Stromberg's ★ *Kids* SEAFOOD   For generous portions of well-prepared seafood and a view of the water, seek out this local favorite at the foot of the bridge to Beverly. You won't care that Beverly Harbor isn't the most exciting spot, especially if it's summer and you're out on the deck. The fish and clam chowders are excellent, daily specials are numerous, and there are more chicken, beef, and pasta options than you might expect. Crustacean lovers in the mood to splurge will fall for the world-class lobster roll.

2 Bridge St. (Rte. 1A). © **978/744-1863**. www.strombergs.com. Reservations recommended for dinner. Main courses $7–$11 lunch, $11–$19 dinner; children's menu $5. AE, DISC, MC, V. Sun and Tues–Thurs 11am–9pm; Fri–Sat 11am–10pm.

5 Cape Ann

Gloucester, Rockport, Essex, and Manchester-by-the-Sea make up Cape Ann, a rocky peninsula so enchantingly beautiful that when you hear the slogan "Massachusetts's *Other* Cape," you may forget what the first one was. Cape Ann and Cape Cod do share some attributes—scenery, shopping, seafood, and traffic. The smaller cape's proximity to Boston and manageable scale make it a wonderful day trip and a good choice for a longer stay.

With the decline of the fishing industry that brought great prosperity to the area in the 19th century, Cape Ann has played up its long-standing reputation as a haven for artists. Along with galleries and crafts shops, you'll find historical attractions, beaches—and oh, that scenery!

Although all four towns have large year-round populations, this is hardly a four-season destination. Many establishments close in fall or early winter through April or May; some open on weekends in December.

The **Cape Ann Transportation Authority** (© 978/283-7916; www.canntran.com) runs buses from town to town on Cape Ann and operates special summer routes.

The **Cape Ann Chamber of Commerce,** 33 Commercial St., Gloucester (© 800/321-0133 or 978/283-1601; www.capeannvacations.com), and the **North of Boston Convention & Visitors Bureau** (© 800/742-5306 or 978/977-7760; www.northofboston.org) provide abundant visitor information.

MANCHESTER-BY-THE-SEA

The scenic route to Gloucester from points south is Route 127, which runs through Manchester-by-the-Sea, a lovely village incorporated in 1645. Now a prosperous suburb of Boston, Manchester is probably best known for **Singing Beach** (see "Life's a Beach . . . With Very Cold Water!," below). The **commuter rail** (© 800/392-6100 outside Mass., or 617/222-3200; www.mbta.com) from Boston costs $11 round-trip and stops in the center of the compact downtown area, where there are many shops and restaurants. Nearby **Masconomo Park** overlooks the harbor.

The home of the Manchester Historical Society is the **Trask House,** 10 Union St. (© 978/526-7230; www.manchesterhistorical.org), a 19th-century sea captain's home. Tours show off the period furnishings, including pieces produced in Manchester, and the society's costume collections. It's specialized, but intriguing to devotees of house tours. Open July and August weekdays from 10am to 4pm, September through June weekdays from 10am to noon, and by appointment. A donation is requested.

MAGNOLIA

Pay close attention as you head north from Manchester or south from Gloucester on Route 127—Magnolia is easy to miss, but the village (technically part of Gloucester) is worth a detour. Notable for its lack of waterfront commercial property, the village center is unremarkable. The homes surrounding it, many of them former summer residences now occupied year-round, are magnificent.

Just up the coast are two noteworthy geological formations. **Rafe's Chasm** is a huge cleft in the shoreline rock, opposite the reef of **Norman's Woe,** which figures in Henry Wadsworth Longfellow's scary poem "The Wreck of the *Hesperus*." About three-quarters of a mile out of the center, look for a small parking area on the right. After a ¼-mile walk through the woods, you'll find a gorgeous panorama of stone and surf.

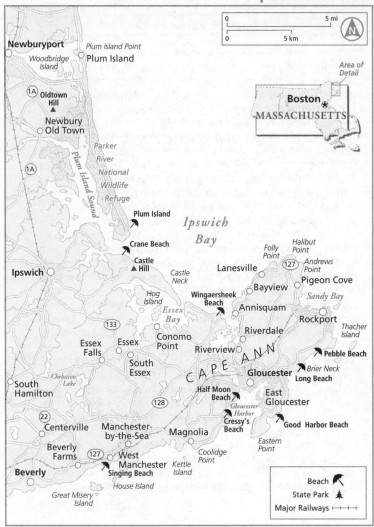

Cape Ann & Environs

0 ____ 5 mi
0 ____ 5 km

Newburyport
Woodbridge Island
Plum Island Point
Plum Island

Area of Detail

Boston
MASSACHUSETTS

1A Oldtown Hill

Newbury Old Town

Parker River National Wildlife Refuge

1A

Plum Island Sound

Plum Island

Crane Beach

Castle Hill

Ipswich

Castle Neck

Hog Island

Essex Bay

Ipswich Bay

Folly Point
Halibut Point
Andrews Point
127
Pigeon Cove

Lanesville

Bayview

Wingaersheek Beach
Annisquam

Sandy Bay

Rockport
Thacher Island

Essex Falls
Essex
133
Conomo Point
South Essex

Riverview

Riverdale

CAPE ANN

Pebble Beach

Gloucester
Brier Neck
Long Beach

South Hamilton
Chebacco Lake

128

Half Moon Beach

Gloucester Harbor

East Gloucester

22
Centerville

Manchester-by-the-Sea

Magnolia

Cressy's Beach

Good Harbor Beach

Eastern Point

Beverly Farms
127
West Manchester
Singing Beach
Coolidge Point
Kettle Island

Beverly

House Island

Great Misery Island

Beach
State Park
Major Railways

ESSEX

West of Gloucester (past Rte. 128) on Route 133 lies a beautiful little town known for Essex clams, salt marshes, a long tradition of shipbuilding, a plethora of antiques shops, and one celebrated restaurant.

Legend has it that **Woodman's of Essex** ★★★, 121 Main St. (© **800/649-1773** or 978/768-6057; www.woodmans.com), was the birthplace of the fried clam in 1916. Today the thriving family business is a great spot to join legions of locals and visitors from around the world for lobster "in the rough," chowder, steamers, corn on the cob, onion rings, and (you guessed it) superb fried clams. Expect the line to be long, even in winter, but it moves quickly and offers a view of the regimented commotion in the food-preparation area. Credit cards aren't accepted, but there's an ATM on the premises. Eat in a booth, upstairs on the

Life's a Beach . . . With Very Cold Water!

Paradoxically, Cape Ann is almost as well known for its sandy beaches as for its rocky coastline. Things to know: First, the water is *cold*. Second, parking can be scarce, especially on weekends, and pricey—as much as $20. If you can't set out before breakfast, wait until midafternoon and hope that the early birds have had enough. During the summer, lifeguards are on duty from 9am to 5pm at larger public beaches. Surfing is generally permitted outside of those hours. The beaches listed here all have bathhouses and snack bars. Swimming or not, watch out for greenhead flies in July and August. They don't sting—they take little bites of flesh. Bring or buy insect repellent.

The best-known North Shore beach is **Singing Beach** ★★, off Masconomo Street in Manchester-by-the-Sea. Because it's accessible by public transportation, it attracts the most diverse crowd—carless singles, local families, and other beach bunnies of all ages. From the train station, they walk about half a mile on Beach Street to find sparkling sand and lively surf. Take the commuter rail (© **800/392-6100** outside Mass., or 617/222-3200; www.mbta.com) from Boston's North Station.

Nearly as famous and popular is **Crane Beach** ★, off Argilla Road in Ipswich, part of a 1,400-acre barrier beach reservation. Fragile dunes and a white-sand beach lead down to Ipswich Bay. The surf is calmer than that at less sheltered Singing Beach, but still quite chilly. Pick up Argilla Road south of Ipswich Center near the intersection of Routes 1A and 133. Also on Ipswich Bay is Gloucester's **Wingaersheek Beach** ★, on Atlantic Street off Route 133. From Exit 13 off Route 128, the beach is about 15 minutes away (mind the speed limits). Wingaersheek has beautiful white sand, a glorious view, and more dunes. Because these beaches are harder to get to, they attract more locals—but also lots of day-tripping families.

Most other good beaches in Gloucester have almost no nonresident parking. Two exceptions are **Half Moon Beach** and **Cressy's Beach,** at Stage Fort Park, off Route 127 near Route 133 and downtown. The sandy beaches and the park snack bar are popular local hangouts.

deck, or out back at a picnic table. You'll want to be well fed before you explore the numerous antiques shops along Main Street.

The water views in town are of the Essex River, a saltwater estuary. Narrated 90-minute tours that put you in prime birding territory are available through **Essex River Cruises** ★, Essex Marina, 35 Dodge St. (© **800/748-3706** or 978/768-6981; www.essexcruises.com), open daily April through October. The pontoon boat, which allows for excellent sightseeing, is screened and has restrooms. Call for reservations.

GLOUCESTER ★★

The ocean has been Gloucester's lifeblood since long before the first European settlement in 1623. The most urban of Cape Ann's communities, Gloucester (which rhymes with "roster") is a working city, not a cutesy tourist town. Miles

of gorgeous coastline surround the densely populated downtown area. Gloucester is home to one of the last commercial fishing fleets in New England, an internationally celebrated artists' colony, a large Portuguese-American community,
and just enough historic attractions. Allow at least half a day, perhaps combined
with a visit to the tourist magnet of Rockport; a full day would be better, especially if you plan a cruise or whale watch.

ESSENTIALS

GETTING THERE   From Boston, the quickest route is I-93 (or Rte. 1, if it's
not rush hour) to Route 128, which ends at Gloucester. From Salem, a slower
but prettier approach is Route 1A across the bridge at Beverly to Route 127. It
runs through Manchester to Gloucester. The Manchester exits from Route 128
allow access to Route 127. There's street parking and a free lot on the causeway
to Rocky Neck. Gloucester is 33 miles northeast of Boston, 16 miles northeast
of Salem, and 7 miles south of Rockport.

The **commuter rail** (© **800/392-6100** outside Mass., or 617/222-3200;
www.mbta.com) runs from Boston's North Station. The trip takes about 1 hour;
the round-trip fare is $11. The station is across town from downtown, about 10
blocks, so allow time for getting to the waterfront. The **Cape Ann Transportation Authority** (© **978/283-7916;** www.canntran.com) runs buses from town
to town as well as special summer routes.

VISITOR INFORMATION   The **Gloucester Tourism Office** (© **800/649-
6839** or 978/281-8865; www.gloucesterma.com) operates the excellent **Visitors
Welcoming Center** at Stage Fort Park, off Route 127 at Route 133. It's open in
summer daily from 9am to 5pm. The **Cape Ann Chamber of Commerce,** 33
Commercial St. (© **800/321-0133** or 978/283-1601; www.capeannvacations.
com), is open year-round (summer weekdays 8am–6pm, Sat 10am–6pm, Sun
10am–4pm; winter weekdays 8am–5pm). It also operates a seasonal information
booth on Rogers Street at Harbor Loop.

GETTING AROUND   Downtown is fairly compact and walkable, but there's
more to Gloucester than that. If you can manage it, travel by car. You'll be able
to make the best use of your time, especially if you plan several stops. The **Cape
Ann Transportation Authority** (see above) serves Gloucester.

SPECIAL EVENTS   Gloucester holds summer festivals and street fairs that
honor everything from clams to schooners. The best known is **St. Peter's Fiesta,**
a colorful 4-day event at the end of June. The Italian-American fishing colony's
festival has more in common with a carnival midway than a religious observation,

---

Moments *The Perfect Storm*

Even 5 years after the release of the blockbuster movie, Sebastian Junger's
best-selling book *The Perfect Storm* remains a popular reason to visit
Gloucester. The thrilling but tragic nonfiction account of the "no-name"
hurricane of 1991 centers on the ocean and a neighborhood tavern. The
Crow's Nest, 334 Main St. (© **978/281-2965**), a bit east of downtown, is a
no-frills place with a horseshoe-shaped bar and a crowd of regulars who
seem amused that their hangout is a tourist attraction. The Crow's Nest
plays a major role in Junger's story, but its ceilings aren't high enough for
it to be a movie set—so the crew built an exact replica nearby.

but it's great fun. There are parades, rides, music, food, sporting events, and, on Sunday, the blessing of the fleet.

EXPLORING THE TOWN

Start at the water, as visitors have done for centuries. The French explorer Samuel de Champlain called the harbor "Le Beauport" in 1604—some 600 years after the Vikings first visited—and its configuration and proximity to good fishing gave it the reputation it enjoys to this day. Fishing is still Gloucester's leading industry (as your nose will tell you), with tourism a close second. The city is exceptionally welcoming—residents seem genuinely happy to see out-of-towners and to offer directions and insider info. The **Gloucester Maritime Trail** brochure, available at visitor centers, describes four excellent self-guided tours.

On Stacy Boulevard (west of downtown) is a reminder of the sea's danger. Leonard Craske's bronze statue of the **Gloucester Fisherman,** known as "The Man at the Wheel," bears the inscription "They That Go Down to the Sea in Ships 1623–1923." To the west is a memorial to the women and children who waited at home. As you take in the glorious view, consider this: More than 10,000 fishermen lost their lives during the city's first 300 years.

Stage Fort Park, off Route 127 near the intersection with Route 133, offers an excellent view of the harbor and has a busy seasonal snack bar. It's a good spot for picnicking, swimming, or playing on the cannons in the Revolutionary War fort.

To reach **East Gloucester,** follow signs as you leave downtown or go directly from Route 128, Exit 9. On East Main Street, you'll see signs for the world-famous **Rocky Neck Art Colony** ★★, the oldest continuously operating art colony in the country. Park in the lot on the tiny causeway and head west along Rocky Neck Avenue, which abounds with studios, galleries, restaurants, and people. The attraction is the presence of working artists, not just shops that happen to sell art. In summer, most galleries are open daily from 10am to 10pm. The prestigious **North Shore Arts Association,** 197 E. Main St. (② **978/283-1857;** www.cape-ann.com/nsaa), founded in 1922, is open from late May to October, Monday through Saturday from 10am to 5pm, Sunday from 1 to 5pm. Admission is free.

Also in East Gloucester, the **Gloucester Stage Company** ★, 267 E. Main St. (② **978/281-4099;** www.cape-ann.com/stageco.html), is one of the best repertory troupes in New England. Founder and artistic director Israel Horovitz, a prizewinning playwright and screenwriter, schedules six plays a season (June to mid-Sept).

Beauport (Sleeper-McCann House) ★★   The Society for the Preservation of New England Antiquities, which operates Beauport, describes it as a "fantasy house," and that's putting it mildly. Interior designer Henry Davis Sleeper accumulated vast stores of American and European decorative arts and antiques in his summer home. From 1907 to 1934, he decorated the 40 rooms, most of which are open to the public, to illustrate literary and historical themes. The entertaining tour concentrates more on the house in general than on the countless objects. You'll see architectural details from other buildings, magnificent arrangements of colored glassware, the "Red Indian Room" (with a majestic view of the harbor), and "Strawberry Hill," the master bedroom. Note that the house is closed on summer weekends.

75 Eastern Point Blvd. ② 978/283-0800. www.spnea.org. Guided tour $10 adults, $9 seniors, $5 students and children 6–12. Tours on the hr. June to mid-Sept Mon–Fri 10am–4pm; mid-Sept to Oct 15 daily

(Kids) A Whale of an Adventure

The waters off the Massachusetts coast are prime **whale-watching** ★★ territory, and Gloucester is a center of cruises. Stellwagen Bank, which runs from Gloucester to Provincetown about 27 miles east of Boston, is a rich feeding ground for the magnificent mammals, which dine on sand eels and other fish that gather on the ridge. The whales often perform by jumping out of the water, and dolphins occasionally join the show. Naturalists on board narrate the trip for the companies listed here, pointing out the whales and describing birds and fish that cross your path.

Whale-watching is not particularly time- or cost-effective, especially if restless children are along, but it's so popular for a reason: The pay-off is, literally and figuratively, huge. This is an experience that kids (and adults) will remember for a long time.

The season runs from April or May to October. Dress warmly—it's much cooler at sea than on land—and wear a hat and rubber-soled shoes. Pack sunglasses, sunscreen, a camera, and plenty of film. If you're prone to motion sickness, take precautions, because you'll be at sea for 4 to 6 hours.

This is an extremely competitive business—they'd deny it, but the companies are virtually indistinguishable. Most guarantee sightings, offer morning and afternoon cruises and deep-sea fishing excursions, honor other firms' coupons, and offer Internet, AARP, and AAA discounts. Check ahead for sailing times, prices ($29–$31 for adults, less for seniors and children), and reservations, which are strongly recommended. In downtown Gloucester, **Cape Ann Whale Watch** (② 800/ 877-5110 or 978/283-5110; www.caww.com), is the best-known operation. Also downtown are **Captain Bill's Whale Watch** (② 800/33-WHALE or 978/283-6995; www.captainbillswhalewatch.com) and **Seven Seas Whale Watch** (② 800/238-1776 or 978/283-1776; www.7seas-whale watch.com). At the Cape Ann Marina, off Route 133, is **Yankee Whale Watch** (② 800/WHALING or 978/283-0313; www.yankeefleet.com).

10am–4pm. Closed Oct 16–May and summer weekends. Take E. Main St. south to Eastern Point Blvd. (a private road), continue ½-mile to house, park on left.

Cape Ann Historical Museum ★ This meticulously curated museum makes an excellent introduction to Cape Ann's history and artists. It devotes an entire gallery to the extraordinary work of **Fitz Hugh Lane** ★★★, the Luminist painter whose light-flooded canvases show off the best of his native Gloucester. The nation's single largest collection of his paintings and drawings is here. Other galleries feature works on paper by 20th-century artists such as Maurice Prendergast and Milton Avery, work by other contemporary artists, and granite-quarrying tools and equipment. There's also an outdoor sculpture court. The maritime and fisheries galleries display entire vessels, exhibits on the fishing industry, ship models, and historic photographs and models of the Gloucester waterfront. The Capt. Elias Davis House (1804), decorated and furnished in Federal style, is part of the museum.

27 Pleasant St. (© **978/283-0455.** www.cape-ann.com/historical-museum. Admission $6.50 adults, $6 seniors, $5 students, free for children under 6. Mar–Jan Tues–Sat 10am–5pm. Closed Feb. Follow Main St. west through downtown and turn right onto Pleasant St.; the museum is 1 block up on right. Metered parking on street or in lot across street.

ORGANIZED TOURS & CRUISES

For information on whale watches, see "A Whale of an Adventure," above.

Moby Duck Tours ⚓ (© **978/281-3825;** www.mobyduck.com) are 55-minute sightseeing expeditions that travel on land before plunging into the water. They're just the right length for kids, who delight in the transition from street to sea. The amphibious vehicles leave from Harbor Loop downtown. Tickets (cash only) cost $16 for adults, $14 for seniors, and $10 for children under 12. Tours operate daily from Memorial Day to Labor Day, plus September weekends.

Also at Harbor Loop, you can tour the two-masted schooner **Adventure** ⚓⚓ (© **978/281-8079;** www.schooner-adventure.org), a 121-foot fishing vessel built in Essex in 1926 and undergoing extensive restoration. It doesn't move, so it's not as thrilling as the *Thomas E. Lannon* (discussed next), but it's quicker and cheaper and can be more interesting, depending on what's being worked on. The "living museum," a National Historic Landmark, is in view all the time and open to visitors from Memorial Day to Labor Day, Thursday through Sunday from 10am to 4pm. The suggested donation is $5 for adults, $4 for children.

The schooner **Thomas E. Lannon** ⚓ (© **978/281-6634;** www.schooner.org) is a lovely reproduction of a Gloucester fishing vessel. The 65-foot tall ship sails from Seven Seas Wharf downtown; 2-hour excursions ($30 for adults, $25 for seniors, $20 for children under 17) leave about four times a day from mid-June to mid-October, less often on weekends from mid-May to mid-June. Reservations are recommended. The company offers music and dining cruises (including Fri lobster bakes) and "storytelling sails."

SHOPPING

Rocky Neck (see "Exploring the Town," above) offers great browsing. If you admired the wardrobe design in *The Perfect Storm,* check out the shirts and caps at **Cape Pond Ice,** 104 Commercial St., near the Chamber of Commerce (© **978/283-0174;** www.capepondice.com). Downtown, Main Street between Pleasant and Washington streets is a good destination. Agreeable stops include **Mystery Train,** 178 Main St. (© **978/281-8911;** www.mystrain.com), which carries used LPs, CDs, tapes, and videos; **Ménage Gallery,** 134 Main St. (© **978/283-6030**), which shows work by artists and artisans; and the **Dogtown Book Shop,** 2 Duncan St. (© **978/281-5599**), noted for its used and antiquarian selection.

WHERE TO STAY

The 40-unit **Vista Motel,** 22 Thatcher Rd. (Rte. 127A), Gloucester (© **866/VISTA-MA** or 978/281-3410; www.vistamotel.com), is a comfortable establishment on a hilltop near the Rockport border. Summer rates run $130 to $140.

Atlantis Oceanfront Motor Inn   This motor inn sits across the street from the water, affording stunning views from every window. It doesn't have the resort feel of the neighboring Bass Rocks Ocean Inn, but the views are the same. The good-size guest rooms are decorated in comfortable, contemporary style. Every unit has a terrace or balcony. The view from second-floor accommodations is a little better.

125 Atlantic Rd., Gloucester, MA 01930. ⓒ **800/732-6313** or 978/283-0014. Fax 978/281-8994. www. atlantismotorinn.com. 40 units (some w/shower only). Late June to Labor Day $150–$180 double; spring and fall $125–$155 double. Children under 13 stay free in parent's room. Extra person $8. Off-season packages available. Closed Nov to mid-Apr. Minimum stay may be required. AE, MC, V. Follow Rte. 128 to the end (Exit 9, East Gloucester), turn left onto Bass Ave. (Rte. 127A), and follow it ½ mile. Turn right and follow Atlantic Rd. **Amenities:** Coffee shop (breakfast only); heated outdoor pool. *In room:* A/C, TV.

Best Western Bass Rocks Ocean Inn   A family operation since 1946, the Bass Rocks Ocean Inn offers gorgeous views and modern accommodations in a traditional setting. The spacious guest rooms take up a sprawling, comfortable two-story motel across the road from the rocky shore. A Colonial Revival mansion built in 1899 and known as the "wedding-cake house" holds the office and public areas, including a billiard room and library. The inn has larger rooms than the neighboring Atlantis. Each unit has a balcony or patio; second-floor rooms have slightly better views. In the afternoon, the staff serves coffee, tea, lemonade, and cookies.

107 Atlantic Rd., Gloucester, MA 01930. ⓒ **800/528-1234** or 978/283-7600. Fax 978/281-6489. www.best western.com/bassrocksoceaninn. 48 units. Late June to Sept $170–$285 double; spring and fall $125–$210 double. Extra person $8; rollaway or crib $12. Children under 12 stay free in parent's room. Rates include continental breakfast. 3-night minimum summer weekends, some spring and fall weekends. Closed Nov to late Apr. AE, DC, DISC, MC, V. Follow Rte. 128 to the end (Exit 9, East Gloucester), turn left onto Bass Ave. (Rte. 127A), and follow it ½ mile; turn right and follow Atlantic Rd. **Amenities:** Heated outdoor pool; free bikes. *In room:* A/C, TV/VCR, dataport, fridge, coffeemaker, hair dryer, iron.

WHERE TO DINE

See "Essex," earlier, for information on the celebrated **Woodman's of Essex,** which is about 20 minutes from downtown Gloucester.

Boulevard Oceanview Restaurant ⭐ PORTUGUESE/SEAFOOD   This is a friendly neighborhood place in a high-tourist-traffic location. Across the street from the waterfront promenade just west of downtown, it's a dinerlike spot with water views from the front windows and the small deck. It serves ultrafresh seafood (crane your neck and you can almost see the processing plants) and lunch-counter sandwiches. Try shrimp *a la plancha* (in irresistible lemon-butter sauce) or one of the several unusual casseroles.

25 Western Ave. (Stacy Blvd.). ⓒ **978/281-2949.** Reservations recommended for dinner in summer. Sandwiches $4–$8; main courses $7–$16; lobster priced daily. DISC, MC, V. Summer daily 11am–10pm; winter daily 11am–9:30pm.

The Franklin Cape Ann ⭐⭐ BISTRO   A sophisticated offshoot of a neighborhood favorite in Boston's South End, the Franklin is a welcome addition to the fried-seafood-focused local dining scene. It does serve seafood, but in inventive preparations such as panko-crusted scallops accompanied by delectable lemon sauce, and pan-seared Atlantic cod with oyster mushrooms, scallions, and ginger. Meat dishes are equally creative. The two-story restaurant also offers fabulous martinis and live jazz at least 1 night a week, making it a popular late-evening destination.

118 Main St. ⓒ **978/283-7888.** Reservations not accepted. Main courses $10–$17. AE, MC, V. Daily 5pm–midnight.

The Gull Restaurant ⭐⭐ *Kids* SEAFOOD/AMERICAN   Floor-to-ceiling windows show off the Annisquam River from almost every seat at the Gull. The big, welcoming restaurant is known for prime rib as well as excellent seafood. It draws locals, visitors, boaters, and families for large portions at reasonable prices. The seafood chowder is famous, appetizers tend toward bar food, and the french fries are terrific. Daily specials run from simple lobster (market price) to sophisticated fish and meat dishes. At lunch, there's an extensive sandwich menu.

75 Essex Ave. (Rte. 133), at Cape Ann Marina. ⓒ **978/281-6060.** Reservations recommended for parties of 8 or more. Main courses $5–$13 lunch, $8–$22 dinner; breakfast items less than $8. DISC, MC, V. Late Apr to Oct daily 6am–9pm. Closed Nov to late Apr. Take Rte. 133 west from intersection with Rte. 127, or take Rte. 133 east from Rte. 128.

Halibut Point Restaurant SEAFOOD/AMERICAN A local legend for its chowders and burgers, Halibut Point is a friendly tavern that serves generous portions of good food. The "Halibut Point Special"—$13 for a cup of chowder, a burger, and a beer—hits the high points. The clam chowder is terrific, and some people come to Gloucester just for the spicy Italian fish chowder. There's also a raw bar. Main courses are simple (mostly sandwiches) at lunch, more elaborate at dinner. Be sure to check the specials board—you didn't come all this way to a fishing port not to have fresh fish, did you?

289 Main St. ⓒ **978/281-1900.** Main courses $5–$12 lunch, $9–$17 dinner. AE, DISC, MC, V. Daily 11:30am–11pm.

ROCKPORT

This lovely little town at the tip of Cape Ann was settled in 1690. Over the years it has been a fishing port, a center of granite excavation, and a thriving summer community whose specialty seems to be selling fudge and refrigerator magnets to out-of-towners. But there's more to Rockport than just gift shops. It's home to a lovely state park, and popular with photographers, sculptors, jewelry designers, and painters. Winslow Homer, Fitz Hugh Lane, and Childe Hassam are among the famous artists who have captured the local color. At times, especially on summer weekends, you'll be hard pressed to find much local color in this tourist-weary destination. But for every year-round resident who seems genuinely startled when people with cameras around their necks descend each June, there are dozens who are proud to show off their town. Rockport makes an entertaining half-day trip, perhaps combined with a visit to Gloucester.

ESSENTIALS
GETTING THERE Rockport is north of Gloucester along Route 127 or 127A. At the end of Route 128, turn left at the signs for Rockport to take 127, which is shorter but more commercial. To take 127A, continue on 128 to the sign for East Gloucester and turn left. Parking is next to impossible, especially on summer Saturday afternoons. Make one loop around downtown, and then head to the free parking lot on Upper Main Street (Rte. 127). The shuttle bus to downtown costs $1. Rockport is 40 miles northeast of Boston, 7 miles north of Gloucester.

The **commuter rail** (ⓒ **800/392-6100** outside Mass., or 617/222-3200; www.mbta.com) runs from Boston's North Station. The trip takes 60 to 70 minutes; the round-trip fare is $12. The station is about 6 blocks from the downtown waterfront. **Cape Ann Transportation Authority** (ⓒ **978/283-7916;** www. canntran.com) buses serve Rockport.

VISITOR INFORMATION The **Rockport Chamber of Commerce and Board of Trade,** 22 Broadway (ⓒ **888/726-3922** or 978/546-6575; www. rockportusa.com), is open in summer Monday through Saturday from 9:30am to 6pm, and in winter Tuesday through Saturday from 11am to 5pm. From mid-May to mid-October, it operates an information booth on Upper Main Street (Rte. 127), about a mile from the town line and a mile from downtown—look for the WELCOME TO ROCKPORT sign. Out of season, from January to mid-April, Rockport is pretty but somewhat desolate, though some businesses stay open and keep reduced hours.

GETTING AROUND　For traffic and congestion, Boston has nothing on Rockport on a summer weekend afternoon. If you can schedule only one week-day trip, make it this one. When you arrive, park and walk, especially downtown. The Cape Ann Transportation Authority (see above) runs within the town.

SPECIAL EVENTS　The **Rockport Chamber Music Festival** (© **978/546-7391;** www.rcmf.org) takes place in June and early July at the Rockport Art Association, 12 Main St. Events include performances, family concerts, lectures, and discussions. The annual **Christmas pageant,** on Main Street in early December, is a kid-friendly event with carol singing and live animals.

EXPLORING THE TOWN

The most famous sight in Rockport has something of an "Emperor's New Clothes" aura—it's a wooden fish warehouse on the town wharf, or T-Wharf, in the harbor. The barn-red shack known as **Motif No. 1** is the most frequently painted and photographed object in a town filled with lovely buildings and sur-rounded by rocky coastline. The color certainly catches the eye in the neutrals of the surrounding seascape, but you may find yourself wondering what the big deal is. Originally constructed in 1884 and destroyed during the blizzard of 1978, Motif No. 1 was rebuilt using donations from residents and visitors. It stands again on the same pier, duplicated in every detail, reinforced to withstand storms.

Nearby is **Bearskin Neck,** named after an unfortunate ursine visitor who washed ashore in 1800. It holds perhaps the highest concentration of gift shops anywhere. The narrow peninsula has one main street (South Rd.) and several alleys crammed with galleries, snack bars, antiques shops, and ancient houses. The peninsula ends in a plaza with a magnificent water view.

Throughout town, more than two dozen **art galleries** ✿ display the work of local and nationally known artists. The **Rockport Art Association,** 12 Main St. (© **978/546-6604**), sponsors major exhibitions and special shows. It's open daily in the summer, Tuesday through Sunday in the winter,

The 1922 **Paper House,** 52 Pigeon Hill St., Pigeon Cove (© **978/546-2629**), is an unusual experience. Everything in it (including the furniture) was built entirely out of 100,000 newspapers. Every item is made from papers of a different period. It's open April through October, daily from 10am to 5pm. Admission is $1.50 for adults, $1 for children. Follow Route 127 north from downtown about 1½ miles until you see signs at Curtis Street pointing to the left.

SHOPPING

Bearskin Neck is the obvious place to start. Dozens of little shops stock clothes, gifts, toys, jewelry, souvenirs, inexpensive novelties, and expensive handmade crafts and paintings. Another enjoyable stroll is along **Main** and **Mount Pleas-ant streets.** Good stops include the nonprofit **Toad Hall Bookstore,** 47 Main St. (© **978/546-7323**); **New England Goods,** 57 Main St. (© **978/546-9677**), where the stock is exclusively local; and **Willoughby's,** 20 Main St. (© **978/ 546-9820**), a women's clothing and accessories shop.

Two favorite stops are retro delights. Downtown, you can watch taffy being made at **Tuck's Candy Factory,** 7 Dock Sq. (© **800/569-2767** or 978/546-6352), a local landmark since the 1920s. Near the train station, **Crackerjacks,**

27 Whistlestop Mall, off Railroad Avenue (© **978/546-1616**), is an old-fashioned variety store with a great crafts department.

A TRIP TO THE EDGE OF THE SEA

The very tip of Cape Ann is accessible to the public, and well worth the 2½-mile trip north on Route 127 to **Halibut Point State Park** ★★ (© **978/546-2997;** www.state.ma.us/dem/parks/halb.htm). The surf-battered point got its name not from the fish, but because sailing ships heading for Rockport and Gloucester must "haul about" when they reach the jutting promontory. This is a great place to wander around and admire the scenery. On a clear day, you can see Maine.

About 10 minutes from the parking area, you'll come to a huge water-filled quarry next to a visitor center, where staffers dispense information, brochures, and bird lists. Swimming in the quarry is absolutely forbidden. There are walking trails, tidal pools, a World War II observation tower, and a rocky beach where you can climb around on giant boulders. Guided quarry tours and stone-splitting demonstrations take place on summer Saturdays at 10am. November through April, there's a guided bird walk on the first Saturday of the month at 9am. The park is open daily, year-round, from dawn to dusk; parking costs $2 from Memorial Day to Columbus Day.

WHERE TO STAY

When Rockport is busy, it's very busy, and when it's not, it's practically empty. The town's dozens of B&Bs fill in good weather and empty or even close in the winter. If you haven't made summer reservations well in advance, cross your fingers and call the Chamber of Commerce to ask about cancellations. Most innkeepers will arrange for guests to be picked up at the train station; if you're not driving, be sure to ask about this service when you reserve.

In Town

Captain's Bounty Motor Inn This modern, well-maintained motor inn is on the water. In fact, it's almost *in* the water, and nearly as close to the center of town as to the harbor. Each rather plain unit in the three-story building overlooks the water and has its own balcony. Rooms are spacious and soundproofed, with good cross-ventilation but no air-conditioning. The best units are on the adults-only top floor. Kitchenette units are available. Although it's hardly plush, you can't beat the location.

1 Beach St., Rockport, MA 01966. © **978/546-9557.** www.captainsbountymotorinn.com. 24 units. Mid-June to early Sept $130 double, $145 efficiency, $160 efficiency suite; spring and fall $83–$100 double, $87–$105 efficiency, $95–$115 efficiency suite. Extra adult $10; $5 for each child over 5. 2- to 3-night minimum weekends and holidays. MC, V. Closed Dec–Mar. *In room:* TV, coffeemaker.

Inn on Cove Hill (Caleb Norwood Jr. House) ★ This attractive Federal-style inn was built in 1771 using the proceeds of pirates' gold found nearby. Although it's just 2 blocks from the town wharf, the inn is set back from the road and has a hideaway feel. Guest rooms are decorated in period style; most have colonial furnishings and handmade quilts, and some have canopy beds. Innkeeper Betsy Eck overhauls one room each winter. Water views from the back of the house are worth the climb on the narrow stairs that lead to the third floor. The generous breakfast is served in the dining room or, in good weather, in the pleasant garden. A harbor-view apartment across the street is available for long-term (1 week or more) stays.

37 Mount Pleasant St., Rockport, MA 01966. © **888/546-2701** or 978/546-2701. Fax 978/546-1095. www.innoncovehill.com. 7 units (some w/shower only). $95–$165 double. Extra person $25. Rates include

continental breakfast. 2-night minimum June–Oct weekends. Off-season discounts available. MC, V. *In room:* A/C, TV, no phone.

Sandy Bay Motor Inn ★ About ½ mile from downtown Rockport, this modern motor inn offers comfortable accommodations and a variety of recreational facilities at a good price. One of the largest lodgings in town, it's a sprawling two-story complex with attractively landscaped grounds on a hill next to Route 127, which is busy during the day but not at night. Still, units that face away from the road are preferable. Guest rooms are large and conventionally furnished—nothing fancy, but well maintained and large enough to hold a cot.

183 Main St. (Rte. 127), Rockport, MA 01966. ℂ 800/437-7155 or 978/546-7155. www.sandybaymotorinn. com. 79 units (some w/shower only). Mid-June to early Sept $115–$160 double; spring and fall $96–$125 double; winter $80–$110 double. Extra adult $15. Each child $4. Cot $6. 2-night minimum summer weekends. AE, MC, V. Pets accepted; $50 deposit. **Amenities:** Restaurant (breakfast only); heated indoor pool; putting green; 2 outdoor tennis courts; whirlpool; saunas. Rooms for travelers with disabilities are available. *In room:* A/C, TV.

On the Outskirts

Emerson Inn by the Sea ★★ Somewhere in an old guest register, you might find Ralph Waldo Emerson's name—the philosopher stayed at the original (1840) inn. He wouldn't recognize it today: The oceanfront building expanded in 1912, and innkeepers Bruce and Michele Coates have transformed it into a mini-resort. Still, the inn retains a relaxing old-fashioned feel, with modern conveniences like a heated outdoor saltwater pool. Traditional furnishings such as four-poster beds grace the rooms, which are nicely appointed but not terribly large. If you can manage the stairs, the view from the top floor is worth the exertion. The best units have private balconies, fireplaces, or hot tubs; the regular oceanview rooms offer the same scenery. A three-bedroom cottage across the street rents for $1,500 to $3,000 a week. The public dining room (ℂ **978/546-9500**) enjoys a growing reputation for contemporary American cuisine. It serves dinner daily in the summer and on weekends in the off season; reservations are required.

1 Cathedral Ave., Rockport, MA 01966. ℂ 800/964-5550 or 978/546-6321. Fax 978/546-7043. www. emersoninnbythesea.com. 35 units (some w/shower only). $179–$379 "best" double; $159–$229 oceanview double; $95–$179 double without view. Extra person $25; crib or cot $25. Rates include full breakfast May–Oct, continental breakfast Nov–Apr. Weekly rates available. 2- or 3-night minimum weekends May–Oct. AE, DC, DISC, MC, V. Follow Rte. 127 north from the center of town for 2 miles; turn right at sign on Phillips Ave. **Amenities:** Dining room; outdoor pool; sauna. *In room:* A/C, TV, dataport, hair dryer.

WHERE TO DINE

Rockport is a "dry" community—no alcoholic beverages can be sold or served—but you can bring your own bottle, usually subject to a corking fee.

A good way to experience the town is to arrive before the tourist hordes descend and enjoy a hearty breakfast. Two tasty destinations are **Flav's Red Skiff,** 15 Mount Pleasant St. (ℂ **978/546-7647**), and **Michael's,** at the Sandy Bay Motor Inn, 183 Main St./Rte. 127 (ℂ **978/546-9665**).

The birthplace of the fried clam, **Woodman's of Essex** (see "Essex," earlier in this chapter), is about half an hour from Rockport.

Brackett's Oceanview Restaurant *Kids* SEAFOOD/AMERICAN The dining room at Brackett's has a gorgeous view of the water. The nautical decor suits the seafood-intensive menu, which offers enough variety to make this a good choice for families—burgers are always available. The service is friendly and the fresh seafood quite good, if not particularly adventurous. Try the moist, plump codfish cakes if you're looking for a traditional New England dish, or something with Cajun spices for variety. The most exciting offerings are on the extensive dessert menu, where anything homemade is a great choice.

29 Main St. ⓒ **978/546-2797**. www.bracketts.com. Reservations recommended for dinner. Main courses $7–$20 lunch, $10–$26 dinner. AE, DC, DISC, MC, V. Mid-Apr to Memorial Day Wed–Sun 11:30am–8pm; Memorial Day to Oct Sun–Fri 11:30am–8pm, Sat 11:30am–9pm. Closed Nov to mid-Apr.

The Greenery ✪ SEAFOOD/AMERICAN   The Greenery could get away with serving so-so food because of its great location near Bearskin Neck—but it doesn't. The cafe at the front serves light fare to stay or go; the dining rooms, at the back, boast great harbor views. The food ranges from tasty crab salad quiche at lunch to lobster at dinner to steamers and fresh-caught fish anytime. As in any town with working fishermen, check out the daily specials. All baking is done in-house, which explains the lines at the front counter for muffins and pastries. When the restaurant is busy, the cheerful service tends to drag. This is a good place to launch a picnic on the beach, and an equally good spot for lingering over coffee and dessert while watching the action around the harbor.

15 Dock Sq. ⓒ **978/546-9593**. www.thegreeneryrestaurant.com. Reservations recommended for dinner. Main courses $7–$12 lunch, $10–$22 dinner; breakfast items $2–$7. AE, DC, DISC, MC, V. Spring–fall daily 8am–9:30pm; call for winter hours.

Portside Chowder House ✪ CHOWDER/SEAFOOD   In an unbelievably touristy location, this busy restaurant on Bearskin Neck is a favorite with locals as well as out-of-towners. The crowds are here for chowder—clam and whatever else looked good that day. Equally enjoyable are seafood platters, burgers, and lobster rolls, all served in a dining room with a great view of the harbor or (seasonally) on the deck.

7 Tuna Wharf, off Bearskin Neck. ⓒ **978/546-7045**. www.portsidechowderhouse.com. Reservations not accepted. Most items less than $9. AE, MC, V. Late June to Labor Day daily 11am–8pm; Labor Day to late June daily 11am–3pm. Off-season hours may vary; call ahead.

6 Newburyport, Ipswich & Plum Island

The area between Cape Ann and the New Hampshire border is magnificent, with outdoor sights and sounds that can only be described as natural wonders, and enough impressive architecture to keep any city slicker happy.

In a part of the world where the word "charming" is used almost as often as "hello," Newburyport is a singular example of a picturesque waterfront city. Downtown Newburyport is on the Merrimack River. On the town's Atlantic coast, Plum Island contains one of the country's top nature preserves. On the other side of Ipswich Bay, Ipswich is a lovely town that's home to Crane Beach, on another wildlife reservation.

NEWBURYPORT ✪✪

To get here directly from Boston, take I-93 (or Rte. 1 if it's not rush hour) to I-95—*not* Route 128, as for most other destinations in this chapter—and follow it to Exit 57, a solid 45-minute ride. Signs point to downtown, where you can park and explore. The **commuter rail** (ⓒ **800/392-6100** outside Mass., or 617/222-3200; www.mbta.com) from North Station takes about 75 minutes and costs $12 round-trip. A $1 **shuttle bus** (ⓒ **978/469-6878;** www.mvrta.com) connects the train station to downtown.

Newburyport has a substantial year-round population that lends it a less touristy atmosphere than its appearance might suggest. Start your visit at the **Greater Newburyport Chamber of Commerce and Industry,** 38R Merrimac

St. (© **978/462-6680;** www.newburyportchamber.org), in the red-brick downtown shopping district. It also runs a seasonal information booth on Merrimac Street near Green Street.

Market Square, at the foot of State Street near the waterfront, is the center of a neighborhood packed with boutiques, gift shops, plain and fancy restaurants, and antiques stores. You can also wander to the water, take a stroll on the boardwalk, and enjoy the action on the river. Architecture buffs will want to climb the hill to High Street, where the **Charles Bulfinch**–designed building (1805) that houses the Superior Court is only one of several Federal-era treasures. Ask at the Chamber of Commerce for the walking-tour map.

If you haven't gone out to sea yet, now is a good time, and here's a good place: **Newburyport Whale Watch** ★★, Hilton's Dock, 54 Merrimac St. (© **800/848-1111** or 978/499-0832; www.newburyportwhalewatch.com), offers 4½-hour cruises on a 100-foot boat with on-board marine biologists as guides. Tickets are $29 for adults, $25 for seniors, and $18 for children 4 to 12; reservations are suggested. (See "A Whale of an Adventure," on p. 175, for more information.)

Or head to the ocean using an inland route: From downtown, take Water Street south until it becomes Plum Island Turnpike and follow it to the Parker River National Wildlife Refuge.

PARKER RIVER NATIONAL WILDLIFE REFUGE ★★

The 4,662-acre refuge (© **978/465-5753;** http://parkerriver.fws.gov) on **Plum Island** is a complex of barrier beaches, dunes, and salt marshes, one of the few remaining in the Northeast. The refuge is flat-out breathtaking, whether you're exploring the marshes or the seashore. More than 800 species of plants and animals (including more than 300 bird species) visit or make their home on the narrow finger of land between Broad Sound and the Atlantic Ocean.

The refuge offers some of the best **birding** ★★★ anywhere, as well as observation of mammals and plants. Wooden boardwalks with observation towers and platforms wind through marshes and along the shore—most lack handrails, so this isn't an activity for rambunctious children. You might see native and migratory species such as owls, hawks, martins, geese, warblers, ducks, snowy egrets, swallows, monarch butterflies, Canada geese, foxes, beavers, and harbor seals.

The ocean beach closes April 1 to allow piping plovers, listed by the federal government as a threatened species, to nest. The areas not being used for nesting reopen July 1; the rest open in August, when the birds are through. The currents are strong and can be dangerous, and there are no lifeguards—swimming is allowed but not encouraged. Surf fishing is popular, though; striped bass and bluefish are found in the area. A permit is required for night fishing and vehicle access to the beach.

The refuge is open from dawn to dusk year-round. The daily entrance fee is $5 for motorists, $2 for bikers and pedestrians. The seven parking lots fill quickly on weekends when the weather is good, so plan to arrive early. South of lot 4 (Hellcat Swamp), the access road is flat and well maintained but not paved.

IPSWICH ★

Across Ipswich Bay from Plum Island is the town of Ipswich. It's accessible from Route 1A (which you can pick up in Newburyport or at Rte. 128 in Hamilton) and from Route 133 (which intersects with Rte. 128 in Gloucester and I-95 in Georgetown). The **visitor center,** in the Hall Haskell House, 36 S. Main St., Rte. 133 (© **978/356-8540**), is open daily from Memorial Day to October, and weekends in May, November, and December. Information is also available from the **Ipswich Business Association** (✆ **978/356-9055;** www.ipswichma.com).

Settled in 1630, Ipswich is dotted with **17th-century houses** ✮—reputedly the largest concentration in the United States. Many are private homes; ask at the visitor center for a map of a tour that passes three dozen of them. House-tour aficionados can go inside the **John Whipple House,** 1 South Village Green

---

(Finds   More Whale Tales: A Trip to New Bedford

The masses that flock to eastern Massachusetts aren't yet swarming the cobblestone streets of New Bedford, which makes it a good destination for families on the verge of crowd-phobia. The **New Bedford Whaling National Historical Park,** which encompasses the downtown historic district, commemorates the city's past as the world's leading whaling port.

The downtown area near the waterfront has been restored, and the attractions are reasonably close together. Start your visit at the **National Park Service Visitor Center,** 33 William St. (✆ **508/996-4095;** www.nps. gov/nebe), open daily from 9am to 5pm. The exhibits include a film about whaling and the city's history. Take a guided walking tour (daily in summer, some off-season weekends) or pick up a brochure that describes self-guided excursions around the historic district.

The centerpiece of the Historical Park is the **New Bedford Whaling Museum** ✮, 18 Johnny Cake Hill (✆ **508/997-0046;** www.whaling museum.org). It's the world's premier whaling museum, which sounds terribly specialized but is actually quite absorbing. On display in the lobby is the skeleton of a 65-foot juvenile blue whale, Kobo (short for "king of the blue ocean"). Admission to the lobby is free, but the rest of the museum is worth a visit. Children love the half-scale model of the whaling bark *Lagoda,* the world's largest ship model. The museum is open daily from 9am to 5pm, until 9pm on the second Thursday of each month. Admission is $10 for adults, $9 for seniors and students, and $6 for children 6 to 14.

The **Seamen's Bethel,** 15 Johnny Cake Hill (✆ **508/992-3295**), a non-denominational chapel described in Herman Melville's classic novel *Moby-Dick,* is across the street. Up the hill from the water, the **Rotch-Duff-Jones House & Garden Museum,** 396 County St. (✆ **508/997-1401**), is an 1834 Greek Revival mansion with magnificent formal gardens. Admission is $5 for adults, $4 for seniors and students, $2 for children 12 and under.

To get there, take the Southeast Expressway south to I-93 (Rte. 128), then Route 24 south. Follow signs to Route 140 south to I-195. From Plymouth, take Route 44 west to Route 24 south. **American Eagle** (✆ **800/453-5040** or 508/993-2040) buses take 75 minutes from Boston's South Station ($20 round-trip). For more information, contact the **New Bedford Office of Tourism** (✆ **508/979-1745;** www.ci.new bedford.ma.us, click "visitors") or the **Bristol County Convention & Visitors Bureau** (✆ **800/288-6263** or 508/997-1250; www.bristol-county.org).

(© **978/356-2811**). Built between 1655 and 1700, it's decorated with period furnishings. May through October, tours start on the hour from 10am to 3pm Wednesday through Saturday, 1 to 3pm Sunday. The price ($7 for adults, $3 for children 12 and under) includes a tour of the nearby Heard House (1795).

Ipswich is also known for two more contemporary structures. The **Clam Box,** 246 High St., Rte. 1A/133 (© **978/356-9707**), is a restaurant shaped like— what else?—a red-and-white-striped takeout clam box. It's a great place to try Ipswich clams, and not easy to sneak past if you have children in the car. Heading south from Newburyport, it's on the right. Closed December through February.

South of Ipswich Center, near the intersection of Routes 1A and 133, look carefully for the Argilla Road sign (on the east side of the street). If you're traveling west on Route 133 from Gloucester and Essex, watch for a sign on the right pointing to Northgate Road, which intersects with Argilla Road. Follow it east to the end, where you'll find the 1,400-acre Crane Estate.

The property is home to **Crane Beach** (see "Life's a Beach . . . With Very Cold Water!," on p. 172), the **Crane Wildlife Refuge** ★★, a network of hiking trails, and **Castle Hill,** 290 Argilla Rd. (© **978/356-4351;** www.thetrustees.org). One of the Boston area's most popular wedding locations, the exquisite Stuart-style seaside mansion known as the Great House was built by Richard Teller Crane, Jr., who made his fortune in plumbing and bathroom fixtures early in the 20th century. If you can't wangle an invitation to a wedding, tours of the house ($7 for adults, $5 for seniors and children 12 and under) are given on Wednesday and Thursday in summer and two Sundays a year, spring and fall. You can also explore the estate ($8 per car on summer weekends, otherwise $5 per car) without entering the house.

Children who can't get excited about a tour might be pacified by a stop just before Castle Hill. **Russell Orchards Store and Winery** ★, 143 Argilla Rd. (© **978/356-5366;** www.russellorchardsMA.com), is open daily May through November. It has a picnic area, farm animals, and an excellent country store. Depending on the season, you might go on a hayride or taste fruit wines. Be sure to try some cider and doughnuts.

7 Plymouth ★★

Everyone educated in the United States knows at least a little about Plymouth— about how the Pilgrims, fleeing religious persecution, left Europe on the *Mayflower* and landed at Plymouth Rock in 1620. Many also know that the Pilgrims endured disease and privation, and that just 51 people from the original group of 102 celebrated the first Thanksgiving in 1621 with Squanto, a Pawtuxet Indian associated with the Wampanoags, and his cohorts.

What you won't know until you visit is how small everything was. The *Mayflower* (a replica) seems perilously tiny, and when you contemplate how dangerous life was at the time, it's hard not to be impressed by the settlers' accomplishments. The *Mayflower* passengers weren't even aiming for Plymouth. They originally set out for what they called "Northern Virginia," near the mouth of the Hudson River. On November 11, 1620, rough weather and high seas forced them to make for Cape Cod Bay and anchor at Provincetown. The captain then announced that they had found a safe harbor, and refused to continue to their original destination. On December 16, Provincetown having proven an unsatisfactory location, the weary travelers landed at Plymouth.

> ### ⌒Tips A Presidential History Twofer
>
> A worthwhile detour en route to Plymouth is the **Adams National Historical Park** in Quincy, about 10 miles south of Boston. The park preserves the birthplaces of Presidents John Adams and John Quincy Adams, the house where four generations of the family lived, and eight other buildings associated with the political dynasty. A trolley connects the buildings, which are open for guided tours daily in season (Patriots Day through Veterans Day) from 9am to 5pm. Admission is $3 for adults, free for children under 16. The grounds and the visitor center, 1250 Hancock St. (© **617/770-1175**; www.nps.gov/adam), are open in the winter Tuesday through Friday 10am to 4pm. The center is across the street from the Quincy Adams stop on the Red Line; call or surf ahead for driving directions.

Today, Plymouth is in many ways a model destination, where the 17th century coexists with the 21st, and most historic attractions are both educational and fun. Tourists jam the downtown area in summer, but the year-round population is so large that Plymouth feels more like the working community it is than like a warm-weather day-trip destination. It's a manageable excursion from Boston, particularly enjoyable if you're traveling with children. It also makes a good stop between Boston and Cape Cod.

ESSENTIALS

GETTING THERE   By car, follow the Southeast Expressway (I-93) from Boston to Route 3. From Cape Cod, take Route 3 north. Take Exit 6A to Route 44 east, and follow signs to the historic attractions. The 40-mile trip from Boston takes 45 to 60 minutes if it's not rush hour. Take Exit 5 to the **Regional Information Complex** for maps, brochures, and information. Take Exit 4 to go directly to **Plimoth Plantation.**

The **commuter rail** (© **800/392-6100** outside Mass., or 617/222-3200; www. mbta.com) serves Cordage Park, on Route 3A north of downtown, from South Station. The round-trip fare is $12. The **Plymouth Area Link bus** (© **508/222-6106;** www.gatra.org/pal.htm) runs between the train station and downtown. The fare is $1.

Plymouth & Brockton buses (© **617/773-9401** or 508/746-0378; www. p-b.com) run more often and cost more than the train: $10 one-way, $18 round-trip. The ride takes about an hour from South Station.

VISITOR INFORMATION   If you haven't visited the Regional Information Complex (see "Getting There," above), pick up a map at the **visitor center** (© **508/747-7525**), open seasonally at 130 Water St., across from the town pier. To plan ahead, contact Plymouth Visitor Information, known as **Destination Plymouth** (© **800/USA-1620** or 508/747-7525; www.visit-plymouth. com). The **Plymouth County Convention & Visitors Bureau** (© **508/747-0100;** www.plymouth-1620.com) publishes a vacation guide.

GETTING AROUND   The downtown attractions are accessible on foot. A shallow hill slopes from the center of town to the waterfront. **Plymouth Rock**

Plymouth

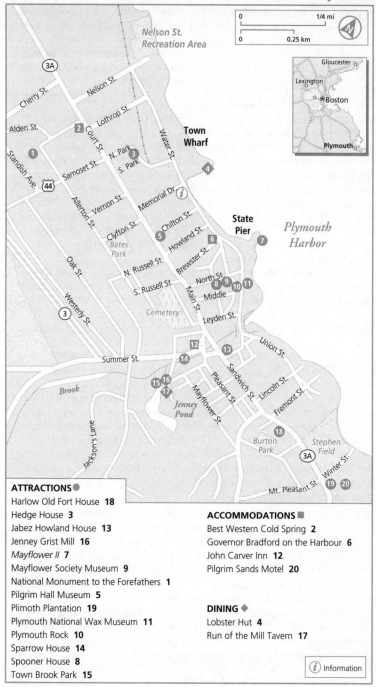

ATTRACTIONS ●
Harlow Old Fort House **18**
Hedge House **3**
Jabez Howland House **13**
Jenney Grist Mill **16**
Mayflower II **7**
Mayflower Society Museum **9**
National Monument to the Forefathers **1**
Pilgrim Hall Museum **5**
Plimoth Plantation **19**
Plymouth National Wax Museum **11**
Plymouth Rock **10**
Sparrow House **14**
Spooner House **8**
Town Brook Park **15**

ACCOMMODATIONS ■
Best Western Cold Spring **2**
Governor Bradford on the Harbour **6**
John Carver Inn **12**
Pilgrim Sands Motel **20**

DINING ◆
Lobster Hut **4**
Run of the Mill Tavern **17**

i Information

Trolley Company (© **800/698-56636** or 508/747-4161; www.plymouthrock
trolley.com) offers a 40-minute narrated tour and unlimited reboarding daily
from Memorial Day to October and weekends until Thanksgiving. It serves
marked stops downtown (every 20 min.) and Plimoth Plantation (once an hour
in summer). Tickets are $15 for adults, $12 for seniors and AAA members, and
$12 for children 5 to 12.

EXPLORING THE HISTORIC SITES

No matter how many times you suffered through elementary-school pageants
wearing a big black hat and paper buckles on your shoes, you can still learn
something about Plymouth and the Pilgrims. The logical place to begin (good
luck talking children out of it) is where the Pilgrims first set foot—at **Plymouth
Rock** ✦✦. The rock, accepted as the landing place of the *Mayflower* passengers,
was originally 15 feet long and 3 feet wide. It was moved on the eve of the Revolution and several times thereafter. In 1867, it assumed its present position at
tide level. The Colonial Dames of America commissioned the portico around
the rock, designed by McKim, Mead & White and erected in 1920. The rock
isn't much to look at, but the accompanying descriptions are interesting, and the
atmosphere curiously inspiring.

To get away from the waterfront crowds, make your way to **Town Brook
Park,** at Jenney Pond, across Summer Street from the John Carver Inn. Near the
tree-bordered pond is the **Jenney Grist Mill,** 6 Spring Lane (© **508/747-3715;**
www.jenneygristmill.com). It's a working museum where you can see a reconstructed water-powered mill that operates daily from April through November.
The self-guided tour is free; admission to a demonstration and corn-grinding
exhibition is $5 adults, $2 children 6 to 12. The specialty shops in the complex,
including the ice-cream shop, are open year-round, daily from 10am to 6pm.
Ducks and geese live in the pond, and there's room to run around.

Also removed from the waterfront is the **National Monument to the Forefathers** (© **508/746-1790**), a granite behemoth inscribed with the names of the
Mayflower passengers. Heading away from the harbor on Route 44, look carefully on the right for the turn onto Allerton Street, and climb the hill. The 81-
foot-high monument is elaborately decorated with figures representing moral
and political virtues and scenes of Pilgrim history. The monument is incongru-
ous in its little park in a residential neighborhood, but it's also quite impressive.
The view from the hilltop is excellent.

Mayflower II ✦ (Kids)   Berthed a few steps from Plymouth Rock, *Mayflower II*
is a full-scale reproduction of the type of ship that brought the Pilgrims from
England to America in 1620. Even at full scale, the 106½-foot vessel seems
remarkably small. Although little technical information about the original
Mayflower survives, William A. Baker, designer of *Mayflower II,* incorporated the
few references in Governor Bradford's account of the voyage with other research
to re-create the ship as authentically as possible. Costumed guides provide interesting first-person narratives about the vessel and voyage. Displays describe and
illustrate the journey and the Pilgrims' experience, including 17th-century navigation techniques.

State Pier. © 508/746-1622. www.plimoth.org. Admission $8 adults, $7 seniors, $6 children 6–12. Plimoth
Plantation (good for 2 consecutive days) and *Mayflower II* admission $22 adults, $20 seniors and students,
$14 children 6–12, $72 families. Apr–Nov daily 9am–5pm.

Pilgrim Hall Museum ✦   This is a great place to get a sense of the day-to-day
lives of Plymouth's first European residents. Many original possessions of the

early Pilgrims and their descendants are on display, including Myles Standish's sword, Governor Bradford's Bible, and an uncomfortable chair (you can sit in a replica) that belonged to William Brewster. Regularly changing exhibits explore aspects of the settlers' lives, such as home construction or the history of prominent families. Among the permanent exhibits is the skeleton of the *Sparrow-Hawk*, a ship wrecked on Cape Cod in 1626 that lay buried in the sand until 1863. (It's even smaller than the *Mayflower II*.)

75 Court St. ℂ 508/746-1620. www.pilgrimhall.org. Admission $6 adults, $5 seniors and AAA members, $3 children 5–17, $16 families. Feb–Dec daily 9:30am–4:30pm. Closed Jan. From Plymouth Rock, walk north on Water St. and up the hill on Chilton St.

Plimoth Plantation ★★ *Kids*   Allow at least half a day to explore this re-creation of the 1627 Pilgrim village, which children and adults find equally interesting. Enter by the hilltop fort that protects the "villagers" and walk down the hill to the farm area, visiting homes and gardens constructed with careful attention to historic detail. The "Pilgrims" are actors who, in speech, dress, and manner, assume the personalities of members of the original community. You can watch them framing a house, splitting wood, shearing sheep, preserving foodstuffs, or cooking a pot of fish stew over an open hearth, all as it was done in the 1600s. Wear comfortable shoes—you'll be walking a lot.

The plantation is as accurate as research can make it. The planners combined accounts of the original colony with archaeological research, old records, and the history written by the Pilgrims' leader, William Bradford (who often used the spelling "Plimoth"). There are daily militia drills with matchlock muskets that are fired to demonstrate the community's defense system. In fact, little defense was needed, because the Native Americans were friendly. Local tribes included the Wampanoags, who are represented near the village at Hobbamock's Homesite (included in plantation admission). Museum staffers show off native foodstuffs, agricultural practices, and crafts.

At the main entrance are two buildings with an interesting orientation show, exhibits, a gift shop, a bookstore, and a cafeteria. There's also a picnic area. Call or surf ahead for information on special events, lectures, tours, workshops, theme dinners, and family programs.

Rte. 3. ℂ 508/746-1622. www.plimoth.org. Admission (good for 2 consecutive days) $20 adults, $18 seniors, $12 children 6–12. Plimoth Plantation and *Mayflower II* admission $22 adults, $20 seniors and students, $14 children 6–12, $72 families. Apr–Nov daily 9am–5pm. From Rte. 3, take Exit 4, Plimoth Plantation Hwy.

Plymouth National Wax Museum ★★ *Kids*   Adults who visited this entertaining museum as children can still tell you all about the Pilgrims. The galleries hold more than 180 life-size figures arranged in scenes. Dramatic soundtracks tell the story of the move to Holland to escape persecution in England, the harrowing trip across the ocean, the first Thanksgiving, and even the tale of Myles Standish, Priscilla Mullins, and John Alden. This museum is a must if children are in your party, and adults will enjoy it, too. On the hill outside is a monument at the gravesite of the Pilgrims who died during the settlement's first winter.

16 Carver St. ℂ 508/746-6468. Admission $7 adults, $6.50 seniors, $2.75 children 5–12. Daily Mar–May and Nov 9am–5pm; June and Sept–Oct 9am–7pm; July–Aug 9am–9pm. Closed Dec–Feb. From Plymouth Rock, turn around and walk up the hill or the steps.

THE HISTORIC HOUSES

You can't stay in Plymouth's historic houses, but they're worth a visit to see the changing styles of architecture and furnishings since the 1600s. Costumed guides explain the homemaking and crafts of earlier generations. Most of the houses are open Memorial Day through Columbus Day, during Thanksgiving celebrations, and around Christmas; call for schedules.

Tip: Unless you have a sky-high tolerance for house tours, pick just one or two from eras that you find particularly interesting. This advice applies especially if you're sightseeing with children.

Six homes are open to visitors. The 1640 **Sparrow House,** 42 Summer St. (© **508/747-1240;** www.sparrowhouse.com; admission $2 adults, $1 children 12 and under), and the 1666 **Jabez Howland House,** 33 Sandwich St. (© **508/ 746-9590;** $4 adults, $2 children), are most engaging for those curious about the original settlers. The other houses are the 1677 **Harlow Old Fort House,** 119 Sandwich St. (© **508/746-0012;** $4 adults, $2 children); the 1749 **Spooner House,** 27 North St. (© **508/746-0012;** $4 adults, $2 children); the 1754 **Mayflower Society House,** 4 Winslow St. (© **508/746-2590;** $2.50 adults, 75¢ children); and the 1809 **Hedge House Museum,** 126 Water St. (© **508/ 746-9697;** $4 adults, $2 children).

ORGANIZED TOURS & CRUISES

To follow in the Pilgrims' footsteps, take a **Colonial Lantern Tour** ★★ (© **800/ 698-5636** or 508/747-4161; www.lanterntours.com). Participants carry pierced-tin lanterns on a 90-minute walking tour of the original settlement under the direction of a knowledgeable guide. It might seem a bit hokey at first, but it's fascinating. Tours run nightly April through Thanksgiving. Tickets are $15 for adults, $12 for children 12 and under; check the meeting place when you call for reservations.

Narrated cruises run from April or May to November. **Splashdown Amphibious Tours** ★ (© **800/225-4000** or 508/747-7658; www.ducktoursplymouth. com) takes you around town on land and water. The kid-friendly 1-hour excursions (half on land, half on water) leave from Harbor Place, near the Governor Bradford motel, on Water Street—and wind up in the harbor. They cost $17 for adults, $11 for children 3 to 12, and $3 for children under 3. **Capt. John Boats,** 10 Town Wharf (© **800/242-2469** or 508/747-2400; www.captjohn.com), offers several tours. The *Pilgrim Belle* paddle-wheeler is the vessel for 75-minute narrated tours of the harbor ($10 for adults, $8 for seniors, $7 for children under 12) leave from State Pier. **Whale watches** ($29 adults, $24 seniors, $18 children) run from April through October. Dining and entertainment cruises are also available.

A LEGENDARY ATTRACTION NEARBY

Edaville USA Family Fun Park ★, 7 Eda Ave., South Carver (© **877/ EDAVILLE** or 508/866-8190; www.edaville.com), is a longtime favorite with young New Englanders. The main attraction is an entertaining 45-minute train ride on a 5½-mile loop of narrow-gauge railroad tracks that takes you past cranberry bogs. Also on the premises are a carousel, kiddie rides, railroad museum, and cafe. It's a retro experience—no high-tech multimedia stuff, just good clean fun.

The railroad, which dates to 1947, reopened in 1999 after being shuttered for 7 years, and management tinkered with its schedule ever since. Definitely call ahead to confirm hours. It's currently open weekends and holidays September through early January. The railroad is extremely crowded when the weather is good; try to arrive when it opens. Admission is $16, free for children under 3. From Plymouth, follow Route 44 west to Route 58 south, continue about 3 miles to Rochester Road, and turn right.

SHOPPING

Water Street, on the harbor, boasts an inexhaustible supply of souvenir shops. A less kitschy destination, just up the hill, is Route 3A, known as Court, Main, and Warren street as it runs through town. **Lily's Apothecary,** 6 Main St. Extension, in the old post office (© 508/747-7546; www.lilysapothecary.com), carries a big-city-style selection of skin- and hair-care products. **Main Street Antiques,** 46 Main St. (© 508/747-8887), is home to dozens of dealers. **Pilgrim's Progress,** 13 Court St. (© 508/746-6033), carries women's and men's clothing. **Great Giraffe Graphic Co.,** 11 Court St. (© 508/830-1990), is an entertaining card and gift shop. Plymouth has a pawnshop, **Peggy's,** 37 Court St. (© 508/746-1952), that sells jewelry, electronic equipment, and power tools.

WHERE TO STAY

Just about every establishment in town participates in a **Destination Plymouth** (© 800/USA-1620; www.visit-plymouth.com) program that piles on the deals and discounts. Especially in the off season, this can represent great savings. On busy summer weekends, it's not unusual for every room in town to be taken; make reservations well in advance.

The 175-unit **Radisson Hotel Plymouth Harbor,** 180 Water St. (© 800/333-3333 or 508/747-4900; www.radisson.com), is the only chain hotel downtown. On a hill across the street from the waterfront, it offers the usual amenities, including a pool in the atrium lobby. Doubles in high season run $180 to $225.

Best Western Cold Spring ⭐ Convenient to downtown and the historic sights, this fastidiously maintained motel and the adjacent cottages surround nicely landscaped lawns. The property gained an outdoor pool in 2003. Rooms are pleasantly decorated and big enough for a family to spread out; if you want some privacy, book a two-bedroom cottage. The location makes the Cold Spring a good deal: The two-story complex is 1 long block inland, set back from the street in a quiet part of town.

188 Court St. (Rte. 3A), Plymouth, MA 02360. © 800/678-8667 or 508/746-2222. Fax 508/746-2744. www.bwcoldspring.com. 58 units (some w/shower only), 2 2-bedroom cottages. $99–$159 double; $139–$199 suite; $109–$159 cottage. Extra person $10. Rollaway $10. Crib $5. Children under 12 stay free in parent's room. Rates include continental breakfast. Packages, AAA and off-season discounts available. AE, DC, DISC, MC, V. Closed Dec–Mar. **Amenities:** Outdoor pool. *In room:* A/C, TV, dataport, coffeemaker, hair dryer, iron.

Governor Bradford on the Harbour This well-maintained motor inn occupies a great location across the street from the waterfront and only a block from Plymouth Rock and the *Mayflower II.* Each attractively decorated room contains modern furnishings; all were redone in 2000. The more expensive units on the top floor offer excellent water views—if that's what you care about, they're worth the money.

98 Water St., Plymouth, MA 02360. © 800/332-1620 or 508/746-6200. Fax 508/747-3032. www.governorbradford.com. 94 units (some w/shower only). From $139 double. Extra person $10. Children under 16 stay free in parent's room. Off-season, AAA, and AARP discounts available. 2-night minimum weekends and holidays. AE, DC, DISC, MC, V. **Amenities:** Small heated outdoor pool; coin laundry. *In room:* A/C, TV, dataport, fridge.

John Carver Inn *Kids* A three-story colonial-style building with a landmark portico, this hotel offers comfortable, modern accommodations and plenty of amenities, including two pools. The indoor "theme pool," a big hit with families, has a large water slide and a Pilgrim ship model. Business features, including meeting space, make this the Radisson's main competition for corporate travelers. The good-size guest rooms are decorated in colonial style. The best units are the lavish suites with private Jacuzzis; "four-poster" rooms contain king beds and sleeper sofas. The inn is within walking distance of the main attractions on the edge of the downtown business district.

25 Summer St., Plymouth, MA 02360. (✆ **800/274-1620** or 508/746-7100. Fax 508/746-8299. www.john carverinn.com. 85 units. Early Apr to mid-June and mid-Oct to Nov $119–$199 double, $229–$259 suite; mid-June to mid-Oct $159–$229 double, $269–$289 suite; Dec to early Apr $99–$179 double, $209–$239 suite. Extra person $20; rollaway $20; cribs free. Children under 19 stay free in parent's room. Packages and senior and AAA discounts available. AE, DC, DISC, MC, V. **Amenities:** Restaurant (American/seafood); outdoor and indoor pools; room service; laundry service; dry cleaning. *In room:* A/C, TV, dataport.

Pilgrim Sands Motel ★★ *Kids* This attractive motel sits on its own private beach 3 miles south of town, within walking distance of Plimoth Plantation. If you want to avoid the bustle of downtown and still be near the water, it's an excellent choice. The good-size rooms are tastefully furnished and well maintained. If you can swing it, book a beachfront room—the view is worth the money, especially when the surf is rough.

150 Warren Ave. (Rte. 3A), Plymouth, MA 02360. (✆ **800/729-7263** or 508/747-0900. Fax 508/746-8066. www.pilgrimsands.com. 64 units. Summer $130–$170 double; spring and early fall $100–$135 double; Apr and late fall $85–$105 double; Dec–Mar $75–$90 double; $140–$275 suite year-round. Extra person $6–$8 (suite $10–$15). 2-night minimum holiday weekends. Rates may be higher on holiday weekends. AE, DC, DISC, MC, V. **Amenities:** Coffee shop; indoor and outdoor pools; access to nearby health club ($10); Jacuzzi; private beach. Rooms for travelers with disabilities are available. *In room:* A/C, TV, dataport, fridge, hair dryer.

WHERE TO DINE

Plimoth Plantation (p. 189) has a cafeteria and a picnic area, and occasionally schedules theme dinners. The family-friendly **Hearth 'n' Kettle** chain has a branch at the John Carver Inn (p. 191), and there's a lively Southwestern restaurant, **Sam Diego's** (✆ **508/747-0048**), at 51 Main St.

Lobster Hut ★ SEAFOOD The Lobster Hut is a busy self-service restaurant with a great view. It's popular with both locals and sightseers. Order and pick up at the counter, then head to an indoor table or out onto the large deck that overlooks the bay. To start, try clam chowder or lobster bisque. The seafood "rolls" (hotdog buns with your choice of filling) are excellent. The many fried seafood options include clams, scallops, shrimp, and haddock. There are also boiled and steamed items, burgers, chicken tenders—and lobster, of course. Beer and wine are served, but only with meals.

25 Town Wharf. (✆ **508/746-2270.** Reservations not accepted. Lunch specials $7–$9; main courses $6–$15; sandwiches $3–$7; lobster priced daily. MC, V. Summer daily 11am–9pm; winter daily 11am–7pm. Closed Jan.

Run of the Mill Tavern ★ AMERICAN This friendly restaurant sits 3 blocks inland, across from Town Brook Park. You won't mind not having a water view—the food is tasty and reasonably priced, making the comfortable tavern a popular hangout. The unconventional clam chowder, made with red potatoes, is fantastic. Other appetizers include nachos, potato skins, and mushrooms. Entrees are well-prepared versions of familiar meat, chicken, and fish dishes, plus sandwiches, burgers, and fresh seafood specials (fried, broiled, or baked).

6 Spring Lane, Jenney Grist Mill Village, off Summer St. (✆ **508/830-1262.** Reservations not accepted. Main courses $6–$16; children's menu $4–$5. AE, DC, DISC, MC, V. Sun–Thurs 11:30am–10pm; Fri–Sat 11:30am–11pm. Bar closes at 1am.

Cape Cod

by Laura M. Reckford

Only 75 miles long, Cape Cod is a curving peninsula encompassing miles of beaches, hundreds of freshwater ponds, more than a dozen richly historic New England villages, scores of classic clam shacks and ice cream shops—and it's just about everyone's idea of the perfect summer vacation spot.

More than 13 million visitors flock to the Cape to enjoy summertime's nonstop carnival. In full swing, the Cape is, if anything, perhaps a bit too popular for some tastes. Connoisseurs are discovering the subtler appeal of the off season, when prices plummet along with the population. For some select travelers, the prospect of sunbathing en masse on sizzling sand can't hold a candle to a long, solitary stroll on a windswept beach with only the gulls as company. Come Labor Day, the crowds clear out—even the stragglers are gone by Columbus Day—and the whole place hibernates until Memorial Day weekend, the official start of "the season."

We've listed mostly summer rates for the accommodations in this chapter, because that's when the vast majority of travelers plan their trips, but if you decide to explore the Cape off season, you'll get the added benefit of lower prices everywhere you go.

The **Cape Cod Chamber of Commerce,** Routes 6 and 132, Hyannis (© **888/332-2732** or 508/862-0700; fax 508/362-2156; www.capecod chamber.org), is a clearinghouse of information. You can also stop in at the Route 25 Visitor Center (© **508/759-3814;** fax 508/759-2146), open daily year-round.

1 The Upper Cape

Because the Upper Cape towns are so close to Boston by car (just over an hour), they've become bedroom as well as summer communities. They are perhaps a bit more staid than those towns further east, but they are also spared some of the fly-by-night qualities that come with a transient populace. Shops and restaurants tend to stay open year-round.

SANDWICH ★★

Sandwich is both the oldest town on the Cape and the most quaint. Towering oak trees, 19th-century churches, and historic houses line its winding Main Street. A 1640 gristmill still grinds corn beside bucolic Shawme Pond. Farther east, Sandy Neck, one of the Cape's most beautiful beaches, extends out into Cape Cod Bay.

Sandwich's claim to fame is its prominence as the home to the nation's first glass factories in the early to mid-19th centuries. The town still supports a number of highly skilled glassmakers.

Cape Cod

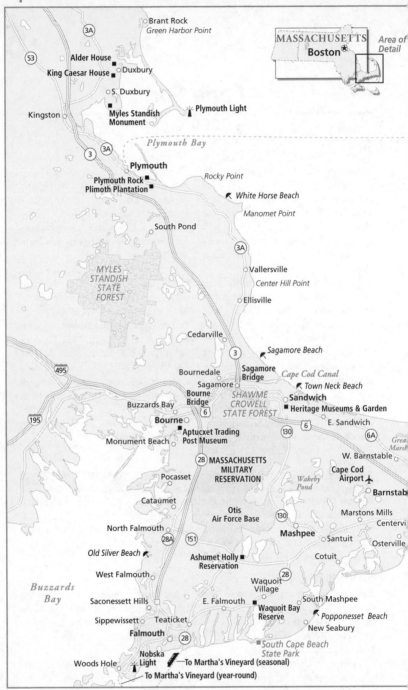

MASSACHUSETTS
Boston
Area of Detail

Brant Rock
Green Harbor Point
3A
53
Alder House
King Caesar House
Duxbury
S. Duxbury
Plymouth Light
Kingston
Myles Standish Monument
3
3A
Plymouth Bay
Plymouth
Rocky Point
Plymouth Rock
Plimoth Plantation
White Horse Beach
Manomet Point
South Pond
3A
MYLES STANDISH STATE FOREST
Vallersville
Center Hill Point
Ellisville
Cedarville
Sagamore Beach
495
3
Bournedale
Sagamore Bridge
Cape Cod Canal
Sagamore
Town Neck Beach
Bourne Bridge
Buzzards Bay
SHAWME CROWELL STATE FOREST
Sandwich
Heritage Museums & Garden
195
Bourne
6
E. Sandwich
6A
Aptucket Trading Post Museum
Great Marsh
Monument Beach
130
W. Barnstable
28
MASSACHUSETTS MILITARY RESERVATION
Cape Cod Airport
Barnstab
Pocasset
Wakeby Pond
Cataumet
Otis Air Force Base
130
Marstons Mills
Centervi
North Falmouth
Mashpee
Santuit
Osterville
28A
151
Old Silver Beach
Ashumet Holly Reservation
Cotuit
West Falmouth
28
Waquoit Village
Buzzards Bay
Saconessett Hills
E. Falmouth
South Mashpee
Sippewissett
Teaticket
Waquoit Bay Reserve
Popponesset Beach
Falmouth
New Seabury
28
South Cape Beach State Park
Nobska Light
To Martha's Vineyard (seasonal)
Woods Hole
To Martha's Vineyard (year-round)

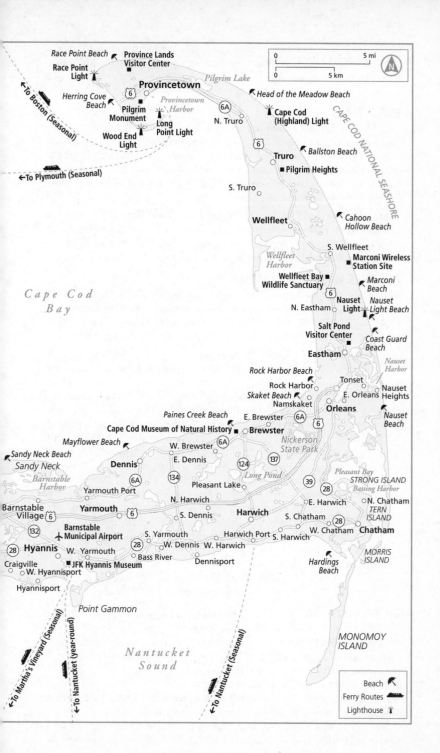

Race Point Beach
Province Lands Visitor Center
Race Point Light
Provincetown
Pilgrim Lake
0   5 mi
0   5 km
Head of the Meadow Beach
To Boston (Seasonal)
Herring Cove Beach
6
Pilgrim Monument
Provincetown Harbor
Long Point Light
N. Truro
6A
Cape Cod (Highland) Light
Wood End Light
CAPE COD NATIONAL SEASHORE
6
Truro
Ballston Beach
To Plymouth (Seasonal)
Pilgrim Heights
S. Truro

Cape Cod Bay

Wellfleet
Cahoon Hollow Beach
S. Wellfleet
Marconi Wireless Station Site
Wellfleet Harbor
Wellfleet Bay Wildlife Sanctuary
Marconi Beach
6
Nauset Light
Nauset Light Beach
N. Eastham
Salt Pond Visitor Center
Coast Guard Beach
Eastham
Nauset Harbor
Rock Harbor Beach
Tonset
Rock Harbor
Skaket Beach
Namskaket
E. Orleans
Nauset Heights
Orleans
Nauset Beach
Paines Creek Beach
E. Brewster
6A
Cape Cod Museum of Natural History
Brewster
6
Mayflower Beach
W. Brewster
6A
Nickerson State Park
Pleasant Bay
Sandy Neck Beach
W. Dennis
E. Dennis
124
137
STRONG ISLAND
Sandy Neck
Dennis
39
Bassing Harbor
Barnstable Harbor
6A
134
Long Pond
Pleasant Lake
28
N. Chatham
TERN ISLAND
Yarmouth Port
N. Harwich
E. Harwich
Barnstable Village
6
Yarmouth
6
S. Dennis
Harwich
S. Chatham
28
132
Barnstable Municipal Airport
S. Yarmouth
Harwich Port
W. Chatham
Chatham
28 **Hyannis**
28
W. Dennis
W. Harwich
MORRIS ISLAND
W. Yarmouth
Bass River
S. Harwich
Craigville
JFK Hyannis Museum
Dennisport
Hardings Beach
W. Hyannisport
Hyannisport
Point Gammon
MONOMOY ISLAND
To Martha's Vineyard (Seasonal)
To Nantucket (year-round)
To Nantucket (Seasonal)
To Nantucket (Seasonal)
Nantucket Sound

Beach
Ferry Routes
Lighthouse

The town is popular with families and nature buffs who will find excellent spots for hiking, biking, and canoeing. Sandwich also makes a convenient base for exploring other parts of the Cape that may offer more lively activities, like the nightlife of Hyannis or the ocean beaches of Wellfleet.

ESSENTIALS

GETTING THERE   Cross the Cape Cod Canal on either the Bourne or Sagamore Bridge. At the Bourne Bridge rotary, take Sandwich Road along the canal; it turns into Route 6A as it nears Sandwich Center. If you cross the Sagamore Bridge, take Exit 1 or 2, and follow Sandwich Road/Route 6A or Route 130, respectively, to Sandwich Center. Sandwich is 3 miles east of the Sagamore Bridge, 16 miles northwest of Hyannis.

VISITOR INFORMATION   The **Cape Cod Canal Region Chamber of Commerce,** 70 Main St., Buzzards Bay (© **508/759-6000;** fax 508/759-6965; www.capecodcanalchamber.org), is open year-round, daily 9am to 5pm. An excellent walking guide is available at most inns in town.

BEACHES & GETTING OUTSIDE

BEACHES   For the beaches listed below, nonresident parking stickers—$40 for the length of your stay—are available at **Sandwich Town Hall Annex,** 145 Main St. (© **508/833-8012**). Note that there's no swimming allowed within the Cape Cod Canal, as the currents are much too swift and dangerous.

- **Sandy Neck Beach** ★★★, off Sandy Neck Road in East Sandwich: This 6-mile stretch of silken barrier beach with low, rounded dunes is one of the Cape's most beautiful beaches; in summer, its parking lot tends to fill up early. It's also popular with endangered piping plovers—and their nemesis, off-road vehicles (ORVs). That means that ORV trails are closed for some of the summer while the chicks hatch. ORV permits ($100 per season for nonresidents) can be purchased at the gatehouse (© **508/362-8300**). ORV drivers must be equipped with supplies like a spare tire, jack, shovel, and tire-pressure gauge. Parking costs $10 per day in season. Up to 3 days of camping in self-contained vehicles is permitted at $10 to $12 per night.
- **Town Neck Beach,** off Town Neck Road in Sandwich: A bit rocky but ruggedly pretty, this narrow beach offers a busy view of passing ships, plus restrooms and a snack bar. Parking costs $10 per day, or you could hike from town (about 1½ miles) via the community-built boardwalk spanning the salt marsh.
- **Wakeby Pond,** Ryder Conservation Area, John Ewer Road (off South Sandwich Rd. on the Mashpee border): The beach, on the Cape's largest freshwater pond, has lifeguards, restrooms, and parking ($10 per day).

BICYCLING   The **Cape Cod Canal bike path** ★★★ is actually two flat 7-mile paths on each side of the canal, maintained by the U.S. Army Corps of Engineers (© **508/759-5991** for recreation hotline). For easy access for the path on the Cape side of the canal, park free at the Bourne Recreation Area, north of the Bourne Bridge, on the Cape side. You can also park free at the Sandcatcher Recreation Area at the end of Freezer Road in Sandwich. For the path on the mainland side of the canal, you can park at the **Cape Cod Canal Region Chamber of Commerce** parking lot at 70 Main St., in Buzzards Bay.

 The closest bike-rental shop is on the mainland side of the canal at **P&M Cycles** at 29 Main St. in Buzzards Bay (© **508/759-2830**), opposite the railroad station. The shop also offers free parking.

BOATING   To explore by canoe, rent one in Falmouth (see below) and paddle around Old Sandwich Harbor, Sandy Neck, or the salt-marsh maze of Scorton Creek, which leads out to Talbot Point.

FISHING   Sandwich has eight fishable ponds; for licenses, inquire at **Town Hall** in the center of town (℃ **508/888-0340**). No permit is required to fish from the banks of the Cape Cod Canal. Call the **Army Corps of Engineers** (℃ **508/759-5991**) for canal tide and fishing information.

NATURE & WILDLIFE AREAS   The **Shawme-Crowell State Forest,** off Route 130 in Sandwich (℃ **508/888-0351**), offers 285 campsites and 742 acres to roam. Entrance is free; parking costs $2. The **Sandwich Boardwalk** links the town and Town Neck Beach by way of salt marshes that attract many birds, including great blue herons.

The 57-acre **Green Briar Nature Center & Jam Kitchen** ✸, 6 Discovery Hill Rd., off Rte. 6A (℃ **508/888-6870**), has a mile-long path crossing marsh and stands of white pine.

MUSEUMS

Heritage Museums and Gardens ✸✸✸ *Finds* *Kids*   This is one of those rare museums that appeals equally to adults and children. The 76 beautifully landscaped acres are crisscrossed with walking paths and riotous with color in late spring, when the museum's famous collection of towering rhododendrons are in bloom. Scattered buildings house a wide variety of collections, from Native American artifacts to Cape Cod Baseball League memorabilia. The high point for most kids will be a ride on the 1912 carousel. There's also a replica Shaker round barn packed with gleaming antique automobiles. Outdoor summer concerts are usually held Sundays around 2pm.

Grove and Pine sts. (about ½ mile SW of the town center). ℃ 508/888-3300. Admission $12 adults, $10 seniors, $6 children 6–16, 5 and under free. AE, DISC, MC, V. May–Oct Fri to Wed 9am–6pm; Thurs 9am–8pm; Nov–April Wed–Sun 10am–4pm.

Sandwich Glass Museum ✸✸ *Finds*   Even if you don't consider yourself a glass fan, make an exception for this fascinating museum, which captures the history of the town above and beyond its legendary industry. A brief video introduces Deming Jarves's brilliant 19th-century endeavor bringing glassware—a hitherto rare commodity available only to the rich—within reach of the middle classes. All went well until Midwestern factories undercut Jarves by using coal to fire their furnaces. Unable to keep up with their level of mass production, Jarves switched back to handblown techniques just as his workforce was ready to revolt. An excellent little gift shop stocks Sandwich-glass replicas and original glassworks. In summer, volunteers demonstrate glass-blowing techniques.

129 Main St. (in the center of town). ℃ 508/888-0251. www.sandwichglassmuseum.org. Admission $3.75 adults, $1 children 6–14, free for children under 6. Apr–Dec daily 9:30am–5pm; Feb–Mar Wed–Sun 9:30am–4pm. Closed Jan, Thanksgiving, and Christmas.

WHERE TO STAY

There are many motels along Route 6A in Sandwich, but the one with the best location is **Sandy Neck Motel** at 669 Rte. 6A, East Sandwich (℃ **800/564-3992** or 508/362-3992; www.sandyneck.com), which sits at the entrance to the road leading to Sandy Neck, the best beach in these parts. Rates are $89 to $99 double and $125 to $225 for one- and two-room efficiencies. Closed November to mid-April.

The Belfry Inne ★★ *Finds*   This Victorian rectory and the church next door have been converted into Sandwich's most stylish lodging. Rooms in the rectory have queen-size antique beds, claw-foot tubs (or Jacuzzis), and a scattering of fireplaces and balconies. The third floor, with its single attic rooms and its delightful *Alice in Wonderland* mural leading up to the belfry, is perfect for families. Next door in the Abbey are six deluxe guest rooms and a very fine **restaurant** (see below). The Abbey rooms are painted vivid colors and tucked cleverly into sections of the old church. The owner recently purchased the Village Inn nearby with eight rooms decorated in a French country style.

8 Jarves St. (in the center of town), Sandwich, MA 02563. ℂ 800/844-4542 or 508/888-8550. Fax 508/888-3922. www.belfryinn.com. 22 units. Summer $95–$195 double. Rates include continental breakfast. AE, MC, V. **Amenities:** Restaurant (New American).

The Dan'l Webster Inn ★★   This large, popular inn is a dependable bet for a comfortable stay or a hearty meal. The main building sits on the site of a colonial tavern favored by Daniel Webster, the famous orator and Boston lawyer. Guest rooms are ample and nicely furnished with reproductions. Deluxe suites, some in nearby historic houses, offer perks like balconies, gas fireplaces, oversize whirlpool tubs, and heated tile bathroom floors. The inn's common spaces are convivial, if bustling; the restaurant is a tour bus lunch spot that turns out surprisingly sophisticated fare.

149 Main St. (in the center of town), Sandwich, MA 02563. ℂ 800/444-3566 or 508/888-3622. Fax 508/888-5156. www.danlwebsterinn.com. 54 units. Summer $159–$229 double; $219–$359 suite. Off-season rates include full breakfast. AE, DC, DISC, MC, V. **Amenities:** Restaurant (New American); tavern/bar; small outdoor heated pool; access to local health club; limited room service. *In room:* A/C, TV, dataport, hair dryer, iron.

Isaiah Jones Homestead ★ *Value*   Of the many B&Bs in Sandwich Center, this one is a particularly good value, though the fancier rooms tend to be more expensive (and more elegant) than those at other small B&Bs in town. Innkeepers Jan and Doug Klapper have carefully appointed this courtly 1849 Victorian with fine antiques and reproductions. Many rooms have additional romantic touches like fireplaces and whirlpool baths. Two mini-suites in the Carriage House have sitting alcoves. The room named for industrial magnate Deming Jarves boasts an inviting floral-curtained half-canopy bed and an oversize whirlpool tub. The gentility that prevails at the candlelight breakfast, served with fine china and crystal, completes the picture.

165 Main St. (in the center of town), Sandwich, MA 02563. ℂ 800/526-1625 or 508/888-9115. Fax 508/888-9648. www.isaiahjones.com. 7 units. Summer $115–$175 double. Rates include full breakfast. AE, DISC, DC, MC, V. Children under 12 cannot be accommodated. *In room:* AC, hair dryer, no phone.

Spring Hill Motor Lodge ★   This motel boasts all sorts of amenities, like the night-lit tennis court and the large pool. The interiors are cheerfully contemporary, the grounds beautifully landscaped. In addition to the motel rooms, there are four cottages that are light, airy, and comfortable.

351 Rte. 6A (about 2½ miles E of the town center), East Sandwich, MA 02537. ℂ 800/647-2514 or 508/888-1456. Fax 508/833-1556. www.sunsol.com/springhill. 24 units (20 tub/shower), 4 cottages (shower only). Summer $95–$150 double; $155–$225 efficiency; $185–$250 or $1,100 weekly for 1-bedroom cottage; $225–$325 or $1,400 weekly for 2-bedroom cottage. AE, DC, DISC, MC, V. **Amenities:** Heated outdoor pool; night-lit tennis court. *In room:* A/C, TV, fridge, coffeemaker.

Wingscorton Farm Inn ★★ *Kids* *Finds*   This colonial farmhouse on 7 acres will delight youngsters and animal lovers of all ages. It's been a working farm since 1758 and still houses a cheerful brood of sheep, goats, dogs, cats, chickens, a pet turkey, and a potbellied pig. The paneled guest rooms have canopy beds, working fireplaces, and braided rugs. Modernists might prefer the carriage house, with its skylight-suffused loft bedroom, kitchen (with woodstove), and private deck. A private bay beach is a short walk down a country lane.

11 Wing Blvd. (off Rte. 6A, about 5 miles E of the town center), East Sandwich, MA 02537. © 508/888-0534. Fax 508/888-0545. 3 units, carriage house, cottage. Summer $175 suite; $200 carriage house; $1,100 weekly cottage. Rates for suites and carriage house include full breakfast. AE, MC, V. Pets welcome. *In room:* A/C, TV, fridge, no phone.

WHERE TO DINE

Aquagrille ☆ SEAFOOD   Overlooking the town's picturesque marina and not-so-picturesque power plant, this place wants to be the premier place for fish in Sandwich. The towering lobster salad with *haricot vert*, tomato, avocado, chives, and crème fraîche is the perfect antidote to a steamy summer night. Those with larger appetites may want to try the baby-back pork spareribs with peach barbecue sauce, which comes with—what else?—potato salad and Boston baked beans. Ask for a table that doesn't face the power plant.

14 Gallo Rd. (next to Sandwich Marina). © 508/888-8889. www.aquagrille.com. Reservations recommended. Main courses $8–$20. AE, DC, MC, V. Apr–Oct Mon–Fri 11:30am–2:30pm and 5–9pm, Sat–Sun noon–9pm; call for off-season hours.

The Bee-Hive Tavern ☆ INTERNATIONAL   A cut above the rather characterless restaurants clustered along this stretch of road, this tavern employs atmospheric old-time touches: Green-shaded banker's lamps illuminate the dark wood booths, and vintage prints convey a clubby feel. The food is good if not spectacular, and well priced for what it is: straightforward but tasty. Steaks, chops, and fresh fish among the pricier choices, while burgers, sandwiches, and salads cater to lighter appetites (and wallets). At lunch, try the lobster roll, one of the Cape's best.

406 Rte. 6A (about ½ mile E of the town center), East Sandwich. © 508/833-1184. Main courses $7–$16. MC, V. Mon–Sat 11:30am–3pm and 5–9pm; Sun 8–11:30am, noon–3pm, 5–9pm.

The Belfry Bistro ☆☆ *Finds* NEW AMERICAN   Sandwich's most romantic dining option is located in a restored 19th-century church (see the Belfry Inne under "Where to Stay," above). Entrees range from delicate shrimp scampi with artichoke hearts to hearty grilled filet mignon served with garlic and leek mashed potatoes on a white bean ragout. Desserts here are clearly a specialty; especially good is the old-fashioned Victorian gingerbread with fresh berries. There is a piano bar Friday and Saturday nights. Because this restaurant hosts many weddings and other events, it is sometimes closed to the public, so be sure to call ahead.

8 Jarves St. (in the center of town). © 508/888-8550. Reservations recommended. Main courses $19–$29. AE, MC, V. Feb–Dec Tues–Sat 5–10pm; call for off-season hours. Closed Jan.

The Dan'l Webster Inn ☆☆ *Kids* AMERICAN   You have a choice of four main dining rooms—from a casual, colonial-motif tavern to a skylight-topped conservatory fronting a splendid garden. The atmospheric Tavern at the Inn, with its own pub-style menu, is the most popular. A restaurant on this scale could probably get away with ho-hum food, but the output is on a par with that of the Cape's best boutique restaurants. Try a classic dish like the *fruits de mer* in white wine.

149 Main St. (in the center of town). © 508/888-3622. Reservations recommended. Main courses $18–$29; Tavern menu $7–$14. AE, DC, DISC, MC, V. Daily 8am–9pm; call for off-season hours.

Marshland Restaurant *Value* DINER Locals have been digging this diner for 2 decades. This is home-cooked grub, slung fast and cheap. You'll gobble up the hearty breakfast and be back in time for dinner.

109 Rte. 6A. ℂ 508/888-9824. Most items under $10. No credit cards. Mon 6am–2pm; Tues–Sat 6am–8pm. Open year-round.

FALMOUTH & WOODS HOLE ★★★

Falmouth is a classic New England town, complete with church steeples encircling the town green and a walkable and bustling Main Street. With over 32,000 year-round residents, it's the second largest town on the Cape, after Barnstable.

Woods Hole ★★★, one of eight villages in Falmouth, has been a world-renowned oceanic research center since 1871, when the U.S. Commission of Fish and Fisheries set up a primitive seasonal collection station. Today the various scientific institutes crowded around—the National Marine Fisheries Service, the Marine Biological Laboratory, and the Woods Hole Oceanographic Institute—employ thousands of scientists. They offer a unique opportunity to get in-depth—and often hands-on—exposure to marine biology. Woods Hole is also one of the hipper communities on the Cape, with a number of restaurants, bars, and shops making crowded Water Street (don't even think of parking here in summer) a very pleasant place to stroll.

Falmouth Heights ★★★, a cluster of shingled Victorian summer houses on a bluff east of Falmouth's harbor, is as popular as it is picturesque; its narrow ribbon of beach is a magnet for all, especially families.

ESSENTIALS

GETTING THERE After crossing the Bourne Bridge, take Route 28 south. It's 18 miles south of the Bourne Bridge, 20 miles southwest of Hyannis.

Falmouth's bus station near the center of town is serviced by **Bonanza Bus Lines** (59 Depot Ave.; ℂ **508/548-7588;** www.bonanzabus.com). There are daily buses from Boston, Providence, and New York.

GETTING AROUND To get around Falmouth and Woods Hole (where parking in summer is a mathematical impossibility due to ferry traffic to Martha's Vineyard), use the **Whoosh Trolley,** which makes a circuit every 20 minutes down Falmouth's Main Street to Woods Hole. You can flag it down anywhere along the route.

The **Sea Line Shuttle** (ℂ **800/352-7155**) connects Woods Hole and Falmouth, with Hyannis year-round (except holidays). The fare ranges from $1 to $3.50, depending on distance.

VISITOR INFORMATION Contact the **Falmouth Chamber of Commerce,** Academy Lane, Falmouth, MA 02541 (ℂ **800/526-8532** or 508/548-8500; fax 508/548-8521; www.falmouth-capecod.com).

SPECIAL EVENTS

The **Falmouth Road Race** (www.falmouthroadrace.com), on the second Sunday in August, is a 7.3-mile run from the Captain Kidd Bar in Woods Hole to the British Beer Company in Falmouth Heights. It all started nearly 30 years ago when two buddies decided to race from one bar to the other. Now the race attracts 10,000 participants from all over the world. Those who want to run need to apply to a lottery in April.

BEACHES & GETTING OUTSIDE

BEACHES While Old Silver Beach, Surf Drive Beach, and Menauhant Beach will sell a day pass, most other Falmouth public beaches require a parking sticker.

Passes to Old Silver are $20 and passes to Surf Drive and Menauhant are $10. Renters can obtain temporary beach parking stickers for $50 per week or $80 per month at **Falmouth Town Hall,** 59 Town Hall Sq. (© 508/548-7611), or at the **Surf Drive Beach Bathhouse** in season (© 508/548-8623). The town beaches for which a parking fee is charged all have lifeguards, restrooms, and concession stands. Falmouth's public shores include:

- **Falmouth Heights Beach** ✷✷✷, off Grand Avenue in Falmouth Heights: Once a rowdy spot, this is now primarily a family beach. Parking is sticker-only. This neighborhood supported the Cape's first summer colony. The grand Victorian mansions still overlook the beach.
- **Grew's Pond** ✷✷, in Goodwill Park off Palmer Avenue in Falmouth: This freshwater pond in a large town forest stays fairly uncrowded, even in the middle of summer. While everyone else is trying to find parking at Falmouth's popular saltwater beaches, here you can park for free and wander shady paths around the pond. There's a playground, picnic tables, barbecue grills, lifeguard, and restrooms.
- **Menauhant Beach** ✷, off Central Avenue in East Falmouth: A bit off the beaten track, Menauhant is a little less mobbed than Falmouth Heights Beach and better protected from the winds. Parking costs $10.
- **Old Silver Beach** ✷✷✷, off Route 28A in North Falmouth: Western-facing (great for sunsets) and relatively calm, this warm Buzzards Bay beach is a popular, often crowded, choice. This is the chosen spot for the college crowd. Families with young children cluster on the opposite side of the street where a shallow pool formed by a sandbar is perfect for toddlers. Parking costs $20.
- **Surf Drive Beach** ✷✷✷, off Shore Street in Falmouth: About a half mile from downtown, this is an easy-to-get-to choice. The tidal beach between the jetties is a shallow, calm area called "the kiddie pool." Parking is limited and costs $10.

BICYCLING   The **Shining Sea Bicycle Path** ✷✷✷ (© 508/548-8500) is a 3.3-mile beauty skirting Vineyard Sound from Falmouth to Woods Hole with plenty of swimmable beach along the way. (Unfortunately, most of the beach along this stretch is rocky.) You can park at the trailhead on Locust Street in Falmouth or at any spot in town (parking in Woods Hole is scarce). The closest bike shop is **Corner Cycle** at Palmer Avenue and North Main Street (© 508/540-4195) near the Village Green.

BOATING   **Patriot Party Boats,** 227 Clinton Ave. (at Scranton Ave. on the harbor), Falmouth (© 800/734-0088 or 508/548-2626; www.patriotparty boats.com, www.TheLiberte.com), offers scenic cruises around Vineyard Sound aboard the three-masted schooner **Liberte** ✷✷. Two-hour sails cost $20 to $25 for adults and $15 to $18 for children 12 and under. Also offered in July and August are 2-hour sunset cruises on the *Patriot Too.*

Cape Cod Kayak (© 508/563-9377; www.capecodkayak.com) rents kayaks and offers lessons and eco-tours. **Waquoit Kayak Company** at **Edward's Boat Yard,** 1209 E. Falmouth Hwy., East Falmouth (© 508/548-9722), rents out canoes for exploring Waquoit Bay (see "Nature & Wildlife Areas," below). **Washburn Island** ✷✷✷, a protected reserve with wooded trails and pristine beaches, is about a 1-hour paddle via canoe.

FISHING   Falmouth has six fishable ponds. A free guide is available from the Falmouth Chamber of Commerce. Freshwater fishing and shellfishing licenses can be obtained at **Falmouth Town Hall,** 59 Town Hall Sq. (℃ **508/548-7611,** ext. 219). Freshwater fishing licenses can also be obtained at **Eastman's Sport & Tackle,** 150 Main St. (℃ **508/548-6900**).

Surf Drive Beach is a great spot for surfcasting, once the crowds have dispersed. Other good locations are the jetties off Nobska Point in Woods Hole and Bristol Beach on Menauhant Road in East Falmouth.

To go after bigger prey, head out with a group on one of the **Patriot Party Boats** (℃ **800/734-0088** or 508/548-2626; www.patriotpartyboats.com). Boats leave twice daily in season. The clunky *Patriot Too,* with an enclosed deck, is ideal for family-style "bottom fishing" (4-hr. sails $30 adults, $20 children under 12; equipment provided).

For sportfishing out of Falmouth Inner Harbor, call Capt. Bob MacGregor of the **Hop-Tuit** (℃ **508/540-7642**), or Captain Dan Junker of **Cool Running Charters** (℃ **508/457-9445**).

NATURE & WILDLIFE AREAS   **Ashumet Holly and Wildlife Sanctuary** ★★, operated by the Massachusetts Audubon Society at 186 Ashumet Rd., off Route 151 (℃ **508/362-1426**), is an intriguing 49-acre collection of more than 1,000 holly trees, along with over 130 species of birds and a kettle pond that's covered with a carpet of Oriental lotus blossoms in summer. The trail fee is $3 for adults and $2 for seniors and children under 16.

Near the center of Falmouth (follow Depot Rd. to the end) is the 650-acre **Beebe Woods** ★★, a treasure for hikers and dog walkers. From here, you can wend your way to the 90-acre **Peterson Farm** ★★ (entrance off Woods Hole Rd.; take a right at the Quisset farm stand) with paths through woods and fields, as well as a flock of sheep and a llama grazing in a meadow. Bluebird boxes (special birdhouses for bluebirds) line the path on the way to a quiet pond.

The 2,250-acre **Waquoit Bay National Estuarine Research Reserve (WBN-ERR),** at 149 Waquoit Hwy. in East Falmouth (℃ **508/457-0495;** www.waquoit bayreserve.org), maintains a 1-mile nature trail. Also inquire about the boat ride to **Washburn Island** ★★★ on Saturdays in season by reservation. After the 20-minute boat trip to the island, naturalist-led guided walks are offered.

WATERSPORTS   Falmouth is something of a sailboarding mecca, prized for its unflagging southwesterly winds. While Old Silver Beach in North Falmouth is the most popular spot for windsurfing, the sport is allowed there only prior to 9am and after 5pm. The Trunk River area on the west end of Falmouth's Surf Drive Beach and a portion of Chapoquoit Beach are the only public beaches where windsurfers are allowed during the day.

SEA SCIENCE

Woods Hole Aquarium ★ *Kids*   A little beat-up after more than a century of service, this aquarium—the first such institution in the country—may not be state of the art, but it's a treasure nonetheless. The displays, focusing on local waters, might make you think twice before taking a dip. Children show no hesitation, though, in getting up to their elbows in the "touch tanks." A key exhibit concerns the effect of plastic trash on the marine environment. The seals who live here are fed at 11am and 4pm.

Albatross St. (off the western end of Water St.), Woods Hole. ℃ **508/495-2001**. Donations accepted. Mid-June to early Sept daily 11am–4pm; mid-Sept to mid-June Mon–Fri 10am–4pm. You need a picture I.D. to enter.

Woods Hole Oceanographic Institution Exhibit Center and Gift Shop
This world-class research organization—locally referred to by its acronym,

WHOI (pronounced "Hooey")—is dedicated to the study of marine science. Kids might enjoy looking through microscopes at organisms or listening to sounds of marine animals on a computer. *Titanic* fans will enjoy the brief video, displays, and a life-size model of the submersible that discovered the wreck. Walking tours of WHOI are offered twice a day on weekdays in July and August, reservations required; call © **508/289-2252.**

15 School St. (off Water St.), Woods Hole. © **508/289-2663.** $2 donation requested. Late May to early Sept Mon–Sat 10am–4:30pm, Sun noon–4:30pm; call for off-season hours. Closed Jan–Mar.

WHERE TO STAY
EXPENSIVE

Coonamessett Inn ★★   A gracious inn built around the core of a 1796 homestead, the Coonamessett Inn is Falmouth's most traditional lodging choice. Set on 7 lush acres overlooking a pond, it has the feel of a country club. Some of the guest rooms, decorated in reproduction antiques, can be a bit somber, so try to get one with good light. Most have a separate sitting room attached. On site is a restaurant featuring a very comfortable tavern room as well as a more formal dining room. The extensive buffet brunch here on Sundays brings out people from all over town.

Jones Rd. and Gifford St. (about ½ mile N of Main St.), Falmouth, MA 02540. © **508/548-2300.** Fax 508/540-9831. www.capecodrestaurants.org. 27 units, 1 cottage. Summer $150–$180 double; $175–$230 2-bedroom suite; $200–$260 cottage. Rates include continental breakfast. AE, MC, V. **Amenities:** 2 restaurants (1 fancy, 1 tavern with entertainment). *In room:* A/C, TV, coffeemaker, hair dryer.

Inn at West Falmouth ★★   One of the loveliest small inns on the Cape, this turn-of-the-century shingle-style house is set high on a wooded hill with distant views to Buzzards Bay. The large living room has heaps of bestsellers begging to be borrowed, while the guest rooms are lavished with custom linens and unusual antiques. Some units have small balconies and whirlpool tubs. After a leisurely breakfast, you might carry off a tome to the small deck pool set in the deck or wander the landscaped grounds. Chapoquoit Beach is about a 10-minute walk away.

66 Frazar Rd. (off Rte. 28A), West Falmouth, MA 02574. © **508/540-7696.** www.innatwestfalmouth.com. 7 units. Summer $250–$345 double. Rates include continental breakfast. AE, MC, V. **Amenities:** Small outdoor heated pool; clay tennis court; billiard room, masseuse on staff (fee). *In room:* AC, cable TV, hair dryer, iron.

Scallop Shell Inn ★★ *Finds*   This deluxe B&B, located just steps from Falmouth Heights Beach, is one of Falmouth's best. Several rooms have wonderful views of Vineyard Sound and Martha's Vineyard, and guests are apt to be found lounging on the wide front porch. Several of the rooms have gas fireplaces and two-person whirlpool tubs. Two units have balconies; several have private entrances. In the billiard and sitting room guests can enjoy a drink from the wet bar; they also have free rein in the guest kitchenette, stocked with beverages and homemade treats. The four-course gourmet breakfast could include an omelet with lobster, asparagus, and Gruyère.

16 Massachusetts Ave., Falmouth Heights, MA 02540. © **800/249-4587** or 508/495-4900. Fax 508/495-4600. www.scallopshellinn.com. 7 units. Summer $225–$330 double. Rates include full breakfast. AE, DISC, MC, V. **Amenities:** Free laundry room. *In room:* A/C, TV/VCR, safe.

MODERATE

For a basic motel with a great location, try the **Tides Motel** (© **508/548-3126**) at the west end of Grand Avenue in Falmouth Heights. The 1950s-style no-frills (no air-conditioning, no phone) motel is a good value. It sits on the beach at the head of Falmouth Harbor facing Vineyard Sound. Rates in season are $140 to $150 double, $195 suite. Closed late October to mid-May.

The **Red Horse Inn** ★ (✆ **508/548-0053;** www.redhorseinn.com) is a family-friendly option just a short walk from Falmouth Harbor in Falmouth Heights. The 22 rooms are priced from $150 to $250, and kids will love the large outdoor pool.

Inn on the Sound ★★ *Finds*   The ambience here is as breezy as the setting, high on a bluff beside Falmouth's premier sunning beach, with a sweeping view of Vineyard Sound from the large front deck. Innkeeper Renee Ross is an interior decorator, and it shows: There's none of the usual frilly/cutesy stuff in these well-appointed guest rooms, most of which have ocean views, several with their own private decks. The focal point of the inn's living room is a handsome boulder hearth (nice for those nippy nights). Most guests enjoy having their breakfast, which features lots of home-baked goodies, served on the front deck.

313 Grand Ave., Falmouth Heights, MA 02540. ✆ **800/564-9668** or 508/457-9666. Fax 508/457-9631. www.innonthesound.com. 7 units (5 tub/shower; 2 shower only). Summer $150–$295 double, $3,500 a week. Rates include continental breakfast. AE, DISC, MC, V. No children under 16. *In room:* TV, hair dryer, robes, no phone.

Sands of Time Motor Inn & Harbor House ★★   This property, across the street from the ferry terminal for Martha's Vineyard, consists of a two-story motel in front of a shingled 1879 Victorian mansion. The motel rooms feature crisp, above-average decor, plus private balconies overlooking the harbor. The rooms in the Harbor House are more lavish—some with four-poster beds and working fireplaces.

549 Woods Hole Rd., Woods Hole, MA 02543. ✆ **800/841-0114** or 508/548-6300. Fax 508/457-0160. www.sandsoftime.com. 36 units (2 with shared bathroom). Summer $130–$200 double. Rates include continental breakfast. AE, DC, DISC, MC, V. Closed Nov–Mar. **Amenities:** Small heated pool; 2 tennis courts. *In room:* A/C, TV.

Wildflower Inn ★★   Though located on a busy stretch of road, this B&B is immaculately appointed and full of welcoming touches, like the row of rocking chairs lining the front porch. Guest rooms are creatively and individually decorated with wicker furnishings and country quilts. A stand-alone apartment features a loft bedroom served by a spiral staircase. The five-course breakfast might include apple-pie French toast garnished with edible flowers. The inn is across the street from the satellite parking lot for the Martha's Vineyard ferries, so you can easily hop a bus down to the terminal in Woods Hole.

167 Palmer Ave. (2 blocks N of Main St.), Falmouth, MA 02540. ✆ **800/294-5459** or 508/548-9524. Fax 508/548-9524. www.wildflower-inn.com. 5 units, 1 cottage (4 tub/shower; 2 shower only). Summer $185–$250 double; $275 cottage. Rates include full breakfast. AE, MC, V. *In room:* A/C, hair dryer, robes, no phone.

INEXPENSIVE

Inn at One Main   Though built back in 1892, this shingled house with Queen Anne flourishes still has a youthful air. The bedrooms embody barefoot romance, rather than the Victorian brand. Lace, chintz, and wicker have been laid on lightly, leaving plenty of room to kick about. The Turret Room, with its big brass bed, is perhaps the most irresistible. Breakfasts feature gingerbread pancakes, orange-pecan French toast, homemade scones—it's a good thing the Shining Sea bike path is right at hand.

1 Main St. (1 block NW of the Village Green), Falmouth, MA 02540. ✆ **888/281-6246** or 508/540-7469. Fax 603/462-5680. www.innatonemain.com. 6 units. Summer $110–$150 double. Rates include full breakfast. AE, DISC, MC, V. *In room:* A/C, hair dryer, no phone.

WHERE TO DINE
EXPENSIVE

La Cucina Sul Mare ✿✿ ITALIAN Locals and tourists alike line up outside this popular Main Street restaurant, craving its hearty Italian fare. The interior features cheerful murals and a tin ceiling, and large picture windows overlook Main Street. Chef/owner Mark Ciflone's signature dishes include classic Italian specialties like lasagna, braised lamb shanks, osso buco, lobster *fra diavlo* over linguine, *zuppa de pesce,* rigatoni a la vodka, chicken Parmesan, and veal piccata, among others. The desserts here are homemade and truly delicious.

237 Main St., Falmouth. ⓒ 508/548-5600. Reservations required. Main courses $15–$25. AE, MC, V. Tues–Sun 11:30am–2pm and 5–10pm. Open year-round.

Fishmonger's Cafe ✿✿ NATURAL This sunny cafe jutting out into the harbor attracts local young people, scientists, and tourists, for an array of imaginatively prepared dishes, with vegetarian choices a specialty. Lunch could be a tempeh burger or a regular beef version. The eclectic, changing dinner menu includes some Thai entrees. Regulars sit at the counter to enjoy a bowl of the Fisherman's Stew while newcomers usually go for the tables by the window, where you can watch boats come and go from Eel Pond.

56 Water St. (at the Eel Pond drawbridge), Woods Hole. ⓒ 508/540-5376. Main courses $15–$25. AE, MC, V. Mid-June to Oct Wed–Mon 7am–10pm; Tues noon–10pm. Call for off-season hours. Closed mid-Dec to mid-Feb.

Phusion Grille ✿✿ NEW AMERICAN/ASIAN This is one of Falmouth's best restaurants, combining excellent food, professional service, and a terrific location on Eel Pond in Woods Hole. The interior is all blond wood and Asian screens, but nothing blocks the views of the wraparound floor-to-ceiling windows. The chef/owner Bin Phu combines his classical training with imaginative innovations nightly. The menu changes nightly depending on the catch of the day, but keep an eye out for the bouillabaisse and the sautéed sea scallops tossed with artichokes and a lobster sherry cream sauce. There's also a sushi bar. The dessert menu here is an all-chocolate affair, with scrumptious homemade items like Key lime pie with chocolate sauce and chocolate mousse.

71 Water St., Woods Hole. ⓒ **508/457-3100.** Reservations not accepted. Main courses $20–$27. AE, MC, V. Daily 11:30am–2pm and 5–10pm. Call for off-season hours.

RooBar ✿✿ NEW AMERICAN RooBar is the top restaurant in town, for service, food, and atmosphere. The arty decor of this stylish bistro features hand-blown glass lamps over the bar and metal sconce sculptures on the walls. The food is exceptionally yummy, if pricey. Creative appetizers include Thai wontons with ginger chicken and a crispy tuna stick with a spicy dipper sauce. As a main course, try the snapper pie, which is a braised snapper in a puff pastry. Pizzas from the wood-burning oven come with unusual toppings like scallop and prosciutto. They don't take reservations, but if you call a half-hour ahead, you can put your name on the waiting list.

285 Main St. (at Cahoon Court.). ⓒ **508/548-8600.** Reservations not accepted. Main courses $11–$26. AE, MC, V. Daily 5–10pm; call for off-season hours.

MODERATE

The Cantina Mexican Bar and Grill ✿ MEXICAN This is Falmouth's only Mexican restaurant and it's a stylish and lively addition to the restaurant scene. In season there is often a long wait for a table because of the no reservations policy. There are usually seats available at the bar, if you don't mind the roar of the blender as it whips up frozen margaritas. The menu features traditional dishes such as burritos, fajitas, and tacos, made with meat, seafood, or vegetarian style. For dessert, there's fried ice cream or drunken plantains topped with vanilla ice cream.

327 Gifford St. (½ mile N of town). © 508/548-9861. Reservations not accepted. Main courses $7–$15. MC, V. Daily 5–10pm.

Chapoquoit Grill ★★ NEW AMERICAN   One of the few worthwhile dining spots in sleepy West Falmouth, this little roadside bistro has Californian aspirations: wood-grilled slabs of fish accompanied by trendy salsas, and crispy personal pizzas delivered straight from the brick oven. People drive here from miles around for the flavorful food. A no-reservations policy means long waits nightly in season and weekends year-round.

410 Rte. 28A, West Falmouth. © 508/540-7794. Reservations not accepted. Main courses $10–$18. MC, V. Daily 5–10pm.

Landfall ★★ AMERICAN   A waterfront setting and good service make this Woods Hole seafood restaurant stand out. Besides the usual fish and pasta dishes, there's "lite fare" like burgers and fish –and chips. This is a great place to bring the kids; a children's menu comes with games and crayons. Or come for a drink at the half-dory bar to enjoy this massive wooden building constructed of salvage, both marine and terrestrial. A large bank of windows looks out onto the harbor, and the Martha's Vineyard ferry, when docking, appears to be making a beeline straight for your table.

Luscombe Ave. (½ block S of Water St.), Woods Hole. © 508/548-1758. Reservations recommended. Main courses $7–$26. AE, MC, V. Mid-May to Sept daily 11:30am–9pm; call for off-season hours. Closed late Nov to mid-Apr.

INEXPENSIVE

Betsy's Diner ★ *Finds* *Kids* AMERICAN   This is hearty food like your mother used to make, if your mother was a variation of June Cleaver. The menu features turkey dinner, breakfast all day, and homemade pies. Some say the fried clams here are the best in town. Each red vinyl booth is equipped with its own jukebox with retro hits.

457 Main St. (in the center of town). © 508/540-0060. No reservations accepted. All items under $11. AE, MC, V. Mon–Sat 6am–9pm; Sun 6am–2pm; call for off-season hours.

The British Beer Company ★ PUB FARE/PIZZA   The view is great at this faux British pub across the street from Falmouth Heights beach. Best choices are the fish and chips, burgers, and pizzas. The lobster bisque is also good and has won local awards. Of course, there is beer, 23 drafts available, like Guinness and John Courage, as well as bottled selections.

263 Grand Ave. (across from the beach), Falmouth Heights. © 508/540-9600. Reservations not accepted. All items under $15. AE, DC, DISC, MC, V. Mon–Sat 11:30am–10pm; Sun noon–10pm.

The Clam Shack ★ *Kids* SEAFOOD   This classic clam shack at the head of Falmouth harbor offers steaming plates of fried seafood that you carry to a picnic table inside, outside, or up on the roof deck. It's basic fare, but the fish is fresh and you can't beat the view.

227 Clinton Ave. (off Scranton Ave., about 1 mile S of Main St.). © 508/540-7758. Reservations not accepted. Main courses $5–$15. No credit cards. Daily 11:30am–7:45pm. Closed early Sept to late May.

FALMOUTH AFTER DARK

The Boathouse (© 508/548-7800) at 88 Scranton Ave. on Falmouth Inner Harbor features live bands in season, from classic rock to jazz, and dancing is popular here. God knows whom you'll meet in the rough-and-tumble old **Cap'n Kidd** ⚓, 77 Water St., in Woods Hole (📞 **508/548-9206**): maybe a lobster-woman, maybe a Nobel Prize winner. Good grub, too. Everyone heads to **Liam Maguire's Irish Pub** ⚓, on 273 Main St. in Falmouth (📞 **508/548-0285**), for a taste of the Emerald Isle. Live music on weekends year-round, often by Liam himself. **Grumpy's**, at 29 Locust St. (📞 **508/540-3930**), is a good old bar/shack with live music (rock, blues, and jazz) Thursday to Saturday nights. Cover is $2 to $10.

2 The Mid-Cape

Visitors who want to be centrally located on Cape Cod choose the Mid-Cape, which is just over an hour from Boston (without traffic), an easy (less than an hour) drive to the Outer Cape, and a 1-hour ferry ride from Nantucket. This is the Cape's most populous area and also the prime location for its cheapest motels, which line Route 28 from Hyannis to Dennis.

Hyannis is the Cape's unofficial capital. It's a sprawling concrete jungle of strip malls and chain stores where the Kennedy mystique of the 1960s had the unfortunate side effect of spurring heedless development over the ensuing decades—a period during which the Cape's year-round population doubled to more than 200,000. The summer population is about three times that, and you'd swear every single person had daily errands to run in Hyannis. And yet this overrun town still has plenty of pockets of charm, especially the waterfront area and Main Street.

The real beauty of the Mid-Cape lies in its smaller places: old-money hide-aways like **Osterville** ⚓ to the west, and charming villages like **West Barnstable** ⚓⚓ and **Yarmouth Port** ⚓⚓, which can be found along the **Old King's Highway** ⚓⚓⚓ (Rte. 6A) on the northern bay side of the Cape. A drive along this winding two-lane road reveals the early architectural history of the region, from humble colonial saltboxes to ostentatious captains' mansions. Scores of intriguing antiques shops subtly compete to draw a closer look, and each village seems a throwback to a kinder, gentler era.

HYANNIS & ENVIRONS ⚓

Hectic Hyannis is the commercial center and transportation hub of the Cape, with the large Cape Cod Mall and busy Barnstable Municipal Airport. It also has a diverse selection of restaurants, bars, and nightclubs. But if you were to confine your visit to this one town, you'd get a warped view of the Cape. Along Routes 132 and 28, you could be visiting Anywhere, USA: The roads are lined with the standard chain stores and mired with maddening traffic.

While Hyannis's impersonal hotels and motels have more beds at better prices than anywhere else on the Cape, there's little reason to choose them unless you happen to have missed the last ferry out to Nantucket. We recommend staying in Hyannisport or heading due north to Barnstable Village, where you'll find myriad charming B&Bs along the scenic Old King's Highway. Once you're settled, you can visit Hyannis to sample some of the Cape's best restaurants and nightlife. See "Barnstable Village & Environs," later in this section.

ESSENTIALS
GETTING THERE   After crossing the Sagamore bridge, head east on Route 6 or 6A. Route 6A passes through Barnstable Village; Route 132 (Exit 6 off Rte. 6) leads to Hyannis. You can also fly into Hyannis, and there is good bus service from Boston and New York.

VISITOR INFORMATION   Contact the **Hyannis Area Chamber of Commerce,** 1481 Rte. 132, Hyannis, MA 02601 (© **800/449-6647,** 877/492-6647, or 508/362-5230; fax 508/362-9499; www.hyannis.com).

BEACHES & GETTING OUTSIDE

BEACHES   Most of the Nantucket Sound beaches are fairly protected and offer little in the way of surf. Parking costs $10 a day, usually payable at the lot; for a weeklong parking sticker ($40), visit the Recreation Department at 141 Basset Lane, at the **Kennedy Memorial Skating Rink** (© **508/790-6345**).

- **Craigville Beach** ★★★, off Craigville Beach Road in Centerville: This broad expanse of sand has lifeguards and restrooms. A destination for the bronzed and buffed, it's known as "Muscle Beach." It's a short walk to Craigville Village, a former Methodist camp meeting site with Carpenter Gothic-style cottages.
- **Kalmus Beach** ★★, off Gosnold Street in Hyannisport: This 800-foot spit of sand stretching toward the mouth of the harbor makes an ideal launching site for windsurfers. The surf is tame, the slope shallow, and the conditions ideal for young kids. There are lifeguards, a snack bar, and restrooms.
- **Orrin Keyes Beach** ★★ (also known as Sea Beach), at the end of Sea Street in Hyannis: This little beach at the end of a residential road is popular with families.
- **Veterans Beach,** off Ocean Street in Hyannis: A small stretch of harborside sand adjoining the John F. Kennedy Memorial, this spot is not tops for swimming. Parking is usually easy, though, and it's walkable from town. The snack bar, restrooms, and playground will see to a family's needs.

FISHING   Among the charter boats berthed in Barnstable Harbor is the 36-foot *Drifter* (© **508/398-2061**), offering half- and full-day trips. **Hy-Line Cruises** offers seasonal sonar-aided "bottom" or blues fishing on boats leaving from its Ocean Street dock in Hyannis (© **508/790-0696**). **Helen H Deep-Sea Fishing** at 137 Pleasant St., Hyannis (© **508/790-0660**), offers year-round expeditions aboard a 100-foot boat with a heated cabin and full galley.

GOLF   The **Hyannis Golf Club,** Route 132 (© **508/362-2606**), offers a 46-station driving range, and an 18-hole championship course. Smaller but scenic is the nine-hole **Cotuit High Ground Country Club,** 31 Crockers Neck Rd., Cotuit (© **508/428-9863**).

WATERSPORTS   **Eastern Mountain Sports,** 1513 Iyannough Rd./Rte. 132 (© **508/362-8690;** www.ems.com), offers rental kayaks—tents and sleeping bags, too—and sponsors free clinics and walks, like a full-moon hike. Kayaks rent for about $40 to $50 a day.

SIGHTSEEING TOURS BY STEAMER

Hy-Line Harbor Cruises   For a fun and informative introduction to the harbor and its residents, take a leisurely 1- to 2-hour tour aboard one of Hy-Line's 1911 steamer replicas. The Sunday "Ice-Cream Float" includes a design-your-own Ben & Jerry's sundae, while the Thursday "Jazz Boat" features a Dixieland band.

Ocean St. Dock, Hyannis. © 508/790-0696. www.hy-linecruises.com. Tickets $12–$21 adults, $19 seniors, $15 children 12 and under. Parking is $3 per car. Late June to Sept departures daily; call for schedule. Closed Nov to mid-April.

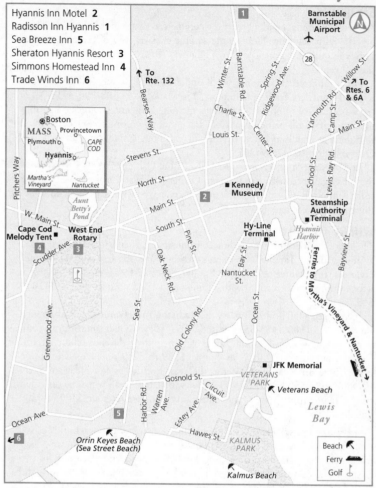

Hyannis

THE KENNEDY LEGACY

Don't even bother trying to track down the Kennedy Compound in Hyannisport; it's effectively screened from view. You'll see more at the following museum. Or if you absolutely must satisfy your curiosity, take a harbor cruise (see "Sightseeing Tours by Steamer," above).

John F. Kennedy Hyannis Museum *Overrated*   This multimedia display captures the Kennedys during the glory days from 1934 to 1963. The death of John F. Kennedy, Jr., in a plane crash in 1999 also caused a spike in the number of visitors. A special exhibit of photos of John, Jr., will be on display for an indefinite period of time.

397 Main St., Hyannis. © **508/790-3077.** Admission $5 adults, $2.50 for children 10–16 and seniors. Mid-Feb to Dec Mon–Sat 9am–4:30pm; Sun and holidays noon–4:30pm; last admission at 3:30pm. Call for off-season hours.

SHOPPING

Although Hyannis is undoubtedly the commercial center of the Cape, the stores here are fairly standard. Head to the wealthy enclaves west of Hyannis, such as Osterville, and along the Old King's Highway (Rte. 6A) to the north, to locate the real gems.

On Main Street in Hyannis, you'll find a world of wonderful kitchen products at **Nantucket Trading Company,** 354 Main St. (© **508/790-3933**).

Ex-Nantucketer Bob Marks fashions the only authentic Nantucket lightship baskets, crafted off-island; as aficionados know, they don't come cheap. You'll find them at **Oak and Ivory,** 1112 Main St., about 1 mile south of Route 28, Osterville (© **508/428-9425**).

At 374 Main St. in Hyannis, **Red Fish, Blue Fish** (© **508/775-8700**) wins the funky-gallery award, hands down. Owner Jane Walsh makes jewelry in the front window, but inside this closetlike space, every inch is covered with something unusual and handmade.

WHERE TO STAY

There are a variety of generic but convenient hotels and motels in Hyannis. Within strolling distance of restaurants, shops, and the ferries is the 77-unit **Hyannis Inn Motel,** 473 Main St. (© **800/922-8993** or 508/775-0255; www.hyannisinnmotel.com), with an indoor pool and summer rates of $110 to $127 double.

If you need a full health club, try the **Radisson Inn Hyannis,** 287 Iyannough Rd./Rte. 28, (© **800/333-3333** or 508/771-1700; www.radisson.com/capecod); it has an uninspiring location, but is within spitting distance of the airport. Summer rates are $179 to $199 double, $239 to $259 suite. Another option is the **Sheraton Hyannis Resort** at the West End rotary just off Main Street (© **800/598-4559** or 508/775-7775; www.sheraton.com), which boasts a golf course, tennis courts, pools, and restaurants. Summer rates are $209 to $309 double.

Sea Breeze Inn ★ *Kids* Within whistling distance of the beach, this classic shingled beach house has been decked out with the totems of small-town America: a picket fence, exuberant plantings, and even a wooden rocker built for two couples. The coast used to be lined with superior guesthouses of this sort, and to find one still in its prime is a real treat.

270 Ocean Ave. (about 1 mile S of the West End rotary), Hyannis, MA 02601. © **508/771-7213.** Fax 508/862-0663. www.seabreezeinn.com. 14 units. Summer $100 double. Rates include continental breakfast. AE, DISC, MC, V. *In room:* A/C, TV.

Simmons Homestead Inn ★★ *Finds* The first thing passers-by notice are all the classic red sports cars: 50 at last count. A former ad exec and racecar driver, innkeeper Bill Putman likes to collect. He's made his sports car collection into a small museum open to the public called Toad Hall, after *The Wind in the Willows.* Each room in this rambling 1820s house has an animal theme represented by stuffed toys, sculptures, even needlepoint and wallpaper. Guests who prefer privacy may book the spiffily updated "servants' quarters," a spacious wing with its own deck. This is the kind of place where you'll find everyone milling around the hearth sipping complimentary wine while they compare notes and nail down dinner plans. To help his guests plan their days, Putman has typed up extensive notes on day trips, bike routes, and his own quirky restaurant reviews.

288 Scudder Ave. (about ¼ mile west of the West End rotary), Hyannisport, MA 02647. © **800/637-1649** or 508/778-4999. Fax 508/790-1342. www.SimmonsHomesteadInn.com. 14 units. Summer $200–$260 double;

$350 2-bedroom suite. Rates include full breakfast. AE, DISC, MC, V. Dogs welcome. **Amenities:** 6-person hot tub; loaner bikes; billiards parlor. *In room:* Hair dryer, iron, no phone.

Trade Winds Inn ★ *Kids* *Finds*   Many rooms in this attractive motel have wonderful views of Craigville Beach. And because it's hard to see the sand once the summer crowds hit, this property also has its own immaculate 500-foot private stretch of beach. On cloudy days, guests may enjoy strolling to the Craigville Campground next door, a compound of 19th-century gingerbread-style cottages that still serves as a Methodist meeting camp preserve.

780 Craigville Beach Rd. (across the street from Craigville Beach), Centerville, MA 02632. Ⓒ 877/444-7966 or 508/775-0365. www.twicapecod.com. 46 units. Summer $199 double; $219–$229 suite. Rates include continental breakfast in season. AE, MC, V. Closed Nov–Apr. **Amenities:** Small bar; putting green. *In room:* A/C, TV.

WHERE TO DINE
Expensive

Alberto's Ristorante ★★ ITALIAN   Alberto's explores the full range of Italian cuisine, and owner/chef Felisberto Barreiro's most popular dishes are his treatments of lobster, rack of lamb, and beef tenderloin. Hand-cut pasta is also a specialty, including the ultra-rich seafood ravioli cloaked in saffron-cream sauce. Though the atmosphere is elegant, it is not one of hushed reverence: People clearly come here to have a good time, and the friendly service and fabulous food ensure that they do. There's live jazz or piano music daily year-round.

360 Main St., Hyannis. Ⓒ 508/778-1770. Reservations recommended. Main courses $11–$27. AE, DC, DISC, MC, V. Mon–Sat 3–11pm; Sun noon–11pm.

The Black Cat ★ NEW AMERICAN   Located less than a block from the Hy-Line ferries, this is a fine place to catch a quick bite while you wait for your boat to come in. The menu is pretty basic—steak, pasta, and, of course, fish—but attention is paid to the details; the onion rings, for instance, are made fresh. The dining room, with its bar of gleaming mahogany and brass, will appeal to chilled travelers on a blustery day; in fine weather, you might prefer the porch. There's live jazz on the weekends in season.

165 Ocean St. (opposite the Ocean Street Dock), Hyannis. Ⓒ 508/778-1233. Reservations not accepted. Main courses $15–$29. AE, DC, DISC, MC, V. Apr–Oct daily 11:30am–10:30pm; call for off-season hours. Closed Jan.

The Regatta of Cotuit at the Crocker House ★★★ NEW AMERICAN One of the best restaurants on Cape Cod, the Regatta serves fine-dining cuisine in the Federal-era rooms of a 1790 Cape. The food and service are always top-notch. Specials might include roasted buffalo tenderloin with blackberry Madeira sauce served with braised fresh greens and a Stilton sage bread pudding. For budget-minded gourmands, the Regatta menu also includes several less expensive "bistro" items, like chicken fricassee and grilled pork loin medallions.

4631 Rte. 28 (near the intersection of Rte. 130), Cotuit. Ⓒ 508/428-5715. Reservations recommended. Main courses $26–$35; bistro menu $16–$17. AE, MC, V. Apr–Dec daily 5–10pm; Jan–Mar Wed–Sun 5–10pm.

Ristorante Barolo ★★ NORTHERN ITALIAN   This is the best Italian restaurant in town. Part of a smart-looking brick office complex, this place does everything right, from offering extra-virgin olive oil for dunking the crusty bread to getting those pastas perfectly al dente. Entrees include a number of tempting veal choices, as well as such favorites as *Linguine al Frutti di Mare,* with little-necks, mussels, shrimp, and calamari. The desserts are brought in daily from Boston's famed North End.

1 Financial Place (297 North St., just off the West End rotary), Hyannis. ℂ 508/778-2878. Reservations recommended. Main courses $10–$27. AE, DC, MC, V. June–Sept Sun–Thurs 4:30–10pm, Fri–Sat 4:30–11pm; call for off-season hours.

Roadhouse Café ★★ AMERICAN/NORTHERN ITALIAN   This is neither a roadhouse nor a cafe but it is a solid entry in the Hyannis dining scene. The menu is split between American standards and real Italian cooking. Among the appetizers are beef carpaccio with fresh-shaved Parmesan, and vine-ripened tomatoes and buffalo mozzarella drizzled with balsamic vinaigrette. The vinaigrette also makes a tasty marinade for native swordfish headed for the grill. A less expensive, lighter-fare menu, including what some have called "the best burger in the world," is served in the snazzy bistro in back, which also features live jazz Monday nights (see "Hyannis & Environs After Dark," below).

488 South St. (off Main St., near the West End rotary), Hyannis. ℂ 508/775-2386. Reservations recommended. Main courses $15–$26. AE, DC, DISC, MC, V. Daily 4pm–midnight.

Moderate

Tugboats ★ *Kids* AMERICAN   Yet another harborside perch for munching and ogling, this one's especially appealing. Forget fancy dining and chow down on blackened-swordfish bites (topping a Caesar salad, perhaps) or lobster fritters. Among the desserts is a Key lime pie purportedly lifted straight from Papa's of Key West.

21 Arlington St. (at the Hyannis Marina, off Willow St.), Hyannis. ℂ 508/775-6433. Reservations not accepted. Main courses $11–$18. AE, DC, DISC, MC, V. Late May to Oct daily 11:30am–10:30pm; Apr to late May Tues–Sun 11:30am–10:30pm. Closed Nov–March.

Inexpensive

Baxter's Boat House ★ *Value* *Kids* SEAFOOD   A shingled shack on a jetty jutting out into the harbor, Baxter's caters to the boating crowd with fried clams and fish virtually any way you like it, served on paper plates at picnic tables.

177 Pleasant St. (near the Steamship Authority ferry), Hyannis. ℂ 508/775-7040. Main courses $8–$14. AE, MC, V. Late May to early Sept Mon–Sat 11:30am–10pm, Sun 11:30am–9pm; hours may vary at the beginning and end of the season. Closed mid-Oct to April.

Collucci Brothers Diner DINER   In the tradition of great diners, this one has a tin ceiling, comfy booths, and a shiny counter. It also has sassy waitresses who pour really good coffee. Selections from the children's menu are under $4. Wash down a tuna melt with a root beer float or splurge on the roast turkey dinner. The diner is a block from Main Street and about a half mile from the Hy-Line ferry terminal with boats to Nantucket.

50 Sea St. (at the corner of South St.). ℂ 508/771-6896. Reservations not accepted. All items under $10. AE, MC, V. Late May to Sept Mon–Sat 6am–3pm, Sun 6am–2pm.

Common Ground Cafe ★ *Value* AMERICAN   Talk about an out-of-body experience: Step off tacky Main Street Hyannis into this New Age-y sandwich shop run by a commune. The barn-board walls and wide-board floors surround alcoves with private booths containing amorphous tree-stump tables. But enough about atmosphere; this place makes the best iced tea on Cape Cod (the house blend—a mixture of mint teas and lemon). The sandwiches and salads are wholesome and delicious, and the burrito with turkey is a winner.

420 Main St., Hyannis. ℂ 508/778-8390. Most items under $6. AE, DC, DISC, MC, V. Mon–Thurs 10am–9pm; Fri 10am–3pm.

HYANNIS & ENVIRONS AFTER DARK

From July to early September, try to catch a show at the **Cape Cod Melody Tent** ★★, West End rotary, Hyannis (© 508/775-9100). Built as a summer theater in 1950, this billowy big top proved even better suited to variety shows. A nonprofit venture since 1990, the Melody Tent has hosted the major performers of the past 50 years, from jazz greats to comedians, crooners to rockers. There's children's theater Wednesday at 11am.

The congenial **Baxter's Boat House,** 177 Pleasant St. (see "Where to Dine," above), Hyannis (© 508/775-7040), with low-key blues piano, draws an attractive crowd. A good place for after-dinner entertainment is **Roadhouse Café** ★, 488 South St. (see "Where to Dine," above), Hyannis (© **508/775-2386**), a dark-paneled bar that stocks 48 boutique beers. Insiders show up Monday nights to hear local jazz great Dave McKenna. **Roo Bar,** 586 Main St., Hyannis (© **508/778-6515**), feels very Manhattan, with ultra-cool servers, a long, sleek bar area, and lots of attitude. The bistro food is good, too.

The cramped dance floor makes for instant camaraderie at **Harry's** ★★, 700 Main St., Hyannis (© **508/778-4188**), which features live blues and rockabilly nightly in season and about 5 nights a week the rest of the year. The cover is $3 to $4 Thursday through Saturday.

BARNSTABLE VILLAGE & ENVIRONS ★★

Just a couple miles from Hyannis, the bucolic village of Barnstable houses the county courthouse and government offices for the region. In this peaceful setting are some of the most charming B&Bs around. The bay area along historic Route 6A, the Old King's Highway, unfolds in a blur of greenery and well-kept colonial houses.

BEACHES & GETTING OUTSIDE

BEACHES   Barnstable's primary bay beach is **Sandy Neck,** accessed through East Sandwich (see "The Upper Cape," earlier in this chapter).

BOATING   You can rent a canoe from **Eastern Mountain Sports** (see "Watersports," under "Hyannis & Environs," earlier in this chapter) and paddle around Scorton Creek, Sandy Neck, and Barnstable Harbor.

FISHING   Barnstable has 11 ponds for freshwater fishing; for permits, visit **Town Hall,** 367 Main St., Hyannis (© **508/790-6240**), or **Sports Port,** 149 W. Main St., Hyannis (© **508/775-3096**). Shellfishing permits are available from the **Department of Natural Resources,** 1189 Phinneys Lane, Centerville (© **508/790-6272**). Surf-casting without a license is permitted on Sandy Neck. Among the charter boats berthed in Barnstable Harbor is the *Drifter* (© **508/398-2061**), a 36-foot boat offering half- and full-day trips.

SHOPPING

Today only one weaver in the United States creates Jacquard designs by hand, and that's Bob Black, who began his trade at age 14 and refined it at the Rhode Island School of Design. He works out of **The Blacks' Handweaving Shop,** 597 Rte. 6A, about ⅔ mile west of Rte. 149, West Barnstable (© **508/362-3955**).

Tao Water Art Gallery, 1989 Rte. 6A, West Barnstable (© **508/375-0428**), is a former garage converted into a very Zenlike space. It features paintings by Chinese artists as well as museum reproductions of Chinese antiques and jade.

Richard Kiusalas and Steven Whittlesey salvage antique lumber and turn it into cupboards, tables, and chairs, among other things at **West Barnstable Tables,** 2454 Meetinghouse Way, off Route 149 near the intersection of Route 6A, West Barnstable (© **508/362-2676**).

WHERE TO STAY

Ashley Manor Inn ✦   A lovely country inn along the Old King's Highway, this 1699 mansion still retains many of its original features, including a hearth with beehive oven and wide-board floors, many of them brightened with Nantucket-style splatter paint. The rooms, all but one with working fireplace, are spacious and inviting. A deluxe unit has a separate entrance, whirlpool bath, and canopy bed. The 2-acre property includes a Har-Tru tennis court. Breakfast on the brick patio is worth waking up for.

3660 Rte. 6A (just E of Hyannis Rd.), Barnstable, MA 02630. © **888/535-2246** or 508/362-8044. Fax 508/362-9927. www.ashleymanor.net. 6 units. Summer $150–$165 double; $200–$215 suite. Rates include full breakfast. AE, DISC, MC, V. **Amenities:** Har-Tru tennis court; loaner bikes. *In room:* A/C, dataport, coffeemaker, hair dryer.

Beechwood Inn ✦✦ *(Finds)*   Look for a butterscotch-colored 1853 Queen Anne Victorian all but enshrouded in weeping beech trees. Admirers of late-19th-century decor are in for a treat: The interior remains dark and rich, with a red-velvet parlor and a tin-ceilinged dining room. Two of the upstairs bedrooms embody distinctive period styles from the 1860s and 1880s. Each affords a distant view of the bay. Rooms range from quite spacious (Lilac) to romantically snug (Garret).

2839 Rte. 6A (about 1½ miles E of Rte. 132), Barnstable, MA 02630. © **800/609-6618** or 508/362-6618. Fax 508/362-0298. www.beechwoodinn.com. 6 units (4 tub/shower, 2 shower only). Summer $160–$180 double. Rates include full breakfast. AE, DISC, MC, V. *In room:* A/C, minifrdge, hair dryer; no phone.

Lamb and Lion Inn ✦   This is an unusual property: part B&B, part motel. From the roadside, it's one of those charming old Cape Cod cottages (ca. 1740) along the Old King's Highway. Inside, it's a motel-like space with units encircling a pool and hot tub. The rooms are all individually decorated, and six rooms have kitchenettes. All rooms in the main inn building are air-conditioned. The multilevel barn suite, with three loft-type bedrooms, is a funky historic space (built in 1740), filled with rustic nooks and crannies.

2504 Main St. (Rte. 6A), Barnstable, MA 02630. © **800/909-6923** or 508/362-6823. Fax 508/362-0227. www.lambandlion.com. 10 units (6 tub/shower, 4 shower only). Summer $145–$250 double. Rates include continental breakfast. MC, V. Well-behaved pets allowed (40-lb. limit). **Amenities:** Pool; hot tub. *In room:* A/C, TV.

WHERE TO DINE

Dolphin Restaurant ✦✦ NEW AMERICAN   Never mind the corny decor in what looks like just another run-of-the-mill eatery. The finesse is to be found in the menu, where amid the more typical fried fish you'll find such delicacies as Chilean sea bass with roasted corn salsa and lime vinaigrette, roast duck with mango glaze and toasted coconut.

3250 Rte. 6A (in the center of town), Barnstable. © **508/362-6610**. Main courses $17–$23. AE, MC, V. May–Oct Mon–Sat 11:30am–3pm and 5–9:30pm; Sun 5–9:30pm.

Mattakeese Wharf ✦ SEAFOOD   This place, with great views and average food, is always packed; don't even bother on summer weekends. The outdoor seating fills up first, and no wonder, with Sandy Neck sunsets to marvel over. The bouillabaisse is always good, and you can't go wrong if you stick to the varied combinations of pasta, seafood, and sauce—from Alfredo to *fra diavolo*. There's live piano music most nights in season.

271 Mill Way (about ½ mile N of Rte. 6A), Barnstable. © 508/362-4511. Reservations recommended. Main courses $14–$28. AE, DC, DISC, MC, V. June to mid-Oct daily 11:30am–10pm; call for off-season hours. Closed mid-Oct to mid-Apr.

YARMOUTH 👬

Yarmouth represents the Cape at its best—and worst. **Yarmouth Port** 👬👬, on Cape Cod Bay, is an enchanting village, whereas the sound-side villages of West and South Yarmouth are a lesson in unbridled development run amuck. This section of Route 28 is a nightmarish gauntlet of mostly tacky accommodations and attractions.

ESSENTIALS

GETTING THERE   After crossing the Sagamore bridge, head east on Route 6 or 6A. The section of Route 6A north of Route 6's Exit 7 passes through the village of Yarmouth Port. The villages of West Yarmouth, Bass River, and South Yarmouth are located along Route 28, east of Hyannis; to reach them from Route 6, take Exit 7 (Yarmouth Rd.) or Exit 8 (Station St.) south.

VISITOR INFORMATION   Contact the **Yarmouth Area Chamber of Commerce,** 657 Rte. 28, West Yarmouth, MA 02673 (© **800/732-1008** or 508/778-1008; fax 508/778-5114; www.yarmouthcapecod.com).

BEACHES & GETTING OUTSIDE

BEACHES   Yarmouth boasts 11 saltwater and two pond beaches open to the public. The body-per-square-yard ratio can be pretty intense along the sound, but so's the social scene, so no one seems to mind. The beachside parking lots charge $10 a day and sell week-long stickers ($45).

- **Bass River Beach** 👬, off South Shore Drive in Bass River (South Yarmouth): Located at the mouth of the largest tidal river on the eastern seaboard, this sound beach offers restroom facilities and a snack bar, plus a wheelchair-accessible fishing pier. The beaches along the south shore (Nantucket Sound) tend to be clean and sandy with comfortable water temps, but they can also be crowded. You'll need a beach sticker to park here.

- **Grays Beach,** off Center Street in Yarmouth Port: This isn't much of a beach, but tame waters make this tiny spit of dark sand good for young children. It adjoins the Callery–Darling Conservation Area with a 2½-mile trail. The Bass Hole boardwalk offers one of the most scenic walks in the Mid-Cape. Parking is free, and there's a picnic area.

- **Parker's River Beach,** off South Shore Drive in Bass River: The usual amenities are available, like restrooms and a snack bar, plus a gazebo for the sun-shy.

- **Seagull Beach** 👬, off South Sea Avenue in West Yarmouth: Rolling dunes, a boardwalk, and all the necessary facilities, like restrooms and a snack bar, attract a young crowd. Bring bug spray, though: Greenhead flies get the munchies in July.

FISHING   Of the five fishing ponds in the Yarmouth area, Long Pond near South Yarmouth is known for its largemouth bass and pickerel; for details and a license (shellfishing is another option), visit **Town Hall** at 1146 Rte. 28 in South Yarmouth (© **508/398-2231**), or **Riverview Bait and Tackle** at 1273 Rte. 28 in South Yarmouth (© **508/394-1036**). Full-season licenses for out-of-state residents cost $39. You can cast for striped bass and bluefish off the pier at Bass River Beach (see "Beaches," above).

NATURE & WILDLIFE AREAS   For a pleasant stroll, follow the 2 miles of trails maintained by the **Historical Society of Old Yarmouth.** Park behind the post office. The in-season trail fee (50¢ adults, 25¢ children) includes a keyed trail guide. Your path will cross the 1873 Kelley Chapel, said to have been built by a Quaker grandfather to comfort his daughter after the death of her child.

MUSEUMS

The Edward Gorey House ★★ *Finds*   The Cape's newest attraction is a museum devoted to the life and works of illustrator Edward Gorey, whose whimsically mischievous works may be most famous as the animated opening to the television series *Mystery!* on PBS. He was also the author of many illustrated books, including *The Doubtful Guest* and *The Gashlycrumb Tinies.* Gorey died in the spring of 2000 and his home on the Yarmouth Port Common off Route 6A (the Old Kings Highway) has been converted into an intimate museum displaying original artworks, photographs, and first editions from his career as an author, playwright, illustrator, and costume and set designer. Gorey's passion for animals is also a focus of the collection.

8 Strawberry Lane (off Rte. 6A, on the Common), Yarmouth Port. ☎ **508/362-3909.** www.edwardgorey house.com. Admission $5 adults, $3 students and seniors, $2 children 6–12, under 6 free. May–Sept Wed–Sat 10am–5pm, Sun noon–5pm; Oct–April Thurs–Sat 11am–4pm, Sun noon–4pm. Closed Feb.

Winslow Crocker House ★★   The only property on the Cape currently preserved by the prestigious Society for the Preservation of New England Antiquities, this house, built around 1780, deserves every honor. Not only is it a lovely example of the shingled Georgian style, it's packed with outstanding antiques collected in the 1930s by Mary Thacher, a descendent of the town's first land grantee. Anthony Thacher and his family had a rougher crossing than most: Their ship foundered off Cape Ann in 1635, and though their four children drowned, Thacher and his wife were able to make it to shore, clinging to the family cradle. You'll come across a 1690 replica in the parlor.

250 Rte. 6A (about ½ mile E of the town center), Yarmouth Port. ☎ **508/362-4385.** www.spnea.org. Admission $5 adults, $4 senior citizens, $2.50 children 6–12, free to Cape Cod residents and SPNEA members. June to mid-Oct Sat–Sun tours hourly 11am–5pm (last tour at 4pm). Closed mid-Oct to May.

SHOPPING

Driving Route 6A, the Old King's Highway, in Yarmouth Port, you'll pass a number of antiques stores and shops for the home. Check out **Town Crier Antiques,** 153 Rte. 6A (in the center of town), Yarmouth Port (☎ **508/362-3138**), for fun stuff including well-priced quilts, glassware, and attendant paraphernalia. The most colorful bookshop on the Cape is **Parnassus Books,** 220 Rte. 6A, Yarmouth Port (☎ **508/362-6420**), housed in an 1858 Swedenborgian church. New stock, including the Cape-related reissues published by Parnassus Imprints, is offered alongside the older treasures. The outdoor racks, maintained on an honor system, are open 24 hours a day.

WHERE TO STAY

There are so many hotels and motels lining Route 28 and along the shore in West and South Yarmouth that it may be hard to make sense of the choices. For those staying on Route 28, the town runs frequent beach shuttles in season. Families looking for a reasonably priced beach vacation may want to consider one of the following options, all near or on the beach.

The attractive 101-unit white clapboard **Tidewater Motor Lodge,** 135 Main St. (Rte. 28), West Yarmouth (© **800/338-6322** or 508/775-6322; www.tide waterml.com), has indoor and outdoor pools. Double rates go for $120 to $136 in summer. The 114-unit **All Seasons Motor Inn,** 1199 Main St. (Rte. 28), South Yarmouth (© **800/527-0359** or 508/394-7600; www.allseasons.com), has a game room and indoor and outdoor pools. Summer rates are $130 to $145 for a double room. The 63-unit **Ocean Mist** ⚓, 97 S. Shore Dr., South Yarmouth (© **800/248-6478** or 508/398-2633; www.capecodtravel.com/oceanmist), is right on the beach. There's also an indoor pool, in case it rains. Doubles range from $189 to $209 double, and suites are $249.

Captain Farris House ⚓⚓ Sumptuous is the only way to describe this 1845 inn, improbably set a block off bustling Route 28. Fine antiques and striking contemporary touches lift this inn's interiors above the average B&B decor. Some suites are apartment-size, with fireplaces and whirlpool tubs. Welcoming touches include chocolates, fresh flowers, and plush robes. Next door, the Elisha Jenkins House contains an additional suite with its own deck.

308 Old Main St. (just west of the Bass River Bridge), Bass River, MA 02664-4530. © **800/350-9477** or 508/ 760-2818. Fax 508/398-1262. www.captainfarris.com. 10 units (9 tub/shower, 1 shower only). Summer $140– $180 double; $185–$250 suite. Rates include full breakfast. AE, DISC, MC, V. *In room:* A/C, TV/VCR, dataport, hair dryer, iron.

Red Jacket ⚓⚓ *(Kids)* Of the huge resort motels lining Nantucket Sound in South Yarmouth, Red Jacket has the best location. It's at the end of the road and borders Parker's River on the west, so sunsets are particularly fine. Families who want all the fixings will find them, though the atmosphere can be a bit impersonal. All rooms have a balcony or private porch.

1 S. Shore Dr. (P.O. Box 88), South Yarmouth, MA 02664. © **800/672-0500** or 508/398-6941. Fax 508/398-1214. www.redjacketinns.com/redjacket. 150 units, 14 cottages. Summer $250–$395 double; $325–$550 cottages. Cottages weekly: $3,000–$5,500. MC, V. Closed Nov to mid-Apr. **Amenities:** Restaurant; bar/lounge; ice cream shop; indoor and outdoor heated pools; putting green; tennis court; exercise room; whirlpool; sauna; full concierge service. *In room:* A/C, TV/VCR, hair dryer, fridge.

Wedgewood Inn ⚓⚓ This elegant 1812 Federal house sits atop its undulating lawn with unabashed pride. In the main house, the formal front bedrooms all have cherry-wood pencil-post beds, Oriental rugs, and wood-burning fireplaces, while the downstairs rooms have screened porches. The two romantic hideaways under the eaves are decorated in a cheerful country-casual style. The picturesque barn contains three very private suites, with canopy beds, fireplaces, and decks. These suites also include phones and TVs.

83 Main St./Rte. 6A (in the center of town), Yarmouth Port, MA 02675. © **508/362-5157** or 508/362-9178. Fax 508/362-5851. www.wedgewood-inn.com. 9 units. Summer $135–$225 double, $205–$225 suites. Rates include full breakfast. AE, MC, V. No children under 10. *In room:* A/C.

WHERE TO DINE

At **Hallett's,** 139 Rte. 6A, Yarmouth Port (© **508/362-3362**), an 1889 drugstore, you can get a float from the original marble soda fountain.

abbicci ⚓⚓⚓ MEDITERRANEAN This sophisticated spot serves cuisine that's a cut above most of the New England-y fare you'll find around these parts. While the exterior is a modest 18th-century Cape, the stylish interior features mosaic floors and mural-covered walls. The menu offers seafood dishes, as well as veal, lamb, and, of course, pasta, all in a delicate Northern Italian style. A taste of the veal *nocciole* (with toasted hazelnuts and a splash of balsamic vinegar), and you'll be transported straight to Tuscany. This small restaurant can get overburdened on summer weekends, so expect a wait even with a reservation.

43 Main St./Rte. 6A (near the Cummaquid border), Yarmouth Port. (C) 508/362-3501. Reservations recommended. Main courses $18–$28. AE, MC, V. Daily 11:30am–2:30pm and 5–10pm.

Inaho ★★ (Finds) JAPANESE   What better application of the Cape's oceanic bounty than fresh-off-the-boat sushi? From the front, Inaho is a typical Cape Cod cottage, but park in the back so you can enter through the Japanese garden. The decor is minimalist with traditional shoji screens and crisp navy-and-white banners softened by tranquil music and service. On chilly days, opt for the tempura or a steaming bowl of shabu-shabu.

157 Main St./Rte. 6A (in the village center), Yarmouth Port. (C) 508/362-5522. Reservations recommended. Main courses $13–$23; sushi pieces and rolls $3–$7. MC, V. Tues–Sun 5–10pm; call for off-season hours.

Jack's Out Back (Finds) (Kids) AMERICAN   This neighborhood diner is hyperactive and full of fun. Chef/owner Jack Braginton-Smith makes a point of dishing out good-natured insults along with the home-style grub, which you bus yourself from the open kitchen. This is a perfect place for impatient children, who'll find lots of familiar, approachable dishes.

161 Main St./Rte. 6A (behind Main St. buildings, in the center of town), Yarmouth Port. (C) 508/362-6690. Reservations not accepted. All items under $7. No credit cards. Daily 6:30am–2pm.

DENNIS ★★

In Dennis, as in Yarmouth, virtually all the good stuff—pretty drives, inviting shops, and restaurants with real personality—are in the north, along Route 6A. Route 28, on the other hand, is chockablock with generic motels and strip malls.

ESSENTIALS

GETTING THERE   After crossing the Sagamore Bridge, head east on Route 6 or 6A. Route 6A passes through the villages of Dennis and East Dennis (which can also be reached via northbound Rte. 134 from Exit 9 off Rte. 6). Route 134 South leads to South Dennis; if you follow Route 134 all the way to Route 28, the village of West Dennis will be a couple of miles to your west, and Dennisport a couple of miles east. Or fly into Hyannis (see "Getting There," in chapter 2).

VISITOR INFORMATION   Contact the **Dennis Chamber of Commerce,** 242 Swan River Rd., West Dennis, MA 02670 ((C) **800/243-9920** or 508/398-3568; www.dennischamber.com).

BEACHES & RECREATIONAL PURSUITS

BEACHES   Dennis harbors more than a dozen saltwater and two freshwater beaches open to nonresidents. The bay beaches are charming and a big hit with families. The beaches on the Sound tend to attract wall-to-wall families, but the parking lots are usually not too crowded, because many beachgoers stay within walking distance. The lots charge $10 per day; for a 1-week permit ($40), visit **Town Hall** on Main Street in South Dennis ((C) **508/394-8300**).

- **Chapin Beach** ★★, off Route 6A in Dennis: A nice, long bay beach pocked with occasional boulders and surrounded by dunes. No lifeguard, but there are restrooms.
- **Corporation Beach** ★★, off Route 6A in Dennis: This bay beach boasts a wheelchair-accessible boardwalk, lifeguards, snack bar, restrooms, and a children's play area.

- **Mayflower Beach** ⚲⚲, off Route 6A in Dennis: This 1,200-foot bay beach has the necessary amenities, plus an accessible boardwalk. The tide pools attract lots of children.
- **Scargo Lake in Dennis:** This large kettle-hole pond (formed by a melting fragment of a glacier) has two pleasant beaches: Scargo Beach, accessible right off Route 6A; and Princess Beach, off Scargo Hill Road, where there are restrooms and a picnic area.
- **West Dennis Beach** ⚲⚲, off Route 28 in West Dennis: This long (½-mile) but narrow beach along the sound has lifeguards, a playground, a snack bar, restrooms, and a special kite-flying area. The eastern end is reserved for residents; the western end tends, in any case, to be less packed.

BICYCLING   The 25-mile **Cape Cod Rail Trail** ⚲⚲⚲ (© **508/896-3491**) starts here, on Route 134, a half mile south of Route 6, Exit 9. Once a Penn Central track, this paved bikeway extends all the way to Wellfleet (with a few on-road lapses), passing through woods, marshes, and dunes. At the trailhead is **Bob's Bike Shop,** 430 Rte. 134, South Dennis (© **508/760-4723**), which rents bikes and in-line skates and does repairs. Rates are $10 for a couple hours and up to $22 for the full day. Another bike path runs along Old Bass Road, 3½ miles north to Route 6A.

FISHING   Fishing is allowed in Fresh Pond and Scargo Lake; for a license (shellfishing is also permitted), visit **Town Hall** on Main Street in South Dennis (© **508/394-8300**), or **Riverview Bait and Tackle** at 1273 Rte. 28 in South Yarmouth (© **508/394-1036**). Plenty of people drop a line off the Bass River Bridge along Route 28 in West Dennis. Several charter boats operate out of the Northside Marina in East Dennis's Sesuit Harbor, including the *Albatross* (© **508/385-3244**).

NATURE & WILDLIFE AREAS   Behind the town hall parking lot on Main Street in South Dennis, a half-mile walk along the **Indian Lands Conservation Trail** leads to the Bass River, where blue herons and kingfishers often take shelter. Dirt roads off South Street in East Dennis, beyond the Quivet Cemetery, lead to Crow's Pasture, a patchwork of marshes and dunes bordering the bay; this circular trail is about a 2½-mile round-trip.

WATERSPORTS   Located on the small and placid Swan River, **Cape Cod Waterways,** 16 Rte. 28, Dennisport (© **508/398-0080**), rents canoes, kayaks, and paddleboats for exploring 200-acre Swan Pond (less than a mile north) or Nantucket Sound (2 miles south). A full-day canoe or kayak rental costs $50.

MUSEUMS

Cape Museum of Fine Arts ⚲⚲   Part of the prettily landscaped Cape Play-house complex, this museum has done a great job of acquiring hundreds of works by representative area artists dating back to the turn of the 20th century.

⟨Kids⟩ Especially for Kids

If the kids get sick of all the miscellaneous go-cart and mini-golf concessions on Route 28, they can take in a show. On Friday mornings in season, at 9:30 and 11:30am, the **Cape Playhouse** ⚲⚲ (© **508/385-3911**), 820 Rte. 6A, Dennis, hosts visiting companies that mount theater geared toward children 4 and up. At only $6 to $7, tickets go fast.

60 Hope Lane (off Rte. 6A in the center of town). ℂ 508/385-4477. www.cmfa.org. Admission $7 adults, free for children under 18. MC, V. Mon–Sat 10am–5pm; Sun noon–5pm; Wednesday between 10am and 1pm is free with a donation.

SHOPPING

There's a growing cluster of flea market-style antiques shops in Dennisport, but you may want to save your time and money for the better shops along Route 6A, where you'll also find fine contemporary crafts.

More than 136 dealers stock the co-op **Antiques Center of Cape Cod,** 243 Rte. 6A, about 1 mile south of Dennis Village center, Dennis (ℂ **508/385-6400**); it's the largest such enterprise on the Cape.

Dennis along Route 6A has become a magnet for interesting small galleries. Among the finest is **Scargo Stoneware Pottery and Art Gallery,** 30 Dr. Lord's Rd. S. (off Rte. 6A, about 1 mile east of the town center), Dennis (ℂ **508/385-3894**).

WHERE TO STAY

Corsair & Cross Rip Resort Motels ☆ *Kids*   Of the many family-oriented motels lining this part of Nantucket Sound, these two neighbors are among the nicest, with fresh contemporary decor, two beach-view pools, and their own chunk of sand. As a rainy-day backup, there's an indoor pool, a game room, and a toddler playroom equipped with toys.

41 Chase Ave. (off Depot St., 1 mile SE of Rte. 28), Dennisport, MA 02639. ℂ **800/201-1072** or 508/398-2279. Fax 508/760-6681. www.corsaircrossrip.com. 47 units (all with tub/shower). Summer $135–$265 double; $175–$295 efficiency. Special packages and family weekly rates available. AE, MC, V. Closed mid-Oct to April. **Amenities:** 2 outdoor pools, indoor pool; outdoor Jacuzzi; game room; toddler playroom and kids' playground; coin-op washers and dryers. *In room:* A/C, TV w/HBO, fax, dataport, fridge, coffeemaker, hair dryer, iron.

Isaiah Hall B&B Inn ☆☆   This inn's location on a quiet side street in a residential neighborhood bodes well for a good night's sleep, but it's also just a short walk to restaurants, entertainment options, and Corporation Beach. Innkeeper Marie Brophy has been entertaining the entertainers from the nearby Cape Playhouse for over 15 years. Breakfasts are served at the long plank table that dominates the 1857 country kitchen. Room styles range from 1940s knotty pine to spacious and spiffy.

152 Whig St. (1 block NW of the Cape Playhouse), Dennis, MA 02638. ℂ **800/736-0160** or 508/385-9928. Fax 508/385-5879. www.isaiahhallinn.com. 10 units (5 with tub/shower, 5 with shower only). Summer $110–$155 double; $185 suite. Rates include continental breakfast. AE, DISC, MC, V. Closed mid-Oct to late Apr. No children under age 7. *In room:* A/C, TV/VCR, dataport, hair dryer.

Lighthouse Inn ☆☆ *Kids*   Set on placid West Dennis Beach on Nantucket Sound, this resort has been welcoming families for over 60 years. In 1938, Everett Stone acquired a decommissioned 1855 lighthouse and built an inn and a 9-acre cottage colony around it. With amusements such as miniature golf and shuffleboard right on the premises, as well as a heated outdoor pool and tennis courts, there's plenty to do. The rooms aren't what you'd call fancy, but some have great views. Lunch is served on the deck overlooking Nantucket Sound, a delightful setting in which to enjoy a club sandwich. The Sand Bar, a classic bar with cabaret-style entertainment, serves as on-site nightspot.

1 Lighthouse Inn Rd. (off Lower County Rd., ½ mile S of Rte. 28), West Dennis, MA 02670. ℂ **508/398-2244**. Fax 508/398-5658. www.lighthouseinn.com. 44 units, 24 cottages (all with tub/shower). Summer $244–$298 double; $447–$650 2-bedroom cottage; $480–$760 3-bedroom cottage. MC, V. Rates include full breakfast and all gratuities. Closed mid-Oct to mid-May. **Amenities:** 2 restaurants (large dining room, pool snack bar);

bar with entertainment; outdoor heated pool with sunning deck, chairs, umbrellas, and pool house/changing rooms; outdoor tennis court; "InnKids," a free supervised play program (ages 3–11) offered July and Aug; game room; shuffleboard; volleyball; and mini-golf. *In room:* A/C, TV, fridge, hair dryer, iron, safe.

WHERE TO DINE

For a time-travel treat, visit **Sundae School** ☀, 381 Lower County Rd., at Sea Street, about ½-mile south of Route 28, Dennisport (ⓒ **508/394-9122**). The spacious barn has been retrofitted with a turn-of-the-century marble soda fountain and other artifacts from the golden age of ice cream.

Bob Briggs' Wee Packet Restaurant and Bakery ☀ *Kids* *Finds* SEAFOOD Since 1949, this tiny joint has served all the requisite seafood staples, plus steak and chicken dishes. Sit at a Formica table for a traditional summer feast topped off by a timeless dessert such as blueberry shortcake.

79 Depot St. (at Lower County Rd., about ⅛ mile S of the town center), Dennisport. ⓒ 508/398-2181. www.weepacket.com. Reservations not accepted. Main courses $6–$15. MC, V. Late June to late Sept daily 8am–8:30pm; early May to late June daily 11:30am–8:30pm. Closed late Sept to early May.

Gina's by the Sea ☀☀ ITALIAN A landmark amid Dennis's "Little Italy" beach community since 1938, this intimate restaurant specializes in traditional Italian comfort food. Save room for Mrs. Riley's Chocolate Rum Cake, made daily by the owner's mother. This popular place fills up fast, so if you want to eat before 8:30pm, arrive before 5:30pm.

134 Taunton Ave. (about 1½ miles NW of Rte. 6A; turn north across from the Public Market and follow the signs). ⓒ 508/385-3213. Reservations not accepted. Main courses $10–$23. AE, MC, V. June to late Aug daily 5–10pm; Apr–May and late Aug to Nov Thurs–Sun 5–10pm. Closed Dec–Mar.

The Marshside ☀ AMERICAN Overlooking a picturesque marsh, this is one of the Cape's best diners. There's a relaxed atmosphere here that comes from having a year-round staff that knows what it's doing (a rarity on the Cape). The food is fresh and tasty, be it a fried-fish platter, cheeseburger, or veggie melt. The homemade desserts are good, too.

28 Bridge St. (at the junction of Routes 134 and 6A), East Dennis. ⓒ 508/385-4010. Reservations not accepted. Main courses $7–$17. AE, DC, DISC, MC, V. Daily 7:30am–9pm. Open year-round.

Olde Inn at West Dennis ☀ *Finds* NEW ENGLAND A walk through the doors of this Irish pub/roadhouse, with wide wooden floorboards and a low beamed ceiling, is a step back in time. Large families of several generations sit at big round tables, and everyone seems to know one another. Later in the evenings, someone takes out a guitar or a fiddle and starts to play and everyone sings along. The food is about as traditional as it gets. Stick with the basics, like the baked scrod, prime rib, or roast chicken.

348 Main St. (Rte. 28), West Dennis. ⓒ 508/760-2627. Reservations not accepted. Main courses $10–$19. MC, V. June–Sept daily 4–9:30pm; call for off-season hours.

The Red Pheasant Inn ☀☀ CONTEMPORARY AMERICAN An enduring Cape favorite since 1977, this handsome space—an 18th-century barn turned chandlery—has managed not only to keep pace with trends, but also to remain a front-runner. Favorites include roast rack of lamb, sole meunière, and in the fall, game specials like venison. Two massive brick fireplaces tend to be the focal point in the off season. In fine weather, you'll want to sit out in the garden room.

905 Main St. (about ½ mile E of the town center). ⓒ 508/385-2133. Reservations required. Main courses $18–$30. DISC, MC, V. Apr–Dec daily 5–10pm; Jan–Mar Wed–Sun 5–10pm.

Scargo Cafe ✦ INTERNATIONAL Formerly a sea captain's house, this lively bistro has a menu split into "traditional" and "adventurous" categories. Traditionalists will find surf and turf, and the popular grilled lamb loins served with mint jelly (talk about traditional!); adventurous dishes include the likes of "wildcat chicken" (a sauté of sausage, mushrooms, and raisins, flambéed with apricot brandy). Serving food until 11pm makes this the perfect (and only) place in the neighborhood to go after a show at the Cape Playhouse across the street.

799 Main St./Rte. 6A (opposite the Cape Playhouse). ✆ **508/385-8200.** Reservations accepted for parties of 6 or more. Main courses $14–$22. AE, DISC, MC, V. Mid-June to mid-Sept daily 11am–3pm, 4:30–11pm; mid-Sept to mid-June 11am–10pm.

Swan River Seafood ✦ SEAFOOD Every town on the Cape has its own version of the "fish place with a fantastic view." Here the scenic vista is a marsh and an old windmill, and the fish is available deep-fried, broiled or sautéed. The difference here is that the fish is unloaded daily at the adjacent market from fishing boats. Go for the scrod San Sebastian, fresh filets poached in a garlic-infused broth.

5 Lower County Rd. (at Swan Pond River, about ⅔ mile SE of the town center), Dennisport. ✆ **508/394-4466.** www.swanriverseafoods.com Reservations for parties of 8 or more only. Main courses $13–$22. AE, DISC, MC, V. June–Aug daily noon–9pm. Call for off-season hours. Closed Oct to late May.

DENNIS AFTER DARK

The oldest continuously active straw-hat theater in the country and still one of the best, the **Cape Cod Playhouse** ✦✦, 820 Rte. 6A (✆ **877/385-3911** or 508/385-3911; www.capeplayhouse.com), was the 1927 brainstorm of Raymond Moore, who'd spent a few summers as a playwright in Provincetown and quickly tired of the strictures of "little theater." Salvaging an 1838 meetinghouse, he plunked it amid a meadow and got his New York buddy, designer Cleon Throckmorton, to turn it into a proper theater. It was an immediate success, and a parade of stars has trod the boards in the decades since, from Humphrey Bogart to Julie Harris. Not all of today's headliners are quite as impressive, but the theater can be counted on for a varied season of polished work. Performances are staged from mid-June to early September. Tickets range from $25 to $45.

The **Cape Cinema** ✦✦, 36 Hope Lane, off Route 6A in the center of town (✆ **508/385-22503** or 508/385-5644; www.capecinema.com), is an Art Deco surprise, with a Prometheus-themed ceiling mural. George Mansour, curator of the Harvard Film Archive, sees to the art-house programming. The setting and seating—black leather armchairs—may spoil you forever.

3 The Lower Cape

The Lower Cape has fewer year-rounders than the Mid and Upper Cape towns, so the communities on this part of Cape Cod are more summer-oriented. There are also several upscale and expensive resorts and restaurants in this section of the Cape.

Located on the easternmost portion of historic Route 6A, **Brewster** still enjoys much the same cachet that it boasted as a high roller in the maritime trade. But for the cars, it looks much as it might have in the late 19th century, with its general store still serving as a social center. Perhaps because excellence breeds competition, Brewster has spawned several fine restaurants and has become something of a magnet for gourmands.

Realtors tout **Chatham,** the Cape's most chi-chi town, as "the Nantucket of the Cape." Its Main Street offers appealing shops and eateries, complemented by a scenic lighthouse and plentiful beaches nearby.

As the gateway to the Outer Cape, where all roads merge, **Orleans** is a bustling town in the summer. The village of East Orleans is a destination itself, offering a couple of fun restaurants and—best of all—a goodly chunk of magnificent, unspoiled Cape Cod National Seashore.

BREWSTER ★★

With miles of placid Cape Cod Bay beaches and acres of state park, Brewster is an attractive place for families. Route 6A, the Old King's Highway, becomes Brewster's Main Street and houses a bevy of B&Bs, pricey restaurants, and the Cape's finest antique shops. The town has managed to absorb a huge development within its borders, the 380-acre condo complex known as Ocean Edge. Brewster also welcomes the tens of thousands of campers and day-trippers headed for Nickerson State Park.

ESSENTIALS

GETTING THERE   After crossing the Sagamore Bridge, head east on Route 6 or 6A. Route 6A on the north side of the Cape passes through the villages of West Brewster, Brewster, and East Brewster. You can also reach Brewster by taking Route 6 to Exit 10 north, along Route 124.

VISITOR INFORMATION   Contact the **Brewster Chamber of Commerce Visitor Center** behind Brewster Town Hall, 2198 Main St./Rte. 6A, Brewster (✆ **508/896-3500;** fax 508/896-1086; www.brewstercapecod.org).

BEACHES & GETTING OUTSIDE

BEACHES   Brewster's eight bay beaches have minimal facilities. When the tide is out, the beach extends as much as 2 miles, leaving behind tide pools to splash in and explore. On a clear day, you can see the whole curve of the Cape, from Sandwich to Provincetown. Purchase a beach parking sticker ($10 per day, $30 per week) at the **Visitor Center** behind Town Hall at 2198 Main St. (Rte. 6A; ✆ **508/896-4511**).

- **Breakwater Beach** ★★, off Breakwater Road, Brewster: Only a brief walk from the center of town, this calm, shallow beach (the only one with restrooms) is ideal for young children.
- **Flax Pond** ★★ in Nickerson State Park (see "Nature & Wildlife Areas," below): This freshwater pond has a bathhouse and offers watersports rentals. The park contains two more ponds with beaches—Cliff and Little Cliff. Access and parking are free.
- **Linnells Landing Beach** ★, on Linnell Road in East Brewster: This is a ½-mile, wheelchair-accessible bay beach.
- **Paines Creek Beach** ★, off Paines Creek Road, West Brewster: With 1½ miles to stretch out on, this bay beach has something to offer sun lovers and nature lovers alike. Your kids will love it if you arrive when the tide's coming in—the current will give an air mattress a nice little ride.

BICYCLING   The **Cape Cod Rail Trail** ★★★ intersects with the 8-mile **Nickerson State Park** trail system at the park entrance, where there's plenty of free parking; you could follow the Rail Trail back to Dennis (about 12 miles) or onward toward Wellfleet (13 miles). In season, **Idle Times** (✆ **508/255-8281**) provides rentals within the park. Another good place to jump in is on Underpass

---

Moments **Biking the Cape Cod Rail Trail**

The 25-mile **Cape Cod Rail Trail** ★★★ is one of New England's longest and most popular bike paths. Once a bed of the Penn Central Railroad, the trail is relatively flat and straight. On weekends in summer, you'll have to contend with dogs, in-line skaters, families, and bikers who whip by you on their way to becoming the next Lance Armstrong. Still, if you want to venture away from the coast and see some of the Cape's countryside without having to deal with motorized traffic, this is one of the best ways to do it.

The trail starts in South Wellfleet on Lecount Hollow Road or in South Dennis on Route 134, depending on which way you want to ride. Beginning in South Wellfleet, the path cruises by purple wildflowers, flowering dogwood, and small maples, where red-winged blackbirds and goldfinches nest. In Orleans, you'll have to ride on Rock Harbor and West roads until the City Council decides to complete the trail. Fortunately, the roads provide a good view of the boats lining Rock Harbor. Clearly marked signs lead back to the Rail Trail. You'll soon enter Nickerson State Park bike trails, or continue straight through Brewster to a series of swimming holes—Seymour, Long, and Hinckleys ponds. A favorite picnic spot is the Pleasant Lake General Store in Harwich. Shortly afterwards, you'll cross over Route 6 on Route 124 before veering right through farmland, soon ending in South Dennis.

—by Stephen Jermanok

Road about a half mile south of Route 6A. Here you'll find **Brewster Bicycle Rental,** 442 Underpass Rd. (© 508/896-8149); and **Brewster Express,** which makes sandwiches to go. Just up the hill is the well-equipped **Rail Trail Bike & Blade,** 302 Underpass Rd. (© 508/896-8200). All three shops offer free parking. Bicycle rentals start at around $13 for 4 hours and go up to about $20 for 24 hours.

BOATING   You can rent a canoe from **Goose Hummock** ★ in Orleans (© 508/255-2620) and paddle around Paines Creek and Quivett Creek, as well as Upper and Lower Mill ponds.

FISHING   Brewster offers more ponds for fishing than any other town: 14 in all. Among the most popular are Cliff and Higgins ponds (within Nickerson State Park). For a license, visit the town clerk at **Town Hall** at 2198 Rte. 6A (© 508/896-3701).

GOLF   The 18-hole championship **Ocean Edge Golf Course** at 832 Villages Dr. (© 508/896-5911) is the most challenging in Brewster, followed closely by **Captain's Golf Course** at 1000 Freemans Way (© 508/896-5100).

NATURE & WILDLIFE AREAS   Admission is free to the two trails maintained by the Cape Cod Museum of Natural History (see below). The **South Trail,** covering a ¾-mile round-trip south of Route 6A, crosses a natural cranberry bog beside Paines Creek to reach a hardwood forest of beeches and tupelos; toward the end of the loop, you'll come upon a "glacial erratic," a huge boulder dropped by a receding glacier. Before heading out on the ¼-mile **North Trail,** stop in at the museum for a free guide describing the local flora. Also accessible from the museum parking lot is the **John Wing Trail,** a 1½-mile network traversing 140 acres of preservation land, including upland, salt marsh, and beach. (*Note:* This can be a soggy trip. Be sure to heed the posted warnings about high tides, especially in spring, or you might very well find yourself stranded.)

As it crosses Route 6A, Paines Creek Road becomes Run Hill Road. Follow it to the end to reach **Punkhorn Park Lands,** an undeveloped 800-acre tract popular with mountain bikers; it features several kettle ponds, a "quaking bog," and 45 miles of dirt paths.

The short jaunt around the **Stony Brook Grist Mill** is especially scenic. In spring, you can watch the alewives (freshwater herring) vaulting upstream to spawn, and in the summer, the millpond is surrounded and scented by honeysuckle.

The 1,955-acre **Nickerson State Park** at Route 6 and Crosby Lane (© **508/ 896-3491**) encompasses 418 campsites (reservations pour in a year in advance, but some are held open for new arrivals willing to wait a day or two), eight kettle ponds, and 8 miles of bicycle paths.

WATERSPORTS   Sailboats, kayaks, canoes, and more are available seasonally at **Jack's Boat Rentals** (© **508/896-8556**) on Flax Pond in Nickerson State Park.

BREWSTER MUSEUMS

Cape Cod Museum of Natural History ★★★ *(Kids)*   Long before "ecology" had become a buzzword, noted naturalist writer John Hay helped found a museum dedicated to Cape Cod's unique landscape. The children's exhibits include a "live hive"—like an ant farm, only with busy bees and marine-room tanks. The bulk of the museum is outdoors, where 85 acres invite exploration (see "Nature & Wildlife Areas," above). There's an on-site archaeology lab on Wing Island, thought to have sheltered one of Brewster's first settlers—the Quaker John Wing, driven from Sandwich in the mid–17th century by religious persecution— and before him, native tribes dating back 10 millennia. The museum sponsors lectures, concerts, marsh cruises, bike tours, seal cruises, and "eco-treks"—including a sleepover on uninhabited Monomoy Island off Chatham.

869 Rte. 6A (about 2 miles W of the town center). © **800/479-3867** (eastern Mass. only), or 508/896-3867. www.ccmnh.org. Admission $7 adults, $6 seniors, $3.50 children 3–12. Open May–Sept Mon–Sat 9:30am– 4:30pm; Sun 11am–4:30pm. Closed Oct–Apr and major holidays.

SHOPPING

Brewster's stretch of Route 6A offers the best antiquing on the entire Cape. The artifacts gathered at **Kingsland Manor Antiques,** 440 Rte. 6A, about 1 mile east of the Dennis border (© **800/486-2305** or 508/385-9741), tend to be on the flamboyant side, which makes browsing all the more fun. Imagine a town dump full of treasures all meticulously arranged, and you'll get an idea of what's in store at **Diane Vetromile's Antiques** at 3884 Rte. 6A in Brewster (no phone). If the sign that reads ANTIQUES is out, it's open. This place is a tad kooky, but any junk aficionado will be thrilled by the pickings: hubcaps, wooden nails, iron rakes, wood shutters—the more peeled paint the better. Owner Diane Vetromile is herself a sculptor, who works with (surprise) found objects, and you'll find her work on view at Jacob Fanning Gallery and Farmhouse Antiques, both in Wellfleet.

No one should miss **The Brewster Store,** 1935 Main St./Rte. 6A, in the center of town (© **508/896-3744**), built as a church in 1852. You'll find everything from penny candy to comics to the bestselling Brewster Store coffee. Neighbors meet on the wide front porch to catch up on village gossip.

WHERE TO STAY

Captain Freeman Inn ★★ This mint-green 1866 Victorian has a terrific location, right next to the Brewster Store and within walking distance of a pretty bay beach. The "luxury rooms" incorporate every extra you could hope to encounter: a canopied, four-poster bed; a fireplace; a TV/VCR; and a private porch with a two-person hot tub. The plainer rooms are just as pretty.

15 Breakwater Rd. (off Rte. 6A, in the town center), Brewster, MA 02631. © 800/843-4664 or 508/896-7481. Fax 508/896-5618. www.captainfreemaninn.com. 12 units (all with tub/shower). Summer $180–$225 double. Rates include full breakfast and afternoon tea. MC, V. No children under age 10. **Amenities:** Outdoor pool; loaner bikes. In room: A/C, hair dryer.

Michael's Cottages ★ (Value) These cottages on an immaculately groomed compound are small yet centrally located. Across the street is Brewster's Drummer Boy Park, which has a playground, historic windmill, and antique house. Brewster's summer band concerts are held there as well. The closest beach is Paines Creek, about 1 mile away. In July and August, rentals are available by the week only.

618 Main St./Rte. 6A, Brewster, MA 02631. © 800/399-2967 or 508/896-4025. Fax 508/896-3158. www.sunsol.com/michaels. 7 units (2 tub/shower, 5 shower only). Summer $100–$150 double. Weekly rates $750–$825 double; $1,350 2-bedroom. B&B rooms include continental breakfast. AE, DISC, MC, V. Open year-round. In room: A/C, TV, fridge, coffeemaker, hair dryer.

Old Sea Pines Inn ★★ (Kids) (Value) This reasonably priced, large historic inn is a great spot for families. The inn's former days as the Sea Pines School of Charm and Personality for Young Women can still be seen in the handful of rather minuscule boarding-school-scale rooms on the second floor. These bargain rooms with shared bathrooms are the only ones in the house without air-conditioning, but at $95 per night in season, who cares? The annex rooms are downright playful, with colorful accoutrements, such as pink TVs. Sunday evenings from mid-June through mid-September, Old Sea Pines is the site of a dinner/theater performance by the Cape Cod Repertory Theatre.

2553 Main St. (about 1 mile E of the town center), Brewster, MA 02631. © 508/896-6114. Fax 508/896-7387. www.oldseapinesinn.com. 24 units, 5 with shared bathroom. Summer $95–$150 double; $135–$155 suite. Rates include full breakfast and afternoon tea. AE, DC, DISC, MC, V. Closed Jan–Mar. In room: TV, hair dryer, iron.

Ruddy Turnstone Bed & Breakfast ★★ (Finds) Bird lovers will be particularly entranced by this cozy 1880s B&B; the salt marsh makes for frequent sightings. The house is beautifully situated up on a knoll and is furnished with antiques, Oriental rugs, and some canopy beds. The 1860s barn, moved here from Nantucket, houses two additional rooms. Your country breakfast served out on the screened porch or in the old keeping room might feature home-baked apple French toast.

463 Main St./Rte. 6A, Brewster, MA 02631. © 800/654-1995 or 508/385-9871. Fax 508/385-5696. www.theruddyturnstone.com 5 units (4 tub/shower, 1 shower only). Summer $125–$195 double. Rates include full breakfast. DISC, MC, V. Closed Nov–Feb. In room: A/C, TV, hair dryer, no phone.

WHERE TO DINE

The Bramble Inn Restaurant ★★★ NEW AMERICAN Often named among the best restaurants on Cape Cod, the Bramble Inn is also one of the most expensive—but worth it for a special night out. Five dining rooms are each imbued with a distinct personality, from sporting (the Tack Room) to best-Sunday-behavior (the Parlor). But the highlight is Ruth Manchester's extraordinary cuisine. Her assorted seafood curry (with lobster, cod, scallops, and shrimp in a light curry sauce with grilled banana, toasted almonds, coconut, and chutney) and her rack of lamb (with deep-fried beet-and-Fontina polenta, pan-seared zucchini, and mustard port cream) have been written up in the *New York Times*.

2019 Main St. (about ⅓ mile E of Rte. 124). ℭ **508/896-7644.** Reservations suggested. Fixed-price dinner $44–$59. AE, DISC, MC, V. June to early Sept daily 5:30–9pm; call for off-season hours. Closed Jan–Mar.

Chillingsworth ★★★ FRENCH   This longtime contender for the title of fanciest restaurant on the Cape has two dining options: formal with jackets suggested for men, and the more casual bistro, which doesn't take reservations. The dining room boasts antique appointments reaching back several centuries and a six-course Francophiliac table d'hôte menu that will challenge the most shameless gourmands. Specialties include steamed lobster over spinach and fennel with sea beans and lobster-basil butter sauce. Finish with warm chocolate cake with pistachio ice cream and chocolate drizzle. Or try the moderately priced Bistro, which serves lunch and dinner daily in season in the adjoining greenhouse or on the shady lawn. There are also three deluxe guest rooms on the premises.

2449 Main St. (about 1 mile E of the town center). ℭ **800/430-3640** or 508/896-3640. www.chillingsworth. com. Reservations suggested. Jacket advised for men in fine-dining section. Fixed-price meals $50–$68. Bistro $13–$24. AE, DC, MC, V. Early May to mid-Oct Tues–Sun noon–2pm and 6–9:30pm (Bistro opens for dinner at 5:30pm), Mon 5:30–9:30pm (dinner in Bistro only on Mon); call for off-season hours. Closed Dec–Apr.

MODERATE

The Brewster Fish House ★★ NEW AMERICAN   Spare and handsome as a Shaker refectory, this small restaurant bills itself as "non-conforming" and delivers on the promise. Its approach to seafood borders on genius: Consider, for instance, squid delectably tenderized in a marinade of soy and ginger; or silky-tender, walnut-crusted ocean catfish accompanied by kale sautéed in Marsala. There are always beef and vegetarian options as well. Better get there early (before 7pm) if you want to get in.

2208 Main St. (about ½ mile E of the town center). ℭ **508/896-7867.** Reservations not accepted. Main courses $14–$26. MC, V. May–Aug Mon–Sat 11am–3pm and 5–9:30pm, Sun noon–3pm and 5–9:30pm; call for off-season hours. Closed mid-Dec to Apr.

INEXPENSIVE

Brewster Inn & Chowder House ★ ECLECTIC   To get the gist of the expression "chow down," just observe the early-evening crowd happily doing so at this century-old restaurant. The draw is hearty staples at prices geared to ordinary people rather than splurging tourists. This place also makes the best martinis in town, and there's a good old bar, **The Woodshed,** out back.

1993 Rte. 6A (in the center of town). ℭ **508/896-7771.** Main courses $12–$18. AE, DISC, MC, V. Late May to mid-Oct daily 11:30am–2:30pm, Sun–Thurs 5–9:30pm, Fri–Sat 5–10pm; call for off-season hours. Open year-round.

Cobie's ★ AMERICAN   Accessible to cars whizzing along Route 6A and within collapsing distance for cyclists exploring the Rail Trail, this picture-perfect clam shack has been dishing out exemplary fried clams, lobster rolls, footlong hot dogs, black-and-white frappés, and all the other beloved staples of summer since 1948.

3260 Rte. 6A (about 2 miles E of Brewster center). ℭ **508/896-7021.** Most items under $15. No credit cards. Late May to early Sept daily 11am–9pm. Closed early Sept to late May.

CHATHAM ★★★

Chatham (say "Chatt-um") is small-town America the way Norman Rockwell imagined it. Roses climb white picket fences in front of shingled Cape cottages, all within a stone's throw of the ocean. The Cape's fanciest town is also its prettiest. As a result, inn rooms are pricier here and rentals are snapped up more quickly. But those looking for a picture-perfect New England town will love Chatham's winding Main Street, filled with pleasing shops and leading to a beautiful beach with lighthouse.

Sticking out like a sore elbow, Chatham was one of the first spots to attract early explorers. Samuel de Champlain stopped by in 1606 but got into a tussle with the prior occupants and left in a hurry. The first colonist to stick around was William Nickerson of Yarmouth, who befriended a local *sachem* (tribal leader) and built a house beside his wigwam in 1656. To this day, listings for Nickersons occupy a half page in the Cape Cod phone book.

Chatham is one of the few areas on the Cape to support a commercial fishing fleet—against increasing odds. Overfishing has resulted in closely monitored limits to give the stock time to bounce back. Boats must now go out as far as 100 miles to catch their fill. Despite the difficulties, it's a way of life few locals would willingly relinquish.

ESSENTIALS

GETTING THERE   After crossing the Sagamore Bridge, head east on Route 6 and take Exit 11 south (Rte. 137) to Route 28. From this intersection, South Chatham is about a half mile west, and West Chatham is about 1½ miles east. Chatham itself is about 2 miles farther east on Route 28. The town lies 32 miles east of Sandwich, 24 miles south of Provincetown.

VISITOR INFORMATION   Visit the **Chatham Chamber of Commerce,** 533 Main St., Chatham, MA 02633 (© **800/715-5567** or 508/945-5199; www.chathaminfo.com); or the new **Chatham Chamber booth** at the intersection of Routes 137 and 28 (no phone).

BEACHES & GETTING OUTSIDE

BEACHES   Chatham has an unusual array of beach styles, from the peaceful shores of the Nantucket Sound to the treacherous, shifting shoals along the Atlantic. For beach stickers ($10 per day, $50 per week), call the **Permit Department** on George Ryder Road in West Chatham (© **508/945-5180**).

- **Chatham Light Beach** ★★: Located directly below the lighthouse parking lot (where stopovers are limited to 30 min.), this narrow stretch of sand is easy to get to: Just walk down the stairs. Currents here can be tricky and swift, though, so swimming is discouraged.
- **Cockle Cove Beach, Ridgevale Beach,** and **Hardings Beach** ★★: Lined up along the sound, each at the end of its namesake road south of Route 28, these family-pleasing beaches offer gentle surf and full facilities. Ridgevale Beach also has kayak and sailboat rentals.
- **Forest Beach** ★: No longer an officially recognized town beach (there's no lifeguard), this Sound landing near the Harwich border is still popular, especially among surfboarders.
- **Oyster Pond Beach,** off Route 28: Only a block from Chatham's Main Street, this sheltered saltwater pond (with restrooms) swarms with children.
- **South Beach** ★★: A former island jutting out slightly to the south of the Chatham Light, this glorified sandbar can be dangerous, so heed posted warnings and content yourself with strolling.

- **North Beach** ★★: Extending all the way south from Orleans, this 5-mile barrier beach is accessible from Chatham only by boat; you can take the **Beachcomber** (© 508/945-5265), a water taxi, which leaves from the fish pier. The round-trip costs $10 for adults, $5 for children 12 and under.

BICYCLING Though Chatham has no separate recreational paths per se, a demarcated biking/skating lane makes a scenic, 8-mile circuit of town, heading south onto "The Neck," east to the Chatham Light, up Shore Road all the way to North Chatham, and back to the center of town. A brochure prepared by the **Chatham Chamber of Commerce** (© 800/715-5567 or 508/945-5199) shows the route. Rentals are available at **Bikes & Blades,** 195 Crowell Rd., Chatham (© 508/945-7600).

FISHING Chatham has five ponds and lakes that permit fishing; Goose Pond off Fisherman's Landing is among the top spots. For saltwater fishing without a boat, try the fishing bridge on Bridge Street at the southern end of Mill Pond. First, though, get a license at **Town Hall** at 549 Main St. in Chatham (© 508/945-5101). If you hear the deep sea calling, sign on with the *Booby Hatch* (© 508/430-2312; www.capecodfishingcharters.com), or the *Banshee* (© 508/945-0403), both berthed in Stage Harbor. Sportfishing rates average around $500 to $600 for 8 hours. Shellfishing licenses are available at the **Permit Department** on George Ryder Road in West Chatham (© 508/945-5180).

NATURE & WILDLIFE AREAS Heading southeast from the Hardings Beach parking lot, the 2-mile, round-trip **Seaside Trail** offers beautiful parallel panoramas of Nantucket Sound and Oyster Pond River. Access to 40-acre Morris Island, southwest of the Chatham Light, is easy: walk or drive across and start right in on a marked ¾-mile trail. Heed the high tides, as advised, though—they can come in surprisingly quickly, leaving you stranded.

The **Beachcomber** ★★ (© 508/945-5265) runs **seal-watching cruises** out of Stage Harbor. Parking is behind the former Main Street School on the left before the rotary. The cruises cost $18 for adults, $16 for seniors, $12 for children 3 to 15, and are free for children under 3.

The uninhabited **Monomoy Islands** ★★, 2,750 acres of brush-covered sand favored by some 285 species of migrating birds, is the perfect pit stop along the Atlantic Flyway. Harbor and gray seals are catching on, too: Hundreds now carpet the coastline from late November through May. Both the **Wellfleet Bay Wildlife Sanctuary,** operated by the Audubon Society (© 508/349-2615), and Brewster's **Cape Cod Museum of Natural History** (© 508/896-3867) offer guided trips. The Audubon's trips take place April through November; the cost is $30 to $60. About a dozen times each summer, the museum organizes sleepovers in the island's only surviving structure—a clapboard "keeper's house" flanked by an 1849 lighthouse.

WATERSPORTS Seaworthy vessels, from surf- and sailboards to paddle craft and Sunfish, can be rented from **Monomoy Sail and Cycle** at 275 Rte. 28 in North Chatham (© 508/945-0811). Pleasant Bay, the Cape's largest bay, is the best place to play for those with sufficient experience; if the winds don't seem to be going your way, try Forest Beach on the South Chatham shore.

SHOPPING

Chatham's tree-shaded Main Street offers a terrific opportunity to shop and stroll. Headed for such prestigious outlets as Neiman Marcus, the handblown glassworks of James Holmes originate at **Chatham Glass Company,** 758 Main

St., just west of the Chatham rotary (℃ **508/945-5547**), where you can literally look over their shoulders as the pieces take shape. At **Chatham Pottery,** 2058 Rte. 28, east of the intersection with Route 137 (℃ **508/430-2191**), striking graphics characterize the collaborative work of Gill Wilson (potter) and Margaret Wilson-Grey (glazer).

WHERE TO STAY

Chatham's accommodations tend to be more expensive than those of neighboring towns, because it's considered a chi-chi place to vacation. But Chatham also has several good inexpensive motel options.

Practically across the street from the Chatham Bars Inn, the very basic **Hawthorne,** 196 Shore Rd. (℃ **508/945-0372;** www.thehawthorne.com), boasts one of the best locations in town: right on the water, with striking views of Chatham Harbor, Pleasant Bay, and the Atlantic Ocean. An additional perk here is phone calls (local and long distance) and Internet access are free. Rates for the 26 rooms are $165 to $195 double.

Chatham Seafarer, 2079 Rte. 28 (about ½ mile east of Rte. 137), West Chatham (℃ **800/786-2772** or 508/432-1739; www.chathamseafarer.com), is a well-run motel on Route 28. Though it does not have a pool, it's only about a half mile from Ridgevale Beach. Rates are $125 to $145 double.

Another inexpensive option is **The Chatham Motel,** 1487 Main St./Rte. 28, Chatham (℃ **800/770-5545** or 508/945-2630; www.chathammotel.com), 1½ miles from Hardings Beach. It has an outdoor pool, and summer rates in the 32 rooms are $135 to $185 double, $305 suites.

VERY EXPENSIVE

Chatham Bars Inn ★★ *Kids*   Set majestically above the beach in Chatham with commanding views out to a barrier beach and the Atlantic Ocean beyond is the grand Chatham Bars Inn. The colonnaded 1914 brick building is surrounded by 26 shingled cottages on 20 acres. This resort also has a heated outdoor pool, tennis courts, and three restaurants. Take in the sweeping ocean views from the breezy veranda, where you can order a drink and recline in an Adirondack chair. Many guest rooms have balconies with views of the beach or the landscaped grounds. Cottage rooms are cheery with painted furniture and Waverly fabrics.

Shore Rd. (off Seaview St., about ½ mile NW of the town center), Chatham, MA 02633. ℃ **800/527-4884** or 508/945-0096. Fax 508/945-5491. www.chathambarsinn.com. 205 units. Summer $320–$550 double; $550–$620 1-bedroom suite; $790–$1,600 2-bedroom suite. AE, DC, MC, V. **Amenities:** 3 restaurants (the formal Main Dining Room, the fireplaced Tavern, and the seasonal Beach House Grill located right on the beach); outdoor heated pool; putting green (Seaside Links, a 9-hole course open to the public, adjoins the resort; guests play for a fee, $18); 3 all-weather tennis courts ($15 an hour); boat to the outer beach for a fee; Wellness Center offering spa and massage services and fitness equipment; complimentary children's program for ages 3½ and up, available morning through night in summer; room service (7am–10pm in season, 7am–9pm off season); babysitting; concierge. *In room:* A/C, TV/VCR, dataport (free unlimited Internet access, hair dryer, iron.

Wequassett Inn Resort and Golf Club ★★★   Fans of golf, sailing and tennis will enjoy this 22-acre resort occupying its own little peninsula sticking out on Pleasant Bay. Adjacent is the private Cape Cod National Golf Club, where inn guests enjoy exclusive privileges. The resort's restaurant, 28 Atlantic, was recently revamped and is now one of the Cape's top dining spots (see below). Tucked amid the woods along the shore, 15 buildings, built in the 1940s, harbor roomy quarters done up in a country style. They cost a bit more than the 56 more modern "villa" rooms because of their beach front locations. All units have either a balcony or a patio. Beachloving guests can choose the calm private bay beach just steps from the rooms or Chatham's North Beach, a 15-minute ride via the inn's Power Skiff ($12).

2173 Rte. 28 (about 5 miles NW of Chatham center, on Pleasant Bay), Chatham, MA 02633. Ⓒ **800/225-7125** or 508/432-5400. Fax 508/432-5032. www.wequassett.com. 104 units. Summer $340–$665 double, $600–$1,100 suites. AE, DC, DISC, MC, V. Closed Dec to Mar. **Amenities:** 2 restaurants (28 Atlantic for fine dining and Outer Bar and Grille for casual fare, both open to the public); golf course next door ($105 a round plus $20 for a cart); pear-shaped heated outdoor pool; 4 all-weather Plexipave tennis courts ($15 an hour per person) plus a pro shop; fitness room (with new machines and weights); rental bikes ($20–$40 per day) and watersports equipment (sailboards, Sunfish, Daysailers, and Hobie Cats) for about $40 an hour; free horse-shoes, basketball, and volleyball equipment; yoga and pilates classes for $15; Children's Fun Club, $25 for half day, $45 for full day; concierge; room service (daily 7am–10pm); yoga and massage; secretarial and babysitting services available. *In room:* A/C, TV, minibar, coffeemaker, hair dryer, iron.

EXPENSIVE

Captain's House Inn ★★★ *Finds*   This 1839 Greek Revival house—along with a cottage and a carriage house—set on 2 meticulously maintained acres is a shining example of 19th-century style. The hospitality and amenities here make this one of the top B&Bs on Cape Cod. Guest rooms are richly furnished, with atmospheric touches like canopied four-posters, beamed ceilings and brick hearths. The inn provides a wonderful array of extras, like robes, bottled water, newspapers, early morning coffee, and room service. Many rooms have mini-fridges and Jacuzzis. The window-walled breakfast room is also the site of a traditional tea. Light lunches can be enjoyed poolside for an extra charge.

369–377 Old Harbor Rd. (about ½ mile N of the rotary), Chatham, MA 02633. Ⓒ **800/315-0728** or 508/945-0127. Fax 508/945-0866. www.captainshouseinn.com. 16 units (14 tub/shower, 2 shower only). Summer $235–$425 double. Rates include full breakfast and afternoon tea. AE, DISC, MC, V. **Amenities:** Outdoor heated pool; exercise room. *In room:* A/C, TV/VCR, dataport, coffeemaker, hair dryer, iron.

Chatham Wayside Inn ★★   Centrally located on Chatham's Main Street, this 1860 stagecoach stop, has undergone a thoroughly modern renovation. Don't expect any musty antique trappings: it's all lush carpeting, Waverly fabrics, and polished reproductions. The prize rooms boast patios or balconies overlooking the town bandstand. The restaurant serves three meals a day and is open to the public.

512 Main St. (in the center of town), Chatham, MA 02633. Ⓒ **800/391-5734** or 508/945-5550. Fax 508/945-3407. www.waysideinn.com. 56 units. Summer $185–$295 double; $325–$375 suite; off-season packages available. DISC, MC, V. **Amenities:** Restaurant/bar; outdoor heated pool. *In room:* A/C, TV/VCR, hair dryer, iron.

Pleasant Bay Village ★★   Across the street from Pleasant Bay, a few minutes' walk from a bay beach, this is one fancy motel. Over the past 25 years, the owner has transformed this property into a Zen paradise, where waterfalls cascade through colorful rock gardens into a stone-edged pool surrounded by whimsical Oriental gardens. Guest rooms, done up in pastels, are unusually pleasant. Many bathrooms feature marble countertops and stone floors. The suites have fully equipped kitchens, including microwave ovens, as well as two televisions, one with a VCR. In summer, the restaurant serves three meals a day. You can order lunch from the grill without having to leave your place at the heated pool.

1191 Orleans Rd./Rte. 28 (about 3 miles N of Chatham center), Chatham Port, MA 02633. Ⓒ **800/547-1011** or 508/945-1133. Fax 508/945-9701. www.pleasantbayvillage.com. 58 units. Summer $135–$275 double; $295–$455 1- or 2-bedroom suite (for 4 occupants). AE, MC, V. Closed Nov–Apr. **Amenities:** Restaurant (breakfast; July and Aug: lunch by the pool and dinner); heated pool and 8-person hot tub; game room (with pinball). *In room:* A/C, TV, dataport, fridge, hair dryer, iron.

MODERATE

The Dolphin of Chatham ★ *Value*   With an 1805 main building, motel units, and cottages, The Dolphin offers a wide range of lodging options in the heart of town. Even on exquisitely groomed Main Street, this property's extensive and colorful gardens stand out. The main inn has seven individually decorated rooms with romantic touches like beamed ceilings, canopied beds, and lacy curtains. These rooms tend to be smaller than the motel rooms, which are in an adjacent building. There is also a "honeymoon suite," which is housed in a whimsical windmill. Several rooms have Jacuzzis. The inn has a bar and restaurant, **Martini's with a Twist,** serving fixed price dinners. Lighthouse Beach is a pleasant stroll away.

352 Main St. (at the E end of Main St.), Chatham, MA 02633-2428. ℰ **800/688-5900** or 508/945-0070. Fax 508/945-5945. www.dolphininn.com. 34 units, 3 cottages. Summer $169–$220 double; $230–$285 2-bedroom suite; $2,000 weekly cottages. Rates include continental breakfast. AE, DC, DISC, MC, V. Open year-round. **Amenities:** Restaurant (Martini's serves dinner only); 2 bars (including pool bar for lunch and drinks); outdoor heated pool; 10-person hot tub. *In room:* A/C, TV, fax, fridge, coffeemaker, hair dryer, iron.

The Moorings Bed and Breakfast ★★   Whether you end up in the main house, a Victorian beauty, or the carriage houses out back, you'll enjoy a breakfast in the gazebo surrounded by flower gardens. Several rooms in the carriage houses are spacious, with kitchenettes and private decks or courtyards. Some units have VCRs and mini-fridges. All are immaculate and quaintly decorated, joined by a central courtyard. In addition, everything you need to enjoy Chatham's winding roads and beautiful beaches is provided: bikes, beach chairs, and umbrellas.

326 Main St. (at the E end of Main St.), Chatham, MA 02633. ℰ **800/320-0848** or 508/945-0848. www.mooringscapecod.com. 15 units, 1 cottage (14 tub/shower; 2 shower only). Summer $148–$215 double; $230–$235 suite; $2,200 weekly cottage. Rates include full breakfast. DISC, MC, V. **Amenities:** Loaner bikes. *In room:* A/C, TV, hair dryer.

WHERE TO DINE

The Blue Coral ★ NEW AMERICAN   This new restaurant features "seaside cuisine" on an outdoor courtyard just off Main Street. Specialties include the three-pound lobster dinner with all the fixins, and sushi-grade blue fin tuna pan-seared with balsamic demi-glaze. One of the most popular dishes is the lobster ravioli served with a brandy cream sauce. There's live entertainment in the form of jazz and blues on Thursday through Sunday nights in season.

483 Main St., Chatham. ℰ **508/348-0485.** Reservations accepted. Main courses $18–$40. AE, DISC, MC, V. Daily 11:30am–2:30pm and 5–10pm. Closed late Sept to late June.

The Impudent Oyster ★ INTERNATIONAL   All but hidden off the main drag, this perennially popular eatery cooks up fabulous fish in exotic guises, ranging from Mexican to Szechuan, but mostly Continental. The flavorful specialties of the house are the *sole picatta* (native sole with lemon, fresh herb, and caper butter sauce) the steak *au poivre,* and the *pesca fra diablo* (local littlenecks, lobster, and other seafood simmered in a spicy sauce over fettuccine). A tavern menu is served at the bar from 3 to 5pm with soup, salads, raw bar, chicken fingers, and burgers. This place is very busy in the summer and if you don't make a reservation, you may be out of luck.

15 Chatham Bars Ave. (off Main St., in the center of town). ℰ **508/945-3545.** Reservations recommended. Main courses $14–$20. AE, MC, V. Mon–Thurs 11:30am–3pm and 5–9:30pm; Fri–Sat 11:30am–3pm and 5–10pm; Sun noon–3pm and 5–9:30pm.

Roo Bar ★ NEW AMERICAN   Like its sister restaurants in Hyannis and Falmouth, this new Roo Bar in Chatham has quickly become the place to see and be seen. Somehow the owners have turned a former Friendly's Restaurant into a sleek and stylish venue that features a garden patio area as well as a welcoming bar. The menu offers a wide range of options, from seafood specialties like seafood jambalaya or fine meat dishes, like herb-grilled Delmonico. You may also opt for a brick-oven pizza like the spicy prawn or the barbecue chicken.

907 Main St., Chatham. ✆ **508/945-9988**. Reservations accepted. Main courses $17–$28. AE, MC, V. Daily 5–10pm. Open year-round.

28 Atlantic ★★★ NEW AMERICAN A major renovation has turned this restaurant on the grounds of the Wequasett Inn resort into one of the top places to eat on Cape Cod. The elegant, spacious dining room overlooks Pleasant Bay through immense floor-to-ceiling glass panels. Service is professional and stylish. And the food stands out as superb, from the *amuse bouche* (a little taste teaser) offered at the start of the meal, to the exceptional desserts served at the end. Menu items use local provender as much as possible, but there are also delicacies from around the world. You might start with the Cape lobster and roasted corn bisque with sherried Devonshire cream; move on to the composed salad of mache, melon, prosciutto, grapes, goat cheese mousse, and tawny port syrup; and then get to your main course, perhaps skillet-seared local bluefish with saffron smoked mussel risotto, wilted Swiss chard, and lobster oil. You're in for a treat here; it's all exquisite.

2173 Rte. 28 (at the Wequasett Inn, about 5 miles NW of Chatham center, on Pleasant Bay). ✆ **508/ 430-3000**. www.wequasett.com. Reservations recommended. Main courses $21–$44. AE, DC, DISC, MC, V. May–Nov daily 7am–10pm. Call for off-season hours. Closed Dec–Mar.

Vining's Bistro ★★ *Finds* FUSION If you're looking for cutting-edge cuisine, venture upstairs at Chatham's mini-mall and into this ineffably cool cafe. The menu offers compelling juxtapositions such as the warm lobster tacos with salsa fresca and crème fraîche, or the spit-roasted chicken suffused with achiote-lime marinade and sided with a salad of oranges and jicama.

595 Main St. (in the center of town). ✆ **508/945-5033**. Reservations not accepted. Main courses $16–$24. AE, DC, MC, V. June to mid-Oct daily 5:30–9:45pm; call for off-season hours. Closed Jan–Mar.

CHATHAM AFTER DARK

Chatham's free **band concerts** ★★ are arguably the best on the Cape and attract crowds in the thousands. This is small-town America at its most nostalgic, as the band plays those standards of yesteryear that never go out of style. Held in Kate Gould Park (off Chatham Bars Ave.) from July to early September, they kick off at 8pm every Friday. Better come early to claim your square of lawn; it'll be checkerboarded with blankets by late afternoon. Call ✆ **508/945-5199** for information.

A great leveler, the **Chatham Squire** ★, 487 Main St. (✆ **508/945-0942**), attracts CEOs, seafarers, and collegians alike. Great pub grub, too! The piano bar **Upstairs at Christian's**, 443 Main St. (✆ **508/945-3362**), has the air of a vintage frat house with scuffed leather couches and movie posters. Live music is offered nightly in season and weekends year-round.

ORLEANS ★★

Orleans is where the "Narrow Land" (the early Algonquin name for the Cape) starts to get very narrow indeed: From here on up—or "down," in paradoxical local parlance—the Cape is never more than a few miles wide from coast to coast. This is also where the oceanside beaches open up into a glorious expanse some 40 miles long, framed by dramatic dunes and serious surf.

The Cape's three main roads (Routes 6, 6A, and 28) converge here, too, so on summer weekends, it acts as a rather frustrating funnel. Nevertheless, Main Street boasts some appealing restaurants and shops. The village of East Orleans, near the entrance to Nauset Beach, may be the best place to base yourself. The 10-mile beach, which is the southernmost stretch of the Cape Cod National Seashore preserve, is a magnet for families and young folks.

ESSENTIALS

GETTING THERE   After crossing the Sagamore Bridge, head east on Route 6 or 6A (the long but scenic route); both converge with Route 28 in Orleans. The town is 35 miles east of Sandwich, 25 miles south of Provincetown.

VISITOR INFORMATION   Contact the **Orleans Chamber of Commerce,** 44 Main St. (P.O. Box 153), Orleans, MA 02653 (© **800/865-1386** or 508/255-1386; www.capecod-orleans.com). There's an **information booth** at the corner of Route 6A and Eldredge Parkway (© **508/240-2484**).

BEACHES & GETTING OUTSIDE

BEACHES   From here all the way to Provincetown on the Cape's eastern side, you're dealing with the wild Atlantic Ocean. Current ocean conditions are clearly posted at the entrance to Nauset Beach. One-week parking permits ($40 for renters; $135 seasonal sticker for transients) may be obtained from **Town Hall** on School Road (© **508/240-3775**). Day-trippers who arrive early enough—better make that before 10am on weekends in July and August—can pay at the gate (© **508/240-3780**).

- **Crystal Lake** ☆, off Monument Road about ¾ mile south of Main Street: Parking—if you can find a space—is free, but there are no facilities here.
- **Nauset Beach** ☆☆☆, in East Orleans (© **508/240-3780**): Stretching southward all the way past Chatham, this barrier beach, which is part of the Cape Cod National Seashore but is managed by the town, has long been one of the Cape's gonzo beach scenes—good surf, big crowds, lots of young people. Full facilities, including a terrific snack bar, can be found within the 1,000-car parking lot. The in-season parking fee is $10 per car, which is also good for same-day parking at Skaket Beach (see below). Substantial waves make for good surfing and boogie-boarding in the special section to the far left reserved for that purpose. In July and August, there are concerts from 7 to 9pm in the gazebo.
- **Pilgrim Lake** ☆, off Monument Road about 1 mile south of Main Street: This small freshwater beach is covered by a lifeguard in season. You must have a beach parking sticker.
- **Skaket Beach** ☆, off Skaket Beach Road to the west of town (© **508/255-0572**): This peaceful bay beach is a better choice for families. When the tide recedes, little kids will enjoy splashing about in the tide pools left behind. Parking costs $10, and you'd better turn up early.

BICYCLING   Orleans presents the one slight gap in the 25-mile **Cape Cod Rail Trail** ☆☆☆ (© **508/896-3491**): Just east of the Brewster border, the trail merges with town roads for about 1½ miles. The best way to avoid vehicular aggravation and fumes is to zigzag west to scenic Rock Harbor. Bike rentals are available at **Orleans Cycle** at 26 Main St. (© **508/255-9115**).

BOATING   Arey's Pond Sailing School, off Route 28 in South Orleans (© **508/255-7900**), offers sailing lessons on Little Pleasant Bay. Individual lessons are $60 per hour; weekly group lessons are around $160 to $250. The **Goose Hummock Outdoor Center** at 15 Rte. 6A, south of the rotary (© **508/255-2620;** www.goose.com), rents out canoes, kayaks, and more, and the northern half of Pleasant Bay is the perfect place to use them.

FISHING   Fishing is allowed in Baker Pond, Pilgrim Lake, and Crystal Lake. For licenses, visit **Town Hall** at Post Office Square in the center of town (© **508/240-3700,** ext. 305) or **Goose Hummock** (see above). Surf-casting—no license needed—is permitted on Nauset Beach South, off Beach Road. **Rock Harbor** ★★, a former packet landing on the bay (about 1¼ miles northwest of the town center), shelters New England's largest sportfishing fleet: some 18 boats at last count. One call (© 800/287-1771 in Mass., or 508/255-9757) will get you information on them all—or go look them over in person. Rock Harbor charter prices range from $450 for 4 hours to $700 for 8 hours. Individual prices are also available ($115 per person for 4 hr.; $140 per person for 8 hr.).

> **Fun Fact   Rock Harbor**
>
> Yes, those are trees in the middle of the harbor at Rock Harbor; and no, they are not live trees. For decades, dead trees have been erected in the harbor in order to mark the channel. At sunset, the row of narrow trees silhouetted against the horizon makes a pretty picture.

WATERSPORTS   The **Pump House Surf Co.** at 9 Rte. 6A (© **508/240-2226**) rents and sells wet suits, body boards, and surfboards. Stop by for up-to-date reports on where to find the best waves. **Nauset Sports** at Jeremiah Square, Route 6A at the rotary (© **508/255-4742**), also rents surfboards, boogie boards, skim boards, kayaks, and wet suits.

SHOPPING

Though shops are somewhat scattered, Orleans is full of great finds for browsers. You'll find some 400 vintage light fixtures at **Continuum Antiques,** 7 S. Orleans Rd., Route 28, south of the junction with Route 6A (© **508/255-8513**). The proprietor of **Countryside Antiques,** 6 Lewis Rd., south of Main Street in the center of East Orleans (© **508/240-0525**), roams the world in search of stylish furnishings. Stop by **Kemp Pottery,** 9 Rte. 6A, just south of the rotary (© **508/255-5853**), and check out the turned and slab-built creations from soup tureens to fanciful sculptures.

WHERE TO STAY
MODERATE

A Little Inn on Pleasant Bay ★★ *Finds*   Set back from a winding road that follows the coast between Orleans and Chatham, A Little Inn on Pleasant Bay sits on a hill next to a cranberry bog and overlooks the water (Pleasant Bay, naturally). The sprawling grounds are a riot of colorful flowers. The four rooms in the peaceful main house, which dates to 1798, have been completely renovated in warm tiles, light woods, and subtle colors that reflect a sort of Zen–Pottery Barn aesthetic. An adjacent building, called the "Paddock," has three additional rooms. There is also a two-bedroom suite. Breakfast (served outside, overlooking either the garden or the bay) is an extravagant affair; the spread of pastries, yogurt, muesli, cereals, fresh fruits and assorted meats and cheeses feels vaguely European. Innkeepers Bernd and Sandra are an excellent source for local restaurant recommendations. Pictures posted in the kitchen chronicle the "wildlife" spotted on the grounds—chief among them the resident Yorkie, Penny, who's a sucker for the love and attention guests routinely shower on her.

654 S. Orleans Rd., South Orleans, MA 02662. © 888/332-3351 or 508/255-0780. www.alittleinnon pleasantbay.com. 9 units. $185–$275 double, $1,000 per week suite. Extra person in room $20 per night. Rates include continental breakfast and evening sherry. AE, MC, V. No children under 10 accepted. *In room:* A/C, TV (in Paddock rooms), hair dryer, no phone.

The Barley Neck Inn Lodge ★ (Kids)   Every room is a little different in this motel, but all boast fluffy designer comforters and stylish appointments. A family suite has two bathrooms, two TVs, and three beds. Three newly renovated rooms have been decorated in a "cottage" style with wicker furniture. Six deluxe rooms have country decor and extra amenities like irons, coffeemakers, and hair dryers. The policy of "adults only" in the upstairs rooms means a quieter atmosphere. Nauset Beach, an ocean beach with heavy surf, is a mile down the road, and the motel provides beach-parking stickers. For those who prefer calmer swimming conditions, there's a pool on site.

5 Beach Rd. (in the center of town), East Orleans, MA 02643. © 800/281-7505 or 508/255-0212. Fax 508/ 255-3626. www.barleyneck.com. 17 units. Summer $129–$179 double. Rates include continental breakfast. Open year-round. AE, DC, MC, V. **Amenities:** 2 restaurants (tavern and more formal); outdoor pool. *In room:* A/C, TV, fridge.

The Cove ★   This well-camouflaged motel complex on busy Route 28 also fronts placid Town Cove, where guests are offered a free mini-cruise in season. The interiors are adequate, if not dazzling, and a small heated pool and a restful gazebo overlook the waterfront. Some rooms have kitchenettes, and balconies with cove views.

13 S. Orleans Rd. (Rte. 28, N of Main St.), Orleans, MA 02653. © 800/343-2233 or 508/255-1203. Fax 508/ 255-7736. www.thecoveorleans.com. 47 units. Summer $119–$189 double; $179–$189 suite or efficiency. Open year-round. AE, DC, DISC, MC, V. **Amenities:** Small heated pool. *In room:* A/C, TV/VCR, fridge, coffeemaker, hair dryer, microwave.

Nauset Knoll Motor Lodge ★★ (Value)   Overlooking Nauset Beach, one of Cape Cod's most popular beaches, this nothing-fancy motel with picture windows will suit beach lovers to a T. The simple, clean rooms are well maintained, and by staying here, you'll save on daily parking charges at Nauset Beach. The whole complex is owned by Uncle Sam and is under the supervision of the National Park Service.

237 Beach Rd. (at Nauset Beach, about 2 miles E of the town center), East Orleans, MA 02643. © 508/ 255-2364. www.capecodtravel.com. 12 units (all with tub/shower). Summer $150 double. MC, V. Closed late Oct to early Apr. *In room:* TV, no phone.

The Orleans Inn ★   You can't miss this mansard-roofed beauty, perched right on the edge of Town Cove. Absolutely, get one of the rooms facing the water. Built in 1875, the inn has been lovingly restored and maintains its central place in the community. The simple rooms, some with twin beds or sleeper sofas, are cheerful with modern amenities and extra touches like a box of chocolates on the bureau. Downstairs is a bar and restaurant with wonderful views of the cove.

Rte. 6A (P.O. Box 188; just S of the Orleans rotary), Orleans, MA 02653. © 508/255-2222. Fax 508/255- 6722. www.orleansinn.com. 11 units. Summer $125–$250 double. Rates include continental breakfast. AE, DC, DISC, MC, V. **Amenities:** Restaurant/bar. *In room:* TV, fridge.

INEXPENSIVE

Nauset House Inn ★★ (Value)   Just a half mile from Nauset Beach, this reasonably priced country inn is a cozy setting for those seeking a quiet retreat. Several

of the rooms in greenery-draped outbuildings feature such romantic extras as a sunken bath or private deck. The most romantic hideaway here, though, is a 1907 conservatory appended to the 1810 farmhouse inn. It's the perfect place to lounge as the rain pounds down, prompting the camellias to waft their heady perfume. Breakfast would seem relatively workaday, were it not for the setting— a pared-down, rustic refectory—and innkeeper Diane Johnson's memorable muffins and pastries.

143 Beach Rd., (P.O. Box 774; about 1 mile E of the town center), East Orleans, MA 02643. ☏ **508/255-2195.** Fax 508/240-6276. www.nausethouseinn.com. 14 units, 6 with shared bathroom (4 tub/shower, 4 shower only). Summer $60 single; $75–$85 shared bathroom; $100–$160 double with private bathroom. Rates include full breakfast. DISC, MC, V. Closed Nov–Mar. No children under 12. *In room:* No phone.

WHERE TO DINE

Academy Ocean Grille NEW AMERICAN   Just the basics here, but it's fresh food prepared simply, and sometimes that's just what you want. Seafood specialties include flounder sautéed and topped with blue crab and a lemon thyme and lavender beurre blanc sauce; and local cod baked and served with a sweet beet and horseradish beurre blanc sauce. There's also veal, steak, and roast duck. On clear summer evenings, dinner is served outside on the trellised patio, which is quite lovely. The interior of the restaurant is on the bland side.

2 Academy Place (in the center of town). ☏ **508/240-1585.** Reservations recommended. Main courses $20–$30. AE, MC, V. Late June to mid-Sept daily 11:30am–2:30pm and 5:30–9:30pm; call for off-season hours. Closed Jan to mid-April.

The Barley Neck Inn ☆☆ NEW AMERICAN   This 1857 captain's house with adjoining tavern, called Joe's Beach Road Bar and Grill, is a favorite with locals. While the front room has a more traditional ambience, the tavern space features a more casual atmosphere with a huge fieldstone fireplace and World War II posters. The 28-foot mahogany bar is a popular meeting place. The menu varies from fancy dishes such as grilled Atlantic salmon filet with a red-pepper coulis and basil vinaigrette to Joe's pizza (with goat cheese, roasted peppers, and spinach) or high-falutin' fish –and chips—beer-battered, with saffron aioli.

At The Barley Neck Inn, 5 Beach Rd. (about ½ mile E of the town center). ☏ **508/255-0212.** www.barleyneck.com Reservations accepted. Main courses $10–$25. AE, DC, MC, V. June to early Sept daily 5–10pm. Call for off-season hours. Open year-round.

Binnacle Tavern ☆ *Kids* AMERICAN   All sorts of strange nautical salvage adorn the barn-board walls of this popular pizzeria, where the pies—reputed to be the Cape's best—come with some very peculiar toppings (Thai pizza with chicken, ginger, cilantro, scallions, and peanut sauce, topped with mozzarella cheese!) for those so inclined. More conservative combos are available, along with traditional Italian fare. Kids love the funky atmosphere. The margaritas are marvelous here, and there are homemade desserts and espresso.

20 S. Orleans Rd./Rte. 28 (N of Main St.). ☏ **508/255-7901.** Reservations not accepted. Most items under $12. AE, MC, V. Mid-May to mid-Oct daily 5–11:30pm; mid-Oct to mid-May Wed–Sun 5–11:30pm.

Cap't Cass Rock Harbor Seafood SEAFOOD   Most tourists figure that a silvered shack sporting this many salvaged lobster buoys has an inside track on the freshest of seafood. The supposition makes sense, but the stuff here is about par for the area and the preparations are plain. Nevertheless, it's fun to eat in a joint left untouched for decades as time—and dining fads—marched on.

117 Rock Harbor Rd. (on the harbor, about 1½ miles NW of the town center). No phone. Most main courses under $12. No credit cards. Late June to mid-Oct Tues–Sun 11am–2pm and 5–9pm. Closed mid-Oct to late June.

The Lobster Claw Restaurant ⍟ (Kids) SEAFOOD   This sprawling family-owned business has been serving up quality seafood for almost 30 years. Get the baked stuffed lobster with all the fixings.

Rte. 6A (just S of the rotary), Orleans. ℂ **508/255-1800.** Main courses $10–$19. AE, DC, DISC, MC, V. Daily 11:30am–9pm. Closed Nov–Mar.

Mahoney's Atlantic Bar & Grill ⍟ NEW AMERICAN   Seafood is the specialty at this casual restaurant. Dishes like tuna sashimi, grilled sea bass, and pan-seared lobster are why you came to Cape Cod. There are also poultry, meat, pasta, and vegetarian dishes. Some nights in season, there's live jazz and blues.

28 Main St. (in the center of town). ℂ **508/255-5505.** www.mahoneysatlantic.com. Reservations recommended. Main courses $12–$21. AE, MC, V. May–Sept daily 5–10pm; Oct–April Tues–Sun 5–10pm.

ORLEANS AFTER DARK

Joe's Beach Road Bar & Grille ⍟ at the Barley Neck Inn (ℂ **508/255-0212;** see "Where to Dine," above) is a big old barn of a bar that might as well be town hall: It's where you'll find all the locals exchanging juicy gossip and jokes. On Sunday evenings in season, there's live "Jazz at Joe's." Other nights feature Jim Turner, a blind piano player who entertains with show tunes and boogie-woogie. There's never a cover charge.

There's live music Thursday through Saturday at the **Land Ho!** ⍟⍟ (ℂ **508/255-5165**), the best pub in town, and on Monday and Tuesday nights as well during high season . There's usually no cover charge.

4 The Outer Cape

It's only on the Outer Cape that the landscape and even the air feel really beachy. You can smell the seashore just over the horizon—in fact, everywhere you go, because you're never more than a mile or two away from sand and surf. You won't find any high-rise hotels along the shoreline or tacky amusement arcades—just miles of pristine beaches and dune grass rippling in the wind. That's because in the early 1960s, 27,000 acres here became the federally protected Cape Cod National Seashore.

WELLFLEET ⍟⍟⍟

With the well-tended look of a classic New England village and surrounded by pristine beaches, Wellfleet is the chosen destination for artists, writers, off-duty psychiatrists, and other contemplative types who hope to find more in the landscape than mere quaintness or rusticity. Distinguished literati such as Edna St. Vincent Millay and Edmund Wilson put this rural village on the map in the 1920s, in the wake of Provincetown's bohemian heyday.

To this day, Wellfleet remains remarkably unspoiled. Once you leave Route 6, commercialism is kept to a minimum, though the town boasts plenty of appealing shops, distinguished galleries, and a couple of very good New American restaurants. It's hard to imagine any other community on the Cape supporting so sophisticated an undertaking as the Wellfleet Harbor Actors' Theatre, or hosting such a wholesome event as public square dancing on the adjacent Town Pier. And where else could you find a thriving drive-in movie theater right next door to an outstanding nature preserve?

ESSENTIALS

GETTING THERE   After crossing the Sagamore Bridge, head east on Route 6 to Orleans, and after the rotary, continue north on Route 6 to Wellfleet. Wellfleet is 42 miles northeast of Sandwich, 14 miles south of Provincetown.

VISITOR INFORMATION   Contact the **Wellfleet Chamber of Commerce,** off Route 6, Wellfleet, MA 02663 (📞 **508/349-2510;** fax 508/349-3740; www. wellfleetchamber.com).

BEACHES & GETTING OUTSIDE

BEACHES   Wellfleet's fabulous ocean beaches tend to sort themselves demographically: LeCount Hollow is popular with families, Newcomb Hollow with high-schoolers, White Crest with the college crowd, and Cahoon Hollow with 30-somethings. Only the latter two permit parking by nonresidents ($15 per day). To enjoy the other two, as well as Burton Baker Beach on the harbor at Indian Neck and Duck Harbor on the bay, plus three freshwater ponds, you'll have to walk or bike in, or see if you qualify for a sticker ($50 per week). Bring proof of residency to the seasonal Beach Sticker Booth on the Town Pier, or call the **Wellfleet Recreation Department** (📞 508/349-9818). Parking is free at all beaches and ponds after 4pm.

- **Marconi Beach** ⭐⭐, off Marconi Beach Road in South Wellfleet: A National Seashore property, this cliff-lined beach (with restrooms) charges an entry fee of $10 per day, or only $30 for the season. *Note:* The bluffs are so high that the beach lies in shadow by late afternoon.
- **Mayo Beach,** Kendrick Avenue (near the Town Pier): Right by the harbor, facing south, this warm, shallow bay beach (with restrooms) is hardly secluded but will please young waders. Parking is free. You could grab a bite (and a paperback) at The Bookstore Restaurant across the street.
- **White Crest & Cahoon Hollow Beaches** ⭐⭐⭐, off Ocean View Drive in Wellfleet: These two town-run ocean beaches—big with surfers—are open to all. Both have snack bars and restrooms. Parking costs $15 per day.

BICYCLING   The end of the 25-mile **Cape Cod Rail Trail** ⭐⭐⭐ (📞 508/896-3491), Wellfleet is also among its most desirable destinations: A country road off the bike path leads right to LeCount Hollow Beach. At the end of the trail, the **Black Duck Sports Shop** at 1446 Rte. 6 in Wellfleet, at LeCount Hollow Road (📞 **508/349-9801**), stocks everything from rental bikes to boogie boards. The deli at the adjoining **South Wellfleet General Store** (📞 **508/349-2335**) can see to your snacking needs.

BOATING   **Jack's Boat Rentals,** located on Gull Pond off Gull Pond Road, about a half mile south of the Truro border (📞 **508/349-9808**), rents out canoes, kayaks, sailboards, and Sunfish, as well as sea cycles and surf bikes. Gull Pond connects to Higgins Pond by way of a placid, narrow channel lined with red maples and choked with water lilies. Needless to say, it's a great place to paddle. If you'd like a canoe for a few days, you'll need to go to the Jack's Boat Rentals location on Route 6 in Wellfleet (next to the Cumberland Farms). In addition to watercraft to go, Jack's is also the place for information about **Eric Gustavson's guided kayak tours** (📞 508/349-1429) of kettle ponds and tidal rivers from Chatham to Truro.

   The Chequessett Yacht & Country Club on Chequessett Neck Road in Wellfleet (📞 **508/349-0198**) offers group sailing lessons. For experienced sailors, **Wellfleet Marine Corp.,** on the Town Pier (📞 **508/349-2233**), rents sailboats in season.

FISHING   For a license to fish at Long Pond, Great Pond, or Gull Pond, visit **Town Hall** at 300 Main St. (📞 **508/349-0301**). Surf-casting, which doesn't require a license, is permitted at the town beaches. Shellfishing licenses—Wellfleet's oysters are world-famous—can be obtained from the **Shellfish Department** on the Town Pier off Kendrick Avenue (📞 **508/349-0300**).

> **Tips** **Recommended Reading**
>
> In *Midnights: A Year with the Wellfleet Police,* frequent *New Yorker* contributor Alec Wilkinson chronicles his stint with the police department in this small Cape Cod town, earning the nickname "Crash." A sense of the Cape, and of New England life, is nicely captured here.

Heading out from Wellfleet Harbor in season is the 60-foot party fishing boat *Navigator* (© 508/349-6003) and three charter boats: the *Erin-H* (© 508/349-9663; www.virtualcapecod.com/erinh), *Jac's Mate* (© 508/255-2978), and *Snooper* (© 508/349-6113).

NATURE & WILDLIFE AREAS   Right in town, the short, picturesque boardwalk known as **Uncle Tim's Bridge,** off East Commercial Street, crosses Duck Creek to access a tiny island crisscrossed by paths.

The Cape Cod National Seashore maintains two spectacular self-guided trails. The 1¼-mile **Atlantic White Cedar Swamp Trail** ★★, off the parking area for the Marconi Wireless Station (see "Cape Cod National Seashore," later in this chapter) shelters a rare stand of the lightweight species prized by Native Americans as wood for canoes; the moss-choked swamp is a magical place, refreshingly cool even at the height of summer. A boardwalk will see you over the muck, but the return trip does entail a calf-testing half-mile trek through deep sand. Consider it a warm-up for magnificent **Great Island,** jutting 4 miles into the bay (off the western end of Chequessett Neck Rd.) to cup Wellfleet Harbor. Before attaching itself to the mainland in 1831, Great Island harbored a busy whaling post. Be sure to cover up, wear sturdy shoes, bring water, and venture to Jeremy Point—the very tip—only if you're sure the tide is going out.

You'll find 6 miles of very scenic trails lined with lupines and bayberries—Goose Pond, Silver Spring, and Bay View—within the **Wellfleet Bay Wildlife Sanctuary** ★★★, off Route 6 north of the Eastham border, in South Wellfleet (© 508/349-2615; fax 508/349-2632; www.wellfleetbay.org). A spiffy, eco-friendly visitor center serves as both introduction and gateway to this 1,000-acre refuge, maintained by the Massachusetts Audubon Society. Passive solar heat and composting toilets are just a few of the waste-cutting elements incorporated into the seemingly simple building. You might see red-winged blackbirds and osprey as you follow the looping trails through pine forests, salt marsh, and moors. The sanctuary offers naturalist-guided tours and workshops for children. Inquire about canoeing, birding, and seal-watching excursions. Trail use is free for Massachusetts Audubon Society members; otherwise, the fee is $5 for adults and $3 for seniors and children 3–12. Trails are open July through August from 8am to 8pm, and September through June from 8am to dusk. The visitor center is open from Memorial Day to Columbus Day daily from 8:30am to 5pm; off season, it's closed Monday.

WATERSPORTS   Surfing is restricted to White Crest Beach, and sailboarding to Burton Baker Beach at Indian Neck during certain tide conditions; ask for a copy of the regulations at the Beach Sticker Booth on the Town Pier.

SHOPPING
A stroll from Main Street down Bank Street and then along Commercial Street will take you past a dozen galleries worth a look. Crafts make a strong showing, too, as do contemporary women's clothing and eclectic home furnishings. But

unlike Provincetown, which has something to offer virtually year-round, Wellfleet pretty much closes up come Columbus Day, so buy while the getting's good.

The **Cove Gallery,** 15 Commercial St., by Duck Creek (© **508/349-2530**)—with a waterside sculpture garden—carries the paintings and prints of many well-known artists, including Barry Moser and Leonard Baskin. John Grillo's work astounds every summer during his annual show in July. **Jules Besch Stationers,** 15 Bank St. (© **508/349-1231**), specializes in stationery products, including papers, gift cards, handmade journals, and unusual gift items.

WHERE TO STAY

Even'tide ★ *Kids* Set back from busy Route 6, this well-run motel is a good base for families. In case of rain, there's a 60-foot, heated indoor pool—a rarity in this part of the Cape. There are seven cottages on the property with one-, two-, and three-bedrooms units. There's a barbecue and picnic area in the pines. The Rail Trail goes right by, and a 1-mile footpath through the woods leads to Marconi Beach.

650 Rte. 6 (about 1 mile N of the Eastham border), South Wellfleet, MA 02663. © **800/368-0007** in Mass. only, or 508/349-3410. Fax 508/349-7804. www.eventidemotel.com. 40 units (39 tub/shower; 1 shower only). Summer $125–$205 double; $155–$200 efficiency; $950–$1,400, weekly for cottages. AE, DISC, MC, V. **Amenities:** Large heated indoor pool; playground; self-service laundromat. *In room:* A/C, TV, fridge, coffeemaker.

The Inn at Duck Creeke *Value* This historic complex is set on 5 woodsy acres overlooking a tidal creek and salt marsh. The 1880s captain's house features wide-board floors and charming but basic rooms, many with shared bathrooms; the carriage house contains a few light and airy cabin-style rooms; and the 1715 saltworks building has smaller, rooms with antique decor. In the main building, each shared bathroom adjoins two rooms, which might not suit those in search of privacy. All rooms have fans, and the third floor rooms have air-conditioning. The carriage house and saltworks building are quieter and can be downright romantic. But there's definitely a no-frills quality to this place—towels are thin, and so are walls. A big plus is that there are two good restaurants on-site: **Sweet Seasons** (see "Where to Dine," below) and the **Duck Creeke Tavern,** with live entertainment in season.

70 Main St. (P.O. Box 364), Wellfleet, MA 02667. © **508/349-9333**. Fax 508/349-0234. www.innatduck creeke.com. 26 units (13 tub/shower; 5 shower only; 8 with shared bathroom). Summer $85–$90, double with shared bath; $90–$125 double with private bath. Rates include continental breakfast. AE, MC, V. Closed Nov–Apr. **Amenities:** 2 restaurants (seafood restaurant and tavern). *In room:* No phone.

Surfside Cottages ★★ *Kids* This is where you want to be: smack dab on a spectacular beach with 50-foot dunes, within biking distance of Wellfleet Center and a short drive from Provincetown. All of the one, two, or three bedrooms have kitchens, fireplaces, barbecues, outdoor showers, and screened porches. Some even have roof decks. From mid-May to mid-October, the cottages rent weekly. Bring your own sheets and towels; renting a set costs $10 per person.

Ocean View Dr. (at LeCount Hollow Rd.; P.O. Box 937), South Wellfleet, MA 02663. ©/fax **508/349-3959**. www.surfsidevacation.com. 18 cottages (showers only). Summer $875–$1,575 weekly; off season $80–$130 per day. MC, V. Pets allowed off season. *In room:* Fridge, coffeemaker. Closed mid-November to early April.

WHERE TO DINE

Hatch's Fish & Produce Market ★, 310 Main St., behind Town Hall (© **508/349-6734** for produce, 508/349-2810 for fish market), is the unofficial heart of

Wellfleet. You'll find the best local bounty, from fresh-picked corn to fruit-juice Popsicles to steaming lobsters. Virtually no one passes through without picking up a little something, along with the latest talk of the town. It's closed from late September until May.

Aesop's Tables ★★ NEW AMERICAN   This delightful restaurant has it all: a historic setting; a relaxed atmosphere; and delectable food. Owner Brian Dunne oversees the sourcing of the superb local provender, even growing some of the edible flowers and delicate greens that go into the "Monet's Garden" salad. The scallops and oysters come straight from the bay. For dessert, try "Clementine's Citrus Tart."

316 Main St. (in the center of town). ✆ 508/349-6450. Reservations recommended. Main courses $16–$26. AE, MC, V. July–Aug daily 5:30–9:30pm; May, June, Sept Thurs–Sun 5:30–9:30pm. Closed Oct–Apr.

Mac's Seafood Market and Harbor Grill Restaurant ★ *Finds* *Kids*   Located on the town pier, this takeout shack with picnic tables features fresh local seafood unloaded from the boats just steps away. Besides grilled fish dinners, there's homemade chowders, sushi, and a raw bar.

Wellfleet Town Pier. ✆ 508/349-9611. MC, V. Daily 7:30am–10pm. Closed mid-Oct to late May.

Moby Dick's Restaurant ★ *Kids* SEAFOOD   This is your typical clam shack. Order your meal at the register, sit at a picnic table, and a cheerful college student brings it to you. Fried fish, clams, scallops, and shrimp are all good here; try the Moby's Seafood Special—a heaping platter of all of the above, plus coleslaw and fries. Then there's the clambake special with lobster, steamers, and corn on the cob. Bring the family and chow down.

Rte. 6, Wellfleet. ✆ 508/349-9795. www.mobydicksrestaurant.com. Reservations not accepted. Main courses $8–$20. MC, V. Mid-June to early Sept daily 11:30am–10pm; call for off-season hours. Closed mid-Oct to Apr.

Sweet Seasons Restaurant ★ NEW AMERICAN   Chef-owner Judith Pihl's Mediterranean-influenced fare is still appealing after 20-plus years, as is this dining room's peaceful pond view. Some of the dishes can be a bit heavy by contemporary standards, but there's usually a healthy alternative: Wellfleet littlenecks and mussels in a golden, aromatic tomato-and-cumin broth, for instance, as opposed to Russian oysters with smoked salmon, vodka, and sour cream. Specialties of the house include creamy sage-and-asparagus ravioli, and Seasons shrimp with feta and ouzo.

At the Inn at Duck Creeke, 70 Main St. (about ¼ mile W of Rte. 6). ✆ 508/349-6535. Reservations recommended. Main courses $19–$26. AE, MC, V. July–Sept Tues–Sun 5:30–10pm. Closed Oct–June.

WELLFLEET AFTER DARK

The Beachcomber ★, 1220 Old Cahoon Hollow Rd., off Ocean View Drive (✆ 508/349-6055; www.beachcomber.com), arguably the best dance club on Cape Cod, is definitely the most scenic. It's right on Cahoon Hollow Beach—so close, in fact, that late beachgoers on summer weekends can count on a free concert of reggae, blues, ska, or rock. Cover varies. Closed early September to late May.

Local talent—jazz, pop, folk, and blues—accompanies the light fare at **Duck Creeke Tavern,** at the Inn at Duck Creeke, 70 Main St. (✆ 508/349-7369). Closed mid-October to late May; no cover.

The cozy attic at the **Upstairs Bar at Aesop's Tables,** 316 Main St. (✆ 508/ 349-6450), is usually inhabited by local blues and jazz performers.

The **Wellfleet Drive-In Theater,** 51 Rte. 6, just north of the Eastham border (© **800/696-3532** or 508/349-2520), built in 1957, is the only drive-in left on Cape Cod and one of a scant half-dozen surviving in the state. The rituals are unbending and endearing as ever: the playtime preceding the cartoons, the countdown plugging the allures of the snack bar, and finally, two full first-run features. It's open daily from late May through mid-September; show time is at dusk. Call for off-season hours.

The principals behind the **Wellfleet Harbor Actors' Theatre,** 1 Kendrick Ave., near the Town Pier (© **508/349-6835**), aim to provoke—and usually succeed, even amid this very sophisticated, seen-it-all summer colony. Performances are given from late May through October, daily at 8pm.

TRURO 🐾🐾

With only 1,600 year-round residents (fewer than it boasted in 1840, when Pamet Harbor was a whaling and shipbuilding port), Truro amounts to little more than a smattering of stores and public buildings, and lots of low-profile houses hidden away in the woods and dunes. Edward Hopper lived in contented isolation in a South Truro cottage for nearly 4 decades. If you find yourself craving cultural stimulation or other kinds of excitement, Provincetown is only a 10-minute drive away.

ESSENTIALS

GETTING THERE   After crossing the Sagamore Bridge, head east on Route 6 or 6A to Orleans and north on Route 6.

VISITOR INFORMATION   Contact the **Truro Chamber of Commerce,** Route 6A (at Head of the Meadow Rd.), Truro, MA 02666 (© **508/487-1288**). Truro is 46 miles east of Sandwich, 10 miles south of Provincetown.

BEACHES & GETTING OUTSIDE

BEACHES   Parking at all of Truro's exquisite Atlantic beaches, except for one Cape Cod National Seashore access point (Corn Hill Beach), is reserved for residents and renters. To obtain a sticker ($20 for 1 week; $30 for 2 weeks), inquire at the beach-sticker office at 14 Truro Center Rd. behind the post office in Truro Center (© **508/487-3635**).

- **Corn Hill Beach** 🐾🐾, off Corn Hill Road: Offering restrooms, this bay beach—near the hill where the Pilgrims found the seed corn that ensured their survival—is open to nonresidents for a parking fee of $10 per day.
- **Head of the Meadow** 🐾🐾🐾, off Head of the Meadow Road: Among the more remote National Seashore beaches, this spot (equipped with restrooms) is known for its excellent surf. A parking lot connected by a short boardwalk to the beach makes this beach more easily accessible than other National Seashore beaches. It is also connected by a short bike path to Pilgrim Heights (see "Bicycling," below). Parking costs $10 per day, or $30 per season.

BICYCLING   Although it has yet to be linked up to the Cape Cod Rail Trail, Truro does have a stunning 2-mile bike path of its own: the **Head of the Meadow Trail** 🐾, off the road of the same name (look for a right-hand turn about a half mile north of where Routes 6 and 6A intersect). Part of the old 1850 road toward Provincetown, it skirts the bluffs, passing Pilgrim and ending at High Head Road.

FISHING   Great Pond, Horseleech Pond, and Pilgrim Lake—flanked by parabolic dunes carved by the wind—are all fishable; for a freshwater fishing license, visit **Town Hall** on Town Hall Road (© **508/487-2702**). You can also call town hall for a shellfishing license. Surf-casting is permitted at Highland Light Beach, off Highland Road.

GOLF   North Truro boasts the most scenic—and historic—nine-hole course on the Cape. Created in 1892, the minimally groomed, Scottish-style **Highland Links** at 10 Lighthouse Rd., off South Highland Road (© **508/487-9201**), shares a lofty bluff with the 1853 Highland Light.

NATURE TRAILS   The Cape Cod National Seashore, comprising 70% of Truro's land, offers three self-guided nature trails. The half-mile **Pamet Trail** 🎯 off North Pamet Road leads you past an old cranberry-bog building and bogs that have reverted to marshland. Park in the lot to the left of the Little America youth hostel (see "Where to Stay," below) and walk back to the fire road entrance about 500 feet down North Pamet Road. The **Pilgrim Spring Trail** 🎯 and **Small Swamp Trail** 🎯 (each a ¾-mile loop) head out from the National Seashore parking lot just east of Pilgrim Lake. Both paths overlook Salt Meadow, a freshwater marsh favored by hawks and osprey.

A MUSEUM & AN ARTS CENTER

Highland House Museum and Highland Lighthouse   Built as a hotel in 1907, the Highland House is a perfect repository of the odds and ends collected by the Truro Historical Society: ship's models, harpoons, primitive toys, a pirate's chest, and so on. In 1996, Highland Lighthouse was moved back from its perilous perch above a rapidly eroding dune. Now the lighthouse is within 800 feet of the museum and is also operated by the Truro Historical Society. Seasonal lighthouse tours run May through October. There is a 51-inch height requirement so, unfortunately, little ones can't climb up the tower.

27 Highland Light Rd. (off S. Highland Rd., 2 miles N of the town center on Rte. 6). © **508/487-1121.** www.trurohistorical.org. Admission to both museum and lighthouse $5 adults, free for children under 12. Admission to museum or lighthouse $3; free for children under 12 at museum only. Museum June–Sept daily 10am–4:30pm. Last ticket sold at 3:30pm. Lighthouse May–Oct daily 10am–6pm. Closed Nov.–May.

WHERE TO STAY

Days Cottages 🎯 (Value   Lined up along the bay beach in North Truro, these identical cottages—named after flowers—are all white clapboard with sea-foam green shutters. Although lacking frills, each has a living room, two small bedrooms, a kitchen, and a bathroom. The downside is that these accommodations are somewhat rough: The bedrooms are minuscule, and in some of the cottages, the fireplace has about 10 years' worth of graffiti written on the brick chimney. There is also the noise of passing cars on this busy stretch of road to contend with. The upside is miles of bay beach for walking and swimming with views of Provincetown's quirky skyline in the distance. In season, beginning June 1, the cottages are rented only by the week, and they usually book up far in advance.

Rte. 6A. (a couple miles S of the Provincetown border), North Truro, MA 02652. © **508/487-1062.** Fax 508/487-5595. www.dayscottages.com. 23 cottages (all with shower only). Summer $920 weekly. No credit cards. Closed mid-Oct to Apr. *In room:* Fridge.

Kalmar Village 🎯🎯 (Kids (Value   Spiffier than many of the motels and cottages between Pilgrim Lake and Pilgrim Beach, this 1940s complex features little white cottages shuttered in black. There are picnic tables, grills, and daily maid service. Some cottages have air-conditioning. The clientele—mostly families— can splash the day away in the 60-foot freshwater pool or on the 400-foot private beach.

Moments   A Vineyard in the Dunes

This pastoral property just off Route 6 in Truro is one of the last working farms in the Outer Cape and the site of an honest-to-goodness vineyard. Horticulturist/innkeepers Kathy Gregrow and Judy Wimer of **Truro Vineyard of Cape Cod** (11 Shore Rd./Rte. 6A, North Truro; 🕐 **508/487-6200**) uncorked their first homegrown chardonnay and Cabernet Franc in the fall of 1996, the muscadet in 1997; the merlot in 1998. Inside the main house, the living room, with its exposed beams, is decorated with interesting oenological artifacts. Late May through October, free wine tastings are held daily from noon to 5pm. Guided tours of the property take place at 1 and 3pm.

---

674 Shore Rd. (Rte. 6A, about ¼ mile S of the Provincetown border), North Truro, MA 02652. 🕐 **508/487-0585.** Fax 508/487-5827. www.kalmarvillage.com. 16 units, 40 cottages. Summer $135 double; $175 2-bedroom suite; $1,295–$1,495 cottages weekly. DISC, MC, V. Closed mid-Oct to late May. **Amenities:** Outdoor pool; coin-op laundry. *In room:* TV, fridge.

WHERE TO DINE

Terra Luna ✦ FUSION   People come from miles around to sample the outstanding breakfasts at this modest restaurant. The muffins and scones emerge fresh from the oven, and "entrees" such as the breakfast burrito or strawberry mascarpone-cheese pancakes call for a hearty appetite. You can start in again in the evening, on well-priced Pacific Rim and/or neo-Italian fare, such as penne prosciutto sautéed with garlic, black pepper, and a splash of vodka. Main courses include local seafood and lobster dishes, like lobster risotto with asparagus and saffron. There's even a creative children's menu here.

104 Shore Rd. (Rte. 6A), North Truro. 🕐 **508/487-1019.** Reservations recommended. Main courses $14–$20. AE, MC, V. Late May to mid-Oct daily 8am–1pm and 5:30–10pm. Closed mid-Oct to late May.

SWEETS & TAKEOUT

Jams *Finds*   Seeing as this deli/bakery/grocery is basically the whole enchilada in terms of downtown Truro, and seasonal to boot, it's good that it's so delightful. It's full of tantalizing aromas: fresh, creative pizzas (from pesto to pupu); rotisseried fowl sizzling on the spit; or cookies straight from the oven. The pastry and deli selections deserve their own four-star restaurant, but are all the more savory as part of a picnic.

14 Truro Center Rd. (off Rte. 6, in the center of town). 🕐 **508/349-1616.** Closed early Sept to late May. Call for hours.

PROVINCETOWN ✦✦✦

You made it all the way to the end of the Cape, to one of the most interesting spots on the eastern seaboard. Explorer Bartholomew Gosnold must have felt much the same thrill in 1602, when he and his crew happened upon a "great stoare of codfysshes" here. The Pilgrims, of course, were overjoyed when they slogged into the harbor 18 years later. Never mind that they'd landed several hundred miles off course.

And Charles Hawthorne, the painter who "discovered" this near-derelict fishing town in the late 1890s and introduced it to the Greenwich Village intelligentsia, was besotted by this "jumble of color in the intense sunlight accentuated by the brilliant blue of the harbor."

He'd probably be aghast at the commercial circus his enthusiasm has wrought—though pleased, no doubt, to find the Provincetown Art Association & Museum, which he helped found in 1914, still going strong. The whole town, in fact, is dedicated to creative expression, both visual and verbal. The general atmosphere of open-mindedness plays a pivotal a role, allowing a very varied assortment of individuals to explore their creative urges.

That same open-mindedness may account for Provincetown's ascendancy as a gay and lesbian resort. In peak season, the streets are a celebration of the individual's freedom to be as "out" as imagination allows. But the street life also includes families, art lovers, and gourmands. In short, Provincetown has something for just about everyone.

ESSENTIALS

GETTING THERE   After crossing the Sagamore Bridge, head east on Route 6 or 6A to Orleans, then continue north on Route 6 to Provincetown. Provincetown is 56 miles northeast of Sandwich, 42 miles northeast of Hyannis.

If you plan to spend your entire vacation in Provincetown, you won't need a car—everything is within walking or biking distance. And because parking is a hassle, consider leaving your car at home and taking a boat from Boston or Plymouth. You'll get to skip the horrendous Sagamore Bridge traffic jams and arrive by sea like the Pilgrims did.

In season, **Bay State Cruises** (© 617/748-1428; www.baystatecruises.com) makes daily round-trips from Boston.

From mid-May to late September, the high-speed *Provincetown Express* boat makes three round-trips daily, taking 1½ hours each way. The regular ferry *Provincetown II* makes one 3-hour trip daily.

Capt. John Boats (© 508/747-2400; www.provincetownferry.com) connects Plymouth and Provincetown daily mid-June through August.

You can also fly into Provincetown. **Cape Air** (© 800/352-0714; www.flycapeair.com) offers flights from Boston and from Nantucket in season. Both trips take about 25 minutes.

As far as getting around once you're settled, you can enjoy the vintage fleet of the **Mercedes Cab Company** (© 508/487-3333).

GETTING AROUND

Parking is at a premium. Illegally parked cars are ticketed (even on Sun), and repeat offenders will be towed. If your inn provides parking, you may want to keep your car there and get around on foot, bicycle, or shuttle. **Provincetown's Summer Shuttle** (© 508/487-8966) loops through town and to the beach daily from late June through October.

VISITOR INFORMATION   Contact the **Provincetown Chamber of Commerce,** 307 Commercial St., Provincetown, MA 02657 (© 508/487-3424; fax 508/487-8966; www.ptownchamber.com), or the gay-oriented **Provincetown Business Guild,** 115 Bradford St., P.O. Box 421, Provincetown, MA 02657 (© 800/637-8696 or 508/487-2313; fax 508/487-1252; www.ptown.org).

BEACHES & GETTING OUTSIDE

BEACHES   With nine-tenths of its territory (basically, all but the downtown area) protected by the Cape Cod National Seashore, Provincetown has miles of beaches. The 3-mile bay beach that lines the harbor, though certainly swimmable, is not all that inviting compared to the magnificent ocean beaches overseen by the National Seashore. The two official access areas (see below) tend to be

Provincetown

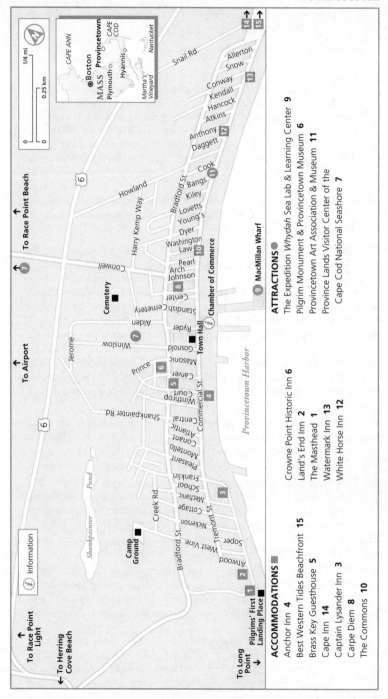

ACCOMMODATIONS

Anchor Inn 4
Best Western Tides Beachfront 15
Brass Key Guesthouse 5
Cape Inn 14
Captain Lysander Inn 3
Carpe Diem 8
The Commons 10
Crowne Point Historic Inn 6
Land's End Inn 2
The Masthead 1
Watermark Inn 13
White Horse Inn 12

ATTRACTIONS ●

The Expedition *Whydah* Sea Lab & Learning Center 9
Pilgrim Monument & Provincetown Museum 6
Provincetown Art Association & Museum 11
Province Lands Visitor Center of the
Cape Cod National Seashore 7

crowded; however, you can always find a less densely populated stretch if you're willing to hike down the beach a bit.

- **Herring Cove** ★★★: This popular west-facing National Seashore beach is known for its spectacular sunsets. The long stretches of pristine sand front a calmer beach than Race Point (see below) because Herring Cove faces Cape Cod Bay. This is a haven for same-sex couples, who tend to gather to the far left side of the beach. Parking costs $10 per day, $30 per season.

- **Long Point:** Trek out over the breakwater at the far west end of Commercial Street and walk about 1½ miles over sand—or catch a water shuttle—$8 one-way, $12 round-trip, hourly in season—from Flyer's Boat Rental (see "Boating," below) to visit this very last spit of land, capped by an 1827 lighthouse. Locals call it "the end of the Earth." Shuttles run hourly in July and August.

- **Race Point** ★★★: Facing the Atlantic Ocean, Race Point offers rougher surf than Herring Cove, and you might actually spot whales en route to Stellwagen Bank. Parking costs $10 per day, $30 per season.

BICYCLING   North of town, nestled amid the Cape Cod National Seashore preserve, is one of the more spectacular bike paths in New England, the 7-mile **Province Lands Trail** ★★, a heady swirl of steep dunes anchored by wind-stunted scrub pines. With its free parking, the **Province Lands Visitor Center** ★ (© **508/487-1256**) is a good place to start: You can survey the landscape from the observation tower to try to get your bearings before setting off amid the dizzying maze. Follow signs to follow a spur path leading to one of the beaches, Race Point or Herring Cove, lining the shore. Rentals are offered in season by **Nelson's Bike Shop** at 43 Race Point Rd. (© **508/487-8849**). It's also an easy jaunt from town, where you'll find plenty of good bike shops—such as **Ptown Bikes** at 42 Bradford St. (© **508/487-8735**); reserve several days in advance.

BOATING   In addition to operating a Long Point shuttle from its own dock (see "Beaches," above), **Flyer's Boat Rental** at 131 Commercial St. in the West End (© **508/487-0898**) offers all sorts of craft, from kayaks and dinghies to sailboats of varying sizes; sailing lessons and fishing-gear rentals are also available.

FISHING   Surf-casting is permitted at Herring Cove Beach (off Rte. 6) and Race Point Beach (near the Race Point Coast Guard Station); many people drop a hand-line or light tackle right off the West End breakwater. For low-cost deep-sea fishing via party boat, board the *Cee Jay* (© **800/675-6724** or 508/487-4330; www.ceejayfishing.com). For serious sportfishing, sign on for the *Shady Lady II* (© **508/487-0182**). Both depart from MacMillan Wharf.

NATURE TRAILS   Within the Province Lands (off Race Point Rd., ½ mile north of Rte. 6), the National Seashore maintains the 1-mile **Beech Forest Trail** ★, a shaded path that circles a shallow freshwater pond blanketed with water lilies before heading into the woods. You can see the shifting dunes gradually encroaching on the forest.

A walk along the **West End breakwater** ★★ out to the end of **Long Point** is about 5 miles round-trip. Walking just to the end of the wide breakwater, located at the end of Commercial Street next to the Provincetown Inn, is quite popular. You'll see all ages maneuvering the layered boulders, about a 30-minute walk each way. If you want to continue to Long Point, the very tip of Cape Cod, it's about a 1½-hour walk across soft sand. At low tide, the distance can be shortened by

Whale-Watching in P-town

Stellwagen Bank, 8 miles off Provincetown, is a rich feeding ground for whales. The **Dolphin Fleet** ★★★, MacMillan Wharf (© **800/826-9300** or 508/349-1900), was the first, and by all accounts still the best, outfitter running whale-watching trips to Stellwagen. Most cruises carry a naturalist to provide running commentary; on the *Dolphin*, these are scientists from the Center for Coastal Studies out doing research crucial to the whales' survival, and part of the proceeds goes to further their worthwhile efforts.

Tickets for the 3½-hour trips are $22 for adults, $20 for seniors, $19 for children 7 to 12, and free for children under 7. Call to reserve. Closed late October through March.

Tips for first-timers: Dress very warmly, in layers, and take along a waterproof windbreaker. If you're prone to seasickness, consider taking a motion-sickness pill at the start of the trip. (They are provided free as you board the vessel.)

cutting across the salt flats. **Wood End Lighthouse** is directly across the spit of sand near the breakwater. **Long Point Lighthouse** is at the end of the point. Hikers determined to reach the end of Long Point will want to bring a hat, water, and sunscreen. The inside of the arm has views of Provincetown and Provincetown Harbor and a couple of shipwrecks.

ORGANIZED TOURS & CRUISES

Art's Dune Tours ★★ is at the corner of Commercial and Standish streets (© **800/894-1951** or 508/487-1950; www.artsdunetours.com). In 1946, Art Costa started driving sightseers out to ogle the decrepit "dune shacks" where such transient luminaries as Eugene O'Neill, Jack Kerouac, and Jackson Pollock found their respective muses. The park service wanted to raze these eyesores, but luckily saner heads prevailed: They're now National Historic Landmarks. The tours typically take about 1 to 1½ hours. Tickets are $15 to $20 for adults, $8 to $10 for children 6 to 11. Additional tours offered include a sunset clambake dune tour ($66), a barbecue tour ($56), and a Race Point Lighthouse tour ($23 adults, $13 children 6–11).

A recommended boat tour is on the ***Bay Lady II*** ★ (© **508/487-9308;** www.sailcapecod.com), which leaves from Macmillan Wharf. The sunset trip aboard this 73-foot reproduction gaff-rigged Grand Banks schooner is especially spectacular. Tickets cost $12 to $16 for adults, $7 for children under 12. There are four 2-hour sails daily from mid-May to mid-October.

MUSEUMS

The Expedition Whydah Sea Lab & Learning Center *Overrated* Though the subject matter here is fascinating, this site is a bit of a tourist trap. Cape Cod native Barry Clifford made headlines in 1984 when he tracked down the wreck of the 17th-century pirate ship ***Whydah*** (pronounced *Wid*-dah, like Yankee for "widow") 1,500 feet off the coast of Wellfleet, where it had lain undisturbed since 1717. Only 10% excavated to date, it has already yielded over 100,000 artifacts. In this museum/lab, visitors can supposedly observe the reclamation work being done, though it's unusual to actually see scientists or scholars at work.

MacMillan Wharf (just past the whale-watching fleet). © 508/487-8899. www.whydah.com. Admission $8 adults, $6 children 6–12. June–Sept daily 9:30am–9pm; Oct–Dec and mid-Apr–May weekends only 10am–5pm. Closed Jan to mid-Apr.

Pilgrim Monument & Provincetown Museum ★★ Anywhere you go in town, this granite tower looms, ever ready to restore your bearings. Climb up the 60 gradual ramps interspersed with 116 steps—a surprisingly easy lope—and you'll get a gargoyle's-eye view of the spiraling coast and, in the distance, Boston against a backdrop of New Hampshire's mountains. Definitely devote some time to the curious exhibits in the museum, chronicling P-town's checkered past as both fishing port and arts nexus. Among the memorabilia, you'll find polar bears brought back from MacMillan's expeditions and early programs for the Provincetown Players.

High Pole Hill Rd. (off Winslow St., N of Bradford St.). © 508/487-1310. www.pilgrim-monument.org. Admission $7 adults, $3 children 4–12. July–Aug daily 9am–7pm; off season daily 9am–5pm. Last admission 45 min. before closing. Closed Dec–Mar.

Province Lands Visitor Center of the Cape Cod National Seashore ★ Though much smaller than the Salt Pond Visitor Center, this satellite does a good job of explicating this special environment, where plant life must fight a fierce battle to maintain its hold amid shifting sands buffeted by salty winds. Be sure to circle the observation deck for great views. Inquire about special events, such as guided walks, family campfires, and canoe programs (reservations required).

Race Point Rd. (about 1½ miles NW of the town center). © 508/487-1256. Free admission. Mid-Apr to late Nov daily 9am–5pm. Closed late Nov to mid-Apr.

Provincetown Art Association & Museum ★★ *Moments* This extraordinary cache of 20th-century American art began with five paintings donated by local artists, including Charles Hawthorne, the charismatic teacher who first "discovered" this picturesque outpost. Founded in 1914, only a year after New York's revolutionary Armory Show, the museum was the site of innumerable "space wars," as classicists and modernists vied for square footage. In today's less competitive atmosphere, it's not unusual to see a tame still life next to an unrestrained abstract. The museum sponsors a full schedule of concerts, lectures, readings, and classes.

460 Commercial St. (in the East End). © 508/487-1750. www.paam.org. Admission: $2 adults, members and children under 12 free. July–Aug daily noon–5pm and 8–10pm; call for off-season hours. Open year-round.

SHOPPING

ART GALLERIES Of the several dozen galleries in town, only a handful are reliably worthwhile. In season, most of the galleries and even some of the shops open around 11am, then take a siesta from around 5 to 7pm, reopening and greeting visitors up to as late as 10 or 11pm. Shows usually open on Friday evenings, prompting a "stroll" tradition spanning the many receptions.

Berta Walker is a force to be reckoned with, having nurtured many top artists through her association with the Fine Arts Work Center, before opening her own gallery in 1990, the **Berta Walker Gallery** ★, 208 Bradford St. in the East End (© 508/487-6411). Closed from late October to late May.

DNA (Definitive New Art) Gallery ★, 288 Bradford St. above the Provincetown Tennis Club in the East End (© 508/487-7700), has attracted such talents as photographer Joel Meyerowitz, Provincetown's favorite portraitist, known for such tomes as *Cape Light;* sculptor Conrad Malicoat, whose free-form brick chimneys and hearths can be seen around town; and local conceptualist/provocateur Jay Critchley. Readings by cutting-edge authors add to the buzz. Closed from mid-October to late May.

Julie Heller started collecting early P-town paintings as a child—and a tourist at that. She chose so incredibly well, her roster at **Julie Heller Gallery** ✸, 2 Gosnold St. on the beach in the center of town (© **508/487-2169**), reads like a who's who of local art. Hawthorne, Avery, Hofmann, Lazzell, Hensche—all the big names from Provincetown's past are here, as well as some contemporary artists. Closed weekdays January to April.

Schoolhouse Center for Art and Design, 494 Commercial St. in the East End (© **508/487-4800**), is an impressive setup with two galleries, studios, arts programs, and an events series.

DISCOUNT SHOPPING

Marine Specialties, 235 Commercial St. in the center of town (© **508/487-1730**), is packed to the rafters with useful stuff, from discounted Doc Martens to cut-rate Swiss Army knives. Hung from the ceiling are some real antiques, including several carillons' worth of ship's bells.

FASHION

Giardelli/Antonelli Studio Showroom, 417 Commercial St. in the East End (© **508/487-3016**), is filled with Jerry Giardelli's unstructured clothing elements in vibrant colors and inviting textures. They demand to be mixed and matched by Diana Antonelli's statement jewelry.

Mad as a Hatter, 360 Commercial St. (© **508/487-4063**), has hats to suit every style and inclination. Closed January to mid-February.

Moda Fina, 349 Commercial St. (© **508/487-6632**), specializes in women's clothing and accessories, including shoes and lingerie, and unique summer dresses.

WHERE TO STAY
VERY EXPENSIVE

Anchor Inn ✸✸ This waterfront property centrally located on Commercial Street recently underwent a multimillion-dollar face-lift. Many feature deluxe showers, whirlpool baths, and fireplaces. Sixteen guest rooms have waterfront balconies overlooking the harbor. Four have separate entrances through private porches. Some of the rooms, called "yacht cabins," are quite small, but have fabulous views. Others are large suites with king-size beds, two-person whirlpool baths, and French doors leading to a private balcony. Breakfast is an elaborate affair that could include quiche or eggs Benedict.

175 Commercial St. (in the center of town), Provincetown, MA 02657. © **800/858-2657** or 508/487-0432. Fax 508/487-6280. www.anchorinnbeachhouse.com. 23 units. Summer $255–$275 double; $375 suite. Rates Include continental breakfast. AE, MC, V. Closed Jan–Mar. *In room:* A/C, TV/VCR, CD player, dataport, fridge, hair dryer.

Brass Key Guesthouse ✸✸✸ Brass Key is the fanciest place to stay in Provincetown. With Ritz-Carlton–style amenities and service in mind, the innkeepers have created a paean to luxury. They've thought of everything: down pillows, jetted showers, and free iced tea and lemonade delivered poolside. Rooms in the 1828 Federal-style Captain's House and the Gatehouse are decorated in a playful country style, while the Victorian-era building is classically elegant, with materials like mahogany, walnut, and marble. Most deluxe guest rooms have gas fireplaces and oversize whirlpool tubs. In high season, the clientele here is primarily gay men, though all are made to feel welcome.

67 Bradford St. (in the center of town), Provincetown, MA 02657. © **800/842-9858** or 508/487-9005. Fax 508/487-9020. www.brasskey.com. 29 units, 4 cottages (9 tub/shower; 22 shower only; 2 with tub and shower). Summer $245–$445 double; $295–$445 cottage. Rates include continental breakfast and afternoon wine-and-cheese hour. AE, DISC, MC, V. Closed late Nov to early Apr. No children under 18. **Amenities:** Outdoor heated pool; 17-ft. hot tub. In room: A/C, TV/VCR, dataport, fridge, hair dryer, safe.

Crowne Pointe Historic Inn ★★ At this newly restored property perched high on Bradford Street, the inn and grounds are exquisitely maintained with deluxe commons areas and attractive gardens. The staff is accommodating and professional. Rooms are spacious and some of the deluxe rooms and suites have fireplaces, wet bars, and whirlpool spas. Buffet breakfast is served in the large living room, which has plenty of overstuffed couches to lounge around on while you plan your day.

82 Bradford St. (in the center of town), Provincetown, MA 02657. © **877/CROWNE1** or 508/487-6767. Fax 508/487-5554. www.crownepointe.com. 40 units. $195–$450 double. Rates include continental breakfast, afternoon tea, and wine-and-cheese hour. AE, MC, V. **Amenities:** Heated outdoor pool; 10-person outdoor spa. In room: AC, TV/VCR, dataport, hair dryer, iron.

EXPENSIVE

Best Western Tides Beachfront ★★ (Kids) Families will be delighted with this beachfront motel, located on 6 acres well removed both from Provincetown's bustle and North Truro's ticky-tacky congestion. Every inch of this complex has been groomed to the max, including the ultra-green grounds, the Wedgwood-blue breakfast room, and the spotless guest rooms decorated in a soothing pastel palette.

837 Commercial St. (near the Truro border), Provincetown, MA 02657. © **800/528-1234** or 508/487-1045. Fax 508/487-1621. www.bwprovincetown.com. 64 units. Summer $159–$289 double; $299–$319 suite. AE, DC, DISC, MC, V. Closed late Oct to mid-May. **Amenities:** Outdoor heated pool; coin-op laundry. In room: A/C, TV, dataport, fridge, coffeemaker, hair dryer, iron.

Land's End Inn ★★★ (Finds) Enjoying a prime perch atop Gull Hill in the far West End of Commercial Street, this whimsical 1907 bungalow is bursting with outlandish antiques. Some rooms would suit a 19th-century sheik. In other words, the place is unique in a way that will delight some guests and overwhelm others. There are three deluxe rooms that make use of the inn's soaring towers. The two-bedroom loft tower suite, entered through an armoire (very Narnia) must be one of the most unusual and spectacular lodging spaces on the Cape. From the spacious living room, climb the ironwork spiral stairway to the bedroom, where an immense stained-glass window serves as your headboard. There's also a wonderful octagonal tower room with bay-view decks on two sides. Some of the other rooms are small, but all are filled with kitschy Victorian and Deco *objets*. Though the inn is predominantly gay, cosmopolitan visitors will feel welcome. The breakfast, an elaborate continental spread, features fresh fruits and homemade baked goods.

22 Commercial St. (in the West End), Provincetown, MA 02657. © **800/276-7088** or 508/487-0706. Fax 508/487-0755. www.landsendinn.com. 16 units. Summer $165–$195 double; $295–$495 tower rooms. Rates include continental breakfast and wine-and-cheese hour. AE, MC, V. Closed Nov–April. In room: AC, no phone.

The Masthead ★★ (Kids) This is one of the few places in town, other than the impersonal motels, that actively welcomes families, and the placid 450-foot private beach will delight young splashers. The cottages are fun, some with wicker furniture and antiques. In the water-view rooms perched above the surf, with their 7-foot picture windows overlooking the bay and Long Point, you may feel like you're onboard a ship.

31–41 Commercial St. (in the West End), Provincetown, MA 02657. © 800/395-5095 or 508/487-0523. Fax 508/487-9251. www.themasthead.com. 21 units (3 tub/shower; 16 shower; 2 with shared bathroom), 4 cottages. Summer $86–$93 double with shared bath; $102–$249 double; $179–$235 efficiency; $265 2-bedroom apt; $1,750–$2,541 cottage weekly. AE, DC, DISC, MC, V. Open year-round. *In room:* A/C, TV, fridge, coffeemaker.

Watermark Inn ★★ *Kids*   If you'd like to experience P-town without being stuck in the thick of it (the carnival atmosphere can get tiring at times), this contemporary inn at the peaceful edge of town is the perfect choice. This beachfront hotel contains dazzling suites; the prize ones, on the top floor, have picture windows and sweeping deck views. Handmade quilts brighten up clean, monochromatic rooms.

603 Commercial St. (in the East End), Provincetown, MA 02657. © 508/487-0165. Fax 508/487-2383. www.watermark-inn.com. 10 units. Summer $130–$270 suite. From mid-May to mid-Sept, suites rent by the week only ($1,200–$2,440 per week). AE, MC, V. Open year-round. *In room:* TV, fridge, coffeemaker.

MODERATE

Cape Inn ★   This no-surprises motel on the waterfront at the far eastern edge of town is a good choice for first-timers not quite sure what they're getting into. Guests in waterfront rooms get a nice view of town. In season free movies are shown in the restaurant/lounge on a 100-foot screen and dinner is served in the restaurant. There's also a poolside bar and grill. Though this motel is a bit of a hike from the town's center, an in-season town shuttle will whisk you down Commercial Street or to the beaches.

698 Commercial St. (at Rte. 6A, in the East End), Provincetown, MA 02657. © 800/422-4224 or 508/487-1711. Fax 508/487-3929. www.capeinn.com. 78 units. Summer $119–$179 double. Rates include continental breakfast. AE, DC, DISC, MC, V. Closed Nov–Apr. Dogs allowed. **Amenities:** Restaurant; outdoor pool. *In room:* A/C, TV, dataport, fridge, coffeemaker, hair dryer, iron.

Carpe Diem ★★   The theme of this stylish B&B is "seize the day." The location, a quiet side street right in the center of town, would suit most P-town habitués to a "T." Guest rooms here are exquisitely decorated with European antiques and brightly painted walls and wallpapers. All rooms have down comforters and pillows, as well as bathrobes, and all but one has a mini-fridge. There are two deluxe garden suites with private entrances, Jacuzzis, and fireplaces. The cottage has a two-person whirlpool, a fireplace, a private patio, and a wet bar. The full breakfast features homemade pastries served at the dining-room table. On clear days, sun worshippers prefer the patio where there's a six-person hot tub.

12 Johnson St. (in the center of town), Provincetown, MA 02657. © 800/487-0132 or 508/487-4242 (also fax). www.carpediemguesthouse.com. 14 units. Summer $140–$185 double; $225–$265 suites; $325 cottage. Rates include full breakfast and wine-and-cheese hour. AE, DISC, MC, V. Open year-round. **Amenities:** 8-person hot tub. *In room:* A/C, TV/VCR, dataport.

Copper Fox ★★   This majestic 1856 captain's house with its large wraparound porch is a short walk from the galleries and restaurants of the East End. From the second floor deck, you have a perfect harbor view. Several of the spacious rooms also have bay views. Two apartments have private entrances and kitchens; one has a private garden, and the other is large enough to accommodate six people comfortably.

448 Commercial St. (in the East End), Provincetown, MA 02657. ©/fax 508/487-8583. www.province town.com/copperfox. 7 units. Summer $140–$179 double; $195 apt. Rates include continental breakfast and afternoon tea. MC, V. Open year-round. *In room:* A/C, TV/VCR, no phone.

INEXPENSIVE

Captain Lysander Inn ✦ *Value*   Set back from the street in the quiet West End, this 1840 Greek Revival captain's house has definite curb appeal. The conservatively furnished rooms are quite nice for the price, and some have partial water views. Tall windows make these rooms feel light and airy. The whole gang can fit in either the apartment or the cottage, both of which sleep six and have TV/VCRs and kitchenettes.

96 Commercial St. (in the West End), Provincetown, MA 02657. © 508/487-2253. Fax 508/487-7579. www. captainlysanderinn.com. 13 units (6 with shared bathroom), 1 cottage. Summer $105 double with shared bathroom, $115 double with private bathroom; efficiency $135 daily, $1,400 weekly; apt $200 daily, $1,200 weekly; cottage $250 daily, $1,400 weekly. Rates include continental breakfast except for apt and cottage. MC, V. Open year-round. *In room:* No phone.

White Horse Inn ✦✦ *Value*   Look for the house with the bright yellow door in the East End. The rates are terrific, especially given the fact that this inn is the very embodiment of Provincetown's bohemian mystique. Frank Schaefer has been tinkering with this late-18th-century house since 1963. The rooms may be a bit austere, but each is enlivened by some of the 300 to 400 paintings he has collected over the decades. A number of his fellow artists helped him cobble together the studio apartments out of salvage: There's an aura of beatnik improv about them still. Guests over the years have embodied a range of low and high art: Cult filmmaker John Waters stayed here often, as did poet laureate Robert Pinsky.

500 Commercial St. (in the East End), Provincetown, MA 02657. © 508/487-1790. 24 units (10 with shared bathroom). Summer $60 single with shared bathroom; $70–$80 double; $125–$140 efficiency. No credit cards. *In room:* No phone.

WHERE TO DINE

Spiritus Pizza, 190 Commercial St. (© **508/487-2808**), is an extravagant pizza parlor open until 2am. The pizza's good, as are the fruit drinks, and premium ice cream. For a peaceful morning repast, check out the little garden in back.

Peruse the scrumptious meat pies and pastries at **Provincetown Portuguese Bakery,** 299 Commercial St. (© **508/487-1803**). Both establishments are closed November to early April.

VERY EXPENSIVE

Chester ✦✦✦ NEW AMERICAN   Step through the columned portico for a singular dining experience. Chester specializes in local seafood, meats, and vegetables prepared simply yet with a flourish. Service is exceptional; the food is beautifully presented. Starters like spinach and scallop risotto take advantage of local provender, as does the main course of Chatham cod with prosciutto and sage. The extensive wine list has won *Wine Spectator* awards. For dessert, look no further than the warm chocolate cake with homemade ice cream.

404 Commercial St. © 508/487-8200. www.chesterrestaurant.com. Reservations recommended. Main courses $19–$34. AE, MC, V. Late June to mid-Sept daily 6–10pm; mid-Apr to late May Thurs–Mon; late May to late June and mid-Sept to Oct Thurs–Tues 6–10pm; call for off-season hours. Closed Jan to mid-Apr, except New Year's Eve.

The Dancing Lobster Cafe Trattoria ✦ MEDITERRANEAN   This waterfront restaurant has a well-known chef and great location, but it's a tad pricey for the offerings. Chef/owner Nils "Pepe" Berg's establishment is a popular place, so expect to wait, even with a reservation. The mainstay here is seafood, but the menu also features Venetian specialties. Main courses may include steak al "Pepe" with green and black peppercorns, brandy, demiglace, and cream. This is a particularly good choice for lunch (try the extra-special lobster rolls), which is served on the outside terrace or on the second floor overlooking the beach.

373 Commercial St. (in the center of town). ℂ **508/487-0900**. Reservations recommended. Main courses $17–$30. MC, V. July–Sept Tues–Sun 11:30am–5pm and 5:30–11pm; May–June and Oct 6–9pm. Closed Nov–Apr.

Martin House ★★★ CONTEMPORARY NEW ENGLAND/INTERNA-TIONAL   Easily one of the most charming restaurants on the Cape, this snuggery of rustic soft-lit rooms happens to contain one of the Cape's most forward-thinking kitchens. The chef favors local delicacies, such as the littlenecks that appear in a kafir-lime–tamarind broth with Asian noodles. Main courses might include local-lobster–stuffed squash blossoms with a warm porcini-saffron vinaigrette. In season, there's seating in the rose-covered garden terrace for both dinner and, on Saturdays and Sundays, breakfast.

157 Commercial St. ℂ **508/487-1327**. www.themartinhouse.com. Reservations recommended. Main courses $16–$33. AE, DC, DISC, MC, V. May–Oct daily 6–11pm, Sat and Sun 9am–12:30pm; Jan–Apr and Nov–Dec Thurs–Mon 6–10pm. Closed mid-Dec.

The Red Inn ★★ NEW AMERICAN   New owners have turned this property at the far west end of Commercial Street into one of the toughest reservations to get in town. The dining room with its wraparound floor-to-ceiling windows has great beach views. The refined atmosphere makes this a favorite for special occasions, when your dinner might begin with a glass of champagne and end with a soufflé. This is fine dining on the calorie-rich side, with entrees like grilled thick pork chops with tomatillo salsa and pepper-crusted filet mignon with truffle mashed potatoes and Jack Daniels sauce. There are always fresh fish and vegetarian main courses on the menu also.

15 Commercial St. ℂ **508/487-7334**. Reservations required. www.theredinn.com. Main courses $21–$38. AE, DC, DISC, MC, V. Mid-June to early Sept daily 5:30–10pm and Sat and Sun 10am–2:30pm; call for off-season hours.

EXPENSIVE

Front Street ★★ MEDITERRANEAN FUSION/ITALIAN   For years, this restaurant has delivered high-quality food and service, and locals consider it a cherished locale. Located in a belowground space on Commercial Street, this cozy restaurant feels most comfortable in the chilly days of spring and summer. Chef Donna Aliperti is constantly improving her menu, inspired by trips to Italy and southern France. The fusion menu, available in season, has creative items like soft shell crabs with corn-studded risotto and Chinese five-spice grilled duckling. There is also a traditional Italian menu with pastas available every night.

230 Commercial St. ℂ **508/487-9715**. www.frontstreetrestaurant.com. Reservations recommended. Main courses $18–$25. DISC, MC, V. June–Sept daily 6–10pm. Call for off-season hours.

Lorraine's ★★ MEXICAN/NEW AMERICAN   Long heralded by year-rounders as a spot for creative food and a festive atmosphere, Lorraine's moved last year to a storefront locale on the far west end of Commercial Street. In its new smaller location, the restaurant continues its tradition of being one of the town's top dining spots. Even those who shy away from Mexican restaurants should try Lorraine's; the food here is truly unique. Maryland soft-shell crabs are lightly dusted in flour with Chimayo chile powder and pan-sautéed and served with a jalapeño aioli. For a main course, consider *viere verde*—sea scallops sautéed with tomatillos, flambéed in tequila, and cloaked in a green-chile sauce. For a treat, check out the extensive tequila menu; shots are served with a wonderful tomato juice-based chaser.

133 Commercial St. (in the West End). 🅒 🅒 **508/487-6074.** Reservations suggested. Main courses $17–$26. DISC, MC, V. June–Sept daily 6–10pm; call for off-season hours. Closed mid-Dec to Mar.

The Mews & Cafe Mews 🅐🅐 INTERNATIONAL/AMERICAN FUSION Bank on fine food and suave service at this beachfront restaurant, an enduring favorite since 1961. Upstairs is the cafe with its century-old mahogany bar and lighter menu. The dining room downstairs sits right on the beach. The best soup in the region is the Mews' scrumptious summertime special, chilled cucumber-miso bisque with curry shrimp timbale. Among the showier entrees is "captured scallops": prime Wellfleet specimens enclosed with a shrimp-and-crab mousse in a crisp wonton pouch and served atop a petite filet mignon with chipotle aioli. Desserts and coffees—take them upstairs in the cafe to the accompaniment of soft-jazz piano—are delectable.

429 Commercial St. 🅒 **508/487-1500.** Reservations recommended. www.mews.com. Main courses $18–$29. AE, DC, DISC, MC, V. Mid-June to early Sept daily 6–10pm and Sun 11am–2:30pm; late Sept to mid-June 6–10pm only. Open year-round.

MODERATE

Bubala's by the Bay 🅐 ECLECTIC   This trendy bistro promises "serious food at sensible prices." And that's what it delivers: from buttermilk waffles to creative focaccia sandwiches to fajitas, Cajun calamari, and pad Thai. This is a big operation for Provincetown, and the huge outdoor patio facing Commercial Street is particularly popular in the morning. In season, there's entertainment nightly from 10pm to 1am.

183 Commercial St. (in the West End). 🅒 **508/487-0773.** Main courses $10–$21. AE, DISC, MC, V. Apr–Oct daily 8am–11pm. Closed late Oct to Apr.

Café Heaven 🅐 AMERICAN   Prized for its leisurely country breakfasts (served till mid-afternoon, for reluctant risers), this modern storefront—adorned with big, bold paintings by acclaimed Wellfleet artist John Grillo—also turns out substantial sandwiches, such as avocado and goat cheese on a French baguette. For dinner, Café Heaven becomes a Thai restaurant.

199 Commercial St. (in the center of town). 🅒 **508/487-9639.** Reservations not accepted. Most items $11–$18. No credit cards. July–Aug daily 8am–3pm and 6:30–10pm; call for off-season hours. Closed Feb–May.

The Commons Bistro & Bar 🅐🅐   ECLECTIC/FRENCH BISTRO   It's a toss-up: The sidewalk cafe provides an optimal opportunity for studying P-town's inimitable street life, whereas the plum-colored dining room affords a refuge adorned with the owners' extraordinary collection of Toulouse-Lautrec prints. Either way, you'll get to partake of tasty and creative fare. At lunch, the lobster club sandwich on country bread is unbeatable. The Commons boasts the only wood-fired oven in town to date, which comes in handy in preparing the popular gourmet pizzas with unique toppings. At dinner, try the paella with roasted chicken, chorizo, clams, mussels, and shrimp. The Commons also serves as an all-day coffee shop, with cappuccinos and baked goods.

386 Commercial St. 🅒 **508/487-7800.** www.commonsghb.com. Reservations recommended. Main courses $10–$26. AE, MC, V. Mid-June to mid-Sept daily 8am–3pm and 6–10:30pm; call for off-season hours. Closed Nov–Mar.

Napi's 🅐🅐 INTERNATIONAL   Restaurateur Napi Van Dereck can be credited with bringing P-town's restaurant scene up to speed—back in the early 1970s. His namesake restaurant still reflects that Zeitgeist, with its rococo-hippie carpentry, select outtakes from his sideline in antiques, and some rather outstanding art. The cuisine is a lot less granola than it was, or maybe we've just caught up—hearty peasant fare never really goes out of style. And these peasants really get around, culling dumplings from China, falafel from Syria, and, from Greece, shrimp feta flambéed with ouzo and Metaxa. Unusual in Provincetown, this restaurant has its own parking lot (around back).

7 Freeman St. (at Bradford St.). ℂ 800/571-6274 or 508/487-1145. Reservations recommended. Main courses $14–$26. DISC, MC, V. May to mid-Sept daily 5–10pm; mid-Sept to Apr daily 11:30am–4pm and 5–9pm.

INEXPENSIVE

Clem and Ursie's 𝕂 *(Kids)* *(Finds)* SEAFOOD & BARBECUE   Grab a picnic table for a big family dinner of fried seafood and barbeque ribs. More elaborate choices include bouillabaisse, and Japanese udon (fish, shellfish, and vegetables in a dashi broth over noodles). The children's menu offers a choice of $5 entrees with fries, drink, dessert, and a surprise. Takeout is popular here, as is the separate ice cream section.

85 Shankpainter Rd. (off Bradford St., a few blocks S of town). ℂ 508/487-2333. Main courses $6–$17. MC, V. Apr to mid-Oct daily 11am–10pm. Closed mid-Oct to Mar.

TAKEOUT & PICNIC FARE

Mojo's 𝕂, 5 Ryder St. Ext. (ℂ **508/487-3140**), a fried-seafood shack is known for its lightly breaded fried fish and hand-cut fries. There are also veggie burgers, burritos, and chicken tenders. Eat at one of the six picnic tables on the patio or take it to the beach. Closed mid-Oct to early May.

The best gourmet shop is **Angel Foods,** 467 Commercial St., in the East End (ℂ **508/487-6666**), which offers Italian specialties and other prepared foods.

The rollwiches—pita bread packed with a wide range of fillings—at **Box Lunch,** 353 Commercial St., in the center of town (ℂ **508/487-6026**), are ideal for a strolling lunch.

CYBER CAFE

To check your email, surf online, or just hang out with techies, stop by **Cyber Cove,** an Internet lounge on the second floor of Whalers' Wharf on Commercial Street (ℂ **508/487-7778;** www.cybercove-ptown.com).

PROVINCETOWN AFTER DARK

To order tickets for any of the shows at Provincetown's nightclubs and cabarets, call **In-Town Reservations** at (ℂ **508/487-2234**).

An on-again, off-again contender for hottest club in town is **Club Euro,** 258 Commercial St., 2nd floor, beside Town Hall (ℂ **508/487-8800**), the current home of "Two Fags and a Drag" and the ever-popular all-star musical comedy drag revue "Big Boned Barbies," starring Kandi Kane. Closed October to May.

Perhaps the nation's premier gay bar, **The Atlantic House** 𝕂, 6 Masonic Place, off Commercial Street (ℂ **508/487-3821**), is open year-round. The "A-House" also welcomes straights, except in the leather-oriented Macho Bar upstairs. In the little bar downstairs, check out the Tennessee Williams memorabilia, including a portrait *au naturel.*

Come late afternoon, if you're wondering where all the beachgoers went, it's a safe bet that a number are attending the gay-lesbian tea dance held daily in season from 3:30 to 6:30pm on the pool deck at the **Boatslip Beach Club** 𝕂, 161 Commercial St. (ℂ **508/487-1669**). The action then shifts to the **Pied,** 193

Commercial St. (📞 **508/487-1527**); www.pied.com), for its After Tea T-Dance from 5 to 10pm, but returns to the Boatslip later in the evening for disco. Closed November through April.

Crown & Anchor 🐾, 247 Commercial St. (📞 **508/487-1430;** www.the crownandanchor.net), houses a number of bars spanning leather, disco, comedy, drag shows, and cabaret. Facilities include a pool bar and game room. Closed November through April.

One of P-town's top clubs, the **Post Office Café and Cabaret,** 303 Commercial St. (📞 **508/487-3892**), despite its cramped space, can be depended on for amusing drag and comedy shows. In recent years, the B-Girlz (Hard Kora, Barbie-Q, and Belle Bottom) have been the featured act. The cover is $20. Closed November to April.

The chic women's bar, **Vixen,** at the Pilgrim House, 336 Commercial St. (📞 **508/487-6424**), features local and national jazz, blues, and comedy acts, including such favorites as Lea DeLaria and Melissa Ferrick a couple times a season. There are also pool tables. Closed November to April.

Governor Bradford, 312 Commercial St. (📞 **508/487-2781**), is a good old bar, featuring pool tables, drag karaoke (summer nights at 9:30pm), and disco.

CAPE COD NATIONAL SEASHORE ★★★

No trip to Cape Cod would be complete without a visit to the **Cape Cod National Seashore** on the Outer Cape. Take an afternoon barefoot stroll along the "The Great Beach," and see why the Cape attracts so many artists and poets. On August 7, 1961, President John F. Kennedy signed a bill designating 27,000 acres in the 40 miles from Chatham to Provincetown as the Cape Cod National Seashore, a new national park. However, as early as the 1930s, the National Park Service had been interested in Cape Cod's ocean beach; back then the land would have cost taxpayers about $10 an acre! Unusual in a national park, the Seashore includes 500 private residences, the owners of which lease land from the park service. Convincing residents that a National Seashore would be a good thing for Cape Cod was an arduous task back then, and Provincetown still grapples with Seashore officials over town land issues.

ESSENTIALS

GETTING THERE   Take Route 6, the Mid-Cape Highway, to Eastham; it's about 50 miles from the Sagamore Bridge.

VISITOR INFORMATION   Pick up a map of the National Seashore at the **Salt Pond Visitor Center,** in Eastham (📞 **508/225-3421**). It's open daily: late May to early September from 9am to 5pm, early September to late May from 9am to 4:30pm. Major renovation work is expected to be completed by the fall of 2004. The center itself will be closed during the renovation, but visitors will still be able to walk the trails and obtain maps at a temporary visitor booth. There is also the **Province Lands Visitor Center** (p. 250), a smaller site, in Provincetown. Both centers have ranger activities, gift shops, and restrooms. Seashore beaches are all clearly marked off Route 6. Additional beaches along this stretch are run by individual towns; you must have a sticker or pay a fee to park.

BEACHES & GETTING OUTSIDE

BEACHES   The Seashore's claim to fame is its spectacular beaches—in reality, one long beach—with dunes 50 to 150 feet high. This is the Atlantic Ocean, so the surf is rough (and cold), but a number of the beaches have lifeguards. A $30 pass will get you into all of them for the season, or you can pay a daily rate of

$10. Most of the Seashore beaches have large parking lots, but you'll need to arrive early (before 10am) on busy summer weekends to claim a spot. If the beach you want to go to is full, try the one next door—most of the beaches are 5 to 10 miles apart. Don't forget your beach umbrella—the sun exposure here can get intense.

- **Coast Guard Beach** ✿✿✿ and **Nauset Light Beach** ✿✿✿, off Ocean View Drive, Eastham: Connected to outlying parking lots by a free shuttle, these pristine beaches have lifeguards and restrooms. With the old Coast Guard building on one and the striped lighthouse on the other, these two strands are among the most scenic in the Seashore.
- **Head of the Meadow Beach** ✿✿, off Head of the Meadow Road, Truro: Among the more remote National Seashore beaches, this spot (with restrooms) is known for its excellent surf. Because beachgoers don't have to traverse steep dunes to get here, Head of the Meadow is easier for seniors or those with disabilities to access.
- **Marconi Beach** ✿✿, off Marconi Beach Road in South Wellfleet: The bluffs are so high here that the beach lies in shadows by late afternoon. Restrooms are available.
- **Race Point Beach** ✿✿✿ and **Herring Cove Beach** ✿✿✿, off Route 6, Provincetown: Race Point has rough surf, and you might even spot a whale on its way to Stellwagen Bank, a breeding ground. Herring Cove, with much calmer waters, is a good place to watch sunsets, and is popular with same-sex couples.

BICYCLING   Some say the best bike path on Cape Cod is the **Province Lands Trail** ✿✿✿, 5 swooping and invigorating miles at Race Point Beach. There is also a 2-mile, relatively flat path linking Head of the Meadow Beach to High Head Beach in Truro.

FISHING   Surf-casting is allowed from the ocean beaches. Race Point is a popular spot.

NATURE TRAILS   The Seashore has a number of walking trails—all free, all picturesque. In Eastham, **Fort Hill** ✿✿✿, off Route 6, has one of the best scenic views on Cape Cod, as well as a popular boardwalk trail through a red maple swamp. Following the trail markers around Fort Hill, you'll pass "Indian Rock" (bearing the marks of untold generations who used it to sharpen their tools) and enjoy scenic vantage points overlooking the channel-carved marsh and out to sea. The Fort Hill Trail hooks up with the ½-mile Red Cedar Swamp Trail, offering boardwalk views of an ecology otherwise inaccessible.

The **Nauset Marsh Trail** ✿ is accessed from the Salt Pond Visitor Center, on Route 6 in Eastham. **Great Island** ✿✿, on the bay side in Wellfleet, is one of the finest places to have a picnic; you could spend the day hiking the trails. On **Pamet Trail** ✿, off North Pamet Road in Truro, hikers pass the decrepit old cranberry-bog building on the way to a trail through the dunes. Don't try the old boardwalk trail over the bogs here; it has flooded and is no longer in use. The **Atlantic White Cedar Swamp Trail** ✿✿ is located at the Marconi Wireless Station site (described below). **Small Swamp** ✿ and **Pilgrim Spring** ✿ trails are found at Pilgrim Heights Beach. **Beech Forest Trail** ✿✿ is located at Race Point in Provincetown.

SEASHORE SIGHTS   The **Old Harbor Lifesaving Station** ✿, Race Point Beach off Race Point Road, Provincetown (✆ **508/487-1256**), was one of 13

Tips **Recommended Reading**

Henry David Thoreau's *Cape Cod* is an entertaining account of the author's journeys on the Cape in the late 19th century. The writer/naturalist walked along the beach from Eastham to Provincetown, and you can follow in his footsteps. Henry Beston's *The Outermost House,* originally published in 1928 (Henry Holt, 2003), describes a year of living on the beach in Eastham in a simple one-room dune shack. The shack washed out to sea about 20 years ago, but "The Great Beach" remains. Michael Cunningham's *Land's End: A Walk in Provincetown* (Crown, 2002) is a brief, engrossing meditation, travelogue, and memoir about the little town at the tip of Cape Cod.

lifesaving stations mandated by Congress in the late 19th century. This shingled shelter with a lookout tower was part of a network responsible for saving some 100,000 lives. Before the U.S. Lifesaving Service was founded in 1872 (it became part of the Coast Guard in 1915), shipwreck victims lucky enough to be washed ashore were still doomed unless they could find a "charity shed"—a hut supplied with firewood—maintained by the Massachusetts Humane Society. The six valiant "Surfmen" manning each life-saving station took a more active approach, patrolling the beach at all hours and rowing out into the surf to save all they could. Their old equipment is on view at this museum. Admission is free; there's a parking fee for Race Point Beach (see "Beaches," above). It's open daily from 3 to 5pm in July and August; call for off-season hours. Closed November through April.

The **Marconi Wireless Station,** on Marconi Park Site Road (off Rte. 6), South Wellfleet (© **508/349-3785**), tells the story of the first international telegraphic communication. It's from this spot that inventor Guglielmo Marconi sent the world's first wireless communiqué: "Cordial greetings from President Theadore [sic] Roosevelt to King Edward VII in Poldhu, Wales." It was also here, in 1912, that news of the *Titanic* first reached these shores. There's scarcely a trace left of this extraordinary feat of technology (the station was dismantled in 1920); still, the outdoor displays convey the leap of imagination that was required.

The **Captain Edward Penniman House** ⍟, at Fort Hill off Route 6 in Eastham, is a grandly ornate 1868 Second Empire mansion. It's open for tours in season, but the exterior far outshines the interior. Call the visitor center (© **508/255-3421**) for times. Check out the huge whale jawbone gate before crossing the street to the trails (see "Nature Trails," above).

Five lighthouses, all automated now, dot the Seashore. In 1996, both Nauset Light, in Eastham, and Highland Light, in Truro, were successfully moved from precarious positions on the edge of dunes in order to save the beloved lighthouses. **Nauset Light** ⍟, with its cheerful red stripe, was originally moved to Eastham from Chatham in 1923. The lighthouse flashes an alternating red and white light that can be seen for 23 miles; public tours are offered.

Highland Light ⍟⍟, also known as **Cape Cod Light,** is the site of the first light in this area, dating back to 1798. The present structure was built in 1857. Follow signs from Route 6 in North Truro to the end of Highland Road. This lighthouse, set high on a cliff, was the first light seen by ships traveling from Europe. Now that the structure has been moved back from the eroding cliff, visitors are allowed to climb the staircase to the top with a guide. *Note:* There's a minimum 4-foot height requirement for climbing the lighthouse. Nearby is the 1907 **Highland House** ★★, home of the collections of the Truro Historical Society. Admission to both lighthouse and museum is $5 for adults, free for children under 12. Both are open June through September, daily from 10am to 5pm.

Wood End Light, on Long Point in Provincetown, is an unusual square lighthouse built as a "twin" to Long Point Light in 1873. Hearty souls can hike first across the breakwater at the west end of Commercial Street and then about ½ mile over soft sand to see this lighthouse.

Long Point Light, established in 1827, is isolated at the very tip of Cape Cod. It's about a 1½-hour walk from the breakwater, or a short boat ride from the center of Provincetown. Its fixed green light can be seen for 8 miles. This lighthouse was once the center of a thriving fishing community in the 1800s. Storms and erosion led the community to float their houses across the bay to Provincetown's West End, where a couple of the houses—some of the oldest in town—are still standing.

Martha's Vineyard & Nantucket

by Laura M. Reckford

Megastars and CEOs, vacationing families, and penniless students all seek refuge on Martha's Vineyard and Nantucket, two picturesque islands off the coast of Cape Cod. Both islands have much to offer families with children and couples seeking a romantic getaway. Their fame as summer resorts doesn't begin to take into account their rich history, diverse communities, and artistic traditions. But the popularity of these islands means that if you must go in the middle of summer, expect crowds and even—yikes!—traffic jams.

While only about 25 nautical miles apart, each island has its own distinct personality. Martha's Vineyard, large enough to support a year-round population spanning a broad socioeconomic spectrum, is not quite as rarefied as Nantucket. Vineyarders pride themselves on their liberal stances. True, a prime oceanside estate might fetch millions here, but the residents still dicker over the price of zucchini at the local farmers' market.

Nantucket, flash-frozen in the mid–19th century through zealous zoning, has long been considered a Republican haven. It's rich and traditional. Social scene aside, Nantucket has more pristine public shores than the Vineyard, as well as the best upscale shopping in the region. But there's something for everyone on both islands, and an island vacation is bound to be one that's cherished for many years.

1 Martha's Vineyard ★★★

With 100 square miles, Martha's Vineyard is New England's largest island, yet each of its six communities is blessed with endearing small-town charm. When the former First Family vacationed here, locals joked that the Clintons tested their reputed nonchalance toward famous faces. But don't visit the Vineyard for the celebrities. Instead, savor the decidedly laid-back pace of this unique place.

Most visitors never take the time to explore the entire island, staying in the "down-island" towns of **Vineyard Haven** ★ (officially called Tisbury), **Edgartown** ★★★, and **Oak Bluffs** ★★★. The "up-island" towns—**West Tisbury** ★★, **Chilmark** ★ (including the fishing village of **Menemsha** ★★★), and **Aquinnah** ★ (formerly known as Gay Head)—tend to be less touristy.

By all means, admire the regal sea captains' homes in Edgartown. Stroll down Circuit Avenue in Oak Bluffs with a Mad Martha's ice-cream cone, then ride the Flying Horses Carousel, said to be the oldest working carousel in the nation. Check out the cheerful "gingerbread" cottages behind Circuit Avenue, where the echoes of 19th-century revival meetings still ring out from the imposing tabernacle.

But don't forget to journey "up-island" to marvel at the red-clay cliffs of Aquinnah, a national historic landmark. Or bike the country roads of West Tisbury and

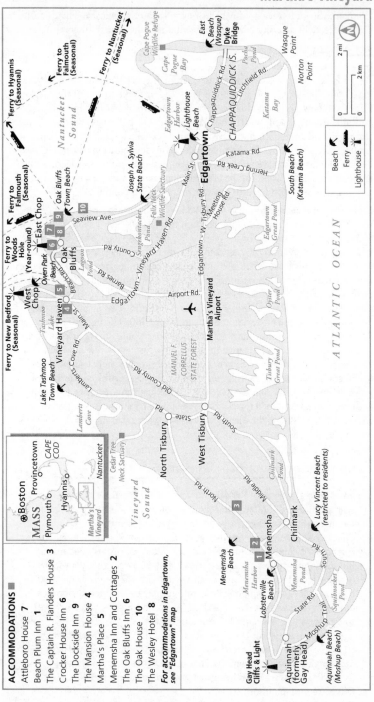

Martha's Vineyard

ACCOMMODATIONS ■
Attleboro House 7
Beach Plum Inn 1
The Captain R. Flanders House 3
Crocker House Inn 6
The Dockside Inn 9
The Mansion House 4
Martha's Place 5
Menemsha Inn and Cottages 2
The Oak Bluffs Inn 6
The Oak House 10
The Wesley Hotel 8
*For accommodations in Edgartown,
see "Edgartown" map*

Beach ↙
Ferry ←➤
Lighthouse ⚓

0 ⟷ 2 mi
0 ⟷ 2 km

Ferry to Nantucket (Seasonal) →

East
Beach
(Wasque)
Dyke
Bridge

Cape Pogue Wildlife Refuge

Cape
Pogue
Bay

Wasque
Point

Norton
Point

Katama
Bay

Pocha
Pond

CHAPPAQUIDDICK IS.
Chappaquiddick Rd.
Litchfield Rd.

Edgartown
Harbor
Lighthouse

Edgartown

Katama Rd.

Herring Creek Rd.

South Beach
(Katama Beach)

Edgartown
Great
Pond

Oyster
Pond

Joseph A. Sylvia
State Beach

Main St.

Edgartown–W. Tisbury Rd.
Meeting
House Rd.

Felix Neck
Wildlife Sanctuary

Sengekontacket
Pond

Ferry to Hyannis (Seasonal)

Ferry to Falmouth (Seasonal)

Ferry to Nantucket (Seasonal)

Nantucket
Sound

Ferry to Falmouth (Seasonal)

East Chop

Oak Bluffs Town Beach

Seaview Ave.

10
9
8
7
6
Owen Park
5
Oak
Bluffs

Beach Rd.

Lagoon
Pond

County Rd.

Barnes Rd.

Ferry to Woods Hole (Year-round)

West Chop

Ferry to New Bedford (Seasonal)

Vineyard Haven

4
Main St.

Lake Tashmoo
Town Beach

Tashmoo
Lake

Lambert's Cove Rd.

Airport Rd.

Edgartown–Vineyard Haven Rd.

Martha's Vineyard
Airport

MANUEL F.
CORRELLUS
STATE FOREST

Old County Rd.

ATLANTIC OCEAN

Tisbury
Great Pond

Boston

Provincetown

CAPE
COD

Plymouth

MASS

Hyannis

Nantucket

Martha's
Vineyard

Cedar Tree
Neck Sanctuary

Lambert's
Cove

Vineyard
Sound

State Rd.

North Tisbury

West Tisbury

South Rd.

North Rd.

Middle Rd.

Chilmark
Pond

Chilmark

Lucy Vincent Beach
(restricted to residents)

3

2
1
Menemsha
Beach

Menemsha
Harbor

Lobsterville
Beach

Menemsha

Menemsha
Pond

State Rd.

South Rd.

Squibnocket
Pond

Moshup Trail

Gay Head
Cliffs & Light

Aquinnah
(formerly
Gay Head)

Aquinnah Beach
(Moshup Beach)

Chilmark. Buy a lobster roll in the fishing village of Menemsha. There's a surprising degree of diversity here, for those who take the time to discover it.

ESSENTIALS
GETTING THERE

BY FERRY   Most visitors take a ferry from the mainland to the Vineyard. You'll most likely catch the ferry from Woods Hole in the town of Falmouth on Cape Cod; however, boats also run from Falmouth Inner Harbor, Hyannis, New Bedford, Rhode Island, and Nantucket. It's easy to get a passenger ticket on almost any of the ferries, but space for cars is extremely limited, especially on summer weekends, when reservations must be made months in advance. Unless you absolutely must have your car with you, leave it on the mainland. Traffic and parking on the island can be brutal in summer, and it's easy to take shuttle buses (see below) from town to town or simply bike around.

From Woods Hole in Falmouth   The state-run **Steamship Authority** (© 508/477-8600 for reservations and information from Apr 4–Sept 7 daily 7am–9pm, and reduced hours the rest of the year; or 508/693-9130 daily 8am–5pm; www.steamshipauthority.com) operates daily, year-round, weather permitting. It maintains the only ferries to Martha's Vineyard that accommodate cars. These large ferries make the 45-minute trip to Vineyard Haven throughout the year; some boats go to Oak Bluffs from late May to late October (call for seasonal schedules). The cost of a round-trip car passage from mid-May to mid-October is $114 to $124; in the off season it drops to $60 to $80. The higher rates are for vehicles more than 16 feet long. Car rates do not include drivers or passengers.

New this year for the **Steamship Authority,** passengers can now buy their tickets online at the boat line's new updated website. No more waiting on hold for an eternity for ferry tickets if you log onto **www.steamshipauthority.com**.

Many people prefer to leave their cars on the mainland, take the ferry (often with their bikes), and then travel around the island by shuttle bus or taxi, or rent a bicycle, car, or Jeep on the island. You can park your car at the Woods Hole lots

Car Passage to Martha's Vineyard

Reservations are required to bring your car to Martha's Vineyard on Friday, Saturday, Sunday, and Monday from mid-June to mid-September, plus Memorial Day weekend. During these months, standby is in effect only on Tuesday, Wednesday, and Thursday. Technically, vehicle reservations can be made up to 1 hour in advance of ferry departure, but in summer ferries are almost always full. Be aware that your space may be forfeited if you have not checked into the ferry terminal 30 minutes prior to sailing time. Reservations may be changed to another date and time with at least 24 hours' notice; otherwise, you will have to pay for an additional ticket for your vehicle.

If you arrive without a reservation on a day that allows standby, come early and be prepared to wait in line for hours. Your passage is guaranteed if you're in line by 2pm on designated standby days. For up-to-date **Steamship Authority** information, check out their website (www.steamshipauthority.com).

(always full in the summer) or at one of the many lots in Falmouth and Bourne that absorb the overflow of cars. Parking costs $10 per day. Free shuttle buses (some equipped for bikes) run regularly from the outlying lots to the Woods Hole ferry terminal. If you're leaving your car on the mainland, plan to arrive at the parking lots at least an hour before sailing time to allow for parking, taking the free shuttle bus to the ferry terminal, and buying your ferry ticket.

The cost of a round-trip passenger ticket on the ferry to Martha's Vineyard is $12 for adults and $6.50 for children 5 to 12. Bringing a bike costs an extra $6 round-trip. You do not need a reservation on the ferry if you're traveling without a car, and there are no reservations needed for parking.

From Falmouth Inner Harbor, you can board the *Island Queen* (© **508/548-4800;** www.islandqueen.com) for a 35-minute cruise to Oak Bluffs (passengers only). The boat runs from late May to mid-October; round-trip fare is $10 for adults, $5 for children under 13, and an extra $6 for bikes. There are seven crossings a day in season (eight on Fri and Sun), and no reservations are needed. Parking runs $10 or $12 a day. Credit cards are not accepted.

The **Falmouth–Edgartown Ferry Service,** 278 Scranton Ave. (© **508/548-9400;** www.falmouthferry.com), operates a 1-hour passenger ferry, called the *Pied Piper,* from Falmouth Harbor to Edgartown. The boat runs from late May to mid-October; reservations are required. In season, there are five crossings a day (six on Fri). Round-trip fares are $30 for adults and $24 for children under 12. Bicycles are $8 round-trip. Parking is $14 per day.

From Hyannis   Early June through late September, **Hy-Line,** Ocean Street Dock (© **508/778-2600;** www.hy-linecruises.com), operates from the Ocean Street dock to Oak Bluffs on Martha's Vineyard. It runs three trips a day; travel time is about 1 hour and 45 minutes. A round-trip costs $27 for adults and $14 for children 5 to 12 ($10 extra for bikes). It's a good idea to reserve a parking spot in Hyannis; the all-day fee is $10.

From Nantucket   From early June to mid-September, **Hy-Line,** Ocean Street Dock (© **508/778-2600;** www.hy-linecruises.com), runs three passenger ferries to Oak Bluffs on Martha's Vineyard. There is no car-ferry service between the islands. The trip time is 2 hours and 15 minutes. The one-way fare is $14 for adults, $6.75 for children 5 to 12, and $5 extra for bikes.

From New Bedford   The *Schamonchi,* at Billy Woods Wharf (© **508/997-1688;** www.mvferry.com), which is also run by the Steamship Authority, makes runs to Vineyard Haven from mid-May to mid-September. Trip time is about 1½ hours. A round-trip ticket is $20 for adults, $10 for children under 12, and $5 extra for bikes. Parking is $8 per calendar day. No reservations are needed.

In the summer of 2004, the *Schamonchi* may be replaced by a fast ferry that will make the trip to Martha's Vineyard in 45 minutes to an hour. While schedule and ferry specifics have not yet been announced, a round-trip ticket on the new ferry would cost about $40. Contact the Steamship Authority for details (© 508/477-8600; www.steamshipauthority.com).

From North Kingstown, Rhode Island   From mid-June through October, the new company **Vineyard Fast Ferry** (© **401/295-4040;** www.vineyardfastferry. com) runs the high-speed catamaran, *Millenium,* to Oak Bluffs two to three round-trips daily. The trip takes 90 minutes. The ferry leaves from Quonset Point, about 10 minutes from Route I-95, 15 minutes from T.F. Green Airport in Providence, and 20 minutes from the Amtrak station in Kingston. There is dockside parking. Rates are $48 round-trip for adults; $36 round-trip for children 4–12; free for children under 4; and $8 round-trip for bikes. Parking next to the ferry port is $8 per day.

BY PLANE   You can fly into **Martha's Vineyard Airport,** also known as Dukes County Airport (© **508/693-7022**), in West Tisbury, about 5 miles outside Edgartown.

Airlines serving the Vineyard include **Cape Air/Nantucket Airlines** (© **800/ 352-0714** or 508/771-6944), which connects the island year-round with Boston (trip time 34 min.; hourly shuttle service in summer costs about $240 round-trip), Hyannis (trip time 20 min., cost $80), Nantucket (15 min., $89), and New Bedford (20 min., $83); and **US Airways** (© **800/428-4322**), which flies from Boston for about $215 round-trip and also has seasonal weekend service from La Guardia (trip time 1 hr. 15 min.), which costs approximately $400 round-trip.

Year-round charter service is offered by **Direct Flight** (© **508/693-6688**). **Westchester Air** (© **800/759-2929**), which runs out of White Plains, New York.

BY BUS   Bonanza Bus Lines (© **888/751-8800** or 508/548-7588; www. bonanzabus.com) connects the Woods Hole ferry port with Boston (from South Station), New York City, and Providence, Rhode Island. The trip from South Station in Boston takes about 1 hour and 35 minutes and costs about $17 one-way, $30 round-trip; from Boston's Logan Airport, the cost is $22 one-way, $40 round-trip; from New York, the bus trip to Woods Hole takes about 6 hours and costs approximately $52 one-way or $93 round-trip.

BY LIMO   King's Coach (© **800/235-5669** or 508/563-5669) will pick you up at Boston's Logan Airport and take you to meet your ferry in Woods Hole (or anywhere else in the Upper Cape area). The trip takes about 90 minutes depending on traffic, and costs about $125 one-way plus a gratuity for a carload or a vanload of people. You'll need to book the service a couple of days in advance. **Falmouth Taxi** (© **508/548-3100**) also runs limo service from Boston and the airport to the Woods Hole ferry terminal.

GETTING AROUND
BY BICYCLE & MOPED   The best way to explore the Vineyard is on two wheels. There's a little of everything for cyclists, from paved paths to hilly country roads (see "Exploring the Vineyard on Two Wheels," later in this chapter, for details on where to ride).

Mopeds are also a way to navigate Vineyard roads, but remember that some roads tend to be narrow and rough—the number of accidents involving mopeds seems to rise every year. You'll need a driver's license to rent a moped. If you rent one, be aware they are considered quite dangerous on the island's busy, winding and sandy roads. Also, there is a lot of negative feeling about mopeds from islanders.

Bike-rental shops are clustered in all three down-island towns. Scooter- and moped-rental shops are only in Oak Bluffs and Vineyard Haven. Bike rentals cost about $15 to $30 a day (the higher prices are for suspension mountain bikes), scooters and mopeds $46 to $85. For bike rentals in Vineyard Haven, try **Strictly Bikes,** Union Street (© **508/693-0782**); or **Martha's Bike Rentals,** Lagoon Pond Road (© **508/693-6593**). For mopeds, try **Adventure/Thrifty Rentals,** Beach Road (© **508/693-1959**). In Oak Bluffs, there's **Anderson's,** Circuit Avenue Extension (© **508/693-9346**), which rents bikes only; **DeBettencourt's Bike Shop,** 31 Circuit Ave. Extension (© **508/693-0011**), which is across from the Island Queen ferry landing; and **Sun 'n' Fun,** Lake Avenue

(© **508/693-5457**). In Edgartown, you'll find bike rentals only at **R. W. Cutler Bike,** 1 Main St. (© **508/627-4052**); **Edgartown Bicycles,** 190 Upper Main St. (© **508/627-9008**); and **Wheel Happy,** 204 Upper Main St. and 8 S. Water St. (© **508/627-5928**).

BY CAR   If you're here for a long visit or you want to do some exploring up-island, you may want to bring a car or rent one on the island. Keep in mind that car-rental rates can soar during peak season, and gas is also much more expensive on the island. Representatives of national car-rental chains are located at the airport and in Vineyard Haven and Oak Bluffs. Local agencies also operate out of all three port towns, and many of them also rent Jeeps, mopeds, and bikes. The national chains include **Budget** (© **800/527-0700** or 508/693-1911), **Hertz** (© **800/654-3131**), and **Thrifty** (© **800/874-4389**).

For local agencies, in Vineyard Haven, you'll find **Adventure Rentals,** Beach Road (© **508/693-1959**); and in Edgartown, try **AAA Island Rentals,** 141 Main St. (© **508/627-6800**). Operating out of the airport is **All Island Rent-a-Car** (© **508/693-6868**).

BY SHUTTLE BUS   In season, shuttle buses run often enough to make them a practical means of getting around. Connecting Vineyard Haven (across from the ferry terminal), Oak Bluffs (near the Civil War statue in Ocean Park), and Edgartown (Church St., near the Old Whaling Church), the **Island Transport** (© **508/693-0058**) yellow school buses cost about $1.50 to $4, depending on distance. From late June to early September, they run from 6am to midnight every 15 minutes or half-hour. Hours are reduced in spring (they start running in Apr) and fall (they stop running in Oct). From late June through August, buses go out to Aquinnah (via the airport, West Tisbury, and Chilmark), leaving every couple of hours from down-island towns.

The **Martha's Vineyard Regional Transit Authority** (© **508/693-9440;** www.vineyardtransit.com) operates shuttle buses daily from mid-May to mid-October (white buses with a purple logo). The Edgartown Downtown Shuttle and the South Beach buses circle throughout town or out to South Beach every 20 minutes in season. They also stop at the free parking lots just north of the town center. Parking here and shuttling to town is a great way to avoid circling the streets in search of a vacant spot on busy weekends. A one-way trip in town is $1; a trip to South Beach (leaving from Edgartown's Church St. visitor center) is also $1.

BY TAXI   Upon arrival, you'll find taxis at all ferry terminals and at the airport, and there are permanent taxi stands in Oak Bluffs (at the Flying Horses Carousel) and Edgartown (next to the Town Wharf). Most taxi outfits operate cars as well as vans for larger groups and travelers with bikes. Cab companies on the island include **Adam Cab** (© **800/281-4462** or 508/693-3332), **Accurate Cab** (© **888/557-9798** or 508/627-9798; the only 24-hr. service), **All Island Taxi** (© **800/693-TAXI** or 508/693-2929); and **Marlene's Taxi** (© **508/693-0037**). Rates from town to town in summer are generally flat fees based on where you're headed and the number of passengers on board. A trip from Vineyard Haven to Edgartown would probably cost around $15 for two people. Late-night revelers should keep in mind that rates double after midnight until 7am.

THE CHAPPAQUIDDICK FERRY   From June to mid-October, the **On-Time ferry** (© **508/627-9427**) runs the 5-minute trip from Memorial Wharf on Dock Street in Edgartown to Chappaquiddick Island. It leaves every 5 minutes from 7am to midnight. Passengers, bikes, mopeds, dogs, and cars (three at a time) are all welcome. The one-way cost is $2 per person, $8 for one car/one driver, $5 for one bike/one person, and $5 for one moped or motorcycle/one person.

VISITOR INFORMATION

Contact the **Martha's Vineyard Chamber of Commerce** at Beach Rd., Vineyard Haven (P.O. Box 1698 Vineyard Haven, MA 02568; ℭ **508/693-0085;** fax 508/693-7589) or visit their website at **www.mvy.com**. There are also information booths at the ferry terminal in Vineyard Haven, across from the Flying Horses Carousel in Oak Bluffs, and on Church Street in Edgartown. For information on current events, check the two local newspapers, the **Vineyard Gazette** (www.mvgazette.com) and the **Martha's Vineyard Times** (www.mvtimes.com), for information on current events.

In case of an **emergency,** call ℭ **911** and/or head for the **Martha's Vineyard Hospital,** Linton Lane, Oak Bluffs (ℭ **508/693-0410**), which has a 24-hour emergency room.

A STROLL AROUND EDGARTOWN ⭐⭐⭐

A good way to acclimate yourself to the pace and flavor of the Vineyard is to walk the streets of Edgartown. This walk starts at the Dr. Daniel Fisher House and meanders along for about a mile; it takes about 2 to 3 hours.

If you're driving, park at the free lots at the edge of town (you'll see signs on the roads from Vineyard Haven and West Tisbury) and bike or take the shuttle bus (it only costs 50¢) to the Edgartown Visitor Center on Church Street.

The **Dr. Daniel Fisher House** ⭐, 99 Main St. (ℭ **508/627-8017**), is a prime example of Edgartown's trademark Greek Revival opulence. A key player in the 19th-century whaling trade, Dr. Fisher amassed a fortune sufficient to found the Martha's Vineyard National Bank. Built in 1840, his proud mansion boasts such classical elements as colonnaded porticos and a delicate roof walk.

Note: The only way to view the interior (now headquarters for the Martha's Vineyard Preservation Trust) is with a guided **Vineyard Historic Walking Tour** (ℭ **508/627-8619**). This tour, which also takes in the neighboring Old Whaling Church, originates next door at the **Vincent House Museum.** Tours are offered June through September, Monday through Saturday noon–3pm. The cost is $7 to $10 for adults, free for children 12 and under.

The **Vineyard House Museum** ⭐, off Main Street between Planting Field Way and Church Street, is a transplanted 1672 full Cape and is considered the oldest surviving dwelling on the island. The **Old Whaling Church** ⭐⭐, 89 Main St., is a magnificent 1843 Greek Revival edifice designed by local architect Frederick Baylies, Jr., and was built as a whaling boat would have been, out of massive pine beams; it boasts 27-ft. windows and a 92-ft. tower. Maintained by the Preservation Trust and still supporting a Methodist parish, the building is now primarily used as a performance venue.

Continuing down Main Street and turning right onto School Street, you'll pass another Baylies monument, the 1839 **Baptist Church,** which, having lost its spire, was converted into a private home with a rather grand, column-fronted facade. Two blocks farther is the **Vineyard Museum** ⭐⭐, 59 School St. (ℭ **508/627-4441**), a fascinating complex assembled by the Dukes County Historical Society. This cluster of buildings contains exhibits of Native American crafts; an entire 1765 house; an extraordinary array of maritime art; and the Gay Head Light Tower's decommissioned Fresnel lens.

Give yourself enough time to explore the museum's curiosities before heading south 1 block on Cooke Street. Cater-corner across South Summer Street, you'll

Edgartown

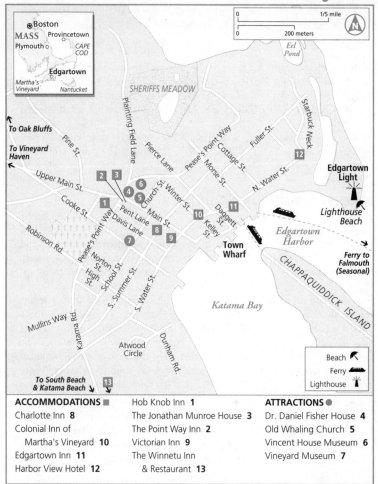

ACCOMMODATIONS ■

Charlotte Inn **8**
Colonial Inn of
    Martha's Vineyard **10**
Edgartown Inn **11**
Harbor View Hotel **12**

Hob Knob Inn **1**
The Jonathan Munroe House **3**
The Point Way Inn **2**
Victorian Inn **9**
The Winnetu Inn
    & Restaurant **13**

ATTRACTIONS ●

Dr. Daniel Fisher House **4**
Old Whaling Church **5**
Vincent House Museum **6**
Vineyard Museum **7**

---

spot the first of Baylies's impressive endeavors, the 1828 **Federated Church.** One block left are the offices of the *Vineyard Gazette,* 34 S. Summer St. (© **508/627-4311**). Operating out of a 1760 house, this exemplary small-town newspaper has been going strong since 1846.

Walk down South Summer Street to Main Street and take a right toward the water, stopping at any inviting shops along the way. Veer left on Dock Street to reach the **Old Sculpin Gallery,** 58 Dock St. (© **508/627-4881**), open from late June to mid-September. The output of the Martha's Vineyard Art Association is displayed. The real draw is the stark old building itself, which started out as a granary and spent the better part of the 20th century as a boat-building shop.

Cross the street to survey the harbor from the second-floor deck at Town Wharf. You can watch the tiny On-Time ferry make its 5-minute crossing to **Chappaquiddick Island** 🦆🦆. Don't bother looking for the original **Dyke Bridge,** infamous scene of the Kennedy/Kopechne scandal; it has been dismantled and, at long last, replaced.

Stroll down North Water Street to admire the many formidable captain's homes, several of which have been converted into inns. Each has a tale to tell. The 1750 **Daggett House** (no. 59), which is now a private inn, started out as a 1660 tavern, and the original beehive oven is flanked by a "secret" passageway. Nathaniel Hawthorne holed up at the **Edgartown Inn** (no. 56) for nearly a year in 1789 while writing *Twice Told Tales*—and, it is rumored, romancing a local maiden who inspired *The Scarlet Letter.* On your way back to Main Street, you'll pass the **Gardner–Colby Gallery** (no. 27), filled with beautiful island-inspired paintings.

After all that walking, stop for a drink at **The Newes from America,** 23 Kelley St., off N. Water St. (✆ **508/627-4397**). This colonial basement pub serves up specialty beers and the best French onion soup on the island (see "Where to Dine").

BEACHES & OUTDOOR PURSUITS

BEACHES Most down-island beaches in Vineyard Haven, Oak Bluffs, and Edgartown are open to the public and are just a walk or a short bike ride from town. In season, shuttle buses make stops at **State Beach** between Oak Buffs and Edgartown. Most of the Vineyard's magnificent up-island shoreline is privately owned or restricted to residents, and thus off-limits to visitors. Renters in up-island communities, however, can obtain a beach sticker (around $35–$50 for a season sticker) for those private beaches by applying with a lease at the relevant **town hall:** West Tisbury, ✆ **508/696-0147;** Chilmark, ✆ **508/645-2115** or 508/645-2100; or Aquinnah, ✆ **508/645-2300.** Also, many up-island inns offer the perk of temporary passes to the beautiful up-island beaches. In addition to the public beaches listed below, you might also track down a few hidden coves by requesting a map of conservation properties from the **Martha's Vineyard Land Bank** (✆ **508/627-7141**). Below is a list of visitor-friendly beaches.

- **Aquinnah Beach** ★★★ (Moshup Beach), off Moshup Trail: Parking costs $20 a day in season at this peaceful half-mile beach just east (Atlantic side) of the colorful cliffs. Although it is against the law, nudists tend to gravitate toward this beach. Because of rapid erosion, climbing the cliffs or taking clay for a souvenir is forbidden. Restrooms are near the parking lot, which is a 10-minute walk from the beach.

- **East Beach** ★★, Wasque (pronounced *Way*-squee) Reservation, Chappaquiddick: Relatively few people bother biking or hiking (or four-wheel driving) this far, so you should be able to find all the privacy you crave. Take the On-Time Ferry to Chappaquiddick, then go straight 2½ miles, and continue straight for another ½ mile on a dirt road. Biking on Chappaquiddick is one of the great Vineyard experiences, but the roads can be quite sandy and are best suited for a mountain bike. Along the dirt road, you'll pass **Mytoi,** a 14-acre Japanese garden open to the public, which is an oasis of flora and fauna. Because of its exposure on the east shore of the island, the surf here is rough. Pack a picnic; there are no stores on Chappy. There is a portable toilet in the parking lot. Most people park their car near the Dike Bridge and walk the couple hundred yards out to the beach. Admission is $3 per person.

- **Joseph A. Sylvia State Beach** ★★★, midway between Oak Bluffs and Edgartown: Stretching a mile and flanked by a paved bike path, this placid beach has views of Cape Cod and Nantucket Sound and is prized for its gentle and (relatively) warm waves, which make it perfect for swimming. The

Moments   Menemsha Beach Sunset

This beach is the ideal place to watch a sunset. Get a lobster dinner to go at the famous **Home Port restaurant** right next to the beach in Menemsha (see "Where to Dine"), grab a blanket and a bottle of wine, and picnic here for a spectacular evening.

drawbridge is a local landmark, and visitors and islanders alike have been jumping off it for years. Be aware that State Beach is one of the Vineyard's most popular; in midsummer, it's packed. The shuttle bus stops here, and roadside parking is also available—but it fills up fast, so stake your claim early. Located on the eastern shore of the island, this is a Nantucket Sound beach, so waters are shallow and rarely rough. There are no restrooms, and only the Edgartown end of the beach, known as Bend-in-the-Road Beach, has lifeguards.

- **Lake Tashmoo Town Beach** ⟨★⟩, off Herring Creek Road, Vineyard Haven: The only spot on the island where lake meets ocean, this tiny strip of sand is good for swimming and surf-casting but is somewhat marred by limited parking and often brackish waters. Nonetheless, this is a popular spot, as beachgoers enjoy a choice between the Vineyard Sound beach with mild surf or the placid lake beach. Bikers will have no problem reaching this beach from Vineyard Haven; otherwise, you have to use a car to get to this beach.
- **Menemsha Beach** ⟨★★⟩, next to Dutchers Dock in Menemsha Harbor: The gentle surf of this small but well-trafficked strand, with lifeguards and restrooms, is popular with families. In season, it's virtually wall-to-wall umbrellas. Nearby food vendors in Menemsha—selling everything from ice cream and hotdogs to shrimp cocktail—are a plus here.
- **Oak Bluffs Town Beach,** Seaview Avenue: This sandy strip extends from both sides of the ferry wharf, which makes it a convenient place to linger while waiting for the next boat. This is an in-town beach, within walking distance for visitors staying in Oak Bluffs. The surf is consistently calm and the sand smooth, so it's also ideal for families with small children. Public restrooms are available at the ferry dock, but there are no lifeguards.
- **Owen Park Beach,** off Main Street in Vineyard Haven: A tiny strip of harborside beach adjoining a town green with swings and a bandstand will suffice for young children, who, by the way, get lifeguard supervision. There are no restrooms, but this is an in-town beach, which is probably a quick walk from your Vineyard Haven inn.
- **South Beach** ⟨★★★⟩ (Katama Beach), about 4 miles south of Edgartown on Katama Road: If you have time for only one trip to the beach and you can't get up-island, go with this popular, 3-mile barrier strand that boasts heavy wave action (check with lifeguards for swimming conditions), sweeping dunes, and, most important, relatively ample parking space. It's also accessible by bike path or shuttle. Lifeguards patrol some sections of the beach, and there are sparsely scattered toilet facilities. The rough surf here is popular with surfers. *Tip:* Families tend to head to the left, college kids to the right.

A word about Aquinnah: Almost every visitor to the Vineyard finds his or her way to the cliffs, and with all the tour buses lined up in the huge parking lot and the rows of tacky concession stands and gift shops, this can seem like a rather outrageous tourist trap. You're right; it's not the Grand Canyon. But the

Tips Exploring the Vineyard on Two Wheels

Biking on the Vineyard is a memorable experience, not only for the smooth, well-maintained paths, but also for the long stretches of virtually untrafficked up-island roads that reveal breathtaking country landscapes and sweeping ocean views.

A triangle of paved bike paths, roughly 8 miles to a side, links the down-island towns of Oak Bluffs, Edgartown, and Vineyard Haven. The Vineyard Sound portion along Beach Road, flanked by water on both sides, is especially enjoyable. From Edgartown, you can also follow the bike path to South Beach. For a more woodsy ride, there are paved paths and mountain-biking trails in the **Manuel F. Corellus State Forest** (© 508/693-2540), a vast spread of scrub oak and pine in the middle of the island. The bike paths are accessible off Edgartown–West Tisbury Road.

The up-island roads leading to West Tisbury, Chilmark, Menemsha, and Aquinnah are a cyclist's paradise, with unspoiled pastureland, old farmhouses, and brilliant sea views reminiscent of Ireland's countryside. But keep in mind that the terrain is often hilly, and the roads are narrow and a little rough around the edges. From West Tisbury to Chilmark Center, try **South Road**—about 5 miles—which passes stone walls rolling over moors, clumps of pine and wildflowers, verdant marshes and tidal pools, and, every once in awhile, an Old Vineyard farmhouse. **Middle Road** is another lovely ride with a country feel and will also get you from West Tisbury to Chilmark. (It's usually less trafficked, too.)

Our favorite up-island route is the 6-mile stretch from Chilmark Center out to Aquinnah via **State Road** and **Moshup Trail** *. The ocean views along this route are spectacular. Don't miss the **Quitsa Pond Lookout,** about 2 miles down State Road, which provides a panoramic vista of Nashaquitsa and Menemsha ponds, beyond which you can see Menemsha, Vineyard Sound, and the Elizabeth Islands. A bit farther, just over the Aquinnah town line, is the Aquinnah spring, a roadside iron pipe where you can refill your water bottle with the freshest and coldest water on the island. At the fork after the spring, turn left on Moshup Trail—in fact, a regular road—and follow the coast, which offers gorgeous views of the ocean and the sweeping sand dunes. You'll soon wind up in Aquinnah, where you can explore the red-clay cliffs and pristine beaches. On the return trip, you can take the handy bike ferry ($7 round-trip) from Aquinnah to Menemsha. It runs daily in summer and on weekends in May.

There are lots of bike-rental operations near the ferry landings in Vineyard Haven and Oak Bluffs, as well as a few rental shops in Edgartown. For information rentals, see "Getting Around," earlier in this chapter.

A very good outfitter out of Boston called **Bike Riders** (© 800/473-7040; www.bikeriderstours.com) runs 6-day island-hopping tours of Martha's Vineyard and Nantucket. The cost is $1,790 per person, including most meals and snacks, plus an additional $110 for bike rental. Stays are at various inns on the islands. It's a perfect way to experience both islands.

observation deck, with its view of the colorful cliffs, the adorable brick light-house, and the Elizabeth Islands beyond, will make you glad you bothered. Instead of rushing away, stop for a cool drink and a clam roll at the snack bar with the deck overlooking the ocean.

FISHING   For shellfishing, get information and a permit from the appropri-ate town hall (for the telephone numbers, see "Beaches," above). Popular spots for surf-casting include **Wasque Point** on Chappaquiddick, South Beach, and the jetty at Menemsha Pond.

The party boat *Skipper* (© 508/693-1238) offers half-day trips out of Oak Bluffs harbor in season. The cost is $35 for adults and $25 for children 12 and under. Deep-sea excursions can be arranged aboard **Big Eye Charters** (© 508/627-3649) out of Edgartown, and **Summer's Lease** (© 508/693-2880) out of Oak Bluffs. Up-island, there are **North Shore Charters** (© 508/645-2993; www.bassnblue.com) and **Flashy Lady Fishing Charters** (© 508/645-2462; www.flashyladycharters.com) out of Menemsha, locus of the island's commercial fish-ing fleet.

International Game Fish Association world-record holder Capt. Leslie S. Smith operates **Backlash Charters** (© 508/627-5894), specializing in light tackle and fly-fishing, out of Edgartown. Cooper Gilkes III, proprietor of **Coop's Bait & Tackle** at 147 W. Tisbury Rd. in Edgartown (© 508/627-3909), which offers rentals as well as supplies, is another acknowledged authority. He's avail-able as an instructor or charter guide.

GOLF   The nine-hole **Mink Meadows Golf Course** off Franklin Street in Vineyard Haven (© 508/693-0600), is open to the general public, while the championship-level 18-hole **Farm Neck Golf Club** off Farm Neck Road in Oak Bluffs (© 508/693-3057) is semi-private.

NATURE TRAILS   About a fifth of the Vineyard's landmass has been set aside for conservation, and it's all accessible to bikers and hikers. The **West Chop Woods,** off Franklin Street in Vineyard Haven, comprise 85 acres with marked walking trails. Midway between Vineyard Haven and Edgartown, the **Felix Neck Wildlife Sanctuary** ✦✦ includes a 6-mile network of trails over varying terrain, from woodland to beach.

The 633-acre **Long Point Wildlife Refuge** ✦✦ off Waldron's Bottom Road in West Tisbury (gatehouse © 508/693-7392) offers heath and dunes, fresh-water ponds, a popular family-oriented beach, and interpretive nature walks for children.

Up-island, along the sound, the **Menemsha Hills Reservation** off North Road in Chilmark (© 508/693-7662) encompasses 210 acres of rocks and bluffs, with steep paths, lovely views, and even a public beach. **The Cedar Tree Neck Sanctuary,** off Indian Hill Road southwest of Vineyard Haven (© 508/693-5207), offers some 300 forested acres that end in a stony beach. Swimming and sunbathing are prohibited.

Some remarkable botanical surprises can be found at the 20-acre **Polly Hill Arboretum** ✦✦, 809 State Rd., West Tisbury (© 508/693-9426). Legendary horticulturist Polly Hill has developed this property over the past 40 years and allows the public to wander the grounds Thursday to Tuesday from 7am until 7pm. This is a magical place, particularly mid-June to July when the Dogwood Allee is in bloom. Wanderers will pass old stone walls on the way to The Tunnel of Love, an arbor of hornbeam. There are also witch hazels, camellias, magno-lias, and rhododendrons. To get there from Vineyard Haven, go south on State

Road, bearing left at the junction of North Road. The arboretum entrance is about a half mile down, on the right. There is a requested donation of $5 for adults.

WATERSPORTS   Wind's Up, 199 Beach Rd., Vineyard Haven (© **508/693-4252**), rents out canoes, kayaks, and various sailing craft, including windsurfers, and offers instruction on a placid pond; it also rents surfboards and boogie boards. Canoes and kayaks rent for $20 per hour.

MUSEUMS & HISTORIC LANDMARKS

Cottage Museum ⭐   This little museum, a cottage in the center of Oak Bluffs' famous "campground," displays 19th-century artifacts, like bulky black bathing costumes and a melodeon used for informal hymnal sing-alongs. The campground consists of a 34-acre circle with more than 300 multicolored, elaborately trimmed Carpenter Gothic cottages, which look very much the way they might have more than a hundred years ago. These adorable little houses were loosely modeled on the revivalists' canvas tents that inspired them. In the 1860s, when many of the cottages were built, campers typically attended three lengthy prayer services daily. Opportunities for worship remain at the 1878 Trinity Methodist Church within the park or, just outside, on Samoset Avenue, at the non-sectarian 1870 Union Chapel, a magnificent octagonal structure with superb acoustics.

At the very center of the Camp Meeting Grounds is the striking **Trinity Park Tabernacle** ⭐⭐. Built in 1879, the open-sided chapel is the largest wrought-iron structure in the country. Thousands can be accommodated on its long wooden benches, which are usually filled to capacity for the Sunday-morning services in summer, as well as for community sings (Wed in July and Aug) and occasional concerts.

1 Trinity Park (within the Camp Meeting Grounds), Oak Bluffs. © 508/693-7784. Admission $1.50 (donation). Mid-June to Sept Mon–Sat 10am–4pm. Closed Oct to mid-June.

Flying Horses Carousel ⭐⭐ *Kids*   You don't have to be a kid to enjoy what is considered to be the oldest working carousel in the country. Built in 1876 at Coney Island, this National Historic Landmark predates the era of horses that "gallop." Lacking the necessary gears, these mounts merely glide smoothly in place to the joyful strains of a calliope. Take a moment to admire the intricate hand carving and real horsehair manes, and gaze into the horses' glass eyes for a surprise: tiny animal charms glinting within.

33 Circuit Ave. (at Lake Ave.), Oak Bluffs. © 508/693-9481. Tickets $1 per ride, or $8 for 10. Late May to early Sept daily 10am–10pm; call for off-season hours. Closed mid-Oct to mid-Apr.

The Martha's Vineyard Historical Society ⭐   All of Martha's Vineyard's colorful history is captured here, in a compound of historic buildings. To acclimate yourself chronologically, start with the pre-colonial artifacts—from arrowheads to colorful Gay Head clay pottery—displayed in the 1845 **Captain Francis Pease House.** The **Gale Huntington Reference Library** houses rare documentation of the island's history, from genealogical records to whaling-ship logs. Some extraordinary memorabilia, including scrimshaw and portraiture, are on view in the adjoining **Francis Foster Maritime Gallery.**

To get a sense of daily life during the era when the waters of the East Coast were the equivalent of a modern highway, visit the **Thomas Cooke House,** a shipwright-built colonial, built in 1765, where the Customs collector lived and worked. The Fresnel lens on display outside the museum was lifted from the

Gay Head Lighthouse in 1952, after nearly a century of service. Though it no longer serves to warn ships of dangerous shoals (that light is automated now), it still lights up the night every evening in summer, just for show.

59 School St. (corner of Cooke St., 2 blocks SW of Main St.), Edgartown. © **508/627-4441**. www.marthas vineyardhistory.org. Admission in season $7 adults, $4 children 6–15. Mid-June to mid-Oct Tues–Sat 10am–5pm. Mid-Oct to late Dec and mid-Mar to mid-June Wed–Fri 1–4pm, Sat 10am–4pm. Early Jan to mid-Mar Wed–Fri by appointment, Sat 10am–4pm.

ORGANIZED TOURS & CRUISES

Hugh Taylor (James's brother) alternates with a couple of other captains in taking the helm of *Arabella* ⚓, docked in Menemsha Harbor at the end of North Road (© **508/645-3511**). This swift 50-foot catamaran makes daily trips to Cuttyhunk Island, and offers sunset cruises around the Aquinnah cliffs. It's a great way to see lovely coves and vistas otherwise denied the ordinary tourist. Daily sails are $60 for adults, $30 for children under 12. From mid-June to mid-September, departures are daily at 10:30am and 6pm (or 2 hr. before sunset). Reservations required.

The Trustees of Reservations, a statewide land conservation group, offers fascinating 2½-hour **Natural History Tours** ⚓⚓⚓ (© **508/627-3599;** www.the trustees.org) by safari vehicle or canoe around Cape Poge on Chappaquiddick Island. The canoe tour on Poucha Pond and Cape Poge Bay is designed for all levels. The cost for the safari tour is $30 for adults and $15 for children 15 and under. The cost for the canoe tour is $35 for adults and $15 for children. There's also a tour of the Cape Poge lighthouse that costs $20 for adults and $12 for children. Two-hour kayak tours around Long Point cost $35 for adults and $18 for children. Call © **508/693-7392** for details on the Long Point trips.

SHOPPING ⚓

ANTIQUES/COLLECTIBLES   For the most exquisite Asian furniture, lamps, porcelains, and jewelry, visit **All Things Oriental** at 123 Beach Rd. in Vineyard Haven (© **508/693-8375**). The owner handpicks the treasures in China.

ARTS & CRAFTS   No visit to Edgartown would be complete without a peek at the wares of scrimshander Thomas J. DeMont, Jr., at **Edgartown Scrimshaw Gallery** at 43 Main St. (© **508/627-9439**). All the scrimshaw in the gallery is hand-carved using ancient mammoth ivory or antique fossil ivory.

The Field Gallery, State Road (in the center of town), West Tisbury (© **508/693-5595**), is where Marc Chagall meets Henry Moore and where Tom Maley's playful figures have enchanted locals and passersby for decades. You'll also find paintings by Albert Alcalay and drawings and cartoons by Jules Feiffer. The Sunday-evening openings are high points of the summer social season. Closed from mid-October to mid-May.

Don't miss the **Granary Gallery at the Red Barn,** Old County Road (off Edgartown–West Tisbury Rd., about ¼ mile north of the intersection), West Tisbury (© **800/472-6279** or 508/693-0455), which displays astounding prints by the late longtime summerer Alfred Eisenstaedt and dazzling color photos by local luminary Alison Shaw.

Another unique local artisans' venue is **Martha's Vineyard Glass Works,** State Road, North Tisbury (© **508/693-6026**). The three resident artists—Andrew Magdanz, Susan Shapiro, and Mark Weiner—have shown nationwide to considerable acclaim. Their output is decidedly avant-garde and may not suit all tastes, but it's an eye-opening array and all the more fascinating once you've witnessed a work in progress.

GIFTS/HOME DECOR **Craftworks,** 149 Circuit Ave. (© **508/693-7463**), is filled to the rafters with whimsical, contemporary American crafts.

Carly Simon's **Midnight Farm,** 18 Water-Cromwell Lane, Vineyard Haven (© **508/693-1997**), offers a world of high-end, imaginative gift items from candles to children's clothes to furniture and glassware.

Paper Tiger, 29 Main St., Vineyard Haven (© **508/693-8970**), is an old-fashioned stationery store with wonderful papers and envelopes, and the best selection of cards anywhere.

WHERE TO STAY

When deciding where to stay on Martha's Vineyard, you'll need to consider the type of vacation you prefer. The down-island towns of Vineyard Haven, Oak Bluffs, and Edgartown provide shops, restaurants, beaches, and harbors within walking distance, and frequent shuttles to get you all over the island. But all three can be overly crowded on busy summer weekends. Vineyard Haven is the gateway for most of the ferry traffic; Oak Bluffs is a raucous town with most of the Vineyard's bars and nightclubs; and many visitors make a beeline to Edgartown's manicured Main Street. Up-island inns provide more peace and quiet, but you'll probably need a car to get around. Also, you may not be within walking distance of the beach.

We've provided only summer rates below, because the Vineyard is so seasonal. If you do visit in the off season, you may find substantial discounts at the establishments that remain open year-round.

EDGARTOWN
Very Expensive

Charlotte Inn ✸✸✸ Ask anyone to recommend the best inn on the island, and this is the name you're most likely to hear. It's one of only two Relais & Châteaux properties on the Cape and Islands. Linked by formal gardens, each of the 18th- and 19th-century houses has a distinctive look and feel, though the predominant mode is English country. All but one of the rooms have TVs; some have VCRs. The bathrooms are luxurious, and some are bigger than most standard hotel rooms. The restaurant onsite is **L'étoile,** the island's best fine-dining restaurant (p. 281).

27 S. Summer St. (in the center of town), Edgartown, MA 02539. © **508/627-4751**. Fax 508/627-4652. 25 units (all with tub/shower). Summer $295–$550 double; $695–$850 suite. Rates include continental breakfast; full breakfast offered for extra charge ($15). AE, MC, V. Open year-round. No children under 14. **Amenities:** Restaurant. *In room:* A/C, TV, hair dryer.

Harbor View Hotel ✸✸ Grander than grand on the outside but hotel-standard on the inside, this shingle-style complex started out as two Gilded Age waterfront hotels, later joined by a 300-foot veranda that overlooks Edgartown Harbor and the lighthouse. Front rooms with that pretty view cost substantially more. In back, there's a large pool surrounded by newer annexes, where some rooms and suites have kitchenettes. The hotel is just far enough from "downtown" to avoid the traffic, but close enough for a pleasant walk past regal captain's houses. **The Coach House** (p. 282) serves three meals in an elegant setting.

131 N. Water St. (about ½ mile NW of Main St.), Edgartown, MA 02539. © **800/225-6005** or 508/627-7000. Fax 508/627-8417. www.harbor-view.com. 124 units (all with tub/shower). Summer $330–$600 double; $490–$675 one-bedroom suite; $725–$850 two-bedroom suite; $900 three-bedroom suite. AE, DC, MC, V. Open year-round. **Amenities:** 2 restaurants (fine dining serving 3 meals daily, more casual bar open daily for lunch and dinner; you can ask to be served by the pool); heated outdoor pool; 2 tennis courts; concierge; room service (seasonal only: breakfast, lunch, and dinner); babysitting; same-day laundry. *In room:* A/C, TV, fridge, hair dryer, iron, safe.

Hob Knob Inn ★★   Owner Maggie White has reinvented this 19th-century Gothic Revival inn as an exquisite destination now vying for top honors as one of the Vineyard's best places to stay. Her style is peppy/preppy, with crisp floral fabrics and striped patterns creating a clean and comfortable look. The farm breakfast is a delight and is served at beautifully appointed individual tables in the sunny, brightly painted dining rooms. Bovine lovers will enjoy the agrarian theme, a decorative touch throughout the inn. The attentive staff will pack a splendid picnic basket or plan a charter fishing trip on Maggie's 27-foot Boston Whaler.

128 Main St. (on upper Main St., in the center of town), Edgartown, MA 02539. ☎ **800/696-2723** or 508/627-9510. Fax 508/627-4560. www.hobknob.com. 20 units; 4-bedroom cottage. Summer $270–$425 double. Rates include full breakfast and afternoon tea. AE, MC, V. Open year-round. **Amenities:** Exercise room; rental bikes ($20 per day); room service; massage (extra charge). *In room:* A/C, TV, hair dryer.

The Winnetu Inn & Resort ★★   This large luxury hotel sits on 11 acres overlooking South Beach in Katama. Guests can walk down a 250-yard path to get to the private beach, which is next to South Beach on the Atlantic Ocean. A 3-mile bike path links the inn to Edgartown, but the inn also runs a shuttle service that can pick up inn guests at the Edgartown ferry. Most rooms are two- and three-bedroom suites with kitchenettes, and there is one deluxe cottage with a four-person hot tub and a roof deck. Some guest rooms have ocean views and washer/dryers. Many have private decks or patios. The fine-dining restaurant, **Opus,** is a treat.

South Beach, Edgartown, MA 02539. ☎ **978/443-1733** (reservations line), 508/627-4747. www.winnetu. com. 48 units. Summer $275 double; $475–$1,140 suite. AE, MC, V. Closed Dec to mid-Apr. **Amenities:** Fine-dining restaurant; outdoor heated pool; putting green; tennis courts with pro (6 Har-Tru, 4 all-weather); fitness room; children's program (late June to early Sept complimentary 9am–noon; fee in evenings for 3-year-olds through pre-teens); concierge; laundry facilities. *In room:* A/C, TV/VCR, fridge, coffeemaker, iron, microwave.

Expensive

Colonial Inn of Martha's Vineyard ★★ *Kids*   This 1911 inn in the center of Edgartown has been transformed into a fine modern hotel and recent extensive renovations have elevated it to what can accurately be described as "affordable luxury." Its lobby serves as a conduit to the Nevins Square shops beyond. The guest rooms are decorated in soothing, contemporary tones with pine furniture, crisp fabrics, hardwood floors, and beadboard wainscoting. Suites have VCRs (complimentary videos) and kitchenettes. Many rooms have gas fireplaces. Be sure to visit the roof deck, ideally around sunset or, if you're up for it, sunrise.

38 N. Water St., Edgartown, MA 02539. ☎ **800/627-4701** or 508/627-4711. Fax 508/627-5904. www. colonialinnmvy.com. 43 units (42 tub/shower; 1 shower only). Summer $215–$415 double; $370–$395 suite or efficiency. Rates include continental breakfast. AE, MC, V. Closed Dec–Mar. Pets allowed in designated rooms for $30 per day. **Amenities:** 2 restaurants; fitness room and spa; shopping arcade. *In room:* A/C, TV, dataport, hair dryer, iron.

The Jonathan Munroe House ★★ *Finds*   With its graceful wraparound, colonnaded front porch, the Jonathan Munroe House stands out from the other inns and captain's homes on this stretch of upper Main Street. Inside, the formal parlor has been transformed into a comfortable gathering room with European flair. Guest rooms are immaculate, antique-filled, and dotted with clever details. Many rooms have fireplaces. At breakfast, don't miss the homemade waffles and pancakes, served on the sunny porch. Request the garden cottage if you are in a honeymooning mood.

100 Main St., Edgartown, MA 02539. ✆ 877/468-6763 or ✆/fax 508/627-5536. 7 units, 1 cottage (5 tub/shower, 2 shower only, 1 tub and shower). Summer $190–$250 double; $300 cottage. Rates include full breakfast and wine and cheese hour. AE, MC, V. Open year-round. No children under 12. *In room:* A/C, hair dryer.

The Point Way Inn ⭐⭐ This inn has recently undergone a multimillion-dollar freshening up and is just as pretty as it could be. While some of the rooms are on the small side, they are cheerfully decorated in a contemporary style. The garden room is an especially cozy first-floor room with a separate entrance. Hearty breakfasts might include crepes, stuffed French toast, or quiche. In the afternoons, there are homemade cookies, and in the evenings, wine and cheese. An unusual feature here is a complimentary guest car available for exploring the island.

104 Main St. (at Pease's Point Way), Edgartown, MA 02539. ✆ 888/711-6633 or 508/627-8633. Fax 508/627-3338. www.pointway.com. 13 units (8 tub/shower, 5 shower only). Summer $250–$425 double; $400–$600 suite. Rates include full breakfast. AE, DISC, MC, V. Closed Jan to mid-Feb. Well-behaved dogs allowed in 2 rooms ($50). *In room:* A/C, TV, hair dryer, no phone.

Victorian Inn ⭐⭐ Do you long to stay at a quaint, reasonably priced inn that is bigger than a B&B but smaller than a Marriott? The Victorian Inn is a freshened-up version of those old-style hotels that used to exist in every New England town. There are enough rooms here so you don't feel like you are trespassing in someone's home, yet there's a personal touch. With three floors of long, graceful corridors, the Victorian could serve as a stage set for a 1930s romance. Several rooms have canopy beds and balconies. The innkeepers are always quick to dispense helpful advice with good humor.

24 S. Water St. (in the center of town), Edgartown, MA 02539. ✆ 508/627-4784. www.thevic.com. 14 units (2 tub/shower, 12 shower only). Summer $165–$385 double. Rates include full breakfast and afternoon tea. MC, V. Open year-round. Dogs welcome Nov–Mar. *In room:* A/C, TV, hair dryer, no phone.

Moderate

Edgartown Inn ⭐ *Value* This centrally located inn offers perhaps the best value on the island. Nathaniel Hawthorne holed up here for nearly a year, and Daniel Webster also spent time here. The lovely 1798 Federal manse is a showplace even here on captain's row. Rooms are no-frills but pleasantly traditional; some have TVs and harbor views. Modernists may prefer the two cathedral-ceilinged quarters in the annex out back, which offer lovely light and a sense of seclusion. Service is excellent; be sure to say hello to Henry King, who has been on the staff for over 50 years.

56 N. Water St., Edgartown, MA 02539. ✆ 508/627-4794. Fax 508/627-9420. www.edgartowninn.com. 20 units, 4 with shared bathroom. Summer $110 shared bathroom; $155–$250 double. No credit cards. Closed Nov–Mar. Children 8 years and older. *In room:* A/C, no phone.

OAK BLUFFS

Those looking for a basic motel with a central location, can try **Surfside Motel** across from the ferry dock on Oak Bluffs Avenue in Oak Bluffs (✆ 800/537-3007 or 508/693-2500). Summer rates are $150 to $220 double; $250 to $300 for suites. Well-behaved pets are allowed.

Expensive

The Oak House ⭐⭐ *Finds* An 1872 Queen Anne bayfront beauty has preserved all the luxury and leisure of the Victorian age. Innkeeper Betsi Convery-Luce trained at Johnson & Wales; her pastries are sublime. The common rooms are furnished in an opulent Victorian mode, as are the 10 guest rooms. Those toward the back are quieter, but those in front have Nantucket Sound views.

This inn is very service oriented, and requests for feather beds, down pillows, or non-allergenic pillows are accommodated. Anyone intent on decompressing is sure to benefit from this immersion into another era—the one that invented the leisure class.

75 Seaview Ave. (on the sound), Oak Bluffs, MA 02557. © **800/245-5979** or 508/693-4187. Fax 508/696-7385. www.vineyardinns.com. 10 units (1 tub/shower; 9 shower only). Summer $195–$250 double; $310–$315 suite. Rates include continental breakfast and afternoon tea. AE, DISC, MC, V. Closed late Oct to early May. *In room:* A/C, TV.

Moderate

The Dockside Inn ★ *Kids*   Set close to the harbor, the Dockside is perfectly located for exploring the town of Oak Bluffs and is geared toward families. The welcoming exterior, with its colonnaded porch and balconies, duplicates the inns of yesteryear. Once inside, the whimsical Victorian touches will transport you into the spirit of this rollicking town. Most of the cheerfully decorated rooms have either garden or harbor views; some have private decks. Location, charm, and flair make this a popular place, so book early.

9 Circuit Ave. Extension (Box 1206), Oak Bluffs, MA 02557. © **800/245-5979** or 508/693-2966. Fax 508/696-7293. www.vineyardinns.com. 22 units. Summer $165–$210 double; $270–$360 suite. Rates include continental breakfast. AE, DISC, MC, V. Closed late Oct to early Apr. *In room:* A/C, TV, hair dryer, iron.

The Oak Bluffs Inn ★   This homey Victorian inn has a fun location at the top of Circuit Avenue, Oak Bluff's main drag. The inn stands out with its colorful Victorian paint scheme and its prominent cupola, from which guests can enjoy a 360-degree view of Oak Bluffs. It's a 2-minute stroll from the inn to all the Oak Bluffs attractions, like the ginger bread cottages, the tabernacle, the Flying Horses Carousel, the waterfront park, and the ferries. Some of the rooms are a tad on the small side, but others are spacious and even have comfortable seating areas.

64 Circuit Ave. (at the corner of Pequot Ave.), Oak Bluffs, MA 02557. © **800/955-6235** or 508/693-7171. Fax 508/693-8787. www.oakbluffsinn.com. 9 units. Summer $195–$255 double. Rates include continental breakfast. AE, MC, V. Closed Nov–Apr. *In room:* A/C, hair dryer, no phone.

Wesley Hotel ★ *Value*   Formerly one of the grand hotels of Martha's Vineyard, this imposing 1879 property, right on the harbor, is now a solid entry in the good-value category, especially with its low off-season rates. It occupies a terrific location in Oak Bluffs, across the street from the harbor, in the center of the action. The only drawback here can be the noise from revelers on the boats in the harbor or traffic on busy Lake Avenue. Most of the rooms are fairly compact and basic, though some are roomy with harbor views. The Wesley Arms, behind the main building, contains 33 air-conditioned rooms with private bathrooms, accessible by elevator. Eight suites and executive suites contain kitchenettes. Reserve early to specify harbor views, which do not cost more than regular rooms. This is also one of the few Vineyard hotels that does not require a minimum stay in season.

70 Lake Ave. (on the harbor), Oak Bluffs, MA 02557. © **800/638-9027** or 508/693-6611. Fax 508/693-5389. www.wesleyhotel.com. 95 units (all with shower only). Summer $195–$215 double; $275 suite. AE, DC, MC, V. Closed late Oct to Apr. *In room:* A/C, TV, no phone.

VINEYARD HAVEN (TISBURY)
Very Expensive

The Mansion House Inn ★★ *Finds*   After a fire burned down the 200-year-old Tisbury Inn several years ago, the owners decided to rebuild, making this one of the island's most full-service inns. The building, occupying a prominent corner location in Vineyard Haven, is already a community hub, with a restaurant, health club, and shops. The three-story hotel is comfortable with generous amenities. The rooms range in size from cozy to spacious and prices vary accordingly. Many have kitchenettes, plasma-screen TVs, and extra-large bathtubs. Some have harbor views. All the rooms are equipped with high-speed Internet service. One of the most unique features of the inn is the 75-foot mineral spring (no chlorine) swimming pool in the health club in the inn's basement. The restaurant, **Zephrus,** is open to the public for lunch and dinner, and also supplies room service for guests until late in the evening.

9 Main St., Vineyard Haven, MA 02568. © 800/332-4112 or 508/693-2200. Fax 508/693-4095. www.mvmansionhouse.com. 32 units. $229–$439 double; $269–$649 suite. Rates include full buffet breakfast. AE, MC, V. Open year-round. **Amenities:** Restaurant (Zephrus, a fine-dining New American–style restaurant); health club and spa with 75-ft. pool. *In room:* AC, TV, fridge.

Martha's Place ★★   Martha's Place is exceptional for its elegance in the heart of this bustling port town; it's across the street from Owen Park, a harbor beach, and a block from the center of Vineyard Haven. The owners have lovingly restored this stately Greek Revival home and surrounded it with rosebushes. Swags and jabots line the windows; every knob has a tassel, every fabric a trim. If you admire neoclassical armoires or antique beds draped in blue velvet, Martha's is the place. Most rooms have harbor views. The bathrooms here are quite luxurious: Ever seen one with a fireplace? One guest room is accessible to guests with disabilities. Breakfast is served at the dining room table set with china and silver, or you may have breakfast in bed.

114 Main St. (across from Owen Park, in the center of town), Vineyard Haven, MA 02568. © 508/693-0253. Fax 508/693-1890. www.marthasplace.com. 6 units. Summer $225–$450 double. Rates include continental breakfast. AE, DISC, MC, V. **Amenities:** 8-person hot tub; loaner bikes. *In room:* A/C, TV, dataport, hair dryer.

CHILMARK (INCLUDING MENEMSHA), WEST TISBURY & AQUINNAH
Very Expensive

Beach Plum Inn ★★ *(Finds)*   This family-owned country inn is set on 8 lush acres, with a lawn sloping gracefully down to Vineyard Sound. The room decor is predominantly cottage-y, though some rooms lean towards elegance. All but one room have decks or patios, some with views of Menemsha Harbor. Some units have canopied beds and are quite romantic. Linens are 275 count and above; towels are Egyptian cotton. Five of the rooms have a whirlpool bath. The inn's restaurant is one of the best fine-dining spots on the island (see "Where to Dine," below).

Beach Plum Lane (off North Rd., ½ mile NE of the harbor), Menemsha, MA 02552. © 877/645-7398 or 508 /645-9454. Fax 508/645-2801. www.beachpluminn.com. 11 units (all with tub/shower). Summer $250–$400 double or cottage. Rates include full breakfast in season; continental off season. AE, DC, DISC, MC, V. Closed Jan–Apr. **Amenities:** Restaurant (fine-dining); private beach passes; tennis court; croquet court; laundry service for a charge. Babysitting and in-room massage by arrangement. *In room:* A/C, TV, dataport, fridge, hair dryer, iron.

Expensive

Menemsha Inn and Cottages ★★   There's an almost Quaker-like plainness to this weathered waterside compound set in the pines near Menemsha Harbor, though many of the rooms are quite inviting. Mostly it's a place to revel in the outdoors (on 11 seaside acres) without distractions. The property is about a half-mile walk through a wooded path to the beach. There's no restaurant—just a restful breakfast room. Cottages have hair dryers, TVs, VCRs, dataports, outdoor showers, barbecue grills, and kitchenettes. The most luxurious suites are located in the Carriage House, which has a spacious common room with a field-stone fireplace. All rooms have private decks; most have water views. Guests have access to complimentary passes and shuttle bus service to the Lucy Vincent and Squibnocket private beaches.

Off North Rd. (about ½ mile NE of the harbor), Menemsha, MA 02552. © 508/645-2521. Fax 508/645-9500. www.menemshainn.com. 15 units, 12 cottages. Summer $225–$290 double; $525 2-bedroom suite daily; $2,100–$2,900 cottages weekly. Rates include continental breakfast for rooms and suites. MC, V. Closed Dec to mid-Apr. **Amenities:** Beach passes; tennis court; fitness room (step machine, treadmill, exercise bike, and free weights). *In room:* TV.

Moderate

The Captain R. Flanders House ★ *Finds* Set amid 60 acres of rolling meadows crisscrossed by stone walls, this late–18th-century farmhouse has remained much the same for 2 centuries. The living room, with its broad-plank floors, is full of astonishing antiques. Two countrified cottages overlook the pond. The owners will provide you with a coveted pass to nearby Lucy Vincent Beach.

North Rd. (about ½ mile NE of Menemsha), Chilmark, MA 02535. © 508/645-3123. www.captainflanders. com. 5 units, 3 with shared bathroom; 2 cottages. Summer $80 single with shared bathroom; $175 double with shared bathroom; $195 double with private bathroom; $275 cottage. Rates include continental breakfast. AE, MC, V. Closed Nov to early May. **Amenities:** Private beach and shuttle bus passes. *In room:* No phone.

WHERE TO DINE

Outside Oak Bluffs and Edgartown, all of Martha's Vineyard is "dry," including Vineyard Haven, so bring your own bottle; some restaurants charge a small fee for uncorking.

EDGARTOWN
Very Expensive

L'étoile ★★★ CONTEMPORARY FRENCH Every signal (starting with the price) tells you that this is going to be one very special meal. To get to the restaurant, you first pass through a pair of sitting rooms before coming to a summery conservatory, sparkling with the light of antique brass sconces and fresh with the scent of potted citrus trees. Everything is perfection, from the table settings (gold-rimmed Villeroy & Boch) to the nouvelle-cuisine menu. Chef Michael Brisson is determined to dazzle with an ever-evolving seven-course menu of delicacies flown in from the four corners of the earth. Sevruga usually makes an appearance—perhaps as a garnish for chilled leek soup. An étouffée of lobster with lobster, cognac, and chervil sauce might come with littlenecks, bay scallops, and roasted corn fritters.

At the Charlotte Inn, 27 S. Summer St. (off Main St.). © 508/627-5187. Reservations required. Collared shirts requested for men. Fixed-price menu $78. Chef's Tasting Menu $120. AE, MC, V. July–Aug seatings daily from 6:30–9:30pm; May, June, Sept, and Oct Tues–Sun 6:30–9:45pm; mid-Feb to Apr and Nov–Dec Thurs–Sat 6:30–9:45pm. Closed Jan to mid-Feb.

Expensive

Alchemy ★★ FRENCH BISTRO This spiffy restaurant is a slice of Paris on Main Street. Such esoteric choices as oyster brie soup and Burgundy Vintners salad share the bill with escargot-and-chanterelle fricassee. As befits a true bistro, there's a large selection of cocktails, liqueurs, and wines. In addition to lunch and dinner, a bar menu is served from 2:30 to 11pm. This choice isn't for everyone, but sophisticated diners will enjoy the Continental flair.

71 Main St. (in the center of town). © 508/627-9999. Reservations accepted. Main courses $22–$33. AE, MC, V. Apr–Nov daily noon–2:30pm, 5:30–10pm; call for off-season hours. Open year-round.

Atria ★★ NEW AMERICAN   This fine-dining restaurant set in an 18th-century sea captain's house gets rave reviews for its gourmet cuisine and high-caliber service. Pronounced with the emphasis on the second syllable (ah-TRE-ah), the name refers to the brightest of three stars forming the Southern Triangle constellation. You can sit in the elegant dining room, the rose-covered wraparound porch, or the brick cellar bar downstairs for more casual dining. The menu offers a variety of creative dishes with influences from around the country and around the world, with stops in the Mediterranean, Middle East, and Asia. It features organic island-grown produce, off-the-boat seafood, local shellfish, and aged prime meats. Popular starters include miso soup with steamed crab dumplings or Thai lemongrass mussels. Unusual main courses include wok fried Martha's Vineyard lobster or cracklin' pork shank with southern collard greens. There is live entertainment in the bar, along the lines of acoustic guitar, on weekends.

137 Main St. (a short walk from the center of town). © **508/627-5850**. www.atriamv.com. Reservations recommended. Main courses $22–$36. AE, MC, V. June–Sept daily 5:30–10pm; call for off-season hours. Open year-round.

The Coach House ★★ NEW AMERICAN   This is a terrific place to have a drink or to dine, with its exquisite view of Edgartown Harbor and the lighthouse. The long and elegant bar is particularly smashing. The menu is simple but stylish. To start, there's soft-shell crab with arugula and teardrop tomatoes. As a main course, try the caramelized sea scallops with a salad of Asian pear and apple. Service is excellent; these are trained waiters, not your usual college surfer dudes. At the end of your meal, you may want to sit on the rockers on the Harbor View Hotel's wraparound porch and watch the lights twinkling in the harbor.

At the Harbor View Hotel (p. 276), 131 N. Water St. © **508/627-7000**. Reservations recommended. Main courses $18–$35. AE, MC, V. Mon–Sat 7–11am and noon–2pm, Sun 8am–2pm; daily 6–10pm; call for off-season hours. Open year-round.

Lattanzi's ★★ NORTHERN ITALIAN   Some say Al Lattanzi cooks the best veal chops on Martha's Vineyard. Lattanzi's would be the ideal place to eat in the dead of winter, by the glow of the paneled living room's handsome fireplace.

Moments **The Quintessential Lobster Dinner**

When the basics—a lobster and a sunset—are what you crave, head to the **Home Port** on North Road in Menemsha (© **508/645-2679**), a favorite of locals and visitors alike. At first glance, prices for the lobster dinners may seem a bit high, but note that they include an appetizer of your choice (go with the stuffed quahog), salad, amazing fresh-baked breads, a nonalcoholic beverage (remember, it's BYOB in these parts), and dessert. The decor is on the simple side, but who really cares? It's the riveting harbor views that have drawn fans to this family-friendly place for over 60 years. Locals not keen on summer crowds prefer to order their lobster dinners for pickup (less than half price) at the restaurant door, then head down to Menemsha Beach for a private sunset supper. Reservations are required. Fixed-price platters range from $25 to $45. The Home Port is open mid-June to Labor Day daily at 5pm with last reservations at 9pm. Closed mid-September to mid-May. Call for off-season hours.

Service is exceptional, and the wine list has a wide range of well-priced bottles. Back to the veal chop. You have two choices: *Piccolo Fiorentina,* which is hickory-grilled veal porterhouse chop with black peppercorns and lemon, or *Lombatina di Vitello al Porcini,* which pairs the chop with porcini-mushroom cream. If it's July, get the striped-bass special; from local waters, it's luscious.

Lattanzi also owns the very good **brick-oven pizza joint** next door (© 508/627-9084).

19 Church St. (Old Post Office Sq., off Main St. in the center of town). © **508/627-8854.** Reservations recommended. Main courses $22–$38. DC, DISC, MC, V. June–Sept daily 6–10pm; call for off-season hours. Open year-round.

Moderate

Among the Flowers Cafe ★★ *Value* AMERICAN   Everything's fresh and appealing at this small outdoor cafe near the dock. The breakfasts are the best around, and the comfort-food dinners are among the most affordable options in this pricey town. There's almost always a wait, not just because it's so picturesque, but because the food is homey, hearty, and kind on the wallet.

Mayhew Lane. © **508/627-3233.** Main courses $10–$18. AE, DC, DISC, MC, V. July–Aug daily 8am–10pm; May–June and Sept–Oct daily 8am–4pm. Closed Nov–Apr.

Chesca's ★★ *Finds* ITALIAN   This modern-decor restaurant at the Colonial Inn is a solid entry, with yummy food at reasonable prices. You're sure to find favorites like paella (with roasted lobster and other choice seafood), risotto (with roasted vegetables), and ravioli (with portobello mushrooms and asparagus). Smaller appetites can fill up on homemade soup and salad.

At the Colonial Inn, 38 N. Water St. © **508/627-1234.** Reservations accepted for parties with 6 or more only. Main courses $13–$32. AE, MC, V. Late June to early Sept daily 5:30–10pm; call for off-season hours. Closed Nov–Mar.

Inexpensive

The Newes from America ★★ *Finds* PUB GRUB   The food is better than average at this subterranean tavern, built in 1742. Beers are a specialty here. Try a rack of five esoteric brews, or let your choice of food—from a wood-smoked oyster "Island Poor Boy" sandwich with linguica (Portuguese-style sausage) relish to an 18-ounce porterhouse steak—dictate your draft; the menu comes handily annotated with recommendations. Don't miss the seasoned fries.

At The Kelley House, 23 Kelley St. © **508/627-4397.** Main courses $7–$10. AE, MC, V. Daily 11:30am–11pm. Open year-round.

OAK BLUFFS
Expensive

Park Corner Bistro ★★★ *Finds* NEW AMERICAN   This superb restaurant in the center of Oak Bluffs is an intimate and cozy bistro that has a definite European aura. With just 10 tables, it's a romantic space for casual fine dining. Favorite appetizers are the beet salad and the Parmesan gnocchi, which is sautéed with chanterelle and black trumpet mushrooms. Move on to the Australian lamb loin with sweet corn flan and champagne corn emulsion. For dessert, don't miss the warm fruit cobbler with vanilla ice cream.

20H Kennebec Ave. (off Circuit Ave., across from the OB Post Office). © **508/696-9922.** Reservations suggested. Main courses $25–$37. AE, MC, V. July–Aug daily 9am–3pm and 6–10pm; call for off-season hours. Open year-round.

Sweet Life Cafe ★★★ FRENCH/AMERICAN   Locals are crazy about this pearl of a restaurant, set in a restored Victorian house on upper Circuit Avenue.

In season, the most popular seating is outside in the gaily lit garden. Fresh island produce is featured, with seafood specials an enticing draw. If the roasted lobster with potato-Parmesan risotto, roasted yellow beets, and smoked-salmon chive fondue is offered, order it.

63 Circuit Ave. ✆ **508/696-0200**. Reservations recommended. Main courses $18–$35. AE, DISC, MC, V. Mid-May to Aug daily 5:30–10pm; Apr to mid-May and Sept–Nov Thurs–Mon 5:30–9:30pm. Closed Dec to mid-May.

Moderate

Lola's Southern Seafood ✮ SOUTHERN   This sultry New Orleans–style restaurant drips with atmosphere: crystal chandeliers; intricate wrought-iron, arched doorways; and starched linens in an ochre palette. Specialties include the chicken-and-seafood jambalaya, and the rib-eye steak spiced either "from heaven or hell." Meals are served family-style, with large helpings of side dishes. There's live entertainment nightly in season, while Sunday brunch also features live music. Off season, there's live music Friday and Saturday nights. A less-expensive pub menu is served in the bar.

At the Island Inn, Beach Rd. ✆ **508/693-5007**. www.lolassouthernseafood.com. Reservations accepted only for 5 or more. Main courses $20–$36. DC, MC, V. Sun 10am–2pm; daily 5–11pm. Open year-round.

Inexpensive

Coup de Ville ✮ SEAFOOD   Of the several open-air harbor-front choices in Oak Bluffs, this one has the best service and food. This outdoor fried-seafood shack serves up tasty beer-battered shrimp, grilled swordfish, lobster salad, and "world famous" chicken wings. It's a fun place to people-watch on sunny summer days as boaters cruise around the harbor.

Dockside Market Place, Oak Bluffs Harbor. ✆ **508/693-3420**. Most items $9–$20. MC, V. June–Aug daily 11am–10pm; call for off-season hours. Closed mid-Oct to Apr.

VINEYARD HAVEN (TISBURY)

Just around the corner from the Black Dog Tavern on Water Street near the ferry terminal is the **Black Dog Bakery** (✆ **508/693-4786**). The doors open at 5am, and from midmorning on, it's elbowroom only as customers line up for freshly baked breads, muffins, and desserts that can't be beat. Don't forget some home-made doggie biscuits for your pooch.

Expensive

Black Dog Tavern ✮ NEW AMERICAN   How does a humble harbor shack come to be a national icon? Location helps. So do cool T-shirts. Soon after *Shenandoah* captain Robert Douglas decided, in 1971, that this hardworking port could use a good restaurant, influential vacationers, stuck waiting for the ferry, began to wander into this saltbox to tide themselves over with a bit of "blackout cake" or peanut-butter pie. The food is still home-cooking good, especially the seafood, and the blackout cake has lost none of its appeal. Though the lines grow ever longer, nothing much has changed at this beloved spot. Eggs Galveston for breakfast at the Black Dog Tavern is still one of the ultimate Vineyard experiences— go early, when it first opens, and sit on the porch, where the views are perfect.

Beach St. Extension (on the harbor), Vineyard Haven. ✆ **508/693-9223**. Reservations not accepted. Main courses $14–$27. AE, MC, V. June to early Sept daily 7–11am, noon–4pm, and 5–9pm; call for off-season hours. Open year-round.

Zephrus at the Mansion House Inn ✮✮ INTERNATIONAL   This hip restaurant is a great place to go for casual fine-dining. Seating is at the sidewalk cafe on Main Street or inside by the hearth in view of the open kitchen.

Main-course winners are pan-roasted pork tenderloin served with sweet 'tater tots; and shrimp and farfalle pasta. Though the menu is in constant flux, there is always a good vegetarian choice like the delicious vegetable risotto with truffle vinaigrette. Bring your favorite wine; the corkage fee is $5 per table.

9 Main St., Vineyard Haven © 508/693-3416. www.zephrus.com. Reservations recommended. Main courses $20–$28. AE, DC, DISC, MC, V. July and Aug daily 11:30am–3pm and 5:30–9pm. Call for off-season hours. Open year-round.

CHILMARK (INCLUDING MENEMSHA) & WEST TISBURY
Very Expensive

The Beach Plum Inn Restaurant ★★★ INTERNATIONAL   This jewel of a restaurant is located in an inn that sits on a bluff overlooking the fishing village of Menemsha. Extensive renovations and attention to quality have made this one of the island's top dining venues. Guests can dine inside in the spare, but elegant, dining room, or outside on the new tiled patio. Chef James McDonough's most popular dishes include hazelnut-encrusted halibut with Marsala wine *beurre blanc* sauce. The most winning appetizer is the blackened lobster tips, served with mango cream sauce and house-cured gravlax with homemade wild rice and corn pancakes. For dessert, you'll flip for the chocolate quadruple-layer cake made with white and dark chocolate mousse and Chambord. In the spring and fall, there is usually an ethereal soufflé on the menu, either Grand Marnier or chocolate.

At the Beach Plum Inn, 50 Beach Plum Lane (off North Road), Menemsha. © 508/645-9454. www.beach pluminn.com. Reservations required. Main courses $32–$40, 4-course fixed-price menu $68; off season only fixed-priced menu $50. AE, MC, V. Mid-June to early Sept daily seatings from 5:30–6:45pm and 8–9:30pm. Call for off-season hours. Closed Dec–Apr.

Ice House Restaurant ★★ NEW AMERICAN   A pricey but popular up-island restaurant, the Ice House is earning raves for the creative menu. It's also a trendy venue, a place for island-insiders who wouldn't be caught dead in the down-island towns. The chef combines unusual ingredients with island produce, meats, and locally caught fish. His specialty appetizer is a golden-fried tomato with a lobster salad and avocado. As a main course, look no further than the pan-roasted halibut with sweet corn and fava bean succotash.

688 State Road, West Tisbury. © 508/645-9329. Reservations recommended. Main courses $25–$36. AE, MC, V. July and Aug Mon–Sat 6–10pm; Sun 11am–2pm and 6–10pm. Call for off-season hours. Closed Jan–Mar.

Moderate

The Bite ★★ *Finds* SEAFOOD   It's usually places like The Bite that you crave when you think of New England. This is your quintessential "chowdah" and clam shack, flanked by picnic tables. The Bite makes superlative chowder, potato salad, fried fish, and so forth.

Basin Rd. (off North Rd., about ¼ mile NE of the harbor), Menemsha. © 508/645-9239. Main courses $18–$30. No credit cards. July–Aug daily 11am–8pm; call for off-season hours. Closed late Sept to Apr.

MARTHA'S VINEYARD AFTER DARK

All towns except Oak Bluffs and Edgartown are dry, and last call at bars and clubs is at midnight. Hit Oak Bluffs for the rowdiest bar scene and best nighttime street life. In Edgartown, you may have to hop around before you find the evening's most happening spot.

Disco lives! As do karaoke and comedy, on occasion at **Atlantic Connection,** 19 Circuit Ave., Oak Bluffs (© 508/693-7129). There's entertainment nightly in season. Cover ranges from free to $25; most nights $5 to $10.

Young and loud are the watchwords at the **Lamppost** and the **Rare Duck,** 111 Circuit Ave., Oak Bluffs (© **508/696-9352**), a pair of clubs in the center of town. The Lamppost features live bands and a dance floor; the Rare Duck, acoustic acts. This is where the young folk go, and the performers could be playing blues, reggae, R&B, or '80s. The cover is $1 to $5.

The Vineyard's first and only brewpub, **Offshore Ale Company,** 30 Kennebec Ave., Oak Bluffs (© **508/693-2626**), is an attractively rustic place, with oak booths and peanut shells strewn on the floor. Local acoustic performers entertain 6 nights a week in season. The cover is $5.

The Ritz Cafe, 1 Circuit Ave., Oak Bluffs (© **508/693-9851**), is a down-and-dirty hole-in-the-wall that features live music nightly in season and on weekends year-round. The cover is $2 to $3.

PERFORMING ARTS

This magnificent 1843 **Whaling Church,** 89 Main St., Edgartown (© **508/627-4442**), functions primarily as a 500-seat performing-arts center offering lectures and symposia, films, plays, and concerts. Ticket prices vary; call for schedule.

The Vineyard Playhouse, 24 Church St., Vineyard Haven (© **508/696-6300** or 508/693-6450; www.vineyardplayhouse.org), is an intimate black-box theater, where Equity professionals put on a rich season of favorites and challenging new work, followed, on summer weekends, by musical or comedic cabaret in the gallery/lounge. Children's theater selections are performed on Saturdays at 10am. Townspeople often get involved in the outdoor Shakespeare production, a 3-week run starting in mid-July at the Tashmoo Overlook Amphitheatre about 1 mile west of town.

2 Nantucket ⋆⋆⋆

Once the whaling capital of the world, this tiny island, 30 miles off the coast of Cape Cod, still counts its isolation as a defining characteristic. At only 3½ by 14 miles in size, Nantucket is smaller and more insular than Martha's Vineyard. But charm-wise, Nantucket stands alone—21st-century amenities wrapped in an elegant 19th-century package.

Sophisticated Nantucket Town features bountiful stores, quaint inns, cobblestone streets, interesting historic sites, and pristine beaches. The rest of the island is mainly residential, but for a couple of notable villages. **Siasconset** (nicknamed 'Sconset), on the east side of the island, is a tranquil community with picturesque, rose-covered cottages and a handful of businesses, including a pricey French restaurant. Sunset aficionados head to **Madaket,** on the west coast of the island, for the evening spectacular.

The lay of the land on Nantucket is rolling moors, cranberry bogs, and miles of exquisite public beaches. The vistas are honeymoon-romantic: an operating windmill, three lighthouses, and a skyline dotted with church steeples.

ESSENTIALS
GETTING THERE

BY FERRY   From Hyannis   Ferry service to Hyannis is fairly hassle-free, unless you're bringing a car in summer. But first-time visitors will find a car more of a nuisance than a convenience, unless they're staying outside of Nantucket Town.

From Hyannis (South St. Dock), the **Steamship Authority** (© **508/477-8600** in Hyannis; © **508/228-3274** in Nantucket; www.steamshipauthority.com) operates year-round ferry service for cars, passengers, and bicycles to Steamship Wharf on Nantucket using both high-speed and conventional ferries.

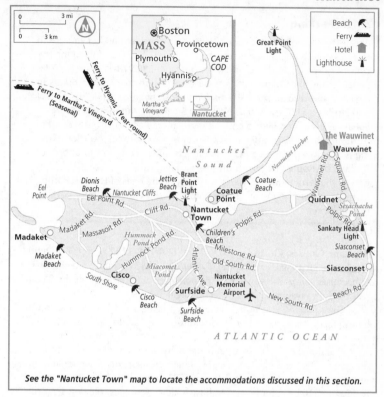

See the "Nantucket Town" map to locate the accommodations discussed in this section.

The Steamship Authority's high-speed ferry to Nantucket, **The Flying Cloud** (© **508/495-3278**), is for passengers only. It takes 1 hour and runs five to six times a day in season. Tickets from mid-March through December cost $28 one-way ($55 round-trip) for adults, $21 one-way ($42 round-trip) for children 5 to 12. From January through mid-March, tickets cost $23 one-way for adults and $17 one-way for children. Parking costs $8 to $10 per day. Watch for the ferry parking signs on Route 6; if lots next to the dock are full, you'll need to take Exit 6 for a satellite lot, instead of Exit 7 for the main lot. Passenger reservations are highly recommended. No pets are allowed on *The Flying Cloud*.

Total trip time on the conventional ferry that carries cars is 2 hours and 15 minutes. A round-trip fare for a car costs $350 to $380 from mid-May to mid-October; $230 to $250 the rest of the year. The higher rates are charged for vehicles more than 16 feet long. Car rates do not include drivers or passengers. Passenger tickets are $14 one-way ($28 round-trip) for adults, $7.25 one-way ($15 round-trip) for children 5 to 12; bikes cost $12 round-trip. Parking costs $8 to $10 per day; you do not need to make parking reservations.

No advance reservations are needed for passengers traveling without their cars on the conventional ferry. But if you bring your car in summer, you must reserve *months in advance*—only six boats make the trip daily and they fill up fast. Arrive at least 1 hour before departure to avoid having your space given away. There is a $10 fee for canceling a reservation.

Tips **Parking**

Because you won't need a car on Nantucket, consider parking your car in Hyannis before boarding the ferry to the island. If you are taking the **Hy-Line** ferry service from Ocean Street Dock (© **888/778-1132** or 508/778-2602) in July and August, it's a good idea to not only reserve tickets in advance, but also to reserve a parking spot ahead of time. The all-day parking fee is $15 in season. Travelers on **Steamship Authority** (© **508/477-8600**) vessels do not need a parking reservation. Parking at the Steamship Authority lots is $8 to $10 per day. For both ferry services, overflow parking is now at the Cape Cod Community College parking lots just north of Route 6 on Route 132 (exit 6 off Rte. 6). Free shuttle buses take passengers to the ferry terminals, which are on opposite ends of Hyannis Harbor. In season, watch signs on Route 6 for up-to-the-minute ferry parking information.

Hy-Line Cruises, Ocean Street Dock (© **888/778-1132** or 508/778-2600; for high-speed ferry reservations, call © **800/492-8082** or 508/778-0404; www.hy-linecruises.com), offers two types of passenger-only ferries from the Ocean Street Dock in Hyannis to Nantucket's Straight Wharf.

The Grey Lady, a year-round high-speed passenger ferry, makes the trip in 1 hour. The cost is $33 one-way ($58 round-trip) for adults, $25 one-way ($41 round-trip) for children 5 to 12, and $5 ($10 round-trip) for bicycles. The boat seats 260 and makes five to six round-trips daily in season; reserve in advance.

From early May through October, Hy-Line runs its standard 1-hour-and-50-minute ferry service. Round-trip tickets are $27 for adults, $14 for children ages 5 to 12, and $10 extra for bikes. On busy holiday weekends, the slow ferry fills up too, so order tickets in advance; buy or pick up your tickets at least half an hour before sailing time.

Hy-Line also runs slow crossings on the **MV *Great Point,*** which has a first-class section with a private lounge, restrooms, bar, and snack bar. The fare is $23 one-way ($46 round-trip) for adults and children. The comfortable seats on the *Great Point* are a far cry from the unforgiving benches on the regular slow ferry. No pets are allowed on the *Great Point.*

Hy-Line's **"Around the Sound" cruise** is a 1-day round-trip excursion from Hyannis with stops on Nantucket and Martha's Vineyard. It runs from early June to late September. The price is $41 for adults, $20 for children 5 to 12, and $15 extra for bikes.

From Martha's Vineyard   From Oak Bluffs on Martha's Vineyard, Hy-Line runs three passenger-only ferries to Nantucket from early June to mid-September (there is no car-ferry service between the islands). The trip time is 2 hours and 15 minutes. The one-way fare is $14 for adults, $7 for children 5 to 12, and $5 extra for bikes.

From Harwich Port   You can avoid the summer crowds in Hyannis by boarding a passenger-only ferry with **Freedom Cruise Line,** 702 Rte. 28 in Harwich Port, across from Brax Landing (© **508/432-8999;** www.nantucketisland ferry.com). From mid-May to mid-October, boats leave from Saquatucket Harbor in Harwich Port; the trip takes 1½ hours. Round-trip tickets are $46 for adults, $37 for children ages 2 to 11, $6 for children under 2, and $10 extra for bikes. Parking is free if you pick up your car the same day, but it's $12 for each night thereafter. Reservations are highly recommended.

BY PLANE   You can fly into **Nantucket Memorial Airport** (© **508/325-5300**), which is about 3 miles south of Nantucket Road on Old South Road. The flight to Nantucket takes 30 to 40 minutes from Boston, 15 minutes from Hyannis, and a little more than an hour from New York City airports.

Airlines providing service to Nantucket include: **Business Express/Delta Connection** (© **800/221-1212**) year-round from Boston and seasonally from New York; **Cape Air/Nantucket Airlines** (© **800/352-0714**) year-round from Hyannis ($79 round-trip), Boston (about $249 round-trip), Martha's Vineyard ($76 round-trip), and New Bedford ($139 round-trip); **Continental Express** (© **800/525-0280**) from Newark, seasonally (about $723 round-trip); **Island Airlines** (© **508/228-7575**) year-round from Hyannis ($79 round-trip); and **Colgan/US Airways Express** (© **800/428-4322**) year-round from Boston ($316) and New York ($535 and up round-trip).

Island Airlines and Nantucket Airlines both offer year-round charter service to the island.

GETTING AROUND

Nantucket is easily navigated on bike, moped, or foot, and also by shuttle bus or taxi. The chamber of commerce strongly suggests that visitors leave their cars behind in order to minimize congestion and environmental impact. If you're staying outside of Nantucket Town, however, or if you plan to explore the outer reaches of the island, you might want to bring your car or rent one here. Keep in mind that if you do opt to travel by car, in-town traffic can reach gridlock in the peak season, and parking can be a nightmare.

BY BICYCLE & MOPED   Biking is a great way to get around Nantucket. The island is relatively flat, and paved bike paths abound—they'll get you from Nantucket Town to Siasconset, Surfside, and Madaket. There are also many unpaved back roads to explore, which make mountain bikes a wise choice. Mopeds are also available, but be aware that local rules and regulations are strictly enforced. Mopeds are not allowed on sidewalks or bike paths. You'll need a driver's license to rent a moped, and state law requires that you wear a helmet.

You can bring your own bike over on the ferries for an additional charge. Otherwise, shops that rent bikes and mopeds (all within walking distance of the ferries) include: **Cook's Cycle Shop, Inc.,** 6 S. Beach St. (© **508/228-0800**); **Nantucket Bike Shops,** at Steamboat Wharf and Straight Wharf (© **508/228-1999**); and **Young's Bicycle Shop,** at Steamboat Wharf (© **508/228-1151**), which also does repairs. Bike rentals average $20 to $25 for 24 hours.

BY SHUTTLE BUS   From June through September, inexpensive shuttle buses, with bike racks and wheelchair lifts, make a loop through Nantucket Town and to outlying spots; for routes and stops, contact the **Nantucket Regional Transit Authority** (© **508/228-7025;** www.nantucket.net/trans/nrta) or pick up a schedule at the visitor center on Federal Street or the chamber of commerce office on Main Street. The cost is $1 to $2, and exact change is required. A 3-day pass can be purchased at the visitor center for $10. Dogs are allowed on the bus as long as they are relatively clean and dry.

BY CAR & JEEP   We recommend a car if you'll be here for more than a week or if you're staying outside Nantucket Town. Remember, though, there are no in-town parking lots; parking, although free, is limited.

Rental agencies on the island include: **Affordable Rentals of Nantucket,** 6 S. Beach Rd. (© **508/228-3501**); **Budget,** at the airport (© **800/527-0700** or 508/228-5666); **Hertz,** at the airport (© **800/654-3131** or 508/228-9421); **Nantucket Windmill Auto Rental,** at the airport (© **800/228-1227** or 508/228-1227); and **Young's 4 X 4 & Car Rental,** Steamboat Wharf (© **508/228-1151**). A standard car costs about $100 per day in season; a four-wheel-drive rental costs about $185 per day (including an Over-Sand Permit).

BY TAXI   You'll find taxis (many are vans that can accommodate large groups or those traveling with bikes) waiting at the airport and at all ferry ports. During the busy summer months, we recommend reserving a taxi in advance to avoid a long wait upon arrival. Rates are flat fees, based on one person riding before 1am, with surcharges for additional passengers, bikes, and dogs. A taxi from the airport to Nantucket Town hotels will cost about $10. Reliable cab companies include **A-1 Taxi** (© **508/228-3330**), **All Point Taxi** (© **508/228-5779**), **Bev's Taxi** (© **508/228-7874**), **Lisa's Taxi** (© **508/228-2223**), and **Val's Cab Service** (© **508/228-9410**).

VISITOR INFORMATION

For information contact the **Nantucket Island Chamber of Commerce** at 48 Main St., Nantucket, MA 02554 (© **508/228-1700;** www.nantucketchamber. org). When you arrive, you should also stop by the **Nantucket Visitors Service and Information Bureau,** 25 Federal St. (© **508/228-0925**). It's open daily from June to September; and Monday to Saturday from October to May. There are also information booths at Steamboat Wharf and Straight Wharf. Always check the island's newspaper, the *Inquirer & Mirror* (known locally as "The Inky"), for information on events and activities around town.

Nantucket Accommodations, P.O. Box 217, Nantucket, MA 02554 (© **508/228-9559;** fax 508/325-7009; www.nantucketaccommodation.com), a 30-year-old private service, arranges advance reservations for inns, cottages, guesthouses, bed-and-breakfasts, and hotels; it has access to 95% of the island's lodging, in addition to houses and cottages available by the night or week (as opposed to most realtors, who will only handle rentals for 2 weeks or more). The charge for the service is $15, assessed only when a reservation is made. Last-minute travelers should keep in mind the **Nantucket Visitors Service and Information Bureau** (© **508/228-0925**), a daily referral service for available rooms. It's not a booking service, but it always has the most updated list of accommodations availability and cancellations.

ATMs can be difficult to locate on Nantucket. **Nantucket Bank** (© **508/228-0580**) has five locations: 2 Orange St., 104 Pleasant St., Amelia Street, the Hub on Main Street, and the airport lobby, all open 24 hours. **Pacific National Bank** has four locations: A&P Supermarket (next to the wharves), the Stop & Shop (open 24 hr. seasonally), the Steamship Wharf Terminal, and Pacific National Bank lobby (open during bank hours only).

In case of a **medical emergency,** the **Nantucket Cottage Hospital,** 57 Prospect St. (© **508/228-1200**), is open 24 hours.

BEACHES & OUTDOOR PURSUITS

BEACHES   In distinct contrast to Martha's Vineyard, virtually all of Nantucket's 110-mile coastline is open to the public.

- **Children's Beach:** This small beach is a protected cove just west of busy Steamship Wharf. Appealing to families, it has a park, a playground, restrooms, lifeguards, a snack bar, and even a bandstand for free weekend concerts.

- **Cisco Beach** ★★: About 4 miles from town, in the southwestern quadrant of the island (from Main St., turn onto Milk St., which becomes Hummock Pond Rd.), Cisco enjoys vigorous waves—great for the surfers who flock here, not so great for the waterfront homeowners. Restrooms and lifeguards are available.

- **Coatue Beach** ★: This fishhook-shaped barrier beach, on the northeastern side of the island at Wauwinet, is Nantucket's outback, accessible only by four-wheel-drive vehicles, watercraft, or the very strong-legged. Swimming is strongly discouraged because of fierce tides.

- **Dionis Beach** ★★★: About 3 miles out of town (take the Madaket bike path to Eel Point Rd.) is Dionis, which enjoys the gentle Nantucket Sound surf and steep, picturesque bluffs. It's a great spot for swimming, picnicking, and shelling, and you'll find fewer children than at Jetties or Children's beaches. Stick to the established paths to prevent further erosion. Lifeguards patrol here, and restrooms are available.

- **Jetties Beach** ★★★: Located about a half mile west of Children's Beach on North Beach Street, Jetties is about a 20-minute walk, or an even shorter bike ride, shuttle bus ride, or drive, from town (there's a large parking lot, but it fills up early on summer weekends). It's another family favorite for its mild waves, lifeguards, bathhouse, and restrooms. Facilities include the town tennis courts, volleyball nets, a skate park, and a playground; watersports equipment and chairs are also available to rent. In August, Jetties hosts an intense sand-castle competition, and the Fourth of July fireworks are held here.

- **Madaket Beach** ★★★: Accessible by Madaket Road, the 6-mile bike path that runs parallel to it, and by shuttle bus, this westerly beach is narrow and subject to pounding surf and sometimes serious crosscurrents. Unless it's a fairly tame day, you might content yourself with wading. It's the best spot on the island for admiring the sunset. Facilities include restrooms, lifeguards, and mobile food service.

- **Siasconset ('Sconset) Beach** ★★: The easterly coast of 'Sconset is as pretty as the town itself and rarely, if ever, crowded, perhaps because of the water's strong sideways tow. You can reach it by car, by shuttle bus, or via the Polpis or Milestone bike paths, about an 8-mile trip. Lifeguards are usually on duty, but the closest facilities (restrooms, grocery store, and cafe) are back in the center of the village.

- **Surfside Beach** ★★★: Three miles south of town via a popular bike/skate path, broad Surfside—equipped with lifeguards, restrooms, and a surprisingly accomplished little snack bar—is appropriately named and very popular. It draws thousands of visitors a day in high season, from college students to families, but the free-parking lot can only fit about 60 cars—you do the math, or better yet, ride your bike or take the shuttle bus.

BICYCLING ★★★   Several paved bike paths radiate out from the center of town to outlying beaches. The **bike paths** run about 6 miles west to Madaket, 3½ miles south to Surfside, and 8 miles east to 'Sconset. To avoid backtracking from 'Sconset, continue north through the charming village, and return on the **Polpis Road bike path** ★★. Strong riders could do a whole circuit of the island in a day, but most will be content to combine a single route with a few hours at a beach.

For a free map of the island's bike paths, stop by **Young's Bicycle Shop,** at Steamboat Wharf (© **508/228-1151**). It's definitely the best place for bike rentals. See "Getting Around," above, for more bike-rental shops.

FISHING   For shellfishing, you'll need a permit from the **harbormaster's office** at 34 Washington St. (© **508/228-7261**). You'll see surf-casters all over the island (no permit is required); for a guided trip, try Mike Monte of **Surf & Fly Fishing Trips** (© **508/228-0529**). Deep-sea charters heading out of Straight Wharf include Capt. Bob DeCosta's *The Albacore* (© **508/228-5074**), Capt. Josh Eldridge's *Monomoy* (© **508/228-6867**), and Capt. David Martin's *Flicka* (© **508/325-4000**).

NATURE TRAILS   Through preservationist foresight, about one-third of Nantucket's shoreline is protected from development. Contact the **Nantucket Conservation Foundation** at 118 Cliff Rd. (© **508/228-2884**) for a map of its holdings ($4), which include the 205-acre **Windswept Cranberry Bog** (off Polpis Rd.), where bogs are interspersed amid hardwood forests; and a portion of the 1,100-acre **Coskata–Coatue Wildlife Refuge** ★★, comprising the barrier beaches beyond Wauwinet (see "Organized Tours," below). The **Maria Mitchell Association** (see "Museums & Historic Landmarks," below) sponsors guided birding and wildflower walks in season.

WATERSPORTS   **Nantucket Community Sailing** manages the concession at **Jetties Beach** (© **508/228-5358**), which offers lessons and rents out kayaks, sailboards, sailboats, and more. **Sea Nantucket,** on tiny Francis Street Beach off Washington Street (© **508/228-7499**), also rents kayaks; it's a quick sprint across the harbor to beautiful Coatue.

MUSEUMS & HISTORIC LANDMARKS

Hadwen House ★★   During Nantucket's most prosperous years, whaling merchant Joseph Starbuck built the "Three Bricks" (nos. 93, 95, and 97 Main St.) for his three sons. His daughter married successful businessman William Hadwen, owner of the candle factory that is now the Whaling Museum, and Hadwen built this grand Greek Revival home across the street from his brothers-in-law in 1845. Although locals (mostly Quakers) were scandalized by the opulence, the local outrage spurred Hadwen on, and he decided to make the home even grander than he had originally intended. It soon became a showplace for entertaining the Hadwens' many wealthy friends. The home has been furnished with period pieces, and the gardens have been maintained in period style.

96 Main St. (at Pleasant St., a few blocks SW of the town center). © **508/228-1894**. www.nha.org. Admission included in Nantucket Historical Association's History Ticket ($15 adults, $8 children under 16, $35 family). AE, MC, V. June–Sept Mon–Sat 10am–5pm, Sun noon–5pm. Call for off-season hours. Closed Dec–Mar.

Jethro Coffin House ★   This 1686 saltbox is the oldest building left on the island. A National Historical Landmark, the brick design on its central chimney has earned it the nickname "The Horseshoe House." It was struck by lightning and severely damaged (in fact, nearly cut in two) in 1987, prompting a long-overdue restoration. It's filled with period furniture such as a trundle bed on wooden wheels.

Sunset Hill Rd. (off W. Chester Rd., about ½ mile NW of the town center). © **508/228-1894**. www.nha.org. Admission included in Nantucket Historical Association's History Ticket ($15 adults, $8 children, $35 families). AE, MC, V. Late May to mid-Oct Mon–Sat 10am–5pm, Sun noon–5pm. Closed mid-Oct to late May.

The Maria Mitchell Association ★★ *Kids*   This is a group of six buildings organized and maintained in honor of distinguished astronomer and Nantucket

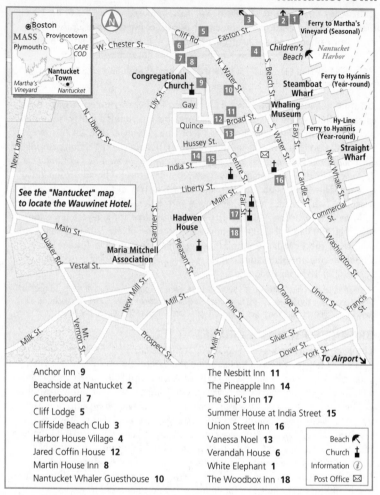

Anchor Inn **9**	The Nesbitt Inn **11**
Beachside at Nantucket **2**	The Pineapple Inn **14**
Centerboard **7**	The Ship's Inn **17**
Cliff Lodge **5**	Summer House at India Street **15**
Cliffside Beach Club **3**	Union Street Inn **16**
Harbor House Village **4**	Vanessa Noel **13**
Jared Coffin House **12**	Verandah House **6**
Martin House Inn **8**	White Elephant **1**
Nantucket Whaler Guesthouse **10**	The Woodbox Inn **18**

Beach
Church
Information
Post Office

native Maria Mitchell (1818–1889). The science center consists of astronomical observatories, with a lecture series, children's science seminars, and stellar observation opportunities (when the sky is clear) from the **Loines Observatory** at 59 Milk St. Extension (✆ **508/228-8690**) and the **Vestal Street Observatory** at 3 Vestal St. (✆ **508/228-9273**).

The **Hinchman House Natural Science Museum** (✆ **508/228-0898**) at 7 Milk St. houses a visitor center and offers lectures, bird-watching, wildflower and nature walks, and discovery classes for children and adults. The **Mitchell House** (✆ **508/228-2896**) at 1 Vestal St., the astronomer's birthplace, features a children's history series and adult-artisan seminars, and has wildflower and herb gardens. The **Science Library** (✆ **508/228-9219**) is at 2 Vestal St., and the tiny, child-oriented **aquarium** (✆ **508/228-5387**) is at 28 Washington St.

4 Vestal St. (at Milk St., about ½ mile SW of the town center). ✆ 508/228-9198. www.mmo.org. Admission to each site: $4 adults, $3 children. Museum pass (for birthplace, aquarium, science museum, and Vestal Street Observatory) $10 adults, $7 children ages 6–14. MC, V. Early June to late Aug Tues–Sat 10am–4pm; call for off-season hours.

Nantucket Life-Saving Museum ★★ *Finds* Housed in a replica of the Nantucket Life-Saving Station, the museum has loads of interesting exhibits, including historic photos and newspaper clippings, as well as one of the last remaining Massachusetts Humane Society surf boats and its horse-drawn carriage.

158 Polpis Rd. (2½ miles E of town) ℂ **508/228-1885**. Admission $5 adults, $2 children. Mid-June to mid-Oct daily 9:30am–4pm.

Whaling Museum ★★★ *Kids* Housed in a former spermaceti (a waxy fluid extracted from sperm whales) candle factory, this museum is a must-visit, if not for the awe-inspiring skeleton of a 43-foot finback whale, then for the exceptional collections of scrimshaw and nautical art. (Check out the action painting, *Ship Spermo of Nantucket in a Heavy Thunder-Squall on the Coast of California 1876*, executed by a captain who survived the storm.) The admission price includes daily lectures on the brief and colorful history of the industry, like the beachside "whalebecue" feasts that natives and settlers once enjoyed.

Note: The Whaling Museum is scheduled to close for a 1-year renovation from fall 2003 to fall 2004. Visitors can see some of the Whaling Museum exhibits at the Friends Meeting House at 7 Fair St., an 1838 former Quaker school, during the renovations. Call the Nantucket Historical Association at ℂ 508/228-1894 for updates.

13 Broad St. (in the center of town). ℂ **508/228-1894**. www.nha.org. Admission $10 adults, $6 children 5–14. Admission is also included in the Nantucket Historical Association's History Ticket ($15 adults, $8 children, $35 families). AE, MC, V. Apr–Nov Mon–Sat 10am–5pm, Sun noon–5pm. Closed Dec–Mar.

ORGANIZED TOURS & CRUISES

The 1926 *Christina* ★★, at Slip 1016, Straight Wharf (ℂ **508/325-4000**), is a classic mahogany catboat. A sail around the harbor is probably the best entertainment bargain on Nantucket ($25 for a 1½-hr. trip). The sunset trips ($35) tend to sell out a day or two in advance. No sailings November through April.

The Trustees of the Reservations, a statewide conservation organization, runs the 3-hour **Coskata–Coatue Wildlife Refuge Natural History Tour** ★★★ (ℂ **508/228-6799**). The trip via Ford Expedition takes you over sand dunes and through rare habitat out to the **Great Point Lighthouse,** a replica of the 1818 original. On the way, you might spot snowy egrets, ospreys, and terns. Tours are offered mid-May to mid-October, daily at 9:30am and 1:30pm. The cost is $30 for adults and $15 for children 15 and under; call to reserve.

Endeavor **Sailing Excursions** ★★, at Slip 15 on Straight Wharf (ℂ **508/228-5585**), offers jaunts around the harbor on the *Endeavor,* a 31-foot replica of a historic Friendship sloop. Skipper James Genthner will gladly drop you off at one the beaches for a bit of sunbathing or beachcombing. Rates are $25 to $35 for a 1½-hour sail; reservations are recommended. No sailings November through April.

SHOPPING

All of the shops listed below are located right in the center of Nantucket Town.

ANTIQUES/COLLECTIBLES **Tonkin of Nantucket,** 33 Main St. (ℂ **508/228-9697**), specializes in English and French antiques. Its offerings include silver, china, ship models, and majolica.

ART & CRAFTS **The Artists' Association of Nantucket** has the widest selection of work by locals, and the gallery at 19 Washington St. (ℂ **508/228-0294**) is impressive. It's open April through January and by appointment only February and March.

Exquisite art glass, as well as ceramics, jewelry, and basketry, can be found at **Dane Gallery,** 28 Centre St. (*©* 508/228-7779).

Sailor's Valentine in the Macy Warehouse on lower Main Street (*©* **508/ 228-2011**) houses a collection of contemporary fine art, folk art, and "outsider art." There are also new versions of the namesake craft, a boxed design of colorful shells, which 19th-century sailors used to bring back from the Caribbean for their sweethearts at home.

FASHION   Martha's Vineyard may have spawned "Black Dog" fever, but this island boasts the inimitable "Nantucket reds"—cotton clothing that starts out tomato-red and washes out to salmon-pink. The fashion originated at **Murray's Toggery Shop,** 62 Main St. (*©* **800/368-2134** or 508/228-0437).

WHERE TO STAY

As with Martha's Vineyard, we've given only summer rates here, because Nantucket is so seasonal. However, if you do visit in the off season, you can find substantial discounts at any of the places that remain open. Note, though, that lodging rates on Nantucket are at high-season levels during the popular Christmas Stroll in December and Daffodil Festival in April.

VERY EXPENSIVE

Cliffside Beach Club ★★★ *Finds*   Right on the beach and a 15-minute walk from town, this is surely the premier lodging on the island. It may not be as fancy as some, but there's a sublime beachy-ness to the whole setup, from the simply decorated rooms and the cheerful, youthful staff to the colorful umbrellas lined up on the beach. All guest rooms have such luxuries as French milled soaps, thick towels, and exceptional linens. Lucky guests on the Fourth of July get a front-row seat for the fireworks staged at Jetties Beach nearby.

46 Jefferson Ave. (about 1 mile from town center), Nantucket, MA 02554. *©* **800/932-9645** or 508/228-0618. Fax 508/325-4735. www.cliffsidebeach.com. 25 units, 1 cottage. Summer $380–$605 double; $695–$1,385 suite; $705 apt; $895 cottage. Rates include continental breakfast. AE. Closed mid-Oct to late May. **Amenities:** Restaurant (The Galley, an elegant French bistro); exercise facility (Cybex equipment and a trainer on staff); indoor hydrotherapy spa; steam saunas; concierge; climate-controlled massage room; babysitting. *In room:* A/C, TV/VCR, fridge, coffeemaker, hair dryer.

Nantucket Whaler Guesthouse ★★   This lodging option, an 1850s sea captain's house, is unique in that all of the rooms are suites with their own entrance and kitchen facilities. Compared to other B&Bs on the island, this one has a particularly private feel, almost like having your own apartment. The entire building has been recently restored and all rooms are comfortably outfitted with cottage-y furnishings including overstuffed couches and stacks of games and books.

8 North Water St. (in the center of town), Nantucket, MA 02554. *©* **800/462-6882** or 508/228-6597. Fax 508/228-6291. www.nantucketwhaler.com. 12 units (8 tub/shower; 4 shower only). Summer $300–$400 double; $575 2-bedroom suite. AE, DC, MC, V. Closed mid-Dec to mid-Mar. No children under age 12. *In room:* A/C, TV/VCR, CD player, dataport, hair dryer, iron.

Vanessa Noel ★   This is Nantucket's trendiest inn. Vanessa Noel, a shoe designer whose shoe store is on the first floor, has decorated the eight rooms in this historic building with boutique hotel features like Philippe Starck fixtures, Bulgari toiletries, 15-inch flat screen plasma televisions, and minibars stocked with the hotel's bottled water. Most of the rooms are tiny, though there are two including a fun attic space that are fairly spacious. **The Vanno Bar,** a caviar and champagne bar on the first floor, has novelties like leopard-print calfskin banquettes, two swings, and food imported from Caviarteria, the New York City caviar emporium.

5 Chestnut St. (in the center of town), Nantucket, MA 02554. © **508/228-5300.** Fax 508/228-8995. www.
VANNO.com. 8 units. Summer $340–$480 double. AE, DISC, MC, V. Open year-round. *In room:* AC, TV, minibar, hair dryer.

The Wauwinet 👀👀👀   This ultra-deluxe beachfront retreat is Nantucket's
only Relais & Châteaux property. The inn is next to a wildlife sanctuary and is
nestled between the Atlantic Ocean and Nantucket Bay. Each lovely room has a
unique decor, with pine armoires, plenty of wicker, exquisite Audubon prints,
and handsome fabrics. Extras include robes, bottled water, and a personalized set
of engraved note cards. If you order up a video from the extensive library, it is
delivered on a tray with a couple of boxes of complimentary hot popcorn. The
staff goes to great lengths to please, ferrying you into town, for instance, in a
1946 "Woody," or dispatching you on a 21-foot launch across the bay to your
own private strip of beach in season.

120 Wauwinet Rd. (P.O. Box 2580), about 8 miles E of Nantucket center, Nantucket, MA 02554. © **800/426-
8718** or 508/228-0145. Fax 508/325-0657. www.wauwinet.com. 25 units. 10 cottages (all with tub/shower).
Summer $450–$800 double; $800–$1,500 cottage. Rates include full breakfast and afternoon wine and
cheese. AE, DC, MC, V. Closed Nov to mid-May. **Amenities:** Restaurant (fine dining); 2 clay tennis courts with
pro shop and teaching pro; croquet lawn; row boats, sail boats, sea kayaks, and mountain bikes on loan;
concierge; room service (8am–9pm). *In room:* A/C, TV/VCR, CD player, hair dryer, iron.

White Elephant 👀👀👀   This luxury property, right on the harbor, is the ultimate in-town lodging and has been newly renovated by the owners of The
Wauwinet (see above). Guest rooms (distributed among one building and 12
cottages) are big and airy (the most spacious rooms on Nantucket), with coun-
try-chic decor. In-room amenities include DVD players. About half the rooms
have working fireplaces, and most have harbor views. The same company owns
Breakers, a 25-room hotel next door that offers a less bustling atmosphere.

50 Easton St. (P.O. Box 1139), Nantucket, MA 02554. © **800/445-6574** or 508/228-2500. Fax 508/325-1195.
www.whiteelephanthotel.com. 52 units, 11 cottages (61 tub/shower, 2 shower only). Summer $350–$630
double; $440–$1,400 cottage. Rates include full breakfast. AE, DC, DISC, MC, V. Closed Nov–Mar. **Amenities:**
Restaurant (lobster and steakhouse serving lunch and dinner daily plus an afternoon raw bar); exercise room;
concierge; business lounge; full room service; fee-based laundry and dry-cleaning service. *In room:* A/C,
TV/VCR, dataport, fridge, hair dryer, iron, safe.

EXPENSIVE

Beachside at Nantucket 👀   No ordinary motel, the Beachside's 90 guest
rooms have been lavished with Provençal prints and handsome rattan and wicker
furniture; the patios and decks overlooking the central courtyard with its heated
pool have been prettified with French doors and latticework.

30 N. Beach St. (about ¾ mile W of the town center), Nantucket, MA 02554. © **800/322-4433** or 508/228-
2241. Fax 508/228-8901. www.thebeachside.com. 90 units (all with tub/shower). Summer $245–$290
double; $535 suite. Rates include continental breakfast. AE, DC, DISC, MC, V. Closed late Oct to late Apr.
Amenities: Heated outdoor pool. *In room:* A/C, TV, fridge, hair dryer.

Centerboard 👀👀   This updated 1886 home boasts parquet floors, Oriental
rugs, lavish fabrics, plush feather mattresses, and lace-trimmed linens. Of the
inn's seven bedrooms, the first-floor suite is perhaps the most romantic, with a
green-marble Jacuzzi and a private living room with fireplace. Other rooms and
bathrooms are small, but all have bathrobes and mini-fridges.

8 Chester St. (in the center of town), Nantucket, MA 02554. © **508/228-9696.** Fax 508/325-4798. www.
centerboard.com. 7 units. Summer $225–$235 double; $325–$425 suite. Rates include continental breakfast.
AE, MC, V. Closed Nov–April. *In room:* A/C, TV, fridge, hair dryer.

Harbor House Village 👀👀 *Kids*   This property, which recently underwent a
multimillion-dollar freshening-up, is now one of Nantucket's most full-service

lodging options, complete with pool and two restaurants. It is located just a 5-minute walk from the center of Nantucket Town. The main building, the 35-room historic Harbor House, was originally built 130 years ago, but there are few vestiges from the days of yore. The rooms are decorated with pine and wicker furniture, and some are quite spacious and have balconies.

South Beach St., Nantucket, MA 02554. © **866/325-9300** or 508/228-1500. Fax 508/228-7639. www. harborhousevillage.com. 104 units. Summer $370–$410 double. AE, DC, DISC, MC, V. Closed early Dec to mid-Apr. **Amenities:** 2 restaurants (a seasonal Chinese restaurant and a breakfast café); bar/lounge (featuring Mon Night Football on the large screen TV in the fall); outdoor heated pool (in season); free children's program in summer; concierge; free shuttle from Steamship Authority ferry; babysitting; laundry service; dry cleaning. *In room:* A/C, TV, dataport, hair dryer, iron, VCR or fridge available on request.

Jared Coffin House ★★ *Kids*   This grand brick manse built in 1845 is the social center of town. Accommodations range from well-priced singles to spacious doubles. The central location does have a drawback: front rooms can be quite noisy and 20-minute breakfasts are not unusual because locals come, too. It's the best breakfast in town, though it is not included in the room rate; we suggest calling ahead and putting your name on the list.

29 Broad St. (at Centre St.), Nantucket, MA 02554. © **800/248-2405** or 508/228-2400. Fax 508/228-8549. www.jaredcoffinhouse.com. 60 units (52 tub/shower; 8 shower only). Summer $290–$375 double. AE, DC, DISC, MC, V. Open year-round. **Amenities:** 2 restaurants (family and tavern); concierge. *In room:* TV, dataport, fridge, coffeemaker, hair dryer, iron.

The Pineapple Inn ★★   This beautifully renovated historic inn has quickly become one of the premier places to stay on the island. The graceful Quaker entrance of the 1838 home leads to spacious guest rooms decorated with fine reproductions and antiques, Oriental rugs, marble bathrooms, and many four-poster canopy beds. Breakfast here is extra deluxe with fresh baked goods, espresso, cappuccino, and freshly squeezed orange juice.

10 Hussey St. (in the center of town), Nantucket, MA 02554. © **508/228-9992**. Fax 508/325-6051. www. pineappleinn.com. 12 units (8 tub/shower; 4 shower only). Summer $195–$325 double. Rates include continental breakfast. AE, MC, V. Closed early Dec to mid-Apr. No children under age 8. *In room:* A/C, TV, dataport, hair dryer, iron.

Summer House at India Street ★   The Summer House management now owns three properties: the very expensive cottages overlooking the beach in Siasconset, an inn on Fair Street, and this property on India Street. The India Street property is the most centrally located and is a handsome historic house, fully renovated with all new furnishings and top-notch amenities. Rooms are equipped with robes and deluxe toiletries. Guests have access to complimentary jitney service to the Summer House beachfront property in 'Sconset and use of the pool there.

31 India St. (in the center of town), Nantucket, MA 02554. © **508/257-4577**. Fax 508/257-4590. www. thesummerhouse.com. 10 units. Summer $200–$250 double. Rates include continental breakfast. AE, MC, V. Closed Jan–Apr. *In room:* A/C, TV, hair dryer.

Union Street Inn ★★ *Finds*   Innkeepers Deborah and Ken Withrow have a terrific location for their 1770s property, just steps from Main Street yet in a quiet, residential section. Ken's experience in big hotels shows in the full concierge service offered here. Many guest rooms have canopied or four-poster beds; half have working wood-burning fireplaces. All are outfitted with antique furniture and fixtures. Unlike many Nantucket inns that are forbidden by zoning laws to serve a full breakfast, this inn's location allows a superb complete breakfast on the garden patio.

7 Union St. (in the center of town), Nantucket, MA 02554. ℂ 800/225-5116 or 508/228-9222. Fax 508/325-0848. www.unioninn.com. 12 units (1 with tub/shower; 11 shower only). Summer $195–$365 double; $395 suite. Rates include full breakfast. AE, MC, V. Closed Jan–Mar. *In room:* A/C, TV, CD player, hair dryer, no phone.

MODERATE

Anchor Inn ⭐ *Value*   This historic gem, an 1806 captain's home, is located next to the Old North Church. This year they have added a new property, 72 Centre St., three doors down, to the inn. Authentic details can be found throughout both houses, in the antique hardware and paneling, wide-board floors, and period furnishings. The five rooms in the 72 Centre St. house are a particularly good value; they are smaller and less expensive.

66 Centre St. (P.O. Box 387, in the center of town), Nantucket, MA 02554. ℂ 508/228-0072. www.anchorinn.net. 16 units (2 tub/shower, 9 shower only). Summer $185–$225 double. Rates include continental breakfast. AE, MC, V. Closed Jan–Feb. *In room:* A/C, TV, hair dryer.

Cliff Lodge ⭐⭐ *Finds*   Debby and John Bennett have freshened up this charming 1771 whaling captain's house with their own countrified style. The cheerful guest rooms feature colorful quilts and splatter-painted floors. Rooms range from a first-floor beauty with king-size bed, paneled walls, and fireplace to the tiny third-floor rooms tucked into the eaves. The spacious apartment in the rear of the house is a sunny delight. Climb up to the widow's walk for a bird's-eye view of the town and harbor.

9 Cliff Rd. (a few blocks from the center of town), Nantucket, MA 02554. ℂ 508/228-9480. Fax 508/228-6308. www.nantucket.net/lodging/clifflodge. 12 units. Summer $135 single; $170–$265 double; $425 apt. Rates include continental breakfast. MC, V. Open year-round. No children under 12. *In room:* A/C, TV.

Martin House Inn ⭐⭐ *Value*   This is one of the lower-priced B&Bs in town, but also one of the most stylish, with a formal parlor and a spacious side porch, complete with hammock. Some guest rooms in this historic 1803 mariner's home have four-poster beds and working fireplaces. The four garret single rooms with a shared bathroom are a bargain.

61 Centre St. (between Broad and Chester sts.; a couple blocks from town center), Nantucket, MA 02554. ℂ 508/228-0678. Fax 508/325-4798. www.nantucket.net/lodging/martinn. 13 units (4 tub/shower, 5 shower only; 4 with shared bathroom). Summer $95 single; $175–$245 double; $260–$320 suites. Rates include continental breakfast. AE, MC, V. Open year-round. *In room:* No phone.

The Ship's Inn ⭐ *Value*   This pretty, historic inn is on a quiet side street, just slightly removed—3 blocks—from Nantucket's center. Rooms are comfortable, spacious, and charming, and offer a good variety of bed arrangements like single rooms and twin beds. The restaurant downstairs holds its own (see "Where to Dine," below).

13 Fair St. (a few blocks from town center), Nantucket, MA 02554. ℂ 888/872-4052 or 508/228-0040. Fax 508/228-6524. www.nantucket.net/lodging/shipsinn. 12 units, 2 with shared bathroom. Summer $110 single with shared bathroom; $235 double. Rates include continental breakfast. AE, DISC, MC, V. Closed late Oct to mid-May. **Amenities:** Restaurant (fine dining) located in the basement. *In room:* A/C, TV, fridge, hair dryer, iron.

The Veranda House ⭐⭐ *Finds*   This newly reopened classic guesthouse, formerly known as the Overlook Hotel, has been in the same family for generations. The inn is located in a quiet neighborhood, a short walk from the center of town. Wraparound porches surround the inn and serve as the communal area for enjoying the sunshine or meeting fellow guests. Inn rooms are on the small side but smartly decorated with antique photos. Beds are made with Frette linens and goosedown comforters. On the top floor, there are seven rooms that share bathrooms. Breakfast, which features hot delicacies like quiches and frittatas, is served on the ample front porch. The entire inn property is covered by a wireless Internet service.

Three Step Lane (a few blocks from town center), Nantucket, MA 02554. © 508/228-0695. Fax 508/374-0406. www.theverandahouse.com. 20 units, 7 with shared bathroom. Summer $155 double with shared bathroom; $195–$250 double; $320–$350 2-bedroom suite. Rates include continental breakfast. AE, MC, V. Closed mid-Oct to late May. *In room:* A/C, hair dryer.

The Woodbox Inn ★ *Value*   Built in 1709, this is Nantucket's oldest inn and it's an atmospheric place. Located in a residential section of the historic district, the inn is a short walk to Main Street. The well-known restaurant on site serves breakfast and dinner and is famous for popovers. The rooms, decorated with period antiques and reproductions, and canopy beds, range from cozy to spacious. Some have refrigerators and phones. There are also one- and two-bedroom suites with working fireplaces. **The Woodbox** is a popular spot for breakfast, but the meal is not included in the room rates.

29 Fair St. (a few blocks from town center) Nantucket, MA 02554. © **508/228-0587.** Fax 508/228-7527. www.woodbox.com. 9 units. Summer $180–$210 double; $210 1-room suite; $310 2-room suite. (Unusual in the area, a 10% "service" fee is added to your bill here, in addition to tax.) No credit cards. Closed early Jan to late Mar. **Amenities:** Fine-dining restaurant serving breakfast and dinner. *In room:* Fridge.

INEXPENSIVE

The Nesbitt Inn *Value*   This Victorian-style inn in the center of town has been run by the same family for 95 years. It's quite old-fashioned and a bargain for Nantucket. All rooms have sinks and share bathrooms. There's a friendly, family atmosphere to the inn, and beloved innkeepers Dolly and Nobby Noblit are salt-of-the-earth Nantucketers.

21 Broad St., P.O. Box 1019, Nantucket, MA 02554. © **508/228-0156** or 508/228-2446. 15 units (13 with shared bathroom). Summer $75 single; $85–$125 double; $1,200 weekly apt. Rates include continental breakfast. MC, V. Closed mid-Dec to Mar. *In room:* No phone.

WHERE TO DINE
VERY EXPENSIVE

Brant Point Grill ★★ NEW AMERICAN   At this lobster, steak, and chops house, many of the signature dishes, like the cedar planked Atlantic salmon and rotisserie of prime rib, are prepared on the Fire Cone grill, a 21st-century interpretation of a Native American technique that cooks food by radiant heat and imparts it with a smoky mesquite flavor. If you can't sit on the terrace, try to snag a seat near one of the windows where you can watch the twilight fade over the harbor. Dinner at this establishment is an expensive proposition. However, the raw bar is open July through Labor Day from 4 to 7pm for light snacks.

At the White Elephant Hotel (Easton and Willard sts.). © 508/325-1320. Collared shirt and long pants requested for gentlemen. Reservations strongly recommended. Main courses $23–$39. AE, DISC, MC, V. Mid-Apr to early Dec daily noon–2:30pm and 6–10pm. Closed Nov–Mar.

Chanticleer Inn ★★★ FRENCH   A contender for the priciest restaurant on the Cape and Islands, this rose-covered cottage-turned-restaurant has fans who insist they'd have to cross an ocean to savor the likes of the classic cuisine. A few glamorous options on the fixed-price menu include a frogs' legs "cake" in a potato crust; a gingered monkfish scaloppini with a lemon-rum sauce and sweet garlic fritters; and a very classy bread pudding with white-chocolate ice cream and apricot sauce. The restaurant's stellar wine cellar is stocked with 38,000 bottles. Unfortunately, this kind of luxury comes with *beaucoup d'attitude*, so whether you are royalty or hoi polloi, prepare to be snubbed.

9 New St., Siasconset. ✆ **508/257-6231** or 508/257-9756. Reservations recommended. Jacket preferred for men. Main courses $42–$45. AE, DC, MC, V. Mid-May to mid-Oct Wed–Sun noon–2:30pm and 6:30–9:30pm. Closed mid-Oct to mid-May.

Club Car ⭐⭐⭐ CONTINENTAL   For decades one of the top restaurants on Nantucket, this posh venue is popular with locals. The menu has classic French influences. Interesting offerings include a first course of Japanese octopus in the style of Bangkok and an entree of roast rack of lamb Club Car (with fresh herbs, honey-mustard glaze, and minted Madeira sauce). Some nights, seven-course tasting menus are available for $65 per person. The lounge area is within an antique car from the old Nantucket railroad.

1 Main St. ✆ **508/228-1101.** Reservations recommended. Main courses $32–$38. MC, V. July–Aug daily 11am–3pm and 6–10pm; call for off-season hours. Closed Jan–Apr.

The Galley on Cliffside Beach ⭐⭐⭐ NEW AMERICAN   With the best setting of any restaurant on the island—on a private beach on the property of Cliffside Beach Club (see "Where to Stay")—this restaurant offers a particularly chic yet beachy fine-dining experience. Given the setting, it's no surprise that the Galley specializes in seafood, caught locally by island fishermen. Produce comes from the restaurant's own organic garden. The menu changes often, but noteworthy menu options include the restaurant's signature New England clam chowder with smoked bacon, or the shrimp tempura served with Asian slaw. As a main course, there might be a luscious lobster risotto, native halibut with forest mushroom strudel, or Black Angus filet, or simply a 2-pound lobster with all the fixings.

54 Jefferson Ave., Nantucket. ✆ **508/228-9641.** Reservations suggested. Main courses $29–$39. AE, MC, V. Open daily noon–2pm and 5–10pm. Closed Oct to late May.

The Pearl ⭐⭐ NEW AMERICAN   It's Miami Beach on Nantucket at this swank establishment with numerous stylish touches: appetizers and desserts served in martini glasses; a contemporary look with bluish lighting and large fish tanks; an extensive champagne list. Skip the *grande deluxe plateau de mer;* it's not a lot of shellfish for a lot of money. But do choose the wild mushroom galette with white truffle cream. As a main course, look no further than the pan-roasted striped bass with citrus tomato infusion.

12 Federal St. ✆ **508/228-9701.** Reservations recommended. Main courses $28–$40. AE, MC, V. Mid-May to mid-Oct daily 6–10pm; call for off-season hours. Closed Jan–Mar.

Straight Wharf ⭐⭐ NEW AMERICAN   Straight Wharf, on the waterfront in the center of town, has long been known for its creative cuisine. Choices may include fancy appetizers like seared beef carpaccio with white truffle oil, and main courses like native lobster *a la nage,* which is prepared with a champagne sauce. Devoted regulars at Straight Wharf swear by the smoked bluefish pâté served with herb focaccia. A more affordable "summer grill" menu, served in the bar area, features simpler fare. Make your reservation for 8pm on the deck so you can watch the sun set over the harbor.

Straight Wharf. ✆ **508/228-4499.** Reservations recommended. Main courses $31–$38; summer grill menu $16–$22. AE, MC, V. July–Aug Tues–Sun 6–9:30pm; call for off-season hours. Closed late Sept to late May.

The Summer House ⭐⭐ *Finds* NEW AMERICAN   The classic 'Sconset-style atmosphere distinguishes this fine-dining experience from others on the island: wicker and wrought-iron, roses and honeysuckle. A pianist plays nightly—often Gershwin standards, and the pounding Atlantic Ocean is just over the bluff. Distinctive main courses include unusual lobster cutlets with coconut-jasmine risotto timbale and mint-tomato relish. If it's in season, end your meal with the blueberry pie.

17 Ocean Ave., Siasconset. (508/257-9976. Reservations recommended. Main courses $33–$39. AE, MC, V. July–Aug daily 11:30am–3pm (weather permitting) and 6–11pm; mid-May to June and Sept to mid-Oct Wed–Sun 6–11pm. Closed mid-Oct to Apr.

Topper's at The Wauwinet ★★★ REGIONAL/NEW AMERICAN   This 1850 restaurant—part of a secluded resort—is a tastefully subdued knockout, with wicker armchairs, splashes of chintz, and a two-tailed mermaid to oversee a chill-chasing fire. Try to sit at one of the cozy banquettes if you can. The menu features the finest regional cuisine: Lobster is a major event (it's often sautéed with champagne beurre blanc), and be on the lookout for unusual delicacies such as arctic char. Desserts are fanciful and fabulous: Consider the toasted brioche with poached pears and caramel sauce. The Wauwinet runs a complimentary launch service from mid-June to mid-September to the restaurant for lunch and dinner; it leaves from Straight Wharf at 11am and 5pm, takes 1 hour, and also makes the return trip.

120 Wauwinet Rd. (off Squam Rd.), Wauwinet. (**508/228-8768.** Reservations required for dinner and the launch ride over. Jacket requested for men. Main courses $34–$56. AE, DC, MC, V. May–Oct Mon–Sat noon–2pm and 6–10pm; Sun 11:30am–2pm and 6–10pm. Closed Nov–Apr.

EXPENSIVE

American Seasons ★★ REGIONAL AMERICAN   This romantic little restaurant has a great theme: Choose your region (New England, Pacific Coast, Wild West, or Down South) and select creative offerings. Start, for instance, with Louisiana crawfish risotto with fire-roasted onion and fried parsnips in a sweet corn purée from Down South; then move on to the Pacific Coast's aged beef sirloin with caramelized shallot and Yukon potato hash.

80 Centre St. (2 blocks from the center of town). (508/228-7111. Reservations recommended. Main courses $24–$30. AE, MC, V. Daily Apr–Nov 6–9pm. Closed early Dec to mid-Apr.

Boarding House ★★ NEW AMERICAN   This centrally located fine-dining restaurant doubles as one of the most popular bars in town. You can dine in the romantic lower-level dining room or upstairs in the hopping bar area. But on clear summer nights, you'll want to get one of the tables outside on the patio. The menu has definite Asian and Mediterranean influences. But the signature dish is the classic gilled lobster tails with grilled asparagus, mashed potatoes, and champagne *beurre blanc.* The award-winning wine list offers a range of prices.

12 Federal St. (508/228-9622. Reservations recommended. Main courses $26–$36. AE, MC, V. July–Aug daily 6–10pm; call for off-season hours. Open year-round.

Company of the Cauldron ★★★ CONTINENTAL   Considered the most romantic restaurant on the island, this candlelit dining room features a classical harpist in season. The menu is unusual in that there is one three- to four-course fixed-price meal each night, so would-be patrons must check the menu out front or call ahead to see which night to go. Dietary preferences can be accommodated with advance notice. The main course could be seafood, a special swordfish preparation, or a meat dish, like beef Wellington.

5 India St. (between Federal and Centre sts.) (508/228-4016. www.companyofthecauldron.com. Reservations required. Fixed-price dinner $50. MC, V. Early July to early Sept Tues–Sun, 2 seatings 6:45 and 8:45pm; call for off-season hours. Closed mid-Oct to mid-May, except Thanksgiving weekend and the first 2 weeks of Dec.

DeMarco ★★ NORTHERN ITALIAN   Come to this frame house carved into a cafe/bar and loft to get the best Italian food on the island. A forward-thinking menu and attentive service ensure a superior meal, which might include *antipasto di salmone* (house-smoked salmon rollatini, lemon-herb cream cheese, cucumber-and-endive salad with chive vinaigrette), and the delicate *capellini con scampi* (capellini with rock shrimp, tomato, black olives, capers, and hot pepper).

9 India St. (between Federal and Centre sts.). © 508/228-1836. Reservations recommended. Main courses $18–$32. AE, MC, V. Mid-June to Sept daily 6–10pm; call for off-season hours. Closed mid-Oct to mid-May.

Òran Mór ★★★ *Finds* INTERNATIONAL This second-floor waterfront venue has quickly become the premier restaurant on the island. The menu changes nightly, and there are always surprising and unusual choices. Appetizer standouts are the lobster risotto and the Thai littleneck clam hot pot with *somen* (thin white Japanese noodles similar to vermicelli) noodles. Intriguing entrees include grilled buffalo tenderloin and sautéed gray sole with sauce puttanesca. Some say the grilled breast of duck with savory tapioca and local nectar jus is the best duck dish on the island.

2 S. Beach St. (in the center of town). © 508/228-8655. Reservations recommended. Main courses $22–$34. AE, MC, V. July–Aug daily 6–10pm; Sept–June Thurs–Sat and Mon–Tues 6–9pm, Sun noon–9pm. Open year-round.

Ropewalk ★ SEAFOOD This open-air restaurant on the harbor is Nantucket's only outdoor raw bar, and it's where the yachting crowd hangs out after a day on the boat. While the food is a bit overpriced, the location is prime. This is a good place to enjoy a light meal or appetizers, such as fried calamari, crab cakes, or fried oysters. The dinner menu includes grilled swordfish with ratatouille and grilled breast of chicken with roasted garlic and rosemary jus.

1 Straight Wharf. © 508/228-8886. No reservations. Main courses $23–$33. MC, V. Apr to mid-Dec daily 11am–10pm. Closed mid-Oct to Apr.

Ship's Inn Restaurant ★★ NEW AMERICAN This intimate restaurant in the brick-walled basement of a 12-room inn is one of the island's most romantic dining options. The waitstaff here is professional and entertaining, a real treat. The menu features a variety of fresh fish, meat, and pasta dishes including several lighter options made without butter or cream. A flavorful starter here is the Roquefort and walnut terrine with Asian pear. As a main course, popular dishes include the pan-roasted Muscovy duck breast and the grilled yellowtail flounder. For a festive dessert, there's always the Grand Marnier soufflé.

13 Fair St. © 508/228-0040. Reservations recommended. Main courses $28–$38. AE, DISC, MC, V. July–Sept Wed–Mon 5–10pm. Call for off-season hours. Closed Nov–Apr.

21 Federal ★★ NEW AMERICAN This restaurant seems to get better every year. For melt-in-your-mouth pleasure, try the appetizer of tuna tartare with wasabi crackers and cilantro aioli. The fish entrees are the most popular here, although you might opt for the fine breast of duck accompanied by pecan wild rice and shiitake mushrooms. We love the pan-crisped salmon with champagne cabbage and beet-butter sauce, which has been a staple of the menu for years.

21 Federal St. (in the center of town). © 508/228-2121. Reservations recommended. Main courses $27–$37. AE, MC, V. Apr to mid-Dec daily 6–9:30pm. Closed mid-Dec to Mar.

MODERATE

Black Eyed Susan's ★★ *Finds* ETHNIC ECLECTIC This is supremely exciting food in a funky bistro atmosphere. Reservations are accepted for the 6pm seating only, and they go fast. Others must line up outside; the line starts forming around 5:30pm. The menu is in constant flux, as chef Jeff Worster's mood and influences change every 3 weeks. We always enjoy the spicy Thai fish cake, and the tandoori chicken with green mango chutney. There's usually a South-western touch like the Dos Equis beer–battered catfish quesadilla with mango slaw, hoppin' john, and jalapeño. There's no liquor license, but you can BYOB.

10 India St. (in the center of town). ℂ 508/325-0308. Reservations accepted for 6pm seating only. Main courses $15–$25. No credit cards. Apr–Oct daily 7am–1pm, Mon–Sat 6–10pm; call for off-season hours. Closed Nov–Mar.

Bluefin ⭐⭐ ASIAN/INTERNATIONAL   This new restaurant, an intimate spot a short walk from the center of town, offers great prices and tasty food, including sushi and tapas. The crispy crab Rangoon comes with the perfect hot-and-sour sauce, and shrimp lo mein is served with wok-crisp vegetables. The lobster ravioli served with sweet basil cream is the ultimate in wretched excess. Keep in mind, there is a bar scene here, too, so if you are sitting near the bar area, it can be loud.

15 South Beach St. ℂ 508/228-2033. Main courses $9–$16. AE, MC, V. June–Aug daily 5:30–10pm; call for off-season hours. Open year-round.

Centre Street Bistro ⭐⭐ NEW AMERICAN   This tiny fine-dining restau-rant in the center of Nantucket town is owned and operated by Ruth and Tim Pitts, who are considered top chefs on the island. This cozy place features won-derful, creative cuisine at reasonable prices, especially compared to other island fine-dining restaurants. The menu is in constant flux, but recent high points included the warm goat cheese tart to start, and the Long Island duck breast with pumpkin and butternut squash risotto as a main course.

29 Centre St. ℂ 508/228-8470. No reservations. Main courses $16–$20. No credit cards. Wed–Sun noon–2:30pm and 6–10pm. Open year-round.

Eat, Fire, Spring ⭐⭐ NEW AMERICAN   Nantucket's newest restaurant, a hip outdoor cafe located past the galleries at the end of Old South Wharf, is get-ting rave revues. This is a casual place, the perfect spot to enjoy a leisurely lunch on a sunny day, or a light dinner on a sultry night. The eclectic menu features standards like blackened tuna, for instance, or steak tips, but prepared with unique sauces and sides. There's live music nightly.

12 Old South Wharf. ℂ 508/228-5756. Reservations not accepted. Main courses $18–$25. AE, MC, V. Late June to early Sept noon–3pm and 6–9pm. Call for off-season hours. Closed early Sept to early June.

Le Languedoc Cafe ⭐⭐ NEW AMERICAN   Nantucket's most authentic French cafe offers a cozy atmosphere and reasonable prices. An expensive dining room is upstairs, but locals prefer the casual bistro atmosphere downstairs and out on the terrace. Soups are superb, as are the Angus-steak burgers with garlic french fries. More elaborate dishes include the roasted tenderloin of pork stuffed with figs and pancetta.

24 Broad St. ℂ 508/228-2552. www.lelanguedoc.com. Reservations not accepted for cafe; reservations recommended for dining room. Main courses $9–$19. AE, MC, V. June–Sept daily 5:30–9:30pm, Tues–Sun noon–2pm; call for off-season hours. Closed mid-Dec to Apr.

Nantucket Lobster Trap ⭐ *Kids* SEAFOOD   When only a bowl of chow-der and a giant lobster roll will do, bring the whole family to this quintessential clam shack where the big game is usually on the TV behind the bar. Seating is on large picnic tables and lobsters and other shellfish come straight from local waters. The prices are kept relatively affordable here.

23 Vestry St. ℂ 508/228-4200. Reservations for parties of 6 or more only. Main courses $12–$30. AE, MC, V. June–Sept daily 5–10:30pm. Call for off-season hours. Closed late Oct to early May.

INEXPENSIVE

Arno's ⭑ *Kids* ECLECTIC   A storefront facing the passing parade of Main Street, this institution packs surprising style between its bare-brick walls. The internationally influenced menu yields tasty, bountiful platters for breakfast, lunch, and dinner. Specialties include grilled sirloin steaks and fresh grilled fish.

41 Main St. ✆ **508/228-7001.** Reservations recommended. Main courses $15–$23. AE, DC, DISC, MC, V. Apr–Dec daily 8am–2pm and 5–9:30pm. Closed Jan–Mar.

Cap'n Tobey's Chowder House ⭑ SEAFOOD   The specialty at this convenient eatery close to the harbor is seafood, obtained on a daily basis from local fishermen. Diners can choose between halibut, yellowfin tuna, and haddock, and have it grilled, baked, or blackened. The raw bar features oysters, littlenecks, and shrimp. Upstairs, called **Off Shore at Cap'n Tobey's,** there's live music in season.

20 Straight Wharf. ✆ **508/228-0836.** Reservations accepted. Main courses $9–$30. AE, MC, V. Late June to Sept daily 11:30am–10pm. Call for off-season hours. Closed Jan–Apr.

The Even Keel Café ⭑ AMERICAN   This low-key cafe in the heart of town serves breakfast, lunch, and dinner both indoors and outside on the patio in the back. Unlike much of Nantucket's dining scene, you'll find reasonable prices and non-exotic fare here, like burgers and sandwiches. There are always vegetarian choices as well as meat and fish dishes, everything from a cheeseburger to grilled salmon to veal osso bucco. There's also a kid's menu, as well as high-speed Internet access. On Sundays, they serve a hearty brunch. There is no alcohol for sale here but you can BYOB.

40 Main St. ✆ **508/228-1979.** Reservations not accepted. Main courses $10–$25. AE, MC, V. July–Aug daily 7am–10pm. Call for off-season hours. Open year-round.

Fog Island Cafe ⭑⭑ NEW AMERICAN   You'll be wowed by the creative breakfasts and lunches at this sassy cafe; they're reasonably priced, with superfresh ingredients. Homemade soups and salads are healthy and yummy. The dinner menu, served June through August only, features fresh seafood, pasta dishes, and a vegetarian alternative among the specialties.

7 S. Water St. ✆ **508/228-1818.** Reservations accepted. Main courses at dinner $10–$20. MC, V. July–Aug Mon–Sat 7am–9:30pm, Sun 7am–1pm; call for off-season hours. Open year-round.

TAKEOUT & PICNIC FARE

You can get fresh-picked produce right on Main Street from the traveling truck from **Bartlett's Ocean View Farm** ⭑, 33 Bartlett Farm Rd. (✆ **508/228-9403**), or head out to this seventh-generation farm where, in June, you get to pick your own strawberries. They also sell sandwiches, quiches, pastries, pies, and more. Closed January through March.

   Henry's Sandwich Shop ⭑, Steamboat Wharf (✆ **508/228-0123**), which opened in 1969, is set a block away from Steamboat Wharf, where the ferries dock. They bake their own sub rolls from scratch every morning. Closed November through May.

   Before you bike out of town to the beach, stop by **Provisions,** 3 Harbor Sq., Straight Wharf (✆ **508/228-3258**), a gourmet sandwich shop. Closed early November to March.

   A terrific value on pricey Nantucket, **Something Natural,** 50 Cliff Rd. (✆ **508/228-0504**), turns out gigantic sandwiches, with fresh ingredients piled atop fabulous bread. Save room for their addictive chocolate-chip cookies. Closed mid-October to March.

The **Juice Bar** ★★, 12 Broad St. (© **508/228-5799**), is a humble hole-in-the-wall that scoops up some of the best homemade ice cream and frozen yogurt around, complemented by superb homemade hot fudge. Closed from mid-October to mid-April.

Juice Guys, 4 Easy St. (© **508/228-4464**), is the spot to get your Nantucket Nectars fix. High-tech blenders mix potent combinations of fresh juice with vitamins, sorbet, yogurt, and holistic enhancers. Closed from late December to April.

NANTUCKET AFTER DARK

Acoustic performers from all over the country hold forth in the **Brotherhood of Thieves,** 23 Broad St., in the center of Nantucket Town (no phone), an atmospheric pub where you'll find live folk music just about every night in season; no cover. Closed in February. The **Chicken Box,** 12 Dave St. (© **508/228-9717**), is the rocking spot for the 20-something crowd. It sometimes seems like the entire population of the island is shoving their way in here. Jimmy Buffett shows up late at night about once a summer, unannounced, and jams with the band. The cover runs from $4 to $15. The **Rose and Crown,** 23 S. Water St. (© **508/228-2595**), draws all ages with its loud music for dancing. The cover for live bands on weekends is $3 to $5. Closed January through March.

The **Nantucket Arts Alliance** (© **800/228-8118** or 508/228-8118) operates Box Office Nantucket, offering tickets for all sorts of cultural events around town. It operates out of the Macy Warehouse on Straight Wharf, in season daily from 10am to 4pm.

Theater buffs will want to spend an evening at the **Actors' Theatre of Nantucket,** Methodist Church, 2 Centre St. (© **508/228-6325;** www.nantucket theatre.com). This shoebox-size theater assays thought-provoking plays as readily as summery farces. The season runs from mid-May to mid-September. Tickets are $12 to $20. You can catch the children's productions ($12) from mid-July to mid-August.

Central & Western Massachusetts

by Herbert Bailey Livesey

While Boston and its maritime appendages of Cape Ann and Cape Cod face the sea and embrace it, inland Massachusetts turns in upon itself. Countless ponds and lakes shimmer in its folds and hollows, often hidden by deep forests and granite outcroppings. Farming and industry grew along the north-south valleys of the Connecticut and Housatonic rivers.

The heartland Pioneer Valley, bordering the Connecticut River, earned its name in the early 18th century, when European trappers and farmers first began to push west from the colonies clinging to the edges of Massachusetts Bay. They were followed by ambitious capitalists who erected red-brick mills along the river for the manufacture of textiles and paper. Most of those enterprises failed or faded in the post–World War II movement to the milder climate and cheaper labor of the South, leaving a miasma of economic hardship that has yet to be remedied. But those

industrialists also helped fund several distinguished colleges for which the valley is now known; their educated populations provide much energy and a rich cultural life.

Roughly the same pattern applied in the Berkshires, the twin ranges of rumpled hills that define the western band of the state. There is only one college of note here, however, and the development of this region in the 19th century was prompted mainly by the construction of the railroad from New York and Boston. Artistic and literary folk made a favored summer retreat of it, followed by wealthy urbanites attracted by the region's reputation for creativity and Bohemianism. Many of their extravagant mansions, dubbed "Berkshire Cottages," still survive, and to this day the region attracts the town-and-country crowd, who support a vibrant summer schedule of the arts, then steal away as the crimson leaves fall and the Berkshires grow quiet beneath 6 months of snow.

1 Worcester

46 miles W of Boston; 55 miles NE of Springfield

A dispirited air clings to Massachusetts's second-largest city, especially around its often dilapidated edges. But that observation applies to many of the region's cities, most of which reached their apogees in the late 19th century, and Worcester has a sufficiency of attractions to justify a stopover or an overnight on the way to or from Boston.

Its citizens support frequent bootstrapping efforts, especially downtown around the Romanesque City Hall. Over the years, local benefactors have invested in a surprising number of museums, historic buildings, and theatrical

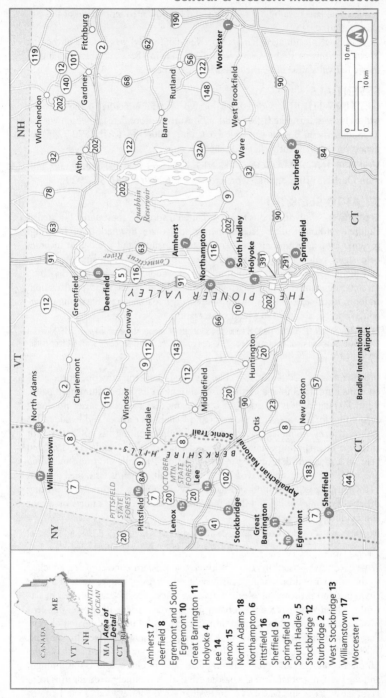

venues. The latest example is the costly and long-awaited renovation of the railroad station.

Worcester (pronounced *Wuss*-ter, or *Woos*-tah locally) was the site of the first National Women's Rights Convention, held here in 1850, and the city's annual music festival claims to be the oldest in the country.

ESSENTIALS

GETTING THERE   Worcester is located near the juncture of the east-west Massachusetts Turnpike (I-90) and I-395. **Amtrak** stops here daily each way on its route between Boston and Chicago. Call ✆ **800/USA-RAIL** (872-7245) for details on the frequently changed schedule.

VISITOR INFORMATION   The **Visitor Center** is at the Worcester Common Outlets, 110 Front St., Worcester, MA -1608 (✆ **508/753-2920**).

WHAT TO SEE & DO

Ecotarium   This ambitious family-oriented institution is primarily directed at children, although their accompanying adults are diverted, too. It brings together a planetarium, an observatory, an aquarium, and a zoo that includes bald eagles, polar bears, barred owls, bobcats, otters, and mountain lions. Ponds and picnic areas dot the 60 hilltop acres of woods, which are traversed by a meandering nature trail. A narrow gauge railroad is yet another attraction. Indoors, interactive displays and computers sugarcoat messages regarding underlying concerns about ecology and conservation.

222 Harrington Way. ✆ 508/791-9211. Admission $8 adults, $6 seniors, students, and ages 3–16. Mon–Sat 10am–5pm; Sun noon–5pm. From exit 14 of I-290, head east on Rte. 122 (Grafton St.), bearing left on Hamilton St., then left again on Harrington Way.

Higgins Armory Museum 🏰   The steel-and-glass structure, one of the earliest of its kind, resembles a Gothic castle shining in its coat of aluminum paint. John W. Higgins was president of a company that processed steel, no doubt accounting for his interest in medieval and Renaissance armor and heraldry. He gathered many examples over his lifetime, supplementing his collection with ancient arms, paintings, stained glass, and tapestries. The results are displayed here, in a museum that opened in 1931. Nearly 100 suits of armor, including one made for a dog, are arrayed in the Great Hall, which is fashioned after an 11th-century castle. A sound-and-light show and various demonstrations bring the age of chivalry to life and there is a room in which visitors can try on armor and clothing of the period.

100 Barber Ave. ✆ 508/853-6015. Admission $7.75 adults, $7 seniors, $6.75 children 6-16. Tues-Sat 10am–4pm; Sun noon–4pm. Take 1-190 to exit 1, onto MA 12 north, then turn right on Barber Ave.

Worcester Art Museum 🏰🏰   With a large modern concrete wing attached to the original building facing Salisbury Street, WAM occupies most of a large city block and is therefore able to contain an unexpectedly large number of artworks. The diverse collections contain pieces from ancient Egypt to 20th-century America, a total of over 30,000 paintings, sculptures, and related objects. Particular strengths are the American wing, housing canvases by Sargent, Whistler, Ryder, and a few memorable works by anonymous Colonial artists; the Europeans on the 2nd floor, including Gauguin, El Greco, and Gainsborough; and the pre-Columbian artifacts on the 4th floor, with finely wrought urns from Peru, Costa Rica, and Mexico's Monte Alban. In the lower level of the 1st floor is a reconstructed 12th-century French chapter house *and* a large floor mosaic from 6th-century Antioch in what is now southeastern Turkey.

55 Salisbury St. (corner of Tuckerman St.) ✆ **508/799-4406.** Admission $8 adults, $6 seniors and students, free under age 17 and to all Sat 10am–noon. Wed–Fri 11am–5pm (until 8pm Thurs); Sat 10am–5pm; Sun 11am–5pm. Closed Sun in July and Aug.

WHERE TO STAY

Pickings are slim for local lodging, which are mostly chain motels. An alternative is staying in nearby Sturbridge, which is less than 20 miles away and has a more interesting choice of accommodations.

Beechwood Hotel The eye-catching feature of this relatively young red-brick building is its round core structure, which resembles a medieval keep. Public spaces and guest rooms are agreeably furnished with pieces that use wood and fabric in nearly equal proportions. A costly recent renovation added fifteen executive level rooms and suites, which are accorded such extra services as continental breakfast and newspaper delivery. High-speed Internet access is available throughout.

363 Plantation St., Worcester, MA 01605. ✆ **800/344-2589** or 508/754-5789. Fax 508/752-2060. www. beechwoodhotel.com. 73 units. $149–$224 double, $194–$234 suite. AE, DC, DISC, MC, V. **Amenities:** Restaurant (New American); bar; limited room service; dry cleaning/laundry service. *In room:* A/C, TV, dataport, coffeemaker, hair dryer, iron.

Crowne Plaza The most desirable lodging in town—at least in terms of location and facilities—this outlet of the well-known chain delivers on most points of expected conveniences. Fireplaces in the lobby and adjacent dining room are warming notes on a winter night, and self-parking is handy in the garage directly opposite the main entrance. Bedrooms provide more than sufficient elbow room, and contain such extras as clock radios and makeup mirrors. Complimentary newspapers are outside the door in the morning. The concierge level has a private lounge serving food and drinks and has unstocked fridges in bedrooms.

10 Lincoln Sq. (corner of Lincoln St. and Belmont St.), Worcester, MA 01608. ✆ **800/227-7963** or 508/791-1600. Fax 508/791-1796. www.crowneplaza.com. 243 units. $92–$145 double. AE, DC, DISC, MC, V. **Amenities:** Restaurant (Italian/Continental); bar; heated indoor/outdoor pool with whirlpool; adequate exercise room; business center; free parking, limited room service; dry cleaning/laundry service. *In room:* A/C, TV w/pay movies, dataport, coffeemaker, hair dryer, iron.

WHERE TO DINE

Flying Rhino Centered in Worcester's major dining and nightlife street, this all-purpose gathering place caters to the tastes of the mostly youngish folks who make that scene. That means a bar that is five deep as the weekend approaches and a pubby menu that is all over the place—Caribbean, Southeast Asia, Mediterranean, and, of course, New England. Typical is the toasted *boule* filled with dense chili or creamy clam chowder, and such designated "wild bites" as tequila shrimp, hot wings, and Thai wraps. The difference is that almost all of it is several times better than bar-hoppers have come to expect. Lobster ravioli, for example, utilizes squid-ink pasta supplemented with shrimp and scallops tossed in a sherry cream sauce, and marinated chicken souvlaki combined with zucchini, onions, and peppers over rice. At lunch, the grilled panini and "rhino" wraps are maddeningly tasty.

278 Shrewsbury St. ✆ **508/757-1450.** Main courses $11–$24. AE, DC, DISC, MC, V. Mon–Sat 11:30am–1am (Thurs until 2am).

Sole Proprietor ✦ In urban legend, Legal Seafoods, the steamrolling seafood restaurant chain, came to Worcester to challenge the local champ. The interloper soon turned tail and fled, vanquished handily by Sole Proprietor. The evidence of that suzerainty is clear even on a cold Tuesday night, when the large parking lot outside is like a bumper car attraction. Part of the reason is the congenial staff, from the hostess who remains unflustered no matter how many would-be diners clog the entrance to waiters who can describe dishes in as much detail as patrons seem to want. But the food is central, with fish as fresh as the dawn and preparations from barebones simple to entrancingly complex. One side of the large rectangular bar is given to a sushi and raw bar, while the kitchen produces such worthy inventions as tuna steak Barcelons, the fish coated with cracked peppercorns, grilled medium rare, sliced, and laid over a bed of feta cheese, sun-dried tomatoes, scallions, and basil leaves. Menus (and prices) are changed daily, and even give stock market, sports, and weather reports. Up to 50 wines, red and white, are available by the glass.

118 Highland St. © **508/798-3474.** Main courses $19–$37 (sushi $6–$8 per piece). AE, DC, MC, V. Mon–Fri 11:30am–10pm; Sat noon–11pm; Sun 4–9:30pm.

2 Sturbridge & Old Sturbridge Village

18 miles SW of Worcester; 32 miles E of Springfield

First things first: Sturbridge and Old Sturbridge Village aren't a single entity. The former is an organic community, populated by working people with real lives. But why are there so many motels and restaurants in a town of fewer than 8,000 residents? That's because of the latter, a fabricated early-19th-century village comprised of authentic buildings moved here from other locations and peopled by docents pretending to follow the pursuits of 170 years past. It is deservedly popular, one of the two most prominent tourist destinations in central Massachusetts.

ESSENTIALS

GETTING THERE   Take the east-west Massachusetts Turnpike (I-90) to Exit 9, or take I-84 to Exit 3B.

VISITOR INFORMATION   The **Sturbridge Area Visitors Center,** 380 Main St. (© **508/347-2761**), is open Monday through Friday during regular business hours.

SPECIAL EVENTS   Highly popular annual occasions are the **Brimfield Antique and Collectible Shows** ★ (© **800/628-8379** or 508/347-2761; www.brimfieldshow.com), when over 6,000 dealers gather along a mile-long strip for up to 6 days (Tues–Sun) in mid-May, mid-July, and early September. Brimfield is an otherwise sleepy village adjoining Sturbridge on the west. Because it has few hotels, most of the dealers and seekers stay in Sturbridge, so you'll need to reserve your room at least 6 months in advance during show periods.

Thanksgiving and Christmas weeks at Old Sturbridge Village bring traditional New England dinners, concerts, and candlelit nights. Call © **800/733-1830** or 508/347-3362 for details.

EXPLORING A 19TH-CENTURY VILLAGE

There is only one sight of significance in this otherwise pleasantly unremarkable town. Expect crowds on holiday weekends in summer and during the October foliage season.

Old Sturbridge Village ★★★ *(Kids*   Only one of the more than 40 restored structures in the complex stands on its original site—the Oliver Wight House, now part of the Old Sturbridge Village Motor Lodges (see below). The rest were transported here from as far away as Maine. All are authentic buildings, not re-creations, and they represent the living quarters and places of trade and commerce of a rural settlement of the 1830s. Among these are a Quaker meetinghouse, sawmill, bank, country store, blacksmith shop, school, cooperage, and printing office. At the edges of the village are a working farm and herb garden.

Costumed docents demonstrate hearth cooking, sheep shearing, heirloom gardening, maple sugaring, musketry, carpentry, and more. "Residents" include children who roll hoops and play games true to the period. At the children's museum, kids 3 to 7 can dress up in costumes and use their imaginations in a pretend farm kitchen and one-room school. Special events mark such dates as the Fourth of July, Thanksgiving, and the Christmas season. Weddings, militia drills, and a harvest fair are staged. The 20-minute boat ride on the adjacent Quinebaug River is popular with younger visitors.

The Village is constantly evolving, with special seasonal events, new activities, and additional buildings. Among the last is the Tavern, at the entrance, opened in 2002. Unlike the structures in the Village proper, it is a re-creation of an early-19th-century New England house, incorporating a full-service restaurant and a museum gallery. It serves lunch on Mondays, and both lunch and dinner Tuesday through Sunday. Village admission isn't required.

1 Old Sturbridge Rd. ℂ **800/733-1830** or 508/347-3362. Fax 508/347-0375. www.osv.org. Admission (2-day pass) $20 adults, $18 seniors, $10 children 6–15. Apr–Oct daily 9:30am–5pm; Nov–Dec daily 9:30am–4pm; Jan–Mar Wed–Sun 9:30am–4pm; but there are frequent exceptions in hours and days of operation, so call ahead. Closed Dec 25. Take Exit 3B off I-84 or Exit 9 off I-90, drive west on Rte. 20, and bear right into the turnaround just before the entrance to the village.

WHERE TO STAY

If the choices below are full, try the **EconoLodge,** 262 Main St. (ℂ **508/347-2324**), the **Colonial Quality Inn,** on Route 20 (ℂ **508/347-3306**), or the **Sturbridge Coach Motor Lodge,** 408 Main St. (ℂ **508/347-7327**). The first two are located near Exit 9 off I-84, the third near the entrance to Old Sturbridge Village.

Old Sturbridge Village Motor Lodges   Six barn-like structures of post–World War II origin are arranged around a common green and swimming pool. Rooms are fresh, spacious, and straightforward, outfitted with colonial reproductions. Exceptions are those in the 200-year-old Oliver Wight House, with sloping wide-board floors and deep fireplaces (nonworking) once meant for cooking. Some rooms have unstocked fridges.

Rte. 20 E., Sturbridge, MA 01566. ℂ **508/347-3327.** Fax 508/347-3018. www.osv.org. 59 units. May–Oct $90–$120 double; Nov–Apr $85–$120 double. Extra person $5. AE, DISC, MC, V. **Amenities:** Heated outdoor pool; access to nearby health club. *In room:* A/C, TV, coffeemaker, hair dryer.

Publick House ⭐   This complex is the high-profile lodging in the Sturbridge area. The main structure is a tavern, heavy on the antique charm, built in 1771. Rooms are rustic, some with canopy beds, rag rugs, and colonial reproductions. A 1786 Federal-style farmhouse called the Colonel Ebenezer Crafts Inn, a mile from the hotel, has its own pool.

Rte. 131 (P.O. Box 187), Sturbridge, MA 01566. ℂ **800/782-5425** or 508/347-3313. Fax 508/347-5073. www.publickhouse.com. 126 units. $99–$165 double. Packages available. AE, DC, DISC, MC, V. From Exit 3B off I-84, drive 1½ miles south of Rte. 20 on Rte. 131. Pets accepted in some rooms of Country Motor Lodge ($5 per night). **Amenities:** 2 restaurants (American); bar; 2 heated outdoor pools; tennis courts; access to nearby health club; dry cleaning. *In room:* A/C, TV, hair dryer.

WHERE TO DINE

In addition to the establishments listed below, you might sample either of the two restaurants associated with the **Publick House** (see above).

Rom's ✿ ITALIAN/AMERICAN   This was once a hot dog and fried-clam roadside stand that has grown over the last half-century like a multigenerational New England farmhouse. Today, it seats 750 diners and remains a near-ideal family restaurant, with something to please everyone, from homemade pastas and pizzas to full seafood dinners. The lobster roll is twice the size but about the same price as those offered on the coast. Buffets at Wednesday dinner and Thursday lunch are crowd pleasers. A takeout window ladles "buckets of rigatoni" and fish and chips.

Rte. 131, 2 miles south of Rte. 20. ✆ **800/ROM-1952** or 508/347-3349. Main courses $6.75–$15. AE, DISC, DC, MC, V. Daily 11:30am–9pm.

Rovezzi's ✿ ITALIAN   This new roadside trattoria is a welcome addition to the area's rather wan dining possibilities. Inside the front door is a long, brightly lit bar populated with people who know each other; the dining room, with its marble fireplace, is an attached wing in back. The two-page menu lists appetizer-size pastas and cold and hot antipasti (you might want to order something other than the two bruschettas, which are made with the same focaccia served with dinner). Pastas can be supplemented with herb-roasted chicken or what are billed as the "world's best meatballs." Every night has a special soup, risotto, filet mignon, cannoli, and crème brulée. Jump for the excellent crab and salmon bisque, if offered. Of the main dish pastas, the ravioli *per lo Invierno* was a good choice, butternut squash and sweet potato envelopes with crumbled sausage and a sage cream sauce.

Rte. 20, 2 miles west of Old Sturbridge Village. ✆ **508/347-0100**. Main courses $17–$19. MC, V. Daily 5–9pm (Fri–Sat until 10pm).

3 Springfield

89 miles W of Boston; 32 miles N of Hartford

Times have been tough in this once-prosperous manufacturing city on the east bank of the Connecticut River. But its loyal citizens haven't given in to the consequences of job flight and high unemployment, and there is evidence of redevelopment throughout downtown, with recycled loft and factory buildings standing beside modern glass towers. Springfield remains the most important city in western Massachusetts and has enjoyed some success in attracting new enterprises. Vacationers can pass a few hours or an overnight here, but Springfield is primarily a stop on the way north or south.

ESSENTIALS

GETTING THERE   Springfield is located near the juncture of the east-west Massachusetts Turnpike (I-90) and north-south I-91.

Bradley International (✆ **203/627-3000**), in Windsor Locks, Conn., is the nearest major airport, about 20 miles to the south. Rent a car here from any of the major companies or catch a bus, cab, or limo into Springfield. Major airlines serving Bradley include **American** (✆ **800/433-7300**), **Continental** (✆ **800/525-0280**), **Delta** (✆ **800/221-1212**), **Northwest** (✆ **800/225-2525**), **United** (✆ **800/241-6522**), and **US Airways** (✆ **800/247-8786**).

Amtrak (✆ **800/USA-RAIL;** www.northeast.amtrak.com) trains stop daily both ways in Springfield on routes between Boston and Chicago; Boston and Washington, D.C.; and New York and St. Albans, Vt. (where there are connecting buses from Montreal), with intermediate stops in Philadelphia, New York, and Hartford, among others.

Fun Fact *... And to Think That I Saw It on Mulberry Street*

Interest in the man who called himself Dr. Seuss spiked with the recent Broadway show, *Seussical,* and the movies *The Cat in the Hat* and *The Grinch.* The grandparents of Theodor Seuss Geisel lived on Springfield's Mulberry Street, and in 1937, the writer and illustrator named the first of his dozens of children's books for the neighborhood. He followed up with such classics as *The Cat in the Hat* and *How the Grinch Stole Christmas.* Over 100 million copies of his books have been sold, and every title is still in print.

Geisel spent most of his adult life in California, the result of a nearly 2-decade career in documentary films, during which he won two Academy Awards. But much of his inspiration for the children's books for which he is remembered can be traced to Springfield. His drawing of Bartholomew Cubbins's castle bears a strong resemblance to the Howard Street Armory, now a community center, and certain of his landscapes look as if they were recalled from his playtimes in Forest Park, near his boyhood home at 74 Fairfield St.

Alas, Mulberry Street is no longer the august avenue it once must have been, its Victorian manses now crowded by undistinguished apartment blocks and commercial strips—and the former Central High School from which Geisel graduated is now a condominium.

VISITOR INFORMATION   The new **Riverfront Visitor Information Center** of the Greater Springfield Convention and Visitors Bureau (© 413/787-1548; www.valleyvisitor.com) is at 1200 West Columbus Ave., next to the Basketball Hall of Fame.

SPECIAL EVENTS   The mid-September **Eastern States Exposition** (© 413/737-2443) is a huge old-fashioned agricultural fair with games, rides, a midway, and entertainment. It's held on a fairground on the opposite side of the Connecticut River in West Springfield. Also on the grounds is the **Old Storrowtown Village,** a collection of restored colonial buildings, accessible by guided tour Monday through Saturday from June to Labor Day, and by appointment the rest of the year.

MUSEUMS & HISTORIC SITES

Naismith Memorial Basketball Hall of Fame ★★   Dr. James Naismith invented basketball in Springfield in 1891, providing the logic for this center. A must for fans, it is painless even for those who regard the game as a blur of 7-foot armpits. It has been so popular an entirely new facility has been built at the opposite end of the parking lot from the original hall. You can't miss it—there's a 136-foot spire holding a 13-foot illuminated basketball. Take one of the glass elevators to the top (third) level and work down. Up there is the Honors Ring, detailing the biographies of the players enshrined in the Hall. Displays there and on lower floors, many of them interactive, feature memorabilia of the sport and the history of the game—remember the Waterloo Hawks, the Indianapolis Kautskys, the Philadelphia Hebrews? On the ground floor are shooting courts where clinics and skill challenges are held. There are two fast-food restaurants in the building.

1000 W. Columbus Ave. (at Union St.). ⓒ 413/781-6500. Fax 413/781-1939. www.hoophall.com. Admission $16 adults, $13 seniors, $11 children 7–15. Daily 10am–6pm. Closed Thanksgiving, Dec 25.

Springfield Museums at the Quadrangle ⭐ *Kids*   Four museums and a library surrounding a quadrangle constitute this worthwhile resource. Enter the library from State Street and walk through to the back. Near that exit is the new **Dr. Seuss National Memorial Sculpture Garden,** with three groups, including the author himself (who was born in Springfield), the Cat in the Hat, and the Grinch. On the right is the first museum; the others around the quad make a counterclockwise circuit. Before setting out, note the somewhat limited hours below.

The **George Walter Vincent Smith Art Museum** is housed in an 1896 Italian Renaissance–style mansion. Upstairs are largely sentimental pastoral scenes, with a few small landscapes by George Inness, Thomas Cole, and Albert Bierstadt. On the main floor are cases of Japanese samurai weaponry surrounding a carved 1805 Shinto shrine.

Kids will enjoy the **Springfield Science Museum,** which contains a 100-seat planetarium, dioramas of African animals, a Dinosaur Hall, and the Solutia Eco-Center.

Enter the **Connecticut Valley Historical Museum** to see examples of weapons made by the city's firearms manufacturers, including a blunderbuss and an unusual 1838 rifle with a revolving cartridge chamber.

The strongest of the lot is the **Museum of Fine Arts** ⭐, with 14 galleries of colonial paintings through Gilbert Stuart and John Copley to early-20th-century realists George Bellows and Reginald Marsh, and culminating with magic realists and Abstract Expressionists—Frank Stella, Helen Frankenthaler, Don Eddy, and George Sugarman. Make a particular effort to view the remarkable serigraph of lower Manhattan by Richard Estes.

220 State St. (at Chestnut St.). ⓒ 413/263-6800. www.quadrangle.org. Combined admission for all 4 museums $7 adults, $5 seniors and college students, $3 children 6–18; $3 extra each for the planetarium and dinosaur hall. Wed–Fri noon–5pm; Sat–Sun 11am–4pm.

WHERE TO STAY

Sheraton Springfield ⭐⭐   Just off the Springfield Center exit of I-91, this can be a treat after a few nights in idiosyncratic New England B&Bs. Predictable, yes, but curl up in a room with all these conveniences, and lack of charm can suddenly seem unimportant—especially when it's combined with room service, a capable restaurant, and an expansive spa and fitness center. Executive-level rooms are sometimes cheaper than standard units, so be sure to inquire.

1 Monarch Place, Springfield, MA 01114. ⓒ 800/426-9004 or 413/781-1010. Fax 413/734-3249. info@ sheratonspringfield.com. 310 units. $149–$210 double. AE, DC, DISC, MC, V. **Amenities:** Restaurant (Continental); bar; heated indoor pool; health club; Jacuzzi; sauna; business center; shopping arcade; limited room service; same-day dry cleaning. *In room:* A/C, TV w/pay movies, dataport, coffeemaker, hair dryer, iron.

Springfield Marriott ⭐⭐   Directly across the street from the Sheraton (see above), this representative of the widespread chain shares, even duplicates, most of its rival's attributes. Among its perks are high-speed Internet access, a concierge level, and poolside food service.

1500 Main St., Springfield, MA 01105. ⓒ 800/228-9290 or 413/781-7111. Fax 413/731-8932. www.marriott hotels.com. 265 units. $99–$139 double. AE, DC, DISC, MC, V. **Amenities:** Restaurant (Continental); 2 bars; heated indoor pool; health club; Jacuzzi; sauna; business center; limited room service; same-day dry cleaning. *In room:* A/C, TV w/pay movies, dataport, coffeemaker, hair dryer, iron.

WHERE TO DINE

Art-é-pasta ITALIAN   This lively *ristorante* is a welcome exception to the largely forlorn dining scene, apart from its ungainly name. The extra-long menu and prodigious servings ensure initial indecision and a subsequent need for doggie bags. The stuffed crostini loaf alone is allegedly an appetizer, but practically a meal–a loaf of bread stuffed with mozzarella, tomatoes, basil, and garlic olive oil. Then on to a second course of pasta with 16 choices of sauce, say the "Vodka Gypsy," comprised of capers, shallots, hot peppers, sun-dried yellow tomatoes, artichokes, kalamata olives, and spinach. After that, the entree, no smaller, of various chicken, beef, veal, or seafood fabrications (the lobster ravioli is super). And dessert? Maybe you'll want to skip it.

272 Worthington St. ✆ 413/732-0008. Main courses $13–$26. AE, DISC, MC, V. Mon–Wed 11am–10pm; Thurs–Fri 11am–2am; Sat 4pm–2am; Sun 4pm–10pm.

Student Prince and the Fort GERMAN/AMERICAN   In 1935, German immigrants opened the Student Prince and began serving schnitzels and sauerbraten. That might not have seemed the precise historical moment to ensure the success of such an enterprise, but it thrived. In 1946, the Fort dining room was added next door. The result is the most popular place in town. Waitresses rush about in sensible shoes, slapping plates down and tolerating no lip from playful patrons. Monster portions are the rule, with veal shanks as thick as a linebacker's forearm. Check out the enormous stein collection at the bar.

8 Fort St. (west of Main St.). ✆ 413/734-7475. Main courses $9.95–$25. AE, DC, DISC, MC, V. Mon–Sat noon–11pm; Sun noon–10pm.

SPRINGFIELD AFTER DARK

Symphony Hall, at Court Street and East Columbus Avenue (✆ **413/788-7033;** tickets@citystage.symphonyhall.com), is the venue for concerts by the Springfield Symphony Orchestra, touring performers and musicals, and productions meant for children.

A bustling strip of beer-and-pool joints, music bars, and hip eateries continues to expand along downtown Worthington and Bridge Streets near our two recommended hotels. Check out the food and weekend live jazz at **Caffeine's Downtown,** 254 Worthington St. (✆ **413/788-6646**); it has outdoor seating in summer. Nearby are **The Fat Cat Bar & Grill,** 232 Worthington (✆ **413/734-0554**), showcasing local bands Wednesday through Sunday, and intimate **All That Jazz,** 254 Worthington St. (✆ **413/788-6646**), with live music, not always jazz, Wednesday through Saturday. They are only three of many.

4 The Pioneer Valley

Low hills and quilted fields channel the Connecticut River as it runs south toward Long Island Sound, forming the Pioneer Valley. The earliest European settlers came here for what proved to be uncommonly fertile soil and were followed in the 19th century by men who harnessed the power of the river and became wealthy textile and paper manufacturers.

These industrialists took the lead in funding the institutions of higher learning that are now the pride of the region. Prestigious Smith, Mount Holyoke, and Amherst are here, as are innovative Hampshire College and the sprawling main campus of the University of Massachusetts, with its enrollment of more than 25,000 students. All five contribute mightily to the cultural life of the valley, and the towns of **Northampton, Amherst,** and **South Hadley** are invigorated by the vitality of thousands of college-age young people.

In the north, near Vermont, the living village of **Deerfield** preserves the architecture and atmosphere of colonial New England, but without the whiff of sterility that often afflicts artificial gatherings of old buildings with costumed docents.

Interstate 91 and Route 5 both traverse the valley from south to north. The trip from edge to edge on the interstate takes less than an hour, while Route 5 tenders more of the flavor of pastoral vistas and colorful mill towns.

There are plenty of motels along the way, but if you're looking for lodgings more representative of the character of the region, contact the **Folkstone Bed & Breakfast Reservation Service** (© 800/762-2751 or 508/480-0380).

ESSENTIALS

GETTING THERE   From Boston and upstate New York, take the Massachusetts Turnpike (I-90) to Springfield, then follow I-91 or Route 5 north. While there are local buses, you'll want a car.

The nearest major airport is **Bradley International** (© 860/292-2000; www.bradleyairport.com), just south of Springfield, in Windsor Locks, Conn. (See "Springfield," earlier in this chapter, for a list of airlines that serve Bradley.) **Valley Transporter** (© 800/872-8752 or 413/549-1350) offers van shuttles between the airport and Amherst, Northampton, Hadley, Holyoke, and Deerfield. **Peter Pan Bus Lines** (© 800/237-8747; www.peterpanbus.com) schedules frequent connections between Springfield and the towns of the Valley.

Amtrak (© 800/USA-RAIL; www.northeast.amtrak.com) *Vermonter* trains stop in Amherst and Northampton on the route between St. Albans, Vt., and Washington, D.C., with connections to New York City and Boston.

VISITOR INFORMATION   The **Pioneer Valley Tourist Information Center** (© 413/665-7333) is at the intersection of Routes 5 and 10 in South Deerfield, at Exit 24 off I-91.

HOLYOKE

Once an important paper-manufacturing center, Holyoke (8 miles north of Springfield, 88 miles west of Boston) has suffered a long economic slide since World War II. Abandoned factories and the dissolute air of the commercial center don't bolster first impressions. Still, there are a couple of modestly worthwhile sights amid some imaginatively recycled old mills.

Canals dug during the city's heyday still cut through downtown. (They were intended to allow access to the mills.) Running beside one of the canals is long and narrow **Heritage State Park** (© 413/534-1723), with its entrance at 221 Appleton St. Its interpretive center offers walking tours and exhibits; a restored antique merry-go-round and the **Volleyball Hall of Fame** (© 413/536-0926; www.volleyhall.org) are also in the park. On most Sundays from mid-June to late August, the ancient locomotive of the **Heritage Park Railroad** pulls train buffs on a 2-hour trip downriver to Holyoke Mall at Ingleside. Call Heritage State Park (see above) for more information.

WHERE TO STAY & DINE

Yankee Pedlar Inn ⚐   If you're looking for a sedate, tranquil country inn, this isn't it. Business is thriving, and the place bustles with weddings, tour groups, and corporate get-togethers. The dining room is highly popular with locals as well as travelers. Of the five buildings in the largely Victorian complex, the 1850 House has the most modern rooms, while the Carriage House has the least expensive. Live music is presented many evenings in the Oyster Bar.

1866 Northampton St. (Rte. 5), Holyoke, MA 01040. ☏ **413/532-9494**. Fax 413/536-8877. www.yankee
pedlar.com. 28 units. May–Oct $85–$140 double; Nov–Apr $80–$136 double. Rates include breakfast. AE,
DC, DISC, MC, V. Take Exit 16 off I-91 and head east 5 blocks. **Amenities:** Restaurant (American); bar; access
to nearby health club; video rentals. *In room:* TV/VCR.

SOUTH HADLEY

Pioneer educator Mary Lyon founded Mount Holyoke Female Seminary, one of
the Seven Sisters group, here in 1836. Strung along the eastern side of Route
116 (College St.), the college is the essential reason for the existence of this small
town (pop. 13,600). It lies 15 miles north of Springfield and 7 miles south of
Amherst.

On the campus is a worthy **Art Museum** ❀ (☏ **413/538-2245**), which
focuses on art of the Orient, Egypt, and the Mediterranean. Renovation and
expansion were recently completed, bringing more of the collection into regular
view. Hours are Tuesday through Friday from 11am to 5pm, Saturday and Sunday from 1 to 5pm. Admission is free. To find it, take Park Street from the east
side of the Y intersection in the center of town and follow the signs.

Joseph Skinner State Park (☏ **413/586-0350**) straddles the border between
South Hadley and Hadley. On its 390 acres are miles of trails, picnic grounds,
and the historic Summit House (open Sat and Sun May–Oct), with panoramic
views of the valley.

NORTHAMPTON ❀❀

Smith College, with its campus sprawling along Main Street slightly west of the
commercial center, is Northampton's dominating physical and spiritual presence. One of the original "Seven Sisters" schools for women, Smith is the largest
female liberal arts college in the United States.

Northampton was long the home of Calvin Coolidge, who pursued his law
practice here before and after his occupancy of the Oval Office. A room maintained by the **Forbes Library,** 20 West St. (☏ **413/584-6037**), contains many
of his papers. Coolidge lived in houses at 21 Massasoit St. and on Hampton Terrace, but the homes are not open to the public.

Much else is open to visitors, however, and Northampton supplies many of the
diversions of a thriving college town. Cultural events range from chamber music
to art exhibitions, the number and diversity of restaurants and bars are far greater
than most cities its size can flaunt, and its many stores are as kicky as any devout
shopper might ask. Try to allow at least a long day and overnight in the area.

Just so you know, some folks like to call the town "NoHo." A well-received
book by Tracy Kidder, *Home Town* (Random House; 1999), profiles Northampton and a number of its people.

SEEING THE SIGHTS

Historic Northampton Among Northampton's most popular attractions are
the Museum Houses—three historic homes still standing on their original sites.
They are the 1730 Parsons House, the 1796 Shepherd House, and the 1812
Isaac Damon House, which contains a furnished parlor true to 1820.

46 Bridge St. (east of the railroad bridge). ☏ 413/584-6011. www.historic-northampton.org. Tours $3
adults, $2 seniors and students, $1 children 12 and under. Museum Tues–Fri 10am–4pm, Sat–Sun noon–4pm;
house tours given Sat–Sun noon–4pm only.

Smith College ❀ To a considerable extent, the campus buildings that line
Elm Street are a testament to the excesses of late-19th-century architecture.
Their often egregious admixtures of Gothic, Greco-Roman, Renaissance, and
medieval esthetic notions lend a Teutonic sobriety to the west end of town. On

the other hand, Frederick Law Olmsted, famed for his design of New York's Central Park, laid out much of the original landscaping, and the campus contains many wooded walks and gardens.

Elm St. (C) 413/584-2700. www.smith.edu.

Smith College Museum of Art ★★   With the conclusion of a 3-year renovation and expansion, this facility steps up to equal footing with New England's finest college art museums, including those at Williams, Harvard, and Yale. It already had an impressive permanent collection of paintings by Degas, Monet, Picasso, and Winslow Homer, among many 19th- and 20th-century Europeans and Americans. Now, there is not only more space to show them, but ample room in addition for an ambitious program of temporary exhibitions. The new third-floor galleries, in addition to fine views of town and campus, allow abundant light for canvases by a substantial number of French Impressionists and Post-Impressionists, including Gauguin, Cézanne, Renoir, and Monet. Americans Sargent, Whistler, and Georgia O'Keefe are also represented. On the second floor, British historical and portrait painters Benjamin West and Joshua Reynolds share space with Greek and Roman glassware, ceramics, and statuary, while the ground floor is given to traveling exhibits. There is an atrium cafe serving drinks and snacks. Parking is a challenge, but worth the effort.

Elm St. and Bedford Terrace. (C) 413/585-2760. www.smith.edu/artmuseum. Admission free. June–Aug Tues–Sun noon–4pm; Sept–May Tues–Sat 10am–4pm; Sun noon–4pm.

GETTING OUTSIDE

Three miles southwest of town on Route 10 is **Arcadia Nature Center and Wildlife Sanctuary,** 127 Combs Rd., Easthampton ((C) **413/584-3009**), a 700-acre preserve operated by the Massachusetts Audubon Society. It contains marshes and woods bordering the Connecticut River, with 5 miles of trails. The sanctuary is open Tuesday through Sunday from dawn to dusk, trails from 9am to 3pm. Admission is $3 for adults, $2 for seniors and children 3 to 15.

The 8½-mile **Norwottuck Rail Trail Bike Path** follows a former railroad bed running between Northampton and Amherst. Access is via Damon Road and at Mount Farms Mall. Bicyclists, skaters, and cross-country skiers are all welcome. Bikes can be rented at **Valley Bicycles,** 319 Main St. ((C) **413/256-0880**), across the river in Amherst.

Look Memorial Park, 300 N. Main St. ((C) **413/584-5457**), is northwest of town off Route 9, with 157 acres of woods, a lake (with boats for rent), miniature golf, tennis, picnic grounds, and a small zoo. Musical and theatrical events, including puppet shows, are held in summer. Admission $3 weekends and $2 weekdays from April to October; free from November to March.

SHOPPING

In a town with a bookstore at every other corner, **Raven Used Books,** 4 Old South St., down the hill from Main Street ((C) **413/584-9868**), shines. Along with the usual categories, it has shelves devoted to shamanism, prophecy, and erotica.

In addition to an abundance of bookstores, Northampton enjoys the most diverse shopping in the valley. The **Antiques Center of Northampton,** 9½ Market St. ((C) **413/584-3600**), contains the stalls of more than 60 dealers; closed Wednesdays. **Ten Thousand Villages,** 82 Main St. ((C) **413/582-9338**), is part of a nonprofit Mennonite program selling handicrafts from more than 30 Third World countries.

A former department store has been reconfigured into **Thorne's Market-place,** 150 Main St. (*C* **413/584-5582**), now containing more than 30 bou-tiques and a box office for theatrical and musical events. Next to the side entrance of the marketplace is **Herrell's,** 7 Old South St. (*C* **413/586-9700**), home base of a mini-chain of New England ice-cream emporia.

Northampton has a reputation as a small town with an unusually vigorous arts community. Burnishing that image is the prestigious **R. Michelson Gallery,** 132 Main St. (*C* **413/586-3964**), which occupies a grand former bank.

WHERE TO STAY

Anticipate higher rates and limited vacancies during graduation and homecom-ing, in addition to the usual holiday weekends.

Clarion Hotel ★ This used to be called the Inn at Northampton, so there's a new sign out by the road. That makes it easier to find, because the hotel is hid-den behind a gas station. Renovations have elevated it from a standard motel to something closer to a modest resort and conference center.

Rte. 5 and I-91 (just west of Exit 18), Northampton, MA 01060. *C* **800/582-2929** or 413/586-1211. Fax 413/586-0630. www.hampshirehospitality.com. 122 units. $88–$140 double; $159 suite. Rates include conti-nental breakfast Mon–Fri. AE, DC, DISC, MC, V. **Amenities:** Restaurant (Steakhouse); bar; heated indoor pool; outdoor pool; lighted tennis court; Jacuzzi; business center; limited room service. *In room:* A/C, TV, dataport, coffeemaker, hair dryer, iron.

Hotel Northampton ★ Built in 1927, this brick building at the center of town looks older. Rooms of varying sizes contain wicker and colonial reproductions, feather duvets, and assorted Victoriana. Many front rooms have balconies over-looking King Street, some have fridges, and a few have Jacuzzis. Downstairs, **Wig-gins Tavern** is a colonial watering hole with dark beams and three stone fireplaces.

36 King St., Northampton, MA 01060. *C* **800/547-3529** or 413/584-3100. Fax 413/584-9455. www.hotel northampton.com. 107 units. Apr–Nov $145–$245 double; Dec–Mar $135–$215 double. Rates include con-tinental breakfast. AE, DC, DISC, MC, V. Free parking. **Amenities:** 2 restaurants (American); bar; exercise room; business center; limited room service; same-day dry cleaning/laundry. *In room:* A/C, TV, dataport, hair dryer, iron.

WHERE TO DINE

Eastside Grill ★★ REGIONAL AMERICAN The consensus choice for tops in town, this white-clapboard building with a nautical look is a refuge for the 40-plus set from the prevailing collegiate tone of Northampton. The far-reach-ing menu has bayou riffs, such as barbecued shrimp with greens, duck étouffée, and shrimp and andouille jambalaya. But while the Cajun/Creole dishes absorb much of the kitchen's attention, there are ample alternatives. Seafood is impres-sive, especially the curried fried oysters and macadamia-crusted halibut.

19 Strong Ave. (1 block south of Main St.). *C* **413/586-3347.** Reservations recommended. Main courses $12–$18. AE, DC, DISC, MC, V. Mon–Thurs 5–10pm; Fri 5–10:30pm; Sat 4–10:30pm; Sun 4–9pm.

Fitzwilly's AMERICAN Occupying an 1898 building, this ingratiating pub makes the most of its stamped-tin ceilings and ample space. Copper brew-ing kettles signal an intriguing selection of beers. Beyond the two bars are cur-tained booths where patrons dive into pizzas, ribs, pastas, and such pub faves as blooming onion and fried calamari. Appetizers are half price during the 4-to-7pm happy hour, and there are blue-plate lunches for only $5.25 to $6.95. Everything is available for takeout.

23 Main St. (near Pleasant St.). *C* **413/584-8666.** Reservations not accepted. Main courses $10–$15. AE, DC, DISC, MC, V. Daily 11:30am–1am.

Green Street Café ★ NEW AMERICAN   Julia Child dined here, and the chef is a graduate of the French Culinary Institute. That accounts for the Gallic tilt of the menu and the excellent baguettes, baked right here. Don't overdose on the bread, though, for there are any number of delectables emerging from the kitchen—salmon with lentils, duck braised in Gewürztraminer, and chicken with apples and hazelnuts, for three. The restaurant grows its own vegetables in season, and the emphasis throughout the year is on fresh ingredients. All that, and there's a fireplace, too. One hitch: it's the most expensive place in town (compare with the prices at the Eastside Grill, above).

64 Green St. ⓒ 413/586-5650. Reservations recommended. Main courses $20–$26. MC, V. Mon–Fri noon–2pm and 5:30–10pm; Sat 5:30–10pm; Sun 10am–2pm and 5:30–10pm. Follow Main St. toward the Smith campus, straight into West St., turning right on Green St.

Osaka JAPANESE   There's no pretending that this new sushi and steakhouse is the equal of similar establishments in New York or Los Angeles, but it's odds-on best of breed in the Valley. Its predecessor was a Mexican restaurant, so some decor changes have been made, including lots of blond wood, a sushi bar at the entrance and a large hibachi in back, which they'll fire up for as few as two people. The menu lists 18 special rolls ($7.95–$13), 28 a la carte sushi and sashimi, and 16 vegetable sushi maki. That's before it takes a deep breath before adding hand rolls, soups, chef's specials, bento boxes, teriyaki, and on. Entrees come with uninspired miso soup and boiled rice. While it's possible to put together a conventional meal, the wiser course is to pick and choose among the many rolls and sushi options—the spicy red snapper, ebi tempura, maki, osaki, and naruto have been good. Once past the taciturn male members of the staff, the waitresses are cheerful and accommodating.

7 Old South St. (1 block south of Main St.). ⓒ 413/587-9548. Main courses $12–$26. AE, DC, DISC, MC, V. Mon–Sat 11:30am–11pm (Fri–Sat until midnight); Sun 12:30–11pm.

Vermont Country Deli & Cafe ECLECTIC   Tantalizing options include sesame chicken, pesto tortellini, and maple-barbecued pork ribs. Nearly 20 imaginative sandwiches, including three of the strictly vegetarian persuasion, are made to order. Also on offer are plump sticky buns and sourdough baguettes.

48 Main St. (near Pleasant St.). ⓒ 413/586-7114. Main courses $5.50–$8.95. MC, V. Mon–Sat 7am–7pm; Sun 8am–6pm.

NORTHAMPTON AFTER DARK

The presence of Smith and four other area colleges only partially accounts for the large number of bars and clubs in town, making Northampton the nightlife magnet of the valley. For a rundown of what's happening, pick up a free copy of the *Valley Advocate*.

Still thriving after 100-plus years, the **Academy of Music,** 74 Main St. (ⓒ 413/584-8435), shows arthouse and foreign films, and provides a venue for opera, ballet, and pop performers on tour.

Another old favorite, the **Iron Horse Music Hall,** 20 Center St. (ⓒ 413/586-8686), has played host to a wide variety of artists, from Bonnie Raitt to Dave Brubeck to folkies and grunge rockers. Cover is typically between $8 and $18.

Live bluegrass, jam rock, and soul-funk alternate with DJs at the **Pearl Street Nightclub,** 10 Pearl St. (ⓒ 413/584-0610). There are often dance nights targeted at teenagers, as well as gay nights. Nearby is the new **Bishop's Lounge,** 41 Strong Ave. (ⓒ 413/584-8513), a sophisticated update of the funky old Bay State Hotel, with live music 6 nights a week. **Harry's,** 140 Pleasant St.

(© 413/586-9155), has music every night, mostly live, largely rock or R&B, with karaoke, open mike, and DJ interludes.

The **Calvin Theatre and Performing Arts Center,** 19 King St. (© **401/586-0851**), offers touring performers as diverse as the Pat Metheny Group, flamenco troupes, and children's theater. Classical and chamber music is the customary fare at Smith's **Sweeney Concert Hall,** Sage Hall (© **413/585-2787**).

AMHERST

Yet another Pioneer Valley town defined by its educational institutions, this one has an even larger student population than most, with distinguished Amherst College occupying much of its center, the large University of Massachusetts campus to its immediate northwest, and Hampshire College off South Pleasant Street. All three—and Smith College and Mount Holyoke, on the other side of the Connecticut River—combine to provide a full September-to-June slate of artistic and musical events.

On the edge of the town green is a seasonal **information booth.** Its hours vary, but if it's closed, visitors can call the **Chamber of Commerce** (© **413/253-0700**) for information.

HISTORIC HOMES & COLLEGES

Most of the historic homes are within a few blocks of the Amity/Main/Pleasant street crossing. Amherst College lies mostly along the east side of the town green. At the northeast corner is the **Town Hall,** another fortress-like Romanesque Revival creation of Boston's H. H. Richardson.

Amherst College   Named for Baron Jefferey Amherst, a British general during the last of the French and Indian Wars, the illustrious liberal-arts college was founded in 1821, with Noah Webster on its first board of trustees. Robert Frost was a member of the faculty for more than a decade.

Amherst's campus cuts through the heart of the town and contains two museums open to the public. The **Pratt Museum** ⭐, at the southeast corner of the main quad (© **413/542-2165**), contains dinosaur tracks collected from sedimentary rocks of the valley, as well as fossils and a mastodon skeleton. The **Mead Art Museum** ⭐, Routes 116 and 9 (© **413/542-2335**), displays sculptures, paintings, photographs, and antiquities. Its strengths lie in the works of 19th- and 20th-century American artists and French Impressionists. Admission to both museums is free.

S. Pleasant and College sts. © 413/542-2000. www.amherst.edu.

Dickinson Homestead ⭐   Designated a National Historic Monument, this is the house where Emily Dickinson was born in 1830 and where she lived until her family moved in 1840. They returned in 1855, and the famous poet stayed here until her death 31 years later. The "Belle of Amherst" was the granddaughter and daughter of local movers and shakers, the source of her support while she produced the poetry that was to be increasingly celebrated even as she withdrew into near-total seclusion.

280 Main St. (2 blocks east of the Town Hall). © 413/542-8161. www.dickinsonhomestead.org. Admission $5 adults, $4 seniors and students, $3 children 6–18, free for children under 6 and students from the 5 area colleges. Guided tours only, Mar to mid-Dec Wed and Sat 1–4pm on the hour; Apr–May and Sept–Oct Wed–Sat 1–4pm on the hour; June–Aug Wed–Sun 1–4pm on the half-hour, Sat 10:30 and 11:30am. Reservations recommended.

University of Massachusetts   Though the university was founded in 1863, this sprawling 1,200-acre campus north of the town center dates mainly from the 1960s. Several of its buildings top out at over 20 stories. Its 25,000 students study for degrees in 90 academic fields. Six art galleries are scattered around the campus; foremost among these is the University Gallery in the **Fine Arts Center** ⭐, beside the pond in the quad. It focuses on 20th-century artists. The center also mounts productions in dance, music, and theater. Call the box office (☎ 413/545-2511) for information on upcoming performances.

Rte. 116. ☎ **413/545-4237** for tour information. Campus tours available daily at 11am and 1:15pm, except Sat–Sun in June–July, Mar break, and most holidays.

GETTING OUTSIDE

An 8½-mile bicycle trail follows an old rail bed from Warren Wright Road in Belchertown, passing through Amherst, and on to Elder Island in the Connecticut River adjacent to Northampton. Bikes can be rented at **Valley Bicycles,** 319 Main St., Amherst (☎ **800/831-5437** or 413/256-0880). It operates a seasonal shop, **Valley Bicycles Trailside,** 8 Railroad St. (☎ **413/584-4466**), directly on the trail.

SHOPPING

Under new ownership, the former Atticus/Albion Bookstore has become **Amherst Books** 8 Main St. (☎ **413/256-1547**). While it has a less rumpled aspect than it did, but the operators are no less committed to books and their patrons. The nearby **Jefferey Amherst Bookshop,** 55 S. Pleasant St. (☎ **413/253-3381**), specializes in Emily Dickinson and academic texts.

WHERE TO STAY

Lord Jeffery Inn ⭐⭐ It's a running battle to keep the principal lodging in a college town from looking a little battered. At the moment, the Lord Jeff is winning, thanks to almost constant renovation and redecorating. So despite the wear and tear of more than 75 years of graduations and homecomings, the inn offers an environment that is as warm as its several fireplaces. The Sorbonne-trained chef has turned the **Windowed Hearth** into Amherst's event restaurant, open for dinner and Sunday brunch.

30 Boltwood Ave. (next to the Town Hall), Amherst, MA 01002. ☎ **800/742-0358** or 413/253-2576. Fax 413/256-6152. www.lordjefferyinn.com. 48 units. $89–$159 double; $129–$209 suite. AE, MC, V. Pets accepted ($15). **Amenities:** 2 restaurants (Creative Regional); bar; access to nearby health club; limited room service. *In room:* A/C, TV, dataport.

WHERE TO DINE

Another option is the **Windowed Hearth,** at the Lord Jeffery Inn, above.

Judie's ⭐⭐ CREATIVE AMERICAN Don't leave Amherst without eating at Judie's. The vivacious owner does her best to suit every taste. Just to keep things ticking, for example, there's a "Munchie Madness" period from 3 to 6pm, with a half-price snacks menu of potato skins, nachos, and such. Throughout the day, folks drop by for a cup of seafood bisque and one of the trademark popovers. Typical dinner entrees are the steak and three-mushroom risotto and seafood gumbo with shrimp, sausage, scallops, salmon, and lobster. This being a college town, portions run from really big to immense, the better to assuage raging young metabolisms.

51 N. Pleasant St. (north of Amity and Main sts.). ☎ **413/253-3491.** Main courses $12–$17. AE, DISC, MC, V. Sun, Tues–Thurs 11:30am–10pm; Fri–Sat 11:30am–11pm.

AMHERST AFTER DARK

Students and other young adults tend to gravitate toward the livelier music scene in Northampton, but Amherst does offer some nighttime entertainment. Close at hand is the **Black Sheep Cafe,** 79 Main St. (© **413/253-3442**), active with singers, readings, chamber music—a broad, unpredictable selection. The beer is good, the food indifferent, and the music varied at the **Amherst Brewing Company,** 24–36 N. Pleasant St. (© **413/253-4400**).

Amherst College's **Buckley Recital Hall** (© **413/542-2195**) and the **Mullins Center** (© **413/733-2500**) at UMass mount a variety of performances that might include, for example, the Cincinnati Symphony, Mummenschantz, or Elton John.

DEERFIELD ★★★

Meadows cleared and plowed more than 330 years ago still surround this historic town between the Connecticut and Deerfield rivers. Every morning, tobacco and dairy farmers leave houses fronting the main street to work their land nearby. Students attend the distinguished prep school, Deerfield Academy, founded in 1797. Deerfield is an invaluable fragment of American history, and it isn't one of those New England village exhibits with costumed performers who go home to their condos at night.

A town still exists here, 16 miles north of Northampton and 16 miles northwest of Amherst, because the earliest English settlers were determined to thrive despite their status as a frontier pressure point in the wars that tormented colonial America. Massacres of Deerfield's settlers by the French and Indian enemies of the British nearly wiped out the town in 1675 and again in 1704. In the latter raid, 47 people were killed and another 112 were taken prisoner and marched to French Québec.

The main thoroughfare, simply called "The Street," is lined with more than 80 houses built in the 17th, 18th, and 19th centuries. Most are private, but 14 of them can be visited through tours conducted by Historic Deerfield, a local tourism organization (see below).

MUSEUMS & HISTORIC HOMES

"The Street" is a mile long, with most of the museum houses concentrated along the long block north of the central town common. There are two buildings operated by organizations other than Historic Deerfield. One is Memorial Hall Museum, east of the town common on Memorial Street, for which a separate admission is charged. (For the slightly higher fee of $12 adults, $5 children and students, tours of the 14 museum houses can be combined with a visit to Memorial Hall through Historic Deerfield.) The other is the Indian House Memorial, north of the Deerfield Inn, also maintained by a separate organization. Because it is only a 1929 reproduction of an earlier house, it is of less interest than the other structures.

Special celebrations in the town are held on Patriot's Day (the 3rd Mon in Apr), Washington's Birthday, Thanksgiving, and the Christmas holidays. Call the information center (© **413/774-5581;** see below) for details.

Historic Deerfield ★★★ Begin with a visit to the Hall Tavern, opposite the post office, where tickets are sold and brochures are available. A particularly useful booklet outlines a walking tour of 88 historic locations in the village. This is also the departure point for guided tours. While there are no charges for simply strolling The Street, the only way to get inside the museum houses is by tour.

The 14 houses on the tour were constructed between 1720 and 1850. They contain furnishings, textiles, ceramics, silver and pewter, and implements used from the early 17th century to 1900. Included are imports from China and Europe as well as items made in the Connecticut River Valley during its prominence as an industrial center.

The judicious selection at the **Museum Store,** between the post office and the Deerfield Inn (© **413/774-5581**), includes weather vanes, hand-dipped candles, and reproductions of light fixtures found in the village houses.

A stone building behind the Dwight House contains the **Flynt Center of Early American Life** 🏛, with galleries for changing exhibitions of paintings, textiles, and decorative arts relevant to the local history.

A free attraction is the **Channing Blake Meadow Walk.** Open from 8am to 6pm in good weather, the interpretive trail begins beside the Rev. John Farwell Moors House, a Historic Deerfield holding on the west side of the Street. It goes through a working farm, past the playing fields of Deerfield Academy, and through pastures beside the Deerfield River. Along the trail, sheep and cattle are seen up close; for that reason, dogs aren't allowed.

Information Center, Hall Tavern, The Street. © 413/774-5581. grace@historic-deerfield.com. Admission to all museum houses (good for 2 consecutive days) $12 adults, $6 children 6–17. Daily 9:30am–4:30pm.

Memorial Hall Museum 🏛   Deerfield Academy's original 1798 building was converted into this museum of village history in 1880. A popular, if suggestively grisly exhibit is the door of a 1698 home that shows the gashes made by weapons of the French and Indian raiders in 1704. Should the point be too muted, a hatchet is also embedded in the door. Five period rooms are also on view. Special events—plays, crafts fairs, lectures, and even ice-cream socials—are held monthly.

8 Memorial St. (between the Street and Routes 5 and 10). © 413/774-3768, or 413/774-7476 off season. Admission $6 adults, $3 children and students, free for children under 6. May–Oct daily 10am–4:30pm.

WHERE TO STAY & DINE

Deerfield Inn 🏛   Built in 1884, this inn is located in the middle of The Street and is one of the best-known stopping places in the valley. The innkeepers restlessly scour the establishment, over the last few years replacing all the bathroom fixtures, refinishing the older furniture, and installing new carpeting. Antiques and reproductions are judiciously mixed throughout. With blazes in the several fireplaces and an atmospheric tavern in which to linger, this is as pleasant a setting as can be found. That said, the food served in the dining room and in the cafeteria, truth to tell, is no better than ordinary.

81 Old Main St., Deerfield, MA 01342. © 800/926-3865 or 413/774-5587. Fax 413/775-7221. www. deerfieldinn.com. 23 units. May–Oct $125–$200 double; Nov–Apr $125–$180 double. Rates include breakfast and afternoon tea. Midweek discounts available. AE, DC, MC, V. **Amenities:** Restaurant (American)' cafeteria; bar. *In room:* A/C, TV, dataport, coffeemaker, hair dryer, iron.

5 The Berkshires

More than hills but less than mountains, the Taconic and Hoosac ranges that define this region at the western end of the state go by the collective name "The Berkshires." The hamlets, villages, and two small cities that have long drawn sustenance from the region's kindly Housatonic River and its tranquil tributaries are as New England as New England can be.

Mohawks and Mohegans lived and hunted here, and while white missionaries established settlements at Stockbridge and elsewhere in an attempt to Christianize the native tribes, the Indians eventually moved on west. Farmers, drawn to the narrow but fertile floodplains of the Housatonic, were supplanted in the 19th century by manufacturers, who erected the brick mills that drew their power from the river.

At the same time, artists and writers were attracted by the mild summers and seclusion that these hills and lakes offered. Nathaniel Hawthorne, Herman

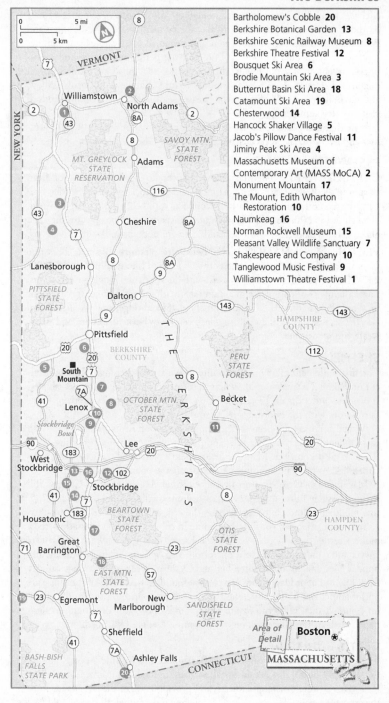

The Berkshires

0   5 mi
0   5 km

VERMONT

NEW YORK

Williamstown
North Adams

MT. GREYLOCK
STATE
RESERVATION

Adams

SAVOY MTN.
STATE
FOREST

Cheshire

Lanesborough

PITTSFIELD
STATE
FOREST

Dalton

Pittsfield

BERKSHIRE
COUNTY

South
Mountain

Lenox

Stockbridge
Bowl

West
Stockbridge

OCTOBER MTN.
STATE
FOREST

Becket

Lee

HAMPSHIRE
COUNTY

PERU
STATE
FOREST

Stockbridge

Housatonic

BEARTOWN
STATE
FOREST

Great
Barrington

OTIS
STATE
FOREST

HAMPDEN
COUNTY

EAST MTN.
STATE
FOREST

Egremont

New
Marlborough

SANDISFIELD
STATE
FOREST

Sheffield

Ashley Falls

CONNECTICUT

BASH-BISH
FALLS
STATE PARK

Area of
Detail

Boston

MASSACHUSETTS

Melville, and Edith Wharton were among those who put down temporary roots. By the late 19th century and the arrival of the railroad, wealthy New Yorkers and Bostonians had discovered the region and begun to erect extravagant summer "cottages." With their support, culture and the performing arts found a hospitable reception. By the 1930s, theater, dance, and music performances had established themselves as regular summer fixtures. Tanglewood, Jacob's Pillow, and the Berkshire and Williamstown Theatre festivals draw tens of thousands of visitors every summer.

Note that many inns routinely stipulate minimum 2- or 3-night stays in summer and over holiday weekends and often require advance deposits.

ESSENTIALS

GETTING THERE   The Massachusetts Turnpike (I-90) runs east-west from Boston to the Berkshires, with an exit near Lee and Stockbridge. From New York City, the scenic Taconic State Parkway connects with I-90 not far from Pittsfield.

Amtrak (© **800/USA-RAIL;** www.northeast.amtrak.com) operates the Lake Shore Limited daily between Boston and Chicago, stopping in Pittsfield each way.

VISITOR INFORMATION   The **Berkshire Visitors Bureau,** Berkshire Common (off South St., near the entrance to the Hilton), Pittsfield (© **800/ 237-5747** or 413/443-9186), can assist with questions and lodging reservations. Local chambers of commerce maintain information booths at central locations in Great Barrington, Lee, Lenox, Pittsfield, Stockbridge, and Williamstown (see the sections that follow). Also check out **www.berkshires.com** and **www. westernmassvisit.net**.

SHEFFIELD ✫

The first settlement of any size encountered when approaching from Connecticut on Route 7 is Sheffield, known as the "Antiques Capital of the Berkshires." It occupies a floodplain beside the Housatonic River, 11 miles south of Great Barrington, with the Berkshires rising to the west.

Agriculture has long been the principal occupation of its residents, and still is, to a degree. Everyone else sells antiques, or so it might seem driving along Route 7 (also known as Main St. or Sheffield Plain). The meticulously maintained houses cultivate an impression of prosperous tranquility.

May through October, stop by the **Colonel Ashley House,** Cooper Hill Road, in Ashley Falls (© **413/298-3239**). Built by the colonel himself in 1735, this modified saltbox is believed to be the oldest house in Berkshire County. Ashley was a person of considerable repute in colonial western Massachusetts, a pioneer settler, an officer in one of the French and Indian Wars, and later a lawyer and a judge. The house is open from 1 to 5pm on Saturday, Sunday, and holiday Mondays in June, September, and October; Wednesday through Sunday from July to Labor Day. Admission to the grounds is free; tours of the house are $3 for adults and $1 for children 6 to 12. To find it, drive south from Sheffield on Route 7, then veer onto Route 7A toward Ashley Falls. Bear right on Rannapo Road. At the Y intersection, turn right on Cooper Hill Road.

GETTING OUTSIDE

The 278-acre nature reservation called **Bartholomew's Cobble** ✫, on Route 7A (© **413/229-8600**), lies beside an oxbow bend in the Housatonic. Its 6 miles of trails cross pastures, penetrate forests, and provide vistas of the river valley from the area's high point, Hurlburt's Hill. Picnicking is permitted. Birders should take binoculars. Trails are open from sunrise to sunset, and the small natural-history

> ### ⌒ *Tips* Sheffield on Stage
>
> From late June to late August, the **Barrington Stage Company** (© 413/528-8888; www.barringtonstageco.org) mounts musicals, comedies, and dramas at the **Consolati Performing Arts Center,** on Berkshire School Road. On five Saturday evenings in July and August, the **Berkshire Choral Festival,** 245 N. Undermountain Rd. (© 413/229-3522; www.chorus.org), performs classical works at the Berkshire School in Sheffield.

museum is open daily from 9am to 4:30pm. Requested donations are $3 for adults and $1 for children 6 to 12. To get here, follow the directions for the Colonel Ashley House (see above), except at the end of Rannapo Road, bear left on Weatogue Road.

ANTIQUING

Sheffield lays justifiable claim to the title of "Antiques Capital of the Berkshires"—no small feat, given what seems to be an effort by half the population of the Berkshires to sell collectibles, oddities, and true antiques to the other half. These are canny, knowledgeable dealers who know exactly what they have, so expect high quality and few bargains.

Darr Antiques and Interiors, 34 S. Main St. (© 413/229-7773), specializes in 18th- and 19th-century English and American furniture. Farther north along Route 7, **Dovetail Antiques,** 440 Sheffield Plain (© 413/229-2628), features American clocks. Continuing along Route 7, on the left at the edge of town, is **Susan Silver** (© 413/229-8169), with meticulously restored 18th- and 19th-century English library furniture (desks, reading stands) and French accessories.

There are at least two dozen other dealers along this route. Most of them stock the **free directory** of the Berkshire County Antiques Dealers Association, which lists member dealers from Sheffield to Cheshire and across the border in Connecticut and New York. Look, too, for the pamphlet called *The Antique Hunter's Guide to Route 7.*

SOUTH EGREMONT

If you're coming to the Berkshires from the Taconic Parkway in New York, you can't help but drive through the town of Egremont. Its larger, busier half is South Egremont, once a stop on the stagecoach route between Hartford and Albany. It retains many structures from that era, including mills that utilized the stream that still rushes by. Those circumstances make it a magnet for antiques dealers and restaurateurs. In the former category, seek out **The Splendid Peasant,** on Route 23 (© 413/528-5755), which specializes in folk art.

GETTING OUTSIDE

HIKING   Scenic **Bash-Bish Falls State Park** 🛠🛠, on Route 23 (© 413/528-0330), makes a rewarding day outing for hiking, birding, and fishing (no picnicking, though). To get here, drive west on Route 23 from town, turning south on Route 41, and immediately right on Mount Washington Road. Watch for signs directing the way to Mount Washington State Forest and Bash-Bish Falls. After 8 miles, a sign indicates a right turn toward the falls; look for it opposite a church with an unusual steeple. The road begins to follow the course of a mountain stream, going downhill. In about 3 miles is a large parking place next to a craggy promontory.

The sign also points off to a trail down to the falls, which should be negoti-
ated only by reasonably fit adults. First, mount the promontory for a splendid
view across the plains of the Hudson Valley to the pale-blue ridgeline of the
Catskill Mountains. The falls can be heard, but not yet seen, down to the left.
If this trail seems too steep, continue driving down the road to another parking
area, on the left. From here, a gentler trail a little over a mile long leads to the
falls. The falls themselves are quite impressive, crashing down from more than
80 feet. The park is open from dawn to dusk. It has 15 campsites.

SKIING   At the western edge of the township, touching the New York border,
is the **Catamount Ski Area,** on Route 23 (✆ **413/528-1262;** www.catamount
ski.com). Only about 2 hours from Manhattan, it is understandably popular
with New Yorkers. It has 28 trails, including the daunting Catapult (the steepest run in the Berkshires) and seven chairlifts, as well as a 400-foot half-pipe for
snowboarders. Night skiing and rentals are available.

WHERE TO STAY

Egremont Inn ⭐   Slip into this friendly former stagecoach stop as easily as
into a favorite old flannel robe. The Egremont has been a tavern and inn since
1780. That longevity shows, in tilting floors and a grand brick fireplace. Dinner
is served Wednesday through Sunday year-round. A singer-guitarist performs
Thursday nights, a jazz ensemble Saturday evenings. Rates are negotiable during
slow periods and for long stays. Kids are welcome.

Old Sheffield Rd. (1 block off Rte. 23), South Egremont, MA 01258. ✆ 413/528-2111. Fax 413/528-3284.
www.egremontinn.com. 19 units. Weekdays $90–$165 double; weekends $110–$190 double. Rates include
breakfast. Weekend packages available. AE, DISC, MC, V. **Amenities:** Restaurant (American); tavern; outdoor
pool; golf course nearby; 2 tennis courts; bike rental. In room: A/C.

Weathervane Inn   An affectionate cat welcomes new arrivals to a building
that began as a 1735 farmhouse, but was renovated in Greek Revival style in
1835. Many guest rooms have four-poster beds with quilts; fireplaces have been
added to two units. In summer, a three-night stay is required on weekends. Children are welcome, but pets aren't.

Rte. 23, South Egremont, MA 01258. ✆ 800/528-9580 or 413/528-9580. Fax 413/528-1713. www.
weathervaneinn.com. 10 units. $135–$165 double; $225–$245 suite. Rates include breakfast and afternoon
tea. Packages available. AE, DC, MC, V. **Amenities:** Unheated outdoor pool; public golf course next door. In
room: A/C, dataport.

WHERE TO DINE

John Andrew's ⭐ CONTEMPORARY BISTRO   This superior farmhouse
restaurant utilizes several rooms, walls sponged a dusky rose, the dim lighting
brightened by candles on white tablecloths. Rows of windows in the rear enclosed
porch let in rays of the fading summer sun. Focaccia squares come with generously proportioned cocktails. Notable appetizers include grilled Hudson River
duck foie gras with currants and greens and lightly breaded sardines (how can
they taste this fresh in the Berkshires?) with tiny white beans on the side. Obviously, a fertile imagination is at work behind the kitchen doors, one that conjures
refreshing twists on bistro standards. Pork shank is especially recommendable,
this version with spinach and carrots over creamy polenta. The breast of the
duck entree is rare and flavorful, the flesh of the leg falling off the bone. The
food is better than the service, which tends to be glum and sometimes forgetful.

Rte. 23 (west of town center). ✆ 413/528-3469. Reservations strongly advised. Main courses $16–$28.
MC, V. Thurs–Tues 5–9pm (until 10pm Fri–Sat).

GREAT BARRINGTON

Even with a population well under 8,000, this pleasant retail center, 7 miles south of Stockbridge, is the largest town in the southern part of the county. Rapids in the Housatonic provided power for a number of mills in centuries past, most of which are now gone, and in 1886 this was one of the first communities in the world to have electricity on its streets and in its homes.

Great Barrington has no sights of particular significance, leaving time to browse its many antiques galleries and specialty shops. Convenient as a home base for excursions to such nearby attractions as Monument Mountain, Bash-Bish Falls, Butternut Basin, Tanglewood concerts, and the historic houses of Stockbridge, it has a number of unremarkable but entirely adequate motels north of the center along or near Route 7 that tend to fill up more slowly on weekends than the better-known inns in the area. It is something of a dining destination, too, with 55 eating places, including *four* sushi bars! *Note:* The local Board of Health has banned smoking in *any* public space in town.

The **Southern Berkshire Chamber of Commerce** maintains an information booth at 362 Main St. (© **413/528-1510;** www.greatbarrington.org), near the town hall. It's open Tuesday through Saturday from 9am to 5pm.

GETTING OUTSIDE

The **Egremont Country Club,** on Route 23 (© **413/528-4222;** www.bcn.net/ ~egremont), is open to the public. Its facilities include an 18-hole golf course, tennis courts, and an Olympic-size pool. Greens fees are modest; tee times required.

Butternut Basin, on Route 23, 2 miles east of town (© **413/528-2000,** or 800/438-7669 for snow conditions; www.butternutbasin.com), is known for its strong family ski programs. There's day care at $8 per hour for kids 2½ to 6 from December 23 until the end of the season, and the Mountaineer program for children 4 to 12 offers packages that include lunch, instruction, and lift tickets for $75 per day. Six double and quad chairlifts provide access to 22 trails. There are also 5 miles of cross-country trails. On weekends, full-day lift tickets cost $45 for adults, $34 for seniors and children 7 to 13, and $10 for children 6 and under. A two-day jazz festival is presented in late August.

A little over 4 miles north of town, west of Route 7, is **Monument Mountain,** with two trails to the summit. The easier route is the Indian Monument Trail, about an hour's hike to the top; the more difficult one, the Hickey Trail, isn't much longer but takes the steep way up. The summit, called Squaw Peak, offers splendid views.

SHOPPING

Head straight for Railroad Street, the town's best shopping strip. Start on the corner with Main Street, at **T. P. Saddle Blanket & Trading Co.** (© **413/528-6500**). An unlikely emporium that looks as if it had been lifted whole from the Rockies, it's packed with boots, hats, Indian jewelry, blankets, and jars of salsa.

Mistral's, 6 Railroad St. (© **413/528-1618**), stocks Gallic tableware, linens, fancy foods, and furniture. Nearby, **Nahuál,** 9 Railroad St. (© **413/528-2423**), offers folk arts and handicrafts, primarily from Africa and Latin America. **Church Street Trading Company,** 4 Railroad St. (© **413/528-6120**), defies easy categorization, with walking sticks, dog collars, and candles all on display. The primary wares are sturdily stylish North Country sweaters, shirts, and pants.

Recently moved from around the corner on Main St., **The Chef's Shop,** 31 Railroad St. (© **413/528-0135**), still features a bounty of gadgets and cookbooks as well as cooking classes. Still on Main Street, near Railroad, is the **Birdhouse Gallery,** 280 Main St. (© **413/528-0984**), with a variety of American folk arts—dolls, quilts, paintings—expertly made to look old. In the other direction, you'll encounter **Sappa,** #306 (© **413/528-6098**), presenting luxury bath products, vases, and flax-filled pillows. Across the street, **La Pace,** 313 Main St. (© **413/528-1888**), is an upmarket "Bed, Bath, and Beyond"-style store with an Italian tilt.

In the north end of town, just before Route 7 turns right across a short bridge, Route 41 goes straight, toward the village of Housatonic. In about 4 miles you'll see a shed that houses the kiln of **Great Barrington Pottery** (© **413/274-6259**). Owner Richard Bennett has been throwing pots according to ancient Japanese techniques for more than 30 years.

Stay on Route 7, going north of the center, and you'll pass a large mall with an anchoring Kmart. In that unlikely location is one of the best (and few) bookstores in the Berkshires, **The Bookloft,** Barrington Plaza (© **413/528-1521**).

WHERE TO STAY

There are several acceptable motels north of town on Route 7, the most desirable being the new **Holiday Inn Express,** 415 Stockbridge Rd. (© **413/528-1810;** www.hiexgb.com), which has an indoor pool and whirlpool, and rooms with Jacuzzis and/or fireplaces; rates include breakfast. The **Chamber of Commerce** operates a lodging hot line at © **800/269-4825** or 413/528-4006.

The Old Inn on the Green & Gedney Farm ★★   This growing establishment comprises a former 1760 tavern/general store and the 18th-century Thayer House, both on the village green; a pair of converted dairy barns; and the latest addition, 1906 Gedney Manor. Among the most desirable units are those in Thayer House, some with fireplaces and all with air-conditioning, and in the barn, where contemporary furnishings are combined with Oriental rugs. All five intimate dining rooms have fireplaces, and the only other illumination at dinner is from candles. Menus are quite sophisticated and reservations are strongly advised, especially on weekends.

Rte. 57, New Marlborough, MA 01230. © 800/286-3139 or 413/229-3131. Fax 413/229-8236. www.oldinn. com. 26 units. $185–$365 double; $245–$325 suite. Rates include breakfast. AE, MC, V. Take Rte. 23 east from Great Barrington, picking up Rte. 57 after 3½ miles. After 5¾ miles, the Old Inn is on the left. Continue to the barns on the left; registration is on the ground floor of the gray barn. **Amenities:** Restaurant (Creative American); courtyard pool at Thayer House. *In room:* A/C, hair dryer.

Windflower Inn   A roadside lodging built in the middle of the last century in Federal style, the Windflower commands a large plot of land opposite the Egremont Country Club, on Route 23 between Great Barrington and South Egremont. The gracious family that has owned and operated the inn through two generations makes everyone welcome. Six rooms have fireplaces; four have canopy beds. The inn is smoke-free.

684 S. Egremont Rd. (P.O. Box 25), Great Barrington, MA 01230. © 800/992-1993 or 413/528-2720. Fax 413/528-5147. www.windflowerinn.com. 13 units. $100–$200 double. Rates include full breakfast and afternoon tea. Children under 16 stay in parent's room for $25. AE. **Amenities:** Unheated outdoor pool. *In room:* A/C, TV, dataport.

WHERE TO DINE

In addition to the places listed below, you might check out the restaurant at the **Old Inn on the Green & Gedney Farm** (see above).

Castle Street Cafe ★★ NEW AMERICAN   This storefront bistro has ruled the Great Barrington roost for some time now, and recently expanded into the next building, installing what it calls a "Celestial Bar," with live jazz piano 6 nights a week in summer and on weekends the rest of the year. While a Francophilic inclination is apparent in the main room, what with duck breast with potato galette and steak *au poivre,* it isn't overpowering—rack of lamb and the grilled vegetable entree are other possibilities. Have a drink at the bar in the new room while you're checking out the night's menu, or stay there for such casual eats as burgers, pizzas, and cheese plates. An award-winning wine list is another reason to stop in.

10 Castle St. (near the Town Hall). ℂ 413/528-5244. Reservations advised on weekends. Main courses $18–$24. AE, DISC, MC, V. Daily 5–9pm (until 10pm Fri–Sat).

Helsinki Tea Company *Finds* ECLECTIC   It looks like an Eastern European tea room run by an eccentric fortuneteller, with mismatched tables and even overstuffed living room armchairs amid the assorted oddments. (In winter, try for a table near the fireplace in the back room.) There are Scandinavian items on the card to justify the name, including Finnish meatballs, "Red Square" smelts, latkes and dilled cucumber, borscht, and blini with gravlax. Refusing the straitjacket, though, the kitchen also puts together a quesadilla du jour, teriyaki ribs, and a blackened catfish po' boy with jalapeño aioli. At least they did, on last sight–expect surprises. There's full bar service.

284 Main St. (in back, down the passageway). ℂ 413/528-3394. Reservations suggested on weekends. Main courses $14–$21. DISC, MC, V. Daily 10am–10pm.

Pearl's ℱ CONTEMPORARY BISTRO   A share of the credit for GB's growing rep as a gastronomic destination has to go to this self-assured enterprise. A follow-up to the owners' stylish Bistro Zinc in Lenox (see below), traditionalists grumble that it's more Manhattan than Berkshires, and it clearly isn't country cookin'. The presence of a floor-to-ceiling painting of a bull of regal bearing and a large print of a resplendent wild turkey rightly imply that beef and game are the way to go. The NY strip, filet mignon, and 24-ounce porterhouse come with *rosti* potatoes, fried onions, haricots vert, and roast tomatoes–all straightforward, and hard to beat for flavor. Barbecued quail with sweet potato fritters and triple-cut lamb chops with mint butter and white bean purée are easily as satisfying. Don't resist the caramel banana strudel as a finisher. Since most of the menu items can be cooked quickly, expect to be in and out within an hour unless you purposely slow down delivery.

47 Railroad St. ℂ 413/528-7767. Reservations suggested. Main courses $17–$31. AE, MC, V. Mon–Sat 5–10pm (until 11pm Fri–Sat); Sun 11am–3pm and 5:30–10pm.

Union Bar & Grill NEW AMERICAN   The industrial-chic interior, with exposed ceiling ducts and brushed-metal trim, has been softened by the new chef-owner. The menu is a little more conservative than it was under the previous proprietors, too, given the evidence of grilled Cornish game hen, grilled salmon, and steak au poivre. While none of this is especially adventuresome, it is, with only a few exceptions, most satisfying. Much of the time, the young and hip mingle easily with seniors and families, accompanied by live jazz Wednesday nights and at Sunday brunch. Subject to change, lunch is only served on weekends.

293 Main St. ℂ 413/528-6228. Main courses $18–$25. MC, V. Mon, Wed–Thurs 5–10pm; Fri 5–11pm; Sat noon–3pm and 5–11pm; Sun noon–3pm and 5–10pm.

Verdura/Dué CONTEMPORARY ITALIAN   It doesn't put on airs, not with wood-only floors, tables, chairs, and ceiling beams, but this is a welcome antidote to the red-sauce-and-pizza joints that usually pass for Italian in the Berkshires. A basket of thick, chewy bread sets the tone, with a fruity olive oil for dipping, following icy, filled-to-the-brim martinis. An excellent starter is the antipasto sampler, with pickled white anchovies, roasted sweet peppers with balsamic vinegar, honeyed cippolini onions, charred leeks, and prosciutto with fig jam. After that, a simple dish of pasta is likely to be more than enough dinner. Short, plump bucatelli tumbled with a rich veal ragout does nicely. Heartier appetites might prefer the braised lamb shank with rosemary polenta or the wood-grilled quail with sweet potato gratin. The bill comes before you ask.

That might explain why the dinner crowd is more often greyheaded than pierced, but that ratio reverses in **Dué,** the new wine bar adjoining the restaurant. The *enoteca* is for conversation with glasses of pinot grigio and tapas, pastas, or panini. Prices are gentler than next door.

44-47 Railroad St. ⓒ 413/528-8969. Reservations advised for Verdura on weekends. Main courses, Verdura $21–$26, Dué $3–$14. AE, MC, V. Verdura Thurs–Tues 5–10pm; Dué Tues–Sun 11:30am–close (summer), 5pm–close (winter).

GREAT BARRINGTON AFTER DARK

A grand old downtown cinema, the **Mahaiwe,** has been restored to some of its 1930s glory and is being transformed into a year-round performing arts center. One of its first tenants was the **Berkshire Opera Company** (ⓒ 413/644-9988; www.berkshireopera.org), which has a June to September season. The **Aston Magna Festival** features classical music performed on period instruments. Concerts are held on five Sundays in July and August at St. James Church, Main Street and Taconic Avenue (ⓒ 800/875-7156 or 413/528-3595).

Live jazz is often presented at the Castle Street Cafe and the Union Bar & Grill (see "Where to Dine," above). **Club Helsinki** (284 Main St.; ⓒ 413/528-3394; www.clubhelsinkiweb.com) is a more regular music venue, with as many as 6 nights a week of rock, pop, bluegrass, reggae, and other forms throughout the year. The **Triplex Cinema,** 70 Railroad St. (ⓒ 413/528-8886), shows a mixed bag of independent and foreign flicks as well as major studio releases.

STOCKBRIDGE 🟊🟊

Stockbridge's ready accessibility to Boston and New York (about 2½ hr. from each and reachable by rail since the mid–19th century) transformed the original frontier settlement into a Gilded Age summer retreat for the rich. The town has long been popular with artists and writers as well. Illustrator Norman Rockwell, who lived here for 25 years, rendered the Main Street of his adopted town in a famous painting. Along and near Main Street are a number of historic homes and other attractions, enough to fill up a long weekend, even without the Tanglewood concert season in nearby Lenox. One of the Berkshires' hottest destinations, Stockbridge is inevitably jammed on warm weekends and during foliage season.

Stockbridge lies 7 miles north of Great Barrington and 6 miles south of Lenox. The **Stockbridge Chamber of Commerce** (ⓒ 413/298-5200; www.stockbridgechamber.org) maintains an information booth opposite the row of stores depicted by Rockwell. It's open May through October.

SEEING THE SIGHTS

Berkshire Botanical Garden These 15 acres of flower beds, ponds, and vegetable and herb gardens are an inviting destination for strollers and picnickers. The first weekend in October features a harvest festival.

Routes 102 and 183. ℭ **413/298-3926**. www.berkshirebotanical.org. Admission $7 adults, $5 seniors, $3 students, free for children under 12. May–Oct daily 10am–5pm. Tours offered Sat–Sun June–Aug. Drive west from downtown Stockbridge on Main St., picking up Church St. (Rte. 102) northwest for about 2 miles.

The Berkshire Theatre Festival ⚹⚹   From June to August, and occasionally at other times during the year, the Berkshire Theatre Festival holds its season of classic and new plays, often with marquee names starring or directing. Kevin Kline and Joanne Woodward have been participants. Its venue is a "casino" built in 1887 to plans by architect Stanford White. A second venue, the Unicorn Theatre, opened in 1996. The Festival celebrated its 75th anniversary in 2003.

P.O. Box 797, Main St. ℭ **413/298-5576**. www.berkshiretheatre.org. Tickets: Main Stage $35–$50, Unicorn Theatre $25–$35.

Chesterwood ⚹   Sculptor Daniel Chester French, best known for the Lincoln Memorial in Washington, D.C., used this estate as his summer home for more than 30 years. His *Minute Man* statue at the Old North Bridge in Concord, completed in 1875 at the age of 25, launched his highly successful career. The 122-acre grounds are used for an annual show of contemporary sculpture.

4 Williamsville Rd. ℭ **413/298-3579**. www.chesterwood.org. Admission $10 adults, $9 seniors and college students, $5 children 6–18. May–Oct daily 10am–5pm. Drive west on Main St., south on Rte. 183 about 1 mile to the Chesterwood sign.

Mission House ⚹   The Rev. John Sergeant had the most benevolent, if paternalistic, of intentions: He sought to build a house among the members of the Housatonic tribe, hoping to convert them to "civilized" (that is, English) ways through proximity to his godly self and his small band of settlers. The weathered Mission House, built in 1739, was the site of this Christianizing process.

Main and Sergeant sts. (Rte. 102). ℭ **413/298-3239**. www.thetrustees.org. Admission $5 adults, $3 children 6–12. Memorial Day to Columbus Day daily 10am–5pm. Visits are by guided tour only.

Naumkeag   In 1886, Stanford White designed this 26-room house for Joseph Hodge Choate, who served as U.S. ambassador to the Court of St. James. The client dubbed it "Naumkeag," a Native American name for Salem, Mass., his childhood home. His house of many gables and chimneys is largely of the New England shingle style, surrounded by impressive gardens. Admission is by guided tour only, worth it for the glimpses of the rich interior.

Prospect Hill. ℭ **413/298-3239**. www.thetrustees.org. Admission $10 adults, $3 ages 6–12. Memorial Day to Columbus Day daily 10am–5pm. From the Cat & Dog Fountain in the intersection next to the Red Lion Inn, drive north on Pine St. to Prospect Hill Rd. about ½-mile.

Norman Rockwell Museum ⚹⚹   This striking building opened in 1993, at a cost of $4.4 million, to house the works of Stockbridge's favorite son. The illustrator used both his neighbors and the town where he lived to tell stories about an America now rapidly fading from memory. Most of Rockwell's paintings adorned covers of the *Saturday Evening Post:* warm and often humorous depictions of homecomings, first proms, and visits to the doctor. He addressed serious concerns, too, notably with his poignant portrait of a little African-American girl being escorted by U.S. marshals into a previously segregated school. Critics long derided his paintings as saccharine and sentimental, but today a revision of sorts has led to widespread appreciation for his deft brushwork. The lovely 36-acre grounds also contain Rockwell's last studio (which is closed Nov–Apr). The museum and grounds remain open year-round.

Rte. 183. ℭ **413/298-4100**. www.nrm.org. Admission $12 adults, $7 students, free for children 18 and under. May–Oct daily 10am–5pm; Nov–Apr Mon–Fri 10am–4pm, Sat–Sun 10am–5pm. Take Main St. (Rte.

102) west to the junction with Rte. 183, then turn left (south) at the traffic signal. In about ½ mile, you'll see the entrance to the museum on the left.

WHERE TO STAY

Inn at Stockbridge ⭐ A mile north of Stockbridge center, this 1906 building with a grandly columned porch is set well back from the road on 12 acres. The innkeepers are eager to please, serving full breakfasts by candlelight and afternoon spreads of wine and cheese. Several bedrooms have fireplaces and whirlpools, and there are four suites in the newly remodeled barn. High-speed Internet access is provided.

30 East St. (Rte. 7), Stockbridge, MA 01262. © **888/466-7865** or 413/298-3337. Fax 413/298-3406. www. stockbridgeinn.com. 16 units. June–Oct $140–$320 double; Nov–May $140–$245 double. Rates include full breakfast and afternoon refreshments. AE, DISC, MC, V. No children under 12. **Amenities:** Heated outdoor pool. *In room:* A/C, TV/VCR, dataport, hair dryer, iron.

The Red Lion Inn ⭐⭐ So well known that it serves as a symbol of the Berkshires, this busy inn had its origins as a stagecoach tavern in 1773. The rocking chairs on the porch are the place to while away an hour reading or people-watching. An ancient birdcage elevator carries guests up to halls and rooms filled with antiques ranging in styles of over 2 centuries. Floors creak and tilt, as might be expected, but modern comforts are provided. Six satellite buildings have gradually been added, all within 3 miles of the inn. Dining choices include the pricey traditional dining room, the casual and marvelously atmospheric **Widow Bingham Tavern,** the **Lion's Den** pub, and, in good weather, the courtyard out back. The basement Lion's Den also has nightly live entertainment, usually of the folkrock variety. Book your room far in advance; for a quieter night, ask for an inside room.

Main St., Stockbridge, MA 01262. © **413/298-5545.** Fax 413/298-5130. www.redlioninn.com. 108 units (14 with shared bathrooms). Mid-Apr to late May $130–$200 double, $200–$305 suite; late May to late Oct $180–$215 double, $270–$355 suite; late Oct to mid-Apr $110–$205 double, $185–$315 suite. Packages available. AE, DC, DISC, MC, V. **Amenities:** 3 restaurants (Eclectic/American); 2 bars; outdoor pool; golf and tennis privileges nearby; recently upgraded fitness room; limited room service; massage; babysitting; laundry; dry cleaning. *In room:* A/C, TV/VCR, dataport, unstocked fridges in suites, hair dryer.

Taggart House ⭐⭐ Ordinarily, an inn with only four guest rooms wouldn't merit space here. But what rooms! The decor of this outwardly sedate 1850 Victorian/colonial mansion provides guests with a breathtaking immersion in the Gilded Age. Start with the theatrical main floor—the inlaid mahogany dining table was once a centerpiece in an Argentine palace. There's a paneled library, a ballroom, a harpsichord, and nine beguiling fireplaces. And upstairs, beds are decorated with fur throws, East Indian silk coverlets, and velvet canopies.

Main St. (1 block west of the Red Lion), Stockbridge, MA 01262. © and fax **413/298-4303.** www.taggart house.com. 4 units. Weekdays $235–$355 double; weekends $265–$355. Rates include breakfast. Packages available. 2- to 3-night minimum stay on summer and fall weekends. MC, V. Young children not accepted. *In room:* A/C, dataport.

WHERE TO DINE

See also the dining options at the **Red Lion Inn,** reviewed above.

The American Craftsman ⭐ A crafts gallery by the same name on Main Street preceded the restaurant (only open since Aug 2003), and so this converted farmhouse is a showcase for fanciful objects and furnishings—articulated wooden turtles, music boxes in shape of pianos, shelves of free-form blown glass and ceramics. All of it is for sale, including your chair and the salt and pepper shakers. The menu sounds fresh and chipper and proves to be exactly that. An open-faced rabbit tart with mushrooms and a truffle cream is something not seen everywhere, as is roasted pork tenderloin with Turkish figs and three-onion marmalade. Lunch sandwiches are equally interesting, such as the duck pastrami Rueben and the sourdough panini composed of arugula, roasted peppers, tomato, and *grana padano* cheese. Weekend brunch is especially popular.

7 South St. (Rte. 7 and Maple St.). ℂ **413/298-0250.** Reservations advised on weekends. Main courses $19–$25. AE, MC, V. Daily noon–4:30pm and 5:30–10pm (closed Mon in winter).

WEST STOCKBRIDGE

The hills around this Stockbridge satellite (just 5 miles to the northwest) are alive with creativity. Potters, painters, writers, sculptors, weavers, and glass blowers pursue their compulsions, selling the results from their studios and several galleries. A pamphlet called *The Art of West Stockbridge,* available in display racks throughout the area, describes the work of some of the more important artisans and where it can be found.

One of the most ambitious enterprises is the **Berkshire Center for Contemporary Glass** ⋆, 6 Harris St. (ℂ **413/232-4666**), in the heart of the village. Kids find the process fascinating and are even allowed to participate. The center is open daily, from 10am to 10pm May through October, from 10am to 6pm November through April.

WHERE TO DINE

La Bruschetta ⋆⋆ NEW ITALIAN The chef/owners grew weary of gearing up for the frantic summer business, then downstaffing and cutting back during the slow winter—so they now operate a fine food and wine store, providing quality takeout stews, rotisserie chicken, osso buco, and the best (and only) pizzas in West Stockbridge.

1 Harris St. ℂ **413/232-7141.** Pizzas and main courses $9–$13. AE, MC, V. Tues–Sun 11am–9pm.

Truc Orient Express ⋆⋆ VIETNAMESE The menu is full of revelatory taste sensations. *Mai tuyet nhi* is a soup adrift with snow mushrooms and lobster meat, a suitable lead-in to the extravaganza called *lauthap cam-chap pin loo,* a hot pot crowded with meatballs, shrimp, squid, scallops, and assorted veggies ladled over rice noodles. Tables are set up on the deck in summer, and takeout is available.

3 Harris St. ℂ **413/232-4204.** Main courses $7.50–$18. AE, DISC, MC, V. Summer daily 11am–3pm and 5–10pm; winter Wed–Mon 5–9:pm.

LEE

While Stockbridge and Lenox were developing into luxurious recreational centers for the upper crust of Boston and New York, Lee was a thriving paper-mill town. That meant that it was shunned by the wealthy summer people and thus remained essentially a town of workers and merchants. It has a somewhat raffish though not unappealing aspect, its center bunched with shops and offices and few of the stately homes that characterize neighboring communities.

The town's contribution to the Berkshire cultural calendar is the Jacob's Pillow Dance Festival, which first thrived as "Denishawn," a fabled alliance between founders Ruth St. Denis and Ted Shawn.

Lee is located 5 miles southeast of Lenox. In summer and early fall, the **Lee Chamber of Commerce** (ℂ **413/243-0852;** www.leechamber.org) operates an **information center** on the town common, Route 20 (ℂ **413/243-4929**). It can help you find lodging, often in guesthouses and B&Bs—rarely as grand as those in neighboring Lenox, but nearly always cheaper. That's something to remember when every other place near Tanglewood is either booked or quoting prices of $250 a night.

SEEING THE SIGHTS

The Jacob's Pillow Dance Festival ✦✦✦   In 1933, Ted Shawn decided to put on a show in the barn, and so was born Jacob's Pillow. After decades of advance and retreat and evolution, Jacob's Pillow is now to dance what Tanglewood is to classical music. Once a regular summer venue for Shawn and famed dancer and choreographer Martha Graham, one of his early disciples, the theater has long welcomed troupes of international reputation, including the Mark Morris Dance Group, Twyla Tharp, and the Paul Taylor Dance Company. The season runs from mid-June to late August, and tickets go on sale April 1.

The more prominent companies are seen in the main Ted Shawn Theatre, while other troupes are assigned to the Doris Duke Studio Theatre. Admission is free to the Inside/Out, an outdoor stage. The growing campus includes a store, pub, dining room, tent restaurant, and exhibition space. Picnic lunches can be pre-ordered 24 hours in advance.

P.O. Box 287, George Carter Rd., Becket. © 413/243-0745. www.jacobspillow.org. Tickets $5–$60. From Lee, take Rte. 20 east about 9 miles, then turn north on Rte. 8 toward Becket.

Santarella ✦   With no obligatory historic homes or museums to see in Lee, visitors often make the short excursion to a curious fairy-tale structure called Santarella, but known by most as the "Gingerbread House." Conical turrets top towers, while the shingled roof rolls like waves on the ocean. It served as a studio for sculptor Henry Hudson Kitson from 1930 to 1947, and now houses galleries showcasing the works of Berkshire artists.

Tyringham Rd. © 413/243-3260. www.berkshireweb.com/santarella. Memorial Day to Oct daily 10am–5pm. Admission $4 adults, free for children under 6. Take Rte. 20 south from Lee to Rte. 102, near the no. 2 interchange of the Massachusetts Tpk. Following the signs through the complicated intersection, pick up Tyringham Rd. on the other side and drive south about 4 miles.

GETTING OUTSIDE

October Mountain State Forest offers 50 campsites (with showers) and more than 16,000 acres for hiking, canoeing, cross-country skiing, and snowmobiling. To get here, drive northwest on Route 20 into town, turn right on Center Street, and follow the signs.

WHERE TO STAY

On the road to Lenox, the lakeside **Best Western Black Swan,** 435 Laurel St./Rte. 20 (© **800/876-7926** or 413/243-2700; www.travelweb.com), has a pool and restaurant; some of the 52 rooms have fireplaces.

Applegate ✦   This B&B utilizes a gracious 1920s Georgian Colonial manse to full advantage. The top unit has a canopy bed, Queen Anne reproductions, sunlight filtering through gauzy curtains, a steam shower, and a fireplace (with real wood). Most rooms have phones with dataports, some have TVs, Jacuzzis, and gas fireplaces. Chocolates and brandy await guests at bedside. Breakfast is by candlelight, and the innkeepers set out wine and cheese in the afternoon. They are "flexible" on children.

279 W. Park St., Lee, MA 01238. © **800/691-9012** or 413/243-4451. www.applegateinn.com. 10 units plus a 2-bedroom cottage. June–Oct $115–$295 double; Nov–May $115–$245 double; carriage house rates on application. MC, V. From Stockbridge, drive north on Rte. 7 about ½ mile; take a right on Lee Rd. The inn is 2¼ miles ahead. No children under 12. **Amenities:** Heated outdoor pool; 9-hole golf course across the street; tennis court; access to nearby health club; bikes. *In room:* A/C.

Chambéry Inn ⭐ This was the Berkshires' first parochial school (1885), named for the French hometown of the nuns who ran it. That accounts for the extra-large bedrooms, which were formerly classrooms. Six of them, with 13-foot ceilings and the original woodwork and blackboards, are equipped with whirlpool tubs and gas fireplaces. Some rooms have TV/VCRs, CD players, and fridges. A breakfast basket is delivered to your door each morning. No children under 18. No smoking.

199 Main St., Lee, MA 01238. ℂ **413/243-2221.** Fax 413/243-0039. www.berkshireinns.com. 9 units. July–Aug and Oct $99–$160 double, $135–$289 suite; Sept and last 2 weeks in June $85–$239 double, $129–$215 suite; Nov to mid-June $85–$135 double, $119–$199 suite. Rates include breakfast. AE, DISC, MC, V. **Amenities:** Limited room service from neighboring restaurant. *In room:* A/C, TV, coffeemaker, hair dryer, iron.

Devonfield From the road, there's no way to tell what this place is. The sign out front reads only "Devonfield," and the large house standing on a rise amid tall hemlocks and 29 acres could as easily be a yoga retreat or a conference center. But an inn it is, of the comfy-casual, rather than elegant, variety. When JFK and Queen Wilhemina stayed here decades ago, they were probably given the house on the other side of the pool, with its large sitting room with fireplace, kitchen, Jacuzzi, and king bedroom. Three rooms in the main house have fireplaces, too. Several common rooms invite guests inclined to cocooning. Children over 12 are welcome.

85 Stockbridge Rd., Lee, MA 01238. [te] **413/243-3298.** Fax 413/243-1360. www.devonfield.com. 10 units. June–Oct $120–$230 double; Nov–May $90–$170. Rates include breakfast. MC, V. **Amenities:** Heated outdoor pool. *In room:* A/C, TV, hair dryer

Federal House Built in 1824 in the Federal style, including a portico with fluted columns, this distinguished inn still sports antiques belonging to the original family in its bedrooms, which are perfectly nice if pricey. Four units have TVs. Breakfast is served by candlelight, the new owners have upgraded bedding and window treatments, and gas fireplaces have been installed in three rooms. Children 12 and over accepted. No smoking.

Main St. (Rte. 102), South Lee, MA 01260. ℂ **800/243-1824** or 413/243-1824. www.federalhouseinn.com. 10 units. Late June to Aug and late Sept to Oct $145–$245 double; early Sept and Nov to late June $100–$175 double. Rates include breakfast. AE, DISC, MC, V. Children over 12 welcome. *In room:* A/C.

LENOX ⭐⭐ & TANGLEWOOD

Stately homes and fabulous mansions mushroomed in this former agricultural settlement from the 1890s until 1913, when the 16th Amendment, authorizing income taxes, put a severe crimp in that impulse. But Lenox remains a repository of extravagant domestic architecture surpassed only in such fabled resorts of the wealthy as Newport and Palm Beach. And because many of the cottages have been converted into inns and hotels, it is possible to get inside some of these beautiful buildings, if only for a cocktail or a meal.

The reason for so many lodgings in a town with a population of barely 5,000 is Tanglewood, a nearby estate where a series of concerts by the Boston Symphony Orchestra is held every summer.

Lenox lies 7 miles south of Pittsfield. The **Lenox Chamber of Commerce** (ℂ **413/637-3646;** www.lenox.org) provides visitor information and lodging referrals.

SEEING THE SIGHTS

Frelinghuysen Morris House & Studio ⭐ Built on 46 acres next to the Tanglewood property in the early 1940s, this Bauhaus-influenced house was the home of abstract artists Suzy Frelinghuysen and George L. K. Morris. Their chosen style was Cubism, which they pursued long after it had been abandoned by better-known practitioners. Works by some of those artists—Braque, Léger, Gris, and Picasso—can be viewed alongside the canvases of the owners. Visits are by tour only.

92 Hawthorne St. ℂ **413/637-0166**. www.frelinghuysen.org. Admission $9 adults, $3 children 5–16. June 19th to Labor Day Thurs–Sun 10am–4pm; Sept–Oct Thurs–Sat 10am–4pm. Drive south from Tanglewood on Rte. 183, turn left on Hawthorne Rd., then left again on Hawthorne St. (note 2 different streets).

The Mount, Edith Wharton Restoration ✮ Wharton, who won a Pulitzer for her novel *The Age of Innocence,* was singularly equipped to write that deftly detailed examination of the upper classes of the Gilded Age and the first decades of the 20th century. She was born into that stratum of society in 1862 and traveled in the circles that made the Berkshires a regular stop on their restless movements between New York, Florida, Newport, and the Continent. Wharton had her villa built on this 130-acre lakeside property in 1902 and lived here 10 years before leaving for France, never to return. She took an active hand in the creation of the Mount, which makes the mansion a notable rarity—one of the few designated National Historic Landmarks designed by a woman. Wharton was, after all, the author of an upscale 1897 how-to guide called *The Decoration of Houses.* A $15-million restoration campaign continues, with work so far completed on the terrace and greenhouse and continuing on the interior and gardens.

2 Plunkett St. (at the intersection of Routes 7 and 7A). ℂ **413/637-1899**. www.edithwharton.org. Admission $16 adults, $8 students, free for children under 12. Guided tours given May–Oct daily 9am–5pm.

Shakespeare & Company ✮✮ The repertory company had long used buildings and amphitheaters on the grounds of the Mount (see above) to stage its May-to-December season of plays by the Bard, works by Chekhov and George Bernard Shaw, and efforts by new American and English playwrights. After increasingly bitter conflict with the custodians of the Wharton property, officials of the company purchased a 63-acre property on Kemble Street, closer to downtown Lenox. With construction of a new Founder's Theatre, the tented Rose Footprint Theatre, an administration building, and planned rehabilitation of other existing buildings, the Company now enjoys its very own campus devoted to the dramatic arts. Walking trails have been developed at the north end of the grounds and a cafe in the theatre lobby serves drinks and light fare. Free outdoor performances are staged before evening curtain times.

70 Kemble St. ℂ **413/637-3353**. www.shakespeare.org. Tickets $12–$50.

Tanglewood Music Festival ✮✮✮ Lenox is filled with music every summer, and the undisputed headliner is the Boston Symphony Orchestra (BSO). Concerts are given at the famous Tanglewood estate, usually beginning in July and ending the weekend before Labor Day. The estate is on West Street (actually in Stockbridge township, although it's always associated with Lenox). From Lenox, take Route 183 1½ miles southwest of town.

While the BSO is Tanglewood's 800-pound cultural gorilla, the program features a menagerie of other performers and musical idioms. These run the gamut from popular artists (like James Taylor and Bonnie Raitt) and jazz musicians (including Dave Brubeck and Wynton Marsalis) to such guest soloists as Itzhak Perlman and Yo-Yo Ma.

The Koussevitzky Music Shed is an open auditorium that seats 5,000, surrounded by a lawn where an outdoor audience lounges on folding chairs and blankets. Chamber groups and soloists appear in the smaller Ozawa Hall. Major performances are on Friday and Saturday nights and Sunday afternoon.

Tentative programs are available after January 1; the schedule is usually locked in by March. Tickets can sell out quickly, so get yours as far in advance as possible. If you decide to go at the last minute, take a blanket or lawn chair and get tickets for lawn seating, which is almost always available. You can also attend open rehearsals during the week, as well as the rehearsal for the Sunday concert on Saturday morning.

The estate itself (℗ **413/637-5165** June–Aug), with more than 500 acres of lawns and gardens, much of it overlooking the lake called Stockbridge Bowl, was put together starting in 1849 by William Aspinwall Tappan. Admission to the grounds is free when concerts aren't scheduled.

In 1851, a structure on the property called the Little Red Shanty was rented to Nathaniel Hawthorne, who stayed here long enough to write a children's book, *Tanglewood Tales,* and meet Herman Melville, who lived in nearby Dalton. The existing Hawthorne Cottage is a replica (and isn't open to the public). On the grounds is the original Tappan mansion, with fine views.

West St., Stockbridge. For recorded information, call ℗ **617/266-1492** from Sept–June 10 (note that information on upcoming Tanglewood concerts is not available until the program is announced in Mar or Apr). www.bso.org (tentative program info available after Jan 1). Tickets $14–$78 Shed and Ozawa Hall, $13–$18 lawn. Lawn tickets for children under 12 are free; children under 5 not allowed in the Shed or Ozawa Hall. Higher prices apply for some special appearances. To order tickets by mail before June, write the Tanglewood Ticket Office at Symphony Hall, 301 Massachusetts Ave., Boston, MA 02115. After June 1, write the Tanglewood Ticket Office, 297 West St., Lenox, MA 01240. Tickets can be charged to a credit card through **Symphony Charge** (℗ **888/266-1200** outside Boston, or 617/266-1200) or at www.bso.org.

GETTING OUTSIDE

Pleasant Valley Wildlife Sanctuary, 472 West Mountain Rd. (℗ **413/637-0320;** www.massaudubon.org), has a small museum and 7 miles of hiking and snowshoeing trails crossing its 1,500 acres. Beaver lodges and dams can be glimpsed from a distance, and waterfowl and other birds are found in abundance—bring binoculars. Hours are Tuesday through Saturday from dawn to sunset; admission is $3 for adults and $2 for children 3 to 15. To get here, drive north about 6½ miles on Routes 7 and 20 and turn left on West Dugway Road.

More extensive trails can be found at **October Mountain State Forest** (see "Getting Outside," under the section on Lee, above) or at **Beartown State Forest,** ℗ **413/528-0904,** 69 Blue Hill Rd., in nearby Monterey. The Appalachian Trail, which runs from Maine to Georgia, connects with a loop trail around a small pond with a nice swimming area. To get here, take Route 7 south for 3½ miles, then turn left onto West Road. After 2½ miles, turn left at the T intersection onto Route 102 east. Turn right over the bridge onto Meadow Street, then turn right onto Pine Street and follow the signs.

SHOPPING

The Bookstore, 9 Housatonic St. (℗ **413/637-3390**), helps fill a yawning need in the Berkshires, which are curiously short on comprehensive bookstores. Those in pursuit of art and antiques, on the other hand, cannot easily exhaust the possibilities. Among them: **Lenox Old Country Store,** 67 Church St. (℗ **413/637-9702**), known for the diversity of its offerings, including crafts, souvenirs, toys, and candy; and the **Hoadley Gallery,** 21 Church St. (℗ **413/637-2814**), which shows American crafts and ceramics. For fashion-forward clothing for men and women, much of it Italian-made, check in at **Casablanca,**

21 Housatonic St. (© **413/637-2680**). L.L.Bean, it isn't. Out on Route 7, heading toward Pittsfield, serious cooks should watch for **Different Drummer's Kitchen,** 374 Pittsfield Rd. (© **413/637-0606**).

WHERE TO STAY

The list of lodgings below is only partial, and most can accommodate only small numbers of guests. The Tanglewood concert season is a powerful draw, so prices are highest in summer as well as during the brief foliage season. Rates are of Byzantine complexity, set according to wildly varying combinations of seasons and days of the week as well as facilities offered. Minimum 2- or 3-night stays are usually required during the Tanglewood weeks, foliage, weekends, and holidays. *Note:* For visits during the Tanglewood season, reserve far in advance—February isn't too soon.

Given the substantial number of lodgings and limited space to describe them, admittedly arbitrary judgments have been made to winnow the list. Some inns, for example, are so rule-ridden and facility-free that they come off as crabby—no kids, no pets, no phones, no credit cards, no breakfast before 9am, shared bathrooms—and they cost twice as much as nearby motels that have all those conveniences. Let them seek clients elsewhere.

Others are open only 6 or 7 months a year and charge the world for a bed or a meal. In this latter category, though, one place demands at least a mention: **Blantyre,** 16 Blantyre Rd. (© **413/637-3556;** fax 413/637-4282), in its 1902 Tudor-Norman mansion, cossets its guests with a soak in undeniable luxury, both in dining room and bedchamber. Rates are $350 to $450 double, up to $950 for the top suite. It's open from early May to early November.

If all the area's inns are booked or if you want to be assured the full quota of 21st-century conveniences, Routes 7 and 20 north and south of town harbor a number of motels, including the **Mayflower Motor Inn** (© **413/443-4468**), the **Susse Chalet** (© **413/637-3560**), the **Lenox Motel** (© **413/499-0324**), and the **Comfort Inn** (© **413/443-4714**).

Very Expensive

Canyon Ranch in the Berkshires ★★★   Resorts successfully melding turn-of-the-last-century opulence and contemporary impulses for fitness and healthy living are rare, so for those with the discretionary income or others who'd like to splurge just once, this is the place. A guard turns away the unconfirmed at the gate, so there's no popping in for a look around. The core facility is the 1897 mansion modeled after Le Petit Trianon at Versailles. A fire in 1949 left only the magnificent library untouched, but that loss has been offset by major renovations. Sweat away the pounds in the huge spa complex, with more than 50 fitness classes and related activities a day, weights, an indoor track, racquetball, squash, and all the equipment you might want. Skiing, snowshoeing, kayaking, canoeing and hiking are added possibilities. The staff includes physicians, nurses, and psychologists, as well as sports and cooking instructors and massage therapists. Guest rooms are in contemporary New England style, with every hotel convenience except tempting minibars. After being steamed, exhausted, pummeled, and showered, the real events of each day are mealtimes: "nutritionally balanced gourmet," naturally.

P.O. Box 2170, 165 Kemble St., Lenox, MA 01240. © **800/726-9900** or 413/637-4100. Fax 413/637-0057. www.canyonranch.com. 126 units. All-inclusive 3- to 7-night packages from $935–$4,540 double. Rates include meals and allowances for health, beauty, and fitness services. Taxes and 18% service charge extra. AE, DC, DISC, MC, V. **Amenities:** Restaurant (Spa Cuisine); heated indoor and outdoor pools; outdoor and indoor tennis courts; extensive health club and spa; bikes; business center; salon; limited room service;

in-room massage; same-day dry cleaning/self-service laundry. *In room:* A/C, TV/VCR/DVD, dataport, hair dryer, iron, safe.

Cranwell Resort ★★★   The main building of this all-season resort looks like a castle in the Scottish Highlands, but no 17th-century laird lived this well. It stands at the center of a 380-acre property, ringed by views of the surrounding hills. That's where the most expensive rooms are; the rest are in four smaller outlying buildings. Accommodations are outfitted with less concern for adherence to a particular style than for surrounding guests in immediate comfort. In addition to the lovely grounds (which serve as cross-country ski trails in winter), there is a 60-acre golf school. Three dining rooms range from formal to pubby, and live jazz is featured Friday and Saturday nights. An enormous 35,000 square foot spa was opened in 2002, with pool, lounges with fireplaces, and 16 spa treatment rooms.

55 Lee Rd. (Rte. 183), Lenox, MA 01240. © **800/272-6935** or 413/637-1364. Fax 413/637-4364. www. cranwell.com. 107 units. May–Oct $265–$415 double, from $365 suite; Nov–Apr $165–$265 double, from $265 suite. Golf, spa, and ski packages available. AE, DC, DISC, MC, V. From Lenox Center, go north to Rte. 20 E. The resort is on the left. **Amenities:** 3 restaurants (Eclectic); bar; heated outdoor and indoor pools; 18-hole golf course; 4 tennis courts; extensive new health club; bike rental; salon; limited room service; in-room massage; babysitting; same-day dry cleaning. *In room:* A/C, TV/VCR, fax, dataport, fridge, coffeemaker, hair dryer, iron, safe.

Wheatleigh ★★   A fountain out front and a lobby fireplace with deeply carved garlands and cherubim set the tone. Beyond, glamorous urbanites often drape themselves in Gatsbyesque poses around the lavishly appointed great hall. Much of the time, they look elaborately bored, no easy feat in this persuasive 1893 replica of a 16th-century Tuscan palazzo, which aspires to the highest standards of the moneyed Berkshires. Happily, the interior decor is muted, not florid, utilizing neutral colors and restrained shapes. Wheatleigh has always been very expensive, even though the cheapest rooms average only 11 by 13 feet. But other places are catching up, and the manager is striving to give requisite value. The dining room rounds out the experience, with painstakingly conceived food in superb presentation.

Hawthorne Rd., Lenox, MA 01240. © **413/637-0610.** Fax 413/637-4507. www.wheatleigh.com. 19 units. $495–$695 double, from $1,155 suite. AE, DC, MC, V. **Amenities:** 2 restaurants (eclectic); lounge; heated outdoor pool; tennis court; exercise room; bike rental; concierge; in-room massage; babysitting; laundry service; dry cleaning. *In room:* A/C, TV/VCR, fax, hair dryer.

Expensive

Cliffwood Inn ★   One of the relatively compact manses of the Vanderbilt era, this inn has a long veranda in back overlooking the pool. Antiques and reproductions of many styles and periods fill the common and private spaces. Six guest rooms have working fireplaces (including one in a bathroom!). Three units have TVs.

25 Cliffwood St., Lenox, MA 01240. © **800/789-3331** or 413/637-3330. Fax 413/637-0221. www.cliffwood. com. 7 units. July to Labor Day and foliage season $159–$254 double; May 15–June 30 and Sept after Labor Day $136–$200; Nov–May 14 $118–$173. Rates include breakfast daily in high season, Sat–Sun only in shoulder season, Sun and holiday weekends only in low season. No credit cards. Children over 10 welcome. **Amenities:** Outdoor pool and indoor counter-current workout pool; Jacuzzi. *In room:* A/C.

Gateways Inn ★★   Harley Procter, who hitched up with a man called Gamble and made a bundle, had this house built in 1912. Its most impressive feature is the staircase that winds down into the lobby. Designed by McKim, Mead & White, it's a stunner, just the thing for a grand entrance. Equally impressive is the suite named for conductor Arthur Fiedler, with not one but two fireplaces, a big four-poster on the sun porch, and a Jacuzzi. Eight rooms have working fire-places. Dining here is one of Lenox's greater pleasures. The once-tiny bar has been expanded—it features 99 single-malt scotches and 55 grappas. Also, a ter-race has been added for after-concert light meals and desserts. Lunch is offered on summer weekends.

51 Walker St., Lenox, MA 01240. © **888/492-9466** or 413/637-2532. Fax 413/637-1432. www.gateways inn.com. 12 units. June–Oct $150–$295 double; $350–$450 suite; Nov–May $100–$190 double, $230–$350 suite. Rates include breakfast. AE, DC, DISC, MC, V. No children under 12. **Amenities:** Restaurant (eclectic); bar. *In room:* A/C, TV, dataport.

Moderate

Candlelight Inn   A folksy gathering place for locals as well as guests, the bar in this 1885 Victorian enjoys a convivial nightly trade, and the dining rooms are often full. In winter, sit beside a crackling fire; in summer, lunch out in the courtyard. On summer weekends, the basement pub is open for after-concert drinks and snacks. While the Candlelight does most of its business on the restaurant side, the upstairs bedrooms are homey and unpretentious.

35 Walker St., Lenox, MA 01240. © **800/428-0580** or 413/637-1555. www.candlelightinn-lenox.com. 8 units. $75–$195 double. Rates include breakfast. AE, DISC, MC, V. Often closed for a week or so in Jan. Accommo-dations unsuitable for children under 10. **Amenities:** Restaurant (eclectic); bar. *In room:* A/C, no phone.

Gables Inn ★★   Edith Wharton, who spent more than 2 decades in Lenox, made this Queen Anne mansion her home for 2 years while her house, the Mount, was being built. That may be enough to interest fans of the novelist, but there's much more to appeal to potential guests, including the canopied four-poster in Edith's bedroom. Meticulously maintained Victoriana and antiques are found in every corner. Many rooms have fireplaces, and suites have VCRs and fridges.

81 Walker St., Lenox, MA 01240. © **800/382-9401** or 413/637-3416. Fax 413/637-3416. www.gableslenox. com. 19 units. $90–$200 double; $160–$250 suite. Rates include breakfast. DISC, MC, V. No children under 12. **Amenities:** Heated outdoor and indoor pools; tennis court. *In room:* A/C, TV.

Village Inn   An inn off and on since 1775, this place hasn't a whiff of pre-tense. Its rooms come in considerable variety and are categorized as Deluxe, Superior, Standard, or Economy. That means four-posters in the high-end rooms, some of which have fireplaces and/or Jacuzzis, and constricted quarters with double beds at the lower prices. Claw-foot tubs are common in all cate-gories. Ask about rooms on the renovated third floor. Afternoon tea and dinner are served in the restaurant, light meals in the tavern. All rooms have VCRs. No smoking and no children under 6.

16 Church St., Lenox, MA 01240. © **800/253-0917** or 413/637-0020. Fax 413/637-9756. www.villageinn-lenox.com. 32 units. Summer–fall $130–$285 double, $530–$590 suite; winter–spring $65–$225 double, $370–$470 suite. Discount of 30% during midweek in winter/spring. Rates include breakfast. AE, DC, DISC, MC, V. **Amenities:** Restaurant; bar; free video library. *In room:* A/C, TV/VCR.

Yankee Inn   Of the several motels strung along Route 20 east of Lenox cen-ter, this is arguably the most desirable, and a place to remember when the area's inns are filled. It is also more congenial for families, for children are welcomed, as they are not in most B&Bs. Housekeeping is of reasonably high standard, and furnishings, while routine in design, are as fresh-looking, as might be expected in a city hotel. Some rooms have gas fireplaces and unstocked fridges. Long, empty corridors don't enhance the experience, but the indoor pool, convenient location, and relatively moderate prices (for the Berkshires) compensate.

461 Pittsfield Rd. (Rte. 20), Lenox, MA 01240. © **800/835-2364** or 413/499-3700. Fax 413/499-3634. www.berkshireinns.com. 96 units. June–Sept $89–$269 double; Oct–May $79–$239. AE, DC, DISC, MC, V.

Amenities: Lounge; heated indoor pool with whirlpool; modest exercise room. *In room:* A/C, TV, dataport, hair dryer, iron.

WHERE TO DINE

See also "Where to Stay," above, as many inns have dining rooms. In particular, **Blantyre** (© 413/637-3556) is worth a splurge. In high season, **Spigalina,** 80 Main St. (© 413/637-4455), serves imaginative Mediterranean cooking. Note that three of the restaurants listed below serve lunch, in a region where most of the better restaurants don't open until evening.

Bistro Zinc ⋆ CONTEMPORARY BISTRO   With its eponymous zinc bar, butcher paper over white tablecloths, tile floor, and waitresses in ankle-length aprons, this now-established entry has leapt in a single bound to the upper echelon of Berkshires dining. That is, if you admire not only the setting but also a cuisine and wine list that adhere with some rigor to the French-bistro canon. Menus have listed such appetizers as boneless quail stuffed with polenta, continuing with rabbit saddle, choucroute, sautéed skate wing, and lobster bouillabaisse. A remarkable 24 wines are available by the glass.

56 Church St. © 413/637-8800. Reservations suggested. Main courses $21–$28. AE, MC, V. Wed–Mon 11:30am–3pm and 5:30–10pm (bar until 12:30am).

Café Lucia ⋆⋆ REGIONAL ITALIAN   Here on Lenox's Restaurant Row, the post-preppie crowd of regulars and weekend refugees from the city is attired in country-casual cashmere and tweed, a taste no doubt honed at campuses of the Ivy League and Seven Sisters. The waitresses display a professionalism rarely experienced in these hills, bringing satisfying starters—carpaccio, bruschetta, and the like—followed by superior renditions of *saltimbocca alla Romana* and eight pastas. Look for the grilled spiedini—cubed leg of lamb marinated in fresh lemon and rosemary. Dine out on the broad deck in warmer months.

80 Church St. © 413/637-2640. Reservations recommended. Main courses $19–$32. AE, DC, DISC, MC, V. Tues–Sun 5:30–10pm. Closed 3 weeks Mar or Apr. Winter hours fluctuate, especially around holiday weekends; call ahead.

Church Street Cafe ⋆⋆ ECLECTIC AMERICAN   The most popular place in town delivers fanciful combinations that please the eye and pique the taste buds. Creative appearances on past menus have included fried oysters with a lemony remoulade sauce, sake and soy marinated and grilled shrimp with crabmeat wontons. Lunch is a busy time here, with quesadillas and crab-cake sandwiches among the favorites. The decor is rudimentary, the service friendly but rushed. A large deck fills up whenever the weather allows.

65 Church St. © 413/637-2745. Reservations recommended on weekends. Main courses $19–$28. MC, V. May–Oct daily 11:30am–2pm and 5:30–9pm; Nov–Feb Tues–Sat 11:30am–2pm and 5:30–8:30pm. Closed Mar and Apr.

Dish ⋆ NEW AMERICAN   Opened only in late 2003, this narrow storefront eatery was packed from the get-go. Since the decor is negligible and the accommodations cramped, the principal discernible reason for its furious popularity is the food. It comes from the kitchen in stuttering intervals, the uncertainty easily compensated by the startlingly high quality of what the creative chef-owner sends forth. At dinner, the pecan-encrusted rainbow trout and herb-roasted baby rack of lamb au jus are stars, preceded by a remarkable shrimp cake with horseradish plum tomato aioli or, perhaps, the pan-seared vegetable dumplings with ginger-soy vinaigrette. Those appetizers appear as "small plates" at lunch, where all the wildly tasty sandwiches are only $7. That's another reason the locals like it—they don't need a bank loan to eat here. And, at the time of this review, at least, the weekenders hadn't discovered it yet. That won't last.

37 Church St. ⓒ 413/637-1800. Reservations strongly advised. Main courses $16–$20. MC, V. Wed–Mon 7:30am–3pm; Thurs–Sat 5:30–9pm.

Firefly AMERICAN/GLOBAL   Previously known as the Roseborough Grill, the once largely unadorned old farmhouse has been given a sleeker, more urbane look. The menu, too, has been overhauled, and often-surprising food issues from the kitchen, sometimes featuring Asian and Mexican inflections, but mostly skipping around the Mediterranean Rim. Upping the chic-ness meter are tapas and martini menus. Past dishes have included pan-seared Chilean sea bass escabeche, lobster linguine, and Spanish-style baked chicken with olives, lemon, and saffron rice, all of which demonstrate that the chefs gambol in many scented fields, usually emerging with dignity intact.

71 Church St. ⓒ 413/637-2700. Main courses $19–$27. AE, DC, DISC, MC, V. Thurs–Mon 11:30am–3pm and 5–9pm (until 10pm Fri–Sat). Call ahead in winter. Closed Feb–Mar.

PITTSFIELD

Berkshire County's largest city (pop. 48,000) gets little attention in most tourist literature, and for good reason. A commercial and industrial center, it presents little of the charm that marks such popular destinations as Stockbridge and Lenox. Still, it is a convenient base for day excursions to attractions elsewhere in the region. In summer, the **Berkshire Black Bears** (ⓒ **413/448-2255**) play minor-league baseball at Wahconah Park, a 1919 stadium with real wooden box seats.

Pittsfield lies 137 miles west of Boston, 7 miles north of Lenox. The **Berkshire Visitors Bureau** (ⓒ **800/237-5747** or 413/443-9186; www.berkshires.org) is located in the same block of buildings as the Crowne Plaza Hotel, on Berkshire Common.

SEEING THE SIGHTS

Arrowhead   Herman Melville bought this 18th-century house in 1850 and lived here until 1863. It was during this time that he wrote *Moby-Dick*. A nature trail and shop are on site. In truth, however, the house is of limited interest to visitors other than literature students and avid readers.

780 Holmes Rd. ⓒ 413/442-1793. www.mobydick.org. Admission $8 adults, $5 students 15 and older, $3 for ages 6–14. From Fri before Memorial Day to Columbus Day daily 9:30am–5pm; rest of year by appointment only. Visits are by guided tour only, given on the hour. Drive east from Park Sq. on East St., turn right on Elm St., and turn right on Holmes Rd.

Berkshire Museum 🖈   It began in 1903 as the "Museum of Natural History and Art," words chiseled in stone above the entrance. The holdings bounce from Babylonian cuneiform tablets to tanks of live fish to archaeological artifacts like a delicate necklace from Thebes dating to at least 1500 B.C. An auditorium seating 300 serves as the "Little Cinema," which shows art and foreign films during the warmer months.

39 South St. (Rte. 7, 1 block south of Park Sq.). ⓒ 413/443-7171. www.berkshiremuseum.org. Admission $7.50 adults, $6.50 seniors, $5 ages 3–18. Mon–Sat 10am–5pm; Sun noon–5pm.

Hancock Shaker Village 🖈🖈🖈   Of the 20 restored buildings that make up the village, its signature structure is easily the 1826 round stone barn. The Shaker preoccupation with functionalism joined with purity of line and respect for materials has never been clearer than it is in the design of this building—its round shape expedited the chores of feeding and milking livestock by arranging

Movers & Shakers in Massachusetts

Mother Ann arrived in 1774 with eight disciples just as the disgruntled American colonies were about to burst into open rebellion. The former Ann Lee, once imprisoned in England for her excess of religious zeal, had anointed herself leader of the United Society of Believers in Christ's Second Coming. The austere Protestant sect was dedicated to simplicity, equality, and celibacy. They were popularly known as "the Shakers" for their spastic movements when in the throes of religious ecstasy. By the time of her death in 1784, Mother Lee had made many converts, who then fanned out across the country to form communal settlements from Maine to Indiana. One of the most important Shaker communities, Hancock, edged the Massachusetts–New York border, near Pittsfield.

Shaker society produced dedicated, highly disciplined farmers and craftspeople whose products were much in demand in the outside world. They sold seeds, invented early agricultural machinery and hand tools, and erected large buildings of several stories and exquisite simplicity. Their spare, clean-lined furniture and accessories anticipated the so-called Danish Modern style by a century and in recent years have drawn astonishingly high prices at auction.

All of these accomplishments required a verve owed at least in part to sublimation of sexual energy, for a fundamental Shaker tenet was total celibacy for its adherents. They kept going with converts and adoption of orphans (who were free to leave, if they wished). But by the 1970s, the inevitable result of this policy left the movement with a bare handful of believers. The string of Shaker settlements and museums that remain is testament to their dictum, "Hands to work, hearts to God."

cows in a circle, and the precise joinery of the roof beams and support pillars is a joy to observe.

The second must-see is the brick dwelling that contained the communal dining room, kitchens, and sleeping quarters. Sexes were separated at meals, work, and religious services, and such features as the opposing staircases leading to male and female "retiring rooms" served equality.

While artisans and docents demonstrate Shaker crafts and techniques, only those in the Schoolhouse and the Trustee's Office and Store dress in period clothing to portray Shaker inhabitants. All are knowledgeable about their subject, though, and dispense such nuggets as explanations of the Shaker discipline that required members to dress the right side first, to button from right to left, and to step with the right foot first.

The museum shop is excellent, and a cafe serves lunches in summer and fall, with some dishes based on Shaker recipes. On Saturday nights from July to October, the village presents tours and Shaker four-course dinners at a cost of about $40. Reservations for these are essential.

Routes 20 and 41, Pittsfield. © **800/817-1137** or 413/443-0188. www.hancockshakervillage.org. Admission Memorial Day to late Oct $15 adults, $6.50 children 6–17; rest of year (by guided tour only) $12 adults, $6 children 6–17. May to Oct daily 9:30am–5pm; rest of year daily 10am–4pm (tours on the hour). Call ahead in winter for hours and events.

GETTING OUTSIDE

Plaine's Bike, Ski, & Snowboard, 55 W. Housatonic St., at Center Street (© 413/499-0294; www.plaines.com), rents bikes and carries equipment for all the sports its name suggests. It's on Route 20, west of downtown.

Pittsfield State Forest, entered on Cascade Street (© 413/442-8992), is a little over 3 miles west of the center of town. Its 10,000 acres have 31 campsites, boat ramps, streams for canoeing and fishing, and trails for hiking, biking, riding, and cross-country skiing. It's open daily from 8am to 8pm. Admission is $2 per car.

BOATING **Onota Boat Livery,** 463 Pecks Rd. (© 413/442-1724), rents canoes and motorboats for use on Onota Lake, conveniently located at the western edge of the city.

SKIING South of the city center, off Route 7 near the Pittsfield city limits, is the **Bousquet Ski Area,** Dan Fox Drive (© 413/442-8316 business office, 413/442-2436 snow phone; www.bousquets.com). Bousquet (pronounced "Bos-kay") has 21 trails, with a vertical drop of 750 feet, two double lifts, and two rope tows. Night skiing is available Monday through Saturday. Rentals and lessons are offered. Lift tickets cost $15 to $25.

About 10 miles north of Pittsfield on Route 7, in New Ashford, is **Brodie Mountain Ski Area** (© 413/443-4752; www.brodiemountain.com), with a vertical drop of 1,250 feet. Night skiing is available, and in summer the ski area offers racquetball, tennis, 150 campsites, and a heated pool. Lift tickets are $29 for adults, $19 for seniors and children 12 and under.

Alternatively, turn west a mile short of Brodie Mountain on Brodie Mountain Road and continue 2 miles to **Jiminy Peak** ☆, Hancock (© 413/738-5500, or 413/738-7325 for ski reports; www.jiminypeak.com). This expanding resort aspires to four-season activity, so skiing on 28 trails (18 open at night) with seven lifts is supplemented the rest of the year by horseback riding, trapshooting, fishing in a stocked pond, a rock-climbing wall, six tennis courts, mountain biking, pools, and golf at the nearby Waubeeka Springs course.

WHERE TO STAY

The Country Inn at Jiminy Peak *Kids* This is one of the better lodging deals in the Berkshires, if your idea of luxury is space. All units are one-to-three bedroom suites with full kitchens and sofa beds. Recent renovations have enhanced the resort's reputation as a family destination, with its on-site downhill skiing and abundant recreational facilities (see "Getting Outside," above). Four- and 8-hour lift tickets start any time. No pets.

⌐*Tips* **Pittsfield on Stage**

The **Berkshire Opera Company,** 297 North St. (© 413/443-7400; www.berkshireopera.org), stages its June productions at the Mahaiwe Threatre in Great Barrington, its July and August productions of both established and new operas at the Koussevitzky Arts Center of Berkshire Community College in Pittsfield. That venue is also employed by the **Albany Berkshire Ballet,** 51 North St. (© 413/445-5382), with up to 14 performances of two ballets from early July to mid-August.

Brodie Mountain Rd. (near Rte. 43), Hancock, MA 01237. © **800/882-8859** or 413/738-5500. Fax 413/738-5513. www.jiminypeak.com. 105 units. $129–$379 1–3 bedroom suite. Winter rates include lift tickets. Children under 19 stay free in parent's room. AE, DC, DISC, MC, V. **Amenities:** 2 restaurants (eclectic); 2 bars; heated outdoor and indoor pools; 6 tennis courts; exercise room; Jacuzzi; sauna; children's programs; game room; babysitting; coin-op washers and dryers. *In room:* A/C, TV/VCR, kitchenette, coffeemaker, hair dryer, iron.

Crowne Plaza   The tallest building in town at 14 stories, this former Hilton isn't hard to find, although it takes a little round-the-block maneuvering to get to the front door. It has the bells and whistles expected of upper-middle chain hotels and is more family-friendly than many smaller lodgings in the region. Kids are welcome, and readily occupied with the heated indoor pool and PlayStations in every room. With this many rooms, there's also a good chance of copping a bed on Tanglewood weekends. Free self-parking is available in the adjacent garage.

1 West St., Pittsfield, MA 01201. © **800/227-6963** or 413/499-2000. Fax 413/442-0449. www.berkshire crowne.com. 175 units. Summer $127–$179 double; off season $102–$165 double. AE, DISC, MC, V. **Amenities:** 2 restaurants (American); bar; heated indoor pool; fitness room with Jacuzzi. *In room:* A/C, TV w/pay movies, dataport, coffeemaker, hair dryer.

WILLIAMSTOWN ★★

This community and its prestigious liberal-arts college were both named for Col. Ephraim Williams, who was killed in 1755 in one of the French and Indian Wars. He bequeathed the land for creation of a school and a town. His college grew, spreading east from the central common along both sides of Main Street (Rte. 2). Over the town's long history, buildings have been erected in several styles of the times. That makes Main Street a virtual museum of institutional architecture, with representatives of the Georgian, Federal, Gothic Revival, Romanesque, and Victorian modes, as well as a few that are yet to be labeled. They stand at dignified distances from one another, so what might have been a tumultuous visual hodgepodge is a stately lesson in historical design. The impressive Clark Art Institute is the best reason to make a special trip, perhaps in conjunction with a performance at the increasingly ambitious Williamstown Theatre Festival.

A free weekly newspaper, the *Advocate* (© 413/664-7900), produces useful guides to both the northern and southern Berkshires. For a copy, write to the *Advocate*, 87 Marshall St., North Adams, MA 01267. An unattended **information booth,** at North Street (Rte. 7) and Main Street (Rte. 2), has an abundance of pamphlets and brochures free for the taking.

SEEING THE SIGHTS

Sterling and Francine Clark Art Institute ★★★   Within these walls are canvases by Renoir (34 of them), Degas, Gauguin, Toulouse-Lautrec, Pissarro, and their predecessor, Corot. Also on display is the famed Degas sculpture *Little Dancer,* believed to be his only three-dimensional piece and a signature work of the Institute. While they are the stars, there are also works by 15th- and 16th-century Dutch portraitists, European genre and landscape painters, and Americans Sargent and Homer, as well as fine porcelain, silver, and antiques. This qualifies as one of the great cultural resources of the Berkshires and of the state.

Apart from the collection itself, the Clarks' farsighted endowment funded the modern wing added to the original neoclassical building and has covered all acquisitions, upkeep, and renovations. His stipulation that there be no admission fee was finally breached, but the charge applies only to adults, 4 months a year. A substantial bookstore in the lobby has been joined by a snack counter and an attractive cafe. An additional wing is being contemplated.

225 South St., Williamstown. ⓒ 413/458-2303. www.clarkart.edu. Admission June–Oct $10 adults, free for students and children; free to all Tues and Nov–June. Sept–June Tues–Sun 10am–5pm; July–Aug daily 10am–5pm.

Williams College Museum of Art ⭐ The second leg of Williamstown's two prominent art repositories exists in large part thanks to the college's collection of almost 400 paintings by the American modernists Maurice and Charles Prendergast. The museum also has works by Gris, Léger, Whistler, Picasso, Warhol, and Hopper.

15 Lawrence Hall Dr., Williamstown. ⓒ 413/597-2429. www.williams.edu/WCMA. Free admission. Tues–Sat (and some Mon holidays) 10am–5pm; Sun 1–5pm.

GETTING OUTSIDE
Waubeeka Golf Links, Routes 7 and 43, South Williamstown (ⓒ **413/458-5869**), is open to the public, with weekday greens fees of $39, weekends $35.

Mount Greylock State Reservation ⭐ contains the highest peak (3,491 ft.) in Massachusetts as well as a section of the Appalachian Trail. A road allows cars almost to the summit, where the War Memorial Tower affords vistas of the Taconic and Hoosac ranges, far into Vermont and New York. The park is open from sunrise until ½ hour after sunset, the visitor center mid-May to mid-October daily from 9am to 5pm, and mid-October to mid-May weekends and holidays from 8am to 4pm. Trails radiate from the parking lot near **Bascom Lodge,** North Main Street off Route 7 in Lanesboro (ⓒ **413/743-1591** or 413/443-0011), a grandly rustic creation of the Civilian Conservation Corps in the New Deal 1930s. Simple dormitory beds and four private rooms accommodating at total of 32 guests are available for rent from mid-May to late October. Family-style dinners are available by reservation.

SHOPPING
In the small downtown shopping district, **Library Antiques,** 70 Spring St. (ⓒ **413/458-3436**), is filled with a wealth of English chess sets, African carvings, Peruvian alpaca sweaters, and antique American fishing lures and creels. South of the town center on Route 7, **Saddleback Antiques,** 1395 Cold Spring Rd. (ⓒ **413/458-5852**), features country, wicker, and Victorian furniture. Slightly north of town on Route 7, **Collectors Warehouse,** 105 North St. (ⓒ **413/458-9686**), has a little bit of everything—jewelry, books, dolls, furniture, and glassware.

WHERE TO STAY
This is a college town, so in addition to the usual Berkshires peak periods of July, August, and the October foliage season, accommodations fill up during graduation and on football weekends. The largest lodging in town is the 100-unit **Williams Inn,** 1090 Main St. (ⓒ **800/828-0133** or 413/458-9371). Despite the name, it is a standard motel, with a dining room, tavern, and indoor pool. Three miles south of town at Routes 2 and 7 is the brookside **Berkshire Hills Motel** (ⓒ **413/458-3950**), with a heated pool. See also the section on North Adams, below.

Field Farm Guesthouse ⭐ After an extended vacation of B&B-hopping, there may come a time when one more tilted floor or wobbly Windsor chair will send even a devout inn lover over the edge. Here's an antidote. This pristine example of postwar modern architecture rose in 1948 on a spectacular 296-acre estate with 4 miles of trails. The living room is equipped with a telescope to view the beavers and waterfowl on the lake. Most guest rooms look over meadows to

Mount Greylock, most of the Scandinavian Modern furniture was made to order for the house, and three units have decks while two have fireplaces. Breakfasts are hearty meals of waffles and five-cheese omelets utilizing fruits, herbs, and vegetables grown on the property. Well-behaved children are welcome.

554 Sloan Rd., Williamstown, MA 01267. ℂ and fax **413/458-3135.** www.thetrustees.org. 5 units. $125–$165 double. Rates include breakfast. DISC, MC, V. Follow Rte. 7 to Rte. 43 and turn west, then make an immediate right on Sloan Rd. Continue 1 mile to the Field Farm entrance, on the right. **Amenities:** Heated outdoor pool; tennis court. *In room:* Hair dryer.

The Orchards ★★ A sedate choice just right for visiting Williams alumni and parents, this has an upscale country-club atmosphere, the sort of place where afternoon tea is an event. Each of its public and private rooms enjoys a mix of antique and reproduction English-style furniture. Even standard rooms are sizeable, all with separate dressing cubicles, and those with working fireplaces have chaise lounges and deeply padded chairs. Some have fridges with soft drinks; safes are hidden in places we can't divulge. A 3-year renovation has benefited every corner, including the exercise room, and the kitchen, too, now surpasses the merely competent operation that preceded it. There is live piano in the lounge on weekends. Providing an international touch is an internship program that brings young people from all over the world to the front desk and dining room.

222 Adams Rd., Williamstown, MA 01262. ℂ **800/225-1517** or 413/458-9611. Fax 413/458-9611. www.orchardshotel.com. 47 units. Mid-Nov to late May $150–$250 double; late May to mid-Nov $175–$275. AE, DC, DISC, MC, V. **Amenities:** Restaurant (International Fusion); bar; heated outdoor pool; exercise room with sauna and whirlpool. *In room:* A/C, TV/VCR, coffeemaker, hair dryer, iron, safe.

WHERE TO DINE

Mezze ECLECTIC The Williamstown dining scene is in constant flux, with seemingly successful restaurants moving or closing overnight, and new ones springing up like April crocuses. Mezze is one of the latter. The clientele is composed primarily of professors, administrators and students with visiting parents in tow. The enthusiasm for "small plates" is addressed in the name and on the menu, with tapas-type starters like steamed mahogany clams and plates of anchovies, prosciutto, olives, and marinated eggplant. Chef James Tracey put in time at the acclaimed Craft in New York, an experience reflected in such dishes as the roasted skate with sautéed arugula, gnocchi, and chanterelles and the roasted spaghetti squash with a lobster curry sauce. Less esoteric choices are beef stroganoff, hanger steak, and a serious cheeseburger. All this proves to be entirely competent but, it must be said, less than dazzling.

16 Water St. ℂ **413/458-0123.** Main courses $13–$26. AE, DISC, MC, V. Sun–Thurs 5–9m; Fri–Sat 5–10pm.

Spice Root INDIAN Catch an irresistible whiff of this Indian newcomer from several storefronts away and thoughts of anything but food vanish. Impecunious students like it for the bargain all-you-can-eat $8.95 lunch buffet, and while it's pretty good, choices are necessarily limited. The a la carte menu is more rewarding, with several starters, breads, curries, nine vegetarian dishes, tandoor specialties, and a half-dozen dishes from Bombay. Standouts are the curried salmon, chicken or lamb tikka masala, fiery shrimp vindaloo, and a veggie delight that involves bell peppers stuffed with mashed potatoes, paneer cheese, and spinach accompanied by yellow lentils. Of the several breads baked on site, plain nan is certainly serviceable, but the version filled with cheese, nuts, and raisins is a particular treat.

23 Spring St. ℂ **413/458-5200.** Main courses $8–$16. AE, DISC, MC, V. Mon–Thurs 5–10pm; Fri–Sat 5–11pm; Sun noon–3pm and 5–10pm.

WILLIAMSTOWN AFTER DARK

The Williams College Department of Music sponsors diverse concerts and recitals. Call its **Concertline** (© **413/597-3146**) to learn of upcoming events. In addition, the Clark Art Institute (see above) hosts frequent classical-music events.

The Williamstown Theatre Festival ★★   Williamstown's premier attraction each summer, the festival performs in the Adams Memorial Theatre. Staging classic and new plays during its season from late June to August, the festival attracts many top actors and directors, among them Gwyneth Paltrow, Frank Langella, Ethan Hawke, and Bebe Neuwirth. The Main Stage presents works by major playwrights, while the Nikos Stage often features more experimental productions. The schedule is usually announced by April. It's not too difficult to get tickets, but if a particular performance is said to be sold out, there are often cancellations in the 30 minutes before curtain.

1000 Main St. (P.O. Box 517). © 413/597-3400 for box office, 413/597-3399 for recorded information. www.wtfestival.org. Tickets $19–$50.

NORTH ADAMS

Eight years ago, there was not a wisp of hope that this comatose mill town could be pulled back from the brink of near-death. Its unemployment rate was the highest in the state, and over two-thirds of its storefronts were empty. A land developer once even suggested that the town be flooded to create lakefront property.

North Adams experienced a whiplash turnaround, many of those storefronts filling up with restaurants and galleries and high-tech start-ups. The unlikely reason, to almost everyone's agreement, is an art museum. An abandoned industrial complex has been converted, despite hoots of derision, into a center for the visual and performing arts. It is called the Massachusetts Museum of Contemporary Art, and it has strikingly altered the socio-economic dynamic of North Adams.

Massachusetts Museum of Contemporary Art ★★   A lot of excitement and anticipation surrounded this ambitious project, the conversion of an empty 27-building textile factory into a center for the arts. Even before its official opening, it had a nickname—MASS MoCA—and hosted performances by David Byrne, Patti Smith, and the Merce Cunningham Dance Company. Works on display are often outsized, crossing traditional esthetic boundaries to marry elements of both performing and visual arts.

Its chief virtue—from the standpoint of those contemporary artists who choose to work on a grand scale—is the vastness of the spaces available. But additionally, the museum has hosted a variety of musical events, experimental films, even dance parties, and is attracting small tenant companies working the vineyards of technology, including software, video, and e-commerce. MASS MoCA has attracted hundreds of thousands of visitors and is certainly worth the short detour east from neighboring Williamstown.

Two restaurants operate on the sprawling museum campus: the snacky **Lickety Split** (© **413/663-3372**), serving coffee, ice cream, and light fare; and **Eleven** (© **413/662-2004**), a New American cafe serving lunch and dinner from late May to the end of October.

87 Marshall St., North Adams. © 413/662-2111. www.massmoca.org. Admission June–Oct $9 adults, $3 children 6–16; Nov–May $9 adults, $7 seniors and students, $3 children 6–16. June–Oct daily 10am–6pm; Nov–May Wed–Mon 11am–5pm.

WHERE TO STAY

Blackinton Manor *⊛*   Music informs this 1849 Greek Revival house, hardly surprising since one of the owners is a classical pianist and his wife an opera singer and invested cantor. They hold a number of chamber concerts throughout the year, many of them to benefit favorite causes, but they don't neglect their hospitality functions for a minute. You'll know after passing an evening before the fire with a glass of sherry. All of the bedrooms are grandly furnished; try for the lavishly appointed Music Room, spacious enough to contain its own piano. A typical breakfast consists of fresh fruit, an herbed omelet, and freshly baked pastries.

1391 Massachusetts Ave., North Adams, MA 01247. © 800/795-8613 or 413/663-5795. www.blackinton-manor.com. 5 units. $110–$190 double. Rates include breakfast. MC, V. Children over 7 welcome, but no pets. Follow Rte. 2 east from Williamstown into North Adams, turn left on Ashton, and turn right after railroad bridge. **Amenities:** Unheated outdoor pool. *In room:* A/C, TV.

The Porches *⊛⊛*   In this entertaining melding of vintage and contemporary, a row of six detached 19th-century workingmen's houses has been stitched together by an uninterrupted streetside veranda, the spaces in between roofed over and fitted with indoor catwalks and patios. Rooms are witty tributes to the past, with kitschy lamps and paint-by-numbers pictures on the walls, but are also equipped with DVD players and high-speed Internet access. A computer is provided for guests' use, and laptop rentals are also available. Down duvets, bathrobes, and cushy sofas add to guests' comfort. Ask for one of the second-floor king rooms with balcony. Although breakfast is the only meal served, cocktails are available.

231 River St., North Adams, MA 01247. © 413/664-0400. Fax 413/664-0401. www.porches.com. 50 units. Late May to early Nov $160–$295 double, $225–$435 suite; early Nov to late May $135–$259 double, $185–$425 suite. Rates include breakfast. Packages available. AE, DC, MC, V. Find it behind the MASS MoCA complex, ½ block west of Marshall St. **Amenities:** Heated outdoor pool; Jacuzzi; sauna; in-room massage; laundry service (Mon–Fri); free DVD library. *In room:* A/C, TV/DVD, dataport, minibar, hair dryer, iron.

9

Connecticut

by Herbert Bailey Livesey

Connecticut resists generalization and confounds spinners of superlatives. It doesn't rank at the top or bottom of any important chart of virtues or liabilities, which makes it impossible to stuff into pigeonholes. The nation's second-smallest state is certainly compact—only 90 miles wide and 55 miles top to bottom—but it is still three times the size of the most diminutive of all, which happens to lie right next door. While parts of it are clogged with humanity, some corners are as empty and undeveloped as inland Maine.

By many measures, Connecticut's citizens are as wealthy as any in the country, but dozens of its towns are only shells of their prosperous 19th-century selves, beset by poverty as intractable as it gets. It can boast no dramatic geographical feature, and its highest elevation is only 2,380 feet. Established in 1635 by disgruntled English settlers who didn't like the way things were going at Plymouth Colony, it has long seemed spiritually divorced from the rest of New England—an appendage of New York, or a place to be traversed on the way to Boston.

All this might appear to constitute an identity crisis and hardly makes Connecticut seem an appealing vacation destination. But a closer look reveals an abundance of reasons to slow down and linger.

To a great extent, the state owes its existence to the presence of water. In addition to having Long Island Sound along its entire southern coast, several significant rivers and their tributaries slice through the hills and coastal plain—the Housatonic, Naugatuck, Quinnipiac, Connecticut, and Thames. They provided power for the mills along their courses and the towns and cities that grew around them. Industry still drives most of the economy, despite the bucolic image that mention of the state often conjures, and the pollution that industry has caused in the rivers and the sound is being scoured away.

Development, too, appears to have slowed, helping to preserve Connecticut's scores of classic colonial villages, from the Litchfield Hills in the northwest to the Mystic coast in the opposite corner. They are as placid and timeless as they have been for more than 3 centuries, or as polished and sophisticated as transplanted urbanites can make them. And the state's salty maritime heritage is palpable in the old boat-building and fishing villages at the mouths of its rivers, especially those east of New Haven.

Connecticut is New England's front porch. Pull up a chair and stay awhile.

1 Fairfield County

Mansions, marinas, and luxury apartment blocks elbow for space right up to the deeply indented Long Island Sound shoreline in the southwestern corner of the state. This is one of the most heavily developed stretches of the coast, and, in

Connecticut

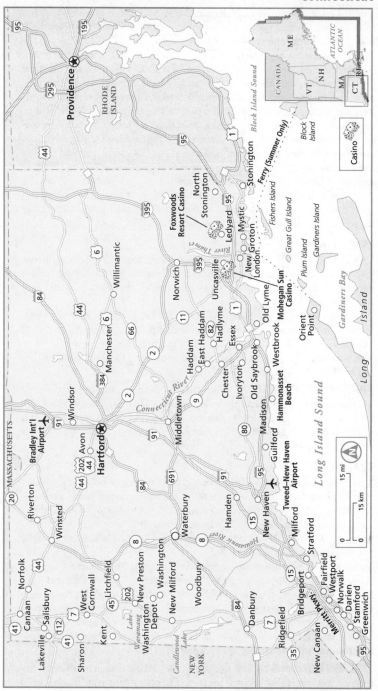

terms of family income, one of the wealthiest. As the land rises slowly inland from the water's edge, woods thicken, roads narrow, and pockets of New England unfold. Yacht country becomes horse country.

The first suburbs began to form in the middle of the last century, when train rails started radiating north and east from New York's Grand Central Terminal into the countryside. This part of the state was made accessible for summertime refugees from the big city, and eventually weekend houses became permanent dwellings. Corporate executives liked the life of the gentry, so after World War II, they started moving their companies closer to their new homes. Stamford became a city; Greenwich, New Canaan, Darien, and Westport were the bedrooms of choice—pricey, haughty, redolent of the good life. (Of course, Fairfield County also contains Bridgeport, a depressed city that once considered filing for bankruptcy and has a penchant for political scandal.)

But for visitors, the fashionable exurbs and their beaches, restaurants, and upscale shops are the draw, along with the villages farther north, especially Ridgefield, that hint of Vermont, all within 1½ hours of Times Square.

ESSENTIALS

GETTING THERE   From New York and points south, take I-95 or, preferably, the Hutchinson and Merritt parkways. From eastern Massachusetts and northern Connecticut, take I-84 south to Danbury, then Route 7 south into Fairfield County.

The **Metro North** (© **800/METRO-INFO** or 212/532-4900; www.mta. nyc.ny.us/mnr) commuter line has many trains daily from New York's Grand Central Terminal, with stops at Greenwich, Stamford, Darien, Norwalk, Westport, and additional stations all the way to New Haven. Express trains make the trip in 45 to 65 minutes.

VISITOR INFORMATION   Information on the northern part of the county is available from the **Housatonic Valley Tourism District** (© **800/841-4488;** www.housatonic.org), while the **Coastal Fairfield County Convention and Visitor Bureau** (© **800/866-7925;** www.coastalCT.com) can provide materials about the coastal towns.

STAMFORD

A trickle of corporations started moving their headquarters from New York 38 miles northeast to Stamford in the 1960s. That flow became a steady stream by the 1980s, and more than a dozen Fortune 500 companies continue to direct their operations from here. They have erected shiny mid-rise towers that give the city of 117,000 residents an appearance more like the new urban centers of the Sun Belt than those of the Snow Belt.

One result is a lively downtown that other, less prosperous Connecticut cities surely envy. Roughly contained by Greylock Place, Tresser Boulevard, and Atlantic and Main streets, it has two theaters, tree-lined streets with many shops and a large mall, pocket parks and plazas, and a number of stylish restaurants, sidewalk cafes, and nightclubs.

For further information, contact the **Greater Stamford Convention & Visitors Bureau,** 1 Landmark Sq. (© **203/359-4761**).

Stamford Museum & Nature Center 🛝 (Kids)   About 5 miles north of the city center is this fine family-oriented resource. The center has a large lake, an open pen with a pair of river otters, and a real working farm with goats, sheep, cattle, and peacocks. May and June mark the arrival of newborn chicks, kids, calves, and lambs. On the grounds are a country store, nature trails, a small planetarium, and an oddball Tudor-Gothic house with galleries of art, natural history, and Indian lore.

39 Scofieldtown Rd. ⓒ 203/322-1646. Admission $6 adults, $5 seniors and children 4–14. Mon–Sat and holidays 9am–5pm; Sun 11–5pm. Feeding time is 9am. The center is 1 mile north of Exit 35 off the Merritt Pkwy. (Rte. 15).

SHOPPING

United House Wrecking (535 Hope St.; ⓒ 203/348-5371; www.unitedhouse wrecking.com) is a find for dedicated antiques hounds, who will want to make time for this sprawling emporium of oddments. The name may not sound promising, but the company got its start selling architectural remnants salvaged from demolitions. For years, it featured such items as 1930s gas pumps, stone pigs, and pagodas. Now it showcases far less bizarre imported antiques and reproductions. It's open Monday through Saturday from 9:30am to 5:30pm, Sunday from noon to 5pm. It's also tough to find. From Exit 9 of I-95, pick up Rte. 1, then Rte. 106 north; make a left on Glenbrook Rd., which becomes Church St., and turn right on Hope St. Be sure you have a map or detailed directions.

WHERE TO STAY

Westin Stamford ★★   This outpost of the always reliable international chain does nothing to diminish the expectations of business travelers. Everything is in place, from the executive floors with club lounge to the airport shuttle van. The more expensive rooms have high-speed Internet connections.

1 Stamford Place (Exit 7, I-95), Stamford, CT 06902. ⓒ 800/937-8461 or 203/967-2222. Fax 203/351-1910. www.westin.com. 481 units. $129–$369 double. AE, DC, DISC, MC, V. **Amenities:** Restaurant (International); heated indoor pool; tennis court; health club; concierge; business center; 24-hr. room service; same-day dry cleaning/laundry. *In room:* A/C, TV, dataport, minibar, coffeemaker, hair dryer, iron, safe.

WHERE TO DINE

Oceans 211 ★ NEW AMERICAN/SEAFOOD   First, know that the hands-on owner put in his apprenticeship at the venerable Oyster Bar in New York's Grand Central Terminal. It shows: The ground-floor bar has a Manhattan sheen, with a curving black marble bar and a long display case of featured wines (mostly from California). The menu is deceptively plain, the entrees listed only by their central ingredients—halibut, Dover sole, wild salmon, shrimp. The delights come with what shows up on the plate. Sea scallops, for example, arrive over black spaghetti with pesto and hot peppers. You might have trouble getting past the delectable appetizers, and a large selection (most nights) of oysters from the raw bar. Upstairs is a less cozy dining room that seats up to 70.

211 Summer St. ⓒ 203/973-0494. Reservations suggested on weekends. Main courses $20–$26. AE, DC, MC, V. Mon–Fri noon–2:30pm and 5:30–9:30pm; Sat 5:30–10:30pm.

Smokey Joe's BARBECUE   This used to be called Buster's, but apart from a paint job and a new sign, nothing much has changed. Smack on the Stamford—Darien line, it wouldn't pass an Amarillo authenticity test, but it's close enough. Upstairs is a down-and-dirty bar with pool table; downstairs is a classic barbecue joint. Stand in the cafeteria line and select from confusing lists of ribs, brisket, pulled pork, sausage, and birds; then retire to the oil-clothed picnic tables to gorge.

1308 E. Main St. (Rte. 1). ⓒ 203/406-0605. Main courses $9.95–$25. Mon–Thurs 11:30am–9:30pm; Fri–Sat 11:30am–10:30pm; Sun 11:30am–9pm (bar daily until 1:30am).

Zanghi on Summer Street ★★ FRENCH/ ITALIAN   Nicola Zanghi first attracted enthusiastic notice with his eponymous restaurant in the Inn at

National Hall in Westport back in the mid-1990s. He resurfaced on Stamford's prime restaurant row and replicated that success. The large bar-lounge in front has a sleek industrial look with bluish-purple ducts overhead, while a softer atmosphere of pale green walls and chairs prevails in the dining rooms beyond. He still places maximum emphasis on seasonal ingredients, so his menu lists almost as many daily specials as regular items. On the fixed side of the card are some favorites that are available both at lunch and at dinner. Notable among these are the oysters with chili-peppercorn mignonette sauce, an unexpectedly earthy lobster carbonara with carmelized onion shreds and pancetta, and seared tuna with a leek-potato skillet cake and shallot pinot noir reduction. His house-made sorbets are bracing, not cloying. It's hard to go wrong here, no matter what you choose. If you're interested in lunch, call ahead—he's thinking about reducing or eliminating it.

201 Summer St. (℃ 203/327-3663. Reservations suggested on weekends. Main courses $19–$29. AE, DC, MC, V. Mon–Sat noon–2:30pm and 5:30–9:30pm (Fri–Sat until 10:30pm).

STAMFORD AFTER DARK

The **Stamford Center for the Arts,** Atlantic Street and Tresser Boulevard (℃ **203/325-4466;** www.onlyatsca.com) has three venues. The **Rich Forum** is the best known, presenting professional productions, with name actors, of successful Broadway and off-Broadway plays as well as musical and dance presentations, while the **Palace Theatre,** 61 Atlantic St. (℃ **203/325-4466;** www.only atsca.com), offers musicals; rotating appearances by the Stamford Symphony Orchestra, the Connecticut Grand Opera and Orchestra, and the Connecticut Ballet; and one-night stands by solo acts and traveling troupes like B.B. King and the Alvin Ailey Dance Theater. Smaller, often experimental plays and related performances are given in **The Studio at Rich Forum.**

Among the handful of downtown clubs is the long-standing **Terrace Club,** 1938 W. Main St. (℃ **203/961-9770**). Claiming to have the largest dance floor in the state, it has both live acts and DJ nights—country, Latin, and ballroom dancing all get their turn. The aptly named **Next Door Cafe,** 1990 W. Main St. (℃ **203/961-9770**), has DJs most nights spinning hip-hop, R&B, and reggae. In summer, there's live Latin music on the patio. Jazz is on tap at the **Lava Lounge,** 184 Summer St. (℃ **203/602-0722**), where the Thursday and Friday happy hours feature half-price martinis and beer and a tantalizing spread of little plates, just the time and place to get a date for the weekend. DJs are on from Thursday through Sunday, and live acts show up Fridays and Sundays.

NORWALK

Given the despair that grips many New England cities, the continuing betterment of this city's once notorious South Norwalk neighborhood gladdens the heart. The rehabilitation of several blocks of 19th-century row houses is transforming the waterfront into a trendy precinct that has come to be called, inevitably, "SoNo." The Norwalk Seaport Oyster Festival, held in early September, attracts over 90,000 visitors to its tall ships and oyster boats, crafts show, and food court. The district, bounded roughly by Washington, Water, and North and South Main streets, is readily accessible from the South Norwalk railroad station.

Lockwood-Mathews Mansion Museum   Erected in 1864, this granite mansion in the Second Empire style is covered with peaked and mansard slate roofs and has 62 rooms arranged around a stunning sky-lit octagonal rotunda. Marble, gilt, marquetry, and frescoes were commissioned and incorporated with abandon. Visits are by guide or audio tour. It has been designated a National Historic Landmark.

295 West Ave. ✆ **203/838-9799.** Admission $8 adults, $5 seniors and students, free for children under 12. Mid-Mar to New Year's Day Wed–Sun noon–5pm. From I-95 southbound, take Exit 15; from I-95 northbound, take Exit 14.

The Maritime Aquarium at Norwalk ★★   This facility remains the centerpiece of revitalized SoNo, so much so that it recently doubled its size. The present name isn't inclusive, as part of the complex includes a section of boatbuilders at work as well as exhibits of model ships and full-size vessels, including the *Tango,* which was *pedaled* across the Atlantic. The main attractions, though, are the marine creatures and mammals on view. Five harbor seals are fed at 11:45am, 1:45pm, and 3:45pm, when they wriggle up on the rocks and even rest their heads in their handler's lap. Additional exhibits include a pair of river otters, an open pool of cow-nosed rays, and tanks alive with creatures found in Sound waters, including sea turtles and sharks. Finally, a giant IMAX screen shows nature films that aren't necessarily confined to the seven seas.

10 N. Water St. ✆ **203/852-0700.** www.maritimeaquarium.org. Admission $9.25 adults, $8.50 seniors, $7.50 children 2–12; IMAX $7.50 adults, $6.50 seniors, $5.50 children; combination packages (aquarium plus IMAX movie) $15 adults, $13 seniors, $11 children. July–Aug daily 10am–6pm; Sept–June daily 10am–5pm.

CRUISES

Excursions to **Sheffield Island** and its historic lighthouse are offered by the *Seaport Islander* (✆ **888/547-6863** or 203/854-4656), a 60-passenger vessel that departs from Hope Dock, near the Maritime Aquarium. Weather permitting, the boat sets out two to four times daily, on Saturdays and Sundays from Memorial Day weekend to late September as well as Monday through Friday from late June to Labor Day. The round-trip takes about 2½ hours, with a 15-minute layover on the island. Fares are $15 for adults, $12 for children 3 to 12, and $5 for children under 3. Special outings include sunset cruises and occasional Sunday picnics. Call ahead for schedule.

Similarly, the research vessel *Oceanic* has "creature cruises" on many winter weekends to spot seals and bird life, as well as marine study cruises at other times, a service of the Maritime Aquarium. Fares are $18 per person. Reserve ahead by calling ✆ **203/852-0700,** ext. 2206.

SHOPPING

Serious shoppers have several choices, primarily among the boutiques and galleries along Washington and Main streets. One shop that may produce a bargain or at least a surprise is **Saga,** 119 Washington St. (✆ **203/855-1900**). It specializes in folk arts and crafts as well as jewelry and furnishings from the southwestern United States, Mexico, and points south. Recently moved here, **And Company, Inc.,** 108 Washington St. (✆ **203/831-8855**), offers bedding and bath products, but carries whimsical Oaxaca carvings and Mata Ortiz pottery, too.

WHERE TO DINE

For a break from shopping and strolling, drop into **SoNo Caffeine,** 133 Washington St. (✆ **203/857-4224**), an eccentric java joint that serves breakfast and lunch, offers live jazz and pop Sunday, Tuesday, Wednesday, and Thursday, and sticks a price tag on virtually every piece of furniture on the place.

Amberjacks ✍ CONTEMPORARY AMERICAN   The room looks as if it was trucked up intact from Key West's Duval Street, with a bar shaped like the prow of a boat and maritime paintings on the walls. The food is boldly flavored, with frequent use of Asian spices and Creole staples. Examples are the popular Thai tuna steak, mixed grill, and shrimp ravioli. About 20 wines are available by the glass. Jazz, blues, and local bands appear Thursdays, Fridays, and some Saturdays. The result is a substantial singles scene for the 20 to mid-30s set, with a lively Friday happy hour that moves out onto the deck in summer. Otherwise, lunch anytime and dinners early in the week are suitable for patrons of all ages.

99 Washington St. (between Broad and Main sts.). © 203/853-4332. Reservations suggested on weekends. Main courses $17–$25. AE, DC, MC, V. Mon–Sat noon–3pm and 5:30–10pm (Fri–Sat until 11pm); Sun noon–10pm.

Barcelona ★★ MEDITERRANEAN   Tapas are the featured attraction here, but the kitchen isn't doctrinaire about recipes, which range all over the Mediterranean and even down to South America for inspiration. Two or three tapas per person, and sharing is inevitable. Start, perhaps, with charcuteria, either an assortment of Spanish cheeses, changed daily, or of cured meats and sausages, usually including nutty Serrano ham. The day's additional delectables might include mussels al Diablo, chorizo with sweet and sour figs, garlic shrimp, or triangular piquillo peppers stuffed with potato-cod brandade. Other options include steaks, roast monkfish, and paella for two to six people. The patio is open year-round.

63–65 N. Main St. (north of Washington St.). © 203/899-0088. Reservations suggested on weekends. Tapas $3.50–$13. Main courses $18–$29. AE, DC DISC, MC, V. Daily 5pm–1am.

WESTPORT

After World War II, the housing crunch had young couples scouring the metropolitan area for affordable housing along the three main routes of what is now known as the Metro North transit system. Some of them wound up in this pretty village beside the Saugatuck River, several miles inland from Long Island Sound (47 miles northeast of New York City, 29 miles southwest of New Haven). Most of the new commuter class found Westport to be too far away from Manhattan (1–1½ hr. each way on the train), and it was deemed the archetype of the far-out bedroom communities that were dubbed the "exurbs"—beyond suburban.

Notable for its large contingent of people in the creative crafts, primarily commercial artists, advertising copywriters, art directors, and their fellows, the town was also appealing to CEOs and higher-level executives, many of whom solved their commuting problem by moving their offices to nearby Stamford. The result is a bustling community with surviving elements of its rural New England past wrapped in a sheen of Big Apple panache.

For further information, contact the **Westport Chamber of Commerce,** 180 Post Rd. E. (© **203/227-9234**).

OUTDOOR PURSUITS

Sherwood Island State Park, Green Farms (© **203/566-2305**), has two long swimming beaches separated by a grove of trees sheltering dozens of picnic tables with grills. Surf fishing is a possibility from designated areas, and the park has concession stands, restrooms, and an amateurish "nature center." The park is open from Memorial Day to Labor Day, daily from 8am to sunset. Pets are not allowed. By car, take Exit 18 off I-95 or U.S. 1, following the road called the Sherwood Island Connector. Admission for out-of-state cars from Memorial Day to September is $8 Monday through Friday, $12 Saturday and Sunday. Cars with CT plates are charged $5 weekdays, $7 weekends.

You can get to Sherwood Island by taking a train to Westport and a taxi from the station to the park. If you don't have a car, you might prefer to use that method to get to **Compo Beach,** the long municipal strand not far from downtown.

West of the town center is the **Nature Center for Environmental Activities,** 10 Woodside Lane (ℰ 203/227-7253). Its 62 acres offer several trails, a wildlife rehab center, and a building with live animals and an aquarium. Open Monday through Saturday from 9am to 5pm, Sunday from 1 to 4pm. Donations are welcome.

The Nature Conservancy oversees **Devil's Den Preserve,** Old Route 7 (ℰ 203/226-4991), in Weston, north of Westport (take Route 7 to Old Route 7). An undeveloped tract of more than 1,500 acres in the heart of densely populated Fairfield County, this is a refuge of rare value. It has 15 miles of trails beside ponds and waterways rich with birds and other wildlife. Cross-country skiing is permitted, but there are no picnic or toilet facilities. Open daily from sunrise to sunset. Admission is free, but donations are welcome.

Rent a sailboat or arrange a lesson at the **Longshore Sailing School,** Longshore Club Park, 260 S. Compo Rd. (ℰ 203/226-4646), about 2 miles south of the Boston Post Road (U.S. 1).

SHOPPING

The long Main Street has plenty of shops, but they are increasingly being taken over by national chains, Talbot's, The Gap, Brooks Brothers, Pottery Barn, and Williams-Sonoma among them. Individuality is more likely to be found in antique shops, such as the two below.

Circa Antiques   Here is as eclectic a selection as two owners from Ontario and west Texas might contrive. They unload containers from France every 3 months or so, most of it furniture from the 19th and early 20th centuries. Biedermeier pieces are increasingly evident. 11 Riverside Ave. ℰ 203/222-8642.

The Stuart Collection   On the west end of the bridge over the Saugatuck is a row of fetching shops. This one trumpets its taste for dazzlingly colorful ceramics and blown glassware, most of it Italian, such as the ornate Venetian chandeliers. 11 Winter St. ℰ 203/221-7102.

WHERE TO STAY

For some years, the luxurious **Inn at National Hall** (2 Post Rd.; ℰ 800/629-4255 or 203/221-1351) was mentioned in the same breath with only a few other Connecticut hostelries. It is still operating (at this writing) but all the signs suggest that it has fallen upon hard times—reduced staff, a closed restaurant, slipping maintenance. Prices, on the other hand, have not declined appreciably, with doubles from $295 to $345 and suites from $495 to $650. Your call.

The Westport Inn   The building housing this motor hotel has been on the scene since 1935, and while it can't claim the style and elegance of the Inn at National Hall (above), it will likely be around a lot longer. With a substantial renovation and expansion in 2000, it now provides more facilities and services than most motels, including an indoor pool, laundromat, and fitness room. Depending upon your anticipated date and time of arrival, the front desk is often flexible on room rates. Guests have access to the town beach and a nearby golf course. Find it east of the town center. No pets.

1595 Post Rd. E., Wesport, CT 06880. ℰ 203/259-5236. Fax 203/254-8439. www.westportinn.com. 116 units. $144–$174 double. Rates include breakfast. AE, DC, DISC, MC, V. **Amenities:** Restaurant (Steakhouse); bar;

small fitness room with sauna; same-day dry cleaning/laundry. *In room:* A/C, TV, dataport, coffeemaker, hair dryer, iron.

WHERE TO DINE

Acqua ✦ MEDITERRANEAN/SEAFOOD   A light touch does wonders with such immaculately fresh ingredients as striped bass, halibut, crab, skate, and clams. Presentations are marvelously inviting, yet without the appearance of excessive pushing and prodding in the kitchen. The decor consists of murals depicting cherubim, aged-looking tiles, and a bar arching around the wood-burning oven, used for terrific designer pizzas and a customer favorite, roasted chicken. Among other possibilities is a horseradish-crusted salmon in a red wine reduction. An express lunch in the street-level bar costs only $10, and the mid-day menu upstairs is far less expensive than dinner.

43 Main St. (near east end of Saugatuck Bridge). ✆ 203/222-8899. Reservations recommended on weekends. Main courses, dinner $14–$38. AE, DC, MC, V. Mon–Thurs noon–2:30pm and 5:30–10pm; Fri–Sat noon–2:30pm and 5:30–10:30pm; Sun noon–3pm and 5:30–9:30pm.

Tavern on Main ✦ AMERICAN BISTRO   Westporters don't come in too many different ages, sizes, or colors, but most of them mount the Tavern's front steps with regularity. Local merchants, widows who lunch, executives, and young moms crowd into the clubby bar to wait for a table. The main room has fragments of the building's earliest years—hand-hewn beams and a brick fireplace. Menu items suffer from neither gushing elaboration nor daring. But the kitchen toys with convention, as with the trademark lobster roll: The center of a seeded roll is scooped out, the cavity filled with warm (not cool) buttery chunks and shreds of the crustacean. Similar turns are taken with house-cured duck confit, five-vegetable couscous, and potato-wrapped sea bass.

146 Main St. ✆ 203/221-7222. Reservations recommended. Main courses, dinner $18–$33. AE, DC, MC, V. Daily 11:30am–10pm (Fri–Sat until 11pm).

WESTPORT AFTER DARK

One of the oldest theaters on the straw-hat circuit, the **Westport Country Playhouse,** 25 Powers Ct. (✆ **203/227-4177;** www.westportplayhouse.com), has passed its 70th year. Revitalized under the leadership of Artistic Director Joanne Woodward and other new administrators, the theater produces comedies, dramas, and musicals from mid-June to mid-September, with performances Monday through Saturday evenings and Wednesday and Saturday matinees. Famous or at least vaguely familiar actors appear in almost every production (Ms. Woodward even persuaded her husband Paul Newman to appear in a production of *Our Town* that went to Broadway). A Sunday music series brings in such diverse acts as Arlo Guthrie, the Preservation Hall Jazz Band, and doo-wop groups. Single tickets go on sale in May, priced from about $18 to $48.

The **White Barn Theatre,** Newtown Avenue (✆ **203/227-3768**), is a respected venue with a slightly shorter summer season than the Playhouse. From late June to August, outdoor musical performances are given at **Levitt Pavilion,** off Jesup Green near the center of town (✆ **203/226-7600**).

RIDGEFIELD

No town in Connecticut has a more imposing main street. Ridgefield's is 132 feet wide, lined with ancient elms, maples, and oaks, and bordered by massive 19th-century houses in largely Classical Revival and Late Victorian styles. Impressive at any time of the year, it is in its glory during the brief blaze of the October foliage season. Only a little over an hour from New York City (58 miles northeast), the town (pop. 24,000) is nonetheless a true evocation of the New England character.

Aldrich Museum of Contemporary Art ★★   Larry Aldrich was a fashion designer who used his superb collection of paintings and sculptures from the second half of the 20th century to establish this museum. The original 18th-century clapboard structure in which he housed his collection was soon doubled in size. But when Aldrich died in 2001, the museum took a sharp turn in another direction. It was decided that it would now be devoted exclusively to young, living artists and to work no more than 5 years old. To that end, the original collection is almost completely sold off, and in April 2003, the museum was closed for the construction of yet another building to carry out the new mission. It is to contain 12 galleries, a screening room, and performance spaces. It should be open as you read this, but call ahead before making a special trip.

258 Main St. (near the intersection of Routes 35 and 33 at the south end of Main St.). © 203/438-4519. www.aldrichart.org.

Keeler Tavern   This 1713 stagecoach inn was providing sustenance to travelers between Boston and New York long before the Revolutionary War, but that conflict provided it with its object of greatest note. A British cannonball is imbedded in one of its walls, presumably fired during the Battle of Ridgefield in 1777. It's now a museum of colonial life, with period furnishings and costumed guides. And the tavern has another claim to fame: It was long the summer home of architect Cass Gilbert (1849–1934), who designed the Supreme Court Building in Washington, D.C., and who was a key figure in the construction of the George Washington Bridge in New York.

132 Main St. © 203/431-0815. Admission $5 adults, $3 seniors, $2 children under 12. Wed and Sat–Sun 1–4pm.

SHOPPING

Apart from the usual antiques shops and the strip malls north of town on Route 35, **Hay Day Market** (21 Governor St. © **203/431-4400**) is a most interesting stop for devoted food lovers. Hidden in a shopping center behind Main Street, it is about as fancy a food market as exists outside of Manhattan. Sections are devoted to produce, prepared foods, baked goods, charcuterie, cheeses, and fresh flowers. It's open Monday to Saturday 8am to 8pm, and until 7pm on Sundays. There are also branches in Westport (1385 Post Rd.; © 293/254-5400) and Greenwich (1050 E. Putnam Ave.; © 203/637-7600).

WHERE TO STAY & DINE

The Elms ★   Ridgefield's oldest (1799) operating inn has the ambience of a small contemporary hotel with the conveniences most travelers desire, as well as newly decorated guest rooms with canopied beds. Included among the 20 units are five suites. The **dining room and tavern** ★★ (© **203/438-9206**) are in the highly capable hands of star chef Brendan Walsh, whose ministrations accomplish fresh twists on recipes utilizing regional ingredients without masking their origins. In the main dining room, Connecticut seafood stew and lobster shepherd pie are staples, and the mixed grill of lamb, venison, and sausage is a Sunday dinner fixture. The tavern serves pub grub on the order of bangers and mash and grilled fish and chicken. Reservations are essential on weekends.

500 Main St. (Rte. 35, at the north end of town), Ridgefield, CT 06877. © and fax **203/438-2541**. www. elmsinn.com. 20 units. $150–$210 double. Rates include breakfast. AE, DC, MC, V. **Amenities:** Restaurant (creative American); tavern. *In room:* A/C, TV.

WHERE TO STAY

West Lane Inn ★★   An inn to fit most images of a romantic country getaway, this also works for businesspeople, as it offers modems, voice mail, and express checkout. For longer stays, there are two rooms with kitchenettes. A couple of rooms have fireplaces, and all have four-poster beds. The 1849 house stands on a property blessed with giant shade trees. Take breakfast on the porch in good weather; the continental version is included, but a la carte hot dishes are extra. Snacks are available until 9pm. Bernard's (below), just across the driveway, serves lunch and dinner.

22 West Lane (off Rte. 35), Ridgefield, CT 06877. ✆ **203/438-7323.** Fax 203/438-7325. www.westlane inn.com. 18 units. $125–$195 double. Rates include breakfast. AE, DC, DISC, MC, V. Driving north from Wilton on Rte. 33, turn west on Rte. 35 at the edge of town. **Amenities:** Concierge; limited room service; laundry service; dry cleaning. *In room:* A/C, TV/VCR, dataport, fridge, coffeemaker, hair dryer.

WHERE TO DINE

Bernard's ★ FRENCH   New proprietors breathed life into the tired old Inn at Ridgefield a few years ago. The piano still stands in the main dining parlor, and it's played Friday and Saturday nights and for the festive Sunday brunch, but the primary interests of the owners clearly lie in the kitchen. Imagine fricassee of snails in a crisp crepe with salsify, fava beans, tomato confit, and a parsley coulis! Main courses are about 50-50 land- and ocean-based proteins. Among the most successful are roasted monkfish osso bucco wrapped in rosemary pancetta and the venison chop and medallion with spätzel and braised cabbage. Several dinner choices appear as half-priced versions at lunch, but the romance of music and flickering lights is in the evenings.

20 West Lane (near the junction with Rte. 7). ✆ **203/438-8282.** Reservations recommended on weekends. Main courses $24–$32. AE, DC, MC, V. Tues–Fri noon–2:30pm and 6–9pm., Sat 6–10pm, Sun noon–2:30pm and 5–8pm.

2 The Litchfield Hills ★★

When the Hamptons got too pricey, too visible, and too chichi back in the 1980s, a lot of stockbrokers, CEOs, and celebs started discovering the Litchfield Hills, arguably the most fetchingly rustic yet sophisticated part of Connecticut.

The topography and, to an extent, the microculture of the region are defined by the river that runs through it, the Housatonic. Broad but not deep enough for vessels larger than canoes, it waters farms and villages and forests along its course, provides opportunities for recreational angling and float trips, and, over the millennia, has helped to shape these foothills, which merge with the Massachusetts Berkshires.

Men in overalls and CAT caps still stand on the porches of general stores, their breath steaming in the bracing autumn air. Churches hold pancake-breakfast fundraisers; neighbors squabble about development. That's one side of these bucolic hills, less than 2 hours from Times Square.

Increasingly, the other side is fashioned by refugees from New York. These chic seekers of tranquility and real estate fled to pre-Revolutionary saltboxes and Georgian colonials on Litchfield's warren of back roads and brought Manhattan-bred expectations with them. Boutiques fragrant with designer coffees and cachets opened in spaces once occupied by luncheonettes and feed stores. Restaurants discovered sushi and sun-dried tomatoes and just how much money they could get away with charging the newcomers.

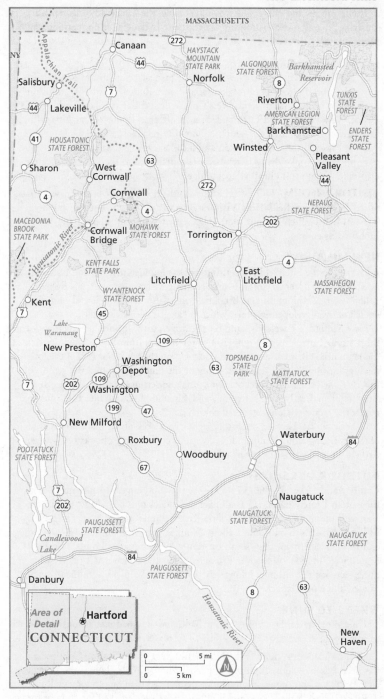

MASSACHUSETTS

NY

Appalachian Trail

Salisbury

Lakeville

Canaan

44

Norfolk

HAYSTACK
MOUNTAIN
STATE PARK

ALGONQUIN
STATE FOREST

Barkhamsted
Reservoir

8

Riverton

AMERICAN LEGION
STATE FOREST

TUNXIS
STATE
FOREST

ENDERS
STATE
FOREST

Barkhamsted

Winsted

Pleasant
Valley

44

272

7

41

HOUSATONIC
STATE FOREST

Sharon

West
Cornwall

63

Cornwall

4

4

Torrington

202

NEPAUG
STATE FOREST

MACEDONIA
BROOK
STATE PARK

Cornwall
Bridge

MOHAWK
STATE FOREST

KENT FALLS
STATE PARK

Litchfield

East
Litchfield

4

NASSAHEGON
STATE FOREST

Kent

7

WYANTENOCK
STATE FOREST

45

Lake
Waramaug

New Preston

109

63

8

TOPSMEAD
STATE
PARK

MATTATUCK
STATE FOREST

7

202

109

Washington
Depot

Washington

199

47

Waterbury

84

New Milford

Roxbury

Woodbury

67

POOTATUCK
STATE FOREST

Naugatuck

7

202

PAUGUSSETT
STATE FOREST

NAUGATUCK
STATE FOREST

NAUGATUCK
STATE FOREST

Candlewood
Lake

84

Danbury

PAUGUSSETT
STATE FOREST

8

63

Housatonic River

Housatonic River

Area of
Detail

Hartford

CONNECTICUT

New
Haven

0   5 mi

0   5 km

N

Compromises and city-country conflicts aside, the Litchfield Hills remain a satisfying all-season destination for day trips and overnights from metropolitan New York and Connecticut.

ESSENTIALS

GETTING THERE From New York City, take the Hutchinson River Parkway to I-684 north to I-84 east, taking Exit 7 onto Route 7 north. Continue on Route 7 for New Milford, Kent, West Cornwall, and Canaan. For Washington Depot, New Preston, and Litchfield, branch off onto Route 202 at New Milford. An especially attractive entrance into the region is Route 44 from the Taconic Parkway, through Millerton and into Lakeville and Salisbury.

From Boston, take the Massachusetts Turnpike west to the Lee exit, picking up Route 7 south from nearby Stockbridge.

VISITOR INFORMATION The useful 40-page *Unwind* brochure is produced by the **Litchfield Hills Visitors Bureau** (© **860/567-4506;** fax 860/567-5214; www.litchfieldhills.com). Also see **www.housatonic.org** and **www.litchfieldcty.com**.

NEW MILFORD

A gateway to the Litchfield Hills, this town was founded in 1703 and functions as a commercial center for the smaller villages that surround it—Roxbury, Bridgewater, Washington, and Brookfield. It is also at the high end of a long stretch of overdeveloped Route 7, which is clogged with strip malls.

New Milford is a welcome stop on the drive north, if only for lunch and a short stroll. Turn right on Route 202 where it splits from Route 7 and crosses the Housatonic River and a railroad track. Up on the left is one end of the long town green. A 1902 fire destroyed many of the buildings around the green, so this isn't one of those picturebook New England settings. Rather, it is a mix of late Victoriana, early Greek Revival, and Eisenhower-era architecture, not to ignore the requisite Congregational church.

Otherwise, there are no obligatory sights, so a walk down Bank Street, west of the green and along Railroad Street, with its crafts shops, a bookstore, and an Art Moderne movie house, won't take long.

OUTDOOR PURSUITS

Candlewood Lake (© **860/354-6928**) is the third-largest man-made lake in the eastern United States. It has a finger that pokes into New Milford, but the area with the most recreational facilities is a few miles to the west. From New Milford, drive north on Route 7 about 2½ miles, turn west on Route 37 toward and through Sherman, then south on Route 39 to **Squantz Pond State Park** (© **203/797-4165**). With over 170 acres along the lakeshore, it offers swimming, ice-skating, fishing, hiking and cycling trails, picnic grounds, rental canoes, and a boat launch.

WHERE TO DINE

There are many dining choices along Bank and Railroad streets and out on nearby Route 7.

The Cookhouse ⋆ SOUTHERN/BARBECUE Inexplicably, Connecticut has been home to some thumpingly good barbecue joints. This is the current champ. It's set, appropriately enough, in a converted barn on often-tacky Route 7. Ribs, chicken, pulled pork, and beef brisket are slow-smoked for 10 hours or more. Heaping portions come with sides such as baked beans, collard greens, and mashed potatoes. Separate menu categories list grills, fish, and "comfort foods", the last including burritos, fajitas, macaroni and cheese, and chicken fried steak. But go for the 'cue.

31 Danbury Rd. (Rte. 7). © 860/355-4111. Main courses $12–$23. AE, DC, MC, V. Daily 11:30am–11pm (Fri–Sat until midnight).

WOODBURY ⭐

The chief distinction of this attractive town strung along Route 6, west of Waterbury, is its number of high-end antiques stores. On weekends in good weather, the main road is clogged with cars trolling for treasures, and progress can be slow.

ANTIQUING

Shoppers are drawn here for antiques and collectibles of every sort, from funky to obscure to elegant. To winnow down the list, pick up the directory produced by the **Woodbury Antiques Dealers Association** (www.antiqueswoodbury.com) at one of the member stores.

Start off in the building at 289 Main St., at the intersection of Routes 6 and 317, which contains **Jennings & Rohn Antiques** (© 203/263-3775). European paintings and furnishings from the 16th century to 1960 are on view, as well as lighting fixtures and some Art Deco. At **Martell & Suffin Antiques** (© 203/263-1913), the owners favor 18th- and early-19th-century European furniture as well as Asian works of art.

Drive south on Main Street (Rte. 6) to the notable **Wayne Pratt Antiques,** 346 Main St. (© 203/263-5676), which specializes in 18th-century American furniture, much of it museum-level Chippendale and Queen Anne pieces. Some items are within reach for the rest of us, like the Chinese porcelain boxes for $12.

Of similar high order are the offerings at **Country Loft Antiques,** 557 Main St. (© 203/266-4500), largely 19th-century French furnishings and *objets* displayed in a fine old barn. Wares run from biscuit tins to armoires, bolts of fabric to 18th-century dining tables. Be sure to look into the basement, outfitted as a wine cellar.

On most Saturdays in decent weather, the **Woodbury Antiques & Flea Market** (© 203/263-2841) sets up in a parking lot at the south end of town.

SEEING THE SIGHTS

Flanders Nature Center   North of Woodbury on Route 6, watch for Flanders Road forking to the left. Three miles along, on the right, is the office building for this nature center. Yearly events include maple syrup and wreath making, along with a fall festival. Maps of hiking trails are available.

Church Hill and Flanders Rd. © 203/263-3711. Free admission. Office Mon–Fri 9am–5pm; trails daily dawn to dusk.

Glebe House   About the only scrap of surviving history worth mentioning in town is this 1750 house of an Episcopal bishop, west of Route 6 on a street of fine 18th-century houses. A *glebe* was a property given to a preacher as partial compensation for his services. Inside are furnishings true to the period; outside is the Gertrude Jekyll Garden.

Hollow Rd. © 203/263-2855. www.glebehouse.org. Admission $5 adults, $2 children 6–12. Apr–Oct Wed–Sun 1–4pm; Nov Sat–Sun 1–4pm.

WHERE TO STAY & DINE

Longwood Country Inn ⚓ South of the town center, this 2-century-old house has been a B&B since 1951, until recently known as Merryvale. One of the current owners is an architect and the other worked in fashion, accounting for the spare good taste evident throughout. The considerably upgraded accommodations include room 3, with a four-poster bed and a fireplace, and the smaller but country-elegant room 2. In addition, the owners have pushed out the walls for a new 48-seat restaurant, **Coriander.** The food is contemporary in aspiration and execution, served at both lunch and dinner from Tuesday through Saturday (reservations ✆ **203/263-7005**). Smoking and pets aren't permitted, and children must be over 10 years old.

1204 Main St. (Rte. 6), Woodbury, CT 06798. ✆ **203/266-0800.** Fax 203/263-4479. www.longwoodcountry inn.com. 5 units. $125–$250 double. Rates include breakfast. AE, DC, MC, V. **Amenities:** Restaurant (creative American). *In room:* A/C, TV.

WHERE TO DINE

Another option is the **Longwood Country Inn,** described above.

Good News Café ⚓⚓ NEW AMERICAN This is a fun spot, with a cheery staff and rooms doused in blazing primary colors. The food? Make it Europe meets Asia, touching down in various parts of the Americas along the way. The results are spirited, but never bizarre. Examples: juniper-scented venison medallions with celery root and parsnip purée with cider sauce, and mussels in Thai coconut broth with leeks, snow peas, carrots and purple rice. Most of the entrees qualify as heart-healthy, and ingredients, whenever possible, are purchased from local farmers. Desserts, however, tend to be rich, gooey, and caloric. Saturday nights feature live jazz, and there's outdoor dining in summer.

694 Main St. (Rte. 6). ✆ **203/266-4663.** Reservations recommended on weekends. Main courses $16–$28. AE, DC, MC, V. Wed–Mon 11:30am–10pm.

WASHINGTON ⚓⚓ & WASHINGTON DEPOT

Settled in 1734, its name changed in 1779 to honor the first American president, Washington occupies the crown of a hill beside Route 47. Its village green, with the impressive 1802 Congregational Meeting House surrounded by white buildings and sheltered by shade trees, is an example of a municipal arrangement found all over New England—but rarely to such near-perfection. The traveling series of musical events known as the **Armstrong Chamber Concerts** (✆ **860/ 868-0522**) usually alights in Washington on four Saturday afternoons in spring and fall (other appearances are in Greenwich, Conn., and Lenox, Mass.). Performances are in the Congregational church.

Adjacent Washington Depot, down the hill beside the Shepaug River, serves as the commercial center, with a bank and a small cluster of shops. Stop in at the beguiling **Hickory Stick Bookshop,** 2 Greenhill Rd. (✆ **860/868-0525**).

Nearby **Steep Rock Reservation** (✆ **860/868-9131**) is a lovely spot for hiking, fly-fishing, or cross-country skiing. (Unfortunately for pet owners, dogs must now be leashed.)

Institute for American Indian Studies A worthwhile detour takes drivers down Curtis Road to this small repository of Native American crafts and artifacts. They are presented with sensitivity and, for the most part, without polemics. Down a nearby path is a re-creation of an Algonquian village. There's a picnic area on the grounds.

38 Curtis Rd. (off Rte. 199). ✆ **860/868-0518.** Admission $4 adults, $3.50 seniors, $2 children 6–16. Mon–Sat 10am–5pm; Sun noon–5pm (closed Mon–Tues Jan–Mar).

WHERE TO STAY

Mayflower Inn ✦✦   Galaxies of stars have already been scattered in abundance over this, one of the state's courtliest manor inns. While the main building is almost entirely new, some elements survive from the original 1894 structure, the most delightful of which is the richly paneled library. Porches look out across manicured lawns to deep woods. Most bedrooms have fireplaces, the bathrooms are done with tapestry rugs and mahogany wainscoting—all is as close to perfection as such an enterprise is likely to be, *almost* justifying the breathtaking prices. The clientele can't be described as youthful.

The accomplished restaurant features top-drawer ingredients drawn from New England producers and Atlantic fisheries. Perhaps needless to say, the cellar is extensive, meticulously chosen, and pricey.

118 Woodbury Rd. (Rte. 47), Washington, CT 06793. © 860/868-9466. Fax 860/868-1497. inn@ mayflowerinn.com. 25 units. $400–$600 double; $650–$1,300 suite. AE, MC, V. Take Rte. 202 north 2 miles past New Preston, turn south on Rte. 47 through Washington Depot and up the hill past Washington Common. The entrance is on the left. Children over 12 welcome. **Amenities:** Restaurant (eclectic); pub; heated outdoor pool; nearby golf course; tennis court; extensive health club; sauna; bike rental; massage; same-day dry cleaning/laundry. *In room:* A/C, TV w/pay movies, fax, dataport, minibar, hair dryer.

WHERE TO DINE

One dining option is the restaurant at the **Mayflower Inn** (see above). For a more casual meal, put together a picnic from the delectable array of quiches, pizzas, and salads at **The Pantry,** 5 Titus Rd., Washington Depot (© **860/868-0258**).

G. W. Tavern ✦ ECLECTIC AMERICAN   The tavern's atmospheric bar has booths and a fireplace, while the simulated attached barn is airier, with a deck that looks down on the Shepaug River. The kitchen is dedicated to interpretations of such robust Americana as crab cakes, meatloaf, and fish-and-chips. There are spins on convention, though, exemplified by the braised veal breast with fennel, mushrooms, and spinach over cavatelli and shavings of asiago cheese. Daily specials nearly outnumber the items on the regular menu (plus a short card of lighter fare between 2:30 and 5:30pm). Weekend brunches are popular, as is live jazz Thursday evenings and a variety of rock, pop, and folk performers on weekends. Find the tavern a block north of the Washington Depot shopping center.

20 Bee Brook Rd. (Rte. 47). © 860/868-6633. Main courses $13–$30. AE, MC, V. Daily 11:30am–10pm (Fri–Sat until 11pm).

NEW PRESTON & LAKE WARAMAUG ✦✦

Never more than a few houses and retailers at the junction of two country roads, the hamlet of New Preston long served primarily as a supplier for locals and, starting in the mid–19th century, the families who summered on nearby Lake Waramaug. More recently, New Preston's small grocery and hardware stores have been converted to antiques emporia of high order, and they find themselves surrounded on weekends by BMWs and Volvos.

EXPLORING THE LAKE WARAMAUG AREA

At the northwest tip of the L-shaped lake, 95-acre **Lake Waramaug State Park** ✦, Lake Waramaug Road (© **860/868-0220**), gives the public access to a beautiful body of water that is otherwise monopolized by the private homes and inns that border it. Canoes and paddleboats are for rent, and there's a swimming beach as well as picnic tables, food concessions, and a total of almost 80 camping and RV sites.

Hopkins Vineyard   A former dairy farm on a promontory above Lake Wara-maug was converted into a vineyard and winery in 1979. Headquartered in a 19th-century barn across the street from the Hopkins Inn (see "Where to Stay & Dine," below), it produces about a dozen bottlings. They won't make anyone forget the Napa Valley, but prices are fair. Overlooking the lake is a wine bar, where selections of pâtés and cheese can accompany samples of the primary product.

25 Hopkins Rd. ℂ 860/868-7954. www.hopkinsvineyard.com. Jan–Feb Sat–Sun 10am–5pm; Mar–Apr Wed–Sat 10am–5pm, Sun 11am–5pm; May–Dec Mon–Sat 10am–5pm, Sun 11am–5pm.

SHOPPING

In no time, the intersecting streets that form the center of the village have gone from sleepy to spiffy. Notable among the shops is **J. Seitz & Co.,** Main Street/East Shore Road (ℂ **860/868-0119**), featuring Indian blankets and clothing. Two doors down is **Cartegna,** selling Italian ceramics and home furnishings.

WHERE TO STAY & DINE

The Birches Inn ✮   Enthusiastic reviews were lavished upon the latest refig-uring of the in-house restaurant before the paint was dry. Less remarked upon were the restored bedrooms, five of them in the main house, up a slope from the road, and more yet in the lakeside cottage and "Birch House." Comfort prevails over quaintness, and the results are superior to those found in most nearby lodg-ings. Take in the vista from the **dining room** ✮✮ or deck, almost a match for the satisfying food. The French-born chef/owner comes up with such worthies as Thai rolls, *fromage blanc* tart, and duck breast in a black cherry port wine glaze, joined with a barley ragout.

233 West Shore Rd., New Preston, CT 06777. ℂ 888/590-7945 or 860/868-1735. Fax 860/868-1815. www.thebirchesinn.com. 8 units. May–Nov 15 $150–$375 double; Nov 16–Apr $125–$350 double. Rates include breakfast. AE, MC, V. Drive to the left of the town beach on West Shore Rd. about a mile. *In room:* A/C, TV.

The Boulders ✮✮   This once rustic lakeside inn, with a private swimming beach, has scrambled steadily upward in both price and quality. With its sale for $4.3 million in 2002, it took a great leap. The outlying "guesthouses"—four buildings with two spacious units each plus a new carriage house—enjoy private decks, fireplaces, Jacuzzis, and refrigerators. These have contemporary furnish-ings, while the tone of the bedrooms in the 1895 main house is set by a massive stone fireplace, an elkhorn chandelier, and country antiques and reproductions. Drinks at the handsome bar or in the large sitting room precede dinner in the main dining room or on the porch, all with lake views. A serious wine cellar complements the acclaimed cuisine, based on seasonal and local ingredients. Children over 12 are welcome, pets are not. Smoking isn't permitted.

E. Shore Rd. (Rte. 45), New Preston, CT 06777. ℂ 800/552-6853 or 860/868-0541. Fax 860/868-1925. www.bouldersinn.com. 20 units. $350–$410 double, from $595 suite. Rates include breakfast, Sunday brunch, and afternoon tea. AE, DISC, MC, V. Drive north from New Preston about 2 miles on Rte. 45. **Amenities:** Restau-rant (New American); golf course nearby; tennis court; spa, small fitness room, lake swimming, free canoes and rowboats; game room; limited room service; in-room massage. *In room:* A/C, TV/DVD/CD, dataport, hair dryer.

Hopkins Inn   A family named Hopkins started farming this land in 1787, and its descendants turned the farm into a vineyard and winery in 1979. The farm-house sits atop a hill with the best views of Lake Waramaug. Food is the main event, since most of the guest rooms are on the spartan side, with phones and TV only in the two-bedroom suite in the annex. Dishes from the Swiss and Aus-trian Alps are served in hefty portions, with Wiener schnitzel and trout bleu among the options. The restaurant is closed from January to late March.

22 Hopkins Rd., New Preston, CT 06777. © **860/868-7295.** Fax 860/868-7464. www.thehopkinsinn.com. 13 units (11 with private bathroom). $90–$160 double. AE, DISC, MC, V. From New Preston, take Rte. 45 north about 2½ miles and look for the sign on the left. **Amenities:** Restaurant (Contemporary Austrian). *In room:* A/C.

WHERE TO DINE

Oliva Although the owners describe it as an "Italian Café", the Palestinian chef touches down at many points around the Mediterranean, from France to Turkey to Tunisia and Morocco. And on a sunny day out on the terrace, with Middle Eastern music on the stereo and dishes of olives on the table, it isn't difficult to allow oneself to be transported to a Greek taverna on Patmos. When it turns cold and slushy out there, withdraw to the small interior of the old house and find a warmth generated by both the simple bistro food and the sense of a gathering of family and friends. It's popular with locals, not least due to the several inventive pizzas ($9.75 to $20) available at table and for takeout. Nothing on the plate will knock your socks off, but you will be seduced by the atmosphere. Bring your own wine.

East Shore Rd. (Rte. 45). © **860/868-1787.** Reservations advised. Main courses $12–$20. Wed–Fri 5:30–9pm; Sat–Sun noon–2:30pm and 5:30–9pm.

LITCHFIELD ★★

Possessed of a long common with stately trees reconfigured around the turn of the 20th century by the Frederick Law Olmsted landscaping firm (designers of New York's Central Park), Litchfield is testimony to the taste and affluence of the Yankee entrepreneurs who built it up in the late 18th and early 19th centuries from a colonial farm community to an industrial center. The factories and mills were dismantled toward the end of the 19th century, and the men who built them settled back to enjoy their riches in their uncommonly large homes.

In recent decades, the town has been discovered by fashionable New Yorkers, who find it less frenetic than the Hamptons. Their influence is seen both in the quality of store merchandise and restaurant fare, as well as in the lofty prices houses command.

A WALK THROUGH HISTORY

Litchfield's houses and tree-lined streets reward leisurely strollers. From the stores and restaurants along West Street, walk east (to the right when facing the common), and then turn right on South Street. On the opposite corner is the **Litchfield History Museum,** at South and East streets (© **860/567-4501**), containing an eclectic array of local historical artifacts, including the world's largest collection of works by the 18th-century portraitist Ralph Earl. It's open from April to mid-November, Tuesday through Saturday from 11am to 5pm and Sunday from 1 to 5pm. Admission is $5 for adults, $3 for seniors, and free for children under 14.

Walking down South Street, on the right, are the **Tapping Reeve House and Law School** (© **860/567-4501**). One of the few historic houses regularly open to the public, the Reeve house was built in 1773, while the adjacent 1784 building was the earliest American law school, established before independence. It counted among its students Aaron Burr and Noah Webster. Hours are the same as those of the Litchfield History Museum, which maintains it; one ticket buys admission to both museums.

When the street starts to peter out into more modern houses, walk back toward the common and cross over to the north side. Over here on the right is the magisterial **First Congregational Church,** built in 1828. Turn left, then right on North Street, where the domestic architecture matches the quiet splendor of South Street.

NEARBY ATTRACTIONS

Haight Vineyard Chardonnays and merlots don't spring to mind as likely Connecticut products, but this establishment, established in 1978, has grown and prospered, presently offering 11 drinkable bottlings. The tasting room is open year-round. There's a second winery in Mystic.

29 Chestnut Hill Rd. (C) 860/567-4045. Mon–Sat 10:30am–5pm; Sun noon–5pm.

OUTDOOR PURSUITS

The **White Memorial Foundation,** Route 202 ((C) **860/567-0857;** www.white memorialcc.org), is a 4,000-acre wildlife sanctuary and nature conservancy about 3 miles southwest of Litchfield. It has campsites and 35 miles of trails for hiking, cross-country skiing, and horseback riding. On the grounds is a small museum of natural history. The Holbrook Bird Observatory looks out on a landscape specially planted to attract birds. The museum is open year-round, Monday through Saturday from 9am to 5pm and Sunday from noon to 4pm. Admission is $4 for adults, $2 for children 6 to 12.

This is horse country, so consider a canter across the meadows and along the wooded trails of **Topsmead State Forest,** Buell Road ((C) **860/567-5694**). The park has a wildlife preserve and a Tudor-style mansion that can be toured the second and fourth weekends of each month from June to October. To get here, follow Route 118 for a mile east of town. The grounds are open from 8am to sunset. Horses can be hired nearby at **Lee's Riding Stables,** 57 East Litchfield Rd., off Route 118 ((C) **860/567-0785**).

SHOPPING

Most of the interesting shops are in the row of late-19th-century brick buildings on the south side of the town green. One such is **Kitchenworks,** 23 West St. ((C) **860/567-5011**) with a good selection of cookware and tableware, as well as some non-culinary gifts. Nearby is **Litchfield Gourmet,** 33 West St. ((C) **860/ 567-4882**), selling quality baked goods, ice cream, smoothies, espresso, and sandwiches at separate stations. Tables are available.

WHERE TO STAY & DINE

Toll Gate Hill Inn ★ The centerpiece of this red-barn complex is a 1745 structure known as the Captain William Bull Tavern in the National Register of Historic Places. It houses the bar and restaurant, and it's as atmospheric as all get out, with random-width floors and walls, a marvelously worn old bar with a fireplace inglenook, and two dining rooms. Empty for 2½ years before purchase by the present owners, it had a number of code violations that required tearing out the kitchen and replacing everything. That done, attention has been turned to the bedrooms in the newer outlying buildings, mostly involving cosmetic updating. Do inspect your room before accepting it, for there are substantial variations in size and configuration. Children and well-behaved pets are welcome. With relatively few local options, the rejuvenated **restaurant** ★★ was instantly in demand, not least because of a chef who has put in years manning stoves from Asia to Alaska to Europe. He conjures up such delights as barbecued pork crostini with crawfish aioli on polenta teacakes. His domain is open Wednesday through Sat for lunch and dinner, for dinner only on Sunday.

571 Torrington Rd. (Rte. 202), Litchfield, CT 06759. ℂ 866/567-1233 or 860/567-1233. Fax 860/567-1230. www.tollgatehill.com. 20 units. $95–$170 double, from $160 suite. AE, DC, MC, V. **Amenities:** Restaurant (creative International); bar; dataport.

WHERE TO DINE

West Street Grill NEW AMERICAN   When this contemporary bistro opened well over a decade ago, it was showered with stars by local and big-city reviewers. Known as an incubator for some of Connecticut's best chefs, several of whom went off to open their own places, it hasn't always merited the raves. But despite several important changes, the restaurant's fortunes have waxed more than waned, and are currently on an upswing with the hiring of a new CIA-trained chef. Entrees tend toward fusion renditions of meats, fowl, and fish, and portions are substantial. It remains the trendiest spot for miles, some of its patrons bearing familiar faces from TV and newspapers.

43 West St. (on the Green). ℂ 860/567-3885. Reservations recommended for dinner, essential on weekends. Main courses $17–$29. AE, MC, V. Mon–Thurs 11:30am–3pm and 5:30–9pm; Fri–Sat 11:30am–4pm and 5:30–10:30pm.

KENT

A prominent prep school of the same name, a history as an iron-smelting center, and a continuing reputation as a gathering place of artists and writers define this town of fewer than 2,000. Noted 19th-century landscape painter George Inness helped establish that assessment, and several galleries represent the works of his creative descendants. They are joined by a multiplicity of antiques shops and bookstores, most of them strung along Route 7. South of town on the same road is the hamlet of Bull's Bridge, named for one of the two remaining covered bridges in the state that can be crossed by cars.

Talk of the town is the recent federal recognition of the barely viable Schaghticoke ("SKAT-a-cokes") Indian tribe. Ten members occupy a 400-acre reservation next to the prestigious Kent School. It is the fourth tribe in Connecticut to receive formal sovereignty, and controversy is rife locally over what it might do with that status. The prospect of yet another casino looms.

Four miles northeast of·Kent is **Kent Falls State Park,** on Route 7 (ℂ 860/ 927-3238). Its centerpiece, a 250-foot cascade, is clearly visible from the road, and picnic tables are set about the grounds. A path mounts the hill beside the falls. Restrooms are available. A parking fee of $10 per out-of-state car ($7 per Connecticut car) is charged on weekends and holidays between June and October.

WHERE TO STAY & DINE

Fife 'n Drum ECLECTIC   Reminiscent of the roadhouses depicted in Hollywood noir, this place is all dark wood and brick. There are two dining rooms (each with its own grand piano) with a big battered bar in between. Apart from daily specials and an appetizer list that bounces all over the place, from sushi to escargots, the set menu could date from the 1940s, too. Settle in for no-surprises herb-crusted pork loin, baked fish, or filet mignon *au poivre.*

A separate building contains eight guest rooms, which adhere to a colonial theme but offer TVs, air-conditioning, and private bathrooms.

53 N. Main St. (Rte. 7). ℂ 860/927-3509. Main courses $14–$30. AE, DC, MC, V. Mon and Wed–Sat 11:30am–3pm and 5:30–9:30pm; Sun 11:30am–8:30pm.

WEST CORNWALL

Not to be confused with Cornwall, 4 miles to the southeast, nor Cornwall Bridge, 7 miles to the south, this tiny village is best known for its picturesque covered bridge, one of only two in the state that still permit the passage of cars. The bridge connects Routes 7 and 128, crossing the Housatonic. With a state forest to the north and a state park to its immediate south, West Cornwall enjoys a piney seclusion that remains welcoming to passersby.

Housatonic Meadows State Park, on Route 7 (© **860/672-6772** in summer, or 860/927-3238 the rest of the year), is comprised of 452 acres bordering both sides of the Housatonic River immediately south of West Cornwall. With 95 campsites, it offers access to fishing, canoeing, and picnicking.

Housatonic Anglers, Route 7 (© **860/672-4457;** www.housatonicanglers. com), offers float trips, fly-fishing schools, and guided fishing trips. **Clarke Outdoors,** 163 Rte. 7, West Cornwall (© **860/672-6365;** www.clarkeout doors.com), offers rentals of kayaks and rafts, as well as instruction and guided trips. Whitewater rafting in the Class IV-V section of the Housatonic costs $85.

Just outside Cornwall proper, off Route 4, is **Mohawk Mountain Ski Area,** 46 Great Hollow Rd. (© **800/895-5222** or 860/672-6100; www.mohawkmtn. com). "Mountain" is an overstatement, but this is the state's oldest ski resort, with five lifts, 23 trails, snowmakers, and night skiing. All-day lift tickets are $30 for adults, $20 for night skiing (6–10pm). Skis and snowboards are available for rent.

SHARON

This hamlet near the New York border is primarily residential, a picturesque village with many houses made of brick or fieldstone in a region where wood-frame houses prevail.

Sharon Audubon Center The 2,000-acre nature preserve has gardens, a shop and interpretive center, and 11 miles of trails. Injured birds are brought to the center for rehabilitation, and there are usually several recuperating raptors in house.

Rte. 4. © 860/364-0520. Trails $3 adults, $1.50 seniors and children under 12. Main building Tues–Sat 9am–5pm, Sun 1–5pm; grounds dawn to dusk.

LAKEVILLE & SALISBURY

These two attractive villages share a main street lined with 19th-century houses stretching along Route 44. The "lake" in question is Wononscopomuc, slightly south of the town center.

The discovery in the area of a particularly pure iron ore led to the development of mines and forges as early as the mid-1700s. One of the ironworkers was the eccentric Ethan Allen, later to become the leader of the Green Mountain Boys and a hero for his capture of Fort Ticonderoga from the British in 1775.

Holley-Williams House One wealthy forge owner, John Milton Holley, bought a 1768 mansion and doubled its size in 1808. The result is a Federal and Greek Revival mix. It contains furnishings assembled by Holley and his descendants over the 173 years the family lived there. There were a lot of them—the outhouse has seven holes.

15 Millerton Rd., (Rte. 44). © 860/435-2878. Free admission; guided tours $3 adults, $2 seniors and students, free for children under 5. Late June to Labor Day Sat–Sun and holidays noon–5pm.

WHERE TO STAY

Interlaken Inn Guest rooms here are divided among five buildings, including Sunnyside, with a B&B feel; Main, with its pleasant-enough double rooms; and the Townhouse Suites, fully equipped with washer/dryers, fireplaces, and kitchens. Room sizes and styles vary, so be clear about your needs before booking. For a splurge, consider the Woodside building's Executive Suite, complete with two TV/VCRs, a granite bathroom, and French doors opening out to a private patio with hot tub. Pets are allowed in some units ($10 per night).

74 Interlaken Rd., (Rte. 112) Lakeville, CT 06039. © 800/222-2909 or 860/435-9878. Fax 860/435-2980. www.interlakeninn.com. 82 units. $139–$249 double, from $269 suite. AE, MC, V. Packages available. **Amenities:** Restaurant (New American); bar; outdoor pool; nearby golf course; 2 tennis courts; health club; 2 saunas; canoes, paddleboats, kayaks, and rowboats; game room; business center; limited room service; massage and facials by reservation; babysitting. *In room:* A/C, TV/VCR, dataport, coffeemaker, hair dryer, iron.

White Hart ✿ This inn's fortunes have fluctuated in its 180-plus years, but the white-clapboard lodging at the end of Salisbury's main street is continuing its recent rise without a bump. The front porch is a prime summertime perch. Apart from the three suites and the large Ford Room, most of the guest rooms are on the small side. Both the dining rooms and the wine cellar have received excellent notices. Rates have remained stable for some time. VCRs and fridges are available for rent.

Village Green (P.O. Box 545), Salisbury, CT 06068. © 800/832-0041 or 860/435-0030. Fax 860/435-0040. www.whitehartinn.com. 26 units. $109–$249 double. AE, DC, DISC, MC, V. Pets allowed ($10). **Amenities:** Restaurant (New American); cafe; bar. *In room:* A/C, TV, hair dryer.

WHERE TO DINE

You may also want to consider a meal at the **White Hart,** reviewed above.

West Main ✿ FUSION The team that started out together in a more modest setting in Sharon picked up and moved here a few years ago. This is a far more attractive venue, with the big beams and old stones of a former barn fitted out with a striking fireplace and what they claim is the longest bar in the state. Such items as summer rolls with sesame-chili-mustard sauce, sensational frites with aioli, and spicy Shandong noodles have caused a lot of *ooh*ing and cross-table sampling. Live jazz is featured Thursday through Saturday nights.

8 Holley Place, Lakeville © 860/435-1450. Main courses $18–$24. AE, MC, V. Wed–Mon 5:30–9pm (Fri–Sat until 10pm). Closed 2 weeks in Mar and 2 weeks in Nov.

NORFOLK

Founded in 1758, Norfolk (pronounced "NOR-fork") was long popular as a vacation destination for industrialists who owned mills and factories along Connecticut's rivers. At the least, drive into the center for a look at the village green. It is highlighted by a monument that involved the participation of two of the late 19th century's most celebrated creative people—sculptor Augustus Saint-Gaudens and architect Stanford White.

At the opposite corner is the 90-year-old "Music Shed," the venue for an eagerly awaited series of summer events, the **Norfolk Chamber Music Festival** ✿ (© 860/542-3000; www.yale.edu/norfolk). Held from July to August, it hosts performances by such luminaries as the Tokyo String Quartet and the Vermeer Quartet.

Two prime recreational areas are near each other on Route 272, north of town. A mile from the village green is **Haystack Mountain State Park,** Route 272 (© 860/482-1817). Its chief feature is a short trail leading to a stone tower at the 1,715-foot crest. On clear days, the views from the top take in a panorama stretching from the Catskill Mountains to Long Island Sound.

Another 5 miles farther north, on the Massachusetts border, enjoy this abundance of streams, rapids, and cascades at **Campbell Falls,** Route 272 (© 860/482-1817). Fishing is a possibility, as are hiking and picnicking.

WHERE TO STAY

Manor House ✰ This gabled 1898 manse doesn't fit into a stylistic cubby-hole; just call it "Late Victorian Bavarian Tudor." Inside, it manages to be both stately and homey, with authentic Tiffany windows and fireplaces in the main salon, dining room, and four bedrooms. The most desirable rooms are on the second floor, notably the English Room, with a king-size bed, and the Lincoln Room, with a half-canopied antique queen bed. The least expensive room is on the third floor, tucked under the eaves—when the owner tells you it's very small, believe her.

69 Maple Ave., Norfolk, CT 06058. ℂ 860/542-5690. Fax 860/542-5690. www.manorhouse-norfolk.com. 9 units. $125–$250 double. Rates include breakfast. AE, DISC, MC, V. *In room:* No phone.

3 New Haven

Much of what is worthwhile about New Haven can be credited to the presence of one of the world's most prestigious universities. Yale both enriches its community and exacerbates the usual town-gown conflicts—a paradox with which the institution and civic authorities have struggled since the colonial period.

While New Haven suffers the generalized afflictions of many of Connecticut's cities—nearly a quarter of its citizens live at or below the poverty line—it also has a great deal to offer the leisure traveler: performing-arts centers and theaters, outstanding museums, autumn renewals of college football rivalries that date back over 120 years, and a variety of ethnic restaurants.

Relatively little serious history has happened here, but there are a number of "firsts" that boosters love to trumpet. Yale awarded the first Doctor of Medicine degree in 1729 to a man who never practiced medicine. Noah Webster compiled his first dictionary here, Eli Whitney perfected his cotton gin, and a local man named Colt invented a revolver in 1836. The first telephone switchboard was made here, necessitated by a Reverend John E. Todd, who was the first person in the world to request telephone service. And, the first hamburger was allegedly made and sold here, as was—even less certainly—the first pizza.

ESSENTIALS

GETTING THERE   Interstate 95 between New York and Providence skirts the shoreline of New Haven; I-91 from Springfield, Mass., and Hartford ends here. Connections can also be made from the south along the Merritt and Wilbur Cross parkways. Downtown traffic isn't too congested, except at the usual rush hours, and there are ample parking lots and garages near the green and Yale University, where most visitors spend their time.

Tweed–New Haven Airport (ℂ 203/466-8888) primarily handles commuter and charter traffic, as well as feeder flights of **US Air Express** (ℂ 800/428-4322). It's located southeast of the city, near Exits 50 and 51 off I-95.

Amtrak (ℂ 800/USA-RAIL; www.amtrak.com) has several trains daily that run between Boston and New York and stop in New Haven. To or from New York takes 1½ hours; to or from Boston, about 3 hours. **Metro North** (ℂ 800/638-7646 or 212/532-4900; www.mta.nyc.ny.us/mnr) commuter trains make many daily trips between New Haven and New York. Metro North tickets are much cheaper than Amtrak's, but its trains take longer.

VISITOR INFORMATION   The **Greater New Haven Convention & Visitors Bureau** (ℂ 203/777-8550) maintains an office at 1 Long Wharf Dr., easily reached from Exit 46 off I-95. It's open from Memorial Day to Labor Day. Downtown, **INFO New Haven** (ℂ 203/773-9494; www.infonewhaven.com)

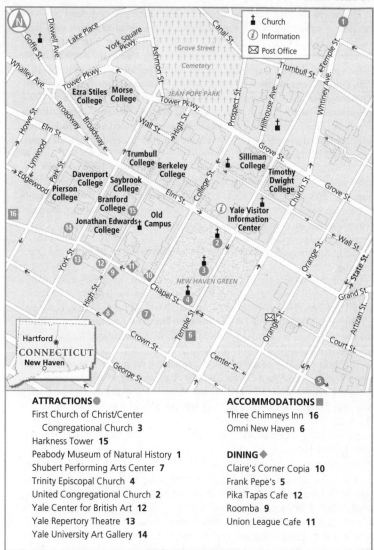

Legend:
- Church
- *i* Information
- ✉ Post Office

Map labels: Dixwell Ave, Lake Place, York Square Pkwy., Ashmun St., Canal St., Grove Street Cemetery, Goffe St., Whalley Ave, Tower Pkwy., Ezra Stiles College, Morse College, JEAN POPE PARK, Tower Pkwy., Trumbull St., Temple St., Prospect St., Hillhouse Ave., Whitney Ave., Broadway, Elm St., Howe St., Park St., Broadway, Wall St., High St., Grove St., Trumbull College, Berkeley College, Silliman College, Timothy Dwight College, Edgewood, Lynwood, Dwight St., Davenport College, Pierson College, Saybrook College, Branford College, Elm St., College St., Church St., Grove St., Jonathan Edwards College, Old Campus, Yale Visitor Information Center, Wall St., Orange St., State St., York St., High St., Chapel St., NEW HAVEN GREEN, Crown St., Temple St., Orange St., Court St., Center St., George St., Grand St., Artizan St., Hartford, CONNECTICUT, New Haven

ATTRACTIONS ●

First Church of Christ/Center Congregational Church **3**
Harkness Tower **15**
Peabody Museum of Natural History **1**
Shubert Performing Arts Center **7**
Trinity Episcopal Church **4**
United Congregational Church **2**
Yale Center for British Art **12**
Yale Repertory Theatre **13**
Yale University Art Gallery **14**

ACCOMMODATIONS ■

Three Chimneys Inn **16**
Omni New Haven **6**

DINING ◆

Claire's Corner Copia **10**
Frank Pepe's **5**
Pika Tapas Cafe **12**
Roomba **9**
Union League Cafe **11**

is open daily, all year. In addition to stocks of useful brochures, there is a terminal at which visitors can check their e-mail.

SPECIAL EVENTS   Important events are the new **International Festival of Arts & Ideas** (www.artidea.org), held at many sites around the city in late June, and a free **jazz festival** on the green from late July to early August. Call the visitor center for details.

EXPLORING YALE & NEW HAVEN

The major attractions are all associated with Yale University, and, except for the Peabody Museum, are within walking distance of one another near the **New Haven Green,** which is bounded by Elm, Church, Chapel, and College streets.

The green, about a third the size of Boston Common, is divided into two unequal parts by north-south Temple Street. Government and bank buildings, including the Gothic Revival City Hall, border it on the east, a retail district on the south, and some older sections of the vast Yale campus to the north and west.

Facing Temple Street are three historic churches, all dating from the early 19th century. Next to Chapel Street is **Trinity Episcopal Church,** a brownstone Gothic Revival structure; the Georgian **First Church of Christ/Center Congregational Church;** and the essentially Federal-style **United Congregational.** The First Church of Christ is of greatest interest, built atop a crypt with tombstones inscribed as early as 1687. Tours are conducted Tuesday through Friday between 10:30am and 2:30pm.

The oldest house in New Haven is now the **Yale Visitor Information Center,** a colonial facing the north side of the green at 149 Elm St., near College Street (② **203/432-2300**). While its primary mission is to familiarize prospective students and their parents with Yale on a 1-hour **guided walking tour,** the center also has an introductory video and maps for self-guided tours. It's open Monday through Friday from 9am to 4pm, Saturday and Sunday from 10am to 4pm. Guided tours are available Monday through Friday at 10:30am and 2pm, Saturday and Sunday at 1:30pm.

It is impossible to imagine New Haven without Yale, so pervasive is its physical and cultural presence. After all, it helped educate our last three presidents, as well as Gerald Ford, William Howard Taft, Noah Webster, Nathan Hale, and Eli Whitney. Established in 1702 in the shoreline town now known as Clinton, the young college was eventually moved here in 1718 and named for Elihu Yale, who made a major financial contribution.

The most evocative quadrangle of the sprawling institution is the **Old Campus,** which can be entered from College, High, or Chapel streets. Inside, the mottled green is enclosed by Federal and Victorian Gothic buildings and dominated by **Harkness Tower,** a 1920 Gothic Revival campanile that looks much older.

A free "trolley" bus takes loops through downtown Monday through Saturday from 11am to 6pm.

Peabody Museum of Natural History ⋆ Head to the third floor and work your way down, especially if a raucous school group has just entered. Up at the top are dioramas with stuffed animals in various environments: bighorn sheep, Alaskan brown bears, bison, and musk oxen. On the same floor is a small but illuminating collection of ancient Egyptian artifacts. The second floor doesn't hold much of general interest, but down on the first is a "bestiary" of large stuffed animals, which leads logically into the Great Hall of Dinosaurs.

170 Whitney Ave. (at Sachem St.). ② **203/432-5050.** www.peabody.yale.edu. Admission $7 adults, $6 seniors, $5 children 3–18, free to all Thurs 2–5pm. Mon–Sat 10am–5pm; Sun noon–5pm.

Yale Center for British Art ⋆⋆ What looks like a parking garage from outside is a great deal more impressive inside. The museum, designed by Louis I. Kahn, claims to be the most important repository of British art outside the United Kingdom, with holdings of more than 1,400 paintings and sculptures. Most of the paintings in the permanent collection are from the 16th through the early 19th century. It's a dazzling array, with canvases by such luminaries as Hogarth, Gainsborough, Joshua Reynolds, and the glorious Turner.

1080 Chapel St. (at High St.). ② **203/432-2800.** www.yale.edu/ycba. Free admission. Tues–Sat 10am–5pm; Sun noon–5pm.

Yale University Art Gallery ★★   The artworks of many epochs and regions are on display, but the museum is most noted for its collections of French Impressionists and American realists of the late 19th and early 20th centuries. It's a satisfying collection for connoisseurs, and won't test the patience of reluctant museum-goers. Architect Louis I. Kahn, responsible for the nearby Center for British Art, also designed the larger of these two buildings. Take the elevator to the fourth floor and work your way down. Asian arts and crafts command the top floor. The tiny Netsuke ivories at the center bear close examination. On the third floor are 14th- to 18th-century Gothic ecclesiastical panels and 16th-century Italian and Dutch portraits, among them paintings by Rubens and Frans Hals. In sharp contrast are adjoining galleries of 20th-century works—Rothko and Rauschenberg as well as Braque, Picasso, and Mondrian.

1111 Chapel St. (at York St.). 🕐 203/432-0600. www.yale.edu/artgallery. Free admission ($5 suggested donation). Tues–Sat 10am–5pm (Thurs until 8pm); Sun 1–6pm.

SHOPPING

Atticus Bookstore & Cafe   It might as easily be listed under "Where to Dine," for half of this store consists of a lunch counter and takeout section, famous for its scones. The rest of the space is devoted to what many call the best bookstore in town. Open daily from 8am to midnight. 1082 Chapel St. 🕐 203/776-4040.

WHERE TO STAY

New Haven lodgings are both limited and, with one notable exception, devoid of either charm or distinctiveness. Still, its motels and hotels fill up far in advance for football weekends, alumni reunions, and graduation.

Among the chains in town are the **Holiday Inn,** 30 Whalley Rd. (🕐 **203/ 777-6221**); **Fairfield Inn,** 400 Sargent Dr. (🕐 **203/562-1111**); and **Residence Inn,** 3 Long Wharf Dr. (🕐 **203/777-5337**). The visitor center has a **hotel reservations service** (🕐 **800/332-7829**).

Omni New Haven ★★   This is a conventional member of the reliable Omni chain. Its location couldn't be improved, next to the green and within walking distance of the theaters, much of the campus, and two of the Yale museums. **Galileo's,** the 19th-floor restaurant, offers fine views of the green and surrounding cityscape.

155 Temple St. (south of Chapel St.), New Haven, CT 06510. 🕐 **800/THE-OMNI** or 203/772-6664. Fax 203/974-6780. www.omnihotels.com. 305 units. $129–$189 double. AE, DC, DISC, MC, V. **Amenities:** Restaurant; bar; exercise room; concierge; business center; limited room service; same-day dry cleaning/laundry. *In room:* A/C, TV/VCR, dataport, minibar, coffeemaker, hair dryer.

Three Chimneys Inn ★★   Once known as the Inn at Chapel West, this 1870 mansion is a favorite of Yalies and their parents. All rooms are outfitted with mahogany four-poster beds. On chilly days, gas fires burn in seven of the bedrooms and in the dining room and parlor, where a tray of cordials is set out. An honor bar and guest pantry are also at hand. Businesspeople are more in evidence than is usual at inns, many of them here to interview Yale students for jobs. The inn is nonsmoking.

1201 Chapel St. (between Park and Howe sts.), New Haven, CT 06511. 🕐 **800/443-1554** out of state, or 203/789-1201. Fax 203/776-7363. www.threechimneysinn.com. 11 units. $195–$245 double. Rates include full breakfast and afternoon tea. AE, DISC, MC, V. Children over 6 welcome. **Amenities:** Exercise room; access to nearby health club; same-day dry cleaning. *In room:* A/C, TV/VCR, dataport, hair dryer.

WHERE TO DINE

Claire's Corner Copia VEGETARIAN   Few college towns are without at least one low-cost vegetarian restaurant. This one has ruled in New Haven since 1975.

Options include curried couscous, eggplant rollatini, BBQ soy chicken, and a number of Mexican entrees, but the stars might well be the award-winning quiches. The operator stops short of vegan purity, with tuna salad and open-faced albacore melt sandwiches on the card. Breakfast brings a bounty of plump scones and massive muffins. Place your order at the counter after perusing the very long blackboard menu, pay the cashier, and claim a table. Presently, someone emerges from the kitchen and shouts your name.

1000 Chapel St. (at College St.). ✆ 203/562-3888. Main courses $5.25–$9.50. No credit cards. Sun–Thurs 8am–9pm; Fri–Sat 8am–10pm.

Frank Pepe ✪ PIZZA On the scene for most of the last century, Pepe's has long claimed the local pizza crown while fighting off perpetual challenges. In exchange for super, almost unimaginably thin-crusted pies, pilgrims put up with long lines, a nothing decor, and a sullen staff the management prefers to think of as "seasoned." A big fave is the white clam pie. There's an annex called **The Spot** (✆ 203/865-7602) next door.

If the wait looks to be especially long, you can do about as well at **Sally's** ✪, 237 Wooster St. (✆ 203/624-5271), just down the street. They accept reservations.

157 Wooster St. (between Olive and Brown sts.). ✆ 203/865-5762. Pizzas $6–$19, depending on toppings No credit cards. Mon and Wed–Thurs 4–10pm; Fri–Sat 11:30am–11pm; Sun 2:30–10:30pm.

Louis' Lunch ✪ SANDWICHES The claim, unprovable but gaining strength as the decades roll on, is that America's very first hamburger sandwich was sold in 1900 at this little luncheonette. It moved from its original location to escape demolition, but not much else has changed. The wooden counter and tables are carved with the initials of a century of patrons. The beef is freshly ground each day, thrust into gas-fired ovens, and then served (medium rare, usually) on two slices of white toast. The only allowable garnishes are slices of tomato, onion, or cheese. There's no mustard and no ketchup, so don't even ask. And there's no fries, either, just potato chips. On the upside, there's soup, and, on Fridays only, tuna sandwiches.

261–263 Crown St. (between High and College sts.). ✆ 203/562-5507. All items under $6. No credit cards. Tues–Wed 11am–4pm; Thurs–Sat noon–2am. Closed Aug.

Roomba ✪✪ NUEVO LATINO What you'll find here, thanks to the highly creative mind of the chef/owner, is the fusion of techniques and ingredients of at least half a dozen Latin American countries. Much of it you will never have seen before, but none of it requires courage to eat. Waiters in guayaberas are happy to explain the menu. They bring plates of marvelously fanciful construction, often utilizing fried strips of plantains and paper umbrellas. Meats and fowl are roasted in a brick oven, ensuring a juicy, tender finish. There's patio seating in summer.

1044 Chapel St. (south of Chapel St.). ✆ 203/562-7666. Main courses $19–$26. AE, MC, V. Tues–Sat noon–2:30pm and 5:30–9:30pm (Fri–Sat until 10:30pm); Sun 11am–3pm and 5:30–8:30pm.

Union League Café ✪✪ CREATIVE FRENCH These grand salons retain an air of their aristocratic origins, which date back to 1854. Even the name fairly shrieks of its former status as a bastion of WASP privilege, the Union League Club. It has loosened up considerably, and denim-clad Yalies, their doting parents, philosophizing profs, and deal-making execs are all equally comfortable here. With waiters in aprons and tables covered with butcher paper, the atmosphere is now closer to an updated brasserie than to that of a gentlemen's sanctuary. The chef routinely tinkers with Gallic culinary tradition. Entrees on the order of mussels steamed in white wine, rabbit terrine, and foie gras-and-chestnut ravioli seem both familiar and fresh. A daily cheese card is proffered instead of, or in addition to, dessert. The wine list is almost exclusively French. Service is informed and proficient.

1032 Chapel St. (between High and College sts.). ℭ **203/562-4299**. Main courses $20–$30. AE, DC, MC, V. Mon–Fri 11:30am–2:30pm and 5–9:30pm; Sat 5–10pm.

NEW HAVEN AFTER DARK

The presence of Yale and a highly educated faction of the general population ensures a cultural life equal to that of many larger cities. A reliable source of information on cultural events and nightlife is the free weekly newspaper, the *New Haven Advocate* (www.newhavenadvocate.com).

THE PERFORMING ARTS   Within a couple of blocks of the green, the **Shubert Performing Arts Center,** 247 College St. (ℭ **800/228-6622** or 203/562-5666; www.shubert.com), presents musicals, opera, plays, cabaret, concerts, and such touring troupes as the Alvin Ailey Dance Theater. The well-regarded **Yale Repertory Theatre** (ℭ **203/432-1234;** www.yalerep.org), which mounts an October-to-May season of modern productions as well as classics by Shakespeare, George Bernard Shaw, and Tennessee Williams. It uses three venues: University Theater (222 York St.), the New Theatre (1156 Chapel St.), and The Rep (1120 Chapel St.)

Away from downtown, but worth the cab fare, is the prestigious **Long Wharf Theatre,** 222 Sargent Dr. (ℭ **203/787-4282,** www.longwharf.org), known for its success in producing new plays that often make the jump to off-Broadway and even Broadway itself. The season runs from October to June. The Long Wharf spawned the smaller **Stage II.**

Several venues on the Yale campus, including **Sprague Memorial Hall,** 470 College St., and **Woolsey Hall,** College and Grove streets, host the performances of many resident organizations, including the New Haven Symphony Orchestra, New Haven Civic Orchestra, Yale Concert Band, Yale Glee Club, Yale Philharmonia, and Yale Symphony Orchestra. For upcoming events, call the **Yale Concert Information Line** (ℭ **203/432-4157**).

THE CLUB SCENE   The biggest and best venue for live rock and pop is **Toad's Place,** 300 York St. (ℭ **203/621-TOAD**), which has welcomed the likes of the Rolling Stones, U2, and Bob Dylan, although the usual fare is tribute bands and regional groups.

For something less frenetic, the popular **BAR,** 254 Crown St. (ℭ **203/495-1111**), has a lounge in front—open to the street on warm nights—and a pool table, terrace, and dance floor in back. On Sundays, listen to live jazz or blues. **The Brü Rm,** a brewpub tacked onto the slightly older nightclub, produces rich beers and poses a naked challenge in the eternal New Haven pizza wars. Its thinnest-crust pies are leading contenders for the crown long held by Frank Pepe's.

4 Hartford

115 miles NE of New York; 103 miles SW of Boston

Dissidents, fleeing the rigid religious dictates of the Massachusetts Bay Colony, founded Hartford in 1636. Three years later, they drafted what were called the "Fundamental Orders," the basis of a subsequent claim that Connecticut was the first political entity on earth to have a written constitution, hence the nickname "Constitution State."

Unfortunately, Connecticut's capital and second-largest city endures a drooping uneasiness it hasn't been able to shake. There was hope for revival a few years ago when it appeared that the governor had persuaded the New England Patriots to move to downtown Hartford. A new stadium was to have been the centerpiece of a $1-billion, 35-acre riverfront development. At the last contractual minute, the Patriots exercised an escape clause, choosing to remain in the Boston area. While it is possible that parts of the plan will yet be realized, there was a great whoosh of despair when the balloon burst.

It was uncertain that even the ambitious original scheme would have reversed decades of decline. Hartford continues to point gamely to its grand edifices—the divinely overwrought gold-domed capitol, the High Victorian Mark Twain House, and the august Wadsworth Atheneum. Worthwhile as these sites certainly are, they don't prevent visitors from noticing the miles of distressed housing, weed-strewn lots, and hollow-eyed office structures that radiate out from the center.

It isn't as if efforts haven't been made to heal the wounds. A civic center was completed in 1975 in an attempt to attract business downtown, and a flyway connects it with the newer 39-story CityPlace. Both venues offer concerts and art exhibits, and the 489-seat Hartford Stage Company has a 10-month theatrical season in its own 1977 building cater-corner from the center. A block away, the gracious Old State House enjoyed a 4-year renovation. Across Main Street, a shed has been provided for a daily farmers' market; a local paper sponsors noontime rock concerts in summer. All these efforts have encouraged the establishment of a few cosmopolitan restaurants and a couple of good hotels, so most of a day trip or overnight visit can be contained within only a few square blocks.

ESSENTIALS

GETTING THERE   Interstates 84 and 91 intersect in central Hartford, halfway between New York and Boston. Downtown Hartford has plenty of convenient parking, including the garage of the Civic Center.

Bradley International Airport, in Windsor Locks, about 12 miles north of the city, is served by several major airlines, including **American** (© 800/433-7300), **Continental** (© 800/525-0280), **Delta** (© 800/221-1212), **Northwest** (© 800/225-2525), **Southwest** (© 800/435-9792), **United** (© 800/241-6522), and **US Airways** (© 800/428-4322). Buses, cabs, and limousines shuttle passengers into the city and to other points in the state.

Amtrak (© 800/USA-RAIL; www.amtrak.com) has several trains daily following the inland route between New York City and Boston, stopping at Hartford and Windsor Locks. The trip to either New York or Boston takes about 2½ hours.

VISITOR INFORMATION   The **Greater Hartford Convention** & **Visitors Bureau** (© 860/728-6789) is at 31 Pratt St., 4th floor, Hartford, CT 06103. A visitors Guide can be downloaded at their website, http://grhartfordcvb.com.

SPECIAL EVENTS   Hartford makes the most of its association with one of America's most beloved authors, Mark Twain. His image is seen everywhere, and the city puts on **Mark Twain Days** in mid-August, with such events as frog jumping, riverboat rides, and performances of plays based on Twain's life or works. In late July, there's a **Festival of Jazz** with free performances at the pavilion in Bushnell Park.

SEEING THE SIGHTS

Harriet Beecher Stowe House   On the adjacent property, across the lawn from the Twain residence, this is a smaller version of its neighbor, built in 1871.

Hartford

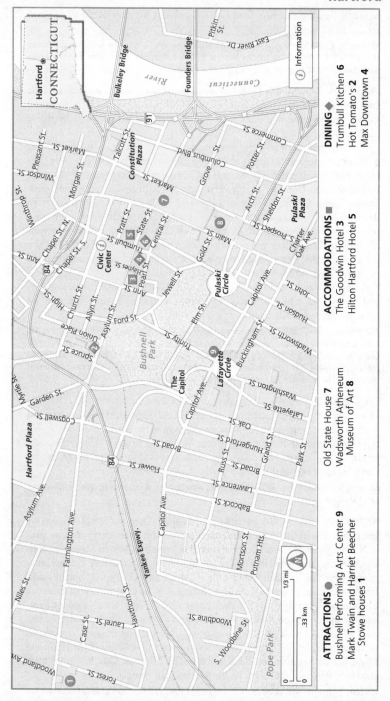

ATTRACTIONS ●
Bushnell Performing Arts Center **9**
Mark Twain and Harriet Beecher
Stowe houses **1**

Old State House **7**
Wadsworth Atheneum
Museum of Art **8**

ACCOMMODATIONS ■
The Goodwin Hotel **3**
Hilton Hartford Hotel **5**

DINING ◆
Trumbull Kitchen **6**
Hot Tomato's **2**
Max Downtown **4**

ⓘ Information

381

Stowe, the author of *Uncle Tom's Cabin,* lived here for most of the time Twain resided in his house.

77 Forest St. ✆ **860/522-9258**. Admission $6.50 adults, $6 seniors, $2.75 children 6–16, free 5 and under. Memorial Day to Columbus Day and Dec Mon–Sat 9:30am–4:30pm; Sun noon–4:30pm. Rest of the year, closed Tues. Visits by guided tour only; last tour begins at 4pm.

Mark Twain House ★★   This 19-room house is a fascinating example of the late-19th-century style sometimes known as "Picturesque Gothic," with several steeply peaked gables and brick walls whose varying patterns are highlighted by black or orange paint.

Samuel Clemens, whose pseudonym was a term used by Mississippi River pilots to indicate a water depth of 2 fathoms, lived here from 1874 to 1891. The High Victorian interior was the work of distinguished designers of the time, including Louis Comfort Tiffany, who provided both advice and stained glass. Twain's enthusiasm for newfangled gadgets—*Life On The Mississippi* is said to be the first novel written on a typewriter—led to the installation of a primitive telephone in the entrance hall. A guided tour takes about an hour and eventually leads to the top floor and the writer's main workroom, a large space that also has a pool table. Twain would often walk across the hall in the middle of the night and wake up his butler to play a few games.

A new education and visitor center houses galleries, a small cinema, a cafe, and a shop. As expected, prices were raised substantially—prohibitively, for some visitors, especially families.

351 Farmington Ave. ✆ **860/247-0998**. www.marktwainhouse.org. Admission $16 adults, $14 seniors, $12 students, $8 children 6–12, free for children 5 and under. May–Dec daily 9:30am–5:30pm (Thurs until 8pm). Rest of the year, closed Tues. Visits by guided tour only; last tour begins at 4:45pm. Take Exit 46 off I-84, turn right onto Sisson Ave., then right onto Farmington Ave. The house is on the right. From downtown, drive west on Asylum St., bearing left on Farmington Ave. The house is on the left.

The Old State House   After a 4-year, $12-million restoration, the 1796 State House opened in time to celebrate its bicentennial. Costumed interpreters stand ready to answer questions. Upstairs on the right is the Senate chamber, with a full-length painting of the first president by the indefatigable Washington portraitist Gilbert Stuart. These days, the building is used for temporary art exhibitions, changed two or three times yearly.

800 Main St. (at Asylum Ave.). ✆ **860/522-6766**. www.ctosh.org. Free admission. Mon–Fri 10am–4pm; Sat 11am–4pm.

Wadsworth Atheneum Museum of Art ★★★   Opened in 1842, this was the first public art museum in the United States and remains a repository with few equals in New England. The strength of the collection lies primarily in its American paintings, spanning the period from landscape artists of the 19th century through luminaries of the New York School of the mid–20th century. On the top floor are works by Thomas Cole, of the Hudson River School, and his contemporaries Frederick Church and Albert Bierstadt. On the balcony are more Americans—Frederic Remington, Andrew Wyeth, Milton Avery, Norman Rockwell. Watch for the shadow box by Joseph Cornell. The first floor contains rule-bending multimedia works, as well as canvases by Abstract Expressionists and pop and op artists of the 1950s and 1960s like de Kooning and Rauschenberg. The **Museum Cafe** has surprisingly good light items and tables out on the terrace in fair weather.

600 Main St. (1 block west of the Old State House). ✆ **860/278-2670**. www.wadsworthatheneum.org. Admission $9 adults, $7 seniors, $5 students, free children 12 and under (free to all until noon Sat); surcharges for some special exhibitions. Tues–Fri 11am–5pm, Sat–Sun 10am–5pm (until 8pm 1st Thurs of most months).

WHERE TO STAY

The Goodwin Hotel ⭐   This quiet hostelry opposite the Civic Center is housed in a Queen Anne–style Victorian built in 1881 as a residence for J. P. Morgan. Its understated public areas are attractive, while its cautiously decorated bedrooms are fully equipped. Valet parking is often slow, but still a blessing along this crowded block. The in-house restaurant has an erratic reputation, but some of the city's best dining options are short walks away.

1 Haynes St. (at Asylum St.), Hartford, CT 06103. ℭ **800/922-5006** or 860/246-7500. Fax 860/244-2669. www.goodwinhotel.com. 124 units. $159–$269 double. Weekend packages available. AE, DC, DISC, MC, V. Valet parking $15. **Amenities:** Restaurant (American); lounge; modest fitness center; concierge; limited room service; same-day dry cleaning. *In room:* A/C, TV w/pay movies, VCR on request, dataport, hair dryer, iron.

Hilton Hartford Hotel ⭐⭐   This 22-story slab used to be a Sheraton. Guests will enjoy the results of the $4 million expended on largely cosmetic renovations. Over a hundred connecting bedrooms make it attractive to families. The hotel connects with the Civic Center and is readily visible to drivers entering the city from I-84.

315 Trumbull St., Hartford, CT 06103. ℭ **800/445-8667** or 860/728-5151. Fax 860/240-7246. www.hartford. hilton.com. 390 units. $109–$282 double. AE, DC, DISC, MC, V. **Amenities:** Two restaurants (International); sports bar; indoor pool; fully equipped health club; Jacuzzi; sauna; limited room service; same-day dry cleaning/laundry. *In room:* A/C, TV, dataport, coffeemaker, hair dryer, iron.

WHERE TO DINE

Hot Tomato's ITALIAN   The renovation of Union Station spawned this popular trattoria in one wing. Dine in the glass-sided dining room or on the terrace. A casually dressed crowd tucks into big bowls of garlicky pasta, the primary offerings here. There is lobster *pinchiori*, for one, heaping chunks of the shellfish with portobellos and asparagus in lobster cream sauce over tagliatelle. Atkins followers have six equally hearty portions of beef and pork to choose among, notably the 18-ounce "Cowboy Cut" rib-eye. Especially spicy dishes are marked with a star. Sides are extra. The bar stays open late.

1 Union Place (corner of Asylum St.). ℭ **860/249-5100.** Reservations advised for patio and on weekends. Main courses $15–$28. AE, DISC, DC, MC, V. Mon–Thurs 11:30am–11pm; Fri 11:30am–midnight; Sat 4pm–midnight; Sun 4–10pm.

Max Downtown ⭐⭐ CONTEMPORARY AMERICAN   Hartford's primetime power epicenter has a crowd that looks essentially interchangeable with the one that frequents the Trumbull Kitchen (see below), albeit with a few more suits at midday and a lot of air-kissing at night. Too bad patrons don't pay much attention to the bar menu, for its treats are along the lines of mulligatawny and mahimahi with mango-papaya sauce. The main room has banquettes arrayed behind expanses of glass, with a flashy mural on the back wall. Diners are indulged with hefty chophouse favorites—thick veal chops and porterhouse steaks for two—and flightier efforts, such as gingered duck breast with a duck confit risotto cake, peas, and Japanese eggplant.

185 Asylum St. (opposite City Center). ℭ **860/522-2530.** Reservations advised on weekends. Main courses $18–$30. AE, DC, MC, V. Mon–Fri 11:30am–10:30pm (Fri until 11:30pm); Sat 5–11:30pm; Sun 4:30–9:30pm.

Trumbull Kitchen ⭐ ECLECTIC   Formerly the Civic Cafe, this latest addition to the highly successful Max chain (see Max Downtown, above) retains its popularity, and appears to be building upon it. Still looking like it belongs in a hipper city, young execs and lawyers continue to frequent it, observing or partaking in the ritual collisions of egos. The menu is sprinkled with such global grazing categories as fondues and tapas-like noshes on the lines of lime-chipotle marinated lamb skewers. Large plates include such possibilities as tuna with tamarind basmati rice and coconut spinach. This is fun, diverting food—tasty enough without distracting from the primary mingling. The bar stays open after the kitchen closes.

150 Trumbull St. (near Asylum St.). (℃ 860/493-7412. Main courses $14–$19. AE, DC, DISC, MC, V. Mon–Wed 11:30am–11pm, Thurs–Fri 11:30am–midnight, Sat 5pm–midnight.

HARTFORD AFTER DARK

The free weekly *Hartford Advocate* (www.hartfordadvocate.com) provides useful information on cultural, sports, and musical events.

The **Bushnell Performing Arts Center,** 166 Capitol Ave. (℃ 860/987-5900; www.bushnell.org), is in the midst of a $45-million expansion, including a new 918-seat theater added to the 2,800-seat main stage. They serve as venues for the Hartford Symphony, Connecticut Opera, Hartford Pops, and smaller traveling groups, when not hosting visiting symphony orchestras or road companies of Broadway plays. The **Hartford Stage,** 50 Church St. (℃ 860/527-5151; www. hartfordstage.org), mounts a variety of mainstream plays.

Several downtown clubs host live bands, usually Thursday through Saturday. At the **Arch Street Tavern,** 85 Arch St. (℃ 860/246-7610), nationally known bands of the second magnitude appear from time to time, but local groups dominate. The **Brickyard Cafe,** 113 Allyn St. (℃ 860/249-2112), contains a bar, dance floor, sports bar, pool tables, and a lot of people looking to hook up. **Black-Eyed Sally's,** 350 Asylum St. (℃ 860/278-7427), known for its ribs and other Southern-style gustatorial treats, presents live blues bands Thursday through Saturday nights.

City Steam Brewery, 942 Main St. (℃ 860/525-1600), serves food that goes well with the dozens of home brews. On the premises are pool tables, frequent live music, and the Brew HA HA Comedy Club (Thurs). For beer by the pitcher along with Monday Night Football or the Final Four, where better than **Coach's,** 187 Allyn St. (℃ 860/522-6224), a place founded by the UConn basketball coach himself. It has 35 TVs, bar snacks, video games, and live music Thursday through Saturday.

5 From Guilford to Old Saybrook

Usually ignored by vacationers anxious to get on to Mystic and Essex and the casinos, the stretch of coast between New Haven and the Connecticut River, known simply as the Shoreline, has its gentle pleasures, enough to justify a short detour for lunch, a walk on a beach, a spell of shopping, or even a proper British high tea (in Madison). When lodgings are difficult to find at the better-known destinations, the Shoreline's inns and resorts are logical alternatives within easy driving distance.

ESSENTIALS

GETTING THERE The Shoreline can be reached from Exit 57 off I-95. Pick up Route 1 (aka the Boston Post Rd.), which serves as the main street of several Shoreline towns.

Several daily **Amtrak** (℃ 800/USA-RAIL; www.amtrak.com) trains stop at Old Saybrook. The **Shore Line East** (℃ 800/255-7433; www.shorelineeast.com) commuter line uses the same tracks to service towns between New Haven and New London, but only Monday through Friday.

VISITOR INFORMATION   Contact the **Connecticut River Valley and Shoreline Visitors Council,** 393 Main St., Middletown (℃ **800/486-3346** or 860/347-0028; www.cttourism.org).

GUILFORD

One of the state's oldest colonial settlements (1639), this village, 13 miles east of New Haven, is embraced by the West and East rivers and has an uncommonly large public green. There are dozens of historic houses to see in town, most of them privately owned and a few others open to the public on a limited basis, typically from Memorial Day to Columbus Day. **Hyland House,** 84 Boston St. (℃ **203/453-9477**), built around 1690, and the **Thomas Griswold House,** 171 Boston St. (℃ **203/453-3176**), from 1774, are two of these.

Henry Whitfield State Museum   The Whitfield Museum bills itself as the oldest house in Connecticut and the oldest stone house in New England. Most of what you see now, though, including the leaded windows, dates from a 1930s reconstruction and not from the mid-1600s, so it is really more a museum than a historic home. It is still worth a brief visit, and the furnishings are authentic to the period.

248 Old Whitfield St. ℃ 203/453-2457. Admission $3.50 adults, $2.50 seniors, $2 children 6–17. Feb 1–Dec 14 Wed–Sun 10am–4:30pm; Dec 15–Jan 30 by appointment only.

WHERE TO DINE

Esteva ⭐   Occupying a space that formerly contained the uneven Bistro on the Green, this fresh entry bears no resemblance to its predecessor. The windows looking out on the town green are larger, the contemporary artwork eye-catching, the staff amiable. Most important, the food takes a giant step toward memorable, finding delectable twists on widely familiar items. That's because Steve Wilkinson, who previously operated a highly regarded cafe in Centerbrook, is at the helm. Fried calamari, a menu staple throughout the Northeast, here comes with a spicy tomato and ancho remoulade dipping sauces and sliced cherry peppers mixed with the squid. The lunch menu is constituted of that trendy division between small plates and large plates–soup and salads among the former, grilled salmon and hefty sandwiches among the latter—while the dinner card is more conventional. The kitchen's dashing creativity is evident in the ravioli simmered in porcini broth and dusted with grated cheese and the roasted monkfish wrapped in prosciutto with chive-mashed potatoes, sautéed spinach, and a portobello vinaigrette.

12 Whitfield St. ℃ 203/458-1300. Reservations advised. Main courses $19–$26. MC, V. Tues–Thurs and Sun 11:30am–2:30pm and 5:30–9pm; Fri–Sat 11:30am–2:30pm and 5:30–9:30pm.

MADISON

Madison, 19 miles east of New Haven, is home to an historic architectural district that stretches west of the business district along the Boston Post Road, from the main green to the town line, and contains many examples of 18th- and 19th-century domestic styles.

The well-to-do town has completed the transition from colony to seaside resort to year-round community, a process begun when the first house was built in 1651. Today, there are two dwellings from the early years that can be visited on limited summer schedules. **Deacon John Grave House,** 581 Boston Post Rd. (℃ **203/245-4798**), dates from 1685, and the **Allis-Bushnell House,** 853 Boston Post Rd. (℃ **203/245-4567**), from 1785.

Off the Boston Post Road east of the town center, also reached from Exit 62 off I-95, is **Hammonasset Beach State Park** (℃ **203/245-2785**), a 900-plus-acre peninsula jutting into Long Island Sound that has the only public swimming beach in the area, and it's over 2 miles long. It has a nature center, picnic areas, campgrounds, fishing, and boating. From Memorial Day to Labor Day, cars with Connecticut plates are charged $5 Monday through Friday, $7 on weekends and holidays; out-of-state plates are charged $8 Monday through Friday, $12 on weekends and holidays.

SHOPPING

Madison's commercial district may look ordinary at first glance, but several shops along Boston Post Road and intersecting Wall Street provide entertaining browsing. **R. J. Julia Booksellers,** 768 Boston Post Rd. (© **203/245-3959**), holds frequent author readings and poetry slams.

The British Shoppe, 45 Wall St. (© **203/245-4521**), stocks such favorites as kippers, pork pies, and sublime cheeses. Classic ploughman's lunches recall those in English pubs. (Tough licensing requirements don't allow for pints of English beer, but you can bring your own.)

Exit 63 off 1-95 west leads directly to **Clinton Crossing,** 20-A Killingsworth Tpk. (© **860/664-0700**), a "premium" outlet mall with more than 80 shops. Clothing by such designers as Calvin Klein, Donna Karan, and Ralph Lauren are augmented by Coach leather goods and Le Creuset cookware.

WHERE TO STAY & DINE

The Inn at Lafayette 🌟 **Cafe Allegre** 🌟🌟   The stately Greek Revival portico in the middle of the business district promises a touch of elegance, and the interior delivers. Since 1998, the ground floor has housed Cafe Allegre, a soothing setting for northern Italian and European food of considerable accomplishment. Fresh regional ingredients are paramount. Main courses, such as lemon chicken and veal saltimbocca, run from $17 to $27. The bar is a low-key gathering place, popular for lunch, with a piano player on Thursday and Friday nights; closed Monday. The owners haven't done much with the guest rooms upstairs, which are clearly secondary to their restaurant, but they're comfortable enough, with marble baths and king- or queen-size beds.

725 Boston Post Rd., Madison, CT 06443. © **866/623-7498** or 203/245-7773. Fax 203/245-6256. www. allegrecafe.com. 5 units. Late May to early Oct $125–$175 double; Columbus Day to late May $95–$150 double. AE, DC, MC, V. Children over 12 welcome. **Amenities:** Restaurant (Italian/European); bar. *In room:* A/C, TV, dataport, hair dryer.

WHERE TO DINE

Lenny & Joe's Fish Tale SEAFOOD   At this rough-and-ready fish shack, fish rules, most of it fried. And while it is sure to elevate triglyceride counts, the nutty coating on super-fresh clams, oysters, shrimp, and calamari is hard to resist. There's another branch at 1301 Boston Post Rd. (© 860/245-7289).

86 Boston Post Rd., Westbrook © **860/669-0767.** Main courses $8.95–$18. Daily 11am–9pm (Fri–Sat until 10pm).

OLD SAYBROOK

Its location at the mouth of the Connecticut River (35 miles east of New Haven, 26 miles west of Mystic) is this otherwise nondescript town's principal lure. Get off Route 1 to see it at its best. Pick up Route 153 south at the western edge, following the nearly circular route as it touches the shore and passes through the hamlets of Knollwood and Fenwick and across the causeway to Saybrook Point before ending up back in the main business district.

WHERE TO STAY & DINE

Saybrook Point Inn & Spa ★★ Resort hotels have existed at this location since the late 19th century, and they've gotten the formula down pat at the current facility. It has one of the largest marinas along the coast, an ingratiating restaurant with a clubby bar and a summer dining terrace, a fully equipped fitness room, and a spa offering a full range of body and skin care services, including mud and seafood wraps. The **Terra Mar Grille** far exceeds the bland country club fare often associated with shore resorts, not with such surprises as chipotle-orange marinated hanger steak and blackened escarole with lobster mashed potatoes and sautéed broccoli rabe. Their definitive versions of clam chowder and lobster roll aren't to be missed. Sunday buffet brunch is especially popular. Bedrooms are spacious, all with wet bars and sitting areas, some of the more expensive with working fireplaces and whirlpool tubs. A shuttle carries guests to and from the Shore Line East railroad station.

2 Bridge St., Old Saybrook, CT 06475. ✆ **800/243-0212** or 860/395-2000. www.saybrook.com. 80 units. Apr–Oct $159–$339 double; Nov–Mar $159–$249; suites from $349. AE, DC, DISC, MC, V. Take Rte. 154 south from the Old Saybrook business district. **Amenities:** Restaurant (New American); bar; limited room service; indoor and outdoor pool; health club and spa. *In room:* A/C, TV, dataport, unstocked fridge, hair dryer, iron.

6 The Connecticut River Valley

New England's longest river originates in the far north near the Canadian border, 407 miles from Long Island Sound. It separates Vermont from New Hampshire, splits Massachusetts in half, then takes a 45-degree turn at Middletown, south of Hartford, to make its final run to the sea.

Native Americans of the region called the river *Quinnetukut,* which, to the tin ears of the English settlers, sounded like "Connecticut." The colonists encroached upon Indian territory as far north as present-day Windsor, which ignited a brief war with the Pequot, who occupied the land.

Because the river was navigable by relatively large ships as far as Hartford, the sheltered lower Connecticut became important for boat-building and industries associated with the international clipper trade. The Connecticut River retains that nautical flavor, and the valley has miraculously avoided the industrialization, development, and decay that afflict most of the state's other rivers.

Cruising, boating, and kayaking are obvious attractions, supplemented by rides on a steam-powered train, a selection of worthy B&Bs, antiques shops, a venerable musical theater, even a bizarre castle on a hilltop.

ESSENTIALS

GETTING THERE Limited-access state highway 9 runs parallel to the river, along the west side of the valley, connecting I-91 south of Hartford with I-95 near Old Saybrook. The lower valley is therefore readily accessible from all points in New England and from the New York metropolitan area and points south.

Amtrak (✆ **800/USA-RAIL;** www.amtrak.com) trains stop at Old Saybrook, at the mouth of the river, several times daily on runs between New York and Boston. In addition, **Shoreline East** (✆ **800/255-7433**) commuter trains operate Monday through Friday between New Haven and New London.

VISITOR INFORMATION The **Connecticut River Valley and Shoreline Visitors Council,** 393 Main St., Middletown (✆ **800/486-3346** or 860/347-0028; www.cttourism.org), is a source of pamphlets, maps, and related materials.

OLD LYME

As quiet a town as the coast can claim, Old Lyme (40 miles east of New Haven, 21 miles west of Mystic) was the favored residence of generations of seafarers and ship captains. Many of their 18th- and 19th-century homes have survived, some as inns and museums. Preservationists and community activists proudly point out that their main street is the only one cut by I-95 that continues to thrive. With its many tree-lined streets largely free of traffic, stressless biking is an attractive option here.

Florence Griswold Museum ⋆   After the shipbuilding and merchant trade had all but flickered out at the end of the 19th century, artists who came to be known as the "American Impressionists" took a fancy to this area. They received encouragement, patronage, and even food and shelter from Ms. Griswold, the wealthy daughter of a sea captain. Falling upon hard times later in life, she decided to open her Georgian-Federalist 1817 mansion to boarders. It became the temporary home for a number of painters, many of whom left samples of their work in gratitude, sometimes painting directly on the walls of the dining room. Among her grateful guests was Childe Hassam, considered the grand master of the American Impressionists. Woodrow Wilson was also a visitor, in 1910, when he was president of Princeton University. Now, The Flo Gris has a new building behind the mansion with three light-filled galleries. The first two spaces are usually devoted to changing exhibits, the third to paintings rotated from the Griswold permanent collection. Visitors can walk across the mansion's 6 acres to the Lieutenant River.

96 Lyme St. (Rte. 1). *©* **860/434-5542.** www.flogris.org. Admission $7 adults, $6 seniors and students, $4 children 6–12. Tues–Sat 10am–5pm, Sun 1–5pm.

OUTDOOR PURSUITS

One of several state parks located at the edge of Long Island Sound, **Rocky Neck State Park,** Route 156 (*©* **860/739-5471**), east of Old Lyme, has a crescent-shaped beach and over 560 acres for camping, picnicking, fishing, and hiking. Take I-95 to Exit 72 and follow Route 156 south. Open daily from 8am to sunset. From Memorial Day to Labor Day, admission is $5 to $7 for cars with CT plates, $8 to $12 for out-of-state vehicles.

WHERE TO STAY & DINE

Bee and Thistle Inn ⋆   Situated on more than 5 acres beside the Lieutenant River, the Bee and Thistle has a core structure that dates from 1756, with the usual later wings and additions. Every corner of the place is an enjoyable jumble of antiques and collectibles. A detached cottage is the best lodging, with the only in-room TV. It has a fireplace, as does one room in the main house. Year after year, the inn's **dining room** ⋆⋆ is voted "best overall" and "most romantic" in the state by reader polls. It's open Wednesday through Monday; reservations are essential. Musicians are on hand weekend evenings; appropriate attire is requested. Kids over 12 are welcome at the inn; pets are not.

100 Lyme St. (Rte. 1), Old Lyme, CT 06371. *©* **800/622-4946** or 860/434-1667. Fax 860/434-3402. www.bee andthistleinn.com. 12 units. $110–$219 double. AE, DC, DISC, MC, V. From the south, take Exit 70 off I-95; turn left, then right on Rte. 1 (Halls Rd.) north. Children over 12 welcome. **Amenities:** Restaurant (creative American). *In room:* A/C.

Old Lyme Inn   Most of the spacious bedrooms in this expansive 1850s farmhouse are furnished in part with attractive Victorian pieces, including four-poster beds. Some have VCRs. There are two dining rooms, but the informal

Grill features an antique Victorian bar and marble-mantled fireplace as well as live music on weekends. Admirers of venerable taverns might not want to leave. New owners are making physical improvements, including making a library-breakfast room out of what used to be a nearly bare corridor. Pets are accepted, a rare policy among New England inns. Breakfast is on the skimpy side.

85 Lyme St. (Rte. 1), Old Lyme, CT 06371. © 800/434-5352 or 860/434-2600. Fax 860/434-5352. www.old lymeinn.com. 13 units. $99–$195 double. Rates include breakfast. AE, DC, DISC, MC, V. To get here, follow directions for the Bee and Thistle, above. **Amenities:** 2 restaurants (creative American); bar. *In room:* A/C, TV, hair dryer.

ESSEX ★★

It is difficult to imagine what improvements might be made to bring this dream of a New England waterside town any closer to perfection. In fact, a published survey, *The 100 Best Small Towns in America,* has ranked the waterside village number one. Among the criteria were low crime rates, per-capita income, proportion of college-educated residents, and numbers of physicians.

Tree-bordered streets are lined with shops and homes that retain an early-18th-century flavor without the unreal frozen-in-amber quality that often afflicts other towns as postcard-pretty as this. People live and work and play here, and bustle busily along a Main Street that runs down to Steamboat Dock and its flotilla of working vessels and pleasure craft.

Clustered along the harbor end of Main Street are three historic houses that are open to the public on limited seasonal schedules. No. 40 is the **Richard Hayden House,** an 1814 brick Federal. Next door, at no. 42, is the **Noah Tooker House,** an 18th-century center-hall colonial. And at no. 51 is the **Robert Lay House,** completed around 1730 and thought to be the oldest original structure in town.

In winter, bald eagles come to the lower reaches of the river, and Essex holds an **Eagle Festival** in mid-February in celebration, with music, Native American dancers, and guided boat and land-based viewing of the raptors. Call © **800/ 714-7201** or log on to www.ctaudubon.org for information and to make tour reservations.

Connecticut River Museum ★   Anglers cast lines from the dock while gulls and ducks hang around hoping for a discarded tidbit. Steamboat service was fully operational here from 1823, and the existing dock dates from 1879. Designated a National Historic Site, the museum proper features model ships, marine paintings, and artifacts that relate the story of shipbuilding in the valley, which began in 1733 and helped make this a center of world trade far into the 19th century. A replica of America's first submarine (1775), the *Turtle* is also on display. The museum usually has walking-tour maps of Essex, too, making this a good first stop on your visit.

Steamboat Dock (at foot of Main St.). © 860/767-8269. www.ctrivermuseum.org. Admission $5 adults, $4 seniors and students, $3 children 6–12. Tues–Sun 10am–5pm.

Essex Steam Train *Kids*   Steam locomotives from the 1920s chug along to a boat landing in the hamlet of Deep River, a diverting excursion of about an hour. It can be combined with an optional cruise on the river. Dinner trains include five-course meals and fare for $60 per person; call for schedule.

1 Railroad Ave. (Rte. 154). © 860/767-0103. www.essexsteamtrain.com. Train and boat $24.00 adults, $12 children 3–11; train only $16 adults, $8 children 3–11. Daily trips mid-June to Labor Day, less frequently Sept–May.

WHERE TO STAY & DINE

Griswold Inn ★★   Nobody doesn't like "The Gris." Gloss over the assertion that it's the oldest inn in America (there are other claimants). What's more important is that some years ago local people rescued the inn from outside buyers. That was a relief, for it is difficult to imagine this corner of New England without the Gris. Rumpled, cluttered, folksy, and forever besieged by drop-in yachtspeople, anglers, locals, and tourists, the main building dates to 1776. The atmospheric taproom started life as a schoolhouse and was moved here in 1800. There's live entertainment every night, be it a Dixieland band or just a man with a banjo. The colorful dining rooms are named for their displays of books, antique weapons, or marine paintings. Food, while still hearty, has taken a turn toward the less conventional, now featuring goose confit risotto, moose tournedos, roasted oysters, and braised rabbit; but the famed 1776 sausages mixed grill is still available. The often plain and unadorned bedrooms scattered throughout six buildings are slowly being upgraded; some have fireplaces. *Viva Gris!*

36 Main St. (center of town), Essex, CT 06426. © 860/767-1776. Fax 860/767-0481. www.originalinns.com. 30 units. June–Oct $105–$140 double, from $165 suite; Nov–May $95–$125 double, from $150 suite. Rates include breakfast. AE, MC, V. **Amenities:** Restaurant (American); bar. *In room:* A/C.

IVORYTON

Once a center for the ivory trade, where factories fabricated piano keys and hair combs, Ivoryton has since subsided into a residential quietude. A virtual suburb of the only slightly larger Essex, a few miles east, the town perks up a bit in summer, when the **Ivoryton Playhouse,** 103 Main St. (© **860/767-7318;** www.river rep.com) conducts its theatrical season. The repertoire runs to revivals of Broadway comedies and mysteries.

WHERE TO STAY & DINE

Copper Beech Inn ★★   Despite comparisons with the Griswold Inn in nearby Essex, these are two very different animals. Where the Gris is decidedly populist and perennially busy, the stately Copper Beech has much less traffic, without a single figurative hair out of place. The rooms in the converted barn have ample elbowroom, TVs, Jacuzzis, and decks, while those in the 19th-century main building have most of the character, with plenty of antiques. All 13 bathrooms have been redone. The Copper Beech was already the home to one of the most honored restaurants in the region, but the new owners have raised the stakes even higher, and the chef they hired is garnering ecstatic reviews. He joins French techniques and recipes with high-quality seasonal ingredients. Service is seamless, the wine list impressive.

46 Main St., Ivoryton, CT 06442. © 888/809-2056 or 860/767-0330. www.copperbeechinn.com. 13 units. $155–$295 double, $315–$335 suite. Rates include breakfast. AE, DC, DISC, MC, V. Closed 1st week in Jan. Take Exit 3 from Rte. 9 and head west on Main St. Children over 10 welcome. **Amenities:** Restaurant (country French); bar. *In room:* A/C, TV (9 units), hair dryers.

CHESTER

Hardly more than a 3-block business center, Chester can be dismissed easily enough. But pause a moment, for this riverside hamlet deserves savoring. Along Main Street are antiques shops, galleries, and several eateries. **Ceramica,** 36–38 Main St. (© **860/526-9978**), an outlet of a small chain, carries a line of uniformly gorgeous hand-painted bowls, pitchers, vases, and teapots.

WHERE TO DINE

The Wheatmarket (© 860/526-9347), next door to Fiddlers (see below), will make up picnic baskets, or you can put together your own from the appetizing array of breads, cheeses, soups, salads, and sandwiches.

Fiddlers ★ SEAFOOD   Have your fish any way you want—poached, sautéed, broiled, baked, or grilled over mesquite—or leave it up to the skillful kitchen staff, for they can come up with some eye-openers. If "lobster au pêché" (fat chunks of lobster meat married to peach nubbins, shallots, mushrooms, cream, and peach brandy) is still on the menu, go for it. Not for lobster purists, certainly, but a revelatory example of what an imaginative chef can do. The dining rooms are cheerfully unremarkable.

4 Water St. (behind Main St.). ℰ 860/526-3210. Main courses $14–$24. DC, MC, V. Wed–Sat 11:30am–2pm and 5:30–9pm; Sun 4–8pm.

EAST HADDAM

Hadlyme (a jurisdiction of the town of East Haddam), hardly more than a wide spot in a country road, wouldn't have attracted much attention at all if a wealthy thespian hadn't decided to build his hilltop redoubt here.

To get here, take the **Chester-Hadlyme Ferry,** at the end of Route 148, slightly less than 2 miles from Chester. A ferry has operated here since 1769, and the current version takes both cars and pedestrians ($2.25 for vehicles plus $1.50 for trailers, 75¢ for walk-on passengers). It operates (when it feels like it) from 7am to 6:45pm Monday through Friday, 10:30am to 5pm Saturday through Sunday from April through November 30th. If it's closed, there will be a sign posted at the intersection of Routes 148 and 154, in which case you'll have to drive north on Route 154 to Haddam and take the bridge.

Gillette Castle State Park ★   William Gillette was a successful actor and playwright known primarily for his portrayals of Sherlock Holmes. He took the money and ran to this hill rearing above the Connecticut River, where he had his castle built. It's difficult to believe that he really thought the result resembled the Norman fortresses that allegedly were his inspiration. Rock gardens by roadside eccentrics in South Dakota or Death Valley are closer relations. Gillette felt it necessary, for one example, to design a dining-room table that slid into the wall, an inexplicable space-saving effort by a bachelor rattling around in 24 oddly shaped rooms.

But whatever Gillette's deficiencies as an architect and designer, no one can argue with his choice of location. The castle sits atop a hill above the east bank, with superlative vistas upriver and down. Nowhere else is the blessed underdevelopment of the estuary more apparent. After 2 years of renovations, which involved replacing rotted ceiling beams and repairing extensive water damage, the castle was reopened in 2002

The 184-acre grounds have picnic areas, nature trails, and fishing sites. Because the terrace of the "castle" can be entered for free, many visitors come just to take in those **views** ★★.

67 River Rd. ℰ 860/526-2336. www.cttourism.org. Admission $4 adults, $2 children 6–11. Grounds daily 8am–sunset; castle Memorial Day to Labor Day Fri–Sun 10am–5pm.

RIVER CRUISES

A voyage on the river is an irresistible outing. Cruises of a variety of lengths, times, and themes are offered by **Camelot Cruises,** 1 Marine Park (ℰ **860/345-8591;** www.camelotcruises.com). The pride of its fleet is the MV *Camelot,* a 160-foot vessel carrying as many as 400 passengers. In addition to dinner and mystery cruises, there are summer and fall excursions to Greenport, Long Island.

A competing company, **Mark Twain Cruises,** River Street, Deep River (ℰ **877/658-9246;** www.marktwaincruises.com), uses six boats for winter eagle-spotting, fall foliage, fireworks, birding, meal, and jazz cruises. Embarkations are from Charter Oak Landing in Hartford as well as from Saybrook Point and other ports along the river.

EAST HADDAM AFTER DARK

From Gillette Castle State Park, turn north on Route 82 and make the short drive to East Haddam proper. The dominant building is a restored 1877 Victorian of splendid proportions that is now the **Goodspeed Opera House** ★★, Goodspeed Landing (© **860/873-8668**; www.goodspeed.org). It mostly stages revivals of Broadway musicals on the order of *Man of La Mancha* and *Very Good Eddie,* but always makes room for more experimental or original shows that have often made it all the way to the Big Apple. The smaller Norma Terris Theatre has an additional schedule of more experimental plays. The season for both runs usually from April into December.

7 Mystic & the Southeastern Coast

Mystic: 55 miles E of New Haven

This section of the shoreline is studded with towns that still bear the stamp of their maritime pasts, a string of fishing ports and inlets that segues into the mainland beach resorts of Rhode Island. Inland are a number of still semi-rural villages, but their futures are unpredictable due to the presence of two enormously successful and steadily expanding Indian casino complexes, Foxwoods and Mohegan Sun. They produce gushers of money that are altering forever the character of this region.

The town of Mystic and its twin attractions, Mystic Aquarium and the living museum that is Mystic Seaport, are the prime reasons for a stay—the Seaport alone can easily occupy most of a day, and the two-part town itself sustains a nautical air, with fun shops and restaurants to suit most tastes.

But that's not a complete list of the region's charms. The tranquil neighboring village of Stonington is home to a small but active commercial fishing fleet, the last in the state; there are several enchanting inns in the area; and many companies offer their vessels for whale-watching, dinner cruises, and deep-sea fishing excursions. And yes, for those with a taste for the adrenaline rush of a winning streak, there are those casinos.

If at all possible, avoid July, August, and weekends from May to Columbus Day, when the crowds are oppressive, restaurants are packed, and rooms are booked months in advance at very high rates.

ESSENTIALS

GETTING THERE   From New York City, take I-95 to Exit 84 (New London), Exit 86 (Groton), Exit 90 (Mystic), or Exit 91 (Stonington). Or, to avoid the heavy truck and commercial traffic of the western segment of I-95, use the Hutchinson River Parkway, which becomes the Merritt Parkway (Rte. 15) and merges with the Wilbur Cross Parkway. Continue to Exit 54, connecting with I-95 for the rest of the trip. From Boston, take the Massachusetts Turnpike to I-395 south to Exit 75, then south on Route 32 to New London and I-95.

Amtrak (© **800/USA-RAIL;** www.amtrak.com) runs several trains daily on its Northeast Direct route between New York, Providence, and Boston, with intermediate stops at New Haven, Old Saybrook, New London, and Mystic.

SEAT (© **860/886-2631**), the regional bus company, connects the more important towns and villages of the district, except for North Stonington.

A new way to get from the metropolitan New York region to New London, and from there to the Foxwoods casino complex, is via the super-fast tri-catamaran ferries operated by **Fox Navigation** (© **888/724-5369;** www.foxnavigation.com). Embarkation is at Glen Cove, on the north shore of Long Island, and the trip takes about 2 hours 15 minutes. Pass the time on reclining airline-type seats with on-board movies and food service. Passengers debark at the State Pier in New London and are transported from there to Foxwoods. There are four round-trips, 4 days per week.

VISITOR INFORMATION   Mystic Coast & Country (✆ **800/692-6278;** www.mycoast.com) can provide vacation planning kits. If the many motels off I-95 aren't for you, ask for the folder describing the loosely affiliated **Bed & Breakfasts of Mystic Coast,** which lists 23 establishments in the area, including four just across the Rhode Island state line.

NEW LONDON

New London's protected deep-draft harbor at the mouth of the Thames River was responsible for its long and influential history as a whaling port. That heritage lingers, although its years of great prosperity seem to be behind it. That may change, for the opening of a global headquarters of the Pfizer Corporation in 2001 has provoked hopes for a rosier economic future.

Possessed of an architecturally interesting but largely somnolent downtown district, New London, which lies 46 miles east of New Haven and 45 miles southeast of Hartford, is of note to travelers primarily because it's a transit point for three ferry lines connecting Block Island, R.I., and Long Island, N.Y., with the mainland, as well as the new high-speed ferries connecting with Martha's Vineyard and Glen Cove, Long Island. **Connecticut College** has a large campus at the northern edge of the city, along Route 32 and Williams Street.

An **information booth** is located downtown at the corner of Eugene O'Neill Drive and Golden Street (✆ **860/444-7264**). It's open June through August, daily from 10am to 4pm; May, September, and October, Friday through Sunday from 10am to 4pm.

Coast Guard Academy   Visitors are directed to a pavilion overlooking the Thames. It doesn't offer much except views of the river and shores. A full-rigged sailing vessel, the *Eagle,* is the academy's principal attraction, with boarding allowed usually only in April and May, Friday to Sunday from 1 to 5pm, when the boat is in port. It was built as a training ship for German Naval cadets in 1936 and taken as a war prize after World War II.

15 Mohegan Ave. (off Williams St., north of Exit 84 off I-95). ✆ 510/444-8270. Free admission. Grounds daily 9am–5pm; Visitors Pavilion May–Oct daily 10am–5pm; Apr Sat–Sun 10am–5pm. Pavilion closed Nov–Mar.

Lyman Allyn Museum of Art   This neoclassical granite pile stands on a hill looking across Route 32 toward the Coast Guard Academy. Its holdings are the result of the enthusiasms of private collectors and therefore stick to no specific curatorial vision. Colonial American paintings are supplemented by landscapes by Hudson River School landscapists Frederic Edwin Church, George Innes, and Albert Bierstadt. Upstairs are exhibits as diverse as Asian temple castings and Japanese lacquerware, along with traveling shows that recently included a substantial exhibit of Louise Nevelson sculptures. Pause a moment for the robustly intricate ship models of a local folk artist. The notable collection of 19th-century dolls and dollhouses, arranged in detailed room settings right down to tiny ladles on the kitchen counter, has been moved to the nearby Deshon-Allyn House.

625 Williams St. ✆ 860/443-2545. Admission $5 adults, $4 seniors and students, free for children under 8. Tues–Sat 10am–5pm; Sun 1–5pm. From Exit 83 off I-95, follow brown signs to museum.

OUTDOOR PURSUITS

Not far from downtown is **Ocean Beach Park,** at the south end of Ocean Avenue (✆ **800/510-7263** or 860/447-3031), a 40-acre recreational facility with a broad sand beach, boardwalk, 50-meter saltwater pool, miniature golf, water slide, bathhouse with lockers and showers, concession stands, and lounge. Open Memorial Day weekend through Labor Day, daily from 9am to 11pm.

The ferries that ply the Long Island Sound from New London have a recreational aspect, as well as simply serving as transport between Block Island and Long Island. **Cross Sound Ferry** (© **860/443-5281** for reservations and information; www.longislandferry.com) provides year-round service to Orient Point on Long Island. Departures are every hour or two during the day, and the one-way voyage takes about an hour and 20 minutes. Call ahead to make reservations, especially when taking a car. The **Fishers Island Ferry** (© **860/443-6851**) also has daily departures for Long Island. From mid-June to early September, **Nelseco Navigation Co.** (© **860/442-7891** or 860/442-9553) operates its ferry once a day (with an extra trip Fri evenings) between New London and the Old Harbor on Block Island. The one-way trip takes about 2 hours. Call ahead to determine fares and sailing times; advance reservations for cars are essential.

WHERE TO STAY

Lighthouse Inn ★★ The former 1902 Sound-side mansion of a steel magnate is at the center of this multi-structure property. It became an inn over 70 years ago and new owners have just poured $1.2 million into its renovation. One of the outbuildings is a day spa providing salon services and massage therapy, another is a large cottage suitable for families, and a third contains 24 rooms—these, in addition to the 27 in the mansion. While the public rooms preserve a late Victorian flavor, all with working fireplaces, the bedrooms are more in country home style, with a variety of antiques and reproductions, including some four-posters with crocheted tops. Eight suites have water views. One of the owners' best moves was persuading Chef Timothy Grills to close his admired downtown restaurant and reopen here (see review below). He ensures that the several dining rooms are forever full. Meals are also served in the atmospheric tavern, where there is live music, mostly jazz, almost every night. Getting there is a challenge; the directions below lead from downtown's Bank Street.

6 Guthrie Place, New London, CT 06320. © **860/443-8411**. Fax 860/437-7027. www.lighthouseinn-ct.com. 52 units. $109–$359 double. Rates include breakfast. Packages available. AE, DC, MC, V. Drive west on Bank St. and turn left (south) on Howard St. This soon arrives at a rotary; take the 3rd exit, which goes under a railroad bridge. At the second traffic circle, take the 1st exit onto Pequot Ave. Follow Pequot about 1½ miles to Guthrie Place. Turn right. **Amenities:** Restaurant (New American); bar; heated outdoor pool; access to nearby health club and golf course. *In room:* A/C, TV, dataport, coffeemaker, hair dryer, iron.

WHERE TO DINE

Timothy's ★★ NEW AMERICAN Chef-owner Timothy Grills (talk about names as predestination) was doing just fine in his original contemporary bistro downtown. He's doing even better now, in his new, more expansive digs in the Lighthouse Inn. While there are always a couple of perky pastas on offer—a recent pasta primavera with scallops was special—his menu now has fewer Italianate touches. In fact, at first glance, it appears to be entirely conventional, with such stalwarts as Long Island duckling, prime rib, and filet mignon. Obviously, he doesn't go in for mind-bending innovation, but shoots instead for a high level of execution. He brought along his signature creamy lobster bisque, hardly a rarity in these parts, but with supernal flavorings. Crab cakes on red pepper coulis and fried calamari with a chipotle dipping sauce are regulars, and very good. All of it is brightly seasoned, with daring combinations of fresh herbs. New London needs more operations like this.

In the Lighthouse Inn, 6 Guthrie Place. ✆ **860/443-8411.** Reservations recommended. Main courses $18–$28. Daily 11:30am–2:30pm and 5:30–9:30pm (Fri until 10pm).

GROTON

The future is uncertain for this naval-industrial town on the opposite side of the Thames from New London. It has long been dependent on the presence of the Electric Boat division of General Dynamics and the Navy's submarine base, and cutbacks in military budgets have adversely affected both. Whatever happens, the principal tourist attraction remains the USS *Nautilus,* the world's first nuclear-powered vessel.

After a visit to the submarine museum, history buffs may wish to stroll around **Fort Griswold Battlefield State Park,** Monument Street and Park Avenue (✆ **860/445-1729** or 860/449-6877). It was here, in 1781, that the traitor Benedict Arnold led a British force against American defenders, ruthlessly ordering the massacre of his 88 prisoners after they had surrendered. The free museum is open from Memorial Day to Labor Day, daily from 10am to 5pm; and from Labor Day to Columbus Day, Saturday and Sunday from 10am to 5pm.

Submarine Force Museum   The entry hall and adjoining galleries display models of submarines, torpedoes, missiles, deck guns, periscopes, and a full-scale cross-section of Bushnell's *Turtle,* the "first submersible ever used in a military conflict," in 1776. Out back, the 362-foot-long USS *Nautilus* itself stands at its mooring, ready for inspection. The claustrophobic walk through the control rooms, attack center, galley, and sleeping quarters is aided by listening devices handed out to each visitor. Passing through, it is difficult to imagine how it could possibly contain a crew of 116 men, especially on its fabled cruises between New London and San Juan and from Pearl Harbor to the North Pole.

Naval Submarine Base, 1 Crystal Lake Rd. ✆ **800/343-0079** or 860/694-3174. www.submarinemuseum. Free admission. May 15–Oct 31 Wed–Mon 9am–5pm, Tues 1–5pm; Nov 1–May 14 Wed–Mon 9am–4pm. Take Exit 86 from I-95, drive north on Rte. 12, and follow signs to the USS *Nautilus.*

FISHING TRIPS

A number of companies offer full- and half-day fishing trips. Typical of the party boats is the 114-foot *Hel-Cat II,* 181 Thames St. (✆ **860/535-2066** or 860/ 535-3200; www.visitconnecticut.com/helcat), operating from its own pier about 2 miles south of Exit 85 north or Exit 86 south off I-95. Trips are from 6 to 8½ hours at fares of $30 to $48. Tackle is available for rent.

Both charter and party boats are available from the **Sunbeam Fleet,** based at **Captain John's Sport Fishing Center,** 15 First St., Waterford (✆ **860/443-7259;** wwwsunbeamfleet.com). Fishing party boats sail twice daily Friday through Sunday in June, Thursday through Tuesday from July to Labor Day. The same firm has whale-watching voyages three times a week in July and August. Nature cruises go eagle-watching in February and March, and search for harbor seals March through May. Adult fares are $33 to $60. Waterford is the town immediately south of New London; the dock is next to the Niantic River Bridge.

WHERE TO STAY

Mystic Marriott Hotel & Spa ⭐⭐   Filling a perceived gap in area lodgings, Marriott brings a measure of big-town pizzazz to an otherwise colorless intersection in a triangle occupied at the other corners by the casinos and Mystic. At a cost of $47 million, they obviously didn't stint, and there is little more that a business or leisure traveler might ask. Rooms adhere to corporate cookie-cutter standards, but are no less comfortable for that. Room safes are large enough for laptop computers; voice mail and high-speed Internet access are standard. On the sixth-floor concierge level, robes, fridges, and cordless phones are among the extras. The big deal is the Elizabeth Arden spa, which shares facilities with the excellent fitness center. In addition to the nail, skincare, and hair salons are two hydrotubs, supplemented by seaweed wraps, herbal mud masks, massages, and stone therapy. Shuttles make frequent trips to both casinos.

625 North Rd. (Rte. 117), Groton, CT 06340. © 866/449-7390 or 860/446-2600. Fax 860/446-2696. www. mysticmarriott.com. 291 units. $179–$259 double. Packages available. AE, DC DISC, MC, V. **Amenities:** 2 restaurants (Steakhouse/Bistro); bar; heated indoor 50m pool; exhaustively equipped health club and spa; business center; 24-hr. room service; same-day dry cleaning/laundry. *In room:* A/C, TV w/pay movies, Sony PlayStation, dataport, coffeemaker, hair dryer, iron, safe.

WHERE TO DINE

Octagon ⭐ STEAKHOUSE   After a stuttering start in its first months as the Mystic Marriott's formal restaurant, this ambitious steakhouse is hitting its stride. Not as heavy-handedly masculine as others of its type, but with its dark, leathery tones it still manages to look as if midtown Manhattan is just beyond the door. Beef is prime and grilled to the requested degree of doneness, but there are options beyond the expected T-bones, porterhouses, and New York strips. An interesting sidebar is the selection of "composed plates" for $17 to $27—various proteins paired with starches or vegetables, such as braised lamb shanks with seared gnocchi and gremolata (a classic Italian garnish of parsley, garlic and lemon zest) and shellfish tossed with linguini and tomatoes. Starters include local oysters and clams from the raw bar, and the beef-phobic find salmon, venison, and pork chops on the card. The short dessert list of cheesecake and cobblers is complemented by a longer selection of ports, cognacs, and single-malt scotches.

In the Mystic Marriott Hotel, 625 North Rd. © 860/326-0300. Reservations recommended. Main courses $17–$32. AE, DC, DISC, MC, V. Daily 7:30–11am; noon–2:30pm; and 6–10pm.

Olio CONTEMPORARY BISTRO   So new at the time of review it didn't appear in the phone book, this spiffy little roadhouse didn't need anything but word-of-mouth to pack in eager diners nightly. From barely legal to decidedly mature, patrons drop by on a whim for an hour or two of leisurely grazing (although it's wise to have a reservation). As in almost all of such enterprises these days, pastas—14 of them—dominate the offerings, but there is an equal number of those international faves that have become all but obligatory. Fill in the blanks—crab cakes, chicken satays, quesadillas, bruschettas, yadda yadda—but tasty and quick for all their familiarity. Can tiramisu be far behind? With bare tables and hard surfaces everywhere, it's loud. And take the reading glasses, because the menu is written in a tiny hand and there are only guttering candles and a few dim pinlights for illumination. The waitstaff is composed of uniformly fetching young women who can be forgiven a lack of efficiency in keeping glasses full.

33 Kings Hwy. (Rte. 395, exit 86N off I-95). © 860/445-6546. Reservations advised. Main courses $9.95–$19. AE, MC, V. Mon–Sat 11:30am–4:30pm and 5–9pm (until 10pm Fri–Sat); Sun 4:30–9pm.

MYSTIC ⭐⭐⭐

The spirit and texture of the maritime life and history of New England are captured in many ports along its indented coast, but nowhere more cogently than beside the Mystic River estuary and its harbor. This was a dynamic whaling and shipbuilding center during the colonial period and into the 20th century, but the discontinuation of the first industry and the decline of the second haven't adversely affected the community. No derelict barges or rotting piers degrade the views and waterways (or at least not many).

Mystic and West Mystic are stitched together by a drawbridge, the raising of which, mostly for sailboats, causes traffic stoppages at a quarter past every hour but rarely shortens tempers, except for visitors who don't leave their urban impatience behind. There are complaints by some that the two-part town has been commercialized, but the incidence of T-shirt shops and related tackiness is limited, and the more garish motels and attractions have been restricted to the periphery, especially up near Exit 90 off I-95.

The town is home to one of New England's most singular attractions, the Mystic Seaport museum village. Far more than the single building the name might suggest, it is a re-created seaport of the mid-1800s, with dozens of buildings and watercraft of that romantic era of clipper ships and the China trade.

A **visitor center** is located in Building 1D of the Olde Mistick Village shopping center, at Route 27 and Coogan Boulevard, near the Interstate (© **860/ 536-1641**).

SEEING THE SIGHTS

Mystic Aquarium ★★ *Kids*   If you've never seen a marine show, the Marine Theater here is the place. In past years, it has housed dolphins and orcas, but the current occupants are no less engaging. Less gimmicky than similar commercial enterprises in Florida and California, the show illuminates as it entertains, and at 15 minutes in length, doesn't test the attention spans of the very young. (The popularity of Disney's *Finding Nemo* hasn't hurt attendance.)

While the rest of the exhibits are in the shadow of the stars, they are enough to occupy at least another hour. In the outdoor "Alaskan Coast," see five beluga whales squeal and twirl and otherwise perform for their trainers at feeding time. Next door is a facsimile of the Bering Strait's Pribilof Islands, home to fur seals and endangered Steller sea lions, and out back are African black-footed penguins, with underwater viewing windows. A $52-million expansion was completed in 1999 under the direction of the legendary undersea explorer Robert Ballard, who discovered the sunken *Titanic.* Even newer is a re-creation of a Louisiana Bayou stocked with "Swamp Things:" frogs, turtles, carp, largemouth bass, and small alligators. Elsewhere, visitors are eye to eye with such creatures as sea horses, jellyfish, and the pugnacious yellow-head jaw fish, which spends its hours digging fortifications in the sand. Dozens of rays flutter like butterflies and translucent jellyfish billow and flex in slow motion dance, a hypnotic display.

55 Coogan Blvd. (at Exit 90 off I-95). © 860/572-5955. www.mysticaquarium.org. Admission $16 adults, $15 seniors, $11 children 3–12. July–Labor Day Sun–Thurs 9am–7pm, Fri–Sat 9am–6pm; Sept–Dec daily 9am–6pm; Jan–Feb Mon–Fri 10am–5pm, Sat–Sun 9am–6pm; Feb–June daily 9am–6pm.

Mystic Seaport ★★★ *Kids*   Few visitors fail to be enthralled by this evocative museum village. It encompasses an entire waterfront settlement, more than 60 buildings on and near a 17-acre peninsula poking into the Mystic River. Plan to set aside at least 2 or 3 hours—if not an entire day—for a visit. A useful map guide is available at the ticket counter in the **visitor center** in the building opposite the museum stores (which stay open later than the village most of the year, so make them your last stop).

Exit the visitor center and bear right along the path leading between the Galley Restaurant and the village green. It bends to the left, intersecting with a street of shops, public buildings, and houses. At that corner is an 1870s hardware and dry-goods store.

Turning right here, you'll pass a schoolhouse, a chapel, and an 1830s home. Stop at the **children's museum,** which invites youngsters to play games characteristic of the seafaring era. It faces a small square that is the starting point for **horse-drawn wagon tours.**

From here, the three-masted barque *Charles W. Morgan,* one of the proudest possessions of the Seaport fleet of over 400 craft, is only a few steps away. It was built in 1841.

If you're a fan of scrimshaw and ship models, continue along the waterfront to the right until you reach the **Stillman Building,** which contains fascinating exhibits of both. Otherwise, head left toward the lighthouse. Along the way, you'll encounter a tavern, an 1833 bank, a cooperage, and other shops and services that did business with the whalers and clipper ships that put in at ports such as this.

The friendly docents in the village are highly competent at the crafts they demonstrate and are always ready to impart as much information as visitors care to absorb. The fact that they aren't dressed in period costumes (except during special events like the Christmas lamplight tours) paradoxically enhances the village's feeling of authenticity by avoiding the contrived air of many such enterprises.

The next vessel encountered is the iron-hulled square-rigger *Joseph Conrad,* which dates from 1881. Up ahead is a small **lighthouse,** which looks out across the water toward the large riverside houses that line the opposite shore. Round the horn, go past the boat sheds, the fishing shacks, and the ketches and sloops that are moored along here in season until you come to the dock for the perky 1908 **SS Sabino.** This working ship gives half-hour river rides from mid-May to early October, daily from 11am to 4pm, and 1½-hour evening excursions Monday through Thursday leaving at 5pm, Friday and Saturday at 7pm. A few steps away is the 1921 fishing schooner *L. A. Dunton.*

And still the village isn't exhausted. A few steps south is the **Henry B. Du Pont Preservation Shipyard,** where the boats are painstakingly restored. One recent project was the re-creation of the schooner *Amistad,* which inspired an exhibit exploring the historical incident.

Also on the grounds are the **Galley Restaurant,** which serves pretty good fish and chips, fried clam strips, and lobster rolls; and **Sprouter's Tavern,** which offers snacks and sandwiches.

When you exit for the day, ask the gatekeeper to validate your ticket so you can come back the next day for free.

Across the brick courtyard with the giant anchor is a building containing several **museum stores** as well as an art gallery. These superior shops stock books, kitchenware, fresh-baked goods, nautical prints and paintings, and ship models.

75 Greenmanville Ave. (Rte. 27). © **888/9-SEAPORT** or 860/572-5315. www.mysticseaport.org. Admission $17 adults, $9 children 6–12 (2nd day included with validation). AE, MC, V. Ships and exhibits Apr–Oct daily 9am–5pm, Nov–Mar daily 10am–4pm; grounds 9am–5pm. Closed Dec 25. Take Exit 90 off I-95, going about 1 mile south on Rte. 27 toward Mystic. Parking lots are on the left, the entrance on the right.

OUTDOOR PURSUITS

For a change from salt air and ship riggings, drive inland to the **Denison Pequotsepos Nature Center,** 109 Pequotsepos Rd. (© **860/536-1216**), a 200-acre property with more than 8 miles of trails. The center building has a thrown-together quality, with dog-eared books beside the live boa constrictor and worm farm. Younger children are nonetheless fascinated. Outside are picnic tables and flight cages of rehabilitating raptors. There are five nature trails, none of which merit special effort—but they can serve as gentle diversion for a half-hour or so. Admission is $6 for adults, $4 for seniors and children 12 and under. Open Monday through Saturday from 9am to 5pm, Sunday from 10 to 4pm (closed

Sun Jan–Apr, Mon Sept–Apr). To get here, take Route 27 north from Mystic, make a right on Mistuxet Avenue, and turn left on Pequotsepos Road.

Several operators offer **sailing and fishing cruises.** One of the most convenient is the *Argia* (© **860/536-0416;** www.voyagermystic.com), a replica of a 19th-century schooner that docks 100 feet south of the drawbridge in Mystic. Fares are $34 to $36 for adults, $31 to $33 for seniors, $24 to $26 for children 5–10. For longer trips, outings on the *Mystic Whaler* (© **800/697-8420;** fax 860/536-4219; www.mysticwhaler.com) include dinner sails, day trips, and extended cruises that can last 2, 3, or 5 days. Corresponding rates go from $75 up to $760. Voyages set out from a pier at 15 Holmes St., off Route 27, 1 mile south of Mystic Seaport.

SHOPPING

Downtown Mystic has limited shopping, a situation made worse by a fire in 2000 that destroyed a 19th-century building with eight storefronts next to the famous drawbridge. Of the survivors, an engaging choice is **Bank Square Books,** 53 W. Main St. (© **860/536-3795**), which has remodeled and expanded since the fire.

WHERE TO STAY & DINE

The Inn at Mystic ✸✸   A variety of lodgings are on offer at this property occupying 13 acres overlooking Long Island Sound. At the crest of the hill is the impressive inn, a 1904 Classical Revival mansion with public rooms as grand as the exterior. Bedrooms are humbler, antique furniture mixed with merely old stuff, but often with four-poster beds. Some have whirlpools. Porches and decks take in both sunrises and sunsets. Down the hill is the intimate Gatehouse, similarly accoutered. Some of the units in the new motel sections are equally well appointed, including a few with balconies; others are modest and conventional.

The complex also incorporates one of the area's best restaurants, **Flood Tide** (© **860/536-8140**). Peel back about 3 decades: They still do tableside preparations here—chateaubriand, bananas Foster, and such—retro performances that remind us why we used to relish this celebratory stuff in the days before Pan-Asian-Fusion food was invented. The room has a new look, with an exhibition kitchen containing a wood-burning grill and oven. Don't miss the sumptuous breakfast buffet, with such offerings as eggs Benedict with lobster. A pianist plinks at the baby grand nightly and at Sunday brunch. The dining rooms look out over the sound, so ask for a table by the window.

Routes 1 and 27, Mystic, CT 06355. © **800/237-2415** or 860/536-9604. www.innatmystic.com. 67 units. $65–$175 motel double; $120–$295 mansion or gatehouse double. Packages available. Rates include afternoon tea. Packages available. AE, DC, DISC, MC, V. Pets accepted in 6 units ($10). **Amenities:** Restaurant (Continental); bar; outdoor pool; 2 putting greens; tennis court; access to nearby health club; free kayaks and boats; limited room service; same-day dry cleaning/laundry. *In room:* A/C, TV, dataport, fridge, coffeemaker, hair dryer.

WHERE TO STAY

There are plenty of ho-hum but adequate area motels that can soak up the traffic at all but peak periods, meaning weekends from late spring to early fall plus weekdays in July and August, when it is necessary to have reservations. Pick of the litter may be the **Best Western Sovereign,** north of Exit 90 (© **800/528-1234** or 860/536-4281), with a pool and restaurant. Nearby competitors are the **Comfort Inn** (© **800/228-5150** or 860/572-8531), **Days Inn** (© **800/325-2525** or 860/ 572-0574), and **Residence Inn** (© **800/331-3131** or 860/536-5150).

Hilton Mystic ✸   Unlike the motels clustered around the I-95 interchange, this is a full-service hotel, providing the amenities expected of its big-city cousins, though without much personality. The front desk is often willing to negotiate prices. A pianist entertains many evenings in the lounge. The hotel is owned by the Pequot tribe, so it's no surprise that there are posters announcing coming attractions at Foxwoods Casino and a shuttle van to take you there. High-speed Internet access is available.

20 Coogan Blvd., Mystic, CT 06355. ℂ **800/445-8667** or 860/572-0731. Fax 860/572-0328. www.hilton mystic.com. 183 units. $99–$219 double. AE, DC, DISC, MC, V. Free valet parking. Take Exit 90 off I-95 and drive south, following signs to the Mystic Aquarium; the hotel is opposite. **Amenities:** Restaurant (Continental); lounge; heated indoor pool; fitness room; bike rental; children's programs; video arcade; limited room service; same-day dry cleaning/laundry. *In room:* A/C, TV w/pay movies, dataport, coffeemaker, hair dryer, iron.

Steamboat Inn 🌟🌟 Mystic's most ingratiating lodging is easily overlooked from land, but readily apparent from the river. Perched on the riverbank, the yellow-clapboard structure has apartment-size downstairs bedrooms, with Jacuzzis and wet bars, while the upstairs units have wood-burning fireplaces. Every room is decorated uniquely—Laura Ashley must have been a muse—and all but one have water views. They are, it must be said, starting to look just a bit tired. A nonsmoking policy is enforced. The inn commissioned the 97-foot luxury yacht, *Valiant,* that is moored at its dock. The five staterooms can be rented when the yacht isn't chartered; log on to www.valiantcharters.com.

73 Steamboat Wharf, Mystic, CT 06355. ℂ **860/536-8300.** Fax 860/536-9528. www.visitmystic.com/ steamboat. 10 units. Late May–Nov $195–$300 double; Dec to late May $125–$245 double. Rates include breakfast. AE, DISC, MC, V. Validated parking available in a gated lot. Look for the sign pointing down an alley on the west bank of the Mystic River, just before the drawbridge. Children over 9 welcome. *In room:* A/C, TV, dataport, fridge, coffeemaker, hair dryer, iron.

Taber Inne 🌟 Not quite an inn but more than a motel, this place has something to suit most tastes and budgets, with seven immaculate buildings containing both simple units and hedonistic suites with fireplaces and decks. A recently erected cottage with a cathedral ceiling has two bedrooms, a sitting room, and a kitchen, and a new building with an indoor pool and fitness center opened in 2004. Most rooms have fireplaces and twenty have whirlpools; high-speed Internet access is now available.

66 Williams Ave. (Rte. 1; 2 blocks east of the intersection with Rte. 27), Mystic, CT 06355. ℂ **860/536-4904.** Fax 860/572-9140. www.taberinn.com. 34 units. Mid-Apr to Nov $155–$169 double, $210–$365 suite; Nov to mid-Apr $95–$139 double, $225–$340 suite. Rates include breakfast. AE, MC, V. **Amenities:** Heated indoor pool; exercise room; access to nearby health club with tennis court. *In room:* A/C, TV, dataport, coffeemaker, hair dryer.

The Whaler's Inn 🌟 Recently acquired by people who also have interests in the estimable Steamboat Inn in Mystic (above) and the Inn at Stonington (below), the previously dispirited aspect of the venerable Whaler's has been banished. The five structures that constitute the property have all been addressed, with fresh fabrics and furnishings and new bathrooms. Best of all (and most expensive) are the eight bedrooms of Hoxie House, all with gas fireplaces, Jacuzzis, and Bose table radios. Sleigh beds and four-posters are common, and some rooms have VCRs. Breakfast is taken in the spacious Hospitality Room, which also has an Internet terminal for guest use.

20 E. Main St., Mystic, CT 06355. ℂ **800/243-2588** or 860/536-1506. Fax 860/572-1250. www.whalersinn mystic.com. Mid-May to late Nov $139–$249 double; Dec to early May $89–$189. Rates include breakfast. *In room:* A/C, TV, dataport, coffeemaker, hair dryer.

WHERE TO DINE

Abbott's Lobster in the Rough 🌟 SEAFOOD   It's as if a wedge of the Maine coast has been punched into the Connecticut shore. This nitty-gritty lobster shack has plenty of picnic tables and not a frill to be found. While there are many options, including hotdogs and chicken, the classic shore dinner rules. That means clam chowder, boiled shrimp, steamed mussels, and a tasty lobster, with coleslaw, chips, and drawn butter thrown in. Bring your own beer. Nearby is **Costello's Clam Co.,** owned by the same family, where scallops and the eponymous bivalves are featured. (Get it? Abbott's? Costello's?)

117 Pearl St., Noank. ✆ 860/536-7719. Reservations not accepted. Main courses $16–$32 (prices subject to market availability). AE, MC, V. First Fri in May to Memorial Day Fri–Sun noon–7pm; Memorial Day to Labor Day weekend daily noon–9pm; after Labor Day weekend to Columbus Day weekend Fri–Sun noon–7pm. From downtown Mystic, go south on Rte. 215 and cross a railroad bridge. At Main St. in Noank, turn left, and take an immediate right on Pearl St. Be prepared to ask for directions anyway.

Bravo Bravo ✿ NEW ITALIAN/AMERICAN   Ask locals about the best restaurant in town, and they'll likely send you here. As a result, it's a money machine for the owners, even on a frigid Tuesday night.. Regulars are families, couples old and young, friends with friends, and men in suits or polo shirts and khakis. On weekends, it can get as noisy as a disco, aided by bare wood tables and floors, and the waitstaff can get a little scattered.

Warm, coarse country bread arrives with drinks, supplemented with marinated olives and a white-bean red pepper spread. Order antipasti and get a plate crowded with salami, provolone, tuna chunks, artichoke hearts, and sliced tomatoes. At least half the entrées involve pasta—lobster ravioli, shrimp with penne, linguine and clams—but cool weather choices usually include braised lamb shanks and osso bucco. One special was sautéed tilapia over a zingy risotto with haricots vert and chopped tomatoes given a drizzle of pesto.

20 E. Main St. ✆ 860/536-3228. Reservations recommended. Main courses $16–$25. AE, DC, MC, V. Sun and Tues–Thurs 5–9pm; Fri–Sat 5–10pm.

Go Fish ✿ SEAFOOD   Brash and boisterous, Go Fish is dominated by a sprawling granite bar at its center, often surrounded by younger drinkers and grazers. At the far end is an enclosed sushi bar, while near the door is a room usually populated by older folks and families. Local or regional fishery products are employed as much as possible, including Stonington sea scallops and Point Judith calamari. A long list of daily specials reflects their freshness. Ask for them cooked just about any way possible—baked, roasted, grilled, deep-fried, or pan-blackened—and they invariably arrive exactly as ordered. Portions are abundant, so you might want to skip appetizers, enticing though they are (the creamy bisque, for one). Each day has featured beers and wines.

Olde Mistick Village, at Exit 90 off I-95. ✆ 860/536-2662. Reservations not accepted. Main courses $16–$24. AE, DC, DISC, MC, V. Sun–Thurs 11:30am–9:30pm; Fri–Sat 11:30am–10:30pm.

Kitchen Little ✿ AMERICAN   Not much more than a shack by the water, this is the sort of place dismissed and passed every day by hundreds of tourists hurrying on to the Seaport. They're missing not only 45 distinct breakfast choices, including at least a dozen three-egg omelets, but also some of the coast's tastiest clam and scallop dishes. At lunch, you must have the definitive clear broth clam chowder, maybe the whole belly clam rolls, and absolutely the fried scallop sandwich. Or the lobster roll, with no fillers, only tail and claw flesh. Expect a wait in summer and tight quarters inside. They serve only breakfast on weekends. Try to snare a table out back, in view of the tall ships.

Rte. 27, 1 mile south of I-95. ✆ 860/536-2122. Reservations not accepted. Main dishes $3.45–$13. MC, V. Mon–Fri 6:30am–2pm; Sat–Sun 6:30am–1pm.

STONINGTON & NORTH STONINGTON

Not much seemed to happen in these slumbering villages, only lightly brushed by the 21st century despite all the thrashing about in heavily touristed Mystic. That suited the residents just fine, explaining why most of them are not thrilled by the continual rumors of projected expansions of the nearby Foxwoods complex, not to mention the federal recognition of a third tribe, the Eastern Pequots, in 2002.

It is difficult to imagine what the flexing of the established gambling empire might do eventually to inland North Stonington, as peaceful a New England hamlet as can be found, with hardly any commercialization beyond a couple of inns. Sound-side Stonington has a pronounced maritime flavor, sustained by the presence of the state's only remaining (albeit dwindling) fishing fleet. Its two lengthwise streets are lined with well-preserved Federal-style and Greek Revival homes.

EXPLORING THE AREA

For an introduction, 'drive south to **Cannon Square** along Stonington's **Water Street.** Standing in the grassy main square are two cannons that were used to fight off an attack by British warships during the War of 1812. Opposite is a lovely old granite house and, on the corner, a neoclassical bank.

Continue south to the end of Water Street, where there's a small **town beach** (admission $2–$3, or $5–$6 per family). The misty blue headland directly south across the sound is Montauk Point, the eastern extremity of New York's Long Island. Return along Main Street, which is almost exclusively residential except for a few government buildings.

You might check out the **Old Lighthouse Museum,** 7 Water St. (© **860/ 535-1440**). Built of stone in 1823, it was moved here from 100 yards away and deactivated. Most of its exhibits relate to the maritime past of the area, with scrimshaw tusks and the export porcelain that constituted much of the 19th-century China trade. Most interesting is the carved ivory pagoda. Admission is $4 for adults, $2 for children 6 to 12. Open May through October, Tuesday through Sunday from 11am to 4pm.

One of the Nutmeg State's handful of earnest wineries, **Stonington Vineyards,** 523 Taugwonk Rd., Stonington (© **860/535-1222**), has a tasting room in a barn beside its vineyard. There are usually six or seven pressings to be sampled, with a chardonnay leading the pack. Open daily from 11am to 5pm, with a cellar tour at 2pm. To get here, take Exit 91 off I-95 and drive north 2½ miles.

WHERE TO STAY & DINE

Randall's Ordinary ⭐ The oldest structure on this 250-acre estate dates from 1685. The three bedrooms upstairs have fireplaces and four-poster or canopied beds, though no TVs or phones. Those conveniences are provided in the rooms in the nearby 1819 barn. All meals are cooked at an open hearth and served by a staff in period costumes. Considering the primitive circumstances under which the food is prepared, it is always hearty, if simple. Go for the romantic setting, not gastronomy.

Rte. 2, North Stonington, CT 06359. © **877/599-4540.** Fax 860/599-3308. www.randallsordinary.com. 18 units. $140–$250 double. Packages available. AE, MC, V. Take Exit 92 off I-95 and head north on Rte. 2. *In room:* A/C.

Stonecroft ⭐⭐ This 1807 inn is home to a gifted chef who works wonders with dishes that have become familiar in the past 2 decades of America's food revolution. His realm is a converted barn, with linen-dressed tables and a fireplace. Wine is generously poured in anticipation of such starters as the trio of shrimp prepared, respectively, with curry-coconut sauce and banana chutney, spicy Rangoon and ginger hoisin sauce, and chili-cilantro seasoning over cukes. A favorite entree is blue cornmeal-crusted salmon with sweet potato and fingerling hash. Other dishes come in a remarkable variety of colors, textures, and ingredients—a touch too many, in some cases—but you'll likely be delighted with most choices. Entrées are $18 to $45; the restaurant is open for dinner Wednesday through Sunday.

There are 10 rooms at the inn, four in the 1807 Georgian main house and six in the converted barn. Many have fireplaces; rates are $150 to $245, from $250 suite.

515 Pumpkin Hill Rd., Ledyard. © 860/572-0771. www.stonecroft.com. Reservations recommended on weekends. Main courses $19–$28. AE, DC, MC, V. Wed–Sun 6–10pm. Take Exit 89 north from I-95, onto Cow Hill Rd., which shortly becomes Pumpkin Hill Rd.

WHERE TO STAY

The Inn at Stonington ⋒⋒   Built on the site of a restaurant leveled by fire a few years ago, this inn harmonizes nicely with its neighbors on the town's main street. Combining the intimacy of a small inn with the comforts of a luxury hotel, it abounds in felicitous flourishes that exceed the expected. Every unit has a gas fireplace, six have balconies, and 10 have Jacuzzis. While rooms reflect a single design sensibility, with tailored contemporary interpretations of country decor, no two are alike.

60 Water St., Stonington, CT 06378. © 860/535-2000. Fax 860/535-8193. www.innatstonington.com. 12 units. Spring/summer $149–$295 double; fall/winter $135–$295 double. Rates include breakfast and evening wine and cheese. AE, DC, MC, V. Take Exit 91 off I-95; follow signs into Stonington village. **Amenities:** Small, well-equipped exercise room; bikes and kayaks available; computer for guests' use. *In room:* A/C, TV, dataport, hair dryer.

WHERE TO DINE

Boom ⋒ NEW AMERICAN   With a spate of closings in recent years, it's a challenge picking new restaurants that have the necessaries to survive. This one, though, not only has a predictably long life span ahead, it has already spawned a sibling by the same name at Brewer's Pilots Point Marina in Westbrook (© 860/399-2322). The original is a companionable, under-decorated little room looking out over a marina. Often, there are irresistible fried oysters among the appetizers, and the roasted tomato bisque with a Bomster scallop (voted the #1 scallop in the world by *Gourmet* magazine) and chevre is a surprise. Seafood is the way to go, as with the sesame-seed-coated "Patty Jo" scallops with wasabi-mashed potatoes. Salmon, tuna, and flounder are regulars, in various guises. In defiance of current super-sizing trends, they come in manageable portions. In good weather, tables are set up outside with a raw bar. Local purveyors are employed for seafood, and the restaurant moves a lot of lobster in summer.

Dodson Boatyard, 194 Water St. © 860/535-2588. Reservations recommended on weekends. Main courses $16–$25. AE, MC, V. Tues–Sat 11:30am–3pm; Sun 10am–3pm; Tues–Sun 5:30–9:30pm. Closed Mar.

FOXWOODS RESORT CASINO

This casino-hotel complex (© 800/752-9244 or 860/885-3000; www.foxwoods.com) is forever changing, adding, renovating, and expanding. There are six cavernous gambling rooms, one of the most popular being the hall containing 4,500 slot machines (out of a total of 6,400). The 3,200-seat Bingo Hall is huge, and the high-tech horse parlor is a dazzler. All the usual methods of depleting wallets are at hand—blackjack, bingo, keno, craps, baccarat, roulette, money wheels, and several variations of poker.

A Casino in the Woods

What has been wrought in the woodlands north of the Mystic coast in the last decade is astonishing. There was little but trees here when the Mashantucket Pequot tribe received clearance to open a gambling casino on their ancestral lands in rural Ledyard. Virtually overnight, the tribal bingo parlor was expanded into a full-fledged casino, and a hotel was built.

That was in 1992. Within 3 years, it had become the single most profitable gambling operation in the world, with a reported 40,000 visitors a day. Money cascaded over the Pequot (pronounced *Pee*-kwat) in a seemingly endless torrent. Expansion was immediate—another hotel, then a third, more casinos, golf courses, and the $139-million **Mashantucket Pequot Museum and Research Center,** devoted to Native American arts and culture. The tribe bought up adjacent lands and at least four nearby inns and hotels, and then opened a shipworks to build high-speed ferries. All that hasn't sopped up the cascades of money, and the tribe has made major contributions to the Mystic Aquarium and Smithsonian Museum of the American Indian.

All this prosperity came to a tribe of fewer than 520 acknowledged members, nearly all of them of mixed ethnicity. Residents of surrounding communities were ambivalent, to put the best face on it. When it was learned that one of the tribe's corporate entities was to be called Two Trees Limited Partnership, a predictable query was, "Is that all you're going to leave us? Two trees?"

But while there is a continuing danger of damage to the fragile character of this authentically picturesque corner of Connecticut, it is also a fact that because of the recent development, thousands of non-Pequots have found employment in their various enterprises.

The complex is reached through forested countryside of quiet hamlets that give little hint of the behemoth rising above the trees in Ledyard township. There are no signs screaming FOXWOODS. Instead, watch

SEEING THE SIGHTS

Mashantucket Pequot Museum and Research Center ✮✮ A $139-million trickle of the floods of cash washing over southeastern Connecticut and its resurgent Indian Nation has been diverted to create this museum. Opened in 1998 to substantial fanfare, it has justified the hoopla with a carefully conceived mix of film, murals, models, dioramas, and re-creations of scenes of Native American life. The Pequot Village exhibit is complete with wigwams and life-size figures shown fishing, hunting, cooking, butchering game, and making baskets and ceramics. An observation tower supplies views of the reservation. Lunch and snacks are served in the restaurant, and there's a shop with books, jewelry, and crafts.

110 Pequot Trail. ℰ 800/411-9671. www.mashantucket.com. Admission $15 adults (16–54), $13 seniors, $10 children 6–15. Daily 9am–5pm.

for plaques with the symbols of tree, wolf, and fire above the word RESERVATION. As you enter the property, platoons of attendants point the way to parking and hotels. Ongoing construction surrounds the glassy, turquoise-and-violet towers of the hotels and casino. Though bustling, it doesn't look like Vegas from the outside—happily, there are no sphinxes, no fake volcanoes, and no neon palm trees.

Inside, the glitz gap narrows, but it is still relatively restrained as such temples to chance go. The gambling rooms have windows, for example, even though the prevailing wisdom among casino designers is that they should not give customers any idea of what time of day or night it is.

And no one is allowed to forget that this whole eye-popping affair is owned and operated by Native Americans. Prominently placed around the main buildings are larger-than-life sculptures by artists of Chiricahua and Chippewa descent, depicting Amerindians in a variety of poses and artistic styles. One other Indian-oriented display is *The Rainmaker,* a glass statue of an archer shooting an arrow into the air. Every hour on the hour, he is the focus of artificial thunder, wind-whipped rain, and lasers pretending to be lightning bolts, the action described in murky prose by a booming voice-of-Manitou narrator. That's as close as the chest thumping gets to going over the top.

The pace of all this is slowing somewhat, at least temporarily. Extravagant proposals for monorails, a Six Flags theme park, and a futuristic train to whisk travelers from Providence's T.F. Green Airport to the casino have been abandoned or set aside. As well, the Pequots monitor closely the younger Mohegan Sun Resort, barely 6 miles away as the crow flies.

Two dozen bus companies provide daily service to Foxwoods from Boston, Hartford, Providence, New York, Philadelphia, and Albany, among many other cities—too many to list here. For information on transit from particular destinations, call © **860/885-3000.**

WHERE TO STAY

The resort has three hotels, the newest and most luxurious of which became operational in 1998, more than doubling Foxwoods' housing capacity. Unlike Las Vegas and other gambling centers, rates aren't kept artificially low as an inducement to gamblers, although that policy may change depending upon competitive pressures from the rival Mohegan Sun Resort.

To get to the resort from Boston, take I-95 south to Exit 92 onto Route 2 west. From New Haven and New York, take I-95 to I-395 north to Exit 79A onto Route 2A east, picking up Route 2 east. Don't bother trying to park your car in the huge garage. It takes forever, and the valet parking at the front door is swift and free.

Grand Pequot Tower ★★   The Grand Pequot Tower handily takes its place among New England's elite resort hotels. The newest of Foxwoods' hotels (so far) is the grandest in space and concept, yet it is also the most tasteful of the three. Polished granite and imported woods and marbles feature extensively in the handsome lobby. The tower's main restaurants, Fox Harbour and Al Dente, surpass all the resort competition. In back is a 50,000-square-foot casino, containing a plush Club Newport International open only to big-money players.

Rte. 2, Mashantucket, CT 06339. ℭ **800/369-9663** or 860/885-3000. Fax 860/312-7474. www.foxwoods.com. 824 units. July–Labor Day $220–$295 double, from $400 suite; Sept–June $145–$270 double, from $400 suite. AE, DC, DISC, MC, V. Free valet parking. **Amenities:** 2 restaurants (seafood, Italian); bars; indoor pool; golf course on property; health club and spa; video arcade; concierge; shopping arcade; 24-hr. room service; babysitting; same-day dry cleaning/laundry. In room: A/C, TV, dataport, hair dryer.

Great Cedar Hotel ⭐ Well maintained despite the heavy foot traffic, this hotel has eight floors adjoining the casinos. Guest rooms are colorful, but not too gaudy (except for the suites for high rollers on the top floor).

Rte. 2, Mashantucket, CT 06339. ℭ **800/369-9663** or 860/885-3000. Fax 860/885-4040. www.foxwoods.com. 312 units. July–Labor Day $160–$220 double, from $500 suite; Sept–June $175–$265 double, from $500 suite. AE, DC, DISC, MC, V. Free valet parking. **Amenities:** Restaurant; bars; indoor pool; golf course on the property; health club and spa; video arcade; shopping arcade; limited room service; babysitting; same-day dry cleaning/laundry. In room: A/C, TV, dataport.

Two Trees Inn This was the first Foxwoods lodging, built in less than 3 months, now a short shuttle-bus ride or 10-minute walk from the casino complex. A conventional motor hotel, it attracts large numbers of bus tours.

240 Lantern Hill Rd. (off Rte. 2), Mashantucket, CT 06339. ℭ **800/369-9663** or 860/312-3000. Fax 860/885-4050. www.foxwoods.com. 280 units. Nov–Mar $99–$225, suites from $210; Apr–June $125–$210, suites from $180; July–Aug $150–$225; suites from $280; Sept–Oct $125–$220, suites from $250. AE, DC, DISC, MC, V. **Amenities:** Restaurant; bar; heated indoor pool; fitness room; sauna; same-day dry cleaning/laundry. In room: A/C, TV.

WHERE TO DINE

Twenty-four restaurants and fast-food operations situated throughout the hotel-casino complex cover the most popular options. Only a couple aspire to even moderately serious culinary achievement, and there are no bargains as found in Atlantic City or Vegas. Expect to pay at least $50 for dinner for two, not including drinks, taxes, or tip.

Cedars Steak House grills Angus beef and native seafood, **Al Dente** does designer pizzas and pastas, and **Paragon** trafficks in French-Asian–influenced cuisine. All three expect guests to be dressed at least a notch better than tank tops and jeans, and they accept reservations. Call ℭ **860/885-3000** and ask for the desired extension.

The most popular dining room is the **Festival Buffet** (ext. 3172), which charges $10 for an all-you-can-eat spread. Other self-explanatory possibilities are **Han Garden** (ext. 4093), **Pequot Grill** (ext. 2690), and **The Deli** (ext. 5481).

FOXWOODS AFTER DARK

Just as in Vegas and Atlantic City, big showbiz names are whisked onto the premises, usually on weekends. Even Wayne Newton makes the scene, as do the likes of Chris Rock, Tony Bennett, Reba McEntire, the Dixie Chicks, and Jay Leno. For information, call ℭ **800/200-2882.**

UNCASVILLE & THE MOHEGAN SUN CASINO

About halfway between New London and Norwich, this blue collar town once provided barely sufficient reason even to downshift your car. That's changed, for good.

Kids A Break from Gambling

If you want to temporarily escape the whirring of slots at Foxwoods, or simply need to occupy underage kids, check out **Cinetropolis,** an entertainment center that looks like a cleaned-up futuristic Gotham. **Turbo Ride** lets you pretend you're experiencing the rumbling takeoffs and powerful G-forces of jets taking off. **Fox Giant Screen Theatre** is an IMAX-like production that features front-row rock concerts and exploding volcanoes, and **Virtual Adventures** lets you take control of an undersea vessel.

In 1996, the barely-extant Mohegan tribe opened its gambling casino, the **Mohegan Sun,** Mohegan Sun Boulevard (© **888/226-7711;** www.mohegan sun.com). Sitting in the middle of a potential $1 billion annual market, it was drawing 20,000 gamblers a day away from Foxwoods within a few weeks of opening. Obviously, the initial outlay of over $300 million for land and construction paid off handsomely, for the tribe announced soon after its inauguration that it was committing another $400 million for a new 1,200-room hotel, a marina, and non-gambling entertainment facilities. Those undertakings were soon completed and the complex now also includes a 10,000-seat sports arena (with its own professional basketball team, the WNBA's Connecticut Sun), a planetarium, and a "Casino of the Sky" to complement the original "Casino of the Earth".

Both casinos bulge with eager gamblers. "Earth" is circular, with four entrances named for the seasons. The core of 150,000 square feet is devoted to the games, everything from blackjack to craps, supplemented by keno, a race book, and thousands of slot machines. In the center is a nightclub, the Wolf's Den, featuring free entertainment with weekend headliners on the order of Seal and Crystal Gayle. Overhead are simulated log constructions meant to suggest ancient lodge houses. It's an aesthetically pleasing space, as casinos go, although few of the avid players seem to notice. They can even park their kids in the childcare center. "Sky" directly adjoins the hotel, and is more splashily Vegas in style. It contains over thirty pricey shops and the 300-seat Cabaret, venue of choice for such headliners as Tony Bennett. The sports arena handles basketball, boxing matches, bull riders, and luminaries on the order of David Bowie and Bette Midler.

The casino is right off I-395, Exit 79A, which makes for easy on/off access for gamblers who don't want to deal with that onerous 20-minute drive to Foxwoods before emptying their bank accounts.

WHERE TO STAY

Mohegan Sun Hotel ★★   This asymmetrical grouping of soaring silver-skinned wedges provokes the *Wow*! response from visitors exactly as intended. Every bit the equal of its rival, the Grand Pequot Tower at Foxwoods, it indulges in jaw-dropping design that begins with the slanting columns arrayed around a reflecting pool in abstract homage to woodland ponds. The front desk is over to the right, the escalators down to the restaurants and shops of the new Casino of the Sky on the far side. Rooms are conventionally attractive, albeit utilizing irregular shapes that echo design that was called "Modern" in the 1950s. Extras include Nintendo and high-speed Internet access through the TV with a wireless keyboard.

1 Mohegan Sun Blvd. (Off Rte. 2A), Uncasville, CT 06382. ⓒ 888/226-7711 or 860/862-8000. www. mohegansun.com. 1,200 units. $150–$375 double. Packages available. AE, DC, DISC, MC, V. Free valet parking. **Amenities:** 9 restaurants (Steakhouse, Fusion, Italian, Seafood, American); 4 bars; large indoor pool; extensive health club and spa; shopping arcade; concierge; 24-hr. room service; babysitting; same-day dry cleaning/laundry. *In room:* A/C, TV w/pay movies, dataport, hair dryer, fridge, coffeemaker, iron.

WHERE TO DINE

Of the score of dining options now available at the expanded complex, those in the new Casino of the Sky are the more impressive. The ambitious **Rain** gets some of the best notices for its fusion cuisine and dazzling setting of cascades, glass, and gleaming metals. It is followed closely by an outpost of **Michael Jordan's Steakhouse** and those of celebrity chefs Jasper White and Todd English with the casual seafood of **Summer Shack** and contemporary Italian edibles of **Tuscany,** respectively. The quality of the food is unexpectedly good, too, within the limits of their missions, at **Big Bubba's BBQ, The Longhouse** (beef and fish), **Bamboo Forest** (Southeast Asian), and **Pompeii and Caesar.** For reservations for Rain, Tuscany, The Longhouse, Pompeii and Caesar, or Bamboo Forest, call ⓒ **888/777-7920;** for Summer Shack, call ⓒ **860/862-9500;** for Michael Jordan's, call ⓒ **860/862-8600;** or for Big Bubba's BBQ, call ⓒ **860/ 862-9800.**

NORWICH

There is tourist potential here, where the Yantic and Shetucket rivers converge to form the Thames. Blocks of Broadway and Union Street are lined with substantial mansions from the city's golden era. There is no pretending, however, that this old mill town isn't in the doldrums, and so far, the presence of the nearby Mohegan Sun casino hasn't had much spillover effect. Until efforts to reverse that decline take hold, the principal reason for a visit is the fine lodging described below.

WHERE TO STAY & DINE

The Spa at Norwich Inn 🏵🏵🏵 After extensive renovations a few years back, this is now an even more desirable property. The complex is set on 40 acres, the main building augmented by outlying "villas" with 160 condo units. A typical suite has a kitchen, a sitting area with fireplace, a separate bedroom, and a deck overlooking the woods and a pond. Inn rooms aren't as large and don't have fireplaces, but they are hardly spartan. Terry robes and nightly turndowns are standard. Kensington's, the dining room, enjoys a versatile kitchen staff capable of producing meals either conventional or fitness-minded. The hotel and full service spa have attracted the diverse likes of Barbra Streisand, Mary J. Blige, Michael Douglas, and Bob Dylan. The property is owned by the Pequot tribal organization, and its Foxwoods Casino, visible from the front door, is about 15 minutes away, making this inn a soothing and convenient respite from the glitz.

607 W. Thames St. (Rte. 32), Norwich, CT 06360. ⓒ **800/275-4772** or 860/886-2401. Fax 860/886-9483. www.thespaatnorwichinn.com. 103 units. Inn $150–$325 double, villas $200–$350 suite. AE, DC, MC, V. From New Haven, take Exit 76 off I-95 onto I-395 north, Exit 79A onto Rte. 2A east, then exit onto Rte. 32 north and drive 1½ miles to the inn. **Amenities:** Restaurant; bar; indoor and outdoor pools; golf course on property; fully equipped health club and spa (with exercise classes, steam rooms, sauna, and massage); bicycle rental, limited room service; babysitting; same-day dry cleaning/laundry. *In room:* A/C, TV, dataport, fridge, coffeemaker, hair dryer, iron.

10

Rhode Island

by Herbert Bailey Livesey

Water defines "Little Rhody" as much as mountain peaks characterize Colorado. The Atlantic thrusts all the way to the Massachusetts border, cleaving the state into unequal halves and filling the geological basin that is Narragansett Bay. That leaves 400 miles of coastline and several large islands.

A string of coastal towns runs in a northeasterly arc from the Connecticut border up to Providence, the capital, which lies at the point of the bay, 30 miles from the open ocean. It was here that Roger Williams, banned from the Massachusetts Bay Colony in 1635 for his outspoken views on religious freedom, established his colony. Little survives from that first century, but a large section of the city's East Side is composed almost entirely of 18th- and 19th-century buildings.

Another group of Puritan exiles established their settlement a couple of years after Providence, on an island known to the Narragansett tribe as "Aquidneck." Settlers thought their new home resembled the Isle of Rhodes in the Aegean, so the official name became "Rhode Island and Providence Plantations," a moniker that was subsequently applied to the entire state and remains the official name.

The most important town on Aquidneck is Newport, and it's the best reason for an extended visit to the state. Its first era of prosperity was during the colonial period, when its ships not only plied the new mercantile routes to China but also engaged in the reprehensible "Triangular Trade" of West Indies molasses for New England rum for African slaves. Their additional skill at smuggling and evading taxes brought them into conflict with their British rulers, whose occupying army all but destroyed Newport during the Revolution.

After the Civil War, the town began its transformation from commercial outpost to resort, with the arrival of the millionaires whose lives spawned what Mark Twain sneeringly described as the "Gilded Age." They built astonishingly extravagant mansions, their contribution to Newport's bountiful architectural heritage. Winning the America's Cup and subsequent defenses of yachting's most famous trophy made the town into a recreational sailing center with a packed summer cultural calendar. As a result, travelers who want nothing more than a deep tan by Monday can coexist with history buffs and music lovers, who come to attend concerts held against a seductive backdrop of waves hissing across packed sand.

Finally, there is Block Island, which is a 1-hour ferry ride from Point Judith. A classic summer resort, it has avoided the imposition of Martha's Vineyard chic and Provincetown clutter. It has also sidestepped history (even though it was first settled in 1661), so there are few mandatory sights. That leaves visitors free simply to explore its lighthouses, hike its cliffside trails, and hit the beach.

1 Providence (★(★

45 miles S of Boston; 55 miles NE of New London

Providence delights in its new sobriquet, "Renaissance City," and was beside itself over the several season run of a recent TV series named for it. No question, this city is moving on up, counter to the trend of so many small and mid-size New England cities. *Money* magazine even declared it the "Best Place to Live in the East." Revival is in the air and prosperity is returning, evident in the resurgent "downcity" business district. Rivers have been uncovered to form canals and waterside walkways; distressed buildings of the last century have been reclaimed; and continued construction has added a new hotel behind Union Station as well as Providence Place, a monster mall that brings national department stores to town for the first time.

Much of the credit for Providence's boom, grudging or exuberant, went to the ebullient six-term mayor, Vincent A. "Buddy" Cianci, Jr. But he is now in prison, having been caught in the net of an FBI probe into the bribery of local officials. A 97-page federal indictment charged Cianci and others with racketeering, extortion, witness tampering, and mail fraud. Buddy tried to laugh it off, right up until the verdict. Called Operation Plunder Dome, the investigation revived Providence's reputation for tolerance of corruption at high levels.

Still, continued local pride in the city's revitalization is palpable. A burgeoning dining scene includes ambitious new restaurants that are nearly always less expensive than their counterparts in Boston and New York. College Hill is one of only 26 National Historic Districts, the calendar is full of special events, and the presence of the young people attending the city's 12 colleges and universities guarantees a lively nightlife.

Roger Williams knew what he was doing. Admired for his fervent advocacy of religious and political freedom in the early colonial period, he obviously had good instincts for town building as well. He planted the seeds of his settlement on a steep rise overlooking a swift-flowing river at the point where it widened into a large protected harbor. That part of the city, called the East Side and dominated by the ridge now known as College Hill, remains the most attractive district of a New England city second only to Boston in the breadth of its cultural life and rich architectural heritage.

College Hill is so named because it is the site of Rhode Island College, which started life in 1764 and was later renamed Brown University. The Hill is further enhanced by the presence of the highly regarded Rhode Island School of Design, whose buildings are wrapped around the perimeter of the Brown campus. In and around these institutions are several square miles of 18th- and 19th-century houses, colonial to Victorian, lining often gaslit streets. At the back of the Brown campus is the funky shopping district along Thayer Street, while at the foot of the Hill is the largely commercial Main Street.

While most points of interest are found on the East Side, the far larger collection of neighborhoods west of the river has its own attractions. The level downtown area is the center for business, government, and entertainment, with City Hall, a new convention center, the three best large hotels, some small parks and historic buildings, and several venues for music, dance, and theatrical productions. To its north, across the Woonasquatucket River, is the imposing State House, as well as the Amtrak station. And to its west, on the other side of Interstate 95, is Federal Hill, a residential area bearing a strong ethnic identity, primarily Italian, but increasingly leavened by numbers of more recent immigrant groups.

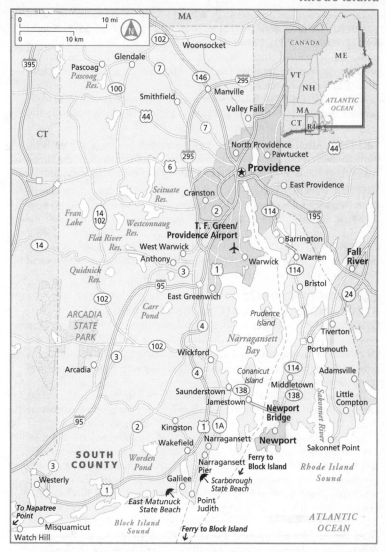

Note: Smoking isn't regulated yet in public places in Rhode Island, at least at this writing, so it is left up to the proprietors of stores, inns, hotels, restaurants, and bars to set their own policies on tobacco use. In practice, this means that owners of restaurants often restrict puffing to their bars and innkeepers prohibit smoking entirely.

ESSENTIALS

GETTING THERE   I-95, which connects Boston and New York, runs right through the city. From Cape Cod, pick up I-195 west.

T. F. Green/Providence Airport (℡ **888/268-7222** or 401/737-8222; www.pvdairport.com) in Warwick, south of Providence (Exit 13, I-95), is served by major airlines such as **American** (© 800/433-7300), **Continental** (© 800/525-0280), **Delta** (© 800/221-1212), **Northwest** (© 800/225-2525), **Southwest** (© 800/435-9792), **United** (© 800/241-6522), and **US Airways** (© 800/428-4322). The Rhode Island Public Transit Authority (RIPTA) provides transportation between the airport and the city center. Taxis are also available, costing about $20 for the 20-minute trip.

Amtrak (© 800/USA-RAIL; www.amtrak.com) runs several trains daily between Boston and New York, stopping at the attractive new station at 100 Gaspee St., near the State House.

GETTING AROUND   Traffic on local streets isn't bad, even at rush hour. Taxis are not easy to come by, with few to be found outside even the largest hotels. They can take 15 minutes to an hour when called from restaurants.

VISITOR INFORMATION   For advance information, contact the **Providence Warwick Convention & Visitors Bureau,** 1 West Exchange St. (© 800/233-1636 or 401/274-1636; www.providencecvb.com). In town, consult the new visitor center in the Rhode Island Convention Center, 1 Sabin St. (© 800/233-1636 or 401/751-1177), or check with the helpful park rangers at the visitor center of the Roger Williams National Park, at the corner of Smith and North Main streets, open daily from 9am to 4:30pm.

EXPLORING PROVIDENCE
STROLLING THE HISTORIC NEIGHBORHOODS
This is a city of manageable size—the population is about 170,000—that can easily occupy 2 or 3 days of a Rhode Island vacation. Two leisurely walks, one short, another longer, pass most of the prominent attractions and offer up a sense of the city's evolution from a colony of dissidents to a contemporary center of commerce and government.

Downtown, chart a route from the 1878 City Hall on Kennedy Plaza along Dorrance Street 1 block to Westminster. Turn left, then right in 1 block, past the Arcade (see "Quick Bites," later in this section), then left on Weybosset.

To extend this into a longer walk, follow Weybosset until it joins Westminster and continue across the Providence River. Turn right on the other side, walking along South Water Street as far as James Street, just before the I-195 overpass. Turn left, cross South Main, and then turn left on Benefit Street. This is the start of the so-called **Mile of History** ★★. Lined with 18th- and 19th-century houses, it is enhanced by gas streetlamps and sections of brick herringbone sidewalks. Along the way are opportunities to visit, in sequence, the 1786 **John Brown House,** the **First Unitarian Church** (1816), the **Providence Athenaeum,** and the **Museum of Art, Rhode Island School of Design.**

SEEING THE SIGHTS
Boosters are understandably proud of their **Waterplace Park & Riverwalk** ★★, which encircles a tidal basin and borders the Woonasquatucket River down past where it joins the Moshassuck to become the Providence River. It incorporates an amphitheater, boat landings, landscaped walkways, and vaguely Venetian bridges that cross to the East Side. Summer concerts and other events are held here, among them the enormously popular **WaterFires** ★★ (© 401/272-3111), when 97 bonfires are set ablaze in the basin of Waterplace Park and along the river on New Year's Eve and on more than 20 other dates July through October, their roar accentuated by amplified music.

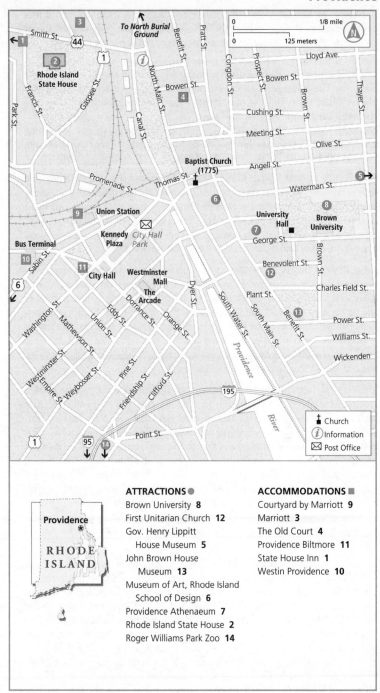

Smith St.
To North Burial Ground
Benefit St.
Pratt St.
Congdon St.
Prospect St.
Lloyd Ave.
Bowen St.
Brown St.
Thayer St.
Rhode Island State House
Gaspee St.
Francis St.
Park St.
North Main St.
Canal St.
Bowen St.
Cushing St.
Meeting St.
Olive St.
Angell St.
Baptist Church (1775)
Thomas St.
Promenade St.
Waterman St.
Union Station
University Hall
Brown University
Kennedy Plaza
City Hall Park
George St.
Bus Terminal
Sabin St.
Benevolent St.
Brown St.
City Hall
Westminster Mall
Charles Field St.
The Arcade
Dyer St.
Plant St.
South Water St.
South Main St.
Benefit St.
Power St.
Washington St.
Mathewson St.
Union St.
Dorrance St.
Eddy St.
Orange St.
Williams St.
Wickenden
Westminster St.
Empire St.
Weybosset St.
Pine St.
Friendship St.
Clifford St.
Providence
195
River
Point St.

0   1/8 mile
0   125 meters

✝ Church
ⓘ Information
✉ Post Office

ATTRACTIONS ●
Brown University **8**
First Unitarian Church **12**
Gov. Henry Lippitt
    House Museum **5**
John Brown House
    Museum **13**
Museum of Art, Rhode Island
    School of Design **6**
Providence Athenaeum **7**
Rhode Island State House **2**
Roger Williams Park Zoo **14**

ACCOMMODATIONS ■
Courtyard by Marriott **9**
Marriott **3**
The Old Court **4**
Providence Biltmore **11**
State House Inn **1**
Westin Providence **10**

Providence
✶
RHODE ISLAND

Nearby, in Kennedy Plaza, the new **Fleet Skating Center** has an ice rink twice the size of the one in New York's Rockefeller Center, fully utilized almost every winter evening. Skate rentals, lockers, and a snack bar are available.

Brown University   The nation's seventh-oldest college was founded in 1764 and has a reputation as the most experimental institution among its Ivy League brethren. The evidence of its pre-Revolutionary origins is seen in **University Hall,** built in 1771. Tours of the campus are intended primarily for prospective students, but anyone can join (call ahead).

Office of Admissions, 45 Prospect St. (corner of Angell St.). 🕐 401/863-1000. Free admission. Tours, late Nov to early Sept Mon–Fri at 10am, 11am, 1pm, 3pm, and 4pm (11am and 3pm only during Christmas and spring vacations); early Sept to late Nov, Sat 10am, 11am, and noon.

Gov. Henry Lippitt House Museum ★   This house is as magnificently true to its grandiose Victorian era as any residence on the Continent. Meticulously detailed stenciling, expanses of stained glass, and inlaid floors make this mansion one of the treasures of College Hill. Visits are by guided tour only.

199 Hope St. (at Angell St.). 🕐 401/453-0688. Admission $4 adults, $2 seniors and students. Tours Apr–Dec Tues–Fri 11am–3pm on the hour; Sat–Sun and Jan–Mar by appointment only.

John Brown House Museum   Quite unlike the fiery 19th-century abolitionist of the same name, *this* John Brown was an 18th-century slave trader who amassed a fortune in the China trade. He contributed much of that fortune to the university that bears the family name. The style of his 1786 mansion is Georgian, although after the Revolution, Brown no doubt preferred to think of it as Federal. Visits are by guided tour only.

52 Power St. (at Benefit St.). 🕐 401/331-8575. Admission $7 adults, $5.50 seniors and students, $4 children 7–17. Tues–Sat 10am–5pm; Sun noon–4pm. Closed Jan–Feb.

Museum of Art, Rhode Island School of Design ★★   Prestigious RISD (pronounced *Riz*-dee) supports this ingratiating center of fine and decorative arts. Of the many fine college and university museums in New England, this ranks near the top for the breadth of its collection. Those holdings include Chinese terra cotta, Greek statuary, and French Impressionist paintings. Probably of greatest interest are the works by such masters as Monet, Cézanne, Rodin, Picasso, and Matisse. But allow time for the American wing, which contains paintings by Gilbert Stuart, John Singleton Copley, and John Singer Sargent. The Gorham silver collection alone is nearly worth the admission.

224 Benefit St. (between Waterman and College sts.). 🕐 401/454-6500. Admission $8 adults, $5 seniors, $3 college students with ID, $2 children 5–18; free to all the 3rd Thurs of the month from 5–9pm. Tues–Sun 10am–5pm (Thurs until 9pm).

Providence Athenaeum   The Providence Athenaeum commissioned this 1838 Greek Revival building to house its lending library, the fourth oldest in the United States and an innovative concept at the time. Edgar Allan Poe courted Sarah Whitman, his "Annabel Lee," between these shelves. Glances through the old card catalog reveal handwritten cards dating well back into the 1800s. Bibliophiles will lose themselves in this marvelous place. Rotating exhibits of rare books and works by local artists are additional attractions. The library has money problems that have contributed to a contretemps over ways to raise funds, specifically a decision to sell off an Audubon folio valued at $7 million.

251 Benefit St. (at College St.). 🕐 401/421-6970. Free admission. Mon–Thurs 9am–7pm; Fri–Sat 9am–5pm; Sun 1–5pm. Closed first 2 weeks in Aug.

Rhode Island State House   Constructed of Georgian marble that blazes in the sun, the 1900 capitol dominates the city center. This near-flawless example of neoclassical governmental architecture (by McKim, Mead & White, 1891–92) boasts one of the largest self-supported domes in the world. The gilded figure on top represents "Independent Man," the state symbol. Inside, a portrait of George Washington is given pride of place, one of many depictions painted by Gilbert Stuart, a Rhode Island native son.

82 Smith St. (between Francis and Hayes sts.). © 401/277-2357. Free admission. Guided tours by appointment Mon–Fri 8:30am–noon.

Roger Williams Park Zoo ★★ *Kids*   Situated in a 430-acre park that also contains a museum of natural history and a planetarium, the zoo is divided into three principal habitats: Tropical America, the Farmyard, and the Plains of Africa. A newer exhibit is devoted to Australia, with the zoo's first saltwater aquarium. A walk-through aviary and underwater viewing areas with polar bears, sea lions, and harbor seals are additional attractions.

1000 Elmwood Ave. (at Exit 17 off I-95). © 401/785-3510. www.rogerwilliamsparkzoo.org. Admission $8 adults, $7 seniors and children 3–12. Mid-May to mid-Oct Mon–Fri 9am–5pm, Sat–Sun 9am–6pm; mid-Oct to mid-May daily 9am–4pm. Driving south on I-95, take Exit 17; driving north, take Exit 16.

SHOPPING

Thayer Street, the main commercial district for the university, is home to the official **Brown Bookstore,** at no. 244 (at the corner of Olive St.)-. Also in the vicinity are **Silverberry's,** at no. 220, with dressy and casual clothes for college-age women, and **Hillhouse,** no. 135, long in the business of providing male Brownies with Ivy dress-up clothes for interview weeks and parents' days.

WHERE TO STAY

The clusters of motels around most of the exits from I-95 and I-195 offer decent value. Among these possibilities are the **Days Hotel,** 220 India St. (© 401/272-5577), and the **Ramada Inn,** 940 Fall River Ave., Seekonk, Mass. (© 508/336-7300).

Alternatives are provided by B&B referral agencies such as **Bed & Breakfast of Rhode Island** (© 800/828-0000 or 401/849-1298). These are rooms in private homes, so sometimes quirky rules apply. Lodgings in the historic districts are required to provide off-street parking, and it's free at the two East Side inns (the Old Court and the State House Inn) recommended below. There's a charge for parking at the big downtown hotels. Rates at most area inns and motels go up on alumni and parents' weekends and during graduation weeks.

Courtyard by Marriott ★   This recent addition to the downcity lodging scene is welcome both for its lower rates and for the extra rooms provided in a city still short on accommodations. It also was built in style and exterior materials to be harmonious with the adjacent former Union Station complex. As a mid-priced entry designed primarily for businesspeople, its rooms are equipped with two-line phones, high-speed Internet access, and well-lit desks. It is just as comfortable for leisure travelers, with several of our recommended restaurants, the new Providence Place mall, and WaterFires only minutes away. While the on-site cafe doesn't serve dinner, meals can be delivered from nearby restaurants.

32 Exchange Terrace, Providence, RI 02903. © 800/321-2211 or 401/272-1191. Fax 401/272-1416. www.courtyard.com. 216 units. $139–$199 double. AE, DC, DISC, MC, V. **Amenities:** Cafe/bar (breakfast and cocktails); indoor pool with whirlpool; exercise room; business center; coin-op laundry; same-day dry cleaning. *In room:* A/C, TV w/pay movies, dataport, coffeemaker, hair dryer, iron.

Marriott   This busy motor hotel is popular with both business and leisure travelers. It's north of downtown, but within a 10-minute drive of most of the city's attractions. Shuttle service to and from the airport and the bus and train stations can be arranged when booking. Parking is free. No pets.

1 Orms St., Providence, RI 02904. ℭ 800/228-9290 or 401/272-2400. Fax 401/273-2686. www.marriott hotels.com/pvdri. 346 units. $199–$318 double. AE, DC, DISC, MC, V. Free parking. **Amenities:** 2 restaurants (American); bar; indoor/outdoor pool; exercise room with Jacuzzi and sauna; concierge; business center; limited room service; dry cleaning. *In room:* A/C, TV w/pay movies, dataport, coffeemaker, hair dryer, iron.

The Old Court   This was once a rectory, built in 1863, and the furnishings reflect that use and period. There are secretaries embellished with marquetry, Oriental rugs, and more familiar Victoriana. Most traces of its tenure as a boardinghouse for students have been expunged. Families or longer-term visitors may be interested in the apartment across the street.

144 Benefit St., Providence, RI 02903. ℭ 401/751-2002. Fax 401/272-4830. www.oldcourt.com. 10 units. $115–$155 double. Rates include breakfast. AE, DISC, MC, V. No children under 12. *In room:* A/C, TV.

Providence Biltmore 🏨🏨   A grand staircase beneath the stunning Deco bronze ceiling dates the centrally located building to the 1920s, and a plaque in the lobby shows the nearly 7-foot-high water level of the villainous 1938 hurricane. From the lobby, the dramatic glass elevator literally shoots skyward, exiting outdoors to scoot up the side of the building. Most guest rooms are large, half of them with more than 600 square feet of floor space; some of the 20 suites have kitchenettes. The entire property has received more than $10 million of overdue attention over the last 3 years, and another 50 rooms have been added.

11 Dorrance St., Providence, RI 02903. ℭ 800/294-7709 or 401/421-0700. Fax 401/455-3127. www. providencebiltmore.com. 291 units. $149–$239 double; from $209 suite. AE, DC, MC, V. Valet parking $16. **Amenities:** Restaurant; bar; fitness center; concierge; business center; limited room service; babysitting; laundry; dry cleaning. *In room:* A/C, TV, VCR available, dataport, coffeemaker, hair dryer.

State House Inn   The neighborhood isn't the best, but it isn't scary, either, and downtown restaurants are only minutes away. In compensation, the owners lay out lower rates and hotel conveniences. Some rooms in the 1889 house have canopy beds or fireplaces, and new and antique furnishings have been added in the last couple years. Children are welcome.

43 Jewett St., Providence, RI 02908. ℭ 401/351-6111. Fax 401/351-4261. www.providence-inn.com. 10 units. May–Oct $129–$159 double; Nov–Apr $139–$189 double. Ask about lower weekday corporate rates. Rates include full breakfast. AE, DISC, MC, V. From the State House, drive west on Smith St., over I-95, then left on Holden and right on Jewett. *In room:* A/C, TV, VCR available, dataport, hair dryer, iron.

Westin Providence 🏨🏨🏨   Easily the city's best hotel, this property does nothing to diminish the solid reputation of the Westin chain, and even with a luxurious interior and downtown location, the rates are lower than those of its siblings in Boston and New York. Skyways connect the hotel with the new Providence Place mall and the convention center. Bedrooms are equipped with the patented "Heavenly Bed" sheets, pillows, and mattresses. The architectural grandeur of the lobby rotunda and other public spaces doesn't seem to dampen the sunny dispositions of the staff. Off the lobby is a lounge with the buffed glow of an exclusive men's club. **Agora,** the main dining room, gets excellent reviews from critics, and serves all meals.

1 West Exchange St., Providence, RI 02903. ℭ 800/937-8461 or 401/598-8000. Fax 401/598-8200. www. westin.com. 364 units. $279–$339 double. Valet parking $18. AE, DC, MC, V. **Amenities:** 2 restaurants

(Eclectic, American); 2 bars; indoor pool; fully equipped health club with Jacuzzi and sauna; concierge; business center; limited room service; babysitting; same-day dry cleaning/laundry. *In room:* A/C, TV w/pay movies, VCR available, Nintendo, dataport, minibar, coffeemaker, hair dryer, iron, safe.

WHERE TO DINE

Providence has a sturdy Italian heritage, resulting in a profusion of tomato-sauce and pizza joints, especially on Federal Hill, the district west of downtown and I-95. Because they are so obvious, the suggestions below focus on restaurants that break away from the red-gravy imperative.

One fruitful strip to explore for lower-cost dining options is that part of **Thayer Street** that borders the Brown University campus. It counts Thai, Tex-Mex, barbecue, and Indian restaurants among its possibilities.

Cafe Nuovo ★★★ MEDITERRANEAN FUSION   This spacious room of glass, marble, and burnished wood occupies part of the ground floor of a downtown office tower that overlooks the confluence of the Moshassuck and Woonasquatucket rivers. Unlike its local competitor, Al Forno, which gets the greater share of largely undeserved ink, Cafe Nuovo takes reservations, is open for lunch *and* dinner, and impresses with every course, from dazzling appetizers to stunning pastries. The fare is grounded in the Italian repertoire, but skips lightly among other inspirations, too—Thai, Greek, and Portuguese among them. That culinary restlessness leads to dishes as the appetizer of seared tuna on black sesame brioche with ginger-lime aioli and the entree of pork tenderloin and clams with a chouriço-studded potato cake. There's music on weekends and outdoor dining in warm weather. Restaurants rise and fall, but Café Nuovo persists, steady and embracing.

1 Citizens Plaza (access is from the Steeple St. bridge). © **401/421-2525.** Reservations advised. Main courses $20–$32. AE, DC, DISC, MC, V. Mon–Fri 11:30am–3pm; Mon–Thurs 5–10:30pm; Fri–Sat 5–11pm. Closed first week in Jan.

CAV ★★ ECLECTIC   No corporate design drudge had a hand in *this* warehouse interior, a Jewelry District pioneer. CAV is an acronym for "Coffee/Antiques/Victuals," and patrons are surrounded by tribal rugs, African carvings, and assorted antiques (most for sale). Turkish kilims under glass cover tables. The resulting Bohemian air is not unlike Greenwich Village in the 1960s, complete with live jazz or blues on weekends ($5 cover). Attractive servers bring dishes prepared by folks quite accomplished at their craft. Select from such strenuous menu swings as Asian chive cakes to the overkill grilled venison filet on black-eyed peas, game sausage, plums, and honeyed carrots. Every day brings a choice of special soup, appetizer, pasta, and a pizza or two. Smoking isn't permitted.

14 Imperial Place (near Basset St.). © **401/751-9164.** Reservations recommended. Main courses $17–$29. DISC, MC, V. Mon–Thurs 11:30am–10pm; Fri–Sat 11:30am–1am; Sun 10:30am–10pm.

The Gatehouse ★★ NEW AMERICAN   Step into a refined room with a green marble bar on the left, a fireplace and elegantly set tables over to the right, all of it shifted around and redecorated by new owners (who also have Mill's Tavern, below). Downstairs is a candlelit lounge where smoking is permitted and a deck perched above the Seekonk River. Jazz musicians perform down here Thursday nights. Service is efficient and polished. Expect no serious surprises on the plate–the kitchen appears to be determined to keep things simple. The excesses of fusion cuisine aren't in evidence. That doesn't mean bland. Amid the currently requisite crab cakes, fried calamari, and raw oysters, find veal tenderloins bathed in a

Tips   Big Tastes Hide in Little Rhody

You'd think, in an age of instant communication, that no ingratiatingly flavorful edible tidbit or preparation would stay unknown for long. Worthy regional specialties fast become national staples—think Buffalo wings, Carolina blooming onions, Texan burritos. But Rhode Islanders are tightfisted about their food secrets, and even residents of neighboring states are in the dark. Check them out:

- **Rhode Island clam chowder** is a clear broth, not cream- or tomato-based, as in the far better-known Manhattan and New England chowders.

- **Stuffies** come in as many versions as there are cooks. At Flo's Clam Shack in Newport, quahog clams are chopped up with hot and sweet peppers and breadcrumbs, packed inside the two shell halves and shut, the whole held together by a rubber band and baked. The mixture assumes the consistency of setting plaster, but is no less tasty for that.

- **Johnnycakes** (aka jonnycakes) are breakfast fodder, some as thin as crepes, others as thick as standard griddlecakes. The difference from the conventional pancakes is the primary ingredient, cornmeal. Honey is a common topping.

- **Clam cakes** are as inaccurately named as Brooklyn egg creams (which have neither eggs nor cream). These aren't cakes, but deep-fried fritters, and the clams therein are notable primarily for their virtual absence.

- **Coffee milk** and **cabinets** are the obligatory beverages to go with Rhody chow. The first is made with sweet coffee syrup, while the second is what the rest of America thinks of as a milkshake.

- **New York System Wieners** have only a passing acquaintance with Big Apple franks. In Rhode Island, the wieners are short—3 or 4 inches long—served on soft steamed buns and topped (usually) with a chili-type meat sauce, minced onion, and mustard. Nobody eats just one—the typical ration is four or more per person.

So step up to the counter and demand "Four all the way, extra sauce, and a coffee milk." You thus commence your initiation into the mysteries of the Rhode Island food culture. Did we mention doughboys and Gray's Ice Cream?

chimichurri sauce with mashed potatoes and a raisin-onion chutney. A variation on the classic Portuguese dish of pork and clams Alentejana has at its center a pork shank rather than cubed meat. About half the dinner entrees involve seafood, from cod loin to swordfish, and much of it is grilled over a wood fire. Presentation is careful but not fussy. Unlike in its previous incarnation, lunch is served.

4 Richmond Sq. (east end of Pitman St.). 🕐 **401/521-9229.** Reservations recommended. Main courses $17–$28. AE, DC, DISC, MC, V. Daily 11:30am–3pm and 5–10pm (Fri and Sat until 11pm).

Mill's Tavern ⭐ NEW AMERICAN   Hip. Hot. Happening. There have to be better words to describe this hugely popular Main Street eatery, but you get the idea. It's not all that tavern-like, a spread-out space with a ceiling crossed with dark beams, a black marble-topped bar straight ahead, and a large exhibition kitchen off to the right. Loaded throughout its hours with attractive young to middle-aged professionals, the tone of the crowd tilts a bit on weekends with an influx of Providence's version of a bridge-and-tunnel crowd. The bartenders are a quick-moving, affable lot, and their number includes the guys operating the raw bar. As in the owners' other enterprise, The Gatehouse (above), the menu is relatively uncomplicated, much of it utilizing wood grilling. Salmon with French lentils and a tomato-citrus jam is typical, as is the open-faced rabbit ravioli with wild mushrooms garnished with sage and truffle essence. The wood-burning oven is employed for slow-braised ribs and pull jerk boar. Free valet parking is offered. Smoking only at the bar, which stays open until midnight or 1am.

101 N. Main St. ℂ **401/272-3331**. Reservations essential. Main courses $16–$34. AE, DC, MC, V. Daily 5–10pm (Fri–Sat until 11pm).

XO Café ⭐ ECLECTIC   A younger, more casual crowd than that drawn to Mill's Tavern (above) keeps the staff moving at a fast evening-long pace. A modest redecoration effort laid new carpets on the floors and nonobjective sculptures on the walls. Behind the copper-topped bar are female mixologists in clothes not meant to conceal their gender. They serve almost as many meals as drinks, and their customers have some interesting choice. A note at the top of the menu insists "Life is short, order dessert first." That would mean crème brulée, tart tatin, and molten chocolate cake, and some diners happily take the advice. Slaves to tradition can order the "Pre Fixe"—their spelling—which on one occasion listed seared foie gras in brioche with candied shallots and citrus-honey glaze. The "Greatest Burger On Earth"—their hyperbole—is ground sirloin stuffed with barbecued duck confit and shaved truffle topped with pâté de foie gras. It is served on grilled brioche with a side of Parmesan truffled fries. There's free valet parking Thursday through Saturday.

125 N. Main St. ℂ **401/273-9090**. Reservations advised. Main courses $20–$29. AE, DC, MC, V. Daily 5–10pm (Fri–Sat until 11pm.)

QUICK BITES

Providence claims the invention of the diner, starting with a horse-drawn wagon transporting food down Westminster Street in 1872. The tradition is carried forward by the likes of the **Seaplane Diner,** 307 Allens Ave. (ℂ **401/941-9547**), a silver-sided classic with tableside jukeboxes, and **Richard's Diner,** 377 Richmond St. (ℂ **401/331-8541**), so small you can walk across it in six strides.

A bona fide National Historic Landmark is an unlikely venue for snarfing up cookies, souvlaki, and egg rolls. But **The Arcade,** 65 Weybosset St. (ℂ **401/598-1199**), is a 19th-century progenitor of 20th-century shopping malls, an 1828 Greek Revival structure that runs between Weybosset and Westminster streets. Its main floor is given over largely to fast-food stands and snack counters of the usual kinds—yes, the Golden Arches, too—while the upper floor is primarily boutiques and souvenir shops.

Another local culinary institution arrives in Kennedy Plaza on wheels every afternoon around 4:30pm. The grungy aluminum-sided **Haven Bros.** (ℂ **401/ 861-7777**) is a food tractor-trailer with a counter and six stools inside and good deals on decent burgers and even better fries sold from its parking space next to City Hall. No new frontiers here, except that it hangs around until way past midnight to dampen the hunger pangs of club-goers, lawyers, night people, and workaholic pols.

PROVIDENCE AFTER DARK

This being a college town, there is no end of music bars, small concert halls, and pool pubs. A good source of information is the free weekly *Providence Phoenix* (www.providencephoenix.com).

THE PERFORMING ARTS The **Opera Providence** (© 401/331-6060) stages three or four productions a season at various locations, including the Veterans Memorial Auditorium. The **Rhode Island Philharmonic** (© 401/831-3123) usually appears at the Providence Performing Arts Center or the Veterans Memorial Auditorium. Big-ticket touring musicals on the order of *Rent, Hairspray,* and *Mamma Mia!* as well as traveling dance companies and other attractions, are showcased at the **Providence Performing Arts Center,** 220 Weybosset St. (© 401/421-ARTS), while new plays share space with Ibsen and Shakespeare at the **Trinity Repertory Company,** 201 Washington St. (© 401/521-1100).

THE CLUB & MUSIC SCENE South of downcity, in the Jewelry District, **The Complex** , 180 Pine St(© 401/751-4263), offers four distinctive dance clubs for only one cover: techno at Liquid Assets, disco at Polly Esta's, Top 40 at Algiers, and dance rock at Club Uranus. It's open Wednesday through Saturday. **The Green Room,** 145 Clifford St. (© 401/351-7665), usually has DJs Wednesdays and Thursdays, live rock Fridays and Saturdays, and a comedy showcase on Sundays.

Lupo's at the Strand, 79 Washington St. (© 401/272-5876), known as Lupo's Heartbreak Hotel when it was at 239 Westminster St., still hosts a variety of live concerts. **The Call,** 15 Elbow St. (© 401/751-2255), showcases mostly regional bands, supplemented by acts in the attached **Century Lounge,** 150 Chestnut St. (same phone). At the **Custom House Tavern,** 36 Weybosset St. (© 401/751-3630), an open mike is on Monday and Wednesday, with live jazz or blues on Saturday and Sunday. Connected to the popular Café Paragon, **Club Viva,** 234 Thayer St. (© 401/272-7600), has food from the same kitchen, but in a lounge environment that turns into dance club on weekends.

Many restaurants in the city engage musical groups 2 or more nights a week. These include the Gatehouse and CAV described under "Where to Dine," above. At the **Trinity Brewhouse,** 186 Fountain St. (© 401/453-2337), live jazz and blues share attention with boutique beers, a pool table, and a deck.

MOVIES For art-house films and midnight cult movies, there is the **Avon Cinema,** 260 Thayer St., near Meeting Street (© 401/421-3315).

2 A Bucolic Detour to Sakonnet Point

As a break from the urbanity of Providence or the concentration of sights and activities that is Newport, a side trip down the length of the oddly isolated southeastern corner of the state is a soothing excursion.

No one has thought to throw a bridge or run a ferry across the water between Newport and Sakonnet Point, prospects the reclusive residents would no doubt resist to the last lawsuit. They have been known to steal away with road signs to discourage summer visitors, and there are almost no enterprises specifically geared to attract tourists. Things are quiet in these parts, and they intend to keep it that way.

To get here from Providence or Boston, pick up I-195 east, then Route 24 south, toward Newport. Take Exit 4 for Route 77 south, just before the Sakonnet River Bridge. From Newport, take Route 138 toward Fall River, and exit on Route 77 south immediately after crossing the bridge.

After a welter of small businesses, most of them involved in some way with the ocean, Route 77 smoothes out into a pastoral Brigadoon, not quite rural, but more rustic than suburban. Colonial farmhouses, real or replicated, bear sidings of weathered shakes the color of wood smoke. They are centered in tidy lawns, bordered by miles of low stone walls. No plastic deer, no tomato plants in front yards—it's as if a requirement of residence were attendance at a school of good taste.

There are a few antiques shops and roadside farm stands along the way, and a cluster of shops and eating places at Tiverton Four Corners, about halfway down the point. The building on the near right corner of that intersection is **Provender** (℗ 401/624-8084), a lunch counter famed for its veggie sandwich, the "Great Garbanzo." It's closed from Christmas until spring. On the far left corner, at the edge of the parking lot, is a destination dear to the hearts of Rhode Islanders. **Gray's Ice Cream** (℗ 401/624-4500) scoops out 32 flavors of the super-premium dessert, along with 11 more sherbets and frozen yogurts. A big cone or cupful costs $2.75; coffee is the best-selling flavor. It's open daily from 6:30am to 7pm in winter, until 9pm in summer.

Another good reason to pull off the road is **Sakonnet Vineyards** ✿, 162 W. Main Rd. (℗ 401/635-8486; www.sakonnetwine.com), with an entrance road on the left, about 3 miles south of Tiverton Four Corners. In operation for more than 20 years, it is one of New England's oldest wineries, and produces 50,000 cases of creditable wines annually. Types range from a popular pinot noir to an honored vidal blanc. Bring along a picnic lunch, then buy a bottle and retire to one of the tables beside the pond. The hospitality center is open daily from 10am to 6pm in summer, 11am to 5pm in winter, with tours on the hour.

Continuing south on Route 77, the road skirts Little Compton and heads on to **Sakonnet Point,** where the inland terrain gives way to stony beaches and coastal marshes. There's a wetlands wildlife refuge, a small harbor with working boats, and not much else.

Now head back north on Route 77, watching for the sign pointing toward Adamsville. Take the right turn at the triangular traffic island just beyond, onto a road that seems to have neither name nor number. Shortly, it arrives at a T intersection surrounded by a church, a general store, and the **Common's** restaurant (see below). This is downtown **Little Compton** ✿. Turn left (north) and you're back in the country. In less than 2 miles, the road ends at Peckham Road. Turn left to return to Route 77, and turn right (north) to return to your original destination.

WHERE TO STAY ALONG THE WAY

Stone House Club   From the last stop in Sakonnet Point, return along Route 77, and you'll shortly note the entrance to this restaurant/tavern/inn. It's open to the public, but it must observe the wink-wink subterfuge of proclaiming itself a private club because it serves spirits and there's a church next door. That means a $25 membership fee for individuals and $40 for couples, in addition to room rates. Furnishings are worn and unstylish, but look oddly right for their location. Two private beaches are available to guests. The cellar Tap Room and the more formal restaurant upstairs traipse all over the gastronomic map, with an emphasis on seafood. They are open Tuesday through Sunday in summer, Friday through Sunday from October to December and March to April.

122 Sakonnet Point Rd., Little Compton, RI 02837. ℂ **401/635-2222.** Fax 401/635-2822. www.stonehouse club.com. 14 units (4 with shared bathroom). Summer $58–$125 double, from $125 suite; Nov–Dec and Mar–Apr $48–$80 double, from $90 suite. Rates include breakfast. *Note:* Additional membership fee as noted above. MC, V. Closed Jan–Feb. **Amenities:** Restaurant; bar. *In room:* No phone.

WHERE TO DINE ALONG THE WAY

Another dining option is the **Stone House Club,** described above.

Common's REGIONAL AMERICAN   This is the place to sample a few Rhode Island specialties: johnnycakes (lacy pancakes of stoneground cornmeal as thin as playing cards) and stuffies (chopped Quahog [*KWAH*-og or *KOE*-hog] clams mixed with minced bell peppers and bread crumbs, and packed into both halves of the shell for baking). A highly satisfying lunch is the chock-full lobster roll, which comes with Quahog chowder and fritters for $14, a bona fide bargain. The most expensive item on the four-page menu is a seafood plate with clams, scallops, fish, shrimp, and fries. Everyone here knows everyone else, filling the place with joshing and laughter.

On the Little Compton Commons. ℂ **401/635-4388.** Main courses $6.95–$16. No credit cards. Daily 5am–6pm (Fri–Sat until 7pm).

---

3 Newport ⋆⋆⋆

75 miles S of Boston; 115 miles NE of New Haven

"City by the Sea" is the singularly unimaginative nickname an early resident unloaded on Newport. At least it was accurate, because for a time during the colonial period it rivaled Boston and even New York as a center of New World trade and prosperity. Newport occupies the southern tip of Aquidneck Island in Narragansett Bay, and is connected to the mainland by three bridges and a ferry.

Wealthy industrialists, railroad tycoons, coal magnates, financiers, and robber barons were drawn to the area in the 19th century, especially between the Civil War and World War I. They bought up property at the ocean's rim to build what they called summer "cottages"—which were in fact mansions of immoderate design and proportions patterned after European palaces.

The principal toys of the Newport elite were equally extravagant yachts meant for pleasure, not commerce, and competition among them established Newport's reputation as a sailing center. In 1851, the schooner *America* defeated a British boat in a race around the Isle of Wight. The prize trophy became known as the America's Cup, which remained in the possession of the New York Yacht Club (with an outpost in Newport) until 1983. In that shocking summer, *Australia II* snatched the Cup away from *Liberty* in the last race of a four-out-of-seven series. An American team regained the cup in 1987, but in 1995 a New Zealand crew won it back. The strong U.S. yachting tradition has endured despite the loss of the Cup, and Newport continues as a bastion of world sailing and a destination for long-distance races.

The perimeter of the city resembles a heeled boot, its toe pointing west, not unlike Italy. About where the laces of the boot would be is the downtown business and residential district. Several wharves push into the bay, providing support and

ACCOMMODATIONS ■
Abigail Sherman Inn **4**
La Farge Perry House **1**
Francis Malbone House **12**
Mill Street Inn **8**
Turner Inn **9**
Vanderbilt Hall **5**
The Viking **7**

See the "Greater Newport" map for additional accommodations.

DINING ◆
Asterix **15**
Black Pearl **11**
Bouchard **14**
Brick Alley Pub **6**
Clarke Cooke House **10**
Salvation Café **2**
Scales & Shells **13**
White Horse Tavern **3**

a lodging-availability service, a cafe, a souvenir stand, restrooms, and panoramic photos showing the locations of mansions, parks, and other landmarks. The building is shared with the bus station.

PARKING & GETTING AROUND   Most of Newport's attractions, except for the mansions, can be reached on foot, so leaving your car at your hotel or inn is wise. Parking lots aren't cheap, especially at the waterfront, and many streets are narrow. The metered parking along Thames Street is closely monitored by police, and fines are steep (although in the off season, the meters are hooded and parking is free for up to 3 hr.). Renting or bringing a bicycle is an attractive option.

The **Rhode Island Public Transit Authority,** or **RIPTA** (© 401/781-9400), has a free shuttle bus that follows a roughly circular route through town, making stops at major sights.

SPECIAL EVENTS   Arrive any day in summer and expect to find at least a half dozen festivals, competitions, or other events in progress. Following is only a partial list. (Call ahead to confirm dates: © **800/263-4636** outside R.I., or 401/848-2000 in R.I.).

While there are a few substantive events in the off season, notably **Christmas in Newport** (© 401/849-6454; www.christmasinnewport.org) and the **February Winter Festival** (© 888/976-5122; www.newportevents.com), which focuses on food and winter sports, the pace ratchets up in June, starting with the **Great Chowder Cook-Off** (© 401/846-1600; www.newportfestivals.com). In the third week of June, the gardens of the Point section of town are open to visitors during the **Secret Garden Tour** (© 401/847-0514; www.secretgardentour.com).

During 2 weeks in July, the **Newport Music Festival** (© 401/846-1133; www.newportmusic.org), offers classical concerts daily at various venues. In the third week is the **Black Ships Festival** (© 401/847-7666; www.newport events.com), a celebration of all aspects of Japanese culture.

August brings the **Apple & Eve Newport Folk Festival** (www.newport folk.com) and the **JVC Jazz Festival** (© 401/847-3700; www.festivalproductions.net), both held at Fort Adams State Park. Things wind down after Labor Day, though there's still the **Waterfront Irish Festival** (© 401/846-1600; www.newportfestivals.com) in early September and the **Bowen's Wharf Seafood Festival** (© 401/849-2120; www.bowenswharf.com) in the third week of October.

THE COTTAGES

That's what wealthy summer people called the almost unimaginably sumptuous mansions they built in Newport in the last decades before the 16th Amendment to the Constitution permitted an income tax.

Say this for the wealthy of the Gilded Age, many of whom obtained their fortunes by less than honorable means: They knew a good place to put down roots when they saw it. These are the same ones, after all, who developed Palm Beach in winter, the Hudson Valley in spring, the Berkshires in autumn, and Newport in summer, sweeping from house to luxurious house with the insouciance of a bejeweled matron dragging her sable down a grand staircase.

When driving or biking through the cottage district (walking its length is impractical for most people), consider the fact that most of these astonishing residences are still privately owned. That's almost as remarkable as the grounds and interiors of the nine that are open to the public.

Also, resolve to visit only one or two estates per day: The sheer opulence of the mansions can soon become numbing. Each residence requires 45 minutes to an hour for its guided tour. If at all possible, go during the week to avoid crowds and traffic.

Six of the mansions are maintained by the **Preservation Society of Newport County,** 424 Bellevue Ave. (© **401/847-1000;** www.newportmansions.org), which also operates the 1748 Hunter House, the 1860 Italianate Chepstow villa, the 1883 Isaac Bell House, and the Green Animals Topiary Gardens in Portsmouth. The Society sells a **combination ticket,** good for a year, to five of its properties; the cost is $31 for adults, $10 for children 6 to 17. Individual tickets for the Breakers are $15 for adults, $10 for children, while individual tickets for Kingscote, the Elms, Chateau-sur-mer, Marble House, Hunter House, and Rose-cliff are $10 for adults, $4 for children. They can be purchased at any of the properties. Credit cards are accepted at most, but not all, of the cottages. Special events, such as the festive Thanksgiving and Christmas celebrations, cost extra. The Society conducts an hour-long walking tour past the mansions, and the price includes a ticket to The Breakers and a second mansion of your choice. Tours are priced at $25 for adults and $9 for ages 6 to 17. Parking is free at all the Society properties.

The mansions that aren't operated by the Preservation Society but are open to the public are Belcourt Castle, Beechwood, and Rough Point.

During the winter, the mansions of the Society take turns each year staying open through the period, with an additional one or two openings on weekends. Following are descriptions of the cottages in the order in which they're encountered when driving south from Memorial Boulevard along Bellevue Avenue, then west on Ocean Drive.

Kingscote ⟨★⟩   This mansion (on the right side of the avenue) is a reminder that well-to-do Southern families often had second homes north of the Mason-Dixon line to avoid the sultry summers of the Deep South. Kingscote was built in 1841, nearly 40 years before the Gilded Age (usually regarded as the era between the end of the Civil War and the beginning of World War I). But it is considered one of the Newport Cottages because it was acquired in 1864 by the sea merchant William Henry King, who furnished it with porcelains and textiles accumulated in the China trade. Architect Richard Upjohn designed the mansion in the same Gothic Revival style he used for Trinity Church in New York. The firm of McKim, Mead & White was commissioned to design the 1881 dining room, notable for its Tiffany glass panels. As you drive down Bellevue, the Isaac Bell House is between Kingscote and the Elms.

Bowery St. (west of Bellevue Ave.). Late Mar–Apr Sat–Sun 10am–5pm; May to Columbus Day daily 10am–5pm. See above for admission details.

The Elms ⟨★★⟩   Architect Horace Trumbauer is said to have been inspired by the Château d'Asnieres outside Paris, and a first look at the ornate dining room of the Elms, suitable for at least a marquis, buttresses that claim. So do the sunken gardens, laid out and maintained in the formal French manner. The owner was a first-generation millionaire, a coal tycoon named Edward J. Berwind. His cottage was completed in 1901, and he filled it with Louis XIV and XV furniture as well as paintings and accessories true to the late 18th century. It was one of the first fully electrified mansions in Newport. Visitors can opt for a self-guided audio tour.

Bellevue Ave. Daily 10am–5pm. Closed Thanksgiving, Dec24–25. See above for admission details.

Chateau-sur-mer ⭐   William S. Wetmore was yet another merchant who made his fortune in the China trade. The entrance to this "Castle by the Sea" is on the left side of Bellevue, driving south. High Victorian in style, which means it drew from many inspirations (including Italian Renaissance and French Second Empire), the Chateau features a central atrium with a skylight and balconies at every level. A park designed in a style true to the period of the cottage has copper beech and weeping willow trees standing around its garden pavilion.

Bellevue Ave. Jan to mid-Apr Sat–Sun and holidays 10am–4pm; mid-Apr–Oct daily 10am–5pm. See above for admission details.

The Breakers ⭐⭐⭐   After Chateau-sur-mer, turn left on Ruggles Avenue, then left again on Ochre Point Avenue. The Breakers is on the right; a parking lot is on the left.

If you have time to see only one of the cottages, make it this one. Architect Richard Morris Hunt was commissioned to create this replica of a generic Florentine Renaissance palazzo, replacing a wood structure that burned down in 1892. He was unrestrained by cost considerations. The high iron entrance gates alone weigh over 7 tons. The 50-by-50-foot great hall has 50-foot-high ceilings, forming a giant cube, and is sheathed in marble. Such mind-numbing extravagance shouldn't really be surprising—Hunt's patron was, after all, Cornelius Vanderbilt II, grandson of railroad tycoon Commodore Vanderbilt.

Had Vanderbilt been European royalty, the Breakers would have provided motive for a peasant revolt. Vanderbilt's small family and their staff of 40 servants had 70 rooms in which to roam. The mansion's foundation is approximately the size of a football field, and the Breakers took nearly 3 years to build (1892–95). Platoons of artisans were imported from Europe to apply gold leaf, carve wood and marble, and provide mural-size baroque paintings. The furnishings on view are original. The bathrooms, far from common at the time, were provided with both fresh and salt running water, hot and cold.

Ochre Point Ave. (east of Bellevue Ave.). ✆ **401/847-1000.** Mid-Apr to Jan 1 daily 10am–5pm (until 6pm Fri–Sat in July–Aug); Nov 24 and Dec 1, 8, 15 and 29 also 6–8pm. See above for admission details.

Rosecliff ⭐   From the Breakers, return to Bellevue Avenue and turn left (south); Rosecliff is on the left. Stanford White thought the Grand Trianon of Louis XVI at Versailles a suitable model for this 1902 commission for the flamboyant Tessie Fair Oelrichs, heiress to the Comstock Lode. With a middling 40 rooms, it doesn't overwhelm, at least not on the scale of the Breakers. But it has the largest ballroom of all the cottages, not to mention a storied heart-shaped grand staircase. All this was made possible by one James Fair, an immigrant who made his fortune after he unearthed the thickest gold and silver vein in Nevada's Comstock Lode and bought this property for his daughters.

In 1941, the mansion and its contents were sold for $21,000. It was used as a setting for some scenes in the Robert Redford movie of Fitzgerald's *The Great Gatsby* (1974) and for a ballroom scene in Arnold Schwarzenegger's *True Lies* (1994). On a humid summer day, keep in mind that the mansion is air-conditioned.

Bellevue Ave. Mid-Apr to late Oct daily 10am–5pm. See above for admission details.

The Astors' Beechwood ⭐⭐   Mrs. William Backhouse Astor—*the* Mrs. Astor, as every brochure and guide feels compelled to observe—was, during her active life, the arbiter of exactly who constituted New York and Newport society.

"The 400" list of socially acceptable folk was influenced or perhaps even drawn up by her, and that roster bore meaning, in some quarters, well into the second half of the 20th century. Being invited to Beechwood was absolutely critical to a social pretender's sense of self-worth, and elaborate machinations were set in motion to achieve that goal.

Rebuilt in 1857 after a fire destroyed the original version, the mansion isn't as large or impressive as some of its neighbors. But unlike those managed by the Preservation Society, it provides a little theatrical pizzazz with a corps of actors who pretend to be friends, children, and servants of Mrs. Astor. In set pieces, they share details about life in the late Victorian era. Frequent special events are held, often replicating those that took place when she held court, including costume balls and specially decorated banquets with Victorian music and dancing.

580 Bellevue Ave. ⓒ 401/846-3772. www.astors-beechwood.com. Admission $10 adults, $8.50 seniors and children 6–12; $30 per family. Mid-May to early Nov daily 10am–5pm (tours every 20 min.); Christmas events Nov–Dec Wed–Sun; Feb to mid-May Fri–Sun 10am–4pm (tours every 30 min.). Closed Jan.

Marble House ★★★   Architect Richard Morris Hunt outdid himself for his clients William and Alva Vanderbilt. Several types of marble were used both outside and in, with a lavish hand that rivals the palaces of the Sun King, especially Le Petit Trianon at Versailles. It reaches its apogee in the ballroom, which is encrusted with three kinds of gold. It cost William $11 million to build and decorate Marble House, but Alva divorced him 4 years after the project was finished. She got the house, which she soon closed after marrying William's friend and neighbor. When her second husband died, Alva discovered the cause of female suffrage, and reopened Marble House in 1913 to hold a benefit for the campaign for women's right to vote. (Dishes in the scullery bear the legend "Votes for Women.")

Bellevue Ave. Mid-Apr to Jan 1 daily 10am–5pm (Fri–Sat until 6pm); Nov Sat–Sun 10am–4pm; Jan–Mar Sat–Sun and holidays 10am–4pm. See above for admission details.

Belcourt Castle ★★   This was the only slightly less grand mansion down the road from Marble House to which Alva Vanderbilt repaired after her second marriage. While the Vanderbilts were avid yachtsmen, her new husband, Oliver Hazard Perry Belmont, was a fanatical horseman. His 60-room house contained extensive stables on the ground floor where his beloved steeds slept under monogrammed blankets (the Belmonts were instrumental in building New York's famed Belmont Racetrack).

The castle, intended to resemble a European hunting lodge, has a ponderously masculine character, understandable in that it was designed for the bachelor Belmont before he won over vivacious Alva. It contains artifacts from the medieval era through the 19th century, including stained glass, Japanese and Chinese cabinetry, a full-size replica of a gaudy Portuguese coronation carriage, and French Renaissance furniture. Thomas Edison designed the lighting. There are 14 secret doors and a tunnel to the kitchens, which were located 2 blocks away for fear of fire.

The castle sold for a mere $25,000 in the early 1940s to the family of Harold B. Tinney, members of which still live here.

657 Bellevue Ave. (at Lakeview Ave.). ⓒ 401/846-0669. Admission $10 adults, $8 seniors and college students, $7 children 13–18, $3.50 children 6–12. Feb–May Sat–Sun and holidays 10am–3pm; Memorial Day to mid-Oct daily 9:30am–4:30pm; mid-Oct to Nov daily 10am–4pm; Dec (special tours) 10am–3pm. Closed Jan.

Rough Point ★★   The fabled 1887 Gothic-Tudor home of the late tobacco heiress Doris Duke made its long-awaited opening in 2000. Only a portion of it 105 rooms are currently open for viewing, and by only 96 visitors per day. They may be greeted by Chairman Mao, the last of Duke's many pets. The heiress's collections include a wealth of Ming-dynasty vases, Flemish and French tapestries, and paintings by Van Dyck and Gainsborough. Watch for the ivory inset side tables bearing the marks of Catherine the Great in what is called the Yellow Room.

While those who knew her reject suggestions that Duke was reclusive or troubled, hers was, at the least, an often darkly eventful life. It was here at Rough Point in 1967 that the story of the tobacco heiress and her interior decorator/companion unfolded. Eduardo Tirella was killed after being crushed against the iron entrance gates by Duke's station wagon. Duke later claimed that Tirella had gotten out of the car to open the gates when she accidentally hit the accelerator. The police chief declared it "an unfortunate accident," but local tongues wagged.

Duke died in 1993, bequeathing Rough Point to the Newport Restoration Foundation, along with all clothing, jewelry, and furniture in the house. To get here from Belcourt Castle, continue south on Bellevue. Rough Point is on the left, just before a sharp turn west along what becomes Ocean Drive. Individual visits aren't allowed. The only source for tickets is the Newport Gateway Visitor Center, where parking is also available (there is no parking at the mansion). Minibuses shuttle visitors to Rough Point every 20 minutes between 10am and 3:20pm; tours are limited to 12 people each and take about 60 minutes.

Bellevue Ave. Ⓒ 401/849-7300. www.newportrestoration.org. Admission $25. Visits by guided tour only; mid-Apr to early Nov Tues–Sat.

ADDITIONAL ATTRACTIONS

Historic Hill is the large district of colonial Newport that rises from America's Cup Avenue, along the waterfront, to Bellevue Avenue, the beginning of Victorian Newport. **Spring Street** ★ serves as the Hill's main drag, and it's a treasure trove of colonial, Georgian, and Federal structures. Chief among its visual delights is the 1725 **Trinity Church** ★, at the corner of Church Street. Said to have been influenced by the work of the legendary British architect Christopher Wren, it certainly reflects that inspiration in its belfry and distinctive spire, seen from all over downtown Newport and dominating Queen Anne Square, a greensward that runs down to the waterfront.

Hammersmith Farm   Built for John W. Auchincloss in 1887, this shingled Victorian mansion was used for the wedding reception of Jacqueline Bouvier (whose mother was married to an Auchincloss), in 1953. It subsequently became the unofficial summer White House of the short Kennedy presidency. Hammersmith was sold in 1997 for over $6.6 million to a Chicago businessman who sold it again 2 years later, and it is no longer open to the public. The house can still be seen from the road, however.

Ocean Dr. (past Castle Hill Ave.).

Hunter House ★   Another property of the Preservation Society, this 1754 Georgian colonial is one of the most impressive dwellings in the neighborhood known as the Point, north of downtown. Above the doorway is a carved wooden pineapple. This symbol of welcome derived from the practice of placing a real pineapple at the door to announce that the sea-captain owner had returned from his long voyage and was ready to receive guests. The interior displays furniture crafted by Newport's famed 18th-century cabinetmakers, Townsend and Goddard.

54 Washington St. (at Elm St.). © **401/847-1000**. See "The Cottages," above, for admission details. Late May to early Oct daily 10am–5pm.

International Tennis Hall of Fame   On Bellevue Avenue, there was (and is) an exclusive men's club called the Newport Reading Room. One member was James Gordon Bennett, Jr., the wealthy publisher of the *New York Herald*. He persuaded a friend to ride a horse into the club. The outraged members reprimanded Bennett, who had an instant snit that they hadn't enjoyed his little jest. He went right out and bought a property on the other side of Memorial Boulevard, and ordered a structure built for his own social and sports club.

McKim, Mead & White produced a shingle-style edifice of lavish proportions, with turrets and verandas and an interior piazza for lawn games, equestrian shows, and a new game called tennis. It is now given to a permanent grass court. As Bennett hoped, his Newport Casino swiftly became the premier gathering place of his privileged compatriots.

Now the pavilion hosts professional tournaments, and its courts are open to the public for play (call ahead to make reservations between May–Oct). The building itself houses the Hall of Fame, of interest primarily to fans of the game. A restaurant (© **401/847-0418**) serves lunch, sunset dinners, and weekend brunch.

194 Bellevue Ave. (at Memorial Blvd.). © **800/457-1144** or 401/849-3990. www.tennisfame.org. Admission $8 adults, $6 seniors and students, $4 children 16 and under; $20 per family. Daily 9:30am–5pm (except during tournaments).

Museum of Newport History   Maintained by the Newport Historical Society, this museum is in the refurbished 1772 Brick Market (not to be confused with the nearby shopping mall Brick Marketplace). The architect was Peter Harrison, also responsible for the Touro Synagogue (see below). The museum houses boat models, marine charts, antique silverware, and a ship figurehead, and also features videos on Newport history.

127 Thames St. (at Touro St.). © **401/841-8770**. www.newporthistorical.org. Admission $5 adults, $4 seniors, $3 children 6–18. Apr–Oct Mon and Wed–Sat 10am–5pm, Sun 1–5pm; Nov–Mar Fri–Sat 10am–4pm, Sun 1–4pm.

Newport Art Museum   Across the avenue from Touro Park, this was the first Newport commission of Richard Morris Hunt, who went on to design many of the cottages along Bellevue Avenue. Unlike most of his later Newport houses, the 1862 main structure is in the Victorian stick style, a wood construction that had origins in earlier Carpenter Gothic. It now mounts art exhibitions and serves as a venue for concerts.

76 Bellevue Ave. (at Old Beach Rd.). © **401/848-8200**. Admission $6 adults, $5 seniors, $4 students, free for children under 5. Only a voluntary donation charged for entrance Sat 10am–noon. Memorial Day to Columbus Day Mon–Sat 10am–5pm, Sun noon–5pm; Columbus Day to Memorial Day Mon–Tues and Thurs–Sat 10am–4pm, Sun noon–4pm.

Touro Park   Opposite the Newport Art Museum, this small park provides a shaded respite. At its center is the Old Stone Mill. Dreamers like to believe that its eight columns were erected by Vikings. Realists say it was built by Benedict Arnold, a governor of the colony long before his great-great-grandson committed his infamous act of treason during the War of American Independence.

Bellevue Ave. (between Pelham and Mill sts.).

Touro Synagogue   The oldest existing synagogue in the United States dates from 1763. A Sephardic Jewish community, largely refugees from Portugal, lived in Newport from the mid–17th century, over 100 years before this building was erected. It was designed by Peter Harrison, who was also responsible for the Brick Market (see Museum of Newport History, above). The synagogue was designated a National Historic Site in 1946.

Next door is the **Newport Historical Society,** 82 Touro St. (© **401/846-0813**), which features displays of colonial furnishings and sponsors walking tours (see "Organized Tours & Cruises," below).

85 Touro St. (Spring St.). © **401/847-4794.** Free admission. July 1 to Labor Day Sun–Fri 10am–5pm; Labor Day to June 30 Sun 11am–3pm, Mon–Fri 1–3pm; Nov 1–Apr 30 Sun 11am–3pm, Mon–Fri at 1pm (groups of 10 or more by appointment only). Guided tours only, beginning every half-hour; call for the current schedule.

OUTDOOR PURSUITS: THE BEACH & BEYOND

Fort Adams State Park, Harrison Avenue (© **401/841-0707**; www.fort adams.org), is on the thumb of land that partially encloses Newport Harbor. It can be seen from the downtown docks and reached by driving or biking south on Thames Street and west on Wellington Avenue (a section of Ocean Dr., which becomes Harrison Ave.). The sprawling 1820s fort for which the park is named is under restoration, work that can be viewed by guided tour. Admission is $6 for adults, $5 for seniors and ages 12 to 18, and $3 for ages 5 to 11. Boating, ocean swimming, fishing, and sailing are all possible in the park's 105 acres. Open from Memorial Day to Labor Day. Also on the grounds is the **Museum of Yachting** (© **401/847-1018**), housed in a stone barracks from the early 19th century. Open from mid-May to October daily from 10am to 5pm, by appointment the rest of the year. Admission is $5 for adults, $4 for seniors and children under 12.

Farther along Ocean Drive, past Hammersmith Farm, is **Brenton Point State Park** 🎀🎀, a scenic preserve that borders the Atlantic, with nothing to impede the waves rolling in and collapsing on the rock-strewn beach. Scuba divers are often seen surfacing offshore, anglers enjoy casting from the long breakwater, and on a windy day the sky is dotted with colorful kites.

There are other beaches more appropriate for swimming. The longest and most popular is **Easton's Beach** 🎀, which lies along Route 138A, the extension of Memorial Boulevard, east of town. There are plenty of facilities, including a bathhouse, eating places, picnic areas, lifeguards, a carousel, and the **Newport Aquarium** (© **401/849-8430**).

On Ocean Drive, less than 2 miles from the south end of Bellevue Avenue, is **Gooseberry Beach** 🎀, which is privately owned but open to the public. Parking costs $8 Monday through Friday, $12 Saturday and Sunday.

Cliff Walk 🎀🎀 skirts the edge of the southern section of town where most of the cottages were built, and provides better views of many of them than can be seen from the street. Traversing its length, high above the crashing surf, is more than a stroll but less than an arduous hike. For the full 3½-mile length, start at the access point near the intersection of Memorial Boulevard and Eustis Avenue. For a shorter walk, start at the Forty Steps, at the end of Narragansett Avenue, off Bellevue. Leave the walk at Ledge Road and return via Bellevue Avenue. Figure 2 to 3 hours for the round-trip, and be warned that there are some mildly rugged sections to negotiate, no facilities, and no phones. The walk is open from 9am to 9pm.

A new enterprise, the outdoor **Børn Family Skating Center,** is set up at the Newport Yachting Center, on America's Cup Avenue (© **401/846-1600**). An oval rink about 40 yards long, it's open from late October into March, depending upon weather. Skate rentals are available.

Biking is one of the best ways to get around town, especially out to the mansions and along **Ocean Drive** ★★. Among several rental shops are **Firehouse Bicycle,** 25 Mill St. (© **401/847-5700**); **Ten Speed Spokes,** 18 Elm St. (© **401/ 847-5609**); and **Scooters,** 411 Thames St. (© **401/619-0573**).

Adventure Sports Rentals, at the Inn on Long Wharf, 142 Long Wharf (© **401/849-4820**), rents not only bikes and mopeds, but also outboard boats, kayaks, and sailboats; parasailing outings can be arranged.

Guided fly-fishing trips and fly-casting instruction are offered by the **Saltwater Edge,** 561 Lower Thames St. (© **401/842-0062;** www.saltwateredge.com). Anglers are taken out on half- and full-day quests for yellowfin tuna, bluefish, striped bass, and white marlin.

ORGANIZED TOURS & CRUISES

Several organizations conduct tours of the mansions and the downtown historic district. Between May 15 and October 15, the **Newport Historical Society,** 82 Touro St. (© **401/846-0813**), offers two itineraries. Tours of Historic Hill leave on Thursday and Friday at 10am and tours of the Point on Saturday at 10am; each takes about 1½ hours. Tours of Cliff Walk leave on Saturday at 10am and take about 2 hours. Tickets cost $7 and can be purchased at the Society or at the Gateway Visitor Center (see "Visitor Information," earlier in this section).

Newport on Foot (© 401/846-5391) leaves the Gateway Visitor Center twice daily on 90-minute tours. Call for details and times. Tickets are $7 per person, free for children under 12.

Viking Tours, based at the Gateway Visitor Center, 23 America's Cup Ave. (© 401/847-6921), has narrated bus tours of the mansions and harbor cruises on the excursion boat *Viking Queen.* Bus tours—daily in summer, Saturdays from November to March—are 1½ to 4 hours and cost $20 to $42 for adults, $12 to $19 for children 5 to 11. Boat tours, from late May to early October, are 1 hour in length and cost $10 for adults, $8 for seniors, and $5 for kids. In July and August, the cruise can be extended to include a stop and tour of Fort Adams; $14 for adults, $13 for seniors, and $8 for children.

Classic Cruises of Newport ★, Bannister's Wharf, schedules narrated cruises on its 72-foot schooner *Madeleine* (© **401/847-0298**) and its classic powerboat *RumRunner II* (© **401/847-0299**). They're offered daily in summer, Saturdays and Sundays in spring and fall.

The *Spirit of Newport* ★, 2 Bowen's Wharf (© **401/849-3575**), offers 1½-hour cruises of the bay and harbor. Another possibility is the *Adirondack* ★, a 78-foot schooner that makes 2-hour cruises from the Newport Yachting Center (© **401/846-3018**). Its ticket booth is on America's Cup Avenue at Commercial Wharf; reservations must be made in advance.

The **Newport Touring Company,** 19 America's Cup Ave. (© **800/398-7427** or 401/841-8700; www.newportdinnertrain.com), features 90-minute round-trip excursions in vintage railroad trains along the edge of the bay. Fares are $15 for adults; kids 10 and under are free, but only one per paying adult; additional kids are charged $7.50. The company also has a **dinner train** that operates Thursdays through Saturdays, mid-April to mid-December. Variations include a rail-and-cruise luncheon, and cabaret and murder mystery dinners; with prices per person from $43 to $60.

SHOPPING

At the heart of the downtown waterfront, **Bannister's Wharf, Bowen's Wharf,** and **Brick Marketplace** have about 60 stores among them, few of them especially compelling.

More interesting, if only for their quirky individuality, are the shops along **Lower Thames Street.** For example, **J. T.'s Ship Chandlery** (no. 364) outfits recreational sailors with sea chests, ship lanterns, and foul-weather gear. **Aardvark Antiques** (no. 475) specializes in salvaged architectural components. Books, nautical charts, and sailing videos are offered at **Armchair Sailor** (no. 543); for vintage clothing, visit **Cabbage Rose** (no. 493).

Spring Street is noted for its antiques shops and purveyors of crafts, jewelry, and folk art. One of these is **MacDowell Pottery** (no. 140), a studio selling ceramics and gifts by Rhode Island artisans; the nearby **J.H. Breakell & Co.** (no. 132) is a good source for handcrafted jewelry. Antique boat models are displayed along with marine paintings and navigational instruments at **North Star Gallery** (no. 105). **The Drawing Room/The Zsolnay Store** (nos. 152–154) stocks estate furnishings and specializes in Hungarian Zsolnay ceramics. Folk art and furniture are the primary goods at **Liberty Tree** (no. 104).

Spring intersects with **Franklin Street,** which harbors even more antiques shops in its short length. **Newport China Trade Co.** (no. 8) deals in export porcelain and objects associated with 19th-century China. Take a fat wallet to the **John Gidley House** (no. 22) for European antiques of high order. **Patina** (no. 26) is another dealer in Americana and folk art.

WHERE TO STAY

The **Gateway Visitor Center** (© 800/976-5122 or 401/849-8040; www.go newport.com) lists vacancies in motels, hotels, and inns. Most can be called from free direct-line phones located nearby. Less impulsive travelers should reserve in advance, especially on weekends (2 months ahead for weekends from Memorial Day to Labor Day).

Newport Reservations (© 800/842-0102 or 401/842-0102; www.newport reservations.com) is a free service representing a number of hotels, motels, inns, and B&Bs. **Bed & Breakfast Newport, Ltd.** (© 800/800-8765 or 401/846-5408; www.bbnewport.com) claims to offer 350 choices of accommodation.

Many of the better motels are located in Middletown, about 2 miles north of downtown Newport. Possibilities include the **Courtyard by Marriott,** 9 Commerce Dr. (© 401/849-8000); **Newport Ramada Inn,** 936 W. Main Rd. (© 401/846-7600); **Newport Gateway Hotel,** 31 W. Main Rd. (© 401/847-2735); and **Howard Johnson,** 351 W. Main Rd. (© 401/849-2000). Newport itself has a **Marriott,** 25 America's Cup Ave. (© 401/849-1000).

The rates given below generally have very wide ranges depending upon seasonal demand, so a $200 room on weekends in July might be half that in spring. The summer season is usually defined as Memorial Day to Columbus Day, with lower prices in effect the rest of the year.

VERY EXPENSIVE

Castle Hill ⭐⭐ The setting—40 oceanfront acres on a near-island—is the overwhelming attraction of this venerable resort. But after sorely needed renovations of the 1874 Victorian mansion and its outbuildings, even a visit in foul weather is a treat. Best values are the Harbor Houses, which have been gutted and overhauled, with new furniture, Jacuzzis, and porches overlooking the bay.

The handsome taproom offers a riveting view (shared by the dining areas, deck, and many of the bedrooms) of sailing ships on Narragansett Bay. Breakfast buffets are expansive, and dinners in the several dining rooms and on the terrace are among the most accomplished and expensive in Newport. The Inn is completely nonsmoking, and pagers and cellphones are verboten in the restaurant.

590 Ocean Dr., Newport, RI 02840. ℂ 888/466-1355 or 401/849-3800. Fax 401/849-3838. www.castle hillinn.com. 27 units. Summer $395–$450 double, from$750 suite; fall–spring $145–$350 double, from $450 suite. Rates include breakfast and afternoon tea. AE, DISC, MC, V. Open weekends only Nov–Apr. Closed Jan. Children under 12 not accepted in main house. **Amenities:** Restaurant (regional); bar; laundry; dry cleaning. *In room:* A/C, TV, hair dryer.

The Chanler ★★★   The innkeepers and hoteliers of Newport keep topping themselves, but it will be a long while before they can best what has been wrought here. A boutique hotel with only 20 units, the main structure dates from 1873. It stands above the northern end of the Cliff Walk, overlooking the surf that rolls through the bay and onto Eaton's Beach. Extensive and very costly renovations have brought the French Empire mansion and six outlying villas to a level of opulence they never knew. All rooms have DVD and CD players, gas fireplaces, two TVs (some are plasma), separate sitting areas, and, except for one suite, double Jacuzzis, supplemented by multi-nozzled shower stalls. Each is decorated to a different theme—Mediterranean, Renaissance, Tudor—but chairs, sofas, and mattresses are uniformly plush, deep, and all-but-impossible to leave. **Spiced Pear,** the restaurant, has received good to ecstatic reviews since its opening; Kobe beef, foie gras, lobster, and caviar figure prominently in the menu. There's a dining terrace in summer with live music, and a short, casual menu is served in the wood-cloaked bar. In peak season, there are about three staff members for every guest.

117 Memorial Blvd., Newport, RI 02840. ℂ 401/847-1300. wwwthechanler.com. 20 units. June–Oct $595–$1,095; Nov–May $295–$795. Rates include breakfast. AE, DC, MC, V. **Amenities:** Restaurant (Fusion); bar; concierge; access to nearby health club; in-room massage; dry cleaning; laundry. *In room:* A/C, TV/DVD, dataport, hair dryer, safe.

Cliffside Inn ★★★   Assuming that money is no object, this tops the list of inns in Newport. All units now have at least one working fireplace, and most have whirlpool baths. A new suite in the Seaview Cottage has a bathroom that has to be seen: The tub features both standard and hand-held showerheads, eight spray nozzles, and a built-in TV and CD player! Antiques are generously deployed, including Eastlake and Tiffany originals and Victorian fancies that include (in room 11) an amusing "bird cage" shower from 1890. A favorite unit is the Garden Suite, a duplex with private garden and big double bathroom with radiant heat beneath the Peruvian tile floors. Coffee, juice, and the newspaper of your choice are delivered to your room even before the full breakfast. From May to October, there is a room surcharge of $50 on weekends, as well as winter holiday weekends. Smoking isn't allowed in the inn.

2 Seaview Ave. (near Cliff Ave.), Newport, RI 02840. ℂ 800/845-1811 or 401/847-1811. Fax 401/848-5850. www.cliffsideinn.com. 16 units. $235–$385 double; from $355 suite. Rates include breakfast and afternoon tea. AE, DISC, MC, V. No children under 13. **Amenities:** Limited room service; laundry; same-day dry cleaning. *In room:* A/C, TV/VCR, dataport, hair dryer, iron.

Francis Malbone House ★★   A few years ago, nine modern rooms were added in a wing attached to the original 1760 colonial house. They are very nice, with king-size beds and excellent reproductions of period furniture. Four of them share two sunken gardens, and three have Jacuzzi tubs built for two. But given a choice, take a room in the old section, where antiques outnumber repros, Oriental rugs adorn buffed wide-board floors, and silks and linens are deployed unsparingly. All but two units enjoy gas fireplaces. The most interesting parts of the waterfront are right outside the door. No smoking.

392 Thames St. (east of Memorial Blvd.), Newport, RI 02840. ✆ **800/846-0392** or 401/846-0392. Fax 401/848-5956. www.malbone.com. 18 units. Apr–Oct $245–$345 double, from $395 suite; Nov–Mar $99–$260 double, from $200 suite. Midweek discounts available. Rates include breakfast and afternoon tea. AE, MC, V. No children under 12. *In room:* A/C, TV/VCR, CD player, dataport, hair dryer, iron.

Hyatt Regency Newport ✿   More than 25 years old, the Hyatt is notable for its complete roster of hotel services, its location on an island at the northern end of Newport Harbor, and its full-service spa. You might expect such a place to be impersonal, but the staff endeavors to be pleasant. There are delightful views of the harbor and town from the restaurant and most of the guest rooms. No pets.

1 Goat Island, Newport, RI 02840. ✆ **800/233-1234** or 401/851-1234. Fax 401/846-7210. www.hyatt.com. 264 units. Summer $290–$365 double; winter $99–$225 double. Parking $12. AE, DC, DISC, MC, V. Valet parking $9. **Amenities:** 2 restaurants (American, regional); bar; indoor freshwater and outdoor saltwater pools; 2 tennis courts; well-equipped health club and spa; concierge; airport courtesy van; business center; limited room service; massage; babysitting; same-day laundry; dry cleaning. *In room:* A/C, TV w/pay movies, dataport, coffeemaker, hair dryer, iron.

La Farge Perry House ✿✿   The first thing you're likely to notice upon entering this 1852 Federal-style home is the pristine standard of housekeeping, and immediately after, the muted elegance of the superb furnishings. Crystal chandeliers, plush fabrics, and nautical artifacts fill both public and private rooms. That isn't to imply early-19th-century austerity: Unlike many of Newport's lesser B&Bs, no sacrifices in new-millennium conveniences are made. All units are suites with poster or sleigh beds; two have double Jacuzzis and one has a fireplace. The lavish breakfasts are memorable. Weekday discounts are often available, starting at $175. No smoking, no pets, and no children under 12.

24 Kay St. (at Bull St.), Newport, RI 02840. ✆ **877/736-1100** or 401/847-2223. www.lafargeperry.com. 5 units. May–Oct $300–$350 suite; Nov–Apr $245–$300 suite. Rates include full breakfast. AE, MC, V. No children under 12. *In room:* A/C, TV/VCR, dataport, fridge, hair dryer.

Vanderbilt Hall ✿✿   After its $11-million renovation, this 1908 Georgian Revival manse gives no hint of its last use as a YMCA (1915–1968). Built with a donation by Alfred Vanderbilt, it would now suit its benefactor as one of his own residences. Public rooms contain antiques and paintings. Bedrooms have armoires, fabrics with period patterns, and, in the older wing, 18-foot ceilings. Rosenthal crystal and Wedgwood china set the tone in the acclaimed **Alva Restaurant,** which calls its food "Creative American." All meals are served there, including inventive twists on chicken potpie and macaroni and cheese. Upgrading continues, with a new martini (and single-malt scotch) bar. You'll be reminded to watch the sunset from the rooftop deck.

41 Mary St. (west of Bellevue), Newport, RI 02840. ✆ **401/846-6200.** Fax 401/846-0701. www.vanderbilt hall.com. 52 units. Spring–summer $295–$550 double, from $600 suite; fall–winter about 40% lower. Rates include afternoon tea. Midweek discounts available. AE, DC, DISC, MC, V. No children under 12. **Amenities:** 2 restaurants (New American); bar; indoor pool; small fitness room with Jacuzzi and sauna; billiards room. *In room:* A/C, TV, dataport, hair dryer.

EXPENSIVE

Abigail Sherman Inn ✿✿   The latest property of the company that also operates the Cliffside Inn (above) and Adele Turner Inn (below), this inn, the smallest of the group, displays trademark fixtures and services of its siblings. These include exquisite decor, marble baths with double Jacuzzis in every room, pre-breakfast room delivery of juice, coffee, and newspaper of your choice, and extraordinary afternoon teas with scones, cakes, and finger sandwiches. But it has its own distinctive touches, too. There is a bar set up like a little pub . . . for designer waters. An intimate room where couples can have tea for just two. And the level of sensuality has been amped up. Separate menus list long rosters of soaps and bath products, dozens of teas, and over 20 different kinds of pillows to add or replace the several all on the bed. In sum, guests who can't relax here need medical help.

A surcharge of $50 applies on weekends and holiday Sundays from May 1 through October. No children under 13, no pets, and no smoking.

102 Touro St., Newport, RI 02840. ⓒ 800/845-1811. www.legendaryinnsofnewport.com. 5 units. $355–$575 double. Rates include breakfast and afternoon tea. AE, DC, DISC, MC, V. **Amenities:** Concierge, limited room service, same-day dry cleaning/laundry. *In room:* A/C, TV/VCR/CD, dataport, hair dryer.

Adele Turner Inn ★★   The 1855 Admiral Benbow Inn was transformed into this sister property of the estimable Cliffside (see above). That meant that sur-roundings and services took an instant upward turn. While it is unlikely that the Adele Turner will ever match its sibling virtue for virtue—its rooms are smaller, for one thing—it comes close enough to merit this high recommendation. And in one area, it is preferable: Once you are here, most of the downtown attrac-tions are within walking distance. Old fireplaces have been restored and new ones installed, and all rooms have one. Some of the units have hot tubs. Full breakfasts and afternoon teas are nothing less than sumptuous. Room rates are $50 higher on weekends from May to October.

93 Pelham St., Newport, RI 02840. ⓒ **800/845-1811** or 401/857-1811. Fax 401/848-5850. www.adeleturner inn.com. 13 units. $185–$335 double, from $315 suite. Rates include breakfast and afternoon tea. AE, DC, MC, V. **Amenities:** Concierge; limited room service; same-day dry cleaning/laundry; free video library. *In room:* A/C, TV/VCR, hair dryer.

MODERATE

Mill Street Inn ★   Something different from most Newport inns, this 19th-century sawmill was scooped out and rebuilt from the walls in. Apart from exposed expanses of brick and an occasional wood beam, all of it is new. An all-suite facility, even the smallest unit has a queen-size bed and a sofa bed. The duplexes have private balconies, but everyone can use the rooftop decks, where breakfast is served on warm days. The inn is smoke-free.

75 Mill St. (2 blocks east of Thames), Newport, RI 02840. ⓒ **800/392-1316** or 401/849-9500. Fax 401/848-5131. www.millstreetinn.com. 23 units. June–Sept $125–$345 suite; Oct–May $65–$265 suite. Rates include breakfast and afternoon tea. Packages available. Children under 16 stay free in parent's room. Packages available. AE, DC, MC, V. Free adjacent parking. **Amenities:** Access to nearby health club; dry clean-ing. *In room:* A/C, TV w/pay movies, dataport, minibar, hair dryer, safe.

The Viking   On the Newport scene since 1926, this neo-Georgian sprawl of a hotel was built to accommodate the summer guests of Newport's wealthiest fami-lies. Today, its assets outnumber deficiencies, although it poses no challenge to Cas-tle Hill or the Chanler, described above. On the plus side, it is cheaper than its rivals, has a modest new fitness room and spa, an indoor pool, a good location, and a pleasant, if sometimes distracted, staff. On the other, its bland Reagan-era fur-nishings and fixtures don't allow for many extras—no VCRs and only 11 channels on the TV. The rooftop bar with views of the harbor is an outstanding feature.

1 Bellevue Ave., Newport, RI 02840. ⓒ 800/556-7126 or 401/847-3300. www.hotelviking.com. 237 units. June–Oct $189–$269; Nov–Mar $99–$119; Apr–May $129–$149 double. Packages available. AE, DC, DISC, MC, V. **Amenities:** Restaurant (Regional); bar; health club and spa; limited room service; laundry/dry cleaning. *In room:* A/C, TV, dataport, hair dryer.

WHERE TO DINE

There are far too many restaurants in Newport to give full treatment even to the best among them. Equal in many ways to those recommended below are **Canfield House,** 5 Memorial Blvd. (ⓒ 401/847-0416); **Yesterday's & the Place,** 28 Washington Sq. (ⓒ 401/847-0116); **The Bistro,** 41 Bowen's Wharf (ⓒ 401/ 849-7778); and **The West Deck,** 1 Waites Wharf (ⓒ 401/847-3610). And for pure bargain dining in pricey Newport, the bountiful pastas of **Salas,** 343 Thames St. (ⓒ 401/845-8772), are a perfect choice for hungry families.

Winter hours and days of operations vary considerably. Call ahead to avoid disappointment.

EXPENSIVE

Asterix ⭐⭐ CONTEMPORARY FRENCH   Named for a famous French cartoon character for no obvious reason, this cheerful place does render classic Gallic bistro dishes. Come and remember how delectable a near-perfect roast herbed chicken or sole meunière can be. To add a note of Lyonnaise authenticity, bluepoints, Wellfleets, and littlenecks are opened to order as starters. Daily specials are considerably more venturesome. A short bar menu lists sandwiches, pizzas, and pastas. What was once a car-repair shop has been given splashes of color, with an open kitchen in back. Sunday dinners are served to live jazz from 7pm. Excellent breads are provided by the chef/owner's **Boulangerie,** 382 Spring St. (ⓒ 401/846-3377).

599 Lower Thames St. ⓒ 401/841-8833. Reservations recommended on summer weekends. Main courses $18–$32. MC, V. Daily 5–10pm (Sat–Sun until 11pm).

Black Pearl ⭐ SEAFOOD/AMERICAN   This long building near the end of the wharf has you covered. The main building is divided into two sections. The Tavern contains an atmospheric bar and a room with marine charts on the walls. The pricier Commodore's Room is more formal, with linens and candles. In either setting, most of the preparations of fish, duck, and beef are familiar but of good quality, with an occasional lurch in exotic directions, such as ostrich steak. In the popular Tavern, don't miss the definitive Newport chowder, followed by a Pearlburger or one of the other overstuffed sandwiches. In summer, the menu is similar at the patio and open-air bar on the wharf, and there is a separate "Hot Dog Clam Chowder Annex."

30 Bannister's Wharf. ⓒ 401/846-5264. Reservations and jackets for men required for dinner in Commodore's Room. Main courses $15–$25 in Tavern, $18–$30 in Commodore's Room. AE, MC, V. Tavern daily 11:30am–1am; Commodore daily 11:30am–3pm and 6–10pm. Closed Jan and 1st 2 weeks in Feb.

Bouchard ⭐⭐ CREATIVE FRENCH   Settle in for the evening on comfortable Empire chairs, while an efficient waiter takes your coat and your cocktail order. It's a polished performance, under the alert eye of the hostess, and what issues from the kitchen validates that promise. Presentations are thoughtfully conceived, attractive without voguish excesses—no heavily embellished towers of food as high as your chin. Here comes roasted wild boar redolent with a peppery currant sauce or sautéed scallops with a delicate red wine and truffle butter sauce. You are asked when you place your order if you'll be having the Grand Marnier soufflé. If you do, you won't regret it. This is dining in a grand tradition. The only silly affectation is menu prices written out, as "Twenty Six dollars."

505 Lower Thames St. ✆ 401/846-0123. Reservations recommended in high season. Main courses $24–$34. AE, DISC, MC, V. Wed–Mon 6–9pm (Sat–Sun until 10pm). Closed 1st 2 weeks in Jan.

Clarke Cooke House ★★★ ECLECTIC For many, this is the quintessential Newport restaurant. The picturesque 19th-century structure was moved to the wharf from America's Cup Avenue in the 1970s. Most of its several levels are open to the air in summer and glassed-in in winter. Several bars lubricate conversation. Up on the formal third floor, the staff sautés your lobster out of the shell while you put away such appetizers as stuffed zucchini blossoms, perhaps moving on to a rack of lamb *persillade* with minted tarragon glaze. If that seems too rich, spare the walk upstairs and stop in at the Grille, which wraps around a fireplace and center bar. Opt, if possible, for the braised lamb shank with black trumpet mushrooms and squash risotto. The main floor, called the Candy Store, serves snacks, sandwiches, and drinks, and below that is the Boom Boom Room, with dancing on weekends from 9pm to whenever. No smoking, and no cellphones in the dining areas.

Bannister's Wharf. ✆ 401/849-2900. Reservations recommended on summer weekends. Main courses $14–$40 in Candy Store and Grille, $28–$44 in the Porch. AE, DC, DISC, MC, V. Candy Store and Grille, summer daily 11:30am–10:30pm, winter Fri–Sun 11:30am–10:30pm; dining rooms, summer daily 6–10pm, winter Wed–Sun 6–10pm.

Twenty-Two Bowen's ★★ STEAKHOUSE On a wharf? Surrounded by water and fishing boats and unlimited tureens of clam chowder? Counter-intuitive though it might seem, that's where the owners of The Castle Hill Inn decided to open their unabashed beef emporium. They guessed right: It's been full since the first day, and unlike many of its competitors, busy enough to stay open straight through the winter. The three rooms and bar have the burnished dark wood and polished brass of an old-time yacht club. Patrons are of an age and apparent prosperity to be comfortable with the steep prices, and possessed of sufficient knowledge to make assured choices from the extensive wine list. Oysters from the raw bar are the preferable starters, light and briny before digging into a pound or two of perfectly charred prime sirloin or porterhouse. Thick veal and lamb chops are possible alternatives, and of course there are lobsters. They are alone on the plate—sides are extra. Service is as professional as can be found in Newport.

22 Bowen's Wharf. ✆ 401/841-8884. Reservations advised for dinner and weekends. Main courses $22–$44. AE, DC, MC, V. Daily 11:30am–3:30pm and 5–10pm (Fri–Sat until 11pm).

White Horse Tavern ★ NEW AMERICAN Still going strong after almost 330 years, the White Horse makes a credible claim to be the oldest operating tavern in America. On the ground floor are a bar and two dining rooms, with a big fireplace once used for cooking. Given the setting, the kitchen could have chosen to coast on New England boiled dinners and Indian pudding. But the food is quite good, from the daily lunch specials to the spice-rubbed venison with pears poached with rosemary. About a third of the dishes involve seafood. Prices are significantly lower on the Tavern menu, available from 5pm Sunday through Thursday.

25 Marlborough St. (at Farewell). ✆ 401/849-3600. Reservations recommended, essential for dinner. Jackets required for men at dinner. Main courses $13–$25. AE, DC, DISC, MC, V. Mon–Fri 6–9pm, Sat–Sun noon–2:30pm and 6–9pm.

MODERATE

Brick Alley Pub ☆ ECLECTIC   Just so you know what you're getting into, the cab of a Chevy pickup truck is next to the soup-and-salad bar. It's loud and good-natured, Newport's favorite hangout. Families, tourists, working stiffs, and yachtsmen squeeze through the doors into the thronged dining rooms, the bar, and the terrace. The voluminous menu is pub grub squared: stuffed clams, Cajun catfish, nachos, burgers, pizzas, and squid-ink spaghetti with cream, scallops, and crabmeat. Entrees include salad or the soup/salad/bread buffet *plus* potatoes and vegetables.

140 Thames St. ℂ **401/849-6334.** Reservations recommended for dinner. Main courses $15–$22. AE, DISC, MC, V. Mon–Fri 11:30am–10pm (Fri until 11pm); Sat 11am–11pm; Sun 11am–10pm.

Salvation Café ☆ ECLECTIC   As funky-hip as Newport gets, this is a gathering place so popular to locals that the tourists who discover it are barely visible. A monster Gulf sign and amateurish oil paintings occupy the walls. The steel-topped bar is given primarily to diners, at least in the early evening hours. The stereo gets your attention, playing 1940s big bands or Tom Jones or Gene Autry, and the menu, too, hops and skips around the map. It plucks pad Thai here, *malai kofta* there, and the no-doubt tasty spinach and tofu concoction from a place not known. But unfocused though it might be, there's a lot of satisfying food to be had here. Linguine with chipotle shrimp gets a nod, as do pork vindaloo over lemon coconut rice and the meltingly tender flesh from long-braised short ribs topped with mole sauce. Truth to tell, though, most people probably wind up with the 10-ounce Salvation burger with bacon and cheddar.

140 Broadway. ℂ **401/847-2620.** Main courses $8.50–$20. AE, DC, MC, V. Mon–Thurs 5–10pm; Fri–Sat 5–11pm; Sun 10am–2:30pm and 5–10pm.

Scales & Shells ☆☆ SEAFOOD   That graceless name reflects the uncompromising character of this clangorous fish house. Diners who insist on a modicum of elegance should head for the upstairs room, called Upscales. Myriad fish and shellfish, listed on the blackboard, are offered in guileless preparations that allow the natural flavors to prevail. Substantial portions, too: The "large" appetizer of fried calamari is enough for four. Swordfish grilled over hardwood and topped with roasted sweet peppers is typical. Expect no meat or fowl, but there are some vegetarian pastas.

527 Lower Thames St. ℂ **401/846-3474** for main floor, 401/847-2000 for Upscales. Reservations recommended May–Sept. Main courses downstairs $11–$21, Upscales $16–$29. No credit cards. Sun–Thurs 5–10pm; Fri–Sat 5–11pm; Sun 4–10pm (slightly shorter hours in winter). Closed Mon Jan–May and from last week in Dec to 1st 2 weeks in Jan.

INEXPENSIVE

Flo's Clam Shack SEAFOOD   Located just past Easton's Beach over the Newport/Middletown line, this old-timer is more than a lopsided strand-side shanty—but not *much* more. Step up to the order window, choose from the handwritten menu, and receive a stone with a number painted on it. What you'll get, if you're wise, are clams, on a plate or on a roll. Cooked swiftly to order, they're as tender as any to which you might have set your teeth. This is the place, also, to sample "chowda" and that Rhode Island specialty, stuffies. The menu also suggests two hotdogs with a bottle of Moët for $50. Few patrons take that opportunity. Upstairs are a raw bar and deck even more happily ramshackle than below. Sundays feature live music from 2 to 6pm.

4 Wave Ave., Middletown, RI ℂ **401/847-8141.** Main courses $7.25–$12. No credit cards. Apr–Dec 11am–9pm. Closed Jan–Mar.

Jack & Josie NEW AMERICAN   Fun is on the menu at this quirky new corner spot, a sort of poolroom-luncheonette-sports-bar-Internet-cafe. Within the airy, well-lit space are five computer terminals ($10 per hour), three black-felt-covered pool tables, plasma TVs, and a free-form sofa defining the eating area, with several brushed aluminum tables. Food? Mostly soups, salads, and sandwiches, along with contemporary twists, as in the warm pear and goat cheese salad and "The Jack," thin slices of sirloin with carmelized onions, fig compote, and arugula saga blue cheese. But the dishy owner—who is neither Jack nor Josie, which are actually the names of her dogs—has added several entrees, including a quiche of the day, roasted pork tenderloin, meat loaf, and a roasted salmon filet wrapped in prosciutto. Bring your own wine or beer. She doesn't have a liquor license and doesn't intend to get one. Herbal teas, smoothies, and specialty coffee drinks are options. She doesn't allow smoking, either.

111 Broadway. ℂ 401/851-6900. Main courses $6.95–$10. AE, MC, V. Daily 10am–11pm (extended hours in summer). Closed 1 week in Mar.

NEWPORT AFTER DARK

The most likely places to spend an evening lie along **Thames Street.** One of the most obvious possibilities, **The Red Parrot,** 348 Thames St., near Memorial Boulevard (ℂ 401/847-3140), has the look of an Irish saloon and features jazz combos Thursday through Sunday. **One Pelham East** ⊛, at Thames and Pelham streets (ℂ 401/847-9460), has a cafe, a small dance floor, a pool table, and another bar upstairs, with mostly college-age patrons attending to rockers on the stage at front. Free pizza is served some evenings. **Park Place Tavern,** at Thames and Church streets (ℂ 401/847-1767), makes room for jazz duos Thursday through Sunday.

A full schedule of live music is on the plate at the **Newport Blues Café** ⊛, 286 Thames St., at Green Street (ℂ 401/841-5510), plus a Sunday gospel brunch. With its fireplace, dark wood, and massive steel back door that used to guard the safe of this former bank, the cafe has a lot more class than most of the town's bars. Meals are available nightly in summer, Thursday through Sunday nights off season. It might close for 2 or 3 months in winter.

The Garden, 206 Thames St. (ℂ 401/849-9300), has pool, foosball, and live rock 3 to 4 nights a week. Folk and rock duos play at **Sully's Pub,** 108 Williams St. (ℂ 401/849-4747), for under-35 singles more interested in each other than in the music. The pool table stays busy. Upstairs is **Señor Frog's,** with a DJ who spins indie rock 6 nights a week. **Mudville,** 8 W. Marlborough St. (ℂ 401/849-1408), is a bar for guys and the women who put up with them. A dozen TVs, including a couple of big-screen plasmas, are fed by both satellite and cable, insuring that no sporting event, anywhere, will be unavailable. A fireplace and fake Tiffany lamps constitute the decor.

Several restaurants occasionally offer music, as with the three-piece combo at Asterix, disco at the Clarke Cooke House's Boom Boom Room, and jazz, folk, and rock at the Rhode Island Quahog Company.

4 South County: From Wickford to Watch Hill

Narragansett: 32 miles SW of Providence; 14 miles W of Newport

Travelers rushing along the Boston–New York corridor inevitably choose I-95 to get from Providence to the Connecticut border. They either do not have the time for a detour or don't know that the nearby shore has some of the best beaches and most congenial fishing and resort villages of New England. This is called South County, a designation that has no official status, but refers to the coast that is the southerly edge of Bristol County. Bypassed by the inland I-95, it has escaped much of the commercial development that besets many parts of the New England coast.

Rhode Islanders certainly know about the beguilements of South County, though, so try to avoid weekends in July and August, when the crush of day-trippers can turn these two-lane roads into parking lots.

Definitions are fuzzy, but for our purposes, South County runs from Wickford, near Providence, to Westerly, nudging Connecticut. See the map on p. 411 to locate towns discussed in this section.

ESSENTIALS

GETTING THERE   To get to South County from Providence or Boston, take I-95 south, leaving it at Exit 9 to pick up Route 4, also a limited-access highway. In about 7 miles, exit onto Route 102 east, and you'll soon arrive in Wickford. From Newport, cross the Newport and Jamestown bridges on Route 138 to Route 1A north, and follow it to Wickford. Narragansett, at the center of South County's beach country, is 32 miles southwest of Providence and 14 miles west of Newport.

VISITOR INFORMATION   The attendants at the **tourist information office** (© **401/783-7121**), in the landmark Towers on Route 1A in Narragansett, can help visitors find lodging. Contact the **South County Tourism Council,** 4808 Tower Hill Rd., Wakefield (© **800/548-4662** or 401/789-4422; www.southcountyri.com), to request the useful brochure *South County Style.*

WICKFORD

Apart from those crowded summer weekends, a day or two in South County is as laid-back as an outing can be. There is nothing that can be regarded as a must-see sight, hardly any museums to speak of, and only a couple of historic houses to divert from serious cafe-sitting, sunbathing, and shopping—and these are the chief pursuits in Wickford, a tidy village that crowds the cusp of a compact harbor.

Sailors and fishermen, artists and craftspeople are among the residents, all of them evident within a block on either side of the **Brown Street** bridge that crosses the narrow neck of the waterway connecting Academy Cove with the harbor. Most of the shopping of interest clusters here, slipping over to adjoining **Main Street.**

One place that catches the eye is **Nautical Impressions,** 16 W. Main St. (© **401/294-7779**), a second-floor shop that features sextants, ships' bells, banded chests, and model yachts. On the ground floor, at the same street address, is **Seaport Tavern** (© **401/294-5771**). Its deck is just the spot for a snack, a light meal, or a glass of iced tea.

Proceed south on Route 1A, known through here as Boston Neck Road. About a mile south of Hamilton, watch for the side street on the right marked for the **Gilbert Stuart Birthplace,** 815 Gilbert Stuart Rd. (© **401/294-3001**). This may be the one historic homestead in South County that is worth a detour, and not because the painter famous for his portraits of George Washington was born here. Rather, it's the setting and the two preserved buildings that reward a visit. First is a weathered gristmill dating from the late 1600s; second, the Stuart birthplace, built over his father's snuff mill. Admission is $5 for adults, $2 for children 6 to 12; visits are by guided tour only between April and October, Thursday through Monday from 11am to 4pm.

Still on Route 1A, on the right, south of Saunderstown, is the **Casey Farm** (*©* **401/295-1030**). The working 300-acre farmstead is a handsome 18th-century complex of barns and houses. Free-range chickens hop along the carefully laid stone walls that section the fields. Visits are by guided tour. The farm is open from June 1 to October 15, Tuesday, Thursday, and Saturday from 1 to 5pm. Admission is $3 for adults, $1.50 for children 6 to 12.

NARRAGANSETT & THE BEACHES ★★

Continuing south on 1A from the Casey Farm, the pace quickens, at least from late spring to foliage season. After crossing the Narrow River Inlet, the road bends around toward **Narragansett Pier.** Along here and several miles on south to Port Judith and Jerusalem are some of the most desirable beaches in New England, with swaths of fine sand, relatively clean waters, and summer water temperatures that average about 70°F (21°C).

After a few blocks, Route 1A makes a sharp right turn (west), but stick to the shore, proceeding south on Ocean Road. Straight ahead is the **Towers,** a massive stone structure that spans the road between cylindrical towers with conical roofs. It is all that remains of the Gilded Age Narragansett Casino, designed by McKim, Mead & White, but lost in a 1900 fire. In the seaward tower is the Narragansett **tourist information office** (see "Essentials," above).

WHERE TO STAY

Village Inn ★   There are several inns and hotels in the vicinity, many of them looking out over the water across wide lawns. This is one of the largest and most obvious, a couple of blocks from the Towers. Despite the humble name, it is large and almost new, part of a complex that incorporates a cinema, a gas station, and a dozen shops. It has an oceanview deck, ready access to the beach, and modest resort facilities.

1 Beach St., Narragansett, RI 02882. *©* **800/843-7437** or 401/783-6767. Fax 401/782-2220. 61 units. Apr to mid-May $85–$120; mid-May to late June and early Sept to late Oct $110–$130; late June to Labor Day $131–$239. Packages available. Closed Nov–Mar. **Amenities:** Restaurant (Continental); bar; heated indoor pool with Jacuzzi. *In room:* A/C, TV, dataport, fridge, coffeemaker, hair dryer, iron, microwave.

WHERE TO DINE

Coast Guard House ★ SEAFOOD/AMERICAN   Adjacent to the Towers is this 1888 former Coast Guard headquarters, now a well-regarded restaurant that enjoys unobstructed views of the beach and breakers crashing a few feet below its windows. Despite the venue, the menu features as many meat dishes as seafood, but all are executed with a measure of sophistication. Seafood stew packs in lobster, fish, mussels, Italian sausage, kale, fennel, and potatoes in a tomato-saffron broth. Lobster comes steamed, broiled, or baked. There's another bar on the deck upstairs.

40 Ocean Rd. *©* **401/789-0700.** Main courses $16–$24. AE, DC, DISC, MC, V. Mon–Thurs 11:30am–3pm and 5–9pm; Fri–Sat 11:30am–3pm and 5–10pm; Sun 10am–2pm and 4–10pm (shorter hours in winter; call ahead). Closed Jan.

Spain ★★ SPANISH   South of Scarborough Beach, this restaurant is deservedly the most popular on this stretch of shore. Partly it's the congenial staff, partly the terraces overlooking the sea. But the greater share of credit goes to the stellar interpretations of the Spanish tapas tradition and such favorites as *paella Valenciana.* Authenticity doesn't head the list of the kitchen's concerns: The irresistible fried calamari are tossed with very un-Spanish hot peppers. Do sample the *espinacas a la Catalana*—spinach sautéed with garlic, raisins, and pine nuts. The nightly land rush suggests that an early arrival is wise.

1144 Ocean Rd. (✆ 401/783-9770. Reservations accepted only for parties of 6 or more. Main courses $13–$22. AE, DC, DISC, MC, V. Tues–Sat 4–10pm (Fri–Sat until 11pm); Sun 1–9pm.

FROM NARRAGANSETT TO POINT JUDITH

Follow scenic Ocean Road south from the Towers, soon arriving at **Scarborough State Beach** ★★. Noticeably well kept, with a row of pavilions for picnicking and changing, it has ample parking and surroundings unsullied by brash commercial enterprises. The beach is largely hard-packed sand. While it has a mild surf that makes it good for families with young children, sections of it are often also jammed with teenagers and college-age folks.

Continuing on Ocean Road to the end, you'll reach the **Point Judith Lighthouse,** 1460 Ocean Rd. (✆ **401/789-0444**). Built in 1816, the brick beacon is a photo op that can be approached but not entered.

GALILEE

Backtrack along Ocean Road, turning left on Route 108, then left again on Sand Hill Cove Road, past the dock of the only year-round ferries to Block Island, and into the Port of Galilee. At the end, past a cluster of restaurants beside the channel connecting Point Judith Pond with the ocean, is the **Salty Brine State Beach.** Though small, it is protected by a breakwater and is a good choice for families with younger children. On the opposite side of the channel is popular **East Matunuck State Beach,** where waves break upon the sand at an angle, producing enough action to permit decent surfing on some summer days.

To get a better sense of the area from the water, consider the 1¾-hour tour on the *Southland* (✆ **401/783-2954;** www.southlandcruises.com), which departs from State Pier in Galilee. Cruises are on Saturday and Sunday only from Memorial Day to mid-June and after Labor Day until mid-October; there are daily departures from mid-June to Labor Day. Prices are $12 to $14 for adults, $6 to $8 for children 4 to 12, free for ages 3 and under.

Numerous **party and charter boats** leave for fishing expeditions from Point Judith. Another possible excursion is a **whale-watching cruise** with the **Frances Fleet,** 2 State St., Point Judith (✆ **800/662-2824** or 401/783-4988; www.francesfleet.com). Cruises are made from July to Labor Day, Monday through Saturday from 1 to about 5:30pm. It isn't cheap, at $32 for adults and $20 for children under 12, but the sight of a monster humpback leaping from the water is unforgettable. Tuesdays and Fridays are "family days," when two parents and two kids under 12 cost $85.

WHERE TO DINE

Very similar in atmosphere, food, and situation, **Champlin's Seafood,** 256 Great Island (✆ **401/783-3152**), is an entirely acceptable alternative to George's of Galilee (below) and only a short walk away. Main courses are $9 to $17, and all food is made to order.

George's of Galilee SEAFOOD/AMERICAN   The impulse to drive as far as you can without winding up in the drink may account for part of the popularity of George's, in business for over 50 years. It can't be the food, which is unexceptional, despite the accolades of enthusiastic readers of regional magazines. Anyway, the decks serve as a good vantage point to watch the boat traffic in the channel. As for food, give the fried smelts, stuffies, fish and chips, and clam and cod cakes a thought, perhaps carrying them over to the picnic tables by the beach.

250 Sand Hill Cove Rd. (✆ 401/783-2306. Main courses $8.95–$30 (market prices for lobster). AE, DISC, MC, V. May–Oct daily noon–10pm; Nov–Apr Thurs–Sun noon–2:30pm and 6–9:30pm.

WATCH HILL ✴

Although much of Westerly township remains peacefully semi-rural, it contains more than a dozen villages, notably the peninsular resort of Watch Hill, and several contiguous public beaches on slender barrier islands enclosing large saltwater ponds.

A beautiful land's-end village that achieved its resort status during the post–Civil War period, Watch Hill has retained it ever since. It helped that it is the closest of South County's beach towns to New York. Many grand summer mansions and Queen Anne gingerbread houses remain from that time. The north side of the point occupied by the village is the harbor, packed with pleasure boats. Stretching from the eastern edge of Westerly township to the southwesternmost tip of the state at Watch Hill are **Dunes Park Beach** ✴ and **Atlantic Beach,** followed by **Misquamicut State Beach** ✴, a gathering place for large numbers of adolescents, and **Napatree Point Barrier Beach** ✴, a wildlife preserve notable for its white crescent beach. While you can enter the Napatree preserve for free, there are no facilities, a reason for its generally sparser crowds. All the beaches are noted for their fine-grained sand and swimming in gentle surf with slow drop-offs.

South of town on Watch Hill Road is the picturesque 1856 **Watch Hill Lighthouse,** open from 1 to 3pm Tuesday and Thursday. Back in town at the small **Watch Hill Beach,** younger kids get a kick out of the nearby **Flying Horse Carousel,** which dates to 1867. Only kids are allowed to ride; tickets are 50¢. The carousel is open daily from mid-June to early September. Parents will have to settle for the more than 50 boutiques that fill the commercial blocks.

To get to Watch Hill from Providence and points north, take Exit 1 off I-95, south on Route 3, which passes through Westerly and continues to Watch Hill. From Connecticut, take Exit 92 from I-95, going south briefly on Route 2, picking up Route 78 (the Westerly Bypass) down along Airport Road into Watch Hill. Free parking is extremely limited, so if you arrive after 8am, expect to pay up to $15 in the commercial lot behind the main street.

Amtrak trains from Boston and New York stop in Westerly several times daily. There is a pull-over **information office** on I-95 near the Connecticut border, and a **Chamber of Commerce** office at 74 Post Rd. in Westerly (✆ **800/ 732-7636**).

WHERE TO STAY

Pleasant View Inn ✴   Two miles east of Watch Hill, this is a small resort with a private strand that adjoins 4 miles of Misquamicut Beach. The front desk can arrange guaranteed tee times at a nearby course. Five categories of rooms are assigned, most of the better ones facing the ocean, with balconies; some have fridges and microwaves. The cheapest rooms overlook a parking lot.

65 Atlantic Inn, Westerly, RI 02891. (✆ 800/782-3224 or 401/348-8200. www.pvinn.com. 112 units. May–June and Sept–Oct $80–$155; July–Aug $140–$257. Closed Nov–Apr. Packages available. AE, MC, V. **Amenities:** 2 restaurants (American); bar; heated outdoor pool and Jacuzzi; fitness room with Jacuzzi and sauna; game room. *In room:* A/C, TV.

Shelter Harbor Inn ★★ If it's time to stop for the night, for dinner, or for a spectacular Sunday brunch (reservations essential), watch for the entrance to this venerable inn off U.S. 1, about 6 miles east of Westerly. Parts of the main building date to 1810, and a genteel tone prevails. Several bedrooms have fireplaces, decks, or both. A shuttle takes guests to the private beach a mile away. A cautiously creative restaurant and honored wine cellar round out the picture, sullied only by uneven service. The inn is more permissive than most: Children are welcome and smoking is allowed.

10 Wagner Rd., Westerly, RI 02891. ✆ 800/468-8883 or 401/322-8883. Fax 401/322-7907. www.shelter harborinn.com. 24 units. May–Oct $126–$176 double; Nov–Apr $92–$156 double. Rates include breakfast. AE, DC, DISC, MC, V. **Amenities:** Restaurant (Regional); bar; rooftop hot tub. *In room:* A/C, TV.

The Villa ★ A Dutch colonial manor with many Italianate overlays on Route 1A outside of town, the Villa is most often recommended for its extensive gardens and warm hospitality. All units are suites—three have Jacuzzi tubs built for two, and a couple have fireplaces. The breakfasts are continental during the week, but enhanced with hot dishes on weekends. Unlike most lodgings in the area, it is open all year. The inn is nonsmoking.

190 Shore Rd., Westerly, RI 02891. ✆ 800/722-9240 or 401/596-1054. Fax 401/596-6268. www.thevilla atwesterly.com. 6 units. Memorial Day to Columbus Day $140–$255 double; Columbus Day to Memorial Day $95–$195 double. Rates include breakfast. Packages available. AE, DISC, MC, V. **Amenities:** Outdoor pool with Jacuzzi. *In room:* A/C, TV/VCR/CD, fridge, coffeemaker, hair dryer.

Watch Hill Inn Savor sunsets from the veranda of this century-old clapboard lodge. Bedrooms are mostly of good size, with nothing special by way of decor, apart from the four-posters and occasional antiques. There's access to a beach. Meals are largely in the seafood-and-pasta tradition, but with superb views, taken in from the Grille Room and four decks.

38 Bay St., Watch Hill, RI 02891. ✆ 800/356-9314 or 401/348-6300. Fax 401/348-6301. www.watchhill inn.com. 16 units. Mid-June to early Sept $175–$275 double; Sept to mid-June $100–$185 double. Rates include breakfast. Packages available. MC, V. **Amenities:** Restaurant. *In room:* A/C, TV, dataport.

WHERE TO DINE

Additional dining options include the restaurants at the **Pleasant View Inn, Shelter Harbor Inn,** and **Watch Hill Inn** (see above).

Olympia Tea Room ★ NEW AMERICAN The genteel tone of Watch Hill is undergirded by the Olympia, long a favorite meet-and-eat retreat. This version of an even older restaurant opened in 1939, and long retained its soda fountains and wooden booths. The fountain is now a full bar, but the kitchen continues to crank out pretty imaginative food. If available, jump for the appetizer of plump, lightly fried oysters on wilted spinach and corn salsa. The stuffies and lobster rolls are as good as you're likely to enjoy in coastal New England.

74 Bay St. ✆ 401/348-8211. Reservations not accepted. Main courses $12–$28. AE, MC, V. June to Columbus Day daily 11am–10pm; mid-Oct to Nov and Apr–May Fri–Sun 11am–9pm. (Hours may vary; call ahead.) Closed Dec–Easter.

5 Block Island ★★

Viewed from above or on a map, Block Island looks like a pork chop with a big bite taken out of the middle. Only 7 miles long and 3 miles wide, it is edged with long stretches of beach lifting at points into dramatic bluffs. The interior is dimpled with undulating hills, only rarely reaching above 150 feet in elevation.

Block Island

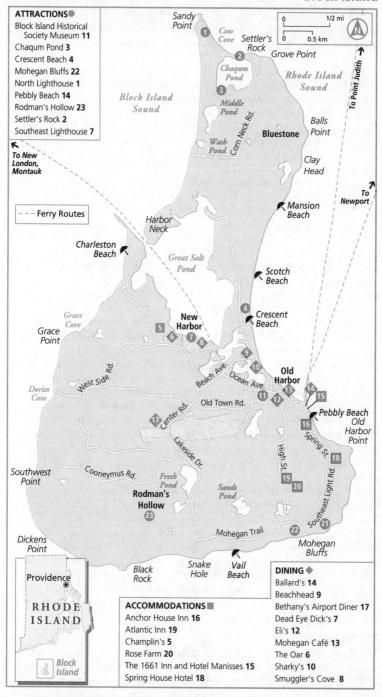

To Point Judith

0   1/2 mi
0   0.5 km

ATTRACTIONS
Block Island Historical
  Society Museum **11**
Chaqum Pond **3**
Crescent Beach **4**
Mohegan Bluffs **22**
North Lighthouse **1**
Pebbly Beach **14**
Rodman's Hollow **23**
Settler's Rock **2**
Southeast Lighthouse **7**

To New
London,
Montauk

--- **Ferry Routes**

To
Newport

Sandy
Point
Cow
Cove
Settler's
Rock
Grove Point

*Rhode Island
Sound*

*Chaqum
Pond*

*Block Island
Sound*

Middle
Pond

Balls
Point

Bluestone

Clay
Head

Wash
Pond

Corn Neck Rd.

Mansion
Beach

Harbor
Neck

Charleston
Beach

*Great Salt
Pond*

Scotch
Beach

Crescent
Beach

*Grace
Cove*

**New
Harbor**

Grace
Point

Beach Ave.   Ocean Ave.

**Old
Harbor**

*Dories
Cove*

West Side Rd.

Old Town Rd.

Pebbly Beach
Old
Harbor
Point

Center Rd.

Lakeside Dr.

High St.

Spring St.

Southeast Light Rd.

*Southwest
Point*

Cooneymus Rd.

*Fresh
Pond*

*Sands
Pond*

**Rodman's
Hollow**

*Dickens
Point*

Black
Rock

Snake
Hole

Vail
Beach

Mohegan Trail

Mohegan
Bluffs

DINING ◆
Ballard's **14**
Beachhead **9**
Bethany's Airport Diner **17**
Dead Eye Dick's **7**
Eli's **12**
Mohegan Café **13**
The Oar **6**
Sharky's **10**
Smuggler's Cove **8**

Providence

*RHODE
ISLAND*

*Block
Island*

ACCOMMODATIONS ■
Anchor House Inn **16**
Atlantic Inn **19**
Champlin's **5**
Rose Farm **20**
The 1661 Inn and Hotel Manisses **15**
Spring House Hotel **18**

Its hollows and clefts cradle over 300 sweet-water ponds, some no larger than a backyard swimming pool. That "bite" out of the western edge of the "chop" is **Great Salt Pond,** which almost succeeds in cutting the island in two, but, as it is, serves as a fine protected harbor for fleets of pleasure boats.

The only significant concentration of houses, businesses, hotels, and people is at **Old Harbor,** on the lower eastern shore, where the ferries from the mainland arrive and most of the remaining fishing boats moor.

Named for Adrian Block, a Dutch explorer who briefly stepped ashore in 1641, the island's earliest European settlement was in 1661, and it has since attracted the kinds of people who nurture fierce convictions of independence, fueled in part by the streaks of paranoia that lead them to live on a speck of land with no physical connection to the mainland. In the past, that has meant farmers, pirates, fishermen, smugglers, scavengers, and entrepreneurs, all of them willing to deal with the realities of isolation, lonely winters, and occasional killer hurricanes. Today, there are about 875 permanent residents of similar pluck and enterprise who tough it out 9 months a year waiting for the sun to stay awhile.

The challenges of island living aren't readily apparent to the tens of thousands of visitors who arrive every summer. They aren't likely to worry that the water supply is fragile or that generator-provided electricity is hugely expensive. Vacationers are wont to describe this as paradise—and they are correct, at least if sun and sea and zephyrs are paramount considerations. Those elements transformed the island from an offshore afterthought into an accessible summer retreat for the urban middle class after the Civil War, in America's first taste of mass tourism.

Unlike other such regions throughout the country that have lost their sprawling Victorian hotels to fire or demolition, Block Island has preserved many of its buildings from that time. They crowd around Old Harbor, providing most of the lodging base. Smaller inns and B&Bs add more tourist rooms, most in converted houses built at the same time as the great hotels. There are only a few establishments that even resemble motels, and building stock is marked, with few exceptions, by tasteful Yankee understatement. Despite the ominous presence of a few houses that resemble those plunked down in potato fields in ultra-chic precincts of New York's Long Island, development so far remains under control, and there are no franchised eateries or shops of any kind—not the place to have a Big Mac attack.

Away from the sand and surf, it is an island of peaceful pleasures and gentle observations. Police officers wear Bermuda shorts and ride bikes. Children tend lemonade stands in front of picket fences and low hedges. Clumps of hydrangeas tangle with beach roses and honeysuckle, hiding the foundations of saltboxes and Victorian farmhouses with shingles scoured gray by sea winds. There are no squirrels, chipmunks, possums, or raccoons on the Block, but the island is in the middle of a prominent flyway for migratory birds, and egrets, ducks, goldfinch, and kingfisher are seen in abundance. Deer were introduced about 30 years ago, to the islanders' current regret, bringing Lyme disease and an enthusiasm for turning flowerbeds into salad bars.

ESSENTIALS

GETTING THERE   The **Nelseco & Interstate Navigation Company,** New London, Conn. (© **401/783-4613;** www.blockislandferry.com), provides most of the surface service, including passenger-only ferries on daily triangular routes between Providence, Newport, and Block Island from late June to early September. Bicycles may be taken on board for a small fee. While reservations aren't required for passengers, get to the dock early, as the boats tend to fill up quickly.

Getting a car to Block Island is something of a hassle and considerably more expensive—at press time, $52.60 per vehicle round-trip in addition to fares of $16.80 per adult and $8.20 for each child under 12, or a total of $102.60 for a family of four. It can be assumed that these fares will continue to increase from year to year. Car ferries depart from the Port of Galilee at Point Judith, R.I. Apart from blacked-out days from Christmas to New Year's, there are daily departures year-round, as few as one or two a day in winter to as many as nine a day from early June to late August. Sailing time is about an hour. Drivers, be prepared: You are expected to *back* your car into the close quarters of the ferry's main deck.

The same company provides service from New London, Conn., daily from early June to Labor Day at 9am (extra trips at 7:15pm on Fri), with a return at 4:30pm. Sailing time is a little over 2 hours; round-trip passenger fare is $19.

Given the cost of taking a car, consider parking in one of the nearby long-term lots at Point Judith or New London. Block Island is small, rental bicycles and mopeds are readily available, there are cabs for longer distances, and most hotels and inns are within a few blocks of the docks. There are even car rental agencies on the island. If you intend to take a car anyway, understand that it's important to make ferry reservations well in advance—2 months isn't too early for weekend departures.

High-speed, passenger-only ferry service from Point Judith was inaugurated in 2001 by **Island Hi-Speed Ferry** (© 877/733-9425; www.islandhighspeed ferry.com). The boat is equipped with airline-style seating and a cash bar; it makes the trip in 30 minutes, putting in at Payne's Dock in New Harbor. Service is available from June 1 to September 3, with five to six departures each day. Round-trip fares are $26 for adults and $12 for children 4 to 12; reservations are recommended.

Finally, service is also provided between Block Island and Montauk, at the eastern end of New York's Long Island, by **Viking Star,** Montauk, N.Y. (© 516/668-5700). From late May to mid-October, there are daily departures at 9am, returning from Block Island at 4:30pm. Despite what the company might say, the trip usually takes over 2 hours, landing at Champlin's Marina in New Harbor. Only passengers and bicycles can be accommodated; parking is available in Montauk. Reservations aren't required, but arrive early to make sure you get onboard. Round-trip fare is $35.

Westerly State Airport, near the Connecticut border, is the base for over a dozen regular flights to and from Block Island by **New England Airlines** (© 800/243-2460, 401/596-2460 in Westerly, or 401/466-5881 on Block Island; www. block-island.com/nea). Flights depart hourly, taking 12 to 15 minutes; the round-trip fare is $69. Make advance reservations and allow for the possibility that not-infrequent coastal fogs or high winds will delay or cancel flights.

VISITOR INFORMATION   The **Block Island Chamber of Commerce** has a year-round information office at the ferry landing at Old Harbor (© 800/383-BIRI or 401/466-2474; www.blockislandinfo.com). Its knowledgeable attendants can answer questions and help visitors find lodging. In the same building are lockers and one of the island's few ATMs. A new building at Corn Neck Road and Ocean Avenue contains the only bank, which also has an ATM.

Most streets on Block Island have no house numbers, and some roads have no names. Leave your dog at home: Hotels, inns, and B&Bs won't accept them, they are banned from the beaches, and they are supposed to be leashed at all times.

GETTING AROUND   Cars are allowed on the island, but roads are narrow, winding, and without shoulders, and drivers must contend with runners and flocks of bicycles and mopeds. Unless your party includes people with mobility problems or small children, we recommend leaving your car on the mainland and joining the two-wheelers. If you'd like to rent a car after you arrive by boat or plane, **Block Island Bike & Car Rental,** on Ocean Avenue (© 401/466-2297), has offices near Payne's Dock and at the airport; reserve ahead. If you decide to bring your car to the island, top off the gas tank before rolling onto the ferry. There is only one rudimentary gas station, behind Sharkey's restaurant.

Rental bikes and mopeds are available at several shops and stands. Convenient sources near Old Harbor include **The Moped Man,** Water Street (© 401/466-5444), on the main business street, renting bikes as well as mopeds; **Old Harbor Bike Shop,** at the ferry dock (© 401/466-2029); and **Island Bike & Moped,** Chapel Street, behind the Harborside Inn (© 401/466-2700). Rates for bikes are typically $18 to $30 a day, less with widely available discount coupons. Moped rates vary, but are usually from $70 to $85 for half to full days. Bargaining often brings prices down, especially early in the week after the weekenders have left, or for 3 or more days. Keep in mind that mopeds aren't allowed on dirt roads, which provide access to many beaches.

Some inns also rent bicycles, so a possible plan is to take a taxi from the ferry or airport to your inn, drop off luggage, and get around by bike after that. Two such inns are the **Seacrest,** 207 High St. (© 401/466-2882), and **Rose Farm,** on Roslyn Road (© 401/466-2034), but inquire about rentals when making room reservations at other places as well.

EXPLORING THE ISLAND

Little on the island distracts from the central missions of sunning, cycling, hiking, lolling, and ingesting copious quantities of lobster, clams, chowder, and alcohol. There is no golf course, and the lone museum takes only about 20 minutes to cover. Add a couple of lighthouses, a wildlife refuge, and three topographical features of note, and that's about it, enough to provide destinations for a few leisurely bike trips. A driving tour of every site on that list takes no more than 2 hours.

A couple of miles south of Old Harbor on what starts out as Spring Street is the **Southeast Lighthouse** (© 401/466-5009). A tablet by the road claims that in 1590, the Manisseans, the Indians of Block Island, drove a war-party of 40 Mohegans over the bluffs. An undeniably appealing Victorian structure, built in 1874, the lighthouse's claim for attention lies primarily in the fact that it had to be moved 245 feet back from the eroding precipice a few years ago to save it. That was expensive, and now another $1 million is desperately needed for renovation. That the building was designated a National Historic Landmark in 1997 might help in fundraising. There's a free small exhibit on the ground floor, but the admission fee to the top is $5.

(Tips   A Note on Accommodations

If you arrive on Block Island without reservations, one approach to getting a bed for the night is to show up at an inn an hour or so after the last ferry has departed, when management will often lower quoted rates if rooms are still available.

Continuing along the same road, which goes through other names and soon makes a sharp right turn inland, watch for the left turn onto West Side Road. In a few hundred yards, pull over near the sign for **Rodman's Hollow,** a geological dent dug by a passing glacier. It's deeper than it looks, the bottom a few feet below sea level and laced with walking trails beneath a thick mantle of low trees. Much of what you see here is designated forever wild, for the Nature Conservancy has purchased about a third of the island's surface to protect it from development. A map of the 12-mile trail network can be purchased for $1.50 at the Chamber of Commerce building at the ferry landing.

From Old Harbor, proceed north on Corn Neck Road, skirting Crescent Beach, on the right. The paved road eventually ends at **Settler's Rock** ★★★, with a plaque naming the English pioneers who landed here in 1661. This is one of the loveliest spots on the island, with mirrored **Chaqum Pond** behind the Rock and a scimitar beach curving out to **North Lighthouse,** erected in 1867. In between is a **national wildlife refuge** that is of particular interest to birders. The lighthouse, best reached by foot along the rocky beach, is now an interpretive center of local ecology and history, open from July 5 to Labor Day daily from 10am to 4pm. Admission is $2.

Back in Old Harbor, the **Block Island Historical Society Museum,** Old Town Road and Ocean Avenue (© 401/466-2481), was an 1871 inn that now contains a miscellany of photos, ship models, and tools. Upstairs is a room set up to reflect the Victorian period.

There are beaches on Block Island to suit every taste. Immediately south of the Old Harbor, past the breakwater, is the northern end of **Pebbly Beach,** a section informally known as **Ballard's Beach** for the popular restaurant located there (see "Where To Dine," below). Crowded with sunbathers and swimmers, it is one of only two on the island with lifeguards. The surf is often rough. Drinks are served at your towel. North of Old Harbor, beyond the Surf Hotel, starts the 3-mile-long **Crescent Beach** (aka Frederick J. Benson Town Beach or simply Town Beach). The southern section, with a sandy bottom that stays shallow well out into the gentle surf, is known as **Kid Beach** because of its relative safety for children. Farther along is the main part, a broad strand served by a pavilion with a snack bar, bathrooms, and showers ($1). Chairs, umbrellas, and boogie boards can be rented. The surf is higher along here and rolls straight in; lifeguards are on duty. Continuing north, and with a small parking lot reached by a dirt road off Corn Neck Road, is **Scotch Beach.** Consider this grown-up and R-rated, dominated by young summer workers and residents. Still further north is **Mansion Beach,** with a dirt road of the same name leading in from Corn Neck Road. Somewhat more secluded, it is usually less crowded than the others. On the west side of the island, running south from the jetty that marks the entrance to New Harbor, is **Charlestown Beach.** Uncrowded and relatively tranquil during the day, it draws anglers from dusk and into the night surfcasting for striped bass.

Apart from sunbathing, the island's most popular pursuit is **bicycling.** The ferries allow visitors to bring their own bikes (for a small fee), but several local agencies rent bikes as well (see "Getting Around," above).

Parasailing has become popular here, and chutes can be seen lifting riders up to heights of 1,200 feet above the ocean. Call **Block Island Parasail** (© 401/864-2474) with questions, but you must make reservations in person at the office near the Old Harbor ferry landing. Fares are $60 to $75, gauged by altitude.

A more old-fashioned form of transportation is provided by **Rustic Rides Farm,** on West Side Road (℄ **401/466-5060**). A walking attendant handles the reins and protects the littlest ones on the trail. A 1-hour slow ride costs $30; a 2-hour beach ride is $70.

Fishing, kayaking, and canoeing are hugely popular, and the name to know is **Oceans & Ponds,** at Ocean and Connecticut avenues (℄ **401/466-5131**). The owners possess encyclopedic knowledge of the island; their quality stock features Orvis clothing and fishing gear. Rental kayaks and canoes put in at the head of the gentle inland ponds off the Great Salt Pond (New Harbor). Charters can be arranged on three sportfishing boats. Another source of boat rentals is **Champlin's Resort,** on Great Salt Pond (℄ **401/466-5811**), which has bumper boats and Zodiacs as well as kayaks.

WHERE TO STAY & DINE

Atlantic Inn ★★   Perched upon 6 rolling acres south of downtown, this 1879 Victorian hotel beguiles with its long veranda and broad views. Bedrooms are furnished mostly with antiques. Drawn by the promise of spectacular sunsets and the restaurant's changing menu of tapas ($4–$12) joined with the most diverse beer and wine selection on the island, people start assembling on the veranda and lawn at 4pm each summer day. President Clinton stopped by for dinner a few years ago, drawn by the reputation of the kitchen, one of the two most accomplished on Block Island. He had no trouble getting a table, it can be assumed, but the rest of us need reservations from June to September. Fish, fowl, and vegetables are smoked on the premises, and the chef comes up with such attractions as grilled striped bass with orzo salad. The inn is nonsmoking.

High St., Box 188, Block Island, RI 02807. ℄ **800/224-7422** or 401/466-5883. Fax 401/466-5678. www.atlantic inn.com. 21 units. Mid-Apr to mid-Oct $142–$259 double; from $197 suite. Rates include breakfast. DISC, MC, V. Closed Nov–Apr. **Amenities:** Restaurant (Eclectic)*; bar; 2 tennis courts; bike rental. *In room:* Dataport.

The 1661 Inn & Hotel Manisses ★★★   Emus, llamas, black swans, and a Scottish Highland ox graze in the meadow behind the Victorian Hotel Manisses, only the most visible part of a small hospitality empire. Other properties include the 1661 Inn & Guest House, up the hill, and the Dodge, Dewey, and Nicholas Ball cottages. (Children are welcome in five of the six buildings; smoking is allowed in one.) Guest rooms in the hotel utilize oak antiques and lots of wicker; some units have TVs and/or fireplaces. The median age in the hotel is noticeably grayer than in the other buildings, where families tend to gather. Common rooms in the 1661 Inn host an afternoon "wine and nibble" hour, while the Manisses parlor serves desserts and flaming coffees in the evening. Stylish dining is featured in the main dining room, with comparable fare in the more casual Gatsby Room. Picnic lunches are also prepared for guests. The inn is now open year-round, although the restaurants are closed in winter.

1 Spring St., P.O. Box 1, Block Island, RI 02807. ℄ **800/626-4773** or 401/466-2421/2063. Fax 401/466-3162. www.blockislandresorts.com. 17 units in hotel, plus 43 units (some with shared bathroom) in satellite buildings. $65–$299 double. Rates include breakfast. MC, V. **Amenities:** 2 restaurants; bar; concierge; babysitting. *In room:* Minibar, hair dryer, no phone.

WHERE TO STAY

Anchor House Inn ★   A huge anchor out front marks this former eyesore. The recently added units don't have as many steep stairs to negotiate. Room decor is spare and restful, avoiding froufrou. Breakfasts are of the hearty continental variety; take your coffee out to one of the rocking chairs on the porch.

253 Spring St., Block Island, RI 02807. ℂ 800/730-0181 or 401/466-5021. Fax 401/466-8887. www.block island.com/anchor. 6 units. Mar–Nov $110–$200 double. Rates include breakfast. AE, MC, V. Parking is limited. Closed Dec–Feb. No children under 12. *In room:* TV.

Champlin's ★★ *Kids*   Families are welcome at this all-inclusive resort, with 225 slips in the marina for visiting yachters. Those who are put off by the idiosyncratic adornments of Victorian inns will be pleased by the simpler lines and muted fabrics of the bedrooms here. There's live music in the bars on weekends, picnic grounds with grills, a pizza bar and ice-cream parlor, even a theater showing first-run movies. Once you've unpacked, there isn't much to compel you to leave, but a shuttle van is provided for trips to other parts of the island. With all that in its favor, the people in the chaotic reception area are annoyingly distracted and offhanded, and there is a slap-dash approach to maintenance.

Great Salt Pond, P.O. Box J, Block Island, RI 02807. ℂ 800/762-4541 or 401/466-7777. Fax 401/466-2638. www.champlinsresort.com. 30 units. $195–$295 double; from $450 suite. AE, MC, V. Closed mid-Oct to early May. From Old Harbor, drive west on Ocean Ave. and turn left on West Side Rd. The entrance road to Champlin's is on the right. The ferry from Long Island docks here. **Amenities:** Restaurant; 2 bars; large outdoor pool; 2 tennis courts; kayak, bumper boat, and paddleboat rentals; moped and bike rentals; game room; car rental; coin-op washers and dryers. *In room:* A/C, TV, fridge.

Rose Farm ★   The 1897 farmhouse that was the original inn is complemented by an additional house across the driveway. Four of the rooms in the new building feature Jacuzzis and decks. Some have canopied beds, most have ocean views, and their furnishings are often antique. Afternoon refreshments, usually iced tea and pastries, are served.

Roslyn Rd., Box E, Block Island, RI 02807. ℂ 401/466-2034. Fax 401/466-2053. www.blockisland.com/ rosefarm. 19 units (2 with shared bathroom). $99–$250 double. Rates include breakfast. AE, DISC, MC, V. Closed Nov–Mar. From Old Harbor, drive west on High St. and turn left on paved driveway past the Atlantic Inn. Children over 12 welcome. **Amenities:** Bike rental; coin-op washers and dryers.

Spring House Hotel ★   Marked by its mansard roof and wraparound porch, the island's oldest hotel (1852) has hosted the Kennedy clan, Ulysses S. Grant . . . and Billy Joel. The young staff is congenial, if occasionally a bit scattered. There are three styles of bedrooms, most of good size, with queen-size beds and pullout sofas. A considerable attraction is the all-you-can-eat barbecue lunch on the veranda. More formal meals are served in the all-white dining room. Swimming is allowed in the freshwater pond on the property. The hotel sponsors concerts of classical and pop music on its grounds in July and August.

902 Spring St., P.O. Box 902, Block Island, RI 02807. ℂ 800/234-9263 or 401/466-5844. springhouse@ids.net. 63 units. Summer $175–$375 double; spring and fall $75–$285. Rates include breakfast. AE, MC, V. Closed mid-Oct to Mar. **Amenities:** Restaurant; bar.

WHERE TO DINE

Expect mostly lobsters, fried and grilled fish and chicken, and routine burgers and beef cuts. Chowders are usually surefire, especially the creamy New England version. Clam cakes appear less frequently on menus than before, but are still a staple. Actually deep-fried fritters containing more dough than clams, they are still fun eating, especially when dipped in tartar sauce.

Several inns and hotels have dining rooms worth noting (see "Where to Stay," above, for reviews of the **Atlantic Inn,** the **1661 Inn & Hotel Manisses,** and **Spring House Hotel**), but even there, neither jackets nor ties are required. Due to the seasonal nature of the resort island, its restaurants can change policies, menus, and, most important, chefs in a twinkling. Keep that in mind if any of the observations below prove to undervalue or overstate a restaurant's virtues.

You can get takeout or eat in at the **Black Rock Café,** in the Figurehead Building at the south end of Water Street (© **401/466-8500**). It has a coffee bar along with an appetizing menu of cheeses, salads, entrees, and fresh baked goods.

Ballard's (A) *(Kids)* AMERICAN/SEAFOOD   Sooner rather than later, everyone winds up at Ballard's. Behind the long front porch is a warehouse-like hall where a monster whale skeleton hangs, and beyond that a terrace beside a crowded beach. Several bars and frequent live bands fuel drinkers and diners from lunch until midnight. The menu is all over the map, with something for everyone. Complementing the lobster rolls and fish –and chips are yellowfin tuna *au poivre* and roasted monkfish medallions with shrimp and sweet pepper dressed in a tarragon hollandaise. Kids have their own menu, and they can make as much noise and mess as they want. It gets pricey for families, though, so you might want to go for lunch, not dinner, and have sandwiches, not entrees.

Old Harbor. © **401/466-2231**. Main courses $8.25–$23. AE, MC, V. Daily 11:30am–11pm. Closed Oct to mid-May.

Beachhead (A) *(Kids)* ECLECTIC   After changes in management, the menu has been expanded from the former tavern limitations to one of the more ambitious slates on the island. The casual atmosphere remains, making this a likely destination for families in afternoon and early evening (dinner prices are steep, though). In peak season, at least, the noise level is high enough to mask childish squeals. There's plenty of seating inside and on the porch. There's a pizza of the day, seafood and meats are prepared in more imaginative ways than before, and the selection of beers and wines is attractive.

Corn Neck Rd. © **401/466-2249**. Main courses $9.95–$21. MC, V. Daily 11:30am–9pm (later in summer).

Bethany's Airport Diner *(Kids)* AMERICAN   "Ramshackle" is too grand a word for this relic of the 1940s. That's good, if your party includes little ones, for even the most destructive 2-year-old can't do much damage, especially out at the tables beside the runway. Decent chili and chowder come in Styrofoam cups, preceding tuna melts and quesadillas. Such specials as the Monte Cristo—a toasted ham and cheese sandwich—are about as fancy as it gets. Apart from the stools at the counter and the wooden benches around the few tables, decor is confined to the model airplanes hanging from the ceiling, several of them fashioned from beer cans.

Center Rd. (at the airport). © **401/466-3100**. All items under $10. Daily 5:30am–5pm (shorter hr. in off season).

Dead Eye Dick's (A) SEAFOOD/AMERICAN   Despite the name and the logo of a shark with an eye patch, which might suggest beer blasts and wet T-shirt contests, this is a PG-rated restaurant with good eats and a welcome for all ages. Swordfish is high on the honors list, often grilled with a tomato-ginger relish. A twist on the Rhode Island stuffie is the minced Quahog crammed back into its shell with andouille sausage and sweet pepper. Lunch is mostly tasty wraps and meat salads. The kids' menu suggests pasta with butter or chicken tenders. Arrive early for a table on the deck.

Water St. (near Payne's Dock). © **401/466-2473**. Main courses $16–$22. AE, MC, V. Memorial Day to Labor Day daily 5–10pm (Sun until 9pm); July–Aug also open noon–3pm. Closed rest of the year.

Eli's ITALIAN/AMERICAN   This place used to be just a spaghetti-and-grinders drop-in, but it's evolved into one of the island's most popular eateries. Problem is, it can serve only 50 voracious diners at a time, and the no-reservations policy

> ## *Tips* DIY Shore Dinners
>
> Should you have housekeeping facilities in your lodging, you might wish to put together a New England shore dinner. Lobster is the central component, of course, and you can buy yours straight off the fishing boats. Each afternoon from about 4 to 5:30pm, boats put in at both Old Harbor and the Great Salt Pond. Depending upon their catches of the day, they charge from $6 to $8 per pound. A more reliable source is **Finn's Fish Market,** at the Old Harbor ferry landing (✆ **401/466-2102**). Its lobster prices are similar, and it also carries oysters, clams, shrimp, and fish.
>
> For the other fixings—corn, tomatoes, bread, sausage, chicken—stop at either the **Block Island Grocery** (known as the B.I.G.) near Ocean Avenue and Corn Neck Road (✆ **401/466-2949**), a conventional supermarket; or **Block Island Depot,** Ocean Avenue (✆ **401/466-2403**), which carries a line of cheeses and organic foods. The best-stocked wine and liquor store is the **Red Bird Package Store,** on Dodge Street (✆ **401/466-2441**), around the corner from the north end of Water Street. **Seaside Market,** toward the other end of Water Street (✆ **401/466-5876**), has a good wine selection and some grocery products.

means waits of up to 2 hours. But it can be worth it. Choices like "Hunter's Dastardly Duck" bring a half of that bird together with apples, pheasant sausage, brandy, and demi-glace. Such combinations are undeniably full-flavored, although the diverse ingredients are often mashed together as if in a thick stew, losing some of their individuality. Huge portions defy anyone to finish.

456 Chapel St. ✆ **401/466-5230.** Main courses $16–$28. AE, MC, V. May–Oct daily 5:30–10pm (Sat–Sun until 11pm); Nov–Dec Sat–Sun 5:30–10pm. Closed Jan–Apr.

Mohegan Café & Brewery ECLECTIC   Walk straight across from the Old Harbor ferry landing to this agreeable tavern—most people do. Featured microbrews are listed on the blackboard. Most of the daytime menu is standard pub fare, with chowder, burgers, burritos, and fried clams featured. That's the time to go, for the kitchen has a sure hand with its luncheon familiars, but looks a little too far afield for dinner ideas (pad Thai and red curried chicken). This is one of the few public places with air-conditioning, something to remember on a muggy July day.

Water St. ✆ **401/466-5911.** Main courses $15–$22. AE, DISC, MC, V. Summer Sun–Thurs 11:30am–9pm, Fri–Sat 11am–10pm; shorter hours during spring and fall shoulder seasons.

The Oar ✦ AMERICAN   This good-time bar is now open for a buffet breakfast and full-service lunch and dinner, and the menu has been plumped up with a few more choices. Grilled swordfish, sirloin, and fried chicken flesh out the old roster of nachos, lobster rolls, and calamari. There's a deck and a bar with a picture window to take in dramatic views of storms over the mainland and of the fleet of pleasure boats in the Great Salt Pond. The ceiling and walls are hung with scores of oars—all of them painted with cartoons, graffiti, and assorted messages of obscure or ribald intent.

West Side Rd. (Block Island Marina). ✆ **401/466-8820.** Main courses $8.25–$28. AE, MC, V. Daily 8am–midnight (bar until 1am). Closed late Oct–May.

Sharkey's AMERICAN   With its kicked-back atmosphere and pub-style menu, this entry opposite Crescent Beach has a clear kinship with at least a dozen casual eateries on the island. Expect the usual burgers and cheesesteak pretenders, but know that the people handling the fried-fish dishes have a superbly light hand— go for the definitive fish –and chips. Start with potstickers or scallops wrapped in bacon. Daily specials lean to the likes of blackened this or that—mako shark, for one—while dinner entrees run to fettuccine and prime rib. Children are welcome.

Corn Neck Rd. © 401/466-9900. Main courses $14–$22. MC, V. Summer daily 11:30am–10pm; hours vary substantially spring and fall. Closed late Oct to mid-May.

Smuggler's Cove AMERICAN   Owned by the same folks who operate the Hotel Manisses and The Oar, this waterside property began life as a recreation center for military personnel during World War I. Choose the indoor dining room with its fireplace and antique ship models or one of the two covered decks. A take-out window hands out chowder, snacks, and some of the best ice cream on the island. While there are few surprises on the menu, what with pizzas, barbecue, burgers, and fish and chips, execution is notches above the island norm. Entrees are served throughout the day, including fried oysters and shrimp, grilled swordfish with red pepper coulis, and a 1-pound T-bone with fried onion "tanglers."

Hog Pen, Ocean Ave. © 401/466-7961. Main courses $9.50–$22. Memorial Day to Columbus Day daily11:30am–11pm. Closed the rest of the year.

BLOCK ISLAND AFTER DARK

Nightlife isn't of the raunchy, rollicking, south Florida variety, but the bars don't close at sunset, either. Among the prime candidates for a potential rockin' good time is **Captain Nick's,** on Ocean Avenue (© **401/466-5670**), opposite the Block Island Grocery. It has pool tables inside, plus live music most nights in season out on the terrace. A block away, **Yellow Kittens,** on Corn Neck Road (© **401/466-5855**), also presents live bands in summer, inside or out on the deck. Darts, pool tables, foosball, and video games help fill the winter nights. Pub food, pool tables, video games, and foosball are also attractions at **Club Soda,** on Connecticut Avenue (© **401/466-5397**), supplemented by live music once or twice a week.

 Ballard's (see "Where to Dine," above) has live rock or pop most afternoons out on the terrace and nightly inside. An occasional live-music venue is the lounge of the **National Hotel,** on Water Street (© **401/466-2901**). Yachtsmen and other sailors docked or moored at Champlin's Marina settle in on the end of the main dock at **Trader Vic's,** at New Harbor (© **401/466-2641**). The bar is downstairs, with a DJ or band out on the deck most afternoons. In addition to the sunset drinks and tapas on the front lawn of the **Atlantic Inn** (see "Where to Stay," earlier in this chapter), many visitors settle in on the porch of the equally well-situated (and less expensive) **Narragansett Inn,** on Water Street (© **401/466-2626**).

 Island residents try to keep **Mahagony Shoals,** on Payne's Dock at the end of Water Street (© **401/466-5572**), to themselves. What they come for is the barbed humor of Wally McDonough. He sings Irish folk ballads and banters with the audience, invariably giving better than he gets. Wally occupies his corner Wednesday, Thursday, Saturday, and Sunday nights, as well as Fridays, when he feels like it. Get there around 10pm.

Vermont

by Paul Karr

Vermont's rolling, cow-spotted hills, shaggy peaks, sugar maples, and towns clustered along river valleys give it a distinct sense of place. Still primarily rural, the state is filled with dairy farms, dirt roads, and small-scale enterprises. The towns here are home to an intriguing mix of old-time Vermonters, back-to-the-landers who showed up in VW buses in the 1960s and stayed (many getting involved with municipal affairs; think Ben and Jerry), and newer, moneyed arrivals from New York or Boston who came to ski or B&B and never could quite leave.

This place captures a sense of America as it once was—because, here, it still *is*. Vermonters continue to share a sense of community, and they respect the ideals of thrift and parsimony above those of commercialism. Locals prize their villages, and understand what makes them special.

Southern and central Vermont are defined by rolling hills, shady valleys, and historic villages. Throughout you'll find antiques shops and handsome inns, fast-flowing streams and inviting restaurants. It's anchored at each corner by the towns of Bennington and Brattleboro; between them and running northward is the spine of the Green Mountains, much of which is part of the Green Mountain National Forest.

Mostly it's rural living, with cow pastures high on the hills, clapboard farmhouses under spreading trees, maple-sugaring operations come spring, and the distant sound of timber being twitched out of a woodlot on the far side of a high ridge. The steep hills also host many of the state's popular ski resorts, such as Okemo, Killington, Sugarbush, and Mount Snow.

Though it's not very far from New York City, southern Vermont has so far mostly resisted overdevelopment, crowds, and the other trappings of a discovered resort area (except at a ski resort on a winter weekend). The area remains a wonderful introduction to one of America's most wonderful states.

1 Bennington, Manchester & Southwestern Vermont

Southwestern Vermont is the turf of Ethan Allen, Robert Frost, Grandma Moses, and Norman Rockwell. As such, it may seem familiar even if you've never been here before. Over the decades, this region has subtly managed to work itself into America's cultural consciousness.

The region is sandwiched between the Green Mountains to the east and the rolling hills along the Vermont–New York border to the west. Bennington is a historic and commercial center that offers up low-key diversions for residents and tourists alike. Northward toward Rutland, the terrain is more intimate, with towns clustered in broad and gentle valleys along rivers and streams. Former 19th-century summer colonies and erstwhile lumber and marble towns exist side by side, offering pleasant accommodations, delightful food, and—in the case of Manchester Center—world-class shopping.

These outposts of sophisticated culture are within easy striking distance of the Green Mountains, enabling you to enjoy the outdoors by day and goose-down duvets by night. The region attracts shoppers, gourmands, and those simply looking for a brief and relaxing detour to the elegant inns and B&Bs for which the region is widely known.

BENNINGTON ✪

Bennington is Vermont's third largest city. Visitors will find two Benningtons. Historic Bennington, with its white clapboard homes, sits atop a hill west of town off Route 9. Modern downtown Bennington is a pleasant if no-frills commercial center with restaurants and stores that still sell what people actually need. Don't miss the stern marble Federal building (formerly the post office), with six fluted columns, at 118 South St. The surrounding countryside, defined by rolling hills, is afflicted with fewer abrupt inclines and slopes than many of Vermont's towns.

ESSENTIALS

GETTING THERE Bennington is at the intersection of Routes 9 and 7. If you're coming from the south, the nearest interstate access is via the New York Thruway at Albany, about 35 miles away. From the east, I-91 is about 40 miles away at Brattleboro. **Vermont Transit** (© **800/642-3133** or 802/442-4808; www.vermonttransit.com) offers bus service to Bennington from Albany, Burlington, and other points. Buses arrive and depart from 126 Washington St.

VISITOR INFORMATION The **Bennington Area Chamber of Commerce,** 100 Veterans Memorial Dr. (© **800/229-0252** or 802/447-3311; www. bennington.com), has an information office on Route 7 North near the veterans' complex. The office is open Monday through Friday from 9am to 5pm mid-May through mid-October; in summer and fall, it's also open Saturday and Sunday from 10am to 4pm.

EXPLORING THE TOWN

One of Bennington's claims to history is the Battle of Bennington, which took place August 16, 1777. Though a relatively minor skirmish, it had major implications for the outcome of the American Revolution. The British were defeated here, clearing the way for another British setback at the Battle of Saratoga and turning the tide for good. That battle is commemorated by northern New England's most imposing monument: the **Bennington Battle Monument** ✪✪ (© **802/447-0550**). This 306-foot obelisk of blue limestone atop a low rise was dedicated in 1891; it's about 6 miles from the site of the actual battle. The monument's viewing platform, which is reached by elevator, is open from 9am to 5pm daily April through October. A fee of $1 is charged.

Moments **"I Had a Lover's Quarrel with the World."**

That's the epitaph on the tombstone of Robert Frost, who's buried in the cemetery behind the 1806 First Congregational Church. (It's where Rte. 9 makes two quick bends west of downtown, and down the hill from the Bennington Monument. Signs point to the Frost family grave.) Travelers often stop to pay their respects to the man many consider the voice of New England. Closer to the church itself, look for early tombstones (some with urns and skulls) of the voiceless and forgotten.

Vermont

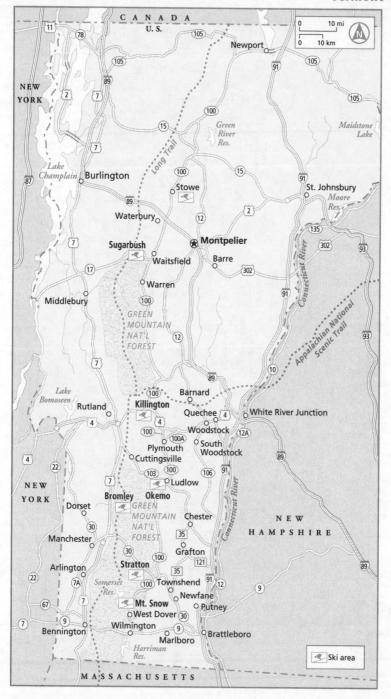

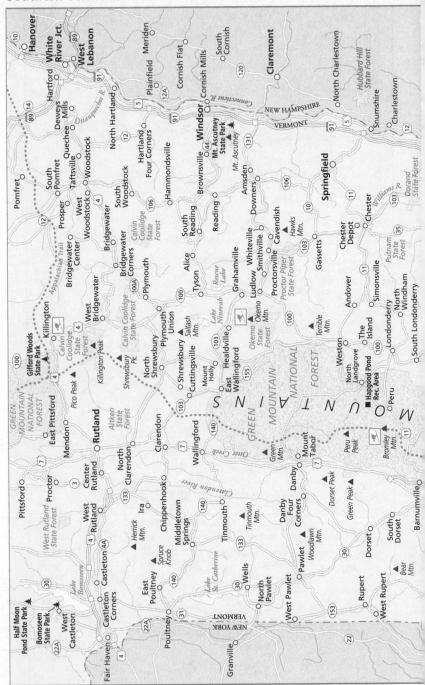

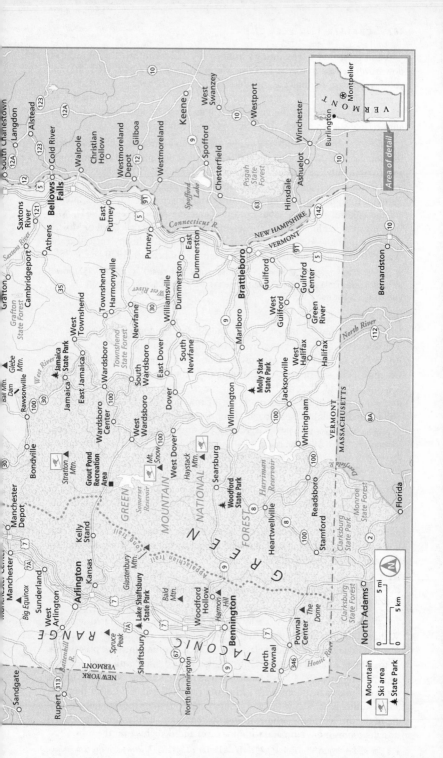

A fun local find is **Hemming's Sunoco** , 222 Main St. (Rte. 9, west of downtown, across from the Paradise Motor Inn); 𝒞 **802/442-3101.** It's not your typical gas station, but also headquarters for *Hemmings Motor News,* a monthly publication bible for vintage car collectors. After you tank up, ask to take an escorted peek at the vintage cars housed in the storage area, and buy auto-related souvenirs such as old Route 66 signs and model cars.

The Bennington Museum   This eclectic and intriguing collection traces its roots back to 1875, although the museum has occupied the current stone-and-column building overlooking the valley only since 1928. The expansive galleries feature a wide range of exhibits on local arts and industry, including early Vermont furniture, glass, paintings, and Bennington pottery. Of special interest are the colorful primitive landscapes by Grandma Moses (1860–1961), who lived much of her life nearby. (The museum has the largest collection of Moses's paintings in the world.) Look also for the glorious 1925 luxury car called the Wasp, 16 of which were handcrafted in Bennington between 1920 and 1925.

W. Main St. (Rte. 9 between Old Bennington and the current town center). 𝒞 802/447-1571. www. benningtonmuseum.com. Admission $7 adults, $6 seniors and students, free for children under 12. Daily 9am–6pm (until 5pm Nov 1–May 31).

WHERE TO STAY

The Four Chimneys Inn   This Colonial Revival building will be among the first to catch your eye as you arrive in Bennington from the west. Set off from Route 7 on an 11-acre, nicely landscaped lot, it's an imposing white, three-story structure with—no surprise—four prominent chimneys. Built in 1912, the inn is at the edge of Historic Bennington; the towering Bennington Monument looms over its backyard. Guest rooms are inviting and homey, but the overall sensibility can be mildly off-putting, as if you're visiting somebody else's relatives.

21 West Rd., Bennington, VT 05201. 𝒞 800/649-3903 or 802/447-3500. Fax 802/447-3692. www.four chimneys.com. 11 units. $105–$205 double. Rates include breakfast. 2-night minimum stay foliage and holiday weekends. AE, DISC, MC, V. Children 12 and over welcome. **Amenities:** Restaurant (Continental). *In room:* A/C, TV, dataport, hair dryer, iron/ironing board.

Paradise Motor Inn *Value*   This is Bennington's best motel, with tidy and generously sized accommodations. Try to reserve the North Building—despite its dated 1980s styling, each room here has an outdoor terrace or balcony. The more up-to-date Office Building has a richer Colonial Revival style. The motel is uncommonly clean and well managed. It's across from the Hemming's gas station and within walking distance of town.

141 W. Main St., Bennington, VT 05201. 𝒞 802/442-8351. Fax 802/447-3889. www.theparadisemotorinn.com. 76 units. $55–$128 double (off-season discounts). DISC, MC, V. **Amenities:** Outdoor pool; 2 tennis courts. *In room:* A/C, TV, Jacuzzis (some).

South Shire Inn   A locally prominent banking family hired architect William Bull in 1880 to design and build this impressive Victorian home. The spacious downstairs has leaded glass on its bookshelves and intricate plasterwork in the dining room. The guest rooms are richly hued, most with canopied beds and working fireplaces (with Duraflame-type logs only). The best of the bunch is the old master bedroom, with a king-size canopied bed, tile-hearth fireplace, and beautiful bathroom with hand-painted tile. Four more modern guest rooms are in the carriage house, whose downstairs rooms are slightly more formal, and upstairs rooms more intimate, with low eaves and skylights over the tubs.

124 Elm St., Bennington, VT 05201. 𝒞 802/447-3839. Fax 802/442-3547. www.southshire.com. 9 units. $110–$190 double. Rates include breakfast. AE, MC, V. Children over 12 welcome. *In room:* A/C, hair dryer.

WHERE TO DINE

Alldays & Onions ECLECTIC   This casual spot was named after an early-20th-century British automobile manufacturer. Locals flock here to enjoy wholesome, tasty sandwiches, deli salads, and tasty soups; the atmosphere is that of a small-town restaurant gussied up for a big night out. Expect Cajun chicken, grilled spicy shrimp, pastrami sandwiches, burgers, tortellini, and the like. (More ambitious entrees might include Southwest cowboy steak with skillet corn sauce and soba and stir-fried vegetables.) Breakfast options include bagels and lox.

519 Main St. (C) 802/447-0043. Reservations accepted for dinner, but not often needed. Breakfast $2–$8; sandwiches $2.50–$7.25; dinner $11–$20. AE, DISC, MC, V. Mon–Sat 7:30–10:30am, 11am–3pm; 5–9pm, Sun 9am–1pm.

Blue Benn Diner ⭐ *Value* DINER   Diner aficionados make pilgrimages to enjoy the ambience of this 1945 Silk City classic. Blue-plate dinner specials include vegetables, rice, soup or salad, rolls, and rice pudding for dessert. A bit incongruously, fancier and vegetarian fare is also available; especially good is the grilled portobello on sourdough. But you come here for diner staples such as turkey with gravy, big slabs of cornbread French toast, or butterscotchy Indian pudding with vanilla ice cream. Of course, the place also offers a great selection of pies, such as blackberry, pumpkin, and chocolate cream.

318 North St. (Rte. 7). (C) 802/442-5140. Breakfast $1.50–$5.95; sandwiches and entrees $1.95–$5.75; dinner specials $7.95–$8.95. No credit cards. Mon–Tues 6am–5pm; Wed–Fri 6am–8pm; Sat 6am–4pm; Sun 7am–4pm.

ARLINGTON ⭐, MANCHESTER ⭐⭐ & DORSET ⭐⭐⭐

The rolling Green Mountains are rarely out of view from this cluster of hamlets. And in midsummer, the lush green hereabouts gives Ireland a good run for its money—verdant hues are found in the forests blanketing the hills, valley meadows, and mosses along the tumbling streams, making it obvious how these mountains earned their name.

This trio of quintessential Vermont villages makes an ideal destination for romantic getaways, aggressive antiquing, and serious outlet shopping. Each of the towns is worth visiting, and each has its own unique charm. **Manchester** ⭐⭐ and **Manchester Center** share a blurred town line, but maintain distinct characters. Manchester has an old-world, old money elegance, with a campus-like town centered around the resplendently columned Equinox Hotel. Just to the north, Manchester Center is a major mercantile center with dozens of national outlets offering discounts on brand-name clothing, accessories, and housewares.

A worthy detour off the beaten track is **Dorset** ⭐⭐, an exquisitely preserved town of white clapboard architecture and marble sidewalks.

ESSENTIALS

GETTING THERE   Arlington, Manchester, and Manchester Center are north of Bennington on Historic Route 7A, which runs parallel to and west of Route 7. Dorset is north of Manchester Center on Route 30, which diverges from Route 7A in Manchester Center. **Vermont Transit** (C) **800/451-3292** or 802/362-1226; www.vermonttransit.com) offers bus service to Manchester.

VISITOR INFORMATION   The **Manchester and the Mountains Chamber of Commerce** (C) **800/362-4144** or 802/362-2100; www.manchestervermont.net) maintains a year-round information center at 5080 Main St. (Rte. 7A) beside the small green in Manchester Center. Hours are Monday through Saturday from 10am to 5pm; Memorial Day weekend through October, it's open Sunday from 10am to 5pm, and to 7pm Fridays and Saturdays.

The **Green Mountain National Forest** maintains a district ranger office (© 802/362-2307) in Manchester on Routes 11 and 30 east of Route 7. It's open Monday through Friday from 8am to 4:30pm.

EXPLORING THE AREA

Arlington has long been associated with painter and illustrator Norman Rockwell, who lived here from 1939 to 1953. Arlington residents were regularly featured in Rockwell covers for *The Saturday Evening Post.*

Visitors can catch a glimpse of this long relationship in a 19th-century Carpenter Gothic–style church in the middle of town, called **The Norman Rockwell Exhibit** (© 802/375-6423). This small museum features a variety of displays, including many of those famous covers, along with photographs of the original models. Sometimes you'll find the models working as volunteers. It's open from 10am to 4pm weekdays, 10am to 5pm weekends in summer; call about winter hours, as it is often closed in the off season. Admission is $2, free for children under 12.

MUSEUMS & HISTORIC HOMES

Hildene ★★   Robert Todd Lincoln was the only son of Abraham and Mary Todd Lincoln to survive to maturity. He earned millions as a prominent corporate attorney, served as secretary of war and ambassador to Britain under three presidents, and was president of the Pullman Company (makers of deluxe train cars) from 1897 to 1911. He also summered in this stately, 24-room Georgian Revival mansion between 1905 and 1926 and delighted in showing off its sweeping staircase and a 1908 Aeolian organ with 1,000 pipes (you'll hear it played on the tour). Lincoln had formal gardens designed after the patterns in a stained-glass window and planted on a gentle promontory with outstanding views of the flanking mountains. The home is viewed on group tours that start at an informative visitor center; allow time following the tour to explore the grounds.

Historic Rte. 7A off Rte 30, Manchester. © 802/362-1788. www.hildene.org. Tours $10 adults, $4 children 6–14, free for children under 6. Grounds only, $5 adults, $2 children 6–14. Tours given mid-May to Oct daily, every ½-hour 9:30am–4pm; grounds close at 5pm. Special holiday tours Dec 27–29.

Southern Vermont Art Center ★★   This fine art center is well worth the short detour from town. Located partly in a striking Georgian Revival home surrounded by more than 400 pastoral hillside acres (it overlooks land that once belonged to Charles Orvis of fly-fishing fame), the center features a series of galleries displaying works from its well-regarded collection, as well as frequently changing exhibits of contemporary Vermont artists. Check the schedule before you arrive; you may be able to sign up for an art class while you're in town.

West Rd. off Rte. 30 (P.O. Box 617), Manchester. © 802/362-1405. www.svac.org. Admission in summer, $6 adults, $3 students, free for children under 13. Tues–Sat 10am–5pm, Sun noon–5pm.

DOWNHILL SKIING

Bromley Mountain Ski Resort ★ *Kids*   Bromley is a great place to learn to ski. Gentle and forgiving, the mountain also features long, looping intermediate runs that are tremendously popular with families; it was recently voted the #2 ski destination for families in the entire nation by a leading ski magazine. The slopes are mostly south-facing, which means they receive the warmth of the sun and some protection from the harshest winter winds. (It also means the snow may melt more quickly than at other ski resorts.) The base lodge scene is mellower than at many resorts, and your experience is almost guaranteed to be relaxing.

3984 Rte. 11, Peru (mailing address: P.O. Box 1130, Manchester Center, VT 05255). © 800/865-4786 for lodging, or 802/824-5522. www.bromley.com. Vertical drop: 1,334 ft. Lifts: 6 chairlifts (including 1 high-speed detachable quad), 3 surface lifts. Skiable acreage: 175. Lift tickets: $34–$54.

Stratton ★★ Founded in the 1960s, Stratton labored in its early days under the belief that Vermont ski areas had to be Tyrolean to be successful—hence, the Swiss chalet architecture and overall feel of being Vail's younger, less affluent sibling. In recent years, Stratton has worked to leave the image of alpine quaintness behind in a bid to attract a younger, edgier set. New owners added $25 million in improvements, mostly in snowmaking, with coverage now up over 80%. The slopes are especially popular with snowboarders, a sport that was invented here when bartender Jake Burton slapped a big plank on his feet and aimed down the mountain. Expert skiers should seek out Upper Middlebrook, a fine, twisting run off the summit.

Stratton Mountain, VT 05155. © **800/843-6867** for lodging, or 802/297-2200. www.stratton.com. Vertical drop: 2,003 ft. Lifts: 1 tram, 9 chairlifts (including two 6-person high-speed), 2 surface lifts. Skiable acreage: 583. Lift tickets: $59–$72.

OTHER OUTDOOR ACTIVITIES

HIKING & BIKING Scenic hiking trails ranging from challenging to relaxing can be found in the hills a short drive from town. At the Green Mountain District Ranger Station (see "Visitor Information," above), ask for the free brochure *Day Hikes on the Manchester Ranger District,* which lists 19 area hikes.

A scenic drive northwest of Manchester Center takes you to the **Delaware and Hudson Rail-Trail.** The southern section of the trail runs about 10 miles from West Pawlet to the state line at West Rupert, over trestles and past vestiges of former industry, such as the old Vermont Milk and Cream Co. Like most rail-trails, this one is perfect for exploring by mountain bike. Drive north on Route 30 from Manchester Center to Route 315, then continue north on Route 153. In West Pawlet, park across from Duchie's General Store and begin across the street.

CANOEING For a duck's-eye view of the rolling hills, stop by **BattenKill Canoe Ltd.** in Arlington (© **800/421-5268** or 802/362-2800; www.battenkill.com). This friendly outfit offers daily canoe rentals for exploring the Battenkill River and surrounding areas. Trips range from 2 hours to a day, but the firm specializes in 5-day inn-to-inn canoe packages. The shop is open daily in season (May–Oct) from 9am to 5:30pm, and limited hours the rest of the year.

FLY-FISHING Aspiring anglers can sign up for fly-fishing classes taught by skilled instructors affiliated with **Orvis** (© **800/548-9548**), the noted fly-fishing supplier and manufacturer. The 2½-day classes include instruction in knot tying and casting, practicing catch-and-release fishing on the company pond and the Battenkill River. Classes are held from mid-April to Labor Day.

SHOPPING ⋆

Manchester Center has the best concentration of high-end **outlets** in New England. Among the noted retailers are Baccarat, Jones New York, Nine West, Giorgio Armani, Coach, and Cole-Haan. Other retailers include Hickey Freeman, Brooks Brothers, Crabtree & Evelyn, Coldwater Creek, Levi's, Timberland, Tommy Hilfiger, J. Crew, and Circa 50 (modernist furnishings). The shops are located in tasteful mini-mall clusters in the heart of Manchester Center.

The **Orvis Company Store** ☆ (© 802/362-3750) is between Manchester and Manchester Center and offers housewares, men's and women's clothing, both for daily wear and sturdy outdoor clothing, and world-famous fly-fishing equipment. Two small ponds outside the shop allow prospective customers to try gear before buying; a Sale Room, with even more deeply discounted items, is directly behind the main store.

Near the middle of Manchester Center, at the intersection of Route 7A and Route 30, is the fine **Northshire Bookstore** (© 800/437-3700 or 802/362-2200; www.northshire.com). It has an excellent selection of current titles, and a recent expansion is doubling shelf space and adding a cafe. It's open 10am to 7pm weekdays, to 9pm weekends. Check the website for author readings.

WHERE TO STAY

Arlington Inn ☆☆ This stout, multi-columned Greek Revival house (1848) would be perfectly at home in the Virginia countryside, but it anchors this village well, set back from Historic Route 7A on a lawn bordered with sturdy maples. Inside, the inn boasts a similarly courtly feel, with unique wooden ceilings adorning the first-floor rooms and a tavern that borrows its atmosphere from an English hunt club. If you prefer modern comforts, ask for a room in the 1830 parsonage next door, where you'll find phones and TVs. The quietest units are in the detached carriage house, most removed from the sound of Route 7A.

Historic Rte. 7A & Rte. 313 West (P.O. Box 369), Arlington, VT 05250. © 800/443-9442 or 802/375-6532. Fax 802/375-6534. www.arlingtoninn.com. 18 units. $90–$310 double. Rates include breakfast. 2-night minimum stay most weekends. AE, DISC, MC, V. **Amenities:** Restaurant (regional); tennis court; babysitting. In room: A/C, TV, dataport.

Barnstead Inn ☆ If you're looking for a bit of history with your lodging but are a bit shell-shocked by area room rates, consider this congenial place within walking distance of Manchester. All but two of the guest rooms are located in an 1830s hay barn; many are decorated in a rustic country style, some with exposed beams. Expect vinyl bathroom floors, industrial carpeting, and a mix of motel-modern and antique furniture. Among the more desirable units are room B, which is the largest and most requested, and the two rooms (12 and 13) above the office, each with two double beds and original round beams. A few rooms are even priced under $100, and all units offer good value.

Rte. 30 (P.O. Box 988), Manchester Center, VT 05255. © 800/331-1619 or 802/362-1619. www.barn steadinn.com. 14 units. $90–$210 double and suites; off season from $80. AE, MC, V. Children over 12 welcome. **Amenities:** Outdoor pool. In room: A/C, TV, dataport, coffeemaker.

Barrows House ☆☆ Within easy strolling distance of Dorset stands this compound of eight early American buildings set on twelve nicely landscaped acres studded with birches, firs, and maples. Built in 1784, the main house has been an inn since 1900. Its primary distinctions are its historic lineage and its convenience to Dorset; the rooms are more comfortable than elegant, though some have gas or wood fireplaces. A few units have phones—ask in advance if it's important to you. This place will please history buffs; those looking for more pampering may prefer the Equinox or the Inn at Ormsby Hill.

Rte. 30, Dorset, VT 05251. © 800/639-1620 or 802/867-4455. Fax 802/867-0132. www.barrowshouse.com. 28 units. Peak season $205–$300 double, off season lower. Rates include breakfast and dinner. B&B rates also available. Midweek and off-season discounts available. 2-night minimum stay on weekends and some holidays. AE, DISC, MC, V. Pets allowed in two cottages. **Amenities:** Restaurant (contemporary New England); outdoor pool; 2 tennis courts; sauna; bicycle rental; game room. In room: A/C, no phone (some)

Dorset Inn ★★ Set in the center of genteel Dorset, this former stagecoach stop was built in 1796 and claims to be the oldest continuously operating inn in Vermont. With 31 rooms, the Dorset Inn is fairly large by Vermont standards but feels far more intimate than comparably sized places. The carpeted guest rooms, some of which are in a well-crafted addition built in the 1940s, are furnished in an upscale country style, with a mix of reproductions and antiques, including canopied and sleigh beds. All rooms are air-conditioned, though only the two suites and a few other rooms have TVs and telephones. The tavern is casual and pubby, paneled in dark wood with a stamped-tin ceiling.

8 Church St. at Rte. 30, Dorset, VT 05251. ⓒ **877/367-7389** or 802/867-5500. Fax 802/867-5542. www.dorset inn.com. 31 units. $95–$200 double; $145–$330 suites. Rates include breakfast. AE, MC, V. Children over 5 welcome. **Amenities:** Restaurant (eclectic). *In room:* A/C, no phone (most).

1811 House ★★★ This inn, one of the best in southern Vermont, is certain to appeal to those drawn to early regional history. This historic home was built starting in the mid-1770s, and began taking guests in 1811 (hence the name). And it seems that not much has changed in the intervening centuries. The cozy, warren-like common rooms are steeped in the past—uneven pine floors, out-of-true doors, and everything painted in earthy, colonial tones. The antique furniture re-creates the feel of the house during the Federal period. A delightful English-style pub lies off the entryway, complete with tankards hanging from the beams. One of the best units is the Robinson Room, with a private deck and great view. The chocolate-chip cookies set out each afternoon are also memorable.

Rte. 7A (P.O. Box 39), Manchester Village, VT 05254. ⓒ **800/432-1811** or 802/362-1811. Fax 802/362-2443. www.1811house.com. 13 units. $140–$280 double. Rates include breakfast. AE, DISC, MC, V. *In room:* A/C.

The Equinox ★★★ Since 2000, the Equinox has been owned and managed by the upscale Rockresorts. It remains a blueblood favorite, with acres of white clapboard behind a long row of stately columns that define lovely Manchester Village. Its roots extend back to 1769, but don't be misled by its lineage: The Equinox is a fully modern resort, complete with the full-service Avanyu spa. You'll find extensive sports facilities scattered about its 2,300 acres, four dining rooms, scheduled events (such as guided hikes up Mount Equinox), and a sense of settled graciousness. The rooms are tastefully appointed, though not terribly large. The restaurants don't quite live up to the near-perfection of the inn, so keep nights open to sample area establishments.

Rte. 7A (P.O. Box 46), Manchester Village, VT 05245. ⓒ **800/362-4747** or 802/362-4700. Fax 802/362-1595. www.equinoxresort.com. 183 units. Peak season $279–$449 double, $449–$639 suite; off season $179–$399 double, $399–$629 suite; Orvis Inn section wing, $609–$899 suite. Ask about packages. AE, DISC, MC, V. **Amenities:** 4 restaurants (contemporary/regional, pub fare); indoor pool; outdoor pool; golf course; 3 tennis courts; spa; sauna; croquet; concierge; shopping arcade; salon; limited room service; babysitting; laundry service; dry cleaning; falconry school. *In room:* A/C, TV, dataport, hair dryer, iron.

Inn at Ormsby Hill ★★ The oldest part of the striking Inn at Ormsby Hill dates to 1764 (the revolutionary Ethan Allen is rumored to have hidden out here). Today, it's a harmonious medley of eras and styles, with inspiring views of the Green Mountains. Guests enjoy those views along with gourmet breakfasts in the dining room, built by prominent 19th-century attorney Edward Isham to resemble the interior of a steamship. Among the best units: the Taft Room, with its vaulted wood ceiling, and the first-floor Library, with many of Isham's books still lining the shelves. Nine rooms feature two-person Jacuzzis and fireplaces.

1842 Main St. (Rte. 7A, near Hildene south of Manchester Village), Manchester Center, VT 05255. ℭ 800/ 670-2841 or 802/362-1163. Fax 802/362-5176. www.ormsbyhill.com. 10 units. Weekdays $205–$265 double; weekends $265–$325 double; foliage season and holidays $320–$380. Rates include breakfast. 2-night minimum stay on weekends. DISC, MC, V. Closed briefly in Apr. Children 14 and older welcome. *In room:* A/C, hair dryer.

Palmer House Resort ⭐ This is actually a motel, but several notches above the run-of-the-mill. Owned and operated by the same family for nearly 50 years, the rooms are furnished with antiques and other niceties you may not expect. Ask for one of the somewhat larger rooms in the newer rear building. There are also eight spacious suites, each with gas fireplace, wet bar, and private deck overlooking a trout-stocked pond and the mountains beyond. The buildings are set on 22 nicely tended acres, and the motel even has its own small golf course. (No charge to play golf or borrow fishing rods.) Rooms tend to book up early in the season, so call ahead to avoid disappointment.

Rte. 7A, Manchester Center, VT 05255. ℭ **800/917-6245** or 802/362-3600. www.palmerhouse.com. 58 units. Summer $75–$175 double, $160–$300 suite. 2-night minimum stay some weekends. **Amenities:** Outdoor pool; golf course; 2 tennis courts; Jacuzzi; sauna; fishing pond. *In room:* A/C, TV, fridge, coffeemaker, hair dryer.

The Reluctant Panther ⭐⭐ A short walk from the Equinox, this location is easy to spot, painted a pale eggplant color with faded yellow shutters, making it stand out in this staid village of white clapboard. This 1850s home is elegantly furnished throughout (as are guest rooms in an adjacent building, built in 1910) and features nice touches, including goose-down duvets in every room. Run with couples in mind, 12 of the rooms have fireplaces (some more than one), and some suites, such as the Mark Skinner, even feature wood-burning fireplaces or double Jacuzzis in the bathrooms. Many visitors plan their stay around a romantic meal at the **restaurant,** which serves European fare prepared by Swiss-German chef Robert Bachofen, a former director at the Plaza Hotel in New York.

39 West Rd. (P.O. Box 678), Manchester Village, VT 05254. ℭ **800/822-2331** or 802/362-2568. Fax 802/ 362-2586. www.reluctantpanther.com. 21 units (1 with detached private bathroom). $139–$339 double, $439 suite; off-season rates lower. Rates include breakfast. AE, DISC, MC, V. Children 14 and older welcome. **Amenities:** Restaurant. *In room:* A/C, TV, hair dryer, iron.

West Mountain Inn ⭐ Sitting atop a grassy bluff at the end of a dirt road ½ mile from Arlington center, this rambling, white-clapboard building dates back a century and a half. It's a perfect place for travelers striving to get away from the irksome hum of modern life. The guest rooms, named after famous Vermonters, are nicely furnished with country antiques and Victorian reproductions. The rooms vary widely in size and shape, but even the smallest has plenty of charm and character. Several rooms in outlying cottages feature kitchenettes and are popular among attendees of family reunions, who also use the 100-year-old post-and-beam barn for gatherings.

River Rd. & Rte. 313, Arlington, VT 05250. ℭ **802/375-6516.** Fax 802/375-6553. www.westmountaininn.com. 18 units. Summer, spring, and winter weekends $198–$275 double; foliage season $228–$305 double; winter midweek $169–$275 double; town houses $131–$299. Rates include breakfast and dinner. 2-night minimum stay on weekends. AE, DISC, MC, V. **Amenities:** Restaurant (contemporary New England); massage (by arrangement); babysitting. *In room:* A/C, no phone.

Wilburton Inn ⭐⭐ This impressive Tudor estate is sumptuously appointed, the common spaces filled with European antiques, Persian carpets, and even a baby grand. Throughout the brick manor house you'll find works from the modern-art collection amassed by the inn's owners, Albert and Georgette Levis. The guest rooms are divided between the main house and several outbuildings of various vintages, sizes, and styles. In the outbuildings, my favorite unit is spacious room 24, with a private deck with views of Mount Equinox and quirky outdoor sculptures. Three rooms have fireplaces; the units in the mansion lack TVs. *Note:* The inn hosts weddings virtually every weekend in summer, so travelers looking for quiet are best off booking midweek.

River Rd., Manchester Village, VT 05254. © 800/648-4944 or 802/362-2500. Fax 802/362-1107. www.wilbur ton.com. 35 units (1 with detached private bathroom). Weekends $125–$260 double; holiday and foliage rates may be higher. Rates include breakfast. 2- to 3-night minimum stay on weekends and holidays. AE, MC, V. **Amenities:** Restaurant (regional contemporary); outdoor pool; 3 tennis courts. *In room:* A/C, TV, hair dryer, iron.

WHERE TO DINE

Most inns listed above offer good-to-excellent dining, often in romantic settings.

Chanteleer *★★★* CONTINENTAL If you like superbly prepared Continental fare but are put off by the stuffiness of highbrow Euro-wannabe restaurants, this is the place for you. Rustic elegance is the best description for this century-old dairy barn. The oddly tidy exterior, which looks as if it could house a chain restaurant, doesn't offer a clue to just how pleasantly romantic the interior is. Swiss-born chef Michel Baumann, who's owned and operated the inn since 1981, changes his menu every 3 weeks. Specializing in game, he may feature veal with a roasted garlic, sage, and balsamic demi-glaze, Swiss air-dried beef, veal chops, Wiener schnitzel, or slow-roasted duck with sesame seeds and hoisin sauce. Especially good is the whole Dover sole, which is filleted tableside. Don't neglect a side of rösti potatoes if they're on the menu.

Rte. 7A (3½ miles north of Manchester Center). © 802/362-1616. Reservations recommended. Main courses $26–$35. AE, MC, V. Wed–Mon 6–9:30pm. Closed Mon in winter and for 2–3 weeks in both Nov and Apr.

Little Rooster Cafe *★* CONTEMPORARY/REGIONAL This appealing spot near the outlets is open only for breakfast and lunch, and it's the best choice in town for either of these meals. Breakfasts include flapjacks served with real maple syrup, a Cajun omelet, and a luscious corned-beef hash (go ahead—your doctor won't know). Lunches feature a creative sandwich selection, such as a commendable roast beef with pickled red cabbage and a horseradish dill sauce.

Rte. 7A South, Manchester Center. © 802/362-3496. Breakfast items $4.50–$6.75; lunch $6.50–$8.25. No credit cards. Daily 7am–2:30pm (closed Wed in off season).

Mistral's at Toll Gate *★★* FRENCH The best tables at Mistral's are along the windows, which overlook a lovely creek that's spotlighted at night. Located in a tollhouse of a long-since-bypassed byway, the restaurant is a romantic mix of modern and old. The menu changes seasonally, with dishes such as salmon cannelloni stuffed with lobster or grilled filet mignon with Roquefort ravioli. The kitchen is run with great aplomb by chef/owner Dana Markey, who does an admirable job ensuring consistent quality. The restaurant has been recognized with the *Wine Spectator* excellence award since 1994.

Toll Gate Rd. (east of Manchester off Rte. 11/30). © 802/362-1779. Reservations recommended. Main courses $22–$32. AE, MC, V. July–Oct Thurs–Tues 6–10pm; Nov–June Thurs–Mon 6–10pm.

2 Brattleboro & the Southern Green Mountains

The hills and valleys around the bustling town of Brattleboro in Vermont's southeast corner contain some of the state's best-hidden treasures. Driving along the main valley floors—on roads along the West or Connecticut rivers, or on

Route 100—tends to be fast and only moderately interesting. To really soak up the region's flavor, turn off the main roads and wander up and over rolling ridges into the narrow folds in the mountains that hide peaceful villages. If it looks as though the landscape hasn't changed all that much in the past 2 centuries, well, you're right. This region is well known for its pristine and historic villages.

BRATTLEBORO ⭑
Set in a scenic river valley, the commercial town of Brattleboro is not just a good spot for provisioning; it has a funky, slightly dated charm that's part 19th century, part 1960s. The rough brick texture of this compact, hilly city has aged nicely, its flavor enhanced since its adoption by ex-flower children, who moved here, grew up, cut their hair, and settled in, operating many of the best local enterprises.

While Brattleboro is very much part of the 21st century, its heritage runs much deeper. In fact, Brattleboro was Vermont's first permanent settlement. Soldiers protecting the Massachusetts town of Northfield built an outpost in 1724 at Fort Dummer, about 1½ miles south of the current downtown. The site of the fort is now a small state park with campground. In later years, Brattleboro became a center of trade and manufacturing, and the home of Estey Organ Co., which once supplied countless home organs carved in ornate Victorian style.

This is the commercial hub of southeastern Vermont, located at the junction of I-89, Routes 5 and 9, and the Connecticut River. It's also the most convenient jumping-off point for those arriving from the south via the interstate. If you're looking for supplies, a strip-mall area with grocery stores is just north of town along Route 5. For more interesting shopping, explore the downtown.

ESSENTIALS
GETTING THERE　From the north or south, Brattleboro is easily accessible by car via Exits 1 and 2 on I-91. From the east or west, Brattleboro is best reached via Route 9. Brattleboro is also a stop on the **Amtrak** (𝓒 **800/872-7245**) line from Boston to northern Vermont.

VISITOR INFORMATION　The **Brattleboro Chamber of Commerce,** 180 Main St. (𝓒 **877/254-4565** or 802/254-4565; www.brattleboro.com), offers travel information year-round, weekdays between 8:30am and 5pm.

EXPLORING THE TOWN
Here's a simple, straightforward strategy for exploring Brattleboro: Park and walk. A town of cafes, bookstores, antiques stores, and outdoor-recreation shops, it invites browsing. One shop of note is **Sam's Outdoor Outfitters,** 74 Main St. (𝓒 **802/254-2933**), filled to the eaves with camping and fishing gear.

Enjoyable for kids and curious adults is the **Brattleboro Museum & Art Center** (𝓒 **802/257-0124**; www.brattleboromuseum.org) at the Union Railroad Station, 10 Vernon St. (downtown near the bridge to New Hampshire). Wonderful exhibits highlight the history of the town and the Connecticut River valley. The museum is open from mid-May to the end of December, Tuesday through Sunday from noon to 6pm. Admission is $3 for adults, $2 for seniors and college students, and free for children under 18.

WHERE TO STAY
Several chain motels flank Route 5 north of Brattleboro. The top choice is **Quality Inn & Suites,** 1380 Putney Rd. (𝓒 **800/228-5151** or 802/254-8701; www.qualityinnbrattleboro.com), featuring a restaurant and indoor/outdoor pool. Double rooms run $49 to $129, depending on size and season.

> ### *Tips* Looking for More Information?
>
> The best source of information on the region is a new state **visitor center** (© 802/254-4593) right off I-91 in Guilford, south of Brattleboro; you can only reach it by traveling north on I-91, not south. This beautiful building, is filled with maps, brochures, and videos. Helpful staff dole out up-to-the-minute information (using the Web if necessary) and make reservations; the vending machines and spotless bathrooms here are a godsend.

Chesterfield Inn ★★ Just a 10-minute drive east of Brattleboro in New Hampshire, this attractive inn sits in a field just off a busy state highway, but inside it's more quiet and refined than you'd imagine. The 1780s farmhouse has been expanded and modernized, possessing a casual contemporary sensibility with antique accents. Nine guest rooms are located in the main inn, and six in cottages nearby. All are spacious and comfortably appointed with a mix of modern and antique furniture. Eight have wood-burning fireplaces, and two have gas fireplaces. The two priciest units feature fireplaces, double Jacuzzis, and a private deck with mountain and meadow views.

Rte. 9, Chesterfield, NH 03443. © 800/365-5515 or 603/256-3211. Fax 603/256-6131. www.chesterfield inn.com. 15 units. $150–$250 double, foliage season and holidays $175–$275 double. 2-night minimum stay foliage season and holidays. Pets allowed with prior permission. AE, DC, DISC, MC, V. **Amenities:** Restaurant (New American); babysitting. *In room:* A/C, TV, dataport, minibar, coffeemaker, hair dryer, iron.

Colonial Motel & Spa *Value* Operated by the same family since 1975, this sprawling compound is well maintained and offers the town's best value. Opt for the back building's larger and quieter rooms, which are furnished with armchairs and sofas. The motel's best feature is the 75-foot indoor lap pool in the spa building. *Note:* Skiers who present their lift tickets enjoy a $20 discount.

Putney Rd., Brattleboro, VT 05301. © 800/239-0032 or 802/257-7733. www.colonialmotelspa.com. 73 units. $48–$130 double and suite. Rates include continental breakfast (served Mon–Fri only). AE, DISC, MC, V. Take Exit 3 off I-91; turn right and proceed ½ mile. **Amenities:** Restaurant (Italian); indoor pool; Jacuzzi; sauna. *In room:* A/C, TV.

Forty Putney Road ★★ Built in the early 1930s, this compact French château–style home features five guest rooms, including one two-room suites in an adjacent cottage. All are attractively appointed with a mix of modern country furnishings and reproductions. Two units feature gas fireplaces; room 4 is a spacious mini-suite. The cottage suite, with a foldaway sofa in the living room, is popular with small families and pairs of couples traveling together. The inn is close enough to town that you can stroll there in a few minutes. The one downside: It's situated along a busy road, diminishing the pastoral qualities.

40 Putney Rd., Brattleboro, VT 05301. © 800/941-2413 or 802/254-6268. Fax 802/258-2673. www.putney. net/40putneyrd. 5 units. $145–$230 double; off season $110–$170. Rates include breakfast. AE, DISC, MC, V. Pets allowed with prior permission. **Amenities:** Pub. *In room:* A/C, TV/VCR, dataport, fridge, hair dryer, iron.

Latchis Hotel ★ *Value* This downtown hotel fairly leaps out in Victorian-brick Brattleboro. Built in 1938 in an understated Art Deco style, the Latchis was once the cornerstone for a small chain of hotels and theaters. It no longer has its own orchestra or commanding dining room (though the theater remains), but it still has an authentic if funky and somewhat outdated flair. That may be one reason construction scaffolding sometimes covers the side. For the most part, the guest rooms are compact and comfortable, if not luxurious. About two-thirds of the rooms have limited views of the river, although those come with the sounds of cars on Main Street. If you want quiet, sacrifice the view and ask for a room in back. From the hotel, it's easy to explore town on foot, or you can wander the first-floor hallways to take in a first-run movie at the historic Latchis Theatre or quaff a pint in the Windham Brewery, where lunch is also served (see below).

50 Main St., Brattleboro, VT 05301. © **802/254-6300.** Fax 802/254-6304. www.brattleboro.com/latchis. 30 units. $65–$105 double, $145–$175 suite. AE, MC, V. **Amenities:** Restaurant (eclectic/brewpub); movie theater. *In room:* A/C, TV, fridge, coffeemaker.

WHERE TO DINE

Backside Cafe 👍 AMERICAN   A great choice for either breakfast or lunch. Nothing fancy here; everything is simple and homemade, and it's less, well, crunchy than the Common Ground (see below). The cafe is located in an open, airy second-floor space with wooden booths in the back of a building that once housed a Chrysler dealership. Lunches include familiar favorites such as grilled ham and Swiss cheese, spicy chili, and homemade soups, and some modest exotica, such as spinach, tomato, and roasted red pepper on focaccia. But even the regular burgers are pretty good. The cafe also offers a small selection of local beer.

Midtown Mall, 22 High St. (between High and Elliot sts., off the public parking lot). © **802/257-5056.** Main courses, breakfast $1.75–$4.75, lunch $3.25–$5.25. AE, DISC, MC, V. Mon–Fri 7:30am–3:30pm; Sat 8am–3:30pm; Sun 9am–3pm.

Brattleboro Food Co-op 👍 DELI   This Co-op has been selling wholesome foods since 1975, and its location, in a small strip mall downtown near the New Hampshire bridge, features plenty of parking (it's a bit tricky to spot from the main road). The huge store features a deli counter great for takeout; snag a quick, filling lunch that won't necessarily be tofu and sprouts—you can get a smoked turkey and Swiss cheese sandwich, or opt for a crispy salad. Check out the eclectic wine selection and the cheeses in the store section, too. Other interesting finds here include a good selection of natural bath products; house-made sausages and hand-cut steaks; and maple syrup and olive oil on tap. (Buy or bring a glass bottle and fill 'er up; you pay by weight at the cash register.)

Brookside Plaza, 2 Main St. © **802/257-0236.** Sandwiches $3.50–$6; prepared foods around $4–$5 per pound. MC, V. Mon–Sat 8am–9pm; Sun 9am–9pm.

Lucca Bistro & Brewery 👍 BISTRO   The Lucca Bistro is located beneath the Latchis Theatre and Latchis Hotel, and it is worth venturing downstairs for a relaxed evening in a comfortable, urbane space featuring informal French and Italian dinners. Sample the excellent homemade ales, stouts, and lagers made by the Windham Brewery, or go a bit more cosmopolitan with the oyster and martini bar near the entrance. The menu includes country French dishes such as a rustic pâté, onion soup au gratin, and escargot. You can also find a meaty "bistro burger" for those disinclined to travel abroad.

6 Flat St. © **802/254-4747.** Reservations recommended. Pasta $5–$8.95, bistro menu $9–$26. AE, DISC, MC, V. Wed–Sun 11:30am–2:30pm and 5:30–9:30pm.

Peter Havens Restaurant 👍👍 REGIONAL/AMERICAN   Chef-owned Peter Havens has been serving up reliable fare since 1989. Situated downtown in a pleasantly contemporary building, Peter Havens may not bowl you over with its menu, but you'll be impressed by what you're served. You're likely to feel instantly at home in this friendly spot, which has just 10 tables. Meals are prepared with choice ingredients and served with panache. Seafood is the specialty, with such offerings as salmon with a chipotle pepper rémoulade. The jazz playing in the background makes a nice accompaniment.

32 Elliot St. (C) **802/257-3333.** Reservations strongly recommended. Main courses $19–$24. MC, V. Tues–Sat 6–9pm.

Shin La (Value) AMERICAN/KOREAN   This is your best bet in Brattleboro for inexpensive spicy food. With wooden booths and mismatched furniture, it has the character of a pizza shop but is usually teeming with locals who come for the consistently good fare. One side of the menu features sandwiches (Reubens, Dagwoods, so forth), but check out the other side, which offers simple Korean country fare such as *bool ko ki* (sliced sirloin) and *shu mai* (steamed dumplings). Meals are tasty and inexpensive; service can be pokey on busy nights, however.

57 Main St. (C) **802/257-5226.** Entrees $5.50–$9.75. MC. V. Mon–Sat 11am–9pm.

T. J. Buckley's 🐸🐸🐸 NEW AMERICAN   Brattleboro's best restaurant, and one of the better choices in all of Vermont, the Lilliputian T. J. Buckley's is housed in a classic old diner on a dim side street. Renovations such as slate floors and golden lighting have created an intimate restaurant that seats about 20. No secrets exist between the chef, the sous chef, and the server, all of whom remain within a couple dozen feet of one another (and you) throughout the meal—the entire place is smaller than the kitchen of many restaurants. The menu is limited, with just four entrees each night—beef, poultry, shellfish, and fish—but the food has absolutely nothing in common with simple diner fare. Ingredients are fresh and select, the preparation more concerned with melding flavors than dazzling with architectural flourishes. If you want to sample chef Michael Fuller's inventiveness, try the fish or shellfish. Vegetarians can request a veggie platter.

132 Elliot St. (C) **802/257-4922.** Reservations strongly recommended. Main courses $25–$32. No credit cards. Winter Thurs–Sun 6–9pm; rest of year Wed–Sun 6–9pm (sometimes later on busy nights).

NEWFANE 🐸 & TOWNSHEND 🐸

These two villages, about 5 miles apart on Route 30, are the picture-perfect epitome of Vermont. Set within the serpentine West River Valley, both are built around town greens. Both towns consist of impressive white-clapboard homes and public buildings that share the grace and scale of the surrounding homes. Both boast striking examples of early American architecture.

Don't bother looking for strip malls, McDonald's, or video outlets hereabouts. Newfane and Townshend have a feel of having been idled on a sidetrack for decades while the rest of America steamed blithely ahead. There is life here. For visitors, however, inactivity is often the activity of choice. Guests find an inn or lodge that suits their temperament, then spend days strolling, undertaking aimless back-road driving tours, soaking in a mountain stream, hunting up, or striking off on foot for one of the rounded, wooded peaks that overlook villages and valleys.

ESSENTIALS
GETTING THERE   Newfane and Townshend are located on Route 30 northwest of Brattleboro. The nearest interstate access is off Exit 3 from I-91.

VISITOR INFORMATION   No formal information center serves these towns. Brochures are available at the **state visitor center** ((C) **802/254-4593**) on I-91 in Guilford, south of Brattleboro.

EXPLORING THE AREA

Newfane was originally founded on a hill a few miles from the current village in 1774; in 1825, it was moved to its present location on a valley floor. Some of the original buildings were dismantled and rebuilt, but most date from the early to mid–19th century. The **National Historic District** 𝒜𝒜 is comprised of some 60 buildings around the green and on nearby side streets. You'll find styles ranging from Federal through Colonial Revival, although Greek Revival appears to carry the day. A strikingly handsome courthouse dominates the shady green. For more details, get a copy of the free walking-tour brochure at the Moore Free Library on West Street or at the Historical Society (see below).

Explore Newfane's history at the engaging **Historical Society of Windham County** 𝒜, located on Route 30 across from the village common. It holds an eclectic assemblage of local artifacts (dolls, melodeons, rail ephemera), along with changing exhibits that feature intriguing snippets of local history. It's open from late May to mid-October, Wednesday through Sunday from noon to 5pm; admission by donation.

More than two dozen **antiques shops** on or near Route 30 in the West River Valley offer good grazing on lazy afternoons; they are also fine resources for serious collectors. Among the best: **Riverdale Antiques Center** 𝒜 (© **802/365-4616**), a group shop in Townshend with about 65 dealers, and **Schommer Antiques** 𝒜 (© **802/365-7777**) on Route 30 in Newfane Village, which carries a good selection of 19th-century furniture and accessories. Treasure hunters might do well to hit the seasonal **Newfane Flea Market** 𝒜 (© **802/365-7771**), which features 100-plus tables of assorted stuff. It operates Sundays, May through October, on Route 30 just north of Newfane Village.

Between Townshend and Jamaica, you'll pass the **Scott Covered Bridge** 𝒜 below the Townshend Dam—the longest single-span bridge in the state.

OUTDOOR PURSUITS

Townshend State Park (© **802/365-7500**) and Townshend State Forest are at the foot of Bald Mountain, 3 miles outside Townshend. Park here to hike **Bald Mountain,** one of the better short hikes in the region. A 3.1-mile loop trail begins behind the ranger station, following a bridle path along a brook. The ascent soon gets steeper, but when you arrive at the 1,680-foot summit, it is not bald. Open ledges offer views toward Mount Monadnock to the east and Bromley and Stratton mountains to the west. Open from early May to Columbus Day; the park charges a small day-use fee, and camping costs $13 to $20 per site. Ask for trail maps at the park office. To get to the park, cross the Townshend Dam (off Rte. 30), then turn left and continue to the park sign.

WHERE TO STAY & DINE

Four Columns Inn 𝒜𝒜   You can't help but notice the Four Columns Inn in Newfane: It's the regal, white-clapboard building with four Ionic columns just off the green. This perfect village setting hides an appealing inn within. Rooms in the Main House and Garden Wing are larger (and more expensive) than those above the restaurant. Four units have been made over as luxury suites, with double Jacuzzis. The best choice in the house might be room 12, with a Jacuzzi, skylight, gas fireplace, sitting area, and private deck with a view of a small pond. Low beams and white damask tablecloths characterize the inn's well-regarded dining room, which features creative New American cooking. Out of doors, the inn owns 150 acres of property interlaced by hiking trails.

21 West St. (P.O. Box 278), Newfane, VT 05345. ℭ **800/787-6633** or 802/365-7713. Fax 802/365-0022. www.fourcolumnsinn.com. 15 units. Weekdays $115–$340 double. Rates include continental breakfast. AE, DISC, MC, V. Pets allowed with prior permission ($10 per pet per night). **Amenities:** Restaurant (New American); outdoor pool; hiking trails; babysitting. *In room:* A/C, hair dryer.

Three Mountain Inn ⋆⋆ The lovely Three Mountain Inn is located in the middle of the appealing village of Jamaica, housed in a historic white clapboard home. It's benefited from a major upgrading under ambitious innkeepers, who are refurbishing the rooms one by one in a restrained country style. Accommodations range from the cozy and basic to the outright sumptuous, with whirlpools, gas fireplaces, and TV/VCRs. The inn is well located as a base for exploring southern Vermont; in winter, skiing at Stratton is a short drive away. Guests can walk from the inn to Jamaica State Park, where there's an easy and serpentine hike along the river on an old rail bed.

Rte. 30 (P.O. Box 180), Jamaica, VT 05343. ℭ **800/532-9399** or 802/874-4140. Fax 802/874-4745. www.three mountaininn.com. 15 units. $145–$285 double; $295 suite; $325 cottage. Rates include breakfast. AE, MC, V. Children 12 and older welcome. Pets allowed with restrictions (call first). **Amenities:** Restaurant (New American). *In room:* A/C, TV/VCR, dataport, hair dryer.

Windham Hill Inn ⋆⋆⋆ This inn is about as good as it gets, especially if you're in search of a romantic getaway. Situated on 160 acres at the end of a dirt road in a high upland valley, the inn was built in 1823 as a farmhouse and remained in the same family until the 1950s, when it was converted to an inn. The inn today melds the best of the old and new. The guest rooms are wonderfully appointed in an elegant country style; 6 have Jacuzzis or soaking tubs, 9 have balconies or decks, 13 have gas fireplaces, and all have views. Especially nice: the Jesse Lawrence Room, with soaking tub and gas woodstove, and Forget-Me-Not, with soaking tub and four-poster bed. The excellent **dining room** features creative cooking with a strong emphasis on local ingredients. Friendly new ownership took over in 2002, who continue the strong tradition set by previous management.

Windham Hill Rd., West Townshend, VT 05359. ℭ **800/944-4080** or 802/874-4080. Fax 802/874-4702. www.windhamhill.com. 21 units. $195–$305 double; foliage season $245–$355. Rates include breakfast. AE, DISC, MC, V. 2- to 3-night minimum stay on weekends and some holidays. Closed the week prior to Dec 27. Children 12 and older welcome. Turn uphill across from the country store in West Townshend and climb 1¼ miles to a marked dirt road; turn right and continue to end. **Amenities:** Restaurant (New American); outdoor heated pool; clay tennis court; game alcove; 6 miles of groomed cross-country ski trails. *In room:* A/C, hair dryer, iron, Jacuzzi (some).

GRAFTON ⋆⋆⋆ & CHESTER ⋆

Lovely **Grafton** was founded in 1763 and grew into a thriving settlement. By 1850, the town was home to 10,000 sheep and provided shelter for guests on the stage between Boston and Montreal. A cheese cooperative and soapstone industry flourished. But the village eventually fell on hard times. In 1963, brothers Hall and Dean Mathey created the Windham Foundation to purchase and restore the village, including an old hotel and the cheese operation. The foundation eventually came to own some 55 buildings and 2,000 acres; today Grafton teems once more, only this time with history buffs and tourists.

Just north, more commercial **Chester** is less pristine and more lived in. The downtown area has a pleasant neighborly feel; you can also find a handful of boutiques and shops along the main road. This is also a great destination for antiquing, with several good dealers in the area.

ESSENTIALS

GETTING THERE Take I-91 to Bellows Falls (Exit 5 or 6), and follow signs to town via Route 5. From here, take Route 121 west for 12 miles to Grafton. For a more scenic route, take Route 35 north from Townshend.

VISITOR INFORMATION The **Grafton Information Center** (© 802/843-2255; www.graftonvermont.org) is located in the Daniels House on Townshend Road, behind the Grafton Inn. For information on Chester, call the **Chester Area Chamber of Commerce** (© 802/875-2939).

EXPLORING GRAFTON

Grafton is best seen on foot. A picnic is a good idea, especially if it involves the excellent local cheddar. No grand historical homes are open for tours; it's more a village to be enjoyed with aimless walks.

Begin at the superb **Grafton Village Cheese Co.** (© 800/472-3866), a small, modern building where you can buy a snack of award-winning cheese and peer through plate-glass windows to observe the process. It's open Monday through Friday from 8:30am to 4pm, Saturday and Sunday from 10am to 4pm.

From here, follow the trail over a nearby covered bridge, then bear right on the footpath along a cow pasture to the **Kidder Covered Bridge.** Head into town via Water Street, and then on to Main Street. By the village center, white clapboard homes and shade trees abound, about as New England as New England gets.

On Main Street, stop by the **Grafton Historical Society Museum** (© 802/843-1010; open 10am to noon and 2 to 4pm weekends only; open daily in foliage season) to peruse photographs, artifacts, and memorabilia of Grafton. The suggested donation is $3 per adult. Then take a look at the **Old Tavern at Grafton,** the impressive building that anchors the town and has served as a social center since 1801, and partake of a beverage at the rustic Phelps Barn Lounge or a meal in one of the dining rooms. From here, make your way back to the cheese company by wandering on pleasant side streets. If you'd like to see Grafton from a different perspective, inquire at the inn about horse-and-buggy rides.

More active travelers, whether visiting in winter or summer, should head for the **Grafton Ponds Nordic Ski and Mountain Bike Center** (© 802/843-2400), just south of the cheese factory on Route 35. Managed by the Old Tavern, Grafton Ponds offers mountain-bike rentals and access to a hillside trails system summer and fall. In winter, it grooms 18 miles of trails and maintains a warming hut near the ponds, where you can sit by a woodstove and enjoy a bowl of soup. The Big Bear loop, running high up the flanks of a hill, is especially appealing; travel counterclockwise to enjoy a longer descent. Ski and snowshoe rentals are available; a trail pass costs $16 for adults, $12 for seniors and students, and $6 for children 7 to 12 (free for ages 6 and under).

WHERE TO STAY & DINE

Fullerton Inn ★ More of a hotel than a country inn, the inn is located in a tall building (well, relatively speaking) smack in the middle of Chester's one-street downtown. The lobby has the feel of an informal old roadhouse, but with its polished maple floors, a handsome fieldstone fireplace, and a piano, it's a welcoming spot. The eclectically furnished guest rooms on the two upstairs floors vary in size and decor, though most have small bathrooms. With little soundproofing, noises from neighbors can carry. Room 17 is quiet, faces the rear of the property, and has a separate sitting area. For the more socially inclined, rooms 8 and 10 have doors onto a balcony that overlooks the street.

40 The Common (P.O. Box 589), Chester, VT 05143. ℂ **866/884-8578** or 802/875-2444. Fax 802/875-6414. www.fullertoninn.com. 21 units. $99–$159 double. Rates include continental breakfast. 2-night minimum stay during foliage season and holiday weekends. AE, DISC, MC, V. Children 13 and older welcome. **Amenities:** Restaurant (traditional New England). *In room:* No phone.

Hugging Bear Inn *✴ Kids* Young kids love this place. A turreted, Queen Anne–style home on Chester's Main Street, it's filled with teddy bears, including a 5-foot teddy in the living room and some 250 of them scattered about the inn. In the attached barn, another *10,000* bears are for sale at the Hugging Bear Shoppe, which attracts serious collectors from around the world. The guest rooms are themed around—no surprise—teddy bears. Expect bear sheets, bear light-switch plates, bear shower curtains, and more. "Pandamonium" has a panda theme; the "Winnie the Pooh Room" is all Winnie, all the time.

244 Main St., Chester, VT 05143. ℂ **800/325-0519** or 802/875-2412. Fax 802/875-3823. www.hugging bear.com. 6 units. $90–$135 double. Rates include breakfast. 2-night minimum weekends and holidays. AE, DISC, MC, V. *In room:* A/C, no phone.

The Old Tavern at Grafton *✴✴* This beautiful, well-managed historic inn is actually a series of rooms spread throughout the town. About a dozen rooms are in the handsome colonnaded main inn building, which dates from 1801, while another few dozen are across the street in the Homestead Cottage. The remaining units are scattered among seven historic guesthouses in and around the village. All are decorated with antiques and an upscale-country sensibility; those in the Homestead Cottage (which is actually two historic homes joined together) have a more modern, hotel-like character—if you want more history, ask for the main inn. The tavern recently consolidated and updated some of its double rooms, converting 15 of them into suites; some even sport Jacuzzis now, making this an even better choice than it was before.

Routes 35 and 121, Grafton, VT 05146. ℂ **800/843-1801** or 802/843-2231. Fax 802/843-2245. www.old-tavern.com. 46 units. $175–$235 double, $285–$350 suite; foliage season, ski season, holidays $10 surcharge. Rates include breakfast. Ask about MAP plan rates. 2- to 3-night minimum stay on winter weekends, some holidays, and in foliage season. AE, MC, V. Closed March to mid-Apr. **Amenities:** Restaurant (contemporary New England); pub; swimming pond; tennis court; Jacuzzi; bicycle rental; game room; cross-country skiing. *In room:* No phone, Jacuzzi (some).

3 Woodstock

For more than a century, the resort community of Woodstock has been considered one of New England's most exquisite villages. You simply can't drive to Woodstock on a route that *isn't* pastoral and scenic, putting one in mind of an earlier, slower-paced era. Few other New England villages can top Woodstock for sheer grace and elegance. The tidy downtown is compact and neat, populated largely by galleries and boutiques. The superb village green is surrounded by handsome homes, creating what amounts to a comprehensive review of architectural styles of the 19th and early 20th centuries.

In addition to Woodstock, the region also takes in White River Junction and Norwich, two towns of distinctly different lineage located along the Connecticut River on the New Hampshire border.

WOODSTOCK *✴✴*

Much of this attractive town is on the National Register of Historic Places, and the Rockefeller family has deeded 500 acres surrounding Mount Tom (see below) to the National Park Service. Woodstock is notable as a historic center of winter outdoor recreation. The nation's first ski tow (a rope tow powered by an old Buick motor) was built in 1933 at the Woodstock Ski Hill near today's Suicide Six ski area. While no longer the skiing center of Vermont, this remains a worthy destination during the winter months for skating, cross-country skiing, and snowshoeing. One caveat: Woodstock's excellent state of preservation hasn't gone unnoticed, and it draws hordes of travelers. During the peak foliage season, the town green is perpetually obscured by tour buses slowly circling around it.

ESSENTIALS

GETTING THERE   Woodstock is 13 miles west of White River Junction on Route 4 (take Exit 1 off I-89). From the west, Woodstock is 20 miles east of Killington on Route 4. **Vermont Transit** (℗ **800/451-3292;** www.vermont transit.com) offers daily bus service to Woodstock, with connections to Boston and Burlington.

VISITOR INFORMATION   The **Woodstock Area Chamber of Commerce,** 18 Central St. (℗ **888/496-6378** or 802/457-3555; www.woodstockvt.com), staffs an information booth on the green, open June through October daily from 9:30am to 5:30pm.

EXPLORING THE TOWN

The heart of the town is the shady, elliptical Woodstock Green, a good place to sit and watch the world go by.

Stop by the **Woodstock Historical Society** ⋆, 26 Elm St. (℗ **802/457-1822**), housed in the Charles Dana House. The lovely home has rooms furnished in Federal, Empire, and Victorian styles, and offers displays of dolls, costumes, and early silver and glass. It and adjoining buildings are open from late May to the end of October, plus weekends in December. Hours are Monday through Saturday from 10am to 5pm and Sunday from noon to 4pm. Admission is $2.

Billings Farm and Museum ★★★   This remarkable working farm offers a striking glimpse of a grander era, as well as an introduction to the oddly interesting history of scientific farming. This extraordinary spot was the creation of Frederick Billings, who is credited with completing the Northern Pacific Railroad. (Billings, Montana, is named after him.) The 19th-century dairy farm was once renowned for its scientific breeding of Jersey cows and its fine architecture, especially the gabled 1890 Victorian farmhouse. A tour includes hands-on demonstrations of farm activities, exhibits of farm life, a look at an heirloom kitchen garden, and a visit to active milking barns.

River Rd. (about ½ mile north of town on Rte. 12), P.O. Box 489, Woodstock. ℗ 802/457-2355. www.billings farm.org. Admission $9 adults, $8 seniors, $7 children 13–17, $4.50 children 5–12, $2 children 3–4; free for children under 3. May–Oct daily 10am–5pm.

Marsh-Billings-Rockefeller National Historic Park ★★   The Billings Farm and the National Park Service have teamed up to manage this new park, the first and only national park focusing on the history of conservation. You'll learn about the life of George Perkins Marsh, the author of *Man and Nature* (1864), considered one of the first and most influential books in the history of the environmental movement. You'll also learn how Woodstock native and rail tycoon Frederick Billings, who read *Man and Nature,* eventually returned and purchased Marsh's boyhood farm, putting into practice many of the principles of good stewardship that Marsh espoused. Visitors can tour the elaborate Victorian mansion and walk the graceful carriage roads surrounding Mount Tom.

Mansion tours can accommodate only a limited number, however; advance reservations are recommended.

54 Elm St. (P.O. Box 178), Woodstock. © 802/457-3368. www.nps.gov/mabi. Free admission to grounds; mansion tour $6 adults, $3 children 16 and under. Late May to Oct daily 10am–5pm.

OUTDOOR PURSUITS

BIKING The terrain around Woodstock is ideal for exploring by bike. Most roads lead to great rides; simply grab a map and go. Mountain bikes are available for rent at **Woodstock Sports,** 30 Central St. (© **802/457-1568**).

HIKING **Mount Tom** ★★ is the prominent hill overlooking Woodstock, and its low summit has great views over the village and to the Green Mountains to the west. (It's part of the Marsh-Billings-Rockefeller National Historic Park.) You can ascend the mountain right from the village: Start at **Faulkner Park** ★. The gentle trail eventually arrives at a clearing overlooking the town. A steeper, rockier, more demanding trail continues 100 yards or so more up to the summit. From the top, follow the carriage path down to Billings Farm or retrace your steps back to the park and village.

HORSEBACK RIDING Experienced and aspiring equestrians head to the **Kedron Valley Stables** ★ (© **800/225-6301** or 802/457-1480; www.kedron. com), about 4½ miles south of Woodstock on Route 106. A full menu of riding options is available, from a 1-hour beginner ride ($35, or $33 per person for parties of 3 or more) to a 5-night inn-to-inn excursion ($1,625 per person, including all meals and lodging, double occupancy; higher in foliage season). Ask about weekend riding programs. The stables also rent horses to experienced riders for local trail rides, offer sleigh and carriage rides, and have an indoor riding ring for inclement weather. They are open daily except Thanksgiving and Christmas, but credit cards are not accepted.

SKIING The area's best cross-country skiing is at **Woodstock Ski Touring Center** ★★ (© **800/448-7900** or 802/457-6674), at the Woodstock Country Club, just south of town on Route 106. The center maintains 36 miles of trails, including 12 miles of trails groomed for skate skiing. And it's not all flat; the high and low points along the trail system vary by 750 feet in elevation. The ski center offers a lounge and restaurant, as well as a large health and fitness center accessible via ski trail. Lessons and picnic tours are available. The full-day trail fee is $12.50 for adults and $8.25 for children under 14.

The ski area **Suicide Six** ★ (© **802/457-6661**) has an intimidating name, but at just 650 vertical feet, it doesn't pose much of a threat to either life or limb. This venerable family-oriented ski resort (it opened in 1934) has two double chairs, a complimentary J-bar for beginners, and a modern base lodge. Beginners, intermediates, and families with young children will be content here. Lift tickets are $44 for adults, $28 for seniors and children under 14. (Inn guests ski free midweek.) The ski area is located 2 miles north of Woodstock on Pomfret Road.

WHERE TO STAY

Jackson House Inn ★★★ A comfortable and elegant choice located a 5-minute drive west of the village center, this home was built in 1890 by a lumber baron who hoarded the best wood for himself; the cherry and maple floors are so beautiful you'll feel guilty for not taking off your shoes. The guest rooms are well appointed with antiques, though some of the older rooms are rather small. A well-executed addition (1997) created four one-room suites with fireplaces and Jacuzzis. The inn welcomes guests with a series of pleasant surprises, including complimentary evening hors d'oeuvres and champagne and a 3-acre backyard with formal English gardens. This inn deserves three stars for its elegance and attentive service; only its location, a stone's throw off a busy stretch of Route 4, detracts from the graceful tranquility the innkeepers have succeeded in creating.

114-3 Senior Lane, Woodstock, VT 05091. ⓒ **800/448-1890** or 802/457-2065. Fax 802/457-9290. www. jacksonhouse.com. 15 units. $195–$260 double; $290–$390 suite. Rates higher in foliage season. Rates include breakfast. 2-night minimum stay most weekends. AE, MC, V. Children 14 and older welcome. **Amenities:** Restaurant (see below); fitness room; steam room; limited room service. *In room:* A/C, hair dryer, no phone (except in suites).

Kedron Valley Inn ⚜⚜   In a complex of Greek Revival buildings at a country crossroads, 5 miles south of Woodstock, the inn is run by Max and Merrily Comins, a cordial couple who offer guests a mix of history and country style. The attractive guest rooms in three buildings are furnished with both antiques and reproductions, and all have heirloom quilts from Merrily's collection; 15 feature wood-burning fireplaces, and 4 have Jacuzzis. The rooms in the newer, motel-like log building by the river are equally well furnished (and less expensive), with canopied beds, custom oak woodwork, and fireplaces. Room 37 even has a private streamside terrace. Rooms 12 and 17 are among the most popular; both suites have fireplaces and double Jacuzzis. Some Frommer's readers have noted that the inn's rooms can be on the cool side in deep winter.

Rte. 106, South Woodstock, VT 05071. ⓒ **800/836-1193** or 802/457-1473. Fax 802/457-4469. www.kedron valleyinn.com. 28 units. $131–$248 double; foliage season and Christmas week $163–$297 double. Rates include breakfast. Discounts available spring and midweek. AE, DISC, MC, V. Closed Apr and briefly prior to Thanksgiving. Pets allowed with prior permission. **Amenities:** Restaurant (contemporary American); swimming pond. *In room:* TV, no phone.

Shire Motel ⚜   The convenient Shire Motel is located within walking distance of the green and the rest of the village, and with its attractive colonial decor, it's better appointed than your average motel. The rooms are bright and have more windows than you might expect, most facing the river that runs behind the property. (The downside: thin sheets and some scuffed walls.) At the end of the second-floor porch is an outdoor kitchen where you can sit on rockers overlooking the river and enjoy a cup of coffee. The yellow clapboard house next door has three spacious and modern suites, all with gas fireplaces and Jacuzzis.

46 Pleasant St., Woodstock, VT 05091. ⓒ **802/457-2211.** www.shiremotel.com. 36 units. Summer $138–$300 double and suite; holidays and foliage season $168–$318; off season $98–$150. AE, MC, V. *In room:* A/C, TV, dataport, fridge.

Three Church St. *Value*   This sturdy brick Greek Revival B&B with a white clapboard ell is located just off the west end of the Woodstock green, and is well situated for launching an exploration of the village. It offers excellent value, especially if you don't mind sharing a bathroom and can overlook small imperfections like the occasional water stain on the ceiling. In the back is a lovely porch overlooking the inn's 3 acres, great for enjoying breakfast or sitting quietly. Guest rooms are furnished comfortably and eclectically with country antiques. A night here feels more like staying with a relative than at a fancy inn.

3 Church St., Woodstock, VT 05091. ⓒ **802/457-1925.** Fax 802/457-9181. 11 units (5 share 2 bathrooms). $75–$105 double. Higher rates during foliage season and Christmas week. Rates include breakfast. MC, V. Closed Apr. Pets allowed ($5 pet per night). **Amenities:** Outdoor pool; tennis court. *In room:* No phone.

Twin Farms ★★★   Twin Farms offers uncommon luxury at an uncommon price. Housed on a 300-acre farm that was once home to Nobel Prize–winning novelist Sinclair Lewis and his journalist wife, Dorothy Thompson, this is a very private, exceptionally tasteful small resort. The compound consists of the main inn, with four guest rooms, and ten outlying cottages—which are quite expensive—each with fireplace. (You can even rent the entire property for $24,000 a night if you're really feeling flush.) The owners are noted art collectors, and some of the work on display includes originals by David Hockney, Roy Lichtenstein, Milton Avery, and William Wegman. Rates here include gourmet meals, open bar, and use of all the resort's recreational equipment.

Barnard, VT 05031. © **800/894-6327** or 802/234-9999. Fax 802/234-9990. www.twinfarms.com. 14 units. $950–$1,100 double; $1,100–$2,600 cottage. Rates include all meals and liquor. AE, MC, V. Closed Apr. No children under 18 accepted. **Amenities:** Restaurant (New American); lake swimming; 2 tennis courts; fitness center; Jacuzzi; water sports equipment rental; bike rental; game room; concierge; car rental; courtesy car; limited room service; in-room massage. *In room:* A/C, TV/VCR, coffeemaker, minibar, hair dryer, iron.

Woodstock Inn & Resort ★★★   This is central Vermont's best full-scale resort. Located in an imposing brick structure off the town green, the inn appears to be a venerable and long-established institution at first glance. But it's not—it wasn't built until 1969. The inn adopted a Colonial Revival look well suited for Woodstock. Inside, guests are greeted by a broad stone fireplace and sitting areas tucked throughout the lobby. Guest rooms are tastefully decorated in either country pine or a Shaker-inspired style. The best units, in the wing built in 1991, feature plush carpeting, fridges, and fireplaces.

14 The Green, Woodstock, VT 05091. © **800/448-7900** or 802/457-1100. Fax 802/457-6699. www.wood stockinn.com. 141 units, 3 suites. Peak season $199–$389 double, $499–$609 suite; off season $129–$248 double, $270–$450 suite. Ask about packages. AE, MC, V. 2-night minimum stay on weekends. **Amenities:** 2 restaurants (traditional/regional, cafe); indoor pool; outdoor pool; golf course; 12 tennis courts; fitness center (squash, racquetball, steam rooms); bike rental; cross-country ski trails; concierge; limited room service; babysitting; laundry service; dry cleaning. *In room:* A/C, TV w/pay movies, dataport, hair dryer, iron, safe.

WHERE TO DINE

Bentley's ★ AMERICAN   Bentley's adopts an affluent English gentleman's club feel and offers Woodstock's best choice for lunch. The dining room, located beyond an Anglophilic bar, affects a Victorian elegance, but not ostentatiously so. Lunch is the time for one of their juicy burgers or creative sandwiches (grilled chicken in mango sauce with almonds, anyone?). The dinner menu leans more toward resort standards such as chicken and shrimp pescatore or steak flambéed with Jack Daniels, but also cracks its doors to slightly more ambitious fare, such as farm-raised duck with apricot and plum sauce. It's very often quite crowded at night, so reserve ahead if you can. At the

> *Tips* **Breadworks**
>
> Right in the village center is **Pane Salute**, 61 Central St. (© **802/457-4882**), a bakery that specializes in delectable Italian breads.

fine brunch on Sunday, order the New England corned beef hash with poached eggs and hollandaise sauce. Stick around late enough on weekend evenings and you might witness a startling transformation: Tables are swept off a dance floor, the ceiling rolls back to reveal high-tech lighting, and Bentley's becomes the place to dance the night away. The adjacent ice-cream parlor makes good milkshakes.

3 Elm St. © 802/457-3232. www.bentleysrestaurant.com. Reservations recommended for parties of 4 or more. Main courses, lunch $7.95–$13; dinner $16–$24. AE, DC, DISC, MC, V. Sun–Thurs 11am–9:30pm; Fri–Sat 11am–10pm. Open later for drinks and dancing on weekends.

Jackson House Inn ★★★ CONTINENTAL   The Jackson House dining room is a modern addition to the original inn (see above). Its centerpiece is a 16-foot-high stone fireplace, and it boasts soaring windows with views of the gardens. Men may feel most comfortable in a sports coat, though a jacket is not required. Once settled, you'll sample some of the most exquisite dishes in New England, ingeniously conceived, deftly prepared, and artfully arranged. The three-course meals begin with offerings such as Maine crabmeat and field greens with shaved fennel. The main courses do an equally good job combining the earthy with the celestial. Expect dishes such as crispy-skin salmon with a shiitake compote, or an Angus filet with creamy white-corn polenta and a three-onion marmalade. For dessert, the banana-walnut soufflé is delicate, and the crème brûlée with a cranberry compote is striking. It's a meal that will linger in memory.

114-3 Senior Lane. ✆ **800/448-1890** or 802/457-2065. Reservations highly recommended. 3-course fixed-price dinner $55 (chef's tasting menu $95). AE, MC, V. Wed–Sun 6–9pm.

The Prince and the Pauper ★★ NEW AMERICAN   It takes a bit of sleuthing to find this place, located down Dana Alley (next to the Woodstock Historical Society's Dana House), but it's worth the effort. This is one of Woodstock's more inviting restaurants, with an intimate but informal setting. (It's a bit more casual than Jackson House.) Begin with a drink in the taproom (open 1 hr. before the restaurant), then move over to the rustic-but-elegant dining room. The menu changes daily, but you might start with a Cuban black bean soup, Vietnamese shrimp rolls in rice paper, a crab custard, house-cured salmon, or a cut of maple-cured rainbow trout, then move on to baked swordfish with a roasted pepper aïoli, crisped duck, grilled New Zealand venison, or a boneless rack of lamb baked in puff pastry with spinach and mushroom *duxelles*. The fixed-price dinner menu offers good value; those on a tighter budget should linger in the lounge and order from the bistro menu, with selections such as crab cakes, meatloaf, pork chops, Texas chili, and tasty wood-fired pizzas.

24 Elm St. ✆ **802/457-1648**. www.princeandpauper.com. Reservations recommended. Dinners (appetizer, salad, entree) $41. AE, DISC, MC, V. Sun–Thurs 6–9pm; Fri–Sat 6–9:30pm. Lounge opens at 5pm.

Simon Pearce Restaurant ★★ NEW AMERICAN   The setting can't be beat. Housed in a restored 19th-century woolen mill with wonderful views of a waterfall (spotlighted at night), Simon Pearce is a collage of exposed brick, pine floorboards, and handsome wooden tables and chairs. Meals are served on Simon Pearce pottery and glassware—if you like your place setting, you can buy it afterward at the sprawling retail shop in the mill. The atmosphere is a wonderful concoction of formal and informal, ensuring that everybody feels comfortable whether in white shirt and tie or (neatly laundered) jeans. Lunch features dishes such as shepherd's pie, beef and Guinness stew, lamb burgers, crispy calamari with field greens, or crab and cod cakes with a red pepper coulis. At dinner, look for entrees such as crispy roast duck with a mango chutney sauce, wild king salmon *en croute*, or filet mignon in port wine sauce with a fig-onion compote and blue cheese butter on the side. The bread and wines are also excellent.

The Mill, Quechee. ✆ **802/295-1470**. www.simonpearce.com. Reservations recommended for dinner. Main courses, lunch $8.75–$13; dinner $22–$28. AE, DC, DISC, MC, V. Daily 11:30am–2:45pm and 6–9pm.

Wild Grass ★ ECLECTIC   Wild Grass is located east of town on Route 4 in a small business complex that lacks the quaintness of much of the rest of Woodstock—yet the food rises above the prosaic surroundings with a menu that contains genuinely creative offerings and good value for this often overpriced town.

Especially appealing are the unique crispy sage leaves with tangy dipping sauces, served as an appetizer. Fish is grilled to perfection here, and sauces are pleasantly zesty. Other entrees include roast duckling with cabernet whipped potatoes, jerked chicken, ancho chili-rubbed filet tenderloin, and, for vegetarians, a rich vegetable ragout with walnut oil and chervil.

Rte. 4 (east of the village). © 802/457-1917. Reservations recommended during peak season. Main courses $11–$17. DISC, MC, V. Tues–Sat 6–9pm (open Sun also in summer).

NORWICH ☆ & WINDSOR

Norwich is a peaceful New England town slightly off the beaten track. The town has a fine selection of woodframe and brick homes, and boasts a superb restaurant and a science museum for kids.

ESSENTIALS

GETTING THERE   Norwich may be reached from Exit 13 on I-91, or by driving north from White River Junction on Route 5. White River Junction is also served by daily **Amtrak** service (© **800/872-7245**).

VISITOR INFORMATION   The **Upper Valley Bi-State Regional Chamber of Commerce,** 100 Railroad Row, White River Junction, VT 05001 (© **802/ 295-6200**), staffs an information center near the railroad station in downtown White River Junction. It's open from 9:30am to 4:30pm daily during the peak season (summer and foliage season).

EXPLORING THE REGION

South of Norwich and White River Junction, in the historic town of Windsor, is the **American Precision Museum** ☆, 196 S. Main St. (© **802/674-5781;** www. americanprecision.org). Its collections commemorate Windsor's role in the machine tool industry and as home to countless inventors and inventions. Asahel Hubbard put Windsor on the map in the early 19th century, when he invented the hydraulic pump. Other inventions followed from Hubbard, his relatives, and other inspired locals: the coffee percolator, the underhammer rifle, the lubricating bullet, an early sewing machine. The museum is open Memorial Day through October daily from 10am to 5pm. Admission is $6 for adults, $4 for seniors and students, and free for children under 6. Families can enter for $18.

Just outside Norwich, on Route 5 a bit south of the interstate exit, is the interesting headquarters, bakery, and baking school run by the **King Arthur Flour** company, which makes some of the best baking flours in America. **The Baker's Store** ☆ (© **802/649-3361** or 800/827-6836) is open 9am to 6pm Monday to Saturday, to 4pm Sunday; in addition to all-natural breads and a program of demonstrations and classes, there's also a good selection of high-quality cookware for sale at the store.

FUN FOR KIDS

Montshire Museum of Science ☆☆ *Kids*   Not your average New England science museum of dusty stuffed animals in a creaky building needing attention, the Montshire is a modern, architecturally engaging, hands-on museum that draws kids back repeatedly. The museum contains some live animals (don't miss the leaf-cutter ant exhibit on the second floor), but it's mostly fun, interactive exhibits that involve kids deeply, teaching them the principles of math and science on the sly. Even preschoolers are entertained here at "Andy's Place," a play area with aquariums, bubble-making exhibits, and other magical things. Outside, a science park masquerades as a playground, and four nature trails wend through this riverside property of tall trees and chirpy birds.

1 Montshire Rd., Norwich. (✆ 802/649-2200. www.montshire.org. $7 adults, $6 children 3–17, children under 3 free. MC, V. Daily 10am–5pm. Use Exit 13 off I-91 and head east; look for museum signs almost immediately.

WHERE TO STAY

If you're craving a fine inn, also try Hanover, New Hampshire, 2 minutes across the Connecticut River bridge; for affordable motels, also drive across the river, to West Lebanon's small airport. See chapter 12 for details on both towns.

Juniper Hill Inn ★★   About 20 miles south of Norwich in Windsor is one of the more inviting retreats I've come across. Set high atop a hill overlooking the Connecticut River Valley, this 1902 manor home is more mannered and elegant than many Vermont inns, taking its architectural inspiration from various Colonial Revivals. Palladian windows, a slate roof, and six chimneys grace the exterior; the richly appointed great hall features coffered paneling. The common rooms are spacious and lovely—especially the library with its leather wingback chairs—and are reason enough to stay. Each of the 16 guest rooms is different, but all feature thoughtful amenities such as chocolates, fresh flowers, hair dryers, CD players and a sample of CDs, and even a decanter of sherry. Room 1 is a bright corner room with four-poster bed and attractive bathroom; the smallest is Room 8, cozy and appealing with its wood-burning fireplace. (Eleven rooms have either wood-burning or propane fireplaces.) Dinner is served by reservation, with 1-day advance notice requested. The lovely dining room is quietly romantic, with classical styling.

Juniper Hill Rd. (RR#1, Box 79), Windsor, VT 05089. (✆ 800/359-2541 or 802/674-5273. Fax 802/674-2041. www.juniperhillinn.com. 16 units. $95–$195 double. Rates include breakfast. 2-night minimum stay during foliage season, holiday weekends, and in fireplace rooms on all weekends. AE, DISC, MC, V. Closed 1st 3 weeks of Apr and 1st 2 weeks of Nov. Children 12 and older welcome. **Amenities:** Restaurant (traditional/regional); outdoor pool. *In room:* A/C, hair dryer, no phone.

Norwich Inn ★   Innkeepers Sally and Tim Wilson bought the once-dowdy Norwich Inn about 10 years ago and have steadily improved the place, most recently re-creating the original tower (with suite) on the front of the building. Many guest rooms at this historic inn, parts of which date back to 1797, feature brass and canopy beds; history buffs should opt for the 16 comfortable rooms in the main inn rather than those in the motel-style annex out back, where rooms are less expensive. The main building is alleged to host one uninvited guest: the ghost of Mary Walker, who according to local lore, atones for the sin of selling bootleg liquor at the inn during Prohibition. Keeping in the tradition of Mary Walker, the inn operates **Jasper Murdock's Alehouse,** certainly one of America's tiniest breweries; Tim, the brewer, loves to talk beer. Tasty burgers and pub fare are served here, plus Tim's delicious handcrafted ales, porters, and stouts.

Main St., Norwich, VT 05055. (✆ 802/649-1143. www.norwichinn.com. 28 units (includes 2 2-bedroom apts). June–Oct $79–$149 double, $149 suite; off season $65–$109 double, $129 suite. Rates include continental breakfast. AE, DC, DISC, MC, V. Dogs allowed in motel only. **Amenities:** Restaurant (New American); pub. *In room:* A/C, TV.

WHERE TO DINE

Polka Dot DINER   Classic diner fare is served up daily in this local institution, a relic of the days when a slew of area diners catered to railwaymen working the freight and passenger trains. (Amtrak still makes a stop across the way.)

The interior is painted a robin's egg blue, and the walls are hung with railroad photos and train models. You can sidle up to the counter and order a fried egg sandwich, or grab one of the booths for a filling, decently prepared meal (think: liver and onions) that's not likely to cost much more than $5 or $6. If you're here for breakfast, try the delicious homemade doughnuts. Architecturally, it's not a classic brushed-steel diner, but the place has all the atmosphere of one.

1 N. Main St. at Joe Reed Dr., White River Junction. © 802/295-9722. Breakfast and lunch $1.25–$4.25; dinner $4.75–$7.50. Daily Tues–Sun 5am–7pm. Closed Thanksgiving and Christmas.

4 Killington & Rutland

The ski resort town of Killington is plainly not the Vermont pictured on calendars and placemats. But the region around the mountain boasts Vermont's most active winter scene, with loads of distractions both on and off the mountain. The area has a frenetic, where-it's-happening feel in winter. Those most content here are skiers who like their skiing BIG, singles in search of aggressive mingling, and travelers who want a wide selection of amenities and are willing to sacrifice the quintessential New England charm for a broader range of diversions.

About a dozen miles to the west, the rough-hewn city of Rutland lacks the immediate charm of other Vermont towns, but has a rich history and an array of convenient services for travelers.

KILLINGTON

Killington lacks a town center, a single place that makes you feel you've arrived. Killington is wherever you park. Since the mountain was first developed for skiing in 1957, dozens of restaurants, hotels, and stores have sprouted along Killington Road to accommodate the legions of skiers who descend upon the area during the skiing season, which typically runs October through May, sometimes into June.

ESSENTIALS

GETTING THERE   Killington Road extends southward from Routes 4 and 100 (marked on some maps as Sherburne). It's about 12 miles east of Rutland on Route 4. Many of the inns offer shuttles to the Rutland airport. **Amtrak** (© 800/USA-RAIL; www.amtrak.com) offers service from New York to Rutland, with connecting shuttles to the mountain and various resorts.

The **Marble Valley Regional Transit District** (© 802/773-3244; www.the bus.com) operates the **Skibus,** offering inexpensive service between Rutland and Killington.

VISITOR INFORMATION   The **Killington Chamber of Commerce** (© 802/ 773-4181; www.killington-chamber.org) has information on lodging and travel packages, and staffs an information booth on Route 4 at the base of the access road, open Monday through Friday from 9am to 5pm, and weekends from 10am to 2pm. For information on accommodations in the area and travel to Killington, contact the **Killington Lodging and Travel Service** (© 877/4KTIMES).

Tips Looking for Classic New England?

If you're in search of classic New England, consider staying in quaint Woodstock (see earlier) and commuting the 20 miles to the slopes.

DOWNHILL SKIING

Killington ★★   A love-it or hate-it kind of place, New England's largest and most bustling ski area offers greater vertical drop than any other New England mountain. You'll find the broadest selection of slopes, with trails ranging from long, narrow, old-fashioned runs to killer bumps high on its flanks. Thanks to this diversity, it's long been the destination of choice for serious skiers. That said, it's also the skier's equivalent of the Mall of America: a huge operation run with efficiency and not much personal touch. It's easy to get lost and separated from friends and family, and seems to attract boisterous groups of young adults. To avoid getting lost, ask about free tours of the mountain, led by ski ambassadors based at Snowshed.

Killington, VT 05751. ℂ 877/4KTIMES for lodging, or 802/422-3261. www.killington.com. Vertical drop: 3,050 ft. Lifts: 2 gondolas, 31 lifts. Skiable acreage: 1,182. Lift tickets: $67 adults, $43 to $54 youth and seniors; holidays $72 adults, $48 to $59 youth and seniors.

CROSS-COUNTRY SKIING

Nearest to the ski area (just east of Killington Rd. on Rte. 100/Rte. 4) is **Mountain Meadows Cross Country Ski Resort** ★ (ℂ **800/221-0598** or 802/775-7077; www.xcskiing.net), with 36 miles of trails groomed for both skating and classic skiing. The trails are largely divided into three pods, with beginner trails closest to the lodge, an intermediate area a bit further along, and an advanced 6-mile loop farthest away. Rentals and lessons are available at the lodge. For adults, a 1-day pass is $18, a half-day (after 1pm) pass is $15. Kids age 6 to 12 pay $8 per day, $6 per half-day.

The intricate network of trails at **Mountain Top Inn** ★★ (ℂ **802/483-6089**) has long had a loyal local following. The 66-mile trail network offers pastoral views through mixed terrain groomed for traditional and skate skiing. The area is often deep with snow owing to its high ridge-top location in the hills east of Rutland, and snowmaking along key portions of the trail ensures that you won't have to walk across bare spots during snow droughts. The resort maintains three warming huts along the way, and lessons and ski rentals are available. The trails have a combined elevation gain of 670 feet. Adults pay $18 for 1-day trail passes, $15 for half-day passes (after 1pm). With more challenging and picturesque terrain, Mountain Top offers the better value of the two options.

OTHER OUTDOOR PURSUITS

MOUNTAIN BIKING   Mountain biking comes in two forms at Killington—organized on the mountain and on-your-own on the back roads. On Killington's mountain, around 45 miles of trails are open for biking, and one eight-passenger gondola line is equipped to haul bikes and riders to the summit, delivering great views. Riders give their forearms a workout applying brakes while bumping down the slopes. A trail pass is $8; a trail pass with a two-time gondola ride is $22; unlimited gondola rides are $32 per day.

The **Mountain Bike Shop** (ℂ 802/422-6232) is located at the Killington Base Lodge and is open from June to mid-October. Bike rentals (with suspension) start at $30 for 2 hours, up to $45 for a full day. Helmets are required ($3 additional per day).

Bikes are also available for rent—along with sound advice on local trails—from **True Wheels Bike Shop** (ℂ 802/422-3234), located in the Basin Ski Shop near the top of the Killington Access Road. Rentals range from $45 a day for a low-end bike to $65 for a bike with rock shocks and disc brakes (half-day rates also available; helmets are included). Bikes are available from April to mid-October; reservations are helpful during holidays and busy times.

GOLF   Vermont is loaded with fine golf courses, public and private, lovely in summer and outstandingly scenic in fall. The acknowledged top course is **Green Mountain National Golf Course** ★★ (© **888/483-4653;** www.greenmountain national.com) in Killington. Greens fees, without cart, are $50 per adult mid-week, $68 weekends and holidays. There are discounts after 3pm and before June 20; rentals, instruction, and a driving range are also available.

HIKING   Area hikers often set their sights on **Deer Leap Mountain** ★★ and its popular 3-hour loop to the summit and back. The trail begins at the Inn at Long Trail off Route 4 at Sherburne Pass. Leave your car across from the inn, then head north through the inn's parking lot onto the Long Trail/Appalachian Trail and into the forest. Follow the white blazes (you'll return on the blue-blazed trail you see entering on the left). In ½ mile, you arrive at a crossroads. The Appalachian Trail veers right to New Hampshire's White Mountains and Mount Katahdin in Maine; Vermont's Long Trail runs to the left. Follow the Long Trail; after some hiking through forest and rock slab for ½ mile or so, turn left at the signs for Deer Leap Height. Great views of Pico and the Killington area await you in less than ½ mile. After a snack break, continue down the steep, blue-blazed descent back to Route 4 and your car. The entire loop is about 2½ miles.

A HISTORIC SITE

President Calvin Coolidge State Historic Site ★★   When told that Calvin Coolidge had died, literary wit Dorothy Parker is said to have responded, "How can they tell?" Even in his death, the nation's most taciturn president had to fight for respect. A trip to the Plymouth Notch Historic District should at least raise Silent Cal's reputation among visitors, who'll get a strong sense of the president reared in this mountain village, a man shaped by harsh weather, unrelieved isolation, and a strong sense of community and family.

Situated in a high upland valley, the historic district consists of a group of about a dozen unspoiled buildings open to the public plus a number of other private residences that may be observed from the outside only. At the Coolidge Homestead (now open for tours) in August 1923, Vice President Coolidge, on a vacation from Washington, was awakened and informed that President Warren Harding had died. His own father, a notary public, administered the presidential oath of office. Coolidge is buried in the cemetery across the road. He remains the only president to have been born on Independence Day, and every July 4th, a wreath is laid at his simple grave in a quiet ceremony.

Be sure to stop by the **Plymouth Cheese Factory** (© **802/672-3650**), just uphill from the Coolidge Homestead. The business was owned by the former president's son until the late 1990s, and makes excellent cheeses. Hours are daily from 9:30am to 5pm; in winter, it's best to call ahead, as the park is closed, but you may be able to visit the factory.

Rte. 100A, Plymouth. © **802/672-3773.** Admission $6.50 adults, free for children 14 and under. Daily 9:30am–5pm. Closed mid-Oct to late May.

WHERE TO STAY

Skiers headed to Killington for a week or so of skiing should consider the condo option. A number of condo developments spill down the hillside and along the low ridges flanking the access road, varying in elegance, convenience, and size.

> (*Value*   **Budget Hints for Skiers**
>
> Skiers on a budget should consider basing in Rutland, at one of the chain motels, and commuting to the mountain via car or the $2 shuttle bus. See the "Rutland" section below for suggestions on motels.

Highridge features units with saunas and two-person Jacuzzis, along with access to a compact health club. **Sunrise Village** is more remote, with a health club and easy access to the Bear Mountain lifts. **The Woods at Killington** are farthest from the slopes (free shuttle) but offer access to the finest health club and the road's best restaurant. Rates fluctuate widely, depending on time of year, number of bedrooms, and number of days you plan to stay. But figure on prices ranging from around $100 to $130 and up per person per day, including lift tickets.

You can line up a vacation—or request more information—by contacting the **Killington Lodging and Travel Bureau** (© 888/4KTIMES; www.killington. com), which also arranges stays at area inns and motels.

Blueberry Hill Inn ★★★   The wonderfully homey Blueberry Hill Inn lies in the heart of the Moosalamoo recreation area, on 180 acres along a quiet road about 45 minutes northwest of Killington (about midway to Middlebury). With superb hiking, biking, canoeing, swimming, and cross-country skiing, it's an extraordinary destination for those inclined toward spending time outdoors and away from the bother of everyday life. (From the inn's brochure: "We offer you no radios, no televisions, no bedside phones to disturb your vacation.") The inn dates to 1813; one graceful addition is the greenhouse walkway, leading to the cozy guest rooms. Family-style meals are served in a rustic dining room, with a great stone fireplace and homegrown herbs drying from the wooden beams.

Goshen-Ripton Rd., Goshen, VT 05733. © 800/448-0707 or 802/247-6735. Fax 802/247-3983. www.blue berryhillinn.com. 12 units. $200–$320 double. Rates include breakfast and dinner. MC, V. **Amenities:** Sauna; bike rental; cross-country ski trails; babysitting. *In room:* No phone.

Butternut on the Mountain Motor Inn   Butternut is a short remove from the access road, just enough to lend a little quiet, although winter guests tend to make up for that with a dose of boisterousness. It's more a recommended budget choice than an especially noteworthy spot. The rooms are motel-size with motel decor, but the inn's unexpected facilities make it a good option. There's a lounge area with fireplace on the second floor and a restaurant with full bar and darts on the first floor. Eleven rooms have air-conditioning.

Killington Rd. (P.O. Box 306), Killington, VT 05751. © 800/524-7654 or 802/422-2000. Fax 802/422-3937. www.butternutlodge.com. 18 units. $56–$120 double. Lower off-season rates. AE, DISC, MC, V. **Amenities:** Restaurant (pub fare); lounge; indoor pool; Jacuzzi; game room. *In room:* A/C (some), TV.

Cortina Inn & Resort ★   The innkeepers here do a fine job making this inn, with nearly 100 rooms, feel like a smaller and more intimate place. Especially appealing is the attention paid to service and detail—the staff even brushes guests' car windows in the morning after a snow. The lodge, set back slightly from busy Route 4 between Pico and Rutland, was built in 1966, with additions in 1975 and 1987. The interior has retro ski chalet charm dating from the original construction—even with a sunken conversation pit with a two-sided fireplace and a spiral staircase twisting up to a second level. Guest rooms vary slightly in their modern country style, but all are nicely furnished.

Rte. 4 (1½ miles west of Pico), Killington, VT 05751. © **800/451-6108** or 802/773-3333. Fax 802/775-6948. www.cortinainn.com. 96 units. $109–$189 double. Rates include breakfast. 5-night minimum stay Christmas week; 3-night minimum stay Columbus and Presidents' Day weekends. AE, DC, DISC, MC, V. Pets allowed ($5 per pet per night). **Amenities:** Restaurant (regional); tavern; indoor pool; 8 tennis courts; fitness room; Jacuzzi; sauna; mountain-biking center; children's center; 2 game rooms; canoeing pond; concierge; courtesy shuttle (ski season only); limited room service; babysitting; laundry service; dry cleaning. *In room:* A/C, TV, data-port, hair dryer, iron.

Inn at Long Trail ✸

The Inn at Long Trail is situated in an architecturally undistinguished building at the intersection of Route 4 and the Long and Appalachian trails (about a 10-min. drive from Killington's ski slopes). The interior of this rustic inn is far more charming than the exterior. Tree trunks support the beams in the lobby, which sports log furniture and banisters of yellow birch along the stairway. The older rooms in this three-floor hotel (built in 1938 as an annex to a long-gone lodge) are furnished simply, in ski-lodge style. Comfortable, more modern suites with fireplaces, telephones, and TVs are offered in a motel-like addition. The **dining room** is fun and appealing, maintaining the Keebler-elf theme with a stone ledge that juts through the wall from the mountain behind. The menu features a selection of hearty meals, including the inn's famed Guinness stew, corned beef and cabbage, and chicken potpie. There's live Irish music in the pub on weekends during the busy seasons.

Rte. 4, Killington, VT 05751. © **800/325-2540** or 802/775-7181. Fax 802/747-7034. www.innatlongtrail.com. 19 units. $89–$118 double; foliage season $190–$250 double; off season $68–$98 double. Rates include breakfast. 2-night minimum stay most weekends and during foliage season. AE, MC, V. Closed late Apr to late June. Pets allowed with prior permission (with damage deposit). **Amenities:** Dining room (rustic/Irish); pub; Jacuzzi; laundry service. *In room:* No phone.

Inn of the Six Mountains ✸

With its profusion of gables and dormers, the Inn of the Six Mountains stands among the more architecturally memorable of the numerous hotels along Killington Road. The lobby is welcoming in a modern, Scandinavian sort of way, with lots of blond wood and stone, and the location is convenient to Killington's base lodge, just a mile up the road. The guest rooms are tastefully decorated in a Shaker-inspired sort of way, but for a luxury hotel that offers only "deluxe" rooms and suites, the attention to detail can come up short, with some routine maintenance that's apparently been put off.

2617 Killington Rd. (P.O. Box 2900), Killington, VT 05751. © **800/228-4676** or 802/422-4302. Fax 802/422-4898. www.sixmountains.com. 103 units (includes 4 suites). Winter $149–$239 double, $199–$250 suite; winter holidays $259–$289 double, $309–$330 suite; foliage season $149–$239 double, $199–$250 suite; spring, summer, and other off season $138–$168 double, $188–$220 suite. Rates include continental breakfast. AE, DC, DISC, MC, V. **Amenities:** Restaurant (American); indoor pool; outdoor pool; tennis court; fitness center; Jacuzzi; sauna; game room; business center; limited room service. *In room:* TV, dataport, fridge, coffeemaker, hair dryer, safe.

Killington Grand Resort Hotel ✸✸

This is a good (though pricey) choice for travelers seeking contemporary accommodations right on the mountain. More than half of the units have kitchen facilities, and most are quite spacious though decorated in a generic country-condo style. Some units can sleep up to six people, and the resort has placed an emphasis on catering to families. You pay a premium for convenience compared with other spots near the mountain, but that convenience is hard to top during ski season. The helpful service is a notch above that typically experienced at large ski hotels.

228 East Mountain Rd. (near Snowshed base area), Killington, VT 05751. © **877/4KTIMES.** Fax 802/422-6881. www.thekillingtongrand.com. 200 units. Fall and winter $336–$395 double, suites from $508; off peak $129–$310 double, suites from $175. Ask about packages. 5-night minimum stay during Christmas and school

holidays; 2-night minimum stay on weekends. AE, DISC, MC, V. **Amenities:** 2 restaurants (upscale American, cafe); outdoor pool; 2 tennis courts; fitness center; Jacuzzi; sauna; children's programs; concierge; limited room service; massage; dry cleaning. *In room:* A/C, TV, coffeemaker, hair dryer, iron.

Mountain Top Inn ★★   Situated on 1,300 ridge-top acres with expansive views of the rolling Vermont countryside (and 65 miles of hiking/cross-country ski trails), the place is modern, yet with country charm. It has the feel of a classic, small Pocono resort hotel, where hosts make sure you have something to do every waking minute. Guest rooms are unremarkable but comfortable, with understated country accents such as quilts and pine furnishings. Rooms are classed as either superior or deluxe—the latter a bit larger with views of the lake. Those who like to be active outdoors and prefer to stay put during their vacation will happily keep busy. The pleasant dining room, with heavy beams and rustic, rawhide-laced chairs, features regional American cuisine with a Continental twist. Note that this is about a 25-minute drive from the slopes.

195 Mountain Top Rd., Chittenden, VT 05737. *C* 800/445-2100 or 802/483-2311. Fax 802/483-6373. www.mountaintopinn.com. 55 units (includes 20 suites with 1–4 bedrooms). $130–$475 double; $230–$1,300 suites/chalet. AE, MC, V. **Amenities:** Restaurant (contemporary American); outdoor pool; golf course; driving range; horseback riding; cross-country skiing trails. *In room:* A/C, dataport.

The Summit Lodge ★   Think plaid carpeting and Saint Bernards. Those two motifs set the tone at this inviting spot on a knoll just off the access road. Though built only in the 1960s, the inn has a more historic character, with much of the common space constructed of salvaged barn timbers. The guest rooms are less distinguished, with clunky pine furniture and little ambience, though all have balconies or terraces. You may not spend much time in your room, however, as the numerous common spaces are so inviting. The Summit has more character than most self-styled resorts along the access road, and offers decent value.

Killington Rd. (P.O. Box 119), Killington, VT 05751. *C* 800/635-6343 or 802/422-3535. Fax 802/422-3536. www.summitlodgevermont.com. 45 units. $64–$210 double. Winter rates include breakfast. AE, DC, MC, V. Minimum-stay policy on holidays. **Amenities:** Restaurant (American); 2 outdoor pools; 5 tennis courts; Jacuzzi; game room; limited room service; massage. *In room:* TV.

WHERE TO DINE

Charity's 1887 Saloon PUB FARE   Rustic, crowded, bustling, and boisterous, Charity's is the place if you like your food big and your company young. The centerpiece of this barn-like restaurant adorned with stained-glass lamps and Victorian prints is a handsome old bar crafted in Italy and then shipped to West Virginia, where it stayed for nearly a century before being dismantled and shipped to Vermont in 1971. The menu offers a selection of burgers, plus a half-dozen vegetarian choices such as veggie stir-fry and red pepper ravioli.

Killington Rd. *C* 802/422-3800. Reservations not accepted. Main courses, lunch $5.95–$8.95; dinner $13–$19. AE, MC, V. Daily 11:30am–10pm.

Choices Restaurant and Rotisserie ★ BISTRO   One of the locally favored spots for consistently good, unpretentious fare is Choices, located on the access road across from the Outback. Full dinners come complete with salad or soup and bread and will amply restore calories lost on the slopes or the trail. Fresh pastas are a specialty (try the Cajun green peppercorn fettuccine); other inviting entrees include meats from the rotisserie. The atmosphere is nothing to write home about and the prices are higher than at nearby burger joints, but the high quality of the food and care taken in preparation make up for that.

Killington Rd. (at Glazebook Center). *C* 802/422-4030. Main courses $13–$22. AE, MC, V. Sun 11am–2:30pm; Sun–Thurs 5–10pm; Fri–Sat 5–11pm.

Hemingway's ★★★ NEW AMERICAN   Hemingway's is an elegant spot—and one that ranks among the best restaurants in New England. Located in the 1860 Asa Briggs House, a former stagecoach stop, Hemingway's seats guests in three formal areas. The two upstairs rooms are sophisticatedly appointed with damask linen, crystal goblets, and fresh flowers. Diners tend to dress causally but neatly (no shorts or T-shirts). The three- or four-course dinners are offered at a price that turns out to be rather reasonable given the quality of the kitchen and the unassailable service. The menu changes often to reflect available stock. A typical meal might start with seared yellowfin tuna and a rice cake, confit of duck strudel with blood oranges, or risotto. Then it's on to the splendid main course: perhaps filet of red snapper with grilled shrimp and a risotto of bacon and chanterelles in fall; cod with lobster, corn, and vanilla in summer; or partridge, roasted Arctic char, or pork tenderloin in winter. Finish with tangerine fruit soup and chocolate sorbet, a poached pear in a port syrup with Vermont cheese, banana bread with maple walnut ice cream, or the chocolate mousse cake.

4988 Rte. 4 (between Rte. 100 N. and Rte. 100 S.). (802/422-3886. www.hemingwaysrestaurant.com. Reservations strongly recommended. Fixed-price menu $48–$65; wine-tasting menu $75–$90. AE, MC, V. Sun and Wed–Thurs 6–9pm; Fri–Sat 6–10pm. (Also open selected Mon–Tues during ski and foliage seasons; call first.) Closed mid-Apr to mid-May and early Nov.

Ppeppers ★ PASTA/ECLECTIC   This 1950s-retro restaurant is a festive, upbeat place—and almost always crowded with visitors and locals who've just enjoyed a long day on the slopes or the trails. Situated in a strip-mallish complex near the top of Killington Road, Ppeppers sets the mood with black-and-white tile floors, red lampshades, and red chili-pepper accent lighting. Take a seat at a genuine Naugahyde booth, or grab a stool at the wooden counter. Despite the name, the food isn't all spicy—the menu is diner fare, expanded for a more sophisticated clientele, but the hamburgers are great, the pasta above average, and the service far friendlier than in many ski mountain establishments.

Killington Rd. (802/422-3177. Reservations not accepted. Main courses, breakfast $3.95–$7.95, lunch $4–$7.95, dinner $9.95–$15. AE, DC, MC, V. Sun–Thurs 7am–9pm; Fri–Sat 7am–midnight.

RUTLAND

Rutland is a no-nonsense, blue-collar town that's never had much of a reputation for charm. Today, it's undergoing a low-grade renaissance, attracting new residents who like the small-city atmosphere and easy access to the mountains, especially nearby Killington in winter. It has the feel of a real place with real people, a good antidote for those who've felt they've spent a bit too much time in tourist-oriented ski resorts.

ESSENTIALS

GETTING THERE   Rutland is at the intersection of Route 7 and Route 4. Burlington is 67 miles to the north; Bennington is 56 miles south. **Amtrak** ((**800/USA-RAIL;** www.amtrak.com) offers daily train service from New York via the Hudson River Valley. Rutland is also served by scheduled air service by **Continental Connection** ((**800/523-FARE;** www.continental.com).

VISITOR INFORMATION   The **Rutland Regional Chamber of Commerce,** 256 N. Main St., Rutland, VT 05701 ((**800/756-8880** or 802/773-2747; www.rutlandvermont.com) staffs an information booth at the corner of Route 7 and Route 4 West from Memorial Day to Columbus Day, open daily from 10am to 6pm. The chamber's main office is open year-round Monday through Friday from 8am to 5pm.

FESTIVALS The **Vermont State Fair** (© 802/775-5200; www.vermont statefair.net) has attracted fairgoers from throughout Vermont for over 150 years. It's held from late August through the first week of September at the fairgrounds on Route 7, south of the city. Gates open at 8am daily.

EXPLORING THE TOWN

A stroll through Rutland's historic downtown will delight architecture buffs. Look for the detailed marblework on many of the buildings, such as the Opera House, the Gryphan's Building, and along Merchant's Row. Note especially the fine marble exterior of the Chittenden Savings Bank at the corner of Merchant's Row and Center Street. Nearby South Main Street (Rte. 7) also has a good selection of handsome homes built in elaborate Queen Anne style.

A stop worth making, especially as a rainy-day diversion, is the **Chaffee Center for the Visual Arts**, 16 S. Main St. (© 802/775-0356). It showcases abundant artistic talent from Rutland and beyond.

OUTSIDE OF TOWN

A worthy detour from Rutland is to the amiable town of **Proctor,** about 6 miles northwest of Rutland center. (Take Rte. 4 west, then follow Rte. 3 north to the town.) This quiet town was once a noted center for its fine-grained marble, which found its way to the U.S. Supreme Court, Lincoln Memorial, and other structures. It is now home to the popular **Vermont Marble Museum** (© 800/427-1396 or 802/459-2300; www.vermont-marble.com). The vast size of this former factory is impressive in itself. The gift shop has a great selection of reasonably priced marble products.

It's open from Memorial Day to late October daily, 9am to 5:30pm (closed the rest of the year). Admission is $6 for adults, $4 for seniors, $3 for students 15 to 18, and free for children under 15. Look for signs to the exhibit from Route 3 in Proctor.

WHERE TO STAY

Rutland has a selection of basic roadside motels and chain hotels, mostly clustered on or along Route 7 south of town. Rates at the **Comfort Inn at Trolley Square,** 19 Allen St. (© 800/432-6788 or 802/775-2200; www.comfortinn.com), include continental breakfast. **The Holiday Inn,** 476 U.S. Rte. 7 South (© 800/462-4810 or 802/775-1911; www.holiday-inn.com), has an indoor pool, hot tub, and sauna. Likewise, the **Howard Johnson Rutland,** 401 U.S. Rte. 7 South (© 802/775-4303; www.hojo.com), features an indoor pool and sauna, with the familiar orange-roofed restaurant next door. The **Best Western Hogge Penny Inn,** on Route 4 East (© 802/773-3200), has a pool and tennis court.

Inn at Rutland Built as a family home in the 1890s by the grain empire Burdett family, the Inn at Rutland is an imposing Victorian B&B overlooking Route 7 on the north side of town. It's elaborate on the outside, and even more so on the inside. Gracefully curving walls, stamped plaster wainscoting, oak trim, and leather wallpaper are among the details worthy of note. The downstairs parlors are formal in an Edwardian sort of way, and guest rooms are unusually spacious. Rooms facing Route 7 are a bit noisier, but the house was solidly wrought and seems to buffer most of the noise. The third-floor rooms are generally less detailed, but among my favorites are Washington and Rutland, which are large and quiet.

70 North Main St. (Rte. 7), Rutland, VT 05701. © 800/808-0575 or 802/773-0575. Fax 802/775-3506. www.innatrutland.com. $135–$205 double; off season from $90 double. Rates include breakfast. *In room:* TV.

WHERE TO DINE

The Coffee Exchange (© 802/775-3337) is a casually hip cafe housed in a former downtown bank at 100 Merchant's Row. You've got your choice here: grab a seat at a sidewalk table or move inside and pick a room. (The bank vault is tiny and painted enchantingly, and you can have a lively conversation with an echo.) A good selection of coffees is available, along with delectable baked goods such as banana-nut tarts, croissants, and cheese Danishes.

Little Harry's ⭐ GLOBAL   This is an offshoot of the popular Harry's outside of Ludlow. It's in downtown Rutland on the first floor and basement of a strikingly unattractive building; but Little Harry's has a wonderfully eclectic menu, with main selections ranging from grilled steak sandwich to duck in a "searing" red Thai curry. (Thurs is Thai night.) Appetizers are equally eclectic, with choices along the lines of marinated green olives, gazpacho, pad Thai, and hummus. As you might guess, the dishes here span the globe and will appeal to anyone with an adventurous palate.

121 West St. © 802/747-4848. Reservations recommended. Main courses $11–$17. AE, MC, V. Daily 5–10pm.

Royal's Hearthside AMERICAN   Royal's Hearthside, a local institution since 1962, falls under the category of "old reliable." At the busy intersection of Route 4 and Route 7, Royal's is calming and quiet on the inside, done up in a sort of Ye Olde Colonial American style. Expect spindle-backed chairs, faux pewter sugar bowls, and Brandenburg concertos playing in the background. Meals don't tax the staff in the creativity department, but are solidly prepared. All the sauces are homemade, as are the popovers, breads, and pastries. They even butcher their own meat. Selections run along the lines of baked stuffed shrimp, grilled rack of lamb, broiled salmon, an assortment of grilled meats, and an array of specials. Lunches include sandwiches, burgers, and omelets. The restaurant is also noted for its traditional puddings, such as grapenut, Indian, and bread. If you're looking for a dinner bargain, arrive before 6:30pm for one of the early-bird specials. "We take care of people who come early," the waitresses say.

37 N. Main St. © 802/775-0856. Reservations recommended on weekends. Main courses, lunch $6.95–$14; dinner $15–$23. AE, MC, V. Mon–Sat 11am–3pm and 5–9:30pm; Sun noon–9pm.

5 Middlebury ⭐⭐

Middlebury is a gracious college town amid rolling hills and pastoral countryside. For many, it provides the perfect combination of small-town charm, access to the outdoors (the Adirondacks and Green Mountains are both close at hand), and a dash of sophistication: the influence of college students and out-of-staters have brought a natural foods store, ethnic restaurants, and more arts, crafts, and books than you would expect to find in a place several times Middlebury's size.

The town centers on an irregular sloping green. Above the green is the commanding Middlebury Inn; shops line the downhill slopes. In the midst of the green is a handsome chapel, and the whole scene is lorded over by a fine, white-steepled Congregational church. Middlebury has some 300 buildings listed on the National Register of Historic Places, including those of Middlebury College, which doesn't so much dominate the village as coexist nicely alongside it.

ESSENTIALS

GETTING THERE   Middlebury is located on Route 7 about midway between Rutland and Burlington. **Vermont Transit** (© 800/451-3292 or 802/388-4373;

www.vermonttransit.com) offers bus service to town. From upstate New York by car, you can short-circuit Lake Champlain by driving to Fort Ticonderoga and taking the cable ferry (© **802/897-7999**) across the lake. The ferry operates from early May to late October; the one-way cost is a steep $7, $12 round-trip per car.

VISITOR INFORMATION Addison County Chamber of Commerce, 2 Court St. (© **800/733-8376** or 802/388-9300; www.midvermont.com), is in a handsome, historic white building just off the green, facing the Middlebury Inn. Brochures and assistance are available Monday through Friday during business hours (9am–5pm), and often on weekends from early June to mid-October. Ask for the map and guide, which lists shops and restaurants around Middlebury, published by the Downtown Middlebury Business Bureau.

EXPLORING THE TOWN

The best place to begin a tour of Middlebury is the Addison County Chamber of Commerce; be sure to request the chamber's self-guided walking-tour brochure.

The **Vermont Folklife Center** ⋒, 3 Court St. (© **802/388-4964;** www.vermontfolklifecenter.org), located in the 1823 Masonic Hall, is a short walk from Middlebury Inn. You'll find a gallery of changing displays featuring various folk arts from Vermont and beyond, including music and visual arts. The small gift shop has intriguing items, such as heritage foods and traditional crafts. Open summers Tuesday through Saturday from 11am to 4pm, Thursday through Saturday (same hours) in spring, late fall, and winter. Admission is by donation.

The historic **Otter Creek** ⋒⋒ district, set on a steep hillside by the rocky creek, is well worth exploring. Here you can peruse top-flight Vermont crafts at the **Vermont State Crafts Center at Frog Hollow** ⋒⋒, 1 Mill St. (© **888/388-3177;** www.froghollow.org). Picturesquely overlooking the tumbling stream, the center is open daily (closed Sun in winter) and features the work of some 300 Vermont craftspeople. Their wares range from extraordinary carved wood desks to metalwork to glass and pottery.

From Frog Hollow, take the footbridge over the river and find your way to **The Marble Works,** an assortment of wood and rough-marble industrial buildings on the far bank, converted to a handful of interesting shops and restaurants.

Atop a low ridge with beautiful views of the Green Mountains to the east and farmlands rolling toward Lake Champlain in the west, prestigious **Middlebury College** ⋒⋒ has a handsome, well-spaced campus of gray limestone and white marble buildings that are best explored by foot. At the edge of campus is the **Middlebury College Center for the Arts,** which opened in 1992. This architecturally engaging center houses the small **Middlebury College Museum of Art** ⋒ (© **802/443-5007**), with a selective sampling of European and American art, both ancient and new. The museum is open Tuesday through Friday from 10am to 5pm, Saturday and Sunday from noon to 5pm. Free admission.

A couple of miles outside Middlebury is the **Morgan Horse Farm** ⋒⋒ (© **802/388-2011**), dating to the late 1800s and now owned and operated by the University of Vermont. Col. Joseph Battell, who owned the farm from the 1870s to 1906, is credited with preserving the Morgan breed, a horse of considerable beauty and stamina that has served admirably in war and exploration. With guided tours May through October daily from 9am to 4pm, the farm also has a picnic area and gift shop. Admission is $5 for adults, $4 for teens, $2 for children 5 to 12, and free for kids under 5. To reach the farm, take Route 125 to Weybridge Street (Rte. 23 North), head north for three-quarters of a mile, turn right at the sign for the farm, and continue on about 2 miles.

OUTDOOR PURSUITS

HIKING   The Green Mountains roll down to Middlebury's eastern edge, enabling easy access to the mountains. Stop by the **U.S. Forest Service's Middlebury Ranger District office,** south of town on Route 7 (℃ **802/388-4362**), for guidance and information on area trails and destinations. Ask for the brochure listing day hikes in the region.

One recommended walk for people of all abilities—and especially those of poetic sensibilities—is the **Robert Frost Interpretive Trail,** dedicated to the memory of New England's poet laureate. Frost lived in a cabin on a farm across the road for 23 summers. (The cabin is now a National Historic Landmark.) Located on Route 125 approximately 6 miles east of Middlebury, this relaxing loop trail is just a mile long, and excerpts of Frost's poems are placed on signs along the trail.

SKIING   Downhill skiers looking for a low-key, low-pressure mountain invariably head to **Middlebury College Snow Bowl** (℃ **802/388-4356**), near Middlebury Gap on Route 125 east of town. Founded in 1939, this ski area has a vertical drop of just over 1,000 feet served by three chairlifts. The college ski team uses the area for practice, but it's also open to the public for about half what you'd pay at Killington. Adult tickets are $26 midweek, $35 on weekends.

Cross-country skiing is nearby at the **Rikert Ski Touring Center** (℃ **802/ 443-2744**), at Middlebury's Bread Loaf Campus about 12 miles away on Route 125. The center offers 24 miles of machine-groomed trails through a lovely winter landscape. Adult ski passes are $10, while students and children under 18 pay $5. Half-day passes are also available ($6 and $3, respectively).

WHERE TO STAY

The outskirts of Middlebury are home to a handful of motels and several inns. The 1960s-era **Blue Spruce Motel,** 2428 Rte. 7 South (℃ **800/640-7671** or 802/ 388-4091), has 22 basic rooms; families lingering in the area for a few days should inquire about Room 122, a large suite with full kitchen, sleeping loft, and carport. Rates run from $75 to $95 for a double room ($135 for the suite). The **Greystone Motel,** 1395 Rte. 7 South (℃ **802/388-4935**), has 10 clean rooms with small bathrooms; rates are $79 to $95 in summer, $65 to $90 in winter.

Inn on the Green ★★★   This handsome village inn occupies a house that dates to 1803 (it was Victorianized with a mansard tower later in the century). It's both historic and comfortable. The rooms are furnished with a mix of antiques and reproductions; wood floors and boldly colored walls of harvest yellow, peach, and burgundy lighten the architectural heaviness of the house. The suites are naturally the most spacious, but all units offer plenty of elbowroom. Those in the front of the house are wonderfully flooded with afternoon light.

71 S. Pleasant St., Middlebury, VT 05753. ℃ **888/244-7512** or 802/388-7512. Fax 802/388-4075. www.innonthegreen.com. 11 units. $98–$190 double, $190–$260 suite. Midweek discounts available. Rates include continental breakfast. 2-night minimum stay on weekends. AE, DC, DISC, MC, V. *In room:* A/C, TV, dataport, hair dryer, iron.

The Middlebury Inn ★   The historic Middlebury Inn traces its roots to 1827, when Nathan Wood built the Vermont Hotel, a brick public house. It now consists of four buildings containing 75 modern guest rooms equipped with most conveniences. Rooms are on the large side, and most are outfitted with a sofa or upholstered chairs, colonial-reproduction furniture, and some vintage bathroom fixtures. Rooms 116 and 246 are spacious corner units entered via a dark foyer/sitting room. Room 129, while smaller, has a four-poster bed, a view of the village green, and a Jacuzzi. The 10 guest rooms in the Porterhouse Mansion next door also have a pleasant, historic feel. An adjacent motel with 20 units is decorated in an early American motif, but underneath the veneer, it's just a standard-issue motel. Stick with the main inn if you're seeking a taste of history.

14 Courthouse Sq., Middlebury, VT 05753. © **800/842-4666** or 802/388-4961. www.middleburyinn.com. 75 units. Midweek $88–$245 double, $235–$240 suite; weekends $98–$270 double, $270–$375 suite. Rates include continental breakfast. AE, DC, MC, V. Pets allowed in some rooms. **Amenities:** Restaurant (traditional New England); tavern (pub fare); laundry service. *In room:* A/C, TV, dataport, hair dryer, iron.

Swift House Inn ✿✿ This historic complex of three whitewashed houses, on a hillside 2 blocks from downtown Middlebury, received a much-needed injection of life in 2003 when new owners Jim and Katrina Kappel purchased the property. Rooms have since been touched up, with the fine dining room refurbished and reopened, and the general friendliness of the place has taken a giant leap forward as well. The five rooms in the roadside gatehouse have a B&B feel (and proximity to the traffic), while 10 rooms in the main, Federal-style house (built in 1814) are imbued with the intriguing history of the place. A Vermont governor lived here at one time, and the story of longtime resident Mrs. Swift is well worth hearing. Inside, it's decorated in a simple, historic style; guest rooms are well appointed with antique and reproduction furnishings. For honeymooners or business travelers, the carriage house's six suites are the most luxurious at the inn, most with Jacuzzis and fireplaces. All the little extras are done right here: free cups of Green Mountain coffee in the bar for guests, unfailingly cheerful service, and landscaped grounds perfect for sipping a drink and watching the sun set over the Adirondacks (in an Adirondack chair, naturally). The Kappels promise further improvements, such as breakfast and additional updating of the rooms; expect it to become even more popular.

25 Stewart Lane, Middlebury, VT 05753. © **802/388-9925.** Fax 802/388-9927. www.swifthouseinn.com. 21 units (1 with detached private bathroom). Main inn $110–$185 double B&B, $160–$245 double MAP; gatehouse $110–$135 double B&B, $170–$195 double MAP; carriage house $235–$255 suite B&B, $295–$315 suite MAP. B&B rates include continental breakfast, MAP rates include breakfast and dinner. 2-night minimum stay some weekends. AE, DISC, MC, V. **Amenities:** Restaurant (eclectic); limited room service (breakfast only). *In room:* A/C, TV, dataport, hair dryer, iron, fireplace (some), Jacuzzi (some).

Waybury Inn ✿ Photos of Bob Newhart with "Larry, his brother Darryl and his other brother, Darryl," (characters on the classic situation comedy based in a Vermont inn) grace the wall behind the desk at this 1810 inn. This inn was featured in the classic "Newhart" show—at least the exterior; the interior was created on a sound stage. The architecturally handsome Waybury has loads of integrity in that simple farmhouse kind of way. Rooms vary in size, as they do in most old inns. The more you pay, the more space you'll get. The inn is close to the road, and the front-facing rooms can be a bit noisy at night; the two attic rooms are cozy, but a bit dark and garret-like.

457 E. Main St. (Rte. 125), East Middlebury, VT 05753. © **800/348-1810** or 802/388-4015. Fax 802/388-1245. www.wayburyinn.com. 14 units (1 with detached private bathroom). Summer and fall $125–$215 double; off season $95–$165 double. Rates include breakfast. Off-season rates available. AE, DISC, MC, V. Pets allowed with restrictions (call first). **Amenities:** Restaurant (New England/New American). *In room:* A/C, no phone.

WHERE TO DINE

In addition to the eateries listed below, Middlebury possesses an abundance of delis, sandwich shops, and the like—perfect for a quick lunch or a picnic.

Among the best are **Noonies Deli** (✆ 802/388-0014), in the Marble Works complex, the locals' choice for sandwiches; **The Taste of India** (✆ 802/388-4856), hidden away down 1 Bakery Lane, with inexpensive lunch specials; and **American Flatbread** (✆ 802/388-3300), also in the Marble Works, open Friday and Saturday evenings only from 5 to 9:30pm and cooking some of the best pizzas I've tasted in New England. All do takeout. There's also a small, good natural foods store, **Middlebury Natural Foods Co-op** (✆ 802/388-7276), at 1 Washington Street just uphill from the Middlebury Inn.

Storm Cafe ✹ NEW AMERICAN   This tiny, casual spot with great river views on the ground floor of a stone mill in Frog Hollow is a chef-owned restaurant popular with locals and travelers alike. The menu is beguilingly simple, but tremendous care is taken in the selection of ingredients and the preparation; salads are especially good. Meal selections could include smoked salmon, jerk chicken, or pasta; there's also a changing fish entree nightly. It's a shame they no longer serve lunches, but as a fine-dining spot for dinner, this is one of the town's best choices.

3 Mill St. ✆ 802/388-1063. Reservations recommended, especially on weekends. Main courses $7–$13. MC, V. Tues–Sat 5–9pm.

Tully and Marie's ✹ NEW AMERICAN/GLOBAL   Tully and Marie's is not Ye Olde New Englande. It's a bright and colorful Art Deco–inspired restaurant overlooking the creek, made all the more appealing by its surprising location down a small, dark alley. It's the kind of fun, low-key place destined to put you in a good mood the moment you walk in. Angle for a table perched over the creek. The menu specializes in New American cuisine, with clear influences from Asia and Mexico. At lunch, expect pad Thai, vegetable linguini, and a variety of hearty meals (for instance, burgers or grilled apple, bacon, and cheddar, served over baked beans). At dinner, you can find chicken saltimbocca, bourbon shrimp, and grilled strip steak with caramelized shallots and leeks.

7 Bakery Lane (on Otter Creek upstream from the bridge in the middle of town). ✆ 802/388-4182. www.tully andmaries.com. Reservations recommended for weekends and college events. Main course, lunch $6.25–$9.50; dinner $13–$20. AE, MC, V. Summer daily 11:30am–3pm and 5–9pm (to 10pm Fri and Sat); winter daily 11:30am–3pm, Sun–Mon and Thurs 5–9pm, Fri–Sat 5–10pm.

6 Mad River Valley ✹✹

The scenic Mad River Valley, one of Vermont's better kept secrets, surrounds the towns of Warren and Waitsfield. Save for a couple of telltale signs, you could drive Route 100 past the sleepy villages of Warren and Waitsfield and not realize that you're close to some of the choicest skiing in the state. The region hasn't fallen prey to unbridled condo or strip-mall developers: development isn't heavily concentrated, even at the base of Sugarbush, the valley's preeminent ski area. Hidden up a winding valley road, Mad River Glen, the area's older ski area, eschews glamour in favor of the rustic. If you love nature, it's a great destination.

The whole valley maintains a friendly and informal attitude, even during peak ski season; residents hope to keep it that way, even in the face of certain growth.

ESSENTIALS
GETTING THERE   Warren and Waitsfield are on Route 100 between Killington and Waterbury. The nearest interstate access is from Exit 10 (Waterbury) on I-89; drive south on Route 100 for 14 miles to Waitsfield.

VISITOR INFORMATION The **Sugarbush Chamber of Commerce** (© **800/828-4748** or 802/469-3409; www.madrivervalley.com) is at 4601 Main St. (Rte. 100) in the General Wait House, next to the elementary school. It's open daily from 9am to 5pm; during slow times, expect limited hours and days.

DOWNHILL SKIING

Mad River Glen ★★★ Mad River Glen is the curmudgeon of the Vermont ski world—just what you'd expect from a place whose motto is "Ski it if you can." High-speed detachable quads? Forget it. The main lift is a 1948 *single*-chair lift that creaks its way 1 mile to the summit. Snowmaking? Don't count on it. Only 15% of the terrain benefits from the fake stuff; the rest is dependent on Mother Nature. Snowboarding? Nope. It's forbidden at Mad River. Mad River's slopes are twisting and narrow and hide some of the steepest drops in New England (nearly half the slopes are classified as expert). Mad River Glen long ago attained the status of a cult mountain among serious skiers, and its fans seem determined to keep it that way. Owned and operated by a cooperative of Mad River skiers since 1995, it's the only cooperative-owned ski area in the country. The owners are proud of the mountain's funky traditions (how *about* that single chair?) and say they're determined to maintain the spirit.

Waitsfield, VT 05763. © **802/496-3551**. www.madriverglen.com. Vertical drop: 2,000 ft. Lifts: 4 chairlifts. Skiable acreage: 115. Lift tickets: $45 adults.

Sugarbush ★★ Sugarbush is a fine intermediate-to-advanced ski resort, comprised of two ski mountains linked by a 2-mile, 10-minute high-speed chairlift that crosses three ridges. (A shuttle bus offers a warmer way to traverse the mountains.) The number of high-speed lifts (four) and excellent snowmaking makes this a desirable destination for serious skiers. While an improved Sugarbush has generated some buzz since large-scale improvements began in the mid-1990s, it remains a low-key area with great intermediate cruising runs on the north slopes and some challenging, old-fashioned expert slopes on Castlerock. Sugarbush is a good choice if you find the sprawl of Killington overwhelming but don't want to sacrifice great skiing for a quieter and more intimate resort.

Warren, VT 05674. © **800/537-8427** for lodging, or 802/583-6100. www.sugarbush.com. Vertical drop: 2,650 ft. Lifts: 14 chairlifts (4 high-speed), 4 surface lifts. Skiable acreage: 432. Lift tickets: $42 to $61 for adults.

EXPLORING THE VALLEY

A unique way to explore the region is atop an Icelandic pony. The **Vermont Icelandic Horse Farm** ★ (© **802/496-7141;** www.icelandichorses.com), on North Fayston Road in Waitsfield (turn west off Rte. 100 near the airport), specializes in tours on these small, sturdy, strong horses. Full- and half-day rides are available daily, but to really appreciate both the countryside and the horses, sign up for a multi-day trek, ranging from 1 to 5 nights and including lodging at area inns, all meals, your mount, and a guide to lead you through the lush hills around Waitsfield and Warren. In winter, try **skijoring,** best described as sort of like water-skiing behind a horse. Call for pricing information and reservations.

BIKING A rewarding 14-mile **bike trip** ★★ along paved roads begins at the village of Waitsfield. Park your car near the covered bridge, then follow East Warren Road past the Inn at Round Barn Farm and up into the hilly, farm-filled countryside. (Don't be discouraged by the unrelenting hill at the outset.) Near the village of Warren, turn right at Brook Road to connect back to Route 100. Return north on bustling but generally safe and often scenic Route 100 to Waitsfield.

Clearwater Sports, at 4147 Main Street (Rte. 100) in Waitsfield north of the covered bridge (*(C)* **802/496-2708;** www.clearwatersports.com), offers mountain-bike rentals from a blue-and-white Victorian-era house. The staff is helpful, with suggestions for other routes and tours.

HIKING   Hikers in search of good exercise and a spectacular view should strike out for **Mount Abraham** *,* west of Warren. Drive west up Lincoln Gap Road (it leaves Rte. 100 just south of Warren Village) and continue until the crest, where you cross the intersection with the Long Trail. Park here and head north on the trail; about 2 miles along, you hit the Battell Shelter. Push on another ⅝ of a mile up a steep ascent to reach the panoramic views atop 4,006-foot Mount Abraham. Allow 4 or 5 hours for the round-trip hike.

WINTER SPORTS   Clearwater Sports (*(C)* **802/496-2708;** www.clearwater sports.com) offers telemark ski rentals and advice in the winter, as well as guided snowshoe hikes into the backcountry. Ask about the Mad River Rocket sled trip, involving snowshoeing up and sledding down a nearby hill.

WHERE TO STAY

While Sugarbush isn't overrun with condos and lodges, it has its share. Some 200 of the condos nearest the mountain are managed by the **Sugarbush Resort** (*(C)* **800/537-8427** or 802/583-6100; www.sugarbush.com), with accommodations ranging from one to four bedrooms. Guests have access to amenities that include a health club and five pools. The resort also manages the 46-unit Sugarbush Inn. Shuttle buses deliver guests to and from the mountain and other facilities. Major winter holidays may require a minimum stay of up to 5 days. Rates vary widely, and most rooms are sold as packages that include lift tickets in winter.

Inn at the Mad River Barn *Value*   This classic 1960s-style ski lodge attracts a clientele that's nearly fanatical in its devotion to the place. It's best not to come here expecting anything fancy—carpets and furniture both tend toward the threadbare. Do come expecting to have some fun once settled. It's all knotty pine; spartan guest rooms and rustic common rooms help visitors feel at home putting their feet up. Accommodations are in the two-story barn behind the white clapboard main house and in an annex building up the lawn, which is a bit fancier but with less character. In winter, dinners are offered ($15), served in boisterous family style. In summer, the mood is slightly more sedate, but enhanced by a beautiful pool a short walk away in a grove of birches.

2849 Mill Brook Rd, Rte. 17, Waitsfield, VT 05673. *(C)* 800/631-0466 or 802/496-3310. Fax 802/496-6696. www.madriverbarn.com. 15 units. $77–$110 double. Midweek discounts available. Rates include breakfast. 2-night minimum stay holiday and winter weekends. AE, DISC, MC, V. **Amenities:** Restaurant (winter only); lounge; outdoor pool; fitness room; sauna; game room. *In room:* TV (most), fridge (some), no phone.

Finds Stop by a Classic

The **Warren General Store** (*(C)* **802/496-3864**) anchors the former bustling timber town of Warren. Set along a stream, the store has uneven floorboards, a potbellied stove, and merchandise updated for the 21st century, including a good selection of gourmet foods and wines. Get coffee or a sandwich at the back deli counter, and enjoy it on the deck overlooking the water. The store is in Warren Village just off Route 100 south of the Sugarbush Access Road.

Inn at Round Barn Farm ★★ You pass through a covered bridge just off Route 100 to arrive at one of my favorite romantic B&Bs in northern New England, a regal barn and farmhouse on 235 sloping acres with views of fields all around. The centerpiece of the inn is the Round Barn, a strikingly beautiful 1910 structure that's used for weddings, art exhibits, and Sunday church services. Each guest room is furnished with an understated country elegance. The less expensive rooms in the older part of the house are comfortable, if small; larger luxury units in the attached horse barn feature stunning soaring ceilings under old log beams and include extras such as steam showers, gas fireplaces, and phones.

1661 E. Warren Rd., Waitsfield, VT 05673. ✆ 802/496-2276. Fax 802/496-8832. www.innattheround barn.com. 11 units. $130–$295 double. Rates include breakfast. 3-night minimum stay during holidays and foliage season. AE, DISC, MC, V. Closed Apr 15–30. Children 15 and older welcome. **Amenities:** Indoor pool; 18-mile cross-country ski center; game room. *In room:* No phone (except luxury rooms), hair dryer.

The Pitcher Inn ★★★ This Relais & Châteaux property is one of Vermont's finest. Set in the timeless village of Warren, the inn was built in the 1990s from the ground up following a fire that leveled a previous home; only the barn is original. Architect David Sellars created an inn that seamlessly blends modern conveniences, whimsy, and classic New England styling. The common areas fuse several styles: a little Colonial Revival, a little Mission, and a little Adirondack sporting camp. With not a bad room in the house, all are designed with such wit that they're more like elegant puzzles. (My favorite feature: The carved goose in flight on the ceiling of the Mallard Room is attached to a weathervane on the roof, and it rotates to indicate wind direction.) Nine units have fireplaces (seven wood-burning, two gas), and five have steam showers.

275 Main St., Warren, VT 05674. ✆ 888/867-8424 or 802/496-6350. Fax 802/496-6354. www.pitcher inn.com. 11 units. $330–$660 double and suite. Rates include breakfast. 2-night minimum stay on weekends, 3 nights on holiday weekends, and 5 nights at Christmas. Children under 16 welcome in suites only. AE, MC, V. **Amenities:** Restaurant (New American/regional); Jacuzzi; spa; game room; limited room service; in-room massage; babysitting. *In room:* A/C, TV/VCR, dataport, hair dryer, Jacuzzi (some).

West Hill House ★ This is among the more casual and relaxed inns in the valley, in part because of its quiet hillside location, and in part because of the easy camaraderie among guests. Set on a lightly traveled country road, the inn offers the quintessential New England experience, just a few minutes from the slopes at Sugarbush. Built in the 1850s, this farmhouse boasts three common rooms, including a bright, modern addition with a handsome fireplace for warmth in winter and an outdoor patio for summer lounging. The guest rooms are decorated in an updated country style, and all have gas fireplaces or gas woodstoves; three are air-conditioned. The more modern units include steam showers and Jacuzzis. Generous country breakfasts are served around a large dining-room table.

1496 West Hill Rd., Warren, VT 05674. ✆ 800/898-1427 or 802/496-7162. Fax 802/496-6443. www.west hillhouse.com. 7 units. $125–$180 double. Rates include breakfast. Check website for specials. 3-night minimum stay for foliage and holiday weekends; 2-night minimum stay on other weekends. AE, DISC MC, V. Children 12 and older welcome. **Amenities:** Honor-system bar; in-room massage; snowshoes. *In room:* TV/VCR, dataport, hair dryer, iron, Jacuzzi (some).

WHERE TO DINE

Friday and Saturday nights in Waitsfield, the **American Flatbread** ★★ bakery (✆ 802/496-8856) on Route 100 serves terrific organic-flour pizzas to the public. Come early to place your name on the waiting list; if you get in, you'll experience founder George Schenk's vision of whole foods.

Bass Restaurant ★★ *Value* NEW AMERICAN   The Bass Restaurant is located in a multi-level former dinner theater with a circular stone fireplace and a blond-wood bar. Light jazz plays in the background, and sculpture enlivens the space. The main courses range from oven-roasted duck with blackcurrant and orange jus to crabmeat-stuffed whole trout to a macadamia-crusted tuna loin on coconut rice. It's a quiet, romantic spot that offers excellent value, delivering more than one would expect for the price. (Most entrees are less than $16.)

527 Sugarbush Access Rd., Warren. © **802/583-3100**. www.bassrestaurant.com. Main courses $13–$25. AE, MC, V. Sun–Thurs 5–10pm; Fri–Sat 5–11pm.

The Common Man ★ EUROPEAN   The Common Man is in a century-old barn, and the interior is soaring and dramatic. Chandeliers, floral carpeting on the walls (weird, but it works), and candles on the tables meld successfully and coax all but cold-hearted guests into a relaxed frame of mind. You'll be halfway through the meal before you notice there are no windows. The menu strives to be as ambitious and appealing as the decor. It doesn't hit the mark as consistently as it once did, and guests often find themselves poking at a bland offering or two. Entrees range from Vermont-raised rabbit braised with white wine and aromatic vegetables to duck with port sauce, trout amandine, and New Zealand lamb roasted and served with a tomato, garlic, and rosemary sauce. The extravagant *Schneeballen* (vanilla ice cream with coconut and hot fudge) makes for a good conclusion if they're serving it.

3209 German Flats Rd., Warren. © **802/583-2800**. www.commonmanrestaurant.com. Reservations recommended in season. Main courses $17–$27. AE, DISC, MC, V. Daily Sun–Fri 6–9pm in ski season, from 6:30pm in spring. Closed as follows: Mon–Tues from mid-Apr to late June; Mon, Wed, Fri from late June to late Oct; Mon from Nov to mid-Dec.

The Den ★ AMERICAN   In a nutshell: good food, decent service, no frills. A local favorite since 1970 for its well-worn, neighborly feel, it's the kind of spot where you can plop down in a pine booth, help yourself to the salad bar while awaiting your main course, then cheer on the Red Sox on the tube over the bar. The menu offers usual pub fare, including burgers, Reubens, roast-beef sandwiches, meal-size salads, and pork chops with applesauce and french fries.

Junction of Routes 100 and 17, Waitsfield. © **802/496-8880**. Main courses, lunch $4.95–$6.95, dinner $8.95–$14. AE, MC, V. Sun–Thurs 11:30am–10pm; Fri–Sat 11:30am–11pm.

John Egan's Big World Pub & Grill ★ GRILL   Gonzo extreme skier John Egan starred in ten Warren Miller skiing films, but *really* took a risk when he opened this restaurant on Route 100 in the valley. In a 1970s-style motel dining room decorated with skiing mementos (including a bar made of ski sections signed by skiing luminaries), the Big World Pub compensates with a small but above-average pub menu that the chef often pulls off with unexpected flair: menu options include snow crab cakes with chipotle sauce, duck-and-scallion wontons, and salads with Vermont chevre, demonstrating a real effort to rise above pub fare. The wood-grilled items are always crowd pleasers, including chicken breast glazed with Vermont cider, ginger, and lime. Also tasty (especially in the winter) is a Hungarian goulash made with pork and sauerkraut.

Rte. 100, Warren. © **802/496-3033**. Main courses $11–$17; burgers and sandwiches $6.50. AE, MC, V. Daily 5–9:30pm.

The Spotted Cow ★★ FRENCH-INSPIRED NEW AMERICAN   Set on the ground floor of a small, rustic retail complex in Waitsfield, the Spotted Cow is a low-ceilinged, modern, natural-wood spot with cherry banquettes and windows facing out onto a walkway. The place has the cozy feel of a bistro that only locals know about, with a more cultivated than funky air. The kitchen shines with creative approaches to old favorites. Venison is always on the menu, as is fresh fish. The duck and lamb cassoulet is a good choice, as is the Bermuda fish chowder, made with a splash of black rum. A vegetarian special is available.

Bridgestreet Marketplace (at corner of Rte. 100 and E. Warren Rd.), Waitsfield. ℂ **802/496-5151.** Reservations recommended. Main courses $18–$24. MC, V. Tues–Sun 5:30–9pm.

The Warren House Restaurant ⚡ NEW AMERICAN With a cozy location in a 1958 sugarhouse, this is a popular and casual spot not far from the slopes. The menu is creative but doesn't stray too far from the familiar—call it eclectic comfort food. Starters include crab cakes made with herbed rémoulade, as well as several salads, including goat cheese wrapped in walnuts and served on baby greens. For main courses, look for filet mignon grilled and served with a fresh pesto aioli, or bouillabaisse with prawns, scallops, clams, and mussels.

2585 Sugarbush Access Rd., Warren. ℂ **802/583-2421.** Reservations recommended. Main courses, $14–$20. AE, MC, V. Wed–Sun 5:30–9:30pm (till 10pm Fri–Sat). Call first in summer and shoulder seasons. Closed first 2 weeks of May and Nov.

7 Montpelier, Barre & Waterbury

Montpelier ⚡⚡ may very well be the most down-home, low-key state capital in the U.S., with a hint of that in every photo of the gold dome of the Capitol. Rising up behind it isn't a bank of mirror-sided skyscrapers, but a thickly forested hill. Montpelier, it turns out, isn't a self-important center of politics, but a small town that happens to be home to state government. It's a quite agreeable place to pass an afternoon, or even stay a night, if you yearn to see just how small-town Vermont really ticks.

Montpelier centers on two main boulevards, State Street and Main Street. The downtown sports a pair of hardware stores next door to each other, good bookstores, and the **Savoy,** 26 Main St. (ℂ **802/229-0509** or 802/229-0598), one of the best art movie houses in northern New England.

Nearby **Barre** (pronounced "Barry") is more commercial and less charming, but shares an equally vibrant past. Barre has more of a blue-collar demeanor than Montpelier. Barre's once-thriving granite industry attracted talented stone workers from Italy and Scotland (it has a statue of Robert Burns), who helped give the turn-of-the-20th-century town a lively, cosmopolitan flavor.

About 10 miles west of Montpelier, **Waterbury** ⚡ is at the juncture of Route 100 and I-89, making it a commercial center by default, if not by design. You'll likely want to hit the Ben & Jerry's factory (ℂ **866/BJTOURS** or 802/882-1240) for its popular tours, which cost $3 per adult, $2 per senior.

ESSENTIALS
GETTING THERE Montpelier is accessible via Exit 7 off I-89. For Barre, take Exit 8. Waterbury is located at Exit 10 off I-89. For bus service to Montpelier, contact **Vermont Transit** (ℂ **800/451-3292** or 802/223-7112; www.vermont transit.com).

For bus service to Waterbury, call **Vermont Transit** (ℂ **802/244-6943**); for train service to Waterbury, contact **Amtrak** (ℂ **800/872-7245;** www.amtrak.com), whose *Vermonter* makes daily departures from New York.

VISITOR INFORMATION   The **Central Vermont Chamber of Commerce** (© 802/229-5711; www.central-vt.com) is on Stewart Road off Exit 7 of I-89. Turn left at the first light; it's a half-mile further on the left. The chamber is open Monday through Friday from 9am to 5pm.

The **Waterbury Tourism Council** (© 802/244-7822) operates a small, unstaffed booth stocked with helpful brochures on Route 100 just north of I-89. It's open daily from 7am to 10pm.

EXPLORING MONTPELIER & BARRE

Start your exploration of Montpelier with a visit to the gold-domed **State House** ★ (© 802/828-2228) at 115 State Street, guarded out front by a statue of Ethan Allen. Three capitol buildings have risen on this site since 1809; the present building retained the portico designed during the height of Greek Revival style in 1836. Modeled after the temple of Theseus in Athens, it's made of Vermont granite. Self-guided tours are offered when the capitol is open, Monday through Friday (except holidays) from 8am to 4pm; in summer, it's also open Saturday from 11am to 3pm. Guided tours are run between July and mid-October, Monday through Friday.

A short stroll from the State House is the **Vermont Historical Society Museum** ★, 109 State St. (© 802/828-2291; www.vermonthistory.org). The museum is housed in a replica of the elegant old Pavilion Building, a prominent Victorian hotel, and contains a number of artifacts, including a gun once owned by Ethan Allen. It's normally open Tuesday to Sunday, from 9am to about 4pm. Admission is $3 for adults, $2 for students or seniors. *Note:* The museum reopened in March 2004 after extensive renovations and expansion; call or log onto the society's website for the latest admissions details.

Rock of Ages Quarry ★★   A free visitor center presents informative exhibits, a video about quarrying, a glimpse of an old granite quarry (no longer active), and a selection of granite gifts. Self-guided tours of the old quarry are free. For a look at the active quarry (the world's largest), sign up for a guided half-hour tour. An old bus groans up to a viewer's platform high above the 500-foot, man-made canyon, where workers cleave huge slabs of fine-grained granite and hoist them out using 150-foot derricks anchored with a spider's web of 15 miles of steel cable. It's an operation to behold.

773 Graniteville Rd. (P.O. Box 482, Barre, VT 05641), Graniteville. © 802/476-3119. www.rockofages.com. Guided tours $4 adults, $3.50 seniors, $1.50 children 6–12. Visitor center (free) May–Oct Mon–Sat 8:30am–5pm; Sun noon–5pm (in foliage season, Sun 8:30am–5:30pm). Guided tours offered June to mid-Sept, Mon–Fri 9:15am–3pm, also Sat during foliage season. Closed July 4. Directions: from Barre, drive south on Rte. 14, turn left at lights by McDonald's; watch for signs to quarry.

HIKING CAMEL'S HUMP

A short drive from Waterbury is **Camel's Hump** ★, the state's fourth highest peak at 4,083 feet. (It's also the state's highest mountain without a ski area.) One popular round-trip loop-hike is about 7½ miles (plan on 6 hr. or more of hiking time), departing from the Couching Lion Farm, 8 miles southwest of Waterbury on Camel's Hump Road (ask locally for exact directions). At the summit, seasonal rangers are on hand to answer questions.

WHERE TO STAY
IN MONTPELIER

Capitol Plaza Hotel ★   The favored hotel of folks on business with the state government, it's also well located (across from the capitol) to serve visitors

Central Vermont & The Champlain Valley

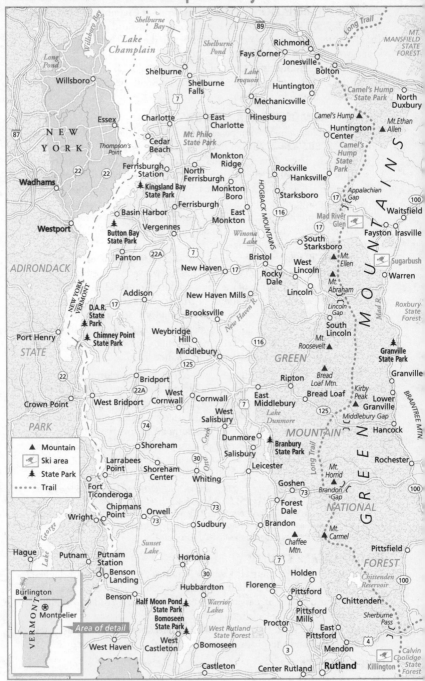

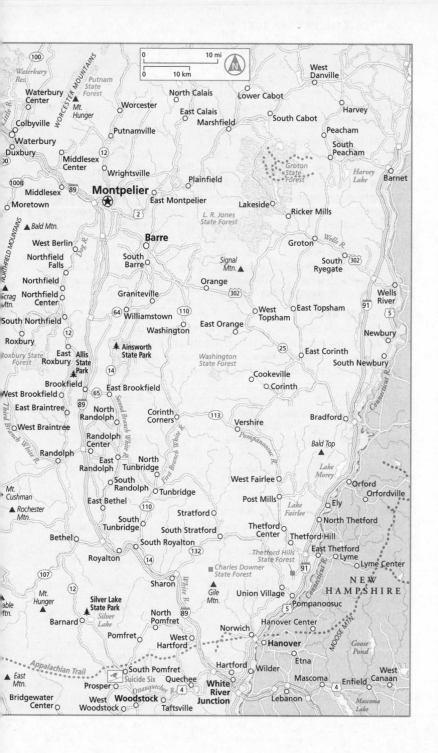

Waterbury Res.

100

Waterbury Center

WORCESTER MOUNTAINS

Mt. Hunger ▲

Colbyville

Waterbury

Duxbury

00

Middlesex Center

Putnam State Forest

North Calais

Worcester

East Calais

Marshfield

Lower Cabot

West Danville

South Cabot

Harvey

Peacham

South Peacham

Putnamville

12

Wrightsville

Plainfield

Groton State Forest

Harvey Lake

Barnet

100B

Middlesex

89

Montpelier ★

East Montpelier

2

Moretown

Lakeside

Ricker Mills

L. R. Jones State Forest

▲ Bald Mtn.

West Berlin

Barre

NORTHFIELD MOUNTAINS

Dog R.

Northfield Falls

South Barre

Groton

Wells R.

South Ryegate

302

Signal Mtn. ▲

Orange

302

Wells River

91

Northfield

Northfield Center

Scrag Mtn.

South Northfield

64

Williamstown

110

West Topsham

East Topsham

5

12

Washington

East Orange

Newbury

Roxbury

Roxbury State Forest

East Roxbury

Allis State Park

▲ Ainsworth State Park

Washington State Forest

25

East Corinth

South Newbury

14

Cookeville

Corinth

Brookfield

65

East Brookfield

Second Branch White R.

West Brookfield

89

East Braintree

North Randolph

Corinth Corners

113

Vershire

Bradford

West Braintree

Randolph Center

Pompanoosuc R.

Bald Top ▲

Randolph

East Randolph

North Tunbridge

First Branch White R.

Lake Morey

Orford

Orfordville

Mt. Cushman

South Randolph

Tunbridge

West Fairlee

Ely

▲ Rochester Mtn.

East Bethel

110

Post Mills

Lake Fairlee

North Thetford

Bethel

South Tunbridge

Stratford

South Stratford

Thetford Center

Thetford Hill

East Thetford

Lyme

107

Royalton

South Royalton

132

Thetford Hills State Forest

91

Lyme Center

NEW HAMPSHIRE

12

Mt. Hunger ▲

Silver Lake State Park

Sharon

White R.

Charles Downer State Forest

Gile Mtn. ▲

Union Village

Pompanoosuc

5

Goose Pond

able Mtn.

Barnard

Silver Lake

North Pomfret

89

Norwich

Hanover Center

Hanover

MOOSE MTN.

Pomfret

West Hartford

Etna

West Canaan

Appalachian Trail

▲ East Mtn.

South Pomfret

Suicide Six

Prosper

Quechee

Hartford

Wilder

Mascoma

Enfield

Bridgewater Center

West Woodstock

Woodstock

Ottauquechee R.

Taftsville

4

White River Junction

Lebanon

Mascoma Lake

exploring the town. The small lobby has a colonial cast to it; guest rooms on the three upper floors adopt a light, faux-colonial tone, and more amenities than you may expect. Bottom line: nothing fancy, but clean, comfortable, and convenient.

100 State St., Montpelier, VT 05602. © 800/274-5252 or 802/223-5252. Fax 802/229-5427. www.capitol plaza.com. 58 units. $98 double, foliage season from $119 double; $118–$168 suite. AE, DISC, MC, V. **Amenities:** Restaurant (steakhouse). *In room:* A/C, TV, dataport, hair dryer, iron.

Inn at Montpelier ⭐ Two historic in-town homes comprise the Inn at Montpelier, and both offer welcoming accommodations and an appeal for those who enjoy historic architecture. The main, cream-colored Federal-style inn, built in 1827, features a mix of historical and up-to-date furnishings, along with a sunny sitting room and deck off the rear of the second floor. (Room 27 is especially pleasant and features a large private deck.) The property is somewhat more sparely furnished than other historic inns in the area (you're better off heading to Waitsfield or Warren if you're in search of the quintessential Vermont inn), but it offers comfortable lodging an easy stroll from downtown.

147 Main St., Montpelier, VT 05602. © 802/223-2727. Fax 802/223-0722. www.innatmontpelier.com. 19 units. $109–$194 double. Rates include continental breakfast. AE, DC, DISC, MC, V. **Amenities:** Bike rental; in-room massage; dry cleaning. *In room:* A/C, TV, dataport.

IN WATERBURY

The Old Stagecoach Inn ⭐ This handsome, gabled home, within walking distance of downtown, is full of wonderful details such as painted wood floors, a pair of upstairs porches to observe the town's comings and goings, an old library with a stamped tin ceiling, and a chessboard awaiting a game. Originally built in 1826, the house was gutted and revamped in 1890 in ostentatious period style by an Ohio millionaire. After some years of quiet disuse, it was converted to an inn in the late 1980s by owners who took care to preserve the historical detailing. Guest rooms are furnished in an understated Victorian style, mostly with oak and pine furniture and a selection of antiques. It's not a polished inn (expect some worn carpeting), but it's quite comfortable. The two third-floor rooms have the original exposed beams and skylights, and are pleasant and open. The three back rooms share a bathroom and offer guests the feel of boarding at a friendly farmhouse; these are a good choice for budget travelers. Room 1 is among the best, with Victorian detailing, a large dressing area, and a marble sink.

18 N. Main St., Waterbury, VT 05676. © 800/262-2206 or 802/244-5056. Fax 802/244-6956. www.old stagecoach.com. 11 units (3 rooms share 1 bathroom). $60–$125 double; foliage season, Christmas week, and President's Day weekend $70–$180 double. Rates include breakfast. 2-night minimum stay during peak periods. AE, DISC, MC, V. Pets allowed ($10 pet per night). **Amenities:** Restaurant (traditional New England).

Thatcher Brook Inn ⭐ On busy Route 100 near the Ben & Jerry's factory, the innkeepers have pulled off the illusion that guests are considerably further away from this major artery. The 1899 white-clapboard building has a pleasing historical character, even though it's undergone significant renovations and expansions. The new additions have kept its Queen Anne–style architectural integrity intact. The common areas downstairs are worn to a nice patina, whether it's the sitting area in front of the fireplace, or the newer bar and grill with its Windsor chairs. The guest rooms are all carpeted, and decorated with furniture varying from Ethan Allen new to flea-market oak, but the overall character takes its cue from a somewhat fussy country look. Four rooms have fireplaces (two wood, two propane), and six have Jacuzzis. Rooms 14 through 17 are a bit larger and more spacious; rooms 8 through 11 have balconies off the back that face a wooded hillside. Only some rooms have air-conditioning; ask if you require it.

Rte. 100, Waterbury, VT 05676. © 800/292-5911 or 802/244-5911. Fax 802/244-1294. www.thatcher brook.com. 22 units. $80–$165 double; foliage season, holidays, Christmas week, and Presidents' Day week- end $125–$195 double. Rates include breakfast. 2-night minimum stay during foliage season; 3-night mini- mum stay during Christmas. AE, DC, DISC, MC, V. **Amenities:** Restaurant (country French); access to fitness center. *In room:* Jacuzzi (some), fireplace (some).

WHERE TO DINE

A creation of the New England Culinary Institute, **La Brioche Bakery & Cafe** (© **802/229-0443**) occupies the corner of Montpelier's State and Main streets. It's a little bit of Europe in one of New England's more Continental cities. (Montpelier could slip into the Black Forest or the Vienna Woods without caus- ing much of a stir.) A deli counter offers baked goods such as croissants and baguettes. Get them to go, or settle into a table in the afternoon sun outdoors.

I've spent many a cold afternoon inside the cleverly named **Capitol Grounds** ★ (© **802/223-7800**) at 45 State Street, a stone's throw from the gold dome of the state capitol. It's one of my favorite coffeehouses in New England: a great, youthful spot for an espresso, hot chocolate, soup, delicious sandwich, or baked good while peering out windows at the goings-on of town, watching the snow fall, or leafing through one of the newspapers or free papers they leave out. You'll find everyone from mothers and their kids to State House interns to Greenpeace members hanging out here.

IN MONTPELIER

Main Street Grill & Bar ★★ AMERICAN/ECLECTIC   This modern, comfortable restaurant serves as classroom and ongoing exam for students of the New England Culinary Institute, just down the block. It's not unusual to see knots of students, toques at a rakish angle, walking between the restaurant and class. You can eat in the first-level dining room, watching street life through the broad windows, or burrow in the homey bar downstairs. Dishes change every 3 months; lunch might include poached pear and Stilton salad to start, followed by a shaved sirloin wrap, sesame-crusted chicken, or sausage and mussel stew. Dinner might feature a short rib terrine, gnocchi, or something more traditional such as leg of venison or pan-seared rainbow trout. Vegetarian dishes are always on the menu.

Also of note is the second-floor **Chef's Table** ★★, which operates on a dif- ferent schedule. (It's open Mon–Fri for lunch and dinner, and Sat for dinner only.) This intimate and well-appointed dining room offers more refined fare, such as a smoked pork chop with apple-fennel salad, rosemary lamb chops, grilled swordfish with an olive tapenade, five-spiced quail, and interesting treat- ments of lobster.

118 Main St., Montpelier. © 802/223-3188 or 802/229-9202 (Chef's Table). Limited reservations accepted. Lunch $6.50–$8.95; dinner $12–$17. AE, DISC, MC, V. Mon–Fri 11:30am–2pm and 5:30–9pm; Sat 11am–2pm and 5:30–9pm; Sun 10am–2pm and 5:30–9pm.

IN WATERBURY

Marsala Salsa ★ INDIAN/MEXICAN   The owner is from Trinidad, was raised on the cuisine of India, and worked at a Mexican restaurant in Nevada. The result? Marsala Salsa, a hybrid that offers two international cuisines, both well prepared at reasonable prices. The restaurant, located in a funky storefront in Waterbury's historic downtown, is decorated with a light and culturally ambiguous touch. Service is friendly and informal. Mexican entrees include carne asada and *bistec picado,* strips of sirloin charbroiled with homemade avocado-lime butter. If you're more tempted by the Asian subcontinent, try the curries or tandoori chicken, or a wonderful shrimp *shaag*—a light curry with sautéed shrimp, spinach, and carrots. Desserts include flan, deep-fried bananas, and coconut-cream caramel. Marsala Salsa is an unexpected oasis deep behind local culinary battle lines manned primarily by cheddar cheese and maple syrup.

13–15 Stowe St. ℂ **802/244-1150.** Reservations recommended on weekends. Main courses $6.95–$13. MC, V. Tues–Sat 5–9:30pm.

8 Stowe

Stowe is a wonderful destination, summer, fall, and winter. One of Vermont's first winter destination areas, it has managed the decades-long juggernaut of growth with patience and aplomb. Condo developments and strip mall–style restaurants are around, to be sure. Yet the village has preserved its essential character nicely, including trademark views of surrounding mountains and vistas across the fertile farmlands of the valley floor. You can actually park your car and explore on foot or by bike, which isn't the case at Vermont's ski resorts. The chief complaint about Stowe is its winter and foliage-season traffic. Fortunately, a free trolley bus connects the village with the mountain during ski season.

ESSENTIALS

GETTING THERE   Stowe is on Route 100 north of Waterbury and south of Morrisville. In summer, Stowe may also be reached via Smugglers Notch on Route 108. This pass, which squeezes narrowly between rocks and is not recommended for RVs or trailers, is closed in winter.

Stowe has no direct train or bus service. Go to Waterbury, 10 miles south of Stowe, via **Vermont Transit** (ℂ 800/451-3292 or 802/244-7689; www.vermont transit.com) or **Amtrak** (ℂ 800/USA-RAIL; www.amtrak.com), then connect to Stowe via a rental car from **Thrifty** (ℂ 802/244-8800; www.thrifty.com), a ride from **Richard's Limousine Service** (ℂ 800/698-3176 or 802/253-5606), or a taxi from **Peg's Pick Up** (ℂ 800/370-9490 or 802/253-9490).

VISITOR INFORMATION   The **Stowe Area Association** (ℂ **877/603-8693** or 802/253-7321; www.gostowe.com) maintains a handy office on Main Street in the village center. It's open Monday through Friday from 9am to 8pm, Saturday and Sunday from 10am to 5pm (limited hr. during slower seasons).

The **Green Mountain Club** (ℂ **802/244-7037**), a venerable statewide association devoted to building and maintaining backcountry trails, has a visitor center on Route 100 between Waterbury and Stowe.

SPECIAL EVENTS   The weeklong **Stowe Winter Carnival** (ℂ **802/253-7321**) has taken place annually, from the middle to the end of January, since 1921. The fest features a number of wacky events involving skis, snowshoes, and skates, as well as nighttime entertainment. Don't miss the snow sculpture contest or "turkey bowling," which involves sliding frozen birds across the ice.

DOWNHILL SKIING

Stowe Mountain Resort ★★★   Stowe was one of the first, one of the classiest, and one of the most noted ski resorts in the world when it opened in the 1930s. It's one of the best places for the full New England ski experience, it's one of the most beautiful ski mountains, and it offers tremendous challenges to

---

(*Fun Fact*) **Maple Syrup & How It Gets That Way**

Two elemental ingredients combine to create maple syrup: sugar-maple sap and fire. Sugaring season slips in between northern New England's long winter and short spring; it usually lasts around 4 or 5 weeks, typically beginning in early to mid-March. When warm and sunny days alternate with freezing nights, the sap in sugar-maple trees begins to run up toward the branches. Sugarers drill shallow holes and insert small taps; buckets or plastic tubing are hung from the taps and collect the sap, bit by bit.

The collected sap is then boiled off. The equipment for this ranges from a simple backyard firepit cobbled together of concrete blocks to elaborate sugarhouses with oil or propane burners. It requires between 32 and 40 gallons of sap to make 1 gallon of syrup, and that means a fair amount of boiling. (The real cost of syrup isn't the sap; it's the fuel to boil it down.)

Vermont is the nation's capital of maple syrup, producing 550,000 gallons a year. You can pick up the real thing in almost any grocery store in the state, but I'm convinced it tastes better straight from the farm. Look for handmade signs touting syrup posted at the end of driveways around the region throughout the year. Drive up and knock on the door.

Some sugarers invite visitors to sample the syrup in early spring. Ask for the brochure "Maple Sugarhouses Open to Visitors," available at information centers or from the **Vermont Agency of Agriculture, Food, and Markets** (Drawer 20, 116 State St., Montpelier, VT 05620; ℂ **802/ 828-2416;** www.vermontagriculture.com). The list is also posted online at **www.vermontmaple.org/sugarhouses.htm**.

---

advanced skiers, with winding, old-style trails. Especially notable are its legendary "Front Four" trails (National, Starr, Lift Line, and Goat), which have humbled more than a handful of skiers attempting to grope their way from advanced intermediate to expert. The mountain has four good, long lifts that go from bottom to top—not the usual patchwork of shorter lifts you find at other ski areas. Beginning skiers can start out across the road at Spruce Peak, which features gentle, wide trails.

Stowe, VT 05672. ℂ **800/253-4754** or 802/253-3000. www.stowe.com. Vertical drop: 2,360 ft. Lifts: 1 gondola, 8 chairlifts (1 high-speed), 2 surface lifts. Skiable acreage: 480. Adult lift tickets: $64 holidays, $62 non-holidays.

CROSS-COUNTRY SKIING

Stowe is an outstanding destination for cross-country skiers, offering three groomed ski areas with a combined total of more than 100 miles of trails traversing everything from gentle valley floors to challenging mountain peaks.

The **Trapp Family Lodge Cross-Country Ski Center,** on Luce Hill Road, 2 miles from Mountain Road (ℂ **800/826-7000** or 802/253-8511; www.trapp family.com), was the nation's first cross-country ski center. It remains one of the most gloriously situated in the Northeast, set atop a ridge with views across the broad valley and into the folds of the mountains flanking Mount Mansfield. The center features 30 miles of groomed trails (plus 60 miles of backcountry trails) on its 2,700 acres of rolling forestland. Rates are $16 for a trail pass, and $20 for equipment rental.

The **Edson Hill Manor Ski Touring Center** (© **800/621-0284** or 802/253-7371) has 33 miles of wooded trails just off Mountain Road ($10 for a day pass). Also offering appealing ski touring are the **Stowe Mountain Resort Cross-Country Touring Center** (© **800/253-4754** or 802/253-3000), with 48 miles at the base of Mount Mansfield ($15 for adults, $8 for children 6–12).

SUMMER OUTDOOR PURSUITS

Stowe's history is linked to winter recreation, but it's also a great fair-weather destination, surrounded by lush, rolling green hills and open farmlands, and towered over by craggy **Mount Mansfield,** Vermont's highest peak at 4,393 feet.

Deciding how to get atop Mount Mansfield is half the challenge. The **toll road** (© **802/253-7311**) traces its lineage back to the 19th century. Drivers now twist their way up this road and park below the summit; a 2-hour hike along well-marked trails will bring you to the top for unforgettable views. The toll road is open from late May to mid-October. The fare is $16 per car with up to six passengers, $3 per additional person. Ascending on foot or by bicycle is free.

Another option is the **Stowe gondola** (© **802/253-7311**), which whisks visitors to within 1½ miles of the summit at the Cliff House Restaurant. Hikers can explore the rugged, open ridgeline, then descend before twilight. The gondola runs from mid-June to mid-October. The round-trip cost is $12 for adults, $7 for children 6 to 12. (It's $15 per ride in winter for all ages.)

The budget route up Mount Mansfield (and the most rewarding) is on foot, with at least nine options for an ascent. Ask for information at your inn, or stop by Green Mountain Club headquarters, on Route 100, 4 miles south of Stowe.

All manner of recreational paraphernalia is available for rent at the **Mountain Sports & Bike Shop** (© **802/253-7919**) on the Rec Path, including full-suspension demo bikes, baby joggers, and bike trailers. Basic bike rentals are $16 for 4 hours, plenty long enough to explore the path. The shop is on Mountain Road (across from the Golden Eagle Resort), open from 9am to 6pm daily in summer. (It's also a good spot for cross-country ski and snowshoe rentals.)

Anglers should allow ample time to peruse **The Fly Rod Shop** (© **802/253-7346**), located on Route 100 2 miles south of the village. This well-stocked shop offers fly and spin tackle, along with camping gear, antique fly rods, and rentals of canoes and fishing videos. Also in town is **Fly Fish Vermont,** 954 S. Main St. (© **802/253-3964**), a retail shop and outfitting operation that can arrange for guides or guided instructional tours.

WHERE TO STAY

Stowe has a number of basic motels to serve travelers who don't require elaborate amenities. The **Sun and Ski Inn & Suites,** 1613 Mountain Rd. (© **800/448-5223** or 802/253-7159; www.sunandski.com), has 26 utilitarian units, all with air-conditioning, phones, TVs, and small fridges. The heated pool is perfect for thawing out after a cold day of skiing. Rates for a double are $72 to $145.

Edson Hill Manor ★★   The Edson Hill Manor sits atop a long, quiet drive 2 miles from Mountain Road and has an ineffably quirky charm. The main lodge dates to the 1940s; the four carriage houses just up the hill are of newer vintage.

The compound is set amid a rolling landscape of lawns, hemlocks, and maples. The comfortable common room in the main house is like a movie set for a country retreat—tapestries, pastels, and oils adorn the walls. Most of the nine guest rooms in the main lodge have pine walls and floors, wood-burning fireplaces, colonial maple furnishings, wingback chairs, and four-poster beds. The 16 carriage-house rooms are somewhat larger, but lack the cozy charm of the main inn and feel more like motel units (*really nice* motel units). Some units have TVs; manor rooms are air-conditioned.

1500 Edson Hill Rd., Stowe, VT 05672. © 800/621-0284 or 802/253-7371. www.stowevt.com. 25 units. $179–$239 double; off season lower. AE, DISC, MC, V. Pets and young children welcome in carriage-house units only. **Amenities:** Restaurant (New American); access to nearby pool; riding stables (private lessons available). *In room:* A/C in some manor house rooms only.

The Gables Inn ✫   This cozy and comfortable inn, housed in a gray farmhouse facing Mountain Road, is a relaxed place—the hot tub next to the front door makes that point clear. The main farmhouse has 13 rooms of varying size and shape, simply furnished with country antiques; the smaller rooms are quite small. A more contemporary "carriage house" in the back offers four nicely sized rooms, mostly with cathedral ceilings, canopy beds, fireplaces, Jacuzzis, and air-conditioning. Two other "Riverview Suites" in an adjacent building are more opulently appointed, and include telephones, TVs, fireplaces, and VCRs.

1457 Mountain Rd., Stowe, VT 05672. © 800/422-5371 or 802/253-7730. Fax 802/253-8989. www.gablesinn.com. 19 units. $78–$235 double; foliage season and holiday rates higher. All rates include breakfast. 2-night minimum stay for weekends, holidays, and foliage season. AE, DC, DISC, MC, V. **Amenities:** Restaurant (American); outdoor pool; Jacuzzi. *In room:* A/C, no phone.

Green Mountain Inn ✫✫✫   This handsome historic structure sits right in the village, and it's the best choice for those seeking a sense of New England history along with a bit of pampering. A sprawling hostelry with 100 guest rooms spread among several buildings old and new, it feels far more intimate, with accommodations tastefully decorated in an early-19th-century motif that befits the 1833 vintage of the main inn. More than a dozen units feature Jacuzzis and/or gas fireplaces, and the Mill House has rooms with CD players, sofas, and Jacuzzis that open into the bedroom from behind folding wooden doors. The *luxe* Mansfield House (which opened in 2000) features double Jacuzzis, marble bathrooms, and 36-inch TVs with DVD players. The most expensive rooms are uniformly superb; some of the lower-priced rooms in the main inn feature minor irritants, such as balky radiators or views of noisy kitchen ventilators.

Main St. (P.O. Box 60), Stowe, VT 05672. © 800/253-7302 or 802/253-7301. Fax 802/253-5096. www.greenmountaininn.com. 100 units. $115–$305 doubles and suites; foliage season $165–$325 doubles and suites; holidays $225–$625 doubles and suites. 2-night minimum stay summer/winter weekends and in foliage season. AE, DISC, MC, V. Pets allowed in some rooms with restrictions (call first; $20 per night). **Amenities:** Restaurant (creative pub fare); heated outdoor pool (year-round); fitness room; Jacuzzi; sauna; steam room; game room; limited room service; in-room massage; laundry service. *In room:* A/C, TV w/pay movies, hair dryer.

Inn at The Mountain ✫   This is the "official" hotel of Stowe Mountain Resort—located near the base of the mountain (but not ski-in-ski-out) and owned and operated by the ski mountain. A low-key casual spot, more like an upscale motel than a fancy lodge, rooms are clean and attractive, more spacious than average motel rooms, with veneer furniture, small refrigerators, and tiny balconies that face the pool and woods. Ask about the 39 nearby condos, suitable for families. Some rooms have air-conditioning and fireplaces.

5781 Mountain Rd., Stowe, VT 05672. © **800/253-4754** or 802/253-3000. www.stowe.com. 33 units (inn rooms, condos also available). $160–$200 double, $240–$500 suites and condos; holidays $230–$275 double, $260–$310 suite, $330–$700 condo; off season $100–$120 doubles and suites; $120–$300 condo. 5-night minimum stay Christmas week. AE, DC, DISC, MC, V. **Amenities:** Restaurant (Continental); outdoor pool; 9 tennis courts; fitness center; Jacuzzi; sauna; limited room service. *In room:* TV, fridge.

Inn at Turner Mill ⚑   Set in a narrow wooded valley along a tumbling stream, this homey 1936 building was built as a residence and inn. In the winter, some of the rooms are combined into suites to accommodate groups, including one with a kitchen, two bathrooms, and a brick fireplace. The inn is eclectic in style, with everything from frightfully orange wall-to-wall carpeting in some areas to attractive and rustic log furniture made by the innkeeper in others. Most memorable may be the monolithic stone walkway outside and the steep staircase to the upper floors. In summer, rooms rent separately (all have private bathroom), and rates include breakfast. The inn is a short trip from the mountain and across the road from the Rec Path, making it a good destination for bike-trippers.

56 Turner Mill Lane, Stowe, VT 05672. © **800/992-0016** or 802/253-2062. www.turnermill.com. 8 units. $110 double, $185–$210 suite; holidays and foliage season, $300–$375 suite. Summer/fall rates include breakfast. AE, MC, V. *In room:* TV, fridge, coffeemaker.

Stone Hill Inn ⚑⚑   With just nine rooms, the contemporary Stone Hill Inn (built in 1998) offers personal service and a handy location, along with room amenities that include in-room VCRs, Egyptian cotton towels, and double-sided gas fireplaces that also front double Jacuzzis in the sizable bathrooms. (*Note:* Rooms don't have phones, but a private phone booth is off the lobby.) Room layouts are roughly the same, each featuring a small sitting area. High-ceilinged common rooms have fireplaces and billiard tables, and there's a well-stocked guest pantry with complimentary beverages and mixers. An outdoor hot tub offers guests a relaxing soak. Breakfast is in a bright morning room where every table is window-side; hors d'ouevres are set out each evening. Stone Hill lacks a patina of age and may strike some visitors as somewhat sterile, but it will please those willing to forego timeworn character in exchange for quiet and luxury.

89 Houston Farm Rd. (just off Mountain Rd. midway between village and ski area), Stowe, VT 05672. © **802/253-6282.** www.stonehillinn.com. 9 units. $250–$325 double; holidays and foliage season $350–$370 double. Rates include breakfast. 2-night minimum stay weekends and foliage season; 3-night minimum stay holiday weekends; 4-night minimum stay Christmas week. Not suitable for children. AE, DC, DISC, MC, V. **Amenities:** Jacuzzi; game room; movie library; snowshoes and toboggan; self-service laundry. *In room:* A/C, TV/VCR, hair dryer, safe.

Stoweflake ⚑⚑   Stoweflake is on Mountain Road 1¾ miles from the village and lately has been playing catch-up with the more upscale Topnotch resort and spa. The newer guest rooms are nicer than those at Topnotch—they're regally decorated and have amenities such as two phones and wet bars. The resort has five categories of guest rooms in two wings; the "superior" rooms in the old wing are a bit cozy. They're okay for an overnight, but you're better off requesting "deluxe" or better if staying a few days. The spa and fitness facilities are adequate, but lack the over-the-top sybaritic elegance of Topnotch (what, no waterfalls?). The fitness facilities include a decent-size fitness room with Cybex equipment, a squash/racquetball court, a coed Jacuzzi, and a small indoor pool. The spa also offers a variety of massages and treatments. Both restaurants offer nearly 50 wines by the glass.

1746 Mountain Rd. (P.O. Box 369), Stowe, VT 05672. © **800/253-2232** or 802/253-7355. Fax 802/253-6858. www.stoweflake.com. 95 units (includes 10 suites), plus 12 town houses. Peak winter season $170–$270 double, $390 suite; holiday season $180–$290 double, suites to $340; off season $150–$250 double, $360 suite. Call for town house or package info. 2-night minimum stay on most weekends; 4-night minimum stay during holidays. AE, DC, DISC, MC, V. **Amenities:** 2 restaurants (pub fare, New American); indoor pool, outdoor pool; 2 tennis courts; racquetball/squash court; health club; spa; bike rental; children's center; game room; business center; salon; limited room service; in-room massage; babysitting; laundry service; dry cleaning. *In room:* A/C, TV, dataport, fridge, coffeemaker, hair dryer, iron.

Stowehof ★ High on a hillside, this inn feels far removed from the hubbub of the valley floor. The exterior architecture features that aggressive neo-Tyrolean ski-chalet styling, but inside, the place comes close to magical—it's pleasantly woodsy, folksy, and rustic, with heavy beams and pine floors, ticking clocks, and maple tree trunks carved into architectural elements. Guests may feel a bit like characters in *The Hobbit.* Furnished without a lot of fanfare, each guest room is decorated individually: some bold and festive with sunflower patterns, others subdued and quiet. Four have wood-burning fireplaces, 24 have air-conditioning, and all have good views. Among the best: rooms 43 and 44, with high ceilings, balconies with expansive views, and sofas. The lodge is next to Wiessner Woods, 80 acres laced with hiking and cross-country ski trails.

434 Edson Hill Rd. (P.O. Box 1139), Stowe, VT 05672. Ⓒ **800/932-7136** or 802/253-9722. Fax 802/253-7513. www.stowehofinn.com. 44 units, 2 guest houses. $83–$240 double; holidays and foliage season $150–$445 double. Rates include breakfast. 2-night minimum stay on some weekends; 4-night minimum stay during holidays. AE, DC, MC, V. **Amenities:** Restaurant (New American); heated outdoor pool; 4 tennis courts; nearby health club; outdoor Jacuzzi; sauna; game room; business center; in-room massage; laundry service; dry cleaning; horseback riding (extra fee); valet parking; safe. *In room:* TV.

Stowe Motel This is one of Stowe's best choices for those traveling on a budget. The motel has 60 units spread among three buildings; rooms are basic but slightly larger than average, and feature some comfortable touches, such as couches and coffee tables. Efficiency units have two-burner stoves.

2043 Mountain Rd., Stowe, VT 05672. Ⓒ **800/829-7629** or 802/253-7629. Fax 802/253-9971 www.stowe motel.com. 30 units. Standard units $64–$89 double, foliage season $94–$120; efficiency units $74–$112 double, holidays and foliage season $110–$146. Ask about ski packages. Pets allowed in some rooms ($10 pet per night). **Amenities:** Outdoor heated pool; Jacuzzi; game room; snowshoes. *In room:* A/C, TV, dataport, fridge.

Topnotch ★★★ A boxy, uninteresting exterior hides a creatively designed interior at this upscale resort and spa. The main lobby is ski-lodge modern, with lots of stone and wood and a huge moose head hanging on the wall. The guest rooms are attractively appointed, most in country pine. Ten units have wood-burning fireplaces; 18 have Jacuzzis; and third-floor rooms have cathedral ceilings. The main attractions here are the resort's spa and activities, which range from horseback riding in summer to cross-country skiing and indoor tennis in winter, with nice touches throughout, such as fireplaces in the spa's locker rooms.

4000 Mountain Rd., Stowe, VT 05672. Ⓒ **800/451-8686** or 802/253-8585. Fax 802/253-9263. www.top notch-resort.com. 92 units. $180–$320 double, $315–$755 suite; holidays $380–$495 double, $500–$860 suite. 6-night minimum stay Christmas week. AE, DC, DISC, MC, V. Pets allowed. **Amenities:** 2 restaurants (Continental, family fare); indoor pool; outdoor pool; tennis courts (4 indoor, 10 outdoor); fitness room; spa; Jacuzzi; sauna; concierge; limited room service; horseback riding. *In room:* A/C, TV/VCR w/pay movies, dataport, fridge, coffeemaker, hair dryer, iron, safe.

Trapp Family Lodge The Trapp family of *Sound of Music* fame bought this sprawling farm high up in Stowe in 1942, just 4 years after fleeing the Nazi takeover of Austria. Descendants of Maria and Baron von Trapp continue to run this Tyrolean-flavored lodge on 2,700 mountainside acres. It's a comfortable resort hotel, though designed more for efficiency than elegance. Guest rooms are a shade or two better than run-of-the-mill hotel rooms, and most come complete with fine valley views and private balconies. Room prices are high; they offer access to nice facilities, but little else. Better value can be found elsewhere in the valley. The restaurant offers well-prepared Continental fare (Wiener schnitzel, lamb tenderloin); Sunday concerts are held in the meadow in summer.

700 Trapp Hill Rd., Stowe, VT 05672. (℗ **800/826-7000** or 802/253-8511. Fax 802/253-5740. www.trapp family.com. 120 units. Winter and summer $245–$275 double, $320–$615 suite; from $180 in off season. Higher rates during holidays and foliage season (includes meals). 3-night minimum stay Presidents' Day week and foliage season; 5-night minimum stay Christmas week. AE, DC, MC, V. Depart Stowe westward on Rte. 108; in 2 miles bear left at fork near white church; continue up hill following signs for lodge. **Amenities:** 2 restaurants (Continental, informal Austrian); heated indoor pool; 2 outdoor pools (1 for adults only); 4 clay tennis courts; fitness center; sauna; children's programs; game room; limited room service; in-room massage; babysitting; coin-op washers/dryers; dry cleaning. *In room:* TV.

WHERE TO DINE

The **Harvest Market,** 1031 Mountain Rd. (℗ **802/253-3800**), is the place for gourmet-to-go. Browse Vermont products and imports, then pick up some fresh-baked goods, such as the pleasantly tart raspberry squares, to bring back to the ski lodge or take for a picnic along the bike path. High prices may cause your eyebrows to arch, but if you're not on a tight budget, it's a good place to splurge.

Blue Moon Cafe ✦✦✦ NEW AMERICAN   Delectable crusty bread on the table, Frank Sinatra crooning in the background, and vibrant local art on the walls offer clues that this isn't your typical ski-area pub-fare restaurant. Located a short stroll off Stowe's main street in a contemporary setting in an older home, the Blue Moon offers the village's finest dining. The menu changes every Friday, but count on lamb, beef, and veggie dishes, plus a couple of seafood offerings. The kitchen staff has superb instincts for spicing and creates inventive dishes such as grilled yellowfin tuna with tomatillo salsa fresca and smoked yellow pepper coulis, a banana leaf-steamed halibut with Thai coconut curry, sweet and sour braised rabbit, grilled lamb loin chops with artichoke purée, or wasabi rice cakes with a stir-fry. Desserts are simple yet pure delights: a Belgian chocolate pot, sorbet with cookies, or a white chocolate mousse with caramelized banana.

35 School St. (℗ **802/253-7006.** Reservations recommended. Main courses $20–$26. AE, DISC, MC, V. Daily 6–9:30pm. In off seasons, usually open weekends only; call first.

Mes Amis BISTRO   The friendly Mes Amis is located in a cozy structure above Mountain Road not far from the village. Once a British-style pub, it was pleasantly converted from half-timber Tudor decor to something more broadly European. A quiet and friendly spot, it lacks even the smallest iota of pretension. The menu is rather limited (usually only five entrees), but the specials round out the offerings. The restaurant has three cozy dining rooms and a bar. Appetizers include smoked salmon on toast points and baked stuffed clams; entrees feature steaks and fish. The house specialty is duck roasted with a hot and sweet sauce.

311 Mountain Rd. (℗ **802/253-8669.** Reservations accepted for 6 or more. Dinner $16–$20. DC, MC, V. Tues–Sun 5:30–10pm (open for appetizers at 4:30pm).

Miguel's Stowe-Away ✦ MEXICAN/SOUTHWEST   In an old farmhouse midway between the village and the mountain, Miguel's packs in folks looking for the tangiest Mexican and Tex-Mex food in the valley. Start off with a margarita or Vermont beer, then order up appetizers such as empanadas, nachos, or jalapenos. Follow up with sizzling fajitas, the good chicken Santa Fe or fish chimichangas, or a filling combo plate. Desserts range from the complicated (apple-mango compote with cinnamon tortilla and ice cream) to the simple (chocolate-chip cookies). Miguel's is popular enough to offer its own brand of chips, salsa, and other products, which turn up in specialty shops around the Northeast. Expect a loud and boisterous atmosphere on busy nights.

3148 Mountain Rd. © 800/254-1240 or 802/253-7574. www.miguels.com. Reservations recommended on weekends and in ski season. Main courses $11–$18 (mostly under $14). AE, DISC, MC, V. Daily 5–10pm (from 5:30pm in summer). Lunch in winter only, noon–3pm.

Mr. Pickwick's ★ BRITISH PUB FARE   Mr. Pickwick's is a pub and restaurant that's part of Ye Old English Inne. It could justly be accused of being a theme-park restaurant, with the theme being, well, ye olde Englande. But it's been run since 1983 with such creative gusto by British ex-pats Chris and Lyn Francis that it's hard not to enjoy yourself here. Start by admiring the Anglo gewgaws while relaxing at handsome wood tables at the booths (dubbed "pews"). Sample from the 150 beers (many British) before ordering house specialties such as bangers and mash (sausages and potatoes), fish and chips, and beef Wellington. The Boathouse Deck offers great additional seating.

433 Mountain Rd. © 802/253-7558. Reservations accepted for parties of 6 or more. Main courses, lunch $6.95–$13; dinner $14–$24. AE, DC, MC, V. Daily 11am–1am.

The Shed ★ PUB FARE   Stowe has plenty of options for pub fare, but The Shed is the most consistently reliable. Since it opened over 3 decades ago, this friendly, informal place has won fans by the sleighload with filling fare and feisty camaraderie. It offers a bar area with free popcorn and a good selection of beverages, ranging from craft beers brewed on the premises to frozen rum drinks to homemade root beer. The dining room has a chain-restaurant feel, but the bright solarium in the rear is a perfect spot to perch during sunny Sunday brunch. Meals are pub-fare eclectic: nachos (a bit soggy), burgers (including veggie burgers), chicken Alfredo, grilled tuna, prime rib, Asian stir-fry noodles, and taco salads.

1859 Mountain Rd. © 802/253-4364. Reservations recommended weekends and holidays. Main courses, lunch $5–$9.95; dinner $11–$19. AE, DC, DISC, MC, V. Sun–Thurs 11:30am–10pm; Fri–Sat 11:30am–11pm.

9 Burlington

Burlington is a vibrant college town—home to the University of Vermont, known as UVM—that's continually, valiantly resisting the onset of middle age. It's the birthplace of hippies-turned-corporation Ben & Jerry's. (Look for the sidewalk plaque at the corner of St. Paul and College streets commemorating the first store.) It elected a socialist mayor in 1981, Bernie Sanders, who's now Vermont's lone representative to the U.S. Congress. Burlington was also the birthplace of the jam rock band Phish.

It's no wonder that Burlington has become a magnet for those seeking an alternative to big-city life. Burlington has a superb location overlooking Lake Champlain and the Adirondacks, and downtown is thriving. The pedestrian mall (Church St.), a creation that has failed in so many other towns, works here. In fact, the city's scale is pleasantly skewed toward pedestrians—park your car and walk to experience the best of Burlington.

ESSENTIALS

GETTING THERE Burlington is at the junction of I-89, Route 7, and Route 2. **Burlington International Airport,** about 3 miles east of downtown, is served by **Continental Connection** (© 800/532-3273; www.continental.com), **Delta Connection** (© 800/221-1212; www.delta.com), **JetBlue** (© 800/538-2583; www.jetblue.com), **United** (© 800/864-8331; www.united.com), and **US Airways Express** (© 800/428-4322; www.usair.com).

The **Amtrak** (© **800/USA-RAIL;** www.amtrak.com) *Vermonter* offers daily departures for Burlington from Washington, Baltimore, Philadelphia, New York, New Haven, and Springfield, Massachusetts.

Vermont Transit Lines (© **802/864-6811;** www.vermonttransit.com), with a depot at 345 Pine St., offers bus connections from Albany, Boston, Hartford, New York's JFK Airport, and other points in Vermont, Massachusetts, and New Hampshire.

VISITOR INFORMATION The **Lake Champlain Regional Chamber of Commerce,** 60 Main St. (© **802/863-3489;** www.vermont.org), maintains an information center in a stout 1929 brick building just up from the waterfront and a short walk from Church Street Market. Hours are Monday through Friday from 8am to 5pm. On weekends, helpful maps and brochures are left in the entryway for visitors. A summer-only information booth is also staffed at the Church Street Marketplace at the corner of Church and Bank streets (no phone).

The free local weekly *Seven Days* (www.sevendaysvt.com) carries topical and lifestyle articles, along with a very good list of events.

SPECIAL EVENTS **First Night Burlington** (© **802/863-6005;** www.first nightburlington.com) turns downtown into a stage on New Year's Eve. Hundreds of performers—from rockers to vaudevillians—play at nearly three dozen venues (mostly indoors) for 10 hours beginning at 2pm. The evening finishes with a bang at the midnight fireworks. Admission is $13 for adults (or $10 if you purchase before Dec 1), $5 for children 12 and under, and covers all performances.

The **Vermont Mozart Festival** (© **802/862-7352;** www.vtmozart.com) takes place in locales in and around Burlington (and further afield) from mid-July to August. (The festival also offers a winter series.) Tickets range from $14 to $30. Call for a schedule and information, or check the website.

EXPLORING BURLINGTON

Ethan Allen Homestead ✪ A quiet retreat on one of the most idyllic, least developed stretches of the Winooski River, the Ethan Allen Homestead is a shrine to Vermont's favorite son. While Allen wasn't born in Burlington, he settled here later in life on property confiscated from a British sympathizer during the Revolution. The reconstructed farmhouse is an enduring tribute to this Vermont hero; an orientation center offers an intriguing multimedia accounting of Allen's life and other points of regional history. The house is open for tours from June 1 to the end of October with tours Monday through Saturday from 10am to 5pm and on Sundays from 1 to 5 pm. The grounds are open year-round daily from dawn to dusk. Park admission is free.

Rte. 127. © **802/865-4556.** Admission $5 adults, $4 seniors, $2.50 children 5–17; $14 per family. May to Oct, daily 9am–5pm; Nov to Apr, Sat–Sun 9am–5pm. Take Rte. 127 northward from downtown; look for signs.

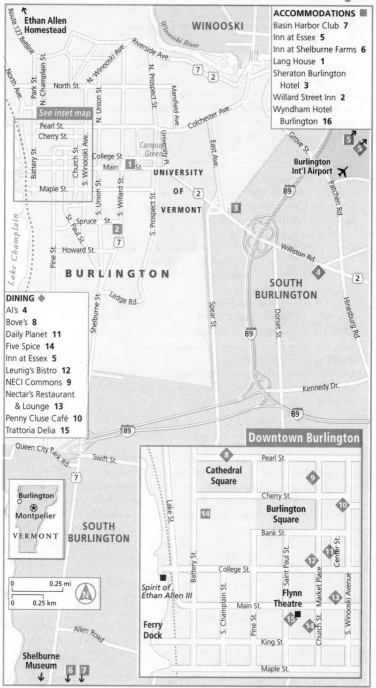

Burlington

WINOOSKI

Winooski River

Ethan Allen
Homestead

Route 127 Beltline

North Ave.

Riverside Ave.

N. Champlain St.

Park St.

N. Winooski Ave.

N. Union St.

N. Prospect St.

Mansfield Ave.

North St.

Colchester Ave.

See inset map

Pearl St.

Cherry St.

Battery St.

Church St.

S. Winooski Ave.

College St.

Campus
Green

University Pl.

Main St.

1

Grove St.

5

Burlington
Int'l Airport ✈

Maple St.

S. Union St.

S. Willard St.

UNIVERSITY

OF

East Ave.

89

Patchen Rd.

Lake Champlain

Pine St.

St. Paul St.

Spruce

S. Willard St.

S. Prospect St.

VERMONT

2

3

Williston Rd.

2

7

Howard St.

B U R L I N G T O N

Ledge Rd.

Shelburne St.

Spear St.

SOUTH
BURLINGTON

4

2

Dorset St.

Hinesburg Rd.

89

Kennedy Dr.

189

89

Queen City Park Rd.

Swift St.

7

Downtown Burlington

8

Pearl St.

Burlington
○
⊛ Montpelier

VERMONT

SOUTH
BURLINGTON

**Cathedral
Square**

9

Cherry St.

Lake St.

14

**Burlington
Square**

10

Bank St.

0   0.25 mi
0   0.25 km
Ⓝ

Battery St.

Saint Paul St.

11

Center St.

12

Market Place

College St.

S. Champlain St.

Pine St.

**Flynn
Theatre**

13

S. Winooski Avenue

*Spirit of
Ethan Allen III*

Main St.

15

Church St.

14

**Ferry
Dock**

King St.

**Shelburne
Museum**
↓

6 **7**

Maple St.

Fun Fact **Ethan Allen: Patriot & Libertine**

In 1749, the governor of New Hampshire began giving away land to settlers willing to brave the howling wilderness of what is now Vermont. Two decades later, New York State courts decreed those grants void, opening the door for New York speculators to flood into the region, vowing to push the original settlers out of the valleys and up into the Green Mountains.

Not surprisingly, this decision didn't sit well with those already there, who established a network of military units, Green Mountain Boys, and promised to drive out the New Yorkers. A hale fellow named Ethan Allen headed up the new militia, which launched a series of effective harrying raids against the impudent New Yorkers. Green Mountain Boys destroyed homes, drove away livestock, and chased the New York sheriffs back across the border.

The American Revolution soon intervened, and Ethan Allen and the Green Mountain Boys took up the revolutionary cause with vigor. They helped sack Fort Ticonderoga in New York in 1775, rallied to the cause at the famed Battle of Bennington, and generally continued to make nuisances of themselves to the British effort throughout the war.

Allen's fame grew as word spread about him and his Green Mountain Boys. A hard-drinking, fierce-fighting, large-living sort of guy, Allen became a legend in his own time. He could bite the head off a nail, one story went; another claimed he was bitten by a rattlesnake, which promptly belched and died. Today you can't drive very far in Vermont without a reminder of Allen's presence—parks are named after him, inns boast he once slept there, and you'll still hear the occasional story about his bawdy doings.

Lake Champlain Ferries ★★   Car ferries chug across the often placid, sometimes turbulent waters of Lake Champlain from Burlington to New York between late spring and foliage season, a good way to cut out miles of driving if you're heading west toward the Adirondacks. It's also a great way to see the lake and mountains on a pleasant, inexpensive cruise. Between June and mid-October, several daily 90-minute narrated lake cruises are also offered; the cost is $8.95 to $13 for adults, and up to $7.95 for children 6 to 12. No reservations are accepted; travelers are advised to arrive 20 to 30 minutes in advance of departure. Call ℂ **802/ 864-9669** for details of these narrated cruises.

Ferries also cross Lake Champlain between Grande Isle, Vermont, and Plattsburgh, New York (year-round), and Charlotte, Vermont, and Essex, New York (Apr to early Jan). Call the number below for more information.

King St. Dock. ℂ **802/864-9804.** www.ferries.com. $14 one-way fare for car and driver from Burlington to Port Kent. Round-trip fares: $7.50 for adults; $3 for children 6–12; free for children under 6. The Burlington ferry operates mid-May to mid-Oct. Frequent departures in summer between 7:30am and 7:30pm. Schedule varies seasonally; call or check website for times.

Shelburne Museum ★★★   Established in 1947 by Americana collector Electra Havenmeyer Webb, the museum contains one of the nation's most singular collections of American decorative, folk, and fine art, occupying some 37 buildings spread over 45 rolling acres 7 miles south of Burlington. The more mundane exhibits include quilts, early tools, decoys, and weather vanes. But the museum also collects and displays *whole* buildings from around New England and New York. These include an 1890 railroad station, a lighthouse, a stagecoach inn, an Adirondack lodge, and a round barn from Vermont. Even a 220-foot steamship is eerily landlocked on the museum's grounds. Additions over the years include a wonderful 1950s ranch house, furnished in period style, and an architecturally engaging Collector's House, made creatively of prefab metal structures and other materials, and featuring folk art displays.

Rte. 7 (P.O. Box 10), Shelburne. © 802/985-3346. www.shelburnemuseum.org. Summer admission $18 adults, $8.75–$13 students with ID, $8.75 children 6–14. May to Oct daily 10am–5pm. Selected buildings open Apr to late May and mid-Oct to Dec 31; call for information.

The Spirit of Ethan Allen ⭐ Accommodating 500 passengers on three decks, the new *Ethan Allen III* (brought to Lake Champlain in 2002 and 40% larger than its predecessor) offers a more genteel touring alternative to the ferry. The vistas of Lake Champlain and the Adirondacks haven't changed much since Samuel de Champlain first explored the area in 1609. The enclosed decks are air-conditioned, and food is available from a full galley, including dinner served nightly and Sunday brunch. The scenic cruise departs daily every other hour from 10am through 4pm. Parking is available at additional cost.

Burlington Boathouse. © 802/862-8300. www.soea.com. Narrated cruises (1½ hr.) $9.95 adults, $3.95 children 3–11. Specialty cruises (dinner, brunch, mystery theater) priced higher; call for details. Daily mid-May to mid-Oct.

SHOPPING

The **Church Street Marketplace** is one of the more notable success stories of downtown development. Situated along 4 blocks that extend southward from the elegant Congregational church, the marketplace buzzes with downtown energy. While the marketplace has been discovered by the national chains, it still makes room for used-book vendors and homegrown shops. In summer, leave time to be entertained by drummers, pan-flutists, buskers, and knots of young folks just hanging out.

OUTDOOR PURSUITS

Burlington is blessed with numerous city parks. Most popular is **Leddy Park** ⭐⭐ on North Avenue, with an 1,800-foot beach, tennis courts, ball fields, walking trails, and a handsome indoor skating rink. **North Beach** ⭐ also features a long sandy beach, plus a campground for those looking to pitch a tent or park an RV. The 68 sites cost $21 to $29 per night.

On the downtown waterfront, look for the **Burlington Community Boathouse** ⭐ (© 802/865-3377), a modern structure built with Victorian flair. You can rent a sailboat or rowboat, sign up for kayak or sculling lessons, or just wander around and enjoy the sunset.

One of Burlington's hidden but beguiling attractions is the **Burlington Bike Path** ⭐⭐⭐, running 9 miles on an old rail bed along picturesque shores of Lake Champlain to the mouth of the Winooski River. Start near the Community Boathouse and head north toward the river; bike rentals are available downtown at **Skirack,** 85 Main St. (© 802/658-3313; www.skirack.com), from 4 hours to a whole day. (Skirack also rents in-line skates, also commonly used on the bike path.) **North Star Cyclery,** at 100 Main St. (© 802/863-3832), rents bicycles at comparable rates.

Ask for the free map *Cycling the City* to help plot a course.

WHERE TO STAY

A number of chain motels are along Route 7 (Shelburne Rd.) in South Burlington, about a 5- to 10-minute drive from downtown. While they lack any trace of New England charm, they're modern, clean, and reliable.

Among the better options are these three, which are clustered together: **Holiday Inn Express,** 1712 Shelburne Rd. (☎ **800/465-4329** or 802/860-1112; www.hojo.com); **Smart Suites,** 1700 Shelburne Rd. (☎ **877/862-1986** or 802/860-9900); and **Howard Johnson,** 1720 Shelburne Rd. (☎ **800/874-1554** or 802/860-6000).

On and around Route 2 near I-89 (west of downtown, near the airport) are several other chain hotels, including the **Holiday Inn,** 1068 Williston Rd. (☎ **800/799-6363** or 802/863-6363; www.holiday-inn.com); and **Best Western Windjammer Inn,** 1076 Williston Rd. (☎ **800/371-1125** or 802/863-1125). My choice for a low-end overnight is the clean, simple **Swiss Host Motel and Village,** 1272 Williston Rd. (☎ **802/862-5734**), which has the excellent good fortune of being across from Al's (see below).

Basin Harbor Club ★★★   On 700 rolling lakeside acres, 30 miles south of Burlington, the Basin Harbor Club offers a detour into a far slower-paced era. Established in 1887, this is the sort of resort where you can spend a week and not get bored—that is, if you're a self-starter and don't need a perky recreational director to plan your day. The property features historic gardens, including the largest collection of annuals in Vermont. The trademark Adirondack chairs are scattered all over the property, inviting the most exquisite indolence (bring books!). The main lodge houses 38 rooms, though I prefer the rustic cottages, tucked along the shore and in shady groves of trees. Nothing's too fancy, yet nothing's shabby; it's all comfortable in a New England old-money kind of way. From art classes to a lecture series, you're never far away from the pleasant sensation that you've stepped into an upscale summer camp for grownups. Staff even caters three meals daily. Living really high off the hog? You're in luck: This place even has its own private airstrip.

Basin Harbor Rd., Vergennes, VT 05491. ☎ **800/622-4000** or 802/475-2311. Fax 802/475-6545. www.basin harbor.com. 105 units. Summer $250 and up double, $350–$425 and up cottage; spring and fall, $238 and up double, $320–$399 and up cottage. Rates include breakfast, lunch, and dinner. Ask about B&B and MAP plans and rates. Closed mid-Oct to mid-May. 2-night minimum stay on weekends. MC, V. Pets allowed in cottages ($6.50 pet per night). **Amenities:** 2 restaurants (traditional American, pub fare); outdoor pool; golf course; 5 tennis courts; fitness center; boat rentals (windsurfers, kayaks, canoes, day sailors, outboards); cruises; bike rentals; children's programs (summer); concierge; limited room service; babysitting; laundry service; dry cleaning. In room: A/C, dataport, hair dryer, iron.

The Inn at Essex ★★   Touted as "Vermont's Culinary Resort," this inn makes a persuasive case for that claim: its chefs come straight from the New England Culinary Institute in Montpelier. The 120 rooms are every bit as impressive, and 20 acres of grounds on a majestic hillside setting enhance the experience of staying here; it's not just about the food. Rooms and suites are fitted with reproduction furniture and decked in flowery wallpaper and bed covers; many are further gussied up by fireplaces, CD players, Jacuzzis, four-poster beds, and even rocking chairs or full kitchens with gas stoves, in some cases. There's also a heated outdoor pool. The inn's two restaurants, **Butler's** and **The Tavern** (see below), offer unparalleled cuisine in both casual and formal settings.

70 Essex Way, Essex, VT 05452. ☎ **800/727-4295** or 802/878-1100. Fax 802/878-0063. www.innatessex.com. 120 units. $96–$235 double; $209–$499 suite. AE, DC, MC, V. **Amenities:** 2 restaurants (American/Continental); outdoor pool; golf course; fitness center; spa; bike rentals; massage. In room: TV, dataport, fridge (some), Jacuzzi (some), fireplace (some).

The Inn at Shelburne Farms ★★   The numbers behind this elaborate mansion on the shores of Lake Champlain tell the story: 60 rooms, 10 chimneys, 1,400 acres of land. Built in 1899, this sprawling Edwardian "farmhouse" is the place to fantasize about the lifestyles of the *truly* rich and famous. From your first glimpse of the mansion from the winding drive, you'll know you've left the grim world behind. That's by design—noted landscape architect Frederick Law Olmsted had a hand in shaping the grounds. The 24 guest rooms vary in terms of decor and upkeep; some are overdue for a makeover. If you're feeling flush, ask for Overlook, with the great views of the grounds. Among the budget units (with shared bathroom), I like the Oak Room with its lake view.

Harbor Rd., Shelburne, VT 05482. (②) 802/985-8498. www.shelburnefarms.org. 24 units (7 units share 4 bathrooms). $100–$380 double. 2-night minimum stay on weekends. Closed mid-Oct to mid-May. AE, DC, DISC, MC, V. **Amenities:** Restaurant (New England regional); lake swimming; tennis court; children's farmyard; babysitting; farm tours.

Lang House ★   This stately, white Queen Anne mansion (1881) sits on the hillside between downtown and the University of Vermont. Not as extravagant as the Willard Street Inn (whose owners are co-owners here), it's very comfortably appointed and lavish, with rich cherry and maple woodwork. Rooms vary, but most have small bathrooms and small TVs. I like two corner units: Room 101, on the first floor, has a wonderfully old-fashioned bathroom with wainscoting; room 202 has a cozy sitting area tucked in the turret, which gets lots of afternoon light.

360 Main St., Burlington, VT 05401. (②) 877/919-9799 or 802/652-2500. Fax 802/651-8717. www.langhouse.com. 11 units. $135–$195 double. Rates include breakfast. AE, DISC, MC, V. *In room:* A/C, TV.

Sheraton Burlington Hotel & Conference Center ★   The largest conference facility in Vermont, the Sheraton also does a decent job catering to individual travelers and families. This sprawling and modern complex (with 15

Moments **No Business Like Snow Business**

If you're a lover of science or nature, one of the more interesting day trips from Burlington is to the little hamlet of **Jericho,** about a 15- to 20-minute drive northeast on Route 15. Once there, find the **Old Red Mill** craft shop and museum ★ ((②) 802/899-3225; www.snowflake bentley.com).

This museum showcases America's finest repository of snowflake photographs, courtesy of Wilson Bentley, the local farmer and amateur naturalist who lived here from 1885 until 1931, devising the world's first camera designed to capture images of snowflakes. He photographed some 5,000 snowflakes in his lifetime, publishing in *National Geographic* and first advancing the idea that no two of them are identical. The story of Bentley's determined pursuit of his studies is as entrancing as the photographs lining the walls, which reveal the amazing variety of crystalline structures created in snowstorms—many of them breathtakingly beautiful.

The free-admission museum is open daily April to December, and from Wednesday to Saturday the rest of the year.

conference rooms) just off the interstate, a 5-minute drive east of downtown, features a sizable indoor garden area. All guest rooms have two phones and in-room Nintendos; rooms in the newer addition are a bit nicer, furnished in a simpler, lighter country style. Ask for a room facing east (no extra charge) to enjoy the views of Mount Mansfield and the Green Mountains.

870 Williston Rd., Burlington, VT 05403. ℂ 800/325-3535 or 802/865-6600. Fax 802/865-6670. 309 units. $89–$229 double. AE, DC, DISC, MC, V. **Amenities:** Restaurant (American); lounge; indoor pool; fitness room; 2 Jacuzzis; concierge; limited room service; laundry service; video rentals (extra charge). *In room:* A/C, TV w/pay movies, dataport, coffeemaker, hair dryer, iron.

Willard Street Inn ⭐⭐ This impressive and historic inn is located in a splendid Queen Anne–style brick mansion a few minutes' walk from the university. The inn has soaring first-floor ceilings, cherry woodwork, and a beautiful window-lined breakfast room. The home was built in 1881 by a bank president and once served as a retirement home before its conversion to an inn. Among the best units are room 12, which boasts a small sitting area and views of the lake, and the spacious room 4, which has a sizable bathroom and lake views.

349 S. Willard St. (2 blocks south of Main St.), Burlington, VT 05401. ℂ 800/577-8712 or 802/651-8710. Fax 802/651-8714. www.willardstreetinn.com. 14 units (1 with detached private bathroom). $125–$225 double. Rates include breakfast. 2-night minimum stay on weekends. AE, DC, DISC, MC, V. *In room:* A/C, TV, dataport.

Wyndham Hotel Burlington ⭐⭐ This nine-story hotel, recently acquired by Wyndham, offers great views (if you spend $20 extra on a lakeside room), as well as the best downtown location. A sleek glass box built in 1976, renovations have kept the weariness at bay. The hotel is located between the waterfront and Church Street Marketplace, both of which are a 5-minute walk away. Five cabana rooms open up to the pool area and are ideal for families.

60 Battery St., Burlington, VT 05401. ℂ 877/999-3223 or 802/658-6500. Fax 802/658-4659. www.wyndham. com. 256 units. Summer $159–$269 double; winter $139–$179 double. Ask about packages. AE, DISC, MC, V. Parking in attached garage $5 per day. **Amenities:** 2 restaurants (family, New American); indoor pool; fitness room; Jacuzzi; concierge; free airport shuttle; limited room service; babysitting; laundry service; dry cleaning. *In room:* A/C, TV w/pay movies, dataport, coffeemaker, hair dryer, iron, safe.

WHERE TO DINE

Al's ⭐ BURGERS & FRIES Al's is where Ben and Jerry (*the* Ben and Jerry) go to sate french fry cravings. This classic roadside joint is both fun and efficient. The vats of fries draw people back repeatedly; the other offerings (hamburgers, hotdogs, sloppy-joe-like barbecue) are okay, but nothing special.

1251 Williston Rd. (Rte. 2, just east of I-89), South Burlington. ℂ 802/862-9203. Sandwiches $1–$3.95. No credit cards. Mon 10:30am–10pm; Tues–Thurs 10:30am–11pm; Fri–Sat 10:30am–midnight; Sun 11am–10pm.

Bove's ⭐ *Value* ITALIAN A Burlington landmark since 1941, Bove's is a classic red-sauce-on-spaghetti joint a couple of blocks from the Church Street Marketplace—and nothing costs more than nine bucks. The facade is black and white, its octagonal windows closed to prying eyes by Venetian blinds. Step through the doors and into a lost era, grab a seat at a vinyl-upholstered booth and browse the menu, which offers spaghetti with meat sauce, spaghetti with meatballs, spaghetti with sausage, and . . . well, you get the idea. The red sauce is rich and tangy, while the garlic sauce packs enough garlic to knock you out of your booth. Cocktails are inexpensive, and include old chestnuts such as stingers, pink ladies, and sloe gin fizzes.

68 Pearl St. ℂ 802/864-6651. www.boves.com. Sandwiches $1.75–$6.95; dinner items $6.50–$8.85. No credit cards. Tues–Sat 11am–8:45pm.

Daily Planet *ECLECTIC   This popular spot is often brimming with college students and downtown workers on evenings and weekends. The mild mayhem adds to the charm, enhancing the eclectic, interesting menu. The meals are better prepared than you may expect from a place that takes its cues from a pub. Look for lamb stew, seafood Newburg, strip steak with a Gorgonzola and green peppercorn sauce, or rainbow trout with peach and red onion relish.

15 Center St. © 802/862-9647. Reservations recommended for parties of 5 or more. Main courses, lunch $5.75–$7.95; dinner $11–$20. AE, DISC, MC, V. Sun–Thurs 5–9:30pm; Fri–Sat 5–10pm.

Five Spice Cafe ** *Finds* PAN-ASIAN   Located upstairs and down in an intimate setting with wood floors and aquamarine wainscoting, Five Spice is a popular spot among college students and professors. But customers are drawn to the exquisite food, not the scene, and the inventive chef here makes this a foodie find. The cuisine is multi-Asian, drawing on the best of Thailand, Vietnam, China, and beyond. Try the superb, spicy hot-and-sour soup. Then gear up for Thai red snapper or the robust kung-pao chicken. The dish with the best name on the menu—Evil Jungle Prince with Chicken—is also one of the best, with a light sauce of coconut milk, chilies, and lime leaves. Or, simply do dim sum. Finish with ginger-tangerine cheesecake or one of the desserts incorporating liqueurs.

175 Church St. © 802/864-4045. Reservations recommended on weekends and in summer. Main courses, lunch $4.50–$9.95; dinner $12–$18. AE, DISC, MC, V. Mon–Thurs 11:30am–3pm and 5–9:30pm; Fri–Sat 11:30am–10pm; Sun 11am–9pm.

Inn at Essex ** REGIONAL/CONTINENTAL   The Inn at Essex, about a 15-minute drive from Burlington, is the auxiliary campus of the Montpelier–based New England Culinary Institute. It offers both formal and informal dining rooms with meals prepared and served by New England's rising culinary stars. Both restaurants are housed in a large faux-farmhouse complex along the fringe of Burlington's suburban sprawl. Inside, the setting is quiet and comfortable. In the light and airy tavern, you may be tempted by the Caribbean grilled chicken with black-bean salsa, chicken puff pie, Tuscan salad, or honey-glazed pork chop. Amid the more intimate, country inn elegance of Butler's, the dinner fare is a bit more ambitious, with entrees such as Dijon–peppered rack of lamb, two kinds of rabbit, pan-seared salmon with a sorrel beurre blanc, or oven-roasted veggies with goat cheese burritos. Ask about the kitchen tours.

70 Essex Way, Essex Junction. © 800/727-4295 or 802/878-1100. www.innatessex.com. Reservations recommended at Butler's; not needed at The Tavern. Tavern: Main courses, lunch $4.50–$6.95, dinner $4.50–$9.95. Butler's: lunch $7–$14, dinner $15–$25. AE, DC, DISC, MC, V. Tavern daily 2:30–11pm; Butler's daily 11:30am–10pm.

Leunig's Bistro ** REGIONAL/CONTINENTAL   This boisterous, fun place on the pedestrian mall has a retro old-world flair, with washed walls, a marble bar, crystal chandeliers, and oversize posters. The inventive, large menu features regional foods prepared with a Continental touch. Brunch is available on weekends; lunch options include sandwiches such as turkey cranberry melt. Dinner offerings change seasonally; in summer, you may find poached asparagus with smoked salmon or soft-shell crabs with a lemongrass and coconut broth; in fall, look for hearty fare like pork chops with green-peppercorn apple-cider sauce.

115 Church St. © 802/863-3759. Reservations recommended on weekends and holidays. Main courses, lunch $5.95–$7.95; dinner $8.95–$28. AE, DISC, MC, V. Mon–Thurs 11am–10pm; Fri 11am–11pm; Sat 9am–11pm; Sun 9am–10pm.

NECI Commons ★★ Value BISTRO Since opening in 1997, NECI Commons has been a popular stop for foodies sniffing out new trends and those who like good value. Yet another in the New England Culinary Institute empire (the Inn at Essex and Montpelier's Main Street Grill & Bar are others), this lively, spacious, and busy spot is a training ground for aspiring chefs and restaurateurs. You can eat upstairs in the main dining room, which has soaring windows overlooking the Church Street Marketplace, or downstairs, where you watch the chef-trainees prepare meals in the open kitchen. At Sunday brunch, look for wood-fired breakfast pizza, with eggs, bacon, tomato, and cheddar. Lunchtime offers delectable pizzas, soups, sandwiches (such as crab cake with chipotle sauce on a toasted roll), and more filling dishes such as salmon cake salad. For dinner, look for sirloin or filet of salmon served with the restaurant's famous Vermont cheddar potatoes, grilled free-range chicken breast, or perhaps a pan-seared halibut with a shrimp-lemongrass broth. Prices are reasonable; service, excellent.

25 Church St. ⓒ **802/862-6324.** Call before arrival for priority seating. Brunch $5.95–$7.95; lunch $6.95–$8.95; bistro $6.50–$8.95; dinner $8.50–$19. AE, DC, DISC, MC, V. Mon–Sat 11:30am–2pm and 5:30–10pm; Sun brunch 11am–3pm and 5:30–9pm.

Nectar's Restaurant and Lounge CAFETERIA Burlington in microcosm parades through Nectar's over the course of a long day. In the morning, you'll find blue-collar workers and elderly gentlemen in ties enjoying heaping plates of eggs and hash browns. Midday finds downtown office workers in for lunch; and late in the evening, it adopts a sort of retro chic as clubbers from nearby clubs and Nectar's own lounge next door file through the cafeteria line for hamburgers, a plate of meatloaf, or a local microbrew and gravy fries, and to hang with friends.

188 Main St. ⓒ **802/658-4771.** Breakfast $1.75–$6; lunch and dinner $2.50–$7.50. No credit cards. Mon–Fri 6am–2am, Sat–Sun 7am–2pm.

Penny Cluse Cafe ★★ CAFE/LATINO This gets my vote as the city's best choice for lunch or breakfast. A block off the Church Street Marketplace, Penny Cluse is a casual, bright, and popular spot decorated in a vaguely Southwestern motif. Among the better breakfasts: the Zydeco breakfast with eggs, black beans, andouille sausage, and corn muffins. Lunch ranges from salads to sandwiches (the veggie Reuben with mushrooms, spinach, and red onions is excellent) to more elaborate fare such as adobo pork chops with plantain cake. Prices are at the high end of the breakfast/lunch scale, but deliver great value.

169 Cherry St. ⓒ **802/651-8834.** Reservations recommended (dinner only). Breakfast $3.50–$6.50; sandwiches and lunch $6.25–$8. MC, V. Breakfast and lunch, Mon–Fri 6:45am–3pm; Sat–Sun 8am–3pm.

Trattoria Delia ★★ ITALIAN Locally foraged mushrooms served over polenta with fontina. If that causes you to sit up and take notice, this is your place. Serving the best Italian food in Burlington, Trattoria Delia is in a low-traffic location, almost hidden through a speakeasy-like door beneath a large building. But locals never fail to find it; be sure to reserve ahead if you're coming. Inside is culinary magic, with wild boar, filet mignon with white truffle butter, and classic pasta dishes, such as tagliattelle alla Bolognese. Then choose from Italian dessert wines and traditional desserts such as tiramisu and pannacotta.

152 St. Paul St. ⓒ **802/864-5253.** Reservations recommended. Main courses $14–$20. DC, MC, V. Daily 5–10pm.

BURLINGTON AFTER DARK
PERFORMING ARTS

Flynn Theatre for the Performing Arts The Flynn is the anchor for the downtown fine arts scene. Run as a nonprofit and housed in a wonderful

Art-Deco theater dating to 1930, the Flynn stages events ranging from touring productions of Broadway shows (Penn & Teller) to concerts (Diana Krall) to dance (Paul Taylor) to performers and writers (Lily Tomlin and David Sedaris). Call or visit their website for the current schedule. 153 Main St. ℂ **802/652-4500** or 802/863-5966. www.flynntheatre.org. Tickets $8–$75.

Royall Tyler Theatre   Plays are performed by the University of Vermont theater department and local theater groups at this handsomely designed performance hall. Shows ranging from Shakespeare to student-directed one-act plays are staged throughout the year; call for a current schedule. University of Vermont campus. ℂ **802/656-2094.** Tickets $8–$20.

UVM Lane Series   This university series brings renowned performers from around the country and the globe to Burlington for performances at the Flynn Theatre, Ira Allen Chapel, and the acoustically superb UVM Recital Hall. The series runs September through April. Performers have included the San Francisco Opera performing *The Marriage of Figaro,* flutist Eugenia Zuckerman, and the Modern Mandolin Quartet. Various venues. ℂ **802/656-4455.** www.uvm.edu/lane series. Tickets $15–$36.

Vermont Symphony Orchestra ⚞   In summer, outdoor pops performances punctuated by fireworks take place at various locations throughout Burlington and Vermont. In winter, the classical series moves indoors, including regular performances at the Flynn Theatre. Call for a current schedule. 2 Church St. ℂ **800/ VSO-9293** or 802/864-5741. www.vso.org. Tickets $9–$37.

10 The Northeast Kingdom

Vermont's Northeast Kingdom has a more wild and remote character than much of the rest of the state. The Kingdom's landscape is open and spacious, with rolling meadows ending abruptly at the hard edge of dense boreal forests. Accommodations and services for visitors aren't as plentiful or easy to find as in the southern reaches of the state, but a handful of inns are tucked among the hills.

If your time is limited, at least stop in St. Johnsbury, which has two good attractions—the Fairbanks Museum and St. Johnsbury Athenaeum. The total tour, from Hardwick to St. Johnsbury by way of Newport, Derby Line, and Lake Willoughby, is approximately 90 miles. Allow a full day, or more if you plan to take advantage of hiking and biking in the region.

Visitor information is available from the **Northeast Kingdom Chamber of Commerce,** 357 Western Ave., Suite 2, in St. Johnsbury (ℂ **800/639-6379** or 802/748-3678; www.nekchamber.com). Additional information on Vermont's northern reaches can be found at **www.vtnorthcountry.com.**

TOURING THE NORTHEAST KINGDOM

Start:	Hardwick
Finish:	St. Johnsbury
Time:	1 full day

➊ Hardwick

A small town with rough edges set on the Lamoille River (at the intersection of Routes 14 and 15, about 23 miles northwest of St. Johnsbury and 26 miles northeast of Montpelier), it has a compact commercial main street, some intriguing shops, a couple of casual, family-style restaurants, and one of Vermont's best natural food co-ops.

From here, head north on Route 14 about 7 miles to the turnoff to Craftsbury and:

➋ Craftsbury Common

An uncommonly graceful village, Craftsbury Common is home to a small academy and a large number of historic homes and buildings spread along a green and the village's main street. The town occupies a wide upland ridge and offers sweeping views to the east and west. Be sure to stop by the old cemetery on the south end of town, where you can wander among historic tombstones of the pioneers, which date back to the 1700s. This is also an excellent destination for mountain biking and cross-country skiing.

From Craftsbury, continue north to reconnect to Route 14. You'll wind through the towns of Albany and Irasburg as you head north. At the village of Coventry, veer north on Route 5 to the lakeside town of:

➌ Newport

This commercial outpost (pop. 4,400) is set on the southern shores of Lake Memphremagog, a truly stunning 27-mile-long lake that's just 2 miles wide at its broadest point and the bulk of which lies across the border in Canada. From Newport, continue north on Route 5, crossing under I-91, for about 7 miles to the border town of Derby Line (pop. 2,000). This outpost has a handful of restaurants and antiques shops; U.S. residents can park and walk across the bridge to poke around the Canadian town of Rock Island with simple ID such as a driver's license. (Foreign travelers must ask at the U.S. Customs

booth about returning before crossing the line.)

Back in Derby Line, look for the:

➍ Haskell Free Library and Opera House

At the corner of Caswell Avenue and Church Street (✆ **802/873-3022**), this handsome neoclassical building contains a public library on the first floor and an elegant opera house on the second that's modeled after the old Boston Opera House. The theater opened in 1904, and it's beautiful, with a scene of Venice painted on the drop curtain and carved cherubim adorning the balcony.

What's most curious about the structure, however, is that it lies half in Canada and half in the U.S. (The Haskell family donated the building jointly to the towns of Derby Line and Rock Island.) A thick black line runs beneath the seats of the opera house, indicating who's in the U.S. and who's in Canada. Because the stage is set entirely in Canada, apocryphal stories abound from its early days of frustrated U.S. officers watching fugitives perform on stage. More recently, the theater has been used for the occasional extradition hearing.

From Derby Line, retrace your path south on Route 5 to Derby Center and the juncture of Route 5A. Continue south on Route 5A to the town of Westmore on the shores of:

➎ Lake Willoughby

This glacier-carved lake is best viewed from the north, with the shimmering sheet of water pinched between the base of two low mountains at the southern end. Route 5A along the eastern shore is lightly traveled and ideal for biking or walking.

Head southwest on Route 16, which departs from Route 5A just north of the lake. Follow Route 16 through the peaceful villages of Barton and Glover. A little over a mile south of Glover, turn left on Route 122. Very soon on your left, look for the farmstead that serves as home to the:

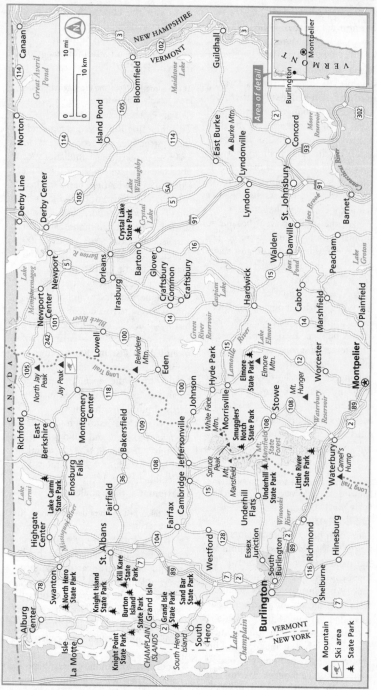

⑥ Bread and Puppet Theater

For nearly 3 decades, until 1998, Polish artist and performer Peter Schumann's Bread and Puppet Theater staged an elaborate annual summer pageant at this farm, attracting thousands. Attendees participated, watched, and lounged about the hillsides as huge, lugubrious, brightly painted puppets crafted of fabric and papier-mâché marched around the farm, acting out a drama that typically featured rebellion against tyranny of one form or another. It was like Woodstock without the music.

Alas, the summer event became so popular it overwhelmed the farm. The troupe periodically travels and stages shows on the road; call for details (© 802/525-3031).

Between June and October, you can still visit the barn, home to the **Bread and Puppet Museum** ⊛, with many of the puppets used in past events. This remarkable display shouldn't be missed. Downstairs, in former cow-milking stalls, smaller displays include mournful washerwomen doing laundry and King Lear addressing his daughters. Upstairs, the vast hayloft is filled with soaring, haunting puppets, some up to 20 feet tall. Admission is free, though donations are encouraged.

From Glover, continue south through serene farmlands to Lyndonville, where you pick up Route 5 south to:

⑦ St. Johnsbury

This town of 7,600 inhabitants is the largest in the Northeast Kingdom and the major center of commerce. The town enjoyed a buoyant prosperity in the 19th century, largely stemming from the success of platform scales (invented here in 1830 by Thaddeus Fairbanks), which are still manufactured here. It has an abundance of fine commercial architecture in two areas, joined by steep Eastern Avenue. The more commercial part of town lies along Railroad Street (Rte. 5) at the base of the hill. The more ethereal part, with the library, St. Johnsbury Academy, and grand museum, is along Main Street at the top of the hill. The north end of Main Street is notable for its grand residential architecture.

At the corner of Main and Prospect streets in St. Johnsbury, look for:

⑧ The Fairbanks Museum

This imposing Romanesque red-sandstone structure was constructed in 1889 to hold the accumulations of obsessive amateur collector Franklin Fairbanks. The soaring, barrel-vaulted main hall, reminiscent of an old-fashioned railway depot, holds four stuffed bears, a huge moose with full antlers, art from Asia, and 4,500 stuffed native and exotic birds. And that's just the tip of the iceberg.

Among the assorted clutter, look for the unique mosaics by John Hampson, who crafted scenes of American history—such as Washington bidding his troops farewell—entirely of mounted insects. In the Washington scene, for instance, iridescent green beetles form the epaulets, and the regal great coat is comprised of hundreds of purple moth wings.

Open Tuesday through Saturday from 9am to 5pm, and Sunday from 1 to 5pm (© 802/748-2372), admission is $5 for adults, $4 for seniors, $3 for children 5 to 17; $12 per family (maximum of three adults).

Also in town, just south of the museum on Main Street, is:

⑨ The St. Johnsbury Athenaeum

In an Edward Hopper-esque brick building with truncated mansard tower and prominent keystones over the windows, the town's public library also houses an extraordinary art gallery dating to 1873. It claims to be the oldest unadulterated art gallery in the nation.

Your first view of the gallery is spectacular: After winding through the cozy library and past its ticking regulator clock, you round a corner and find yourself gazing across Yosemite National Park. This luminous 10-by-15-foot oil painting was created by noted Hudson River School painter Albert Bierstadt, and the gallery was built specifically to accommodate this work. Natural light flooding in from a skylight above nicely enhances the painting.

Some 100 other works fill the walls. Most are copies of other paintings (a common teaching tool in the 19th century), but look for originals by other Hudson River School painters, including Asher B. Durand, Thomas Moran, and Jasper Cropsey.

The Athenaeum, 1171 Main St. (© **802/748-8291**), is open Monday and Wednesday from 10am to 8pm; Tuesday, Thursday, and Friday from 10am to 5:30pm; and Saturday from 9:30am to 4pm. Admission is free, but donations are encouraged.

DOWNHILL SKIING

Jay Peak ★★   Just south of the Canadian border, Jay is Vermont's best choice for those who prefer to avoid all the modern-day glitz and clutter that seem to plague ski resorts elsewhere. While some new condo development has been taking place at the base of the mountain, Jay still has the feel of a remote, isolated destination, accessible by a winding road through unbroken woodlands. Thanks to its staggering snowfall (an average of 340 in., more than any other New England ski area), Jay has developed extensive glade skiing; the ski school also specializes in running the glades, making it a fitting place for advanced intermediates to learn how to navigate these exciting, challenging trails.

Rte. 242, Jay, VT 05859. © **800/451-4449** or 802/988-2611. www.jaypeakresort.com. Vertical drop: 2,153 ft. Lifts: 1 60-person tram, 4 chairlifts, 2 surface lifts. Skiable acreage: 385 acres. Lift tickets: $54 adults.

OTHER OUTDOOR PURSUITS

CROSS-COUNTRY SKIING   The same folks who offer mountain biking at the Craftsbury Outdoor Center also maintain 61 miles of groomed cross-country trails through the gentle hills surrounding Craftsbury. The forgiving, old-fashioned trails, maintained by **Craftsbury Nordic Center** ★★ (© **800/729-7751** or 802/586-7767), emphasize pleasing landscapes rather than fast action. Trail passes are $14 for adults, $7 for children 6 to 12, and $9 for seniors. Another option is **Highland Lodge** ★ (© **802/533-2647**) on Caspian Lake, offering 36 miles of trails (about 10 miles groomed) through rolling woodlands and fields.

MOUNTAIN BIKING   The Craftsbury ridge features several excellent variations for bikers in search of easy terrain. Most of the biking is on hard-packed dirt roads through sparsely populated countryside. Views are sensational, and the sense of being well out in the country very strong. The **Craftsbury Outdoor Center at Craftsbury Common** (© **800/729-7751** or 802/586-7767; www.craftsbury.com) rents mountain bikes and is an excellent source for maps and local information about area roads. Bike rentals are $25 to $35 per day. A small fee is charged for using bikes on the cross-country ski trail network.

WHERE TO STAY

Comfort Suites ★   Built in 2000, the property consists of more than 100 units and has a number of nice touches, such as granite vanity counters and high-backed desk chairs. The rooms are pleasantly appointed (more like an inn than a motel), and the basement houses an appealing, if small, pool and fitness room, along with a game room outfitted with air hockey and a pool table. The hotel is located just off I-91 about a mile south of downtown St. Johnsbury.

703 Rte. 5 South (off Exit 20 of I-91), St. Johnsbury, VT 05819. © **800/228-5150** or 802/748-1500. Fax 802/748-1243. 107 units. Summer $109–$169 double; foliage season from $139; off season from $99. Rates include continental breakfast. AE, DISC, MC, V. **Amenities:** Indoor pool; fitness room; game room; coin-op washers/dryers. *In room:* A/C, TV, dataport, coffeemaker, hair dryer, iron.

Highland Lodge ⚘

Built in the mid–19th century, this lodge has been accommodating guests since 1926. Located just across the road from lovely Caspian Lake, it has 11 rooms furnished in a comfortable country style. Nearby are 11 cottages, 9 of which are equipped with kitchenettes. A stay here is supremely relaxing—the main activities include swimming and boating in the lake in summer, along with tennis on a clay court; in winter, the lodge maintains its own cross-country ski area with 30 miles of groomed trails. Behind the lodge is an attractive nature preserve, which invites quiet exploration.

Caspian Lake, Greensboro, VT 05841. © **802/533-2647.** Fax 802/533-7494. www.thehighlandlodge.com. 22 units, including 11 cottages. Winter $203–$260 double, $270–$290 cottage. Call for summer rates. Rates include breakfast and dinner. DISC, MC, V. Closed mid-Mar to May and mid-Oct to Christmas. From Hardwick, take Rte. 15 east 2 miles to Rte. 16; drive north 2 more miles to East Hardwick. Head west and follow signs to the inn. **Amenities:** Restaurant (traditional New England); tennis court; cross-county ski trails; water-sports/equipment rental; bike rental; children's program; game room; babysitting; laundry service. *In room:* No phone.

Inn on the Common ⚘⚘⚘

This exceedingly handsome complex of three Federal-era buildings anchors the charming ridge-top village of Craftsbury Common, one of the most quintessential of New England villages. This is a stunning inn, and offers just the right measures of history and pampering. It tends to be a rather social place, attracting both families and couples seeking a romantic getaway. Dinner starts with cocktails at 6pm, guests seated family-style amid elegant surroundings at 7:30pm. The menu changes nightly, but includes well-prepared contemporary American fare. Some deluxe guest rooms have fireplaces.

Craftsbury Common, VT 05827. © **800/521-2233** or 802/586-9619. Fax 802/586-2249. www.innonthe common.com. 16 units. $240–$340 double, including breakfast and dinner; $149–$199 double, including breakfast. 2-night minimum stay during foliage season, weekends, and Christmas week. AE, MC, V. Pets allowed with prior permission ($25 per visit). **Amenities:** Outdoor pool; tennis court; croquet; massage; babysitting. *In room:* Hair dryer, no phone.

Willoughvale Inn ⚘⚘

An elegant inn on a low rise at the north end of Lake Willoughby, it has stunning views across the water to the twin mountains at the south end of the lake. This is an ideal location for a quiet retreat, especially in one of four cottages with kitchens right on the lake. (They are available only by the week in July and Aug.) The 11 rooms in the lodge are tastefully appointed, with much of the furniture crafted in Vermont. The cottages tend to have more of a rustic Adirondack-lodge feel. It's hard to imagine a better place to spend a few days with books and a bicycle. The restaurant is unpretentious, serving well-prepared meals before a superb view of the lake.

793 Rte. 5A, Orleans, VT 05860. © **800/594-9102** or 802/525-4123. Fax 802/525-4514. www.willough vale.com. 15 units (including 4 lakeside cottages). Summer, fall, and holidays $129–$234 double, $229–$249 cottage; spring, late fall, and winter $79–$199 double, $149–$209 cottage. Rates include continental break-fast. Ask about ski packages. AE, MC, V. 2-night minimum stay July and Aug, as well as foliage weekends. 1 pet with restrictions (call ahead) permitted per room or cottage ($20 per night). **Amenities:** Restaurant (American); lake swimming; bike rentals; water-sports equipment (canoes and kayaks). *In room:* A/C, TV.

New Hampshire

by Paul Karr

Okay, I admit it. I love New Hampshire. Oh, I know it's not as postcard-pretty as Vermont, nor as tourist-friendly as Maine. But that's what makes it so wonderful to visit: its authenticity. You'll hear real accents, and witness real ingenuity and parsimony. New Hampshire savors its reputation as an outpost of plucky, heroic independent citizens fighting the good fight against intrusive laws and irksome bureaucrats—the same sort of folks who took up arms and thumbed their noses at King George way back when.

But it's not all about flannel shirts and rifle racks. You will also find wonderfully diverse terrain—from beaches to broad lakes to impressive hills and mountains. Without leaving the state's borders, you can toss a Frisbee on a sandy beach, ride bikes along quiet country lanes, hike rugged granite hills blasted by some of the most severe weather in the world, or canoe on a placid lake in the company of moose and loons. You'll also find good food and country inns.

Most of all, you'll find a strong taste of the independence that has defined New England since the first settlers ran up their flags 3½ centuries ago.

1 Portsmouth & the Seacoast

Portsmouth ★★ is a civilized little seaside city of bridges, brick, and seagulls, and quite a little gem. Filled with elegant architecture that's more intimate than intimidating, this bonsai-size city projects a strong, proud sense of its heritage without being overly precious. Part of the city's appeal is its variety: Upscale coffee shops and art galleries stand alongside old-fashioned barbershops and tattoo parlors. Despite a steady influx of money in recent years, the town still retains an earthiness that serves as a tangy vinegar for more saccharine coastal spots.

For the past 3 centuries, the city has been the hub for the region's maritime trade. In the 1600s, Strawbery Banke (it wasn't renamed Portsmouth until 1653) was a major center for the export of wood and dried fish to Europe. Today, Portsmouth's maritime tradition continues with a lively trade in bulk goods; the city's de facto symbol is the tugboat, one or two of which are almost always tied up near the waterfront's picturesque "tugboat alley."

Visitors to Portsmouth will find a lot to see in such a small space, including good shopping in the boutiques that now occupy much of the historic district, good eating at many small restaurants and bakeries, and plenty of history to explore among the historic homes and museums set on almost every block.

ESSENTIALS
GETTING THERE Portsmouth is served by Exits 3 through 7 on I-95. The most direct access to downtown is via Market Street (Exit 7), which is the last New Hampshire exit before crossing the river to Maine.

In 2000, discount airline **Pan Am** (© **800/359-7262;** www.flypanam.com) launched operations out of a former military base on Portsmouth's outskirts. The only airline that serves Portsmouth (don't expect onward connections), it has flights to a limited but growing roster of second-tier airports, including Gary, Indiana; Sanford, Florida; and Baltimore. Call or check the carrier's website for an updated list of airports currently served.

Amtrak (© **800/872-7245;** www.amtrak.com) operates four trains daily from Boston's North Station to downtown Dover, New Hampshire; a one-way ticket is about $15 per person, and the trip takes about 1¼ hours. You then take the #2 **COAST** bus (© **603/743-5777;** www.coastbus.org) to the center of downtown Portsmouth, a 40-minute trip that costs just $1.

Greyhound (© **800/229-9424;** www.greyhound.com), **C&J Trailways** (© **800/258-7111;** www.cjtrailways.com), and **Vermont Transit** (© **800/552-8737;** www.vermonttransit.com) all run about five buses daily from Boston's South Station to downtown Portsmouth, plus one to three daily trips from Boston's Logan Airport. The one-way cost for each service is about $15. A one-way Greyhound trip from New York City's Port Authority bus station to downtown Portsmouth is about $44 and takes about 6½ hours.

VISITOR INFORMATION The **Greater Portsmouth Chamber of Commerce,** 500 Market St. (© **603/436-1118;** www.portcity.org), has an information center between Exit 7 and downtown. From Memorial Day to Columbus Day, it's open Monday through Wednesday, 8:30am to 5pm; Thursday and Friday, 8:30am to 7pm; and Saturday and Sunday, 10am to 5pm. The rest of the year, hours are Monday through Friday, 8:30am to 5pm. In summer, a second booth is at Market Square in the middle of the historic district. A good website with extensive information on the region may be found at **www.seacoastnh.com**.

PARKING Most of Portsmouth can be easily reconnoitered on foot, so you need park only once. Parking can be tight in and around the historic district in summer. The municipal parking garage nearly always has space and costs just 50¢ per hour; it's located on Hanover Street between Market and Fleet streets. Strawbery Banke Museum (see below) also offers limited parking for visitors.

There's also now a free "**trolley**" (© **603/743-5777**) circulating central Portsmouth in a one-way loop from July to early September. It hits all the key historical points. Catch it at Market Square, Prescott Park, or Strawbery Banke.

A MAGICAL HISTORY TOUR

Portsmouth's 18th-century prosperity is evident in the Georgian-style homes that dot the city. Strawbery Banke occupies the core of the historic area and is well worth visiting. And a helpful map and brochure, *The Portsmouth Trail: An Historic Walking Tour,* is available free at information centers.

Tired? Take a break at **Prescott Park** ★★, between Strawbery Banke and the water. It's one of my favorite municipal parks in New England. Water views, lemonade vendors, benches, grass, and occasional festivals make it worth a visit.

John Paul Jones House ★★ Revolutionary War hero John Paul ("I have not yet begun to fight") Jones lived in this 1758 home during the war. He was here to oversee the construction of his sloop, *Ranger,* believed to be the first ship to sail under the U.S. flag (a model is on display). Immaculately restored and maintained by the Portsmouth Historical Society, costumed guides offer tours.

43 Middle St. © 603/436-8420. Admission $5 adults, $4.50 seniors, $2.50 children 6–14, free for children under 6. Thurs–Tues 11am–5pm. Closed mid-Oct to mid-May.

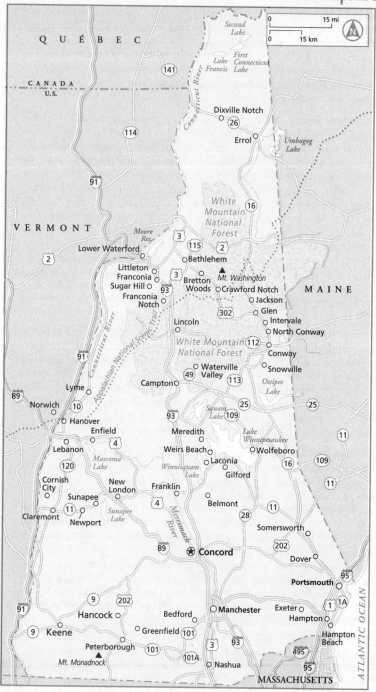

New Hampshire

QUÉBEC

CANADA
U.S.

Second
Lake

First
Connecticut
Lake

Lake
Francis

141

114

Dixville Notch
26

Errol

Umbagog
Lake

VERMONT

Moore
Res.

White
Mountain
National
Forest

16

Lower Waterford

115
2

Bethlehem

Littleton
Franconia

3

Bretton
Woods

▲ Mt. Washington

Crawford Notch

Jackson

Sugar Hill

93

Franconia
Notch

Glen

302

Intervale

Lincoln

North Conway

MAINE

White Mountain
National Forest

112

Conway

Snowville

Waterville
Valley

49

113

Ossipee
Lake

Campton

25

25

Lyme

10

Squam
Lake

109

93

Meredith

Lake
Winnipesaukee

11

Norwich

89

Hanover

Enfield

4

Lebanon

Weirs Beach

Wolfeboro

120

Mascoma
Lake

Winnisquam
Lake

Laconia

16

109

Gilford

11

Cornish
City

New
London

Franklin

Sunapee

4

Belmont

11

Claremont

11

Sunapee
Lake

28

Newport

Somersworth

202

89

★ Concord

Dover

95

Portsmouth

9

202

Hancock

Bedford

Manchester

Exeter

1 1A

Hampton

9

Keene

Greenfield

101

Hampton
Beach

Peterborough

101

93

101A

3

495

▲ Mt. Monadnock

Nashua

95

MASSACHUSETTS

ATLANTIC OCEAN

15 mi

15 km

Moffat-Ladd House ★★ Built for a family of prosperous merchants and traders, the elegant garden is as notable as the 1763 home, with its great hall and elaborate carvings. The home belonged to one family between 1763 and 1913, when it became a museum; many furnishings have never left the premises. The house will appeal to aficionados of early American furniture and painting.

154 Market St. © 603/436-8221. Admission $5 adults, $2.50 children under 12. Mon–Sat 11am–5pm; Sun 1–5pm. Closed Nov–May.

Strawbery Banke ★★★ In 1958, the city planned to raze this neighborhood, first settled in 1653, to make way for urban renewal. A group of local citizens resisted and won, establishing an outdoor history museum that's become one of the largest in New England. Today it consists of 10 downtown acres and 46 historic buildings. Ten buildings have been restored with period furnishings; eight others feature exhibits. (The remainder may be seen from the exterior only.) The neighborhood surrounds an open lawn (formerly an inlet) and has a settled, picturesque quality. At three working crafts shops, watch coopers, boat builders, and potters are at work. The most intriguing home is the split-personality Drisco House, half of which depicts life in the 1790s and half of which shows life in the 1950s, nicely demonstrating how houses grow and adapt.

Hancock St. © 603/433-1100. www.strawberybanke.org. Admission $12 adults, $11 seniors, $8 children 7–17, free for children under 6; $28 per family. May–Oct Mon–Sat 10am–5pm, Sun noon–5pm. Winter (except Jan) Mon–Sat 10am–2pm, Sun noon–2pm. Closed Jan. Look for directional signs posted around town.

Warner House ★ This house, built in 1716, was the governor's mansion in the mid–18th century when Portsmouth was the state capital. After a time as a private home, it has been open to the public since the 1930s. This stately brick structure with graceful Georgian architectural elements is a favorite among architectural historians for its wall murals (said to be the oldest murals still in place in the U.S.), early wall marbleizing, and original white pine paneling.

150 Daniel St. © 603/436-5909. www.warnerhouse.org. Admission $5 adults, $2.50 children 7–12, free for children 6 and under. Mon–Sat 11am–4pm; Sun noon–4pm. Closed Nov to early June.

Wentworth-Gardner House ★★★ Arguably the most handsome mansion in the Seacoast region, this is considered one of the nation's best examples of Georgian architecture. The 1760 home features many period elements, including pronounced *quoins* (blocks on the building's corners), pedimented window caps, plank sheathing (to make the home appear as if made of masonry), an elaborate doorway with Corinthian pilasters, a broken scroll, and a paneled door topped with a pineapple, the symbol of hospitality. Perhaps most memorable is its scale—though a grand home of the colonial era, it's modest in scope; some circles today may not consider it much more than a pool house.

50 Mechanic St. © 603/436-4406. Admission $4 adults, $2 children 6–14, free for children 5 and under. Tues–Sun 1–4pm. Closed mid-Oct to May. Directions: From rose gardens on Marcy St. across from Strawbery Banke, walk south 1 block, turn left toward bridge, make a right before crossing bridge; house is down the block on your right.

BOAT TOURS

The **Isle of Shoals Steamship Co.** ★★ (© **800/441-4620** or 603/431-5500; www.islesofshoals.com) sails from Barker Wharf on Market Street, offering a variety of tours on the 90-foot, three-deck *Thomas Laighton* (a modern replica of a late-19th-century steamship) and the 70-foot *Oceanic,* designed for whale-watching. One popular excursion is to the Isle of Shoals, at which passengers can

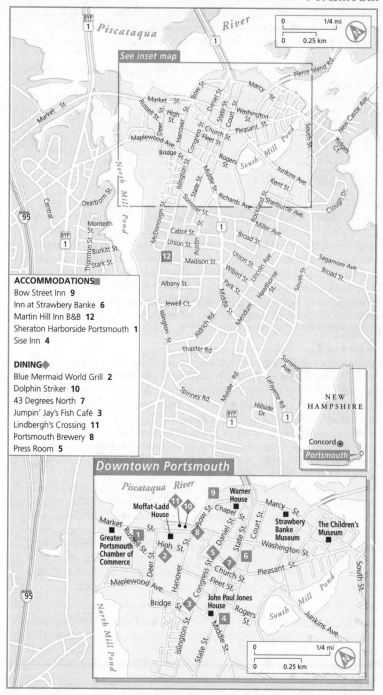

Portsmouth

See inset map

Piscataqua River

BYP 1

Market St.

Russell St.

Deer St.

Maplewood Ave.

Bridge St.

Market St.
Bow St.
Daniel St.
High St.
State St.
Court St.
Washington St.
Pleasant St.
Church St.
Fleet St.
Congress St.
Rogers St.

Marcy St.

Pierce Island Rd.

South Mill Pond

South St.

New Castle Ave.

Ridges Ct.

North Mill Pond

Dearborn St.

Central

95

Monteith St.

BYP 1

Thornton St.

Burkitt St.

Stark St.

Islington St.

State St.

Middle St.

Richards Ave.

Rockland St.

Sherburne Ave.

Junkins Ave.

Kent St.

Clough Dr.

McDonough St.

Sumner St.

Cabot St.

Union St.

Austin

1

Broad St.

Miller Ave.

Sagamore Ave.

Broad St.

12

Madison St.

Union St.

Wibird St.

Lincoln Ave.

Hawthorne St.

South St.

Albany St.

Park St.

Jewell Ct.

Middle St.

Mendum

Aldrich Rd.

Islington St.

Thaxter Rd.

Middle Rd.

Lafayette Rd.

Summit Ave.

Spinney Rd.

BYP 1

Hillside Dr.

1

ACCOMMODATIONS

Bow Street Inn **9**
Inn at Strawbery Banke **6**
Martin Hill Inn B&B **12**
Sheraton Harborside Portsmouth **1**
Sise Inn **4**

DINING

Blue Mermaid World Grill **2**
Dolphin Striker **10**
43 Degrees North **7**
Jumpin' Jay's Fish Café **3**
Lindbergh's Crossing **11**
Portsmouth Brewery **8**
Press Room **5**

NEW HAMPSHIRE

Concord ⊛

Portsmouth

0   1/4 mi
0 0.25 km

Downtown Portsmouth

Piscataqua River

9 Warner House

11 Moffat-Ladd House **10**

Market St.

Greater Portsmouth Chamber of Commerce **1**

8

Bow St.

Chapel St.

Daniel St.

State St.

Court St.

Marcy St.

Strawbery Banke Museum

The Children's Museum

Washington St.

High St.

2

Russell St.

Deer St.

Hanover St.

Congress St.

5

6

Pleasant St.

South Mill Pond

South St.

Maplewood Ave.

Church St.

Fleet St.

3

John Paul Jones House

7

4

Rogers St.

Junkins Ave.

Bridge St.

Islington St.

State St.

Middle St.

95

North Mill Pond

0   1/4 mi
0 0.25 km

disembark and wander about dramatic, rocky Star Island. Reservations are strongly encouraged. Other popular trips include 6-hour whale-watching voyages and a sunset lighthouse cruise. Fares range from $25 to $30 round-trip for adults, $15 to $20 round-trip for children 12 and under, with reduced admission also available for students and military personnel. Parking costs an additional charge.

Portsmouth Harbor Cruises ✦ (© 800/776-0915 or 603/436-8084; www.portsmouthharbor.com) specializes in tours of the historic Piscataqua River aboard the *Heritage,* a 49-passenger cruise ship with plenty of open deck space. Cruise by five old forts or enjoy the picturesque tidal estuary of inland Great Bay, a scenic trip upriver from Portsmouth. Trips run daily; reservations are suggested. Fares are $11 to $18 for adults, $9.50 to $17 for seniors, and $7 to $10 for children 12 and under.

ESPECIALLY FOR KIDS

The Children's Museum of Portsmouth ★★ *Kids*   The Children's Museum is a bright, lively arts and science museum that offers a morning's worth of hands-on exhibits of interest to younger artisans and scientists (it's designed to appeal to children between 1 and 11). Popular displays include exhibits on earthquakes, dinosaur digs, and lobstering, along with the miniature yellow submarine and space shuttle cockpit, both of which invite clambering.

280 Marcy St., 2 blocks south of Strawbery Banke. © 603/436-3853. www.childrens-museum.org. Admission $5 adults and children; $4 seniors; free for ages 1 and under. Tues–Sat 10am–5pm; Sun 1–5pm. Also open Mon during summer and school vacations.

SHOPPING

Portsmouth's historic district is home to dozens of boutiques offering unique items. The **N. W. Barrett Gallery,** 53 Market St. (© 603/431-4262), features the work of area craftspeople, offering a selection of ceramic sculptures, glassware, woodworking, and handmade jewelry. The **Robert Lincoln Levy Gallery,** operated by the New Hampshire Art Association, 136 State St. (© 603/431-4230), is a good destination for art produced by New Hampshire artists.

Bibliophiles should plan a detour to the **Portsmouth Bookshop,** #1–7 Islington St. (© 603/433-4406), which specializes in old and rare books and maps; it's open daily. The **Book Guild** (© 603/436-1758) at 58 State St. holds a more general selection of used travel guides, geographies, sports books, poetry, novels, and more. **Chaise Lounge,** 104 Congress St. (© 603/430-7872), offers a wonderfully eclectic range of home furnishings. **Nahcotta,** 110 Congress St. (© 603/433-1705), is a gallery that boasts "cool goods," including high-end paintings and sculptures, many quietly edgy. **Paradiza,** 63 Penhallow St. (© 603/431-0180), has an array of clever greeting cards, along with exotica such as soaps and bath products from Israel and Africa. **Macro Polo,** 89 Market St. (© 603/436-8338), specializes in retro-chic gifts, toys, magnets, and gadgets.

WHERE TO STAY

For budget accommodations, head for chain hotels along I-95 including **Anchorage Inn & Suites,** 417 Woodbury Ave. (© 603/431-8111); the **Fairfield Inn,** 650 Borthwick Ave. (© 603/436-6363); and the **Holiday Inn of Portsmouth,** 300 Woodbury Ave. (© 603/431-8000).

Bow Street Inn   This is an adequate destination for travelers willing to give up charm for convenience. The former brewery was made over in the 1980s in a bit of inspired recycling: condos occupy the top floor, while the **Seacoast**

Repertory Theatre (© 603/433-4472) occupies the first. The second floor is the Bow Street Inn, a ten-room hotel that offers good access to historic Portsmouth. Guest rooms, set off a rather sterile hallway, are clean, comfortable, small, and, for the most part, unexceptional. Only rooms 6 and 7 feature good views of the harbor, and a premium is charged for these. Parking is on the street or at a nearby paid garage; a parking pass is included with harborview rooms.

121 Bow St., Portsmouth, NH 03801. © 603/431-7760. Fax 603/433-1680. 10 units. Peak season (summer and holidays) $119–$175 double; off season $99–$155 double. Rates include continental breakfast. 2-night minimum stay on some holidays. AE, DISC, MC, V. *In room:* A/C, TV, dataport, hair dryer.

Inn at Strawbery Banke 🏕

This historic inn, located in an 1814 home tucked away on Court Street, is ideally located for exploring Portsmouth: Strawbery Banke is a block away, and Market Square (the center of the action) is 2 blocks away. The friendly innkeepers have done a nice job of taking a cozy antique home and making it comfortable for guests. Rooms are tiny but bright and feature stenciling, wooden shutters, and beautiful pine floors; one has a bathroom down the hall. Common areas include two sitting rooms with TVs, lots of books, and a dining room where a full breakfast is served each morning.

314 Court St., Portsmouth, NH 03801. © 800/428-3933 or 603/436-7242. www.innatstrawberybanke.com. 7 units. Spring, summer, and early fall $145–$150 double; off season $100–$115 double. Rates include breakfast. 2-night minimum stay Aug and Oct weekends. AE, DISC, MC, V. Children 10 and older welcome. *In room:* A/C, no phone.

Martin Hill Inn Bed & Breakfast ★★

Innkeepers Paul and Jane Harnden keep things running smoothly and happily at this friendly B&B in a residential neighborhood a short walk from downtown, and that's why I like it so much. The inn consists of two period buildings: a main house (built around 1815) and a second guesthouse built 35 years later. All rooms have queen-size beds, writing tables, and sofas or sitting areas, and are variously appointed with distinguished wallpapers, porcelains, antiques, love seats, four-poster or brass beds, and the like. Each has its own character—from the master bedroom, with pine floors, to the Victorian Rose Room to the mahogany-lined Library Room (the only room with two beds). There's also a relaxing greenhouse—a suite, really, with sitting room, solarium, and access to the outdoors. A stone path leads to a small, beautiful garden, and the gourmet breakfast is a highlight: It usually consists of blueberry-pecan pancakes, served with Canadian bacon and real maple syrup, or delicious apple Belgian waffles topped with a nutmeg-ginger sauce. The Harndens gladly share their encyclopedic knowledge of local sights and restaurants.

404 Islington St., Portsmouth, NH 03801. © 603/436-2287. 8 units. Summer $125–$145 double, off season $98–$125 double. Holiday rates higher. Rates include full breakfast. MC, V. Children 16 and over are welcome. *In room:* A/C.

Sheraton Harborside Portsmouth ★★

This five-story, in-town brick hotel is nicely located—the attractions of downtown Portsmouth are virtually at your doorstep (Strawbery Banke is about a 10-minute walk), and with parking underground and across the street, a stay here can make for a relatively stress-free visit. It's a modern building inspired by the low brick buildings of the city, and wraps around a circular courtyard. This is a well-maintained, well-managed property popular with business travelers, as well as leisure travelers looking for the amenities of a larger hotel. Some rooms have views of the working harbor.

250 Market St., Portsmouth, NH 03801. © 877/248-3794 or 603/431-2300. Fax 603/431-7805. 200 units. Summer $200–$255 double; ask about off-season discounts. Suites higher. AE, DISC, MC, V. **Amenities:**

Restaurant (American); fitness center; business center; limited room service; executive rooms. *In room:* A/C, TV w/pay movies, dataport, minibar, coffeemaker, hair dryer, iron.

Sise Inn 🌾🌾   A modern, elegant hotel in the guise of a country inn, this solid Queen Anne–style home was built for a prominent merchant in 1881; the hotel addition was constructed in the 1980s. The effect is happily harmonious, with antique stained glass and copious oak trim meshing well with the more contemporary elements. An elevator serves the three floors; modern carpeting is throughout, but many rooms feature antique armoires and updated Victorian styling. I like room 406, a suite with soaking tub and private sitting room, and room 216, with a sauna and lovely natural light. An elaborate continental breakfast is served in the huge old kitchen and adjoining sunroom. This is a popular hotel for business travelers, but if you're on holiday you won't feel out of place.

40 Court St. (at Middle St.), Portsmouth, NH 03801. ℂ 877/747-3466 or 603/433-1200. Fax 603/433-1200. www.siseinn.com. 34 units. Summer and fall $189 double, $229–$269 suite; off season $129 double, $159–$199 suite. Rates include continental breakfast. AE, DISC, MC, V. **Amenities:** Laundry service. *In room:* A/C, TV, iron, Jacuzzis (some).

Three Chimneys Inn 🌾🌾   About 20 minutes northwest of Portsmouth at the edge of the pleasant university town of Durham, the Three Chimneys Inn is a wonderful retreat. The main part of the inn dates back to 1649, but later additions and a full-scale renovation in 1997 have given it more of a regal Georgian feel. All units are above average in size and lushly decorated with four-poster or canopied beds, mahogany armoires, and Belgian carpets. Seventeen rooms have either gas or Duraflame–log fireplaces. One favorite is the William Randolph Hearst Room, with photos of starlets on the walls and a massive bed that's a replica of one at San Simeon. Five rooms are on the ground-floor level beneath the restored barn and have outside entrances, Jacuzzis, and gas fireplaces; these tend to be a bit more cavelike than the others, but also more luxurious. Note that the inn is a popular spot for weddings on summer weekends, and University of New Hampshire events such as graduation and homecoming weekend book it full.

17 Newmarket Rd., Durham, NH 03824. ℂ 888/399-9777 or 603/868-7800. Fax 603/868-2964. www.three chimneysinn.com. 23 units. May to mid-Nov $169–$249 double ($30 less midweek); off season $169–$219 double. Rates include breakfast. 2-night minimum stay on weekends. AE, DISC, MC, V. Children 6 and older welcome. **Amenities:** 2 restaurants (upscale regional, tavern fare). *In room:* A/C, TV, coffeemaker.

Wentworth by the Sea 🌾🌾🌾   The reopening of this historic resort in 2003 was a major event in seacoast hospitality. The photogenic grand hotel, which opened on New Castle Island in 1874 but later shut down due to neglect, was refurbished by the Ocean Properties group (owners of the Samoset in Rockland, Maine) and is operated jointly with Marriott in professional, luxurious fashion. As befits an old hotel, room sizes vary from cozy to big, but most rooms offer good views of the ocean or harbor. Eighteen rooms contain gas-powered fireplaces, while 15 include private balconies; all feature luxury bath amenities, new bathroom fixtures, and beautiful detailing and furnishings. Families should note that many units here contain two queen beds, making it a good choice for them. (Though not open at press time, 17 additional bi-level luxury suites in an adjacent facility known as "The Ship" were scheduled to open in 2004.) The full-service spa features a full range of treatments, while the adjacent privately operated country club is reserved for hotel guests. The **dining room** 🌾 fare here is also wonderful, served beneath a remarkable frescoed dome; entrees might include grilled swordfish, tournedos of yellowfin tuna, a clambake, a lobster pie, or something more Continental. There is a moderate dress code (men must wear a collared shirt).

Wentworth Rd (P.O. Box 860), New Castle NH 03854. ℭ **866/240-6313** or 603/422-7322. Fax 603/422-7329. www.wentworth.com. 164 units. Peak season midweek double from $259, suite from $419; weekend double $349–$369, suite $489–$659. Off-season midweek double from $169, suite from $219; weekend double from $179, suite from $229. AE, DISC, MC, V. Ask about packages. **Amenities:** 2 restaurants (American/Continental); indoor pool; outdoor pool; spa. *In room:* AC, TV, hair dryer, coffeemaker.

WHERE TO DINE

Portsmouth has perhaps the best cafe scene in northern New England; my favorites are **Breaking New Grounds** (ℭ **603/436-9555**), off Market Square, with outstanding espresso shakes and good tables for chatting; **Caffe Kilim** (ℭ **603/436-7330**) at 79 Daniel St., across from the post office, a bohemian choice; and **Me and Ollie's** (ℭ **603/436-7777**) at 10 Pleasant St., well known locally for its bread and homemade granola.

If you want a bit more of a bite with your coffee, three outstanding places leap to mind. The tie-dyed **Friendly Toast** (ℭ **603/430-2154**), at 121 Congress St., serves a variety of eggs and other breakfast dishes all day long, plus heartier items such as burgers. Funky **Ceres Bakery,** 51 Penhallow St. (ℭ **603/436-6518**), on a side street, has a handful of tiny tables; you may want to get a cookie or slice of cake to go and walk to the waterfront rose gardens. **Cafe Brioche,** 14 Market Sq. (ℭ **603/430-9225**), is the most high-profile hangout, often crowded with folks attracted by its central location and delectable French baked goods.

Blue Mermaid World Grill ⋆⋆ GLOBAL/ECLECTIC The Blue Mermaid is a Portsmouth favorite for its good food, good value, and refusal to take itself too seriously. A short stroll from Market Square, in a historic area called the Hill, it's not pretentious—locals congregate here, Tom Waits drones on in the background, and the service is casual but professional. The menu is adventurous in a low-key global way—you might try lobster and shrimp pad Thai, Bimini chicken with walnuts and a bourbon-coconut sauce, or crispy duck with guava and andouille stuffing. Other items include seafood, burgers, pasta, and pizza from the wood grill, plus a fun cocktail menu (mojitos, Goombay smash, and a dozen different margaritas) and homemade fire-roasted salsa.

The Hill (at Hanover and High sts., facing the municipal parking garage). ℭ **603/427-2583.** www.bluemermaid.com. Reservations recommended for parties of six or more. Main courses: lunch $5.95–$14, dinner $13–$21 (most around $15–$17). AE, DISC, MC, V. Sun–Thurs 11:30am–9pm; Fri–Sat 11:30am–10pm.

Dolphin Striker ⋆ NEW ENGLAND In a historic brick warehouse in Portsmouth's most charming area, the Dolphin Striker offers reliable if unexciting traditional New England seafood dishes, such as haddock filet piccata and lobster with ravioli. Seafood loathers can find refuge in one of the grilled meat dishes, such as grilled beef tenderloin, rack of lamb, and duck breast. The main dining room features a rustic, public house atmosphere with wide pine-board floors and wooden furniture; or order meals downstairs in a comfortable pub.

15 Bow St. ℭ **603/431-5222.** www.dolphinstriker.com. Reservations recommended. Main courses: lunch $6.95–$11, dinner $17–$28. AE, DC, DISC, MC, V. Tues–Sun 11:30am–2pm and 5–10pm.

43 Degrees North ⋆⋆⋆ ECLECTIC Right off the city's main square, Portsmouth's newest fancy eatery of note pulls off the neat trick of managing to be both a classy restaurant and a capable wine bar. Chef Evan Hennessey works magic with local seafood, Continental sauces, and game meats. You can fill up on a selection of his small plates, such as cumin-fried oysters, seared Maine crabs, or blackberry-juniper braised short ribs; or go straight to a main course, such as chili-spiced tuna steak, grilled tenderloin of pork, rabbit, boar, or even ostrich, or a grilled five-spice duck in a blood orange reduction with a duck confit crepe. Beguiling side dishes could be anything from applewood bread pudding to andouille-scallion potato cake. And of course, you can get plenty of wines by the glass or half-bottle. In December, lunch is served 3 days a week.

75 Pleasant St. ⓒ 603/430-0225. Reservations recommended. Small plates $7–$10, entrees $18–$28. AE, MC, V. Mon–Sat 5–9pm.

Jumpin' Jay's Fish Café ★★ SEAFOOD   One of Portsmouth's more urbane eateries, Jay's is a welcome destination for those who like their seafood more sophisticated than simply deep-fried. A sleek and spare spot dotted with splashes of color, it also features an open kitchen and a polished steel bar. Jay's attracts a younger, culinary-attuned clientele. The day's fresh catch is posted on blackboards; you pick the fish, and pair it up with sauces, such as salsa verde, ginger-orange, or roasted red pepper. Pasta dishes are also an option—add scallops, mussels, or chicken, as you like. The food's great, and the attention to detail by the kitchen and waitstaff is admirable.

150 Congress St. ⓒ 603/766-3474. Reservations recommended (call by Wed for weekends). Dinner $14–$23. AE, DISC, MC, V. Mon–Thurs 5:30–9:30pm (closes at 9pm in winter); Fri and Sat 5–10pm; Sun 5–9pm.

Lindbergh's Crossing ★ BISTRO   For exotic comfort food, head to this restaurant, which serves what it calls hearty French country fare. Located in an old waterfront warehouse, this intimate, two-story restaurant has a bistro menu that's subtly creative without calling too much attention to itself. You can partake of starters such as seared rare tuna with white beans, then move on to main courses like pan-roasted cod with beet polenta, a Moroccan bouillabaisse, or braised beef short ribs with a Guinness and molasses sauce over baked polenta. They also offer steaks and $14 burgers of mixed lamb and tenderloin. If you don't have reservations, ask about sitting in the bar; they may have room.

29 Ceres St. ⓒ 603/431-0887. Reservations recommended. Main courses $16–$27. AE, DC, MC, V. Sun–Thurs 5:30–9:30pm; Fri–Sat 5:30–10pm. Bar opens 4pm daily, with a limited menu.

Portsmouth Brewery PUB FARE   In the heart of the historic district (look for the tipping tankard suspended over the sidewalk), New Hampshire's first brewpub opened in 1991 and draws a clientele loyal to the superb beers. The tin-ceilinged, brick-wall dining room is open, airy, echoey, and redolent of hops. Brews are made in 200-gallon batches and include specialties such as Old Brown Ale and a delightfully creamy Black Cat Stout. An eclectic menu complements the robust beverages, with selections including burgers, veggie jambalaya, hickory-smoked steak, grilled pizza, and bratwurst. Recently, the kitchen has become more adventurous, with offerings such as cioppino and London broil with white-bean cassoulet. The food's okay, but the beer is excellent.

56 Market St. ⓒ 603/431-1115. www.portsmouthbrewery.com. Reservations accepted for parties of 10 or more. Main courses: lunch $5.25–$8.95, dinner $11–$22. AE, DC, DISC, MC, V. Daily 11:30am–12:30am.

Press Room TAVERN FARE   Locals flock here more for the convivial atmosphere and the easy-on-the-budget prices than for creative cuisine. An in-town favorite since 1976, the Press Room likes to boast that it was the first in the area to serve Guinness stout, so it's appropriate that the atmosphere is rustic Gaelic charm. On cool days, a fire burns in the woodstove, and quaffers flex their elbows at darts amid brick walls, pine floors, and heavy wooden beams overhead.

Choose your meal from a basic bar menu of inexpensive selections, including a variety of burgers, fish and chips, stir-fries, and salads.

77 Daniel St. ℂ **603/431-5186.** Reservations not accepted. Sandwiches $3.50–$6.50; main courses $7.50–$13. AE, DISC, MC, V. Sun–Thurs 5–11pm; Fri–Sat 11:30am–11pm.

2 The Connecticut River Valley ⟨★

New Hampshire's side of the Connecticut River Valley is a pastoral region of rolling hills, small villages, rustic farmsteads, and winding back roads. What the area lacks in major attractions it makes up for in peacefulness and bucolic charm. The inns here tend to be more basic and less elegant than those across the river in southern Vermont, but prices appeal more to budget travelers looking for a taste of history with their room and board.

For most visitors, chief activities in the valley include woodland walks, porch sitting, and idle drives to nowhere in particular. In fact, the best strategy for exploring the area may be to put away the map and turn randomly on a side road to see where you'll end up. Wherever it is, odds are good you'll find a gentle Currier & Ives quality.

PETERBOROUGH & ENVIRONS ★★

Peterborough (pop. 5,000), settled in 1749, is no quaint colonial town gathered primly around a village green. Rather, it has the feel of a once-prosperous commercial center, where the hum of industry provided harmony for a thriving economy. While the hum is a bit quieter these days, Peterborough is still a beautiful town with diverse architecture, set in a valley at the confluence of the Contoocook and Nubanusit rivers. Improbably enough, Peterborough has carved out a niche in the high-tech world as a publishing center for computer magazines.

ESSENTIALS

GETTING THERE   Peterborough is between Keene and Nashua on Route 101. A decent map is essential for exploring the outlying villages and towns on winding state and county roads . . . unless, of course, you choose to get lost.

VISITOR INFORMATION   The **Greater Peterborough Chamber of Commerce,** P.O. Box 401, Peterborough, NH 03458 (ℂ **603/924-7234;** www.peterboroughchamber.com), provides advice either over the phone or at a year-round information center at the intersection of Route 101 and Route 202.

EXPLORING THE REGION

Exploring the area's villages by car (or, for the more ambitious, by bike), could easily eat up a day or two. **Peterborough ★★** itself offers fine browsing, with art galleries, bookstores, antique shops, and boutiques, with most of the wares outside the orbit of the usual mass-market trinketry. Notable is the **Sharon Arts Center,** Depot Square (ℂ **603/924-7256**), with a great selection of eclectic local crafts (pottery, glasswork, paintings, and ironwork) in an attractive gallery.

Fitzwilliam, about 16 miles southwest of Peterborough at the intersection of Route 12 and Route 119, is presided over by the columned Fitzwilliam Inn and is home to several antiques stores. The village has a triangular green with Civil War obelisk; a cast-iron Victorian fountain; some wonderful Greek Revival homes facing the green; and an impressively columned 1817 church, now the town hall.

Hancock ★ is picture-postcard-perfect New England, with a quiet street of early homes. A former cotton-farming center, Hancock is home to one of the oldest operating inns in the region (see "Where to Stay," below).

Between Rindge and Jaffrey on Cathedral Road (look for signs along Rte. 124) is the unique **Cathedral of the Pines** ⚐ (© **603/899-3300**). This outdoor "cathedral" is on an open knoll amid a stately grove of swaying pines, with views toward Mt. Monadnock. It's a quietly spectacular spot, with wooden benches and fieldstone altars and pulpits. May through October, it's open daily from 9am to 5pm; donations are encouraged.

OUTDOOR PURSUITS

Mount Monadnock stands impressively amid the gentler hills of southern New Hampshire. Some 40 miles of trails lace the slopes of the mountain. The most popular (and best-marked) trails leave from near the entrance to **Monadnock State Park** ⚐⚐ (© **603/532-8862**), about 4 miles northwest of Jaffrey Center. (Head west on Rte. 124; after 2 miles, follow the park signs to the north.) A round-trip on the most direct routes will take someone in decent shape 3 to 4 hours. Admission to the park is $3 for adults and children 12 and older; free for children 11 and under. No pets are allowed in the park.

WHERE TO STAY

Hancock Inn ⚐   The austere and simple Hancock Inn, built in 1789, sits on Main Street of a small town that doesn't appear to have changed much since then. You'll find classic Americana inside, from creaky floors and braided oval rugs to guest rooms appointed in understated Colonial decor. The Rufus Porter Room has an evocative wall mural from the inn's early days. Three rooms have gas fireplaces; three have soaking tubs. The inn has four suites, including the new Ballroom and the Bell Tower Room, the former with a domed ceiling, the latter with a cannonball king bed and gas fireplace; both have soaking tubs. The inn has the historic charm of other inns mentioned here, but with a more upscale sensibility.

33 Main St., Hancock, NH 03443. © 800/525-1789 or 603/525-3318. Fax 603/525-9301. www.hancockinn. com. 15 units. $105–$250 double. Rates include breakfast. AE, DC, DISC, MC, V. Children 12 and older welcome. Pets allowed with prior permission. **Amenities:** Restaurant (traditional New England). *In room:* A/C, TV.

The Inn at Jaffrey Center ⚐   In the middle of one of New Hampshire's most gracious villages, this historic, architecturally eclectic inn was built in 1830. After years of turnover and decline, the inn got a much-needed makeover in 2000, with the rooms updated in traditional New England style, some with four-poster or canopy beds. Rooms that formerly shared a bathroom got their own, and fixtures such as old claw-foot tubs (in some rooms) were refurbished and reinstalled. Some rooms have TVs; all have goose-down comforters.

379 Main St., Jaffrey Center, NH 03452. © 877/510-7019 or 603/532-7800. Fax 603/532-7000. www.the innatjaffreycenter.com. 11 units. $100–$150 double; off season $60-$100 double. Rates include continental breakfast. MC, V. Minimum stay policy during foliage and holiday weekends. **Amenities:** Restaurant (upscale New England). *In room:* No phone.

WHERE TO DINE

Acqua Bistro ⚐⚐ MEDITERRANEAN/BISTRO   Hidden off Peterborough's main thoroughfares (near Twelve Pine and the Sharon Arts Center), Acqua is a modern, agreeable restaurant overlooking a river (more a stream, really) and offering a contemporary Mediterranean twist on regional fare. Founded by a Boston restaurant consultant who had wearied of telling other people what to do, Acqua is Peterborough's best choice for a well-crafted meal. Entrees may include the likes of cavatelli with braised artichokes and arugula, along with a veal meatloaf. Creative pizzas (think: lamb sausage) are also offered nightly. Sunday mornings feature a rustic, country brunch.

9 School St., Peterborough. ℂ **603/924-9905.** Reservations accepted for parties of 5 or more. Main courses $12–$25. MC, V. Tues–Sat 5–11pm; Sun 11am–2pm and 5–8pm.

Peterborough Diner ⋆ DINER   This classic throwback to the 1940s is hidden on a side street. Behind the faded yellow and green exterior is a beautiful interior of wood, aluminum, tile, and ceiling fans, along with one of the best

---

Tips Exploring Newport & Lake Sunapee

While visiting Hanover, Concord, or Cornish, don't neglect the Newport–Lake Sunapee region. The commercial center of the area is **Newport** ⋆, a former mill town with grit, character, and substantial history in a valley setting. This is the town that produced Sarah Josepha Hale, authoress of the children's poem "Mary Had a Little Lamb" and creator of the Thanksgiving holiday; President Lincoln was sufficiently impressed by her persistence to make it so. Hale was also one of the first women in the United States to serve as editor of a national publication.

Today the town's historical attractions include a quilt project documenting Newport's industrial past and the immigrants (including healthy numbers of Finns, Polish, Greeks, and Italians) who pitched in to turn the engines of commerce; an antique 1815 Hunnemen "hand-tub," a wheeled apparatus built by an apprentice of Paul Revere and originally used by town firemen to pump water while fighting blazes (on display at the Lake Sunapee Bank); and a wooden covered bridge painstakingly built by a craftsman to replace the priceless original, torched by an unknown arsonist.

Drop by the town's **Richards Free Library** ⋆ ℂ **603/863-3430** on North Main Street to get oriented; for my money, it's one of the best small-town libraries in America. Contact the Newport Chamber of Commerce ℂ **603/863-1510** for more details on the area; there's a good volunteer-run kiosk beside the town green in summer months.

Six miles away, big **Lake Sunapee** ⋆ is said to be one of the purest in the nation (it's much deeper than it looks, which helps), and offers excellent swimming, boating, and fishing. It's a longtime favorite summer resort of Bostonians. The short, steep mountain across the way—also part of **Sunapee State Park** (ℂ **603/763-5561**)—is a fine place to hike, ski, snowboard, or catch a gondola ride for expansive foliage and lake views. There's a $3 charge to enter either the beach or mountain portion of the park; rent skis at **Skinner's Ski & Sports** ℂ **603/763-2303.** August brings an outstanding arts event, the weeklong **Craftsman's Fair** ⋆ ℂ **603/224-3375,** to the park: Expect quality handcrafted art pieces. Two-day admission tickets cost $5 to $7 per adult, free for children under 12.

On the back side of the lake, pretty **New London** is an attractive college town with more than its share of fine homes and upscale restaurants. Settle down for a full meal at the tony **Millstone** (ℂ **603/526-4201**), relax over java at **Jack's Coffee** (ℂ **603/526-8003**), or try an English-style board of bread, cheese, and beer at **Peter Christian's Tavern** (ℂ **603/526-4042**).

easy-listening jukeboxes in New England. The meals are just what you'd expect: filling, cheap, and basic. Look for the great hot oven grinders (served with cheese and chips), Reubens, burgers, and grilled cheese and bacon at lunchtime. (Although blasphemous to diner aficionados, croissant sandwiches are also on the menu.) Dinner selections are what you'd expect: Yankee pot roast, meatloaf, chicken Kiev, pasta, and fried fish.

10 Depot St., Peterborough. © 603/924-6202. Breakfast $2.95–$12; lunch and dinner $1.95–$13. AE, DISC, MC, V. Daily 6am–9pm.

Twelve Pine ☞ UPSCALE DELI   This inviting deli and market is in an airy former railroad building behind Peterborough's main street. It's a great place to nosh and linger; you select a pre-made meal (say, chicken burritos or one of four homemade soups) from a deli counter, and it is popped in a microwave if need be. You bring it to a table. You enjoy it. Simple . . . as lunch should be. Sandwiches are on homemade bread and contain heaping fillings; excellent cheeses are available by the pound, and fresh juices round out a meal. It's a relaxed place where you'll find value for the dollar.

11 School St. (Depot Sq.), Peterborough. © 603/924-6140. Sandwiches around $5; other items priced by the pound, generally $6–$8 for a meal. MC, V. Mon–Fri 8am–7pm; Sat–Sun 9am–4pm.

HANOVER ☞☞ & ENVIRONS

If your idea of New England involves a sweeping green edged with stately brick buildings, be sure to visit Hanover, a thriving university town in the Connecticut River Valley. First settled in 1765, the town was home to early colonists who were granted a charter by King George III to establish a college. The school was named after the second Earl of Dartmouth, its first trustee. Since its founding, Dartmouth College has had a large hand in shaping the community.

Today, a handsome, oversize village green marks the permeable border between college and town. In summer, the green is an ideal destination for strolling and lounging. The best way to explore Hanover is on foot, so your first endeavor is to park your car, which can be trying during peak seasons (fall foliage and whenever school is in session). Try the municipal lots west of Main Street.

ESSENTIALS

GETTING THERE   Hanover is north of Lebanon, New Hampshire, and I-89 via Route 10 or Route 120. Amtrak serves White River Junction, Vermont, across the river.

VISITOR INFORMATION   Dartmouth College alumni and chamber volunteers maintain an **information center** on the green in summer. It's open daily from 10am to 5pm in June and September, daily from 9:30am to 5pm in July and August. In the off season, head to the **Hanover Chamber of Commerce** (© **603/643-3115**) located on Main Street across from the post office. It's open Monday through Friday from 9am to 4:30pm.

SPECIAL EVENTS   In mid-February, look for the fantastic and intricate ice sculptures of the annual **Dartmouth Winter Carnival;** call Dartmouth College (© **603/646-1110**) for more information on this traditionally beer-soaked event.

EXPLORING HANOVER

Hanover is a superb town to explore on foot, by bike, and even by canoe. Start by picking up a map of the campus, available at the Dartmouth information center on the green or at the Hanover Inn. (Free guided tours are also offered in summer.) The expansive, leafy campus is a delight to walk through.

Finds Orozco Art at Dartmouth

Dartmouth's **Baker Memorial Library** houses a wonderful treasure: a set of murals by Latin American painter José Orozco, who painted *The Epic of American Civilization* while teaching here between 1932 and 1934. The huge paintings wrap around a basement study room and are as colorful as they are metaphorical. Ask for a printed interpretation at the front desk.

South of the green next to the Hanover Inn is the modern **Hopkins Center for the Arts** ✪ (© **603/646-2422;** http://hop.dartmouth.edu). The center attracts national acts to its 900-seat concert hall and stages top-notch performances at the Moore Theater. Wallace Harrison, the architect who later went on to fame for his Lincoln Center in New York, designed the building.

You can also shop nicely in Hanover's compact downtown. In addition to excellent gift and clothing shops, two outstanding bookstores stand nearly shoulder-to-shoulder. The huge **Dartmouth Bookstore** (© **800/624-8800** or 603/643-5170; www.dartbook.com) at 33 South Main St. is a maze of good rooms of children's and travel books, calendars, and a bargain-basement section heavy on poetry, literature, and foreign language titles. The newspaper and magazine selection is exemplary, and staff is unfailingly helpful—there's even an information desk for tracking down or ordering titles.

Good as it is, though, I'm partial to **Left Bank Books** (© **603/643-4479**) just up the street at 9 South Main St. (go up the stairs). Owner Corlan Johnson runs this one-woman show, stuffing a small space (with a good Hanover view) with a changing selection of mostly used poetry, fiction, philosophy, art books, cookbooks, and more. The leftward tilt of the place is unmistakable, and so is Johnson's eye for a good read; I never leave empty-handed.

See chapter 11 for the good, family-oriented **Montshire Museum of Science,** located just across the river in Norwich, Vermont.

Hood Museum of Art ✪ This modern, open building next to the Hopkins Center houses one of the oldest college museums in the nation. Its current incarnation—an austere and modern three-story structure—was built in 1986 and features special exhibits as well as examples from the permanent collection, which includes a superb selection of 19th-century American landscapes.

Wheelock St. © **603/646-2808.** http://hoodmuseum.dartmouth.edu. Free admission. Tues and Thurs–Sat 10am–5pm; Wed 10am–9pm; Sun noon–5pm.

Ledyard Canoe Club ✪✪ An idyllic way to spend a lazy afternoon is to drift along the Connecticut River in a canoe. Dartmouth's historic boating club is just down the hill from the campus. While much of the club's focus is on competitive racing, it's a good place for travelers to rent a boat for a few hours and explore the tree-lined river. Instruction is also available.

Off West Wheelock St. (turn upstream at the bottom of the hill west of bridge; follow signs to the clubhouse). © **603/643-6709.** www.dartmouth.edu/~lcc. Canoe and kayak rentals $5 per hr., $15 per day ($25 on weekends). Summer Mon–Fri 10am–8pm; Sat–Sun 9am–8pm. Spring and fall Mon–Fri noon–6pm; Sat–Sun 10am–6pm. Open when river temperature is higher than 50°F(10°C).

Enfield Shaker Museum ✪✪ This cluster of historic buildings on Lake Mascoma is about a 20-minute drive southeast of Hanover. "The Chosen Vale," as its first inhabitants called it, was founded in 1793; by the mid-1800s, it had 350 members and 3,000 acres. From that peak, the community dwindled, and by 1927, the Shakers abandoned the Chosen Vale and sold the village—lock, stock, and barrel. Today, much of the property is owned by either the state of New Hampshire or the museum.

Dominating the village is the **Great Stone Dwelling,** an austere but gracious granite structure erected between 1837 and 1841. When constructed, it was the tallest building north of Boston, and it remains the largest dwelling house in any of the Shaker communes. The Enfield Shakers lived and dined here, with as many as 150 Shakers at once eating at trestle tables. In 1997, the museum acquired the stone building, and in 1998, a new restaurant and inn opened to the public (see below). The self-guided walking tour of the village is free with admission. The historic feel is compromised by a recent condominium development along the lakeshores, although the scale and design of these structures are sympathetic to the original village.

Rte. 4A, Enfield. © 603/632-4346. www.shakermuseum.org. Admission $7 adults, $6 seniors, $3 students or children 10–18, free for children under 10. Memorial Day to Halloween Mon–Sat 10am–5pm; Sun noon–5pm. Winter and spring Sat 10am–4pm; Sun noon–4pm.

A ROAD TRIP TO MOUNT KEARSARGE

Mount Monadnock to the south is the most heavily visited peak in the area, but 2,931-foot **Mount Kearsarge** ranks among the most accessible. In the Sunapee Lake region southeast of Lebanon, Kearsarge can be ascended most of the way by car along a paved carriage road. The entrance is just outside the town of Warner (Exit 9 on I-89). State park rangers collect a toll at the base ($2.50 per person over age 12), and drivers snake their way 3½ miles past dramatic vistas to a gravel parking lot high on the mountain's shoulder. From here, it's a simple half-mile hike to the summit along a well-marked, rocky trail with remarkable views to the south and southwest along the way.

The rocky, knobby summit offers superb panoramas of south-central New Hampshire's lakes and hills, though the views are cluttered slightly by an old fire tower and several small buildings bristling with antennae and other visual pollution of the information age. *Note:* On crisp fall weekends, the summit of Mount Kearsarge has all the seclusion of Christmas Eve at the mall. You're better off avoiding it then and looking for your own peaks away from the crowds.

WHERE TO STAY

Several hotels and motels are just off the interstate in Lebanon and West Lebanon, about 5 miles south of Hanover. Try the **Airport Economy Inn** (© 800/433-3466 or 603/298-8888), at 45 Airport Road (Exit 20 off I-89); **Days Inn** (© 603/448-5070; www.daysinn.com), at 135 Route 120 (Exit 18 off I-89); **Fireside Inn and Suites** (© 603/298-5906), at 25 Airport Road (Exit 20 off I-89); or **Sunset Motor Inn** (© 603/298-8721), at 305 N. Main Street (Rte. 10, 4 miles off Exit 19 off I-89).

There are also lodgings in Norwich, Vermont (across the river) and White River Junction, Vermont (just upriver and across it). See chapter 11 for details.

Alden Country Inn Ten miles north of Hanover is the pretty, quiet crossroads village of Lyme, with its tidy commons and handsome church. Overlooking the commons is this 1809 inn, a regal four-story building with a high triangular gable. Over the years, it has served as a stagecoach stop and Grange Hall. Guest rooms are varied, and decorated with light historic styling; some are simply furnished with white walls and stenciling, others are more floral in character. Most feature painted floors that show off the wide boards. Room 9 has mustard-yellow floors and a somewhat larger bathroom. (Common to many old inns, bathrooms here are on the small side, often tucked into closets.) Be aware that stairs get narrower and steeper the higher your room is in the building.

On the Common, Lyme, NH 03768. ✆ **800/794-2296** or 603/795-2222. Fax 603/795-9436. www.alden countryinn.com. 15 units. Summer and fall $130–$160 double; off season $95–$130 double. Rates include breakfast or Sun brunch. 2-night minimum on weekends Apr to mid-Oct. AE, DC, DISC, MC, V. **Amenities:** Restaurant (classic New England). *In room:* A/C, TV, hair dryer, iron.

The Hanover Inn 🎭🎭🎭   The Hanover Inn is the Upper Connecticut Valley's best managed and up-to-date hotel, perfectly situated for exploring both the campus and the town. Established in 1780, most of the current five-story inn was added later—1924, 1939, or 1968—and this large, modern hotel now features professional service, attractive rooms, excellent dining, and subterranean walkways to the art museum and theater. Yet the inn somehow manages to maintain an old-world graciousness, informed by that mildly starchy neo-Georgian demeanor trendy in the 1940s. Most rooms have canopy or four-poster beds and down comforters; some overlook the green.

Wheelock St. (P.O. Box 151), Hanover, NH 03755. ✆ **800/443-7024** or 603/643-4300. Fax 603/643-4433. www.hanoverinn.com. 92 units. $259 double, $309 suite. AE, DISC, MC, V. Valet parking $12 per day. Pets allowed ($15 per night). **Amenities:** 2 dining rooms (see below); access to fitness equipment; limited room service; massage; babysitting; dry cleaning. *In room:* A/C, TV, dataport, coffeemaker, hair dryer, iron.

Shaker Inn at the Great Stone Dwelling 🎭🎭   Part of the Enfield Shaker Museum, this inn offers a unique destination for those curious about Shakers and American history. Rooms are spread among the upper floors of the massive stone dwelling house built by the community in the 1830s, when it was the tallest building north of Boston. All units are furnished with simple, attractive Shaker reproductions. Some rooms have original built-in cabinets (you can stow your socks in something that would bring five figures at a New York auction house). Room 1 boasts the most original detail (it's also the most expensive). A restaurant in the dining hall features upscale regional fare that draws on Shaker traditions.

Rte. 4, Enfield, NH 03748. ✆ **888/707-4257** or 603/632-7810. Fax 603/632-7922. www.theshakerinn.com. 24 units. $105–$155 double. Rates include breakfast. AE, DC, DISC, MC, V. **Amenities:** Restaurant (Shaker-inspired cuisine); lake swimming. *In room:* Dataport.

WHERE TO DINE

Daniel Webster Room 🎭🎭 CONTEMPORARY AMERICAN   The Daniel Webster Room of the Hanover Inn appeals to those looking for fine dining in a formal New England atmosphere. The inn's Colonial Revival dining room is reminiscent of a 19th-century resort hotel, with fluted columns, floral carpeting, and regal upholstered chairs. The dinner menu isn't extensive, but that doesn't make it any less appealing. Produce from the college's organic farm is used seasonally. The changing entrees are eclectic and creative and may include braised rabbit leg with truffled pappardelle. Off the lobby is **Zins,** a more informal wine bistro offering 30 wines by the glass (open daily from 11:30am to 10pm).

Hanover Inn, Wheelock St. ✆ **603/643-4300.** Reservations recommended. Main courses: breakfast $3.95–$10.95, lunch $4.50–$13, dinner $20–$30. AE, DISC, MC, V. Mon 7–10:30am and 11:30am–1:30pm; Tues–Fri 7–10:30am, 11:30am–1:30pm, and 6–9pm; Sat 7–10:30am and 6–9pm; Sun 11am–1:30pm.

Lou's 🎭 *(Value* BAKERY/COMFORT FOOD   Lou's has been a Hanover institution since 1947, attracting hungry crowds for breakfast on weekends and a steady local clientele for lunch throughout the week. The mood is no-frills New Hampshire, with a black-and-white linoleum checkerboard floor, maple-and-vinyl booths, and a harried but efficient crew of waiters. Breakfast is served all day (real maple syrup on your pancakes is extra—go ahead and splurge), and the sandwiches, served on fresh-baked bread, are huge and delicious.

30 S. Main St. ⓒ **603/643-3321.** Breakfast $3–$7; lunch $5–$8. AE, MC, V. Mon–Fri 6am–3pm; Sat–Sun 7am–3pm (opens 8am Sun in winter). Bakery open for snacks until 5pm.

3 The Lake Winnipesaukee Region ⟨★

Lake Winnipesaukee is the state's largest lake, convoluted with coves and dotted with islands. Yet when you're out on the lake, it rarely seems all that huge. The 180-mile shoreline is edged with dozens of inlets, coves, and bays, and further fragmented by 274 islands. As a result, intermittent lake views from shore give the illusion of a chain of smaller lakes and ponds rather than one massive body of water that measures 12 by 20 miles at its broadest points.

If time is limited, a driving tour around the lake with a few well-chosen stops such as Meredith or Wolfeboro will give you a nice taste of the region's flavor.

MEREDITH

The village of Meredith sits at the northwest corner of Winnipesaukee, with views across a nice bay throughout the town. It lacks the quaintness and selection of activities that many travelers seek—a busy road cuts off the tidy downtown from the lakeshore, and strip malls have intruded—but it has good services and is home to several desirable inns. Foremost among its qualities is its superb location. I'd choose Meredith as a home base to explore the lakes area and the White Mountains in just 2 or 3 days, as both are within striking distance for day trips (Franconia Notch is about 50 miles north).

ESSENTIALS

GETTING THERE　Interstate access to Meredith is via Exit 23 off I-93. Drive 9 miles east on Route 104 to Route 3, then turn left down the hill into town.

VISITOR INFORMATION　The **Meredith Area Chamber of Commerce** (ⓒ **603/279-6121**) maintains an office in the white house on Route 3 (on the left when driving down the hill from Rte. 104). It's open daily in summer from 9am to 5pm; closed weekends in winter.

EXPLORING THE AREA

Meredith's attractive if now largely bypassed Main Street ascends a hill from Route 3 at an elbow in the middle of town. A handful of shops, galleries, and boutiques offer low-key browsing. The creative re-adaptation of an early mill at the **Mill Falls Marketplace** ★ (ⓒ **800/622-6455** or 603/279-7006) features 18 shops, including a well-stocked bookstore. It's connected to the Inns at Mill Falls, at the intersection of Route 3 and Route 25.

An excellent fair-weather trip is an excursion to 112-acre **Stonedam Island** ★★, one of the largest protected islands in the lake. Owned by the Lakes Region Conservation Trust (ⓒ **603/279-7278**), the island has a trail that winds through wetlands and forest. Approximately 2½ miles southeast of downtown Meredith, it's an ideal destination for a picnic, though it takes some doing to get there. Rent a canoe or kayak at **Sports & Marine Parafunalia,** Route 25, Meredith Shopping Center (ⓒ **603/279-8077**), and make a day of it.

Note that the **M/S _Mt. Washington_** makes a stop once weekly in Meredith.

WHERE TO STAY

The Inns at Mill Falls ★★　This ever-expanding complex is gradually dominating Meredith, but it has managed its growth with considerable flair. The accommodations are spread among three buildings (with a fourth slated to open in 2004), each subtly different, but all uncommonly well tended and comfortable. The main inn is in a former mill complex (a small, tasteful shopping mall is adjacent) and features attractive but simple rooms. All rooms in the more upscale Chase House have gas fireplaces; most have balconies and porch rockers with views of the lake. The Inn at Bay Point is on 2,000 feet of lakefront, and most rooms feature balconies with sensational views of Winnipesaukee. Ten rooms have Jacuzzis. The inn is not especially well suited for kids. In 2004, the inn unveils its latest expansion, Church Landing. The converted church, right on the lakefront and in front of two beaches, offers 58 rooms and suites with gas fireplaces (some also sport double Jacuzzis and balconies). Hallelujah! A pool and health club with massage services, Jacuzzi, and sauna are included in this new section, as well as marina space for 25 boats and a restaurant. The church wing will be connected to the other inns by a lakeside walking path.

Rte. 3, Meredith, NH 03253. ℂ **800/622-6455** or 603/279-7006. www.millfalls.com. 101 units. Main inn: $159–$239 double, winter $99–$179; Inn at Bay Point: summer $199–$189 double, winter $149–$249; Chase House: summer $189–$289 double, winter $139–$259. Call for Church Landing rates. AE, DC, DISC, MC, V. Minimum stay required some weekends. **Amenities:** 5 restaurants (casual dining); indoor pool; fitness center; shopping arcade; limited room service; massage; babysitting; laundry service; dry cleaning. *In room:* A/C, TV, dataport, hair dryer, iron.

Manor on Golden Pond ★★★ This regal stucco-and-shingle mansion, 9 miles north of Meredith in Holderness, was built between 1903 and 1907 and sits on a low hill overlooking Squam Lake. The Manor is wonderfully situated on 14 landscaped acres studded with white pines. Inside, it has the feel of an English manor house, with oak paneling and leaded windows; the options to play croquet and horseshoes add to the summery feel. Larger, more expensive guest rooms are creatively furnished and far more inviting than the motel-size units along the first-floor wing. Most rooms have wood-burning fireplaces. Among the best rooms: Savoy Court, Buckingham, and Stratford, all lavishly appointed. Four recently constructed annex suites have French doors that open onto views of the lake. The top-notch **dining room** is "dressy casual" (no shorts or jeans).

Rte. 3, Holderness, NH 03245. ℂ **800/545-2141** or 603/968-3348. Fax 603/968-2116. www.manorongolden pond.com. 27 units. Summer $210–$375 double; winter $180–$375. Rates include breakfast. AE, DISC, MC, V. 2-day minimum stay weekends and foliage season. Children 12 and older welcome. **Amenities:** Restaurant (New American); outdoor pool; lake swimming; tennis court; watersports equipment rental; limited room service; massage. *In room:* A/C, TV, dataport, fridge (some), coffeemaker (some), hair dryer, iron.

WHERE TO DINE

Abondante ✶ ITALIAN/DELI This casual storefront market and deli has a delightful atmosphere—maple floors, copper-topped tables, herbs drying from the joists overhead, classical music. Both table service and to-go orders are available, with an inviting selection of fresh pastas (the lobster ravioli is popular) and rustic breads, not to mention imported chocolates. This is a good spot for a casual dinner, or to pick up a lunch for a boating picnic.

30 Main St., Meredith. ℂ **603/279-7177**. Main courses $8–$19. AE, DISC, MC, V. Summer daily 5–9pm (until 10pm Fri–Sat); off season Wed–Sat 5–9pm, Sun 4–8pm.

Hart's Turkey Farm Restaurant TURKEY/AMERICAN Hart's Turkey Farm Restaurant is bad news if you're a turkey. On a typically busy day, this place dishes up over a ton of America's favorite bird. Judging by name alone, Hart's Farm sounds more rural than it is. In fact, it's in a nondescript building on busy

The White Mountains & Lake Winnipesaukee

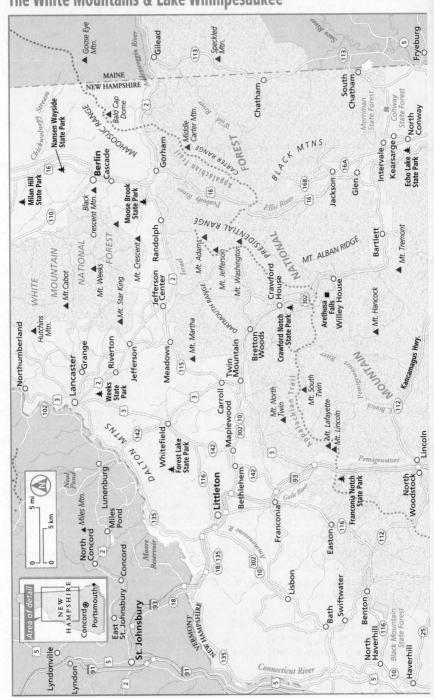

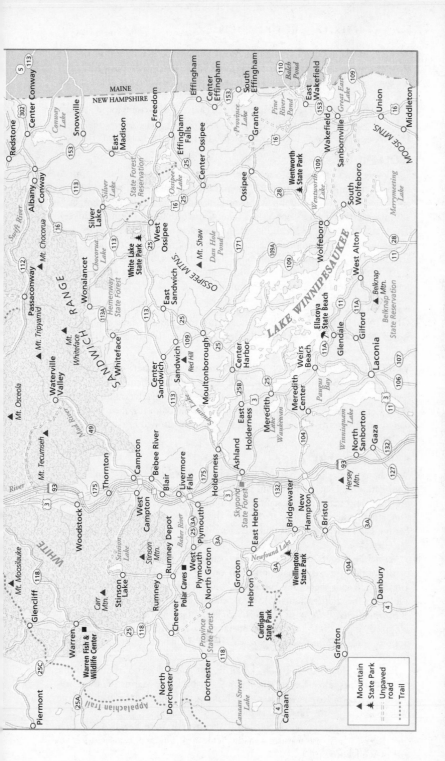

Route 3. Inside, it's comfortable in a faux–Olde New Englande sort of way—a classic family restaurant (founded 1954) that borders on kitsch, but with turkey too good to write off as merely a retro experience. The service is afflicted with that sort of rushed efficiency found in places that attract bus tours. But diners don't return time and again to Hart's for the charm—they come for the turkey.

Junction of Routes 3 and 104, Meredith. © 603/279-6212. www.hartsturkeyfarm.com. Main courses $9.50–$22 (mostly $13–$15). AE, DISC, MC, V. Summer daily 11:15am–9pm; fall–spring daily 11:15am–8pm.

WOLFEBORO ⚜⚜

The lovely town of Wolfeboro on Lake Winnipesaukee's eastern shore claims to be the first summer resort in the U.S., and the documentation makes a pretty good case for it. In 1763, John Wentworth, nephew of a former governor, built a summer estate on what's now called Lake Wentworth (east of Winnipesaukee). The house burned in 1820, and its site now attracts largely archaeologists.

Where western Winnipesaukee tends to be more raucous, with the populist attractions of Weirs Beach, Wolfeboro has more of a blue-blood sensibility. You'll find impeccably maintained 19th-century architecture, attractive downtown shops, and a more refined sense of place.

ESSENTIALS

GETTING THERE Lake Winnipesaukee's east shore is best explored on Route 28 (from Alton Bay to Wolfeboro) and Route 109 (from Wolfeboro to Moultonborough).

VISITOR INFORMATION The **Wolfeboro Chamber of Commerce** (© **800/516-5324** or 603/569-2200; www.wolfeborochamber.com) offers regional information and advice from its offices in a converted railroad station at 32 Central Ave., a block off Main Street in Wolfeboro. It's open in summer daily from 10am to 5pm, in the off season Monday through Friday from 10am to 3pm.

EXPLORING THE AREA

Wolfeboro (pop. 2,800) has a vibrant, homey downtown, easily explored on foot. Park near Depot Square and the Victorian train station, and stock up on brochures and maps at the Chamber of Commerce office. Behind the train station, running along the former tracks of the rail line, is the **Russell C. Chase Bridge-Falls Path** ⚜, a rail-trail that runs along Back Bay to a set of small cascades.

Several boat tours depart from docks behind the shops of Main Street. The best: a wind-in-the-face, half-hour tour on the *Millie B.* ⚜⚜ (© **603/569-1080**), a 28-foot mahogany speedboat constructed by Hacker-Craft ($10 for adults, $5 for children under 5). Also available are 1½-hour excursions on the *Winnipesaukee Belle* ⚜ (© **603/569-3796**), a faux 65-foot steamship with a canopied upper deck, owned and operated by the Wolfeboro Inn. And the impressive **M/S *Mount Washington*** sails out of Wolfeboro four times weekly in summer.

For a self-propelled afternoon, kayak rentals and guided tours are available from **Winnipesaukee Kayak** ⚜, 17 Bay St., at Back Bay Marina (© **603/569-9926**). On a relatively windless day, little beats exploring by paddle from Wolfeboro Bay to the cluster of islands just to the south.

Quieter lake swimming is available at **Wentworth State Beach** ⚜ (© **603/569-3699**), which also features a shady picnic area. The park is located 5 miles east of Wolfeboro on Rte. 109.

Castle in the Clouds ★★ About 15 miles north of Wolfeboro is a rather unusual sight. Cranky millionaire Thomas Gustav Plant built an eccentric stone edifice atop a mountain overlooking Lake Winnipesaukee in 1913, at a cost of $7 million. The home is a sort of rustic, smaller San Simeon East, with cliff-hugging rooms, stained-glass windows, and unrivaled views of surrounding hills and lakes. Park at the carriage house; from there you are taken through the house by knowledgeable guides. If the castle holds no interest, the 5,200-acre grounds are worth the admission. The long access road is harrowingly narrow and winding, with wonderful vistas and turnouts for stopping along the way. Take time to explore on the way; a separate exit road is fast, straight, and uninteresting.

Rte. 171 (4 miles south of Rte. 25), Moultonborough. © 800/729-2468 or 603/476-2352. www.castlesprings. com. Admission $12 adults, $10 seniors, $8 students, free for children under 6. Grounds only: $6 adults, free for children. Mid-May to mid-June Sat–Sun 9am–4:30pm; mid-June to mid-Oct daily 9am–4:30pm. Closed mid-Oct to mid-May.

New Hampshire Antique and Classic Boat Museum Winnipesaukee is synonymous with classic wooden powerboats—sleek wooden Chris-Crafts and other icons of a more genteel era. This newly established museum hopes to bring that era to life with a collection of early boats and artifacts. The museum is located in a barn about 2 miles from downtown Wolfeboro. (Drive north on Rte. 109/28 from downtown.) Plan your trip to coincide with one of the summer regattas, which bring boat restorers and aficionados out of the woodwork to show off their obsessions. Check the website for upcoming events.

397 Center St., Wolfeboro. © 603/569-4554. www.nhacbm.org. Admission $5 adults, $4 seniors, $3 students, free for children under 13. Summer Mon–Sat 10am–4pm, Sun noon–4pm.

WHERE TO STAY & DINE

Wolfeboro Inn ★★ This small, elegant resort hotel strives to mix modern and traditional, and succeeds admirably. Within an easy stroll of downtown Wolfeboro, the inn dates back to 1812 but was expanded and updated in the mid-1980s. The modern lobby features a small atrium with wood beams, a slate floor, and a brick fireplace, but retains an old-world elegance. Most of the comfortable guest rooms are furnished with Early American reproductions and quilts. Deluxe rooms have better views, and a dozen have balconies as well. The downside: For an inn of this price and quality, it has only a disappointing sliver of lakeshore and just a tiny beach for guests.

90 N. Main St. (P.O. Box 1270), Wolfeboro, NH 03894. © 800/451-2389 or 603/569-3016. Fax 603/569-5375. www.wolfeboroinn.com. 44 units. Summer $180–$225 double, $245–$295 suite; spring and fall $135–$225 double, $195–$295 suite; winter $90–$155 double, $135–$195 suite. Rates include continental breakfast. 2-night minimum stay in peak season. AE, MC, V. **Amenities:** 2 restaurants (steakhouse, pub fare); watersports/equipment rental; concierge; limited room service; babysitting; laundry service; dry cleaning. *In room:* A/C, TV, coffeemaker, hair dryer, iron.

(*Tips* **Worthwhile Views**

Enjoy a sweeping view of Winnipesaukee's eastern shore at the Abenaki Tower, 7 miles north of Wolfeboro on Route 109. Look for a parking lot and wooden sign on the right side of the road at the crest of a hill. From the lot, it's an easy 5-minute hike to a sturdy log tower, rising about 80 feet, with a steep staircase to climb (not a good destination for acrophobes). Those who go to the top are rewarded with excellent views of nearby coves, inlets, and the Belknap Mountains southwest of the lake.

4 The White Mountains 🎖🎖🎖

The White Mountains are northern New England's outdoor-recreation capital. This cluster of ancient mountains is a sprawling, rugged playground that attracts kayakers, mountaineers, rock climbers, skiers, mountain bikers, birdwatchers, and especially hikers.

White Mountain National Forest encompasses 773,000 acres of rocky, forested terrain, over 100 waterfalls, dozens of backcountry lakes, and miles of clear brooks and cascading streams. An elaborate network of 1,200 miles of hiking trails dates to the 19th century. The centerpiece of the forest, in spirit if not in geography, is 6,288-foot **Mount Washington,** an ominous, brooding peak that's often cloud-capped and mantled with snow both early and late in the season. This blustery peak is accessible by cog railroad, car, and foot, making it one of the more popular destinations in the region. You won't find utter wilderness here, but you will find abundant natural drama.

Flanking this peak is the brawny **Presidential Range** of the White Mountains, a series of wind-blasted granite peaks named after U.S. presidents and offering spectacular views. Surrounding these, many other rocky ridges lure hikers looking for challenges and a place to experience nature at its most elemental.

If your idea of fun doesn't involve steep cliffs or icy dips in mountain streams, you can still enjoy the mountain scenery via spectacular drives. Route 302 carries travelers through Crawford Notch to the pleasant towns of Bethlehem and Littleton. Route 16 travels from southern New Hampshire through congested North Conway before twisting up dramatic Pinkham Notch at the base of Mount Washington. Wide and fast Route 2 skirts the northern edge of the mountains, with wonderful views en route to the town of Jefferson. I-93 may be the most scenic interstate in northern New England, passing through spectacular Franconia Notch as it narrows to two lanes in deference to its natural surroundings (and local political will). The most scenic drive, though, is the **Kancamagus Highway,** which links Conway with Lincoln and provides frequent roadside pull-offs to admire cascades, picnic along rivers, and enjoy sweeping mountain views.

North Conway is the region's motel capital, with hundreds of rooms—mostly charmless but reasonable. Jackson, Franconia Notch, Crawford Notch, and the Bethlehem-Littleton area are the best places for old-fashioned hotels and inns.

BACKCOUNTRY FEES

The White Mountain National Forest requires anyone using the backcountry— whether for hiking, mountain biking, picnicking, skiing, or any other activity— to pay a recreation fee. Anyone parking at a trailhead must display a backcountry permit on the car dashboard. Those lacking a permit face a fine. Permits are available at ranger stations and many stores in the region. An annual permit costs $20, and a 7-day pass is $5. You can also buy a day pass for $3, but it covers only one site. If you drive somewhere else later in the afternoon and park, you'll have to pay $3 again. You're much better off with a 7-day pass. For information, contact the **Forest Service's White Mountains office** (© **603/528-8721;** www.fs.fed.us/r9/white).

RANGER STATIONS & INFORMATION

The Forest Service's **central White Mountains office** is at 719 N. Main St. in Laconia (© **603/528-8721**), near Lake Winnipesaukee. Your best general source of information is the **Saco Ranger Station,** 33 Kancamagus Hwy., 100 yards west of Route 16, Conway (© **603/447-5448**). Other district offices are **Androscoggin Ranger Station,** 300 Glen Rd., Gorham (© **603/466-2713**); **Ammonoosuc Ranger Station,** 660 Trudeau Rd., Bethlehem (© **603/466-2713**); and **Pemigewasset Ranger Station,** Route 175, Holderness, near the Plymouth town line (© **603/536-1310**). The **Evans Notch Ranger Station** (© **207/824-2134**), which covers the Maine portion of the White Mountains (about 50,000 acres), is in Bethel, 18 Mayville Rd., off Route 2 north of town.

Additional info and advice on recreation in the White Mountains are available at the **AMC's Pinkham Notch Visitor Center** (© **603/466-2727**), on Route 16 between Jackson and Gorham. The center is open daily from 6am to 10pm.

CAMPING

The White Mountain National Forest maintains 19 drive-in campsites scattered throughout the region, with the number of sites at each ranging from 7 to 176. Campsites are $12 to $18 per night, plus an additional fee if you reserve in advance. Reservations are accepted at about half of these through the **National Recreation Reservation Service** (© **877/444-6777;** www.reserveamerica.com). Most campsites are basic (some with pit toilets only), but all are well maintained.

Of these national forest campgrounds, **Dolly Copp Campground** (© **603/466-2713**), near the base of Mount Washington, is the largest and least personal,

---

⟨Tips Guides to Exploring the White Mountains

For serious exploration of the White Mountains, you'll need supplemental guides and maps to keep you on track. Here's a short list of recommended guides, most of which are available at area bookstores:

- *AMC White Mountain Guide* (Appalachian Mountain Club, 1998). This comprehensive 576-page book is full of detailed information on all the hiking trails in the White Mountains; it is the definitive hiker's bible for the region.

- *White Mountains Map Book* (Map Adventures, 2000). This colorful, sharply printed map features 386 hiking trails, distances, and a GPS grid. The text offers an overview of what you'll find on 76 day-hikes, along with info on camping. It's a good choice for those planning 2 or 3 day hikes.

- *50 Hikes in the White Mountains* (Backcountry Publications, 1997). The fifth edition of this popular guide, written by Daniel Doan and Ruth Doan MacDougall, offers a good selection of mountain rambles in the high peaks region around Mount Washington. You'll find everything from easy strolls to overnight backpacking trips.

- *Ponds & Lakes of the White Mountains* (Backcountry Publications, 1998). The White Mountain high country is studded with dramatic tarns (many left by retreating glaciers). This 350-page guide by Steven D. Smith offers 68 trips to help get you there.

- *Waterfalls of the White Mountains* (Backcountry Publications, 1999). Waterfall lovers will get their money's worth from Bruce and Doreen Bolnick's guide to 100 mountain waterfalls, including roadside cascades and backcountry cataracts.

but has a superior location and great views from the open sites. It costs $18 per night. Along the Kancamagus Highway, I'm partial to the **Covered Bridge Campground** (© 603/447-5448), which is adjacent to an 1858 covered bridge and a short drive to delightful river swimming at the Rocky Gorge Scenic Area; it costs $16 per night. Both are open from mid-May until mid-October.

NORTH CONWAY & ENVIRONS

North Conway is the commercial heart of the White Mountains. Shoppers are drawn by the outlets along Routes 302 and 16. (The two state highways overlap through town.) Outdoor purists abhor it, considering it a garish interloper to be avoided at all costs, except when seeking pizza and beer.

Sprawl notwithstanding, North Conway is beautifully situated along the eastern edge of the broad and fertile Saco River valley (also called the Mount Washington Valley). Gentle, forest-covered mountains, some with sheer cliffs that suggest the distant, stunted cousins of Yosemite's rocky faces, border the bottomlands. Northward up the valley, the hills rise in a triumphant crescendo to the blustery, tempestuous heights of Mount Washington.

The village is trim and attractive (if often congested), with an open green, some colorful shops, Victorian commercial architecture, and a distinctive train station. It's a good place to park, stretch your legs, and get a cup of coffee or snack.

ESSENTIALS

GETTING THERE North Conway and the Mount Washington Valley are on Route 16 and Route 302. Route 16 connects to the Spaulding Turnpike, which intersects with I-95 outside of Portsmouth, N.H. Route 302 begins in Portland, Maine. **Concord Trailways** (© 800/639-3317; www.concordtrailways.com) provides service from points south, including Boston.

Traffic can be vexing in the Mount Washington Valley on holiday weekends in summer and foliage weekends in fall, when backups of several miles are common.

VISITOR INFORMATION Contact the **Mount Washington Valley Chamber of Commerce** (© 800/367-3364 or 603/356-3171; www.mtwashingtonvalley.org), which operates a seasonal information booth opposite the village green. Staff can help arrange local accommodations. It's open in summer daily from 9am to 6pm, in winter Saturday and Sunday only. The chamber's main office is at 2617 Main St.

The state of New Hampshire also operates an **information booth** with restrooms and phones at a vista with fine views of Mount Washington on Routes 16 and 302 north of North Conway.

RIDING THE RAILS

The **Conway Scenic Railroad** ★★ (© 800/232-5251 or 603/356-5251; www.conwayscenic.com) offers mountain excursions in comfortable rail cars (including a dome car) pulled by either steam or early diesel engines. Trips depart from a distinctive 1874 train station, off the village green. The 1-hour excursion heads south to Conway; you're better off signing up for the more picturesque 1¾-hour trip northward to the village of Bartlett. For the best show, select the 5½-hour excursion through dramatic Crawford Notch, with stupendous views of the mountains from high along this beautiful glacial valley. Ask also about the railway's dining excursions.

The train runs from mid-April to mid-December, with more frequent trips scheduled daily in midsummer. Coach and first-class fares are available; first-class passengers sit in an 1898 parlor car with wicker and rattan chairs, mahogany woodwork, and an observation platform. Tickets are $10 to $21 for adults ($36–$56 for the Crawford Notch trip), $7.50 to $15 for children ages 4 to 12 ($20–$34 for Crawford Notch). Kids under 4 ride free in coach on the two shorter trips, but there's a charge of $6 to $24 for toddlers who take the Crawford Notch trip. Reservations are accepted for the dining car and the Crawford Notch train.

SHOPPING

North Conway was one of northern New England's first major outlet centers. As many as 200 shops are located along the strip, which extends about 3 miles northward from the junction of Route 302 and Route 16 in Conway into the village of North Conway itself. The keystone is **Settlers' Green Outlet Village Plus** (℮ **603/356-7031;** www.settlersgreen.com), with more than 50 shops, including J. Crew, Harry & David, Nike, Levi's, and Orvis.

Nearby is the popular **L.L.Bean** (℮ **603/356-2100**) factory outlet at the Tanger Outlet Center (one of three Tanger centers in North Conway), located just north of Settler's Green. Next to L.L.Bean is **Chuck Roast** (℮ **800/533-1654**), a notable local manufacturer of fleece that's well worth a browse.

Also of note is **Yield House** (℮ **800/659-2211** or 603/447-8500), the nationally known manufacturer of colonial reproduction furniture. The showroom and discount warehouse is on Route 3 (at Hobbs St.) at the south end of the strip, where it merges with Route 302. You can find some excellent discounts in the warehouse next to the main showroom.

Three good outdoor equipment suppliers are in and around North Conway. **International Mountain Equipment** (℮ **603/356-7013**) and **Eastern Mountain Sports** (℮ **603/356-5433**) are on Main Street, north of the green. My favorite for its selection and friendly staff is **Ragged Mountain Equipment** (℮ **603/356-3042**), 3 miles north of town in Intervale on Routes 16 and 302.

DOWNHILL SKIING

Cranmore Mountain Resort ☆ *Value*   Mount Cranmore is the oldest operating ski area in New England. The slopes are unrepentantly old-fashioned, but the mountain has restyled itself as a snow-sports mecca—look for snow tubing, snow-scooters, and ski-bikes. The slopes aren't likely to challenge advanced skiers, but the resort will delight beginners and intermediates, as well as those who like a little diversion with the ski toys. It's highly recommended for families, thanks to the relaxed attitude, range of activities, and budget ticket prices ($15 for kids 6–12).

North Conway Village, NH 03860. ℮ **603/356-5544.** www.cranmore.com. Vertical drop: 1,200 ft. Lifts: 10. Skiable acreage: 192. Lift tickets: $35.

WHERE TO STAY

Route 16 through North Conway is packed with basic motels, reasonably priced in the off season (around $40–$50), but more expensive in peak travel times such as summer and ski-season weekends and fall foliage season. Fronting the commercial strip, these motels don't offer much in the way of a pastoral environment, but most are comfortable and conveniently located. Try the budget **School House Motel** (℮ **603/356-6829**), with a heated outdoor pool; **The Yankee Clipper Motor Lodge** (℮ **800/343-5900** or 603/356-5736), with a pool and miniature golf (the cheaper rooms lack phones); or the slightly pricier **Green Granite Inn** (℮ **800/468-3666** or 603/356-6901), with 88 rooms, suites with whirlpool, and a free continental breakfast.

Briarcliff Motel   Among North Conway's dozens of roadside motels, the Briarcliff is one of the better options. A basic U-shaped motel with standard-size rooms, all units have recently been redecorated in rich colors, more like B&B rooms. A $10 premium is necessary for a room with a "porch" and mountain view, but these are a little peculiar—the porches are really part of a long enclosed sitting area with each unit separated from its neighbor by cubicle-height partitions. (Save your money.) Get over the traffic noise and the nagging signs, and the Briarcliff offers decent value.

Rte. 16 (½ mile south of village center, P.O. Box 504), North Conway, NH 03860. © **800/338-4291** or 603/356-5584. www.briarcliffmotel.com. 30 units. Summer and fall $59–$156 double; off season $59–$112. 2-night minimum stay holidays and foliage season. AE, DISC, MC, V. **Amenities:** Outdoor pool. *In room:* A/C, TV, fridge.

The Buttonwood Inn ★★   Just a couple minutes' drive from the outlets and restaurants, the Buttonwood has more of a classic country-inn feel than any other North Conway inn. It's set on 17 quiet acres on the side of Mount Surprise in an 1820s-era home, and has a tastefully appointed interior inspired by the Shaker style. Most guest rooms tend toward the small and cozy, but two common rooms (one with TV) allow guests plenty of space to unwind. Two units have gas fireplaces, and one has a large Jacuzzi as well. The hosts are uncommonly helpful with the planning of day trips, no matter your interests. Breakfasts tend toward the country-elegant: think cornmeal waffles with strawberry-rhubarb sauce.

Mt. Surprise Rd., North Conway, NH 03860. © **800/258-2625** or 603/356-2625. Fax 603/356-3140. www.buttonwoodinn.com. 10 units (2 with detached private bathroom). Peak season $115–$235 double; off season $95–$175. Rates include breakfast. AE, DISC, MC, V. 2- to 3-night minimum stay on weekends and holidays. Closed Apr. Children 6 and older are welcome. **Amenities:** Outdoor pool; cross-country ski trails. *In room:* A/C, dataport.

Comfort Inn & Suites ★ (Kids)   This tidy chain hotel features all "suites" (mostly large single rooms, actually) spread among three stories, giving travelers a bit more elbow room than most area motels. It's a good choice for families: close to outlet shopping and with its own elaborate pirate-themed miniature golf course on the property (slight discount for hotel guests). Four executive suites have separate sitting areas; two rooms have gas fireplaces.

2001 White Mountain Hwy. (Rte. 16), North Conway, NH 03860. © **800/228-5150** or 603/356-8811. Fax 603/356-7770. 58 units. $99–$199 double; executive suites to $249. Rates include continental breakfast. AE, DISC, MC, V. **Amenities:** Indoor pool; fitness room. *In room:* A/C, TV, dataport, fridge, coffeemaker, hair dryer, iron.

Cranmore Inn ★   The Cranmore Inn has the feel of a 19th-century boardinghouse—which is appropriate, as that's what it is. Open since 1863, this three-story Victorian home is a short walk from North Conway's village center. Its heritage—it's the oldest continuously operating hotel in North Conway—adds charm and quirkiness, but comes with drawbacks, such as sometimes uneven water pressure in the showers. That said, it offers good value thanks to its handy location and the hospitality of the innkeepers.

80 Kearsarge St., North Conway, NH 03860. © 603/356-5502. www.cranmoreinn.com. 21 units (includes 3 kitchen units with private bathroom). $74–$99 double, $99–$119 kitchen unit; foliage season and ski weekends $89–$119 double, $139–$159 kitchen unit; off season $59–$79 double, $99–$119 kitchen unit. Rates include breakfast except in kitchen units. AE, DISC, MC, V. 2-night minimum stay weekends, holidays, foliage season. **Amenities:** Outdoor pool.

The Forest Country Inn ★   Just 10 minutes north of North Conway is a spur road that leads through the village of Intervale, which has several lodges and a feeling removed from the clutter of the outlet shops. The Forest Country Inn was built in 1850, with a mansard-roofed third floor added in 1890. Typical for the era, the rooms are more cozy than spacious, and today are decorated mostly with reproductions and some country Victorian antiques. The best units are the two in the nearby stone cottage; ask for the Cottle Room, with its wood-burning fireplace, wing chairs, and small porch with Adirondack chairs.

Rte. 16A (P.O. Box 37), Intervale, NH 03845. © **877/854-6535** or 603/356-9772. Fax 603/356-5652. www. forest-inn.com. 11 units. $75–$170 double. AE, DISC, MC, V. Rates include breakfast. 2-night minimum stay most weekends and holidays. Closed Apr. Children 6 and older welcome. **Amenities:** Outdoor pool. *In room:* A/C.

North Conway Grand ⋆ If you're looking for convenience, amenities, and easy access to outlet shopping, this former Sheraton is your best bet. Built on the site of North Conway's former airfield, the Grand is a four-story, gabled hotel adjacent (and architecturally similar) to Outlet Village Plus, one of the outlet centers based in North Conway. The Grand offers clean, comfortable, basic hotel rooms with the usual chain hotel amenities, and a brick-terraced indoor pool.

Rte. 16 at Settler's Green (P.O. Box 3189), North Conway, NH 03860. © **800/648-4397** or 603/356-9300. 200 units. Summer $99–$229 double; off season $69–$199. AE, DC, DISC, MC, V. **Amenities:** Restaurant (American and tavern fare); indoor pool; outdoor pool; tennis court; fitness room; Jacuzzi; executive rooms. *In room:* A/C, TV w/pay movies, dataport (some), fridge, coffeemaker (some), hair dryer, iron.

Stonehurst Manor ⋆ This imposing, architecturally eclectic Victorian stone-and-shingle mansion, originally built for the family that owned Bigelow carpet, is set amid white pines on a rocky knoll above Route 16, 1 mile north of North Conway. It wouldn't seem at all out of place in either the south of France or the moors of Scotland. One's immediate assumption is that it caters to the stuffy and affluent, but the main focus here is on outdoor adventures, and it attracts a youngish crowd. Request one of the 14 rooms in the regal 1876 mansion (another 10 are in a comfortable but less elegant wing built in 1952).

Rte. 16 (1¼ miles north of North Conway Village; P.O. Box 1937), North Conway, NH 03860. © **800/525-9100** or 603/356-3113. Fax 603/356-3217. www.stonehurstmanor.com. 24 units (2 with shared bathroom). $90–$170 double; $116–$196 double with breakfast and dinner included. Fuel and energy surcharge in winter; $20 surcharge weekends; $20–$30 surcharge foliage season. MC, V. 2-night minimum stay on weekends. Pets allowed in some rooms ($25/pet per night). **Amenities:** Restaurant (wood-fired pizza/eclectic); outdoor pool; tennis court; Jacuzzi. *In room:* A/C, TV, Jacuzzi (some), no phone.

White Mountain Hotel and Resort ⋆⋆ This contemporary resort has the best location of any hotel close to North Conway. Sited at the base of dramatic White Horse Ledge near Echo Lake State Park amid a contemporary golf-course community, the White Mountain Hotel was built in 1990, but its style borrows from classic area resorts. Its designers have managed to take some of the more successful elements of a friendly country inn—a nice deck with a view, comfortable seating in the lobby, a clubby tavern area—and incorporate them into a thoroughly modern resort. The comfortably appointed guest rooms are a solid notch or two above standard hotel furnishings.

West Side Rd. (5½ miles west of North Conway; P.O. Box 1828), North Conway, NH 03860. © **800/533-6301** or 603/356-7100. Fax 603/356-7100. www.whitemountainhotel.com. 80 units. $89–$199 double; $119–$249 suite. AE, DISC, MC, V. 2-night minimum stay on weekends. **Amenities:** Dining room (Continental/regional); tavern; outdoor pool; golf course; 2 tennis courts; fitness center; Jacuzzi; sauna; limited room service; babysitting; laundry service; dry cleaning. *In room:* A/C, TV, dataport, coffeemaker, hair dryer, iron.

WHERE TO DINE

If you want more refined dining, you're best off heading for the Inn at Thorn Hill in Jackson, about 10 minutes north (see below).

Bellini's ⚡SOUTHERN ITALIAN Bellini's has a fun, quirky interior that's more informal than its Victorian exterior might suggest. It's run by the third generation of the Marcello family, who opened their first place in Rhode Island in 1927. The food runs the gamut from fettuccine chicken pesto to *braciola*, and most everything is homemade—soups, breads, pastas, and desserts. Particularly good are the toasted ravioli appetizers.

33 Seavey St., North Conway. © 603/356-7000. Reservations not accepted. Main courses $12–$22. AE, DISC, MC, V. Sun and Wed–Thurs 5–10pm; Fri–Sat 5–11pm.

Chinook Café ⚡ECLECTIC The Chinook Café opened in 1998 in Conway (a 10-min. drive south of North Conway) as a small, mostly takeout place, but its popularity led it to move down the street and expand. You'll find healthy fare for breakfast and lunch, with a good selection of vegetarian items. The chicken wraps are delicious (try Thai style with peanut sauce), the smoothies nicely sippable while driving, and the homemade baked goods a fitting conclusion to a hike. The more upscale dinners, served with fresh-baked bread and the "daily grain," could include baked salmon filet, lamb tenderloin, maple-smoked duck breast, or seared sea scallops with braised leeks and toasted pecans.

80 Main St. (across from fire station), Conway. © 603/447-6300. Main courses, breakfast $1.75–$3.75, lunch $4.85–$6.25, dinner $12–$18. MC, V. Mon–Tues 8am–4pm; Wed–Sat 8am–9:30pm.

Horsefeathers PUB FARE In a town where pub food is the rule, Horsefeathers has been leading the pack since 1976. Set in the village, across from the train station, this local hangout is often loud and boisterous, filled with everyone from families to off-duty bartenders. The fare is hard to pin down, ranging from tortilla soup to eggplant ravioli with a red pepper cream sauce, but tends to gather strength in the middle, with burgers, chicken wings, grilled steaks, and the like. The apple-smoked bacon cheddar burger is a good choice, as is the smoked chicken ravioli.

Main St., North Conway. © 603/356-6862. www.horsefeathers.com. Reservations not accepted. Main courses $6.95–$18. AE, MC, V. Daily 11:30am–11:45pm.

Moat Mountain Smoke House and Brewing Co. ⚡BARBECUE/PUB FARE Moat Mountain is the place for fresh beer, smoked meat, and wood-fired pizza. It's casual and relaxed, and has a more intriguing variety of eats than other North Conway beer joints. You can choose from a selection of barbecued meats; several other dishes feature smoked trout and salmon. Other options include burgers, quesadillas, and wraps. A dozen beers are on tap, including six house-brewed. There's also a children's menu.

3378 White Mountain Hwy. (Rte. 16), North Conway (about 1 mile north of the village). © 603/356-6381. www.moatmountain.com. Reservations not accepted. Main courses $12–$24. AE, MC, V. Daily 11:30am–9pm (until 10pm Fri–Sat).

Shalimar of India ⚡NORTHERN INDIAN Shalimar is a pleasant surprise in a town where adventurous ethnic cuisine once meant "nachos fully loaded." Shalimar offers a wide variety of tasty, tangy dishes of northern India. The meals are well prepared, and the chef is very accommodating in ensuring just the right spice level for your palate. The restaurant, a short walk from the village green, offers several tandoori dishes and a wonderfully tangy lamb vindaloo.

27 Seavey St., North Conway. © 603/356-0123. www.shalimarofindia.com. Reservations recommended in peak summer and winter seasons. Main courses, lunch $5.95–$7.25, dinner $11–$13. DISC, MC, V. Mon 5–9:30pm; Tues–Fri 11am–2:30pm and 5–9:30pm; Sat and Sun noon–3pm and 5–9:30pm.

JACKSON & ENVIRONS ⋆⋆

Jackson is a quiet village in a picturesque valley off Route 16 about 15 minutes north of North Conway. The village center, approached on a single-lane covered bridge, is tiny, but touches of old-world elegance remain—vestiges of a time when Jackson was a favored destination for the East Coast upper middle class, who fled the summer heat to relax at rambling wooden hotels or country homes.

With the Depression and the rise of the motel trade in the 1940s and 1950s, Jackson and its old-fashioned hostelries slipped into a lasting slumber. Then along came the 1980s, which brought condo projects sprouting in fields where cows once roamed, vacation homes flanking the hills, and the resuscitation of the two vintage wooden hotels that didn't burn or collapse during the dark ages.

Thanks to a revamped golf course and one of the most elaborate and well-maintained cross-country ski networks in the country, Jackson is again a thriving resort in summer and winter. While no longer undiscovered, it still feels a shade out of the mainstream and is a peaceful spot, especially when compared to commercial North Conway.

ESSENTIALS

GETTING THERE   Jackson is just off Route 16, about 11 miles north of North Conway. Heading north, look for the covered bridge on the right.

VISITOR INFORMATION   The **Jackson Chamber of Commerce** (*(C)* **800/ 866-3334** or 603/383-9356; www.jacksonnh.com), based in offices at the Jackson Falls Marketplace, can answer questions about area attractions and make lodging reservations.

ASCENDING MOUNT WASHINGTON

Mount Washington, just north of Jackson amid the national forest, is home to numerous superlatives. At 6,288 feet, it's the highest mountain in the Northeast. It's said to have the worst weather in the world outside of the polar regions. It holds the world's record for the highest surface wind speed ever recorded—231 miles per hour in 1934. Winds over 150 miles per hour are routinely recorded every month except June, July, and August, in part the result of the mountain's location at the confluence of three major storm tracks.

Mount Washington may also be the mountain with the most options for getting to the summit. Visitors can ascend by cog railroad (see the "Crawford Notch" section, later in this chapter), by car, by guide-driven van, or on foot.

Despite the raw power of the weather, Mount Washington's summit is not the best destination for those seeking wilderness wild and untamed. The summit is home to a train platform, a parking lot, a snack bar, a gift shop, a museum, and a handful of outbuildings, some of which house the weather observatory, which is staffed year-round. And there are the crowds, which can be thick on a clear day. Then again, on a clear day the views can't be beat, with vistas extending into four states and to the Atlantic Ocean.

The best place to learn about Mount Washington and its approaches is rustic **Pinkham Notch Visitor Center** (*(C)* **603/466-2721**), operated by the Appalachian Mountain Club. At the crest of Route 16 between Jackson and Gorham, the center offers overnight accommodations and meals (see below), maps, a limited selection of outdoor supplies, and plenty of advice from the helpful staff. A number of hiking trails also depart from here, offering several loops and side trips: About a dozen trails in all lead to the mountain's summit, ranging in length from about 4 to 15 miles. (Detailed information is available at the visitor center.) The most direct and dramatic is the **Tuckerman Ravine Trail** 𝆏𝆏𝆏, which departs from Pinkham Notch. It's a full day's endeavor: Healthy hikers should allow 4 to 5 hours for the ascent, an hour or two less for the return trip. Be sure to allow enough time to enjoy the dramatic glacial cirque of Tuckerman Ravine, which attracts extreme skiers to its snowy chutes and sheer drops as late as June, and often holds patches of snow well into summer.

The **Mount Washington Auto Road** 𝆏𝆏 (𝄐 603/466-3988; www.mount washingtonautoroad.com) opened in 1861 as a carriage road and has since remained one of the most popular White Mountain attractions. The steep, winding 8-mile road (with an average grade of 12%) is partially paved and incredibly dramatic; your breath will be taken away at one curve after another. The ascent will test your iron will; the descent will test your car's brakes. The trip's not worth doing if the summit is in the clouds; wait for a clear day.

If you'd prefer to leave the driving to someone else, van tours ascend throughout the day, enabling you to relax, enjoy the views, and learn about the mountain from informed guides. The cost is $24 for adults, $22 for seniors, and $10 for children 5 to 12, and includes a half-hour stay on the summit.

The Auto Road, on Route 16 north of Pinkham Notch, is open from mid-May to late October from 7:30am to 6pm (limited hours early and late in the season). The cost for cars is $18 for vehicle and driver, $7 for each additional adult ($4 for children 5 to 12), and $10 for a motorcycle and its operator. The fee includes audiocassette narration pointing out sights along the way (available in English, French, and German). Management has imposed some curious restrictions on cars; for example, Acuras and Jaguars with automatic transmissions must show a "1" on the shifter to be allowed on the road, and no Lincoln Continentals from before 1969 are permitted.

One additional note: The average temperature atop the mountain is 30°F (1°C). (The record low was -43°F [-6°C], and the warmest temperature ever recorded atop the mountain, in August, was 72°F [22°C].) Even in summer, visitors should come prepared for blustery, cold conditions.

EXPLORING PINKHAM NOTCH 𝆏𝆏𝆏

The Pinkham Notch Visitor Center is at the height of land on Route 16. Just south, look for signs for **Glen Ellis Falls** 𝆏𝆏, a worthwhile 10- to 15-minute stop. From the parking area, you'll pass through a pedestrian tunnel and walk along the Glen Ellis River for a few minutes until it seemingly falls off the face of the earth. The stream plummets 64 feet down a cliff; observation platforms are at the top and near the bottom of the falls, one of the region's most impressive after a torrential rain. From the parking lot to the base of the falls is less than a half mile.

From the visitor center, it's about 2½ miles up to **Hermit Lake and Tuckerman Ravine** 𝆏𝆏𝆏 via the Tuckerman Ravine Trail (see above). Even if you're not planning to continue on to the summit, the ravine, with its sheer sides and lacey cataracts, may be the most dramatic destination in the White Mountains. It's well worth the 2-hour ascent in all but the most miserable weather. The trail is wide and only moderately demanding. Bring a picnic and lunch on the massive boulders strewn about the ravine's floor.

In summer, an **enclosed gondola** 𝆏 at Wildcat ski area (see below) hauls passengers up the mountain for a view of Tuckerman Ravine and Mount Washington's summit. The lift operates Saturday and Sunday from Memorial Day to mid-June, then daily through October. The base lodge is just north of Pinkham Notch on Route 16.

DOWNHILL SKIING

Black Mountain ⭐ Dating back to the 1930s, Black Mountain is one of the White Mountains' pioneer ski areas. It remains the quintessential family mountain—modest in size, thoroughly non-threatening, ideal for beginners—although there's also glade skiing for more advanced skiers. A day here feels a bit as though you're trespassing onto a farmer's unused hayfield, which adds to the charm. The ski area also offers two compact terrain parks for snowboarders, as well as lessons, rentals, a nursery, and a base lodge with cafeteria and pub.

Jackson, NH 03846. © 800/ISKINOW or 603/383-4490. www.blackmt.com. Vertical drop: 1,100 ft. Lifts: 2 chairlifts, 2 surface lifts. Skiable acreage: 143. Lift tickets: $20 Mon–Fri; $32 Sat–Sun.

Wildcat ⭐⭐ Set high within Pinkham Notch, Wildcat Mountain has a rich heritage as a venerable New England ski mountain, with the best views of any ski area in the White Mountains. Wildcat has a bountiful supply of intermediate trails, as well as some challenging expert terrain. This is skiing as it used to be—no base area clutter, just a lodge. While that also means no on-slope accommodations, an abundance of options are within a 15-minute drive. Skiers can save a few dollars by purchasing advance tickets online.

Rte. 16, Pinkham Notch, NH 03846. © 888/SKI-WILD or 603/466-3326. www.skiwildcat.com. Vertical drop: 2,100 ft. Lifts: 4 chairlifts (1 high-speed lift). Skiable acreage: 225. Lift tickets: Mon–Fri $42 adults; Sat–Sun and holidays $52 adults.

CROSS-COUNTRY SKIING

Jackson regularly ranks among the top five cross-country ski resorts in the nation. The reason is the nonprofit **Jackson Ski Touring Foundation** ⭐⭐⭐ (© 800/XC-SNOWS or 603/383-9355; www.jacksonxc.com), which created and now maintains the extensive trail network of 93 miles (55 miles of which are regularly groomed). The terrain is wonderfully varied; many of the trails are rated "most difficult," which will keep advanced skiers from getting bored. Novice and intermediate skiers have good options spread out along the valley floor.

Start at the base lodge near the Wentworth Resort in the center of Jackson. There's parking, and you can ski through the village and into the hills. Gentle trails traverse the valley floor, with more advanced trails winding up the mountains. One-way ski trips with shuttles back to Jackson are available; ask if you're interested. Given how extensive and well maintained the trails are, passes are a good value at $14 for adults, $12 for seniors, $7 for children 10 to 15, children under 10 are free.. Rentals are available in the ski center. Ticket/rental packages are available, as are snowshoe rentals and trails specifically for snowshoers.

ESPECIALLY FOR KIDS

Parents with young children (10 and under) can buy peace of mind at **Story-Land** ⭐⭐, situated at the northern junction of Routes 16 and 302 (© **603/383-4186;** www.storylandnh.com). This old-fashioned (around 1954) fantasy village is filled with 30 acres of improbably leaning buildings, magical rides, fairy-tale creatures, and other enchanted beings. A "sprayground" features a 40-foot water-spurting octopus—if so inclined, kids can get a good summer soaking. StoryLand is open from Memorial Day to mid-June, Saturday and Sunday only from 10am to 5pm; from mid-June to Labor Day, daily from 9am to 6pm; and from Labor Day to Columbus Day, Saturday and Sunday only from 10am to 5pm. Admission is a flat $20 for all visitors 4 and older, $15 from Memorial Day to mid-June.

WHERE TO STAY

Covered Bridge Motor Lodge ★ *Value*   This pleasant, family-run motel, on 5 acres between Route 16 and the burbling river, is next to Jackson's covered bridge. Rooms are priced well for this area. The best units have balconies that overlook the river; the noisier rooms facing the road are a bit cheaper. Ask about the two-bedroom apartment units with kitchen and fireplace. While basic, the lodge features gardens and other appealing touches that make this a good value.

Rte. 16, Jackson, NH 03846. © 800/634-2911 or 602/383-9151. www.jacksoncoveredbridge.com. 32 units (includes 6 apartment suites). $79–$139 double, $109–$229 suite. Rates include continental breakfast. AE, DISC, MC, V. **Amenities:** Outdoor pool; tennis court; Jacuzzi. *In room:* A/C, TV.

Eagle Mountain House ★★   The Eagle Mountain House is a handsome relic that happily survived the ravages of time, fire, and the capricious tastes of tourists. Built in 1916, this five-story gleaming white wooden classic is set in an idyllic valley above Jackson. The guest rooms are furnished in a country pine look with stenciled blanket chests, armoires, and feather comforters. You'll pay a premium for rooms with mountain views, but it's not really worth the extra cash. Just plan to spend your free time lounging on the wide porch with the views across the golf course toward the mountains beyond.

Carter Notch Rd., Jackson, NH 03846. © 800/966-5779 or 603/383-9111. Fax 603/383-0854. www.eaglemt. com. 96 units. Summer, fall, and Christmas $89–$169 double, $109–$199 suite; winter and spring $69–$129 double, $79–$159 suite. Ask about packages. AE, DISC, MC, V. **Amenities:** Dining room (New England); tavern; outdoor pool; golf course; 2 tennis courts; health club; Jacuzzi; sauna; massage, dry cleaning. *In room:* TV.

Inn at Thorn Hill ★★★   This elegant inn is a great choice for a romantic getaway. The classic shingle-style home (now swathed in yellow siding) was designed by Stanford White in 1895, and sits just outside the village center surrounded by wooded hills. Inside is a comfortable Victorian feel. Rooms are luxuriously appointed; you'll rarely want to leave. My favorites include Catherine's Suite, with a fireplace and two-person Jacuzzi, and Notch View Cottage, with a screened porch and a Jacuzzi with a view of the forest. The hospitality is warm and top-notch, and the meals are among the best in the Mount Washington Valley.

Thorn Hill Rd. (P.O. Box A), Jackson, NH 03846. © 603/383-4242. www.innatthornhill.com. 19 units. Main inn: $190–$300 double; foliage season, Christmas, and Valentine's $240–$340. Carriage house: $125–$190 double; foliage season, Christmas, and Valentine's $175–$240. Cottages: $250–$290; foliage season, Christmas, and Valentine's $300–$340. Rates include breakfast and dinner. 2- to 3-night minimum stay on weekends and some holidays. AE, DISC, MC, V. Children 8 and older welcome. **Amenities:** Restaurant (see below); outdoor pool; Jacuzzi; limited room service; babysitting; laundry service. *In room:* A/C, TV.

Joe Dodge Lodge at Pinkham Notch   Guests come to the Pinkham Notch Visitor Center more for the camaraderie than the accommodations. Situated spectacularly at the base of Mount Washington, far from commercial clutter and with easy access to many hiking and skiing trails, the center is operated by the Appalachian Mountain Club like a tightly run youth hostel, with guests sharing spartan bunk rooms, dorm-style bathrooms, and meals at family-style tables in the main lodge. (Some private rooms offer double beds or family accommodations.) The pluses: a festive atmosphere and a can't-be-beat location.

Rte. 16, Pinkham Notch, NH. (Mailing address: AMC, P.O. Box 298, Gorham, NH 03581.) © 603/466-2727. www.outdoors.org. 108 beds in bunkrooms of 2, 3, and 4 beds (all with shared bathroom). $74 double. Bunkrooms: peak season $55 per adult, $37 per child 15 and under (discount for AMC members); off season $52 per adult, $35 per child. Rates include breakfast and dinner. MC, V. Children 3 and older welcome. **Amenities:** Cafeteria; weekend activities. *In room:* No phone.

⌒ *Value* **Gorham: Budget Beds, Low-Cost Lunches**

White Mountain travelers on a lean budget would do well to look at **Gorham** as a base for mountain explorations. This tidy commercial town 10 minutes north of Pinkham Notch lacks charm, but has a great selection of clean mom-and-pop motels and family-style restaurants. After all, if you're planning to spend your days hiking or canoeing, where you rest your head at night won't much matter.

The top motel choice is the **Royalty Inn,** 130 Main St. (🕿 **800/437-3529** or 603/466-3312; www.royaltyinn.com), which has a restaurant, larger-than-average, if plain, rooms, two pools, and a large fitness club; rates for a double are $70 to $82 in summer. **Top Notch Inn,** 265 Main St. (🕿 **800/228-5496** or 603/466-5496), has an outdoor pool and hot tub and in-room fridges. Rates start at $69 for a double; small pets are accepted.

For basic family dining, **Wilfred's,** 117 Main St. (🕿 **603/466-2380**), serves steaks, chops, and a variety of seafood. For healthier fare, try the **Loaf Around Bakery,** 19 Exchange St. (🕿 **603/466-2706**), open for breakfast and lunch (a visit to the antique bathroom is mandatory). **Libby's Bistro,** at 115 Main Street (🕿 **603/466-5330**), is located in a handsomely renovated bank and serves dinners better than any in North Conway.

Moriah Sports, 101 Main St. (🕿 **603/466-5050**), sells a wide range of sporting equipment (bikes, cross-country skis, rain gear) and is a good stop for suggestions on area activities.

Wentworth Resort Hotel ⭐⭐ The venerable Wentworth sits in the middle of Jackson Village, all turrets, eaves, and awnings. Built in 1869, this Victorian shingled inn once had 39 buildings (including a dairy and electric plant) but edged to the brink of deterioration in the mid-1980s. The seven remaining buildings were refurbished and added to with a number of condominium clusters around the expanded and upgraded golf course. The inn upgraded again recently, and the owner and chef were both formerly with the respected Four Seasons hotel group. The large standard and superior double rooms are decorated with Victorian-inspired furnishings. Suites (all with king beds) add such amenities as propane fireplaces, whirlpools, outdoor hot tubs, and claw-foot tubs. Those of stouter constitution can stroll up the road and plunge into the waters of Jackson Falls.

Jackson, NH 03846. 🕿 **800/637-0013** or 603/383-9700. Fax 603/383-4265. www.thewentworth.com. 76 units. $175–$305 double and suite. Rates include full breakfast and 5-course dinner. Higher rates during foliage season and Christmas week. AE, DC, DISC, MC, V. **Amenities:** Restaurant (New England); outdoor pool; golf course; tennis court; cross-country ski center. *In room:* A/C, TV, Jacuzzi (some).

Wildcat Inn & Tavern ⭐ The Wildcat Inn occupies a three-story farmhouse-style building in the middle of Jackson. A comfortable, informal place better known for its cozy restaurant and tavern than for its accommodations, most guest rooms are small two-room suites, carpeted and furnished with a mish-mash of furniture. Sitting rooms typically contain contemporary sofas, chairs, and pine furniture, and offer cozy sanctuary after a day of hiking or skiing. The downstairs dining room resembles a traditional country farmhouse, with old wood floors and pine furniture. In the winter, stake out a toasty spot in front of the tavern fireplace—one of the most popular gathering spots in the valley—to sip soothing libations and order from the bar menu.

Rte. 16A, Jackson, NH 03846. ℂ **800/228-4245** or 603/383-4245. www.wildcattavern.com. 14 units (2 with shared bathroom). $89–$119 double, suites to $129. Rates include breakfast. $10 surcharge during foliage season. AE, DC, MC, V. *In room:* A/C, TV.

WHERE TO DINE

Inn at Thorn Hill ★★★ NEW AMERICAN   The romantic Inn at Thorn Hill is a great choice for a memorable meal. The candlelit dining room faces the forested hill behind the inn. Start with a glass of wine (the restaurant has won the *Wine Spectator* award of excellence), then browse the menu selections, which change weekly but often feature Asian accents. Appetizers may include Nigerian prawn pad Thai, a lobster vichyssoise, bacon-wrapped scallops over truffled polenta, or coconut-steamed mussels. Entrees feature options such as lobster and scallop risotto in lobster cream with wasabi caviar, sake-marinated Halibut over crispy noodles, lamb loin poached in olive oil, or Peking duck. If quail or pheasant's on the menu, it's a great choice.

Thorn Hill Rd., Jackson. ℂ **603/383-4242.** www.innatthornhill.com. Reservations recommended. Main courses $23–$30. AE, DISC, MC, V. Daily 6–9pm.

Thompson House Eatery ★★ ECLECTIC   This friendly, old-fashioned spot in a 19th-century farmhouse at the edge of Jackson's golf course attracts crowds not only for its well-prepared fare but also for its reasonable prices. Dining is indoors and out, with lunches including six different salads (the curried chicken and toasted almonds is great), knockwurst, frittatas, and basic sandwiches (tuna, grilled cheese). Dinner offers fresh fish, steak, and several vegetarian entrees. Thompson House has an adjacent ice-cream parlor that's worth a stop.

Rte. 16A, Jackson (near north intersection with Rte. 16). ℂ **603/383-9341.** Reservations recommended for dinner. Main courses lunch $4.95–$7.95; dinner $6.95–$19. AE, DISC, MC, V. Sun–Mon 5:30–9pm; Wed–Thurs 11:30am–3:30pm and 5:30–9pm; Fri–Sat 11:30am–3:30pm and 5:30–10pm.

CRAWFORD NOTCH ★★★

Crawford Notch is a wild, rugged mountain valley that angles through the heart of the White Mountains. Within the notch itself is a surplus of legend and history. For years after its discovery by European settlers in 1771, it was an impenetrable wilderness, creating a barrier to commerce by blocking trade between the upper Connecticut River Valley and harbors in Portland and Portsmouth. This was eventually surmounted by a plucky crew who hauled the first freight through.

The notch is accessible via Route 302, which is wide and speedy on the lower sections, becoming steeper as it approaches the narrow defile of the notch itself. Stop from time to time to enjoy the panoramas. The views up the cliffs from the road can be spectacular on a clear day; on a drizzly day, the effect is nicely foreboding.

ESSENTIALS

GETTING THERE   Route 302 runs through Crawford Notch for approximately 25 miles between the towns of Bartlett and Twin Mountain.

VISITOR INFORMATION   The **Twin Mountain Chamber of Commerce** (ℂ **800/245-8946** or 603/846-5520; www.twinmountain.org) offers general information and lodging referrals at its booth near the intersection of Routes 302 and 3. Open year-round; hours vary.

WATERFALLS & SWIMMING HOLES

Much of the mountainous land flanking Route 302 falls under the jurisdiction of **Crawford Notch State Park** ★★. The headwaters of the Saco River form in the notch, and what's generally regarded as the first permanent trail up Mount Washington also departs from here. Several turnouts and trailheads invite a more leisurely exploration of the area. The trail network on both sides of Crawford Notch is extensive; consult the *AMC White Mountain Guide* or *White Mountains Map Book* for detailed information.

Up the mountain slopes that form the valley, hikers will spot a number of lovely waterfalls, some more easily accessible than others.

Arethusa Falls ★★ has the highest single drop of any waterfall in the state, and the trail to the falls passes several attractive smaller cascades, especially beautiful in the spring or after a heavy rain, when the falls are at their fullest. The trip can be a 2.6-mile round-trip to the falls and back on Arethusa Falls Trail, or a 4.5-mile loop that includes views from Frankenstein Cliffs (named not after the creator of the monster, but after a noted landscape painter). If arriving from the south, look for signs to the trail parking area after passing the Crawford Notch State Park entrance sign. From the north, the trailhead is a half mile south of the Dry River Campground.

Continue north on Route 302 to the trailhead for tumultuous **Ripley Falls** ★. It's an easy walk. Look for the sign to the falls on Route 302 just north of the trailhead for Webster Cliff Trail. (If you pass the Willey House site, you've gone too far.) Park at the site of the Willey Station. Follow signs, allowing a half-hour to reach the cascades. The best swimming holes are at the top of the falls.

A HISTORIC RAILWAY

Mount Washington Cog Railway ★★   The cog railway was a marvel of engineering when it opened in 1869, and it remains so today. Part moving museum, part slow-motion roller-coaster ride, the cog railway steams to the summit with a determined "I think I can" pace of about 4 miles per hour. But you'll feel a bit of excitement on the way up and back, especially when the train crosses Jacob's Ladder, a rickety-seeming trestle 25 feet high that angles upward at a grade of more than 37%. Passengers enjoy the expanding view on the 3-hour round-trip. A 20-minute stop at the summit enables you to browse around. Be aware that the ride is noisy; also, dress warmly and expect to get a bit sooty.

Rte. 302, Bretton Woods. ✆ **800/922-8825** or 603/278-5404. www.thecog.com. Fare $49 adults, $45 seniors, $35 children 6–12, free for children 5 and under. MC, V. Runs daily Memorial Day to late Oct, plus weekends in May. Frequent departures; call for schedule. Reservations recommended.

DOWNHILL SKIING

Attitash Bear Peak ★★   Attitash Bear Peak is a good mountain for families and skiers at the intermediate-edging-to-advanced level; look for great cruising runs and a handful of more challenging drops. The ski area includes two peaks, 1,750-foot Attitash and the adjacent 1,450-foot Bear Peak, and is among New England's most scenic ski areas—dotted with rugged rock outcroppings, with sweeping views of Mount Washington and the Presidentials (an observation tower is on the main summit). The base area tends to be sleepy in the evenings; those looking for nightlife can head 15 minutes away to North Conway.

Rte. 302, Bartlett, NH 03812. (✆ **877/677-SNOW** or 603/374-2368. www.attitash.com. Vertical drop: 1,750 ft. Lifts: 12 chairlifts (including 2 high-speed quads), 3 surface lifts. Skiable acreage: 280. Lift tickets: $43–$49 adults, $19–$39 children 6–18.

Bretton Woods ⭐ Bretton Woods continues its expansion of lifts and expert glade skiing; the resort has also added Olympic medalist Bode Miller to its staff, tapping him as director of skiing. These newer trails and lifts and young blood bring a welcome vitality and edge to the mountain, which has long been popular with beginners and families. The trails include glades and wide cruising runs, along with more challenging options for advanced skiers. The resort continues to do a fine job with kids and offers a low-key attitude that families adore. Accommodations are available on the mountain and nearby, notably at the Mount Washington Hotel, but evening entertainment tends to revolve around hot tubs, TVs, and going to bed early. For those so inclined, there's also an excellent cross-country ski center located nearby.

Rte. 302, Bretton Woods, NH 03575. (✆ **800/258-3320** or 603/278-3307. www.brettonwoods.com. Vertical drop: 1,500 ft. Lifts: 8 chairlifts (including 2 high-speed quads), 2 surface lifts. Skiable acreage: 375. Lift tickets: $49 Mon–Fri; $57 Sat–Sun and holidays.

WHERE TO STAY & DINE

The Bernerhof ⭐ Overlooking busy Route 302 en route to Crawford Notch, The Bernerhof occupies a century-old home that's all gables and squared-off turrets on the outside. Inside, the guest rooms are eclectic and fun, crafted with odd angles and corners. All are tastefully furnished in a simple country style that's sparing with the frou-frou. Spacious Room 7 (a suite) is tucked under the eaves on the third floor and has a two-person Jacuzzi and in-room sauna. Room 8 (not a suite) is also romantic and appealing, with a Jacuzzi under a skylight, wood floors, a brass bed, and a handsome cherry armoire.

Rte. 302, Glen, NH 03838. (✆ **800/548-8007** or 603/383-9132. Fax 603/383-0809. www.bernerhofinn.com. 9 units. Midweek $79–$145 double; weekends $99–$179. Rates include breakfast. 2-night minimum stay peak season and weekends. AE, DISC, MC, V. **Amenities:** Restaurant (Middle European, regional); pub. *In room:* A/C, TV, hair dryer.

Mount Washington Hotel ⭐⭐ This five-story resort, with its gleaming white clapboards and cherry-red roof, was built in 1902. In its heyday, the resort attracted luminaries such as Babe Ruth, Thomas Edison, and Woodrow Wilson. Guest rooms vary in size and decor; many have grand views of the surrounding mountains and countryside. A 900-foot-long veranda makes for relaxing afternoons. Meals are enjoyed in an impressive octagonal dining room. (Men should wear jackets at dinner.) A house orchestra provides entertainment during the meal, and guests often dance between courses. The decor isn't lavish, and while the innkeepers are making overdue improvements, the hotel can feel a bit unfinished in parts. However, it remains a favorite spot in the mountains, partly for the sheer improbability of it all, and partly for its direct link to a lost era.

Rte. 302, Bretton Woods, NH 03575. (✆ **800/258-0330** or 603/278-1000. www.mtwashington.com. 200 units. $115–$455 double; $260–$850 suite. Rates include breakfast and dinner. Minimum stay during holidays. AE, DISC, MC, V. **Amenities:** 2 restaurants (Continental, pub fare); indoor pool; outdoor pool; 2 golf courses; 12 tennis courts; Jacuzzi; sauna; bike rental; children's programs (summer); concierge; shopping arcade; room service; babysitting. *In room:* TV.

Notchland Inn ⭐⭐ Located off Route 302 in a wild section of Crawford Notch, this inn looks every bit like a redoubt in a Sir Walter Scott novel. Built of hand-cut granite in the mid-1800s, Notchland is classy yet informal, perfectly situated for exploring the wilds of the White Mountains. Guest rooms are outfitted with antiques, wood-burning fireplaces, high ceilings, and individual thermostats. Three suites have Jacuzzis; two units are located in the adjacent schoolhouse, where the upstairs room has a wonderful soaking tub. (All but three rooms have air-conditioning.) The inn is also home to affable Bernese mountain dogs and llamas. You may want to add the five-course dinner to your plan ($30 per person). Not just good value, the closest restaurant is a long, dark drive away.

Rte. 302, Hart's Location, NH 03812. © 800/866-6131 or 603/374-6131. Fax 603/374-6168. www.notchland. com. 13 units. $185 double, $215–$245 suite; foliage season and holidays $235 double, $265–$295 suite. Rates include breakfast. 2- to 3-night minimum stay weekends, foliage season, and some holidays. AE, DISC, MC, V. Children 12 and older welcome. **Amenities:** Restaurant (global fare); Jacuzzi; babysitting. *In room:* Hair dryer, iron, no phone.

WATERVILLE VALLEY

In the southwestern corner of the White Mountains is Waterville Valley, occupies a lovely, remote valley at the head of a 12-mile dead-end road. The "village" is reasonably compact (though you need to drive or take a shuttle to the ski slopes): Modern lodges, condos, and a handful of restaurants are all located within a loop road. In the center is the "Town Square," itself a mall complex with a restaurant and a few shops. This is a reasonable choice for a weeklong family vacation—the resort is practiced at planning activities for kids—but those in search of the real New England won't miss a thing by skipping it.

ESSENTIALS

GETTING THERE Waterville Valley is located 12 miles northwest of Exit 28 or Exit 29 off I-93 via Route 49.

VISITOR INFORMATION **Waterville Valley Chamber of Commerce** (© 800/237-2307 or 603/726-3804; www.watervillevalleyregion.com) staffs a year-round information booth on Route 49 in Campton, just off Exit 28 of I-93.

DOWNHILL SKIING

Waterville Valley Waterville Valley is a classic intermediate skier's mountain. The trails are uniformly wide and well groomed, and the ski area is compact enough that no one will get confused and end up staring down a double-diamond trail. Improvements in recent years have made it a fine place to learn to ski or brush up on your skills. Advanced skiers have a selection of black-diamond trails, but the selection and steepness don't rival that of the larger ski mountains to the north. A new terrain park served by a Poma lift above the base lodge is popular with both advanced and beginning boarders. Recently, Waterville Valley bucked trends and lowered regular ticket prices by $10; whether this welcome change sticks beyond one season remains to be seen.

Waterville Valley, NH 03215. © 800/468-2553 or 603/236-8311. www.waterville.com. Vertical drop: 2,020 ft. Lifts: 11. Skiable acreage: 255. Lift tickets: Non-holiday (including most weekends) $39 adults; holiday $47 adults.

WHERE TO STAY

Guests in Waterville Valley pay a 15% resort tax (13% in winter) on hotel bills.

Golden Eagle Lodge This dominating, contemporary condominium project is centrally located in the village, and from the outside, the five-story shingle-and-stone edifice looks like one of the grand White Mountain resorts of the 19th century. Inside it's also regal in a cartoon-Tudor kind of way, with lots of stained wood, columns, and tall windows to let in the views. The hotel accommodates two to six people in each one- or two-bedroom unit, which have kitchens and basic cookware (very handy given the dearth of available eateries during crowded times). While outwardly grand, some of the furnishings and construction feel low budget, which compromises the experience somewhat.

6 Snow's Brook Rd., Waterville Valley, NH 03215. ✆ **888/703-2453** or 603/236-4600. Fax 603/236-4947. www.goldeneaglelodge.com. 118 units. Summer $103–$198; winter $103–$281; spring $88–$158. Resort fee of 13%–15%. Premium charged on holidays. Minimum stay on certain holidays. AE, DC, DISC, MC, V. **Amenities:** Indoor pool; outdoor pool; Jacuzzi; sauna; bike rental. *In room:* TV, dataport, coffeemaker.

Snowy Owl Inn ✪   The Snowy Owl will appeal to those who like the amiable character of a country inn but prefer modern conveniences such as in-room hair dryers. A modern, four-story resort project near Town Square, the inn offers a number of nice touches, such as a towering fieldstone fireplace in the lobby, a handsome octagonal indoor pool, and a rooftop observatory reached via spiral staircase. The rooms are a notch above basic motel-style units in size and decor; five feature kitchens.

Village Rd., Waterville Valley, NH 03215. ✆ **800/766-9969** or 603/236-8383. Fax 603/236-4890. www. snowyowlinn.com. 80 units. $89–$259 double; holidays $199–$309 double. Rates include continental breakfast. AE, DISC, MC, V. **Amenities:** Indoor pool; outdoor pool; Jacuzzi; sauna. *In room:* TV, dataport, hair dryer.

The Valley Inn   This inn is one of the smaller complexes in the valley, and thus somewhat more intimate than its neighbors. Most rooms feature a sitting area and tiny dining table in a bay window, as well as a wet bar; suites have kitchenettes. Conveniently located near the village center and in walking distance of the Athletic Club and Town Square, it offers a shuttle to the slopes in winter.

Tecumseh Rd. (P.O. Box 1), Waterville Valley, NH 03215. ✆ **800/343-0969** or 603/236-8336. Fax 603/236-4294. www.valleyinn.com. 52 units. Fall and summer $75–$158 double, $130–$218 suite; foliage season and Columbus Day weekend $88–$174 double, $146–$250 suite; off season $64–$136 double, $108–$185 suite. AE, DISC, MC, V. Minimum stay during certain holidays. **Amenities:** 2 restaurants (American and pub fare); indoor pool, outdoor pool; 2 tennis courts; Jacuzzi; sauna; game room; limited room service. *In room:* A/C, TV.

WHERE TO DINE

Waterville Valley's accommodations often include kitchens, so you can prepare your own meals. The village has a limited selection of restaurants; the Athletic Club has its own restaurant, the **Wild Coyote Grill** (✆ **603/236-4919**), which offers regional favorites such as potato-crusted salmon, seared tuna, and grilled steaks. Basic pub fare can be enjoyed in the **Red Fox Tavern** (✆ **603/236-8336**), in the basement of the Valley Inn.

LINCOLN, NORTH WOODSTOCK ✪ & LOON MOUNTAIN

Some 25 miles north of Waterville Valley are the towns of Lincoln and North Woodstock, as well as the Loon Mountain ski resort (just east of Lincoln). These towns are also the start (or end) of the Kancamagus Highway, a 35-mile route that's one of the White Mountains' most scenic drives.

Other towns of the White Mountains are much more distinct and interesting than these three, and you're better off pressing onward. Just don't miss the Kancamagus Highway, one of New England's most scenic drives.

ESSENTIALS

GETTING THERE   Lincoln is accessible off I-93 on exits 32 and 33.

VISITOR INFORMATION   The **Lincoln-Woodstock Chamber of Commerce** (✆ **603/745-6621;** www.lincolnwoodstock.com) has an information office open daily at Depot Plaza on Route 112 in Lincoln. A better, more comprehensive information source is the **White Mountains Visitor Center**

(© **800/346-3687** or 603/745-8720), located just east of Exit 32 on I-93. It's open year-round, daily from 9am to 5pm.

THE KANCAMAGUS HIGHWAY ★★★

The Kancamagus Highway—locally called "the Kanc"—is among the White Mountains' most spectacular drives. Officially designated a national scenic byway by the U.S. Forest Service, the 34-mile roadway joins Lincoln and Conway through the 2,860-foot Kancamagus Pass. When the highway was built in the early 1960s, it opened up 100 square miles of wilderness, irking wilderness advocates but very popular with folks who prefer their sightseeing by car.

The route begins and ends along wide, tumbling rivers on fairly flat plateaus. The two-lane road rises steadily to the pass. Several rest areas with sweeping vistas allow visitors to pause and enjoy mountain views. The highway also makes a good destination for hikers; any number of day and overnight trips may be launched from the roadside. One simple, short hike along a gravel path (less than ⅛ of a mile each way) leads to **Sabbaday Falls** ★★, a cascade that's especially impressive after a downpour. Six national forest campgrounds are also located along the highway.

To get the most out of the road, take your time and make frequent stops. Think of it as a scavenger hunt as you look for a covered bridge, cascades with good swimming holes, a historic home with a quirky story behind it, and spectacular mountain panoramas. All of these things and more lie along the route.

DOWNHILL SKIING

Loon Mountain ★   Located on U.S. Forest Service land, Loon had long been stymied in expansion efforts by environmental concerns regarding land use and water withdrawals from the river. The ski mountain has been slowly reshaped, adding uphill capacity, 15 acres of glade skiing, and improved snowmaking. The expansion has reduced some of the congestion of this popular area, but it's still very crowded on weekends. Most of the trails cluster toward the bottom, and most are solid intermediate runs. Experts head to the north peak, with a challenging selection of advanced trails served by a triple chairlift. Kids have a new snow-tubing park off the Little Sister chairlift.

Rt. 112, Lincoln, NH 03251. © **800/227-4191** or 603/745-8111. www.loonmtn.com. Vertical drop: 2,100 ft. Lifts: 10. Skiable acreage: 250. Lift tickets: $49 Mon–Fri; $54 to $56 Sat–Sun.

WHERE TO STAY

In addition to the places listed below, Lincoln offers a range of motels that appeal to budget travelers. Among them: **Kancamagus Motor Lodge** (© **800/346-4205** or 603/745-3365), **Mountaineer Motel** (© **800/356-0046** or 603/745-2235), and **Woodward's Resort** (© **800/635-8968** or 603/745-8141).

Mountain Club at Loon ★★   Set at the foot of Loon Mountain's slopes, the Mountain Club is a contemporary resort of prominent gables and glass built during the real estate boom of the 1980s. Managed for several years as a Marriott, the inoffensive but unexciting decor tends to reflect its chain-hotel heritage. Guest rooms are designed to be rented individually or as two-room suites. The high rates reflect the proximity to the slopes and the excellent health club facilities connected to the hotel via covered walkway.

Rte. 112 (R.R. #1; Box 40), Lincoln, NH 03251. © **800/229-7829** or 603/745-2244. Fax 603/745-2317. www.mtnclubonloon.com. 234 units. $99–$230 double; $134–$461 suite. AE, DISC, MC, V. **Amenities:** 2 restaurants (New England, pub fare); indoor pool; outdoor pool; 2 tennis courts; fitness center; Jacuzzi; sauna; concierge; limited room service. *In room:* A/C, TV, coffeemaker, hair dryer.

Wilderness Inn ⚶★ The Wilderness Inn is located at the southern edge of North Woodstock village—not quite the wilderness that the name suggests. It's a friendly, handsome bungalow-style home that dates to 1912, and the interior features heavy timbers in classic Craftsman style, a spare mix of antiques and reproductions, and games to occupy an evening. Five rooms have TVs, the second-floor units are air-conditioned, and the living room has a VCR and TV. The nearby cottage is a fine spot to relax, with a gas fireplace and Jacuzzi. If you're arriving by bus in Lincoln, the innkeepers will pick you up at no charge.

Rte. 3 (just south of Rte. 112), North Woodstock, NH 03262. ✆ **888/777-7813** or 603/745-3890. www. thewildernessinn.com. 8 units. $65–$165 double; $85–$165 suite. Rates include breakfast. AE, MC, V. *In room:* TV, no phone.

Woodstock Inn The Woodstock Inn has a Jekyll-and-Hyde thing going on. In the front, it's a white Victorian set in Woodstock's commercial downtown area—one of the few older inns in the land of condos and modern resorts. In the back, it's a modern, boisterous brewpub, serving up hearty fare along with robust ales. The inn's guest rooms are spread among three houses. If on a tight budget, go for the shared-bathroom units in the main house and nearby Deachman house; the slightly less personable Riverside building across the street offers rooms with private bathrooms. Rooms are individually decorated in a country Victorian style, furnished with both reproductions and antiques. Three units have Jacuzzis.

Main St. (P.O. Box 118), North Woodstock, NH 03262. ✆ **800/321-3985** or 603/745-3951. Fax 603/745-3701. www.woodstockinnnh.com. 24 units (2 with shared bathroom). Peak season $94–$172 double; off season $63–$139. Rates include breakfast. AE, DISC, MC, V. **Amenities:** 2 restaurants (see below). *In room:* A/C, TV, dataport.

WHERE TO DINE

Clement Room Grille/Woodstock Station AMERICAN/PUB FARE Dine in the casually upscale Clement Room on the enclosed porch of the Woodstock Inn, or head to the brewpub out back, in an old train station. The Clement Room has an open grill and fare that aspires for originality (venison with wild mushrooms, for instance). The pub has high ceilings, knotty pine, and a decor that draws on vintage winter recreational gear. The pub menu rounds up the usual suspects, such as nachos, chicken wings, burgers, and pasta. Better are the porters, stouts, and brown and red ales brewed on the premises.

Main St. ✆ 603/745-3951. Reservations recommended for Clement Room only. Main course, breakfast $3.95–$9.50; lunch and dinner $9.25–$23. AE, DISC, MC, V. Clement Room daily 7–11:30am and 5:30–9:30pm; Woodstock Station daily 11:30am–10pm.

FRANCONIA NOTCH ★★★

Franconia Notch is rugged New Hampshire writ large: flanking mountain ranges press in on either side. Plan on a leisurely trip through the notch, allowing enough time to get out of the car and explore forests and craggy peaks. Note that Franconia Notch is more developed for recreation (and thus more crowded with day-trippers) than equally rugged Crawford Notch to the northeast (see earlier in this chapter).

ESSENTIALS

GETTING THERE I-93 runs through Franconia Notch, reducing from four lanes to two (becoming the Franconia Notch Parkway) in the most scenic and sensitive areas of the park. Several scenic roadside pull-offs dot the route.

Finds   **All Aboard! For Dinner, That Is**

Surprisingly, the best dining hereabouts is aboard **Café Lafayette** ★★, in three restored Pullman rail cars that chug along a scenic tour through the western White Mountains while diners enjoy a five-course meal amid white tablecloths and fresh flowers. The evening tour lasts a little more than 2 hours and includes homemade dinner rolls, salad, sorbet, entree, and dessert. (Wine and cocktails are available at extra cost.) Meals are prepared on board, and main courses include New American fare such as grilled salmon with cranberry walnut salsa or pork tenderloin with pinot noir demi-glaze. The train runs from mid-May through October. Boarding is at 5:15pm Tuesdays, Thursdays, and Saturdays and 4:30pm Sundays at the Eagle's Nest on Route 112 in North Woodstock; reservations are advised, but not essential. Cost is $55 per adult, $35 for children 6 to 11 (© **800/699-3501** or 603/745-3500; www.cafelafayette.com).

VISITOR INFORMATION   Information on the park and surrounding area is available at the **Flume Information Center** (© **603/745-8391**), at Exit 1 off the parkway, open daily in summer from 9am to 4:30pm. North of the notch, the **Franconia Notch Chamber of Commerce** (© **603/823-5661;** www. franconianotch.org) on Main Street next to town hall is open spring through fall, Tuesday through Sunday from 10am to 5pm (days and hours often vary).

EXPLORING FRANCONIA NOTCH STATE PARK ★

Franconia Notch State Park's 8,000 acres, nestled within the surrounding White Mountain National Forest, host an array of scenic attractions easily accessible from I-93 and the Franconia Notch Parkway. At the Flume Information Center (see above), a free 15-minute video summarizes the park's attractions. For information on the following, contact the park offices (© **603/823-8800**).

The **Flume** ★★ is a rugged 800-foot gorge through which the Flume Brook tumbles. A popular attraction in the mid–19th century, it's 800 feet long, 90 feet deep, and as narrow as 20 feet at the bottom; visitors explore by means of a network of boardwalks and bridges on a 2-mile walk. Early photos of the chasm show a boulder wedged in overhead; this was swept away in an 1883 avalanche. If you're looking for easy, quick access to natural grandeur, it's worth the money. Otherwise, set off into the mountains and seek your own drama with fewer crowds and less expense. Open May through October, admission is $8 for adults, $5 for children 6 to 12. You can walk or snowshoe the grounds for free in the off season.

Echo Lake ★ is a picturesquely situated recreation area, with a 28-acre lake, a handsome swimming beach, and picnic tables scattered about all within view of Cannon Mountain on one side and Mount Lafayette on the other. A bike path runs alongside the lake and meanders up and down the notch for a total of 8 miles. (Mountain bikes, canoes, and paddleboats may be rented at the park for $10 per hr.) Admission to the park is $3 for all visitors over 12.

For a high-altitude view of the region, set off for the alpine ridges on the **Cannon Mountain Tramway** ★★ (© **603/823-8800**). The old-fashioned cable car serves skiers in winter; in summer, it whisks up to 80 travelers at a time to the summit of the 4,180-foot mountain. Be prepared for cool, gusty winds. The tramway, at Exit 2, costs $10 round-trip for adults, $6 for children 6 to 12.

HIKING

A pleasant woodland detour of 2 hours or so can be found at the **Basin-Cascades Trail** (look for well-marked signs off I-93 about 1½ miles north of the Flume). The popular roadside waterfall and natural pothole known as the Basin attracts crowds who come to see pillows of granite scoured smooth by glaciers and water; yet few visitors continue to the cascades beyond. Look for signs for the trail, then head off into the woods. After about a half mile of easy hiking, you'll reach **Kinsman Falls,** a beautiful 20-foot cascade. Continue another half mile beyond that to **Rocky Glen,** where the stream plummets through a craggy gorge.

For a more demanding hike, set off for **Mt. Lafayette,** with its spectacular views of the western White Mountains. Hikers should be well-experienced, well-equipped, and in good condition. Allow 6 to 7 hours to complete the hike. A popular and fairly straightforward ascent begins up the **Old Bridle Trail,** which departs from the Lafayette Place parking area off the parkway. This trail climbs steadily to the AMC's **Greenleaf Hut** (about 3 miles), with expanding views along the way. From here the **Greenleaf Trail** covers rocky terrain and can be demanding and difficult, especially if the weather turns on you.

DOWNHILL SKIING

Cannon Mountain　One of New England's first ski mountains, Cannon remains famed for its challenging runs and exposed faces, and the mountain still attracts skiers serious about getting down the hill in style. (During skiing's formative years, this state-run ski area was *the* place to ski in the East.) Many of the old-fashioned New England–style trails are narrow and fun (if often icy, scoured by the notch's winds), and the enclosed tramway is an elegant way to get to the summit. With no base scene to speak of, skiers retire to inns around Franconia or retreat southward to the condo villages of Lincoln.

Franconia Notch Pkwy., Franconia. *℡* **603/823-8800.** www.cannonmt.com. Vertical drop: 2,146 ft. Lifts: 70-person tram, 5 chairlifts, 1 surface lift. Skiable acreage: about 175. Lift tickets: $34 Mon–Fri; $45 Sat–Sun.

A HISTORIC HOME

The Frost Place　Robert Frost lived in New Hampshire from the time he was 10 until he was 45. The Frost Place is a humble farmhouse, where Frost once lived with his family; today, appropriately, it's an arts center and a gathering place for writers. Wandering the grounds, it's not hard to see how his granite-edged poetry evolved at the fringes of the White Mountains. First editions of Frost's works are on display; a nature trail in the woods nearby is posted with excerpts from his poems.

Ridge Rd., Franconia. *℡* **603/823-5510.** Admission $3 adults, $2 seniors, $1.25 children 6–15, free for children under 6. Late May to June Sat–Sun 1–5pm; July to mid-Oct Wed–Mon 1–5pm. Head south on Rte. 116 from Franconia 1 mile to Ridge Rd. (gravel); follow signs a short way to the house; park in lot below the house.

WHERE TO STAY & DINE

Franconia Inn　This welcoming inn is set on a quiet road in a bucolic valley 2 miles from the village of Franconia. Built in 1934 after a fire destroyed the original 1886 structure, the inn has an informal feel, with wingback chairs around the fireplace in one common room, and jigsaw puzzles half completed in the paneled library. Guest rooms are appointed in a relaxed country fashion; three have gas fireplaces and four have Jacuzzis. The inn is a haven for cross-country skiers—38 miles of groomed trails start right outside the front door.

1300 Easton Rd., Franconia, NH 03580. © **800/473-5299** or 603/823-5542. Fax 603/823-8078. www.
franconiainn.com. 32 units. $105–$235 double, $160–$235 suite. Rates include breakfast. MAP rates available. AE, MC, V. 3-night minimum stay on holiday weekends. Closed Apr to mid-May. **Amenities:** Restaurant
(traditional/New American); outdoor pool; 4 tennis courts; Jacuzzi; sauna; free bikes; bridle trails; horse
rentals; cross-country ski trails. *In room:* No phone.

Sugar Hill Inn ★★   A classic inn, with wraparound porch and sweeping
mountain panoramas occupying 16 acres on lovely Sugar Hill, this welcoming,
comfortable spot is a great base for exploring the western White Mountains.
Rooms are graciously appointed in antique country style, some influenced by
Shaker sensibility. Most have gas Vermont Castings stoves for heat and atmosphere. The restaurant, one of the area's best, features upscale regional fare.

Rte. 117, Franconia, NH 03580. © **800/548-4748** or 603/823-5621. Fax 603/823-5639. www.sugar
hillinn.com. 18 units. $100–$320 double; $175–$380 suite. Rates include breakfast. AE, MC, V. Closed Apr.
Children 12 and older welcome. **Amenities:** Restaurant (New England). *In room:* No phone.

BETHLEHEM ★ & LITTLETON ★

More than a century ago, **Bethlehem** was as populous as North Conway to the
south, and home to numerous resort hotels, summer retreats, and even its own
semiprofessional baseball team. (Joseph Kennedy, patriarch of the Kennedy clan,
once played for the team.) Bethlehem subsequently lost the race for the riches,
and today is again a sleepy town high on a hillside.

Nearby **Littleton,** set in a valley along the Ammonoosuc River, is the area's
commercial hub, but it still has plenty of small-town charm. The long main
street has an eclectic selection of shops—you can buy a wrench, a foreign magazine or literary novel, locally brewed beer, pizza, whole foods, or camping
supplies.

Neither town offers much in the way of must-see attractions, but both have
good lodging, decent restaurants, and pleasing environs.

ESSENTIALS

GETTING THERE   Littleton is best reached via I-93; get off at Exit 41 or 42.
Bethlehem is about 3 miles east of Littleton on Route 302. Get off I-93 at
Exit 40 and head east. From the east, follow Route 302 past Twin Mountain to
Bethlehem.

VISITOR INFORMATION   The **Bethlehem Chamber of Commerce**
(© **603/869-3409;** www.bethlehemchamber.com) has an information booth
on Bethlehem's Main Street across from town hall. Its hours vary. The **Littleton
Area Chamber of Commerce** (© **603/444-6561;** www.littletonareachamber.
com) offers information at 120 Main St.

EXPLORING BETHLEHEM

Bethlehem consists of Main Street and a handful of side streets. Several antiques
stores clustered in what passes for downtown are worth browsing. Bethlehem
once was home to 38 resort hotels; little evidence of them remains. For a better
understanding of the town's history, pick up a copy of *An Illustrated Tour of Bethlehem, Past and Present,* available at shops around town. Bethlehem also offers
two well-maintained 18-hole golf courses amid beautiful scenery. Call for hours
and greens fees. Both the municipal **Bethlehem Country Club** (© **603/869-
2176**) and private **Maplewood Country Club** (© **603/869-3335**) are on
Route 302 (Main St.).

West of Bethlehem on Route 302 is **The Rocks** ★★ (© **603/444-6228;** www.
therocks.org), a classic Victorian gentleman's farm that today is the headquarters

for the Society for the Protection of New Hampshire Forests. This 1883 estate on 1,200 acres has a well-preserved shingled house, a handsome barn, and hiking trails that meander through meadows and woodlands. It's a peaceful spot, perfect for a picnic. Admission is free; open daily from dawn to dusk.

WHERE TO STAY

Worth noting is the restoration of a grand old North Country classic. The **Mountain View Grand Resort & Spa** (© **800/438-3017** or 603/837-2100; www.mountainviewgrand.com) in Whitefield, a short drive north of Littleton and Bethlehem. After years of abandonment, the hotel has benefited from a $20 million overhaul. There are 145 rooms and suites, each with a mountain view and oversize TV. The resort also includes a dining room and lounge, indoor and outdoor pools, a fitness center, a golf course, and spa offerings. Summer rates run from about $310 to $490 double, $640 to $700 for suites; winter rates are lower.

Adair ★★★ Adair opened a decade ago, yet remains one of New England's better-kept secrets. The peaceful Georgian Revival home dates from 1927 and is set on 200 acres. Its **Granite Tap Room** is a huge, informal, granite-block-lined rumpus room with VCR, antique pool table, and fireplace. The guest rooms are impeccably well furnished with a mix of antiques and reproductions; six feature fireplaces. The best is the Kinsman suite, with a Jacuzzi the size of a small swimming pool, small library, gas woodstove, and petite balcony looking out to the Dalton Range. Service is hospitable and top-rate. Cocktail lovers should bring their own liquor; set-ups and mixers are free.

80 Guider Lane (off Exit 40 on Rte. 93), Bethlehem, NH 03574. © **888/444-2600** or 603/444-2600. Fax 603/444-4823. www.adairinn.com. 10 units. $175–$295 double; $355 cottage. Rates include breakfast, tax, and gratuity. AE, DISC, MC, V. 2-night minimum stay weekends and foliage season. Children 12 and older welcome. **Amenities:** Restaurant (see Tim-Bir Alley, below); tennis court. *In room:* A/C, hair dryer, no phone.

Hearthside Village Cottage Motel ★ *(Kids)* A little weird and a little charming, Hearthside claims to be the first motor court built in New Hampshire. A colony of steeply gabled miniature homes, the village was constructed by a father and son in the 1930s and late 1940s. The six 1940s-era cottages are of somewhat better quality, with warm knotty-pine interiors. Many cottages have fireplaces (Duraflame–style logs only), some have kitchenettes, and several are suitable for small families. An indoor playroom is filled with toys for tots, and another rec room offers video games and Ping-Pong for older kids.

Rte. 302 (midway between Bethlehem Village and I-93), Bethlehem, NH 03574. © **603/444-1000**. www.hearthsidevillage.com. 16 cottages. $60–$70; foliage season $65–$75. 2- to 3-night minimum stay in foliage season. MC, V. Closed mid-Oct to mid-May. **Amenities:** Outdoor pool. *In room:* A/C, TV, fridge, coffeemaker (on request), no phone.

Rabbit Hill Inn ★★ A short hop across the Connecticut River from Littleton is the lost-in-time Vermont village of Lower Waterford, with its 1859 church and tiny library. Amid this cluster of buildings is the Rabbit Hill Inn, constructed in 1795. With prominent gabled roof and imposing columns, this romantic retreat ranks among the most refined structures in the Connecticut River Valley. More than half of the rooms have gas fireplaces, and several feature Jacuzzis. Rates include breakfast and dinner in the dining room, where proper attire is expected (jacket and tie are "appropriate"). The inn is halfway between Littleton and St. Johnsbury, Vermont, enabling guests to explore both states.

Rte. 18, Lower Waterford, VT 05848. © **800/762-8669** or 802/748-5168. Fax 802/748-8342. www.rabbithillinn.com. 19 units. $275–$315 double; $385–$400 suite. Rates include breakfast, afternoon tea, dinner, and gratuities. 2- to 3-night minimum stay on weekends and holidays. AE, MC, V. Closed early Apr and early Nov. From I-93, take Rte. 18 northwest from Exit 44 for approximately 2 miles. Children 12 and older welcome. **Amenities:** Massage. *In room:* A/C, coffeemaker, hair dryer, iron, Jacuzzi (some).

Thayers Inn 🌟 *Value*   Thayers may offer the best value of any White Mountains inn. It's a clean, well-run hostelry in an impressive Greek Revival downtown building that dates to 1850. A mix of rooms is furnished comfortably if eclectically with high-quality flea-market furniture. The $60 rooms aren't especially spacious but are adequate and comfortable. The top floor is a bit of a hike—but room 47 ($45) is a true bargain for travelers on a budget, with air-conditioning, in-room sink, and shared bathroom. The inn has a free video library of 140 movies. The cupola has a panoramic view of the town.

Main St., Littleton, NH 03561. ✆ **800/634-8179** or 603/444-6469. www.thayersinn.com. 48 units (3 with shared bathroom). $45 double with shared bathroom; $65–$125 double with private bathroom. Rates include continental breakfast. AE, DISC, MC, V. Pets allowed if not left alone in room. **Amenities:** Restaurant (casual dining). *In room:* A/C, TV, no phone.

WHERE TO DINE

Tim-Bir Alley 🌟🌟 REGIONAL/CONTEMPORARY   Some of the region's best dining is at Tim-Bir Alley, housed in the area's most gracious country inn. In this romantic setting, owners Tim and Biruta Carr (hence the name) prepare meals from wholesome, basic ingredients. The menu changes weekly, but diners may start with chicken and pecan dumplings with a honey/soy/balsamic glaze or salmon-brie ravioli. Afterwards, tuck into a main course that might run to salmon with a sunflower-seed crust, spicy tournedos of beef, rosemary-garlic lamb chops, or cinnamon pork tenderloin. Save room for the superb desserts; offerings may include a maple cheesecake, plum-almond tart, or banana-almond bread pudding with Kahlua sauce. Expect a leisurely meal.

Adair Country Inn, 80 Guider Lane, Bethlehem. ✆ **603/444-6142.** Reservations required. Main courses $16–$22. No credit cards. Summer Wed–Sun 5:30–9pm; winter Wed–Sat 5:30–9pm. Closed Apr and Nov.

5 The North Country

New Hampshire's North Country is an ideal destination for those who find the White Mountains too commercialized. Tiny communities—such as **Errol,** at a crossroads of two routes to nowhere—regard change with high suspicion, even during the go-go '80s. The land surrounding the town is an outpost of rugged, raw grandeur that has been little compromised.

But you *can* find plenty to do if you're self-motivated and oriented toward the outdoors, including white-water kayaking on the Androscoggin River, canoeing on Lake Umbagog, and bicycling along the wide valley floors. Or visit one of the Northeast's grandest, most improbable historic resorts. The piney shoreline around spectacular Lake Umbagog was protected as a National Wildlife Refuge in the 1990s, and should remain in its more-or-less pristine state for all time.

ESSENTIALS

GETTING THERE   Errol is at the junction of Route 26 (accessible from Bethel, Maine) and Route 16 (accessible from Gorham, New Hampshire). **Concord Trailways** (✆ **800/639-3317**) provides service to Berlin from points south, including Boston.

VISITOR INFORMATION   The **Northern White Mountains Chamber of Commerce,** 164 Main St., Berlin (✆ **800/992-7480** or 603/752-6060; www.northernwhitemountains.com), offers information Monday through Friday between 8:30am and 4:30pm.

OUTDOOR PURSUITS

Dixville Notch State Park ★ (© 603/323-2087) has several hiking trails, including a 2-mile round-trip to Table Rock. Look for the parking area east of the Balsams Resort on the edge of Lake Gloriette. The loop hike (it connects with a half-mile return along Route 26) ascends a scraggy trail to an open rock with fine views of the resort and the flanking wild hills. The day-use fee for the park is $3.

Excellent lake canoeing may be found at Lake Umbagog, which sits between Maine and New Hampshire. The lake, home to the newly created **Umbagog Lake State Park** ★★ (© 603/482-7795), has some 40 miles of shoreline, most of which is wild and remote. The day-use fee is $3.

WHERE TO STAY & DINE

Balsams Grand Resort Hotel ★★★   The Balsams is a grand gem deep in the northern forest. On 15,000 acres in a remote valley surrounded by 800-foot cliffs, it's one of a handful of great 19th-century New England resorts still in operation. What makes this Victorian grande dame even more exceptional is its refusal to compromise on style. Bathing suits and jeans are prohibited in public areas, you'll be ejected from the tennis courts or golf course if not neatly attired, and men are *required* (not requested) to wear jackets at dinner. The resort maintains strict adherence to the spirit of the "American plan"—everything but booze is included in room rates, including greens fees, boats on Lake Gloriette, and evening entertainment in the lounges. (Even ski tickets at the inn's downhill area are included.) Meals are an event—especially the summer luncheon buffet.

Dixville Notch, NH 03576. © **800/255-0600,** 800/255-0800 in N.H., or 603/255-3400. Fax 603/255-4221. www.thebalsams.com. 204 units. Summer $219–$259 double; fall and winter $189–$215 double; off season $149–$199 double. Ask about MAP plan rates and packages. AE, DISC, MC, V. 4-night minimum July–Aug weekends. Closed Apr–May and mid-Oct to mid-Dec. **Amenities:** Restaurant (American/Continental); 3 lounges; outdoor pool; 2 golf courses; 6 tennis courts; health club; Jacuzzi; sauna; free watersports equipment; bike rental; cross-country ski trails; downhill ski area; children's programs (summer); concierge; shopping arcade; salon; limited room service; massage; babysitting; laundry service; dry cleaning. *In room:* TV (some), dataport, iron.

Philbrook Farm Inn ★★ *(Finds*   This New England period piece traces its lineage to the 19th century, when farmers opened their doors to summer travelers to earn extra cash. Set on 1,000 acres between the Mahoosuc Range and Androscoggin River, it has been owned and operated by the Philbrook family since 1853, with additions in 1861, 1904, and 1934. The cozy rooms are eclectic; some have a farmhouse feel, others a more Victorian flavor. Guests can swim, play croquet or badminton, explore trails in the hills, or simply read on the porch. This is a relaxing retreat, well out of the mainstream and worthy of protection as a local cultural landmark. *Note:* They don't accept credit cards.

881 North Rd. (off Rte. 2 between Gorham, N.H., and Bethel, Maine), Shelburne, NH 03581. © **603/466-3831.** www.philbrookfarminn.com. 24 units (6 with shared bathroom). $120–$150 double (including breakfast and dinner). No credit cards. Closed Apr and Nov–Dec 25. Pets allowed in cottages. **Amenities:** Restaurant (traditional New England); outdoor pool; badminton; shuffleboard. *In room:* No phone.

13

Maine

by Paul Karr

Professional funny guy Dave Barry once suggested that Maine's state motto should be "Cold, but damp."

Cute, but true. Spring tends to last a few blustery, rain-soaked days; November has Arctic winds that alternate with gray sheets of rain; and winter brings a character-building mix of blizzards and ice storms to the fabled coast and rolling mountains.

Ah, but summer. Summer in Maine brings osprey diving for fish off wooded points, gleaming cumulus clouds building over steely-blue rounded peaks of western mountains, the haunting whoop of loons echoing off the dense forest walls bordering the lakes. Summer brings languorous days when the sun rises well before most visitors; by 8am, it seems like noon. Maine summers offer a measure of tranquillity; a stay in the right spot can rejuvenate the most jangled nerves.

The trick is finding that right spot. Maine is roughly as large as the other five New England states combined. It has 5,500 miles of coastline, some 3,000 coastal islands, and millions of acres of undeveloped woodland. With all this space and a little planning, you'll be able to find your piece of Maine.

1 The Southern Maine Coast

Maine's southern coast runs roughly from the state line at Kittery to Portland, and is the destination of most travelers to the state (including many day-trippers from the Boston area). While it takes some doing to find privacy and remoteness here, you'll find at least two excellent reasons for a detour: long, sandy beaches, the region's hallmark; and a sense of history in some of the coastal villages.

Thanks to quirks of geography, nearly all of Maine's sandy beaches are in this 60-mile stretch of coastline. It's not hard to find a relaxing sandy spot, whether you prefer dunes and the lulling sound of the surf or the carnival-like atmosphere of a festive beach town. Waves depend on the weather—during a good Northeast blow (especially prevalent in spring and fall), they pound the shores and threaten beach houses built decades ago. During balmy midsummer days, the ocean can be as gentle as a farm pond, barely audible waves lapping timidly at the shore.

One thing all the beaches share in common, however: They're washed by the chilled waters of the Gulf of Maine. Expect a shock.

KITTERY & THE YORKS

Kittery ⚓ is the first town to appear when entering Maine by car from the south. Once famous for its (still operating) naval yard, it's now better known for dozens of factory outlets. Maine has the second-highest number of outlet malls in the nation (after California), and Kittery is home to a good many of them.

"The Yorks," just to the north, are three towns that share a name but little else. In fact, it's rare to find three such well-defined and diverse New England archetypes within such a compact area. **York Village** ⋆ is full of early (17th century) American history and architecture, and has a good library. **York Harbor** ⋆⋆ reached its zenith during America's late Victorian era, when wealthy urbanites constructed cottages at the ocean's edge; it's the most relaxing and scenic of the three. But it's **York Beach** ⋆⋆ I like the best: a beach town with amusements, taffy shops, a small zoo, gabled summer homes set in crowded enclaves, a great lighthouse, and two good beaches—a long one perfect for walking or tanning, plus a shorter one within a minute's walk of restaurants, souvenir shops, candy shops, an arcade, and even a palm reader.

Just outside York Village, the protrusion of land known as **Cape Neddick** ⋆⋆ is an excellent back-road route to Ogunquit, with views, secluded estates, and excellent lobster, *if* you can find it (go past the police station in Short Sands, and then bear right at the sign for the lobster restaurant).

ESSENTIALS

GETTING THERE   Kittery is accessible from **I-95** or **Route 1,** with well-marked exits. The Yorks are reached most easily from Exit 1 of the Maine Turnpike. Just south of the turnpike exit, look for Route 1A, which connects all three York towns.

Amtrak (☎ **800/872-7245;** www.amtrak.com) operates four trains daily from Boston's North Station to southern Maine, stopping outside Wells, about 10 miles away from the Yorks; a one-way ticket is $17, and the trip takes 2 hours. You'll need to phone for a taxi or arrange for a pickup to get to your destination if you arrive by train.

Greyhound (☎ **800/229-9424**), **C&J Trailways** (☎ **800/258-7111**), and **Vermont Transit** (☎ **800/552-8737**) all run a few buses daily from Boston's South Station to southern Maine, but they only stop in Wells, and not even in the beach or commercial area. Bus fare is comparable to train fare; the trip can be up to a half-hour shorter. Buses also run a bit more frequently from South Station to downtown Portsmouth, New Hampshire, which is close to Kittery and a more convenient place to get off. Taking a Greyhound from New York City's Port Authority to Portsmouth is about $44 one-way and takes about 6½ hours.

VISITOR INFORMATION   The **Kittery Information Center** (☎ 207/439-1319) is located at a well-marked rest area on I-95. It's open daily from 8am to 6pm in summer, from 9am to 5:30pm the rest of the year.

The **York Chamber of Commerce** (☎ 207/363-4422) operates an information center at 571 Rte. 1, a short way from the turnpike exit. It's open in summer daily from 9am to 5pm (until 6pm Fri); limited days and hours the rest of the year.

SHOPPING

Kittery's consumer mecca is 4 miles south of York on Route 1. Some 120 **factory outlets** flank the highway, scattered among more than a dozen strip malls. Retailers include J. Crew, Coach, Eddie Bauer, Anne Klein, Le Creuset, Calvin Klein, Crate & Barrel, Polo/Ralph Lauren, Tommy Hilfiger, and Brookstone.

Navigating the area can be frustrating in summer owing to four lanes of often heavy traffic and capricious restrictions on turns. (A free shuttle bus links the outlets and lessens some of the frustration.) The selection of outlets is slightly more diverse than in Freeport, a little more than an hour north, which is more clothing oriented. But Freeport's quaint village setting is far more appealing than the congested sprawl zone of Kittery. Information is available from the **Kittery Outlet Association** (☎ 888/548-8379; www.thekitteryoutlets.com).

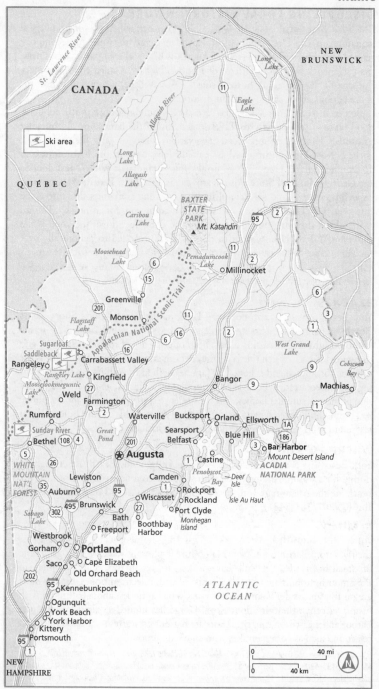

Maine

Ski area

CANADA

NEW BRUNSWICK

QUÉBEC

St. Lawrence River

Long Lake

Eagle Lake

Allagash River

Long Lake

Allagash Lake

Caribou Lake

BAXTER STATE PARK

▲ *Mt. Katahdin*

Pemadumcook Lake

○ Millinocket

Moosehead Lake

Appalachian National Scenic Trail

Greenville

Flagstaff Lake

Monson

West Grand Lake

Sugarloaf

Saddleback

Rangeley

Rangeley Lake

Carrabassett Valley

Kingfield

Mooselookmeguntic Lake

Weld

Farmington

Rumford

Sunday River

Bethel

Bangor

WHITE MOUNTAIN NAT'L FOREST

Lewiston

Auburn

Brunswick

Sabago Lake

Westbrook

Gorham

Saco

Portland

Cape Elizabeth

Old Orchard Beach

Kennebunkport

Ogunquit

York Beach

York Harbor

Kittery

Portsmouth

NEW HAMPSHIRE

Waterville

Bucksport

Orland

Ellsworth

Searsport

Blue Hill

Belfast

Bar Harbor

Mount Desert Island

ACADIA NATIONAL PARK

☆ **Augusta**

Castine

Great Pond

Camden

Penobscot Bay

Deer Isle

Wiscasset

Rockport

Rockland

Bath

Port Clyde

Isle Au Haut

Boothbay Harbor

Monhegan Island

Freeport

Machias

Cobscook Bay

West Grand Lake

ATLANTIC OCEAN

0   40 mi

0   40 km

DISCOVERING LOCAL HISTORY IN YORK

Old York Historical Society ★★ John Hancock is famous for his oversize signature on the Declaration of Independence and the insurance company named after him. What's not so well known is his checkered past as a business-man. Hancock was the proprietor of Hancock Wharf, a failed enterprise that's but one of the intriguing historic sites in York Village, a fine destination for those curious about early American history.

Settled in 1624, York Village has several early buildings open to the public. A good place to start is **Jefferds Tavern,** across from the handsome old **burying ground.** Changing exhibits document various facets of early life. Next door is the **School House,** furnished as it might have been in the 19th century. A 10-minute walk on Lindsay Road brings you to **Hancock Wharf,** next door to the **George Marshall Store.** Also nearby is the **Elizabeth Perkins House,** with its well-preserved Colonial Revival interior. The one don't-miss structure is the intriguing **Old Gaol,** built in 1719 with musty dungeons for criminals. (The jail is the oldest surviving public building in the U.S.) Just down the knoll is the **Emerson-Wilcox House,** built in the mid-1700s. Added to periodically over the years, it's a virtual catalog of architectural styles and early decorative arts.

5 Lindsay Rd., York. © 207/363-4974. Admission $7 adults, $3 children 4–16, free for children under 4. Tues–Sat 10am–5pm; Sun 1–5pm (last tour at 4pm). Closed mid-Oct to mid-June.

BEACHES

York Beach consists of two beaches—**Long Sands Beach** ★ and **Short Sands Beach**—separated by a rocky headland and a small island capped by scenic **Nubble Light** ★. When tide is out, both offer plenty of room for sunning and throwing Frisbees. When tide is in, they're both cramped. Short Sands fronts the town of York Beach and is better for families with kids, with its candlepin bowl-ing and video arcades. Long Sands runs along Route 1A, across from a profu-sion of motels, summer homes, and convenience stores. Changing rooms, public rest rooms, and metered parking (50¢ per hr.) are available at both beaches; local restaurants and vendors provide other services, including snacks.

WHERE TO STAY

York Beach has a number of motels facing Long Sands Beach. Reserve ahead during high season. Among those with simple accommodations on or near the beach are the **Anchorage Inn** (© **207/363-5112**) and the **Long Beach Motor Inn** (© **207/363-5481**).

In Kittery

Inn at Portsmouth Harbor ★★ This 1899 home is just a half-mile across the river from Portsmouth, New Hampshire (a pleasant walk). Guests get a taste of small-town life, yet still have access to restaurants and shopping in Portsmouth. Rooms are tastefully furnished with eclectic antiques, though most are on the small side. Valdra has ruby-red walls, antiques, and a bathroom with historic accents; the third-floor Royal Gorge has limited skylight views of the harbor and a cast-iron tub. Breakfasts are flat-out great: fresh-squeezed juice and selections such as corn pancakes with smoked salmon.

6 Water St., Kittery, ME 03904. © 207/439-4040. Fax 207/438-9286. www.innatportsmouth.com. 5 units. May–Oct $135–$209 double; Nov–Apr $129–$189. Rates include breakfast. 2-night minimum stay summer and holidays. MC, V. Children 12 and older are welcome. *In room:* A/C, TV, dataport, hair dryer, iron.

In the Yorks

Dockside Guest Quarters ★ David and Harriet Lusty established this quiet retreat in 1954; recent additions haven't changed its friendly, maritime flavor.

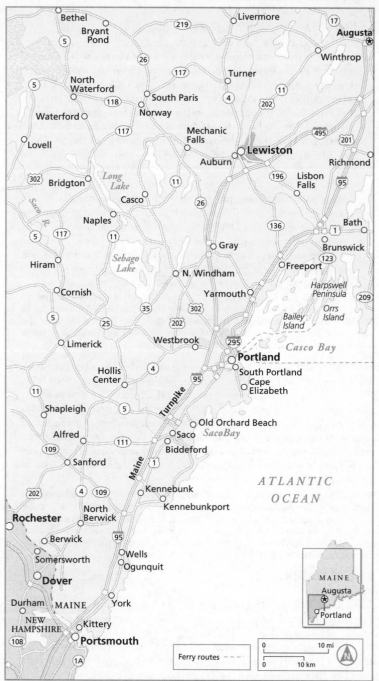

Bethel
Bryant
Pond
5
219
Livermore
17
Augusta
26
Winthrop
5
North
Waterford
117
Turner
11
118
South Paris
4
202
Waterford
Norway
495
201
117
Mechanic
Falls
Lewiston
Lovell
Auburn
Richmond
302
Bridgton
Long
Lake
196
Lisbon
Falls
95
Saco R.
Casco
26
136
Bath
5
117
Naples
11
Sebago
Lake
Gray
Brunswick
123
Hiram
N. Windham
Freeport
Cornish
Yarmouth
Harpswell
Peninsula
209
35
302
Orrs
Island
5
25
202
Bailey
Island
Limerick
Westbrook
295
Casco Bay
Hollis
Center
4
Portland
11
Shapleigh
5
South Portland
Cape
Elizabeth
Turnpike
95
Alfred
111
Old Orchard Beach
Saco Bay
109
Saco
Sanford
Biddeford
Maine
1
202
4
109
Kennebunk
ATLANTIC
OCEAN
Rochester
North
Berwick
Kennebunkport
Berwick
95
Somersworth
Wells
Dover
Ogunquit
Durham
MAINE
York
NEW
HAMPSHIRE
Kittery
108
Portsmouth
1A

Ferry routes - - -

| 0 | | 10 mi |
| 0 | | 10 km |

MAINE
Augusta
Portland

> ⸤*Finds* **Sayward-Wheeler House**
>
> For those who'd like a taste of local history but lack the stamina for the full-court Old York visit, stop by the Sayward-Wheeler House ⚵ in York Harbor, run by the Society for the Preservation of New England Antiquities. A well-preserved merchant's home dating to 1760, you'll see china captured during the 1745 Siege of Louisbourg, which routed the French out of Nova Scotia. It's open weekends only, June through mid-October. Tours are given hourly from 11am to 4pm. Admission is $5, free for SPNEA members and York Harbor residents. For information, call the SPNEA's office in New Hampshire at ✆ **603/436-3205.**

The inn occupies nicely landscaped grounds on a 7-acre peninsula shaded with maples and white pines, off the beaten track between Kittery and the Yorks. Five rooms are in the main house (1885), but most of the accommodations are in small, modern town house–style cottages (suites have kitchenettes), which are bright and airy and have private decks overlooking the entrance to York Harbor. You can also swim in the ocean here, or play badminton or croquet.

Harris Island (P.O. Box 205), York, ME 03909. ✆ **207/363-2868.** Fax 207/363-1977. www.docksidegq.com. 25 units. Feb–Apr $95–$120 double; May–Oct $110–$240 double; Nov–Dec (closed weekdays in May, last week of Oct, and Dec to early Feb; see website for exact dates). $85–$120 double. Continental breakfast $4. DISC, MC, V. 2-night minimum stay July–Sept. Drive south on Rte. 103 from Rte. 1A in York Harbor; after bridge over York River, turn left and follow signs. **Amenities:** Restaurant (New England/seafood); watersports equipment rental; bike rental; laundry service. *In room:* TV, dataport, iron.

Stage Neck Inn ⚵⚵   A hotel in one form or another has housed guests on this windswept bluff between the harbor and the open ocean since about 1870. The most recent incarnation, constructed in 1972, is furnished with an understated, country club–like elegance. Rooms were last renovated in 2000, with fridges and CD players added. The hotel is modern, yet offers an old-fashioned sense of intimacy lacking in other modern resorts. Almost every unit has a view of the water. Pretty York Harbor Beach is but a few steps away, where you can sun or swim (if you dare), and the two clay oceanside tennis courts—reserved for guests—are quite popular as well.

Stage Neck (P.O. Box 70), York Harbor, ME 03911. ✆ **800/340-1130** or 207/363-3850. www.stageneck.com. 58 units. May to Labor Day $235–$345 double; early fall $185–$255 double; winter $135–$185 double; spring $165–$210 double. Ask about off-season packages. AE, DC, DISC, MC, V. Head north on Rte. 1A from Rte. 1; make second right after York Harbor post office. **Amenities:** 2 dining rooms (fine dining, pub fare); indoor pool; outdoor pool; 2 tennis courts; fitness room; Jacuzzi; sauna; limited room service; in-room massage; dry cleaning. *In room:* A/C, TV/VCR, dataport, fridge, coffeemaker, hair dryer.

WHERE TO DINE
In Kittery
Bob's Clam Hut ⚵ FRIED SEAFOOD   In business since 1956 (take-out only until 1989), Bob's has an old-fashioned flavor—despite being surrounded by slick factory outlet malls—while serving up heaps of fried clams and other diet-busting enticements with great efficiency. ("Our suppliers marvel at the amount of Fryolator oil we order.") Order at the front window, get a soda from a vending machine, then stake out a table inside or on the deck with a Route 1 view, waiting for your number to be called. The fare is surprisingly light, cooked in cholesterol-free vegetable oil; onion rings are especially good. To ensure that your diet has been irrevocably violated, Bob's also offers Ben & Jerry's ice cream.

Rte. 1, Kittery. ✆ **207/439-4233**. Reservations not accepted. Sandwiches $1.50–$4.95; dinners $5.25–$19. AE, MC, V. Daily Memorial Day to Labor Day 11am–7pm (Sat–Sun till 8pm). Open year-round, hours vary in off season; call ahead. Just north of the Kittery Trading Post.

Chauncey Creek Lobster Pier ★★ LOBSTER POUND   Chauncey's is one of the best lobster pounds in the state, not least because the Spinney family, which has been selling lobsters here since the 1950s, takes such pride in the place. You reach the pound by walking down a wooden ramp to a broad deck on a tidal inlet, where some 42 festively painted picnic tables await. Lobster is the specialty, of course, but steamed mussels (in wine and garlic) and clams are also available. Want a drink? BYOB. In fact, feel free to bring along your own cooler full of beer, wine, soda, chips, watermelon, and what-have-you. Everyone does.

Chauncey Creek Rd. (between Kittery Point and York off Rte. 103; watch for signs), Kittery Point. ✆ **207/ 439-1030**. Reservations not accepted. Market-priced lobsters; other items $1.50–$13. MC, V. Daily 11am– 8pm (until 7pm during shoulder seasons); closed Mon after Labor Day. Closed Columbus Day to Mother's Day. Limited parking.

In The Yorks

Cape Neddick Inn Restaurant ★★ CONTEMPORARY AMERICAN This is the best choice for an exquisite meal south of Ogunquit. In an elegant structure on a quiet stretch of Route 1, the inn has an open dining area that deftly mixes traditional and modern. Owner Johnathan Pratt has worked in France and at such noted establishments as Restaurant Daniel and Jean George in New York City. His menu is French-inspired American fare, with dishes such as poached lobster in vermouth cream and venison stew in dried red-currant sauce. The wine list has about 125 selections, many of which offer good value.

1233 Rte. 1, Cape Neddick. ✆ **207/363-2899**. Reservations recommended. Main courses $18–$28. DISC, MC, V. Tues–Sun 5:30–10pm; closed Mar.

Goldenrod Restaurant ★ AMERICAN   This beach-town classic is the place for local color—it's been a summer institution in York Beach since 1896. It's easy to find: Look for visitors gathering at the plate-glass windows watching ancient taffy machines churn out saltwater taffy in volumes large enough (9 million candies a year) to keep busloads of dentists wealthy. Be sure to take home a box of the taffy or birch bark as a souvenir. The restaurant, behind the taffy and fudge operation, is short on gourmet fare, long on atmosphere. Diners sit around a stone fireplace or at an antique soda fountain. Meals are basic and filling: waffles, griddle cakes, club sandwiches, egg and bacon sandwiches.

Railroad Rd. and Ocean Ave., York Beach. ✆ **207/363-2621**. www.thegoldenrod.com. Main courses: breakfast $2.75–$5.50, lunch and dinner $2.95–$8. MC, V. Memorial Day to Labor Day daily 8am–10pm (until 9pm in June); Labor Day to Columbus Day Wed–Sun 8am–3pm. Closed Columbus Day to Memorial Day.

THE KENNEBUNKS

"The Kennebunks" consist of the side-by-side villages of **Kennebunk** and **Kennebunkport,** both situated along the shores of small rivers, and both claiming a portion of rocky coast. The region was first settled in the mid-1600s and flourished after the American Revolution, when ship captains, boat builders, and prosperous merchants constructed imposing, solid homes. The Kennebunks are famed for their striking historical architecture and expansive beaches.

ESSENTIALS

GETTING THERE   Kennebunk is off Exit 3 of the Maine Turnpike. Kennebunkport is 3½ miles southeast of Kennebunk on Port Road (Rte. 35).

VISITOR INFORMATION The **Kennebunk-Kennebunkport Chamber of Commerce** (© **800/982-4421** or 207/967-0857; www.visitthekennebunks.com) can answer questions year-round by phone or at its office on Route 9 next to Meserve's Market. The **Kennebunkport Information Center** (© **207/967-8600**), operated by an association of local businesses, is off Dock Square (next to Ben & Jerry's) and open daily throughout summer and fall.

GETTING AROUND A local "trolley" service (© **207/967-3686;** www.intowntrolley.com)—actually, it's a bus with a tour narrator—makes stops in and around Kennebunkport and also serves the beaches. The fare is a steep $9 per adult ($5 for children age 2–14) per day, but you do get unlimited trips.

EXPLORING KENNEBUNKPORT

Kennebunkport is the summer home of President George Bush the Elder, whose family has summered here for decades, and it has the tweedy, upper-crust feel that one might expect. The tiny historic downtown, whose streets were laid out during days of travel by boat and horse, is subject to monumental traffic jams. If the municipal lot off the square is full, go north on North Street a few minutes to the free long-term lot and catch the trolley back into town. Or go about on foot—it's a pleasant walk of 10 or 15 minutes from the satellite lot to Dock Square.

Dock Square ☆ has an architecturally eclectic wharf-like feel, with low buildings of mixed vintages and styles, but the flavor is mostly clapboard and shingles. Today, it's *haute tourist,* with boutiques featuring some arts and crafts and a lot of trinkets. Kennebunkport's deeper appeal is found in the surrounding blocks, where the side streets are lined with one of the nation's best-preserved assortments of early American homes. Neighborhoods are especially ripe with Federal-style homes, many converted to B&Bs (see "Where to Stay," below).

For a clear view of the coast, sign up for a 2-hour sail aboard the **Schooner Eleanor** ☆☆ (at the Arundel Wharf Restaurant, Kennebunkport; © **207/967-8809**), a 55-foot gaff-rigged schooner, built in Kennebunkport in 1999 after a classic Herreshoff design. If the weather's willing, you'll have a perfect view of the Bush compound and Cape Porpoise. Fare is $38 per person.

A bit further afield, in the affluent neighborhood around the Colony Hotel (about 1 mile east of Dock Square on Ocean Ave.), is a fine collection of homes of the uniquely American shingle style. It's worth a detour on foot or by bike to ogle these icons of the 19th- and early-20th-century leisure class.

Ocean Drive from Dock Square to **Walkers Point** ☆ and beyond is lined with opulent summer homes overlooking surf and rocky shore. You'll likely recognize the Bush family compound right out on Walkers Point when you arrive

---

Tips **Beach Parking**

Finding a spot is often difficult, and all beaches require a parking permit, which you can get at the town offices or from your hotel. You can avoid the hassle by renting a bike and leaving your car at your inn or hotel. A good spot for rentals is **Cape Able Bike Shop** (© **800/220-0907** or 207/967-4382), offering three-speeds for $10 a day or $40 a week. The bike shop, which also claims to be Maine's only 100% solar business, is at 83 Arundel Rd., north of Kennebunkport. The trolley also offers beach access (see above); the fare is $9 per adult per day for unlimited trips.

(look for the shingle-style Secret Service booth at the head of a drive). There's nothing to do here but park for a minute, snap a picture, and then push on.

The Seashore Trolley Museum ★★★ *finds*   Just north of Kennebunkport is a local marvel: a scrap yard masquerading as a museum. This quirky museum was founded in 1939 to preserve a disappearing way of life, and today contains one of the largest trolley collections in the world—more than 200, including specimens from Glasgow, Moscow, San Francisco, and Rome. (Naturally, it has a streetcar named "Desire" from New Orleans.) About 40 cars still operate, and admission includes rides on a 2-mile track. An intriguing spot, at times it feels like a scrap yard come to life. Other cars are displayed outdoors and in vast storage sheds. Not until you drive away will you likely realize how much you've learned about how Americans got around before a car was in every garage.

195 Log Cabin Rd., Kennebunkport. ⓒ 207/967-2712. www.trolleymuseum.org. Admission $7.50 adults, $5.50 seniors, $5.75 children 6–16, free for children 5 and under. May 24–Oct 12 daily 10am–5pm; May 3–18 and Oct 18–26 Sat–Sun 10am–5pm. Closed Nov to early May. Drive north from Kennebunkport on North St. for 1¾ miles; look for signs.

BEACHES

The coastal area around Kennebunkport is home to several of the state's best beaches. Southward across the river (technically, this is Kennebunk, though it's much closer to Kennebunkport) are **Gooch's Beach** ★★ and **Kennebunk Beach** ★★. Head eastward on Beach Street (from the intersection of Routes 9 and 35) and you'll soon wind into a handsome colony of eclectic shingled summer homes. The narrow road twists past sandy beaches and rocky headlands. It may be congested in summer; avoid gridlock by exploring on foot or by bike.

Goose Rocks Beach ★★★ is north of Kennebunkport off Route 9 (watch for signs), a good destination if you like your crowds light and prefer actual beaches to beach scenes. An enclave of beach homes is set amid rustling oaks off a fine-sand beach. Offshore, a narrow barrier reef often attracts flocks of geese.

WHERE TO STAY

Beach House Inn ★★   The best choice if you want to be amid the activity of Kennebunk Beach, this 1891 inn has been extensively modernized and expanded; in 1999, the owners of the legendary White Barn Inn (see below) purchased and upgraded it. The rooms aren't necessarily historic, but most are furnished comfortably with Victorian or casual beach cottage accents. Its main draw is a lovely porch, where you gaze out at the pebble beach across the road and idly watch bikers and skaters. The inn provides beach chairs and towels.

211 Beach Ave., Kennebunk Beach, ME 04043. ⓒ 207/967-3850. Fax 207/967-4719. www.beachhseinn. com. 35 units. Peak season $240–$490; off season $145–$400. Rates include continental breakfast. AE, MC, V. 2-night minimum stay on weekends. **Amenities:** Watersports equipment; free bikes. *In room:* TV/VCR, dataport.

Captain Jefferds Inn ★★   Fine antiques abound in this 1804 Federal home; you may need persuading to leave your rooms once you've settled in. Among the best are Manhattan, with four-poster bed, fireplace, and beautiful afternoon light; and Assisi, with restful indoor fountain and rock garden (weird, but it works). Winterthur is the only unit with a TV (the common room also has one); Winterthur and Santa Fe have whirlpools. Prices reflect varying room sizes, but even the smallest rooms are comfortable. An elaborate breakfast is served before a fire on cool days, and on the terrace when summer weather permits.

5 Pearl St. (P.O. Box 691), Kennebunkport, ME 04046. ⓒ 800/839-6844 or 207/967-2311. Fax 207/967 0721. www.captainjefferdsinn.com. 15 units. $165–$340 double; off season $110–$285. Rates include

breakfast. AE, MC, V. 2-night minimum stay on weekends. Pets allowed with prior permission ($30 per night). *In room:* A/C, hair dryer, no phone.

Captain Lord ★★★   Housed in a Federal-style home that peers down a shady lawn toward the river, this is one of the most architecturally distinguished inns in New England. You know this is the genuine article once you spot the grandfather clocks and Chippendale highboys in the front hall. Guest rooms are furnished with antiques—all with gas fireplaces—and not a single one is unappealing (though the Union is a bit dark). Among my favorites: Excelsior, a large corner unit with a massive four-poster bed, a gas fire, and two-person Jacuzzi; Hesper, the best of the lower-priced rooms; and Merchant, a spacious first-floor suite with a large Jacuzzi.

Pleasant St. and Green St. (P.O. Box 800), Kennebunkport, ME 04046. © **207/967-3141.** Fax 207/967-3172. www.captainlord.com. 20 units. Summer and fall $214–$499 double; winter and spring from $175 midweek, from $199 weekends. Rates include breakfast. DISC, MC, V. 2- or 3-night minimum stay weekends and holidays. Children 12 and older are welcome. *In room:* A/C, dataport, minibar, hair dryer, iron.

The Colony Hotel ★★   One of a handful of oceanside resorts that have preserved the classic New England vacation experience, this mammoth white Georgian Revival (1914) lords over the ocean and the mouth of the Kennebunk River. All rooms in the three-story main inn have been renovated over the last 3 years (still no air-conditioning or TVs in most rooms). They're bright and cheery, simply furnished with summer cottage antiques. Rooms in two of the three outbuildings carry over the rustic elegance of the main hotel; the exception is the East House, a 1950s-era hotel at the back of the property with 20 motel-style rooms that are uninspiring but do have televisions. A staff naturalist leads guided coastal ecology tours on Saturdays in July and August; Fridays feature a lobster buffet dinner. The shuffleboard court, putting green, and heated saltwater pool are also popular diversions.

140 Ocean Ave. (P.O. Box 511), Kennebunkport, ME 04046. © **800/552-2363** or 207/967-3331. Fax 207/967-8738. www.thecolonyhotel.com/maine. 123 units. $180–$435 double July–Aug; off-season rates available. Rates include breakfast. 3-night minimum stay summer weekends and holidays in main hotel. AE, MC, V. Closed mid-Oct to mid-May. Pets allowed ($25 per night). **Amenities:** Restaurant (American/seafood); lounge; outdoor pool; tennis courts; bike rental; limited room service. *In room:* Dataport, hair dryer, iron.

Franciscan Guest House *Value*   This former dormitory on the 200-acre grounds of St. Anthony's Monastery is a unique budget choice. The rooms in five buildings are institutional, basic, and clean, with industrial carpeting, inexpensive paneling, and no daily maid service. On the other hand, all have private (if small) bathrooms, and guests can stroll the lovely riverside grounds or walk over to Dock Square, about 10 minutes away. A Lithuanian breakfast is served downstairs (cheese, oatmeal, salami, fruit, juice, and homemade bread), and payment is by donation. Though one of the most spartan lodges in Maine, the fact that reservations are often needed a year in advance tells the story: it's popular.

28 Beach Ave. (P.O. Box 980), Kennebunk, ME 04046. © **207/967-4865.** www.franciscanguesthouse.com. 60 units. $65–$88 double. No credit cards. Closed mid-Sept to mid-June. *In room:* A/C, TV.

Old Fort Inn ★★   This sophisticated inn is in a quiet and picturesque neighborhood of magnificent late-19th-century summer homes, 2 blocks from the ocean and not far from the Colony Hotel. Guests check in at a tidy antique shop; most park in back at the large carriage house, an interesting amalgam of stone, brick, shingle, and stucco. The 14 rooms are modern (once inside you could be in a building constructed last year) but solidly wrought and delightfully decorated with antiques and reproductions. Most rooms have in-floor heated tiles in the bathrooms; all have welcome amenities such as robes, Neutrogena products, and a reasonably priced self-serve snack bar. Two 500-sq.-ft. suites are in the main house; suite 216, flooded with morning light, faces east and the pool. A full buffet breakfast is served in the main house; in nice weather, guests often take waffles, pancakes, croissants, or fresh fruit on wicker trays outside to enjoy the morning sun.

8 Old Fort Rd. (P.O. Box M), Kennebunkport, ME 04046. ✆ 800/828-3678 or 207/967-5353. Fax 207/967-4547. www.oldfortinn.com. 16 units (includes 2 suites). $160–$375 double; from $325 suite; off season $99–$295. Rates include breakfast. AE, DC, DISC, MC, V. **Amenities:** Outdoor pool; tennis court; dry cleaning. *In room:* A/C, TV, dataport, minibar, fridge, coffeemaker, hair dryer, iron.

The Tides Inn ✸   The best bet in the region for a quiet getaway, located just across the street from Goose Rocks Beach, the Tides Inn is a yellow-clapboard and shingle affair dating from 1899 that retains a seaside boarding-house feel while providing up-to-date comfort. (Past guests have included Teddy Roosevelt and Arthur Conan Doyle.) Rooms tend toward the small side, as they often do in historic hostelries, but are comfortable, and you can hear the lapping of the surf from all of them. Among the brightest and most popular are rooms 11, 15, 24, and 29, some of which have bay windows and all of which have ocean views. The parlor has old wicker, TV, and chess for those rainy days. The pub is cozy and features a wood stove and dartboard. The first-floor **Belvedere Room** offers upscale dining in a Victorian setting, with options such as crab cakes with Asian slaw, scallops with ginger chive polenta, and boiled lobster with roasted corn on the cob. Breakfast is also offered, but not included in room rates.

252 Kings Highway, Goose Rocks Beach, Kennebunkport, ME 04046. ✆ 207/967-3757. www.tidesinnbythesea.com. 22 units (4 share 2 bathrooms). Peak season $195–$325 double with private bathroom (off season from $135); $155 with shared bathroom (off season from $135). 3-night minimum July–Aug. AE, MC, V. Closed mid-Oct to mid-May. **Amenities:** Restaurant (New American). *In room:* No phone.

White Barn Inn ✸✸✸   Part of the exclusive Relais & Châteaux group, the White Barn Inn pampers its guests like no other in Maine. Upon checking in, guests are shown to one of the parlors and offered port or brandy while valets gather luggage and park cars. The atmosphere is distinctly European, with an emphasis on service. The rooms are individually decorated in an upscale country style. I know of no other inn of this size that offers as many unexpected niceties, such as robes, fresh flowers in the rooms, and turndown service at night. Nearly half the rooms have wood-burning fireplaces, while the suites (in a separate facility across from the main inn) are truly spectacular; each is themed with a separate color, and most have LCD televisions, whirlpools, or similar perks. Guests can avail themselves of the inn's free bikes (including a small fleet of tandems) to head to the beach, take a cruise on its Hinckley charter yacht, or stroll across the street to explore the grounds of St. Anthony's Franciscan Monastery. You might also lounge around the beautiful outdoor pool. In 2003, the inn acquired a handful of cottages on the Kennebunk River, a bit down the road from the main inn, and will develop a wharf on that site to encourage boating interests. The cottages are cozy, nicely equipped with modern kitchens and bathrooms, and will continue to see future upgrades; an adjacent "friendship cottage" is stocked at all times with snacks, wine, and the like. They are a wonderful addition to a property that previously lacked nothing except water views.

37 Beach Ave. (¼ mile east of junction of Routes 9 and 35; P.O. Box 560-C), Kennebunkport, ME 04046. ✆ 207/967-2321. Fax 207/967-1100. www.whitebarninn.com. 25 units, 4 cottages. $320–$370 double; $500–$725 suite. Rates include continental breakfast and afternoon tea. AE, MC, V. 2-night minimum stay on weekends; 3-night minimum on holiday weekends. **Amenities:** Restaurant (New American); outdoor pool; spa; watersports equipment; bikes (free); concierge; limited room service; massage. *In room:* A/C, TV/VCR.

The Yachtsman Lodge & Marina ★★ The White Barn Inn took over this riverfront motel in 1997 and made it an appealing base for exploring the southern Maine coast. Within walking distance of Dock Square, nice touches abound, such as down comforters, granite-topped vanities, high ceilings, CD players, and French doors that open onto patios just above the river. Every room is a first-floor room and basically the same, but while standard motel size, their simple, classical styling is far superior to anything you'll find at a chain motel.

Ocean Ave. (P.O. Box 2609), Kennebunkport, ME 04046. © 207/967-2511. Fax 207/967-5056. www. yachtsmanlodge.com. 30 units. Peak season $195–$255; off season $129–$253. Rates include continental breakfast. AE, MC, V. 2-night minimum stay on weekends and holidays. *In room:* A/C, TV/VCR, dataport, fridge, coffeemaker, hair dryer, iron.

WHERE TO DINE

Prices for lobster in the rough tend to be a bit more expensive around Kennebunkport than at other casual lobster joints further up the coast. But if you can't wait and are willing to pay the price, **Nunan's Lobster Hut** (© 207/967-4362), on Route 9 north of Kennebunkport at Cape Porpoise, is a good choice. It's a classic lobster shack, often crowded with diners and full of atmosphere, which helps make up for sometimes lackluster food and disappointments such as potato chips (rather than a baked potato) served with the lobster dinner. It's open daily for dinner, starting at 5pm in summer.

Grissini ★★ TUSCAN Run by the folks at White Barn Inn, Grissini is a handsome trattoria that's offers good value. The mood is elegant but rustic Italian writ large: Oversize Italian advertising posters line the walls of the soaring, barn-like space, and burning logs in the handsome stone fireplace take the chill off a cool evening. The menu changes weekly but includes a wide range of pastas and pizza, served with considerable flair. More far-ranging entrees include osso buco served over garlic mashed potatoes, and fried calamari with grilled vegetables, served with a spicy tomato sauce. Expect an exceedingly pleasant experience.

27 Western Ave., Kennebunkport. © 207/967-2211. www.restaurantgrissini.com. Reservations recommended. Main courses $12–$23. AE, MC, V. Sun–Fri 5:30–9:30pm; Sat 5–9pm (closed Wed Jan–Mar).

Pier 77 Restaurant ★★ CONTEMPORARY NEW ENGLAND Long a tony restaurant with a wonderful ocean view, Pier 77 was recently renovated and renamed by husband-and-wife team Peter and Kate Morency. The food, drawing on Peter's training at the Culinary Institute of America and 20 years in top kitchens in Boston and San Francisco, is more contemporary and skillful than most anything else in Maine. The menu offers traditional favorites along with more adventurous dishes such as cashew-crusted Chilean sea bass served with citrus-tamari sauce. The restaurant has earned *Wine Spectator's* award of excellence annually since 1993.

77 Pier Rd., Cape Porpoise, Kennebunkport. © 207/967-8500. www.pier77restaurant.com. Reservations recommended. Main courses $14–$25. Tues–Sat 11:30am–2:30pm and 5–10pm; Sun 10am–2pm.

White Barn Inn ★★★ REGIONAL/NEW AMERICAN The White Barn Inn's (see above) classy dining room attracts gourmands from New York and Boston, who make repeat trips up the Maine Turnpike to dine here. The restaurant is housed in a rustic barn attached to the inn, with a soaring interior and eclectic collection of country antiques displayed in a hayloft; this setting is magical. One window throws in coastal light, and staff gussies it up with changing window dressings (bright pumpkins, corn stalks, and other reminders of the harvest in fall, for example). Chef Jonathan Cartwright's menu also changes frequently, nearly always incorporating local ingredients: You might start with a lobster spring roll of daikon, carrots, snow peas, and Thai sauce or pan-seared diver scallops; glide through an *intermezzo* course of fruit soup or sorbet; then graduate to a roasted New England duck with a juniper sauce, roasted halibut filet with Matsutake mushrooms with sautéed shrimp and a champagne foam, or a simply steamed Maine lobster over fettuccine with cognac coral butter sauce. The tasting menu runs to seasonal items such as three variations of Maine oyster, sautéed veal over butternut squash ragout, and smoked haddock rarebit. The White Barn's service is attentive and knowledgeable, capping the experience; anticipate a meal to remember. It's no surprise this was recently selected one of America's finest inn restaurants by the readers of *Travel + Leisure* magazine.

Beach Ave., Kennebunkport. © 207/967-2321. Reservations recommended. Fixed-price dinner $85, tasting menu $105 per person. AE, MC, V. Mon–Thurs 6:30–9:30pm; Fri–5:30–9:30pm. Closed 2 weeks in Jan.

2 Portland ⓕ

Maine's largest city, Portland sits on a peninsula extending into scenic Casco Bay. It's easy to drive right past on I-295, admire the skyline at 60 miles per hour and be on your way to the villages and headlands further up the coast. After all, urban life isn't what one usually thinks of when one thinks of Maine.

But Portland is well worth an afternoon detour or overnight. This historic city has plenty of charm—especially the renovated Old Port, with its brick sidewalks and cobblestone streets. In addition, travelers who stop here are rewarded with ferries to islands, boutique shops, some top-notch historic homes, graceful neighborhoods—and the food. Portland is a culinary mecca of Maine, blessed with an uncommonly high number of excellent restaurants for a city its size (65,000, roughly half that of Peoria, Illinois).

ESSENTIALS

GETTING THERE   Coming from the south by car, downtown Portland is most easily reached by taking Exit 6A off the Maine Turnpike (I-95), then following I-295. Exit at Franklin Street and continue straight uphill and downhill until you arrive at the ferry terminal. Turn right onto Commercial Street, and continue several blocks to the visitor center on the right (see below).

In December 2001, **Amtrak** © 800/872-7245; www.amtrak.com) finally launched its long-delayed Downeaster service from Boston's North Station to Portland. The train makes four round-trips daily, for $21 one-way. Take a short METRO bus ride to reach downtown from the station.

Concord Trailways (© 800/639-3317 or 207/828-1151) and **Vermont Transit** (© 800/451-3292 or 207/772-6587) offer bus service to Portland from Boston and Bangor. The Vermont Transit bus terminal (next to the Amtrak terminal) is located at 950 Congress St. Concord Trailways, which is slightly more expensive, offers movies and headsets on its trips; its terminal is on Sewall Street (a 35-min. walk from downtown).

Portland International Jetport (© 207/774-7301; www.portlandjetport. org) is served by **Air Nova** (© 902/873-5000; www.airnova.ca), **American Airlines** (© 800/433-7300; www.aa.com), **Delta/Business Express** (© 800/638-7333; www.delta-air.com), **Continental** (© 800/525-0280; www.flycontinental. com), **Northwest** (© 800/225-2525; www.nwa.com), **US Airways** (© 800/428-4322; www.usairways.com), and **United** (© 800/241-6522; www.ual.com). The airport is across the Fore River from downtown. Local METRO buses ($1) connect the airport to downtown; cab fare runs about $15.

VISITOR INFORMATION   The **Convention and Visitor's Bureau of Greater Portland,** 245 Commercial St. (© **207/772-5800** or 207/772-4994; www.visitportland.com), stocks a large supply of brochures and is happy to dispense information. The center is open in summer, Monday through Friday, 8am to 6pm, and Saturday and Sunday, 10am to 5pm; hours are shorter in the off season. Ask for the *Greater Portland Visitor Guide,* which includes a map. Portland's two free, weekly alternative newspapers—the *Casco Bay Weekly* and the *Portland Phoenix*—offer listings of local events, films, nightclubs, and the like. The daily *Portland Press Herald* also publishes arts listings in its Thursday paper.

PARKING   Parking is notoriously tight in the Old Port area, and the city's parking enforcement is efficient. Several garages are convenient to the Old Port, with parking fees around $1 per hour. Be careful when parking in residential neighborhoods; restrictions are complicated, and sometimes change. You *will* get towed if you run afoul of them. (Don't ask how I know. I just do.)

EXPLORING THE CITY

Any visit to Portland should start with a stroll around the historic **Old Port.** Bounded by Commercial, Congress, Union, and Pearl streets, this area near the waterfront contains the city's best commercial architecture, a mess of boutiques, fine restaurants, and one of the thickest concentrations of bars on the eastern seaboard. (The Old Port tends to transform as night lengthens, the crowds growing younger and rowdier.) Its narrow streets and intricate brick facades reflect the mid-Victorian era; most of the area was rebuilt following a devastating fire in 1866. Leafy, quaint Exchange Street is the heart of the Old Port, with other attractive streets running off of and around it.

Just outside the Old Port, don't miss the **First Parish Church** ✦, at 425 Congress St., a beautiful granite meeting house with an impressively austere interior that's changed little since 1826. A few doors down the block, Portland's **City Hall** is at the head of Exchange Street. Modeled after New York's City Hall, Portland's seat of government was built of granite in 1909. In a similarly regal vein is the **U.S. Custom House** ✦, at 312 Fore St. During business hours, wander inside to view its woodwork and marble floors dating back to 1868.

The city's finest harborside stroll is along the **Eastern Prom Pathway** ✦✦, which wraps for about a mile along the waterfront beginning at the Casco Bay Lines ferry terminal (corner of Commercial and Franklin sts.). The paved pathway is suitable for walking or biking, and offers expansive views of the islands and boat traffic on the harbor. The pathway skirts the lower edge of the **Eastern Promenade** ✦✦, a 68-acre hillside park with broad, grassy slopes extending down to the water. Tiny East End Beach is here, but the water is often off-limits for swimming (look for signs). The pathway continues on to Back Cove Pathway, a 3½-mile loop around tidal Back Cove.

Atop Munjoy Hill (above the Eastern Promenade) is the distinctive **Portland Observatory** ✦, 138 Congress St. (© **207/774-5561**), a shingled tower dating from 1807 and used to signal the arrival of ships into port. Exhibits provide a quick glimpse of Portland past, but the real draw is the view of the city and harbor from the top. Open daily from Memorial Day to Columbus Day from 10am to 5pm; admission is $4 for adults, $2 for children.

On the other end of the Portland peninsula is the **Western Promenade** ✦. (From the Old Port, follow Spring St. west to Vaughan; turn right and then take the first left on Bowdoin St.) A narrow strip of lawn atop a forested bluff is the actual promenade; it has views across the Fore River, which is lined with

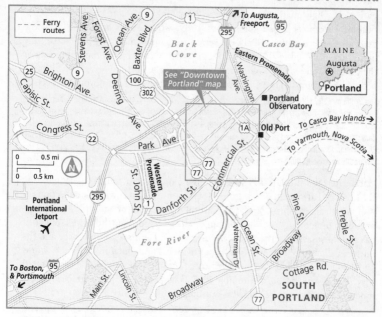

less-than-scenic light industry and commercial buildings, the White Mountains in the distance. The surrounding neighborhood is called the "Western Prom." A walk through here reveals the grandest and most imposing houses in the city, in a wide array of architectural styles, from Italianate to shingle to stick.

Children's Museum of Maine ★★ *Kids*   The centerpiece exhibit here is the *camera obscura,* a room-size "camera" on the top floor of this stout, columned building next to the art museum. Children gather around a white table in a dark room, where they see magically projected images that include cars driving on city streets, boats plying the harbor, and seagulls flapping by. That's just one attraction; others range from running a supermarket checkout counter to a firehouse pole that kids can slide down. It's a fun place for the little ones.

142 Free St. (next to the Portland Museum of Art). ℂ 207/828-1234. www.kitetails.com. Admission $6 adults and children, free for children under 1. Mon–Sat 10am–5pm; Sun noon–5pm. Closed Mon fall through spring. Discounted parking at Spring St. Parking Garage.

Maine Narrow Gauge Railroad Co. & Museum ★ *Kids*   In the late 19th century, Maine was home to several narrow-gauge railways, operating on rails 2 feet apart. Most of these versatile trains have disappeared, but this nonprofit organization is dedicated to preserving the examples that remain. Admission is free, with a charge for a short ride on a train that chugs on a rail line along Casco Bay at the foot of the Eastern Prom. Views of the islands are outstanding; the ride itself is slow-paced and somewhat yawn-inducing unless you're very young.

58 Fore St. ℂ 207/828-0814. www.mngrr.org. Museum admission free; train fare $6 adults, $5 seniors, $4 children 4–12, free for children under 4. Daily 10am–4pm; trains run on the hour from 11am. Closed Jan to mid-Feb. From I-295, take Franklin St. exit and follow to Fore St.; turn left, continue to museum, on the right.

Portland Head Light & Museum ★★★   Just a 10-minute drive from downtown Portland is this 1794 lighthouse, easily one of the most picturesque in the nation. The light marks the entrance to Portland Harbor, and was occupied continuously from its construction until 1989, when it was automated and the graceful keeper's house (1891) converted to a small museum. Still active, the lighthouse is closed to the public, but visitors can stop by the museum, wander the grounds, and watch sailboats and cargo ships come and go. The park has a pebble beach, grassy lawns, and picnic areas well suited for informal barbecues.

Fort Williams Park, 1000 Shore Rd., Cape Elizabeth. ℭ 207/799-2661. www.portlandheadlight.com. Free entrance to park grounds; museum admission $2 adults, $1 children 6–18, free for children under 6. Park grounds open year-round, daily from sunrise to sunset (until 8:30pm in summer); museum open June–Oct daily 10am–4pm, spring and late fall Sat–Sun 10am–4pm. From Portland, follow State St. across the Fore River; continue straight on Broadway. At third light, turn right on Cottage Rd., which becomes Shore Rd.; follow until you arrive at the park, on your left.

Portland Museum of Art ★★

This bold, modern museum, designed by I. M. Pei & Partners in 1983, features selections from its own fine collections as well as touring exhibits. Particularly strong in American artists with Maine connections, including Winslow Homer, Andrew Wyeth, and Edward Hopper, it has good displays of early American furniture and crafts. Colby College and the museum share the Joan Whitney Payson Collection, which includes fine works by Renoir, Degas, and Picasso. A recent addition to the complex is the restored McLellan-Sweat House, a stunning 1801 Federal-style building attached to the modern wing, where the museum was once entirely housed.

7 Congress Sq. (corner of Congress and High sts.). ℭ 207/775-6148. Fax 207/773-7324. www.portland museum.org. Admission $8 adults, $6 students and seniors, $2 children 6–17, free for children under 6. Tues–Thurs and Sat–Sun 10am–5pm; Fri 10am–9pm; June to mid-Oct also open Mon 10am–5pm. Guided tours daily at 2pm.

Victoria Mansion ★★

Widely regarded as one of the most elaborate brownstones ever built in the U.S., this mansion (also known as the Morse-Libby House) is a remarkable display of high Victorian style. Built between 1858 and 1863, the towering home is a prime example—some say America's finest—of the opulent Italianate style. It offers an engaging look at a bygone era. Inside, it appears not a square inch of wall space was left untouched by craftsmen or artisans; 11 painters were hired to create the murals. The most comprehensive tours are given the first and third Friday of each month from June to October; December is a particularly special time here, with a month of holiday events, decorations, and festivities.

109 Danforth St. ℭ 207/772-4841. www.victoriamansion.org. Admission $10 adults, $9 seniors, $3 children 6–17, free for children under 6. May–Oct Tues–Sat 10am–4pm; Sun 1–5pm; tours offered at quarter past and quarter of each hour. Closed Nov–Apr, except for holiday tours from late Nov to mid-Dec. From the Old Port, head west on Fore St., veer right on Danforth St. at light near Stonecoast Brewing; go 3 blocks to the mansion, at the corner of Park St.

Wadsworth-Longfellow House & Center for Maine History ★

The Maine Historical Society's "history campus" on Congress Street includes the austere brick Wadsworth-Longfellow House (1785), built by Gen. Peleg Wadsworth, father of poet Henry Wadsworth Longfellow. It's furnished in an early-19th-century style, with many pieces of Longfellow family furniture. Adjacent is the Maine History Gallery, in a garish postmodern building. Exhibits here explore the rich texture of Maine history, and the library is outstanding.

489 Congress St. ℭ 207/879-0427. www.mainehistory.com. Gallery and Longfellow house tour $7 adults, $3 children 5–18, free for children under 5. Gallery only $4 adults, $2 children. Longfellow House open June–Oct daily 10am–4pm, gallery daily 10am–5:30pm; Nov–May gallery only Wed–Sat noon–4pm.

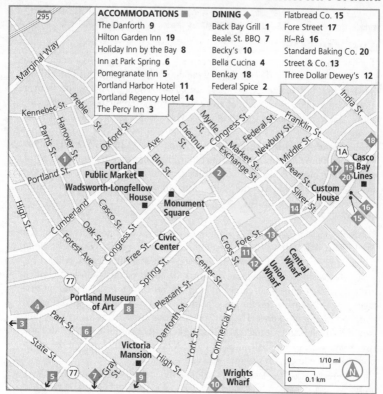

ACCOMMODATIONS ■
The Danforth **9**
Hilton Garden Inn **19**
Holiday Inn by the Bay **8**
Inn at Park Spring **6**
Pomegranate Inn **5**
Portland Harbor Hotel **11**
Portland Regency Hotel **14**
The Percy Inn **3**

DINING ◆
Back Bay Grill **1**
Beale St. BBQ **7**
Becky's **10**
Bella Cucina **4**
Benkay **18**
Federal Spice **2**

Flatbread Co. **15**
Fore Street **17**
Rí~Rá **16**
Standard Baking Co. **20**
Street & Co. **13**
Three Dollar Dewey's **12**

BOAT TOURS

Casco Bay Lines ✯✯ Six Casco Bay islands have year-round populations and are served by ferries from downtown Portland. Except for Long Island, the islands are part of the city of Portland. The ferries offer a reasonably priced way to view the harbor and get a taste of island life. Trips range from a 20-minute (one-way) excursion to Peaks Island (the closest thing to an island suburb, with 1,200 year-round residents) to a 5½-hour cruise to Bailey Island (connected by bridge to the mainland south of Brunswick) and back. All of the islands are well suited for walking; Peaks Island has a rocky back shore that's easily accessible via a paved perimeter road (bring a picnic lunch). Cliff Island is the most remote.

Commercial and Franklin sts. Ⓒ 207/774-7871. www.cascobaylines.com. Fares vary depending on the run and season, but round-trip summer rates are typically $6–$19. Frequent departures 6am–10pm.

Eagle Island Tours ✯✯ Eagle Island was the summer home of Arctic explorer and Portland native Robert E. Peary, who claimed in 1909 to be the first person to reach the North Pole. (His accomplishments have been the subject of exhaustive debate among Arctic scholars.) In 1904, Peary built a home on a remote, 17-acre island at the edge of Casco Bay; in 1912, he added two low stone towers. After his death in 1920, his family kept up the home before donating it to the state. The home is open to the public, and remains much the way it was when Peary lived here. Eagle Tours offers one trip daily from Portland. The 4-hour excursion includes a 1½-hour stopover on the island.

Long Wharf (Commercial St.). ☎ 207/774-6498. Tour $18 adults, $14 seniors, $10.50 children under 12 (includes state park fee of $1.50 adults, 50¢ children). One departure daily at 10am.

WHERE TO STAY

If you're simply looking for something central, Hilton has unveiled a brand-new waterfront hotel across the street from the city's island ferry dock. The **Hilton Garden Inn** (65 Commercial St. ☎ 207/780-0780), though made from a cookie-cutter plan, is convenient to the Old Port's restaurants, bakeries, and pubs—not to mention the islands of Casco Bay. Double rooms run $89 to $289 per night.

The **Holiday Inn by the Bay** ⚬, 88 Spring St. (☎ 207/775-2311), offers great views of the harbor from half the rooms. Peak-season rates run about $150 to $170 per night. Budget travelers seeking chain hotels can head toward the area around the Maine Mall in South Portland, about a 10-minute drive from downtown. Try **Days Inn** (☎ 207/772-3450) or the no-frills **Coastline Inn** (☎ 207/772-3838).

Black Point Inn ⚬⚬⚬   A 15-minute drive from downtown Portland, the Black Point is a Maine classic. Situated on 9 acres on a point with views along the coast both north and south, the inn was built as a summer resort in 1873, in an area enshrined in some of the work of noted painter Winslow Homer. Sixty rooms are in the main shingled lodge; the others are spread about four cottages. Even the smaller rooms are generously sized, with enough space for two wingback chairs and a desk. The cottage units have more of a rustic feel; my pick would be the Sprague Cottage, with its flagstone floors in the common area and five rooms with private balconies, some with ocean views. Note that the inn is popular for weddings on summer weekends.

510 Black Point Rd., Prouts Neck, ME 04074. ☎ 800/258-0003 or 207/883-2500. Fax 207/883-9976. www. blackpointinn.com. 80 units. July to Labor Day $420–$780 double; spring and fall from $290; winter from $250. Rates include breakfast and dinner. AE, DC, DISC, MC, V. **Amenities:** Restaurant (New England); outdoor pool; indoor pool; fitness room; Jacuzzi; sauna; children's programs (summer); shuttle; limited room service; massage; babysitting; laundry service; dry cleaning. *In room:* A/C, TV, VCR (on request), dataport, fridge (on request), hair dryer, iron.

The Danforth ⚬⚬   Located in an unusually handsome brick home constructed in 1821, this is one of Portland's more desirable small inns. The extra touches are welcome throughout, from working wood-burning fireplaces in all guest rooms but one to the richly paneled billiards room. Especially appealing is room 1, with a sitting area and private deck, and room 2, with high ceilings and abundant morning light. The inn is located at the edge of the Spring Street Historic District, a 10-minute walk from downtown. It's popular for weddings, so if you're in search of a quiet weekend retreat, ask if anything is planned.

163 Danforth St., Portland, ME 04102. ☎ 800/991-6557 or 207/879-8755. Fax 207/879-8754. www.danforth maine.com. 9 units. Summer $139–$329 double; off season $119–$249 double. Rates include continental breakfast. AE, MC, V. Pets sometimes allowed ($10 per night). **Amenities:** Bike rentals; massage. *In room:* A/C, TV, dataport, hair dryer, iron.

Inn at Park Spring ⚬   This small, tasteful B&B is on a downtown street in a historic brick home dating from 1835. It's well located for exploring the city on foot: The Portland Museum of Art is just 2 blocks away, the Old Port is 10 minutes by foot, and great restaurants are within easy walking distance. Guests can linger or watch TV in the front parlor or chat at the table in the kitchen. Every room is a corner room; most are bright and sunny. Especially nice is "Spring," with its great morning light and wonderful views of the historic row houses on Park Street, and "Gables," on the third floor, which gets abundant afternoon light and has a nice bathroom. The new owners promise to gradually upgrade the inn.

135 Spring St., Portland, ME 04101. ⓒ **800/437-8511** or 207/774-1059. www.innatparkspring.com. 6 units. Apr 16–May 15 $129–$165 double; May 16–June 15 $139–$165 double; June 16–Oct 31 $149–$175 double; Nov 1–Apr 15$109–$135 double. Rates include breakfast and off-street parking. 2-night minimum stay weekends. AE, DISC, MC, V. *In room:* A/C, dataport, hair dryer.

The Percy Inn ★★ The Percy Inn, at the edge of Portland's West End, is housed in a pair of handsome early-19th-century brick town houses in an up-and-coming but not-quite-there-yet area. Close to good restaurants, it's about a 15-minute walk to the Old Port. Guest rooms in the main building are reached via a narrow, twisting staircase. The Henry W. Longfellow Room has wonderful random-width floorboards, a small snack room with fridge, and a corner sitting area with marble cafe table. In 2001, the inn expanded into the adjacent town house; at 1,000 square feet, Pine Suite 1 is the largest unit, a two-bedroom suite in a former art gallery. For families, another two-bedroom suite is in the carriage house. Nice touches abound: All rooms have weather radios, CD players, VCRs, complimentary soft drinks, and coolers with beach blankets for day trips.

15 Pine St., Portland ME 04102. ⓒ **207/871-7638.** Fax 207/775-2599. www.percyinn.com. 8 units. June–Oct $129–$259 double; Nov–May $89–$229 double. (Rates higher in foliage season and for special events). Rates include continental breakfast. MC, V. Limited off-street parking. *In room:* A/C, TV/VCR.

Pomegranate Inn ★★★ This imposing 1884 Italianate home in the architecturally distinctive Western Prom neighborhood surprises guests with interiors that are both whimsical and elegant—a fatally cloying combination when attempted by anyone without impeccably good taste. Expect bold artwork and eclectic antique furniture. (Some readers have reported that the decor is a bit too bustling for them.) Most units have gas fireplaces; the best is the carriage house, with its own terrace, kitchenette, and fireplace. Tea and wine are served upon arrival, and the sit-down breakfasts are tasty. The inn is well situated for exploring Western Prom; downtown is a 20-minute walk away.

49 Neal St., Portland, ME 04102. ⓒ **800/356-0408** or 207/772-1006. Fax 207/773-4426. www.pomegranate inn.com. 8 units. Summer and fall $175–$265 double; winter and spring $95–$165 double. Rates include breakfast. 2-night minimum stay summer weekends; 4-night minimum stay Christmas and Thanksgiving. AE, DISC, MC, V. On-street parking. Children 16 and older are welcome. From the Old Port, take Middle St. (which turns into Spring St.) to Neal St. in the West End (about 1 mile); turn right and proceed to inn. *In room:* A/C, TV, dataport, hair dryer.

Portland Harbor Hotel ★★★ This new luxury hotel opened in the popular Old Port district in 2003, steps from a clutch of bars and restaurants. All rooms and suites are top-drawer: Even standard rooms are outfitted with big, deep baths in granite-faced bathrooms; armoires; queen and king beds done up in comfy duvets and down coverlets; two-line phones; and big TVs offering 70 channels of digital television with Internet access. Deluxe rooms and suites add Jacuzzis, and many units look out onto an attractive central garden area where guests dine or sip drinks in good weather. (Other rooms offer views of the Old Port's brick skyline.) Turndown service with chocolates is always available. The **restaurant** is excellent, and there's also a bar.

468 Fore St. ⓒ **888/798-9090** or 207/775-9090. Fax 207/775-9990. www.portlandharborhotel.com. 100 units. Mid-May to mid-Oct $229–$249 double, $329 suite; off season $159–$179 double, $259 suite. AE, DC, DISC, MC, V. Valet parking on premises $15 per night. **Amenities:** Restaurant (contemporary American/Continental); bar; indoor pool; fitness center; spa; concierge; laundry service; dry cleaning. *In room:* A/C, TV, hair dryer.

Portland Regency Hotel ✦✦✦ On a cobblestone courtyard in the Old Port, the Regency boasts the city's premier hotel location. But it's got more than location going for it—this is also one of the most architecturally striking and well-managed hotels in the state. Sitting in an 1895 brick armory, the hotel is thoroughly modern within, offering attractive rooms appointed with many amenities. The architects had to work within the quirky layout of the building; as a result, the top-floor rooms lack windows but have skylights, and windows are at knee-height in some units. The hotel has several different types of rooms and suites; for a splurge, try one of the corner units, offering gas fireplaces, CD players, sitting areas, and newly added Jacuzzis. Staff is extremely professional, the health club is very good, and the hotel is also home to both a good downstairs restaurant (**The Armory;** fine dining) and a **bar** ✦ that's the best quiet place in Portland to sip a drink and talk business, hold hands, or watch a ballgame on the TV. The only complaint I've heard is that some walls are a bit thin; on weekends, Old Port revelry may penetrate even the dense brick outer walls. But that's a small price to pay for such luxury, location, and professionalism.

20 Milk St., Portland, ME 04101. ℂ 800/727-3436 or 207/774-4200. Fax 207/775-2150. www.theregency. com. 95 units. Summer $199–$349 double; off season $139–$239 double. AE, DC, DISC, MC, V. Valet parking ($8 daily). **Amenities:** Restaurant (contemporary American); health club; Jacuzzi; sauna; courtesy car to airport; limited room service; massage; babysitting; dry cleaning. *In room:* A/C, TV, dataport, minibar, hair dryer, iron.

WHERE TO DINE
EXPENSIVE

Back Bay Grill ✦✦ NEW AMERICAN Back Bay Grill has long been one of Portland's best-regarded restaurants, offering an upscale, contemporary ambience in a somewhat downscale neighborhood. The innovative menu is revamped seasonally. Diners may start with the popular terrine of house-cured gravlax and smoked salmon with marinated red onions (it's almost always on the menu), or perhaps local mussels or sautéed foie gras. Among main courses, look for heavenly dishes such as rack of lamb with butter-braised potatoes and fava beans; Casco Bay cod with a champagne-and-olive oil sauce, filet mignon with gnocchi, or lavender-marinated duck breast served with a duck confit, lingonberry sauce, and a risotto of English peas and Vidalia onions.

65 Portland St. ℂ 207/772-8833. www.backbaygrill.com. Reservations recommended. Main courses $22–$34. AE, DC, DISC, MC, V. Mon–Thurs 5–9pm; Fri–Sat 5–9:30pm.

Fore Street ✦✦✦ CONTEMPORARY/GRILL Fore Street has emerged to take its place as one of New England's most celebrated restaurants—chef Sam Hayward has been profiled in *Saveur* and *House Beautiful,* and the restaurant has been listed in *Gourmet's* 100 best list. Its secret is simplicity: Local ingredients are used when possible (note the rustic vegetable cooler overflowing with what's fresh), and the kitchen shuns fussy presentations. The room is equally honest: Light floods in through huge windows in the loft-like space, and a sprawling open kitchen is in the middle of it all, a team of chefs stoking the wood-fired brick oven and grilling fish and meats. The menu changes nightly; some of the most memorable meals are prepared over an applewood grill, such as Maine pheasant, or two-texture duckling with grilled pears. Lobster and rabbit courses never fail to disappoint. Though it can be mighty hard to snag a reservation here, particularly on a summer weekend, Fore Street sets aside a few tables each night for walk-ins. Smart move. Now, you make one: Get there.

288 Fore St. ℂ 207/775-2717. Reservations recommended. Main courses $15–$26. AE, MC, V. Mon–Thurs 5:30–10pm; Fri–Sat 5:30–10:30pm; Sun 5:30–9:30pm. Parking in lot off Commercial St.

Street & Co. ⭐⭐⭐ MEDITERRANEAN/SEAFOOD Dana Street's intimate, brick-walled bistro on cobblestoned Wharf Street (in the Old Port) specializes in seafood that's fresh as can be (the docks are close by) and cooked just right. Diners sit at copper-topped tables, designed so that the waiters can deliver steaming skillets directly from the stove. Looking for lobster? Try it grilled and served over linguini in a butter-garlic sauce. If you're partial to calamari, they know how to cook it here so that it's perfectly tender, a knack that's been lost elsewhere. Otherwise, go for seared tuna, fresh mussels, or a grilled piece of whatever's come in (swordfish, perhaps). This place often fills up early, so reservations are strongly recommended. But, like Fore Street (see above), one-third of the tables are reserved for walk-ins; it can't hurt to check if you're in the neighborhood. In summer, outdoor seating is available at a few tables on the alley.

33 Wharf St. ⓒ 207/775-0887. Reservations recommended. Main courses $14–$24. AE, MC, V. Sun–Thurs 5:30–9:30pm; Fri–Sat 5:30–10pm.

MODERATE

Beale Street BBQ ⭐ *Finds* BARBECUE Beale Street BBQ owner Mark Quigg once operated a takeout grill on Route 1 outside Freeport, but he chucked that life when notables such as author Stephen King got wind of his cooking; soon he was catering movie shoots, joining forces with his two brothers, and the Quiggs have never looked back. Of all the 'cue joints in Maine, this is my favorite, with its appealing roadhouse atmosphere, friendly staff, and great smoked meats. Though I like everything here—check the board for intriguing daily specials, which usually include a fish preparation as well as Creole or Cajun offerings—I usually order the $15 barbecue sampler (subtitled "All You Really Need to Know About BBQ"). This entitles you to a choice of pulled pork, chicken, or beef brisket (go with the brisket); ample sweet and crunchy cornbread; a half slab of ribs; a quarter chicken; and delicious spicy smoked links that remind me of East Texas, plus a mound of barbecued beans and coleslaw. Two people could comfortably split it. This location, in South Portland's commercial Mill Creek and Knightville neighborhoods, is a bit hard to find (it's almost beneath the Casco Bay Bridge). There's another fancier location (ⓒ 207/442-9514) at 215 Water St. in the gritty maritime town of Bath, a short drive north on Route 1.

90 Waterman Dr., South Portland. ⓒ 207/767-0130. Reservations not accepted. Main courses $9–$18. MC, V. Mon–Sat 11:30am–10pm; Sun 11:30am–9pm.

Bella Cucina ⭐⭐ RUSTIC ITALIAN Situated in one of Portland's less elegant neighborhoods, Bella Cucina sets an inviting mood with rich colors, stylized fish sculptures, soft lighting, and pinpoint spotlights over the tables that carve out alluring islands of light. The menu changes frequently but dances deftly between rustic Italian and regional, with options such as a robust cioppino with haddock and lobster, and a mélange of veal, pork, and chicken served with a prosciutto and mushroom ragout. Vegan entrees are also always offered. About half the seats at Bella Cucina are kept open for walk-ins, so take a chance and stop by even if you don't have reservations. The wine selection is good, and there's free parking evenings in a lot just off Congress St.

653 Congress St. ⓒ 207/828-4033. Reservations recommended. Main courses $12–$19. AE, DISC, MC, V. Sun and Tues–Thurs 5–9pm; Fri–Sat 5–10pm.

Flatbread Company ⭐ PIZZA This upscale, hippie-chic pizzeria—an offshoot of the original Flatbread Company in Waitsfield, Vermont—may have the best waterfront location in town. It sits on a slip overlooking the Casco Bay

Lines terminal, so you can watch fishermen at work while you eat. (Picnic tables are on the deck in fair weather.) The inside brings to mind a Phish concert, with Tibetan prayer flags and longhaired staffers stoking wood-fired ovens and slicing nitrate-free pepperoni and organic vegetables. The laid-back atmosphere makes the place; the pizza is quite good, though toppings tend to be skimpy.

72 Commercial St. © 207/772-8777. Reservations accepted for parties of 10 or more. Pizzas $12–$15. AE, MC, V. Mon–Tues 5–9pm; Wed–Sun 11:30am–9pm.

INEXPENSIVE

Don't neglect Portland's bakeries and coffee shops while trolling for budget eats. My favorite bakery in New England is **Standard Baking Company** ★★★ at 75 Commercial St. (© **207/773-2112**), across from the ferry terminal and behind the new Hilton hotel. Allison Bray and Matt James bake the best sticky buns (with or without nuts) and focaccia I've tasted in America, plus top-rate breads, brioche, cookies, and more. There's good coffee, too. The bakery is open 7am to 6pm weekdays, to 5pm weekends.

Among the many coffee shops around the city, I frequent both **Arabica** at 16 Free St. (© **207/879-0792**), with house-roasted beans, a good choice of teas, plus bagels, scones, and even toast with peanut butter, and **Portland Coffee Roasting Co.** (© **207/761-9525**) at 111 Commercial St., with inventive coffee drinks, a daily trivia quiz, and a display case of fun snacks such as sushi and energy bars.

Finally, for takeout or a picnic, I'm crazy about **Supper at Six** ★ (© **207/761-6600**), at 16 Veranda St., near Back Cove and Washington Avenue. Their sandwiches, made with Standard Baking Company breads (see above), are the best in the city; they also do a variety of to-go gourmet meals.

Becky's ★★ *Value* BREAKFAST/LUNCH   A glowing write-up from Jane and Michael Stern in *Gourmet* magazine in 1999 obviously hasn't gone to the proprietor's head. This local institution in a squat concrete building on the non-quaint end of the waterfront has drop ceilings, fluorescent lights, and scruffy booths and tables. It's populated very early by local fishermen grabbing a plate o' eggs before setting out; later in the day, it attracts students and businessmen. The menu offers about what you'd expect, such as inexpensive sandwiches (fried haddock and cheese, corn dogs, tuna melt). It's most noted for breakfast, which includes 13 different omelets. Where else can you find five different types of home fries? Dinners include favorites such as lobster rolls and fried clams.

390 Commercial St. © 207/773-7070. www.beckysdiner.com. Main courses: breakfast $2.25–$7.50; sandwiches $1.95–$5.25; dinners $2.25–$7.95. AE, DISC, MC, V. Sun–Mon 4am–3pm; Tues–Sat 4am–9pm.

Silly's ★★ *Finds* *Value* ECLECTIC & TAKE-OUT   Silly's is the favored cheap-eats joint among even jaded Portlanders, and despite moving to a new location in the '90s, it has never lost favor. Situated on a ragged commercial street, the interior is bright and funky, with mismatched 1950s dinettes and an equally hodgepodge back terrace beneath improbable trees. The menu is creative, with everything made fresh and from scratch. The place is noted for its roll-ups ("fast Abdullahs"), a series of tasty fillings piled into fresh tortillas. Among the best: the shish kebab with feta and the sloppy "Diesel," made with pulled pork barbecue and coleslaw. The fries here are hand-cut, the burgers big and delicious, and the milkshakes thick and good. The rotating selection of homemade ice creams varies, but tend to be, shall we say, unique (such as cinnamon-basil or avocado and lime).

40 Washington Ave. © 207/772-0117; www.sillys.com. Main courses: lunch and dinner $3.25–$7.50; pizza $8.50–$11. MC, V. Tues–Thurs 11:30am–9pm; Fri–Sat 11:30am–10pm; Sun 11:30am–8pm.

PORTLAND AFTER DARK

Portland is usually lively in the evenings, especially on summer weekends when hormone levels in the Old Port seems to rocket into the stratosphere, with young men and women prowling dozens of bars and spilling out onto the streets. As is common in cities with more venues than attendees, clubs come and go, sometimes rapidly. Check one of the two free weekly newspapers, the *Casco Bay Weekly* or the *Portland Phoenix,* for current venues, performers, and showtimes.

Among the Old Port bars favored by locals are **Three-Dollar Dewey's,** at the corner of Commercial and Union streets (the popcorn is free), **Gritty McDuff's Brew Pub** , on Fore Street near the foot of Exchange Street, and **Brian Ború,** on Center Street. All three bars are casual and pubby, with guests sharing long tables with new companions.

Portland still has downtown movie houses, enabling travelers in the mood for a flick to avoid the disheartening slog out to the boxy, could-be-anywhere mall octoplexes. **Nickelodeon Cinemas,** 1 Temple St. (© **207/772-9751**), has six screens and offers an eclectic mix of first- and second-run films at slightly lower prices than you'll find at the malls. **The Movies,** 10 Exchange St. (© **207/772-9600**), is a compact art-film showcase in the heart of the Old Port, featuring a line-up of foreign and independent films of recent and historic vintage.

3 Mid-Coast Maine

Veteran Maine travelers contend that this part of the coast is fast losing its native charm—it's too commercial, too developed, too much like the rest of the United States. The grousers do have a point, especially regarding Route 1's roadside, but get off the main roads and you'll find pockets where you can catch glimpses of another Maine. Back-road travelers will stumble upon quiet inland villages, dramatic coastal scenery, and a rich sense of history, especially maritime history.

The best source of information for the region in general is at the **Maine State Information Center** (© **207/846-0833**), off Exit 17 of I-95 in Yarmouth. This state-run center is stocked with hundreds of brochures and a selection of free newspapers, and is staffed with a helpful crew who can provide information on the entire state, but are particularly well informed about the mid-coast region.

FREEPORT

If Freeport were a mall (not a far-fetched analogy), L.L.Bean would be the anchor store. It's the business that launched Freeport, elevating its status from just another town off the interstate to one of the two outlet capitals of Maine (the other is Kittery). Freeport still has the form of a classic Maine village, but it's a village that's been largely taken over by the national fashion industry. Most of the old homes and stores have been converted to upscale shops, and now sell name-brand clothing and housewares.

Strict planning guidelines have managed to preserve much of the local charm, at least in the village section. However, bring a lot of patience and expect teeming crowds if you come at a busy time.

ESSENTIALS

GETTING THERE   Freeport is on Route 1 but is most commonly reached via I-95 from either Exit 19 or 20.

VISITOR INFORMATION   The **Freeport Merchants Association,** 23 Depot St. (© **800/865-1994** or 207/865-1212; www.freeportusa.com), publishes a free map and directory of businesses, restaurants, and accommodations; it's widely available around town.

SHOPPING

With more than 100 retail shops between Exit 19 of I-95, at the far lower end of Main Street, and Mallett Road, which connects to Exit 20, shops have begun to spread south of Exit 19 toward Yarmouth. If you don't want to miss a single shopping opportunity, take Exit 17 and head north on Route 1. Bargains can vary from extraordinary to "huh?" Plan to rack up some mileage if you're intent on finding fantastic deals. The national chains in Freeport include Abercrombie & Fitch (in a former Carnegie library!), Banana Republic, The Gap, Levi's, Calvin Klein, Patagonia, North Face, Nike, Chaudier Cookware ("the cookware of choice aboard Air Force One"), Mikasa, Nine West, Timberland, and Maidenform, among others. Many others.

L.L.Bean ★★★   Monster outdoor retailer L.L.Bean traces its roots to the day Leon Leonwood Bean decided that what the world really needed was a good weatherproof hunting shoe. He joined a watertight gumshoe with a laced leather upper. Hunters liked it. The store grew. An empire was born.

Today, L.L.Bean sells millions of dollars worth of clothing and outdoor goods to customers nationwide through its well-respected catalogs, and it still draws hundreds of thousands through its doors. This modern, multilevel store keeps expanding and is now the size of a regional mall, but it's tastefully done with an indoor trout pond, lots of natural wood, a separate kid's shop (L.L.Kids), and a space for live summer performances out back. Don't worry about arriving when it's open, which is 365 days a year, 24 hours a day (note the lack of locks or latches on the front doors); it's popular even in the dead of night, especially in summer and around holidays. Selections include their trademark clothing, home furnishings, books, shoes, and outdoor gear for camping, fishing, and hunting.

L.L.Bean also stocks an outlet shop ★ with a relatively small but rapidly changing inventory at discount prices. It's located in a back lot between Main Street and Depot Street—ask at the front desk of the main store for walking directions. Main and Bow sts. ⓒ 800/221-4221. www.llbean.com.

WHERE TO STAY

Harraseeket Inn ★★   The Harraseeket deftly mixes traditional and modern in a personable property 2 blocks north of L.L.Bean. A late-19th-century home is the soul of the hotel, but most rooms are in modern additions. Guests can relax in the well-regarded dining room, read the paper in the common room during afternoon tea, or sip a cocktail in the rustic **Broad Arrow Tavern** and order snacks from its wood-fired oven. Guest rooms are quite large, and tastefully appointed with quarter-canopy beds and a mix of contemporary and antique furniture. About a quarter have fireplaces; more than half feature single or double whirlpools.

162 Main St., Freeport, ME 04032. ⓒ 800/342-6423 or 207/865-9377. www.harraseeketinn.com. 84 units. Summer and fall $195–$265 double; spring and early summer $140–$235 double; winter $110–$215 double. Rates include breakfast. AE, DC, DISC, MC, V. Take Exit 20 off I-95 to Main St. **Amenities:** 2 restaurants (New American, grill); indoor pool; concierge; limited room service; laundry service; dry cleaning. *In room:* A/C, TV, dataport, coffeemaker, hair dryer.

Kendall Tavern ★   This cheerful yellow farmhouse is out of the bustle of Freeport, but only half a mile from downtown shopping. Rooms are decorated in a bright and airy style with a mix of antique and new furniture. Those facing Route 1 (Main St.) are noisier than others, but the traffic isn't likely to be too disruptive. A piano is in one of the two parlors, and a hot tub occupies a spacious private room in the back. Breakfasts are served in the pine-floored dining room.

213 Main St., Freeport, ME 04032. ⓒ **800/341-9572** or 207/865-1338. 7 units. $95–$155 double. Rates include breakfast. AE, DISC, MC, V. **Amenities:** Jacuzzi. *In room:* No phone.

Maine Idyll Motor Court ⭐ *Value* This 1932 motor court is a Maine classic—20 cottages scattered about a grove of beech and oak trees. Each has a tiny porch, modest kitchen facilities (no ovens), and timeworn furniture. Fourteen have fireplaces, with birch logs provided more for atmosphere than warmth. The cabins are not lavishly sized, but are comfortable and clean. The only disruption is the omnipresent sound of traffic; Interstate 95 lurks just through the trees on one side of the cottages, Route 1 on the other, so you're the filling in an auto sandwich.

1411 U.S. Rte. 1, Freeport, ME 04032. ⓒ **207/865-4201.** www.freeportusa.com/maineidyll. 20 units. $46–$90 double. Rates include continental breakfast. No credit cards. Closed early Nov to mid-Apr. Pets allowed. *In room:* TV, kitchenette, no phone.

WHERE TO DINE

A short walk from L.L.Bean is **Chowder Express & Sandwich Shop,** 2 Mechanic St. (ⓒ **207/865-3404**), a hole-in-the-wall with counter seating for about a dozen. Fish, lobster, and clam chowder are served in paper bowls with plastic spoons. It's convenient for a quick bite between shops.

Harraseeket Lunch & Lobster ⭐⭐ *Finds* LOBSTER POUND Located at a boatyard on the Harraseeket River about a 10-minute drive from Freeport's main shopping district, this lobster pound is a popular destination on sunny days—though with its heated dining room, it's a worthy destination any time. Take in the river view from the dock while waiting for your number to be called. Be prepared for big crowds; a good alternative is to come in late afternoon between the crushing lunch and dinner hordes.

Main St., South Freeport. ⓒ **207/865-4888.** Lobsters market price (typically $8–$12). No credit cards. Daily 11:30am–8:30pm. Closed mid-Oct to May 1. From I-95, take Exit 17 and head north on Rte. 1; turn right on S. Freeport Rd. at the large Indian statue; continue to stop sign in South Freeport; turn right to waterfront. From Freeport, take South St. (off Bow St.) to Main St. in South Freeport; turn left to water.

Jameson Tavern ⭐ REGIONAL In a handsome, historic farmhouse literally in the shadow of L.L.Bean, this tavern touts itself as Maine's birthplace. In 1820, papers were signed here legally separating Maine from Massachusetts. Today, it's a two-part restaurant under single ownership. The historic Tap Room offers crab-cake burgers, lobster croissants, and a variety of build-your-own burgers (sit outside on the brick patio if the weather's good). The other part of the house is the Dining Room, more formal in a country-colonial sort of way. Meals are more sedate and gussied up, emphasizing steak and hearty fare.

115 Main St. ⓒ **207/865-4196.** Reservations recommended. Tap Room main courses $7.95–$18; Dining Room main courses: lunch $5.95–$12, dinner $12–$23. AE, DC, DISC, MC, V. Tap Room daily 11am–11pm; Dining Room summer daily 11am–10pm, winter daily 11:30am–9pm.

BRUNSWICK & BATH

Brunswick and Bath are two handsome and historic towns that share a strong commercial past. Many travelers heading up Route 1 usually pass through both towns eager to reach the areas with higher billing on the marquee. That's a shame, for both are well worth the detour to sample two distinctive Maine towns.

Along the Androscoggin River, **Brunswick** was once home to several mills, which have been converted to offices and the like, but its broad Maine Street still bustles with activity. (Idiosyncratic traffic patterns can lead to traffic snarls in the late afternoon.) Brunswick is also home to Bowdoin College, one of the nation's most respected small colleges. Founded in 1794, it has an illustrious roster of prominent alumni, including writer Nathaniel Hawthorne, poet Henry Wadsworth Longfellow, President Franklin Pierce, and arctic explorer Robert E. Peary. Civil War hero Joshua Chamberlain was college president after the war.

Eight miles to the east, **Bath** is a noted center of shipbuilding, situated on the broad Kennebec River. The first U.S.-built ship was constructed downstream at the Popham Bay colony in the early 17th century; in the years since, shipbuilders have constructed more than 5,000 ships here. Architecture buffs will find a detour here worthwhile. (Look for the free brochure *Architectural Tours: Walking and Driving in the Bath Area,* available at information centers listed below.) The Victorian era in particular is well represented. Washington Street, lined with maples and impressive homes, is one of the best-preserved displays in New England of late-19th-century homes. The compact downtown, on a rise overlooking the river, is also home to notable Victorian commercial architecture.

ESSENTIALS

GETTING THERE   Brunswick and Bath are both on Route 1. Brunswick is accessible via Exits 22 and 23 off I-95. If you're bypassing Brunswick and heading north up Route 1 to Bath or beyond, continue up I-95 and exit at the "coastal connector" exit in Topsham, which avoids some of the slower going through Brunswick.

For bus service from Portland or Boston, contact **Vermont Transit** (© 800/451-3292) or **Concord Trailways** (© 800/639-3317).

VISITOR INFORMATION   The **Bath-Brunswick Region Chamber of Commerce,** 59 Pleasant St., near downtown Brunswick (© 207/725-8797 or 207/443-9751), offers information and lodging assistance Monday through Friday from 8:30am to 5pm. The chamber also staffs a summer-only information center on Route 1 between Brunswick and Bath; open daily from 10am to 7pm.

EXPLORING THE AREA

Collectors flock to **Cabot Mill Antiques,** 14 Maine St., in downtown Brunswick (© 207/725-2855; www.cabotiques.com), on the ground floor of a restored textile mill. The emporium features the stuff of 140 dealers.

Bowdoin College Museum of Art ★★   This stern, neoclassical building on the Bowdoin campus was designed by the prominent architectural firm of McKim, Mead & White in 1894. While the collections are relatively small, they include a number of exceptional paintings from Europe and America, along with early furniture and artifacts from classical antiquity. The artists include Andrew and N. C. Wyeth, Marsden Hartley, Winslow Homer, and John Singer Sargent.

Walker Art Building, Bowdoin College, Brunswick. © 207/725-3275. Free admission. Tues–Sat 10am–5pm; Sun 2–5pm.

Maine Maritime Museum & Shipyard ★★   This museum on the banks of the Kennebec River (just south of the Bath Iron Works shipyard) features a wide array of displays and exhibits related to the boat builder's art. It's at the former shipyard of Percy and Small, which built some 42 schooners in the late 19th and early 20th centuries. The largest wooden ship built in the U.S.—the 329-foot *Wyoming*—was constructed on this lot in 1909. The Maritime History Building houses exhibits of maritime art and artifacts. The 10-acre property contains a fleet of other displays, including a comprehensive exhibit on lobstering and a boat-building shop. You can watch wooden boats take shape here. Kids enjoy the play area, where they can search for pirates from the crow's nest of the play boat. Occasional river cruises ($30) are offered from the riverside dock, including lighthouse tours and excursions up the river to Merrymeeting Bay.

243 Washington St., Bath. © 207/443-1316. www.bathmaine.com. Admission $9.50 adults, $6.50 children 6–17, free for children under 6; $27 per family. Daily 9:30am–5pm.

Peary-MacMillan Arctic Museum ☆ While Admiral Robert E. Peary (class of 1887) is well known for his accomplishments (he landed at the North Pole in 1909), Donald MacMillan (class of 1898) also racked up an impressive string of achievements in Arctic research and exploration. You can learn about both men in this intriguing museum on the Bowdoin College campus. The front room features mounted animals from the Arctic, including polar bears. A second room outlines Peary's 1909 expedition, complete with excerpts from his journal. The last room includes displays of Inuit arts and crafts, some historic, some modern. This compact museum can be visited in about 20 minutes; the art museum (see above) is just next door.

Hubbard Hall, Bowdoin College, Brunswick. © 207/725-3416. Free admission. Tues–Sat 10am–5pm; Sun 2–5pm.

BEACHES

This part of Maine is better known for rocky cliffs and lobster pots than swimming beaches, with two notable exceptions.

Popham Beach State Park (© 207/389-1335) is located at the tip of Route 209 (head south from Bath). This handsome park has a long and sandy strand, plus great views of knobby offshore islands such as Seguin Island, capped with a lonesome lighthouse. Parking and basic services, including changing rooms, are available. Admission is $2 for adults, 50¢ for children 5 to 11.

At the tip of the next peninsula to the east is **Reid State Park** (© 207/371-2303), an idyllic place to picnic on a summer day. Arrive early enough and you can stake out a picnic table among the wind-blasted pines. The mile-long beach is great for strolling and splashing around. Services include changing rooms and a small snack bar. Admission is $3 for adults, 50¢ for children 5 to 11. To reach Reid State Park, follow Route 127 south from Bath and Route 1.

WHERE TO STAY

Driftwood Inn & Cottages ☆ *Value* The Driftwood Inn dates back to 1910, and not a lot seems to have changed since then. A family-run rustic retreat on 3 acres at the end of a dead-end road, the inn is a compound of four shingled buildings and a handful of housekeeping cottages on a rocky, oceanside property. The spartan rooms have a simple turn-of-the-last-century flavor that hasn't been gentrified in the least. Most units share bathrooms, but some have private sinks and toilets. Cottages are set along a small cove, and are furnished in a budget style. It's nothing fancy: Expect industrial carpeting, plastic shower stalls, and a few beds that could stand replacing. Bring plenty of books and board games.

Washington Ave., Bailey Island, ME 04003. © 207/833-5461, or 508/947-1066 off season. 30 units (most share hallway bathrooms). $80–$120 double; cottages $600–$650 per week. No credit cards. Open late May to mid-Oct; dining room open late July to Labor Day. **Amenities:** Dining room (traditional New England). *In room:* No phone.

Galen C. Moses House ☆ This 1874 inn is an extravagant, three-story Italianate home done up in exuberant colors by innkeepers Jim Haught and Larry

Keift. The whole of the spacious first floor is open to guests and includes a TV room, lots of loudly ticking clocks, and an appropriately cluttered Victorian double parlor. Note the old friezes and stained glass original to the house. Guest rooms vary in decor and size, but all are quite welcoming. The Victorian Room occupies a corner and gets a lot of afternoon light, though the bathroom is dark; the Suite is ideal for families, with two sleeping rooms and a small kitchen.

1009 Washington St., Bath, ME 04530. © 888/442-8771. www.galenmoses.com. 5 units (1 suite). $99–$199 double. Rates include breakfast. 2-night minimum stay on summer weekends. AE, DISC, MC, V. *In room:* A/C, hair dryer, iron.

Grey Havens ★★ This is the inn first-time visitors to Maine fantasize about. Located on Georgetown Island southeast of Bath, this graceful 1904 shingled home with turrets sits on a high, rocky bluff overlooking the sea. Inside is richly mellowed pine paneling; you can relax in a chair in front of the common room's cobblestone fireplace. Guest rooms are simply but comfortably furnished. Oceanfront units command a premium, but are worth it. (Save a few dollars by requesting an oceanfront room with private bathroom across the hall.) *One caveat:* The inn has been only lightly modernized, which means rather thin walls.

Seguinland Rd., Georgetown Island, ME 04548. © 207/371-2616. Fax 207/371-2274. www.greyhavens. com. 13 units (2 with detached private bathrooms). $135–$230 double. Rates include continental breakfast. MC, V. Closed Nov–Apr. Children 12 and older are welcome. From Rte. 1, head south on Rte. 127 and follow signs for Reid State Park; watch for inn on left. **Amenities:** Watersports equipment; bikes. *In room:* No phone.

WHERE TO DINE

Five Islands Lobster Co. ★ LOBSTER POUND The drive alone makes this lobster pound a worthy destination. It's about 12 miles south of Route 1 down winding Route 127, past bogs and spruce forests with glimpses of ocean inlets. (Head south from Woolwich, just across the bridge from Bath.) Drive until you pass a cluster of clapboard homes, then keep going until you can go no farther. It's a down-home affair, owned by local lobstermen and proprietors of the Grey Havens inn (see above). While waiting for your lobster, wander next door to the Love Nest Snack Bar for extras such as soda or (recommended) onion rings. Settle in at a picnic table or head for a grassy spot at the edge of the parking lot. Despite its edge-of-the-world feel, the lobster pound can be crowded on weekends.

Rte. 127, Georgetown. © 207/371-2990. Reservations not accepted. Market price (typically $8–$10) per lobster. MC, V. July–Aug daily 11am–8pm; shorter off-season hours. Closed Columbus Day to Mother's Day.

Robinhood Free Meetinghouse ★★ NEW AMERICAN Chef Michael Gagne's menu features between 30 and 40 wildly eclectic entrees, from scallops Niçoise in puff pastry to two-texture duck to Wiener schnitzel with lingonberries. Ordering from the menu is like playing stump the chef: Let's see you make *this!* And Gagne almost always hits his notes. He has attracted legions of dedicated local followers, who appreciate his extraordinary attention paid to detail, such as the foam baffles glued discreetly to the underside of the seats to dampen the echoes in the sparely decorated, immaculately restored 1855 Greek Revival meetinghouse. Even the sorbet served between courses is homemade. While not a budget restaurant, the Meetinghouse offers good value for the price.

Robinhood Rd., Robinhood. © 207/371-2188. www.robinhood-meetinghouse.com. Reservations recommended. Main courses $18–$25. AE, DISC, MC, V. May–Oct daily 5:30–9pm; limited days in the off season (call first).

Star Fish Grill ★★ *(Finds* SEAFOOD   Rising above a lackluster location (in a strip mall across from the Miss Brunswick Diner), the Star Fish Grill serves up great seafood, excellent service, and an atmosphere that's fun, upbeat, whimsical, and (naturally) maritime. This intimate restaurant has just 50 seats, but provides big-restaurant food and service. The emphasis is on seafood, and you can find whatever's fresh (scallops, pompano, grouper, trout, mahi-mahi) cooked up professionally and well. I'd recommend the lobster paella if it's available. Don't let the unlovely setting throw you off. This is a favorite restaurant in southern Maine, especially if you're a fan of seafood.

100 Pleasant St., Brunswick. ✆ 207/725-7828. Reservations recommended. Main courses $14–$26. MC, V. Tues–Sat 5–9pm.

WISCASSET ★★ & THE BOOTHBAYS ★

Wiscasset is a lovely riverside town on Route 1, and it's not shy about letting you know: THE PRETTIEST VILLAGE IN MAINE boasts the sign at the edge of town and on many brochures. Whether or not you agree, the town *is* attractive (though the sluggish line of traffic snaking through diminishes the charm) and makes a good stop en route to coastal destinations further along.

The Boothbays, 11 miles south of Route 1 on Route 27, consists of several small and scenic villages—**East Boothbay, Boothbay Harbor,** and **Boothbay,** among them—that are closer than Wiscasset to the open ocean. Wealthy rusticators who retreated here each summer in the 19th century discovered the former fishing port of Boothbay Harbor. Having embraced the tourist dollar, the harborfront village never really looked back, and in more recent years, it has emerged as one of the premier destinations of travelers in search of classic coastal Maine. The obvious impact is a village that's a mandatory stop for bus tours, which have in turn attracted kitschy shops and a slew of mediocre restaurants serving baked stuffed haddock. However, if you avoid the touristy claptrap of the downtown harbor area itself, some of the outlying areas are strikingly beautiful.

ESSENTIALS

GETTING THERE   Wiscasset is on Route 1 midway between Bath and Damariscotta. Boothbay Harbor is south of Route 1 on Route 27. Coming from the west, look for signs shortly after crossing the Sheepscot River at Wiscasset.

VISITOR INFORMATION   Wiscasset lacks a tourist information booth, but you can get questions answered by calling the **Wiscasset Regional Business Association** (✆ 207/882-9617). The Boothbay area has three visitor centers in and around town, reflecting the importance of the travel dollars to the region. At the intersection of Routes 1 and 27 is a center that's open May through October and is a good place to stock up on brochures. A mile before you reach the village is the seasonal **Boothbay Information Center** on your right, open June through October. The year-round **Boothbay Harbor Region Chamber of Commerce** (✆ 207/633-2353) is at the intersection of Routes 27 and 96.

EXPLORING WISCASSET

Aside from enjoying the town's handsome architecture and vaunted prettiness, you'll find a handful of worthwhile shops that range from sparely adorned art galleries to antiques shops cluttered with architectural salvage.

Castle Tucker ★   This fascinating mansion overlooking the river at the edge of town was built in 1807, then radically added to in a more ostentatious style in 1860. The home remains more or less in the same state it was when reconfigured by cotton trader Capt. Richard Tucker; his descendant Jane Tucker still lives on the top floor. The Society of New England Antiquities offers tours of the lower floor. The highlight is the detailing; be sure to note the extraordinary elliptical staircase and the painted plaster trim (it's not oak).

Lee and High sts. ☎ 207/882-7364. Admission $5 adults, $2.50 children. Tours leave every hr. June to mid-Oct Wed–Sun 11am–4pm. Closed mid-Oct to May.

Musical Wonder House ✪   Danilo Konvalinka has collected music boxes grand and tiny for decades; nothing seems to delight him more than to show them off. The collection ranges from massive music boxes as resonant as an orchestra (an 1870 Girard from Austria) to the tinnier sounds of smaller contraptions. Music boxes are displayed in four rooms in a stately 1852 home. A full tour is pricey; if you're undecided, visit the gift shop and sample some of the coin-operated 19th-century music boxes in the adjoining hallway. Intrigued? Sign up for the next tour.

18 High St. ☎ 207/882-7163. Tours $15 for full downstairs; $8 for half downstairs; $30 for full house. Late May to Oct daily 10am–5pm. Closed Nov to late May.

EXPLORING THE BOOTHBAY REGION

Summer parking in Boothbay Harbor requires either great persistence or forking over a few dollars. A popular local attraction is the long, narrow **footbridge** across the harbor, built in 1901. It's more of a destination than a link—other than a couple of unnotable restaurants and motels, not much is on the other side. The winding streets that weave through town are filled with shops catering to tourists. Don't expect much merchandise beyond the usual trinkets and souvenirs.

If dense fog or rain socks in the harbor, bide your time at the vintage **Romar Bowling Lanes** ✪ (☎ 207/633-5721). This log-and-shingle building near the footbridge has a harbor view and has been distracting travelers with traditional New England candlepin bowling since 1946.

In good weather, stop by a Boothbay region information center (see above) and request a free guide to the holdings of the **Boothbay Region Land Trust** ✪✪ (☎ 207/633-4818). Eight pockets of publicly accessible lands dot the peninsula, most with quiet, lightly traveled trails good for a stroll or a picnic. Among the best: **Linekin Preserve,** a 95-acre parcel en route to Ocean Point (drive south from Route 1 in Boothbay Harbor on Route 96 for 3.8 miles; look for parking on the left) with 600 feet of riverfront. A hike around the loop trail (about 2 miles) will occupy a pleasant hour.

Coastal Maine Botanical Garden   This 128-acre waterside garden remains a work in progress, but makes for a peaceable oasis. It's not a fancy, formal garden, but rather a natural habitat that's being coaxed into a more mannered state. Those overseeing this nonprofit have blazed several short trails through the mossy forest, good for half an hour's worth of exploring the quiet, lush terrain.

Barters Island Rd., Boothbay (near Hogdon Island). ☎ 207/633-4333. Free admission. Open daylight hours. From Rte. 27 in Boothbay Center, bear right at the monument at the stop sign, then make the first right on Barters Island Rd.; drive 1 mile; look for the stone gate on your left.

Marine Resources Aquarium ✪ *Kids*   Operated by the state's Department of Marine Resources, this aquarium offers context for life in the sea around Boothbay and beyond. Kids will be enthralled by rare albino and blue lobsters and can get their hands wet in a 20-foot touch tank. Parking is scarce at the aquarium, on a point across the water from downtown Boothbay Harbor, so visitors are urged to use the free shuttle bus (look for the Rocktide trolley) that connects to downtown.

McKown Point Rd., West Boothbay Harbor. © 207/633-9542. Admission $3 adults, $2.50 children 5–18, free for children under 5. Daily 10am–5pm. Closed late Oct to Memorial Day weekend.

BOAT TOURS

The best way to see the timeless Maine coast around Boothbay is on a boat tour. Nearly two dozen tour boats berth at the harbor or nearby, offering a range of trips ranging from an hour's outing to a full-day excursion to Monhegan Island. You can even observe puffins at their rocky colonies far offshore.

Balmy Days Cruises ⭐ (© **800/298-2284** or 207/633-2284; www.balmy dayscruises.com) runs several trips from the harbor, including an excursion to Monhegan Island on the 65-foot *Balmy Days II,* which allows passengers about 4 hours to explore the island before returning (see the section on Monhegan Island, below). The cost is $30 for adults, $18 for children 3–11. If you'd rather sail, ask about the 90-minute cruises on the 15-passenger *Bay Lady* ($18). It's a good idea to make reservations.

A more intimate way to tour the harbor is via sea kayak. **Tidal Transit Kayak Co.** ⭐ (© **207/633-7140**) offers morning, afternoon, and sunset tours of the harbor for $30 (sunset's the best bet). Kayaks may also be rented for $15 per hour or $50 per day. Tidal Transit is open daily in summer (except when it rains), located on the waterfront at 47 Townshend Ave. (walk down the alley).

WHERE TO STAY

Five Gables Inn ⭐⭐   This handsome inn, amid a colony of summer homes on a quiet road above a peaceful cove, is nicely isolated from the hubbub of Boothbay Harbor. Room 8 is a corner unit with brilliant morning light; most requested is room 14, with a fine view and a fireplace with marble mantle. (Note that some first-floor rooms open onto a common deck and lack privacy, and all but five have showers only.) The breakfast buffet is sumptuous, with offerings such as tomato-basil frittata and blueberry-stuffed French toast.

207 Murray Hill Rd. (P.O. Box 335), East Boothbay, ME 04544. © 800/451-5048 or 207/633-4551. www.five gablesinn.com. 16 units. $130–$195 double. Rates include breakfast. MC, V. Closed Nov to mid-May. Drive through East Boothbay on Rte. 96; turn right after crest of hill on Murray Hill Rd. Children 12 and older are welcome. *In room:* Hair dryer.

Lobsterman's Wharf Inn & Restaurant ⭐ *(Value*   This is my budget pick for the Boothbay region. A clean, no-frills place adjacent to a working boatyard, this inn was originally a coal depot and later a boardinghouse. It still has some board-inghouse informality to it (though all rooms now have small private bathrooms), but you get a lot for your money. Seven rooms face the water; the Hodgon Suite is the largest, located under the eaves with a view of the boatyard.

Rte. 96, East Boothbay. © 207/633-3443. 9 units. $60–$90 double. Rates include continental breakfast. MC, V. Closed Columbus Day to mid-May. Some pets allowed. **Amenities:** Restaurant (see below). *In room:* TV, no phone.

Newagen Seaside Inn ⭐   This small 1940s-era resort has seen more glam-orous days, but it's still a superb, low-key establishment with great ocean views and walks through a seaside spruce forest. The low, wide, white-shingled Colo-nial Revival–style inn is furnished simply in country pine, with a classically aus-tere dining room, narrow hallways with pine wainscoting, and a lobby with a fireplace. Innkeepers Corinne and Scott Larson, who bought the place in 2000, have been updating the place, long known (even favored) for its plain, occa-sionally threadbare rooms. Guests return each year to the 85-acre grounds filled with decks, gazebos, and walkways that border on the magical. It's hard to con-vey the magnificence of the ocean views, maybe the best of any inn's in Maine.

Rte. 27 (P.O. Box 29), Cape Newagen, ME 04576. ✆ **800/654-5242** or 207/633-5242. Fax 207/633-5340. www.newagenseasideinn.com. 26 units. $140–$240 double. Rates include breakfast. Ask about off-season discounts. AE, MC, V. Closed mid-Oct to mid-May. Take Rte. 27 from Boothbay Harbor and continue south to the tip of Southport Island; look for sign. **Amenities:** Restaurant (New England); 2 outdoor pools; 2 tennis courts; Jacuzzi; watersports equipment rental; bike rental. *In room:* TV/VCR on request.

Spruce Point Inn ✿✿ *Kids*   The Spruce Point Inn, built as a hunting and fishing lodge in the 1890s, became a summer resort in 1912. Those looking for historic authenticity may be disappointed. Those seeking modern facilities with some historic accents will be delighted. (Those who prefer gentility a bit less glossy should consider the Newagen Seaside Inn; see above.) Rooms in the main inn are basic, mid-size, and comfortable; the newer wings are somewhat more condo-like. A great choice for families, it offers plenty of activities to fill a day.

Atlantic Ave. (P.O. Box 237), Boothbay Harbor, ME 04538. ✆ **800/553-0289** or 207/633-4152. www.sprucepointinn.com. 93 units. Mid-July to Aug $165–$335 double; fall $140–$235 double; spring $125–$215 double; early summer $150–$265 double. Cottages and condos $450–$550 per night. 2-night minimum stay on weekends; 3-night minimum stay on holidays. AE, DISC, MC, V. Closed late Oct to mid-May. Turn seaward on Union St. in Boothbay Harbor; go 2 miles to inn. Pets allowed ($50 deposit, $100 cleaning fee). **Amenities:** Restaurant (upscale New England); 2 outdoor pools; 2 tennis courts; fitness center; Jacuzzi; concierge; boat tours; shuttle; massage; babysitting; laundry service; dry cleaning. *In room:* TV, fridge, coffeemaker, iron.

Topside   An old gray house on a hilltop looming over dated motel buildings may bring to mind the Bates Motel, especially when a full moon is overhead. But get over it. Topside offers spectacular ocean views at a reasonable price from a hilltop compound right in downtown Boothbay. The inn—a former boarding house for shipyard workers—features several comfortable rooms, furnished with a somewhat discomfiting mix of antiques and contemporary furniture. At the edge of the inn's lawn are two outbuildings with basic motel units, a bit on the small side, furnished simply with dated paneling and furniture. (You won't find this hotel in *House Beautiful*.) Rooms 9 and 14 have the best views, but most rooms offer a glimpse of the water, and many have decks or patios. All guests have access to the wonderful lawn and endless views; and the Reed family, which owns and operates the inn, is accommodating and friendly.

60 McKown Hill, Boothbay Harbor, ME 04538. ✆ **877/486-7466** or 207/633-5404. Fax 207/486-7466. www.gwi.net/topside. 21 units. Peak season $75–$140 double; off-season rates lower. Rates include continental breakfast. AE, DISC, MC, V. Closed mid-Oct to early Apr. *In room:* TV.

WHERE TO DINE
In Wiscasset

Red's Eats ✦ LOBSTER ROLLS/SANDWICHES   This roadside stand in downtown Wiscasset has received more than its share of media ink about its famous lobster rolls. (They often crop up in "Best of Maine" surveys.) And they *are* good, consisting of moist chunks of chilled lobster placed in a roll served with a little mayo on the side. Be aware they're at the pricey end of the scale—you can find less expensive (though less meaty) versions elsewhere.

Water St. (Rte. 1 just before the bridge). ✆ 207/882-6128. Sandwiches $2.50–$5.75; lobster rolls typically around $12. No credit cards. Mon–Thurs 11am–11pm; Fri–Sat 11am–2am; Sun noon–6pm. Closed Oct–Apr.

Sarah's ✦ SANDWICHES/TRADITIONAL   This hometown favorite overlooks Sheepscot River and is usually crowded for lunch, offering pita pockets, croissant sandwiches, wraps, burritos, and a "whaleboat" (a two-cheese turnover, like a calzone). Lobsters are fresh, hauled in daily by Sarah's brother and father. It's the best choice for an informal lunch break on Route 1.

Water St. and Rte. 1 (across from Red's). ✆ 207/882-7504. Sandwiches $4.45–$6.25; pizzas $4.95–$17. AE, DISC, MC, V. Daily 11am–8pm (until 9pm Fri–Sat).

In the Boothbays

In Boothbay Harbor, look for **"King" Brud** and his famous hotdog cart. Brud started selling hotdogs in 1943, and he's still at it. June through October, he's usually at the corner of McKown and Commercial streets from 10am to 4pm.

Boothbay Region Lobstermen's Co-op SEAFOOD "WE ARE NOT RESPONSIBLE IF THE SEAGULLS STEAL YOUR FOOD" reads the sign at the ordering window of this lobster joint. And that sets the casual tone pretty well. Situated across the harbor from downtown Boothbay, the lobstermen's co-op offers no-frills seafood served at picnic tables on a dock and inside a crude shelter. This is the best pick from the lobster-in-the-rough places that line the waterfront. Lobsters are priced to market (figure $8–$12). The salty atmosphere is the draw here; it's a fair-weather destination that should be avoided in rain or fog.

Atlantic Ave., Boothbay Harbor. *C* **207/633-4900.** Fried and grilled foods $2–$10; dinners $7.50–$12. DISC, MC, V. May to mid-Oct daily 11:30am–8:30pm. On foot, cross footbridge and turn right; follow road for ⅓ mile to co-op.

Christopher's Boathouse ☆☆ NEW AMERICAN/WOOD GRILL A happy exception to generally unexciting fare in this town, this bright and modern restaurant is located at the head of the harbor (and has deck dining.) The chef has a deft touch with spicy flavors, melding the expected with the unexpected (such as lobster and mango bisque with spicy lobster won tons). Meals from the grill are excellent, including a rum-and-spice salmon with shrimp and ginger strudel and a grilled venison flank with wild mushroom sauce. The restaurant is also noted for its lobster succotash, which is better than it sounds.

25 Union St., Boothbay Harbor. *C* **207/633-6565.** Reservations recommended in peak season. Main courses about $25. DISC, MC, V. Mon–Sat 5:30–9:30pm; Sun 5:30–9pm.

Lobsterman's Wharf ☆ SEAFOOD On the waterfront in East Boothbay, this place has the comfortable feel of a popular neighborhood bar, complete with pool table. If the weather cooperates, sit at a picnic table on the dock and admire the views of a spruce-topped peninsula across the Damariscotta River; or grab a table inside amid the festive nautical decor. Entrees include a mixed-seafood grill, a barbecued shrimp-and-ribs platter, and succulent fresh lobster.

Rte. 96, East Boothbay. *C* **207/633-3443.** Reservations accepted for parties of 6 or more. Main courses: lunch $4.50–$14; dinner $14–$23 (mostly $14–$16). AE, MC, V. Daily 11:30am–midnight. Closed mid-Oct to mid-May.

PEMAQUID PENINSULA ☆☆☆

Pemaquid Peninsula is an irregular, rocky wedge driven deep into the Gulf of Maine. Far less commercial than Boothbay Peninsula across the Damariscotta River, it's more inviting for casual exploration. Inland areas are leafy with hardwood trees and laced with narrow, twisting back roads perfect for bicycling. As you near the southern tip where small harbors and coves predominate, the region takes on a more remote, maritime feel. Rugged and rocky Pemaquid Point, at the extreme southern tip of the peninsula, is one of the most dramatic destinations in Maine when the ocean surf pounds the shore.

ESSENTIALS

GETTING THERE The Pemaquid Peninsula is accessible from the west by turning southward on Route 129/130 in Damariscotta, just off Route 1. From the east, head south on Route 32 just west of Waldoboro.

VISITOR INFORMATION The **Damariscotta Region Chamber of Commerce,** P.O. Box 13, Main Street, Damariscotta, ME 04543 (*C* **207/563-8340**) is a good source of local information and maintains a seasonal information booth on Route 1 during the summer months.

EXPLORING THE PEMAQUID PENINSULA

Pemaquid Point (© 207/677-2494) is the place to while away an afternoon. Bring a picnic and a book, and settle in on the dark, fractured rocks. Ocean views are superb, interrupted only by somewhat tenacious seagulls that may take an interest in your lunch. While here, visit the **Fishermen's Museum** (© 207/ 677-2726) in the lighthouse. Informative exhibits depict the whys and wherefores of the local fishing trade. A small fee ($2 for ages 12 and over, 50¢ for seniors; children under 12 free) allows use of the park in summer; admission to the museum is by donation.

From New Harbor, you can get an outstanding view of the coast with **Hardy Boat Cruises** (© 800/278-3346 or 207/677-2026; www.hardy boat.com). Tours aboard the 60-foot *Hardy III* include a 1-hour sunset and lighthouse cruise ($10 adults, $7 children 12 and under), 90-minute puffin tours to Eastern Egg Rock ($18 adults, $11 children), and full-day ocean safaris, with puffin sightings and 90-minute visit to Monhegan Island ($27 adults, $15 children). Extra clothing for warmth is strongly recommended.

> **Tips Lobster Pricing**
>
> Travelers may be in for a rude surprise when they get the bill for a meal at a casual wharfside lobster restaurant. Prices posted for lobsters are per *pound,* not per *lobster*. This can be inadvertently misleading, as a range of prices is often posted—for example, $7 for 1¼-lb. lobsters, $8 for 1½-lb. lobsters, and so on. That's the price per pound, not the total price, so you'll need do a little math to figure out the final price of your lobster.

Route 32 strikes northwest from New Harbor and is the most scenic way to leave the peninsula if you plan to continue eastward on Route 1. Along the way, look for signs pointing to the **Rachel Carson Salt Pond Preserve** . Pull off your shoes and socks and wade through the cold waters at low tide looking for starfish, green crabs, periwinkles, and other creatures.

WHERE TO STAY

Bradley Inn   The Bradley Inn is easy walking or biking distance to the point, but it offers plenty of reasons to lag behind. Start by wandering the nicely landscaped grounds or enjoying a game of croquet in the gardens. If the fog moves in for a spell, settle in for a game of Scrabble at the pub, decorated with a nautical theme. Rooms are tastefully appointed; just three have televisions. Third-floor rooms are my favorites, despite the hike, thanks to distant glimpses of John's Bay. Seafood is served in the inn's restaurant, and is quite good.

3063 Bristol Rd., Rte. 130, New Harbor, ME 04554. © 800/942-5560 or 207/677-2105. Fax 207/677-3367. www.bradleyinn.com. 16 units. Summer and fall $125–$225 double; winter and spring $105–$165 double. Rates include breakfast. AE, MC, V. **Amenities:** Restaurant (American); bikes; limited room service. *In room:* TV, hair dryer, iron.

WHERE TO DINE

Shaw's Fish and Lobster Wharf   LOBSTER POUND   Shaw's attracts hordes of tourists, but it's no trick to figure out why: It's one of the best-situated lobster pounds, with postcard-perfect views of the harbor and the boats coming and going through the inlet that connects to the open sea. While waiting for your order, stake out a seat on the open deck or in the indoor dining room (my advice: go for the deck), or order some appetizers from the raw bar. This is one of the few lobster joints with a full liquor license.

On the water, New Harbor. ℭ **207/677-2200.** Lobster market-priced (typically $8–$12). MC, V. Mid-June to Labor Day daily 11am–9pm; call for shoulder season hours. Closed mid-Oct to late May.

MONHEGAN ISLAND ✸✸✸

Monhegan Island is Maine's premier island destination. Visited by Europeans as early as 1497, the wild, remote island was settled by fishermen attracted to the sea's bounty in offshore waters. In the 1870s, artists discovered the island and stayed for a spell, including Rockwell Kent (the artist most closely associated with the island), George Bellows, Edward Hopper, and Robert Henri. The artists gathered in the lighthouse kitchen to chat and drink coffee; it's said that the lighthouse keeper's wife accumulated quite a valuable collection of paintings. Jamie Wyeth, scion of the Wyeth clan, claims the island as his part-time home.

It's not hard to figure out why artists have been attracted to the place, with its mystical quality, from the thin light to the startling contrasts of dark cliffs and foamy white surf. One finds a remarkable sense of tranquillity here, which can only help focus one's inner vision. In addition, it's a superb destination for hikers, as most of the island is undeveloped and laced with trails.

Be aware that this is not Martha's Vineyard—no ATMs, few pay phones, even electricity is scarce. That's what repeat visitors like about it. An overnight at one of the several hostelries is strongly recommended. Day trips are easily arranged, but the island's true character doesn't start to emerge until the last day boat sails away and the quiet, rustic appeal of the place percolates to the surface.

ESSENTIALS

GETTING THERE   Access to Monhegan Island is via boat from New Harbor, Boothbay Harbor, or Port Clyde. The picturesque trip from Port Clyde is the favored route of longtime island visitors; the boat passes the Marshall Point Lighthouse and by a series of spruce-clad islands before reaching the open sea.

Two boats make the run from Port Clyde. The *Laura B.,* which takes 70 minutes, is a doughty workboat (building supplies and boxes of food are loaded first; passengers fill in the available niches on deck and in the small cabin). The newer, faster (50 min.), passenger-oriented *Elizabeth Ann* has a large heated cabin and more seating. You leave your car behind, so pack light and wear sturdy shoes. Round-trip fare is $27 for adults, $14 for children 2 to 12, and $2 for pets. Reservations are advised; contact **Monhegan Boat Line** (ℭ **207/372-8848; www.monheganboat.com**). Parking is available near the dock for $4 per day.

VISITOR INFORMATION   Monhegan Island has no formal visitor center; it's small and friendly enough that you can ask just about anyone you meet on the island pathways. The clerks at the ferry dock in Port Clyde are also quite helpful. Be sure to pick up the inexpensive map of the island's hiking trail at the boat ticket office or at the various shops around the island.

Note: Because wildfire could destroy this breezy island in short order, smoking is prohibited outside the village.

EXPLORING MONHEGAN

Walking is the chief activity on the island; it's genuinely surprising how much distance you can cover on these 700 acres (about 1½ miles long and ½ mile wide). The village clusters tightly around the harbor; the rest of the island is mostly wildland, laced with 17 miles of **trails** ✸✸✸. Much of the island is ringed with high, open bluffs atop fissured cliffs. Pack a picnic lunch, hike the perimeter trail, and plan to spend much of the day just sitting and reading, or enjoying the surf rolling in against the cliffs.

The inland trails are appealing in a far different way. Deep, dark **Cathedral Woods** ☆☆ is mossy and fragrant; sunlight only dimly filters through the evergreens to the forest floor.

Birding is a popular spring and fall activity. The island is on the Atlantic flyway, and a wide variety of birds stop at the island along their migration routes.

The sole formal attraction on the island is the **Monhegan Museum** ☆, next to the 1824 lighthouse on a point above the village. The museum, open July through September, has a quirky collection of historic artifacts and provides some context for this rugged island's history. Also near the lighthouse is a small and select art museum featuring the works of Rockwell Kent and other island artists.

The spectacular view from the grassy slope in front of the lighthouse is the real prize. The vista sweeps across a marsh, past one of the island's most historic hotels, past melancholy Manana Island, and across the sea beyond. Get here early if you want a good seat for the sunset; most island visitors seem to congregate here after dinner for the view.

Artists are still attracted here in great number, and many open their **studios** to visitors during posted hours in summer. Look for the bulletin board along the main pathway in the village for walking directions to the studios and a listing of the days and hours they're open.

WHERE TO STAY & DINE

Monhegan House ☆ Handsome Monhegan House has accommodated guests since 1870, and it has the comfortable, worn patina of a venerable lodging house. Rooms at this four-floor walk-up are austere but comfortable; all share clean, dormitory-style bathrooms. The lobby with fireplace is a welcome spot to sit and take the fog-induced chill out of your bones (even Aug can be cool here), while the front deck is the place to lounge and keep an eye on the comings and goings of the village.

Monhegan Island, ME 04852. © 800/599-7983 or 207/594-7983. Fax 207/596-6472. www.monhegan house.com. 33 units (all with shared bathroom). $119–$125 double. Rates include breakfast. AE, DISC, MC, V. Closed Columbus Day to Memorial Day. **Amenities:** Restaurant (casual dining). *In room:* No phone.

Trailing Yew ☆ This friendly, informal place, popular with hikers and birders, has been taking in guests since 1929. Guest rooms are eclectic and simply furnished in a pleasantly dated summer-home style. Only one of the four buildings has electricity (most but not all bathrooms have electricity); those staying in rooms without electricity are provided a kerosene lamp (bring a small flashlight—just in case). Rooms are also unheated, so bring a sleeping bag if the weather's chilly. The Trailing Yew has more of an easy-going, youth-hostel camaraderie; if you're the private type, opt for the Monhegan House.

Monhegan Island, ME 04852. © 800/592-2520 or 207/596-0440. 37 units (all but 1 share bathrooms). $134 double. Rates include breakfast, dinner, taxes, and tips. No credit cards. Closed mid-Oct to mid-May. **Amenities:** Restaurant (New England/family style). *In room:* No phone.

4 Penobscot Bay

Traveling east along the Maine coast, those who pay attention to such things will notice they're suddenly heading almost due north around **Rockland**. The culprit behind this geographic quirk is Penobscot Bay, a sizable bite out of the

Maine coast that forces a lengthy northerly detour to cross the head of the bay where the Penobscot River flows in at Bucksport.

You'll find some of Maine's most distinctive coastal scenery in this region, which is dotted with broad offshore islands and high hills rising above the mainland shores. Though the mouth of Penobscot Bay is occupied by two large islands, its waters can still churn with vigor when the tides and winds conspire.

The Penobscot Bay's western shore gets a heavy stream of tourist traffic, especially on Route 1 through **Camden.** It's still a good drive to get a taste of the Maine coast. Services for travelers are abundant, though during peak season, you need a small miracle to find a weekend guest room without a reservation.

ROCKLAND ⚐
On the southwest edge of Penobscot Bay, Rockland has long been proud of its brick-and-blue-collar waterfront reputation. Built around the fishing industry, Rockland historically dabbled in tourism on the side, but with the decline of fisheries and the rise of Maine's tourist economy, the balance has shifted. In the last decade, Rockland has been colonized by creative restaurateurs, innkeepers, and other small-business folks who paint it with an unaccustomed gloss.

The waterfront boasts a small park, from which windjammers come and go, but more appealing than Rockland's waterfront is its commercial downtown—it's basically one long street lined with sophisticated historic brick architecture. If you're seeking picturesque harbor towns, head to Camden, Rockport, Port Clyde, or Stonington; but Rockland makes a great base for exploring this beautiful coastal region, especially if you like your towns a bit rough around the edges.

ESSENTIALS
GETTING THERE   Route 1 passes directly through Rockland. Rockland's tiny airport is served by **Colgan Air** (✆ **800/428-4322** or 207/596-7604), with daily flights from Boston and Bar Harbor. **Concord Trailways** (✆ **800/639-3317**) offers bus service from Rockland to Bangor and Portland.

VISITOR INFORMATION   The **Rockland/Thomaston Area Chamber of Commerce** (✆ **800/562-2529** or 207/596-0376) staffs an information desk at Harbor Park. It's open from Memorial Day to Labor Day, daily from 9am to 5pm; the rest of the year, Monday through Friday from 9am to 5pm.

EVENTS   The **Maine Lobster Festival** (✆ **800/562-2529** or 207/596-0376) takes place at Harbor Park the first weekend in August (plus the preceding Thurs and Fri). Entertainers and vendors of all sorts of Maine products—especially the local crustacean—fill the waterfront parking lot and attract thousands of festivalgoers who enjoy this pleasant event with a sort of buttery bonhomie. The event includes the Maine Sea Goddess Coronation Pageant.

MUSEUMS
Farnsworth Museum ⚐⚐   Rockland, for all its rough edges, has long and historic ties to the arts. Sculptor Louise Nevelson grew up here, and in 1935, philanthropist Lucy Farnsworth bequeathed a fortune large enough to establish the Farnsworth Museum, which has since joined the ranks of the most respected art museums in New England. The Farnsworth has a superb collection of paintings and sculptures by renowned American artists with a connection to Maine. This includes not only Nevelson and three generations of Wyeths (N. C., Andrew, and Jamie) but also Rockwell Kent, Childe Hassam, and Maurice

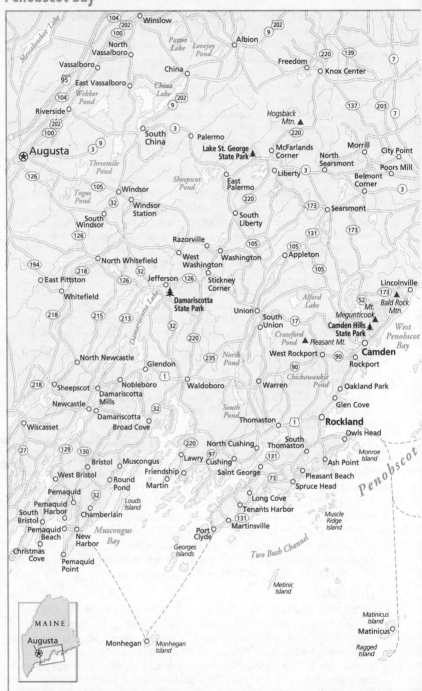

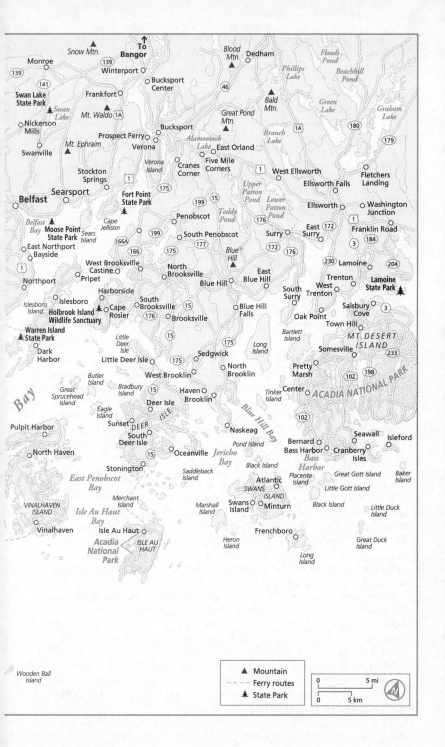

Snow Mtn.

To Bangor

Monroe

139

Winterport

Swan Lake State Park

141

Frankfort

Bucksport Center

Blood Mtn.

Dedham

Floods Pond

Phillips Lake

Beachhill Pond

46

Bald Mtn.

Green Lake

Graham Lake

Nickerson Mills

Mt. Ephraim

Swan Lake

Mt. Waldo

1A

Great Pond Mtn.

Branch Lake

1A

180

179

Swanville

Prospect Ferry

Bucksport

Alamoosook Lake

East Orland

Stockton Springs

Verona

Verona Island

Cranes Corner

Five Mile Corners

West Ellsworth

1

Fletchers Landing

Searsport

Belfast

1

175

Fort Point State Park

199

15

Penobscot

Upper Patton Pond

Lower Patton Pond

Ellsworth Falls

Ellsworth

Washington Junction

Toddy Pond

176

Belfast Bay

Moose Point State Park

Cape Jellison

Sears Island

199

South Penobscot

177

Surry

East Surry

172

Franklin Road

3

184

230

Lamoine

204

166A

166

175

Blue Hill

172

176

East Northport

Bayside

West Brooksville

Castine

North Brooksville

Blue Hill

East Blue Hill

South Surry

West Trenton

Trenton

Lamoine State Park

1

Northport

Pripet

Harborside

South Brooksville

15

Blue Hill Falls

Oak Point

Salsbury Cove

3

Islesboro Island

Islesboro

Cape Rosier

176

Brooksville

Bartlett Island

Town Hill

Somesville

MT. DESERT ISLAND

233

Holbrook Island Wildlife Sanctuary

Little Deer Isle

15

175

Sedgwick

Long Island

Pretty Marsh

102

198

Warren Island State Park

Dark Harbor

Little Deer Isle

175

West Brooklin

North Brooklin

Center

102

ACADIA NATIONAL PARK

Butler Island

Bradbury Island

15

Haven

Brooklin

Tinker Island

Bay

Great Sprucehead Island

Eagle Island

Deer Isle

Blue Hill Bay

Pulpit Harbor

Sunset

DEER ISLE

Naskeag

Bernard

Bass Harbor

Seawall

Isleford

North Haven

South Deer Isle

15

Oceanville

Jericho Bay

Pond Island

Black Island

Cranberry Isles

Baker Island

Stonington

Saddleback Island

Atlantic

SWANS ISLAND

Placenta Island

Bass Harbor

Great Gott Island

VINALHAVEN ISLAND

Merchant Island

Isle Au Haut Bay

Marshall Island

Swans Island

Minturn

Black Island

Little Gott Island

Little Duck Island

East Penobscot Bay

Vinalhaven

Isle Au Haut

Acadia National Park

ISLE AU HAUT

Heron Island

Frenchboro

Great Duck Island

Long Island

Wooden Ball Island

▲ Mountain

---- Ferry routes

★ State Park

0   5 mi

0   5 km

Prendergast. The **Farnsworth Center for the Wyeth Family** is housed just down the block in the former Pratt Memorial Methodist Church, where you'll find Andrew and Betsy Wyeth's personal collection of Maine-related art.

The Farnsworth also owns two other buildings open to the public. The **Farnsworth Homestead,** located behind the museum, offers a glimpse into the life of prosperous coastal Victorians. A 25-minute drive away in the village of Cushing is the **Olson House,** perhaps Maine's most famous home, which was immortalized in Andrew Wyeth's noted painting *Christina's World.* Ask at the museum for directions and information (closed in winter).

356 Main St., Rockland. (© 207/596-6457. www.farnsworthmuseum.org. Admission $9 adults, $8 seniors, $5 students 18 and over, free for children 17 and under (all prices discounted $1 in winter). Summer daily 9am–5pm; winter Tues–Sat 10am–5pm, Sun 1–5pm.

Owls Head Transportation Museum ☆ You don't have to be a car buff or plane nut to enjoy this museum. It has an extraordinary collection of cars, motorcycles, bikes, and planes, displayed in a hangar-like building at the edge of the Knox County Airport. Look for the early Harley-Davidson and the sleek 1929 Rolls-Royce Phantom. The museum is a popular destination for hobbyists, who drive and fly their classic vehicles here for frequent weekend rallies in summer.

Rte. 73 (3 miles south of Rockland), Owls Head. (© 207/594-4418. www.ohtm.org. Admission $7 adults, $6 seniors, $5 children 5–12, free for children under 5, $18 family. Apr–Oct daily 10am–5pm; Nov–Mar daily 10am–4pm.

WINDJAMMER TOURS ☆☆☆

During the long transition from sail to steam, captains of fancy new steamships belittled old-fashioned sailing ships as "windjammers." The term stuck; through a curious metamorphosis, the name evolved into one of adventure and romance.

Today, windjammer vacations combine adventure with limited creature-comforts—such as lodging at a backcountry cabin on the water. Guests typically bunk in small two-person cabins, which usually offer cold running water and a porthole to let in fresh air, but not much else. (You know it's not like a fancy inn when one ship's brochure boasts "standing headroom in all 15 passenger cabins" and another crows that all cabins "are at least 6 feet by 8 feet.")

Maine is the windjammer cruising capital of the U.S., and the two most active Maine harbors are **Rockland** and **Camden** on Penobscot Bay. Cruises last from 3 days to a week, during which these handsome, creaky vessels poke around tidal inlets and small coves that ring the beautiful bay. It's a superb way to explore the coast the way it's historically been explored—from the water, looking inland. Rates run between about $110 and $150 per day per person, with modest discounts early and late in the season.

Cruises vary from ship to ship and from week to week, depending on the inclinations of captains and the vagaries of Maine weather. The "standard" cruise often features a stop at one or more of the myriad spruce-studded Maine islands (perhaps with a lobster bake on shore), hearty breakfasts enjoyed sitting at tables below decks (or perched cross-legged on the sunny deck), and a palpable sense of maritime history as these handsome ships scud through frothy waters. A windjammer vacation demands you use all your senses, to smell the tang of the salt air, to hear the rhythmic creaking of the masts in the evening, and to feel the frigid ocean waters as you leap in for a bracing dip.

More than a dozen windjammers offer cruises in the Penobscot Bay region during summer (some migrate south to the Caribbean for the winter). The ships vary widely in size and vintage, and accommodations range from cramped and rustic to reasonably spacious and well appointed. Ideally, you'll have a chance to look at a couple of ships to find one that suits you before signing up.

If that's not practical, call ahead to the **Maine Windjammer Association** (𝄢 **800/807-9463**) and request a packet of brochures, which enables you to comparison shop. The association's website is **www.sailmainecoast.com**.

Note: If you're hoping for a last-minute windjammer cruise, stop by the chamber of commerce office at the Rockland waterfront (see above) and inquire after any open berths.

WHERE TO STAY

Capt. Lindsey House Inn 𝄢𝄢   This three-story brick house (1835) is just a couple minutes' stroll from the Farnsworth Museum. Guests enter through a doorway a few steps off Main Street, then pass into a first-floor common area with a well-selected mix of antique and contemporary furniture. The rooms are tastefully decorated in a contemporary country style; bold modern colors meld with traditional design. Even the smaller units (such as room 4) are comfortable; the rooms on the third floor feature yellow pine floors and antique Oriental carpets. Rooms facing the street can be noisy.

5 Lindsey St., Rockland, ME 04841. 𝄢 **800/523-2145** or 207/596-7950. Fax 207/596-2758. www.lindsey house.com. 9 units. Peak season $120–$175 double; Columbus Day to Memorial Day $65–$110. Rates include continental breakfast. AE, DISC, MC, V. **Amenities:** Restaurant (pub fare). *In room:* A/C, TV, dataport, hair dryer.

East Wind Inn 𝄢   This low-key inn is south of Rockland in the sleepy town of Tenants Harbor. It's right on the water, with harbor views from all rooms and the long porch. It's a classic seaside hostelry, with simple Colonial reproduction furniture and tidy if small rooms. (The 10 rooms across the way at a former sea captain's house have most of the private bathrooms.) The atmosphere is relaxed almost to the point of ennui, and the service good.

P.O. Box 149, Tenants Harbor, ME 04860. 𝄢 **800/241-8439** or 207/372-6366. Fax 207/372-6320. www.east windinn.com. 26 units (7 with shared bathroom). Summer $159 double; $129 double with shared bathroom; $179–$299 suite or apt. Off season $89–$199 double. Rates include breakfast. AE, DISC, MC, V. 2-night minimum stay in suites and apts. Pets allowed with prior permission ($10 per night). Children 12 and older are welcome. **Amenities:** Restaurant (traditional New England). *In room:* No phone.

LimeRock Inn 𝄢𝄢   This beautiful Queen Anne–style inn is on a side street just 2 blocks from Rockland's Main Street. Originally built for U.S. Rep. Charles Littlefield in 1890, it served as a doctor's residence from 1950 to 1994, after which it was renovated into a gracious inn. The innkeepers have done a commendable job converting what could be a gloomy manse into one of the region's better choices for accommodation. Attention has been paid to detail throughout, from country Victorian furniture to Egyptian cotton bedsheets. All guest rooms are welcoming, but among the best is the Island Cottage Room, a bright and airy chamber wonderfully converted from an old shed and featuring a private deck and Jacuzzi. The Turret Room has French doors into the bathroom, which features a claw-foot tub. If it's big elegance you're looking for, opt for the Grand Manan Room, with large four-poster bed, fireplace, and double Jacuzzi.

96 Limerock St., Rockland, ME 04841. 𝄢 **800/546-3762** or 207/594-2257. www.limerockinn.com. 8 units. $100–$215 double. Rates include breakfast. MC, V. *In room:* Jacuzzi (some), no phone.

Samoset Resort 𝄢𝄢   The Samoset is something of a Maine coast rarity—a modern, self-contained resort with contemporary styling, ocean views from

many rooms, and lots of golf. On 230 acres at the mouth of Rockland Harbor, a handsome 18-hole golf course surrounds the hotel and town houses. Golfers love the place—it's been called Pebble Beach East—and families will find plenty of activities for kids. The lobby is constructed of massive timbers, and all guest rooms have balconies or terraces, which is a big plus when you're this close to the ocean. The expansive new fitness center features a pool, spa, workout rooms, fitness and wellness classes, and additional sports facilities. This resort also has the best sunset stroll in the state—ramble across the golf course to a breakwater that leads to a picturesque lighthouse.

Rockport, ME 04856. ⓒ 800/341-1650 or 207/594-2511. www.samoset.com. 178 units. $139–$319 double, $209–$549 suite. AE, DISC, MC, V. Valet parking available. **Amenities:** 4 restaurants (casual/American, Continental/fine dining); indoor pool; outdoor pool; golf course; 4 tennis courts; health club; Jacuzzi; sauna; children's programs; concierge; courtesy car; business center; room service; massage; babysitting; laundry service; dry cleaning. *In room:* A/C, TV w/pay movies, iron.

WHERE TO DINE

Cafe Miranda 🎄🎄 *Value* WORLD CUISINE   Hidden away on a side street, this tiny contemporary restaurant draws liberally from cuisine from around the globe ("Italian, Thai, Mex, Armenian, More!"); given its wide-ranging culinary inclinations, it's something of a surprise just how well everything is prepared. You can share a large entree, or order from a menu of sometimes dozens of small plates—anything from a plate of grapes and brie to a fish tostada, a roasted ear of corn, a soft-shell crab, or even a roasted banana in cumin sauce. On a big plate, char-grilled pork and shrimp cakes with a ginger-lime-coconut sauce are superb. Other creative entrees have included barbecued pork ribs with a smoked jalapeño sauce, and sautéed shredded duck with roasted shallots, garlic, green peppercorns, and veloute sauce—yet they also do great barbecue brisket and macaroni and cheese as entrees here. They pull it all off; you never know what the kitchen's going to whip up next, but you can't wait to see. Cafe Miranda provides real value for your buck of any restaurant in Maine. Beer and wine are also available.

15 Oak St., Rockland. ⓒ 207/594-2034. www.cafemiranda.com. Reservations recommended. Main courses $17–$20. DISC, MC, V. Tues–Sat 5:30–9:30pm (until 8:30pm in winter).

Cod End 🎄 LOBSTER POUND   Part of Cod End's allure is its hidden and scenic location—as if you've stumbled upon a secret. Situated between the Town Landing and the East Wind Inn, Cod End is a classic lobster joint with fine views of tranquil Tenants Harbor. Walk through its fish market (where you can buy fish or lobster to go, as well as various lobster-related souvenirs), then place your order at the outdoor shack. While waiting, check out the dock at the marina or sit and relax in the sun. (If it's raining, the market has limited seating.) Lobsters are the draw, naturally, but you've plenty to choose from, including chowders, stews, linguini with seafood, and simple sandwiches for young tastes (even peanut butter and jelly). As with most lobster pounds, the less complicated and sophisticated your meal, the better the odds you'll be satisfied.

Next to the Town Dock, Tenant's Harbor. ⓒ 207/372-6782. Main courses: lunch entrees $1.75–$8; dinner $6.95–$13 (more for larger lobsters). DISC, MC, V. July–Aug daily 7am–9pm; limited hours in June and Sept; closed Oct–May.

Market on Main 🎄 CONTEMPORARY DELI   Run by the folks at Cafe Miranda, lively and hip Market on Main is a great choice for a midday break or easy dinner if you're driving up the coast or spending the day at the Farnsworth Art Museum down the block. Half deli, half restaurant, it's casual—with brick walls, exposed heating ducts, and galvanized steel tabletops. Selections range from sandwiches (including choices like baked eggplant) to burgers to seafood, as well as salads and a children's menu (including peanut butter and honey).

315 Main St. © 207/594-0015. Main courses $5.50–$14. DISC, MC, V. Mon–Thurs 11am–7pm; Fri–Sat 11am–8pm; Sun 10am–3pm.

Primo ★★★ MEDITERRANEAN/NEW AMERICAN   Primo has been a "buzz" restaurant since it opened in 2000. Executive chef Melissa Kelly trails behind her a string of accolades: She graduated first in her class at the Culinary Institute of America and won the 1999 James Beard Foundation award for "best chef in the Northeast." The restaurant occupies two deftly decorated floors of a century-old home a short drive south of downtown Rockland. The menu reflects the seasons and draws from local products wherever available: start with foie gras, scallops, or wood oven-roasted Raspberry Point oysters with creamy leeks, tomato, bacon, and tarragon. For the main course, you might choose from among grilled Long Island duck breast with polenta and radicchio, pan-roasted cod over saffron risotto, two styles of pheasant, a lamb shank cassoulet, or pepper-crusted venison with a rosemary spaetzle. Or just order one of the great wood-fired pizzas. Finish with one of co-owner/pastry chef/maitre d' Price Kushner's desserts: espresso float, Belgian chocolate cake, homemade cannolis, or an apple crostata made from local apples and sided with pinenut-caramel ice cream. This place has made such a splash that there's now a second Primo in Orlando, FL; keep that in mind next time you've got a date with Mickey and Minnie.

2 South Main St. (Rte. 173), Rockland. © 207/596-0770. www.primorestaurant.com. Reservations recommended. Main courses $16–$30. AE, DISC, MC, V. Thurs–Sun 5:30–9:30pm; call for days and hours in off season.

CAMDEN ★★

A quintessential coastal Maine village at the foot of wooded Camden Hills on a picturesque harbor, the affluent village of Camden has attracted the gentry of the eastern seaboard for more than a century. The mansions of the moneyed set still dominate the shady side streets (many are now bed-and-breakfasts), and Camden is possessed of a grace and sophistication that eludes many other coastal towns.

The best way to enjoy Camden is to park your car as soon as you can—which may mean driving a block or two off Route 1. The village is of a perfect scale to reconnoiter on foot, allowing a leisurely browse of boutiques and galleries. Don't miss the hidden town park (look behind the library), designed by the landscape firm of Frederick Law Olmsted, the nation's most lauded landscape architect.

ESSENTIALS

GETTING THERE   Camden is on Route 1, and from the south, you can shave a few minutes off your trip by turning left onto Route 90, 6 miles past Waldoboro, bypassing Rockland. The best traffic-free route from southern Maine is to Augusta via the Maine Turnpike, then via Route 17 to Route 90 to Route 1.

Concord Trailways (© **800/639-3317**) offers bus service from Camden to Bangor and Portland.

VISITOR INFORMATION   The **Rockport-Camden-Lincolnville Chamber of Commerce,** P.O. Box 919, Camden, ME 04843 (© **800/223-5459** or 207/236-4404) dispenses helpful information from its center at the Public Landing in Camden. It's open year-round weekdays from 9am to 5pm and Saturdays 10am to 5pm. In summer, it's also open Sundays 10am to 4pm.

EXPLORING CAMDEN

Camden Hills State Park ★★ (© **207/236-3109**) is located about 1 mile north of the village center on Route 1. This 6,500-acre park features an ocean-side picnic area, camping at 112 sites, a winding toll road up 800-foot Mt. Battie (with spectacular views from the summit), and a variety of well-marked hiking trails. The day-use fee is $2 for adults, 50¢ for children 5 to 11.

Make an ascent to the ledges of **Mt. Megunticook** ★★, best early in the morning before crowds have amassed and when mist still lingers in the valleys. Leave from near the campground and follow the well-maintained trail to these open ledges, about 30 to 45 minutes' exertion. Spectacular, almost improbable, views of the harbor await, plus glimpses inland to the gentle vales. Depending on your stamina and desire, you can continue on the trail network to Mount Battie or into the less-trammeled woodlands on the east side of the Camden Hills.

The 57-foot windjammer **Surprise** ★★ (© **207/236-4687;** www.camden mainesailing.com), launched in 1918, departs on 2-hour cruises from the Camden Public Landing. Four daily excursions ($28) are offered in July and August, three daily in June, September, and October. Reservations are recommended; and children must be 12 or older.

The **Schooner Lazy Jack** ★★ (© **207/230-0602;** www.schoonerlazyjack. com) has plied the waters since 1947, modeled after the Gloucester fishing schooners of the late 19th century. It has a maximum of 13 passengers; children must be 10 or older. The 2-hour tours cost $25 per person.

WHERE TO STAY

Despite the preponderance of B&Bs, Camden's total number of guest rooms (only about 300) is limited relative to the number of visitors, and during peak season, lodging is tight. It's best to reserve well in advance. You may also try **Camden Accommodations and Reservations** (© **800/344-4830** or 207/236-6090; www.camdenac.com), which offers assistance with everything from booking rooms at local B&Bs to finding cottages for seasonal rental.

South of the village center are the **Cedar Crest Motel,** 115 Elm St. (© **800/422-4964** or 207/236-4839), a handsome compound with a shuttle-bus connection downtown ($109–$132 in peak season); and long-time mainstay **Towne Motel,** 68 Elm St. (© **207/236-3377**), within walking distance of the village ($99–$115). Also right in town, just across the footbridge, is the **Best Western Camden Riverhouse Hotel,** 11 Tannery Lane (© **800/755-7483** or 207/236-0500), which has an indoor pool and fitness center ($159–$209). Note that High Street is a-rumble with cars and RVs during summer months, and you may find that the steady hum of traffic diminishes the small-town charm of the establishments that flank this otherwise stately, shady road. Restless sleepers should request rooms at the rear of the property.

Blue Harbor House ★   On busy Route 1 just south of town, this pale blue 1810 farmhouse has been an inn since 1978, decorated throughout with a sprightly country look. Guest rooms vary in size; some are rather small and noisy with traffic (earplugs and white-noise machines are in some rooms). Room 3 is especially nice, with wood floors, a handsome quilt, a bright alcove with plants, and a small TV. (Seven rooms have TVs, and two have Jacuzzis). The quietest and most spacious quarters are the two suites in the rear of the house, which offer the best value. Guests tend to return to this B&B not so much for the elegance of the accommodations, as for the congeniality of the hosts (they're especially good at helping plan day trips), and the familiar, familial feel of the place.

67 Elm St., Camden, ME 04843. ☎ **800/248-3196** or 207/236-3196. Fax 207/236-6523. www.blueharbor house.com. 10 units. $115–$205 double. Rates include breakfast. AE, DISC, MC, V. Pets allowed in suite with prior permission. Closed mid-Oct to mid-May. **Amenities:** Dining room (by reservation only). *In room:* A/C, TV, hair dryer.

Camden Windward House ★★   This handsome 1854 inn features welcoming common rooms decorated with a light Victorian touch; the library has a guest refrigerator and afternoon refreshments. Rooms vary in size, four with gas fireplaces; a suite features private balcony, cathedral ceiling, and Jacuzzi. Guests choose from a number of breakfast entrees, served in a pleasant dining room. The property is on Route 1, but the innkeepers have tamed traffic noise by adding a sound-muffling facade and installing multiple windows.

6 High St., Camden, ME 04843. ☎ **877/492-9656** or 207/236-9656. Fax 207/230-0433. www.windward house.com. 8 units. Peak season $169–$250 double; off season $99–$189 double ($10 less midweek). Rates include breakfast. AE, MC, V. Children 12 and older are welcome. *In room:* A/C, TV, dataport, hair dryer.

Cedarholm Garden Bay ★★   Cedarholm began years ago as a small cottage court with four simple cottages north of Camden on Route 1, operated more or less as a hobby. When Joyce and Barry Jobson took over in 1995, they built a road to the 460 feet of dramatic cobblestone shoreline and constructed two modern, steeply gabled cedar cottages, each with two bedrooms, with great detailing such as pocket doors, cobblestone fireplaces, handsome kitchenettes, and Jacuzzis. In 2001, they built two more cottages, Osprey and Tern, smaller and with fewer amenities than the originals, but no less dramatically sited. (The two-star rating reflects the unique appeal of the shorefront cottages.) Guests staying up the hill in smaller and older (but updated) cottages can still wander to the shore and lounge on a common deck overlooking the upper reaches of Penobscot Bay. It's noisier up above, closer to Route 1, and prices reflect that.

Rte. 1, Lincolnville Beach, ME 04849. ☎ **207/236-3886.** 8 units (includes 3 with 2 bedrooms). Oceanfront cottages $275–$295 double; oceanview cottages $85–$155 double. Rates include breakfast. 2-night minimum stay in some cottages. MC, V. *In room:* TV, kitchenette (some), Jacuzzi (some).

Inn at Sunrise Point ★★★   This peaceful sanctuary 4 miles north of Camden Harbor is a world apart from the bustling town. The service is helpful, and the setting can't be beat. Situated on the edge of Penobscot Bay down a long, tree-lined road, the inn consists of a cluster of contemporary yet classic shingled buildings. The predominant sounds here are birds singing and waves lapping at the cobblestone shore. A granite bench and Adirondack chairs on the front lawn enable guests to enjoy the bay view; breakfasts are served in a sunny conservatory. The rooms are spacious, comfortable, and full of amenities, including fireplaces, VCRs, and individual heat controls. The cottages are at the deluxe end of the scale, all featuring double Jacuzzis, fireplaces, wet bars, and private decks.

Rte. 1 (P.O. Box 1344), Camden, ME 04843. ☎ **800/435-6278** or 207/236-7716. Fax 207/236-0820. www. sunrisepoint.com. 7 units, including 4 cottages. $165–$250 double; $245–$395 cottage. Rates include breakfast. AE, MC, V. Closed Nov to late May. No children. *In room:* TV/VCR, fridge (some), coffeemaker (some), hair dryer, Jacuzzi (some).

Maine Stay ★★   The Maine Stay is known for its congenial hospitality. This classic slate-roofed New England home (dating back to 1802 but expanded in 1840) is set in a shady yard within walking distance of both downtown and Camden Hills State Park. All rooms have ceiling fans and antiques; four have TVs as well. The best is the downstairs Carriage House Room, which is away from the buzz of traffic on Route 1 and boasts its own stone patio. Innkeepers Bob and Juanita Topper continue the sociable tradition set by the previous operators.

22 High St., Camden, ME 04843. © 207/236-9636. www.mainestay.com. 8 units. $115–$165 double. Rates include breakfast. AE, MC, V. Children 10 and older are welcome. *In room:* Coffeemaker, hair dryer, no phone.

Norumbega ★★★   This Victorian-era stone castle is big enough to ensure privacy, but intimate enough that you can get to know other guests—mingling often occurs at breakfast and in the afternoon, when the innkeepers put out fresh-baked cookies. Overlooking the bay, the Norumbega has remarkable architectural detailing—extravagant carved-oak woodwork and a stunning oak-and-mahogany inlaid floor. Guest rooms are large and furnished with antiques. Five units have fireplaces, while the three "garden-level rooms" (off the downstairs billiards room) have private decks. Most have TVs. Two rooms rank among the finest in New England—the Library Suite, with interior balcony, and the sprawling Penthouse, with its superlative views.

63 High St., Camden, ME 04843. © 207/236-4646. Fax 207/236-0824. www.norumbegainn.com. 13 units. July to mid-Oct $160–$475 double; mid-May to June and late Oct $125–$375 double; Nov to mid-May $95–$295 double. Rates include breakfast. 2-night minimum stay summer, weekends, and holidays. AE, DISC, MC, V. Children 7 and older are welcome. *In room:* Dataport, hair dryer.

Whitehall Inn ★   The Whitehall is a distinguished and understated New England resort, listed on the National Register of Historic Places, where you half expect to find a young Cary Grant in a blue blazer tickling the ivories on the lobby's 1904 Steinway. Set at the edge of town in a structure dating to 1834, this three-story inn has a striking architectural integrity with its columns, gables, and long roofline. (Ask for a room away from the Rte. 1 noise.) Accommodations are simple but appealing. The Whitehall occupies a minor footnote in the annals of American literature—a young local poet recited her poems here for guests in 1912, stunning the audience with her eloquence. Her name? Edna St. Vincent Millay. The inn is quite popular with a more mature blueblood clientele, many of whom have been coming each summer for generations.

52 High St., Camden, ME 04843. © 800/789-6565 or 207/236-3391. Fax 207/236-4427. www.whitehall-inn. com. 50 units (8 units share 4 bathrooms). July to mid-Oct $135–$165 double with private bathroom; $105–$115 double with shared bathroom. Rates include breakfast. Discounts available in late May and June. AE, MC, V. Closed mid-Oct to late May. **Amenities:** Restaurant (traditional New England); tennis court; tour desk; babysitting.

WHERE TO DINE

You can snack surprisingly well in this blueblood town. Some of the best doughnuts in New England, for instance, are fried up at **Boynton-McKay** (© 207/ 236-2465) at 30 Main Street—also a superlative spot for lunch, coffee, or a sandwich. Just up the street, south of the main drag, pick up a bag of gourmet groceries at **French & Brawn** (© 207/236-3361) or buy some organic, fair-trade coffee at the tiny nook known as **Ortolan** (© 207/236-7025).

Atlantica ★★ CONTEMPORARY AMERICAN   Atlantica gets high marks for its innovative seafood menu and well-prepared fare. On the waterfront with a small indoor seating area and an equally small outdoor deck, Atlantica features creative fare such as pan-seared tuna served with wok-fired vegetables and a wasabi foam, scallops sautéed in ginger and plum wine sauce, rack of lamb in spearmint sauce, and seared halibut with preserved lemon. Of course, there's always lobster as a main course—but be sure to start with a cup or bowl of the famous lobster-corn chowder in any case.

1 Bayview Landing. © 888/507-8514 or 207/236-6011. www.atlanticarestaurant.com. Reservations recommended. Main courses: lunch $8–$14; dinner $18–$25. AE, MC, V. Summer Tues–Sun 10:30am–2pm and 5:30–9pm; off season Thurs–Sat 10:30am–2pm and Tues–Sat 5:30–9pm. Closed Nov.

Cappy's Chowder House SEAFOOD/AMERICAN   Cappy's is a local institution more memorable for its lively atmosphere than its fare, which includes prime rib, hearty seafood stew flavored with kielbasa, and their famous chowder (which has gotten a nod from *Gourmet* magazine). "Old-time sodas" are a specialty. The Crow's Nest upstairs is a bit quieter.

1 Main St. (C) **207/236-2254**. www.cappyschowder.com. Main courses $5.95–$15. MC, V. Daily 7:30am–midnight.

Peter Ott's ★★ AMERICAN   Peter Ott's opened in 1974 and has satisfied customers ever since with its no-nonsense fare. While it resembles a steakhouse with its wood tables and manly meat dishes (such as char-broiled Black Angus), it's grown beyond that to satisfy more diverse tastes. In fact, it offers some of the better prepared seafood in town, including grilled salmon with a lemon caper sauce. Leave room for the lemon-almond crumb tart.

16 Bayview St. (C) **207/236-4032**. Main courses $12–$20. MC, V. Daily 5:30–9:30pm.

Sea Dog Brewing Co. ★ PUB FARE   One of a handful of brewpubs that found immediate acceptance in Maine, Sea Dog is a friendly destination for quick pub food such as nachos or hamburgers. It won't set your taste buds dancing, but it will satisfy basic cravings. On the ground floor of a renovated old woolen mill, the restaurant has a pleasing, comfortable atmosphere with booths, a handsome bar, and views of the old millrace. Beers are consistently excellent.

43 Mechanic St. (C) **207/236-6863**. Main courses $6.95–$14. AE, DISC, MC, V. Daily 11:30am–midnight. Located at Knox Mill 1 block west of Elm St.

The Waterfront ★ SEAFOOD   The Waterfront disproves the theory that "the better the view, the worse the food." Here you can watch yachts and windjammers come and go (angle for a seat on the deck) and still be reasonably pleased with what you're served. Look for fried clams, crab cakes, and boiled lobster, or—on the adventurous side—roasted Gulf shrimp with mango and arugula, aïoli-encrusted haddock, and seared salmon with *herbes de Provence*. More earthbound fare here includes burgers, pitas, and strip steaks, and a lighter pub menu is served between 2:30 and 5pm.

Bayview St. on Camden Harbor. (C) **207/236-3747**. www.waterfrontcamden.com. Main courses: lunch $6.95–$14; dinner $13–$25. AE, MC, V. Daily 11:30am–2:30pm and 5–10pm (closes earlier in off season).

5 The Blue Hill Peninsula

The Blue Hill Peninsula is a back-roads paradise. If you like to get lost on country lanes that dead-end at the sea or inexplicably start to loop back on themselves, this is the place. In contrast to the western shores of Penobscot Bay, the Blue Hill Peninsula has more of a lost-in-time character. The roads are hilly, winding, and narrow, passing through forests, along saltwater farms, and touching on the edge of an inlet here or there. By and large, it's overlooked by the majority of Maine's visitors, especially those who like their itineraries well structured and their destinations clear and simple.

CASTINE ★★

Castine is one of Maine's most gracious villages. It's not so much the stunningly handsome and meticulously maintained mid-19th-century homes, or its location on a quiet peninsula, 16 miles south of RV-clotted Route 1.

No, what lends Castine its charm are splendid, towering elm trees that still overarch many of the village streets. Before Dutch elm disease ravaged the nation's tree-lined streets, much of America looked like this, and it's easy to slip into a debilitating nostalgia for this most graceful tree, even if you're too young to remember America of the elms. Castine has managed to keep several hundred regal elms alive, and it's worth the detour for these alone.

For American history buffs, Castine offers much more. This outpost served as a strategic town in various battles between British, Dutch, French, and feisty colonials in the centuries following its settlement in 1613. It was occupied by each of those groups at some point, and historical personages such as Miles Standish and Paul Revere passed through during one epoch or another. The town has a dignified, aristocratic bearing, and it somehow seems appropriate that Tory-dominated Castine welcomed the British with open arms during the Revolution.

Castine is likely to appeal most to those who can entertain themselves. It's a peaceful place to sit and read, or take an afternoon walk. If it's outlet shopping you're looking for, you're better off moving on.

ESSENTIALS

GETTING THERE   Castine is 16 miles south of Route 1. Turn south on Route 175 in Orland (east of Bucksport) and follow it to Route 166, which winds its way to Castine. Route 166A offers an alternate route along Penobscot Bay.

VISITOR INFORMATION   Castine lacks a formal information center, but the clerk at the **Town Office** (© 207/326-4502) is helpful with local questions.

EXPLORING CASTINE

One of the town's more intriguing attractions is the **Wilson Museum** (© 207/ 326-9247) on Perkins Street, an attractive, quirky anthropological museum constructed in 1921. This small museum contains the collections of John Howard Wilson, an archaeologist and collector of prehistoric artifacts. His gleanings are neatly arranged in a staid, classical arrangement of the sort that proliferated in the late 19th and early 20th centuries. The museum is open from the end of May to the end of September daily except Monday from 2 to 5pm; admission is free.

Next door is the **John Perkins House,** Castine's oldest home. It was occupied by the British during the Revolution and War of 1812, and a tour features demonstrations of old-fashioned cooking techniques. The Perkins House is open July and August, Wednesday and Sunday only from 2 to 5pm. Admission is $2.

Castine is also home to the **Maine Maritime Academy** (© 207/326-2206), which trains sailors for the rigors of life at sea. The campus is on the western edge of the village, and the S.S. *Maine,* the hulking training ship, is often docked in Castine, almost overwhelming the village with its size. When it's in port, free, half-hour tours of the ship are offered in summer from 10am to noon, and 1 to 4pm.

Also worth exploring is **Dyce's Head Light** at the extreme western end of Battle Avenue. While the 1828 light itself is not open to the public, it's well worth scrambling down the trail to the rocky shoreline along the Penobscot River just beneath the lighthouse. A small sign indicates the start of the public trail.

WHERE TO STAY

Castine Harbor Lodge ⭐ *Kids*   Housed in a grand 1893 mansion (the only inn on the water in Castine), this place is run with an informal good cheer that enables kids to feel at home amid the regal architecture. The main parlor is dominated by a pool table, with Scrabble and Nintendo for the asking. The front porch, with views that extend across the bay to the Camden Hills, offers one of the best places in the state to unwind. The spacious guest rooms are eclectically appointed with both antiques and modern furnishings. All rooms in the main inn have private baths; families may consider the annex, where four rooms share two baths. The family dog is also welcome here. It's a great spot if you prefer well-worn comfort to high-end elegance. There's also a 250-foot dock and three guest moorings for guests who arrive by sea.

Perkins St. (P.O. Box 215), Castine, ME 04421. ⓒ **207/326-4335.** www.castinemaine.com. 14 units (4 units share 2 bathrooms in annex). $85–$245 double. Rates include continental breakfast. DC, DISC, MC, V. Pets allowed ($10 per night). **Amenities:** Wine bar (pub fare).

Castine Inn ⭐ The Castine Inn is a Maine coast rarity—a hotel originally built (in 1898) as a hotel, not a residence that was later converted. This handsome village inn, designed in an eclectic Georgian-Federal–Revival style, has a fine front porch and attractive gardens. Inside, the lobby takes its cue from the 1940s, with wingback chairs and loveseats. The guest rooms on the two upper floors (no elevator) are simply if unevenly furnished in a Colonial Revival style. Note that the innkeepers have revamped several units, adding luxe touches, which are markedly more inviting than other rooms and worth the extra splurge.

Main St. (P.O. Box 41), Castine, ME 04421. ⓒ **207/326-4365.** Fax 207/326-4570. www.castineinn.com. 19 units (including 3 suites). $90–$150 double; $215 suite. Rates include breakfast. 2-night minimum stay July–Aug. MC, V. Closed Nov–Apr. Children 8 and older are welcome. **Amenities:** Restaurant (see below); sauna. *In room:* No phone.

Pentagöet Inn ⭐⭐ This quirky 1894 structure with prominent turret is comfortable but not overly fussy, professional but not chilly, personal but not overly intimate. The owners give it a touch of travel exotica, with decor that includes an intriguing photo of Gandhi that once hung in the Indian embassy in Zaire and an oil painting of Lenin liberated from a flea market in Tajikistan. Guest rooms on the upper two floors of the main house are furnished with a similarly eclectic eye and a splash of romance. The five rooms in the adjacent Perkins Street building—a more austere Federal-era house—have also been done over and have a smattering of period antiques. The inn has no air-conditioning, but all rooms have ceiling or window fans.

Main St. (P.O. Box 4), Castine, ME 04421. ⓒ **800/845-1701** or 207/326-8616. Fax 207/326-9382. www. pentagoet.com. 16 units. $85–$195 double. Rates include breakfast. MC, V. Closed Nov–Apr. Pets allowed with prior permission. Children 12 and older are welcome. **Amenities:** Restaurant (regional and global fare). *In room:* No phone.

WHERE TO DINE

Castine Inn ⭐⭐ NEW AMERICAN This handsome hotel dining room has Castine's best fare and some of the better food in the state. Chef/owner Tom Gutow served stints at Bouley and Verbena in New York, and isn't timid about experimenting with local meats and produce. Expect dishes such as lobster with vanilla butter, mango mayonnaise, and tropical-fruit salsa; or lamb loin with eggplant, green lentils, tomatoes, and rosemary jus. One night each week, the restaurant offers a buffet; that night, you're better off heading to Dennett's Wharf.

Main St. ⓒ 207/326-4365. Reservations recommended. Main courses $26–$33. MC, V. Daily 6–9pm. Closed mid-Dec to May.

Dennett's Wharf PUB FARE In a soaring waterfront sail loft, Dennett's Wharf offers upscale bar food amid a lively setting leavened with a good selection of microbrews. If the weather's decent, outdoor dining has superb harbor views. Look for grilled sandwiches, roll-ups, and salads at lunch; dinner includes lobster, stir-fry, and steak teriyaki.

Sea St. (next to the Town Dock). © 207/326-9045. www.dennettswharf.com. Reservations recommended in summer and for parties of 6 or more. Main courses: lunch $5.50–$18; dinner $8.95–$24. AE, DISC, MC, V. Daily 11am–midnight. Closed mid-Oct to Apr 30.

DEER ISLE ⭐

Deer Isle is well off the beaten path but worth the long detour from Route 1 if your tastes run to pastoral countryside with a nautical edge. Looping, winding roads cross through forest and farmland, and travelers are rewarded with sudden glimpses of the sun-dappled ocean and mint-green coves. An occasional settlement crops up now and again.

Deer Isle doesn't cater exclusively to tourists, as many coastal regions do. Still occupied by fifth-generation fishermen, farmers, longtime rusticators, and artists who prize their seclusion, the village has a handful of inns and galleries, but its primary focus is to serve locals and summer residents, not transients. The village of **Stonington,** on the southern tip, is a rough-hewn sea town. Despite serious incursions the past 5 years by galleries and enterprises dependent on tourism, it remains dominated in spirit by fishermen and the occasional quarryworker.

ESSENTIALS

GETTING THERE   Deer Isle is accessible via several winding country roads from Route 1. Coming from the west, head south on Route 175 off Route 1 in Orland, then connect to Route 15 to Deer Isle. From the east, head south on Route 172 to Blue Hill, where you can pick up Route 15. Deer Isle is connected to the mainland via a high, narrow, and graceful suspension bridge built in 1938, which can be somewhat harrowing to cross in high winds.

VISITOR INFORMATION   The **Deer Isle–Stonington Chamber of Commerce** (© **207/348-6124**) staffs a seasonal information booth just beyond the bridge on Little Deer Isle. The booth is open daily in summer from 10am to 4pm, depending on volunteer availability.

EXPLORING DEER ISLE

Deer Isle, with its network of narrow roads to nowhere, is ideal for rambling— a pleasure to explore by car and inviting to travel by bike, though hasty and careening fishermen in pickups can make this unnerving at times.

Stonington, at the southern tip of Deer Isle, consists of one commercial street that wraps along the harbor's edge. While B&Bs and boutiques have made inroads here recently, it's still a mostly rough-and-tumble waterfront town.

Haystack Mountain School of Crafts ⭐   The 40-acre oceanside campus of this respected summer crafts school is stunning. Designed in the 1960s, Edward Larrabee Barnes set the buildings on a hillside overlooking the waters of Jericho Bay. Barnes managed to play up the views while respecting the landscape by constructing a series of small structures on pilings that seem to float above the earth. Classrooms and studios are linked by boardwalks, many connected to a wide central staircase ending at the Flag Deck, a sort of open-air commons just above the shoreline. Buildings and classrooms are closed to the public; summer visitors are welcome to walk to the Flag Deck and stroll the nature trail adjacent to campus. The drive to the campus is outstanding.

Sunshine Rd. © 207/348-2306. www.haystack-mtn.org. Donations appreciated. Summer daily 9am–5pm; tours Wed 1pm. Head south of the village of Deer Isle on Rte. 15; turn left on Greenlaw District Rd. and follow signs to the school, approximately 7 miles.

WHERE TO STAY

You'll find standard motel rooms at **Eggemoggin Landing** (© **207/348-6115**) on Route 15, at a great location on the shores of Eggemoggin Reach at the south end of the bridge from the mainland to Little Deer Isle. Open May through October, rates are $67 to $85 in peak season. Pets are allowed in spring and fall. Amenities include a restaurant, kayak and bike rentals, and sailboat cruises.

Goose Cove Lodge ★★ *Kids*　This rustic compound next to a nature preserve is a superb destination for families and lovers of the outdoors. Exploring the grounds offers an adventure every day. Hike out to Barred Island at low tide, or take a guided nature hike on any of five trails. Mess around in boats in the cove, or borrow a bike for an excursion. Twenty rooms offer fireplaces or Franklin stoves; two cottages sleep six and are available through winter. My favorites? Elm and Linnea, cozy cabins in the woods on a rise overlooking the beach. Meals are far above what you'd expect to find at the end of a remote dirt road.

Goose Cove Rd. (P.O. Box 40), Sunset, ME 04683. © **800/728-1963** or 207/348-2508. Fax 207/348-2624. www.goosecovelodge.com. 23 units. Peak season $150–$320 double; off season $124–$274 double. Ask about off-season packages. Rates include breakfast. 2-night minimum stay July–Aug (1-week minimum in cottages); some units have a 3-person minimum in peak season. MC, V. Closed mid-Oct to mid-May. **Amenities:** Restaurant (New American); watersports equipment; bikes. *In room:* No phone.

Inn on the Harbor ★　This quirky waterfront inn has the best location in town—perched over the harbor and on the main street, ideal for resting up before or after a kayak expedition, and a good base for day trips to Isle au Haut. Ten rooms overlook the harbor, nicely appointed with antiques and sisal carpets. Most units have phones. Complimentary sherry and wine are served in the reception room or on the waterfront deck. Breakfast includes homebaked muffins and breads. The inn operates **Cafe Atlantic** (© **207/367-6373**), a short walk away, featuring seafood, pasta, and beef (prime rib on weekends). Parking on the street or at nearby lots can be inconvenient during busy times.

Main St. (P.O. Box 69), Stonington, ME 04681. © **800/942-2420** or 207/367-2420. Fax 207/367-5165. www.innontheharbor.com. 13 units. $110–$175 double; from $60 in off season. Rates include continental breakfast. AE, DISC, MC, V. On-street parking. Children 12 and older are welcome. **Amenities:** Espresso bar. *In room:* TV, dataport.

Oakland House Seaside Resort/Shore Oaks ★★　On the mainland just north of the bridge to Deer Isle is a classic summer resort that's been in the same family since the American Revolution. For the past half-century, its main draw has been tucked among 50 acres and a half-mile of shorefront with superb water views: a cluster of shoreside cottages that are mostly set aside for weeklong stays (Sat–Sat). The cottages are of varying vintages but most have fireplaces (wood delivered daily). For shorter visits, a grand 1907 shorefront home has been converted to a 10-room inn called Shore Oaks; innkeepers Jim and Sally Littlefield have turned it into a comfortable Arts-and-Crafts–inspired hostelry. In peak season, guests take their meals at the old 1889 hotel, with tasty but basic options such as lamb chops with apple and mint chutney and cod with an herbed crust. Boat charters and a lobster bake are options in the summer, or simply swim. There's a handy plug-in for laptops in the business center.

435 Herrick Rd., Brooksville, ME 04617. © **800/359-7352** or 207/359-8521. www.oaklandhouse.com. 25 units (15 cottages; 3 inn rooms share 1 bathroom.) Summer $159–$295 double, including breakfast and dinner. 1-, 2-, 3-, and 4-bedroom cottages $475–$5,400 per week including breakfast and dinner; off season $475 and up per week w/o meals. 2-night minimum stay for inn on weekends. MC, V. Inn closed mid-Oct to early May; cottages closed Feb–Mar. No children in inn. **Amenities:** Restaurant (American); swimming; water sports equipment rental; business center. *In room:* Kitchenette (some), coffeemaker (some), iron (some), no phone.

Pilgrim's Inn ★★ Set at the edge of the village between an open bay and a millpond, this is a handsomely renovated inn in a lovely setting. The four-story structure, built in 1793, will appeal to history buffs. The interior is appointed in a style that's informed by early Americana, but not beholden to uncomfortable authenticity. The guest rooms are nicely sized, filled with antiques and painted in muted colonial colors; especially intriguing are the rooms on the top floor, with original diagonal beams. Also available are three nearby cottages, which are equipped with TVs, phones, air-conditioning, irons, and coffeemakers.

Deer Isle, ME 04627. ☎ 207/348-6615. www.pilgrimsinn.com. 15 units. Summer $125–$195 double (from $90 in off season); cottages $215–$225. Rates include breakfast. AE, MC, V. Closed mid-Oct to mid-May (cottages open year-round). Children 10 and older are welcome at the inn; younger children and pets permitted in cottages only. **Amenities:** Dining room (regional/fine dining); bike rental; babysitting. *In room:* A/C (some), TV (some), coffeemaker (some), hair dryer, iron (some), no phone.

WHERE TO DINE

For fine dining, **Goose Cove Lodge** and the **Pilgrim's Inn** serve meals to the public; both require reservations (see above.)

Fisherman's Friend ★ SEAFOOD This is a lively and boisterous place where you'll easily get your fill of local color. Simple tables fill a large room, while long-experienced waitresses hustle to keep up with demand. The menu features basic home-cooked meals, with a wide range of fresh fish prepared in a variety of styles. It's been justly famous for its lobster stew since opening in 1976. Dessert selections, including berry pies and shortcake, are extensive and tend toward traditional New England. It's BYOB.

School St., Stonington. ☎ 207/367-2442. Reservations recommended in peak season and on weekends. Sandwiches $2.50–$6.50; dinner entrees $6.95–$16. DISC, MC, V. July–Aug daily 11am–9pm; June and Sept–Oct daily 11am–8pm; Apr–May Tues–Sun 11am–8pm. Closed Nov–Mar. Located up the hill from the harbor past the Opera House.

BLUE HILL ★

Blue Hill (pop. 1,900) is fairly easy to find—look for the gently domed, eponymous Blue Hill Mountain, which lords over the northern end of Blue Hill Bay. Set between the mountain and the bay is the quiet and historic town of Blue Hill, which clusters along the bay shore and a burbling stream. The town never seems to have much going on, which may be exactly what attracts summer visitors time and again—and may explain why two excellent independent bookstores are located here. Many old-money families still maintain retreats along the water or in the rolling inland hills, but Blue Hill offers several excellent options for lodging if you're not well endowed with local relatives. A good destination for an escape, it especially appeals to those deft at crafting their own entertainment.

ESSENTIALS

GETTING THERE Blue Hill is southeast of Ellsworth on Route 172. Coming from the west, take Route 15 south 5 miles east of Bucksport (it's well marked with road signs).

VISITOR INFORMATION Blue Hill does not have a visitor information booth; contact the **Blue Hill Peninsula Chamber of Commerce,** P.O. Box 520, Blue Hill, ME 04614 (☎ 207/374-3242; www.bluehillme.com).

EXPLORING BLUE HILL

From the open summit of **Blue Hill Mountain** ★★ are superb views of the bay and the rocky balds on Mount Desert Island just across the way. To reach the trailhead from the village, drive north on Route 172, then turn west (left) on

---

Tips **Community Radio**

When in the area, tune to the local community radio station, WERU at 89.9 FM. Started by Noel Paul Stookey (the Paul in Peter, Paul and Mary) in a chicken coop, its idea was to spread good music and provocative ideas. It's slicker and more professional in recent years, but still maintains a pleasantly homespun flavor, with an eclectic range of music and commentary.

Mountain Road at the Blue Hill Fairgrounds. Drive .8 mile and look for the marked trail. An ascent of the "mountain" (elevation 940 ft.) is about a mile and requires about 45 minutes. Bring a picnic and enjoy the vistas.

Blue Hill has attracted more than its fair share of artists—especially, it seems, potters. On Union Street, stop by **Rowantrees Pottery** ☆☆ (© 207/374-5535), which has been a Blue Hill institution for more than 50 years. The pottery is richly hued, and the glazes made from local resources. The family-run **Rackliffe Pottery** ☆, on Ellsworth Road (© 207/374-2297), uses native clay and lead-free glazes. The bowls and vases have a lustrous, silky feel. Visitors are welcome to watch the potters at work. Both shops are open year-round.

The **Parson Fisher House** ☆ (© 207/374-2459) was home to Blue Hill's first permanent minister, who settled here in 1796. A rustic Renaissance man, educated at Harvard, Fisher delivered sermons in six different languages and was a gifted writer, painter, and inventor. On a tour of his home, which he built in 1814, you can see a clock with wooden works he made, as well as samples of the books he not only wrote but also published and bound himself. The house is on Routes 176 and 15 a half-mile west of the village. It's open from July to mid-September, Monday through Saturday from 2 to 5pm. Admission is $5 for adults, free for children under 12.

The **Big Chicken Barn** (© 207/667-7308) is a sprawling antiques shop and bookstore unlike any other. The first floor features a mix of antiques in dozens of stalls (literally) maintained by local dealers. Upstairs are some 90,000 (you read correctly) books, well organized by category, as well as a forest's worth of old magazines in plastic sleeves—if nothing else, they make for good browsing on a rainy afternoon). The shop is on Route 1 between Ellsworth and Bucksport (9 miles west of Ellsworth, 11 miles east of Bucksport).

WHERE TO STAY

Blue Hill Farm Country Inn ☆   Comfortably situated on 48 acres, this inn's strength is in its common areas. The first floor of a sprawling barn has been converted to a living room for guests. In the adjoining antique farmhouse, you can curl up in the cozy common room, which is amply stocked with a good selection of books. In contrast, the guest rooms are rather small and lightly furnished. The more modern units, upstairs in the barn loft, are nicely decorated in a country farmhouse style, but these are a bit motel-like, with rooms set off a central hallway. The three older rooms in the farmhouse have more character, but share a single bathroom with a small tub and hand-held shower.

Rte. 15, 2 miles north of the village (P.O. Box 437), Blue Hill, ME 04614. © 207/374-5126. www.bluehill farminn.com 14 units (7 with shared bathroom). June–Oct $85–$99 double; off season $75–$85 double (no shared bathroom in off season). Rates include continental breakfast. AE, MC, V. *In room:* No phone.

Blue Hill Inn ☆☆   The handsome Blue Hill Inn has hosted travelers with aplomb since 1840. Situated on one of Blue Hill's main thoroughfares and within walking distance of village attractions, this Federal-style inn is colonial America throughout, its authenticity enhanced by creaky floors and doorjambs slightly out of true. Guest rooms are furnished with antiques and down comforters; four units feature wood-burning fireplaces. In an adjacent building is a more contemporary luxury suite, which features cathedral ceiling, fireplace, kitchen, and deck.

Union St. (P.O. Box 403), Blue Hill, ME 04614. © 207/374-2844. Fax 207/374-2829. www.bluehillinn.com. 12 units. $138–$195 double. Rates include breakfast. 2-night minimum stay in summer. Ask about activities packages. DISC, MC, V. Closed Dec to mid-May. Children 13 and older are welcome. **Amenities:** Dining (New American/organic). *In room:* No phone.

WHERE TO DINE

Jean-Paul's Bistro ⭐ UPSCALE SANDWICHES You get a lot of atmosphere for a moderate price at Jean-Paul's, which serves only lunch and tea. This is an excellent choice on a sunny day; head for the tables and Adirondack chairs on the stone terraces and lawn that overlook the bay. Lunches tend toward quiche, croissant sandwiches, and salads. The walnut tarragon chicken salad is tasty; the delicious desserts make liberal use of local blueberries.

Main St. (at the intersection of Routes 172 and 15). © 207/374-5852. Main courses $6.95–$9.95. MC, V. Daily 11am–3pm. Closed mid-Sept to June.

6 Mount Desert Island & Acadia National Park ⭐⭐⭐

Mount Desert Island is home to spectacular Acadia National Park, and for many visitors, the two places are one and the same. Yet the park holdings are only part of the appeal of this popular island, connected to the mainland via a short, two-lane causeway. Beyond the parklands are scenic harborside villages and remote backcountry roads, lovely B&Bs and fine restaurants, oversize 19th-century summer "cottages," and the historic tourist town of Bar Harbor.

Mount Desert (pronounced "des*sert*," like what you have after dinner) is divided into two lobes separated by Somes Sound, the only true fjord—that is, a valley carved out by a glacier and then subsequently filled in with rising ocean water—in the continental U.S. Most of the parkland is on the east side of the island, though large swaths of park exist on the west, too. The east side is much more heavily developed, with Bar Harbor the center of commerce and entertainment. The west side has a more quiet, settled air, and teems more with wildlife than tourists. This island isn't huge—about 15 miles from the causeway to the southernmost tip at Bass Harbor Head—yet you can do an awful lot of adventuring in such a compact space. The best plan is to take it slowly, exploring whenever possible by foot, bicycle, canoe, or kayak, and giving yourself up to a week to do it. You'll be glad you did.

ACADIA NATIONAL PARK ⭐⭐⭐

It's not hard to fathom why Acadia is one of the biggest draws in the national park system. Its landscape offers a rich tapestry of rugged cliffs, restless ocean, and quiet woods. Acadia's terrain, like so much of the rest of northern New England, was carved by glaciers 18,000 years ago. A mile-high ice sheet shaped the land, scouring valleys into U shapes, rounding many of the once-jagged peaks, and depositing boulders around the landscape, including the famous 10-foot-high Bubble Rock, which appears to be perched precariously on the side of South Bubble Mountain.

Its more recent roots go back to the 1840s, when Hudson River School painter Thomas Cole brought his sketchbooks and easels to this remote island, then home to a small number of fishermen and boat builders. His stunning renditions of the surf pounding against coastal granite were displayed in New York, triggering an early tourism boom as urbanites flocked to the island to "rusticate." By 1872, national magazines were touting Eden (Bar Harbor's name until 1919) as a desirable summer resort. It soon became summer home to Carnegies, Rockefellers, Astors, and Vanderbilts, who built massive "cottages" with dozens of rooms.

By the early 1900s, the island's popularity and growing development began to concern its most ardent supporters. Boston textile heir and conservationist George Dorr and Harvard president Charles Eliot, aided by the largesse of John D. Rockefeller, Jr., started acquiring large tracts for the public's enjoyment. These parcels were eventually donated to the government, and in 1919, the land was designated Lafayette National Park, the first national park east of the Mississippi. Renamed Acadia in 1929, the park has grown to encompass nearly half the island, with holdings scattered about piecemeal here and there.

It was Rockefeller who built the elaborate 57-mile system of private carriage roads, featuring a dozen gracefully handcrafted stone bridges. These roads, open today to pedestrians, bicyclists, and equestrians, are concentrated most densely around Jordan Pond, but also wind through wooded valleys and ascend to some of the most scenic open peaks.

ESSENTIALS

GETTING THERE   Acadia National Park is reached from the town of Ellsworth via Route 3. If you're driving from southern Maine, avoid the coastal congestion along Route 1 by taking the Maine Turnpike to Bangor, picking up I-395 to Route 1A, then continuing south on Route 1A to Ellsworth. It's the quickest route in summer, and you're not missing much scenery.

Daily flights from Boston to the airport in Trenton, just across the causeway from Mount Desert Island, are offered year-round by US Air affiliate **Colgan Air** (© **800/523-3273** or 207/667-7171; www.colganair.com). In summer, **Concord Trailways** (© **888/741-8686** or 207/942-8686; www.concordtrailways. com) offers van service between Bangor (including an airport stop), Ellsworth, and Bar Harbor. Reservations are required. You can also catch the free #1 shuttle bus (see below), which stops by the island airport once to twice an hour from late June through October and brings you directly downtown.

GETTING AROUND   A wonderful, free **shuttle bus** service known as the *Island Explorer* was inaugurated as part of an experiment to reduce the number of cars on island roads. It's working. The propane-powered buses, equipped with racks for bikes, serve seven routes that cover nearly the entire island and will stop anywhere you request outside the village centers, including trailheads, ferries,

---

⎛Tips Packing a Picnic in Acadia

Before you set out to explore, pack a lunch and keep it handy. Once in, the park has few places (other than Jordan Pond House) to stop for lunch or snacks. Having drinks and snacks at hand will prevent breaking up your day backtracking into Bar Harbor or elsewhere to fend off starvation. The more food you bring, the more your options for the day will expand, so hit one of the charming general stores in any of the island's villages for a wedge of cheese, fresh sandwich, chips, and bottled water.

villages, and campgrounds. All routes begin or end at the Village Green in Bar Harbor, but you're encouraged to pick up the bus wherever you're staying, whether motel or campground, to minimize the number of cars in town. Route 3 goes from Bar Harbor along much of the Park Loop, offering easy access to some of the park's best hiking trails. The buses operate from late June to mid-October.

GUIDED TOURS **Acadia National Park Tours** (© 207/288-3327) offers 2½-hour park tours departing twice daily (10am and 2pm) from downtown Bar Harbor. The bus tour includes three stops (Sieur De Monts Springs, Thunder Hole, and Cadillac Mountain) and plenty of park trivia courtesy of the driver. This is an easy way for first-time visitors to get a quick introduction to the park before setting out on their own. Tickets are available at Testa's Restaurant, 53 Main St., Bar Harbor; $20 for adults, $10 for children under 12.

ENTRY POINTS & FEES A 1-week park pass, which includes unlimited trips on Park Loop Road, costs $10 per car; no additional charge per passenger. (No daily pass is available.) The main point of entry to Park Loop Road, the park's most scenic byway, is the visitor center at **Hulls Cove** (see below). Mount Desert Island consists of an interwoven network of park and town roads, allowing visitors to enter the park at numerous points. A glance at a park map (available free at the visitor center) will make these access points self-evident. The entry fee is collected at a tollbooth on Park Loop Road a half-mile north of Sand Beach.

VISITOR CENTERS & INFORMATION Acadia staffs two visitor centers. The **Thompson Island Information Center,** on Route 3 (© 207/288-3411), is the first you'll pass as you enter Mount Desert Island. The local chambers of commerce maintain this center; park personnel are usually on hand to answer inquiries. Open from mid-May to mid-October, it's the best stop for general lodging and restaurant information.

For more information on park attractions, continue on Route 3 to the National Park Service's **Hulls Cove Visitor Center,** about 7½ miles beyond Thompson Island. This attractive stone-walled center includes park service displays, such as a large relief map of the island, natural-history exhibits, and a short film. You can request brochures on trails and carriage roads or purchase postcards and guidebooks. The center is open mid-April to October. Plans are afoot to build a new visitor center; park funding and other considerations make a timetable uncertain, but disruptions may be likely in coming years.

Information is also available year-round, by phone or in person, from the park's **headquarters** (© 207/288-3338; www.nps.gov/acad), on Route 233 between Bar Harbor and Somesville.

DRIVING TOUR **DRIVING THE PARK LOOP ROAD**

The 20-mile **Park Loop Road** ★★★ is to Acadia what Half Dome is to Yosemite—the park's premier attraction, and magnet for the largest crowds. This remarkable roadway starts near the Hulls Cove Visitor Center and follows the high ridges above Bar Harbor before dropping down along the rocky coast. Here, earthy tones and spires of spruce and fir cap, and dark granite contrast sharply with frothy white surf and steely blue sea. After following the picturesque coast and touching on several coves, the road loops back inland along Jordan Pond and Eagle Lake, with a detour to the summit of the island's highest peak.

Ideally, visitors make two circuits on the loop road. The first is for the sheer exhilaration of it and to discern the lay of the land. On the second trip, plan to stop frequently and poke around on foot by setting off on trails or scrambling along the coastline. Scenic pull-offs are staggered at frequent intervals. The two-lane road is one-way along coastal sections; the right-hand lane is set aside for parking, so you can stop wherever you'd like to admire the vistas.

From about 10am to 4pm in July and August, anticipate large crowds along the loop road when the sun is shining. Expect parking lots to fill early at the more popular destinations.

From the Hulls Cove Visitor Center, the Park Loop initially runs atop

❶ Paradise Hill

The tour starts with sweeping views eastward over Frenchman Bay. You'll see the town of Bar Harbor far below, and just beyond it the Porcupines, a cluster of islands that look like, well, porcupines.

Following the Park Loop Road clockwise, you'll dip into a wooded valley and come to

❷ Sieur de Monts Spring

Here you'll find a rather uninteresting natural spring, unnaturally encased, along with a botanical garden with some 300 species showcased in 12 habitats. The original **Abbe Museum** (© 207/288-3519) is here, featuring a small but select collection of Native American artifacts. Open daily from mid-May to mid-October; admission is $2 for adults, $1 for children 6–15. A larger, more modern branch is open in Bar Harbor itself, featuring more and better-curated displays (see later in this chapter).

The Tarn is the chief reason to stop here; a few hundred yards south of the springs via footpath, it's a slightly medieval-looking and forsaken pond sandwiched between steep hills. Departing from the south end of the Tarn is the fine **Dorr Mountain Ladder Trail** (see "Hiking," below).

Continue the clockwise trip on the loop road; views eastward over the bay soon resume, almost uninterruptedly.

❸ The Precipice Trail

The park's most dramatic trail ✿, this ascends sheer rock faces on the east side of Champlain Mountain. Only about .8 of a mile to the summit, it's rigorous, and involves scrambling up iron rungs and ladders in exposed places (those with a fear of heights or under 5 ft. tall should avoid this trail). The trail is often closed midsummer to protect nesting peregrine falcons. Rangers are often on hand in the trailhead parking lot to point out the birds and suggest alternative hikes.

Between the Precipice Trail and Sand Beach is a tollbooth where visitors pay the park fee of $10 per car, good for 1 week.

Picturesquely set between the arms of a rocky cove is

❹ Sand Beach

Sand Beach ✿ is the only sand beach on the island, although swimming these cold waters (about 50°F/10°C) is best enjoyed on extremely hot days or by those with a freakishly robust metabolism. When it's sunny out, the sandy strand is crowded midday, often with picnickers and pale waders. (*Tip:* The water at the far end of the beach—where a gentle stream enters the cove—is often a few degrees warmer than the end closer to the access stairs.)

Two worthwhile hikes start near the beach. **The Beehive Trail** overlooks Sand Beach (see "Hiking," below); it starts from a trailhead across the loop road. From the east end of Sand Beach, look for the start of the **Great Head Trail,** a loop of about 2 miles that follows on the bluff overlooking the beach, then circles back along the shimmering bay before cutting through the woods back to Sand Beach.

About a mile south of Sand Beach is
⑤ Thunder Hole

Thunder Hole ✦ is a shallow ocean-side cavern into which surf surges, compresses, and bursts out (a walking trail on the road lets you leave your car parked at the beach). When the bay is as quiet as a millpond (it often is during the lulling days of summer), it's a drive-by. Spend your time elsewhere.

But on days when the seas are rough and large swells roll in off the Bay of Fundy, it's a must-see, three-star attraction; you can feel the ocean's power and force resonating under your sternum. (*Tip:* The best viewing time is 3 hours before high tide.)

Parents with overly inquisitive toddlers (or teenagers) needn't fear: Visitors walk to the cusp of Thunder Hole on a path girded with stout steel railings; on the most turbulent days, rangers gate off parts of the walk to keep visitors away from rogue waves.

Just before the road curves around Otter Point, you'll be driving atop
⑥ Otter Cliffs

This set of 100-foot-high precipices is capped with dense spruce that plummet down into roiling seas. Look for whales spouting in summer; in early fall, thousands of eider ducks can sometimes be seen floating in flocks just offshore. A footpath follows the brink of the crags.

At Seal Harbor, the loop road veers north and inland back toward Bar Harbor. On the route is
⑦ Jordan Pond

Jordan Pond ✦✦ is a small but uncommonly beautiful body of water encased by gentle, forested hills. A 3-mile hiking loop follows the pond's shoreline (see "Hiking," below), and a network of splendid carriage roads converge at the pond. After a hike or mountain-bike excursion, spend some time at a table on the lawn of the Jordan Pond House restaurant (see "Where to Dine," below).

Shortly before the loop road ends, you'll pass the entrance to
⑧ Cadillac Mountain

Reach this mountain ✦ by car, ascending an early carriage road. At 1,528 feet, it's the highest peak on the Eastern Seaboard between Canada and Brazil. During much of the year, it's also the first place in the U.S. touched by the sun. But because Cadillac Mountain is the only mountaintop in the park accessible by car, and because it's also the island's highest point, the parking lot at the summit can be jammed, and drivers testy. Views are undeniably great, but the shopping-mall-at-Christmas atmosphere can put a serious crimp in your enjoyment of the place.

OUTDOOR PURSUITS

HIKING Acadia National Park has 120 miles of hiking trails, plus 57 miles of carriage roads suitable for walking. The park is studded with low "mountains" (they'd be called hills elsewhere), and almost all have trails with superb views of the ocean. Many pathways were crafted by stonemasons and others with high aesthetic intent, and thus the routes aren't the most direct—but they're often the most scenic, taking advantage of fractures in the rocks, picturesque ledges, and sudden vistas.

The Hulls Cove Visitor Center offers a brief chart of area hikes; combined with the park map, this is all you'll need to explore the well-maintained, well-marked trails. It's not hard to cobble together loop hikes to make your trips more varied. Coordinate your hiking with the weather; if it's damp or foggy, you'll stay drier and warmer strolling the carriage roads. If it's clear and dry, head for the highest peaks with the best views.

Among the best difficult hikes is the **Dorr Mountain Ladder Trail** ☾☾☾, which departs from near the south end of the Tarn, a pond near Sieur de Monts Spring. (Park at the spring or just off Rte. 3 south at the Tarn.) This trail begins with a series of massive stone steps that ascend along a vast slab of granite, then passes through crevasses and up ladders affixed to the rock face. The views east and south are superb. The trip to the summit of Dorr Mountain is .6 mile; though short, it's quite demanding. Allow about 1½ hours round-trip.

The **Beehive Trail** ☾☾☾ departs from Park Loop Road just across from Sand Beach. The trail begins with a fairly gentle climb of .2 mile and then turns right and begins a demanding ascent up a series of vertiginous ledges, some linked with iron ladders set in the rock. (The layers of ledges give the hill its beehive look.) From the top (a half-mile from the road), hikers get splendid views of Sand Beach and the ocean beyond. Those in dubious physical shape or fearful of heights should steer clear. Allow about 45 minutes for a round-trip hike.

The loop around **Jordan Pond** ☾☾, which departs from the Jordan Pond House, is more like a long stroll. The east side of the pond features a level trail; the west side is edged by a carriage road. The total loop measures just over 3 miles. At the north end of the pond is **The Bubbles,** a pair of oddly symmetrical mounds. Detours to atop these peaks add about 20 minutes each to the loop; look for signs for these spur pathways off the Jordan Pond Shore Trail. Finish up your hike with tea and popovers at the Jordan Pond House (see "Where to Dine," below).

For an easier hike, find the parking lot at **Day Mountain,** between Seal Harbor and the Blackwoods campground. Views of the Cranberry Islands are good and you can glimpse the carriage roads as you gradually ascend.

On the island's west side, an ascent and descent of **Acadia Mountain** ☾☾ takes about 1½ hours, but hikers should allow plenty of time for enjoying the view of Somes Sound and the smaller islands off Mount Desert's southern shores. This 2½-mile loop begins off Route 102 at a trailhead 3 miles south of Somesville. Head eastward through rolling mixed forest, then begin an ascent over ledgy terrain. Of the two peaks, the east peak has better views.

MOUNTAIN BIKING   The 57 miles of **carriage roads** ☾☾☾ built by John D. Rockefeller, Jr., are among the park's most extraordinary hidden treasures. These were maintained by Rockefeller until his death in 1960, after which they became shaggy and overgrown. A major restoration effort was launched in 1990, and today the roads are superbly restored and maintained. With their wide hard-packed surfaces, gentle grades, and extensive directional signs, they make for very smooth biking. Note that bikes are also allowed on the island's free shuttle buses (see "Getting Around," above).

A useful map of the roads is available free at visitor centers; more detailed guides may be purchased at area bookshops but aren't necessary. Where carriage roads cross private land (generally between Seal Harbor and Northeast Harbor), they're closed to mountain bikes, which are also banned from hiking trails.

Two areas are especially well suited for launching mountain-bike trips. Near **Jordan Pond,** a number of carriage roads converge, allowing for a series of loops; several famous stone bridges are in this area. Afterward, enjoy tea at the Jordan Pond House (see "Where to Dine," below).

At the north end of **Eagle Lake,** parking is off Route 223. From here, carriage roads loop around Eagle Lake to the south, with gentle hills and fine views. To the north of the parking area is a wooded loop around Witch Hole Pond; one of the finest stone bridges is over a small gorge just off the loop's southeast corner.

Mountain bikes may be rented along Cottage Street in Bar Harbor, with rates around $15 to $17 per day. Ask about closing times, as you may be able to get in a couple of extra hours of peddling with a later-closing shop.

CANOEING ✰ Mount Desert's ponds offer scenic if limited canoeing; most have public boat access. Canoe rentals are available at the north end of Long Pond (the largest pond on the island, at 3 miles long) in Somesville from **National Park Canoe Rentals** (✆ 207/244-5854). The cost is $22 for 4 hours. Much of the west shore and southern tip are within park boundaries.

CARRIAGE RIDES ✰✰ Carriage rides are offered by **Wildwood Stables** (✆ 207/276-3622; www.acadia.net/wildwood), about a half-mile south of Jordan Pond House. The 1-hour trip departs three times daily and takes in sweeping ocean views; it costs $13.50 for adults, $7 for children 6 to 12, and $4 for children 2 to 5. Longer tours are available, as is a special carriage designed to accommodate passengers with disabilities. Reservations are recommended.

SEA KAYAKING ✰✰ Sea kayaking has boomed around Mount Desert Island over the past decade. Experienced kayakers arrive in droves with their own boats. Novices sign up for guided tours, which are offered by several outfitters. Many new paddlers have found their inaugural experiences gratifying; others have complained that the quantity of paddlers on quick tours in peak season makes the experience a little too much like a cattle drive to truly enjoy.

A variety of options can be found on the island, ranging from a 2½-hour harbor tour to a 7-hour excursion. Details are available from the following outfitters: **Acadia Outfitters,** 106 Cottage St. (✆ 207/288-8118); **Coastal Kayaking Tours,** 48 Cottage St. (✆ 800/526-8615 or 207/288-9605); and **National Park Sea Kayak Tours,** 39 Cottage St. (✆ 800/347-0940 or 207/288-0342). Rates range from approximately $40 to $50 per person for a 2- to 3-hour harbor or sunset tour, up to $75 for a 1-day excursion.

Sea-kayak rentals are available from **Loon Bay Kayaks,** located in summer at Barcadia Campground, at the junction of Routes 3 and 102 (✆ 888/786-0676 or 207/288-0099), which will deliver a boat to you; and from **Aquaterra Adventures,** 1 West St., Bar Harbor (✆ 207/288-0007). Solo kayaks rent for $25 to $40 per day. With unpredictable weather and squirrelly tides, kayakers are advised to have some prior experience before attempting to set out on their own.

CAMPING

The national park itself offers no overnight accommodations other than two campgrounds. (See the "Bar Harbor" and "Elsewhere on the Island" sections, later in this chapter, for inns, hotels, and motels.) Both campgrounds are extremely popular; in July and August, expect them to fill by early to mid-morning.

Blackwoods (✆ 207/288-3274), on the island's eastern side, tends to fill first. With a better location—bikers and pedestrians are just off Park Loop Road and the rocky shore via a short trail—it's the only one that accepts reservations (required mid-May to mid-September). On the downside, sites here are rather gloomy and dour, set in a dense forest of scrappy fir and spruce. No public showers are available, but an enterprising business just outside the campground entrance offers clean showers for a small fee. Blackwoods is open year-round; late fall through spring, sites are easy to come by. You can reserve up to 5 months in advance by calling ✆ 800/365-2267. (This is a national reservations service whose contract is reviewed from time to time by the park service; if it doesn't work, call the campground directly to ask for the current toll-free reservation number.) Reservations may also be made online, between 10am and 10pm only, at reservations.nps.gov. Fees are $18 per night.

First-come, first-served **Seawall** (© **207/244-3600**) is on the island's quieter western half, near the village of Bass Harbor. This is a good base for road biking, and several short coastal hikes are within easy distance. Many tent sites are walk-ins, which require carrying gear a hundred yards or so. Drive-in RV sites are available, but none have hookups. The campground is open late May to September. In general, if you're here by 9 or 10am, you'll have little trouble securing a site, even in midsummer (especially true for tent campers). Fees are $20 for a site with vehicle, $14 for walk-ins. There are no on-site showers, but they're available within a half-mile.

Private campgrounds handle the overflow. The region south of Ellsworth has 14 private campgrounds; the **Thompson Island Information Center** (© **207/ 288-3411**) posts up-to-the-minute information on vacancies. In my opinion, two private campgrounds stand above the rest. **Bar Harbor Campground,** Route 3, Salisbury Cove (© **207/288-5185**), is on the main route between the causeway and Bar Harbor and doesn't accept reservations; it has 300 sites both wooded and open. At the head of Somes Sound is the attractive, though pricey, **Mount Desert Campground** ⭐ on Route 198 (© **207/244-3710**); it's well suited for tent campers, who should inquire about walk-in sites at the water's edge.

WHERE TO DINE

Jordan Pond House ⭐⭐ *(Finds* AMERICAN   The only full-service restaurant within the park, it occupies a delightful location on a lawn looking north up Jordan Pond. Originally a teahouse on an old farm, the birch-bark-lined dining room was destroyed by fire in 1979, replaced by a modern two-level dining room. Though with less charm, it still has the island's best location. Afternoon tea with popovers is a Jordan Pond House tradition. Lunching ladies sit next to mountain bikers; everyone feasts on huge, tasty popovers and strawberry jam served with a choice of teas or fresh lemonade. Lobster and crab rolls are abundant and filling; lobster stew is expensive but very, very good. Dinners include classic resort fare such as prime rib, steamed lobster, and baked scallops with a crumb topping.

Park Loop Rd. (near Seal Harbor), Acadia National Park. © 207/276-3316. www.jordanpond.com. Reservations not accepted; call before arriving to hold a table. Main courses: lunch $7.50–$15; afternoon tea $7.25–$8.50; dinner $14–$20. AE, DISC, MC, V. Mid-May to late Oct daily 11:30am–8pm (until 9pm July–Aug).

BAR HARBOR ⭐

Bar Harbor provides most meals and beds to travelers coming to the island, as it has since the grand resort era of the late 19th century. Wealthy rusticators discovered the region then; later, sprawling hotels and boardinghouses cluttered the shores and hillsides as the newly affluent middle class flocked here by steamboat and rail from Eastern Seaboard cities. At its zenith near the turn of the 20th century, Bar Harbor had rooms enough to accommodate 5,000 visitors.

Bar Harbor was dealt a blow in 1947, when a fire leveled many opulent cottages and much of the rest of the town. In all, some 17,000 acres of the island were burned, though downtown Bar Harbor and many in-town mansions along the oceanfront were spared. Yet Bar Harbor has been revived and rediscovered by both visitors and entrepreneurs. Crowds spill off the sidewalk and into the street in midsummer, and the traffic can be appalling. Yet Bar Harbor's history, distinguished architecture, and beautiful location on Frenchman Bay make it a desirable base for exploring the island, and it offers the best selection of lodging, meals, supplies, and services.

ESSENTIALS

GETTING THERE   Bar Harbor is on Route 3 about 10 miles southeast of the causeway. **Concord Trailways** (© **800/639-3317;** www.concordtrailways.com) offers seasonal bus service from Boston and Portland. They also operate a seasonal four-times-daily van shuttle between Bar Harbor and Bangor International Airport; for details, call © **888/741-8686.**

Daily flights from Boston to the airport in Trenton, across the causeway from Mount Desert Island, are offered year-round by US Air affiliate **Colgan Air** (© **800/523-3273** or 207/667-7171; www.colganair.com). From here, call a taxi or ride the free shuttle bus (late June to mid-October only) to downtown Bar Harbor.

VISITOR INFORMATION   The **Bar Harbor Chamber of Commerce,** P.O. Box 158, Bar Harbor, ME 04609 (© **207/288-5103;** www.acadia.net/bhcc), stockpiles a huge arsenal of information about local attractions at its offices at 93 Cottage St. Write, call, or e-mail in advance for a full guide to area lodging and attractions. The website is chock-full of information and helpful links.

EXPLORING BAR HARBOR

The best water views in town are from the foot of Main Street at grassy **Agamont Park,** which overlooks the town pier and Frenchman Bay. From here, set off past the Bar Harbor Inn on the **Shore Path** ★★, a wide, winding trail that follows the shoreline for half a mile along a public right of way. The pathway passes in front of many elegant summer homes (some converted to inns), offering a superb vantage point to view the area's architecture.

From the path is a fine view of **The Porcupines,** a cluster of spruce-studded islands just offshore. This is a good spot to note the powerful force of glacial action; a south-moving glacier ground away at the islands, creating a gentle slope facing north. On the south shore, away from the glacial push, is a more abrupt, clifflike shore. The islands look like a small group of porcupines migrating southward—or so early visitors imagined.

The **Abbe Museum** ★, 26 Mount Desert St. (© **207/288-3519;** www.abbe museum.org), opened an extensive 17,000-square-foot gallery in late 2001, showcasing a top-rate collection of Native American artifacts. (The original museum, next to Sieur de Monts Spring within the park itself, remains open and unchanged.) The new museum features an orientation center and a glass-walled lab where visitors can see archaeologists at work preserving recently recovered artifacts, along with changing exhibits and videos that focus largely on Maine

---

Tips Parking in Bar Harbor

If parking spaces are scarce downtown, head to the end of Albert Meadow (a side street across from the Village Green). At the end of the road is a small waterfront park with free parking, great views of the bay, and foot access to Shore Path. It's not well marked or publicized, so you can often find a place to park when much of the rest of town is filled up.

Bar Harbor

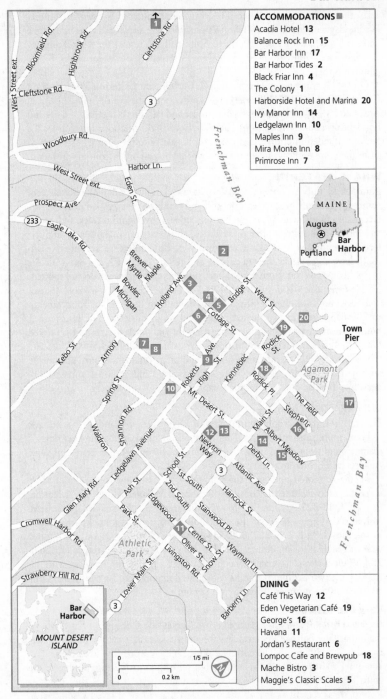

ACCOMMODATIONS ■

Acadia Hotel **13**
Balance Rock Inn **15**
Bar Harbor Inn **17**
Bar Harbor Tides **2**
Black Friar Inn **4**
The Colony **1**
Harborside Hotel and Marina **20**
Ivy Manor Inn **14**
Ledgelawn Inn **10**
Maples Inn **9**
Mira Monte Inn **8**
Primrose Inn **7**

MAINE

Augusta
⊛
Portland   **Bar Harbor**

DINING ◆

Café This Way **12**
Eden Vegetarian Café **19**
George's **16**
Havana **11**
Jordan's Restaurant **6**
Lompoc Cafe and Brewpub **18**
Mache Bistro **3**
Maggie's Classic Scales **5**

Bar Harbor

MOUNT DESERT ISLAND

| 0 | | 1/5 mi |
| 0 | 0.2 km | |

and other New England tribes. The year-round museum is open in summer Wednesday to Sunday from 10am to 9pm, Monday and Tuesday to 5pm; June and September, daily from 10 am to 5pm; and the rest of the year, Thursday through Sunday only from 10am to 5pm. Admission is $4.50 for adults, $2 for children 6 to 15.

One of downtown's quiet attractions is the 900-seat **Criterion Theater** ★ on Cottage Street (© 207/288-3441; www.criteriontheatre.com), built in 1932 in Art Deco style. The theater, open in summer and fall, shows first-run movies and hosts the occasional live concert. The place is worth the price of admission for the fantastic if faded interiors. As at most movie palaces in the past, it costs extra to sit in the more exclusive loges upstairs, where you can order from a light menu.

WHALE-WATCHING

Humpback, finback, minke, and (occasionally) right whales migrate to cool summer waters offshore to feast on krill and plankton that well up near the surface thanks to idiosyncratic ocean bottom topography, vigorous tides, and strong currents. Two outfitters offer tours aboard sleek, fast catamarans, reaching the feeding grounds with speed and comfort. With little difference between the two (both have three decks, heated cabins, and full galleys), pick the one with the best schedule for you. Both refund half the ticket price if no whales are spotted.

The *Friendship V* ★ (© 800/942-5374 or 207/288-2386; www.whalesrus. com) operates from the municipal pier in downtown Bar Harbor. Tours take up to 200 passengers in two heated cabins and on open decks. The tours run 3 hours plus; the cost is $39 per adult. (A puffin and whale-watch tour is offered for $43.) **Acadian Whale Adventures,** 55 West St. (© 888/533-WHAL or 207/288-9800; www.whalesadventures.com), also offers catamaran tours, aboard the jet-powered *Royal Miss Belmar.* Tours last between 3 and 3½ hours, and cost $37 per adult. Free on-site parking is available.

WHERE TO STAY

Bar Harbor is the bedroom community for Mount Desert Island, with hundreds of hotel, motel, and inn rooms. They're invariably filled during the busy days of summer, and even the most basic of rooms can be quite expensive in July and August. It's essential to reserve as early as possible.

Reputable motels in or near town that offer at least some rooms under $100 in peak season include the conveniently located **Villager Motel,** 207 Main St. (© 207/288-3211), with 63 rooms; the in-town, pet-friendly **Rockhurst Motel,** 68 Mount Desert St. (© 207/288-3140); and the smoke-free **Highbrook Motel,** 94 Eden St. (© 800/338-9688 or 207/288-3591). About 4 miles west of Bar Harbor on Route 3 is **Hanscom's Motel and Cottages** (© 207/288-3744; www.hanscomsmotel.com), an old-fashioned motor court with 12 units (some two-bedroom) that have been well maintained. Its rates range from $88 to $120 in summer; from $68 off season.

Very Expensive

Balance Rock Inn ★★★   Tucked down a quiet side alley just off Bar Harbor's main drag, the Balance Rock reaches for and achieves a gracefully upscale Long Island beach house feel. The entrance alone is nearly worth the steep rack rates: You enter a sitting room, which looks out onto the sort of azure outdoor pool you'd expect to find in a Tuscan villa, and just beyond looms the Atlantic. Rooms are as elegant as any on the island, with a variety of layouts, some with sea views; some also have whirlpools and saunas, while the penthouse suite adds a full kitchen as well. The comfortable king beds are adjustable using controls and have been fitted with both feather beds and quality linens. The poolside bar, piano room, gracious staff, and fragrant flowers lining the driveway all enhance and complete the romance of the experience; it seems a perfect place for a honeymoon.

21 Albert Meadow Rd., Bar Harbor, ME 04609. ℂ 800/753-0494 or 207/288-2610. Peak season (mid-June to mid-Oct) $255–$525 double, $455–$625 suite, off season $115–$295 double, $195–$595 suite. Rates include full breakfast. AE, DISC, MC, V. Closed late Oct to early May. **Amenities:** Bar; outdoor pool. *In room:* A/C, TV, hair dryer, iron/ironing board, Jacuzzi (some).

Expensive

The Bar Harbor Inn 🐝🐝 This large, handsome complex, a combination of inn and motel, has the best location in Bar Harbor. On shady waterfront grounds off downtown Agamont Park, at the start of the Shore Path, it offers both convenience and charm. The rambling shingled inn dates to the turn of the 20th century and has a settled, old money feel. Guest rooms in the Oceanfront and Main Inn feature sweeping views of the bay, many with private balconies. The less expensive Newport building lacks views but is comfortable and up-to-date.

Newport Dr. (P.O. Box 7), Bar Harbor, ME 04609. ℂ 800/248-3351 or 207/288-3351. www.barharborinn. com. 153 units. Peak season $185–$355 double; spring $75–$159 double; late fall $99–$249 double. Rates include continental breakfast. AE, DISC, MC, V. Closed Dec to late Mar. **Amenities:** 2 restaurants (formal dining room, outdoor grill); outdoor pool; fitness room; Jacuzzi; limited room service; babysitting; laundry service. *In room:* A/C, TV, coffeemaker, hair dryer.

Bar Harbor Tides 🐝🐝 This accommodation features just four guest rooms in a sprawling 1887 cream-colored mansion. It's at the head of a long, lush lawn that descends to the water's edge, all on 1½ in-town acres in a neighborhood of imposing homes within easy strolling distance of the village center. When you enter, it's as if you're visiting someone's great aunt—someone's very rich great aunt. But soon enough it feels like home, as you unwind in one of two spacious living rooms (one upstairs, one down) or on the veranda with outdoor fireplace. Breakfast is served on the porch in good weather; otherwise, it's in the dining room with polished wood floors and views out to Bar Island. Plan to return by sunset to wander to the foot of the lawn and watch twilight settle in.

119 West St., Bar Harbor, ME 04609. ℂ 207/288-4968. www.barharbortides.com. 4 units. $225–$395 double. Rates include breakfast. AE, DISC, MC, V. Closed Nov to mid-June. *In room:* A/C, TV, dataport, hair dryer.

Harborside Hotel & Marina 🐝🐝 Once a family-style motel known as the Golden Anchor, the Harborside is the town's newest luxury property—and it's got great water views to boot. When completed, a renovation will transform the formerly mid-level lodging into something else: a wide variety of studios and two- and three-bedroom suites sporting fancy bathrooms, business-hotel amenities, and large televisions. The priciest suites are more like condominium units, with various combinations of Jacuzzis, fireplaces, balconies, water views, and even—in a few cases—full kitchens and dining rooms. The large swimming pool and hot tub will be big drawing cards, and a new marina was also in the works at press time. There's a family-style restaurant, **The Pier,** as well.

55 West St., Bar Harbor, ME 04609. ℂ 800/328-5033 or 207/288-5033. www.theharborsidehotel.com. 160 units. $139–$259 double; $225–$850 suite. Off-season rates sometimes lower. DISC, MC, V. Closed Nov–Apr. **Amenities:** Outdoor pool. *In room:* A/C, TV, dataport.

Ivy Manor Inn 🐝🐝 In a 1940s-era Tudor-style house across from the Village Green, the Ivy Manor offers gracious hospitality with an understated French Victorian style. Rooms are larger than average, most furnished with antiques.

Some units have claw-foot tubs; others have small outdoor sitting decks (none with views). Among my favorites are room 6, a small suite with a private sitting room and fireplace; and room 1, the honeymoon room, with an imposing walnut headboard and matching armoire. Evening cocktails are served in a cozy first-floor lounge.

194 Main St. Bar Harbor, ME 04609. © **888/670-1997** or 207/288-2138. www.ivymanor.com. 8 units. Peak season $200–$375; off season $185–$275. Rates include breakfast. AE, DISC, MC, V. 2-night minimum stay on holiday weekends. Closed late Oct to early May. Children 12 and older are welcome. **Amenities:** Restaurant (French/New England). *In room:* A/C, TV.

Moderate

Acadia Hotel ★ The Acadia Hotel is nicely situated overlooking the Village Green, easily accessible to in-town activities and free shuttles to elsewhere on the island. This handsome, simple home dating from the late 19th century has a wraparound porch and guest rooms decorated with busy floral motifs. Rooms vary widely in size and amenities; two have whirlpools, two have phones, one has a kitchenette. Ask for the specifics when you book. The smaller rooms offer good value for those who don't plan to spend much time inside.

20 Mt. Desert St., Bar Harbor, ME 04609. © **207/288-5721.** www.acadiahotel.com. 10 units. Peak season $100–$160 double; off season $55–$100 double. MC, V. *In room:* A/C, TV, no phone.

Black Friar Inn ★ This shingled structure with quirky pediments and an eccentric air offers good value for Bar Harbor. A former owner "collected" interiors and installed them throughout the house. Among them are a replica of the namesake Black Friar Pub in London, complete with elaborate carved-wood paneling (it serves as a common room); stamped tin walls in the breakfast room; and a doctor's office (now a guest room). Guest rooms, most quite small, are furnished with a mix of antiques. The least expensive are the two garret rooms on the third floor, each with a detached private bathroom down the hall.

10 Summer St., Bar Harbor, ME 04609. © **207/288-5091.** Fax 207/288-4197. www.blackfriar.com. 7 units (2 with detached private bathroom). $105–$150 double. Rates include breakfast. DISC, MC, V. 2-night minimum stay mid-June to mid-Oct. Closed Dec–Apr. Children 12 and older are welcome. *In room:* A/C, hair dryer, no phone.

Ledgelawn Inn ★ If you want great location with considerably more flair than a motel, this is a good bet. This hulking cream and maroon 1904 "cottage" sits on a village lot amid towering oaks and maples and has an early-20th-century elegance, updated with modern amenities (some rooms are air-conditioned); on the property, you'll also find a small, no-frills pool. The Ledgelawn first gets your attention with a handsome sun porch lounge with full bar, and when you set foot here, you half expect to find Bogart flirting with Bacall in a corner. Guest rooms vary somewhat in size and mood, but all are comfortably if not stylishly furnished with antiques and reproductions. Room 221 has a working fireplace, a shared balcony, and a pair of oak double beds; room 122 has an appealing sitting area with fireplace. Some rooms have bathrooms shoehorned into small spaces.

66 Mt. Desert St., Bar Harbor, ME 04609. © **800/274-5334** or 207/288-4596. Fax 207/288-9968. www. ledgelawninn.com. 33 units. July and Aug $125–$275 double; off-season discounts. Rates include breakfast. AE, DISC, MC, V. Closed late Oct to early May. Pets allowed ($15 per day). *In room:* TV.

Maples Inn ★★ A popular destination with outdoor enthusiasts, you'll often find guests swapping stories of the day's adventures on the front porch or lingering over breakfast to compare notes on trails. The architecturally modest (by Bar Harbor standards) farmhouse-style inn is tucked away on a leafy side street among other B&Bs and homes; it's an easy walk downtown. The innkeepers make guests feel comfortable, with board games and paperbacks scattered about. Guest rooms aren't huge, but you're not likely to feel cramped, either. The two-room White Birch has a fireplace and is the largest; White Oak has a private deck. Breakfasts are appropriately filling for a full day outdoors.

16 Roberts Ave., Bar Harbor, ME 04609. (*C*) 207/288-3443. www.maplesinn.com. 6 units (including 1 suite). Mid-June to mid-Oct $110–$160 double; off season $70–$110 double. Rates include breakfast. DISC, MC, V. 2-night minimum stay mid-June to mid-Oct. No small children. *In room:* A/C, no phone.

Primrose Inn ☆   This handsome pale-green and maroon Victorian stick-style inn, built in 1878, is one of the more noticeable properties on mansion row on Mount Desert Street. Comfortable and furnished with functional antiques and more modern reproductions, many rooms have a floral theme and thick carpets. It's not a stuffy place—it has a distinctly informal air that encourages guests to mingle and relax in the common room, decorated in a light country Victorian style, complete with a piano. Two guest rooms feature whirlpools or fireplaces. The suites in the rear are spacious and comfortable, and the efficiencies make sense for families who could benefit from a kitchen (for rent by the week only).

73 Mt. Desert St., Bar Harbor, ME 04609. (*C*) 877/846-3424 or 207/288-4031. www.primroseinn.com. 10 units (includes 5 efficiencies). Peak season $110–$210 double, shoulder seasons $85–$165 double; efficiencies $800–$1,150 per week. Daily rates include breakfast. AE, DISC, MC, V. Closed late Oct to Apr. Pets allowed in 1 efficiency (one-time fee of $75). *In room:* TV.

Inexpensive

The Colony ☆ *Value*   The Colony is a classic motor court with a handful of motel rooms and a battery of cottages around a long green. It will be most appreciated by those with a taste for authentic retro; others may decide to look for something with updated amenities. The rooms are furnished in a simple 1970s style that won't win any awards for decor, but all are comfortable, and many have kitchenettes. Just across Route 3 from a cobblestone beach, and a 10-minute drive from Bar Harbor, it offers one of the better values on the island.

Rte. 3 (P.O. Box 56), Hulls Cove, ME 04644. (*C*) 800/524-1159 or 207/288-3383. www.acadia.net/thecolony. 55 units. $65–$105 double. AE, DC, DISC, MC, V. Closed mid-Oct to early June. *In room:* A/C, TV.

WHERE TO DINE

If you're wanting a light bite or breakfast, my local favorite is **Cottage Street Bakery and Deli** ☆ (*C* **207/388-1010**) at 59 Cottage St. Egg dishes, omelets, blueberry pancakes, and baked goods are all well done, and there are plenty of coffee drinks; I also like the outdoor patio. The kid's menu is fun and welcome.

Café This Way ☆☆ NEW AMERICAN   Café This Way has the feel of a casually hip coffeehouse; bookshelves line one wall, and a small (but full) bar is tucked in a nook. Unusually, they serve breakfast and dinner but no lunch. The breakfasts are excellent and mildly sinful—it's more like an everyday brunch—with offerings such as eggs Benedict with spinach, artichoke, and tomato, big breakfast burritos, and a range of omelets. The red-skinned potatoes are crispy and delicious; the robust coffee requires two creamers to lighten it. Dinners are equally appetizing, with starters that might run to a spicy Portuguese stew of mussels and sausages or a flatbread pizza of pears and blue cheese, followed by main courses such as lemon-vodka lobster, a Thai seafood pot, grilled tuna served with apples and smoked shrimp, or grilled and peppered lamb chops.

14½ Mount Desert St. (*C*) 207/288-4483. Reservations recommended for dinner. Main courses: breakfast $3.95–$7.50; dinner $14–$23. MC, V. Mon–Sat 7–11am and 6–9pm; Sun 8am–1pm and 6–9pm. Closed Nov to mid-Apr.

Eden Vegetarian Café ⭐ *Finds* VEGETARIAN   Have you ever seen a vegetarian restaurant where people dress up for dinner? Right across the street from the bay, chef Mark Rampacek operates Bar Harbor's only vegetarian eatery, bringing high culinary flair and atmosphere to the cause; most dishes here use organic and/or locally grown ingredients, and you'll even possibly want to dress up a bit if you dine here. The changing daily menu could include lunches of faux tuna salad, a Thai salad of tofu, coconut, and vegetables, vegan mac-and-"cheese," grapefruit gazpacho, or chickpea burritos. Dinners are more elaborate, beginning with starters such as roasted fig bruschetta, seared crab-like vegetable cakes, ratatouille-stuffed mushroom caps, fresh local salads, or a beet tartare with capers and a delicate arrangement of "stained glass" potato. The main course might be a bento box of tofu, edamame, seaweed salad, and the like; grilled vegetables, tempeh, or seitan; roasted portobello mushroom with polenta cake; or bright red lentil dal paired with eggplant. For dessert, try chocolate fondue for two, dairy-free ice cream with caramel and coconut, or sponge cake with lemon curd and blueberries. There's a full range of coffees and teas, and a full bar.

78 West St. ⓒ 207/288-4422. www.barharborvegetarian.com. Reservations strongly recommended. Main courses $9–$17. MC, V. April–Sept, Mon–Sat 11am–9:30pm; Oct–Nov, Mon–Sat 5–9pm. Closed Dec–Mar.

George's ⭐⭐⭐ CONTEMPORARY MEDITERRANEAN   For more than 2 decades, this Bar Harbor classic has offered fine dining in elegant yet informal surroundings. The original owner (George) sold the place, but the new owners have kept up the traditions, with help from George himself. In a clapboard cottage tucked away behind Main Street's First National Bank, this place captures the joyous feel of summer with four smallish dining rooms (and plenty of open windows) and additional seating on the terrace. The service is upbeat, the meals wonderfully prepared. All entrees sell for one price, including appetizer and potato or rice. Everything's wonderful. You won't go wrong with basic options such as grilled lobster or steak, but you're better off opting for more adventurous fare such as lobster strudel or mustard shrimp. The house specialty is lamb, including a great char-grilled tenderloin served with a bean ragout. Finish with something sweet, such as the coconut pannacotta with rhubarb caramel, a piece of speckled chocolate cake with orange Bavarian cream and chocolate *ganache*, a pear tart, some blackcurrant sorbet, or the maple sugar crème brûlèe.

7 Stephens Lane. ⓒ 207/288-4505. www.georgesbarharbor.com. Reservations recommended. Entrees $25; 3-course meal $37–$40. AE, DC, DISC, MC, V. Daily 5:30–10pm; shorter hours after Labor Day. Closed Nov to early May.

Havana ⭐⭐⭐ LATINO/FUSION   Havana set a new creative standard for Bar Harbor when it opened in 1999. The spare but sparkling decor in the old storefront is as classy as any place in downtown Boston; the menu could compete in any major urban area. Though not specifically Cuban, it does lean toward South America in its accents: Expect appetizers such as jicama-and-coconut-stuffed shrimp, monkfish ceviche, and cakes of crab and roasted corn served with cilantro sour cream. Entrees could include filet mignon with a Cuban coffee and pepper rub, spicy "dragon" grilled tuna, a sesame-and-ginger salmon served over poblano mashed potatoes, or a Chilean black bean stew. Diners never go home unsatisfied. Finish with guava mousse in a chocolate waffle cone, coconut ice cream, or a pecan tart served with cinnamon gelato.

318 Main St. ⓒ 207/288-2822. www.havanamaine.com. Reservations recommended. Main courses $16–$33. AE, DC, DISC, MC, V. Daily 5:30–10pm. Closed Mar.

Jordan's Restaurant _Value_ DINER   This unpretentious breakfast and lunch joint has been dishing up filling fare since 1976, and offers a glimpse of old Bar Harbor before the economy was dominated by T-shirt shops. It's a popular haunt of local working folks in town on one errand or another, but the staff is genuinely friendly to tourists. (Still, with its atmosphere of senior citizens at coffee klatch and rockbottom prices, this is not a gourmet experience.) Diners can settle into one of the booths or at a laminated table and order off the placemat menu, choosing from fare such as grilled cheese with tomato or a slight but serviceable hamburger. Soups and chowders are all homemade. Breakfast is the specialty, with a broad selection of three-egg omelets. But everyone comes here for the huge blueberry muffins and pancakes, all made with wild Maine blueberries.

90 Cottage St. ☎ 207/288-3586. Breakfast and lunch $1.95–$7.95. MC, V. Daily 5am–2pm. Closed Feb–Mar.

Lompoc Cafe and Brewpub ✦ AMERICAN/ECLECTIC   The Lompoc Cafe has a well-worn, neighborhood bar feel; it's little wonder that waiters and other workers from around Bar Harbor congregate here after hours. The adjacent microbrewery produces several unique beers, including a blueberry ale (intriguing concept, but ask for a sample before ordering a full glass) and the smooth Coal Porter, available in sizes up to the 20-oz. "fatty." The menu has some pleasant surprises, such as the Persian plate (hummus and grape leaves), Szechwan eggplant wrap, and crab and shrimp cakes. Vegetarians will find a decent selection. Live music is offered some evenings, with a small cover charge.

36 Rodick St. ☎ 207/288-9392. www.lompoccafe.com. Reservations not accepted. Lunch items $5.75–$12.95; dinner $14–$20. MC, V. May–Nov daily 11:30am–1am. Closed Dec–Apr.

Mache Bistro ✦✦ BISTRO   This small restaurant (just nine tables), with soothing but plain decor, hides a sophisticated kitchen. (You wouldn't expect an imported cheese course in a place with plywood floors, but that's what you get.) The menu changes monthly; appetizers may include a salad with bleu cheese, apples, and truffle oil. Main courses could feature anything from a seared steak with black trumpet-infused jus to a Brittany fisherman's soup of local seafood.

135 Cottage St. ☎ 207/288-0447. Reservations recommended. Main courses $15–$19. AE, MC, V. Daily 6–10pm. Closed Mon–Tues in off season.

Maggie's Classic Scales ✦ SEAFOOD   Maggie's slogan is "notably fresh seafood," and the place delivers on that understated promise (using only locally caught fish). A casually elegant spot off Cottage Street, it's good for a romantic evening with soothing music and attentive service. Appetizers have included smoked salmon, lobster tail cocktail, and steamed mussels. Main courses might range from basic boiled lobster and grilled salmon to more adventurous offerings such as Maine seafood Provençal and sautéed scallops with fresh corn, bacon, and peppers. Desserts are homemade and well worth leaving room for.

6 Summer St. ☎ 207/288-9007. Reservations recommended in July and Aug. Main courses $16–$22. DISC, MC, V. Daily 5–10pm; closed mid-Oct to mid-June.

ELSEWHERE ON THE ISLAND ✦✦

You'll find plenty to explore outside of Acadia National Park and Bar Harbor. Quiet fishing villages, deep woodlands, and unexpected ocean views are among the jewels that turn up when one peers beyond the usual places.

ESSENTIALS

GETTING AROUND   The east half of the island is best navigated on Route 3, which forms the better part of a loop from Bar Harbor through Seal Harbor and past Northeast Harbor before returning up the eastern shore of Somes Sound. Route 102 and Route 102A provide access to the island's western half. See information on the free island shuttle service under "Getting Around" in the section on Acadia National Park, earlier in this chapter.

VISITOR INFORMATION   The best source of information on the island is at the **Thompson Island Information Center** (✆ 207/288-3411), on Route 3 just south of the causeway connecting Mount Desert Island with the mainland. Another source of local information is the **Mount Desert Chamber of Commerce** (✆ 207/276-5040).

EXPLORING THE REST OF THE ISLAND

On the tip of the eastern lobe of Mount Desert Island is the staid, prosperous community of **Northeast Harbor,** long a favored retreat among the Eastern Seaboard's upper crust. Situated on a scenic, narrow harbor, with the once-grand Asticou Inn at its head, Northeast Harbor possesses a refined sense of elegance that's best appreciated by finding a vantage point, and then sitting and admiring.

One of the best, least publicized places for enjoying views of the harbor is from the understatedly spectacular **Asticou Terraces** ✦ (✆ 207/276-5130). Finding the parking lot can be tricky: Head ½ mile east (toward Seal Harbor) on Route 3 from the junction with Route 198, and look for the small gravel lot on the water side of the road with a sign reading ASTICOU TERRACES. Park here, cross the road on foot, and set off up a magnificent path made of local rock that ascends the sheer hillside, with expanding views of the harbor and the town. This pathway, with its precise stonework and the occasional bench and gazebo, is one of the nation's hidden marvels of landscape architecture.

Continue on the trail at the top of the hillside and you'll soon arrive at the designer's cabin (open to the public daily in summer), behind which lies the formal **Thuya Gardens,** which are as manicured as the terraces are natural. They are well worth the trip. A donation of $2 is requested of visitors to the garden; the terraces are free.

From the harbor, visitors can take a seaward trip to the beguilingly remote **Cranberry Islands.** Either travel with a national park guide to Baker Island, the most distant of this small cluster of low islands, and explore the natural terrain; or hop one of the ferries to either Great or Little Cranberry Island and explore on your own. On Little Cranberry, a small historical museum run by the National Park Service is worth seeing. Both islands feature a sense of being well away from it all, but neither offers much in the way of shelter or tourist amenities.

WHERE TO STAY

Asticou Inn ✦   The once-grand Asticou Inn, which dates to 1883, occupies a still-prime location at the head of Northeast Harbor. Its weathered gray shingles and layered eaves give it a slightly stern demeanor, but it also has elements of mild eccentricity. The Asticou's exterior is more elegant than its interior, though it has been spruced up a bit. Despite some incipient shabbiness, a wonderful old-world gentility seems to seep from the creaking floorboards and through the thin walls, especially at mealtime. The rooms are simply furnished in a pleasing summer-home style, as if a more opulent decor were somehow too ostentatious. The dinner dance and elaborate "grand buffet" on Thursday nights in summer remain hallowed island traditions and worth checking out. (Expect smoked seafood, lobster Newburg, salads and relishes, a dessert tray, and more.)

Rte. 3, Northeast Harbor, ME 04662. (✆ 800/258-3373 or 207/276-3344. www.asticou.com. 47 units. Summer $302–$402 double, including continental breakfast and dinner (from $225 without meals); spring and fall from $150 double. MC, V. Closed Nov to mid-May. Children 6 and older are welcome. **Amenities:** Outdoor pool; tennis court; concierge; business center; limited room service; babysitting; laundry service.

The Claremont ★★   The Claremont offers nothing frilly or fancy—just simple, classic New England grace. Early prints of the 1884 building show an austere four-story wooden structure with a single gable overlooking Somes Sound from a grassy rise. It hasn't changed much. It seems appropriate that the state's most combative croquet tournament takes place here annually in early August; all those folks in their whites are right at home. Common areas are appointed in a spare country style. A library offers rockers, a fireplace, and jigsaw puzzles waiting to be assembled. Most guest rooms are bright and airy, furnished with antiques and some furniture that's simply old; bathrooms are modern. Guests opting for the full meal plan are given preference in reserving rooms overlooking the water; it's almost worth it, though dinners tend toward the lackluster.

P.O. Box 137, Southwest Harbor, ME 04679. ℂ **800/244-5036** or 207/244-5036. Fax 207/244-3512. www. theclaremonthotel.com. 42 units (including 14 cottages). July to Labor Day $170–$250 double; off season $95–$135 double. All rates include breakfast. Cottages: June to Labor Day $169–$230; off season $100–$155. 3-night minimum stay in cottages. No credit cards. Closed Nov to mid-May. **Amenities:** Tennis court; water sports equipment rental; bikes (free); babysitting. *In room:* Hair dryers.

Inn at Southwest ★   This architecturally quirky inn is a mansard-roofed Victorian marvel at the edge of the village, and is a thoroughly hospitable place. With a decidedly late-19th-century air to this elegant home, it's restrained on the frills. Guest rooms are named after Maine lighthouses and are furnished with both contemporary and antique furniture. All rooms have ceiling fans and down comforters. Among the most pleasant is Blue Hill Bay on the third floor, with its large bathroom, sturdy oak bed and bureau, and glimpses of the scenic harbor.

371 Main St. (P.O. Box 593), Southwest Harbor, ME 04679. ℂ **207/244-3835**. www.innatsouthwest.com. 7 units (including 2 suites). Summer and early fall $110–$185 double; off season $75–$135. Rates include breakfast. MC, V. Closed Nov–Apr.

Lindenwood Inn ★★   The Lindenwood is a refreshing change from the fusty, overly draperied inns often found on Maine's coast. Housed in a handsome 1902 Queen Anne–style home at the harbor's edge, rooms are clean and uncluttered, colors simple and bold. The adornments are few (those that exist are mostly from the innkeeper's collection of African and Pacific art), but simple lines and bright natural light create a relaxing mood. The spacious suite, with its great harbor views, is especially appealing. Eight rooms have fireplaces. A small but relaxing pool is in the back; the boat dock is a pleasant stroll down the lawn.

118 Clark Point Rd. (P.O. Box 1328), Southwest Harbor, ME 04679. ℂ **207/244-5335**. www.lindenwood inn.com/. 15 units. June to mid-Oct $105–$275 double; mid-Oct to June $95–$225 double. Rates include breakfast. AE, MC, V. **Amenities:** Outdoor pool; Jacuzzi. *In room:* TV.

WHERE TO DINE

The Burning Tree ★★ REGIONAL/ORGANIC   On Route 3 between Bar Harbor and Northeast Harbor, this is an easy restaurant to speed by, but that would be a mistake. This low-key place, with its bright, open, and sometimes noisy dining room, serves the freshest food in the area. Much of the produce and herbs come from its own gardens; the rest of the ingredients are supplied locally whenever possible. Seafood is the specialty, and it's prepared with imagination and skill. The menu changes often to reflect local availability. Typical entrees might include prosciutto-wrapped sea scallops, Maryland-style crab cakes with a roasted jalapeño tartar sauce, or squash ravioli with rosemary cream.

Rte. 3, Otter Creek. ℂ 207/288-9331. Reservations recommended. Main courses $18–$23. Aug daily 5–9pm; mid-June to July and early fall Wed–Mon 5–9pm. Closed Columbus Day to mid-June.

7 The Western Lakes & Mountains ⭐

Maine's western mountains comprise a rugged, brawny region that stretches northeast from the White Mountains to the Carrabassett Valley. Maine's coast is more commercialized, and villages here aren't as quaint as in Vermont's Green Mountains, but you'll find azure lakes, forests of spruce, fir, and lichens, and hills and mountains that take on a sapphire hue during summer hiking season.

Moosehead Lake and Baxter State Park in the North Woods offer numerous outdoor pursuits. About half of Maine is made up of northern forest lands with no formal government—"unorganized townships." While timber companies own and maintain much of the land, visitors will find a lot to explore on foot or by canoe.

Cultural amenities are few; natural amenities are legion. Hikers have the famed Appalachian Trail, which crosses into Maine in the Mahoosuc Mountains (near where Route 26 enters New Hampshire) and follows rivers and ridgelines northeast to Bigelow Mountain and beyond. Canoeists and anglers head to the Rangeley Lakes area, a chain of deepwater ponds and lakes that has attracted sportsmen for over a century; in winter, skiers can choose among several down-hill ski areas, including the state's two largest, Sunday River and Sugarloaf.

BETHEL ⭐⭐

Until recently, Bethel was a sleepy resort town with one of those family-oriented ski areas that seemed destined for extinction. But then the Sunday River ski area was bought and dusted off by a brash young entrepreneur, who turned it into one of New England's most vibrant and challenging ski destinations.

With the rise of Sunday River, the white-clapboard town of Bethel (located about 7 miles from the ski area) has been dragged into the modern era, though it hasn't (yet) taken on the artificial, packaged flavor of many other New England ski towns. The village (pop. 2,500) is still defined by the stoic buildings of the respected prep school Gould Academy, the broad village common, and the Bethel Inn, a sprawling, old-fashioned resort that's managed to stay ahead of the tide by adding condos without losing its pleasant, timeworn character.

ESSENTIALS

GETTING THERE   Bethel is located at the intersection of Routes 26 and 2. It's accessible from the Maine Turnpike by heading west on Route 26 from Exit 11. From New Hampshire, drive east on Route 2 from Gorham.

VISITOR INFORMATION   The **Bethel Area Chamber of Commerce,** 30 Cross St., Bethel, ME 04217 (ℂ **800/442-5826** or 207/824-2282; www.bethel maine.com), has offices behind the Casablanca movie theater. It's open year-round Monday through Friday from 8am to 8pm, Saturday from 10am to 6pm, and Sunday from noon to 5pm.

EXPLORING LOCAL HISTORY

Bethel's stately, historic homes ring the **Bethel Common,** a long, rectangular greensward created in 1807 atop a low, gentle ridge. (It was originally laid out as a street broad enough for the training of the local militia.) The town's **historic district** encompasses some 27 homes, which represent a wide range of architectural styles popular in the 19th century.

The oldest home is the **1813 Moses Mason House,** now a museum housing the collections and offices of the **Bethel Historical Society** (© 207/824-2908). The museum, at 14 Broad Street, is open in July and August Tuesday through Sunday from 1 to 4pm. Admission is $3 for adults and $1.50 for children 6–12.

DOWNHILL SKIING

Ski Mt. Abram   Mount Abram is a welcoming and friendly intermediate mountain, perfect for families still ascending skiing's learning curve. It has an informal atmosphere that sharply contrasts with bustling and impersonal Sunday River nearby. It's suffered from the usual financial ups and downs of small ski areas in recent years, but its current owners seem to have put it on a good course, adding a 500-foot snow tube park for kids, and capitalizing on its popularity among telemark skiers by offering telemark rentals and weekend lessons. The day care and other family programs are worth noting.

P.O. Box 240, Greenwood, ME 04255. © 207/875-5002. www.skimtabram.com. Vertical drop: 1,030 ft. Lifts: 2 chairlifts, 3 T-bars. Skiable acreage: 135. Lift tickets: $21 Mon–Fri; $37 Sat–Sun.

Sunday River Ski Resort ★★★   Sunday River has grown at stunning speed and has swiftly become one of the best ski mountains in New England for its terrain and conditions. (The resort scene, however, sorely lags, and staff can be brusque.) Unlike ski areas that have developed around a single tall peak, Sunday River expanded along an undulating ridge some 3 miles wide that encompasses seven peaks. Just traversing the resort, stitching runs together with chairlift rides, can take an hour or more. As a result, you're rarely bored making the same run repeatedly. The descents offer something for virtually everyone, from deviously steep bump runs to wide, wonderful intermediate trails. Sunday River is also blessed with plenty of water for snowmaking, and makes tons of the stuff using a proprietary snowmaking system. The superb skiing conditions are, alas, offset by an uninspiring base area. The lodges and condos (total capacity 6,000) tend toward the architecturally dull, and the less-than-delicate landscaping is of the sort created by bulldozers. Sunday River's trails are often crowded on weekends; weekdays, you'll pretty much have the place to yourself.

P.O. Box 450, Bethel, ME 04217. © 800/543-2754 for lodging, or 207/824-3000. www.sundayriver.com. Vertical drop: 2,340 ft. Lifts: 15 chairlifts (4 high-speed), 3 surface lifts. Skiable acreage: 654. Lift tickets: $52 Mon–Fri; $56 Sat–Sun.

OTHER OUTDOOR PURSUITS

Grafton Notch State Park ★★ straddles Route 26 as it angles northwest from Newry toward Errol, New Hampshire. The 33-mile drive is one of my favorites, both picturesque and dramatic. You pass through farmland in a fertile river valley before ascending through bristly forest to a glacial notch hemmed in by rough, gray cliffs on the hillsides above. Foreboding Old Speck Mountain towers to the south; views of Lake Umbagog open to the north as you continue into New Hampshire. This route attracts few crowds, though it's popular with Canadians headed to the Maine coast.

Public access to the park consists of a handful of roadside parking lots near scenic areas. The best of the bunch is dramatic **Screw Auger Falls.** Picnic tables dot the forested banks upriver of the falls, and kids seem inexorably drawn to splash and swim in the smaller pools on warm days. Admission to the park is $1; look for self-pay stations at the parking lot.

GOLF   Head for the **Bethel Inn and Country Club** (© 207/824-2175), an unusually scenic 18-hole golf course next to the inn, if you feel the urge to play 9. Equipment and golf carts are available for rent, and the club also features a driving range.

HIKING The **Appalachian Trail** 🏃🏃 crosses the Mahoosuc mountains northwest of Bethel. Many who have hiked the entire 2,000-mile trail say this stretch is the most demanding on knees and psyches. The trail doesn't forgive; it generally foregoes switchbacks in favor of sheer ascents and descents. It's also hard to find water along the trail during dry weather. Still, it's worth the knee-pounding effort for the views and the unrivaled sense of remoteness.

One stretch crosses Old Speck Mountain, Maine's third highest peak. Views from the summit are all but non-existent since the old fire tower closed, but an easy-to-moderate spur trail on the lower end of the trail ascends an 800-foot cliff called "The Eyebrow," and provides a good vantage point for Bear River Valley and the rugged terrain of Grafton Notch. Look for the well-signed parking lot where Route 26 intersects the trail in Grafton Notch State Park. Park your car and then head south on the A.T. toward Old Speck; in one-tenth of a mile, you'll intersect the Eyebrow Trail, which you can follow to the overlook.

The Appalachian Mountain Club's *Maine Mountain Guide* is highly recommended for detailed information about other area hikes.

WHERE TO STAY

The Bethel Inn 🏃 A classic, old-fashioned resort set on 200 acres in the village, this inn has a quiet, settled air, which is appropriate because it was built to house patients of Dr. John Gehring, who put Bethel on the map by treating nervous disorders through a regimen of healthy country living. (Bethel was once known as "the resting place of Harvard" for the legions of faculty treated here.) The quaint, homey rooms aren't terribly spacious, but they are pleasingly furnished with country antiques. More luxurious are the 16 modern rooms and suites added to the inn in the late 1990s. You give up some of the charm of the old inn, but gain elbowroom. The dining room remains the resort's Achilles' heel—the preparation and service often fail to live up to the promise of the surroundings.

On the Common, Bethel, ME 04217. ℂ **800/654-0125** or 207/824-2175. www.bethelinn.com. 62 units. Summer $198–$418 double; winter $158–$454 double. Rates include breakfast and dinner. 2-night minimum stay summer weekends and ski season; 3-night minimum stay during winter school vacations. Ski packages available. AE, DISC, MC, V. Pets allowed ($10 per night). **Amenities:** Dining room (Continental); outdoor pool; golf course; tennis court; fitness center; Jacuzzi; sauna; water sports equiment rental; cross-country skiing; shuttle to ski areas; babysitting; laundry service. *In room:* TV, hair dryer, iron.

Jordan Grand Resort Hotel 🏃 The anchor for expanded development in the far-flung Jordan Bowl area, this hotel feels miles away from the rest of the resort, largely because it is—even the staff makes *The Shining* jokes about its remoteness. A modern if sprawling hotel, it offers little personal touch or flair, but boasts a great location for skiers who want to be first on untracked slopes each morning. Owing to the quirky terrain, parking is inconvenient; you often have to walk some distance to your room (opt for valet parking). Rooms are simply furnished in a durable condo style. Many are quite spacious and most have balconies. It's a popular destination with families, so not the best choice for couples seeking a quiet getaway. Sunday River improved its food service; its two restaurants, though not outstanding, are a notch above typical ski-area hotel fare.

Sunday River Rd. (P.O. Box 450), Bethel, ME 04217. ℂ **800/543-2754** or 207/824-5000. Fax 207/824-2111. www.sundayriver.com. 195 units. $117–$332 double. AE, DC, DISC, MC, V. **Amenities:** 2 restaurants (fine dining, pub fare); outdoor pool; fitness room; Jacuzzi; sauna; steam room; children's center; concierge; business center; limited room service; in-room massage; babysitting; dry cleaning; valet parking. *In room:* A/C, TV, data-port, coffeemaker.

WHERE TO DINE

Great Grizzly/Bart Steakhouse ☆ STEAKHOUSE   These two restaurants share a handsome timber-frame structure a couple of minutes from the ski area. It's casual and relaxed, with pinball, pool table, and bar. The food is significantly better than at the Sunday River Brewing Company, and the beer-on-tap selection is pretty good.

Sunday River Rd. ℂ **207/824-6271** or 207/824-6836. Pizzas $7.95 and up; other entrees $6.95–$17. MC, V. Pizza menu daily 3–10pm; steakhouse menu from 5pm. Open only during ski season.

Sunday River Brewing Company PUB FARE   This modern and boisterous brewpub, on prime real estate at the corner of Route 2 and the Sunday River access road, is a good choice if your primary objective is to quaff robust ales and porters. The brews are very good; the food (burgers, nachos, and chicken wings) doesn't strive for any culinary heights, and certainly doesn't achieve any. If you want good pub fare, you're better off heading up Sunday River Road to try the Great Grizzly (see above). Come early if you're looking for a quiet meal; it gets loud later in the evening when bands take the stage.

Rte. 2 (at Sunday River Rd.), Bethel. ℂ **207/824-4253**. Reservations not accepted. Main courses, $5.95–$17. AE, MC, V. Daily 11:30am–12:30am.

The Victoria ☆☆ NEW AMERICAN   The dining room on the first floor of Bethel's classiest inn serves the town's best dinners. Guests are seated in one of two intimate rooms, where they choose from a menu that's simple but generally delivers on its high aspirations. Starters might be lobster cakes, smoked salmon, or a salad; entrees could include lobster ravioli in a pink vodka sauce, or filet mignon served with a blueberry and port demiglace. Desserts are a treat, both visually and to the taste. This is Bethel's best room for a romantic dinner.

32 Main St. ℂ **888/774-1235** or 207/824-8060. www.thevictoria-inn.com. Reservations recommended on weekends. Main courses $9.95–$18. AE, MC, V. Wed–Mon 5:30–9pm.

CARRABASSETT VALLEY ☆☆

The region in and around the Carrabassett Valley can be summed up in six words: big peaks, wild woods, deep lakes. The crowning jewel of the region is **Sugarloaf Mountain,** Maine's second-highest peak at 4,237 feet. Distinct from nearby peaks because of its pyramidal shape, the mountain has been developed for top-notch skiing and offers the largest vertical drop in Maine, the best selection of winter activities, and a wide range of accommodations.

While Sugarloaf draws the lion's share of visitors, it's not the only game in town. Nearby **Kingfield** is an attractive, historic town with a venerable old hotel; it has more of the character of an Old West outpost than of classic New England. Other valley towns offering limited services for travelers include **Eustis, Stratton,** and **Carrabassett Valley.**

Outside the villages and ski resort, it's all rugged hills, tumbling streams, and spectacular natural surroundings. The muscular mountains of the **Bigelow Range** provide terrain for some of the state's best hiking, and Flagstaff Lake is the place for flatwater canoeing amid majestic surroundings.

ESSENTIALS

GETTING THERE   Kingfield and Sugarloaf are on Route 27. Skiers debate over the best route from the turnpike. Some exit at Auburn and take Route 4 north to Route 27; others exit in Augusta and take Route 27 straight through.

It's a toss-up time-wise, but exiting at Augusta is marginally more scenic. **Airport Car Service** (✆ **800/649-5071**) offers a private shuttle service from the Portland Jetport and other state airports to the mountain.

VISITOR INFORMATION For information on skiing or summer activities in the Sugarloaf area, contact the Sugarloaf resort at ✆ **800/843-5623** or 207/ 237-2000. A seasonal information booth on Route 27 is staffed in summer and winter.

DOWNHILL SKIING

Sugarloaf/USA ★★★ Sugarloaf is Maine's big mountain, with the highest vertical drop in New England after Vermont's Killington. And thanks to quirks of geography, it feels bigger than it is. From the high, open snowfields or the upper advanced runs such as Bubblecuffer or White Nitro, skiers develop vertigo looking down at the valley floor. Sugarloaf attracts plenty of experts to its hard-core runs, but it's also a fine intermediate mountain. Sugarloaf may be the friendliest resort in New England—the staff on the lifts, in the restaurants, and at the hotels seem genuinely glad you're there. It's also a very welcoming family mountain, with lots of activities for kids. The main drawback? Wind. Sugarloaf seems to get buffeted regularly, with higher lifts often closed because of gusting.

RR #1, Box 5000, Carrabassett Valley, ME 04947. ✆ **800/843-5623** or 207/237-2000. www.sugarloaf.com. Vertical drop: 2,820 ft. Lifts: 15 chairlifts, including 2 high-speed quads; 2 surface lifts. Skiable acreage: 1,400 (snowmaking on 475 acres). Lift tickets: $56.

CROSS-COUNTRY SKIING

The **Sugarloaf Outdoor Center** ★ (✆ **207/237-6830**) has 63 miles of groomed trails that weave through the village at the base of the mountain and into the low hills and scrappy woodlands along the Carrabassett River. The trails are impeccably groomed for striding and skating, and wonderful views open here and there to Sugarloaf Mountain and the Bigelow Range. The base lodge is simple and attractive, all knotty pine with a cathedral ceiling, featuring a cafeteria, towering stone fireplace, and well-equipped ski shop. Snowshoes are available for rent. Trail fees are $16 for adults, $10 for seniors and children under 13 (half-day tickets are also available). The center is on Route 27 about a mile south of the Sugarloaf access road. A shuttle bus serves the area in winter.

HIKING

The 12-mile Bigelow Range has some of the most dramatic high-ridge hiking in the state, a close second to Mount Katahdin. It consists of a handful of lofty peaks, with Avery Peak (the east peak) offering the best views. On exceptionally clear days, hikers can see Mount Washington to the southwest and Mount Katahdin to the northeast.

A strenuous but rewarding hike for fit hikers is the 10-mile loop that begins at the **Fire Warden's Trail.** (The trailhead is at the washed-out bridge on Stratton Brook Pond Rd., a rugged dirt road that leaves eastward from Rte. 27 about 2.3 miles north of the Sugarloaf access road.) Follow the Fire Warden's Trail up the ridge to the junction with the **Appalachian Trail.** Head south on the A.T., which tops the West Peak and South Horn, two open summits with stellar views. A quarter-mile past Horns Pond, turn south on **Horns Pond Trail** and descend back to the Fire Warden's Trail to return to your car. Allow about 8 hours for the loop; a topographical map and hiking guide are strongly recommended.

A less rigorous hike that still yields supremely rewarding views is to **Cranberry Peak,** the Bigelow peak furthest west. Plan on 4 to 5 hours to complete this hike along Bigelow Range Trail, which runs about 6.5 miles. The trailhead is just south of the town of Stratton (from the south, turn right ¼ mile after crossing Stratton Brook, then drive on a dirt road ½ mile to a clearing). Follow the trail through woods and over a series of ledges to the 3,213-foot Cranberry Peak. Retrace your steps to your car.

Detailed directions for these hikes and many others in the area may be found in the AMC's *Maine Mountain Guide.*

OTHER OUTDOOR PURSUITS

Sugarloaf's 18-hole **golf course** (© 207/237-2000) is often ranked the number-one golf destination in the state by experienced golfers, who are lured here by the Robert Trent Jones, Jr., course design and dramatic mountain backdrop. Sugarloaf hosts a well-respected golf school during the season.

Other outdoor activities are located in and around the **Sugarloaf Outdoor Center** (© 207/237-6830). Through the center, you can arrange for fly-fishing lessons, mountain-bike excursions at the resort's mountain-bike park (rentals available), or hiking or white-water rafting in surrounding mountains and valleys.

A MUSEUM FOR AUTO & PHOTO BUFFS

Stanley Museum ★★   The Stanley Steamer—a steam-powered automobile— is an anachronistic footnote and prized collectible, but when manufactured between 1897 and 1925, it was state-of-the-art transportation, literally and figuratively smoking the competition. The Stanley Steamer was the first car to reach Mount Washington's summit, the first car to break the 2-miles-in-1-minute barrier with a land-speed record of 127 mph in 1906, and the winner of numerous hill-climb competitions. The Stanley Museum, housed in a handsome, yellow Georgian former schoolhouse in Kingfield, chronicles the rise of the Steamer and the background of the two local-born inventors, twins F. O. and F. E. Stanley. Three working Steamers are on display. You'll learn that the Stanleys invented the car as a hobby—they established their first fortune inventing the dry-plate photographic process and building a company that was eventually purchased by George Eastman, the founder of Kodak. Also on display are extraordinary early photographs taken by their sister, Chansonetta Stanley, who documented life in rural Maine and South Carolina at the turn of the last century—a sort of self-appointed precursor to the WPA photographers.

School St., Kingfield. © 207/265-2729. www.stanleymuseum.org. $4 adults, $2 children under 12, $3 seniors over 65. June–Oct, Tues–Sun 1–4pm; Nov–May, Tues–Fri 1–4pm.

WHERE TO STAY

For convenience, nothing beats staying on the mountain in winter. Many base-area condos are booked through the **Sugarloaf/USA Inn** (© 800/843-5623 or 207/237-2000). **Sugarloaf** also operates a lodging reservation service, booking guest rooms and private homes, mostly off the mountain (© 800/843-2732).

Grand Summit Hotel ★★   A great choice for skiers who want to be in the thick of it, this attractive, contemporary hotel is pretty sleepy in the summer. Next to the lifts in the heart of the Sugarloaf base area, it offers three types of guest rooms. Standard rooms are tucked under sharply angled gables and are a bit dark; one-bedroom suites (with full kitchens) are divided between two floors, with an upstairs bedroom connected by a narrow spiral staircase. Superior rooms (best value) are brightest and most open, with kitchenettes and small sitting areas. The odd-numbered rooms face the slopes, while even-numbered rooms face across the valley with views of distant hills. The ground floor features a lively pub; a free winter shuttle service connects to other restaurants around the resort.

Sugarloaf base area (RR 1, Box 2299), Carrabassett Valley, ME 04947. © **207/237-2222.** Fax 207/237-2874. www.sugarloaf.com. 119 units. Peak ski season $145–$250 double, to $675 suite; off season from $120. AE, MC, V. Minimum stay required some holiday weekends. **Amenities:** Restaurant (pub fare); golf course; health club; Jacuzzi; sauna; babysitting. *In room:* A/C, TV, coffeemaker, hair dryer, iron.

The Herbert The Herbert has the feel of a classic North Woods hostelry— sort of Dodge City by way of Alaska. Built in downtown Kingfield in 1918, the three-story hotel featured the finest accouterments when it was built, including fumed oak paneling and incandescent lights in the lobby (look for the original brass fixtures), a classy dining room, and comfortable guest rooms. It's had ups and downs since then (with some downs more recently). Since new owners purchased it in 2004, it has been getting a gradual makeover (including a new restaurant). The Herbert is about 15 miles from Sugarloaf/USA.

246 Main St. (P.O. Box 67), Kingfield, ME 04947. © **888/656-9922** or 207/265-2000. Fax 207/265-4594. www.herbertgrandhotel.com. 27 units. $110–$175 double. Rates include continental breakfast. AE, DISC, MC, V. **Amenities:** Restaurant (family style). *In room:* TV, no phone.

Three Stanley Avenue ✿ *Value* Three Stanley Avenue is the bed-and-break-fast annex to the well-known restaurant next door, One Stanley Avenue (see below). Set on a shady knoll just across the bridge from downtown Kingfield, this B&B has an old-fashioned Victorian boarding house feel to it, complete with an elaborate stained-glass window at the bottom of the stairs. The rooms are comfortably if not luxuriously appointed; three rooms share two baths, the other three have private baths.

3 Stanley Ave. (P.O. Box 169), Kingfield, ME 04947. © **207/265-5541.** www.stanleyavenue.com. 6 units (3 share 2 bathrooms). Dec–March $65–$70 double; Apr–Nov $60–$65 double. Rates include breakfast. 2-night minimum stay on winter weekends. DISC, MC, V. **Amenities:** Restaurant (see below). *In room:* No phone.

WHERE TO DINE

Hug's ✿ NORTHERN ITALIAN This is a small place, just off the highway in a fairy-tale cottage, and the food is better than one would expect for a ski-area Italian restaurant. Dinner is preceded by a tasty basket of pesto bread, and entrees go beyond red sauce, offering a broad selection of pastas. (The wild-mushroom ravioli with walnut-pesto Alfredo is quite good.)

Rte. 27 (¾ of a mile south of the Sugarloaf access road), Carrabassett Valley. © **207/237-2392.** Reservations recommended. Main courses $11–$20. DISC, MC, V. Winter daily 5–9pm; late summer and early fall Wed–Sun 5–9pm. Closed May to late July and mid-Oct to early Dec.

One Stanley Avenue ✿✿ This small, well-regarded restaurant is open dur-ing ski season only. The chef claims the cuisine is "classical in nature, regional in execution," and he delivers nicely on that claim. You might find roast duckling with rhubarb glaze or sweetbreads with cream sauce flavored with chives and applejack. Northern New England flavors—such as berries and fiddleheads— tend to be well represented.

1 Stanley Ave., Kingfield. © **207/265-5541.** www.stanleyavenue.com Reservations recommended. Main courses $20 to $31. DISC, MC, V. Tues–Sun 6–9pm. Closed mid-Apr to mid-Dec.

8 The North Woods

There are two versions of the Maine Woods. There's the grand and unbroken forest threaded with tumbling rivers that unspools endlessly in the popular perception, and then there's the reality: This forestland is a massive plantation, largely owned and managed by a handful of international paper and timber companies. An extensive network of small timber roads feeds off major arteries and opens the region to extensive clear-cutting.

While the North Woods are not a vast, howling wilderness, the region still has fabulously remote enclaves where moose and loon predominate, and where the turf hasn't changed all that much since Thoreau paddled through in the mid–19th century and found it all "moosey and mossy." If you don't arrive expecting utter wilderness, you're less likely to be disappointed.

MOOSEHEAD LAKE REGION ⭒⭒

Thirty-two miles long and 5 miles across at its widest, Moosehead Lake is Maine's largest lake, a great destination for hikers, boaters, and canoeists. The lake was historically the center of the region's logging activity, a history that preserved the lake and kept it largely unspoiled by development. The second-home building frenzy of the 1980s had an impact on the southern reaches of the lake, but the woody shoreline has absorbed most of the boom rather gracefully.

ESSENTIALS

GETTING THERE   Greenville is 158 miles from Portland. Take the Maine Turnpike to the Newport exit (Exit 39) and head north on Route 7/11 to Route 23 in Dexter, following it northward to Route 6/15 near Sangerville. Follow this to Greenville.

VISITOR INFORMATION   The **Moosehead Lake Chamber of Commerce** (© 207/695-2702; www.mooseheadlake.org) maintains a helpful information center. In addition to a selection of brochures, the center maintains files and bookshelves full of maps, trail information, wildlife guidebooks, and videos. From Memorial Day to mid-October, it's open Wednesday through Monday, 10am to 4pm; it's on your right as you come into Greenville, next to the Indian Hill Trading Post. Call for hours during the rest of the year.

OUTDOOR PURSUITS

BOATING   Open daily, **Northwood Outfitters** on Main Street in Greenville (© 207/695-3288; www.maineoutfitter.com) can help with planning a trip up the lake or into the woods, as well as load you up with enough equipment to stay out for weeks. They rent complete adventure equipment sets, which include canoe, paddles, life jacket, tent, sleeping bag, pad, camp stove, axe, cook kit, and more. Shuttle service and individual pieces of equipment are also available for rent, with canoes running $20 a day, and mountain bikes from $20 to $25 a day.

In Rockwood, **Moose River Landing** (© 207/534-7577) has motorboats for rent to explore the lake. A 20-foot pontoon boat is $125 per day (gas extra); aluminum and fiberglass outboards are $45 to $65 per day, with the first tank of gas free. (Canoes are also available at $15 per day.) The proprietor can make suggestions for beaches and quiet coves to visit along the huge lakeshore.

CANOEING   Follow Thoreau's footsteps into the Maine woods on a canoe excursion down the **West Branch of the Penobscot River** ⭒. This 44-mile trip is typically done in 3 days. Put in at Roll Dam, north of Moosehead Lake and east of Pittston Farm, and paddle northward on the generally smooth waters of the Penobscot. Pick one of several campsites along the river and spend the night, watching for moose as evening descends. On the second day, paddle to huge, wild Chesuncook Lake. Near where the river enters the lake is the Chesuncook Lake House, a farmhouse dating from 1864 and open to guests. Spend the night here (© **207/745-5330**). The final day brings a paddle down Chesuncook Lake with its views of Mount Katahdin to the east and take-out near Ripogenus Dam.

Allagash Canoe Trips (summers: P.O Box. 932, Greenville 04441, © **207/ 695-3668;** winters: 2314 G St., Carrabassett Valley, ME 04947, © **207/237- 3077;** www.allagashcanoetrips.com) has been offering guided canoe trips in the North Woods—including the Allagash, Moose, Penobscot and St. John's rivers—since 1953, with the next generation now taking over this family-run business. A 5-day guided camping trip down the West Branch—including all equipment, meals, and transportation—costs $500 for adults, $395 for children under 18.

HIKING   One of my favorite hikes in the region is **Mount Kineo** ⭑⭑, marked by a massive, broad cliff that rises from the shores of Moosehead. This hike is accessible via water; near the town of Rockwood, look for signs advertising shuttles across the lake to Kineo from the town landing (folks offering this service seem to change from year to year, so ask around; it usually costs about $5 round-trip). Once on the other side, you can explore the grounds of the famed old Kineo Mountain House (alas, the grand, 500-guest-room hotel was demolished in 1938), then cut across the golf course and follow the shoreline to the trail that leads to the 1,800-foot summit.

WHITE-WATER RAFTING   Big waves and roiling drops await rafters on the heart-thumping run through Kennebec Gorge at the headwaters of the **Kennebec River,** located southwest of Greenville. Most of the excitement is over in the first hour; after that, it's a lazy trip down the river, interrupted only by lunch and the occasional water fight with other rafts.

Commercial white-water outfitters offer trips in summer at a cost of about $85 to $115 per person (usually at the higher end on weekends). **Northern Outdoors** (© **800/765-7238;** www.northernoutdoors.com) is the oldest of the bunch and offers rock-climbing, mountain biking, and fishing expeditions as well, plus snowmobiling in winter. Other reputable rafting companies include **Wilderness Expeditions** (© **800/825-9453**), which is affiliated with the rustic Birches Resort, and the **New England Outdoor Center** (© **800/766-7238**).

MOOSEHEAD BY STEAMSHIP & FLOAT PLANE

During the lake's golden days of tourism in the late 19th century, visitors could come to the lake by train from New York or Washington, then connect with steamship to the resorts and boarding houses around the lake. A vestige of that era is found at the **Moosehead Marine Museum** (© **207/695-2716**) in Greenville. A handful of displays in the small museum suggest the grandeur of life at Kineo Mountain House, a sprawling Victorian lake resort that once defined elegance; but the museum's showpiece is the S.S. *Katahdin,* a 115-foot steamship that's been cruising Moosehead's waters since 1914. The two-deck ship (now run by diesel, rather than steam) offers a variety of sightseeing tours, including a twice-a-week excursion up the lake to the site of the former Kineo Mountain House. Fares vary depending on the length of the trip, ranging from $20 to $26 for adults and $12 to $15 for children 6 and over (free for children under 6).

Moosehead from the air is a memorable sight. Stop by **Folsom's Air Service** (© **207/695-2821**) on the shores of the lake in Greenville just north of the village center on Lily Bay Road. Folsom's has been serving the North Woods since 1946 and has a fleet of five float planes, including a vintage canary-yellow DeHavilland Beaver. A 15-minute tour of the southern reaches of the lake costs $20 per person; longer flights over the region run up to about $60.

WHERE TO STAY & DINE

Blair Hill Inn ★★★   This unexpectedly classy inn amid the wilds occupies an 1891 hilltop Queen Anne mansion with dazzling views of Moosehead Lake and the surrounding hills. It's been sparely and elegantly decorated with a mix of rustic and classic appointments, such as Oriental carpets and deer-antler lamps. The bright first-floor common rooms, the drop-dead-gorgeous porch, and the handsome guest rooms invite loafing. All units feature terry robes, spring water, and locally made soaps. Room 1 is the best—the former master bedroom, featuring a panoramic sunset view and fireplace (Duraflame logs only). All guests can enjoy the outdoor Jacuzzi, Adirondack chairs on the lawn, and a small catch-and-release trout pond (ask about fly-fishing workshops).

Lily Bay Rd. (P.O. Box 1288), Greenville, ME 04441. © 207/695-0224. www.blairhill.com. 8 units. June–Oct $195–$395 double. Rates include breakfast. DISC, MC, V. 2-night minimum stay on weekends. Closed Nov and Apr. Children 10 and older are welcome. **Amenities:** Restaurant (fine dining); Jacuzzi. *In room:* Hair dryer, no phone.

Greenville Inn ★★   This handsome 1895 Queen Anne lumber baron's home sits regally on a hilly side street above Greenville's commercial district. The interiors are sumptuous, with wonderful cherry and mahogany woodworking and a lovely stained-glass window over the stairwell. At the handsome small bar, you can order a cocktail or Maine beer, then sit in front of the fire or retreat to the front porch to watch the evening sun slip over Squaw Mountain and the lake.

Norris St., Greenville, ME 04441. © 888/695-6000 or 207/695-2206. www.greenvilleinn.com. 12 units. $250–$425 double. Rates include continental breakfast. DISC, MC, V. 2-night minimum stay on holiday weekends. Children 8 and older are welcome. **Amenities:** Restaurant (Continental/regional). *In room:* No phone.

Little Lyford Pond Camps ★   This venerable backwoods logging camp is one of the more welcoming spots in the North Woods—at least for those looking to rough it a bit. Built in the 1870s to house loggers, each rustic cabin contains a small woodstove, a propane lantern, cold running water, and its own outhouse. At mealtimes, guests gather in the main lodge, which has books to browse and board games for evenings. During the day, activities aren't hard to find, from fishing for native brook trout (fly-fishing lessons available) and hiking with the lodge's llamas to canoeing at two nearby ponds or wandering on the Appalachian Trail to Gulf Hagas, a scenic gorge 2 miles away. In winter, cross-country skiing on the lodging's private network is superb, and time spent in the sauna will make you forget the cold weather. Access is via a rough logging road in summer (ski or snowmobile in winter), so factor in extra time in getting there.

P.O. Box 340, Greenville, ME 04441. © 603/466/2727. 8 units. $90–$120 double. Rates include all meals. No credit cards. 2-night minimum stay on weekends and holidays. **Amenities:** Sauna; canoes. *In room:* No phone.

The Lodge at Moosehead Lake ★★★   The Lodge at Moosehead Lake is a regal 1917 home on a hillside outside of town built for a wealthy summer rusticator. The inn offers a mix of woodsy and modern and is swiftly upgrading both its facilities and its image to reflect an upscale rustic elegance. Though guest rooms are carpeted, Adirondack-style stick furnishings are mixed in with wingback chairs and antique English end tables. The dining room, where a full breakfast is served year-round (dinner is only served once or twice weekly), has a brisk, modern feel in contrast to much of the rest of the inn. Beds in the main lodge are hand-carved, and the five rooms here are themed to North Woodsian creatures such as bears, trout, and moose; the three luxurious suites in the carriage house feature unique swinging beds—suspended from the ceiling by old logging chains—as well as chandeliers, sunken living rooms, and whirlpools fashioned from river stones. One suite, the Katahdin, even has a fireplace in the bathroom.

Lily Bay Rd. (P.O. Box 1167), Greenville, ME 04441. (C) **207/695-4400.** Fax 207/695-2281. www.lodgeat mooseheadlake.com. 8 units. $205–$475 double. Rates include breakfast. 2-night minimum stay. AE, MC, V. Located 2½ miles north of Greenville on Lily Bay Rd. (head north through blinker). Children 14 and older are welcome. **Amenities:** Concierge. *In room:* A/C, TV/VCR, coffeemaker, hair dryer, iron, Jacuzzi.

Maynard's-in-Maine 🐾 Maynard's has long been one of my favorite places in the North Woods. This is the real thing—nothing the least faux, cute, or neo-rustic about it, sitting at the edge of Rockwood on the Moose River. While the sound of logging trucks can be a bit jarring, the more memorable sounds are wooden screen doors slamming and the clank of horseshoes. Chickens wander the grounds, and guests idle in birch and hickory chairs on cedar-post porches. Photos suggest that nothing has moved, much less been replaced, in the main lodge over the past 50 years. The compound has a handful of rustic cabins edging a lawn, most furnished eclectically with some classic camp furniture, as well as cheesy flea-market finds. Wildwood Cottage has three bedrooms, all sharing a bathroom, woodstove, and large screened porch; Birch Cottage is smaller and appropriate for a couple, and is less modernized than others. Note that not only are there no in-room phones, there's not even a pay phone on the premises.

Rockwood, ME 04478. (C) **207/534-7703.** www.maynardsinmaine.com. 14 units. $110 double. Rates include all meals (bag lunch). AE, DISC, MC, V. Pets allowed. Drive across the bridge over Moose River in Rockwood, make first left, and continue to lodge. **Amenities:** Water sports equipment rental. *In room:* No phone.

BAXTER STATE PARK ★★★

Baxter State Park is one of Maine's crown jewels, even more spectacular in some ways than Acadia National Park. This 204,000-acre state park in the remote north-central part of the state is unlike more elaborate state parks you may be accustomed to elsewhere—don't look for fancy bathhouses or groomed picnic areas. When you enter Baxter State Park, you enter near-wilderness.

Former Maine governor and philanthropist Percival Baxter single-handedly created the park, using his inheritance and investment profits to buy the property and donate it to the state in 1930. Baxter stipulated that it remain "forever wild." Caretakers have done a good job fulfilling his wishes.

You won't find paved roads, RVs, or hook-ups at the eight drive-in campgrounds. (Size restrictions keep RVs out.) Even cellphones are banned. You will find rugged backcountry and remote lakes. You'll also find Mount Katahdin, a lone and melancholy granite monolith that rises above the sparkling lakes and severe boreal forest of northern Maine.

ESSENTIALS

GETTING THERE   Baxter State Park is 86 miles north of Bangor. Take I-95 to Medway (Exit 56) and head west 11 miles on Route 11/157 to the mill town of Millinocket, the last major stop for supplies. Head northwest through town and follow signs to Baxter State Park. The less-used entrance is near the park's northeast corner. Take I-95 to the exit for Route 11, drive north through Patten and then head west on Route 159 to the park. The speed limit in the park is 20 mph; motorcycles and ATVs are not allowed.

VISITOR INFORMATION   Baxter State Park offers maps and information from its **headquarters,** 64 Balsam Dr., Millinocket, ME 04462 ((C) **207/723-5140;** www.baxterstateparkauthority.com). Note that no pets are allowed in Baxter State Park, and all trash you generate must be brought out.

For information on canoeing and camping outside of Baxter State Park, contact **North Maine Woods, Inc.,** P.O. Box 421, Ashland, ME 04732 (*©* **207/ 435-6213;** www.northmainewoods.org). Get help finding cottages and outfitters from the **Katahdin Area Chamber of Commerce,** 1029 Central St., Millinocket, ME 04462 (*©* **207/723-4443**).

FEES   Baxter State Park visitors with out-of-state license plates are charged a per-day fee of $12 per car. (It's free to Maine residents.) The day-use fee is charged only once per stay for those camping overnight. Camping reservations are by mail or in person only (see below). Private timberlands managed by North Maine Woods levy a per-day fee of $4 per person for Maine residents, $7 per person for nonresidents. Camping fees are additional (see below).

GETTING OUTDOORS

BACKPACKING   Baxter State Park maintains about 180 miles of backcountry hiking trails and more than 25 backcountry sites, some accessible only by canoe. Most hikers coming to the park are intent on ascending 5,267-foot Mount Katahdin; but dozens of other peaks are well worth scaling, and just traveling through the deep woods is a sublime experience. Reservations are required for backcountry camping; many of the best spots fill up shortly after the first of the year. Reservations can be made by mail or in person, but not by phone. Descriptions are available from the **Appalachian Trail Conference,** P.O. Box 807, Harpers Ferry, WV 25425 (*©* **304/535-6331;** www.appalachian trail.org).

CAMPING   Baxter State Park has eight campgrounds accessible by car and two backcountry camping areas, but don't count on finding anything available if you show up without reservations. The park starts taking reservations in January, and dozens of die-hard campers traditionally spend a cold night outside headquarters the night before the first business day in January to secure the best spots. Many of the most desirable sites sell out well before the snow melts from Mount Katahdin. The park is stubbornly old-fashioned about its reservations, which must be made either in person or by mail, with full payment in advance. No phone reservations are accepted. Don't even mention e-mail. The park starts processing summer camping mail requests on a first-come, first-served basis the first week in January; call well in advance for reservations forms. Camping at Baxter State Park costs $6 per person ($12 minimum per tent site), with cabins and bunkhouses available for $7 to $17 per person per night.

CANOEING   The state's premier canoe trip is the Allagash River, starting west of Baxter State Park and running northward for nearly 100 miles, finishing at the village of Allagash. The **Allagash Wilderness Waterway** (*©* **207/941-4014**) was the first state-designated wild and scenic river in the country, protected from development in 1970. The river runs through heavily harvested timberlands, but a buffer strip of at least 500 feet of trees preserves forest views along the entire route. The trip begins along a chain of lakes involving light portaging. At Churchill Dam, a stretch of Class I–II white-water runs for about 9 miles, then it's back to lakes and a mix of flatwater and mild rapids. Toward the end is a longish portage (about 150 yards) around picturesque Allagash Falls before finishing up above the village of Allagash. (Leave enough time for a swim at the base of the falls.) Most paddlers spend between 7 and 10 days making the trip from Chamberlain Lake to Allagash. Eighty campsites are maintained along the route; most have outhouses, fire rings, and picnic tables. The camping fee is $4 per night per person for Maine residents, $5 for nonresidents.

Several outfitters offer Allagash River packages, including canoes, camping equipment, and transportation. **Allagash Wilderness Outfitters,** Box 620, Star Route 76, Greenville, ME 04441 (they don't have a direct phone line in summer; call Folsom's Air Service at © **207/695-2821** and an operator will relay messages/requests via shortwave radio), rents a complete outfit (including canoe, life vests, sleeping bags, tent, saw, axe, shovel, cooking gear, first-aid kit, and so on) for $23 per person per day. **Allagash Canoe Trips** (© **207/695-3668;** www.allagashcanoetrips.com) in Greenville offers 7-day guided descents of the river, including all equipment and meals, for $650 adults, $500 children under 18.

HIKING   With 180 miles of maintained backcountry trails and 46 peaks (including 18 over 3,000 ft.), Baxter State Park is the destination of choice in Maine for serious hikers.

The most imposing peak is 5,267-foot **Mount Katahdin** ☆☆☆—the northern terminus of the Appalachian Trail. An ascent up this rugged, glacially scoured mountain is a trip you'll not soon forget: The raw drama and grandeur of the rocky, windswept summit is equal to anything you'll find in the White Mountains of New Hampshire. Allow at least 8 hours for the round-trip, and be prepared to abandon your plans for another day if the weather takes a turn for the worse while you're en route. The most popular route leaves and returns from Roaring Brook Campground. This trail is not for acrophobes or the squeamish: Along the ridgeline, the trail narrows to 2 or 3 feet with a drop of hundreds of feet on either side. It's also not a place to be if high winds or thunderstorms threaten.

Appendix: New England in Depth

by Paul Karr

Reduced to simplest terms, New England consists of two regions: Boston and Not-Boston.

Boston, of course, is in the same league as other major metropolitan areas, and boasts first-class hotels, restaurants, and historic and modern architecture. Of all U.S. cities, Boston has perhaps the richest history, ranging from the days of America's settlement in the 17th century through the War of Independence in 1776 and on into the nation's cultural renaissance in the mid- and late 19th century. The Boston area is also a national seat of education, with dozens of prestigious colleges and universities. The presence of so many august institutions lends the city a youthful air in contrast to its staid heritage.

The extensive territory of Not-Boston arcs widely, from the Connecticut and Rhode Island shoreline through the rolling Berkshire Mountains of western Massachusetts on through the Green and White mountains and into the vast state of Maine. This region, while widely spread, traces it roots back to a Puritan ethic, and its longtime residents still tend to display shared traits and values such as a stubborn independence, a respect for thrift and straight-shooting, and an almost genetic mistrust of outsiders.

New England's legendary aloofness is important to keep in mind when visiting the area, because getting to know the region requires equal amounts of patience and persistence. New England doesn't wear its attractions on its sleeve. It keeps its best destinations hidden in valleys and on the side streets of small villages. Your most memorable experience might come in cracking open a boiled lobster at a roadside lobster pound marked only with a scrawled paper sign, or exploring a cobblestone Boston alley that's not on the maps. There's no Disneyland or Space Needle or Grand Canyon here. New England is the sum of dozens of smaller attractions, and resists being defined by a few big ones.

Which isn't to say that New England lacks attractions. It has the mansions of Newport, the endless beaches of Cape Cod, the rolling Green Mountains of Vermont, the craggy White Mountains of New Hampshire, and magnificent Acadia National Park on the Maine coast. It has wonderful, lost-in-time towns like New Preston, Conn., and Woodstock, Vt. But attempting to explore New England as a "connect-the-dots" endeavor, linking the major sights with long drives, is a surefire recipe for disappointment. It's better to plan a slower itinerary that allows you to enjoy the desultory trips between destinations and explore the little villages and quiet byways.

Some writers maintain that New England's character is still informed by a Calvinist doctrine, which decrees nothing will change one's fate and that hard work is a virtue. The New Englander's dull acceptance that the Boston Red Sox will never be victorious is often trotted out as evidence of the region's enduring Calvinism, as is the inhabitants' perverse celebration of the often-brutish climate.

But that's not to say travelers should expect rock-hard mattresses and nutritional but tasteless meals. Luxurious country inns and restaurants serving food rivaling what you'll find in Manhattan have become part of the landscape in the past 2 decades. Be sure to visit these places. But also set aside enough time to spend an afternoon rocking and reading on a broad inn porch, or to wander out of town on an abandoned county road with no particular destination in mind.

"There's nothing to do here," an inn manager in Vermont once explained. "Our product is indolence." That's an increasingly rare commodity these days. Take the time to savor it.

1 New England Today

It's a common question, so don't be embarrassed about asking it. You might be on Martha's Vineyard, or traveling through a pastoral Vermont valley, or exploring an island off the Maine coast. You'll see houses and people. And you'll wonder: "What do these people do to earn a living?"

As recently as a few decades ago, the answer was probably this: living off the land. They might have fished the seas, harvested timber, or managed a gravel pit. Of course, many still do operate such businesses, but this work is no longer the economic mainstay it once was. Today, scratch a rural New Englander and you're just as likely to find an editor for a magazine that's published in Boston or New York, a farmer who grows specialized produce for gourmet restaurants, or a banking consultant who handles business by fax and e-mail. And you'll find lots of folks whose livelihood is dependent on tourism.

This change in the economy is but one of the tectonic shifts facing the region. The most visible and wracking change involves development and growth. For a region long familiar with economic poverty, a spell of recent prosperity and escalating property values has threatened to bring to New England that curious homogenization already marking much of the rest of the nation. Once a region of distinctive villages, green commons, and courthouse squares, New England's landscape in certain places is beginning to resemble suburbs everywhere else—a pastiche of strip malls dotted with fast food chains, big-box discount and home-improvement stores, and the like.

This change pains longtime residents. New England towns have long maintained their identities in the face of considerable pressure. The region has always taken pride in its low-key, practical approach to life. In smaller communities, town meetings are still the preferred form of government. Residents gather in a public space to speak out about—sometimes rather forcefully—and vote on the issues of the day, such as funding for their schools, road improvements, fire trucks, or even symbolic gestures such as declaring their towns nuclear-free. "Use it up, wear it out, make do, or do without" is a well-worn phrase that aptly sums up the attitude of many long-standing New Englanders—and it's the polar opposite of the designer-outlet ethos filtering in.

It's still unclear how town meetings and that sense of knowing where your town starts and the next one begins will survive the slow but inexorable encroachment of Wal-Marts and Banana Republics. Of course, suburban Connecticut communities in the orbit of New York City and Boston have long since capitulated to sprawl, as have pockets elsewhere in the region—including mall-heavy areas outside Hartford, Conn.; Portland, Maine; and Burlington, Vt., not to mention Maine's Route 1 or the outlets along interstate highways in Massachusetts and Connecticut. Here, little regional identity can still be found.

But the rest of New England is still figuring out how best to balance the principles of growth and conservation—how to allow the economy to edge into the modern age, without sacrificing those qualities that make New England such a distinctive place.

Development is a hot but not necessarily inflammatory issue—this isn't like the property rights movement in the West, where residents are manning the barricades and taking hostages for the cause. (At least not yet.) Few seem to think that development should be allowed at all costs. And few seem to think that the land should be preserved at all costs.

Pinching off all development means the offspring of longtime New England families will have no jobs, and New England will be fated to spend its days as a sort of quaint theme park. But if development continues unabated, many of the characteristics that make New England unique—and attract tourist dollars—will vanish. Will the Berkshires or the Maine coast be able to sustain their tourism industries if they're blanketed with strip malls and fast-food joints, making them look like every other place in the nation? Not likely. The question is how to respect the conservation ethic while leaving room for growth. And that question won't be resolved in the near future.

Except for a several-year slump in the early 1990s, New England has been enjoying a generally rosy period of economic growth since the mid-1980s; even when the economy has nosed back downward, as it has done of late, property values continue to rise as city folks increasingly seek a piece of whatever makes rural New England special. Commentators point out that this change, while welcome after decades of slow growth, will bring new conflicts. The rise of the information culture will make it increasingly likely that telecommuters and info-entrepreneurs will settle in New England's most remote and pristine villages, running their businesses via modem or satellite. How will these affluent newcomers adapt to clear-cutting in the countryside or increasing numbers of tour buses cruising their village greens?

Change doesn't come rapidly to New England. But there's a lot to sort out, and friction will certainly continue to build, one strip mall at a time.

2 History 101

Viewed from a distance, New England's history mirrors that of its namesake, England. The region rose from nowhere to gain tremendous historical prominence, captured a good deal of overseas trade, and became an industrial powerhouse and center for creative thought. And then the party ended relatively abruptly, as commerce and culture sought more fertile grounds to the west and south.

To this day, New England refuses to be divorced from its past. Walking through Boston, layers of history are evident at every turn, from the church

Dateline

- 1000–15 Viking explorers land in Canada, and may or may not have sailed southward to New England. Evidence is spotty.

- 1497 John Cabot, seeking to establish trade for England, reaches the island of Newfoundland in Canada and sails south as far as Maine.

- 1602 Capt. Bartholomew Gosnold lands on the Massachusetts coast. Names Cape Cod, Martha's Vineyard, and other locations.

continues

steeples of colonial times (dwarfed by glass-sided skyscrapers) to verdant parklands that bespeak the refined sensibility of the late Victorian era.

History is even more inescapable in off-the-beaten-track New England. Travelers in Downeast Maine, northern New Hampshire, Connecticut's Litchfield Hills, the Berkshires, and much of Vermont will find clues to what Henry Wadsworth Longfellow called "the irrevocable past" every way they turn, from stone walls running through woods to Federal-style homes.

Here's a brief overview of some historical episodes and trends that shaped New England:

INDIGENOUS CULTURE Native Americans have inhabited New England since about 7000 B.C. While New York's Iroquois Indians had a presence in Vermont, New England was inhabited chiefly by Algonquins who lived a nomadic life. Connecticut was home to some 16 Algonquin tribes, who dubbed the region Quinnetukut.

After the arrival of the Europeans, French Catholic missionaries succeeded in converting many Native Americans, and most tribes sided with the French in the French and Indian Wars in the 18th century. Afterward, the Indians fared poorly at the hands of the British, and were quickly pushed to the margins. Today, they are found in greatest concentration at several reservations in Maine. The Pequots have established a thriving gaming industry in Connecticut. Other than that, the few clues left behind by Indian cultures have been more or less obliterated by later settlers.

THE COLONIES In 1604, some 80 French colonists spent a winter on a small island on what today is the Maine–New Brunswick border. They did not care for the harsh weather of their new home and left in spring to resettle in present-day Nova Scotia. In 1607, 3 months after the celebrated

- **1604** French colonists settle on an island on the St. Croix River between present-day Maine and New Brunswick. They leave after a single miserable winter.
- **1614** Capt. John Smith maps the New England coast, names the Charles River after King Charles I of England, and calls the area a paradise.
- **1616** Smallpox kills large numbers of Indians between Maine and Rhode Island.
- **1620** The *Mayflower*, carrying some 100 colonists (including many Pilgrims, fleeing religious persecution in England), arrives at Cape Cod.
- **1630** Colonists led by John Winthrop establish the town of Boston, named after an English village.
- **1635–36** Roger Williams is exiled from Massachusetts for espousing liberal religious ideas; he founds the city of Providence, R.I.
- **1636** Harvard College is founded to educate young men for the ministry.
- **1638** America's first printing press is established in Cambridge.
- **1648** First labor unions are established by coopers and shoemakers in Boston.
- **1675–76** Native Americans attack colonists in New England in what is known as "King Philip's War."
- **1692** The Salem witch trials take place. Twenty people (including 14 women) are executed before the hysteria subsides.
- **1704** America's first regularly published newspaper, the *Boston News Letter*, is founded.
- **1713** The first schooner, a distinctively American sailing ship, is designed and built in Gloucester, Mass.
- **1764** "Taxation without representation" is denounced in reaction to the Sugar Act.
- **1770** Five colonists are killed outside what is now the Old State House in an incident known as the Boston Massacre.
- **1773** British ships are raided by colonists disguised as Indians during the Boston Tea Party. More than 300 chests of tea are dumped into the harbor from three British ships.

Jamestown, Va. colony was founded, a group of 100 English settlers established a community at Popham Beach, Maine. The Maine winter demoralized these would-be colonists as well, and they returned to England the following year.

The colonization of the region began in earnest with the arrival of the Pilgrims at Plymouth Rock in 1620. The Pilgrims—a religious group that had split from the Church of England—established the first permanent colony, although it came at a hefty price: Half the group perished during the first winter. But the colony began to thrive over the years, in part thanks to helpful Native Americans.

The success of the Pilgrims lured other settlers from England, who established a constellation of small towns outside of Boston that became the Massachusetts Bay Colony. Roger Williams was expelled from the colony for his religious beliefs; he founded the city of Providence, R.I. Other restless colonists expanded their horizons in search of lands for settlement. Throughout the 17th century, colonists from Massachusetts pushed northward into what is now New Hampshire and Maine, and southward into Connecticut. The first areas to be settled were lands near protected harbors along the coast and on navigable waterways.

The more remote settlements came under attack in the 17th and early 18th centuries in a series of raids by Indians conducted both independently and in concert with the French. These proved temporary setbacks; colonization continued throughout New England into the 18th century.

THE AMERICAN REVOLUTION
Starting around 1765, Great Britain launched a series of ham-handed economic policies to reign in the increasingly feisty colonies. These included a direct tax—the Stamp Act—to pay for

- **1775** On April 18, Paul Revere and William Dawes spread the word that the British are marching toward Lexington and Concord. The next day the "shot heard round the world" is fired. On June 17, the British win the Battle of Bunker Hill but suffer heavy casualties.
- **1783** Treaty of Paris is signed, formally concluding the American Revolution.
- **1788** Connecticut becomes the fifth, Massachusetts the sixth, and New Hampshire the ninth state to formally join the union.
- **1790** Rhode Island becomes the 13th state and the final colony to ratify the constitution.
- **1791** The short-lived Republic of Vermont (1777–91) ends and the state of Vermont joins the union.
- **1812** War of 1812 with England batters New England economy.
- **1814** The nation's first textile mill is built, in Waltham, Mass.
- **1820** Maine, formerly a district of Massachusetts, becomes a state.
- **1835** Samuel Colt of Connecticut develops the six-shooter pistol.
- **1861** Massachusetts Institute of Technology is founded.
- **1892** America's first gasoline-powered automobile is built in Chicopee, Mass.
- **1897** First Boston Marathon is run; Boston completes first American subway.
- **1903** The first World Series is played; Boston Red Sox win.
- **1918** The Red Sox celebrate another World Series victory. For the next 8 decades (and counting), they fail to repeat this feat.
- **1930** America's Cup sailing race is first held in Newport, R.I.
- **1930s** The Great Depression devastates New England's already reeling industrial base.
- **1938** A major hurricane sweeps into New England, killing hundreds and destroying countless buildings and trees.

continues

a standing army. The crackdown provoked strong resistance. Under the banner of "No taxation without representation," disgruntled colonists engaged in a series of riots, resulting in the Boston Massacre of 1770, when five protesting colonists were fired upon and killed by British soldiers.

In 1773, the most infamous protest took place in Boston. The British had imposed the Tea Act (the right to collect duties on tea imports), which prompted a group of colonists dressed as Indians to board three British ships and dump 342 chests of tea into the

- 1942 A fire at Boston's Cocoanut Grove nightclub kills 491 people.
- 1946 John F. Kennedy is elected to Congress to represent Boston's first congressional district.
- 1957 Boston Celtics win their first NBA championship, laying the groundwork for a reign that will eventually include 16 championships.
- 1963 New Hampshire becomes first state to establish a lottery to support education.
- 1966 Edward Brooke of Massachusetts becomes the first African American elected to the U.S. Senate since Reconstruction.

A Literary Legacy

New Englanders have generated whole libraries, from the earliest days of hellfire-and-brimstone Puritan sermons to Stephen King's horror novels set in fictional Maine villages.

Among the more enduring writings from New England's earliest days are the poems of Massachusetts Bay Colony resident **Anne Bradstreet** (ca. 1612–1672) and the sermons and essays of **Increase Mather** (1639–1723) and his son, **Cotton Mather** (1663–1728).

After the American Revolution, Hartford dictionary writer **Noah Webster** (1758–1843) issued a call to American writers: "America must be as independent in literature as she is in politics, as famous for arts as for arms." He struck an early blow for pragmatism by taking the "u" out of British words like "labour" and "honour."

The tales of **Nathaniel Hawthorne** (1804–1864) captivated a public eager for a native literature. His most famous story, *The Scarlet Letter*, is a narrative about morality set in 17th-century Boston, but he wrote numerous other books that wrestled with themes of sin and guilt, often set in the emerging republic.

Henry Wadsworth Longfellow (1807–1882), the Portland poet who settled in Cambridge, caught the attention of the public with evocative narrative poems focusing on distinctly American subjects. His popular works included "The Courtship of Miles Standish," "Paul Revere's Ride," and "Hiawatha." Poetry in the mid–19th century was the equivalent of Hollywood movies today—Longfellow could be considered his generation's Steven Spielberg (apologies to literary scholars).

The zenith of New England literature occurred in the mid- and late 19th century with the Transcendentalist movement. These exalted writers and thinkers included **Ralph Waldo Emerson** (1803–1882), **Bronson Alcott** (1799–1888), and **Henry David Thoreau** (1817–1862). They fashioned a way of viewing nature and society that was uniquely American. They rejected the rigid doctrines of the Puritans, and found sustenance harbor. This well-known incident was dubbed the Boston Tea Party.

Hostilities reached a peak in 1775, when the British sought to quell unrest in Massachusetts. A contingent of British soldiers was sent to Lexington to seize military supplies and arrest two high-profile rebels—John Hancock and Samuel Adams. The militia formed by the colonists exchanged gunfire with the British, thereby igniting the revolution ("the shot heard round the world").

Notable battles in New England included the Battle of Bunker Hill

- 1972 Maine's Indians head to court, claiming the state illegally seized their land in violation of a 1790 act. They settle 8 years later for $81.5 million.
- 1974 In Connecticut, Ella Grasso becomes the first elected woman governor.
- 1991 The Big Dig begins in Boston. Scheduled completion date: 2005.
- 2002 The New England Patriots win the Super Bowl, stunning New Englanders long accustomed to stinging pro sports defeats.
- 2004 The Patriots win Super Bowl XXXVIII, becoming NFL champions for the second time in 3 years.

in self-examination, the glories of nature, and a celebration of individualism. Perhaps the best known work to emerge from this period was Thoreau's *Walden*.

Among other regional writers who left a lasting mark on American literature was **Emily Dickinson** (1830–1886), a native of Amherst, Mass., whose precise and enigmatic poems placed her in the front rank of American poets. **James Russell Lowell** (1819–1891), of Cambridge, was an influential poet, critic, and editor. Later poets were imagist **Amy Lowell** (1874–1925), from Brookline, Mass., and **Edna St. Vincent Millay** (1892–1950), from Camden, Maine.

The bestselling *Uncle Tom's Cabin*, the book Abraham Lincoln half-jokingly accused of starting the Civil War, was written by **Harriet Beecher Stowe** (1811–1886) in Brunswick, Maine. She lived much of her life as a neighbor of **Mark Twain** (himself an adopted New Englander) in Hartford, Conn. Another bestseller was the children's book *Little Women,* written by **Louisa May Alcott** (1832–1888), whose father, Bronson, was part of the Transcendentalist movement.

New England's later role in the literary tradition may best be symbolized by the poet **Robert Frost** (1874–1963). Though born in California, he lived his life in Massachusetts, New Hampshire, and Vermont. In the New England landscape and community, he found a lasting grace and rich metaphors for life. (Among his most famous lines: "Two roads diverged in a wood, and I—I took the one less traveled by, / And that has made all the difference.")

New England continues to attract writers drawn to the noted educational institutions and the privacy of rural life. Prominent contemporary writers and poets who live in the region at least part of the year include **John Updike, Nicholson Baker, Christopher Buckley, P.J. O'Rourke, Bill Bryson, John Irving,** and **Donald Hall.** Maine is also the home of **Stephen King,** who is considered not so much a novelist as Maine's leading industry.

outside Boston, which the British won but at tremendous cost; and the Battle of Bennington in Vermont, in which the colonists prevailed. Hostilities formally ended in February 1783, and in September, Britain recognized the United States as a sovereign nation.

FARMING & TRADE   As the new republic matured, economic growth in New England followed two tracks. Residents of inland communities survived by farming, and trading in furs. Vermont in particular has always been an agrarian state, and remains a prominent dairy producer to this day.

On the coast, boatyards sprang up from Connecticut to Maine, and ship captains made tidy fortunes trading lumber for sugar and rum in the Caribbean. Trade was dealt a severe blow following the Embargo Act of 1807, but commerce eventually recovered, and New England ships could be encountered everywhere around the globe.

The growth of the railroad in the mid–19th century was another boon. The train opened up much of the interior, and led to towns springing up overnight, such as White River Junction, Vt. The rail lines allowed local resources—such as the fine marbles and granites from Vermont—to be easily shipped to markets to the south.

INDUSTRY   New England's industrial revolution found seed around the time of the embargo of 1807. Barred from importing English fabrics, Americans built their own textile mills. Other common household products were also manufactured domestically, especially shoes. Towns like Lowell, Mass.; Lewiston, Maine; and Manchester, N.H., became centers of textile and shoe production. In Connecticut, the manufacture of arms and clocks emerged as major industries. Today, industry no longer plays the prominent role it once did—manufacturing first moved to the South, then overseas.

TOURISM   In the mid- and late 19th century, New Englanders discovered a new cash crop: the tourist. All along the Eastern Seaboard, it became fashionable for the gentry and eventually the working class to set out for excursions to the mountains and the shore. Regions such as the Berkshires, the White and Green mountains, and Block Island were lifted by the tide of summer visitors. The tourism wave crested in the 1890s in Newport, R.I., and Bar Harbor, Maine, both of which were flooded by the affluent. Several grand resort hotels from tourism's golden era still host summer travelers in the region.

ECONOMIC DOWNTURN   While the railways allowed New England to thrive in the mid–19th century, the train played an equally central role in undermining its prosperity. The driving of the Golden Spike in 1869 in Utah, linking America's Atlantic and Pacific coasts by rail, was heard loud and clear in New England, and it had a discordant ring. Transcontinental rail meant farmers and manufacturers could ship goods from the fertile Great Plains and California to faraway markets, making it harder for New England's hardscrabble farmers to survive. Likewise, the coastal shipping trade was dealt a fatal blow by this new transportation network. And the tourists set their sights on the Rockies and other stirring sites in the West.

Beginning in the late 19th century, New England lapsed into an extended economic slumber. Families commonly walked away from their farmhouses (there was no market for resale) and set off for regions with more promising opportunities. The abandoned, decaying farmhouse became almost an icon for New England, and vast tracts of open farmland were reclaimed by forest. With the rise of the automobile, the grand resorts further succumbed, and many closed their doors as inexpensive motels siphoned off their business.

BOOM TIMES In the last 2 decades of the 20th century, much of New England rode an unexpected wave of prosperity. A massive real-estate boom shook the region in the 1980s, driving land prices sky-high as prosperous buyers from New York and Boston acquired vacation homes or retired to the most alluring areas. In the 1990s, the rise of high-tech also sent ripples from Boston into the hinterlands. Tourism rebounded as harried urbanites of the Eastern Seaboard opted for shorter, more frequent vacations closer to home.

Travelers to the more remote regions will discover that many communities never benefited from the boom at all; they're still waiting to rebound from the economic malaise earlier in the century. Especially hard-hit have been places like northeastern Vermont and far Downeast Maine, where many residents still depend on local resources—timber, fisheries, and farmland—to eke out a living.

3 New England Style

You can often trace the evolution of a town by its architecture, as styles evolve from basic structures to elaborate Victorian mansions. The primer below should aid with basic identification.

- **Colonial** (1600–1700): The New England house of the 17th century was a simple, boxy affair, often covered in shingles or rough clapboards. Don't look for ornamentation; these homes were designed for basic shelter from the elements, and are often marked by prominent stone chimneys. You can see examples at Plimoth Plantation and in Salem, near Boston.
- **Georgian** (1700–1800): Ornamentation comes into play in the Georgian style, which draws heavily on classical symmetry. Georgian buildings were in vogue in England at the time, and were embraced by affluent colonists. Look for Palladian windows, formal pilasters, and elaborate projecting pediments. Deerfield (in the Pioneer Valley) is a good destination for seeing early Georgian homes; and Providence, R.I. and Portsmouth, N.H. have abundant examples of later Georgian styles.
- **Federal** (1780–1820): Federal homes (sometimes called Adams homes) may best represent the New England ideal. Spacious yet austere, they are often rectangular or square, with low-pitched roofs and little ornament on the front, although carved swags or other embellishments are frequently seen near the roofline. Look for fan windows and chimneys bracketing the building. Excellent Federal-style homes are found throughout the region in towns such as Kennebunkport, Maine.
- **Greek Revival** (1820–1860): The most easy-to-identify Greek Revival homes feature a projecting portico with massive columns, like a part of the Parthenon grafted onto an existing home. The less dramatic homes may simply be oriented such that the gable faces the street, accenting the triangular pediment. Greek Revival didn't catch on in New England the way it did in the South, but some fine examples exist, notably in Newfane, Vt.
- **Carpenter Gothic** and **Gothic Revival** (1840–1880): The second half of the 19th century brought a wave of Gothic Revival homes, which borrowed their aesthetic from the English country home. Aficionados of this style and its later progeny featuring gingerbread trim owe themselves a trip to Oak

Bluffs at Martha's Vineyard, where cottages are festooned with scrollwork and exuberant architectural flourishes.

- **Victorian** (1860–1900): This is a catchall term for the jumble of mid- to late-19th-century styles that emphasized complexity and opulence. Perhaps the best-known Victorian style—almost a caricature—is the tall and narrow Addams-Family-style house, with mansard roof and prickly roof cresting. You'll find these scattered throughout the region.

  The Victorian style also includes squarish **Italianate** homes with wide eaves and unusual flourishes, such as the outstanding Victoria Mansion in Portland, Maine.

  Stretching the definition a bit, Victorian can also include the **Richardsonian Romanesque** style, which was popular for railroad stations and public buildings. The classic Richardsonian building, designed by H. H. Richardson himself in 1872, is Trinity Church, in Boston.

- **Shingle** (1880–1900): This uniquely New England style quickly became preferred for vacation homes on Cape Cod and the Maine coast. They're marked by a profusion of gables, roofs, and porches, and are typically covered with shingles from roofline to foundation.

- **Modern** (1900–present): Outside of Boston, New England has produced little in the way of notable modern architecture. In the 1930s, Boston became a center for the stark **International Style** with the appointment of Bauhaus veteran Walter Gropius to the faculty at Harvard. Some intriguing experiments in this style are found on the MIT and Harvard campuses, including Gropius's Campus Center and Eero Saarinen's Kresge Auditorium.

4 A Taste of New England

All along the coast you'll be tempted by seafood in its various forms. You can get fried clams by the bucket at divey shacks along remote coves and busy highways. The more upscale restaurants offer fresh fish, grilled or gently sautéed.

Live lobster can be bought literally off the boat at lobster pounds, especially along the Maine coast. The setting is usually rustic—maybe a couple of picnic tables and a shed where huge vats of water are kept at a low boil.

Inland, take time to sample the local products. This includes delectable maple syrup, sold throughout the northern reaches. Check the label for Grade A syrup certification. Cheese is a Vermont specialty, especially cheddar. Look also for Vermont's famed apple cider, and Maine's wild blueberries.

In summer, small farmers across New England set up stands at the end of their driveways offering fresh produce straight from the garden. You can usually find berries, fruits, and sometimes home-baked breads. These stands are rarely tended; just leave your money in the coffee can.

Restaurateurs haven't overlooked New England's bounty. Many chefs serve up delicious meals consisting of local ingredients—some places even tend their own gardens. Some of the fine dishes we've enjoyed while researching this guide include curried pumpkin soup, venison medallions with shiitake mushrooms, and wild boar with juniper berries.

But you don't have to have a hefty budget to enjoy the local foods. A number of regional classics fall under the "road food" category. Here's an abbreviated field guide:

- **Beans:** Boston is forever linked with baked beans (hence the nickname "Beantown"), which are popular throughout the region. A Saturday-night supper traditionally consists of baked beans and brown bread.

- **Lobster rolls:** Lobster rolls consist of lobster meat plucked from the shell, mixed with just enough mayonnaise to hold it all together, then served on a hotdog roll.
- **Moxie:** Early in this century, Moxie outsold Coca-Cola. Part of its allure was the fanciful story behind its 1885 creation: A traveler named Moxie was said to have observed South American Indians consuming the sap of a native plant, which gave them extraordinary strength. The drink was "re-created" by Maine native and Massachusetts resident Dr. Augustin Thompson. It's still popular in New England, although some folks liken the taste to a combination of medicine and topsoil.
- **Necco wafers:** Still made in Cambridge by the New England Confectionery Company, these powdery wafers haven't changed a bit since 1847. The candies are available widely throughout New England.

Finally, no survey of comestibles would be complete without mention of something to wash it all down: beer. New England has more microbreweries than any other region outside of the Pacific Northwest. Popular brewpubs that rank high on the list include the Great Providence Brewing Co., the Commonwealth Brewing Co. (Boston's first brewpub), the Portsmouth Brewery, Federal Jack's Brewpub (Kennebunkport), Vermont Pub & Brewery (Burlington), the Windham Brewery at the Latchis Hotel (Brattleboro), and Portland, Maine's clutch of mini-breweries—at least a half-dozen, at last count, all making mighty good beer.

Index

FROMMER'S® COMPLETE TRAVEL GUIDES

Alaska
Alaska Cruises & Ports of Call
American Southwest
Amsterdam
Argentina & Chile
Arizona
Atlanta
Australia
Austria
Bahamas
Barcelona, Madrid & Seville
Beijing
Belgium, Holland & Luxembourg
Bermuda
Boston
Brazil
British Columbia & the Canadian Rockies
Brussels & Bruges
Budapest & the Best of Hungary
Calgary
California
Canada
Cancún, Cozumel & the Yucatán
Cape Cod, Nantucket & Martha's Vineyard
Caribbean
Caribbean Cruises & Ports of Call
Caribbean Ports of Call
Carolinas & Georgia
Chicago
China
Colorado
Costa Rica
Cuba
Denmark
Denver, Boulder & Colorado Springs
England
Europe
Europe by Rail
European Cruises & Ports of Call

Florence, Tuscany & Umbria
Florida
France
Germany
Great Britain
Greece
Greek Islands
Halifax
Hawaii
Hong Kong
Honolulu, Waikiki & Oahu
India
Ireland
Israel
Italy
Jamaica
Japan
Kauai
Las Vegas
London
Los Angeles
Maryland & Delaware
Maui
Mexico
Montana & Wyoming
Montréal & Québec City
Munich & the Bavarian Alps
Nashville & Memphis
Newfoundland & Labrador
New England
New Mexico
New Orleans
New York City
New York State
New Zealand
Northern Italy
Norway
Nova Scotia, New Brunswick & Prince Edward Island
Oregon
Ottawa
Paris

Peru
Philadelphia & the Amish Country
Portugal
Prague & the Best of the Czech Republic
Provence & the Riviera
Puerto Rico
Rome
San Antonio & Austin
San Diego
San Francisco
Santa Fe, Taos & Albuquerque
Scandinavia
Scotland
Seattle
Shanghai
Sicily
Singapore & Malaysia
South Africa
South America
South Florida
South Pacific
Southeast Asia
Spain
Sweden
Switzerland
Texas
Thailand
Tokyo
Toronto
USA
Utah
Vancouver & Victoria
Vermont, New Hampshire & Maine
Vienna & the Danube Valley
Virgin Islands
Virginia
Walt Disney World® & Orlando
Washington, D.C.
Washington State

FROMMER'S® DOLLAR-A-DAY GUIDES

Australia from $50 a Day
California from $70 a Day
England from $75 a Day
Europe from $70 a Day
Florida from $70 a Day
Hawaii from $80 a Day

Ireland from $80 a Day
Italy from $70 a Day
London from $90 a Day
New York from $90 a Day
Paris from $90 a Day
San Francisco from $70 a Day

Washington, D.C. from $80 a Day
Portable London from $90 a Day
Portable New York City from $90 a Day
Portable Paris from $90 a Day

FROMMER'S® PORTABLE GUIDES

Acapulco, Ixtapa & Zihuatanejo
Amsterdam
Aruba
Australia's Great Barrier Reef
Bahamas
Berlin
Big Island of Hawaii
Boston
California Wine Country
Cancún
Cayman Islands
Charleston
Chicago
Disneyland®
Dominican Republic
Dublin

Florence
Frankfurt
Hong Kong
Las Vegas
Las Vegas for Non-Gamblers
London
Los Angeles
Los Cabos & Baja
Maine Coast
Maui
Miami
Nantucket & Martha's Vineyard
New Orleans
New York City
Paris

Phoenix & Scottsdale
Portland
Puerto Rico
Puerto Vallarta, Manzanillo & Guadalajara
Rio de Janeiro
San Diego
San Francisco
Savannah
Vancouver
Vancouver Island
Venice
Virgin Islands
Washington, D.C.
Whistler

Frommer's® National Park Guides

Algonquin Provincial Park
Banff & Jasper
Family Vacations in the National
  Parks

Grand Canyon
National Parks of the American
  West
Rocky Mountain

Yellowstone & Grand Teton
Yosemite & Sequoia/Kings
  Canyon
Zion & Bryce Canyon

Frommer's® Memorable Walks

Chicago
London

New York
Paris

San Francisco

Frommer's® With Kids Guides

Chicago
Las Vegas
New York City

Ottawa
San Francisco
Toronto

Vancouver
Walt Disney World® & Orlando
Washington, D.C.

Suzy Gershman's Born to Shop Guides

Born to Shop: France
Born to Shop: Hong Kong,
  Shanghai & Beijing

Born to Shop: Italy
Born to Shop: London

Born to Shop: New York
Born to Shop: Paris

Frommer's® Irreverent Guides

Amsterdam
Boston
Chicago
Las Vegas
London

Los Angeles
Manhattan
New Orleans
Paris
Rome

San Francisco
Seattle & Portland
Vancouver
Walt Disney World®
Washington, D.C.

Frommer's® Best-Loved Driving Tours

Austria
Britain
California
France

Germany
Ireland
Italy
New England

Northern Italy
Scotland
Spain
Tuscany & Umbria

The Unofficial Guides®

Beyond Disney
Central Italy
Chicago
Cruises
Disneyland®
England
Florida
Florida with Kids
Inside Disney

Hawaii
Las Vegas
London
Maui
Mexico's Best Beach Resorts
Mini Las Vegas
Mini-Mickey
New Orleans
New York City

Paris
San Francisco
Skiing & Snowboarding in the
  West
Walt Disney World®
Walt Disney World® for
  Grown-ups
Walt Disney World® with Kids
Washington, D.C.

Special-Interest Titles

Athens Past & Present
Cities Ranked & Rated
Frommer's Best Day Trips from London
Frommer's Caribbean Hideaways
Frommer's China: The 50 Most Memorable Trips
Frommer's Exploring America by RV
Frommer's Gay & Lesbian Europe
Frommer's Best RV and Tent Campgrounds
  in the U.S.A.

Frommer's Road Atlas Europe
Frommer's Road Atlas France
Frommer's Road Atlas Ireland
Frommer's Wonderful Weekends from
  New York City
The New York Times' Guide to Unforgettable
  Weekends
Retirement Places Rated
Rome Past & Present

Travel Tip: He who finds the best hotel deal has more to spend on facials involving knobbly vegetables.

Hello, the Roaming Gnome here. I've been nabbed from the garden and taken round the world. The people who took me are so terribly clever. They find the best offerings on Travelocity. For very little cha-ching. And that means I get to be pampered and exfoliated till I'm pink as a bunny's doodah.

✳✳ travelocity

1-888-TRAVELOCITY / travelocity.com / America Online Keyword: Travel

Travel Tip: Make sure there's customer service for any change of plans — involving friendly natives, for example.

One can plan and plan, but if you don't book with the right people you can't seize le moment and canoodle with the poodle named Pansy. I, for one, am all for fraternizing with the locals. Better yet, if I need to extend my stay and my gnome nappers are willing, it can all be arranged through the 800 number at, oh look, how convenient, the lovely company coat of arms.

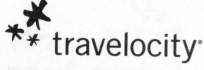

Travel Tip: He who finds the best hotel deal has more to spend on facials involving knobbly vegetables.

Hello, the Roaming Gnome here. I've been nabbed from the garden and taken round the world. The people who took me are so terribly clever. They find the best offerings on Travelocity. For very little cha-ching. And that means I get to be pampered and exfoliated till I'm pink as a bunny's doodah.

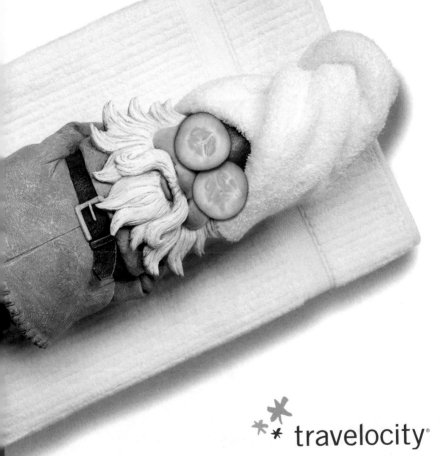

travelocity®

1-888-TRAVELOCITY / travelocity.com / America Online Keyword: Travel